wwnorton.com/nawr

The StudySpace site that accompanies *The Norton Anthology of World Religions* is FREE, but you will need the code below to register for a password that will allow you to access the copyrighted materials on the site.

WRLD–RLGN

THE NORTON ANTHOLOGY OF

WORLD RELIGIONS

ISLAM

THE NORTON ANTHOLOGY OF

WORLD RELIGIONS

ISLAM

Jane Dammen McAuliffe

JACK MILES, *General Editor*
DISTINGUISHED PROFESSOR OF ENGLISH AND RELIGIOUS STUDIES,
UNIVERSITY OF CALIFORNIA, IRVINE

W · W · NORTON & COMPANY
NEW YORK · LONDON

W. W. Norton & Company has been independent since its founding in 1923, when William Warder Norton and Mary D. Herter Norton first published lectures delivered at the People's Institute, the adult education division of New York City's Cooper Union. The firm soon expanded its program beyond the Institute, publishing books by celebrated academics from America and abroad. By midcentury, the two major pillars of Norton's publishing program—trade books and college texts—were firmly established. In the 1950s, the Norton family transferred control of the company to its employees, and today—with a staff of four hundred and a comparable number of trade, college, and professional titles published each year—W. W. Norton & Company stands as the largest and oldest publishing house owned wholly by its employees.

Printed in the United States of America
First Edition

Manufacturing by LSC Communications Crawfordsville
Composition by Westchester Book
Book design by Jo Anne Metsch
Production Manager: Sean Mintus

LIBRARY OF CONGRESS CATALOGING-IN-PUBLICATION DATA

The Norton anthology of world religions / Jack Miles, General Editor, Distinguished Professor of English and Religious Studies, University of California, Irvine; Wendy Doniger, Hinduism; Donald S. Lopez, Jr., Buddhism; James Robson, Daoism. — First Edition.
volumes cm
Includes bibliographical references and index.
ISBN 978-0-393-91898-4 (hardcover)
1. Religions. 2. Religions—History—Sources. I. Miles, Jack, 1942– editor. II. Doniger, Wendy, editor. III. Lopez, Donald S., 1952– editor. IV. Robson, James, 1965 December 1– editor.
BL74.N67 2014
208—dc23

2014030756

Islam (978-0-393-35502-4): Jack Miles, General Editor; Jane Dammen McAuliffe, Editor

W. W. Norton & Company, Inc.
500 Fifth Avenue
New York NY 10110
wwnorton.com

W. W. Norton & Company Ltd.,
15 Carlisle Street, London W1D 3BS

1 2 3 4 5 6 7 8 9 0

Contents

GENERAL INTRODUCTION
How the West Learned to Compare Religions

JACK MILES

ISLAM
Introduction: Submission to God as the Wellspring of a Civilization

JANE DAMMEN MCAULIFFE

The Foundational Epoch, 610–750

QUR'AN: GOD'S CULMINATING GIFT TO HUMANKIND

The Classical Synthesis Encounters Modernity, 1765 to the Present   505

Maps and Illustrations

MAPS

ILLUSTRATIONS

Preface

Welcome to *The Norton Anthology of World Religions*. The work offered to you here is large and complex, but it responds to a simple desire—namely, the desire that six major, living, international world religions should be allowed to speak to you in their own words rather than only through the words of others about them. Virtually all of the religious texts assembled here are primary texts. Practitioners of Hinduism, Buddhism, Daoism, Judaism, Christianity, and Islam have written and preserved these texts over the centuries for their own use and their own purposes. What is it like to read them, gathered as they are here like works of religious art in a secular museum?

For practitioners of any of these six religions, who number in the hundreds of millions, this anthology is likely to provide some of the surprise and fascination of a very large family album: some of one's religious ancestors trigger an immediate flash of recognition, while others look very distant and perhaps even comical. For an army of outsiders—those whose religion is not anthologized here, those who practice no religion, those who are "spiritual but not religious," and those who count themselves critics or antagonists of religion—the experience will be rewarding in different ways. No propaganda intrudes here on behalf either of any given religion or of religion in general. The goal at every point is not conversion, but exploration. The only assumptions made are that the most populous and influential of the world's religions are here to stay, that they reward study best when speaking to you in their own words, and that their contemporary words make best sense when heard against the panoramic background of the words they have remembered and preserved from their storied pasts.

Many of the texts gathered here have been translated from foreign languages, for the religions of the world have spoken many different languages over the course of their long histories. A few of the works—the Bhagavad Gita, the *Daode jing*, the Bible, the Qur'an—are readily available. Many more are available only in the libraries of a few major research universities or, though physically available, have not been intellectually available without detailed guidance that was impossible for the lay reader to come by. Bibliographic information is always provided for previously published translations, and a number of translations have been made especially for this anthology. A central concern throughout has been that the anthologized texts should be not just translated but also framed by enough editorial explanation to make them audible and intelligible across the barriers of time and space even if you are coming to them for the first time. When those explanations require the use of words in a foreign language with a non-Roman writing system, standard academic modes of transliteration have sometimes been simplified to enhance user-friendliness.

Globalization, including international migration in all its forms, has brought about a large-scale and largely involuntary mingling of once-separate religious communities, and this historic change has created an urgent occasion for a deeply grounded effort at interreligious understanding. Yes, most of the world's Hindus still live in India, yet the Hindu Diaspora is enormous and influential. Yes, many Jews have migrated to Israel, but half of the world's Jews still live in deeply rooted Diaspora communities around the world. Conventionally, Islam is thought of as a Middle Eastern religion, yet the largest Muslim populations are in South and Southeast Asia, while the Muslim minority in Europe is growing rapidly. By the same token, Christianity is not thought of as an African religion, yet the Christian population of sub-Saharan Africa is growing even more rapidly than the Muslim population of Europe. In a bygone era, the six religions treated here might have been divided geographically into an "Eastern" and a "Western" trio, but we do not so divide them, for in our era they are all everywhere, and none is a majority. Religiously, we live and in all likelihood will continue to live in a world of large and mingling minorities.

This involuntary mingling has created a state of affairs that can be violently disruptive. Terrorism in the name of religion, more often within national borders than across them, has turned many minds against religion in all forms. And yet, paradoxically, religious violence during the twenty-first century has persuaded many that, contrary to innumerable past predictions, religion is by no means fading from modern life. And though the threat of religious violence is a dark challenge of one sort, the bright new opportunities for cross-cultural and interreligious learning present an unprecedented challenge of a different and, in the end, a more consequential sort. On the one hand, whatever some of us might have wished, religious violence has made religion a subject that cannot be avoided. On the other, for those who engage the subject in depth, the study of religion across cultural and political borders builds a uniquely deep and subtle form of cosmopolitan sophistication.

In all its formal features—the format of its tables of contents; its use of maps and illustrations; its handling of headnotes, footnotes, glossaries, and bibliographies; its forty-eight pages of color illustration in six inserts—*The Norton Anthology of World Religions* announces its membership in the venerable family of Norton anthologies. As was true of *The Norton Anthology of English Literature* upon its first publication more than half a century ago, this anthology is both larger and more rigorously realized than any prior anthology published in English for use by the general reader or the college undergraduate. It opens with a generous introduction addressing a set of basic questions not linked to any single tradition but affecting all of them. Each of the six religious traditions is then presented chronologically from its origins to the present (the Buddhism volume also uses a geographical organizing principle). Each presentation begins with a substantial overview of the tradition being anthologized. Each is also punctuated by period introductions tracing the history of the tradition in question. And yet this work is not a history merely enlivened by the inclusion of original texts. No, history here is simply the stage. The texts themselves are the performance, displaying as only they can the perennial and subversive power of religious literature. The difference might be compared to the difference between English history with a bit of Shakespeare and Shakespeare with a bit of English history. The histories come and go, but Shakespeare is irreplaceable. Shakespeare is, to use a term that originated in the church, *canonical*.

Derived from the Greek word for a ruler or measuring rod, *canon* came to mean a rule or criterion of any kind. By extension, the same word came to mean the church rule or "canon" law governing the contents of the Bible: which books were to be included and which excluded. And by yet a further extension, canon came to refer to the understood list of acknowledged masterpieces in English or some other literature. So, the Bible has a canon. English literature has a canon (however endlessly contested). But what works of religious literature constitute the world religious canon?

Aye, dear reader, there was the rub as plans were laid for this anthology. In 2006, when the editorial team began work in earnest, no canons existed for the literatures of the world's major religions. There were limited canons within that vast expanse of written material, the Bible itself being the paradigmatic example. But the literature of Christianity is larger than the Bible, and the situation grows only more complicated as one ranges farther afield into traditions whose concentric canons are more implicit than explicit. Even though more than one canon of the Bible exists, Bible scholars can easily handle that limited variety and still quite literally *know what they are talking about*: they can deal with a clearly delimited body of material within which evidence-based historical interpretation can go forward. But what canon of religious texts exists to help define the entire field of religious studies for religion scholars? The field has never had an agreed-upon answer to that question, and some of the most sweeping theoretical statements about religion turn out, as a result, to rest on an astonishingly small and vague empirical base.

Granted that no master canon in the original religious sense of that term can ever be devised for the religions of the world, the lack of a limited but large and serious study collection of texts is one major indication that the study of religion remains at an early stage of its development as a discipline. For the religions of Asia, especially, it has been as if the Elizabethan theater were being studied without ready access by students to the plays of Shakespeare or with, at most, access to *Hamlet* alone. This lack has been particularly glaring in the United States for reasons that deserve a brief review. Until the early 1960s, the study of religion was largely confined to private colleges and universities, where, thanks to the country's Protestant intellectual heritage, it consisted overwhelmingly of biblical studies and Christian theology. Often, the department of religion was a department of philosophy and religion. Often, too, there was a close relationship between such departments and the college chaplaincy. In public colleges and universities, meanwhile, the situation was quite different. There, the traditional constitutional separation of church and state was understood to preclude the formal study of religion, perhaps especially of the very religions that the student body and the faculty might turn out to be practicing.

But then several events, occurring at nearly the same moment in both the public and the private spheres, created a new climate for the study of religion, and "religious studies" emerged as a new academic discipline distinct from philosophy or theology, on the one hand, and even more distinct from the chaplaincy, on the other. We are still reckoning with the consequences of this shift.

In 1963, Associate Justice Arthur Goldberg wrote for the Supreme Court of the United States in a concurring opinion in *Abington v. Schempp* (374 U.S. 203, 306): "It seems clear to me . . . that the Court would recognize the propriety of . . . the teaching *about* religion, as distinguished from the teaching *of* religion, in the public schools," language that seemed to clear a path for the study of religion in tax-supported schools. Significantly, Goldberg was a Jew; just three years earlier, Americans had elected John F. Kennedy as their first Roman Catholic president. American religious pluralism was becoming increasingly inescapable at the highest levels in American public life; and as it came to be understood that university-level religious studies was to be the study of various religions at once, including but by no means confined to the religions of the United States, the Founding Fathers' fear of an imposed, national religion began to recede from the national consciousness. American pluralism was now as powerful a factor in American religious life as the Constitution itself.

This anthology is published on the fiftieth anniversary of an event little noticed in the cultural ferment of the 1960s but of great importance for the study of religion—namely, the 1964 reincorporation of the National Association of Biblical Instructors (NABI), the principal association of college professors teaching these subjects, as the American Academy of Religion (AAR), whose current mission statement focuses pointedly on "the understanding of religious traditions, issues, questions, and values"—all in the plural. The formal incorporation of the AAR was intended first as a quiet but magnanimous gesture of invitation by a Protestant academic establishment toward the scholars of America's Catholic and Jewish communities, but this was just the beginning. Others would soon be drawn into a conversation whose animating academic conviction is well captured in a dictum of the great nineteenth-century scholar Max Müller: "He who knows one religion knows none."

Catholics and Jews had had their own seminaries and their own institutions of higher learning, but scholarship produced in them tended to remain in them—partly, to be sure, because of Protestant indifference but also because of defensive or reactively triumphalist habits of mind among the residually embattled minorities themselves. But this was already changing. Optimism and openness in the Roman Catholic community had been much assisted in the earlier 1960s by the Second Vatican Council, whose byword was the Italian *aggiornamento*—roughly, "updating"—as employed by the benignly bold Pope John XXIII. American Jews, meanwhile, profoundly traumatized as they had been during and after World War II by the Shoah, or Holocaust, Nazi Germany's attempted genocide, breathed a collective (if premature) sigh of relief in 1967 after Israel's stunning victory over its Arab opponents in the Six-Day War. During the same period, the Reverend Dr. Martin Luther King, Jr., had spearheaded a revolution in American race relations, as segregation ended and the social integration began that would lead to the election of a black president, Barack Obama, in 2008. In short, the mood in the early 1960s was in every way one of barred doors swung open, locked windows flung up, and common cause undertaken in moral enterprises like the interfaith campaign to end the war in Vietnam.

One influential scholar saw the shift occurring in the study of religion as cause for academic jubilation. Writing in 1971 in the *Journal of the American Academy of Religion* (which had been, until 1966, *The Journal of Bible and Religion*), Wilfred Cantwell Smith clearly welcomed the change that was taking place:

> Perhaps what is happening can be summed up most pithily by saying that the transition has been from the teaching of religion to the study of religion. Where men used to instruct, they now inquire. They once attempted to impart what they themselves knew, and what they hoped (of late, with decreasing expectation) to make interesting; now, on the contrary, they inquire, into something that both for them and for their students is incontrovertibly interesting, but is something that they do not quite understand.

And yet there was a shadow across this scene. The newborn American Academy of Religion had bitten off rather more than it could chew. The spread of religious studies to the state university campuses that were proliferating in the late 1960s and the 1970s was vigorously pluralist. Jewish studies experienced an enormous growth spurt, and so did Hindu studies, Buddhist studies, Islamic studies, and so forth. Smith, a scholar of comparative religion who had made his first mark as a specialist in Islam, could only welcome this in principle. But others, writing later, would be troubled by growth that seemed to have spun out of control.

Recall that in 1971, *globalization* was not the byword that it has since become. The Hindu Diaspora in the United States was still tiny. Christian Pentecostalism, though well established, had not yet achieved critical mass in Africa. Europe's Muslim minority, if already substantial, was relatively dormant. Mainland China's population was still in Maoist lockdown. And in the United States, Americans had not yet begun to grasp the coming effects of the passage of the Immigration and Nationality Act of 1965, which removed quotas that had been in place since the 1920s; the resulting explosive growth in Hispanic and Asian immigration would by 1990 make non-Hispanic Caucasians a minority in Los Angeles, America's second-largest city. Americans still saw themselves as a colonized people who had achieved independence, rather than as a colonizing people. The rhetoric of European postcolonialism had not yet been applied to the United States, a superpower whose world hegemony was quasi-imperial in its reach and neocolonialist in its effects. Worldwide, the transformative interrogation of religious traditions by women and about women had barely begun.

While all of these changes, as they have brought about the multiplication and intensification of religious encounters, have made the study of world religions more important than ever, they have not made it easier. They have not, in particular, lent it any internal intellectual coherence. They have not created for it a new study canon to replace the narrowly Protestant study canon, as the founding of the AAR seemed in principle to require. The creation of religious studies as a field had been an academic gamble on a barely perceived religious future. Had the bet paid off? An eminent senior scholar, Jonathan Z. Smith, wrote in 1995 of the change that had taken place: "The field made a decision to give up a (limited) coherence for a (limitless) incoherence."

That limitless incoherence was the context in which we took up the challenge to produce *The Norton Anthology of World Religions.* How ever were we to begin?

There came first the recognition that we would be creating for the field of religious studies a first draft of the very canon that it lacked—a canon covering nearly four thousand years of history in a score of different languages, aspiring not to be authoritative regarding belief or practice but to be plausibly foundational for the study of the subject.

There came second the recognition that though canons, once achieved, are anonymous, they do not begin anonymously. They begin with somebody who declares this in and that out and defends his or her choice. This realization shifted the decision to be made from *What?* to *Who?*

There came third the question of whether the answer to the question *Who?* would come in the singular or in the plural and if in the plural, how multitudinously plural. For each of the traditions to be anthologized, would a large board of specialist advisers be assembled to determine what would be included? Would the selections be formally approved by some kind of plebiscite, as in the verse-by-verse ratification by translators of the language included in the King James Version of the Bible? Would the work of annotating the resulting selections be divided among committees and subcommittees and so forth? Would some governing board formulate a set of topics that each editor or team of editors would be required to address so as to confer a sturdy structure upon the whole? Would there be, for example, a different board of consultants for each period in the long history of Judaism or each language across the geographic breadth of Buddhism?

Our decision was to reject that kind of elaboration and gamble instead on six brilliant and creative individuals, each with a distinct literary style and a record of bold publication, and then to impose no common matrix of obligatory topics or categories on them, nor even a common set of chronological divisions. (Does China have its own Middle Ages? When does modernity begin in Turkey?) It was understood, however, playing to an institutional strength at W. W. Norton & Company, that the prose of these editors, formidable though they were, would be edited very heavily for explanatory clarity even as we second-guessed very lightly indeed their actual anthological choices. To what end this blend of laxity and severity? Our aim has been simply to enhance the intelligent delight of students in religious literature both as literature and as religion. "Intelligent" delight does not mean the delight of intelligent people. The reference is rather to the delight that a strange and baffling ancient text can provide when a great scholar, speaking in his or her own voice, renders it intelligible for you and you recognize, behind it, a human intelligence finally not all that unlike your own.

If that has been our aim for students, our aim for professors has been rather different. Professors of religious studies often find themselves called upon to teach insanely far beyond their area of trained academic competence. For them, we hope to have provided both an invaluable reference tool and a rich reservoir of curricular possibilities. For their graduate students, we hope to have provided breadth to complement the depth of doctoral study at its best. A student studying in depth and probably in the original language some particular religious text can discover here what *else* was being written in the same tradition at the same time. What preceded that text in the life of the religious tradition? What followed it? Who celebrated it? Who attacked it? The fine art of page flipping, crucial to the unique operating system of an ink-on-paper anthology, enables just this kind of exploratory learning. Over time, by repeated forays backward and forward in the evolution of a religious tradition, a serious student can come to know its literature like the interior of a large residence. But this is just the beginning. Comparable forays into the development of other traditions can by degrees situate the target religious tradition in the global religious context. Finally, to further aid all users, the companion website to *The Norton Anthology of World Religions* will provide, over time, both supplementary substantive content—other religious traditions, to begin with—not included in the print anthology and an array of aids for the use of teachers and students.

Beyond these conventional services, however, lies something riskier. We acknowledge that we have provided the professoriate a target to shoot at: "How could you *possibly* omit X?" some will exclaim. And others: "Why on *earth* did you ever bother with Y?" We welcome all such objections. They betray nothing more than the real, existential condition of a field still in many ways struggling to be born. Disciplines do not spring into existence overnight. They are negotiated into existence over time through trial and error. The more vigorously our colleagues find fault with this first draft of a canon for their field, the more productive will be the ensuing negotiation.

Intuition based on deep scholarship and teaching experience has surely played a role in the choices made by the six associate editors responsible, respectively, for anthologizing the six religious literatures covered: Wendy Doniger (Hinduism), Donald S. Lopez, Jr. (Buddhism), James Robson (Daoism), David Biale (Judaism), Lawrence S. Cunningham (Christianity), and Jane Dammen McAuliffe (Islam). They have all sought to include those incipiently canonical texts that few of their colleagues would dare exclude. More intuitively, they have sought to include neglected works of beauty and power whose very appearance here might help them become canonical. The editors have even included occasional attacks on the religious traditions anthologized—for example, excerpts from Kancha Ilaiah, "Why I Am Not a Hindu," in the Hinduism anthology and from Bertrand Russell, "Why I Am Not a Christian," in the Christianity anthology. As these two contrarian entries nicely demonstrate, the canon of texts regarded as permanent and irreplaceable in a religious tradition does not coincide exactly with the canon of texts arguably crucial for the study of the tradition. Coping with all these complications, the editors have coped in every case as well with the painful space limitations that we have had to impose on them even after allowing the anthology to grow to nearly twice its originally envisioned size.

One large question remains to be addressed in this brief preface: *By what criteria did you choose to anthologize these and only these six religions?* This question has a theoretical as well as a practical dimension. How, to begin with, do we distinguish that which is religious from that which is not? Is atheism a religion, or at least a "religious option"? Whatever atheism is, it is certainly no modern novelty. *The Cambridge Companion to Atheism* (2007) begins with a substantial chapter, "Atheism in Antiquity," by the distinguished Dutch classicist Jan Bremmer. Whether atheism in a given ancient or modern form should be considered a strictly religious option may depend on how a given atheist "plays" it. The novelist Alain de Botton, nothing if not playful, dreams or artfully feigns dreaming of a floridly religious enactment of atheism in his *Religion for Atheists: A Non-believer's Guide to the Uses of Religion* (2012). Meanwhile, a 2010 survey by the Pew Forum suggests that the religiously unaffiliated might actually be both more interested in and better informed about religion than the affiliated. But back to the question at hand: If we cannot clearly distinguish religion from irreligion or the "strictly" from the "casually" religious, how can we be sure that we are choosing six versions of the same thing? Arcane and obscure as this question may sound, it did bear rather directly on one of our six key choices, as will be explained below.

In the end, in making our choices, we fell back to an infra-theoretical, practical, or "working" criterion for inclusion: we required that the religions anthologized should be the six most important *major, living, international* religions, a rubric in which each of the three italicized words counted.

Because we anthologize only *living* religions, we do not anthologize the religions of ancient Mesopotamia, Greece, and Rome, despite the fact that these religious traditions loom large in the history of the study of religion in the West, thanks to the dominance of the Bible and of the Greco-Roman classics in Western higher education.

Because we anthologize only *international* religions, we do not anthologize folkloric or indigenous religions, which are typically and symbiotically confined to a single locale, despite the fascination that these religions have had for the sociological or anthropological study of religion, from Johann Gottfried Herder and Émile Durkheim in the late eighteenth and nineteenth century to Clifford Geertz in the twentieth.

Geography, except as the difference between national and international, is not the principle of organization in this anthology. One consequence, however, of our anthologizing only literary religions and then applying a mostly demographic criterion in choosing among them has been the omission of indigenous African religion. While it is true that Yoruba religion is now international and that some texts for it are now available, no such text has become canonical even for practitioners themselves. Rather than saying anything about the limitations of African or other indigenous religious traditions, notably the rich array of Amerindian religions, our decision says something about the inherent limitations of any text-based approach to the study of religion. Texts can indeed teach much, but they cannot teach everything about everybody.

As for the key criterion *major*, we apply it demographically with one glaring exception. Religious demography tends to overstate or understate the size of a religion depending on whether and how that religion counts heads. Roman Catholicism, which counts every baptized baby as a member, probably ends up with somewhat overstated numbers. Daoism, by contrast, probably ends up with its adherents undercounted because formal affiliation is not a recognized criterion for basic participation in it.

Yet even after these difficulties have been acknowledged, there can be no quarrel that Christianity and Islam are demographically major as well as living and international. The same goes at almost equal strength for Hinduism and Buddhism. The obvious exception is Judaism, whose numbers worldwide, though far from trivial, are small even when the question "Who is a Jew?" is given its most broadly inclusive answer. Too small to be reckoned major by a head count, Judaism is too important on other counts to be reckoned less than major. It is the exception that breaks the rule. Its categories, its legends, and many of its practices have been decisive not only for Christianity and Islam but also, arguably, for Western secularism.

As many readers will have noticed by now, this grid of six does not stray very far from the textbook areas of religious studies, as is only right and proper in a reference work, yet this claim of relative "normality" calls for qualification in two final regards if only to provide the occasion for a pair of disclaimers.

First, this anthology does not deal with several religious traditions that, though fully literary and indeed of great intrinsic interest, do not meet its stated criteria. Three that might be named among these are Sikhism, Jainism, and Shinto, but several other traditions commonly enough included in textbooks might easily be added to the list. No judgment of intrinsic worth or importance should be inferred from their exclusion, just as none should be inferred from the omission of indigenous African or Amerindian religion. A less ample presentation of a larger number of religious traditions would always have been possible. Our choice, and all such choices come at a cost, has been to produce ampler presentations of plausibly canonical texts for those most populous religions traditions that the world citizen is likeliest to encounter in the new religious environment that we all inhabit.

To name a second perhaps surprising choice, our grid of six, though generally familiar, has "Daoism" where most textbooks have "Chinese religion." The usual textbook grid resorts to geography or ethnicity as a naming criterion in and only in the Chinese case. Why so? Though, as noted, the designations "Eastern" and "Western" do still have some textbook currency, no one speaks of Christianity as "European religion" or of Islam as "Afro-Asiatic religion." Why proceed otherwise in the Chinese case alone?

Our decision, breaking with this practice, has been, in the first place, to anthologize Chinese Buddhism within the Buddhism anthology, allowing that sub-anthology to become, by the inclusion of its Chinese material, the longest of the six. Our decision, in the second place, has been not to anthologize Chinese Confucianism at all. We have a secondary and a primary reason for this second decision.

The secondary reason not to anthologize Confucianism is that the People's Republic of China does not regard it as a religion at all. The government recognizes only five religions: Buddhism, Daoism, and Islam plus (as separate religions) Catholicism and Protestantism. Confucianism it simply defines as altogether out of the category *religion*.

Properly so? Is Confucianism a religion, or not? This question is notoriously one that "the West has never been able to answer and China never able to ask," and we do not presume to give a definitive answer here. It is true, on the one hand, that at many points during its long history, Confucianism has seemed to be neither a religion nor quite a philosophy either but rather a code of wisdom and conduct for the Chinese gentleman scholar—or, perhaps better, the aspiring Chinese statesman. Yet at other points in Confucian history, it must be noted, Confucius has been accorded the honor of a virtual god. We choose to leave that question in abeyance.

Our primary reason, in any case, to set Confucianism aside and dedicate our limited space to Daoism is that while the Confucian canon has been widely translated and, as ancient religious texts go, is relatively accessible, the Daoist canon has only recently been rescued from near death and has never before been presented for the use of nonspecialists in an overview of any historical completeness.

While two pre-Daoist classics—the gnomic *Daode jing* of Laozi and the tart wisdom of Zhuangzi—have been endlessly translated and are in no danger of disappearance, their relationship to the Daoist canon as a whole is, to borrow from an observation quoted in James Robson's introduction to the Daoism anthology, like the real but distant relationship of Plato and Aristotle to the Christian canon. What would we know of Christianity if Paul, Augustine, Dante, Luther, Milton, and so on down the hallowed list had all been lost and only Plato and Aristotle survived?

Such a fate did indeed very nearly befall Daoism. In the nineteenth century, leading up to the establishment of the first Republic of China in 1912, Qing dynasty authorities systematically confiscated Daoist temples and turned them into schools and factories. Having begun as an underground movement in the second century, Daoism—long out of official favor—was largely forced underground only again and more deeply so after the establishment of the Republic, which condemned it as superstition.

For the Daoist canon, the cost of this persecution was nearly outright extinction. By the early twentieth century, few copies of Daoism's canon of eleven hundred religious texts survived in all of China. But then, remarkably, circumstances eased enough to permit the reprint in 1926 of a rare surviving copy of the full 1445 Ming dynasty canon. This had been the last great effort at canon formation in Daoist history before Daoism's long decline commenced. As this reprint reached the West, scholarship on the history of Daoism and the interpretation of its texts slowly began. Nonetheless, particularly after the establishment of the Communist People's Republic of China in 1949, with its aggressive early persecution of all religions, many in the West believed that the actual practice of Daoism had finally died out in its birthplace.

They were mistaken. Over the past few decades, reliable reports have made it clear that Daoism is still alive and indeed is growing steadily stronger, having survived as if by taking Mao Zedong's advice to his guerrillas that they "move among the people as a fish swims in the sea." Just as the fish in the sea are not easily counted, so the Daoists of China escape the usual forms of Western quantification and Communist surveillance alike. But the Daoist fish are numerous, even if they have reason to swim deep.

Meanwhile, the work of translating and contextualizing the recovered texts has attracted a growing corps of Western scholars—initially in France and more recently in other Western countries, including the United States. As their work has gone forward, the world has begun to hear of Daoist messiahs and utopian dreams of peace; Daoist confession rituals and community liturgies; Daoist alchemy and proto-scientific experimentation; Daoist medicine, bodily cultivation (as distinct from asceticism), and sexual practices; Daoist prayer, including Daoist letter-writing to the gods; and Daoist pageantry, costume, magic, and music. In short, a lost religious world—the central, popular, indigenous, full-throated religious world of China—has been brought back to textual life. Our decision was to bring our readers a major sampling from this remarkable recovery.

The major religions of the world are probably better grasped, many scholars now insist, as a set of alternative customs and practices in loose organization—worship liturgies, pilgrimages, dietary restrictions, birth and burial practices, art, music, drama, dance, and so forth—than as a set of contending ideologies. Millions of men and women, even when they practice religions that we rightly regard as literary, are themselves illiterate. Yet when writing remade the world, it did remake religion as well. The major religious traditions of the world would not be major today had they not become literary traditions as well.

Because it is *written*, religious literature can be and has been shared, preserved through wars and persecutions, transmitted over time and space, and, most important of all, *taught* with ease and delight. When all else perishes, the written word often survives. The work before you is a self-contained, portable library of religious literature. You may read it on a plane, in the park, or in a waiting room and trust that every foreign or otherwise strange term will be explained on or near the page where it occurs. No foreign alphabets are used. Transliterations have been simplified to serve pedagogical utility rather than philological perfection. Diacritical marks have been kept to the absolute minimum. Though, as noted, a few of the large theoretical considerations that religion raises as a subject for human inquiry will be addressed in the general introduction, the emphasis in this work is overwhelmingly pragmatic rather than theoretical. For in this domain, more perhaps than in any other, outsiders have historically been as important as insiders, and beginners as welcome as veterans. So, to conclude where we began, whether you are an outsider or an insider, a beginner or a veteran, we welcome you to the pages of *The Norton Anthology of World Religions*.

JACK MILES
IRVINE, CALIFORNIA

Acknowledgments

The Norton Anthology of World Religions would not have been possible without the help of many generous and able friends. We are grateful for the help of those named below as well as of others too numerous to list.

From W. W. Norton & Company, we wish to thank Roby Harrington, head of the college division, who conceived this volume; Pete Simon, its first editor, who contributed its title; Carly Fraser Doria, who has managed the assembly of illustrations and ancillary materials with intelligence and taste; developmental editors Alice Falk, Carol Flechner, and Kurt Wildermuth, who have tamed its prose to the demanding Norton standard; Adrian Kitzinger, who created the beautiful maps; Megan Jackson and Nancy Rodwan, permissions experts; art directors Debra Morton Hoyt and Ingsu Liu, designer Chin-Yee Lai, and artist Rosamond Purcell; production managers Sean Mintus and Julia Druskin; managing editor Marian Johnson, whose project-editorial wisdom is quietly evident on every page; and, most of all, Julia Reidhead, editorial director, whose taste and managerial finesse have preserved and advanced this work sagaciously for fully seven years.

Wendy Doniger wishes to thank Velcheru Narayana Rao for finding "Sita Lost in Thought" for her, and for finding and translating "Kausalya in Fury"; Vasudha Naranayan and Richard Fox for the Southeast Asian materials; Eleanor Zelliot, Gail Omvedt, and Dilip Chitre for the Dalit materials; her student assistants, Jeremy Morse and Charles Preston, for assembling all the texts; and Anne Mocko for help with the pronouncing glossaries.

James Robson wishes to thank Stephen R. Bokenkamp, for helping to get this project started; Alice Falk, for helping to get it completed; and Billy Brewster, for help with the pronouncing glossaries.

David Biale wishes to thank Ariel Evan Mayse and Sarah Shectman for research assistance beyond the call of duty.

Lawrence S. Cunningham wishes to thank his beloved wife, Cecilia, and their two daughters, Sarah and Julia.

Jane Dammen McAuliffe wishes to thank her splendid research associates, Carolyn Baugh, Sayeed Rahman, Robert Tappan, and Clare Wilde, and to recognize with appreciation both Georgetown University and Bryn Mawr College for their support of this work.

For generous financial support of this project, Jack Miles wishes to thank the John T. and Catherine D. MacArthur Foundation, the Getty Research Institute, and the University of California, Irvine. He thanks, in addition, for early editorial consultation, his publishing colleague John Loudon; for generous technical assistance, Steve Franklin and Stan Woo-Sam of UCI's information technology office; for invaluable assistance with the initial enormous delivery of texts, his former student Matthew Shedd; for helpful counsel on Asian Christianity, his colleague Tae Sung; for brilliant assistance in editorial rescue and rewrite, his irreverent friend and colleague Peter Heinegg; and for her sustaining and indomitable spirit, his irreplaceable Catherine Montgomery Crary.

This work is dedicated—in gratitude for all that they have preserved for our instruction—to the scribes of the world's great religions.

THE NORTON ANTHOLOGY OF

WORLD RELIGIONS

ISLAM

The relation of the various peoples of the earth to the supreme interests of life, to God, virtue, and immortality, may be investigated up to a certain point, but can never be compared to one another with absolute strictness and certainty. The more plainly in these matters our evidence seems to speak, the more carefully must we refrain from unqualified assumptions and rash generalizations.

—Jacob Burckhardt,
The Civilization of the Renaissance in Italy (1860)

GENERAL INTRODUCTION

How the West Learned to Compare Religions

BY JACK MILES

How to Read This Book: A Poetic Prelude

The Norton Anthology of World Religions is designed to be read in either of two ways. You may read it from start to finish, or you may pick and choose from the table of contents as in a museum you might choose to view one gallery rather than another or one painting rather than another.

Imagine yourself at the entrance to a large museum containing a great many strange works of religious art. If you enter, what will you do? Will you devote equal time or equal intensity of attention to every work in the huge museum? Or will you skip some works, linger over others, and shape as you go a kind of museum within the museum? In the latter case, what will be your criteria? Those, too, you may well shape as you go. You may not entirely know even your own mind as you begin. You may not know exactly what you're after. You may be detached, and yet—disinterested? No, you are not exactly disinterested. You're looking around, waiting for something to reach you, some click, some insemination, a start. Entering is sometimes enough. You do not need a briefing by the curator to begin your visit.

So it is with this anthology. Take the works assembled here as lightly as you wish. You will still be taking them properly: you will be taking them for what they are. A new path begins to open into the consideration of religion when it is regarded as unserious, un-adult—but only in the way that art, poetry, and fiction in all its forms (including the theatrical and the cinematic) are so regarded. They all deal with made-up stuff. And yet will we ever be so adult as to outgrow them?

The Western cast of mind has undeniably had an intrusive and distorting effect in many parts of the world as Western culture has become a world culture, and yet that cast of mind has also had a liberating and fertilizing effect. It has opened a space in which the once incomparable has become comparable. Looking at the religions of others even from the outside but with a measure of openness, empathy, and good will can enable those of any religious tradition or none to see themselves from the outside as well, and that capacity is the very foundation of human sympathy and cultural wisdom.

In church one morning in the eighteenth century, the poet Robert Burns spotted a louse on a proper lady's bonnet and started thinking: If only she could see herself as he saw her! He went home and wrote his wonderfully earthy and witty "To a Louse, On Seeing One on a Lady's Bonnet, at Church 1786." The fun of the poem is that it is addressed to the louse in a mock "How dare you!" tone almost all the way to the end. At that point, however, it becomes suddenly reflective, even wistful, and Burns concludes, in his Scots English:

O wad some Pow'r the giftie gie us
To see oursels as ithers see us!
It wad frae monie a blunder free us,
An' foolish notion:
What airs in dress an' gait wad lea'e us,
An' ev'n Devotion!

Burns dreams, or half-prays, that some power would "the giftie gie us" (give us the gift) to see "oursels" (ourselves) as others see us—to see, as it were, the lice on our bonnets. Our fine and flouncing airs then "wad lea'e us" (would leave us). But it might not be simply vanity that would depart. The last words in the poem are "an' ev'n Devotion!" (and even devotion). Even our religious devotions might be affected if we could see ourselves at that moment just as others see us. So many of the cruelest mistakes in religion are made not out of malice but out of simple ignorance, blunders we would willingly avoid could we but see ourselves as others see us. Looking at other traditions, you need to see the bonnet and not just the louse. Looking at your own, however you define it, you need to see the louse as well as the bonnet.

Can Religion Be Defined?

What is religion? The word exists in the English language, and people have some commonsense notion of what it refers to. Most understand it as one kind of human activity standing alongside other kinds, such as business, politics, warfare, art, law, sport, or science. Religion is available in a variety of forms, but what is it, really? What makes it itself?

Simple but searching questions like these may seem to be the starting point for the study of religion. Within the study of religion, they are more precisely the starting point for the *theory* of religion. And readers will not be surprised to learn that academic theoreticians of religion have not been content with the commonsense understanding of the subject.

The theoretical difficulties that attend any basic element of human thought or experience are undeniable. What is mathematics? What is art? What is law? What is music? Books have been written debating number theory, aesthetic theory, legal theory, and music theory. It should come as no surprise then that the theory of religion is no less actively debated than are those other theories. Some definitions of religion are so loose as to allow almost anything to qualify as a religion. Others are so strict as to exclude almost everything ordinarily taken to be a religion (prompting one recent contributor to the *Journal of the American Academy of Religion* to give his article the wry or rueful title "Religions: Are There Any?").[1]

The inconvenient truth is that no definition of religion now enjoys general acceptance. In *The Bonobo and the Atheist* (2013), the primatologist Frans de Waal writes:

> To delineate religion to everyone's satisfaction is hopeless. I was once part of a forum at the American Academy of Religion, when

> someone proposed we start off with a definition of religion. However much sense this made, the idea was promptly shot down by another participant, who reminded everyone that last time they tried to define religion half the audience had angrily stomped out of the room. And this in an academy named after the topic![2]

A survey of competing theories, if we were to attempt one here, could quickly jump to twenty-three entries if we simply combined the contents of two recent handbooks—the eight in Daniel L. Pals's *Eight Theories of Religion* (2006) and the fifteen in Michael Stausberg's *Contemporary Theories of Religion: A Critical Companion* (2009).[3]

Though no one writing on religion can entirely escape theoretical commitments, *The Norton Anthology of World Religions* is foremost an anthology of primary texts. By the term *primary* we understand texts produced by the practitioners of each of the anthologized religions for their fellow practitioners. Such an anthology does not collect theories of religion, for the simple reason that such theories are secondary texts. They belong not to the creation and practice of religion but, retrospectively, to its study and analysis. Accordingly, they have rarely been of much interest to religious practitioners themselves.

Religious practitioners are far from unique in this regard. "Philosophy of science is about as useful to scientists as ornithology is to birds," Richard Feynman (1918–1988), a Caltech physicist, famously quipped.[4] The philosophy (or theory) of religion is of as little use to, say, the Buddhist as philosophy of science is to the scientist. Just as the scientist is interested in her experiment rather than in the philosophy of science and the painter in his painting rather than in the philosophy of art, so the Buddhist is interested in the Buddha rather than in the philosophy of religion. The term *religion* itself, as an academic term comprising—as indeed it does in this work—many different religious traditions, may not be of much practical utility to the practitioner of any one of the traditions.

And yet we who have assembled this work may not excuse ourselves altogether from addressing the question "What is religion?" simply on the grounds that our pages are filled with primary texts, for introducing, framing, and contextualizing these texts are the words of our six anthologizing editors as well as the general editor. The seven of us speak in these pages not as practitioners of the religions anthologized here but as scholars writing *about* those religions. Scholarship at its most empirical cannot escape theory, because, to quote a dictum from the philosophy of science, all data are theory-laden. A theory of some sort will be found operative even when no explicit theoretical commitment has been made.

If, then, some tacit theory or theories of religion must necessarily have informed the choices made by our associate editors, given the general editor's decision to impose no single theory, has any silent theoretical convergence occurred? Now that the results are in and the editors' choices have actually been made, do they reflect a working answer to the question "What is religion?"

As general editor, I believe that they do, though it would take some rather elaborate spelling out to explain just *how* they do. Something more modest but more readily discernible must suffice for this introduction—namely, the claim that the choices made by the respective associate editors reflect a common method or, more modestly still, a common approach to the task of presenting a major religious literature with some coherence. In brief, the six associate editors have approached the six religions whose texts they anthologize as six kinds of practice rather than as six kinds of belief. In common usage, religious and unreligious people are divided into "believers" and "unbelievers." The editors have departed from this common usage, proceeding instead on the silent and admittedly modest premise that religion is as religion *does*. Even when speaking of belief, as they do only occasionally, they generally treat it as embedded in practice and inseparable from practice. Monotheism in the abstract is a belief. "Hear, O Israel, the Lord is our God, the Lord alone" as sung by a cantor in a synagogue is a practice.

When religion is approached as practice, what follows? Clearly, Daoist practice, Muslim practice, Christian practice, and so on are not identical, but the substantial differences *within* each of them can loom as large as the differences from one to another among them. *The goal of this anthology is to present through texts how this variety has developed and how the past continues to shape the present.* Thus, the body of material put on exhibit here serves less to answer the question "What is religion?" in any theoretically elaborate or definitive way than to question the answers others have given to that question—answers such as those offered by, for example, the twenty-three theories alluded to above. Whatever fascinating questions a given theory of religion may have posed and answered to its own satisfaction, it must also, we submit, be able to account for the complexity of the data that these primary texts exhibit. Rather than serving to illustrate some fully developed new theory of religion, in other words, the texts gathered here constitute the empirical evidence that any such theory must cope with. In the meantime, the working focus is squarely on practice.

Each of the religions anthologized here has contained multiple versions of itself both over time and at any given time, and the anthology does not attempt to drive past the multiplicity to the singular essence of the thing. Practitioners, of course, have not always been so neutral. Many have been or still are prepared to deny the legitimacy of others as Hindu, Muslim, Christian, Jewish, and so on. But for the purposes of this anthology, those denials themselves simply become a part of the broader story.

Syncretism, moreover—namely, the introduction of a feature from one religion into the life of another—is in itself an argument that the borrower and the lender are, or can be, related even when they are not, and never will be, identical. Multiple religious belonging—double or triple affiliation—sometimes takes syncretism a step further. And while borrowings across major borders are an additive process, adjustments within borders can often be a subtractive process, as seen in many statements that take the form "I am a Buddhist, but . . . ," "I am a Catholic, but . . . ," "I am a Muslim, but . . . ," and so forth. In such statements, the speaker takes the broad term as a starting point and then qualifies it until it fits properly.

Yet we do not claim anything more than practical utility for this default approach to the subject, knowing as we do that a great many scholars of religion decline to define the essence of religion itself but do not find themselves inhibited by that abstention from saying a great deal of interest about one religious tradition or another. Rather than name at the outset the one feature that establishes the category *religion* before discussing the particular religion that interests them, they make the usually silent assumption that the full range of beliefs and practices that have been conventionally thought of as religious is vast and that each religion must be allowed to do as it does, assembling its subsets from the vast, never-to-be-fully-enumerated roster of world religious practices. Having made that assumption, the scholars take a deep breath and go on to talk about what they want to talk about.

Twenty-first-century religion scholars are prepared to acknowledge coherence when they find it but determined never to impose it. They are aware that the entries made under the heading *religion* may not all be versions of just the same thing, but they are equally aware that the overlaps, the innumerable ad hoc points of contact, are also there and also real—and so they find the continued use of the collective term *religion* justified for the enriching and enlightening comparisons that it facilitates. All knowledge begins with comparison.

In telling the life stories of six major, living, international religions through their respective primary texts, the editors of *The Norton Anthology of World Religions* have neither suppressed variability over time in service to any supposedly timeless essence of the thing nor, even when using the word *classical*, dignified any one age as truly golden. Each of the stories ends with modernity, but modernity in each case is neither the climax nor the denouement of the story. It is not the last chapter, only the latest.

How Christian Europe Learned to Compare Religions

Most people, we said earlier, understand religion as "one kind of human activity standing alongside other kinds, such as business, politics, warfare, art, law, sport, or science." Another way to say this is that they understand religion to be one domain among many, each separate from the others. Broadly compatible with this popular understanding is a widely influential definition of religion formulated by the anthropologist Clifford Geertz (1926–2006).

In "Religion as a Cultural System," first published in 1966, Geertz defined religion as

> *(1) a system of symbols which acts to (2) establish powerful, pervasive, and long-lasting moods and motivations in men by (3) formulating conceptions of a general order of existence and (4) clothing these conceptions with such an aura of factuality that (5) the moods and motivations seem uniquely realistic.*[5]

Geertz does not claim that all cultures are equally religious. In fact, toward the end of his essay he observes that "the degree of religious articulateness is not a constant even as between societies of similar complexity."[6] However, he does tacitly assume that religion is if not universal then at least extremely widespread and that it is a domain separate from others, such as—to name two that he explores—science and ideology.[7]

But just how widespread is religion, and is it truly a domain separable from the rest of culture? Can religion really be distinguished from ideology? In Geertz's terms, wouldn't Marxism qualify as a religion? In recent decades, some have argued that even a thoroughly secular anthropologist like Geertz, in whose definition of religion neither God nor Christ is mentioned, can be seen as carrying forward an ideological understanding of religion that originated in the Christian West and has lived on in Western academic life as a set of inadequately examined assumptions. That religion is a domain separate from either ethnicity or culture is one of two key, historically Christian assumptions. That religion is a universal phenomenon—in some form, a part of every human society and even every human mind—is the other key assumption.

Perhaps the most widely cited historical critique of these assumptions is Tomoko Masuzawa's revealing *The Invention of World Religions, Or, How European Universalism Was Preserved in the Language of Pluralism* (2005). Masuzawa's book is not about the invention of the world's religions themselves but about the invention of *world religions* as a phrase used in the West to talk about them, postulating their parallel existence as separable and separate realities, available as an indefinitely expandable group for academic discussion.[8]

When and how, she asks, did this omnibus-phrase *world religions* come into the general usage that it now enjoys? She concludes her influential investigation with the candid confession that the invention and, especially, the very widespread adoption of the phrase remain something of a puzzle—but her analysis traces the usage back only to the nineteenth century. Our claim below is that though the phrase *world religions* may be recent, its roots run much deeper than the nineteenth century, as deep in fact as early Christianity's peculiar and unprecedented self-definition.

To say this is not to undercut the strength of the criticism. Christian explorers, traders, missionaries, and colonists encountering non-Western societies, especially after the discovery of the Americas and the colonial expansion of the West into Asia, have often isolated and labeled as "religions" behaviors that they took to be the local equivalents of what they knew in the West as Christianity. This process of isolating and labeling was a mistake when and if the societies themselves did not understand the behaviors in question as constituting either a separate domain or merely one instance of a more general phenomenon called religion. Moreover, when those purporting to understand non-Western societies in these historically Christian terms were invaders and imperialists, a perhaps unavoidable theoretical mistake could have grievous practical consequences. And when, in turn, ostensibly neutral, secular theories of religion—not imposed by conquerors or missionaries but merely proffered by Western academics—are alleged to make the same historically Christian assumptions, the entire project of comparative religious study may be faulted as Christian imperialism.

Because the viability and indeed the enormous value of such study are premises of this anthology, the challenge calls for a significant response, one that necessarily includes substantial attention to just how Christianity influenced the study of what the West has defined as world religions. The intention in what follows, however, is by no means to make a case for Christianity as inherently central or supreme among the world's religions. We intend rather, and only, to trace how, in point of fact, Christianity began as central to the Western *study* of religions and then, by degrees, yielded its position as more polycentric forms of study emerged.

Let us begin by stipulating that Christians did indeed acquire very early and thereafter never entirely lost the habit of thinking of their religion as a separate domain. Once this is conceded, it should come as no great surprise that as a corollary of this habit, they should have adopted early and never entirely lost the habit of thinking of other religions, rightly or wrongly, as similarly separate domains. This would be simply one more instance of the human habit of beginning with the known and with the self and working outward to the unknown and to the others.

But we must stipulate further that Christians made a second assumption—namely, that theirs should become humankind's first-ever programmatically "world" religion. The idea of universally valid religious truth was not new in itself. Ancient Israel had long since been told that its vocation was to be the light of the world. In the book of Isaiah, God says to his people through the prophet (49:6):

> It is too light a thing that you should be my servant to raise up the tribes of Jacob and to restore the preserved of Israel; I will give you as a light to the nations, that my salvation may reach to the end of the earth.[9]

In the Gospel of Matthew, Jesus turns this latent potential into a radically intrusive program for action. His final words to his apostles are

> Go therefore, and make disciplines of *all nations*, baptizing them in the name of the Father and of the Son and of the Holy Spirit, teaching them to observe all that I have commanded you; and, lo, I am with you always, even to the close of the age. (Matthew 28:19–20; emphasis added)

How ever did this instruction, as the first Christians put it into practice, lead to the secular study of "world religions" as we know it today?

The Social Oddity of the Early Church

In the earliest centuries of its long history, the Christian church defined its belief as different from the official polytheism of the Roman Empire, on the one hand, and from the monotheism of Rabbinic Judaism, on the other, inasmuch as the rabbinic Jews did not recognize Jesus as God incarnate. But if the church was thus, to borrow a convenient phrase from contemporary American life, a faith-based organization, it was not just a school of thought: it was also an *organization*. As faith-based, it undeniably placed unique and unprecedented stress on belief (and indeed set the pattern by which today all those religiously active in any way are routinely called *believers*, even when not all regard belief as central to their practice). Yet as an organization, the church depended not just on a distinct set of beliefs but also on a social identity separate, on the one hand, from that of the Roman Empire (or any other empire) and equally separate, on the other, from that of the Jewish nation (or any other nation). As a faith-based, voluntary, nonprofit, multiethnic, egalitarian, nongovernmental organization, the Christian church was a social novelty: nothing quite like it had ever been seen before. And as Christians, growing steadily in number, projected their novel collective self-understanding upon Roman and Jewish social reality alike, the effect was profoundly disruptive. Though many others would follow, these were the first two instances of Christian projection, and an analysis of how they worked is especially instructive.

By encouraging Roman polytheists to *convert* to Christianity while maintaining that they did not thereby cease to be Romans, the Christians implicitly invented religious conversion itself as an existential possibility. The term *religion* did not exist then in Greek, Latin, or Aramaic as a fully developed universal category containing both Roman polytheism and Christianity, but in the very action of conversion the future category was already implicit. By seeking to convert Roman polytheists to Christianity, the early Christians implied that Roman religiosity was a domain both separate from the rest of Roman life and replaceable. You could exchange your Roman religiosity for this modified Jewish religiosity, as the very act of conversion demonstrated, while bringing the rest of your Roman identity with you.

In the first century, conversion thus defined was an unprecedented and socially disruptive novelty. Until the destabilizing intrusion of Christianity, respect for the Roman gods had always been inseparable from simply being Roman: religious identity and civic identity had always constituted an unbroken whole. Christianity encouraged Romans to split that single identity into a double identity: religion, on the one hand; culture and ethnicity, on the other. In this sequestration of the religiously meaningful from the religiously neutral or meaningless was born the very possibility of secular culture, as well as religion as Western modernity has come to understand it—religion as involving some semblance of faith and some form of collective identity separable from ethnicity or culture.

In by far the most important instance of this division of social identity, the original Christian Jews, having adopted a minority understanding of Jewish tradition, denied that they were any less Jewish for that reason. Writing of his Jewish critics, St. Paul fumed (2 Corinthians 11:22): "Are they Israelites? So am I!" Much of first-century Jewry would not have disagreed with him had the matter stopped there, for there were many peacefully coexisting Jewish views about Jewish belief and practice. As no more than the latest variation on the old themes, the Christian Jews would not have created anything structurally new. But they did create something new by taking the further step of bringing themselves, with their recognizably Jewish religious views (views indeed unrecognizable as anything except Jewish), into an unprecedented social relationship with non-Jews—namely, into the Christian church. By linking themselves to non-Jews in this way, without renouncing their Jewish identity, the Christian Jews—enjoying particular success in the Roman Diaspora—demonstrated that as they conceived their own Jewish religiosity to be distinguishable from the rest of what was then the Jewish way of life, so they conceived the same two components of identity to be likewise distinguishable for all other Jews.

Rabbinic Judaism, dominant in Palestine and the Mesopotamian Diaspora, would eventually repudiate this Christian projection and reassert that Jewish religiosity and Jewish identity are one and indistinguishable. In the rabbinic view that became and has remained dominant in world Judaism, there are no "Judaists," only Jews. But this reassertion did not happen overnight: it took generations, even centuries. Neither the Romans nor the Jews nor the Christians themselves immediately understood the full novelty of what was coming into existence.

Through most of world history, in most parts of the world, what we are accustomed to call religion, ethnicity, culture, and way of life have been inextricable parts of a single whole. How did Christianity begin to become an exception to this general rule? On the one hand, it appropriated a set of Jewish religious ideas—including monotheism, revelation, covenant, scripture, sin, repentance, forgiveness, salvation, prophecy, messianism, and apocalypticism—without adopting the rest of the highly developed and richly nuanced Jewish way of life. On the other hand, it universalized these Jewish religious ideas, creating a new social entity, the church, through which non-Jews could be initiated into an enlarged version of the ancestral Jewish covenant with God. The Jews had believed for centuries God's declaration, "I am the LORD your God, who have separated you from the peoples" (Leviticus 20:24) and "you are a people holy to the LORD your God" (Deuteronomy 7:6). In effect, the Christian Jews split the idea of covenanted separateness and holiness from what consequently became the relatively secularized idea of nationality. The Jews were still a people, they maintained, but God had now revised and universalized the terms of his covenant. In the words of Jesus' apostle Peter, "Truly I perceive that God shows no partiality, but in every nation any one who fears him and does what is right is acceptable to him" (Acts 10:34–35).

The original Greek word for church, *ekklēsia*, suggests a collective understanding of church members as "called out" from other kinds of religious, ethnic, or political membership into this new—and now, in principle, universal—"people set apart as holy." The *ekklēsia* offered its members a sense of sacred peoplehood, but it tellingly lacked much else that ordinarily maintains a national identity. It had no ancestral land, no capital city, no language of its own, no literature at the start other than what it had inherited from the Jews, no distinct cuisine, no standard dress, and no political or governmental support beyond the organizational management of the church itself. Moreover, this ethnically mixed and socially unpromising group was atheist in its attitude toward all gods except the God of Israel as they had come to understand him—God as incarnate in Jesus the Messiah. Within the political culture of the Roman Empire, this rejection of the empire's gods was a seditious and rebellious rejection of Roman sovereignty itself. When, unsurprisingly, the empire recognized it as such and began intermittently to persecute the church, the Christian sense of separateness only grew.

In this form, and despite intermittent persecution, the church grew quietly but steadily for more than three centuries. At that point, with perhaps a fifth of the population of the Roman Empire enrolled in separate local Christian churches under relatively autonomous elected supervisors (bishops), the emperor Constantine (r. 312–37) first legalized Christianity and then stabilized its doctrine by requiring the Christian bishops—ordered to convene for the first time as a council at Nicaea, near his eventual capital city of Constantinople—to define it. In 381, the emperor Theodosius (r. 379–95) made this newly defined Christianity the official religion of the Roman Empire, and the new religion—no longer persecuted but now operating under a large measure of imperial control—began a fateful reversal of course. It began to fuse with the political governance and the Hellenistic culture of imperial Rome, compromising the character of the *ekklēsia* as a domain separate from nationality or culture. In a word, it began to normalize.

The establishment of Christianity as the state religion of the Roman Empire ushered in a period of rapid growth, pushed by the government, within the borders of the empire. Beyond them, however, most notably in the Persian Empire just to the east, its new status had the opposite effect.

Once relatively unhindered as a social movement taken to be as compatible with Persian rule as with Roman, Christianity now became suspect as the official religion of the enemy.

Meanwhile, in Rome itself—the "First Rome," as historically prior to the Eastern Empire's capital, Constantinople—and in the western European territories that it administered, a partial but significant return to the original separation of domains occurred just a century later. In 476, Odoacer, king of an invading Germanic tribe, deposed the last Roman emperor, Romulus Augustulus, without effectively assuming authority over the Christian church. Instead, the power of the bishop of Rome—the highest surviving official of the old imperial order—over the church in western Europe began to grow, while the power of kings and feudal lords over all that was not the church steadily grew as well. The nominally unified imperial authority over the empire and its established religion thus split apart. To be sure, for centuries the pope claimed the authority to anoint kings to their royal offices, and at certain moments this was a claim that could be sustained. But gradually, a sense that civilian and religious authority were different and separate began to set in. At the same time, the identity of the church as, once again, detached or disembedded from the state and from culture alike—the church as a potentially universal separate domain, a holy world unto itself—began to consolidate.

The Four-Cornered Medieval Map of Religion

Wealth, power, and population in the world west of India were concentrated during the sixth century in the Persian Empire and in the Eastern Roman or Byzantine Empire. Western Europe during the same century—all that had once been the Western Roman Empire—was far poorer, weaker, more sparsely populated, and culturally more isolated than the empires to its east. Then, during the seventh and eighth centuries, a third major power arose. Arabia had long provided mercenary soldiers to both of the then-dominant empires; but religiously inspired by the Islam newly preached by Muhammad (ca. 570–632) and militarily unified under his successors, it became a major world power in its own right with stunning speed. Arab armies conquered the entirety of the Persian Empire within a generation. Within a century, they had taken from the Eastern Roman Empire its Middle Eastern and North African possessions (half of its total territory) as well as the major Mediterranean islands. From what had been the Western Roman Empire, they had subtracted three-quarters of Spain and penetrated deep into France until driven back across the Pyrenees by the unprecedented European alliance that defeated them in the 732 Battle of Poitiers.

The political map of the world had been redrawn from India to the Atlantic, but what of the religious map? How did western European Christians now understand themselves among the religions of the world? The symbolic birth date of Europe as Christendom has long been taken to be Christmas Day of the year 800. On that date, Pope Leo III crowned Charles the Great, better known as Charlemagne—the grandson of Charles Martel, who had unified the European forces at Poitiers—as the first "Holy Roman Emperor." The Muslim invasion from distant Arabia had shocked an isolated and fragmented region into an early assertion of common religious and geographical identity. As a result, there was a readiness to give political expression to a dawning collective self-understanding. The lost Western Roman Empire was by no means reconstituted: Charlemagne was an emperor without much of an empire, his coronation expressing a vision more than a reality. But the vision itself mattered decisively in another way, for what came into existence at about this time was an understood quadripartite map of the world of religion that would remain standard in Europe for centuries.

There was, first and foremost for Christians, Christianity itself: the Christian church understood to be the same single, separate domain wherever it was found, with the same distinct relationship to national and cultural identity. To the extent that it rested on common faith, the church could be divided by heresy; but even heretical Christians, of whom there would be fewer in the early ninth century than there had been in earlier Christian centuries, were still understood to be Christians. They were practicing the right religion in a wrong way, but they were not practicing another religion altogether.

There was, second, Judaism: the Jews of Europe, a population living among Christians, disparaged but well known, whose relationship to Christianity was well remembered and whose religious authenticity rested on a recognized if more or less resented prior relationship with the same God that the Christians worshipped. Christian understanding of Jewish religious life as the Jews actually lived it was slender, and Christian knowledge of the vast rabbinic literature that had come into existence between the second and the ninth century, much of it in far-off Mesopotamia, was virtually nonexistent. Knowledge of Greek had been lost in Latin Europe, and knowledge of the Hebrew and Aramaic that the Jews of Europe had managed to preserve (despite recurrent persecution) was confined to them alone. Yet, this ignorance notwithstanding, Christian Europe was well aware that the Jews practiced a religion different from their own. And the implicit Christian understanding of religion as a separate domain of potentially universal extent was reinforced by the fact that from the outside, Jewish religious practice appeared to be at least as deeply divorced from national and cultural practices as was Christian religious practice: the Jews, who had lost their land and were dispersed around the world, lived in Europe much as Europe's Christians lived.

The third corner of Europe's four-cornered understanding of world religion was Islam, though the terms *Islam* and *Muslim* would not come into European usage until centuries later. Even the term *Arab* was not standard. The multinational religious commonwealth that we now call world Islam has been traditionally referred to by the Muslims themselves with the Arabic expression *dar al-islam*, the "House of Islam" or the "House of Submission" (because *islam* means "submission"—that is, submission to God). Whether it was *Saracen*, *Moor*, *Turk*, *or Arab*, the ethnic terms used by Christians to refer to the Muslims who faced them in the south and the east depended on time and place. Christendom as the Holy Roman Empire had become a domain geographically separate from the House of Islam. Similarly, Christianity as distinct from Christendom was evidently a domain of belief and practice separate from that of Islam. But among Christians, the further inference was that as Christian identity was separate from Bavarian or Florentine identity, so Muslim identity must be separate from Arab or Turkish identity. To some extent, this was a false inference, for obligatory Arabic in the Qur'an and obligatory pilgrimage to Mecca did much to preserve the originally Arab identity of Islam. Yet the tricontinental distribution and ethnic variability of the House of Islam fostered among Europeans an understanding of Islam as, like Christianity, a potentially universal religion separable from the ethnicity of any one of its component parts.

As Christian anxiety mounted that the year 1000 might mark the end of the world (an outcome that some Christians saw predicted in the New Testament book of Revelation), Muhammad came to be seen by some as the Antichrist, a destructive figure whose appearance during the last apocalyptic period before the end had been foretold (again in the book of Revelation). Yet gradually, albeit as "Mohammedanism," Islam came to be differentiated from Christianity in theological rather than in such floridly mythological terms. The Qur'an was translated into Latin in 1142. The High Middle Ages began to witness various forms of religious and cultural encounter—some as an unintended consequence of the Crusades; others through the influence of large Christian minorities living under Muslim rule and, over time, substantial Muslim minorities living under Christian rule, notably in Spain and Sicily. Finally, there was the mediating influence of a cross-culturally significant Jewish population residing on either side of the Muslim–Christian border and communicating across it. One result of these minglings was a gradually growing overlap in the techniques in use in all three communities for the exegesis of the sacred scriptures that for each mattered so much.

As Muslim monotheism came gradually into clearer focus, medieval Christianity came to recognize Muslims as worshippers of the same God that Jews and Christians worshipped. Meanwhile, Islam was, like Christianity, a religion that actively sought converts who were then made part of a separate quasi-national, quasi-familial, yet potentially universal social entity. The genesis of the Western understanding of religion as such—religion as a separate but expandable social category—was thus significantly advanced by Christianity's encounter with another social entity so like itself in its universalism and its relative independence from ethnic or cultural identity.

The fourth corner of the world religion square was occupied by a ghost—namely, the memory of long-dead Greco-Roman polytheism. Christianity was born among the urban Jews of the Roman Empire and spread gradually into the countryside. Even in largely rural Europe, monasteries functioned as surrogate cities and Christianity spread outward from these centers of structure and literacy. *Pagus* is the Latin word for "countryside," and in the countryside the old polytheisms lingered long after they had died out in the cities. Thus, a rural polytheist was a *paganus*, and *paganismus* (paganism) became synonymous with polytheism. In England, pre-Christian polytheism lingered in the inhospitable heath, and so *heathenism* became an English synonym for *paganism*. Though polytheism is not necessarily idolatrous (one may believe in many gods without making a single idol), polytheistic belief and idolatrous practice were generally conflated. More important for the centuries that lay ahead, the increasingly jumbled memory of what Greco-Roman polytheism—remembered as "paganism"—had been in the Christian past was projected upon the enormous and almost entirely unknown world beyond the realms occupied by Christians, Muslims, and Jews.

The quadripartite typology just sketched was only one long-lived stage in the development of the comparative study of religion in Christian Europe. We may pause to note, however, that as of the year 800 Judaism and Islam were operating under similar typologies. The Qur'an, definitive for all Islamic thought, takes frequent and explicit note of Judaism and Christianity, while the place occupied by the memory of Greco-Roman polytheism in Christianity is occupied in the Qur'an by the memory of polytheism as it existed in Arabia at the time when Muhammad began to receive his revelations. World Jewry, as a minority maintaining its identity and its religious practice in both Christendom and the House of Islam, had a richer experience of both Christians and Muslims than either of those two had of the other. Yet what functioned for Jews in the way that the memory of Greco-Roman polytheism functioned for Christians and the memory of Arabian polytheism functioned for Muslims was the memory of ancient Canaanite, Philistine, and Babylonian polytheism as recorded in the Bible and used thereafter as a template for understanding all those who were the enemies of God and the persecutors of his Chosen People.

Now, the comparison of two religions on terms set by one of them is like the similarly biased comparison of two nationalities: the outcome is a predictable victory for the side conducting the comparison. In fact, when religion and ethnicity are fused, religious comparison is commonly stated in ethnic terms rather than in what we would consider religious terms. Thus, in the Hebrew Bible, apostasy from the religion of Israel is called "*foreign* worship" (*'avodah zarah*) rather than simply false worship, though falsehood or worse is unmistakably implied. To the extent that ethnicity is taken to be a matter of brute fact, and therefore beyond negotiation, religion bound to ethnicity has seemed a nonnegotiable matter of fact as well.

In this regard, however, the condition of medieval Christian Europe was interestingly unstable. Demographically, the two largest religious realities it knew—Islam and Christianity itself—were consciously and ideologically multinational in character, and both actively sought converts from all nations. Judaism was not evangelistic in this way, but world Jewry was uniquely the world's first global nation: the bulk of its population was distributed internationally in such a way that Jews were accustomed in every place to distinguish their ethnicity from the ethnicity of the locale and their religion from its religion. Christian prejudice often prevented Jewish acculturation (not to suppose that Jews always wished to acculturate), but it did not always do so. And so during extended periods of Christian toleration, even the generally firm Jewish sense that religion, ethnicity, and culture were a seamless whole may have become more difficult to sustain. This three-sided—Christian, Muslim, and Jewish—embrace of the notion that religion was a separate domain set the stage in Europe for the comparison of the three on terms derived from a neutral fourth entity that was not to be equated with any one of them.

This fourth entity was Aristotelian philosophy as recovered in Europe during the eleventh and twelfth centuries. Of course, the philosophical discussions that began to be published—such as Abelard's mid-twelfth-century *Dialogue among a Philosopher, a Jew, and a Christian*, in which the philosopher of the title often appears to be a Muslim—always ended in victory for the imagined Christian. Yet Abelard (1079–1142) was eventually condemned by the church because his dialogue clearly recognized reason, mediated by philosophy, as independent of the religions being discussed and as capable of rendering judgments upon them all. Philosophy as that fourth, neutral party would be joined over time by psychology, sociology, anthropology, economics, evolutionary biology, cognitive science, and other analytical tools. But these enlargements lay centuries in the future. As the Middle Ages were succeeded by the Renaissance, philosophy had made a crucial start toward making neutral comparisons, even though Europe's quadripartite map of the world's religions was still quite firmly in place, with most comparisons still done on entirely Christian and theological terms.

The Renaissance Rehearsal of Comparative Religion

The Italian Renaissance—beginning in the fourteenth century and flourishing in the fifteenth and sixteenth—is commonly taken to be more important as a movement in art and literature than in philosophy or religion. To be sure, it did not attempt a transformation of European Christianity comparable to that of the Protestant Reformation of the sixteenth century. But the kind of religious comparison that began in the early eighteenth century, in the aftermath of Europe's devastating seventeenth-century Protestant–Catholic Wars of Religion, was foreshadowed during the Renaissance by the revival of classical Greek and Latin and by the recovery of masterpieces of world literature written in those languages.

First of all, perfected knowledge of Latin and the recovered knowledge of Greek enabled Italian scholars to publish critical editions of the texts of classical antiquity as well as philologically grounded historical criticism of such later Latin texts as the Donation of Constantine, exposed as a papal forgery by the Italian humanist Lorenzo Valla (1407–1457). It was in Renaissance Italy, too, that Christian Europe first recovered knowledge of biblical Hebrew. The earliest chair of Hebrew was established late in the fifteenth century at the University of Bologna. Despite repeated persecutions, ghettoizations, and expulsions, the Jewish population of Italy grew substantially during the Renaissance, enthusiastically embracing the then-new technology of printing with movable type. The first complete publication of the Hebrew Bible in the original, with Jewish commentaries, appeared in Venice in 1517 and proved highly instructive to Christian Europe; by the end of the following century, Italian scholars were even starting to read both the postbiblical rabbinic literature and the Kabbalah, writings in a later extra-rabbinic Jewish mystical tradition that fascinated some of them. Little by little, Christian Europe was beginning to learn from Europe's Jews.

As the Renaissance began to introduce Christian Europe by slow degrees to the critical examination of ancient texts as well as to the inner religious life of Judaism, it accomplished something similar in a more roundabout way for the lost religions of Greece and Rome. The humanists of the Renaissance did not believe in the gods and goddesses of Olympus as they believed in God the Almighty Father of Christianity, but even as they read the classical literature only as literature, they nonetheless were taken deep inside the creedal, ritual, imaginative, and literary life of another religion—namely, the lost Greco-Roman polytheism. During the Italian Renaissance, the term *humanist* (Italian *umanista*), we should recall, was not used polemically, as if in some sort of pointed contrast to *theist*. Rather, it was a declaration of allegiance to the humanizing, civilizing power of art and imaginative literature. Renaissance humanism's imaginative engagement with the religions of classical Greece and Rome thus constituted an unplanned rehearsal for the real-world, real-time imaginative engagements with non-Christian religions and cultures that lay immediately and explosively ahead for Europe. When the Spanish *conquistadores* encountered the living polytheism of Aztec Mexico, their first interpretive instinct was to translate the gods of Tenochtitlán into their nearest Greek and Roman equivalents. This was an intellectually clumsy move, to be sure, but less clumsy than interpreting them exclusively in monotheist Christian terms would have been. Moreover, because neither classical paganism nor Aztec polytheism was taken to be true, the two could be compared objectively or, if you will, humanistically—and from that early and fumbling act of comparison many others would follow.

In the study of philosophy, the Renaissance added Plato and various ancient Neoplatonists to the Aristotle of the medieval universities. More important, perhaps, it began to read late-classical moral philosophies—notably Stoicism and Epicureanism—whose frequent references to the gods made them in effect lost religions. Sometimes inspiring, sometimes scandalous, these recovered moral philosophies introduced personality and inner complexity into the inherited category of paganism. Philosophical recoveries of this sort could remain a purely academic exercise, but for that very reason their influence might be more subtly pervasive. Often, those who studied these texts professed to be seeking only their pro forma subordination to the truth of Roman Catholic Christianity. Nonetheless, the ideas found their way into circulation. To be sure, the few who took the further step of propagating pagan worldviews as actual alternatives to Christian faith or Aristotelian cosmology could pay a high price. The wildly speculative Neoplatonist Giordano Bruno (1548–1600) was burned at the stake as a heretic. But others, scarcely less speculative, spread their ideas with little official interference and in response to widespread popular curiosity.

Comparative Christianity in the Protestant Reformation

Important as the Renaissance was to the development in Europe of a capacity for religious comparison, the Protestant Reformation was surely even more important, for it forced Europeans in one region after another to compare forms of Christianity, accept one, and reject the others. Frequently, this lacerating but formative experience required those who had rejected Catholicism to reject one or more contending forms of Protestantism as well. This was clearly the case during the English Civil War (1642–51), which forced English Christians to side either with the Anglican king or with the Puritan rebels who beheaded him; but there were other such choices, some of them much more complicated.

Tentative moves toward tolerance during these struggles were far less frequent than fierce mutual persecution and, on either side, the celebration of victims as martyrs. The Catholics tried to dismiss and suppress the Protestants as merely the latest crop of Christian heretics. The Protestants commonly mythologized Rome as Babylon and compared Catholics to the ancient Babylonians, viewing them as pagans who had taken the New Israel, the Christian church, into exile and captivity. The century and a half of the reformations and the Wars of Religion certainly did not seem to promise a future of sympathetic, mutually respectful religious comparison. And yet within the religious game of impassioned mutual rejection then being played, each side did develop formidable knowledge of the practices, beliefs, and arguments of the other. To the extent that the broader religious comparison initiated during the Enlightenment of the late seventeenth and the eighteenth centuries called for close observation, firsthand testimony, logical analysis, and preparatory study of all kinds, its debt to both the Protestant Reformation and the Catholic Counter-Reformation is enormous.

Particularly important was the historical awareness that the Protestant Reformation introduced into Christian thought. Protestantism took the New Testament to be a historically reliable presentation of earliest Christianity and, using that presentation as a criterion, proceeded to reject the many aspects of Roman Catholic practice that appeared to deviate from it. To be sure, the Roman church had been reading, copying, and devotedly commenting on the Bible for centuries, but it had not been reading it as history. Here the Renaissance paved the way for the Reformation, for the Bible that Rome read was the Bible in a Latin translation; and the Renaissance, as it recovered the knowledge of Hebrew and Greek, had recovered the ability to read the original texts from which that Latin translation had been made. In 1516, the Dutch humanist Desiderius Erasmus published a bilingual, Greek-Latin edition of the New Testament, correcting the received Latin to bring it into conformity with the newly recovered Greek. Armed with this new tool, the many educated Europeans who knew Latin but not Greek could immediately see that the Latin on which the church had relied for a thousand years was at many points unreliable and in need of revision. In this way, Erasmus, a child of the Renaissance, took a first, fateful step toward historicizing the Bible.

The Reformation, launched just a year later with the publication by Martin Luther of "Ninety-Five Theses on the Power and Efficacy of Indulgences," would take the further, explosive step of historicizing the church itself. To quote a famous line from Reformation polemics, Erasmus "laid the egg that Luther hatched." Thus, two epoch-making historical tools of Protestantism as it would dynamically take shape became integral parts of the later comparative study of non-Christian religions as undertaken by Christian scholars: first, the reconstruction of the composition history of the original texts themselves by scholars who had mastered the original languages; and second, the comparison of later religious practice to earlier through the study of the recovered and historically framed original texts.

In one regard, finally, Protestantism may have indirectly contributed to the comparative study of religion by setting in motion a gradual subversion of the very understanding of religion as a domain separate from ethnicity and culture that had been constitutive of Christian self-understanding almost from its start. Mark C. Taylor argues brilliantly in *After God* (2007) that what is often termed the disappearance of God or the disappearance of the sacred in modernity is actually the integration of that aspect of human experience with the rest of modern experience—a process whose onset he traces to Martin Luther's and John Calvin's sanctification of all aspects of human life as against medieval Christianity's division of the religious life of monks and nuns from the worldly (secular) life of laypeople.[10]

This progressive modern fusion of once separate domains would explain the spread in the West of the experience of the holy in ostensibly secular contexts and of the aesthetic in ostensibly religious contexts. Clearly the earlier Christian sense of religion as a separate domain has lingered powerfully in the West. Yet if Taylor is right, then post-Protestant religious modernity in the West, though deeply marked by Protestantism, may be a paradoxical correction of Christianity to the world norm. Or, to put the matter more modestly, the diffuse post-Christian religiosity of the modern West may bear a provocative similarity to the much older but equally diffuse religiosity of South and East Asia or indeed of pre-Christian world Jewry.

Toleration, Science, Exploration, and the Need for a New Map

After decades of controversy climaxing in all-out war, it became clear to exhausted Protestants and Catholics alike that neither could dictate the religious future of Europe. The Wars of Religion came to a close in 1648 with the Peace of Westphalia, which, though it by no means established individual freedom of religion, did end international religious war in Europe. Its key principle—*Cuius regio, eius religio* (literally, "Whose the rule, his the religion")—allowed the king or the government of each nation to establish a national religion, but effectively banned any one nation from attempting to impose its religion upon another. At the international level, in other words, there was agreement to disagree. Christian religious fervor itself—at least of the sort that had burned heretics, launched crusades, and so recently plunged Europe into civil war—fell into relative disrepute. The latter half of the seventeenth century saw what Herbert Butterfield (1900–1979), a major historian of Christianity in European history, once called "the Great Secularization." [11]

The old religious allegiances remained, but by slow degrees they began to matter less, even as national allegiance and national devotion—patriotism, as it came to be called—began to take on the moral gravity and ceremonial solemnity of religious commitment and the fallen soldier began to supplant the martyr. In 1689, John Locke published *A Letter Concerning Toleration*, in which he advanced the idea that a state would better guarantee peace within its borders by allowing many religions to flourish than by imposing any one of them. Locke favored a division of the affairs of religion as essentially private from the affairs of state as essentially public, capturing an attitudinal shift that was already in the air during the Enlightenment and would significantly mark the comparative study of religion as it took lastingly influential shape in the following century.

More intensely than by nascent toleration, the mood of the late seventeenth century was marked by wonder at the discoveries of natural science, above all those of Isaac Newton, whose major work establishing the laws of motion and universal gravitation was published in 1687. The poet Alexander Pope captured the popular mood in a famous couplet, written as Newton's epitaph (1730): "Nature, and Nature's Laws lay hid in Night. / God said, *Let Newton be!* and All was *Light*." Light was the master image of the Enlightenment—light, light, and "more light" (the legendary last words of Johann Wolfgang von Goethe [1749–1832]). Though the notion of natural law did not begin with Newton, his vision of the vast, calm, orderly, and implicitly benign operation of the laws of motion and gravity was unprecedented and gave new impetus to the search for comparable natural laws governing many other phenomena, including religion. Was there such a thing as a natural religion? If so, how did Christianity or any other actual religion relate to it? This idea, too, was pregnant with the promise of a future comparative study of religion.

While northern European Christianity was fighting the Wars of Religion, southern European Christianity had been transforming both the demography of Christendom and its understanding of the physical geography of the planet. The globe-spanning Portuguese and Spanish empires came into existence with speed comparable only to the Arab conquests of the seventh and eighth centuries. In evangelizing the Americas, the Portuguese and the Spaniards may have made Christianity for the first time the world's largest religion. In any case, their success in establishing colonial trading outposts along the African, Indian, Japanese, and Chinese coasts as well as founding the major Spanish colony of the Philippine Islands (named for the king of Spain) meant that European trade with India and China, above all the lucrative spice trade, no longer needed to pass through Muslim Central Asia or the Muslim Middle East.

Catholic missionaries did not have the success in Asia that they enjoyed in the Americas, yet the highly educated and culturally sophisticated Jesuit missionaries to Asia and the Americas became a significant factor in the evolving religious self-understanding of Europe itself. As extensive reports on the religions of Mexico, Peru, and above all India, China, and Japan reached Europe, they were published and read by many others besides the religious superiors for whom they had been written. Portugal and Spain had opened Europe's doors to a vastly enlarged world. The centuries-old quadripartite European division of the world's religions—Christianity, Judaism, Islam, and Paganism—was still generally in place in European minds. But from that point forward, as the sophistication of the religions of Asia and the Americas as well as the material and social brilliance of their civilizations came into focus, the inadequacy of *paganism* as a catchall term became evident, as did the need for new ways to speak of the newly recognized reality.

A New Reference Book Defines a New Field of Study

If any occasion can be singled out as the juncture when all these factors coalesced and produced a powerful new engagement with *world religions* in a way that approached the modern understanding of that phrase, it is the publication in Amsterdam between 1723 and 1737 of an epochal reference work, one that should indeed be seen as a direct ancestor of *The Norton Anthology of World Religions.* Appearing in seven sumptuous volumes comprising more than 3,000 pages with 250 pages of engravings, this encyclopedic production was *Religious Ceremonies and Customs of All the Peoples of the World* (*Cérémonies et coutumes religieuses de tous les peuples du monde*) by Jean Frédéric Bernard and Bernard Picart. Here, for the first time, was a presentation in one large work of all the religions of the world then known to Europe. Here, for the first time, was an attempt to reckon with how Europe's religious self-understanding would have to change in light of the previous two centuries of exploration, far-flung evangelization, and colonization.

It is important to note that this work, which was an immediate success and went through many editions and translations (and plagiarizations and piracies) over the next two hundred years, did not begin in the academic world and spread outward to the general public. Its address was directly to the general literate public—to the French public first, but quickly to other publics reading other languages. Jean Frédéric Bernard, brilliant but far from famous, was not just its behind-the-scenes research director, editor, and author: he was also its entrepreneurial publisher. It was a masterstroke on his part to secure the collaboration of Bernard Picart, already famous as an engraver producing reproductions of masterpiece paintings in an era before public art museums and long before photography, when what the public knew about art was limited to what they saw in church or what they acquired as engravings. By enabling the European public to see Picart's depictions of Aztec and Asian temples, costumes, and ceremonies, reconstructed from missionaries' descriptions, Bernard and Picart introduced the stimulating possibility of visual comparison. Where visual comparison led, philosophical and other critical comparison were intended to follow—and did.

As noted above, in the latter decades of the seventeenth century and the first of the eighteenth John Locke and a few other thinkers began to argue forcefully for religious toleration. Like Locke, Bernard and Picart were radical Calvinists as well as early "freethinkers," and the Netherlands was unique in their lifetimes as a haven for refugee dissidents and minorities of various kinds. Locke himself took refuge in the Netherlands during a turbulent and threatening period in England. Bernard's Huguenot (French Calvinist) family had fled to the Netherlands when Jean Frédéric was a boy. Picart, having abandoned Catholicism, moved there permanently as an adult, joining a large émigré French or French-speaking population in Amsterdam. The Peace of Westphalia, though it had imposed mutual forbearance in religious matters at the international level, had not done so at the national level. Protestants were still severely persecuted in France, as were Catholics in England. In the Netherlands, by contrast, though Calvinists were overwhelmingly dominant in public life, the private practice of Catholicism was indulged, while Jews were allowed public worship, and even deists or atheists had little to fear from the government. So it happened that though their great work was written in French, Bernard and Picart had good reason to publish it in the Netherlands.

In their magisterial account of the making of this work, *The Book That Changed Europe: Picart and Bernard's "Religious Ceremonies of the World,"* the historians Lynn Hunt, Margaret C. Jacob, and Wijnand Mijnhardt speculate about another possible consequence of its publication in the Netherlands—namely, the relative oblivion that overtook it in the twentieth century. The most populous European nations have tended to understand the intellectual history of the West through the minds of their own most influential thinkers, then through those of their major rivals, and only then through authors, however important, whose works were written or published in the smaller nations. Be that as it may, "Picart," as the work was commonly called, had two lasting effects far beyond the borders of the Netherlands. First, by discussing and illustrating the religions of Asia and of the Americas at length, it ended forever the quadripartite division of the world's religions that had structured European thought for eight hundred years. Second, it further solidified the conception of religion as a domain separable from culture and ethnicity. To quote *The Book That Changed Europe*, "This global survey of religious practices effectively *disaggregated and delimited* the sacred, making it specific to time, place, and institutions."[12]

There was now a greatly enlarged universe of religions to reckon with, to be sure, and Christian "teach ye all nations" missionary universalism had already mobilized to engage it. But also now, more strongly than ever, there was "religion" as an incipiently secular category capable of growth: it had lately been expanded by several new members and conceivably could be expanded further as further reports came in. The universalism of this emergent understanding of religion explains in part why the French Revolution, at the end of the eighteenth century, could presume to declare the "Rights of Man" rather than merely "of the [French] Citizen."

Bernard's and Picart's personal libraries suggest two favorite areas of reading: the ancient classics and travel books. The three historians note that 456 travel books were published in Europe in the fifteenth century, 1,566 in the seventeenth, and 3,540 in the eighteenth.[13] The co-creators' reading in the classics put them in touch with that pluralism of the mind made possible by the Renaissance recovery of classical moral philosophy and by the humanists' imaginative participation in the beliefs that figure so largely in classical literature. Their avid reading of travel reports gave them the enlarged geographical awareness made possible by the age of exploration.

As an early theorist of religion in this transformed mise-en-scène, Bernard blended elements of deist "natural religion" with classic Protestantism. His discussion of the religious customs of the world was scholastically Protestant in its combination of meticulous footnotes and sometimes-strenuous argumentation. More important for its later influence, Bernard's discussion was structurally Protestant in that it cast contemporary religious practice, wherever it was observed around the world, as the corruption of an earlier purity. But where sixteenth-century Protestantism had seen the purity of primitive Christianity, Bernard, writing in the full flush of eighteenth-century enthusiasm for natural science, saw the purity of an early, universal, natural, and "true" religion corrupted by the variously scheming priests of the religions reviewed. Despite this structural Calvinism in their philosophy of religion, Bernard and Picard were indebted to John Locke as well as to John Calvin; and especially when the non-Christian religions were under discussion, their manner was more often expository than forensic.

There is no doubt that Bernard discusses and Picart illustrates the religious customs and ceremonies of the world on the assumption both that each religion is, like Christianity, a separate, practice-defined domain and that these domains are all comparable. For better and for worse, the two of them contributed massively to the establishment of "religion" as a category projecting elements of Christian identity upon the vast, newly discovered worlds that lay beyond Christendom. Discussing Bernard and Picart's treatment of indigenous American religion, Hunt, Jacobs, and Mijnhardt declare:

> In short, Picart's images, especially when read alongside Bernard's text, *essentially created the category "religion."* Whereas the text sometimes wandered off on tangents about the sources of particular ceremonies, the similarities between rituals across space (Jewish and Catholic) and time (Roman antiquity and American Indian), or the disputes between scholars on the origins of different peoples, the images kept the focus on the most commonly found religious ceremonies—birth, marriage, death rituals, and grand processions—or on the most strikingly different practices,

> which could range from the arcane procedures for the election of popes in Rome to human sacrifice in Mexico. Implicitly, the images transformed religion from a question of truth revealed to a select few of God's peoples (the Jews, the Catholics, and then the Protestants) to an issue of comparative social practices.[14]

The charge of Christian projection can plausibly be lodged against Picart and Bernard's interpretation of particular non-Christian rituals through their nearest equivalents in Christianity or Western antiquity. And yet if such habits of mind were limiting, they were scarcely crippling; and for Picart and Bernard themselves, they were evidently enabling and energizing. Is it true to say that between them, these two "essentially created the category 'religion'"? If they did so, we would claim, they did so largely through the convergence in their work and in themselves of the complex heritage that we have tried to sketch above.

Picart and Bernard carry forward the age-old, often suppressed, but never entirely forgotten understanding of the church as a thing in itself, not to be confounded with any nation or any set of cultural habits or practices. They carry forward the relatively subversive late medieval assumption that philosophy provides a neutral standpoint from which all religions may be compared. When considering religions remote from them in space rather than in time, they carry forward the Renaissance habit of drawing freely on classical paganism interpreted with textual sophistication and literary sympathy. They collate, as no one before them had yet done, the reports streaming into Europe about the religions of Asia and the Americas and, in their most brilliant stroke, they make these the basis for a major artistic effort to *see* what had been reported. They apply to their undertaking a distinct blend of moral seriousness, commercial enterprise, and erudite documentary attention to the particulars of religious practice that is their legacy from French Calvinist Protestantism. Finally, as sons of the Enlightenment, they bring a pioneering openness and breadth of vision to what they study.

Bernard can seem genuinely and intentionally prophetic when he writes:

> All religions resemble each other in something. It is this resemblance that encourages minds of a certain boldness to risk the establishment of a project of universal syncretism. How beautiful it would be to arrive at that point and to be able to make people with an overly opinionated character understand that with the help of charity one finds everywhere *brothers*.[15]

The place of good will—the sheer *novelty* of good will—in the study of religion has received far less attention than it deserves. Bernard's dream may seem commonplace now, when courteous interfaith dialogue is familiar enough in much of the West, but it was far from commonplace when he dreamed it.

Like *The Norton Anthology of World Religions*, Bernard and Picart's great work attended first and foremost to rituals and practices, considering beliefs only as expressed or embedded in these. Their work was path-breaking not just as a summary of what was then known about the religions of the world but also as an early demonstration of what sympathetic, participative imagination would later attain in the study of religion.

In painting their portraits of the religions of the world and in dreaming Bernard's dream ("How beautiful it would be . . . !"), Bernard and Picart were at the same time painting their own intellectual self-portrait as representative Europeans—neither clerics nor philosophers but thoughtful professionals—avid to engage in the comparison of the religions of the world on the widest possible scale. Religious comparison did not begin with them, nor had they personally created the intellectual climate in Europe that welcomed religious comparison once they so grandly attempted it. But it is not too much to say that in their day and to some significant degree because of them, Christian Europe finally learned how to compare religions.

Broadening the Foundation, Raising the Roof: 1737–1893

In 1737, when Picart and Bernard completed their work, Europe had barely discovered Australia. The peoples of the Arctic and of Oceania were living in nearly unbroken isolation. And even among peoples well-known to Europe, Japan was a forbidden kingdom, while China's first engagement with the West had only recently come to a xenophobic close. India was becoming relatively familiar, yet the doors of many smaller nations or regions remained barred. Europe had not yet lost its North and South American colonies to revolution; its later, nineteenth-century colonialist "scramble for Africa" had not yet begun. Russia had not yet expanded eastward to the Pacific. The English colonies in North America had not yet become the United States or expanded westward to the Pacific. The enlarged world that Bernard and Picart had sought to encapsulate in their illustrated reference work had many enlargements ahead, with corresponding consequences for the study of religion.

Though the intellectual framework for a global and comparative study of religion was essentially in place among an intellectual elite in Europe by the middle of the eighteenth century, much of even the known religious world remained culturally unexplored because the local languages were not understood. The accepted chronology within which Europeans situated new cultural and religious discoveries did not extend to any point earlier than the earliest events spoken of in the Old Testament. All this was to change during the century and a half that separates the publication of Picart from the convocation of the first World's Parliament of Religions at the 1893 Columbian Exposition in Chicago. That date may serve to mark the entrance of the United States of America into the story we have been telling and will bring us to the more immediate antecedents of *The Norton Anthology of World Religions.*

Broadening the Textual Base

Of special relevance for our work as anthologists is the enormous broadening of the textual foundation for religious studies that occurred during this long period. To review that transformation, we will consider the pivotal roles played by four European linguistic prodigies: F. Max Müller (1823–1900), James Legge (1815–1897), Sir William Jones (1746–1794), and Eugène Burnouf (1801–1852). One may grasp at a glance the scope of the documentary change that took place during the 150 years that followed the publication of Bernard and Picart's *Religious Ceremonies and Customs of All the Peoples of the World* by looking forward to the London publication between 1879 and 1910 of *The Sacred Books of the East* in no fewer than fifty volumes.

This enormous reference work, a superlative and in some regards still unsurpassed academic achievement, was produced under the general editorship of F. Max Müller, a German expatriate long resident in England. Müller's role in the nineteenth-century evolution of the disciplines of both comparative linguistics and comparative religious studies is large, but for the moment what concerns us is the sheer scope of the landmark reference work that he edited: two dozen volumes on Hinduism and Jainism translated into English from Sanskrit; nine on Buddhism alike from Sanskrit, from Pali (the canonical language of Indian Buddhism), and from other Asian languages; seven from Chinese on Confucianism, Daoism, and Chinese Buddhism; eight from Persian on Zoroastrianism; and two from Arabic on Islam. The range is astonishing, given that at the time when Bernard and Picart were writing and engraving, knowledge of *any* of these languages, even Arabic, was rare to nonexistent in Europe. How did Europeans learn them over the intervening century and a half? What motivated them to do so? The story blends missionary daring, commercial ambition, and sheer linguistic prowess in different proportions at different times.

Let us begin with Chinese. The first two modern Europeans known to have mastered Chinese were the Italian Jesuit missionaries Michele Ruggieri (1543–1607) and the preternaturally gifted Matteo Ricci (1552–1610), who entered China from the Portuguese island colony of Macao. Over time, as French Jesuits largely succeeded their Italian brethren in the Jesuit mission to China, the reports that they sent back to France about Qing dynasty (1644–1912) culture and the Confucian scholars they encountered stimulated French and broader European curiosity both about China itself and about the Chinese language. Though the Vatican terminated the Jesuits' Chinese mission on doctrinal grounds and though the Qing dynasty suppressed further Christian missionary work and expelled the missionaries themselves in 1724, a seed had been planted. In retirement on Macao, the French Jesuit Joseph Henri Marie de Prémare would compose the first-ever Chinese grammar in 1729. Later, during the nineteenth century, as Britain forced a weakening Qing dynasty to sign a treaty establishing coastal enclaves or "treaty ports" under British control, British Protestants commenced a new round of missionary activity in China, including the first attempt to translate the Bible into Chinese.

James Legge, originally a Scottish missionary to China, building on de Prémare's grammar and working with the help of Chinese Christians, undertook a major effort to translate the principal Confucian, Daoist, and Chinese Buddhist classics into English, always with the ultimate intention of promoting Christianity. Meanwhile, in 1814, Europe's first chair of Chinese and Manchu was established at the Collège de France. In 1822, Jean-Pierre Abel-Rémusat published in France a formal grammar of Chinese intended not for missionaries alone but for all interested European students. Legge himself became Oxford University's first professor of Chinese in 1876, and near the end of his life he was F. Max Müller's principal collaborator for Chinese texts in *The Sacred Books of the East*.

European penetration into China proceeded almost entirely from offshore islands or coastal enclaves under European colonial control; China as a whole never became a Western colony. India, by contrast, did indeed become a Western colony—specifically, a British colony—and the West's acquisition of the Indian languages and first encounter with the Indian religious classics is largely a British story. From the sixteenth through the early eighteenth century, Portuguese, Dutch, French, and British commercial interests vied for primacy in the lucrative Indian market. By late in the eighteenth century, however, Britain had overtaken all European rivals and established India, including what is now Pakistan, as its most important future colony—more lucrative at the time than the thirteen North American colonies that would become the United States of America. Britain's colonial motives were originally commercial rather than either evangelical or academic, but after British commercial and political control was firmly established in the Indian subcontinent, first cultural and linguistic explorations and then Christian missionary activity would follow.

In the launch of Sanskrit studies in the West, no figure looms larger than Sir William Jones, an Anglo-Welsh jurist in Calcutta who was at least as prodigiously gifted in language study as Matteo Ricci or James Legge. Fascinated by all things Indian, Jones founded an organization, the Asiatic Society, to foster Indian studies; and in 1786, on its third anniversary, he delivered a historic lecture on the history of language itself. In it, he expounded the thesis that Sanskrit, Greek, Latin, most of the European vernacular languages, and probably Persian were all descendants of a vanished common ancestor. Today, linguistic scholarship takes for granted the reality of "Proto-Indo-European" as a lost ancient language whose existence is the only conceivable explanation for the similarities that Jones may not have been the very first to chart but was certainly the first to bring to a large European public.

Jones's lecture detonated an explosion of European interest in studying Sanskrit and in tracing the family tree of the Indo-European, or "Aryan," languages, including all the languages mentioned in the previous paragraph but notably excluding Hebrew and Arabic—descendants of a different linguistic ancestor, later postulated as Proto-Semitic. (In the Bible, it is from Noah's son Shem—*Sēm* in Greek—that the peoples of the Middle East are descended—whence the term *Sem*-itic.) Now, the New Testament had been written in Greek rather than Hebrew or Aramaic, and Western Christianity had quickly left its Aramaic-speaking Palestinian antecedents behind and become a Greek-speaking Mediterranean religion. Did that mean that Christianity was actually Indo-European, or "Aryan," rather than Semitic, even though Jesus and Paul were Jews? This became one cultural strand within the European enthusiasm for Sanskrit studies, as further discussed below. Suffice it to say for now that it was during this period that *Semitic* and *Semitism* were coined as linguistic terms and the anti-Jewish *anti-Semitic* and *anti-Semitism* were coined as prejudicial, pseudo-anthropological counterterms.

Of greater immediate importance for the broadening of the study of religion was the window that Sanskrit opened on an almost unimaginably vast Indian literature whose most ancient and venerated texts, the Vedas, may be as old as, or even older than, the oldest strata of the Old Testament. Sanskrit is the classical language of India, no longer spoken and perhaps artificially perfected as a sacred language at some unrecoverable point in the past. But India has in addition a great many vernacular languages, more of them than Europe has, and in a number of these languages, other extensive Hindu literatures exist. These, too, gradually came to light in the nineteenth and the early twentieth century as knowledge of the relevant languages gradually spread to Europe.

India, for all its immense internal variety, did and does have a sense of itself as a single great place and of its gods as the gods of that place. Siddhartha Gautama, the Buddha, was born in India, and Indian Buddhism was the first Buddhism. Buddhist texts in Sanskrit are foundational for all students of Buddhism. But after some centuries had passed, Buddhism largely died out in India, living on in Sri Lanka, Southeast Asia, China, Korea, Japan, Mongolia, and Tibet. The linguistic and cultural variety of these countries was enormous. The Buddha was not called by the same name in all of them (in China, for example, he was called "Fo"). Western travelers, not knowing the languages of any of the countries where Buddhism was dominant, were slow to recognize even such basic facts as that the Buddha himself was a historical personage and not simply one among the many deities and demons whose statues they saw in their travels.

Donald S. Lopez, Jr., Buddhism editor for *The Norton Anthology of World Religions*, has written or edited several books telling the fascinating tale of how the puzzle of international Buddhism slowly yielded to the painstaking Western acquisition of several difficult languages and the related gradual recovery of a second, astoundingly large multilingual religious literature standing alongside that of Hinduism. In his *From Stone to Flesh: A Short History of the Buddha* (2013), Lopez allows what we might call the statue story—the gradual realization that sculptures of the Buddha represented a man, not a god—to become the human face on this much larger and less visible story of literary and historical recovery.[16]

In the story of how a broad textual foundation was laid for the study of Buddhism, a third linguistic genius stands between the Anglo-Welsh William Jones and the expatriate German F. Max Müller—namely, the French polymath Eugène Burnouf, the last of the four gifted linguists mentioned near the start of this section. Because of the enthusiasm for Sanskrit studies that Jones had touched off in Europe, copies of texts in Sanskrit began reaching European "orientalists" during the first decades of the nineteenth century. Those that arrived from India itself, as they were translated, would enable the assembly of the twenty-one volumes of Hindu texts that open Müller's *Sacred Books of the East.* Initially, however, no Sanskrit texts dealing with Buddhism were forthcoming from the Indian subcontinent. This situation would change, thanks to the fortuitous posting of an energetic and culturally alert English officer, Brian Houghton Hodgson (1801?–1894), to Nepal, where Buddhism thrived. Hodgson collected dozens of Nepalese Buddhist texts in Sanskrit, including the crucially important *Lotus Sutra*, and arranged for copies to be shipped to Europe.

Burnouf had been appointed to the Sanskrit chair at the Collège de France five years before the first shipment from Hodgson arrived. Thanks in part to earlier work he had done in the study of Pali, the Indian language in which the oldest Buddhist texts survive, Burnouf seems to have quickly grasped that what he had before him was the key to the historical roots of Buddhism in India. But this recognition was father to the further insight that Buddhism was the first true world religion (or, as he was inclined to think, the first internationally embraced moral philosophy) in human history. Burnouf was among the first, if not the very first, to see Buddhism whole. His 1844 *Introduction à l'histoire du Buddhisme indien* (*Introduction to the History of Indian Buddhism*) was the first of a projected four volumes that, had he lived to write them, would surely have been his greatest work. The one lengthy volume that he did bring to completion was already of epoch-making importance, particularly in light of his influence on his student F. Max Müller.

What the discovery and European importation of the classical religious literatures of India and China meant for the comparative study of religion in the West can be signaled concisely in the terms *Confucianism*, *Daoism* (earlier, *Taoism*), *Hinduism*, and *Buddhism*. They are all Western coinages, hybrids combining an Asian word at the front end and the Greek morpheme *–ism* at the back end, and each represents the abstraction of a separate domain of religious literature and religious practice from the cultural and ethnic contexts in which it originated. The coinage of these terms themselves may not coincide exactly with the recovery of the respective literatures; but to the extent that nineteenth-century Western scholarship viewed the texts as the East's equivalent of the Bible, it all but unavoidably engaged them on structurally Christian and even Protestant terms, thereby furthering the European conception of each related *–ism* as a religion in Europe's now consolidated and universalist sense of the word.

Structurally, Protestant influence was apparent again whenever, in the manner of Bernard and Picart, the great nineteenth-century linguist-historians judged the early texts to be superior to the later ones. Thus, in the interpretation of newly available Chinese texts, the earlier, more interior or "philosophical" versions of Daoism and Confucianism were often judged superior to the later, more ceremonial or "religious" versions, in which Laozi or Kongzi (Confucius) seemed to be deified or quasi-deified. Similarly, in the nineteenth-century interpretation of Hindu literature, India's British colonial rulers celebrated the supposed nobility and purity of the early Vedas and Upanishads while disparaging later Hindu religious texts and especially actual nineteenth-century Hindu practice. In the Buddhist instance, Eugène Burnouf set the early, human, historical Indian Buddha—whom he understood to have preached an ethics of simplicity and compassion—against the later, superhuman metaphysical Buddha. Consciously or unconsciously, Burnouf's contrast of the historical and the metaphysical Buddha coincided strikingly with the contrast then being drawn for a wide Christian audience between the historical Jesus of Nazareth and the divine God incarnate of Christian faith.

In short, as this new, broadened textual foundation was laid for the documentary study of Hinduism, Buddhism, and Daoism, a Christian theology of scripture and a post-Protestant philosophy of history were often projected upon it by the brilliant but Eurocentric scholars who were shaping the field. However, once primary texts are in hand, their intrinsic power can exert itself against any given school of interpretation. Thus, for example, late twentieth-century scholarship began to foreground and valorize the late and the popular over the early and the elite in several traditions, dignifying texts and practices once thought unworthy of serious scholarly attention.

Though nineteenth-century scholars might shudder at such a shift, it is essentially to them that we owe the availability of the key texts themselves. To be sure, the full recovery and the translation of these literatures are works in progress; nonetheless, knowledge of their great antiquity and their scope—barely even dreamed of by Picart and Bernard—was substantially complete by the end of the nineteenth century. The literary foundation had been put in place for an enormously enlarged effort at comparative study.

Enlarging the Chronological Frame

As already noted, Europeans as late as the early nineteenth century situated new cultural and religious discoveries, including all the texts whose recovery we have been discussing, in a chronology of religion understood to commence no earlier than the earliest events spoken of in the Old Testament. This framework led to efforts, comical in retrospect, to link newly discovered places and newly encountered legends or historical memories in Asia and the Americas to place-names in the book of Genesis, to the Noah story of Genesis 6–9, and to legends about the eastward travels of the apostles of Christ. All this would change with a discovery that might be described as blowing the roof off recorded history.

During Napoleon Bonaparte's occupation of Egypt in 1798–99, a French soldier stationed near the town of Rosetta in the Nile delta discovered a large stone bearing an inscription in three scripts: first, ancient Egyptian hieroglyphics, a script that no one then could read; second, another unknown script, which turned out to represent a later form of the Egyptian language; and finally, a third script, Greek. It took two decades of work, but in 1822, Jean-François Champollion deciphered this "Rosetta Stone." In the ensuing decades, his breakthrough enabled later scholars to translate hundreds of ancient Egyptian hieroglyphic inscriptions recovered from the ruins of ancient Egypt's immense tombs and temples and to discover, as they did so, that the Egyptians had maintained a remarkably complete chronology stretching back millennia before the oldest historical events recorded in the Bible. Decades of archaeological excavation in Egypt further enabled the construction of a chronological typology of Egyptian pottery. And then, since Egyptian pottery and pottery fragments are found all over the ancient Near East in mounds (tells) left by the repeated destruction and reconstruction of cities on the same sites, Egyptian pottery could be used to date sites far removed from Egypt. Over time, the Egyptian chronology would become the anchor for a chronological reconstruction of the entire lost history of the Near East, much of it written on thousands of archaeologically recovered clay tablets inscribed in the Mesopotamian cuneiform script that at the start of the eighteenth century was as undecipherable as Egyptian hieroglyphic.

The cuneiform (literally, "wedge-shaped") writing system was used as early as the late fourth millennium B.C.E. for the representation of Sumerian, a mysterious language without known antecedents or descendants. Sumeria, the oldest civilization of the ancient Near East—situated near the southern tip of Iraq, just north of the Persian Gulf—appears to have invented cuneiform writing. Most extant cuneiform texts, however, survive as small tablets representing several ancient Semitic languages rather than Sumerian. Starting in the mid-nineteenth century, hundreds of thousands of cuneiform tablets were recovered by archaeological excavations nearly as important as those in Egypt.

Cuneiform was deciphered thanks to the discovery in Persia in 1835 of a trilingual set of incised cuneiform wall inscriptions in Behistun (Bisitun, Iran) that, like the Rosetta Stone, included one already-known language—in this case ancient Persian—that scholars were eventually able to recognize behind the mysterious script. The challenge lay in going beyond the Persian of that inscription to decipher the language—now known to be the Mesopotamian Semitic language Akkadian—represented by one of the other two inscriptions. Though Eugène Burnouf played almost as important a role in this decipherment as he played in the recovery of Indian Buddhism, it is Henry Rawlinson, the British East India Company officer who first visited the Behistun inscriptions in 1835, whose name is usually linked to the recovery for European scholarship of the lost cuneiform literatures of Mesopotamia.

None of the now-extinct religions whose literatures survive in cuneiform is anthologized in *The Norton Anthology of World Religions*; we have chosen only major, living international religions. But the recovery of these lost literatures significantly affected the evolving historical context for all religious comparison. What these texts made clear was that recorded history had not dawned in Athens and Jerusalem. The religion of ancient Israel, in particular, was relocated from the dawn of history to a late morning hour, and thus could no longer be seen as in any sense the ancient ancestor of all the religions of the world. On the contrary, it now became possible to study the Bible itself comparatively, as a text contemporaneous with other texts, produced by a religion contemporaneous with and comparable to other ancient Semitic religions. And since the Bible is an anthology produced over a millennium, it became possible and even imperative to study each stratum within the Bible as contemporaneous with differing sets of non-Israelite religions and their respective texts.

European Protestantism, accustomed since the Reformation to employing the Bible as a historically reliable criterion for criticizing and revising the inherited practices of Christianity, was deeply affected by the discovery of both prebiblical and contemporaneous extrabiblical literatures, for they were clearly a way to deepen the historical understanding of the Bible. But the recovery of these literatures, set alongside related evidence from archaeological excavation, was a threat as well as an opportunity. It was an opportunity because it enabled illuminating comparisons of key motifs in Hebrew mythology with their counterparts in other ancient Near Eastern mythologies; it was a threat because though it corroborated the historicity of some biblical events, it undermined that of others.

Arguably, religious truth can be conveyed as well through fiction as through history. Patristic and medieval Christianity had been content for centuries to search the Bible for moral allegories rather than for historical evidence. Where history was not a central concern, comparative Semitic studies could and did enrich the linguistic and literary interpretation of the Bible without impugning its religious authority. But because Protestantism, rejecting allegorical interpretation, had consistently emphasized and valorized the historical content of the Bible, Protestant Christianity had particular trouble entertaining the notion that the Bible could be historically false in some regards and yet still religiously valid. A desire to defend the Old Testament as historically valid thus arose as a second motivation for Semitic studies. In the process, the prestige of the study of history itself as an intellectual discipline able to produce authoritative judgments about religion was significantly enhanced if not indeed somewhat inflated.

The discovery of the Rosetta Stone and the Behistun inscriptions affected the comparative study of Islam as well, though less directly. The recovery of lost Semitic languages and their lost literatures invited comparative linguistic study of the now-increased number of languages clearly related to Aramaic, Hebrew, and Arabic—the three principal languages of this family that were already known at the end of the eighteenth century. This study led to the postulated existence of a lost linguistic ancestor, Proto-Semitic, from which they were all plausibly descended. Proto-Semitic then began to play a role in the study of the religions practiced by the peoples who spoke these languages, somewhat like the role that Proto-Indo-European was playing in the study of the religions practiced by the peoples who spoke Sanskrit, Greek, Latin, German, and the other languages of that linguistic family.

As Proto-Semitic was reconstructed, moreover, it became clear to scholars that classical Arabic, the Arabic of the Qur'an, resembled it very closely and thus was an extremely ancient language that preserved almost the entire morphology of the lost ancestor of all the Semitic languages. Classical Hebrew, by contrast, was shown to be a much younger Semitic language. In an era of so much speculation about the relationship between ancient religions and ancient languages, the near-identity of classical Arabic and Proto-Semitic suggested to some that Islam might have preserved and carried forward ancient features of a Semitic proto-religion that was the lost ancestor of all the Semitic religions, just as Proto-Semitic was the lost ancestor of all the Semitic languages.

Orientalism, Neo-Hellenism, and the Quest for the Historical Jesus

The emergence of "Semitic languages" and "Semitic religions" as groups whose members were identifiable through comparison meant that biblical studies and Qur'anic studies—or more generally the study of ancient Israel and that of pre- and proto-Islamic Arabia—were more closely linked in the nineteenth century than they usually are in the twenty-first. Julius Wellhausen (1844–1918), a major German biblical scholar, reconstructed the formative stages of both. Historical linguists in Wellhausen's day who engaged in such comparative study of languages and history were called "orientalists." *Orientalism* is a term now associated with cultural condescension to the peoples of a region extending from Turkey through Persia to the borders of Afghanistan; but when first coined, it connoted primarily a stance of neutral comparison across that large cultural realm, a realm that the study of the languages, ancient and modern, had now thrown open for historical study as never before.

Interest in the language and history of classical Greece also grew enormously in nineteenth-century Europe, fed both by Hellenic revivalism and by Christian anxiety. The upper class generally celebrated Greek literature and thought as expressing a humane ideal distinct from and even superior to that of Christianity. In the late eighteenth century, in his *The History of the Decline and Fall of the Roman Empire* (1776–88), the English historian Edward Gibbon had already presented the emergence of Christianity as in itself the key factor in the decline of a superior classical civilization; Gibbon elevated the nobility and civic virtue of republican Rome above the faith, hope, and charity of Pauline Christianity as celebrated by classic Protestantism.

In the nineteenth century, it was Greece rather than Rome that defined the cultural beau ideal for an intellectual elite across western Europe. The German philosopher Friedrich Nietzsche (1844–1900), a classicist by training, was steeped in this philo-Hellenic tradition and drew heavily upon it for his well-known critique of Christianity. In its devout classicism, nineteenth-century European culture thus continued and intensified a celebration of an idealized and indeed a more or less mythologized Greece that had begun during the Renaissance and continued during the Enlightenment.

This European cultural identification with Greece, whether or not tinged with antipathy toward Christianity, sometimes worked symbiotically with a larger geographical/cultural identification already mentioned—namely, Europe's identification with the larger world of the Indo-European peoples as distinct from and superior to the disparaged Semitic peoples, most notably the Jews. Religiously motivated Christian prejudice against Jews had by no means disappeared, but it was now joined by a form of pseudo-scientific racism that made more of national than of religious difference. Because nationalist self-glorification linked to invidious anti-Semitism had a seriously distorting effect on the comparative study of religion in nineteenth-century Europe, the full enfranchisement of Europe's Jews as fellow scholars would have, as we will see, a comparably important corrective effect.

A second motivation for classical studies, especially in Lutheran Germany, was Christian: an urgently felt need to write the still-unwritten history of the New Testament in the context of first-century Hellenistic Judaism. The historical reliability of the New Testament had been the foundation of the Lutheran critique of sixteenth-century Catholicism. But nineteenth-century New Testament scholars now claimed to recognize adulterations by the church within the Gospels themselves. To exaggerate only slightly, the challenge that nineteenth-century Protestant scholars saw themselves facing was to recover the historical Jesus from the church-corrupted Gospels in the same way that they understood the sixteenth-century reformers to have recovered the historical practice of Christianity from the corrupted church practice of their day.

"Historical Jesus" scholarship of this sort grew enormously in scope and erudition during the first decades of the nineteenth century, fed by the growing prestige of history as a social science and climaxing with the publication in 1835–36 of David Friedrich Strauss's massive, learned, sensationally successful, but scandalously skeptical *Life of Jesus, Critically Examined*, a German work that appeared in English in 1846 in an anonymous translation by the aspiring English novelist George Eliot (Marian Evans). Decades of further scholarship followed, some of it indirectly stimulated once again by archaeology. As the excavations by Heinrich Schliemann (1822–1890) proved that there was a Troy and that a great war had occurred there, thus allegedly proving the historical reliability of the *Iliad*, so, it was hoped, further archaeological and historical research might yet demonstrate the historical reliability of the New Testament.

A denouement occurred in 1906 with the publication of the German first edition of Albert Schweitzer's epoch-making *The Quest of the Historical Jesus.*[17] Schweitzer believed that the quest for the historical Jesus had actually succeeded as history. Yet the recovered historical Jesus was more a problem for contemporary Christianity than a solution, the renowned scholar ruefully concluded. Schweitzer's work continues to haunt historical Jesus scholarship, even though fresh quests and fresh alleged recoveries of the lost historical Jesus, both learned and popular, have continued to appear.

In sum, narrowly Christian though the quest for the historical Jesus may seem, it did much to establish historical study as the default mode of religious study. Its shadow lies across studies of the historical Buddha, the historical Laozi, and the historical Muhammad, among others, stamping them all with the assumption that in the study of any religious tradition, historical truth will prove the indisputable form of truth.

The Haskalah and Its Impact on the Comparative Study of Religion

The character of the literature of religious studies is determined as much by who is writing as by what is written about. So far, we have concentrated on changes in what was available as subject matter to be written about, thanks to the recovery of religious literatures either lost in time or remote in place. We turn now to a new line of inquiry and a new question: Who was to be commissioned to conduct the study, to do the writing, to tell the story of the religions of the world? In the late eighteenth and the nineteenth centuries, above all in Germany, a Jewish religious, cultural, and intellectual movement called the *Haskalah* emerged, one of whose effects would be the historic enfranchisement of Jews as, for the first time, full participants in Europe's comparative study of religion. Before saying more about the impact of the Haskalah upon secular religious studies in Europe, we should briefly review its direct and complex impact upon the Jews of Europe themselves.

Religiously, thanks in good measure to the pathbreaking work of the Jewish-German philosopher Moses Mendelssohn (1729–1786), the Haskalah gave rise to Reform Judaism as a revised form of Jewish belief and practice more attentive to the Tanakh, or Hebrew Bible (Christianity's Old Testament), than to the Talmud. However uncontroversial it may seem in the twenty-first century for the reformers to honor the biblical prophets rather than the Talmudic sages as the ethical pinnacle of the Jewish tradition, the shift was highly disruptive in the late eighteenth and the nineteenth centuries, for the emphasis in Jewish religious practice until then had been squarely on the Talmud and on the rabbinical sages whose debates, preserved in the Talmud, had made the rabbinate the final authority in Jewish religious observance. In the rabbinic tradition, the Talmud is the heart of the "Oral Torah" that Moses, the original rabbi (teacher), received from God and conveyed in speech to his first (rabbinical) students, beginning a teacher-to-student chain that legitimated the rabbinate as authoritative. To undercut the Talmud, Rabbinic Judaism's foundational second scripture, was thus to undercut the rabbis themselves.

Reform Judaism was religiously unsettling in another way because by going back to the Bible, thereby setting aside centuries of venerable Jewish tradition and subverting established rabbinical religious authority, its founders, beginning with Moses Mendelssohn, delivered a critique that bore a striking structural resemblance to German Lutheranism's back-to-the-Bible critique of Roman Catholicism. The Jewish reformation looked rather like the Christian, to the exhilaration of many Jews at the time in Lutheran northern Germany but to the consternation of others.

Religiously disruptive in these ways, the Haskalah—often referred to as the Jewish Enlightenment—represented as well a major turning point in Jewish European cultural life, away from oppressive and once inescapable social restriction and confinement. The *Maskilim*, as the leaders of the Haskalah were called, recognized that the dawn of a culture of toleration in Christian Europe might just light the path to an escape for Jews who were willing to acculturate in certain manageable ways. Mendelssohn himself, for example, became an acknowledged master of literary German as written by the intellectual elite of Berlin. German culture was then entering its most brilliant century. In an earlier century, German Jews would have had to become Christians to exit the ghetto and take part. But absent the requirement to convert, perhaps German Jews could become Jewish Germans. Such was the tacit hope of the Haskalah.

As Reform Judaism grew in popularity, thousands of Jews gambled that the ghetto walls were indeed coming down, and ultimately they were not mistaken. Despite the murderous anti-Semitism that would rise in the later nineteenth century and the genocide that would so profoundly scar the twentieth, a page had been turned for good in Western academic life—not least in the comparative study of religion.

For this anthology, the Haskalah mattered in one further, only slightly narrower regard: while no longer deferring to the immense corpus of rabbinic literature as authoritative, the Maskilim did not ignore it. On the contrary, they began to apply to it the same techniques of critical scholarship that the Renaissance had pioneered and that Protestantism and the Enlightenment had further developed for the interpretation of the Bible and other classical texts. The process of critically editing and translating the rabbinic literature, which placed yet another major religious literature within the reach of secular study, began very slowly and approached completion only in the twentieth century. Yet were it not for the Maskilim, that great work would not have been undertaken.

Most important of all, however, was the inclusion of Christianity's original "other" in the corps of those attempting in the West to make comparative sense of the religions of the world. This inclusion was truly a watershed event, for it foreshadowed a long list of subsequent, cumulatively transformative inclusions of the previously excluded. Religious studies in the twenty-first century is open to all qualified participants, but such has not always been the case. Broadening the textual basis for religious studies and exploding the temporal frame around it were important nineteenth-century developments. Broadening the composition of the population that would engage in religious studies was even more important.

The gradual inclusion of non-Christian scholars in the Western discussion of world religions has not entailed retiring the historically Christian but now secularized concept of religion (or the related concept of world religions), but Christian or Western scholars have lost any presumptive right to serve as moderators or hosts of the discussion. The overcoming of insufferable condescension, not to speak of outright prejudice, has played a part, but so too, and more importantly, have matters of perception, perspective, and the "othering" of Christianity: the rest had long been accustomed to see themselves through the eyes of the West; now the West has begun to see itself through the eyes of the rest.

The dynamic entry of Europe's Jews not just into the European study of religion but also into many other areas of European life brought about a massive backlash in the late nineteenth century, then the Nazi genocide in the twentieth, the post–World War II triumph of Zionism, and belatedly, among other consequences, a distinct mood of remorse and repentance in late twentieth-century European Christianity.[18] Somewhat analogous emotions accompanied the end of European colonialism during the same late twentieth-century decades amid exposés of the exploitation and humiliation suffered by the colonized. The comparative study of religion has both influenced and been influenced by these ongoing revisionist shifts of mood and opinion, but, to repeat, the first steps down this long path were taken by and during the Haskalah.

Evolution and the Comparative Study of Religion

While the decipherment of Egyptian hieroglyphic and Mesopotamian cuneiform were still throwing new light on the earliest centuries of recorded history, Charles Darwin's *On the Origin of Species by Means of Natural Selection* in 1859 and *The Descent of Man, and Selection in Relation to Sex* in 1871 shone a beam into the deeper darkness of the unrecorded, biological prehistory of the human species. At the time, no one, including Darwin, knew just how old *Homo sapiens* was as a species; the technique of absolute dating by the measurement of radioactive decay would not be developed until the mid-twentieth century. What Darwin could already demonstrate from the fossil record, however, was that the human species had evolved from earlier species in a process that antedated recorded history. The implications of this discovery for all forms of scientific and historical investigation were enormous and are still being explored. For the study of religion, the discovery meant that behind the religions of recorded history, there now stood in principle all the religions of human prehistory. At what point in human evolution did religion first appear, or was that even the right question? Should the question rather be about precursors to religion—earlier behaviors that would evolve into what we now call religion? How, if at all, could the practitioners of these prehistoric proto-religions or precursors to religion be studied?

Answers to that question are still being devised, but none involves their texts, for they left none. Tempting as it would be to explore new work being done on the evolution of religion before the invention of writing, such work is not properly a part of the study of religion to which *The Norton Anthology of World Religions* contributes, for ours is, after all, a collection of texts. We know that the human species emerged some two hundred thousand years ago in southwest Africa and migrated from there eastward and then northward through the Great Rift Valley in what appear to be two noteworthy spikes. One spike proceeded by way of Lake Victoria up the Nile River to where its delta empties into the Mediterranean Sea. The other spike crossed from Africa to Arabia at the Strait of Bab el Mandeb and then proceeded along the southeast coast of Arabia to the Strait of Hormuz, where it crossed into Asia. From there, one stream of human migrants veered northward to the delta of the Tigris River at the upper end of the Persian Gulf, while the other moved southward to the delta of the Indus River. The Indus delta and the river system above it cradled the civilization that, as it moved south into the Indian subcontinent, would produce the Vedas, written in Sanskrit, the earliest scriptures of ancient India. The Nile and the Tigris deltas and the river systems that lay above them would together define the "Fertile Crescent" within which ancient Israel would produce the earliest Hebrew scriptures. The invention of writing in the Tigris delta (Sumer) and the Nile Valley (Egypt) does not antedate the late fourth millennium B.C.E. The oldest works honored as scripture by Hinduism or by Judaism may be a full millennium younger than that. As recoverable from surviving texts, the story of the world's major, living, international religions can reach no further back in time than this.

To concede this much is not to concede that the earlier evolution of religion cannot be reconstructed at all or indeed even reconstructed in a way that would link it to the story told here. It is to concede only that that reconstruction would call for another kind of book than this one, assembling very different kinds of evidence than are assembled here.

The First World's Parliament of Religions

We may close this review of the development of religious studies between 1737 and 1893 with a visit to the World's Parliament of Religions at the World's Columbian Exposition in Chicago in 1893. The vast exposition, which ran for six months and attracted millions of visitors, was a celebration of progress—scientific, political, and cultural—during the five hundred years since Columbus had discovered America. (The exposition missed its intended 1892 opening by a few months.) Though the organizers often seemed to tacitly assume that the latest and greatest chapter in world progress was the American chapter and that thriving, optimistic Chicago was the epitome of American progress, nonetheless an exuberant, generally benevolent and inclusive curiosity characterized much on display. And though there was condescension in the presentation of model villages from "primitive" societies as natural history exhibits, there was also an acknowledgment that many fascinating and once entirely unknown societies were now no longer unknown and could be presented for the instruction of the interested.

As for the World's Parliament of Religions, it seemed to reflect a contemporary, enlightened, Protestant American view that there existed—or there could come into existence—something like a generic religion whose truth all specific religions could acknowledge without renouncing their respective identities. This view may have owed something to the many translations and plagiarizations of *The Religious Ceremonies and Customs of All the Peoples of the World* that for a century and a half had been steadily propagating Bernard and Picart's confidence that a pure, "natural" religion underlay the variously corrupted historical religions of the world. It may have owed something as well to the 1890 publication of James Frazer's *The Golden Bough*, a romantic and enormously popular work that marshaled classical mythology and selected early anthropological studies of primitive tribes in a grand evolutionary march from magic to science.[19] It may have reflected in addition the gradual influence on American Protestants of the Enlightenment ideas underpinning the United States Constitution. Under the Constitution, since there was no "religious test" for public office, a Muslim or even an atheist could legally become president.[20] The legal leveling explicit in the Constitution implicitly encouraged a comparable leveling in American society, first among Protestants but later extended to Catholics and Jews, and gradually to the adherents of other religions. The process was slow, but its direction was unmistakable.

What is most remarkable about the Parliament, however, is the simple fact that when the organizers invited representatives of Hinduism, Buddhism, Daoism, Confucianism, Shinto, Jainism, Islam, and Zoroastrianism to come together and deliberate with Christians and Jews, everyone accepted the invitation. Swami Vivekananda (1863–1902) accepted both the invitation and the idea behind it—namely, that Hinduism was a world religion. He did not object that there was no such thing as "Hinduism," that the religious life of India was not a separate province within a postulated empire named "religion," that Indians who honored the Vedas did not see themselves as en route to any brighter collective religious future, and so forth and so on. Objections like this are legitimate, but Vivekananda agreed to attend anyway, gave a sensationally well-received speech, and went on to found the Vedanta Society as an American branch of Hinduism. Plainly enough, he had begun to construe Hinduism as potentially a global religion, separable from Indian ethnicity. The Sri Lankan Buddhist Anagarika Dharmapala (1864–1933) did something similar. In the real world of religious practice, these were important ratifying votes for a vision of world religious pluralism.

"How beautiful it would be," Jean Frédéric Bernard had written, "to arrive at that point and to be able to make people with an overly opinionated character understand that with the help of charity one finds everywhere *brothers*." If the organizers of the World's Parliament of Religions thought that they had arrived at that blessed point when Swami Vivekananda thrilled his American audience with the opening words of his oration, "Sisters and Brothers of America," they were mistaken. And yet something was happening. A change was taking place. In various related European and American venues, a subtle but distinct shift of attitude was under way.

Is it possible to contemplate beliefs that one does not share and practices in which one does not engage and to recognize in them the shaping of a life that one can recognize as human and even good? When attitudes shift on a question as basic as that one, novelists and poets are often the first to notice. The novelist Marcel Proust wrote as follows about the Hindu and Buddhist concepts of *samsara* and *karma*—though without ever using those words—in his early twentieth-century masterpiece *In Search of Lost Time* (1913–27):

> He was dead. Dead for ever? Who can say? . . . All that we can say is that everything is arranged in this life as though we entered it carrying a burden of obligations contracted in a former life; there is no reason inherent in the conditions of life on this earth that can make us consider ourselves obliged to do good, to be kind and thoughtful, even to be polite, nor for an atheist artist to consider himself obliged to begin over again a score of times a piece of work the admiration aroused by which will matter little to his worm-eaten body, like the patch of yellow wall painted with so much skill and refinement by an artist destined to be for ever unknown and barely identified under the name Vermeer. All these obligations, which have no sanction in our present life, seem to belong to a different world, a world based on kindness, scrupulousness, self-sacrifice, a world entirely different from this one and which we leave in order to be born on this earth, before perhaps returning there to live once again beneath the sway of those unknown laws which we obeyed because we bore their precepts in our hearts, not knowing whose hand had traced them there[.][21]

Marcel Proust was not a Hindu, he was a Frenchman of Jewish descent. Like not a few writers of his day, he may have been influenced by Frazer's *The Golden Bough*, but *In Search of Lost Time* is in any case a novel, not a work of science, philosophy, or theology. And yet we might say that in the words quoted, Proust is a Hindu by sympathetic, participative imagination and thus among the heirs of Jean Frédéric Bernard and Bernard Picart. This kind of imaginatively participant sympathy was taking hold in a new way.

In the United States, the World's Parliament of Religions reflected the same *Zeitgeist* and heralded, moreover, an organizational change that would occur in the latter third of the following century, building on all that had transpired since Bernard dreamed his dream. That change—the decision of the National Association of Biblical Instructors to reincorporate in 1964 as the American Academy of Religion—reflected the emergent conviction that some knowledge of the world's religions was properly a part of every American's education.[22]

If American intellectual culture is distinctive in any regard, it is distinctive in its penchant for popularization or for the democratization of knowledge. The intellectual leadership of the country has generally assumed that the work of intellectual discovery is not complete until everybody has heard the news. But judgment about what constitutes "news"—that is, what subjects constitute the core of education for all people—has changed over time, and knowledge of the world's religions has not always been on the list. It was during the twentieth century that it made the list, and so for the study of religion we may regard the World's Parliament of Religions as opening the twentieth century.

In the comparative study of religion, Europe was America's teacher until the end of World War II. The secular, neutral comparative study of religion was a European inspiration. The heavy lifting necessary to assemble linguistic and archaeological documentary materials for such study—the story we have been reviewing here—was almost entirely a European achievement as well. But a distinctive aspect of the American contribution to the story has been the impulse to share inspirations, achievements, and knowledge gained in the study of religion with the general public. A work like *The Norton Anthology of World Religions*, intended for the college undergraduate or the willing general reader, is a work entirely in the American grain. If you find the texts assembled in the collection that now follows surprising, if you find the editorial frame around them instructive, please know that you are cordially invited to explore the remaining five anthologies that with this one constitute the full *Norton Anthology of World Religions*.

Notes

The intellectual debts incurred in the foregoing introduction are far greater than could be registered even in a far longer list of footnotes than appears here. The subject matter touched upon could obviously command a far longer exposition than even so lengthy an introduction as this one has allowed. I beg the indulgence alike of the students I may have overburdened and of the scholars I have failed to acknowledge. JM

1. Kevin Schilback, "Religions: Are There Any?" *Journal of the American Academy of Religion* 78.4 (December 2010): 1112–38.
2. Frans de Waal, *The Bonobo and the Atheist: In Search of Humanism among the Primates* (New York: Norton, 2013), p. 210.
3. Daniel L. Pals, *Eight Theories of Religion*, 2nd ed. (New York: Oxford University Press, 2006); Michael Stausberg, ed., *Contemporary Theories of Religion: A Critical Companion* (London: Routledge, 2009). Strikingly, they do not overlap on a single entry.
4. Feynman is quoted in Dennis Overbye, "Laws of Nature, Source Unknown," *New York Times*, December 18, 2007.
5. Clifford Geertz, "Religion as a Cultural System," in *The Interpretation of Cultures: Selected Essays* (New York: Basic Books, 1973), p. 90 (emphasis his).
6. Ibid., p. 125.
7. Ibid., pp. 193–233.
8. Tomoko Masuzawa, *The Invention of World Religions, Or, How European Universalism Was Preserved in the Language of Pluralism* (Chicago: University of Chicago Press, 2005).
9. All Bible quotations in this introduction are from *The Holy Bible, Revised Standard Version* (New York: Thomas Nelson & Sons, 1952).
10. Mark C. Taylor, *After God* (Chicago: University of Chicago Press, 2007).
11. Herbert Butterfield, *The Englishman and His History* (Cambridge: The University Press, 1944), p. 119.
12. Lynn Hunt, Margaret C. Jacob, and Wijnand Mijnhardt, *The Book That Changed Europe: Picart and Bernard's "Religious Ceremonies of the World"* (Cambridge, Mass.: Belknap Press of Harvard University Press, 2010), p. 2 (emphasis added).
13. Ibid., p. 5.
14. Ibid., pp. 155–57 (emphasis added).
15. Jean Frédéric Bernard, quoted in ibid., p. 241 (emphasis in original).
16. Donald S. Lopez, Jr., *From Stone to Flesh: A Short History of the Buddha* (Chicago: University of Chicago Press, 2013).
17. *The Quest of the Historical Jesus* is the colorful title of the English translation first published in 1910; Schweitzer's sober German title was *Von Reimarus zu Wrede: Eine Geschichte der Leben-Jesu-Forschung* (From Reimarus to Wrede: A History of Research into the Life of Jesus). Hermann Reimarus and William Wrede were earlier scholars.
18. For the background in World War II and its aftermath, see John Connelly, *From Enemy to Brother: The Revolution in Catholic Teaching on the Jews, 1933–1965* (Cambridge, Mass.: Harvard University Press, 2012).
19. James Frazer, *The Golden Bough: A Study in Magic and Religion: A New Abridgment from the Second and Third Editions* (Oxford: Oxford University Press, 2009). Frazer's extravaganza eventually grew to twelve volumes, now out of print. For a more recent and more richly informed account of the evolution of religion, see Robert M. Bellah, *Religion in Human Evolution: From the Paleolithic to the Axial* Age (Cambridge, Mass.: Belknap Press of Harvard University Press, 2011).
20. See Denise A. Spellberg, *Thomas Jefferson's Qur'an: Islam and the Founders* (New York: Knopf, 2013).
21. Marcel Proust, *In Search of Lost Time*, vol. 5, *The Captive; The Fugitive*, trans. C. K. Scott Moncrieff and Terence Kilmartin, rev. D. J. Enright (New York: Random House, 1993), 5:245–46.
22. See Preface, p. xx.

This was the common hymn of Rabe'eh:
"O God, who knows all secrets, she would pray,
"May fortune favor all my enemies,
And may my friends taste heaven's ecstasies;
It is not this world or the next I crave
But, for one moment, to be called your slave—
With passion I embrace this poverty;
Such endless blessings flow from You to me
If I desire this world or shrink from hell,
I am not better than an infidel."
A man has everything who knows his Lord—
The world and all its seven seas afford.
All that the universe has ever shown
Can find its match but God, who is alone;
And only He, wherever you may seek,
Is absolute, abiding, and unique.

—FARID AL-DIN 'ATTAR,
The Conference of the Birds

ISLAM

EDITED BY

Jane Dammen McAuliffe

INTRODUCTION
Submission to God as the Wellspring of a Civilization

In tenth-century Baghdad, an Iraqi scholar published a book about books. In its initial chapters, he tells us how the Arabs began to write and how they created a calligraphy for literary composition. He also celebrates the scripts of other peoples—the Greeks, the Russians, the Chinese, and the Armenians. He extols the instruments of writing—"The pen is the ambassador of the mind, its apostle, its furthest reaching tongue, and its best interpreter"—and sketches the history of writing materials, beginning with Adam, who composed on clay. He notes that Adam's descendants used copper and stone and that after the Flood people turned to wood and bark and the leaves of trees. Later, the Egyptians mastered papyrus manufacture and the Persians employed animal skins. The Arabs adopted stones and bones and palm stems, and the Chinese invented paper. Our Baghdadi author, Ibn al-Nadim, lived during the early period of Islamic paper production; the Chinese technology had been imported through Samarkand and gradually spread throughout the Muslim world. His enthusiasm for the process of book production shines through his prefatory chapter. A quote that he takes from Socrates (*Suqrat* in Arabic) can serve as a fitting prelude to the rich selection of Islamic religious literature here assembled. When asked if he feared that reading many books would ruin his eyes, Socrates replied, "If I save my insight, I don't attend to weakness of eyesight."

The Foundational Epoch (610–750)

The Qur'an: God's Culminating Gift to Humankind

Muslims revere the Qur'an as God's own word. That deceptively simple statement supports the entire edifice of Muslim theology and spirituality. The Islamic doctrine of revelation thus functions as a doctrine of divine dictation rather than a doctrine of divine inspiration. The role of Muhammad (ca. 570–632) in revelation was to convey, not to compose. Addressed by the angel of revelation, usually identified as Gabriel, the Prophet received God's words, in Arabic, and transmitted them verbatim to his friends and early followers. These words are God's culminating gift to humankind. They conclude a chronology of countless prior revelations, including such noteworthy instances as the Torah and the Gospel. Each calls forth the foundational response of *islam*, "submission," to the sovereignty and the supreme mystery of God, and each proceeds from the primordial archetype of all scripture, "the mother of the Book." For Muslims, however, the Qur'an presents God's full and final guidance on all aspects of human life.

Reverence for the Qur'an expresses itself in multiple modes. Since the physical text embodies God's own words, it is protected from pollution. For example, it is set on a stand well above the ground; many menstruating women will not touch it; copies that can no longer be used are stored away or disposed of with care. But the physical text remains secondary to the primary form of conveying the Qur'an: oral recitation. The Arabic word *qur'an* means "recitation," and recited verses form part of the fivefold daily prayer sequence. More extended recitations occur during marriages, naming ceremonies, circumcisions, and funerals and throughout the fasting month of Ramadan. Modern media, such as radio, television, CDs, and iPods, have made the oral Qur'an available everywhere, day and night, so that the believer can be constantly bathed in the blessing, or *baraka*, of God's verbal presence.

Tiled calligraphic roundel in the Suleymaniye Mosque in Istanbul, Turkey. The mosque, designed by the famed architect Sinan, was completed in 1558. The tiles are inscribed with the verses of the opening chapter of the Qur'an, the *Fatiha*.

Traditional Muslim schooling begins with the Qur'an, as small children are introduced to its shorter chapters and verses. They learn these by rote and always in Arabic, regardless of their native tongues. The ubiquity of such elementary Qur'an schools in all Muslim societies was an important form of transnationality in the premodern Muslim world, and it has continued as such even in modern times. American Muslim children of all ethnicities learn the same verses in their mosque "Sunday school" as do their counterparts in Indonesia and Nigeria.

Some students follow these studies to the point of professionalization. They learn the intricate skills of *tajwid*, the traditional art of Qur'an cantillation that involves precise elisions and prolongations of particular vowels and consonants. Many Muslims also commit the entire Qur'an to memory, an act of piety that earns them the honorific "protector" (*hafiz*) of the Qur'an. Indirectly, this intense and widespread engagement with the text of the Qur'an contributes to the maintenance of a sense of unity and shared identity in the world Muslim community, or umma.

The sacrality of the text encourages its use in amulets encasing scriptural fragments or even in potions made from inked verses dipped in water. Devotion to the word manifests itself in the splendid public epigraphy of mosques, shrines, and tombs and in the exquisite calligraphy of classical and medieval manuscripts. The omnipresence of qur'anic words and phrases marks the material culture of Muslim societies around the globe.

The History of the Qur'anic Text

Conventional accounts of the history of the qur'anic text ordinarily begin with its oral conveyance in the Prophet's initial preaching. Then they move to the period after his death, the decades of the early caliphs. During this era, the Qur'an was "collected" from the memories of its first recipients and from whatever written fragments could be found. A small team of scribes set down the collected portions in an assemblage of chapters, or suras, arranging them roughly from longest to shortest. At this early stage the orthography of the text was rudimentary, lacking the precise specification of Arabic vowels and consonants that would develop over the next several centuries. Orality remained the primary mode of dissemination, and the written Qur'an functioned largely as an aid for memorization. Consequently, some textual variation developed and by the early tenth century was codified as an acceptable range of readings. These canonical readings have long been a subject of Muslim scholarship, and teams of European and North African scholars are currently seeking to build on efforts begun in the twentieth century to collect additional textual variants both from medieval scholarly works that cited the Qur'an and from extant manuscripts of the Qur'an itself.

Like other important scriptural traditions, the Qur'an has generated a vast library of exegetical literature. Commentary on the Qur'an, in the rudimentary form of verbal glosses and narrative embellishments, probably began during Muhammad's lifetime—sometime after 610, when his biographies indicate that he first began to receive revelations. The compilation of these initial explanations eventually evolved into fully developed works of interpretation. An early entry of enduring importance is that of Abu Ja'far ibn

Jarir al-Tabari (ca. 839–923), whose more than thirty volumes of commentary continue to be republished on a regular basis. As commentaries proliferated, they became more varied and specialized. Some emphasized mystical understandings of the Qur'an, while others focused on those verses that carried legal implications. Still others brought philosophical and theological reflection to bear on the sacred text.

Alongside this vast library of exegetical materials, another library could be built to house the countless Qur'an translations that have been produced in the past fourteen centuries. While always acknowledging that the Qur'an was truly the Qur'an only in Arabic, scholars in all the lands to which Islam eventually spread have sought to render the Qur'an's meaning into indigenous languages. The earliest such effort was a Persian paraphrase, but contemporary bibliographies of Qur'an translations now list versions in hundreds of languages. Such translation activity has not been the purview of Muslim scholars alone. In the twelfth century a Latin translation was produced by Robert of Ketton at the request of Peter the Venerable, the abbot of Cluny (ca. 1092–1156). Four centuries later, Martin Luther (1483–1546) wrote the introduction to the republication by Theodore Bibliander (1505–1564) of this translation in Basel. Renderings into European languages, including English, testify to the enduring influence of Ketton's work. In 1734, however, George Sale (ca. 1696–1736) was the first to translate the Qur'an into English directly from Arabic. Since then, dozens of English translations have been produced and new versions continue to appear.

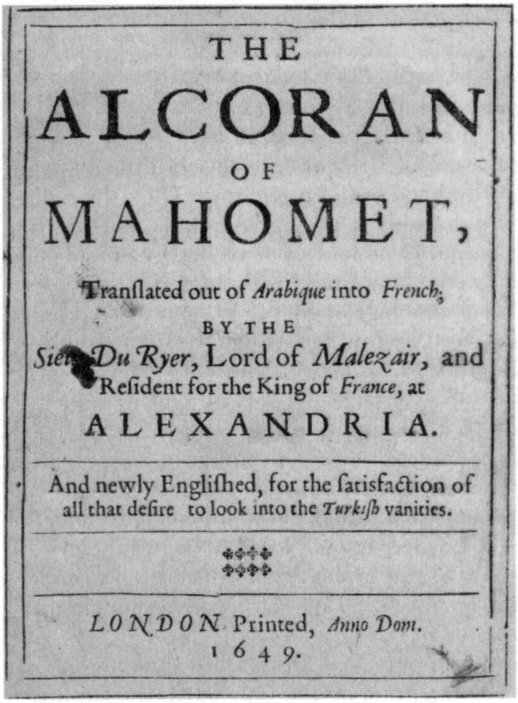
THE
ALCORAN
OF
MAHOMET,
Tranſlated out of *Arabique* into *French*;
BY THE
Sieur Du Ryer, Lord of *Malezair*, and
Reſident for the King of *France*, at
ALEXANDRIA.
And newly Engliſhed, for the ſatisfaction of
all that deſire to look into the *Turkiſh* vanities.
LONDON. Printed, *Anno Dom.*
1649.

Title page of a rare edition of the first English version of the Qur'an held in the Bryn Mawr College Library. This version, made in 1649 by the British schoolteacher Alexander Ross, was based on the French translation by Andre du Ryer and differs in many ways from the original Arabic.

The Qur'an, roughly the size of the Christian New Testament, is divided into 114 chapters or suras, some long and some quite short. It is not easy to read, particularly for those whose expectations of scripture have been shaped by the Bible, because unlike the Bible it is organized by neither chronology nor genre; moreover, except for the twelfth sura, it contains no sustained narratives. The longer suras combine genres as diverse as prayer, preaching, instructions for rituals, parables, prescriptive passages with legal implications, didactic stories, and visionary images.

The thematic range is equally broad, encompassing attestation to God's oneness—or, to use a term favored in Islamic scholarship, divine unicity; denunciation of idolatry; celebration of God's creative activity; warnings of final judgment and eternal damnation; divinely mandated proscriptions and prescriptions; admonitory accounts of previous prophets and the people who rejected them; and arguments against the competing theologies of Jews and Christians.

Sira: *The Life Story of the Prophet*

The final decades of the twentieth century witnessed a renewed scholarly interest in the history of Muhammad and the earliest era of the Muslim community. What we know of the Prophet's life must be drawn from several genres of Islamic literature, including the Qur'an, hadith, commentaries on both, fragmentary accounts of early military expeditions and campaigns, and the initial efforts at biographical accounts of his life. These last-mentioned are known collectively as the *sira*, an Arabic word that means "way of living" or "noteworthy action." Both meanings are subsumed in the classical efforts to create narrative accounts of Muhammad's life. The most noted, especially for English-language readers, is that of Ibn Ishaq (ca. 704–767) as revised by Ibn Hisham (d. 833; see below). Ibn Ishaq, in a portion of his work now lost, situated Muhammad within the long history of preceding prophets, both those mentioned in the Bible and others from traditional Arab lore. Ibn Hisham, however, restricted this frame story to the era of ancient Arabia. Works by al-Waqidi (747–822), Ibn Sa'd (d. 845), and al-Baladhuri (d. ca. 892; see below) contribute varying emphases and additional material. By the early tenth century, the monumental history of al-Tabari had expanded the prehistory of Muhammad from a lineage of previous prophets to one that also included the emperors of Byzantium as well as the kings of Persia.

This biographical literature on the Prophet and his early conquests offers a medley of genres. Stories of military expeditions are interwoven with panegyric poetry, with speeches and sermons, and with letters and other documents. Extended genealogies combine with long lists of those who fought on the side of the Prophet, were his first converts, emigrated to Medina with him, and stood among his "Helpers" in Medina. These Prophet biographies are also an important source of Qur'an commentary, providing narrative elaboration and contextualization for many of its verses.

The Classical Synthesis (750–1756)

Hadith *and* Sunna: *The Perfect Man Remembered as the Perfect Guide to Life*

Qur'an 33:21, "You have a good example in the Messenger of God," encourages the enterprise of hadith, the second form of textual authority in Islam. The Arabic term *hadith* is a singular noun and properly refers to the individual report of something that the Prophet, or one of the early Muslims, said or did. Frequently, however, the term is used in a collective sense to mean the entire body of such reports or a particular subset of them. As a body of written texts, the hadith are different from and far larger than the Qurʾan, but their collection, assessment, and study have generated a remarkably similar scholarly literature. The written hadith record the Prophet's *sunna* or "way," his behavior and practice. While a sunna can be set by anyone—the pre-Islamic Arabs followed the sunna of their ancestors—the Qurʾan presents the sunna of the Prophet as in harmony with "God's way." As the recorded memory of the Prophet's practice, hadith derive their importance from the key conviction that Muhammad was the most perfect human being and that his behavior best exemplifies the divinely guided life. The Prophet's practice is the primary tool for interpreting and understanding qurʾanic directives, and modeling oneself on Muhammad is the ideal way to be a Muslim.

The Prophet's sunna was originally transmitted orally through eyewitness accounts of what he said, did, or tacitly accepted. Each account is a *hadith*, a term that literally means "something that is said." An individual account has two parts: (1) the narrative of the actual event or episode or statement and (2) the list of people who have transmitted the account from one generation to another. The latter is actually the object of more searching analysis than the former. Because the Prophet's legacy was so important for guiding Muslim life, great care was taken to assess the reliability of those who conveyed it from one generation to another. The guiding questions were quite simple and straightforward: Did the lifetimes of transmitters A and B actually overlap? Are we sure if they were ever in the same city? What can be known about the lives of each individual in the chain? Were these upright men (and women)? Were they respected for their integrity and truthfulness? Vast biographical dictionaries that detail the character, educational attainments, and scholarly accomplishments of the thousands of names found in the chains of transmission testify to the serious efforts undertaken to ensure the fidelity of the Prophet's legacy. The motivation for hadith, familiar enough in the histories of other religions, is double. On the one hand is the desire to sustain the memory of inspired adaptations of God's revelation to human circumstances. On the other hand is the desire not to lose the coherence and integrity of revelation in a welter of dubiously warranted modifications.

The three centuries following Muhammad's lifetime saw an exponential proliferation of hadith, not because new material about the Prophet and his Companions was discovered but because ever more widespread transmission multiplied versions of existing accounts as well as their chains of conveyance. Certainly, some hadith were fabricated and forged, the consequence of efforts to create a retrospective prophetic ratification for certain ideas and social practices. Also, some Jewish and Christian material was imported into apparently prophet-sanctioned formats. Eventually, however, efforts to collect, to codify, and to organize the ever-increasing accumulation of hadith began to take effect—and out of these attempts to establish order, the initial anthologies emerged.

At first, the groupings were loosely organized around questions of law and ritual and included not only statements from the Prophet but also reports of current practice and the compiler's own judgments. As attention to the full chains of transmission grew more pronounced, some hadith collections became people-focused, grouping together all the accounts that originated from a particular Companion. Like the twelve apostles of Jesus or the fabled first followers of the Buddha, the *sahaba* or early Companions of Muhammad became in later years celebrated sources of remembered tradition about his words and wisdom. The most famous of anthologies arranged in this way is credited to Ahmad ibn Hanbal (780–855); it contains about 27,700 hadith, many of which are repetitions ordered in different narrative sequences. While arrangement by source reinforced the authority of particular Companions, culling through such collections to find material germane to a specific subject was laborious. The next stage of hadith codification combined the two principles of organization—by subject matter and by sources of transmission. Produced in the ninth and tenth centuries, the six main hadith collections are multivolume works that remain an indispensable form of spiritual and religious guidance for the Muslim community: *Sahih* of Muhammad ibn Isma'il al-Bukhari (810–870; see below), *Sahih* of Muslim ibn al-Hajjaj al-Naysaburi (821–875; see below), *Kitab al-Sunan* of Abu Da'ud al-Sijistani (817–889), *Sahih* of Ahmad ibn Shu'ayb al-Nasa'i (d. 915), *Jami'* of Muhammad ibn 'Isa al-Tirmidhi (d. ca. 892), and *Kitab al-Sunan* of Muhammad ibn Yazid ibn Majah (813–887).

These hadith collections are deemed canonical by most Muslims who identify as Sunni (self-designated followers of the "sunna" of the Prophet). In the Shi'i community—a name derived from the *shi'a*, or "party," of 'Ali ibn Abi Talib (ca. 599–661), the Prophet's first cousin, son-in-law, and (in the view of his partisans) rightful successor (caliph)—a parallel attention to the Prophet's words and actions developed but was supplemented by transmission via 'Ali (the first Shi'i leader, or imam) and those who succeeded him. While there is considerable overlap between Shi'i and Sunni hadith collections, as is evident in the monumental collection of al-Majlisi (1627–1699; see below), there is also dogmatic divergence. The Sunni hadith reflect the view of that community that after the death of Muhammad, leadership of the Muslim community, the caliphate, was properly to be awarded by acclamation within the community itself. Doctrines specific to Shi'ism, such as the infallibility of the imams and the genealogical primacy of 'Ali's claim to the caliphate, receive prominent attention in Shi'i hadith. Yet a pronounced devotion to the family of the Prophet, a hallmark of Shi'ism, is shared by both traditions.

Later centuries saw the production of a large commentary and critical literature on both the major Sunni and the Shi'i collections, as well as the creation of countless summaries and supplements. Within medieval Muslim universities, the technical study of hadith became part of the standard curriculum, and the tools of the discipline, such as concordances and biographical assessments of the transmitters, proliferated. As the six canonical collections of the Sunni traditions were added to and abridged, both digests and encyclopedias were created. A popular sort of summary collection is the "forty hadith" (*arba'un*) book. Motivated by a (perhaps unreliable) hadith in which the Prophet urges all believers to memorize at least forty hadith, these epitomes took various forms. They could be displays of esoteric scholarship or compilations on a single theme or, like the contribution of al-Nawawi (1233–1277; see below), primers on the principles of religion.

Initially, the interest in hadith was driven more by spiritual than by legal concerns. Early legal manuals cite relatively few prophetic sayings, relying more heavily on the opinions of notables or accepted customs. Law developed erratically in different areas of the Muslim world as the young Muslim community began its fast-paced expansion beyond the Arabian Peninsula, encountering cultures and contexts much different than its own. The wide extent of legal variation and interpretation proved alarming for Muslim rulers and bureaucrats. As part of an effort to achieve legal unity and clarity, the ninth-century jurist Muhammad ibn Idris al-Shafiʿi (767–820; see below) insisted that the Prophet's sunna should become the major enduring element in the Islamic jurisprudential exercise. His legal treatise, the *Risala*, called for the preeminence of the hadith over custom, the opinions of judges, or local consensus. Al-Shafiʿi argued that everything needed for making an informed legal decision existed in the Qur'an and the Prophet's sunna. The latter both explained the Qur'an and set behavioral precedents. Hadith collection moved beyond the pious inquiry into Muhammad's conduct to become a reference tool for busy jurists. Yet by themselves, these texts are not a sufficient warrant for all the matters that religious law must address.

Shariʿa *and* Fiqh: *Divine Will and Human Interpretation*

The past three decades have brought terms and categories of Islamic law, *shariʿa* in Arabic, to the attention of the English-speaking public as never before. In 1979 the Iranian Revolution created a theocratic government, and words like *ayatollah* and *mullah* entered the language of foreign policy analysis. As several Muslim nations experienced a rise in popular Islamist sentiments, awareness of "Shariʿa governments" increased in the West, as did a confused sense of the idea of *jihad*, Arabic for "striving," "struggle," or "effort," including military effort. Too often, media sound bites and ill-informed political commentators have offered inaccurate or simplistic understandings of this vocabulary, creating confusion and misunderstanding. Law and legal reasoning are among the most complex topics within Islamic religious literature but also the most central. Moreover, few areas have generated as much scholarly discussion and discord as those that deal with the sources and early development of the Islamic legal tradition. Although there is much in the Qur'an that shapes the ethos of legal reasoning, relatively few verses convey explicitly legal content. Such content that does exist is unevenly distributed across the potential range of human behaviors. The Qur'an, for example, provides some detail on matters of marriage, divorce, and inheritance but almost no guidance on the specifics of commercial transactions.

The Arabic word *shariʿa* has a humble origin. According to the standard classical dictionaries, it is the term for a watering place used by either people or animals and, by extension, the pathway or access point by which one reaches the watering place. Just as water is essential to the sustenance of life, so the Shariʿa addresses not only religious duties and obligations but, at least theoretically, every aspect of human existence. It is the pathway by which humans are guided to God, and via which God is understood to extend his care to humans. The Shariʿa's primary source, the Qurʾan, is often obscure; humans must earnestly endeavor to discern what God desires them to do.

That human endeavor is known as *fiqh,* which derives from a verb meaning "to understand." Fiqh is the human attempt to understand the divine will, or the intellectual exercise that translates the sources of divine guidance into prescriptive and proscriptive stipulations. When Muslim writers produce legal manuals and treatises, then, they are producing not works of Shariʿa but works of fiqh. Within the developed literature of fiqh, there is a major division between actions and duties that govern human behavior toward God (*ʿibadat*) and those that regulate interaction among humans (*muʿamalat*). In both categories, actions are ranked along a fivefold spectrum of moral value, from obligatory to forbidden.

The challenges of constructing a comprehensive legal system from a limited number of proof texts and precedents required the early jurists to draw analogies from a known case or situation to a new one. Such analogical reasoning (*qiyas*) became accepted, at least by Sunnis, as a third source of Muslim jurisprudence. But, of course, human reason, even when guided by precise jurisprudential procedures, always entails differences and divergent interpretations. Out of this diversity, how can the community discern the truth? The answer involved patience and a prolonged time frame. Juridical consensus would eventually emerge, but it could be recognized only retroactively. The recognition of this emergent consensus (*ijmaʿ*) is the final source or root of Islamic jurisprudence in Sunni Islam. For the Shiʿis, as already mentioned, the divinely inspired imam was the sole interpreter of the divine will (after the Prophet), and it was the task of jurists to study the imam's opinions and effectively communicate them to the community.

The theoretical consistency implied by this concept of juristic consensus is tempered, however, by the historical reality of various schools (*madhahib*; sing. *madhhab*) of law. Within the first few centuries, four emerged as centers of Sunni orthodoxy, signaling the acceptance of a bounded range of legal diversity. Of the four classical schools, the earliest bears the name of its eponymous founder, Malik ibn Anas (ca. 715–795), a noted scholar of eighth-century Medina. Subsequent schools are associated with Abu Hanifa (699–767; see below), from Kufa in southern Iraq; Muhammad ibn Idris al-Shafiʿi, also connected to Medina; and Ahmad ibn Hanbal of Baghdad. A parallel development within Shiʿi Islam established similar forms of legal orthodoxy. Over time, each of these schools became dominant in particular geographical areas: the Hanafi school was concentrated in the Middle East and South Asia; the Maliki, in North and West Africa, as represented in the work of al-Qayrawani (922–996; see below); the Hanbali, in Saudi Arabia; and the Shafiʿi, in East Africa and Southeast Asia.

Although these geographical concentrations still exist, the changes wrought by colonialism and emigration have transformed actual legal practice in much of the Muslim world. They have also stimulated and influenced the continuing tradition of Muslim jurisprudence, as evidenced in the works of Rashid Ahmad Gangohi (1829–1905; see below) and Mahmud Shaltut (1897–1963; see below). Following the imposition of foreign control in many Muslim nations, Islamic law became increasingly relegated to matters of personal status, such as marriage, divorce, and inheritance. The legal systems of European colonial occupiers came to dominate commercial and criminal procedures, particularly in countries with large non-Muslim minorities. But foreign occupation in many Muslim-majority countries ended in the twentieth century, and legal changes and reform have continued, sometimes in the direction of accelerating secularization and sometimes with a reassertion of an expanded Shariʿa.

The Intellectual Elaboration of the Classical Synthesis

Kalam: *Theology*

Within the Islamic tradition, theology was no armchair exercise. Frequently, dogmatic positions were forged in conflict or wreaked havoc in the lives of those who held them. The split between Sunni and Shiʿi itself manifests this foundational contention. Arguments about who should lead the community after the Prophet's death or about whether grave sin warranted immediate expulsion from the umma created early divisions with lasting consequences. As contact and conversion proceeded beyond the confines of the Arabian Peninsula and into the Roman and Persian empires—where Christianity and Zoroastrianism, respectively, were the dominant religious traditions—other questions, some of them conditioned by the questioners' earlier religious experiences, emerged. How can human free will coincide with God's omnipotence? Is divine justice bound by dictates of human rationality? Must the words of the Qurʾan, particularly those that speak anthropomorphically about God, be understood literally?

Debate and disputation, both within the Muslim community and beyond, constituted the crucible within which doctrinal positions were defined. Polemical exchanges with hellenized Christians and with Iranian dualists, whether Zoroastrian or Manichaean, offered opportunities to refine and sharpen arguments. The very word for theology in Arabic, *kalam*, means "discussion" or "conversational exchange." Those who participated were the *mutakallimun*, the speculative theologians of the classical Islamic world. A key point of contention was the notion of God's oneness. Clearly, Iranian dualism as well as Christian understandings of the Trinity represented a challenge to the radical monotheism of Islam.

Though Iran was completely subdued militarily by Muslim expansionism, culturally the Persians asserted themselves without reserve, recasting their vast intellectual heritage into Arabic and entering every arena of thought and debate. During the first century of the ʿAbbasid (750–1258) caliphate, lively disputations over the nature of monotheism took place, and a central focus was the relation of God's essence to his revelation: Is the Qurʾan, like God, eternal? In what sense can it be considered "the speech of God"? Is speech an essential divine attribute, and is the Qurʾan thereby coexistent with God? The ʿAbbasids, loosely descended from the Prophet's uncle al-ʿAbbas, could well have been influenced by Persian ideas of kingship when they sought to increase caliphal authority while minimizing the power of the scholarly establishment. If the Qurʾan was eternal, as most Sunni

Tower of the al-Mutawakkili Mosque, Samarra' (built 842–52). The powerful 'Abbasid caliph al-Mutawakkil (r. 847–61) put an end to the Muslim "inquisition" and established the uncreated (or eternal) nature of the Qur'an as Muslim dogma.

theologians asserted, its edicts could not be adjusted or overruled according to the exigencies of the era. If, instead, the Qur'an was created for a particular moment in history, then later interpretations, such as those of a caliph, might hold sway. The ʿAbbasid rulers lost this battle, but not without a fierce attempt to impose their theological position on the scholars; as a result of the triumph of the scholars, the caliphate could never hope to achieve total religious and political authority. The caliph al-Maʾmun (r. 813–33) sided with those theologians who argued that the doctrine of an eternally coexistent Qurʾan compromised the concept of divine oneness. He not only rejected this doctrine himself but, in a period that is often dubbed the Muslim "inquisition," he forced all jurists and judges to do the same. Eventually, al-Maʾmun's dogmatic despotism was reversed, and the uncreatedness of the Qurʾan—the doctrine that he had rejected—became an established tenet of Muslim orthodoxy.

Efforts to express the evolving understandings of God's nature, of his attributes, and of his relation to the created world have continued through the entire course of Islamic intellectual history. Early formulations, such as those of Abu Hanifa, were followed by the more developed expositions of Sunni theologians such as al-Ashʿari (874–935; see below), al-Ghazali (1058–1111; see below), and the Shiʿi Ibn Babawayh (d. 991). This cumulative classical achievement was both replicated and elaborated in the centuries that followed. Because kalam was never isolated from the intellectual currents of a particular era and area, the expanding literature of philosophical theology reflected these encounters and the new questions and issues that they prompted. This diversification accelerated as the Islamic world entered the period of modernity. Represented in this volume are some of the responses generated by that encounter, as exemplified in the work of the Indian scholar Shah Wali Allah Dihlavi (1703–1762), the Saudi Arabian preacher Ibn ʿAbd al-Wahhab (1703–1792), and the Egyptian professor Muhammad ʿAbduh (1849–1905).

Falsafa: *Philosophy*

Although philosophy, *falsafa* in Arabic, operates as a separate intellectual domain within Islamic religious literature, it would be hard to overestimate the extent to which it has influenced—and been influenced by—theological discourse. Following Greek precedents, philosophy developed as a form of systematic and structured reasoning. Conclusions followed from explicit premises, and truth could be distinguished from falsity on the basis of valid and adequate arguments. Such reasoning was, of course, not confined to philosophical writings alone. In addition to theological works, those of law and jurisprudence, of polemic and apologetic, and of science and medicine are indebted to methods of rigorous reasoning. While philosophical discourse in Arabic and Persian has multiple sources and influences, a major one is the ninth-century translation movement centered in Baghdad, which stimulated the rendering of many Greek scientific and philosophical texts into Arabic. This movement, in turn, built on an earlier translation of Greek texts into Syriac, and the Baghdadi translators themselves were often Christians or Jews. Important works of Plato and Aristotle became available in Arabic, as well as those of such Neoplatonists as Plotinus and Proclus. From this effort a nascent philosophical vocabulary emerged for the first time in Arabic; so too did certain key stipulations of Aristotelian reasoning, such as the autonomy of nature and the eternity of the world, that conflicted with qur'anic teachings. Much of the debate between *falsafa* and kalam centers on arguments about creation in time, God's knowledge of particulars, and the resurrection of the body. Charges of infidelity (*kufr*) and unwarranted innovation (*bid'a*) were directed at those who, on the grounds of rational incompatibility, opposed these and other tenets of the faith.

Islamic philosophy, as represented here in the work of al-Farabi (ca. 870–950), Ibn Sina (ca. 980–1037), and Ibn Rushd (1126–1198), testifies to an enduring belief in the unity of knowledge and the ultimate reconciliation of reason and revelation. Whether in their metaphysical manifestations or in their ethico-political applications, classical Islamic philosophers argued for the intrinsic rationality of religious truths and teachings. They saw themselves as heirs to an ancient tradition of wisdom and reasoning, and frequent references to the great thinkers of antiquity characterize their writings. The unity and the continuity of knowledge did not, however, make it universally accessible. Not everyone possessed the intellectual acuity demanded by philosophical reasoning. Rather, an emergent psychology of aptitude levels paralleled the increasing philosophical sophistication. Some minds could comprehend a complex argument and draw from it necessary and valid conclusions. Others could be satisfied with probabilities and logical demonstrations. But most minds were content with—and only capable of—persuasive rhetoric and appeals to the imagination.

At this juncture the distinction between philosopher and prophet presents itself. The prophet is uniquely endowed with the capacity to convey ultimate truth in an accessible manner. Similarly, the revelation accorded to the prophet, the Qur'an, is miraculously available to all mentalities. Some can grasp its literal sense, others can plumb its ambiguities. Still others can probe depths of meaning that the text conceals from all but the most intellectually astute and spiritually prepared. Clearly, a psychology of varying human aptitudes opens the door to religious misunderstandings and dangers. Philosophers were quick to caution against allowing full access to those who were incapable or unprepared for it.

'Ulum al-Qur'an: *Scripture Scholarship or "Qur'anic Sciences"*

The odd-sounding phrase "qur'anic sciences" attempts an English rendering of the Arabic *'ulum al-Qur'an*. The singular form *'ilm* encompasses far more than our word "science," at least in its contemporary connotations. Its plural, *'ulum*, signifies fields of knowledge, areas of study—what we might normally call "academic disciplines." Like all of the world's major scriptural traditions, the Qur'an generated a huge commentary literature and an affiliated array of scholarly activities that support the exhaustive study and analysis of the sacred text. These ancillary aspects include topics as diverse as rules for the proper recitation of the Qur'an and designation of those verses within the text that abrogate the prescriptive force of other verses. Two major medieval compendia have collected and classified the full range of these qur'anic sciences. They were written about a century apart, and *The Proof in the Qur'anic Sciences*, by Badr al-Din al-Zarkashi (d. 1392), serves as a prelude to *The Perfection in the Qur'anic Sciences*, by Jalal al-Din al-Suyuti (d. 1505). Neither of these works has yet been fully translated into English, as is also true of most of the commentaries written on the Qur'an over the centuries.

That literature, taken as a whole, runs to thousands of volumes and encompasses most of the languages into which the Qur'an has been translated. The typical commentary on the Qur'an is a multivolume work—published editions can run to thirty or forty volumes—that begins with the first chapter and first verse of the scripture and proceeds systematically to the very last. Within this framework the commentator takes the words or phrases of a verse in sequence and discusses their meaning, the occasions in the life of the Prophet that may have prompted their revelation, and, most importantly, how they apply to living a life under the guidance of God. Qur'an commentaries tend to accrete. Each new exegete includes the work of earlier masters while adding his own well-supported understandings. Consequently, as a genre, commentary has a conservative character, whether it is formed within a Sunni or a Shi'i or a Sufi tradition of exegesis. Authors as distant in time and place as those represented in this anthology, Fakhr al-Din al-Razi (1149/50–1210), Ibn Taymiyya (1263–1328), and Muhammad 'Abduh, would nevertheless recognize each other as engaged within the same exegetical exercise. Their perspectives differ, as do their areas of emphasis, but all three would see themselves as part of a much larger and longer intellectual conversation—one that seeks to understand God's very own words as a necessary prerequisite for thinking and acting in accordance with his will.

Today the conversation continues unabated and takes advantage of multiple new media. Famous contemporary commentators on the Qur'an make TV appearances in Muslim countries and record lectures that can be purchased on cassettes or DVDs or downloaded to an iPhone. Websites that replicate classical sources proliferate, as do those that feature new interpretations, both scholarly and amateur. A broader dissemination of the major commentaries has been undertaken by large translation projects, such as that currently being funded by the Jordanian government. Recognizing that most of the world's Muslims do not speak or read Arabic, such efforts serve to open an important intellectual tradition to those who cannot access it in the original language.

'Ilm al-akhlaq: *Private Ethics and Public Governance*

If understood in the general sense of "moral discourse," the concept of ethics in Islam covers a broad literary range. While closely related to law and legal reasoning, it is less systematized and more focused on the cultivation of human character. The ethical ideals of pre-Islamic Arabia stressed self-control, valor, generosity, and personal and tribal honor. With the rise of Islam, the God–human relationship and community-based virtues such as justice, compassion, and self-sacrifice came to the fore.

The Qur'an functions as the primary source of ethical injunctions, providing frequent exhortations to do good, to forbid evil, to act with honor and generosity. As represented in the hadith, the prophet Muhammad stands as the ideal human being, the one who must be both honored and emulated. Much of the narrative material that entered Islam from earlier cultures and was reshaped in classical prose works, like those of al-Jahiz (ca. 776–868/69), has an ethically instructive purpose. Works of moral instruction, frequently presented in the form of amusing anecdotes, represent important elements of both Arabic and Persian literature and an area of cultural fusion.

As was true of philosophy, ethics in Islam became deeply influenced by the ancient Greek tradition. The works of Plato and Aristotle, the treatises of Galen, and the commentaries of the Neoplatonists were foundational sources for what came to be called "the science of morals" (*'ilm al-akhlaq*). Its primary concern was virtue and the formation of human character. The most prominent works, like those of Miskawayh (ca. 932–1030) and al-Mawardi (d. 1058) excerpted below, elaborate religious understandings of full human development within the context of Greek philosophical psychology.

Precepts for the proper management of one's person could expand to include the qualities required to run a well-regulated household and, by extension, to successfully supervise the affairs of state. The relevance of, in particular, skill in the management of relations between husbands and wives to skill in affairs of state was understood far more broadly than in modern Western culture, where generally private and public life are allowed to function as separate spheres. A body of literature on governance, known as "mirrors for princes," expounded on the appropriate behavior of the ruler toward those whom he governed. In the works of authors such as Nizam al-Mulk (ca. 1019–1092; see below) and Nasir al-Din Tusi (1201–1274; see below), greater emphasis was placed on political practice than on philosophical theory. The rightfulness of rulership was divinely sanctioned, and its responsibilities devolved from the fundamental importance of ensuring a civic and social space in which God's law could be fully enacted. An integration of ancient Persian traditions of government with Arab-Islamic understandings of the caliphate is characteristic of the more developed forms of this literature. Because they offered exemplary legends of earlier prophets and kings, as well as pragmatic guidance about comportment and conduct, these works won a popular reception with kings, governors, and other high officials.

Akhbar: *History, Geography, and Travel Writing*

Islamic history, particularly of the earliest period, poses controversial questions for scholars. No works survive that can be indisputably dated to the initial and mid-decades of the seventh century, the period that they purport to represent. And because knowledge of these years must be retrieved from fragments found in much later works, their reliability is open to constant question. Scholars who attempt a hypothetical reconstruction of the initial stages of historical writing in Islam imagine a continuation of earlier literary forms and the emergence of new ones. Thus the pre-Islamic poetry performances that glorify raids and battles, exalt and eulogize leading figures, and embellish a tribal genealogy with precursive connections to the Prophet contained the seeds of later developed narratives.

The pious stories in circulation, often centered on biblical figures or those from Arab folklore, constitute another possible source, as do the sermons preached by Muhammad's followers and their successors. Material of this sort eventually found its way into more organized compilations and these, in turn, were the probable prototypes of those early works that have come down to us. In the years following the Prophet's death, the early Muslim community aggressively pushed its frontiers outward, conquering regions and regimes that would decisively shape its political and cultural contours.

While the English word "history" derives from Greek *histōr*, meaning a sage or judge, the Arabic term *akhbar* refers to records of events. Early Arabic history was anecdotal, existing in a narrative style similar to that of the hadith: each anecdote was accompanied by a legitimizing chain of transmitters. Muslim historiographers were compilers and collectors, lending their personal integrity to the content they conveyed. Like hadith, the earliest historical anecdotes frequently survive only as citations in later compilations, many of which were eventually subsumed in yet larger works. Unlike hadith, historical accounts were not systematically subjected to intense scrutiny so that they might be verified or discarded as fraudulent.

Most of what can be known of the earliest periods of historiography, and particularly any sense of the transition from the oral to the written, must be gleaned from works compiled centuries later. These later works often sought to discern a shape and meaning in the events recounted. They tried to make sense of momentous changes, recording them for posterity and honoring those involved. At their core stood a clear conception of God's hand in human events. A theology of history that firmly countered assertions of randomness or fate would be an abiding mark of this Muslim literary genre.

Interest in a pre-Islamic past was also present. The *Book of Idols* by Hisham ibn al-Kalbi (ca. 737–821; see below) catalogues the deities of "pagan" Arabia, detailing rituals of worship and pilgrimage and interspersing these descriptions with excerpts of poetry. The Qur'an itself mentions biblical figures as well as those that belong to Arab lore, instigating the investigation of both by commentators and historians. As Muslim writers shaped and reflected an emerging community identity, they created connections and disjunctions with earlier cultures. Continuities with biblical periods of prophecy and conquest situated nascent Islam within the sequence of divine revelation and guidance. Likewise, a positioning as heir to Persian achievements in statecraft framed works of local and regional dynastic history in post-Sassanian territories.

The late ninth century witnessed the emergence of two author-compilers whose efforts had enduring influence. Al-Baladhuri focused his work on the first Islamic centuries, emphasizing the regional reach of the era's expansive conquests and their subsequent administrative organization. He supplemented this military-political history with a lineage-based assemblage of biographies of the major figures of these first centuries of Islamic history. Abu Jaʿfar ibn Jarir al-Tabari placed his account of these same centuries in a much larger framework. Beginning with creation, he compiled a chronicle that included a large cast of pre-Islamic prophets and peoples, all of whom formed a backdrop to the decisive moment: Muhammad's life and mission. With the advent of Muhammad, al-Tabari tightened his focus to a year-by-year recording of major events up to the final decades of his own life.

Those accustomed to histories written as a single narrative flow may find al-Tabari's work hard to read. His aim is not interpretive synthesis; he seeks instead encyclopedic compilation and conveyance. For a given event, he collects an assemblage of reports, each with a prefatory list of the persons who transmitted it, without much regard for the coordination or consistency of these accounts. So successful was his effort that subsequent generations of historians transmitted but did not transform his accomplishment. Those later generations did, however, add other historical genres to the annalistic chronicle. They wrote urban and regional histories or, in the case of Ibn Munqidh (1095–1188; see below), more personally focused reflections. They charted the dynastic reigns of caliphs, sultans, princes, and governors. They updated the earlier chronicles by incorporating more recent material, both written and oral. They collected the biographies of famous Muslims and organized these by generation or geography. They supplemented biography with bibliography and, in the case of Ibn al-Nadim (before 935–990; see below), catalogued the extant literature of Islamic intellectual life.

As the Muslim world continued to expand through campaigns and expeditions, cross-cultural contact opened new areas of historical and geographical investigation. Initially the information gathered from such exploration found its way into collections of curiosities and anecdotes, of which the *Meadows of Gold* by al-Masʿudi (d. 956) is a noted example. Travelers' accounts, such as those of Ibn Jubayr (1145–1217; see below) and Ibn Battuta (1304–ca. 1368; see below), depicted in more detail places far away and little known. Eventually, collection and compilation pushed toward synthesis, as in Ibn Khaldun's (1332–1406; see below) monumental *Book of Examples* and its famous *Introduction*.

His efforts to ground a science of history drew on an assessment of societies, both Muslim and non-Muslim, both ancient and contemporary. Knowledge of more geographically remote societies expanded continuously in the centuries after Ibn Khaldun, as the Ottoman, Safavid and Mughal empires absorbed ever more territory into the "abode of Islam." With the advent of European incursions and eventual colonization, cultural confrontation was inevitable. The account by al-Jabarti (1753–1825/26; see below) of the Napoleonic invasion and the consequent disruptions of Egyptian life adopted the traditional chronicle format but recognized that these events were a decisive turning point.

Though much historical writing in Islam foregrounds the grand sweep, the big event, and the famous figure, the individual focus and the small scale have their place. Next to chronicles that cover centuries stands the episodic anecdote. Next to biographical dictionaries that capture a millennium of Muslim notables stands the single autobiography of an al-Ghazali, foreshadowing (in a very different era) the autobiography of Malcolm X (1925–1965; see below). The former provided a unique perspective on medieval thought and devotion, while the latter was to celebrate the modern Muslim world as a beacon of brotherhood.

Tray from Syria, mid-13th century. The outstanding feature of this tray, otherwise a typical object of Islamic functional art, is its integration of Christian saints amid the Islamic design. The combination of Muslim and Christian artistic styles was possible only in a milieu in which the two communities interacted closely.

Travel writing plays a special role in the history of Islamic literature. Certainly, journey as a religious duty contributes to this prominence. Every adult Muslim must undertake the pilgrimage to Mecca at least once a lifetime, unless prevented by financial or physical incapacity. Consequently, the thought of extended and arduous travel is familiar to Muslim cultures. A famous hadith of the Prophet supports this orientation, urging Muslims to travel in search of knowledge even as far as China. The world that lay before Muslim travelers, however, was divided between the countries with the religious and cultural connections that united the House of Islam (*dar al-islam*) and the lands that lay beyond that unity, the House of War (*dar al-harb*).

While information gleaned from voyages in both realms can be culled from early geographical and historical literature, much of it is cited anonymously and, presumably, at second or third hand. But from the early tenth century, we have the contemporaneous account of Ibn Fadlan's diplomatic mission for the caliph al-Muqtadir up the Volga River to the king of Bulghar. Fresh translations vividly convey the sense of astonishment and repugnance that the author felt as he encountered social and cultural practices that were utterly foreign. Nevertheless, this work continues to be a fruitful source for scholars of northern Eurasia. Centuries later, first Ibn Jubayr and then Ibn Battuta vastly expanded the scope and sophistication of this genre. Still later, in the sixteenth century, Leo Africanus, born al-Hasan ibn Muhammad al-Wazzan al-Fasi (between 1489 and 1496–ca. 1554; see below), made a significant contribution to the historical geography of Africa.

Tasawwuf: *The Mystical Interiority of Sufism*

Long before terms such as "Sunni" or "Shariʿa" had entered the contemporary American vocabulary, urban bookstores often had a section labeled "Sufism." The poetry of Rumi (1207–1273; see below) and the paperback essays of Idris Shah (1924–1996) were frequently found in the backpacks of American college students and on the shelves of the beatnik generation. What little many Americans knew of Islam was filtered through such popular publications and their rendering of a universalist wisdom attractive to generations of spiritual seekers.

Like the word "Islam" itself, "Sufism" is a label that gained wide currency only after its deployment by nineteenth-century Orientalists—scholars who devoted themselves to the editing and translation of religious manuscripts in Arabic, Persian, Turkish, and Urdu. Sufism is indeed the form in which Islam has most profoundly engaged other religious cultures. Accordingly, as a term—and as a body of thought and practice—Sufism remains a source of ambivalence and tension for many contemporary Muslims. Some will fervently declaim that "Sufism has nothing to do with Islam," while others, equally zealous, find within Sufism the spiritual source of their personal religious lives.

The word "Sufism" is the translation of an Arabic word whose core meaning is "wool" and whose verbal form (*tasawwuf*) connotes a process of taking on or becoming. At base, it means "to put on wool" and, by extension, to adopt various ascetic disciplines such as wearing that scratchy, uncomfortable fabric. Later etymological elaborations that sought to emphasize the early genesis of Sufism connected it with the Arabic word for bench (*suffa*) and with the historical memory of ascetic disciples of Muhammad who gathered on benches near the mosque of Medina.

In the third volume of his *Introduction*, Ibn Khaldun captures the centuries-long core of Sufism as "based upon constant application to divine worship, complete devotion to God, aversion to the false splendor of the world, abstinence from the pleasure, property, and position to which the great mass aspires, and retirement from the world into solitude for divine worship" (chapter 6, section 16). Echoes of Christian monasticism are evident in this description, and scholars attempting to discern the earliest emergence of Sufi attitudes and actions note the presence of monastic establishments in those places, such as Egypt and Syria, where Islamic conquest occurred.

Sufi practice centers on the individual and on the ways in which the individual can cultivate a closer connection to God. By its very nature, such instruction involves an intimate teacher–student, or master–disciple, relationship. Those men, and some women, who became noted for their lives of simplicity, frugality, generosity, and compassion inevitably attracted others who wished to emulate them. Followers affiliated themselves with these spiritual adepts and sought their counsel and guidance. Their prayers and teachings, like those of Zayn al-ʿAbidin (ca. 658–ca. 713) and Abu Yazid al-Bistami (d. 875) included in this anthology, were collected and venerated.

It is no surprise, then, that the exaltation of particular individuals assumes great prominence in Sufism. Hagiography—the literature of the lives of holy people—proliferated, and as the works of al-Hakim al-Tirmidhi (d. between 907 and 912; see below) and al-Sulami (937–1021; see below) reveal, women are well represented. The tombs of these saints became places of pilgrimage and prayer. Those that housed the more widely renowned developed into vast shrine complexes with residential compounds and religious schools. But the attention, acclaim, and posthumous aggrandizement that saints attracted also fed the anti-Sufi sentiments of reformist ideologues from Ibn Taymiyya to Ibn ʿAbd al-Wahhab, who viewed such veneration as antithetical to the strict monotheism that Islam professes.

As modes of affiliation and instruction became more regular and more regulated, a literature of Sufi instruction manuals emerged. Spiritual training, like physical training, involved lifestyle modifications and ever-higher levels of intensity. In this literature, as in analogous literatures of other religious traditions, metaphors of the journey abound. The Sufi seeker embarks on a path charted by his shaykh, or mystical guide. Repentance, repetition of prayer formulas, and ascetic forms of physical discipline reorient the disciple's inner life and prepare him for incessant struggle (*jihad*) with the lower soul. By completely surrendering to the shaykh's direction, the disciple progresses through a sequence of spiritual stations marked by intensifying acts and attitudes of renunciation and abstinence. These prepare the ground for varieties of mystical experience, captured in a descriptive vocabulary that is rich and varied: ecstasy, intoxication, personal annihilation, self-effacement, and union with the divine. Some of the most cherished Sufi authors, such as al-Ghazali and Ibn al-ʿArabi (1165–1240; see below), give expression to their own spiritual crises and moments of ineffable joy.

Trying to express the ineffable, trying to find words that could convey the intensity of spiritual union, drove Sufi mystics to poetry. Love poetry that can be read on multiple levels comprises an enduring heritage of the Sufi quest. Persian literature in particular abounds in mystical love poetry, and the works of such poets as Rumi and Hafiz (1325/26–1390; see below) continue to stand at the center of Iranian culture.

While Sufi thought and practice always remained focused on the individual's cultivating a more intimate connection with the divine, in some instances the small bands of disciples who gathered themselves around a particularly prominent shaykh eventually evolved into large fraternal organizations. Ordinarily, these came to be designated by the name of the venerated shaykh from whom a spiritual lineage was traced. Through succeeding generations, differences in teaching or practice could create divergent lineages that broke off from the main line. Over time, these fraternal organizations or "orders" developed elaborate rituals and regulations. The initiation of new novices frequently involved ceremonial investiture with a woolen garment that signaled their commitment to highly regulated forms of daily life, including the performance of individual and communal prayers. Some of the latter, such as the formalized dance prayers of the Turkish Mawlawiyya, popularly known as the "whirling dervishes," have become modern tourist attractions.

Women have been affiliated with Sufi practices from the earliest periods and some, such as Rabiʿa al-Adawiyya (ca. 714–801), have attracted disciples and followers, both during their lifetimes and beyond. In the later periods, some women were connected to orders and some lived communally in sex-segregated Sufi convents. For both women and men, such organized forms of Sufi lifestyle and practice, and their architectural embodiments, existed simultaneously with independent and individual manifestations of devotion.

The social architecture of Sufi life expanded from its earliest contexts but did not eliminate them. The first generations of Sufis gathered in mosques or in the homes of their masters for spiritual practice and religious teaching, and such settings continued to flourish as sites of Sufi life even as more elaborate venues evolved. From the tenth century onward, communal lodgings were built to house the Sufi shaykh, his family, and his most dedicated followers or sprang up around tomb shrines. As they became larger and more functionally differentiated, these conventual settlements frequently developed a charitable function as housing for travelers and the indigent. The need to support such establishments and their operations created opportunities for pious philanthropy, and rulers could win public approval by endowing and sustaining them.

The geographical spread and the intellectual expansion of Sufism continued unabated through the medieval and early modern periods of Islamic history. Prayer practices evolved and adapted to new settings and cultures. The devotional songs of South Asian Ismaʿili Muslims provide an example of intercultural adaptation. In his philosophical contributions to Shiʿism, Mulla Sadra (ca. 1571–1640; see below) draws heavily on earlier Sufi metaphysical poetry.

Belles Lettres: *The Fine Arts of Poetry and Prose*

In the spring of 2009, news media around the world broadcast the story of a Saudi semifinalist on *Million's Poet*, a wildly popular TV show viewed across the Arab world that has been compared to *American Idol*. Those showcased, however, are not amateur singers hoping for professional careers but poets yearning for a place in the pantheon of Arabic poetry. Contestants are recruited from all Arabic-speaking countries, but the Saudi semifinalist earned particular attention because she was the first woman to reach an advanced stage of the contest. The phenomenal success of this TV program testifies to the enduring esteem of poetry and poets within Arab culture.

Qasida: *The Arabic Ode*

Arabic poetry, with its roots in the pre-Islamic period, has been a living tradition from the sixth to the twenty-first century. Works from the earliest period have kept their renown and continue to set a standard that has been emulated for centuries. Pre-Islamic poetry is expressive and lyrical, filled

Hissa Hilal, a Saudi poetess whose verses challenging violent interpretations of religion earned her death threats, takes the stage of the popular televised poetry competition *Million's Poet*. She won third place and prize money totaling $817,000.

with vivid imagery that celebrates the rugged natural environment of Bedouin life and the ideals that inform that culture. The primary form is the ode (*qasida*), which can vary in length from about thirty to a hundred verses; each line comprises two metrically equivalent half-verses and concludes with a repeated rhyme. A repertoire of themes characterized the genre in its early stages; usually the prelude finds the poet—for example, ʿAlqama (fl. sixth century; see below)—contemplating a deserted campsite and recalling the ecstasies and agonies of a lost love. As the ode unfolds, it often describes the heroic austerities of desert life and the dangers of desert journeys. Wanderings to find pasture, the blessings of rain, and the buffeting of windstorms combine with riveting descriptions of camels, horses, and wild animals to portray the rough reality of Bedouin existence. The exploits of the "hero-poet" and those of his tribe, panegyrics that exalt tribal chiefs and genealogies, satires directed at tribal adversaries: all these are recurring themes in pre-Islamic poetry.

The language of this poetry was not that of daily speech but was a more elevated and inflected form of Arabic with a rich and unusual vocabulary. Its creation and transmission were oral, and theories of oral-formulaic composition have greatly influenced the modern study of this genre. Poetic contests, with public performances at tribal gatherings and market fairs, were a cultural feature of the Arabian Peninsula. In later periods, these took place in the presence of a king or caliph but they continued to include both recitation and improvisation.

Religious ideas and elements were not a prominent part of this tribal poetry, but poets were frequently linked with magic and preternatural powers. Like soothsayers, some were thought to be possessed by jinn and able to forecast the future. It is in the context of these perceptions that the qurʾanic condemnation of poets (Qurʾan 26:221–227) should be read. Clearly, some of the polemic directed at Muhammad's preaching placed him in these categories, a charge that the Prophet vigorously and vehemently denied. Yet such suspicions did not prevent commentators with questions about qurʾanic vocabulary and syntax from extensively consulting poetical texts. The vast lexicon of Arabic poetry helped exegetes seeking to identify and explain unusual qurʾanic vocabulary and grammatical usages.

Persian Lyricism and Further Poetic Permutations

While the ode continued to hold pride of place in later periods of Arabic literary history, it was complemented by other genres more suited to the sensibilities of urban and courtly life. The Umayyad dynasty (661–750), whose conquests were wide-ranging, witnessed the rising urbanization of Arab life and its much more frequent contact with other civilizations. A more lighthearted love poetry emerged, as did schools of singing and other accoutrements of courtly life. As the ʿAbbasids (750–1258) assumed power, the cultural center moved from Damascus to Baghdad and poetic diversification increased. Famous names from this long era include Abu Nuwas (ca. 750–ca. 813) and his wine poetry; al-Mutanabbi (915–965), whose panegyrics graced the court of Sayf al-Dawla (d. 967) in Aleppo; and Abu al-ʿAlaʾ al-Maʿarri (973–1058), the blind Syrian whose work is marked by philological erudition and rhetorical ornament.

As Islam spread across the known world, it touched or transformed the cultures it encountered. Often the influence was reciprocal—and nowhere more so than in the case of Persia. Like the Arabs, Iranians have a proud poetic heritage and continue to embrace poetry as a core cultural value. Firdawsi (ca. 935–ca. 1020) chronicled the story of Iran from creation to the Islamic conquest in the 50,000 lines of his *Shah-nama*, the national epic. Within the tradition of lyrical, romantic poetry, Nizami (ca. 1141–1202; see below) is usually offered pride of place, and his five-part *Khamsa* inspired painters of miniatures for centuries. In the writings of Saʿdi (ca. 1208–early 1290s; see below), storytelling and aptly phrased moral exhortation come to the fore, and quotations from his witty verses continue to be part of common parlance.

Beyond Persia and the lands that lie closest to the Arabian Peninsula, traders, warriors, and preachers carried Islam to the western shores of the Mediterranean, to South and Southeast Asia, to sub-Saharan Africa, and to the regions of China and inner Asia. In every venue, local literary production was reshaped and reoriented through the transformative power of Islamic ideas and ideals. The works of Nana Asmaʾu (1793–1864; see below) in Nigeria and Muhammad Iqbal (1877–1938; see below) in India bear continuing testimony to this impact.

Adam and Eve leaving Paradise from a *Book of Omens* (*Falnama*), used in sixteenth- and seventeenth-century Iran and Turkey to foretell future events. Qazvin, Iran, mid 1550s.

Adab: *Fable, Aphorism, and Essay*

Given the qur'anic attitude toward poetry, Muslim scholars have ordinarily drawn a sharp distinction between poetry and prose. The latter emerged later in the Arabic literary tradition but quickly developed a repertoire that ranged from sober philosophical analysis to elaborate reworkings of age-old fables. The contemporary Arabic term for "literature" is *adab*, a word that in earlier centuries covered a much broader range of material. Classical *adab* works were often collections of verses, aphorisms, and anecdotes on an astonishing array of topics. Regardless of subject, however, the importance of literary merit predominates, with an emphasis on the interesting and the entertaining. One example is the encyclopedic *Book of Animals* by al-Jahiz, the literary polymath whose name means "goggle-eyed." As prose literature expanded and matured, it became closely connected with the court circles and literary salons of ʿAbbasid urban life. The *Book of Songs* by Abu al-Faraj al-Isfahani (879–ca. 972), for example, tells us much about the poets, musicians, and personalities of those societies. Life in the ʿAbbasid era was increasingly influenced by the much older and more established culture of Persia in every aspect of material and artistic production. Proponents of this assimilation, known as the Shuʿubis, argued that Arab descent should not be a mark of social superiority while their opponents insisted on the preeminence of the Arabic literary heritage.

The cities and courts of Andalusia could boast of their own celebrated literary figures, including the prominent legal scholar and belletrist Ibn Hazm (994–1064; see below). He penned the Muslim world's most famous treatise on the theory and practice of love, a work that may well have influenced the notions of courtly love that developed in medieval Europe. Other forms of Islamic literature were also finding an audience in Europe. Via translations into Arabic made during the ʿAbbasid caliphate, the writings of Plato and Aristotle transformed medieval Christian theology and philosophy. But nothing has captured the popular imagination of the West as completely as the tradition of storytelling conveyed in the collection widely known as *The Thousand and One Nights*. With their Indian and Persian roots, these Arabian tales in their eighteenth-century French, English, and Spanish translations and elaborations made Scheherazade and Sinbad, Ali Baba, and Aladdin household names across Europe and the Americas.

The Classical Synthesis Encounters Modernity (1756–2012)

With the shattering events of September 11, 2001, the Muslim world unexpectedly erupted into American consciousness. Terms and names—*Sunni, Shiʿi, jihad*, and *Ramadan*, as well as Usama bin Ladin (1957–2011; see below), Sayyid Qutb (1906–1966; see below), and others—that had been the purview of a few scholars and diplomats suddenly tumbled off the tongues of countless media "experts." Misinformation about Islam and Muslims fanned popular fears and competed with the outreach undertaken by academics and foreign-service professionals who were inundated with requests for interviews, speaking engagements, and editorial comments. For months the statement "Islam means peace" was relentlessly repeated, capturing the spirit of an honest effort at instant education but masking the complexity of the contemporary world of Islam.

The Impact of European Colonialism on World Islam

The Islamic world of the classical synthesis gave way to today's Islamic world during a period that stretches from the final decades of the eighteenth century to the middle decades of the twentieth. Large areas that had been under Muslim rule were seized by other powers. By the mid-eighteenth century, Britain had already consolidated its control over much of India, Russia had

Pakistani women look through peace signs during a demonstration against terrorism on October 24, 2009, in Islamabad, Pakistan.

already expanded deep into Central Asia, and France was poised to launch a more lasting expansion into North Africa than the storied Crusades had brought about in the Levant. These and later European expansions would redraw the map of much of the Muslim world, creating a web of colonial empires and outposts that transformed local societies. Conditions of subjugation and dependency provoked responses that combined religious fervor with a nearly unprecedented kind of political mobilization. Building on the premise that social failure and the loss of autonomy were a consequence of religious decline, reformist ideologies began to appear in diverse places across the Muslim world. The mid-eighteenth-century Wahhabi movement in the Arabian Peninsula, the mid-nineteenth-century jihadist movements in West Africa, and the late-nineteenth-century Mahdist uprising in Sudan—all these and various others sought, in diverse ways, to reorient their societies to a more pristine form of Islamic practice, devoid of the popular accretions that threatened a pure monotheism. The life of the Prophet and his earliest followers was idealized as the perfect community, one that all subsequent Muslim societies should seek to emulate.

Reacting both to the increasing intrusion of Western material culture and social values and to a sense of intellectual stagnation, reformist thinkers such as Sayyid Ahmad Khan (1817–1898; see below), Muhammad ʿAbduh, and Jamal al-Din al-Afghani (1838–1897) called for a revitalization of Islamic thought and practice with a vigorous, reason-based response to modern challenges. As colonial regimes installed educational systems that produced several generations of Westernized elites, the gulf between the uneducated majorities and these elites widened. They became vulnerable to charges of co-option and accommodation as nationalist, counter-colonial initiatives began to gather strength.

These liberation movements gained momentum after World War II as, under pressure, Britain, France, and other European powers withdrew from their former colonies. The nationalist movements that swept through the Muslim world in Asia, Africa, and the Middle East, infused with the euphoria of independence, devised progressive plans for modernization and rapid economic development. But questions about political legitimacy, as well as the damage wrought by colonialism, plagued these efforts and derailed the dreams of rapid transformation. The artificial boundaries of a number of these new nations helped foster a geopolitical instability, which continues to drive regional rivalries. The most enduring of these rivalries are those focused on the state of Israel, created in 1947 by the United Nations' partition of what had been British-ruled Palestine, and on the disputed border between India and Pakistan, created in the same year by the British Parliament's partition of what had been British-ruled India.

The Demise of the Secularization Thesis

The thesis that increasing modernization in these newly independent nations would lead to increasing secularization was demolished with the Iranian Revolution of 1979. The sudden emergence of a theocracy that put political authority in the hands of religious leaders like Ruhollah Khomeini (1902–1989; see below) stunned the political theorists who had assumed that the Shah's Western-oriented and Western-supported regime was the wave of the future and who seemed unaware of the impact that writers like ʿAli Shariʿati (1933–1977; see below) were having. To recognize religion, particularly Islam, as a potential global force, academics had to rethink prevailing positions. Renewed interest in "fundamentalism" as an explanatory category captured academic attention in the aftermath of the Iranian Revolution, even though the term itself remains a poor match for the varieties of sociopolitical reformist efforts that have sped across the Muslim world in the past several decades.

The impacts of these efforts and their ideological underpinnings have differed, depending on context and culture. The Wahhabi-inspired society of Saudi Arabia does not exhibit the religious and demographic diversity of Indonesia or the linguistic and ethnic tensions of the Uighur-speaking, Muslim-majority Xinjiang Province of China, where that immense country abuts Central Asia along its western border. Conflicting interpretations of Islam compete for public support and are manifest in different sectors of the social order across several spectrums, from liberal to conservative, from extremist violence to peaceful pluralism, from internal reform to revolutionary upheaval. The "Arab Spring" of late 2010 and 2011, which led to the overthrow of several dictators reviled equally by religious and secular elements in their societies, became the occasion—most notably in Egypt—for a searching debate about the relationship between multiple religious and secular, Muslim and non-Muslim, values and voices in the writing of new national constitutions. Yet even within this multiplicity some overriding emphases emerge. Islam is seen ideally as an all-encompassing religious and social vision in which authentic autonomy, whether as a nation or a worldwide umma, depends on the religious renewal of individuals—their genuine embrace of Islamic values and practices. History, especially that of the modern period, demonstrates conclusively that other ideologies, whether nationalism, secularism, socialism, Westernization, or pan-Arabism, have failed. They have not delivered on their promise of economic advancement and a more just society. Only Islam is the answer. It is not an option: it is a divine imperative. Countering this widely prevalent conceptualization with a more nuanced understanding of modernity has been the task of such contemporary Muslim intellectuals as Mohammed Arkoun (1928–2010) and Ebrahim Moosa (b. 1957), both included in this anthology. Though well-schooled in the traditional sources, thinkers such as these probe the complexities of Muslim life and thought within the very different social and cultural contexts of modern life.

The Pivotal Role of Muslim Women in a Cultural Transformation

Throughout the period that witnessed the genesis of contemporary Islam, gender concerns have been key. Independence movements that emphasized egalitarian ideals drew educated women into the public sphere and opened a discourse about gender bias and sexual inequalities. More than a century ago, the Egyptian proto-feminist Huda Shaʿrawi (1879–1947) sought to establish that veiling and seclusion are not religious mandates but cultural practices. Her successors, in Egypt and elsewhere, pushed for women's access to education and employment, as well as for fuller participation in the political process. They sought legal reforms, particularly to the statutes governing personal status. Many educated women across the Middle East and North Africa abandoned traditional forms of dress, earned advanced degrees, and secured professional positions. Though they justified their actions on religious grounds, their primary objective was socioeconomic advancement rather than religious equality.

By the final decades of the twentieth century, female sexuality and forms of violence against women became an important focus. Feminist movements in Europe and North America drew international attention to instances of honor killing, to socially sanctioned wife beating, and to female genital mutilation. The Moroccan sociologist Fatima Mernissi (b. 1940; see below) published a best-selling study of female sexuality in the Qur'an and hadith, arguing that it is represented as a force that must be constrained to prevent social chaos. During the same decades, while Islamist reform movements gathered strength in many parts of the Muslim world, women found themselves again pushed to the periphery and their hard-won political and educational gains abrogated. The history of Afghanistan under the Taliban is but one instance of this trend. Many commentators fear that developments after the Arab Spring may provide another.

As global communication enabled women to network from Manhattan to Mindanao and as women in the worldwide Muslim diaspora gained easier access to education, a new form of scholarly activism emerged. It centers on fresh interpretations of the Qur'an and hadith by Muslim feminists who have the linguistic and legal training needed to relate their exegesis to the centuries-long traditions of commentary on these texts. A groundbreaking work of this sort by Amina Wadud (b. 1952; see below) was initially published in Malaysia, and women's organizations in nearby Indonesia have also fostered productive forms of activism by female intellectuals. In North and West Africa, Shariʿa-educated women have successfully intervened in Shariʿa court cases as well as in secular legislative procedures that address gender inequities. In a curious echo of earlier assumptions about the connection between modernity and secularism, some Western observers of Muslim feminism have assumed that social and economic advancement would result in the renunciation of all forms of Islamic dress. Quite the opposite has happened, as the hijab controversies in France and elsewhere demonstrate. Around the world, many young women have donned the headscarf and other markers of Muslim identity, sometimes in the face of family opposition, to publicly manifest their religious affiliation and to visually mark their separation from non-Islamic vices and values.

Will Islam Be Reshaped as World Religious Pluralism Expands?

Although Islam was born within an environment of multiple religions, its earliest exchanges with other religions were chiefly confrontational. The medieval period generated a large literature of polemics and apologetics, aimed especially at combating the theological errors of Judaism and Christianity and at persuading adherents of those faiths that Islam was indeed the final, conclusive divine revelation. Centuries of conflict, both ideological and military, between Muslims and Christians sharpened antagonisms and left a bitter legacy. Efforts on both sides to achieve a more informed understanding of the other were made, but they were minor brushstrokes on the overall canvas. In the modern era, however, the same imperial operations that colonized much of the Muslim world stimulated interest in that world and its cultural and textual heritage. Post-Enlightenment scholars in both Europe and North America embarked on large translation projects and serious academic investigation of the "sacred books of the East." Grand events like the 1893 World's Parliament of Religions in Chicago gave these texts a human face and generated enormous public curiosity.

In the twentieth century—a period marked by migrations and displacements of populations around the globe—Muslims more frequently found themselves living and working in non-Muslim countries and societies. As experiences of religious plurality became far more common, theological reflection within particular religious traditions began to address it. Largely as a consequence of Christian initiatives after World War II, dialogues between Muslims and Christians began to take place. Initially these were formal, bilateral conversations between religious authorities such as the Vatican and the World Muslim League. Later they expanded to national, regional, and even local efforts, a phenomenon that has accelerated exponentially in the post-9/11 period.

In addressing the issues raised by social pluralism and religious interaction, Muslim scholars and activists have drawn on the traditional sources of Islamic faith and learning, but in so doing they have offered new insights and interpretations prompted by contemporary contexts. An early Sufi work by Dara Shukoh (1615–1659; see below) that sought to harmonize Islam and Hinduism serves as a provocative prelude to later attempts to engage with other faiths. Nurcholish Majid (1939–2005; see below) attracted a large following with lectures and publications that developed an Islamic understanding of the forms of religious freedom enshrined in Indonesia's state philosophy of religious pluralism known as Pancasila (Five Principles). The Turkish scholar Fethullah Gulen (b. 1941; see below) has created an international network of schools that are open to Muslims and non-Muslims alike. Tariq Ramadan (b. 1962; see below), whose family roots are Egyptian but whose education was European, writes about the need for Muslims living in Europe and North America to construct their own identities as citizens of Western democracies. Inevitably, this effort will involve an openness to interreligious dialogue and to interfaith actions that operate to promote the common social good.

These thinkers represent but scattered instances of the vast currents of change that are sweeping the Muslim world. Conflicting interpretations and ideologies compete for the attention of an audience whose demographic midpoint grows younger every year and whose access to new media enables it to ignore borders that constrained older generations. As young Muslims from Minneapolis, Madrid, and Manila, from Cape Town, Cairo, and Caracas connect with each other, they will create and re-create a worldwide umma that reflects the grandeur of Islam's past and the dynamism of its future.

A NOTE ON TRANSLITERATION

In the material written especially for this anthology, i.e., the introductions, headnotes, and footnotes, words of foreign origin have been transcribed in accord with the now-standard system of transliteration used by many monographs, reference works, and scholarly journals, minus, however, the markings for long vowels and dotted letters. But the transliteration symbols for the Arabic letters *'ayn* and *hamza* have been retained in order to distinguish these letters from English punctuation, such as single quotation marks and apostrophes.

Within the anthologized texts themselves, the transliteration systems used in the original publication remain intact, with the exception of the standardization of the treatment of *'ayn* and *hamza* for the above-stated reason. Texts of more recent publication ordinarily use the now-standard system detailed below. Older texts deploy a variety of systems, such as representing a long vowel with a caret (^) or transcribing the Arabic letter *jim* with a "dj" instead of a "j." Often, *al-* (the Arabic definite article) is represented with *ar-* or *ad-*, etc., to produce the proper elision of the class of Arabic letters known as the "sun letters." In the pronunciation glossary for each text, words have been listed as they appear in the text itself and the appropriate pronunciation provided.

ARABIC LETTER	TRANSLITERATED ENGLISH
ء	ʾ
ب	b
ت	t
ث	th

ARABIC LETTER	TRANSLITERATED ENGLISH
ج	j
ح	ḥ
خ	kh
د	d
ذ	dh
ر	r
ز	z
س	s
ش	sh
ص	ṣ
ض	ḍ
ط	ṭ
ظ	ẓ
ع	ʿ
غ	gh
ف	f
ق	q
ك	k
ل	l
م	m
ن	n
ه	h
و	w
ي	y
ة	-a
ال	al- or ’l

VOWELS	
long ا or ى	ā
long و	ū
long ي	ī
doubled يّ	iyy (final form ī)
doubled وُّ	uww (final form ū)
diphthong وَ	au or aw
diphthong يَ	ai or ay
short َ	-a
short ُ	-u
short ِ	-i

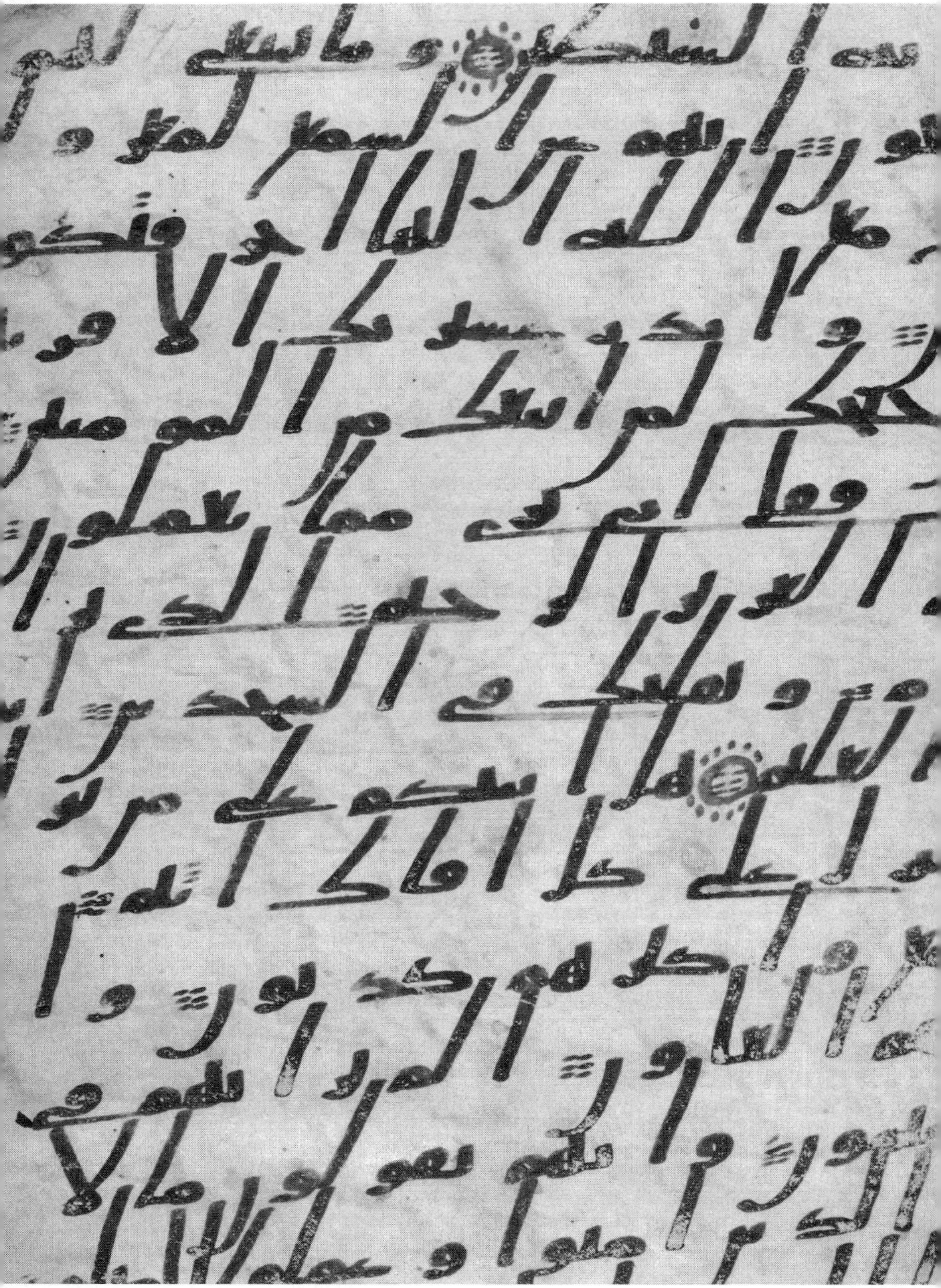

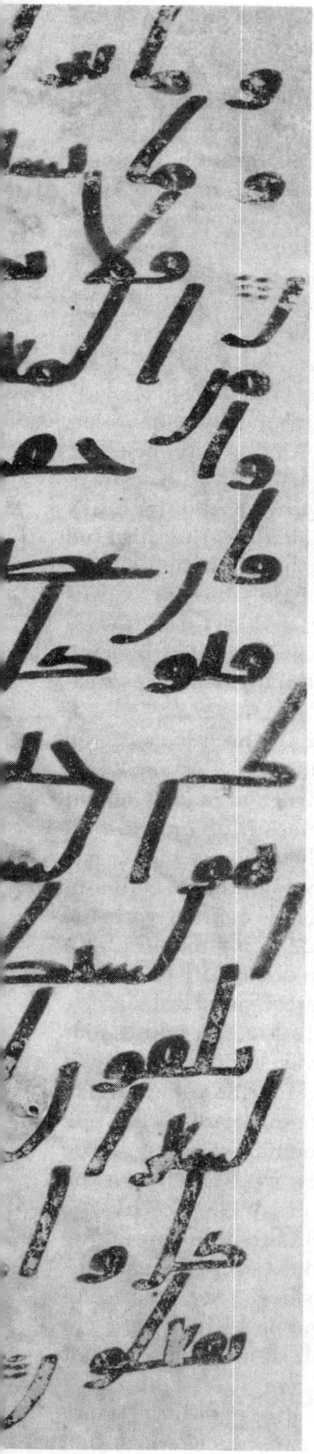

The Foundational Epoch

610–750

THE QUR'AN AND THE EARLY MUSLIM COMMUNITY IN ARABIA

In this anthology of classical Muslim texts, the Qur'an precedes the *Sira*, or life story of the Prophet Muhammad, because, as Muslims believe, the Qur'an precedes Muhammad in reality. In a conventional literary anthology, readers naturally enough are provided biographical information before any discussion of the author's works. But it is only a slight exaggeration to say that in developed Muslim thought, the Qur'an is the author of Muhammad rather than he of it. By its own repeated and self-conscious claims, the Qur'an is a divine book, eternal with the eternity of God the Author, whose guidance it reveals as "the mother of the Book" (Qur'an 3:7) and the ultimate source of all earlier divine self-revelation.

Muhammad was born in 570 C.E. in the town of Mecca in west-central Arabia into a clan of the Banu Hashim within the tribe of the Quraysh. Orphaned at an early age, he was raised by his uncle, Abu Talib, a caravan merchant, and he prepared to follow his uncle's profession. At about the age of twenty-five, he met a well-to-do widow, Khadija, who became his employer in the caravan trade as well as his wife—until her death, his only

Folio from a late 7th- or early 8th-century Qur'an that contains the concluding verses of Sura 26, The Poets, and the initial ones of Sura 27, The Ant (26:183–27:3). Its early script, known as Hijazi, is characterized by thin, slanting strokes. This Qur'an, the oldest in the British Library, has been the subject of several recent studies. One example is Keith E. Small, *Textual Criticism and Qur'an Manuscripts* (2012).

wife (a notable detail, in a polygamous society)—and the mother of his daughter Fatima.

The foundational epoch of Islam begins, however, not with the birth of Muhammad but with the moment during the month of Ramadan in 610 when he first heard the command "Recite!"—the command that gives the Qur'an ("Recitation") its name. The voice—God speaking through the angel Gabriel, Muslims believe—would visit Muhammad at intervals for more than twenty years, until his death in 632. Though "recite" is a translation sanctioned by long usage, the effective meaning of the Arabic word in context is sometimes "proclaim," when the message is a proclamation of the greatness of God, and not infrequently "tell" or "tell them," when the commission to Muhammad as the messenger of God is to correct the errors of Jews, Christians, tribal polytheists, or others. Historians infer that the religious culture of Mecca included all of these worshippers. Mecca was, in fact, a shrine city, where violence was restrained by long-standing custom and religious tolerance was the rule—to the considerable profit of the Meccans themselves, since with this peace came lucrative opportunities for trade.

Not surprisingly, the tribe that ruled Mecca, the Quraysh, did not relish being told by God's messenger or "warner" (in Arabic, *nadhir*) that his God was the only deity and that the social arrangement that so benefited the tribe was inimical to the divine will. Yet the eloquence of the Qur'an was such that Muhammad made powerful converts. One of these, originally a polytheist and an aggressive opponent, was ʿUmar ibn al-Khattab, who said, according to a later account, "When I heard the Qur'an, my heart was softened and I wept, and Islam entered into me."

Islam, "submission" to God as unique and supreme in the universe, had been God's requirement of his creatures from Adam and Eve on down through the centuries, the Qur'an clearly implied, and a good many had met it. There had been Muslims, in other words, long before Muhammad first heard the voice of Gabriel; Abraham was an especially celebrated instance. Henceforth, however, submission to God was to entail recognition of Muhammad as God's messenger as well. On that issue above all, conflict with the Meccan authorities escalated to the point that in 622 Muhammad and a group of key companions fled for their lives to the town of Yathrib, later to be called the City (in Arabic, *medina*) of the Prophet, or more simply Medina.

Muhammad's flight (in Arabic, *hijra*) from Mecca to Medina marks year one of the Muslim calendar not because the flight was so great a glory in itself but because in that year Muhammad became, far from a mere refugee, the judge and governor of Medina. Evidently recognizing his charisma, the Medinans had asked him to adjudicate and mediate chronic strife among their tribes, some of them Arab and others Jewish. Thus began the long decade in which Muhammad would model wise governance for the community—the *umma* ("nation" or "people")—of believers that was taking shape around him. His words of explanation and adjudication in a great variety of circumstances were preserved, and his followers began the practice of recalling and repeating them and of emulating his example—the practice of following the Prophet's sunna, which would ground Muslim custom and law for centuries after his death.

Judge, governor, and prophet, Muhammad was also a military commander, leading the Medinan Muslims through six years of armed conflict

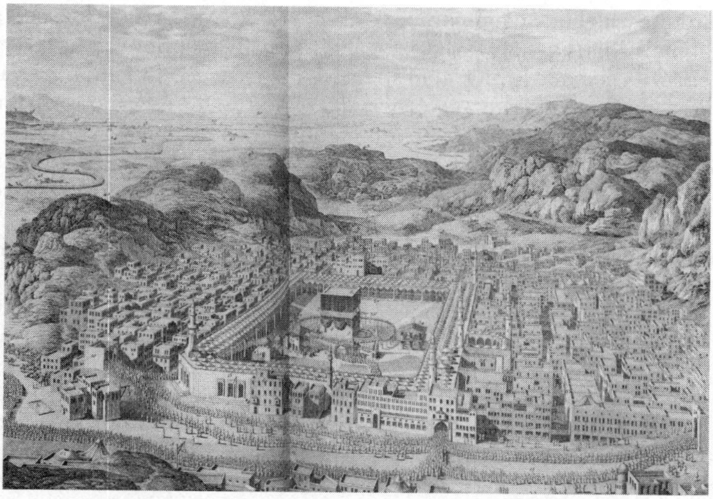

View of Mecca, 18th century. This image comes from the *Tableau general de l'Empire othoman* (Paris, 1788) by Ignace Mouradgea d'Ohsson, an Armenian born in Constantinople who worked for the Swedish legation as charge d'affairs in the Ottoman Porte. The first volume of his history of the Ottoman Empire was concerned with explaining the religion of Islam.

with the Quraysh of Mecca. But in 628, the Meccans abandoned further resistance, Muhammad returned in triumph, and Islam thereafter spread so rapidly—both by conversion and by conquest—through much of the Arabian Peninsula that the umma quickly became an Arabian confederacy.

ESTABLISHMENT OF THE CALIPHATE AND FIRST ARAB CONQUESTS

At the time of his death in 632, Muhammad had neither left a male heir nor appointed a successor to his leadership role. The result was immediate: troubling signs that the Arabian confederacy, which had been held together not by Muslim belief alone but also by the charismatic authority of the Prophet himself, might break apart. While it was inevitable that the umma would somehow be governed one way or another, it was far from clear to what extent the governor would exercise religious rather than mere administrative or military authority. The office that first emerged was that of caliph (in Arabic, *khalifa*, meaning "successor" or "representative"), and Muslim tradition has honored the first four caliphs as "rightly guided" (*rashidun*; sing. *rashid*).

Abu Bakr, the first of these *rashidun*, was the father of 'A'isha, Muhammad's favorite among the many wives he took after Khadija's death, when the umma was being transformed into a confederacy or supertribe built to a large measure around dynastic alliances. Abu Bakr died a natural death (the only one of the *rashidun* to do so) after just two years, but during that brief time he forcefully consolidated and extended Muslim rule through much of Arabia. After his death, the Muslim elite, made up especially of those

Companions who had accompanied Muhammad to Medina in 622, acclaimed ʿUmar ibn al-Khattab—an early convert, as already mentioned, and the father of Hafsa, another of Muhammad's wives—as the second caliph in 634.

It was ʿUmar, more than any other, who laid the foundation for Islam as a global rather than a national religion. Arabia lay between two empires—the Roman or Byzantine empire to the west, and the Persian empire to the east—and Arab border tribes had served both of these empires as mercenaries, learning the respective military practices of their employers while doing so. Though the Arab conquests did not impose Islam, the Muslim fervor of the Arab warriors was undoubtedly a factor in the military success of ʿUmar's ten-year caliphate (634–44). Under his inspired generalship, the Arab tribes, who had long engaged in raids against one another, became an all-but-irresistible fighting force as their formidable military energies were combined and directed outward. In short order, they seized control of Palestine, Syria, and Mesopotamia—all the territory that had most frequently been contested in the endless wars fought by the Romans and the Persians. The Roman (Byzantine) empire's Egyptian province fell soon after. And the Persian (Sassanid) empire's loss of its western provinces to ʿUmar's army proved a blow from which it would never recover.

After his assassination by a Persian prisoner of war, ʿUmar was succeeded by ʿUthman ibn ʿAffan, a wealthy friend whom he himself had converted to Islam and who had later married Ruqayya, another of Muhammad's daughters. During the twelve years of ʿUthman's caliphate, the Arabs extended their empire in the north to include Armenia; in the west to include Cyprus and Tunis; and, crucially, in the east as far as the Oxus River in Central Asia. Moreover, ʿUthman is honored in Islamic history for having promulgated a definitive edition of the many qurʾanic revelations that Muhammad had received during his lifetime. Initially transcribed in various ad hoc ways, these revelations were compiled after the Prophet's death in several collections. During ʿUthman's caliphate (644–56), most Muslim scholars still believe, they were codified as essentially the canonical Qurʾan that we read today.

Toward the end of his caliphate, however, his religious leadership and his military success were compromised by grievous domestic strife. Though in many ways an able administrator, ʿUthman was resented for his nepotism. He belonged to the Banu Umayya clan, a larger and more powerful clan within the tribe of the Quraysh than the Banu Hashim clan to which Muhammad had belonged. Umayyad nepotism was viewed by some of the Muslims of Medina as the revenge of Mecca, an outrageous displacement of the loyal Medinans who had stood by Muhammad during his early struggles and fought alongside him for control of Arabia.

In 656, a group of disgruntled anti-Umayyad soldiers from the Egyptian province assassinated ʿUthman and installed ʿAli ibn Abi Talib (ca. 599–661) as caliph. ʿAli was Muhammad's first cousin, the husband of Muhammad's daughter Fatima, and the son of the very Abu Talib who had raised the orphaned Muhammad. Muhammad and ʿAli had grown up as brothers, though ʿAli was much the younger of the two, and ʿAli had seemed to be Muhammad's most trusted confidant and comrade-in-arms. Many had expected him to succeed his cousin and spiritual brother in what could have established, in effect, a true sacred dynasty. Some went further and doubted the legitimacy of any other outcome. As ʿAli assumed the caliphate, it appeared briefly as if the Umayyad ascendancy had come to a violent end.

But this was not to be. The Umayyads rallied around Muʿawiya, a nephew of ʿUthman's whom he had installed as governor of Syria, and civil war ensued between his supporters and ʿAli's. After an inconclusive attempt at arbitration in 657, Muʿawiya was emboldened to declare ʿAli deposed. Suspecting collaboration, a defector from the party of ʿAli then assassinated him in 661. Abandoning the struggle, ʿAli's son Hasan, the Prophet's grandson, acquiesced in Muʿawiya's victory and retired to Medina.

The Umayyad victory now seemed complete. Yet when Muʿawiya died in 680, the struggle broke out again, this time between Muʿawiya's son Yazid and ʿAli's son Husayn, Hasan's younger brother. The outcome was another victory for the Umayyad party, and a violent one: Husayn was slain at the Battle of Karbalaʾ, and the Umayyads, having moved the caliphate to Damascus in the interim, were established as a dynasty that would rule until 750.

Defeat notwithstanding, the partisans of ʿAli, Hasan, and Husayn retained their belief that the prophetic line of succession through the Prophet's family was the only proper authority in the umma. Thus was born, on the Plain of Karbalaʾ, a deep division in the umma between the Shiʿi, the "partisans" of ʿAli and his descendants (from the Arabic *shiʿa*, "party"), and the Sunni, whose attachment was in their own eyes not to the Prophet's genealogical line but to his *sunna,* his practice or "way." In their different ways, each group intended only fervent loyalty to the Prophet, but the mutual antagonism between them, though quiescent for long periods, has never yielded to true reconciliation; to our own day, it has repeatedly flared into violence. All the same, the era of the *rashidun*—linked to Muhammad as they were by shared, powerful religious experience; by shared struggle against heavy odds; and by complex familial and marital bonds—was now definitively at an end.

THE FOUNDATIONAL SIGNIFICANCE OF THE UMAYYAD DYNASTY

Whatever the justice of Muʿawiya's personal claim to world Muslim leadership, Arab military success continued through the remainder of the Umayyad dynasty, extending the Arab empire as far as Spain's Atlantic coast to the west and as far into the Indian subcontinent as the Indus River to the east. And although, to repeat, the Arabs did not impose Islam upon their subjects at the point of a sword, the quasi-miraculous speed of their conquests did assume for them, in retrospect, a foundational religious significance. Historians have sought secular explanations for that speed, arguing for the role of the deadly spread of the plague and of the exhaustion to which the Byzantine Romans and Sassanid Persians had reduced one another by their long, debilitating wars. Muslims, for their part, Arab or not, could only wonder that a century after the hijra, the Arabs, who had been first to embrace the Qurʾan, were no longer a scorned and marginal collection of tribes but an empire that stretched from the Pyrenees to the Himalayas. How could the hand of God not be seen in something so utterly without parallel in human history? Quite strikingly, Muhammad had worked no miracles. His early followers had made no miraculous claims for themselves nor attracted converts with any such promises. But at the end of the foundational epoch in Islamic history, the Umayyad empire seemed to stand alongside the Qurʾan as God's founding gift to his Muslim people.

Chronology

THE FOUNDATIONAL EPOCH, 610–750

All dates represent the common era.

ca. 570 Birth of the prophet Muhammad

ca. 570 Death of ʿAlqama

610 First Qurʾanic revelations

615 Persecuted Muslims seek refuge with Abyssinian Christian king

622 Muhammad and his followers emigrate from Mecca to Medina to escape increasing persecution (the Hijra)

624 Battle of Badr

625 Battle of Uhud

627 Battle of the Trench

628 Treaty of Hudaybiyya

630 Meccans surrender their city to Muhammad

632 Last pilgrimage and death of the prophet Muhammad

632–634 Caliphate of Abu Bakr al-Siddiq. Wars of Ridda

634 Death of Abu Bakr, the first of the caliphs to succeed Muhammad

634–644 Caliphate of ʿUmar ibn al-Khattab

636 or 637 Battle of Qadisiyya, in which the Sassanid empire suffers pivotal defeat

638 Jerusalem, third holiest city in Islam, comes under Muslim control

644 Assassination of the caliph ʿUmar by a Persian slave

644–656 Caliphate of ʿUthman ibn ʿAffan

ca. 653 Official collection of the Qurʾan under the caliph ʿUthman

656 Assassination of ʿUthman and appointment of ʿAli ibn Abi Talib as caliph. Battle of the Camel

657 Battle of Siffin and ascent of Muʿawiya ibn Abi Sufyan (d. 680)
Secession of the Kharijis

658 or 659–ca. 713 Zayn al-ʿAbidin ʿAli ibn al-Husayn, pious great-grandson of Muhammad and fourth Shiʿi imam

661 A Khariji assassinates ʿAli

661–750 Umayyad dynasty. Capital moves from Medina to Damascus

674 Earliest evidence of Arab settlement in Sumatra

680 Yazid, son of Muʿawiya, takes power after his father's death
Yazid's Umayyad forces defeat Shiʿi revolutionaries at Karbalaʾ, precipitating the martyrdom of al-Husayn, grandson of the Prophet and son of ʿAli
ʿAbdallah ibn al-Zubayr launches a revolution at Mecca and declares a counter-caliphate

683–685 Caliphate of Marwan ibn al-Hakam

685–705 Caliphate of ʿAbd al-Malik ibn Marwan

692 Umayyads defeat and kill Ibn al-Zubayr. Dome of the Rock mosque is completed in Jerusalem

ca. 699–767 Abu Hanifa, legal scholar and eponymous founder of the Hanafi school of law

ca. 704–767 Ibn Ishaq, early biographer of the Prophet

711 Muslim forces enter Spain and Sind

713 Zaydi sect of Shiʿism begins upon death of Zayd ibn ʿAli ibn al-Husayn's father (Zayn al-ʿAbidin)

728 Al-Hasan al-Basri, scholar and jurist, dies

732 Muslim advance on France is halted by Charles Martel

737–821 Ibn al-Kalbi, historian and genealogist

742 Mosque of Xian is built in China

750 ʿAbbasids wrest power from the Umayyads in Syria

750–1258 ʿAbbasid dynasty

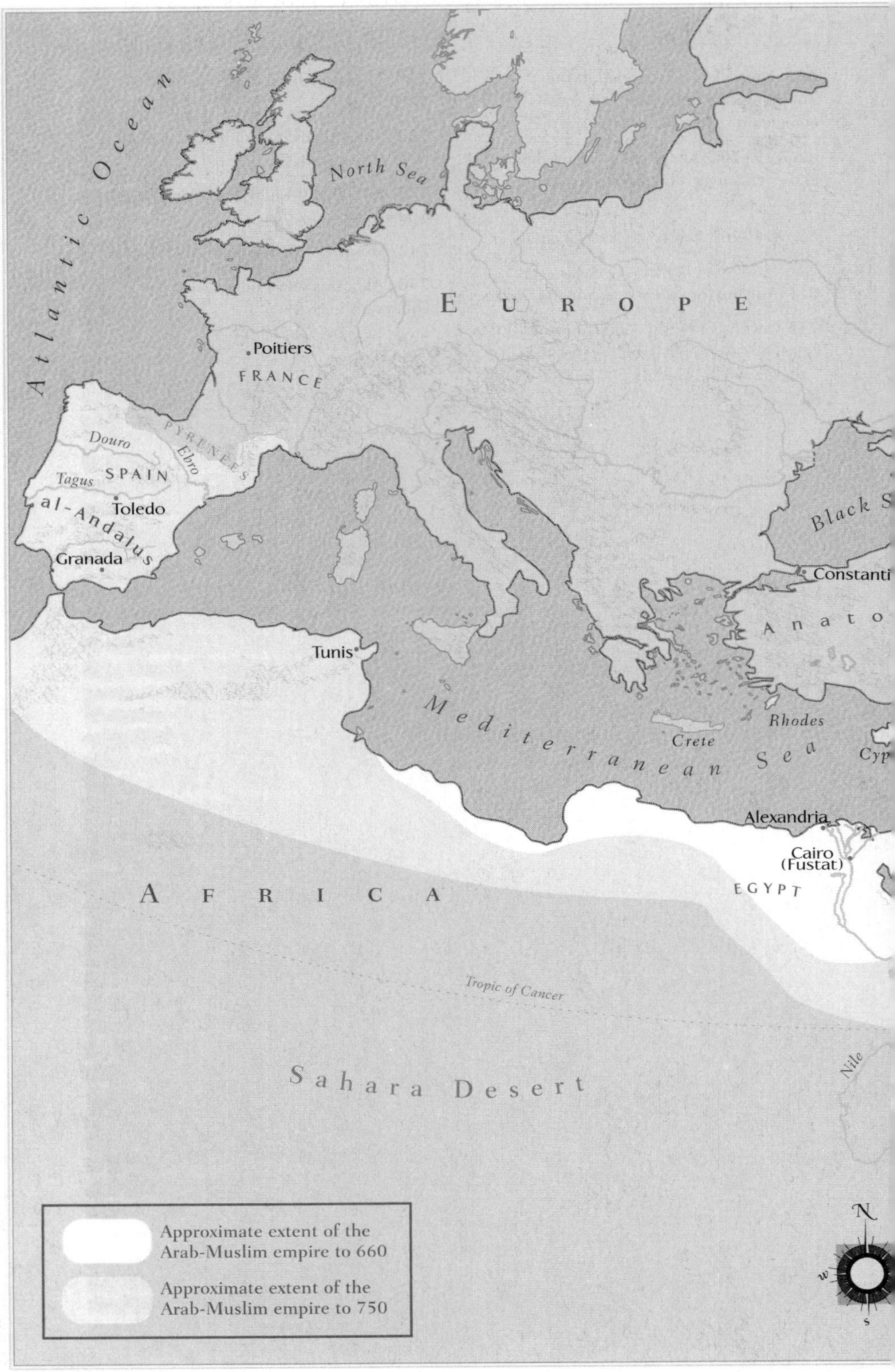

Atlantic Ocean
North Sea
EUROPE
Poitiers
FRANCE
PYRENEES
Douro
Ebro
Tagus
SPAIN
al-Andalus
Toledo
Granada
Tunis
Black S
Constanti
Anato
Mediterranean Sea
Rhodes
Crete
Cyp
Alexandria
Cairo (Fustat)
EGYPT
AFRICA
Tropic of Cancer
Nile
Sahara Desert
Approximate extent of the Arab-Muslim empire to 660
Approximate extent of the Arab-Muslim empire to 750
N
W
S

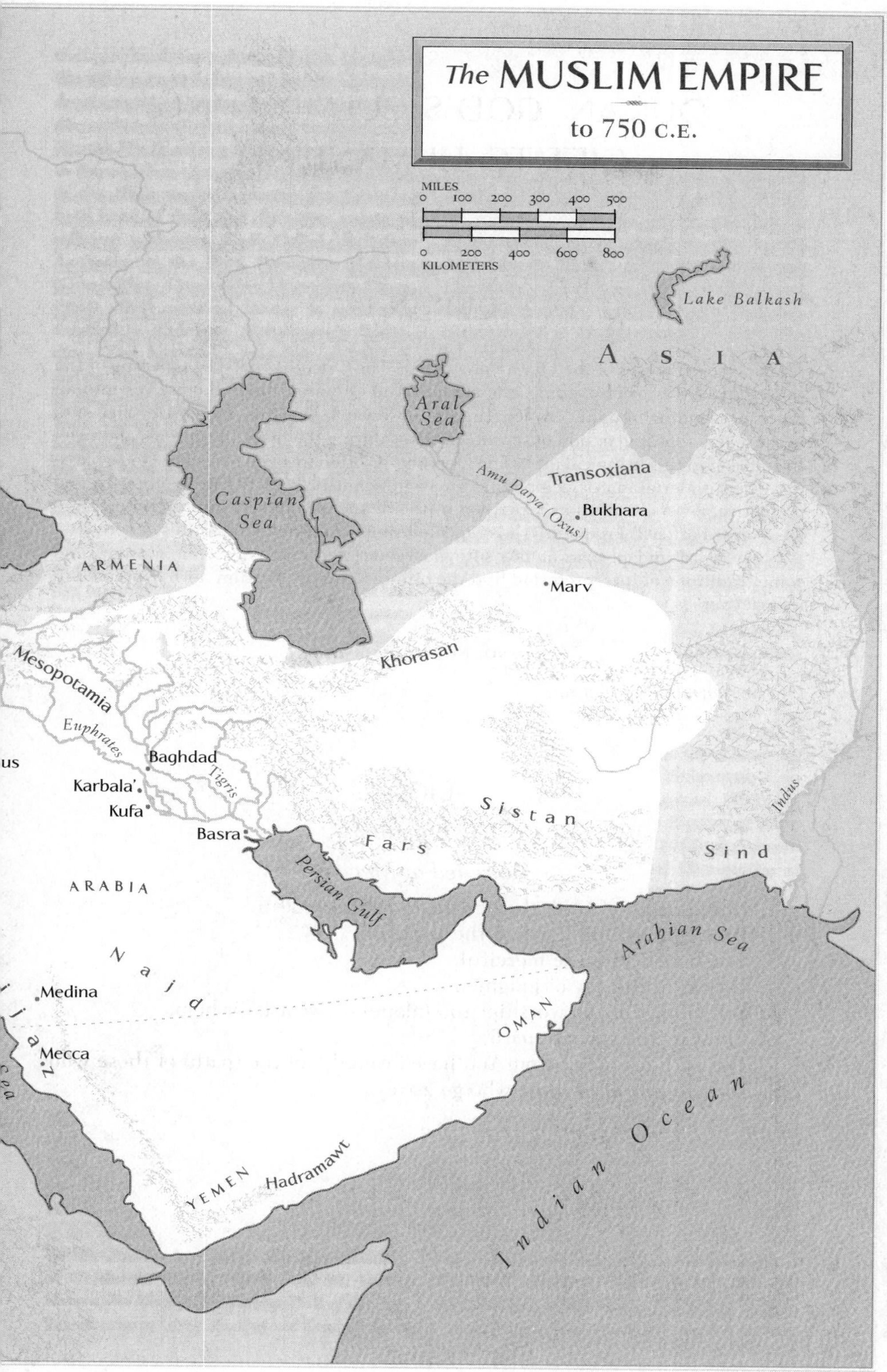

The MUSLIM EMPIRE
to 750 C.E.
MILES
0 100 200 300 400 500
0 200 400 600 800
KILOMETERS
Lake Balkash
A S I A
Aral Sea
Caspian Sea
Amu Darya (Oxus)
Transoxiana
Bukhara
ARMENIA
Marv
Khorasan
Mesopotamia
Euphrates
Baghdad
Tigris
Karbala'
Kufa
Basra
Sistan
Fars
Indus
Sind
Persian Gulf
ARABIA
Arabian Sea
Najd
Medina
OMAN
Mecca
Indian Ocean
YEMEN
Hadramawt

QURʾAN: GOD'S CULMINATING GIFT TO HUMANKIND

QUR'AN 1

The first seven verses of the Qur'an are called "The Opening" or "The Opening of the Book." After this brief opening, the suras of the Qur'an arrange themselves into an order descending roughly by length. All observant Muslims memorize this sura because it is repeated a total of seventeen times during the five daily periods of prayer. In addition to this liturgical use, "The Opening" is often invoked to secure God's blessing when undertaking or completing any significant task. Belief in its curative and protective powers inspires its repetition by the ill and prompts its inscription on amulets to ward off evil. Frequently, it is repeated simply to thank God for his generosity.

Every word and phrase of the sura has generated extensive commentary, and some traditions of interpretation find the quintessence of Muslim faith expressed in its brief verses.

PRONOUNCING GLOSSARY

Qur'an: *qor-ahn'* (not *ko-ran'*)

SŪRA 1

The Opening

Revealed at Mecca

1. In the name of God, the beneficent, the merciful.[1]
2. Praise be to God, Lord of the worlds,
3. The beneficent, the merciful.
4. Owner of the day of judgment,
5. You (alone) do we worship; You (alone) do we ask for help.
6. Show us the straight path,
7. The path of those whom You have favored; not the (path) of those who earn Your anger nor of those who go astray.

TRANSLATED BY Marmaduke Pickthall; revised by Jane Dammen McAuliffe.

1. Known as the *basmala*, this phrase occurs at the beginning of each sura except the ninth. Scholars differ about the scriptural status of the *basmala*: some consider it to be a Qur'anic verse; some do not, but still deem it part of the Qur'an. Others insist that it simply serves as a divider between suras or as a benediction before suras. Muslim scholarly consensus holds that the *basmala* counts as a verse in this sura.

QUR'AN 4

The aptly named fourth chapter (sura) of the Qur'an, "Women" (*al-Nisa'*), addresses several issues involving women but does not restrict itself solely to these. It also touches on other topics, such as the ritual prayer and relations with non-Muslims in Arabia.

According to classical Muslim sources, the sura's revelation began in 626, about four years after Muhammad's emigration to Medina, and shortly after the Muslim defeat at the Battle of Uhud (625). With regard to gender relations, this sura defines the conditions of polygamy (Qur'an 4:3), allots male heirs a larger share than females (4:11), delineates permissible marriages (4:23–24), positions men as caretakers of women (4:34), and allows the disciplining of a disobedient wife (4:34). Understandably, it has generated endless exegetical debate among generations of premodern and modern scholars, such as Sayyid Ahmad Khan (1817–1898), ʿAli Shariʿati (1933–1977), Fatima Mernissi (b. 1940), and Amina Wadud (b. 1952), who seek to reconcile the text of the Qur'an with contemporary societal norms.

Muslim scholarship explains some of the thematic emphases of this sura in light of the losses suffered by the Muslims in the Battle of Uhud. The exhortations to treat orphans kindly (Qur'an 4:1–10) and the account of inheritance law (4:11–12) are thus motivated by the daunting number of battleground deaths. The context of battle also explains the reference to a shortened form of the ritual prayer if an attack was feared and the dispensation to perform ritual purification with earth when no water is available. Finally, this sura inveighs against hypocrites who accept Islam for personal gain but lack true faith in their hearts (e.g., 4:88, 4:137–145).

PRONOUNCING GLOSSARY

Muhammad: *moo-ham'-mad* (not *moh-ha'-med*; heavy *h*)

Uhud: *oo'-hood* (not *oo-hood'*; heavy *h*)

SŪRA 4

Women

Revealed at Medina

In the name of God the beneficent, the merciful.

1. O mankind! Be careful of your duty to your Lord who created you from a single soul and from it created its mate and from the two has spread abroad a multitude of men and women. Be careful of your duty toward God in whom you claim (your rights) of one another, and toward the wombs (that bear you). God has been a watcher over you.

2. Give to orphans their wealth. Do not exchange the good for the bad (in your management of it) nor absorb their wealth into your own wealth. That would be a great sin.

3. And if you fear that you will not deal fairly by the orphans, marry of the women, who seem good to you, two or three or four; and if you fear that you cannot do justice (to so many) then one (only) or (the captives) that your right hands possess.[1] Thus it is more likely that you will not do injustice.

1. This has typically been understood as referring to female slaves made to serve as concubines.

4. And give to the women (whom you marry) free gift of their marriage portions; but if they of their own accord remit to you a part of it, then you are welcome to absorb it (in your wealth).

5. Do not give to the foolish (what is in) your (keeping of their) wealth, which God has given you to maintain; but feed and clothe them from it, and speak kindly to them.

6. Test orphans until they reach the marriageable age; then, if you find them of sound judgment, deliver over to them their fortune; and do not devour it by squandering and in haste for fear that they should grow up. Whoever (of the guardians) is rich, let him abstain generously (from taking of the property of orphans); and whoever is poor let him take of it in reason (for his guardianship). And when you deliver up their fortune to orphans, have (the transaction) witnessed in their presence. God suffices as a reckoner.

7. To the men (of a family) belongs a share of what parents and near kindred leave, and to the women a share of what parents and near kindred leave, whether it be little or much—a legal share.

8. And when relatives and orphans and the needy are present at the division (of the heritage), bestow on them from it and speak kindly to them.

9. And let those fear (in their behavior toward orphans) who if they left behind them weak offspring would be afraid for them. So let them mind their duty to God, and speak justly.

10. Those who devour the wealth of orphans wrongfully, they only swallow fire into their bellies, and they will be exposed to burning flame.

11. God charges you concerning (the provision for) your children: to the male the equivalent of the portion of two females, and if there be more than two women, then theirs is two-thirds of the inheritance, and if there be one (only) then the half. And to each of his[2] parents a sixth of the inheritance, if he has a son; and if he has no son and his parents are his heirs, then to his mother appertains the third; and if he has brothers, then to his mother appertains the sixth, after any legacy he may have bequeathed, or debt (has been paid). Your parents or your children: You do not know which of them is nearer to you in usefulness. It is an injunction from God. God is knower, wise.

12. And to you belongs a half of what your wives leave, if they have no child; but if they have a child then to you the fourth of what they leave, after any legacy they may have bequeathed, or debt (they may have contracted, has been paid). And to them belongs the fourth of what you leave if you have no child, but if you have a child then the eighth of what you leave, after any legacy you may have bequeathed, or debt (you may have contracted, has been paid). And if a man or a woman has a distant heir (having left neither parent nor child), and he (or she) has a brother or a sister (only on the mother's side) then to each of the two (the brother and the sister) the sixth, and if they are more than two, then they shall be sharers in the third, after any legacy that may have been bequeathed or debt (contracted) has been paid, not injuring (the heirs by willing away more than a third of the heritage). A commandment from God. God is knower, indulgent.

13. These are the limits (imposed by) God. Whoever obeys God and His messenger, He will make him enter gardens underneath which rivers flow, where such will dwell for ever. That will be the great success.

2. The deceased [Pickthall's note].

14. And whoever disobeys God and His messenger and transgresses His limits, He will make him enter fire, where such will dwell for ever; his will be a shameful doom.

15. As for those of your women who are guilty of lewdness, call to witness four of you against them. And if they testify (to the truth of the allegation) then confine them to the houses until death take them or (until) God appoint for them a way (through new legislation).[3]

16. And as for the two of you who are guilty of it, punish them both. And if they repent and improve, then let them be. God is relenting, merciful.

17. Forgiveness is only incumbent on God toward those who do evil in ignorance (and) then turn quickly (in repentance) to God. These are they toward whom God relents. God is ever knower, wise.

18. The forgiveness is not for those who do ill deeds until, when death attends upon one of them, he says: "I repent now"; nor yet for those who die while they are disbelievers. For such We have prepared a painful doom.

19. O you who believe! It is not lawful for you forcibly to inherit the women (of your deceased kinsmen), nor (that) you should put constraint upon them that you may take away a part of what you have given them, unless they be guilty of flagrant lewdness. But consort with them in kindness, for if you hate them it may happen that you hate a thing in which God has placed much good.

20. And if you wish to exchange one wife for another and you have given to one of them a sum of money (however great), take nothing from it. Would you take it by the way of calumny and open wrong?

21. How can you take it (back) after one of you has gone in to[4] the other, and they have taken a strong pledge from you?

22. And do not marry those women whom your fathers married, except what has already happened (of that nature) in the past. It was ever lewdness and abomination, and an evil way.

23. Forbidden to you are your mothers, and your daughters, and your sisters, and your father's sisters, and your mother's sisters, and your brother's daughters and your sister's daughters, and your foster-mothers, and your foster-sisters, and your mothers-in-law, and your step-daughters who are under your protection (born) of your women to whom you have gone in—but if you have not gone in to them, then it is no sin for you (to marry their daughters)—and the wives of your sons who (spring) from your own loins. And (it is forbidden to you) that you should have two sisters together, except what has already happened (of that nature) in the past. God is ever forgiving, merciful.

24. And all married women (are forbidden to you) except those (captives) whom your right hands possess. It is a decree of God for you. Lawful to you are all beyond those mentioned, so that you seek them with your wealth in honest wedlock, not debauchery. And those of whom you seek enjoyment (by marrying them), give to them their portions as a duty. And there is no sin for you in what you do by mutual agreement after the duty (has been done). God is ever knower, wise.

25. And whoever is not able to afford to marry free, believing women, let them marry from the believing slave girls whom your right hands possess.

3. See Q 24:2–10 [Pickthall's note].

4. Has had sexual intercourse with.

God knows best (concerning) your faith. You (proceed) one from another;[5] so wed them by permission of their people, and give to them their portions in kindness, they being honest, not debauched nor of loose conduct. And if when they are honorably married they commit lewdness they shall incur the half of the punishment (prescribed) for free women (in that case). This is for him among you who fears to commit sin. But to have patience would be better for you. God is forgiving, merciful.

26. God would explain to you and guide you by the examples of those who were before you, and would turn to you in mercy. God is knower, wise.

27. And God would turn to you in mercy; but those who follow vain desires would have you go tremendously astray.

28. God would make the burden light for you, for man was created weak.

29. O you who believe! Do not squander your wealth among yourselves in vanity, except it is a trade by mutual consent, and do not kill one another. God is ever merciful to you.

30. Whoever does that through aggression and injustice, We shall cast him into fire, and that is ever easy for God.

31. If you avoid the great (things) which you are forbidden, We will remit from you your evil deeds and make you enter at a noble gate.

32. And do not covet the thing in which God has made some of you excel others. To men a fortune from what they have earned, and to women a fortune from what they have earned. (Do not envy one another) but ask God of His bounty. God is ever knower of all things.

33. And to each We have appointed heirs of what parents and near kindred leave; and as for those with whom your right hands have made a covenant, give them their due. God is ever witness over all things.

34. Men are in charge of women, because God has made the one of them to excel the other,[6] and because they spend of their property (for the support of women). So good women are the obedient, guarding in secret what God has guarded. As for those from whom you fear rebellion, admonish them and banish them to beds apart, and scourge them.[7] Then if they obey you, do not seek a way against them. God is ever high exalted, great.

35. And if you fear a breach between the two (the man and wife), appoint an arbiter from his people and an arbiter from her people. If they desire amendment God will make them of one mind. God is ever knower, aware.

36. And serve God. Ascribe nothing as partner to Him. (Show) kindness to parents, and to near kindred, and orphans, and the needy, and to the neighbor who is related (to you) and the neighbor who is not related, and the fellow-traveller and the wayfarer and (the slaves) whom your right hands possess. God does not love such as are proud and boastful,

37. Who hoard their wealth and enjoin avarice on others, and hide what God has bestowed on them of His bounty. For disbelievers We prepare a shameful doom;

5. This expression, which recurs in the Qur'an, is a reminder to men that women are of the same human status as themselves [Pickthall's note].
6. Interpretations of male "excelling" include greater physical strength, greater financial capacity, and ontological superiority.
7. This is ordinarily understood as a gradual series of chastisements. "Scourging" or "beating" is a physical reprimand, variously interpreted as ranging from slight to severe.

38. And (also) those who spend their wealth in order to be seen of men, and do not believe in God or the last day. Whoever takes Satan for a comrade has a bad comrade.

39. What have they (to fear) if they believe in God and the last day and spend (rightly) of what God has bestowed upon them, when God is ever aware of them (and all they do)?

40. God does no wrong even of the weight of an ant; and if there is a good deed, He will double it and will give (the doer) from His presence an immense reward.

41. But how (will it be with them) when We bring of every people a witness, and We bring you (O Muhammad) as a witness against these?

42. On that day those who disbelieved and disobeyed the messenger will wish that they were level with the ground, and they can hide no fact from God.

43. O you who believe! Do not draw near to prayer when you are drunken,[8] until you know what you utter, nor when you are polluted, except when journeying on the road, until you have bathed. And if you are ill, or on a journey, or one of you comes from the toilet, or you have touched women, and you do not find water, then go to high clean soil and rub your faces and your hands (with it). God is benign, forgiving.

44. Do you not see those to whom a portion of the scripture has been given, how they purchase error, and seek to make you (Muslims) err from the right way?

45. God knows best (who are) your enemies. God is sufficient as a friend, and God is sufficient as a helper.

46. Some of those who are Jews change words from their context and say: "We hear and disobey; hear as one who hears not" and "Listen to us!"[9] distorting with their tongues and slandering religion. If they had said: "We hear and we obey: hear, and look at us" it would have been better for them, and more upright. But God has cursed them for their disbelief, so they do not believe, except a few.

47. O you to whom the scripture has been given, believe in what We have revealed confirming what you possess, before We destroy countenances so as to confound them, or curse them as We cursed the sabbath-breakers. The commandment of God is always executed.

48. God does not forgive that a partner should be ascribed to Him. He forgives (all) except that to whom He will. Whoever ascribes partners to God, he has indeed invented a tremendous sin.

49. Have you not seen those who praise themselves for purity? No, God purifies whom He will, and they will not be wronged even the hair on a date-stone.[1]

50. See, how they invent lies about God! That of itself is flagrant sin.

51. Have you not seen those to whom a portion of the scripture has been given, how they believe in idols and false deities, and how they say of those

8. The prohibition of alcohol is generally understood to have been implemented gradually in the Qur'an. Islamic law extends the prohibition to all intoxicants.

9. Devices of some of the Jews of Medina to annoy the Muslims by distorting words of Scripture. *Raina* (meaning "listen to us"), by which the Muslims used to call the Prophet's notice, they turned by slight mispronunciation into a Hebrew word of insult [Pickthall's note].

1. The Qur'an mentions dates and the date palm frequently. Here the Arabic expression means "the tiniest amount."

(idolaters) who disbelieve: "These are more rightly guided than those who believe?"

52. Those are they whom God has cursed, and he whom God has cursed, you (O Muhammad) will find for him no helper.

53. Or have they even a share in the sovereignty? Then in that case, they would not give mankind even the speck on a date-stone.

54. Or are they jealous of mankind because of what God of His bounty has bestowed on them? For We bestowed on the house of Abraham (of old) the scripture and wisdom, and We bestowed on them a mighty kingdom.

55. And of them were (some) who believed in it and of them were (some) who turned away from it. Hell is sufficient for (their) burning.

56. Those who disbelieve Our revelations, We shall expose them to the fire. As often as their skins are consumed We shall exchange them for fresh skins that they may taste the torment. God is ever mighty, wise.

57. And as for those who believe and do good works, We shall make them enter gardens underneath which rivers flow—to dwell there for ever; there for them are pure companions—and We shall make them enter plentiful shade.

58. God commands you that you restore deposits to their owners, and, if you judge between mankind, that you judge justly. How good is this which God admonishes you! God is ever hearer, observer.

59. O you who believe! Obey God, and obey the messenger and those of you who are in authority;[2] and if you have a dispute concerning any matter, refer it to God and the messenger if you are (in truth) believers in God and the last day. That is better and more seemly in the end.

60. Have you not seen those who pretend that they believe in what is revealed to you and what was revealed before you, how they would go for judgment (in their disputes) to false deities when they have been ordered to abjure them? Satan would mislead them far astray.

61. And when it is said to them: "Come to what God has revealed and to the messenger," you see the hypocrites turn from you with aversion.

62. How would it be if a misfortune struck them because of what their own hands have sent before (them)? Then they would come to you, swearing by God that they were seeking nothing but harmony and kindness.

63. Those are they, the secrets of whose hearts God knows. So oppose them and admonish them, and address them in plain terms about their souls.

64. We sent no messenger except that he should be obeyed by God's permission. And if, when they had wronged themselves, they had only come to you and asked forgiveness of God, and asked forgiveness of the messenger, they would have found God forgiving, merciful.

65. But no, by your Lord, they will not believe (in truth) until they make you judge of what is in dispute between them and find within themselves no dislike of what you decide, and submit with full submission.

66. And if We had decreed for them: "Lay down your lives or go forth from your dwellings," only a few of them would have done it; though if they did what they are exhorted to do it would be better for them, and more strengthening;

2. The Arabic *ulu l-amr*, "those of you who are in authority," has often been understood by Sunnis to mean scholars, military commanders, Muhammad's companions, the four caliphs, or the actual rulers of Muslim lands. For Shi'is it usually means the infallible imams.

67. And then We would bestow on them from Our presence an immense reward,

68. And would guide them to a straight path.

69. Whoever obeys God and the messenger, they are with those to whom God has shown favor, of the prophets and the true-hearted and the martyrs and the righteous. The best of company are they!

70. Such is the bounty of God, and God suffices as knower.

71. O you who believe! Take your precautions, then advance the proven ones, or advance all together.

72. Among you there is he who loiters; and if disaster overtook you, he would say: "God has been gracious to me since I was not present with them."

73. And if a bounty from God befell you, he would surely cry, as if there had been no love between you and him: "Oh, would that I had been with them, then I should have achieved a great success!"

74. Let those fight in the way of God who sell the life of this world for the other. Whoever fights in the way of God, be he slain or be he victorious, on him We shall bestow a vast reward.

75. How should you not fight for the cause of God and of the feeble among men and of the women and the children who are crying: "Our Lord! Bring us forth from this town[3] of which the people are oppressors! Oh, give us from Your presence some protecting friend! Oh, give us from Your presence some defender!"

76. Those who believe do battle for the cause of God; and those who disbelieve do battle for the cause of idols. So fight the minions of the devil. The devil's strategy is ever weak.

77. Have you not seen those to whom it was said: "Withhold your hands, establish worship and pay the poor tax," but when fighting was prescribed for them behold! a party of them fear mankind even as they fear God or with greater fear, and say: "Our Lord! Why have you ordained fighting for us? If only You would give us respite for a while!" Say (to them, O Muhammad): "The comfort of this world is scant; the hereafter will be better for him who wards off (evil); and you will not be wronged the down upon a date-stone.

78. Wherever you may be, death will overtake you, even though you were in lofty towers." Yet if a happy thing befalls them they say: "This is from God"; and if an evil thing befalls them they say: "This is of your doing (O Muhammad)." Say (to them): "All is from God." What is amiss with these people that they do not come near to understand a happening?[4]

79. Whatever of good befalls you (O man) it is from God, and whatever of ill befalls you it is from yourself. We have sent you (Muhammad) as a messenger to mankind and God is sufficient as witness.

80. Whoever obeys the messenger obeys God, and whoever turns away: We have not sent you as a caretaker over them.

81. And they say: "(It is) obedience"; but when they have gone forth from you a party of them spend the night in planning other than what you say. God records what they plan by night. So oppose them and put your trust in God. God is sufficient as trustee.

3. Mecca [Pickthall's note].

4. The reference is to the reverse which the Muslims suffered at Mt. Uhud which was caused by their own disobedience to the Prophet's orders [Pickthall's note].

82. Will they not then ponder on the Qur'ān? If it had been from other than God they would have found in it much incongruity.

83. And if any tidings, whether of safety or fear, come to them, they spread it abroad, whereas if they had referred it to the messenger and such of them as are in authority, those among them who are able to think out the matter would have known it. If it had not been for the grace of God upon you and His mercy you would have followed Satan, except a few (of you).

84. So fight (O Muhammad) in the way of God—You are not taxed (with the responsibility for anyone) except for yourself—and urge on the believers. Perhaps God will restrain the might of those who disbelieve. God is stronger in might and stronger in inflicting punishment.

85. Whoever intervenes in a good cause will have the reward of it, and whoever intervenes in an evil cause will bear the consequence of it. God oversees all things.

86. When you are greeted with a greeting, greet with one better than it or return it. God takes count of all things.

87. God! There is no god except Him. He gathers you all to a day of resurrection of which there is no doubt. Who is more true in statement than God?

88. What ails you that you are two parties regarding the hypocrites,[5] when God cast them back (to disbelief) because of what they earned? Do you seek to guide him whom God has sent astray? He whom God sends astray, for him you (O Muhammad) can not find a road.

89. They long that you should disbelieve even as they disbelieve, that you may be upon a level (with them). So do not choose friends from them until they forsake their homes in the way of God; if they turn back (to enmity) then take them and kill them wherever you find them, and choose no friend nor helper from among them,

90. Except those who seek refuge with a people between whom and you there is a covenant, or (those who) come to you because their hearts forbid them to make war on you or make war on their own people. Had God willed He could have given them power over you so that assuredly they would have fought you. So, if they hold aloof from you and do not wage war against you and offer you peace, God allows you no way against them.

91. You will find others who desire that they should have security from you, and security from their own people. So often as they are returned to hostility they are plunged into it. If they keep not aloof from you nor offer you peace nor hold their hands, then take them and kill them wherever you find them. Against such We have given you clear warrant.

92. It is not for a believer to kill a believer unless (it be) by mistake. He who has killed a believer by mistake must set free a believing slave, and pay the blood-money to the family of the slain, unless they remit it as a charity. If he (the victim) is of a people hostile to you, and he is a believer, then (the penance is) to set free a believing slave. And if he comes of a people between whom and you there is a covenant, then the blood-money must be paid to his people and (also) a believing slave must be set free. And whoever

5. According to tradition, the reference here is not to the lukewarm section of the Muslims of Medina, but to a particular group of alleged converts from among the Arabs, who afterwards relapsed into idolatry, and concerning whom there were two opinions among the Muslims [Pickthall's note].

does not have the wherewithal must fast two consecutive months. A penance from God. God is knower, wise.

93. Whoever slays a believer of set purpose, his reward is hell forever. God is angry against him and He has cursed him and prepared for him an awful doom.

94. O you who believe! When you go forth (to fight) in the way of God, be careful to discriminate, and do not say to one who offers you peace: "You are not a believer," seeking the chance profits of this life (so that you may despoil him). With God are plenteous spoils. Even thus (as he now is) were you before; but God has since then been gracious to you. Therefore take care to discriminate. God is ever informed of what you do.

95. Those of the believers who sit still, other than those who have a (disabling) hurt, are not equal with those who strive in the way of God with their wealth and lives. God has conferred on those who strive with their wealth and lives a rank above the sedentary. To each God has promised good, but He has bestowed on those who strive a great reward above the sedentary;

96. Degrees of rank from Him, and forgiveness and mercy. God is ever forgiving, merciful.

97. As for those whom the angels take (in death) while they wrong themselves, (the angels) will ask: "In what were you engaged?" They will say: "We were oppressed in the land." (The angels) will say: "Was not God's earth spacious that you could have migrated there?" As for such, their habitation will be hell, an evil journey's end;

98. Except the feeble among men, and the women, and the children, who are unable to devise a plan and are not shown a way.

99. As for such, it may be that God will pardon them. God is ever clement, forgiving.

100. Whoever migrates for the cause of God will find much refuge and abundance in the earth, and whoever forsakes his home, a fugitive to God and His messenger, and death overtakes him, his reward is then incumbent on God. God is ever forgiving, merciful.

101. And when you go forth in the land, it is no sin for you to curtail (your) worship if you fear that those who disbelieve may attack you. In truth the disbelievers are an open enemy to you.

102. And when you (O Muhammad) are among them and arrange (their) worship for them, let only a party of them stand with you (to worship) and let them take their arms. Then when they have performed their prostrations let them fall to the rear and let another party come that has not worshipped and let them worship with you, and let them take their precaution and their arms. Those who disbelieve long for you to neglect your arms and your baggage that they may attack you once for all. It is no sin for you to lay aside your arms, if rain impedes you or you are sick. But take your precaution. God prepares for the disbelievers shameful punishment.

103. When you have performed the act of worship, remember God, standing, sitting and reclining. And when you are in safety, observe proper worship. Worship at fixed hours has been enjoined on the believers.

104. Do not relent in pursuit of the enemy. If you are suffering, they suffer even as you suffer and you hope from God that for which they cannot hope. God is ever knower, wise.

105. We reveal to you the scripture with the truth, that you may judge between mankind by what God shows you. And do not be a pleader for the treacherous;

106. And seek forgiveness of God. God is ever forgiving, merciful.

107. And do not plead on behalf of (people) who deceive themselves. God does not love one who is treacherous and sinful.

108. They seek to hide from men and do not seek to hide from God. He is with them when by night they hold discourse displeasing to Him. God ever surrounds what they do.

109. You are they who pleaded for them in the life of the world. But who will plead with God for them on the day of resurrection, or who will then be their defender?

110. Yet whoever does evil or wrongs his own soul, then seeks pardon of God, will find God forgiving, merciful.

111. Whoever commits sin commits it only against himself. God is ever knower, wise.

112. And whoever commits a delinquency or crime, then throws (the blame) of it on the innocent, has burdened himself with falsehood and a flagrant crime.

113. But for the grace of God on you (Muhammad), and His mercy, a party of them had resolved to mislead you, but they will mislead only themselves and they will not hurt you at all. God reveals to you the scripture and wisdom, and teaches you what you knew not. The grace of God toward you has been infinite.

114. There is no good in much of their secret conferences except (in) him who enjoins almsgiving and kindness and peace-making among the people. Whoever does that, seeking the good pleasure of God, We shall bestow on him a vast reward.

115. And whoever opposes the messenger after the guidance (of God) has been manifested to him, and follows other than the believer's way, We appoint for him that to which he himself has turned, and expose him to hell—an unfortunate journey's end!

116. God does not pardon that partners should be ascribed to him. All except that He pardons to whom He will. Whoever ascribes partners to God has wandered far astray.

117. They invoke in His stead only females,[6] they pray to none else than Satan, a rebel

118. Whom God cursed, and he said: "I will take of Your servants an appointed portion,

119. And I will lead them astray, and I will arouse desires in them, and I will command them and they will cut the cattle's ears, and surely I will command them and they will change God's creation." Whoever chooses Satan for a patron instead of God is a loser and his loss is manifest.

120. He promises them and stirs up desires in them, and Satan promises them only to beguile.

121. For such, their habitation will be hell, and they will find no refuge from it.

122. But as for those who believe and do good works We shall bring them into gardens underneath which rivers flow, in which they will abide

6. The idols which the pagan Arabs worshipped were all female [Pickthall's note].

for ever. It is a promise from God in truth; and who can be more truthful than God in utterance?

123. It will not be in accordance with your desires, nor the desires of the People of the Scripture.[7] He who does wrong will have the recompense of it, and will not find against God any protecting friend or helper.

124. And whoever does good works, whether of male or female, and he (or she) is a believer, such will enter paradise and they will not be wronged the speck on a date-stone.

125. Who is better in religion than he who surrenders his purpose to God while doing good (to men) and follows the tradition of Abraham, the upright? God (Himself) chose Abraham for friend.

126. To God belongs whatever is in the heavens and whatever is in the earth. God ever surrounds all things.

127. They consult you concerning women. Say: "God gives you decree concerning them, and the scripture which has been recited to you (gives decree), concerning female orphans to whom you do not give what is ordained for them though you desire to marry them,[8] and (concerning) the weak among children, and that you should deal justly with orphans." Whatever good you do, God is ever aware of it.

128. If a woman fears ill-treatment from her husband, or desertion, it is no sin for the two if they make terms of peace between themselves. Peace is better. But greed has been made present in the minds (of men). If you do good and keep from evil, God is ever informed of what you do.

129. You will not be able to deal equally between (your) wives, however much you wish (to do so). But do not turn altogether away (from one), leaving her as in suspense. If you do good and keep from evil, God is ever forgiving, merciful.

130. But if they separate, God will compensate each out of His abundance. God is ever all-embracing, all-knowing.

131. To God belongs whatever is in the heavens and whatever is in the earth. And We charged those who received the scripture before you, and (We charge) you, that you keep your duty toward God. And if you disbelieve, to God belongs whatever is in the heavens and whatever is in the earth, and God is ever absolute, owner of praise.

132. To God belongs whatever is in the heavens and whatever is in the earth. And God is sufficient as defender.

133. If He will, He can remove you, O people, and produce others (in your stead). God is able to do that.

134. Whoever desires the reward of the world, (let him know that) with God is the reward of the world and the hereafter. God is ever hearer, observer.

135. O you who believe! Be staunch in justice, witnesses for God, even though it be against yourselves or (your) parents or (your) kindred, whether (the case be of) a rich man or a poor man, for God is nearer to both (than you are). So do not follow passion for fear that you lapse (from truth) and if you lapse or fall away, then God is ever informed of what you do.

136. O you who believe! Believe in God and His messenger and the scripture which He has revealed to His messenger, and the scripture which

7. Or "People of the Book": Jews and Christians.

8. The Qur'an often speaks about the duty to be just in dealings with orphans, addressing particularly those in charge of an orphan's property. Here the warning is to guardians who would unjustly hold on to a female orphan's wealth either by refusing to allow her to marry or by marrying her themselves.

He revealed before. Whoever disbelieves in God and His angels and His scriptures and His messengers and the last day, he has wandered far astray.

137. Those who believe, then disbelieve and then (again) believe, then disbelieve, and then increase in disbelief, God will never pardon them, nor will He guide them to a way.

138. Bear to the hypocrites the tidings that for them there is a painful doom;

139. Those who choose disbelievers for their friends instead of believers! Do they look for power at their hands? All power belongs to God.

140. He has already revealed to you in the scripture that, when you hear the revelations of God rejected and derided, (you) do not sit with them (who disbelieve and mock) until they engage in some other conversation. In that case (if you stayed) you would be like them. God will gather hypocrites and disbelievers, all together, into hell;

141. Those who wait upon occasion in regard to you and, if a victory comes to you from God, say: "Are we not with you?" and if the disbelievers meet with a success say: "Had we not the mastery of you, and did we not protect you from the believers?" God will judge between you at the day of resurrection, and God will not give the disbelievers any way (of success) against the believers.

142. The hypocrites seek to beguile God, but it is God who beguiles them. When they stand up to worship they perform it languidly and to be seen by people, and are but little mindful of God;

143. Swaying between this (and that), (belonging) neither to these nor to those. He whom God causes to go astray, you (O Muhammad) will not find a way for him:

144. O you who believe! Do not choose disbelievers for (your) friends in place of believers. Would you give God a clear warrant against you?

145. The hypocrites (will be) in the lowest deep of the fire, and you will find no helper for them;

146. Except those who repent and amend and hold fast to God and make their religion pure for God (only). Those are with the believers. And God will bestow on the believers an immense reward.

147. What concern has God for your punishment if you are thankful (for His mercies) and believe (in Him)? God was ever responsive, aware.

148. God does not love the utterance of harsh speech except by one who has been wronged. God is ever hearer, knower.

149. If you do good openly or keep it secret, or forgive evil, God is forgiving, powerful.

150. Those who disbelieve in God and His messengers, and seek to make distinction between God and His messengers, and say: "We believe in some and disbelieve in others, and seek to choose a way in between";

151. Such are disbelievers in truth; and for disbelievers We prepare a shameful doom.

152. But those who believe in God and His messengers and make no distinction between any of them, to them God will give their wages; and God was ever forgiving, merciful.

153. The People of the Scripture ask of you that you should cause an (actual) book to descend on them from heaven. They asked a greater thing of Moses before, for they said: "Show us God plainly." The storm of lightning

seized them for their wickedness. Then (even after that) they chose the calf (for worship) after clear proofs (of God's sovereignty) had come to them.[9] And We forgave them that! And We bestowed on Moses evident authority.

154. And We caused the mount to tower above them at (the taking of) their covenant: and We bade them: "Enter the gate, prostrate!" and We bade them: "Do not transgress the Sabbath!" and We took from them a firm covenant.

155. Then because of their breaking of their covenant, and their disbelieving in the revelations of God, and their slaying of the prophets wrongfully, and their saying: "Our hearts are hardened"—No, but God has set a seal upon them for their disbelief, so that only a few of them believe—

156. And because of their disbelief and of their speaking against Mary a tremendous calumny;[1]

157. And because of their saying: "We slew the Messiah Jesus son of Mary, God's messenger"—They did not kill him nor crucify him, but it appeared so to them; and those who disagree concerning it are in doubt of it; they have no knowledge of it except pursuit of a conjecture; for certain they did not slay him,

158. But God took him up to Himself. God was ever mighty, wise.

159. There is not one of the People of the Scripture but will believe in Him before his death, and on the day of resurrection He will be a witness against them—

160. Because of the wrongdoing of the Jews We forbade them good things which were (before) made lawful to them, and because of their much hindering from God's way,

161. And of their taking usury when they were forbidden it, and of their devouring people's wealth by false pretences. We have prepared for those of them who disbelieve a painful doom.

162. But those of them who are firm in knowledge and the believers believe in what is revealed to you, and what was revealed before you, especially the diligent in prayer and those who pay the poor-due, the believers in God and the last day. Upon these We shall bestow immense reward.

163. We inspire you as We inspired Noah and the prophets after him, as We inspired Abraham and Ishmael and Isaac and Jacob and the tribes, and Jesus and Job and Jonah and Aaron and Solomon, and as we imparted to David the Psalms;

164. And messengers We have mentioned to you before and messengers We have not mentioned to you; and God spoke directly to Moses;

165. Messengers of good cheer and of warning, in order that mankind might have no argument against God after the messengers. God was ever mighty, wise.

166. But God (Himself) testifies concerning what He has revealed to you; in His knowledge has He revealed it; and the angels also testify. And God is sufficient witness.

167. Those who disbelieve and hinder (others) from the way of God, they have wandered far astray.

9. See Exodus 32.
1. This passage criticizes the Jews for insulting the chastity of Mary.

168. Those who disbelieve and deal in wrong, God will never forgive them, neither will He guide them to a road,

169. Except the road of hell, in which they will abide for ever. And that is ever easy for God.

170. O mankind! The messenger has come to you with the truth from your Lord. Therefore believe; (it is) better for you. But if you disbelieve, still, to God belongs whatever is in the heavens and the earth. God is ever knower, wise.

171. O People of the Scripture! Do not exaggerate in your religion nor utter anything concerning God except the truth. The Messiah, Jesus son of Mary, was only a messenger of God, and His word which He conveyed to Mary, and a spirit from Him. So believe in God and His messengers, and say not "Three"[2]—Cease! (it is) better for you!—God is only one god. Far is it removed from His transcendent majesty that He should have a son. His is all that is in the heavens and all that is in the earth. And God is sufficient as defender.

172. The Messiah will never scorn to be a servant to God, nor will the favored angels. Whoever scorns His service and is proud, all such will He assemble to Him;

173. Then, as for those who believed and did good works, to them will He pay their wages in full, adding to them of His bounty; and as for those who were scornful and proud, them will He punish with a painful doom.

174. And they will not find for them, against God, any protecting friend or helper.

175. O mankind! Now has a proof from your Lord come to you, and We have sent down to you a clear light;

176. As for those who believe in God, and hold fast to Him, them He will cause to enter into His mercy and grace, and will guide them to Him by a straight road.

177. They ask you for a pronouncement. Say: "God has pronounced for you concerning distant kindred. If a man die childless and he has a sister, hers is half the heritage, and he would have inherited from her had she died childless. And if there are two sisters, then theirs are two-thirds of the heritage, and if they are brothers, men and women, to the male is the equivalent of the share of two females." God expounds to you, so that you do not err. God is knower of all things.

2. That is, the Father, the Son, and the Holy Spirit.

QUR'AN 12

This sura offers the longest sustained narrative in the Qur'an as it presents the story of Joseph (in Arabic, *Yusuf*), who is also a famous figure in the Hebrew Bible.

The story tells the trials that Joseph endures in fulfilling a childhood vision, one in which eleven stars, the sun, and the moon prostrate before him. When informed of it, his father, Jacob, understands the dream as a sign of God's favor on Joseph but warns him not to reveal it to his brothers (Qur'an 12:4–5). Although he follows Jacob's advice, Joseph's brothers envy him, believing him to be their father's favorite son. While together one day, they cast him into a well and fake his death (12:15). Joseph is rescued by a traveling caravan, taken to Egypt, and sold into slavery.

Two episodes define Joseph as an adult character. The first finds him rejecting the sexual advances of his master's wife (12:23–32), unnamed in the Qur'an but identified as Zulaykha in the commentary literature. He is cast into prison, where his gift for dream analysis reveals itself and wins him the Pharaoh's favor. He is appointed to a high administrative post after successfully interpreting the Pharaoh's dreams (12:47–55). Sometime later, Joseph's brothers arrive in Egypt but fail to recognize him. Joseph, however, engineers a plan to reunite his family, and they are all reconciled. At the end of the chapter, Joseph's vision is realized: the celestial objects were his eleven brothers and two parents, who now bow before Joseph out of respect (12:100).

Joseph's story has provided a thematic treasure trove for poets and writers throughout the Muslim world. The patience with which Joseph endures his trials, his constant devotion to God, and his ultimate success are oft-repeated motifs. Similarly, Jacob's grief at the loss of Joseph, a grief that literally blinds him (12:84), is often drawn on by writers exploring loss and separation. The brief account of Joseph's rejection of Zulaykha's advances generated countless expansions and amplifications. Both exegetical and literary works embellished the story to explore the meaning of virtue and the nature of love. Many authors celebrated Joseph's self-control, while others memorialized Zulaykha's intoxication at the very sight of him.

PRONOUNCING GLOSSARY

Alif Lām Rā: *a´-lif lam rah* (not *a-leef´*)

SŪRA 12
Joseph
Revealed at Mecca

In the name of God the beneficent, the merciful.

1. Alif. Lām. Rā.[1] These are verses of the scripture that makes plain.

2. We have revealed it, a Qur'an in Arabic, that you may understand.

3. We narrate to you (Muḥammad) the best of narratives in that We have inspired in you this Qur'an, though before you were of the heedless.

4. When Joseph said to his father: "O my father! I saw in a dream eleven planets and the sun and the moon, I saw them prostrating themselves to me."[2]

5. He said: "O my dear son! Do not tell your brothers of your vision, for fear that they plot a plot against you. Satan is for man an open foe.

6. Thus your Lord will prefer you and will teach you the interpretation of events, and will perfect His grace upon you and upon the family of Jacob as He perfected it upon your forefathers, Abraham and Isaac. Your Lord is knower, wise."

7. In Joseph and his brothers are signs (of God's sovereignty) for the inquiring.

8. When they said: "Joseph and his brother are dearer to our father than we are, many though we be. Our father is in plain error."

1. Twenty-nine suras begin with letters of the Arabic alphabet; there is no consensus on their significance.

2. Compare Genesis 37:9–11 (more generally, see Genesis 37–46).

9. (One said:) "Kill Joseph or cast him to some (other) land, so that your father's favor may be all for you, and (that) you may afterward be righteous people."

10. One among them said: "Do not kill Joseph but, if you must be doing, fling him into the depth of the pit; some caravan will find him."

11. They said: "O our father! Why will you not trust us with Joseph, when we are good friends to him?

12. Send him with us to-morrow that he may enjoy himself and play. We shall take good care of him."

13. He said: "In truth it saddens me that you should take him with you, and I fear that the wolf may devour him while you are heedless of him."

14. They said: "If the wolf should devour him when we are (so strong) a band, then surely we should have already perished."

15. Then, when they led him off, and were of one mind that they should place him in the depth of the pit, We inspired in him: You will tell them of this deed of theirs when they know (you) not.

16. And they came weeping to their father in the evening.

17. Saying: "O our father! We went racing one with another, and left Joseph by our things, and the wolf devoured him, and you do not believe our saying even when we speak the truth."

18. And they came with false blood on his shirt. He said: "No, but your minds have beguiled you into something. (My course is) becoming patience. And God it is whose help is to be sought in that (predicament) which you describe."

19. And there came a caravan, and they sent their waterdrawer. He let down his pail (into the pit). He said: "Good luck! Here is a youth." And they hid him as a treasure, and God was aware of what they did.

20. And they sold him for a low price, a number of silver coins; and they attached no value to him.

21. And he of Egypt who purchased him said to his wife: "Receive him honorably. Perhaps he may prove useful to us or we may adopt him as a son." Thus We established Joseph in the land that We might teach him the interpretation of events. And God was predominant in his career, but most of mankind did not know.

22. And when he reached his prime We gave him wisdom and knowledge. Thus We reward the good.

23. And she, in whose house he was, asked of him an evil act. She bolted the doors and said: "Come!" He said: "I seek refuge in God! He is my Lord, who has treated me honorably. Wrong-doers never prosper."

24. She desired him, and he would have desired her if it had not been that he saw the illumination from his Lord. Thus it was, that We might ward off from him evil and lewdness. He was of Our chosen servants.

25. And they raced with one another to the door, and she tore his shirt from behind, and they met her lord and master at the door. She said: "What shall be his reward, who wishes evil to your people, except prison or a painful doom?"

26. (Joseph) said: "It was she who asked of me an evil act." And a witness of her own people testified: "If his shirt is torn from before, then she speaks truth and he is of the liars.

27. And if his shirt is torn from behind, then she has lied and he is of the truthful."

28. So when he [Pharaoh] saw his shirt torn from behind, he said: "This is of the guile of you women. The guile of you is very great.
29. O Joseph! Turn away from this, and you, (O woman), ask forgiveness for your sin. You are of the sinful."
30. And women in the city said: "The ruler's wife is asking of her slave-boy an ill deed. Indeed he has smitten her to the heart with love. We behold her in plain error."
31. And when she heard of their sly talk, she sent to them and prepared for them a cushioned couch (to lie on at the feast) and gave to every one of them a knife and said (to Joseph): "Come out to them!" And when they saw him they exalted him and cut their hands, exclaiming: "God forbid! This is not a human being. This is no other than some gracious angel."
32. She said: "This is he on whose account you blamed me. I asked of him an evil act, but he proved continent, but if he does not do my bidding he shall be imprisoned, and shall be of those brought low."
33. He said: "O my Lord! Prison is more dear than that to which they urge me, and if You do not fend off their wiles from me I shall incline to them and become of the foolish."
34. So his Lord heard his prayer and fended off their wiles from him. He is hearer, knower.
35. And it seemed good to them (the men) after they had seen the signs (of his innocence) to imprison him for a time.
36. And two young men went to prison with him. One of them said: "I dreamed that I was pressing wine." The other said: "I dreamed that I was carrying upon my head bread of which the birds were eating. Announce to us the interpretation, for we see you of those good (at interpretation)."
37. He said: "The food which you are given (daily) shall not come to you but I shall tell you the interpretation before it comes to you. This is of what my Lord has taught me. I have forsaken the religion of people who do not believe in God and are disbelievers in the hereafter.
38. And I have followed the religion of my fathers, Abraham and Isaac and Jacob. It never was for us to attribute anything as partner to God. This is of the bounty of God to us (the seed of Abraham) and to mankind; but most men do not give thanks.
39. O my two fellow-prisoners! Are diverse lords better, or God the one, the almighty?
40. Those whom you worship beside Him are but names which you have named, you and your fathers. God has revealed no sanction for them. The decision rests with God only, Who has commanded you that you worship none except Him. This is the right religion, but most men know not.
41. O my two fellow-prisoners! As for one of you, he will pour out wine for his lord to drink; and as for the other, he will be crucified so that the birds will eat from his head. Thus is the case judged concerning which you did inquire."
42. And he said to him of the two who he knew would be released: "Mention me in the presence of your lord." But Satan caused him to forget to mention it to his lord, so he (Joseph) stayed in prison for some years.
43. And the king said: "I saw in a dream seven fat cows which seven lean were eating, and seven green ears of corn and another (seven) dry. O notables! Expound for me my vision, if you can interpret dreams."

44. They answered: "Jumbled dreams! And we are not knowledgeable in the interpretation of dreams."

45. And he of the two who was released, and (now) at length remembered, said: "I am going to announce to you the interpretation, therefore send me forth."

46. (And when he came to Joseph in the prison, he exclaimed): "Joseph! O you truthful one! Expound for us the seven fat cows which seven lean were eating and the seven green ears of corn and another (seven) dry, that I may return to the people, so that they may know."

47. He said: "You shall sow seven years as usual, but that which you reap, leave it on the ear, all except a little which you eat.

48. Then after that will come seven hard years which will devour all that you have prepared for them, except a little of that which you have stored.

49. Then, after that, will come a year when the people will have plenteous crops and when they will press (wine and oil)."

50. And the king said: "Bring him to me." And when the messenger came to him, he (Joseph) said: "Return to your lord and ask him what was the case of the women who cut their hands. My lord knows their guile."

51. He (the king) (then sent for those women and) said: "What happened when you asked an evil act of Joseph?" They answered: "God forbid! We know no evil of him." The wife of the ruler said: "Now the truth is out. I asked of him an evil act, and he is surely of the truthful."

52. (Then Joseph said: "I asked for) this, that he (my lord) may know that I did not betray him in secret, and that surely God does not guide the snare of the betrayers.

53. I do not exculpate myself. The (human) soul enjoins to evil, except that on which my Lord has mercy. My Lord is forgiving, merciful."

54. And the king said: "Bring him to me that I may attach him to my person." And when he had talked with him he said: "You are today in our presence established and trusted."

55. He said: "Set me over the storehouses of the land. I am a skilled custodian."

56. Thus We gave power to Joseph in the land. He was the owner of it where he pleased. We reach with Our mercy whom We will. We do not lose the reward of the good.

57. And the reward of the hereafter is better, for those who believe and ward off (evil).

58. And Joseph's brothers came and presented themselves before him, and he knew them but they knew him not.

59. And when he provided them with their provision he said: "Bring to me a brother of yours from your father. Do you not see that I fill up the measure and I am the best of hosts?

60. And if you do not bring him to me, then there shall be no measure for you with me, nor shall you draw near."

61. They said: "We will try to win him from his father: that we will surely do."

62. He said to his young men: "Place their merchandise in their saddlebags, so that they may know it when they go back to their people, and so will come again."

63. So when they went back to their father they said: "O our father! The measure is denied us, so send with us our brother that we may obtain the measure, surely we will guard him well."

64. He said: "Can I entrust him to you except as I entrusted his brother to you before? God is better at guarding, and He is the most merciful of those who show mercy."

65. And when they opened their belongings they discovered that their merchandise had been returned to them. They said: "O our father! What (more) can we ask? Here is our merchandise returned to us. We shall get provision for our people and guard our brother, and we shall have the extra measure of a camel (load). This (that we bring now) is a light measure."

66. He said: "I will not send him with you until you give me an undertaking in the name of God that you will bring him back to me, unless you are surrounded." And when they gave him their undertaking he said: "God is the warden over what we say."

67. And he said: "O my sons! Do not go in by one gate; go in by different gates. I can avail you nothing as against God. The decision rests with God only. In Him do I put my trust, and in Him let all the trusting put their trust."

68. And when they entered in the manner which their father had enjoined, it would have availed them nothing as against God; it was but a need of Jacob's soul which he thus satisfied;[3] and he was a lord of knowledge because We had taught him; but most of mankind do not know.

69. And when they went in before Joseph, he took his brother to himself, saying: "I, even I, am your brother, therefore do not sorrow for what they did."

70. And when he provided them with their provision, he put the drinking-cup in his brother's saddlebag, and then a crier cried: "O camel-riders! You are surely thieves!"

71. They cried, coming toward them: "What is it you have lost?"

72. They said: "We have lost the king's cup, and he who brings it shall have a camel-load," and "I" (said Joseph) "am answerable for it."

73. They said: "By God, well you know we did not come to do evil in the land, and are no thieves."

74. They said: "And what shall be the penalty for it, if you prove liars?"

75. They said: "The penalty for it! He in whose bag (the cup) is found, he is the penalty for it. Thus we requite wrong-doers."

76. Then he (Joseph) began the search with their bags before his brother's bag, then he produced it from his brother's bag. Thus did We contrive for Joseph. He could not have taken his brother according to the king's law unless God willed. We raise by grades (of mercy) whom We will, and over every lord of knowledge there is one more knowing.

77. They said: "If he steals, a brother of his stole before." But Joseph kept it secret in his soul and did not reveal it to them. He said (within himself): "You are in worse case, and God knows best (the truth of) that which you allege."

78. They said: "O ruler of the land! He has an aged father, so take one of us instead of him. We behold you to be of those who do kindness."

79. He said: "God forbid that we should seize anyone but him with whom we found our property; then truly we should be wrong-doers."

3. There is a prevalent superstition in the East that the members of a large family ought not to appear all together, for fear of the ill luck that comes from envy in the hearts of others [Pickthall's note].

80. So, when they despaired of (moving) him, they conferred together apart. The eldest of them said: "Do you not know how your father took an undertaking from you in God's name and how you failed in the case of Joseph before? Therefore I shall not go forth from the land until my father gives leave or God judges for me. He is the best of judges.

81. Return to your father and say: 'O our father! Your son has stolen. We testify only to that which we know; we are not guardians of the unseen.

82. Ask the township where we were, and the caravan with which we travelled here. We speak the truth.'"

83. (And when they came to their father and had spoken thus to him) he said: "No, but your minds have beguiled you into something. (My course is) becoming patience! It may be that God will bring them all to me. He, only He, is the knower, the wise."

84. And he turned away from them and said: "Alas, my grief for Joseph!" And his eyes were whitened with the sorrow that he was suppressing.

85. They said: "By God, you will never cease remembering Joseph until your health is ruined or you are of those who perish!"

86. He said: "I expose my distress and anguish only to God, and I know from God what you know not.

87. Go, O my sons, and ascertain concerning Joseph and his brother, and do not despair of the spirit of God. None despairs of the spirit of God except disbelieving people."

88. And when they came (again) before him (Joseph) they said: "O ruler! Misfortune has touched us and our people, and we bring but poor merchandise, so fill for us the measure and be charitable to us. God will requite the charitable."

89. He said: "Do you know what you did to Joseph and his brother in your ignorance?"

90. They said: "Is it indeed you who are Joseph?" He said: "I am Joseph and this is my brother. God has shown us favor. He who wards off (evil) and endures (finds favor); for God does not lose the wages of the kindly."

91. They said: "By God, God has preferred you above us, and we were indeed sinful."

92. He said: "Have no fear this day! May God forgive you, and He is the most merciful of those who show mercy.

93. Go with this shirt of mine and lay it on my father's face, he will become (again) one who sees; and come to me with all your people."

94. When the caravan departed their father had said: "Truly I am conscious of the scent of Joseph, though you call me a foolish babbler."

95. (Those around him) said: "By God, you are in your old error."

96. Then, when the bearer of glad tidings came, he laid it on his face and he became one who sees once more. He said: "Did I not say to you that I know from God what you know not?"

97. They said: "O our father! Ask forgiveness of our sins for us, for we were sinful."

98. He said: "I shall ask forgiveness for you of my Lord. He is the forgiving, the merciful."

99. And when they came in before Joseph, he took his parents to him, and said: "Come into Egypt safe, if God will!"

100. And he placed his parents on the daïs and they fell down before him prostrate, and he said: "O my father! This is the interpretation of my dream of old. My Lord has made it true, and He has shown me kindness, since He took me out of the prison and has brought you from the desert after Satan had made strife between me and my brethren. My Lord is tender to whom He will. He is the knower, the wise.

101. O my Lord! You have given me (something) of sovereignty and have taught me (something) of the interpretation of events—creator of the heavens and the earth! You are my protecting friend in the world and the hereafter. Make me to die submissive (to You), and join me to the righteous."

102. This is of the tidings of the unseen which We inspire in you (Muhammad). You were not present with them when they fixed their plan and they were scheming.

103. And though you try much, most men will not believe.

104. You ask them no fee for it. It is nothing else than a reminder to the peoples.

105. How many a sign is there in the heavens and the earth which they pass by with face averted!

106. And most of them do not believe in God except that they attribute partners (to Him).

107. Do they think themselves secure from the coming on them of a pall of God's punishment, or the coming of the hour suddenly while they are unaware?

108. Say: "This is my way: I call on God with sure knowledge, I and whoever follows me—Glory be to God!—and I am not of the idolaters."

109. We did not send before you (any messengers) except men whom We inspired from among the people of the townships—Have they not travelled in the land and seen the nature of the consequence for those who were before them? And the abode of the hereafter, for those who ward off (evil), is best. Have you then no sense?—

110. Until, when the messengers despaired and thought that they were denied, then Our help came to them, and whom We would was saved. And Our wrath cannot be warded from the guilty.

111. In their history there is a lesson for men of understanding. It is no invented story but a confirmation of the existing (scripture) and a detailed explanation of everything, and a guidance and a mercy for people who believe.

QUR'AN 55

Sura 55 takes its name from its first verse, which is simply the divine name, "The Beneficent" (*al-Rahman*). When recited in Arabic its repetitive rhymes create a mesmerizing effect, an effect heightened by the constant refrain: "Which is it, of the favors of your Lord, that you deny?" This chapter of the Qur'an is unusual both in having a pervasive refrain and in using a dual address throughout.

The refrain accounts for more than a third of the sura's seventy-eight verses. It begins at verse 13 and repeats every second or third verse until verse 44. It then alternates with every subsequent verse until the end of the sura. Such repetition is rare in the Qur'an; indeed, only three other suras, Qur'an 26, 57, and 77, have comparable refrains. Their recitative quality has sparked considerable scholarly interest.

Scholars undertaking intertextual study of the Bible and the Qur'an have noted the resonance between numerous passages of the Qur'an and of the Psalms. Psalm 136 and Qur'an 55, for example, are alike in their antiphonal structure, and in Psalm 136 the refrain "For his kindness endures forever" appears at the end of every verse. Like Qur'an 55, Psalm 136 begins with the glorification of God (Psalm 136:1–3; Qur'an 55:1), moves to the creation of heaven and earth (Psalm 136:5–6; Qur'an 55:7, 10), and then continues to the creation of celestial objects (Psalm 136:7–8; Qur'an 55:5–6).

Qur'an 55's use of a dual form for the pronoun "you"—impossible to convey in English translation—opens another line of analysis and interpretation. It must be remembered that the Qur'an addresses not only humans but also a second species of creation who, like humans, are called to obey the qur'anic message. These are the jinn, who occupy a rich and fascinating place in Islamic lore; they also give their name to a chapter title of the Qur'an (Qur'an 72).

Unlike humans, who are created from clay, and the angels, who are made of light, the jinn are composed of a smokeless fire (Qur'an 55:14). Muslim writers often drew on these differences in composition to sharpen their descriptions of each group. The jinn are generally invisible to humans, and although they possess no knowledge of future events (34:14), their mental and physical abilities easily outstrip those of normal humans. Some jinn can ascend to the heavens (72:8–9); others are incredibly strong or can speed across vast distances (27:39–40). Yet despite the jinns' strength and their status as creatures of the divine, whether obedient or disobedient (72:1–14), God clearly favors humans, designating them as his representatives on the earth (2:30; 6:165; 33:72). While other qur'anic passages address humans and jinn (e.g., 6:130), Sura 55 is unique in addressing both for an extended series of verses.

Commentators on this sura have usually concluded that its use of the dual is grammatically mandated by the combined address to humans and jinn. A contemporary German scholar, Angelika Neuwirth, finds a deeper rationale, suggesting that the dual here mirrors an underlying theme of the sura: the balanced symmetry of creation. The expressive clarity of God's speech mimics the harmonious order of material existents. Both creation and revelation manifest the divine, and both can be read as God's text. The use of the dual throughout the sura reflects this deeper meaning, one that is reinforced in its description of heaven and earth (Qur'an 55:7–12) and its reference to sunrise and sunset at the summer and the winter solstice (55:17).

SŪRA 55

The Beneficent

Revealed at Mecca

In the name of God, the beneficent, the merciful.

1. The beneficent
2. Has made known the Qur'an.
3. He has created man.
4. He has taught him utterance.
5. The sun and the moon are made punctual.
6. The stars and the trees adore.
7. And the sky He has uplifted; and He has set the measure,

8. That you exceed not the measure,
9. But observe the measure strictly, nor fall short of it.
10. And the earth He has appointed for (His) creatures,
11. In which are fruit and sheathed palm-trees,
12. Husked grain and scented herb.
13. Which is it, of the favors of your Lord, that you deny?
14. He created man of clay like the potter's,
15. And the jinn he created of smokeless fire.
16. Which is it, of the favors of your Lord, that you deny?
17. Lord of the two easts,[1] and Lord of the two wests![2]
18. Which is it, of the favors of your Lord, that you deny?
19. He has loosed the two seas.[3] They meet.
20. There is a barrier between them. They do not encroach (one upon the other).
21. Which is it, of the favors of your Lord, that you deny?
22. There comes forth from both of them the pearl and coral-stone.
23. Which is it, of the favors of your Lord, that you deny?
24. His are the ships displayed upon the sea, like banners.[4]
25. Which is it, of the favors of your Lord, that you deny?
26. Everyone that is on it will pass away;
27. There remains but the countenance of your Lord of might and glory.
28. Which is it, of the favors of your Lord, that you deny?
29. All that are in the heavens and the earth entreat Him. Every day He exercises (universal) power.
30. Which is it, of the favors of your Lord, that you deny?
31. We shall dispose of you, O you two dependents (man and jinn).
32. Which is it, of the favors of your Lord, that you deny?
33. O company of jinn and men, if you have power to penetrate (all) regions of the heavens and the earth, then penetrate (them)! You will never penetrate them except with (Our) sanction.
34. Which is it, of the favors of your Lord, that you deny?
35. There will be sent, against you both, heat of fire and flash of brass, and you will not escape.
36. Which is it, of the favors of your Lord, that you deny?
37. And when the heaven splits asunder and becomes rosy like red hide—
38. Which is it, of the favors of your Lord, that you deny?—
39. On that day neither man nor jinn will be questioned of his sin.
40. Which is it, of the favors of your Lord, that you deny?
41. The guilty will be known by their marks, and will be taken by the forelocks and the feet.
42. Which is it, of the favors of your Lord, that you deny?
43. This is hell which the guilty deny.
44. They go circling round between it and fierce, boiling water.
45. Which is it, of the favors of your Lord, that you deny?

1. The two points where the sun rises in winter and in summer [all notes in this sura are Pickthall's].
2. The two points where the sun sets in winter and in summer.
3. That is, the salt water and the sweet.
4. The usual explanation of the commentators is "built into the sea like mountains."

46. But for him who fears the standing before his Lord there are two gardens.
47. Which is it, of the favors of your Lord, that you deny?
48. Of spreading branches.
49. Which is it, of the favors of your Lord, that you deny?
50. In which are two fountains flowing
51. Which is it, of the favors of your Lord, that you deny?
52. In which is every kind of fruit in pairs.
53. Which is it, of the favors of your Lord, that you deny?
54. Reclining upon couches lined with silk brocade, the fruit of both the gardens near to hand.
55. Which is it, of the favors of your Lord, that you deny?
56. Therein are those of modest gaze, whom neither man nor jinn will have touched before them,
57. Which is it, of the favors of your Lord, that you deny?
58. (In beauty) like the jacinth and the coral-stone.
59. Which is it, of the favors of your Lord, that you deny?
60. Is the reward of goodness other than goodness?
61. Which is it, of the favors of your Lord, that you deny?
62. And beside them are two other gardens,
63. Which is it, of the favors of your Lord, that you deny?
64. Dark green with foliage.
65. Which is it, of the favors of your Lord, that you deny?
66. In which are two abundant springs.
67. Which is it, of the favors of your Lord, that you deny?
68. In which is fruit, the date-palm and pomegranate.
69. Which is it, of the favors of your Lord, that you deny?
70. In which (are found) the good and beautiful—
71. Which is it, of the favors of your Lord, that you deny?—
72. Fair ones, close-guarded in pavilions—
73. Which is it, of the favors of your Lord, that you deny?—
74. Whom neither man nor jinn will have touched before them—
75. Which is it, of the favors of your Lord, that you deny?—
76. Reclining on green cushions and fair carpets.
77. Which is it, of the favors of your Lord, that you deny?
78. Blessed be the name of your Lord, mighty and glorious!

QUR'AN 78–114

Although the basic units of the Qur'an are chapter (suras) and verses (*ayat*), Muslims have devised others for recitational and liturgical purposes. Most notable is the division of the Qur'an into thirty equal parts (*ajza'*, sing. *juz'*), which is helpful for those wishing to complete the recitation of the Qur'an in a single month. It becomes particularly useful during Ramadan, the month of fasting, when many Muslims recite a *juz'* per night.

The most famous *juz'* of the Qur'an is the final one, named *juz' 'amma*. It comprises chapters 78–114 and takes its name from the first words of chapter 78: "About what (*'amma*) do they question one another?" While few Muslims memorize the entire Qur'an, almost all try to commit all or most of this *juz'* to memory. Indeed, the first chapters that Muslim children learn are from this section. Most of these suras are short, with easily memorized rhyming verses, and date to the Meccan period of Islam—that is, before Muhammad emigrated to Medina in 622.

Much of this *juz'* captures the Prophet's early preaching, which contained calls to repentance before the prospect of final judgment. Moral exhortations abound, with threats of divine retribution for those who cheat and oppress and the promise of divine favor for those who give charity, look after orphans, and reflect on God's signs in creation. The stories of ancient Arabian tribes and of people who ignored their prophets are presented as evidence that those who ignore God's warnings will suffer fearsome consequences.

Special qualities adhere to the last three suras of this *juz'*. Sura 112, "The Unity" (*al-Tawhid*), is seen as expressing the essence of Islamic theology—that there is one God. For many pious Muslims, reciting this sura is equivalent to the reward gained from reciting a third of the Qur'an. Suras 113 ("The Daybreak," *al-Falaq*) and 114 ("Mankind," *al-Nas*) begin, respectively, with the phrases "I seek refuge in the Lord of the daybreak" and "I seek refuge in the Lord of mankind." For this reason, they are referred to collectively as "the two prayers of refuge" (*al-mu'awwidhatan*), and according to numerous reports Muhammad urged his companions to recite these two suras, sometimes in conjunction with Sura 112, to ward off malevolent forces, magic, the evil eye, and general harm.

PRONOUNCING GLOSSARY

Abu Lahab: *a-boo la´-hab*
'Illiyin: *il-lee-yeen´*
Iram: *i´-ram*
Quraysh: *qoo-raysh´*
Sijjin: *sij-jeen´*
Tasnim: *tas-neem´*
Thamud: *tha-mood´*
Tuwa: *too-wa´*

SŪRA 78

The Tidings

Revealed at Mecca

In the name of God, the beneficent, the merciful.

1. About what do they question one another?
2. (It is) of the awful tidings,
3. Concerning which they are in disagreement.
4. No, but they will come to know!
5. No, again, but they will come to know!
6. Have We not made the earth an expanse,
7. And the high hills bulwarks?
8. And We have created you in pairs,
9. And have appointed your sleep for repose,
10. And have appointed the night as a cloak,
11. And have appointed the day for livelihood.
12. And We have built above you seven strong (heavens),

13. And have appointed a dazzling lamp,
14. And have sent down from the rainy clouds abundant water,
15. Thereby to produce grain and plant,
16. And gardens of thick foliage.
17. The day of decision is a fixed time,
18. A day when the trumpet is blown, and you come in multitudes,
19. And the heaven is opened and becomes as gates,
20. And the hills are set in motion and become as a mirage.
21. Hell lurks in ambush,
22. A home for the rebellious.
23. They will abide there for ages.
24. Therein they taste neither coolness nor (any) drink
25. Except boiling water and a paralyzing cold:
26. Reward proportioned (to their evil deeds).
27. For they did not look for a reckoning;
28. They called Our revelations false with strong denial.
29. Everything have We recorded in a book.
30. So taste (of what you have earned). No increase do We give you except of torment.
31. For the dutiful is achievement—
32. Gardens enclosed and vineyards,
33. And maidens for companions,
34. And a full cup.
35. There they hear neither vain discourse, nor lying—
36. Requital from your Lord—a gift in payment—
37. Lord of the heavens and the earth, and (all) that is between them, the beneficent; with whom none can converse.
38. On the day when the angels and the spirit stand arrayed, they do not speak, except him whom the beneficent allows and who speaks right.
39. That is the true day. So whoever will should seek recourse to his Lord.
40. We warn you of a doom at hand, a day in which a man will look on that which his own hands have sent before, and the disbeliever will cry: "Would that I were dust!"

SŪRA 79

Those Who Drag Forth

Revealed at Mecca

In the name of God, the beneficent, the merciful.

1. By those who drag forth to destruction,
2. By the meteors rushing,
3. By the lone stars floating,[1]
4. By the angels hastening,

1. Some commentators take verses 2 and 3 also as referring to angels and explain them thus: "By those who console (the spirits of the righteous) tenderly." "By those who come floating (down from heaven with their Lord's command)." The rendering given in the text above is the more obvious [Pickthall's note].

5. And those who govern the event,
6. On the day when the first trumpet resounds
7. And the second follows it,
8. On that day hearts beat painfully
9. While eyes are downcast
10. (Now) they are saying: "Shall we really be restored to our first state
11. Even after we are crumbled bones?"
12. They say: "Then that would be a vain proceeding."
13. Surely it will need but one shout,
14. And they will be awakened.
15. Has there come to you the history of Moses?
16. How his Lord called him in the holy valley of Tuwa,[2]
17. (Saying:) "Go you to Pharaoh—he has rebelled—
18. And say (to him): 'Have you (will) to grow (in grace)?
19. Then I will guide you to your Lord and you shall fear (Him).'"
20. And he showed him the tremendous sign.
21. But he denied and disobeyed,
22. Then turned he away in haste,
23. Then gathered he and summoned
24. And proclaimed: "I (Pharaoh) am your lord the highest."
25. So God seized him (and made him) an example for the after (life) and for the former.
26. Here is indeed a lesson for him who fears.
27. Are you the harder to create, or is the heaven that He built?
28. He raised its height and ordered it;
29. And He made dark its night, and He brought forth its morn,
30. And after that He spread the earth,
31. And from it produced its water and its pasture,
32. And He made fast the hills,
33. A provision for you and for your cattle.
34. But when the great disaster comes,
35. The day when man will call to mind his (whole) endeavor,
36. And hell will stand forth visible to him who sees,
37. Then, as for him who rebelled
38. And chose the life of the world,
39. Hell will be his home.
40. But as for him who feared to stand before his Lord and restrained his soul from lust,
41. The garden will be his home.
42. They ask you about the hour: "When will it come to port?"
43. Why (ask they)? What have you to tell of it?
44. To your Lord belongs (knowledge of) its term.
45. You are but a warner to him who fears it.
46. On the day when they behold it, it will be as if they had but tarried for an evening or the morning of it.

2. Commentators differ on this reference; some suggest that it denotes a valley near Mount Sinai.

SŪRA 80

He Frowned

Revealed at Mecca

In the name of God, the beneficent, the merciful.

1. He frowned and turned away
2. Because the blind man came to him.
3. What could inform you but that he might grow (in grace)
4. Or take heed and so the reminder might avail him?
5. As for him who thinks himself independent,
6. To him you pay regard.
7. Yet it is not your concern if he does not grow (in grace).
8. But as for him who comes to you with earnest purpose
9. And has fear,
10. From him you are distracted.
11. No, but it is an admonishment,
12. So let whoever wishes pay heed to it,
13. On honored leaves
14. Exalted, purified,
15. (Set down) by scribes
16. Noble and righteous.
17. Man is (self-)destroyed: how ungrateful!
18. From what thing does He create him?
19. From a drop of seed He creates him and proportions him,
20. Then makes the way easy for him,
21. Then causes him to die, and buries him;
22. Then, when He will, He brings him again to life.
23. No, but (man) has not done what He commanded him.
24. Let man consider his food:
25. How We pour water in showers
26. Then split the earth in clefts
27. And cause the grain to grow in it
28. And grapes and green fodder
29. And olive-trees and palm-trees
30. And garden-closes of thick foliage
31. And fruits and grasses:
32. Provision for you and your cattle.
33. But when the shout comes
34. On the day when a man flees from his brother
35. And his mother and his father
36. And his wife and his children,
37. Every man that day will have concern enough to make him heedless (of others).
38. On that day faces will be bright as dawn,
39. Laughing, rejoicing at good news;
40. And other faces, on that day, with dust upon them,
41. Veiled in darkness,
42. Those are the disbelievers, the wicked.

SŪRA 81

The Overthrowing

Revealed at Mecca

In the name of God, the beneficent, the merciful.

1. When the sun is overthrown,
2. And when the stars fall,
3. And when the hills are moved,
4. And when the camels big with young are abandoned,
5. And when the wild beasts are herded together,
6. And when the seas rise,
7. And when souls are reunited,
8. And when the girl-child who was buried alive is asked
9. For what sin she was slain,
10. And when the pages are laid open,
11. And when the sky is torn away,
12. And when hell is lighted,
13. And when the garden is brought near,
14. (Then) every soul will know what it has made ready.
15. Oh, but I call to witness the planets,
16. The stars which rise and set,
17. And the close of night,[1]
18. And the breath of mornings[2]
19. That this is in truth the word of an honored messenger,
20. Mighty, established in the presence of the Lord of the throne,
21. (One) to be obeyed, and trustworthy;
22. And your comrade is not mad.
23. Surely he beheld him[3] on the clear horizon.[4]
24. And he is not a withholder of the unseen.
25. Nor is this the utterance of a devil worthy to be stoned.
26. Then where do you go?
27. This is nothing else than a reminder to creation,
28. To whoever of you wills to walk straight.
29. And you do not will, unless (it be) that God wills, the Lord of creation.

SŪRA 82

The Cleaving

Revealed at Mecca

In the name of God, the beneficent, the merciful.

1. When the heaven is cleft asunder,
2. When the planets are dispersed,

1. Lit. "And the night when it closes" [Pickthall's note].
2. Lit. "And the morning when it breathes" [Pickthall's note].
3. Usually understood to be the angel Gabriel.
4. The reference is to the Prophet's vision at Mt. Hira' [Pickthall's note].

3. When the seas are poured forth,
4. And the sepulchres are overturned,
5. A soul will know what it has sent before (it) and what left behind.
6. O man! What has made you careless concerning your Lord, the bountiful,
7. Who created you, then fashioned, then proportioned you?
8. Into whatever form He wills, He casts you.
9. No, but you deny the judgment.
10. There are above you guardians,
11. Generous and recording,
12. Who know (all) that you do.
13. The righteous will be in delight.
14. And the wicked will be in hell;
15. They will burn there on the day of judgment,
16. And will not be absent from it.
17. Ah, what will convey to you what the day of judgment is!
18. Again, what will convey to you what the day of judgment is!
19. A day on which no soul has power at all for any (other) soul. The (absolute) command on that day is God's.

SŪRA 83

Defrauding

Revealed at Mecca

In the name of God, the beneficent, the merciful.
1. Woe to the defrauders:
2. Those who when they take the measure from mankind demand it full,
3. But if they measure for them or weigh for them, they cause them loss.
4. Do such (men) not consider that they will be raised again
5. To an awful day,
6. The day when (all) mankind stand before the Lord of the worlds?
7. No, but the record of the vile is in Sijjin[1]—
8. Ah! what will convey to you what Sijjin is!—
9. A written record.
10. Woe to the repudiators on that day!
11. Those who deny the day of judgment
12. Which none denies except each criminal transgressor,
13. Who, when you read to him Our revelations, say: "(Mere) fables of the men of old."
14. No, but that which they have earned is rust upon their hearts.
15. No, but surely on that day they will be covered from (the mercy of) their Lord.
16. Then they will burn in hell,
17. And it will be said (to them): "This is that which you used to deny."
18. No, but the record of the righteous is in 'Illiyin[2]—

1. A pit in which the register of the deeds of the wicked is kept. Also, the registry itself.

2. A celestial realm and, by extension, the register in which the deeds of the pious are written.

19. Ah, what will convey to you what 'Illiyin is!—
20. A written record,
21. Attested by those who are brought near (to their Lord).
22. The righteous are in delight,
23. On couches, gazing,
24. You will know in their faces the radiance of delight.
25. They are given to drink of a pure wine, sealed,
26. Whose seal is musk—For this let (all) those strive who strive for bliss—
27. And mixed with water of Tasnim,[3]
28. A spring from which those brought near (to God) drink.
29. The guilty used to laugh at those who believed,
30. And wink one to another when they passed them;
31. And when they returned to their own people, they returned jesting;
32. And when they saw them they said: "These have gone astray."
33. Yet they were not sent as guardians over them.
34. This day it is those who believe who have the laugh of disbelievers,
35. On high couches, gazing.
36. Are not the disbelievers paid for what they used to do?

SŪRA 84

The Sundering

Revealed at Mecca

In the name of God, the beneficent, the merciful.

1. When the heaven is split asunder
2. And attentive to her Lord in fear,
3. And when the earth is spread out
4. And has cast out all that was in her, and is empty
5. And attentive to her Lord in fear!
6. You, O man, are working toward your Lord a work which you will meet (in His presence).
7. Then whoever is given his account in his right hand
8. He truly will receive an easy reckoning
9. And will return to his folk in joy.
10. But whoever is given his account behind his back,
11. He surely will invoke destruction
12. And be thrown to scorching fire.
13. He lived joyous with his folk,
14. He thought that he would never return (to God).
15. No, but his Lord is ever looking on him!
16. Oh, I swear by the afterglow of sunset,
17. And by the night and all that it enshrouds,
18. And by the moon when she is at the full,
19. That you shall journey on from plane to plane.
20. What ails them, then, that they do not believe

3. A well or fountain in paradise.

21. And, when the Qur'an is recited to them, do not worship (God)?
22. No, but those who disbelieve will deny;
23. And God knows best what they are hiding.
24. So give them tidings of a painful doom,
25. Except those who believe and do good works, for theirs is a reward unfailing.

SŪRA 85

The Mansions of the Stars

Revealed at Mecca

In the name of God, the beneficent, the merciful.

1. By the heaven, holding mansions of the stars,
2. And by the promised day.
3. And by the witness and that to which he bears testimony,
4. (Self-)destroyed were the owners of the ditch
5. Of the fuel-fed fire,
6. When they sat by it,
7. And were themselves the witnesses of what they did to the believers.[1]
8. They had nothing against them except that they believed in God, the mighty, the owner of praise,
9. Him to whom belongs the sovereignty of the heavens and the earth; and God is of all things the witness.
10. They who persecute believing men and believing women and do not repent, theirs will be the doom of hell, and theirs the doom of burning.
11. Those who believe and do good works, theirs will be gardens underneath which rivers flow. That is the great success.
12. The punishment of your Lord is stern.
13. He it is who produces, then reproduces,
14. And He is the forgiving, the loving,
15. Lord of the throne of glory,
16. Doer of what He will.
17. Has there come to you the story of the hosts
18. Of Pharaoh and (the tribe of) Thamud?[2]
19. No, but those who disbelieve live in denial
20. And God, all unseen, surrounds them.
21. No, but it is a glorious Qur'an.
22. On a guarded tablet.

1. Or it might be: "(Self-)destroyed were the owners of the trench of fuel-fed fire (*i.e.,* hell) when they took their ease on earth and were themselves the witnesses," etc. [Pickthall's note].

2. A once-prominent Arabian tribe; according to traditional Islamic accounts, they were destroyed because they refused to worship Allah.

SŪRA 86

The Morning Star

Revealed at Mecca

In the name of God, the beneficent, the merciful.

1. By the heaven and the morning star[1]
2. —Ah, what will tell you what the morning star is!
3. —The piercing star!
4. Every human soul has a guardian over it.
5. So let man consider from what he is created.
6. He is created from a gushing fluid
7. That issued from between the loins and ribs.
8. He is able to return him (to life)
9. On the day when hidden thoughts shall be searched out.
10. Then he will have no might nor any helper.
11. By the heaven which gives the returning rain,
12. And the earth which splits (with the growth of trees and plants)
13. This (Qur'an) is a conclusive word,
14. It is no pleasantry.
15. They plot a plot (against you, O Muhammad)
16. And I plot a plot (against them).
17. So give a respite to the disbelievers. Deal gently with them for a while.

SŪRA 87

The Most High

Revealed at Mecca

In the name of God, the beneficent, the merciful.

1. Praise the name of your Lord the most high,
2. Who creates, then disposes;
3. Who measures, then guides;
4. Who brings forth the pasturage,
5. Then turns it to russet stubble.
6. We shall make you read (O Muhammad) so that you shall not forget
7. Except that which God wills. He knows the disclosed and that which still is hidden;
8. And We shall ease your way to the state of ease.
9. Therefore remind (men), for of use is the reminder.
10. He who fears will heed,
11. But the most wretched will flout it,
12. He who will be flung to the great fire
13. In which he will neither die nor live.
14. He is successful who grows,
15. And remembers the name of his Lord, so prays.

1. The Arabic word means originally "that which comes at night" or "one who knocks at the door" [Pickthall's note].

16. But you prefer the life of the world
17. Although the hereafter is better and more lasting.
18. This is in the former scrolls,
19. The scrolls of Abraham and Moses.

SŪRA 88
The Overwhelming
Revealed at Mecca

In the name of God, the beneficent, the merciful.

1. Have there come to you tidings of the overwhelming?
2. On that day (many) faces will be downcast,
3. Toiling, weary,
4. Scorched by burning fire,
5. Drinking from a boiling spring,
6. No food for them but bitter thorn-fruit
7. Which does not nourish or release from hunger.
8. In that day other faces will be calm,
9. Glad for their effort past,
10. In a high garden
11. Where they hear no idle speech,
12. In which is a gushing spring,
13. In which are couches raised
14. And goblets set at hand
15. And cushions ranged
16. And silken carpets spread.
17. Will they not regard the camels, how they are created?
18. And the heaven, how it is raised?
19. And the hills, how they are set up?
20. And the earth, how it is spread?
21. Remind them, for you are but a reminder,
22. You are not at all a warder over them.
23. But whoever is averse and disbelieves,
24. God will punish him with direst punishment.
25. To Us is their return
26. And Ours their reckoning.

SURA 89
The Dawn
Revealed at Mecca

In the name of God, the beneficent, the merciful.

1. By the dawn
2. And ten nights,[1]

1. Of the month of pilgrimage [Pickthall's note].

3. And the even and the odd,
4. And the night when it departs,
5. There surely is an oath for a thinking man.
6. Do you not consider how your Lord dealt with (the tribe of) ʿAd,[2]
7. With many-columned[3] Iram,
8. The like of which was not created in the lands;
9. And with (the tribe of) Thamud,[4] who clove the rocks in the valley;
10. And with Pharaoh, firm of might,
11. Who (all) were rebellious (to God) in these lands,
12. And multiplied iniquity in them?
13. Therefore your Lord poured on them the disaster of His punishment.
14. Your Lord is ever watchful.
15. As for man, whenever his Lord tests him by honoring him, and is gracious to him, he says: "My Lord honors me."
16. But whenever He tests him by restricting his means of life, he says: "My Lord despises me."
17. No, but you (for your part) do not honor the orphan
18. And do not urge the feeding of the poor,
19. And you devour heritages with devouring greed
20. And love wealth with abounding love.
21. No, but when the earth is ground to atoms, grinding, grinding,
22. And your Lord shall come with angels, rank on rank,
23. And hell is brought near that day; on that day man will remember, but how will the remembrance (then avail him)?
24. He will say: "Ah, would that I had sent before me (some provision) for my life!"
25. None punishes as He will punish on that day!
26. None binds as He then will bind.
27. But ah! you soul at peace!
28. Return to your Lord, content in His good pleasure!
29. Enter among My bondmen!
30. Enter My garden!

SŪRA 90
The City
Revealed at Mecca

In the name of God, the beneficent, the merciful.

1. No, I swear by this city—
2. And you are an indweller of this city[1]—

2. An ancient tribe to whom the prophet Hud was sent (Qur'an 11:50–60); they ruled from Iram.

3. I had written "many-columned," following the run of commentators, who take the word *ʿimad* to mean columns, pillars, when I happened upon Ibn Khaldun's diatribe against that rendering and all the legends to which it has given rise, in the preface to the *Prolegomena*. The word meant "tent-poles" to the Arabs of the Prophet's day, as Ibn Khaldun points out. In view of recent discoveries in the Yemen, however, I prefer the usual rendering [Pickthall's note; on Ibn Khaldun (1332–1406), see below].

4. Nabatean descendants of ʿAd who left rock inscriptions in their settlements in northern Arabia.

1. Or "when you have control over this city" (prophetically) [Pickthall's note].

3. And the begetter and that which he begat,
4. We have created man in an atmosphere:[2]
5. Does he think that none has power over him?
6. And he says: "I have destroyed vast wealth,"
7. Does he think that none beholds him?
8. Did We not assign to him two eyes
9. And a tongue and two lips,
10. And guide him to the parting of the mountain ways?
11. But he has not attempted the ascent—
12. Ah, what will convey to you what the ascent is!—
13. (It is) to free a slave,
14. And to feed in the day of hunger
15. An orphan near of kin,
16. Or some poor wretch in misery,
17. And to be of those who believe and exhort one another to perseverance and exhort one another to pity.
18. Their place will be on the right hand.
19. But those who disbelieve our revelations, their place will be on the left hand.
20. Fire will be an awning over them.

SŪRA 91

The Sun

Revealed at Mecca

In the name of God, the beneficent, the merciful.

1. By the sun and its brightness,
2. And the moon as it follows it,
3. And the day when it reveals it,
4. And the night when it enshrouds it,
5. And the heaven and Him who built it,
6. And the earth and Him who spread it,
7. And a soul and Him who perfected it
8. And inspired it (with conscience of) what is wrong for it and (what is) right for it.
9. He is indeed successful who causes it to grow,
10. And he is indeed a failure who stunts it.
11. (The tribe of) Thamud denied (the truth) in their rebellious pride,
12. When the basest of them broke forth
13. And the messenger of God said: "It is the she-camel of God, so let her drink!"
14. But they denied him, and they hamstrung her, so their Lord doomed them for their sin and razed (their dwellings).
15. He does not dread the sequel (of events).

2. Or "in affliction" [Pickthall's note].

SŪRA 92

The Night

Revealed at Mecca

In the name of God, the beneficent, the merciful.

1. By the night enshrouding
2. And the day resplendent
3. And him who has created male and female,
4. Your effort is dispersed (toward diverse ends).
5. As for him who gives and is dutiful (toward God)
6. And believes in goodness;
7. Surely we will ease his way to the state of ease.
8. But as for him who hoards and thinks himself independent,
9. And denies goodness;
10. Surely we will ease his way to adversity.
11. His riches will not save him when he perishes.
12. Ours it is (to give) the guidance
13. And to Us belong the latter portion and the former.
14. Therefore have I warned you of the flaming fire
15. Which only the most wretched must endure,
16. He who denies and turns away.
17. Far removed from it will be the righteous
18. Who gives his wealth that he may grow (in goodness),
19. And none has with him any favor for reward,
20. Except as seeking (to fulfill) the purpose of his Lord most high.
21. He will be content.

SŪRA 93

The Morning Hours

Revealed at Mecca

In the name of God, the beneficent, the merciful.

1. By the morning hours
2. And by the night when it is stillest,
3. Your Lord has not forsaken you nor does He hate you,
4. And the latter portion will be better for you than the former,
5. And your Lord will give to you so that you will be content.
6. Did He not find you an orphan and protect (you)?
7. Did He not find you wandering and direct (you)?
8. Did He not find you destitute and enrich (you)?
9. Therefore do not oppress the orphan,
10. Therefore do not drive away the beggar,
11. Therefore of the bounty of your Lord be your discourse.

SŪRA 94

Solace

Revealed at Mecca

In the name of God, the beneficent, the merciful.

1. Have We not caused your breast to dilate,
2. And eased you of the burden
3. Which weighed down your back;
4. And exalted your fame?
5. But with hardship goes ease,
6. With hardship goes ease;
7. So when you are relieved, still toil
8. And strive to please your Lord.

SŪRA 95

The Fig

Revealed at Mecca

In the name of God, the beneficent, the merciful.

1. By the fig and the olive,
2. By Mount Sinai,
3. And by this land made safe;
4. Surely We created man of the best stature
5. Then We reduced him to the lowest of the low,
6. Except those who believe and do good works, and theirs is a reward unfailing.
7. So who henceforth will give the lie to you about the judgment?
8. Is not God the most conclusive of all judges?

SŪRA 96

The Clot

Revealed at Mecca

In the name of God, the beneficent, the merciful.

1. Read: In the name of your Lord who created,
2. Created man from a clot.
3. Read: And your Lord is the most bounteous,
4. Who teaches by the pen,
5. Teaches man what he knew not.
6. No, but truly man is rebellious
7. That he thinks himself independent!
8. To your Lord is the return.
9. Have you seen him who dissuades
10. A servant (of God) when he prays?

11. Have you seen if he relies on the guidance (of God)
12. Or enjoins piety?
13. Have you seen if he denies (God's guidance) and turns away?
14. Is he then unaware that God sees?
15. No, but if he does not cease We will seize him by the forelock—
16. The lying, sinful forelock—
17. Then let him call upon his henchmen!
18. We will call the guards of hell.
19. No! Do not obey him. But prostrate yourself, and draw near (to God).

SŪRA 97

Power

Revealed at Mecca

In the name of God, the beneficent, the merciful.

1. We revealed it on the night of power.
2. Ah, what will convey to you what the night of power is!
3. The night of power is better than a thousand months.
4. The angels and the spirit[1] descend in it, by the permission of their Lord, with all decrees.
5. (That night is) peace until the rising of the dawn.

SŪRA 98

The Clear Proof

Revealed at Medina

In the name of God, the beneficent, the merciful.

1. Those who disbelieve among the People of the Book[1] and the idolaters could not have left off (erring) until the clear proof came to them,
2. A messenger from God, reading purified pages
3. Containing correct scriptures.
4. Nor were the People of the Book divided until after the clear proof came to them.
5. And they are ordered only to serve God, keeping religion pure for Him, as men by nature upright, and to establish worship and to pay the poor-tax. That is true religion.
6. Those who disbelieve, among the People of the Book and the idolaters, will abide in hell's fire. They are the worst of created beings.
7. (And) those who believe and do good works are the best of created beings.
8. Their reward is with their Lord: gardens of Eden underneath which rivers flow, in which they dwell forever. God has pleasure in them and they have pleasure in Him. This is (in store) for him who fears his Lord.

1. That is, Gabriel or, as some commentators think, a general term for angels of the highest rank [Pickthall's note].

1. Jews and Christians.

SŪRA 99

The Earthquake

Revealed at Mecca

In the name of God, the beneficent, the merciful.

1. When earth is shaken with her (final) earthquake
2. And earth yields up her burdens,
3. And man says: "What ails her?"
4. That day she will relate her chronicles,
5. Because your Lord inspires her.
6. That day mankind will issue forth in scattered groups to be shown their deeds.
7. And whoever does an atom's weight of good will see it then,
8. And whoever does an atom's weight of ill will see it then.

SŪRA 100

The Coursers

Revealed at Mecca

In the name of God, the beneficent, the merciful.

1. By the snorting coursers,[1]
2. Striking sparks of fire
3. And scouring to the raid at dawn,
4. Then, therewith, with their trail of dust,
5. Cleaving, as one, the center (of the foe),[2]
6. Man is an ingrate to his Lord
7. And he is a witness to that;
8. And in the love of wealth he is violent.
9. Does he not know that, when the contents of the graves are poured forth
10. And the secrets of the breasts are made known,
11. On that day will their Lord be perfectly informed concerning them.

SŪRA 101

The Calamity

Revealed at Mecca

In the name of God, the beneficent, the merciful.

1. The calamity!
2. What is the calamity?
3. Ah, what will convey to you what the calamity is!
4. A day in which mankind will be as thickly-scattered moths

1. Fast-running horses.
2. The meaning of the first five verses is by no means clear. The above is a probable rendering [Pickthall's note].

5. And the mountains will become as carded wool.
6. Then, as for him whose scales are heavy (with good works),
7. He will live a pleasant life.
8. But as for him whose scales are light,
9. The bereft and hungry one will be his mother.
10. Ah, what will convey to you what she is!—
11. Raging fire.

SŪRA 102

Rivalry in Worldly Increase

Revealed at Mecca

In the name of God, the beneficent, the merciful.

1. Rivalry in worldly increase distracts you
2. Until you come to the graves.
3. No, but you will come to know!
4. No, but you will come to know!
5. No, would that you knew (now) with a sure knowledge!
6. For you will behold hell-fire.
7. Yes, you will behold it with sure vision.
8. Then, on that day, you will be asked concerning pleasure.

SŪRA 103

The Declining Day

Revealed at Mecca

In the name of God, the beneficent, the merciful.

1. By the declining day,
2. Man is in a state of loss,
3. Except those who believe and do good works, and exhort one another to truth and exhort one another to endurance.

SŪRA 104

The Traducer

Revealed at Mecca

In the name of God, the beneficent, the merciful.

1. Woe to every slandering fault-finder,
2. Who has gathered wealth (of this world) and arranged it.
3. He thinks that his wealth will render him immortal.
4. No, but he will be flung to the consuming one.
5. Ah, what will convey to you what the consuming one is!
6. (It is) the fire of God, kindled,

7. Which leaps up over the hearts (of men).
8. It is closed in on them
9. In outstretched columns.

SŪRA 105

The Elephant

Revealed at Mecca

In the name of God, the beneficent, the merciful.

1. Have you not seen how your Lord dealt with the owners of the elephant?[1]
2. Did he not bring their stratagem to nothing,
3. And send against them swarms of flying creatures,
4. Which pelted them with stones of baked clay,
5. And made them like green crops devoured (by cattle)?

SŪRA 106

"Winter" or "Quraysh"

Revealed at Mecca

In the name of God, the beneficent, the merciful.

1. For the taming[1] of Quraysh[2]
2. For their taming (We cause) the caravans to set forth in winter and summer.
3. So let them worship the Lord of this house,
4. Who has fed them against hunger
5. And has made them safe from fear.

SŪRA 107

Small Kindnesses

Revealed at Mecca

In the name of God, the beneficent, the merciful.

1. Have you observed him who denies religion?
2. That is he who repels the orphan,
3. And does not urge the feeding of the needy.
4. Ah, woe to worshippers
5. Who are heedless of their prayer;
6. Who would be seen (at worship)
7. Yet refuse small kindnesses!

1. The Abyssinians, who were attempting to attack Mecca; Abraha, their leader, unsuccessfully directed his elephant to destroy the Kaʿba (the sacred cubical shrine in Mecca).

1. That is, "civilizing" [Pickthall's note].
2. The tribe that ruled Mecca.

SŪRA 108

Abundance

Revealed at Mecca

In the name of God, the beneficent, the merciful.

1. We have given you abundance;
2. So pray to your Lord, and sacrifice.
3. It is your insulter (and not you) who is without posterity.

SŪRA 109

The Disbelievers

Revealed at Mecca

In the name of God, the beneficent, the merciful.

1. Say: O disbelievers!
2. I do not worship what you worship;
3. Nor do you worship what I worship.
4. And I shall not worship what you worship.
5. Nor will you worship what I worship.
6. To you your religion, and to me my religion.

SŪRA 110

Succour

Revealed at Medina

In the name of God, the beneficent, the merciful.

1. When God's help and the triumph comes
2. And you see mankind entering the religion of God in bands,
3. Then hymn the praises of your Lord, and seek forgiveness of Him. He is ever ready to show mercy.

SŪRA 111

Palm Fibre

Revealed at Mecca

In the name of God, the beneficent, the merciful.

1. The power of Abu Lahab[1] will perish, and he will perish.
2. His wealth and gains will not exempt him.
3. He will be plunged in flaming fire,

1. An uncle of the Prophet but not a supporter. Abu Lahab and his wife tormented Muhammad.

4. And his wife, the wood-carrier,
5. Will have upon her neck a halter of palm-fibre.

SŪRA 112

The Unity

Revealed at Mecca

In the name of God, the beneficent, the merciful.

1. Say: He is God, the one!
2. God, the eternally besought of all!
3. He begets not nor was begotten.
4. And there is none comparable to Him.

SŪRA 113

The Daybreak

Revealed at Mecca

In the name of God, the beneficent, the merciful.

1. Say: I seek refuge in the Lord of the daybreak
2. From the evil of that which He created;
3. From the evil of the darkness when it is intense,
4. And from the evil of malignant witchcraft,[1]
5. And from the evil of the envier when he envies.

SŪRA 114

Mankind

Revealed at Mecca

In the name of God, the beneficent, the merciful.

1. Say: I seek refuge in the Lord of mankind,
2. The king of mankind,
3. The God of mankind,
4. From the evil of the sneaking whisperer,
5. Who whispers in the hearts of mankind,
6. Of the jinn and of mankind.

1. Lit. "from the evil of blowers (feminine) upon knots," it having been a common form of witchcraft in Arabia for women to tie knots in a cord and blow upon them with an imprecation [Pickthall's note].

SIRA: THE LIFE STORY OF THE PROPHET

IBN HISHAM
d. 833

Muhammad ibn Ishaq (ca. 704–767) was a historian whose biography of Muhammad has become his most famous work. Yet this biography comes to us not directly from his pen but in the recension of a later scholar, Muhammad ibn Hisham. Though their lives are separated by several generations, their names are forever linked to a book that remains Islam's most trusted source for the life of the Prophet.

Ibn Ishaq was born in Medina, where his father and paternal uncles, like many scholars of their time, devoted themselves to collecting and transmitting as many accounts (in Arabic, *akhbar*) of Islam's early history as possible. Their tastes were catholic and their range was broad. They were interested in the history of Arabia before Islam and in the fables and folktales that circulated among the peninsula's tribes. They questioned local Jews and Christians, including those who followed Muhammad, about earlier prophets and the biblical stories that spoke of them. They sought out those who could recall the expeditions and early battles of the first generation of Muslims.

Ibn Ishaq continued in this family tradition, initially studying and then teaching in Medina. For reasons that are not clear, he ran afoul of some local scholars, most notably Malik ibn Anas (ca. 715–795), the eponymous founder of the Maliki legal school. Though the basis for Malik's strong dislike of Ibn Ishaq is uncertain, stories abound. According to one, when Malik completed his *The Well-Trodden Path*, Ibn Ishaq asked that the work be presented to him so that he could examine it. Malik apparently took offense at Ibn Ishaq's arrogance and called him an "anti-Christ" (in Arabic, *dajjal*). Another account stresses methodological differences. During Ibn Ishaq's lifetime, those who, like Malik, assessed traditions (*hadith*) for authenticity were gaining ascendency over those who rather indiscriminately amassed early historical reports. Malik may well have objected to the reliability of Ibn Ishaq's collection (no longer extant) of traditions about Muhammad.

Prompted by this animosity or other reasons, Ibn Ishaq left Medina and eventually settled in Baghdad. There, the ʿAbbasid caliph al-Mansur (r. 754–75) asked him to write a universal history commencing with the creation of Adam. To fulfill this request, Ibn Ishaq produced four volumes. The first, titled *The Beginning*, starts with the creation of the world and then covers the prophets before Muhammad and the pre-Islamic history of Arabia. The second volume, *The Mission*, recounts the life of Muhammad until his hijra to Medina. The third volume, *Battles*, focuses on the Medinan phase of Muhammad's career and preserves the earliest covenant in Islamic history, the so-called Constitution of Medina. Ibn Ishaq's final volume carries us through the reigns of the early caliphs who led the Muslim community following Muhammad's death.

Later scholars, most notably Ibn Hisham and the historians al-Tabari (d. 923; see below) and Ibn Kathir (ca. 1300–1373), edited and incorporated Ibn Ishaq's material into their own compositions, and it is through their work and that of other later authors that Ibn Ishaq's writings survive. Their use of this material involved considerable selection and shaping, however. For example, in his own biography of Muhammad, Ibn Hisham draws on Ibn Ishaq's material on the Prophet's life in Mecca and Medina but excises what he considers extraneous or objectionable, glosses difficult words, corrects mistakes in the poetry recorded by Ibn Ishaq, and adds narratives and genealogical descriptions. Al-Tabari's *History* preserves such

A leaf from a Turkish translation of Ibn Ishaq's life of the Prophet, undertaken by al-Zarīr, Mustafa ibn Yusuf ibn ʿUmar al-Mawlawi al-Erzurumi (fl. 14th c.) for a Mamluk sultan. It depicts Muhammad's bodily ascension into heaven, where, according to the biographical and hadith literature, he encountered previous prophets such as Jesus and Moses, and then spoke at length with God, with whom he bargained for leniency for the believing Muslims. Muhammad related that a magical horse called Buraq, here pictured, carried him by night from Mecca to the site of Solomon's Temple in Jerusalem, from which the ascension is to have occurred. That site—and the mosque that was subsequently built there, the Dome of the Rock—is the third holiest place in Islam, after the Arabian mosques at Mecca and Medina.

large parts of Ibn Ishaq's first volume, *The Beginning*, that it is now the primary source for Ibn Ishaq's lost work. Al-Tabari also preserved much of what Ibn Ishaq wrote about Muhammad's life, but the material is repurposed and redistributed. Notably, al-Tabari retains two incidents that Ibn Hisham omits—a moment when Muhammad may have contemplated suicide and the episode in which Muhammad apparently attempted to curry favor with the pagan Meccans by relating verses that extolled their goddesses. These so-called satanic verses were later retracted.

The passages below from Ibn Hisham's edition of Ibn Ishaq's biography of Muhammad begin with Muhammad's call to prophethood and the revelation of the Qur'an. They vividly re-create Muhammad's visionary and auditory experiences during this period of prayerful seclusion on the outskirts of Mecca. They capture the drama of Gabriel's appearance and forceful intervention, the Prophet's terror, and his wife Khadija's fervent testimony to his prophethood. They recount how Khadija tested his spirit by disrobing and unveiling. These scenes and episodes from the earlier years of Muhammad's public life are supplemented by the final selection, which is dated to the concluding years of his life in Medina. It reproduces the Constitution of Medina, which lays out the terms of Muhammad's leadership and delineates the responsibilities of Arab and Jewish tribes of the city. While frequently described in Western sources as a constitution, it is more accurately a covenant or a compact. The document has received significant scholarly attention. For the most part, scholars have accepted its authenticity and studied it closely, believing that it represents the earliest extant example of the terms of an alliance among Muslims themselves and between Muslims and non-Muslims.

The translator of the passages included here, Dr. Alfred Guillaume, sought to reconstruct Ibn Ishaq's original biography by making two changes to Ibn Hisham's recension. First, he eliminated Ibn Hisham's additions, which were clearly marked by the editor himself, and moved them to the end of the work in a section titled "Ibn Hisham's notes." Second, turning to other authors, such as al-Tabari and Ibn Kathir, who had also preserved Ibn Ishaq's writings, Guillaume inserted additional material that was not present in Ibn Hisham's edition of Ibn Ishaq's biography. In the excerpts below, places where material has been excised from Ibn Hisham are marked by a number in parentheses, elements added from al-Tabari are signified by a capital "Ṭ," and Ibn Kathir's version is set off by brackets and the designation "I.K."

PRONOUNCING GLOSSARY

ʿĀʾisha: *ah'-i-shuh*
ʿAbdu Manāf: *ab-doo ma-naf'*
ʿAbdu Shams: *ab-doo shams'*
ʿAbdu'l-Malik ibn ʿUbaydullah ibn Abū Sufyān ibn al-ʿAlāʾ ibn Jāriya: *ab-dul-ma'-lik ibn oo-bay'-dul-lah ibn a-boo soof-yan' ibn al-ah-la' ibn jah'-ree-yuh*
ʿAbdu'l-Muṭṭalib: *ab-dul-mut-tah'-lib*
ʿAbdullah ibn ʿAbbās: *ab-dul-lah' ibn ab-bas'*
ʿAbdullah ibn Abū Najīḥ: *ab-dul-lah' ibn a-boo na-jeeh'* (heavy *h*)
ʿAbdullah ibn al-Ghaffār ibn al-Qāsim: *ab-dul-lah' ibn al-gaf-far' ibn al-qah'-sim*
ʿAbdullah ibn al-Ḥārith ibn Naufal ibn al-Ḥārith ibn ʿAbdu'l-Muṭṭalib: *ab-dul-lah' ibn al-ha'-rith* (heavy *h*) *ibn naw'-fal ibn al-ha'-rith* (heavy *h*) *ibn ab-dul-mut-tah'-lib*
ʿAbdullah ibn al-Zubayr: *ab-dul-lah' ibn az-zoo-bayr'*
ʿAbdullah ibn Ḥasan: *ab-dul-lah' ibn ha'-san* (heavy *h*)
ʿAbdullah ibn Jaʿfar ibn Abū Ṭālib: *ab-dul-lah' ibn ja'-far ibn a-boo tah'-lib*
Abū Bakr ibn Abū Quḥāfa: *a-boo bakr ibn a-boo qoo-ha'-fuh*
Abū Jaʿfar Muḥammad ibn ʿAlī ibn al-Ḥusayn: *a-boo ja'-far moo-ham'-mad* (heavy *h*) *ibn ah'-lee ibn al-hoo-sayn'* (heavy *h*)
Abū Jahl ʿAmr: *a-boo jal' ahmr*
Abū Lahab: *a-boo la'-hab*
Abū Sufyān ibn Ḥarb: *a-boo soof-yan' ibn harb* (heavy *h*)

Abū Ṭālib: *a-boo tah'-lib*
Abū'l-Bakhtarī: *a-bool-bach'-ta-ree* (guttural *ch*)
Abū'l-Ḥakam ibn Hishām ibn al-Mughīra: *a-bool-ha'-kam* (heavy *h*) *ibn he-sham' ibn al-moo-gee'-ruh*
Abū'l-Jald: *a-bool-jald'*
Abū'l-Qāsim: *a-bool-qah'-sim*
ʿAfīf: *a-feef'*
al-ʿAbbās ibn ʿAbdu'l-Muṭṭalib: *al-ab-bas' ibn ab-dul-mut-tah'-lib*
al-ʿAṣ ibn Hishām ibn al-Ḥārith ibn Asad: *al-ahs' ibn he-sham' ibn al-ha'-rith* (heavy *h*) *ibn a'-sad*
al-ʿĀṣ ibn Wā'il: *al-ahs' ibn wa'-il*
al-ʿUzza: *al-uz'-zuh*
al-Ashʿath ibn Qays al-Kindī: *al-ash'-ath ibn qays al-kin'-dee*
al-Aswad ibn al-Muṭṭalib ibn Asad: *al-as'-wad ibn al-mut-tah'-lib ibn a'-sad*
al-Ḥajjāj ibn ʿĀmir ibn Ḥudhayfa: *al-haj-jaj* (heavy *h*) *ibn ah'-mir ibn hoo-dhay'-fuh* (heavy *h*)
al-Ḥasan ibn Abū'l-Ḥasan: *al-ha'-san* (heavy *h*) *ibn a-bool-ha'-san* (heavy *h*)
al-Ḥusayn: *al-hoo-sayn'* (heavy *h*)
al-Lāt: *al-lat'*
al-Minhāl ibn ʿAmr: *al-min-hal' ibn ahmr*
al-Muṭʿim ibn ʿAdīy: *al-mut'-im ibn a-dee'*
al-Walīd: *al-wa-leed'*
al-Walīd ibn al-Mughīra: *al-wa-leed' ibn al-moo-gee'-ruh*
al-Zubayr: *az-zoo-bayr'*
al-Zuhrī: *az-zuh'-ree* (light *h*)
ʿAlī ibn Abū Ṭālib: *ah'-lee ibn a-boo tah'-lib*
ʿAlī ibn Mujāhid: *ah'-lee ibn moo-ja'-hid*
ʿAmr: *ahmr*
ʿAmr ibn ʿUbayd: *ahmr ibn oo-bayd'*
ʿAqīl: *ah-qeel'*
ʿAtīq: *ah-teeq'*
Badr: *badr*
Banū (= B.) ʿAuf: *ba-noo awf'*
Banū (= B.) al-Aus: *ba-nool-aws*
Banū (= B.) al-Muṭṭalib: *ba-nool-mut-tah'-lib*
Banū (= B.) al-Nabīt: *ba-noon-na-beet'*
Banū (= B.) al-Najjār: *ba-noon-naj-jahr'*
Banū (= B.) al-Shuṭayba: *ba-noosh-shoo-tay'-buh*
Banū (= B.) Jusham: *ba-noo joo-sham'*
Banū (= B.) Sāʿida: *ba-noo-sa'-e-duh*
Banū (= B.) Thaʿlaba: *ba-noo tha'-la-buh*
Banū Hāshim: *ba-noo ha'-shim*
Banū Taym: *ba-noo taym'*
Chosrhoes: *chos'-row-es* (guttural *ch*)
Dhū ʿAlaq: *dhoo a'-lahq*
Fāṭima: *fah'-te-muh*
furqān: *fur-qahn'*
Ḥamza: *ham'-zuh* (heavy *h*)
Ḥirā': *hi-ra'* (heavy *h*)
Hishām ibn ʿUrwa: *he-sham' ibn ur-wuh*
Ibn Ḥamīd: *ibn ha-meed'* (heavy *h*)
Ismāʿīl ibn Abū Ḥakīm: *is-ma-eel' ibn a-boo ha-keem'* (heavy *h*)
Ismāʿīl ibn Iyās ibn ʿAfīf al-Kindī: *es-mah-eel' ibn ee-yas' ibn a-feef' al-kin'-dee*
Jaʿfar: *ja'-far*
Jafna: *jaf'-nuh*
Kaʿba: *ka'-buh*
Khadīja: *cha-dee'-juh* (guttural *ch*)
Khuwaylid: *choo-way'-lid* (guttural *ch*)
Kūfa: *koo'-fuh*
Makhzūm: *mach-zoom'* (guttural *ch*)
Minā: *mee-na'*
Muḥammad ibn ʿAbdullah: *moo-ham'-mad* (heavy *h*) *ibn ab-dul-lah'*
Muḥammad ibn ʿAbdullah ibn ʿAbdu'l-Muṭṭalib: *moo-ham'-mad* (heavy *h*) *ibn ab-dul-lah' ibn ab-dul-mut-tah'-lib*
Muḥammad ibn Isḥāq: *moo-ham'-mad* (heavy *h*) *ibn is-hawq'* (heavy *h*)
Mujāhid ibn Jabr Abū'l-Ḥajjāj: *moo-ja'-hid ibn jabr a-bool-haj-jaj'* (heavy *h*)
Munabbih: *moo-nab'-bih* (light *h*)
Nāfīʿ ibn Jubayr ibn Muṭʿim: *na'-fi ibn joo-bayr' ibn mut'-im*
nāmūs: *na-moos'*
Naufal: *naw'-fal*
Nubayh: *noo-bayh'* (light *h*)
qaṣab: *qah'-sahb*
Qatāda ibn Dīʿāma al-Sadūsī: *qah-ta'-duh ibn dee-a'-muh as-sa-doo'-see*
Quraysh: *qoo-raysh'*
Quṣayy: *qoo-say'*
Rabīʿa ibn ʿAbdu Shams: *ra-bee'-uh ibn ab-doo shams'*
Ramaḍān: *ra-ma-dawn'*
Saʿd ibn Abū Waqqāṣ: *sad ibn a-boo waq-qahs'*

Saʿid ibn Abū ʿArūba: *sa-eed' ibn a-boo a-roo'-buh*
Salama ibn al-Faḍl: *sa'-la-muh ibn al-fahdl'*
Ṣāliḥ ibn Kaisān: *sah'-lih* (heavy *h*) *ibn kay-san'*
Shayba: *shay'-buh*
Tʿabarī: *tah'-ba-ree*
taḥannuth: *ta-han'-nuth* (heavy *h*)
Thabīr: *tha-beer'*
Thaur: *thawr*
ʿUbayd ibn ʿUmayr ibn Qatāda: *oo-bayd' ibn oo-mayr' ibn qah-ta'-duh*
ʿUmāra ibn al-Walīd ibn al-Mughīra: *oo-mah'-ruh ibn al-wa-leed' ibn al-moo-gee'-ruh*
umma: *oom'-muh*
ʿUrwa ibn Zubayr: *ur'-wuh ibn zoo-bayr'*
ʿUtba: *ut'-buh*
ʿUtba ibn Muslim: *ut'*-buh ibn mus'-lim
ʿUthmān ibn ʿAmir ibn ʿAmr ibn Kaʿb ibn Saʿd ibn Taym ibn Murra ibn Kaʿb ibn Luʾayy ibn Ghālib ibn Fihr: *uth-man' ibn ah'-mir ibn ahmr ibn kab ibn sad ibn taym ibn mur'-ruh ibn kab ibn loo-ay' ibn gah'-lib ibn fihr* (light *h*)
Wahb ibn Kaisān: *wahb* (light *h*) *ibn kay-san'*
Waraqa ibn Naufal ibn Asad ibn ʿAbdu'l-ʿUzza ibn Quṣayy: *wa'-ra-quh ibn naw'-fal ibn a'-sad ibn ab-dul-uz'-zuh ibn qoo-say'*
Yaʿqūb ibn ʿUtba ibn al-Mughīra ibn al-Akhnas: *ya-qoob' ibn ut'-buh ibn al-moo-gee'-ruh ibn al-ach'-nas* (guttural *ch*)
Yaḥyā ibn Abū'l-Ashʿath al-Kindī: *yah'-ya* (heavy *h*) *ibn a-bul-ash'-ath al-kin'-dee*
Yathrib: *yath'-rib*
Yūnus ibn Bukayr: *you'-nus ibn boo-kayr'*
Zayd ibn Ḥāritha: *zayd ibn ha'-ri-thuh* (heavy *h*)
Zuhra: *zuh'-ruh* (light *h*)

FROM IBN ISHAQ'S *THE LIFE OF MUHAMMAD*

The Prophet's Mission

When Muhammad the apostle of God reached the age of forty, God sent him in compassion to mankind, 'as an evangelist to all men'.[1] Now God had made a covenant with every prophet whom he had sent before him that he should believe in him, testify to his truth and help him against his adversaries, and he required of them that they should transmit that to everyone who believed in them, and they carried out their obligations in that respect. God said to Muhammad, 'When God made a covenant with the prophets (He said) this is the scripture and wisdom which I have given you, afterwards an apostle will come confirming what you know that you may believe in him and help him.' He said, 'Do you accept this and take up my burden?' i.e. the burden of my agreement which I have laid upon you. They said, 'We accept it.' He answered, 'Then bear witness and I am a witness with you.'[2] Thus God made a covenant with all the prophets that they should testify to his truth and help him against his adversaries and they transmitted that obligation to those who believed in them among the two monotheistic religions.

(Ṭ. One whom I do not suspect told me from Saʿīd b. Abū ʿArūba from Qatāda b Diʿāma al-Sadūsi from Abū'l-Jald: 'The Furqān[3] came down on the 14th night of Ramaḍān. Others say, No, but on the 17th; and in support of

Translated by Alfred Guillaume.

1. Qur'an 34:28.
2. Qur'an 3:81.
3. A name given to the Qur'an, meaning "the proof."

this they appeal to God's word: 'And what we sent down to our servant on the day of al-Furqān, the day the two companies met'[4] which was the meeting of the apostle and the polytheists at Badr,[5] and that took place on the morning of Ramaḍān 17th.)

Al-Zuhrī related from ʿUrwa b. Zubayr that ʿĀʾisha[6] told him that when Allah desired to honour Muhammad and have mercy on His servants by means of him, the first sign of prophethood vouchsafed to the apostle was true visions, resembling the brightness of daybreak, which were shown to him in his sleep. And Allah, she said, made him love solitude so that he liked nothing better than to be alone.

ʿAbdu'l-Malik b. ʿUbaydullah b. Abū Sufyān b. al-ʿAlāʾ b. Jāriya the Thaqafite who had a retentive memory related to me from a certain scholar that the apostle at the time when Allah willed to bestow His grace upon him and endow him with prophethood would go forth for his affair and journey far afield until he reached the glens of Mecca and the beds of its valleys where no house was in sight; and not a stone or tree that he passed by but would say, 'Peace unto thee, O apostle of Allah.' And the apostle would turn to his right and left and look behind him and he would see naught but trees and stones. Thus he stayed seeing and hearing so long as it pleased Allah that he should stay. Then Gabriel came to him with the gift of God's grace whilst he was on Ḥirāʾ[7] in the month of Ramaḍān.

Wahb b. Kaisān a client of the family of al-Zubayr told me: I heard ʿAbdullah b. al-Zubayr say to ʿUbayd b. ʿUmayr b. Qatāda the Laythite, 'O ʿUbayd tell us how began the prophethood which was first bestowed on the apostle when Gabriel came to him.' And ʿUbayd in my presence related to ʿAbdullah and those with him as follows: The apostle would pray in seclusion on Ḥirāʾ every year for a month to practise *taḥannuth* as was the custom of Quraysh in heathen days. *Taḥannuth* is religious devotion. Abū Ṭālib said:

By Thaur and him who made Thabīr firm in its place[8]
And by those going up to ascend Ḥirāʾ and coming down (147).

Wahb b. Kaisān told me that ʿUbayd said to him: Every year during that month the apostle would pray in seclusion and give food to the poor that came to him. And when he completed the month and returned from his seclusion, first of all before entering his house he would go to the Kaʿba[9] and walk round it seven times or as often as it pleased God; then he would go back to his house until in the year when God sent him, in the month of Ramaḍān in which God willed concerning him what He willed of His grace, the apostle set forth to Ḥirāʾ as was his wont, and his family with him. When it was the night on which God honoured him with his mission and showed mercy on His servants thereby, Gabriel brought him the command of God. 'He came to me,' said the apostle of God, 'while I was asleep, with a coverlet of brocade whereon was some writing, and said, "Read!" I said, "What shall I read?" He pressed me

4. Qurʾan 8:41.
5. The Battle of Badr (624 C.E.), a decisive victory for the followers of Muhammad over his Meccan opponents (Badr is between Mecca and Medina).
6. Muhammad's favorite wife among the many he took after the death of his first wife, Khadija.
7. A mountain about 2 miles from Mecca. "Gabriel": the angel.
8. Thaur [Thawr] and Thabīr are mountains near Mecca [translator's note].
9. Literally, "the Cube," a stone shrine in Mecca—according to tradition, built by Abraham—that became the most important site in Islam (Muslims around the world face it when they pray).

with it so tightly that I thought it was death; then he let me go and said, "Read!" I said, "What shall I read?" He pressed me with it again so that I thought it was death; then he let me go and said "Read!" I said, "What shall I read?" He pressed me with it the third time so that I thought it was death and said "Read!" I said, "What then shall I read?"—and this I said only to deliver myself from him, lest he should do the same to me again. He said:

> "Read in the name of thy Lord who created,
> Who created man of blood coagulated.
> Read! Thy Lord is the most beneficent,
> Who taught by the pen,
> Taught that which they knew not unto men."[1]

So I read it, and he departed from me. And I awoke from my sleep, and it was as though these words were written on my heart. (Ṭ. Now none of God's creatures was more hateful to me than an (ecstatic) poet or a man possessed: I could not even look at them. I thought, Woe is me poet or possessed—Never shall Quraysh[2] say this of me! I will go to the top of the mountain and throw myself down that I may kill myself and gain rest. So I went forth to do so and then) when I was midway on the mountain, I heard a voice from heaven saying, "O Muhammad! thou art the apostle of God and I am Gabriel." I raised my head towards heaven to see (who was speaking), and lo, Gabriel in the form of a man with feet astride the horizon, saying, "O Muhammad! thou art the apostle of God and I am Gabriel." I stood gazing at him, (Ṭ. and that turned me from my purpose) moving neither forward nor backward; then I began to turn my face away from him, but towards whatever region of the sky I looked, I saw him as before. And I continued standing there, neither advancing nor turning back, until Khadīja[3] sent her messengers in search of me and they gained the high ground above Mecca and returned to her while I was standing in the same place; then he parted from me and I from him, returning to my family. And I came to Khadīja and sat by her thigh and drew close to her. She said, "O Abū'l-Qāsim,[4] where hast thou been? By God, I sent my messengers in search of thee, and they reached the high ground above Mecca and returned to me." (Ṭ. I said to her, "Woe is me poet or possessed." She said, "I take refuge in God from that O Abū'l-Qāsim. God would not treat you thus since he knows your truthfulness, your great trustworthiness, your fine character, and your kindness. This cannot be, my dear. Perhaps you did see something." "Yes, I did," I said.) Then I told her of what I had seen; and she said, "Rejoice, O son of my uncle, and be of good heart. Verily, by Him in whose hand is Khadīja's soul, I have hope that thou wilt be the prophet of this people."' Then she rose and gathered her garments about her and set forth to her cousin Waraqa b. Naufal b. Asad b. ʿAbdu'l-ʿUzzā b. Quṣayy, who had become a Christian and read the scriptures and learned from those that follow the Torah and the Gospel. And when she related to him what the apostle of God told her he had seen and heard, Waraqa cried, 'Holy! Holy! Verily by Him in whose hand is Waraqa's soul, if thou hast spoken to me the truth, O Khadīja, there hath come unto him the greatest Nāmūs[5] (Ṭ. meaning Gabriel) who came to

1. Qur'an 96:1–5.
2. The tribe that ruled Mecca.
3. Muhammad's first wife.
4. Muhammad's *kunya* ("title" or "nickname").
5. Literally, "Law" or "Revealed Law."

Moses aforetime, and lo, he is the prophet of this people. Bid him be of good heart.' So Khadīja returned to the apostle of God and told him what Waraqa had said. (Ṭ. and that calmed his fears somewhat.) And when the apostle of God had finished his period of seclusion and returned (to Mecca), in the first place he performed the circumambulation of the Kaʿba, as was his wont. While he was doing it, Waraqa met him and said, 'O son of my brother, tell me what thou hast seen and heard.' The apostle told him, and Waraqa said, 'Surely, by Him in whose hand is Waraqa's soul, thou art the prophet of this people. There hath come unto thee the greatest Nāmūs, who came unto Moses. Thou wilt be called a liar, and they will use thee despitefully and cast thee out and fight against thee. Verily, if I live to see that day, I will help God in such wise as He knoweth.' Then he brought his head near to him and kissed his forehead; and the apostle went to his own house. (Ṭ. Waraqa's words added to his confidence and lightened his anxiety.)

Ismāʿīl b. Abū Ḥakīm, a freedman of the family of al-Zubayr, told me on Khadīja's authority that she said to the apostle of God, 'O son of my uncle, are you able to tell me about your visitant, when he comes to you?' He replied that he could, and she asked him to tell her when he came. So when Gabriel came to him, as he was wont, the apostle said to Khadīja, 'This is Gabriel who has just come to me.' 'Get up, O son of my uncle,' she said, 'and sit by my left thigh.' The apostle did so, and she said, 'Can you see him?' 'Yes,' he said. She said, 'Then turn round and sit on my right thigh.' He did so, and she said, 'Can you see him?' When he said that he could she asked him to move and sit in her lap. When he had done this she again asked if he could see him, and when he said yes, she disclosed her form and cast aside her veil while the apostle was sitting in her lap. Then she said, 'Can you see him?' And he replied, 'No.' She said, 'O son of my uncle, rejoice and be of good heart, by God he is an angel and not a satan.'

I told ʿAbdullah b. Ḥasan this story and he said, 'I heard my mother Fāṭima, daughter of Ḥusayn, talking about this tradition from Khadīja, but as I heard it she made the apostle of God come inside her shift, and thereupon Gabriel departed, and she said to the apostle of God, "This verily is an angel and not a satan."'

The Beginning of the Sending Down of the Qurān

The apostle began to receive revelations in the month of Ramaḍān. In the words of God, 'The month of Ramaḍān in which the Qurān was brought down as a guidance to men, and proofs of guidance and a decisive criterion.[6] And again, 'Verily we have sent it down on the night of destiny, and what has shown you what the night of destiny is? The night of destiny is better than a thousand months. In it the angels and the spirit descend by their Lord's permission with every matter. It is peace until the rise of dawn.'[7] Again, 'H.M. by the perspicuous book, verily we have sent it down in a blessed night. Verily, we were warning. In it every wise matter is decided as a command from us. Verily we sent it down.[8] And again, 'Had you believed in God and what we sent down to Our servant on the day of decision, the day on which the two parties met',[9]

6. Qur'an 2:185.
7. Qur'an 97.
8. Qur'an 44:1–5. This sura, like twenty-eight others, begins with a grouping of Arabic letters; there is no consensus on their significance.
9. Qur'an 8:41.

i.e. the meeting of the apostle with the polytheists in Badr. Abū Jaʿfar Muhammad b. ʿAlī b. al-Ḥusayn told me that the apostle of God met the polytheists in Badr on the morning of Friday, the 17th of Ramaḍān.

Then revelation came fully to the apostle while he was believing in Him and in the truth of His message. He received it willingly, and took upon himself what it entailed whether of man's goodwill or anger. Prophecy is a troublesome burden—only strong, resolute messengers can bear it by God's help and grace, because of the opposition which they meet from men in conveying God's message. The apostle carried out God's orders in spite of the opposition and ill treatment which he met with.

Khadīja, Daughter of Khuwaylid, Accepts Islam

Khadīja believed in him and accepted as true what he brought from God, and helped him in his work. She was the first to believe in God and His apostle, and in the truth of his message. By her God lightened the burden of His prophet. He never met with contradiction and charges of falsehood, which saddened him, but God comforted him by her when he went home. She strengthened him, lightened his burden, proclaimed his truth, and belittled men's opposition. May God Almighty have mercy upon her!

Hishām b. ʿUrwa told me on the authority of his father ʿUrwa b. al-Zubayr from ʿAbdullah b. Jaʿfar b. Abū Ṭālib that the apostle said, 'I was commanded to give Khadīja the good news of a house of *qaṣab*[1] wherein would be no clamour and no toil' (148).

Then revelations stopped for a time so that the apostle of God was distressed and grieved. Then Gabriel brought him the Sūra of the Morning,[2] in which his Lord, who had so honoured him, swore that He had not forsaken him, and did not hate him. God said, 'By the morning and the night when it is still, thy Lord hath not forsaken nor hated thee,' meaning that He has not left you and forsaken you, nor hated you after having loved you. 'And verily, the latter end is better for you than the beginning, i.e. What I have for you when you return to Me is better than the honour which I have given you in the world. 'And your Lord will give you and will satisfy you,' i.e. of victory in this world and reward in the next. 'Did he not find you an orphan and give you refuge, going astray and guided you, found you poor and made you rich?' God thus told him of how He had begun to honour him in his earthly life, and of His kindness to him as an orphan poor and wandering astray, and of His delivering him from all that by His compassion (149).

'Do not oppress the orphan and do not repel the beggar.' That is, do not be a tyrant or proud or harsh or mean towards the weakest of God's creatures.

'Speak of the kindness of thy Lord,' i.e. tell about the kindness of God in giving you prophecy, mention it and call men to it.

So the apostle began to mention secretly God's kindness to him and to his servants in the matter of prophecy to everyone among his people whom he could trust.

1. A house made of pearls.
2. Qur'an 93, the source of all the quotations that follow in this section.

The Prescription of Prayer

The apostle was ordered to pray and so he prayed. Ṣāliḥ b. Kaisān from ʿUrwa b. al-Zubayr from ʿĀʾisha told me that she said, 'When prayer was first laid on the apostle it was with two prostrations for every prayer: then God raised it to four prostrations at home while on a journey the former ordinance of two prostrations held.'

A learned person told me that when prayer was laid on the apostle Gabriel came to him while he was on the heights of Mecca and dug a hole for him with his heel in the side of the valley from which a fountain gushed forth, and Gabriel performed the ritual ablution as the apostle watched him. This was in order to show him how to purify himself before prayer. Then the apostle performed the ritual ablution as he had seen Gabriel do it. Then Gabriel said a prayer with him while the apostle prayed with his prayer. Then Gabriel left him. The apostle came to Khadīja and performed the ritual for her as Gabriel had done for him, and she copied him. Then he prayed with her as Gabriel had prayed with him, and she prayed his prayer.

ʿUtba b. Muslim freedman of B. Taym from Nāfiʿ b. Jubayr b. Muṭʿim (who was prolific in relating tradition) from I. ʿAbbās told me: 'When prayer was laid upon the apostle Gabriel came to him and prayed the noon prayer when the sun declined. Then he prayed the evening prayer when his shadow equalled his own length. Then he prayed the sunset prayer when the sun set. Then he prayed the last night prayer when the twilight had disappeared. Then he prayed with him the morning prayer when the dawn rose. Then he came to him and prayed the noon prayer on the morrow when his shadow equalled his height. Then he prayed the evening prayer when his shadow equalled the height of both of them. Then he prayed the sunset prayer when the sun set at the time it had the day before. Then he prayed with him the last night prayer when the first third of the night had passed. Then he prayed the dawn prayer when it was clear but the sun was not shining. Then he said, "O Muhammad, prayer is in what is between your prayer today and your prayer yesterday."' (Ṭ. Yūnus b. Bukayr said that Muhammad b. Isḥāq told him that Yaḥyā b. Abū'l-Ashʿath al-Kindī of the people of Kūfa said that Ismāʿil b. Iyās b. ʿAfīf from his father from his grandfather said, 'When I was a merchant I came to al-ʿAbbās during the days of pilgrimage; and while we were together a man came out to pray and stood facing the Kaʿba; then a woman came out and stood praying with him; then a young man came out and stood praying with him. I said to ʿAbbās, "What is their religion? It is some thing new to me." He said, "This is Muhammad b. Abdullah who alleges that God has sent him with it and that the treasures of Chosrhoes and Caesar[3] will be opened to him. The woman is his wife Khadīja who believes in him, and this young man is his nephew ʿAlī who believes in him." ʿAfīf said, "Would that I could have believed that day and been a third!"'

(Ṭ. Ibn Ḥamīd said that Salama b. al-Fadl and ʿAlī b. Mujāhid told him. Salama said, Muhammad b. Isḥāq told me from Yaḥyā b. Abū'l-Ashʿath—Ṭabarī said, 'It is in another place in my book from Yaḥyā b. al-Ashʿath from Ismāʿil b. Iyās b. ʿAfīf al-Kindī, ʿAfīf being the brother of al-Ashʿath b. Qays al-Kindī by the same mother and the son of his uncle—from his father, from

3. That is, of the Sassanid (Persian) and the Roman empires.

his grandfather ʿAfīf: ʿAl-Abbās b. ʿAbdu'l-Muṭṭalib was a friend of mine who used to go often to the Yaman[4] to buy aromatics and sell them during the fairs. While I was with him in Minā there came a man in the prime of life and performed the full rites of ablution and then stood up and prayed. Then a woman came out and did her ablutions and stood up and prayed. Then out came a youth just approaching manhood, did his ablutions, then stood up and prayed by his side. When I asked al-ʿAbbās what was going on, he said that it was his nephew Muhammad b. ʿAbdullah b. ʿAbdu'l-Muṭṭalib who alleges that Allah has sent him as an apostle; the other is my brother's son ʿAlī b. Abū Tālib who has followed him in his religion; the third is his wife Khadīja d. Khuwaylid who also follows him in his religion.' ʿAfīf said after he had become a Muslim and Islam was firmly established in his heart, "Would that I had been a fourth!"'

ʿAlī b. Abū Ṭālib the First Male to Accept Islam

ʿAlī was the first male to believe in the apostle of God, to pray with him and to believe in his divine message, when he was a boy of ten. God favoured him in that he was brought up in the care of the apostle before Islam began.

ʿAbdullah b. Abū Najīḥ on the authority of Mujāhid b. Jabr Abu'l-Ḥajjāj told me that God showed His favour and goodwill towards him when a grievous famine overtook Quraysh. Now Abū Ṭālib had a large family, and the prophet approached his uncle, Al-ʿAbbās, who was one of the richest of B. Hāshim, suggesting that in view of his large family and the famine which affected everyone, they should go together and offer to relieve him of the burden of some of his family. Al-ʿAbbās agreed, and so they went to Abū Ṭālib offering to relieve him from his responsibility of two boys until conditions improved. Abū Ṭālib said, 'Do what you like so long as you leave me ʿAqīl' (150). So the apostle took ʿAlī and kept him with him and Al-ʿAbbās took Jaʿfar. ʿAlī continued to be with the apostle until God sent him forth as a prophet. ʿAlī followed him, believed him, and declared his truth, while Jaʿfar remained with Al-ʿAbbās until he became a Muslim and was independent of him.

A traditionist mentioned that when the time of prayer came the apostle used to go out to the glens of Mecca accompanied by ʿAlī, who went unbeknown to his father, and his uncles and the rest of his people. There they used to pray the ritual prayers, and return at nightfall. This went on as long as God intended that it should, until one day Abū Ṭālib came upon them while they were praying, and said to the apostle, 'O nephew, what is this religion which I see you practising?' He replied, 'O uncle, this is the religion of God, His angels, His apostles, and the religion of our father Abraham.' Or, as he said, 'God has sent me as an apostle to mankind, and you, my uncle, most deserve that I should teach you the truth and call you to guidance, and you are the most worthy to respond and help me,' or words to that effect. His uncle replied, 'I cannot give up the religion of my fathers which they followed, but by God you shall never meet with anything to distress you so long as I live.' They mention that he said to ʿAlī, 'My boy, what is this religion of yours?' He answered, 'I believe in God and in the apostle of God, and I declare that what he has brought is true, and I pray to God with him and

4. The southwestern part of the Arabian Peninsula, largely included in what is now Yemen; a trading crossroads, it dominated the trade in Asian spices and aromatics.

follow him.' They allege that he said, 'He would not call you to anything but what is good so stick to him.'

Zayd the freedman of the apostle was the first male to accept Islam after ʿAlī (151). Then Abū Bakr b. Abū Quḥāfa whose name was ʿAtīq became a Muslim. His father's name was ʿUthmān b. ʿĀmir b. ʿAmr b. Kaʿb b. Saʿd b. Taym b. Murra b. Kaʿb b. Luʿayy b. Ghālib b. Fihr. When he became a Muslim, he showed his faith openly and called others to God and his apostle. He was a man whose society was desired, well liked and of easy manners. He knew more about the genealogy of Quraysh than anyone else and of their faults and merits. He was a merchant of high character and kindliness. His people used to come to him to discuss many matters with him because of his wide knowledge, his experience in commerce, and his sociable nature. He began to call to God and to Islam all whom he trusted of those who came to him and sat with him (152).

[I.K. iii, 24. The following day ʿAlī b. Abū Ṭālib came as the two of them were praying and asked, 'What is this, Muhammad?' He replied, 'It is God's religion which He has chosen for Himself and sent His apostles with it. I call you to God, the One without an associate, to worship Him and to disavow al-Lāt and al-ʿUzzā.'[5] ʿAlī said, 'This is something that I have never heard of before today. I cannot decide a matter until I have talked about it with Abū Ṭālib.' Now the apostle did not want his secret to be divulged before he applied himself to the publication of his message, so he said, 'If you do not accept Islam, then conceal the matter.' ʿAlī tarried that night until God put Islam into his heart. Early next morning he went to the apostle and asked him what his orders were. He said, 'Bear witness that there is no god but Allah alone without associate, and disavow al-Lāt and al-ʿUzzā, and renounce rivals.' ʿAlī did so and became a Muslim. He refrained from coming to him out of fear of Abū Ṭālib and concealed his Islam and did not let it be seen.

Zayd b. Ḥāritha became a Muslim and the two of them tarried nearly a month. (Then) ʿAlī kept coming to the apostle. It was a special favour to ʿAlī from God that he was in the closest association with the apostle before Islam.]

The Apostle's Public Preaching and the Response

People began to accept Islam, both men and women, in large numbers until the fame of it was spread throughout Mecca, and it began to be talked about. Then God commanded His apostle to declare the truth of what he had received and to make known His commands to men and to call them to Him. Three years elapsed from the time that the apostle concealed his state until God commanded him to publish his religion, according to information which has reached me. Then God said, 'Proclaim what you have been ordered and turn aside from the polytheists.'[6] And again, 'Warn thy family, thy nearest relations, and lower thy wing to the followers who follow thee.'[7] And 'Say, I am the one who warns plainly' (164).[8]

(Ṭ. Ibn Ḥamīd from Salama from Ibn Isḥāq from ʿAbdullah b. al-Ghaffār b. al-Qāsim from al-Minhāl b. ʿAmr from ʿAbdullah b. al-Ḥārith b. Naufal b. al-Ḥārith b. ʿAbdu'l-Muṭṭalib from ʿAbdullah b. ʿAbbās from ʿAlī b. Abū Ṭālib said: When these words 'Warn thy family, thy nearest relations' came down

5. Two pre-Islamic goddesses.
6. Qur'an 15:94.
7. Qur'an 26:214–215.
8. Qur'an 15:89.

to the apostle he called me and said, 'God has ordered me to warn my family, my nearest relations and the task is beyond my strength. I know that when I made this message known to them I should meet with great unpleasantness so I kept silence until Gabriel came to me and told me that if I did not do as I was ordered my Lord would punish me. So get some food ready with a leg of mutton and fill a cup with milk and then get together the sons of ʿAbdu'l-Muṭṭalib so that I can address them and tell them what I have been ordered to say.' I did what he ordered and summoned them. There were at that time forty men more or less including his uncles Abū Ṭālib, Ḥamza, al-ʿAbbās, and Abū Lahab. When they were assembled he told me to bring in the food which I had prepared for them, and when I produced it the apostle took a bit of the meat and split it in his teeth and threw it into the dish. Then he said, 'Take it in the name of God.' The men ate till they could eat no more, and all I could see (in the dish) was the place where their hands had been. And as sure as I live if there had been only one man he could have eaten what I put before the lot of them. Then he said, 'Give the people to drink', so I brought them the cup and they drank until they were all satisfied, and as sure as I live if there had been only one man he could have drunk that amount. When the apostle wanted to address them Abū Lahab got in first and said, 'Your host has bewitched you'; so they dispersed before the apostle could address them. On the morrow he said to me, 'This man spoke before I could, and the people dispersed before I could address them, so do exactly as you did yesterday.' Everything went as before and then the apostle said, 'O Sons of ʿAbdu'l-Muṭṭalib, I know of no Arab who has come to his people with a nobler message than mine. I have brought you the best of this world and the next. God has ordered me to call you to Him. So which of you will co-operate with me in this matter, my brother, my executor, and my successor being among you?' The men remained silent and I, though the youngest, most rheumy-eyed, fattest in body and thinnest in legs, said: 'O prophet of God, I will be your helper in this matter.' He laid his hand on the back of my neck and said, 'This is my brother, my executor, and my successor among you. Hearken to him and obey him.' The men got up laughing and saying to Abū Ṭālib, 'He has ordered you to listen to your son and obey him!')

(Ṭ. 1173. Ibn Ḥamīd from Salama from Ibn Isḥāq from ʿAmr b. ʿUbayd from al-Ḥasan b. Abū'l-Ḥasan said: When this verse came down to the apostle, he stood in the vale and said, 'O Sons of ʿAbdu'l-Muṭṭalib; O Sons of ʿAbdu Manāf; O Sons of Quṣayy.'—Then he named Quraysh tribe by tribe until he came to the end of them—'I call you to God and I warn you of his punishment.')

When the apostle's companions prayed they went to the glens so that their people could not see them praying, and while Saʿd b. Abū Waqqāṣ was with a number of the prophet's companions in one of the glens of Mecca, a band of polytheists came upon them while they were praying and rudely interrupted them. They blamed them for what they were doing until they came to blows, and it was on that occasion that Saʿd smote a polytheist with the jawbone of a camel and wounded him. This was the first blood to be shed in Islam.

When the apostle openly displayed Islam as God ordered him his people did not withdraw or turn against him, so far as I have heard, until he spoke disparagingly of their gods. When he did that they took great offence and resolved unanimously to treat him as an enemy, except those whom God had protected by Islam from such evil, but they were a despised minority. Abū

Ṭālib his uncle treated the apostle kindly and protected him, the latter continuing to obey God's commands, nothing turning him back. When Quraysh saw that he would not yield to them and withdrew from them and insulted their gods and that his uncle treated him kindly and stood up in his defence and would not give him up to them, some of their leading men went to Abū Ṭālib, namely ʿUtba and Shayba, both sons of Rabīʿa b. ʿAbdu Shams . . . and Abū Sufyān (165) b. Ḥarb . . . and Abū'l-Bakhtarī whose name was al-ʿĀṣ b. Hishām b. al-Ḥārith b. Asad . . . and al-Aswad b. al-Muṭṭalib b. Asad . . . and Abū Jahl (whose name was ʿAmr, his title being Abū'l-Ḥakam)[9] b. Hishām b. al Mughīra . . . and al-Walīd b. al-Mughīra . . . and Nubayh and Munabbih two sons of al-Ḥajjāj b. ʿĀmir b. Ḥudhayfa . . . and al-ʿĀṣ b. Wāʾil (166). They said, 'O Abū Ṭālib, your nephew has cursed our gods, insulted our religion, mocked our way of life and accused our forefathers of error; either you must stop him or you must let us get at him, for you yourself are in the same position as we are in opposition to him and we will rid you of him.' He gave them a conciliatory reply and a soft answer and they went away.

The apostle continued on his way, publishing God's religion and calling men thereto. In consequence his relations with Quraysh deteriorated and men withdrew from him in enmity. They were always talking about him and inciting one another against him. Then they went to Abū Ṭālib a second time and said, 'You have a high and lofty position among us, and we have asked you to put a stop to your nephew's activities but you have not done so. By God, we cannot endure that our fathers should be reviled, our customs mocked and our gods insulted. Until you rid us of him we will fight the pair of you until one side perishes,' or words to that effect. Thus saying, they went off. Abū Ṭālib was deeply distressed at the breach with his people and their enmity but he could not desert the apostle and give him up to them.

Yaʿqūb b. ʿUtba b. al-Mughīra b. al-Akhnas told me that he was told that after hearing these words from the Quraysh Abū Ṭālib sent for his nephew and told him what his people had said. 'Spare me and yourself,' he said. 'Do not put on me a burden greater than I can bear.' The apostle thought that his uncle had the idea of abandoning and betraying him, and that he was going to lose his help and support. He answered, 'O my uncle, by God, if they put the sun in my right hand and the moon in my left on condition that I abandoned this course, until God has made it victorious, or I perish therein, I would not abandon it.' Then the apostle broke into tears, and got up. As he turned away his uncle called him and said, 'Come back, my nephew,' and when he came back, he said, 'Go and say what you please, for by God I will never give you up on any account.'

When the Quraysh perceived that Abū Ṭālib had refused to give up the apostle, and that he was resolved to part company with them, they went to him with ʿUmāra b. al-Walid b. al-Mughīra and said, according to my information, 'O Abū Ṭālib, this is ʿUmāra, the strongest and most handsome young man among Quraysh, so take him and you will have the benefit of his intelligence and support; adopt him as a son and give up to us this nephew of yours, who has opposed your religion and the religion of your fathers, severed

9. ʿAmr b. al-Hisham b. al-Mughira originally held the *kunya* of Abu al-Hakam, indicating that he possessed wisdom. When he rejected Islam and persecuted Muhammad, his *kunya* changed to Abu Jahl, a title that referred to his ignorance.

the unity of your people, and mocked our way of life, so that we may kill him. This will be man for man.' He answered, 'By God, this is an evil thing that you would put upon me, would you give me your son that I should feed him for you, and should I give you my son that you should kill him? By God, this shall never be.' Al-Muṭʿim b. ʿAdīy said, 'Your people have treated you fairly and have taken pains to avoid what you dislike. I do not think that you are willing to accept anything from them.' Abū Ṭālib replied, 'They have not treated me fairly, by God, but you have agreed to betray me and help the people against me, so do what you like,' or words to that effect. So the situation worsened, the quarrel became heated and people were sharply divided, and openly showed their animosity to their opponents. Abū Ṭālib wrote the following verses, indirectly attacking Muṭʿim, and including those who had abandoned him from the ʿAbdu Manāf, and his enemies among the tribes of Quraysh. He mentions therein what they had asked of him and his estrangement from them.

Say to ʿAmr and al-Walīd and Muṭʿim
Rather than your protection give me a young camel,
Weak, grumbling and murmuring,
Sprinkling its flanks with its urine
Lagging behind the herd, and not keeping up.
When it goes up the desert ridges, you would call it a weasel.
I see our two brothers, sons of our mother and father,
When they are asked for help, say 'It is not our business.'
Nay, it is their affair, but they have fallen away,
As a rock falls from the top of Dhū ʿAlaq.[1]
I mean especially ʿAbdu Shams and Naufal,
Who have flung us aside like a burning coal.
They have slandered their brothers among the people;
Their hands are emptied of them.
They shared their fame with men of low birth,
With men whose fathers were whispered about;
And Taym, and Makhzūm, and Zuhra, are of them
Who had been friends of ours when help was sought;
By God, there will always be enmity between us
As long as one of our descendants lives.
Their minds and thoughts were foolish,
They were entirely without judgement (167).

Then the Quraysh incited people against the companions of the apostle who had become Muslims. Every tribe fell upon the Muslims among them, beating them and seducing them from their religion. God protected His apostle from them through his uncle, who, when he saw what Quraysh were doing, called upon B. Hāshim and B. al-Muṭṭalib to stand with him in protecting the apostle. This they agreed to do, with the exception of Abū Lahab, the accursed enemy of God.

Abū Ṭālib was delighted at the response of his tribe and their kindness, and began to praise them and to bring to men's memory their past. He mentioned the superiority of the apostle among them and his position so that he might strengthen their resolve and that they might extend their kindness to him. He said:

1. A mountain in the territory of the Banu Asad tribe. The Banu Asad lived in northeastern Najd and inhabited the area southeast of the Jabal Shammar mountain range in Saudi Arabia.

If one day Quraysh gathered together to boast,
ʿAbdu Manāf would be their heart and soul;
And if the nobles of ʿAbdu Manāf were reckoned,
Amongst Hāshim would be their noblest and chief;
If they boast one day, then Muhammad
Would be the chosen noble and honourable one.
Quraysh summoned everyone against us;
They were not successful and they were beside themselves.
Of old we have never tolerated injustice;
When people turned away their faces in pride we made them face us.
We protected their sanctuary whenever danger threatened
And drove the assailant from its buildings.
Through us the dry wood becomes green,
Under our protection its roots expand and grow.

The Covenant between the Muslims and the Medinans and with the Jews

The apostle wrote a document concerning the emigrants and the helpers in which he made a friendly agreement with the Jews and established them in their religion and their property, and stated the reciprocal obligations, as follows: In the name of God the Compassionate, the Merciful. This is a document from Muhammad the prophet [governing the relations] between the believers and Muslims of Quraysh and Yathrib,[2] and those who followed them and joined them and laboured with them. They are one community (*umma*) to the exclusion of all men. The Quraysh emigrants according to their present custom shall pay the bloodwit[3] within their number and shall redeem their prisoners with the kindness and justice common among believers.

The B. ʿAuf according to their present custom shall pay the bloodwit they paid in heathenism; every section shall redeem its prisoners with the kindness and justice common among believers. The B. Sāʿida, the B. 'l-Ḥārith, and the B. Jusham, and the B. al-Najjār likewise.

The B. ʿAmr b. ʿAuf, the B. al-Nabīt and the B. al-Aus likewise.

Believers shall not leave anyone destitute among them by not paying his redemption money or bloodwit in kindness (283).

A believer shall not take as an ally the freedman of another Muslim against him. The God-fearing believers shall be against the rebellious or him who seeks to spread injustice, or sin or enmity, or corruption between believers; the hand of every man shall be against him even if he be a son of one of them. A believer shall not slay a believer for the sake of an unbeliever, nor shall he aid an unbeliever against a believer. God's protection is one, the least of them may give protection to a stranger on their behalf. Believers are friends one to the other to the exclusion of outsiders. To the Jew who follows us belong help and equality. He shall not be wronged nor shall his enemies be aided. The peace of the believers is indivisible. No separate peace shall be made when believers are fighting in the way of God. Conditions must be fair and equitable to all. In every foray a rider must take another behind him. The believers must avenge the blood of one another shed in the way of God.

2. Earlier name for Medina.

3. A fine for the shedding of blood.

The God-fearing believers enjoy the best and most upright guidance. No polytheist shall take the property or person of Quraysh under his protection nor shall he intervene against a believer. Whosoever is convicted of killing a believer without good reason shall be subject to retaliation unless the next of kin is satisfied (with blood-money), and the believers shall be against him as one man, and they are bound to take action against him.

It shall not be lawful to a believer who holds by what is in this document and believes in God and the last day to help an evil-doer or to shelter him. The curse of God and His anger on the day of resurrection will be upon him if he does, and neither repentance nor ransom will be received from him. Whenever you differ about a matter it must be referred to God and to Muhammad.

The Jews shall contribute to the cost of war so long as they are fighting alongside the believers. The Jews of the B. 'Auf are one community with the believers (the Jews have their religion and the Muslims have theirs), their freedmen and their persons except those who behave unjustly and sinfully, for they hurt but themselves and their families. The same applies to the Jews of the B. al-Najjār, B. al-Ḥārith, B. Sāʿida, B. Jusham, B. al-Aus, B. Thaʿlaba, and the Jafna, a clan of the Thaʿlaba and the B. al-Shuṭayba. Loyalty is a protection against treachery. The freedmen of Thaʿlaba are as themselves. The close friends of the Jews are as themselves. None of them shall go out to war save with the permission of Muhammad, but he shall not be prevented from taking revenge for a wound. He who slays a man without warning slays himself and his household, unless it be one who has wronged him, for God will accept that. The Jews must bear their expenses and the Muslims their expenses. Each must help the other against anyone who attacks the people of this document. They must seek mutual advice and consultation, and loyalty is a protection against treachery. A man is not liable for his ally's misdeeds. The wronged must be helped. The Jews must pay with the believers so long as war lasts. Yathrib shall be a sanctuary for the people of this document. A stranger under protection shall be as his host doing no harm and committing no crime. A woman shall only be given protection with the consent of her family. If any dispute or controversy likely to cause trouble should arise it must be referred to God and to Muhammad the apostle of God. God accepts what is nearest to piety and goodness in this document. Quraysh and their helpers shall not be given protection. The contracting parties are bound to help one another against any attack on Yathrib. If they are called to make peace and maintain it they must do so; and if they make a similar demand on the Muslims it must be carried out except in the case of a holy war. Every one shall have his portion from the side to which he belongs; the Jews of al-Aus, their freedmen and themselves have the same standing with the people of this document in pure loyalty from the people of this document (284).

Loyalty is a protection against treachery: He who acquires aught acquires it for himself. God approves of this document. This deed will not protect the unjust and the sinner. The man who goes forth to fight and the man who stays at home in the city is safe unless he has been unjust and sinned. God is the protector of the good and God-fearing man and Muhammad is the apostle of God.

The Classical Synthesis

750–1756

In the mid-seventeenth century, in Isfahan, then the capital of Persia, a great mosque was built that remains to this day one of the architectural treasures of the world. The Shah Mosque, as it has come to be called, evoked the serenity and perfection of heaven itself with its soaring dome and the starry blue tiles that covered its columns and walls. And woven into the decorative motifs on those walls was another evocation of eternity: verses from the Qurʾan in elegant Arabic calligraphy.

In the eyes of believers, the Qurʾan had existed from all eternity and was merely revealed at last in its full perfection to Muhammad by the grace of a compassionate God. The human architecture of a building begun in 1611, a full millennium after Muhammad first heard the voice of the angel Gabriel, could evoke the eternal architecture of God's universe most powerfully by binding itself to the Qurʾan. God had created the universe, and it was he who, moment to moment, held it in existence. Humankind could come no closer to that mystery, or to paradise itself, than in the verses of the Qurʾan.

While Shah ʿAbbas was building the Great Mosque of Isfahan, an even more sublime building was rising thousands of miles away in India: a mausoleum for Shah Jahan's beloved third wife, Mumtaz Mahal. The Taj Mahal of Agra is meant

The Imam Mosque (or the Shah Mosque) was completed in 1629 as the centerpiece for a new Safavid capital, Isfahan. The Shah, ʿAbbas I, or ʿAbbas the Great, died that same year.

not just to memorialize Jahan's undying devotion to his lost love but also, like the Great Mosque of Isfahan, to evoke the paradise in which, as he devoutly believed, he would be reunited with her forever. Here, just as in Isfahan, verses from the Qur'an are inscribed upon the walls. Here, in addition, the stately and elegant gardens visible from the mausoleum's windows and porches call to mind passages from the Qur'an in which paradise is described as comprising just such gardens.

Agra, as noted, lies thousands of miles to the east of Isfahan. How does it happen that the two shared an architectural tradition in the seventeenth century? How does it happen that despite living so far from Persia (Iran), Jahan's subjects referred to him by the Persian (Farsi) title for "king"—namely, *shah*? The answer to those questions and many more is found in the international Islamic culture that had come into existence during the millennium between the fall of the Umayyad caliphate in 750 and establishment of British Bengal, the first European colony in the "House of Islam," in 1765—a culture that was a remarkably stable synthesis of elements drawn from even further west than Isfahan and even further east than Agra. Politically and militarily, this millennium may have been as full of turbulence and change as the century of far-reaching Arab conquests that preceded it. Culturally and artistically, however, the story was different. Quite early, Islam developed a set of forms that retained their integrity for centuries. The Shah Mosque and the Taj Mahal are an architectural demonstration of this cultural stability across a vast domain. And so it was also in literature. The seven genres that together constitute the long central section of this anthology demonstrate their own manner of stability and continuity. The texts, many of which were written around the same time, represent still-living genres; the kinds of discussion they contain continue to take place in the Muslim world of today. While it would be an exaggeration to suggest that a religious (and partly secular) literature so vast could have sprung instantaneously to life and thereafter never changed, its striking stability provides important insights into both the religion and the culture of Islam.

In religious terms, in a way already hinted at above, Islamic literature does not thirst for novelty because Islam itself does not do so. God's revelation to Muhammad was not a new revelation but the blessed retrieval of a lost, original revelation. The term *bid'a*—"novelty" or "innovation," in Arabic—is synonymous in popular Muslim usage with "heresy." Suspicion of novelty in religion need not automatically translate into suspicion of novelty in all literary pursuits, much less in all other pursuits, but one should not be surprised to find a certain conservatism of literary forms in a self-consciously conservative religion. Arguably, all religious literature tends to conserve and cherish a precious legacy of expression as well as of belief rather than to avidly devise alternatives. But among the religious literatures of the world, the literature of Islam must surely be viewed as a remarkable instance of blooming in many soils.

To recognize that the major genres of Islamic literature remained relatively stable for a millennium is not to say that the Umayyad empire, in all its vastness, was culturally homogeneous. It was not. We must note, first, that the conquering Arabs had not imposed Islam on the Christians, Jews, Zoroastrians, and others whom they now ruled. Second, when conversions had occurred, innumerable features of diet, language, dress, and many social practices remained untouched. Even, finally, in the realm of literature, the variety that we see on display in the selections assembled here did take some time to mature. Nonetheless, east of Arabia, in the former Persian Empire, a set of cultural conditions rapidly coalesced that helped stabilize that variety. Indeed, the fusion of Arab religion and Persian culture was largely responsible for turning Islam into a world religion with a literature to match. West of Arabia, in the former Roman Empire, the same cultural coalescence did not occur, at least not to nearly the same degree.

This point must not be exaggerated. Muslim rule, Arab or Moorish, lasted for 250 years in Toledo, Spain, and for another 250 in Seville. Al-Andalus, as Spain is called in Arabic, achieved its own noteworthy cultural synthesis and had its own golden literary moments. In the eleventh and into the twelfth century, Cairo, with a fabled library assembled by the Fatimid dynasty, became, as it has largely remained, the intellectual capital of the Arab world. But more of the most important Islamic texts assembled in this book originated in the lands of the former Persian empire—now utterly defeated—than in those of the reduced but embattled and recalcitrant Roman empire. A further word on this east/west difference in world Islam during the first centuries of the millennium of classical synthesis may be helpful.

The Roman Empire at its greatest extent had stretched from the Euphrates River in the east, westward along both shores of the Mediterranean Sea, and northward to include France, much of the Low Countries, and Britain. Religiously, the empire had been officially Christian from the year 385 on, though a large Jewish diaspora lived on as a formally if grudgingly tolerated minority. Politically, the empire had been divided since the late fourth century into two administrative divisions—Latin-speaking in the west, Greek-speaking in the east—each with its own emperor. By the time of the Arab conquests, however, only the eastern half of the Roman Empire, with its capital at Constantinople, existed as such. The western half, with its capital at Rome, had fallen in 476; it was succeeded by a set of smaller successor kingdoms populated by Romanized and Christianized Celtic and Germanic tribes whose power had become too strong for Rome to resist.

By 750, when the Umayyad caliphate ended, the Arabs had taken the southern and eastern half of the Eastern Roman Empire (Syria, Palestine, Egypt, and Libya) and the southern third of the original Western Roman Empire (Tunisia, Algeria, Morocco, and Spain). These Muslim holdings would grow in some areas and shrink in others during the centuries that followed. Thus, the major Mediterranean islands—Cyprus, Sicily, and Sardinia—would fall to the Umayyads' successors, the early 'Abbasid caliphate. Later, the Seljuk Turks and then the Ottoman Turks—after having converted to Islam, in both cases—would expand westward through Asia Minor (modern Turkey) and into Greece and the eastern Balkans. Conversely, the boundaries set by the Umayyad empire would contract as the Mediterranean islands mentioned above and most of Spain reverted to Spanish or other European control by the end of the Crusades.

From a political perspective, the Crusades were no more than a failed effort to retake lost Roman domains in Palestine and Syria, and as such they had much in common with successful contemporaneous efforts in Spain and the Mediterranean islands. Viewed as a religious undertaking, however, the Crusades were a divinely mandated war to recover the lost "Holy Land"

and, above all, the "Holy Cross" of Christ, from which the Crusaders derived their name and their cross-adorned garb. They were a source and an emblem of the greater religious volatility of western than eastern Islam. In the west, when territory changed hands, religion usually changed as well. East of Baghdad, this was simply not the case—and the difference matters considerably. That the Persian empire fell entirely, not just in part, to the invading Arabs and that subsequent invasions by the Turks and the Mongols did not entail any change of religion powerfully aided the cultural and literary stability that was achieved east of Baghdad.

The Arab conquest of the Persian empire, coming just five years after the death of the prophet Muhammad, was stunning indeed, but the complete replacement of Persia's age-old Zoroastrian religion was still more impressive. The ruling Sassanid dynasty, whose armies fell to those of Caliph ʿUmar at the battle of Qadisiyya in 636, had dominated a territory larger than that of the mighty Roman empire—it extended from southern Iraq and eastern Arabia in the west to the Indus River in the east (comprising the modern countries of southern Iraq, all of Iran, Afghanistan, Uzbekistan, Tajikistan, and Turkmenistan, as well as half of Kyrgyzstan and Pakistan). Because these lands, especially those lying furthest to the east, are so exotic for Europeans and Americans, the Arab conquest of them looms smaller in the Western imagination than does the relatively smaller Arab victory over Spain, much less the brief Arab penetration as far north as Poitiers, France. Back in the seventh century, however, and for a number of centuries thereafter, the lands once held by the Sassanid empire were rich and culturally advanced—imperial assets that a dynasty might well covet if it could but control them.

Persia, moreover, had become a cultural legend, fascinating not least to the Greeks, centuries before the rise of Rome. The Sassanids were merely the most recent of several storied dynasties. And the influence of an ancient and venerable empire is exerted not just outward but is ever attractive as well. Just as the Celtic and Germanic tribes had been fascinated by the glamour of Rome and had Romanized themselves, making the Latin language and elements of Roman law their own well before they took over the Roman Empire itself, so also the Turkic tribes lying beyond or just within the outer territories of the Persian empire felt drawn to Persianize themselves.

It was to this Persian sphere of cultural influence, then, and not just to a body of territory, that the Muslim Arabs fell heir when their victory at Qadisiyya led in short order to the fall of Ctesiphon, the Sassanid capital. Despite the speed and brilliance of the initial Arab *coup d'empire*, the Arabs were simply not numerous enough to ethnically colonize all of the territory that they now nominally ruled. But because the religious conversion of Persia to Islam was—by comparison with the only partial conversion of the Roman (Byzantine) empire—so far-reaching, Islam thenceforth would go wherever Persian influence went, even to Agra, where the Muslim king would be called *shah* in audible acknowledgment of the ongoing fusion of Persian culture and Muslim faith.

Zoroastrianism would live on under Muslim rule, as would Christianity and Judaism, but it would do so only weakly. The Christians of the Persian empire were largely Nestorian refugees, so named for Nestorius, a fifth-century patriarch (bishop) of Constantinople whose heterodox understanding of the essential humanity of Christ, condemned by the orthodox Roman church, was surprisingly compatible with Islam. The Jews of the Persian Empire were eastern Jews who revered Babylonian rabbis above any from Palestine or points west. But the Qur'an did not explicitly enjoin tolerance of Zoroastrians, the "Majus" of Qur'an 22:17, as it did of these Jews and Christians. Centuries of exegetical debate swirled around whether they could be included among the Qur'an's "People of the Book." This difference had to matter, and so, perhaps, did the fact that Zoroastrianism, distinguished by a hereditary and aristocratic priesthood, may have enjoyed less popular support than Judaism or Christianity. The emigration of some segment of the Zoroastrian leadership to Hindu India, where Zoroastrians to this day are called Parsees (literally, "Persians"), may have further promoted the religious triumph of Islam. Triumph, in any case, there surely was. And the more this triumph was consolidated, the more striking was the degree to which the swirl of rising and falling caliphates and national dynasties seemed to leave it untouched.

The first of these changes and perhaps the most important was the replacement of the Umayyad by the ʿAbbasid caliphate, whose founding caliph, Abu al-ʿAbbas al-Saffah (r. 750–54), claimed descent from a much earlier ʿAbbas who was an uncle of the prophet Muhammad. Just as the Umayyads (or *banu Umayya*, "sons of Umayya") had come to power by violently suppressing the claims of the Hashimids (or *banu Hashim*, "sons of Hashim") in the persons of the Prophet's son-in-law ʿAli and of ʿAli's son, the Prophet's grandson Husayn, so the ʿAbbasids came to power by an unprecedented tribal slaughter of the Umayyads. The Arab faction that had put Abu al-ʿAbbas al-Saffah in power demonstrated by its inaugural ruthlessness that ʿAbbasid rule would be absolute, on the model of the Sassanid and earlier Persian emperors of legend. But at the same time, though the ʿAbbasids were themselves Arabs, they recognized that concessions to non-Arabs would be necessary if their power was to be effectively wielded. In deference to the growing Persian presence in the umma, they moved their capital from Damascus in Syria eastward first to Kufa, west of the Euphrates in southern Iraq, and then to Baghdad, where the Tigris and the Euphrates loop closest together—a point not far from Ctesiphon, the old Persian capital.

And these symbolic moves were followed by more substantive strategic adjustments on the part of the ʿAbbasids. They extended class privileges once enjoyed exclusively by Arabs to all Muslims, including converts, and they induced disaffected Shiʿis to adopt a stance of pious acquiescence and withdrawal from public life. Their imposition of peace had undeniably been violent, but over time they delivered a major peace dividend. Foreign trade and domestic investment both flourished. Under the ʿAbbasid caliph Harun al-Rashid (r. 786–809), during the generation when the caliphate was at its peak, Baghdad—now beautifully rebuilt and expanded to exceed even Constantinople in population and area—became a true world capital, materially enriched by immigration from its vast empire and culturally enlivened by the active translation and study of Greek philosophy and medicine and Indian mathematics. Dhimmis—unconverted Jews, Christians, and some Zoroastrians who in exchange for the payment of a tribute or tax, called the jizya, were allowed to practice their religions with considerable freedom—took part energetically in many of these cross-cultural endeavors.

The Qalʿa Madrasa in Iraq (ca. 1230), close to the Tigris River in Baghdad. Very little is left of the structure that once functioned as a *madrasa*, or Muslim institution of higher learning, built using the techniques and styles of the Seljuk Turkish dynasty that ruled vast areas of Muslim lands from the 11th to the 14th centuries. Under the Seljuks, madrasas such as this one flourished with state support, and were able to provide lodging for students who traveled from great distances. This model—of students living in dormitories, devoting themselves solely to study, serving as teaching assistants, and eventually receiving diplomas—was later taken up by Western institutions of learning.

The historical and cultural conditions that sustained the classical Islamic synthesis were not called seriously into question until the Mongol conquests of the thirteenth century, which conventionally mark the end of ʿAbbasid rule. Dwarfing in the scope and rapidity of their advance even the first generations of the Arab conquest, the Mongols—horse warriors from the Far East—swept south and east into China, west across Central Asia and on into eastern Europe, and southwest from the Himalayan massif into the Muslim heartlands of Mesopotamia and Iran. The Persian and Persianate Turkish kingdoms that had gradually overwhelmed the ʿAbbasid caliphate were no match for the invading hordes under Genghis Khan (ca. 1162–1227). The devastating sack of Baghdad in 1258 by Hulegu Khan, Genghis Khan's grandson, has often been viewed as marking the sunset of Arab cultural and military glory.

But what would the spectacular Mongol triumph mean for Islam? For half a century, that remained an open question. The Mongols had a shamanistic religion of their own as well as a cultural code, *Yasa*, that functioned in the same way as Islamic Shariʿa. They were attracted both to the Buddhism of China, adjacent to their homeland, and to Christianity as they had encountered it in the now vanished churches of Central Asia. As khanates (*khan*, the Mongol word for "king," replaced the Persian *shah*) were established over the larger part of Asia, some contemporary observers clearly believed, or hoped, that Islam had at last met its military, political, cultural, and religious match.

In the end, however, the Mongols not only adopted Islam in all the realms where Islam was dominant but acculturated in other ways as well—in dress, in language, and in conduct. Despite linguistic and ethnic differences from the Turkic peoples of Central Asia, the Mongols were culturally akin to them as horse nomads and fearless warriors, and the groups intermarried freely. It was probably in Central Asia, among the Turks, that the balance bar tipped for the Mongols in Islam's favor; thus, rather than overturning the classical synthesis they embraced it and brought to it a distinctive and lasting contribution.

The element—elusive but powerful—that the Mongols contributed was a new emphasis on government. The Mongol political ethos coincided neither with the charismatic chieftain model favored by the Arabs nor with the imperial autocracy model of the Persians: it consisted, instead, of a regionally administered but centrally monitored and policed negotiation among the constituent political elements of a given realm. One might even suggest that despite a record of mass atrocity that bears comparison with the worst horrors of the twentieth century, the Mongols, once in power, introduced something of the Chinese appetite for harmony into the Islamic political equation.

Perhaps it is this blend of ruthless authority when challenged but negotiated management when respected that accounts for the durability of the Ottoman empire, the latest of the great Muslim empires to arise and the first to do so under the impact of the immense, if ebbing, wave of Mongol conquest. The Ottoman Turks, named like the Seljuk Turks for a legendary ancestor, first became a force in Islamic history at the end of the thirteenth century; at that time, they began to replace the Seljuks in Anatolia (eastern Turkey), a region rather densely populated with Christian Armenians and Muslim Kurds. From this Anatolian base, Ottoman power rapidly spread northward into the Caucasus, eastward and southward into Mesopotamia,

Mihrab in the Jamiʿ ("Friday") Mosque of Isfahan. One of Iran's oldest surviving mosques, it was continuously renovated from its first use in 771 through the 20th century. The mosque is an intriguing example of accretion and a wide range of building styles characteristic of dynasties ranging from the Seljuks to the Safavids. This mihrab, a focal point indicating the direction toward Mecca and thus of prayer, was built especially for the Mongol Oljaytu Khodabendeh in the 14th century.

and westward into Greece and the Balkans. A victory of great symbolic importance came in 1453 when the Ottoman Turks finally achieved what had eluded eight centuries of earlier Arab and Turkish effort—namely, the conquest of the near-impregnable fortress that was Constantinople (today's Istanbul), the last bastion of the old Roman Empire. During the ensuing two centuries, having in the interim established its control over Arabia and over North Africa from Egypt to Morocco, the Ottoman empire constituted an existential threat to the Hapsburg empire, which had its capital at Vienna. Only after a last effort to take Vienna failed in 1683 did the Ottoman empire enter its long and at first almost imperceptibly slow decline.

Meanwhile, to its east, a major neo-Persian empire, the Safavid, had taken shape between the Tigris River in the west and the Indus River in the east. Starting in the sixteenth century, the Safavid empire had made Shiʿi Islam its state religion. Though different in this respect from the stoutly Sunni Ottoman empire, the Safavid empire seems to have been, like it, the heir to the post-Mongol Islamic governance model. It, too, enjoyed a degree of internal stability unknown in the centuries of the ʿAbbasid caliphate and its successor states. Finally, east of the Indus River, the Mughal empire, whose capital was at Delhi, had negotiated control of much of Hindu as well as of Muslim India. The name *Mughal*, a version of *Mongol*, bespeaks a sense of political continuity with the khanates of an earlier day, but culturally and linguistically the Mughal empire's kinship with Persian tradition was much deeper and more complex.

In a sense, then, at the time when the Shah Mosque and the Taj Mahal were being built, the bipartite division of the world as Caliph ʿUmar knew it in the seventh century had reconstituted itself, with Mesopotamia once again as the dividing line. To the west of Mesopotamia now lay not the Roman but the Ottoman empire. But western Islam now included not just the Ottoman empire but also the east coast of Africa as far south as Kenya, the west coast of Africa as far south as the Gambia, and the sub-Saharan interior of Africa as far south as the Hausa regions of northern Nigeria. To the east now lay not the Sassanid but the Safavid empire. But eastern Islam now included not just the Safavid empire but also the autonomous Turkic states of Central Asia that lay within its sphere of cultural influence; more important, it contained India as far east as the Bay of Bengal and, further east, Malaya and the rich and populous islands of Indonesia.

The spread of Islam to these last-mentioned regions had not, by and large, been preceded by conquest; it had come about through trade and through diverse paths of cultural diffusion and religious enthusiasm. Was Islam destined—by these paths, or by some mix of them and perhaps a gradual Ottoman expansion into Europe—to gain overwhelming dominance among the world's religions? In 1611, when ground was broken in Isfahan for the Shah Mosque, there were many more Muslims in the world than there were Christians, and some such expectation would have seemed quite natural. Islam had expanded steadily from its Arabian starting point to encompass more than half of Asia, the world's largest and most

Mosque lamp, Ottoman Turkey, ca. 1557.

This 48 cm high lamp, from the Suleymaniye mosque complex in Istanbul, is emblematic of a shift in ceramics production at that time. Colors became more brilliant, and a greater range of them was employed. Reds became common, and special clay was used to produce them. The use of Iznik fritware also became standard in the tile decorations of the time.

populous continent, and there seemed no reason to suppose that its steady advance southward into Africa, the second-largest continent, would ever stop. Christianity, by contrast, though it had initially expanded eastward as well as westward from its Palestinian starting point, had been overwhelmed in the East and seemed destined to survive only as the isolated and well-contained regional faith of Europe.

Left out of this equation was, of course, the discovery of the Americas, whose wealth was already fueling a spurt in the world population of Christians of European descent even as the hemisphere's indigenous and mestizo converts were adding to Christianity's numbers. Ignored as well was the impact of open-sea sailing. Motivated in part by Muslim domination of West Asia and the Mediterranean, and aided by navigational tools borrowed from the Arabs, Europeans took their ships around the Horn of Africa to India, Indochina, Indonesia, China, and Japan. European colonization of the Americas, when Asian Muslims thought about it at all, was inconsequential to them, concerning only Europeans and indigenous Americans. European colonization of India was another matter altogether, for India, though its population was still mostly Hindu, had become a Muslim domain under the great and spreading roof of *dar al-islam*, the House of Islam. Asian Muslims found themselves directly confronted with European Christians, many thousands of miles from what had long seemed the safe and manageable border between the two groups.

One line of sorts was crossed in 1757 when, through a treaty negotiated by Robert Clive, the East India Company—Britain's quasi-commercial, quasi-diplomatic, quasi-military trading corporation—was able to install a puppet ruler of its choice in Bengal. A more important line was crossed in 1765 when it wrested full authority over Bengal, including the authority to tax the population, from a weakened Mughal emperor. Far from Europe, direct European rule over an erstwhile Muslim domain had now begun. Where it would end, no one then could have guessed. An accurate prediction of the outcome would have been even less likely a century and a half earlier, in the first decades of the seventeenth century, as the Taj Mahal was being built in the ostensible tranquillity of India while a religiously divided Britain was embroiled in its bloody civil war, its vast colonial empire in Asia and Africa as yet undreamed of.

Back then, what were the world's Muslims reading, reciting, or hearing read or recited? *That* question—with its immense potential to open our eyes to new worlds—is what animates and motivates this anthology of Muslim texts. The real answer to it is detailed in the pages that follow. But a preliminary and summary answer is that the world's Muslims were reading works written in a wide array of literary forms, many of them only distantly related to Western forms, and that to a remarkable extent this array of forms remained stable for them through all the political and military vicissitudes that we have just surveyed. Islam became the cornerstone of a religious and cultural synthesis—a true classical synthesis, in that the umma of today still pays the homage of repetition and memorial cultivation to what was achieved then, just as the West pays homage to its own set of classics drawn from Israel, Greece, and Rome. Just how this Islamic synthesis was both disturbed and stimulated by its encounter with Western, secular modernity will be the subject documented in the final section of this anthology.

Chronology

THE CLASSICAL SYNTHESIS, 750–1756

756–1031 Surviving branch of Umayyad family continues the dynasty in Spain

762 ʿAbbasid capital moves from Damascus to Baghdad

765 Death of Jaʿfar al-Sadiq, sixth Shiʿi imam

767–820 Al-Shafiʿi, eponymous founder of the Shafiʿi school of law and architect of early legal methodology

ca. 776–868 or 869 Al-Jahiz, polymath and litterateur

780–855 Ahmad ibn Hanbal, traditionist, jurist, and eponymous founder of the Hanbali school of law

786–809 Caliphate of Harun al-Rashid, famed ruler immortalized in the *Thousand and One Nights*

796 Death of Malik ibn Anas, eponymous founder of the Maliki school of law

801 Death of Rabiʿa al-Adawiya, renowned female ascetic

809–813 Devastating civil war between Harun al-Rashid's sons, al-Maʾmun and al-Amin

810–870 Al-Bukhari, traditionist and historian

813 Caliphate of al-Maʾmun, victor in the civil war

819–1005 Persian Samanid dynasty rules much of Central Asia

821–875 Muslim ibn al-Hajjaj, scholar of hadith

833–847 The *Mihna*, or Inquisition, in which rulers struggle to exert religious influence, but finally lose out to the scholars

833 Death of Ibn Hisham, genealogist and biographer of the Prophet
Caliphate of al-Muʿtasim. Capital moves to Samarra

839–923 Al-Tabari, scholar, exegete, and historian

847 Caliphate of al-Mutawakkil, who dismantles the Inquisition, supports Sunni scholars, and persecutes other sects

868–905 Tulunid dynasty rules Egypt and Syria

ca. 870–950 Al-Farabi, political philosopher and music theorist

873 or 874–935 Al-Ashʿari, early theologian

874 Occultation of twelfth Shiʿi imam, Muhammad al-Qaʾim

875 Death of al-Bistami, ecstatic Sufi

ca. 890–1037 Ibn Sina (Avicenna), polymath and philosopher

ca. 892 Death of al-Baladhuri, historian

ca. 907–912 Death of al-Hakim al-Tirmidhi, eminent Sufi

909–1171 Shiʿi Fatimids found dynasty in North Africa

ca. 921–991 Ibn Babawayh (Shaykh Saduq), Shiʿi theologian

922–996 Ibn Abi Zayd al-Qayrawani, Maliki jurist

ca. 932–1030 Miskawayh, historian and philosopher

932–1055 Shiʿi Buyid dynasty takes effective control of many eastern Islamic lands

937–1021 Al-Sulami, prolific Sufi author

969 Fatimids found Cairo

late 10th century *Thousand and One Nights* tales enter Arabic-speaking milieu from Persianate culture

970 Construction of al-Azhar University begins in Cairo

974–1058 Al-Mawardi, judge, political philosopher, and diplomat

977–1186 Ghaznavids arise in Central Asia (replacing Samanids) and then expand into India

990 Death of Ibn al-Nadim, Baghdadi bookseller and cataloguer

992–1211 Qarakhanid dynasty of Sunni Turkic rulers

994–1064 Ibn Hazm, Andalusian poet, jurist and theologian

996–1021 Caliphate of the Fatimid al-Hakim bi-Amr Allah in Egypt. Druze movement emerges after his mysterious death

early 11th c.–1147 Almoravid dynasty rules North Africa and Spain

ca. 1019–1092 Nizam al-Mulk, vizier and political philosopher

1038–1194 Turkish Seljuk dynasty takes power in Baghdad, eventually stretching to Isfahan

1058–1111 Al-Ghazali, professor, mystic, and Ashʿari theologian

1065 Nizamiyya madrasa is built in Baghdad

1071 The Battle of Manzikert. Capture of the Byzantine emperor leads to eventual Muslim control of Anatolia

1085 Toledo is taken by Reconquista forces in Andalusia

1090 Almoravids of Morocco take Granada

1095 Pope Urban II calls for the First Crusade after the Byzantine emperor entreats Western Christians for help resisting the Seljuk incursions

1095–1188 Usama ibn Munqidh, Syrian poet and warrior gentleman

1099 Jerusalem is captured by Crusader forces

1126–1198 Ibn Rushd (Averroes), Andalusian philosopher

1127–1173 Zangid dynasty attempts to unite greater Syria against Crusader incursions

1147–1269 Sunni Almohads establish reformist dynasty in western Islamic lands

1140 or 1141–1202 Nizami, Persian epic poet

1143 Qurʾan is translated into Latin

1145–1217 Ibn Jubayr, Andalusian travel-writer

1149 or 1150–1210 Fakhr al-Din al-Razi, Ashʿari theologian, philosopher, jurist and exegete

1165–1240 Ibn al-ʿArabi, mystical philosopher

1166 ʿAbd al-Qadir al-Jilani dies, having founded Qadiriyya order of Sufism

1171–1250 Ayyubid dynasty in Syria and Egypt, founded by Salah al-Din (Saladin), wrests power from the Fatimids and makes Sunnism preeminent in the region

1187 Salah al-Din retakes Jerusalem, allowing the Jews who had been expelled by the Franks to resettle there; a new crusade is organized for its recapture

1192 Salah al-Din signs peace treaty with Richard the Lionheart

1200 Islam reaches southeast Asia

1201–1274 Nasir al-Din Tusi, Shiʿi philosopher and polymath

1204 Islam is established in North Sumatra with accession of Johan Shah as first Sultan

1207–1273 Rumi, mystic and poet; eponymous founder of the Mevlevi Sufi order

ca. 1208–ca. 1290 Sa'di, Persian literary master

1220 Mongol invasions of Muslim-held lands begin

1227 Death of Genghis Khan

1233–1277 Al-Nawawi, Shafi'i jurist and expert traditionist

1249 Main phase of the Reconquista ends; Granada is Andalusia's sole Muslim outpost

1250–1517 Mamluk dynasty of slave soldiers is founded in Egypt

1258 'Abbasid rule, long largely symbolic, ends with Baghdad's fall to the Mongols

1260 Mamluk forces end Mongol advances at the Battle of 'Ayn Jalut

1263–1328 Ibn Taymiyya, outspoken Hanbali jurist

1269 Berber Marinids consolidate power by taking Marrakesh, ruling the Maghrib until 1465

1281–1922 Ottoman empire

1312–1337 Mansa Musa rules Mali

1325–1390 Hafiz, master of Persian lyric poetry

1304–1368 Ibn Battuta, Moroccan jurist and world-traveler

1332–1406 Ibn Khaldun, jurist and social theorist

1334 Construction begins on the Alhambra, fortress and palace for Granadan Muslim rulers

1370–1506 Timurid dynasty is founded in Central Asia by the Mongol conqueror Timur Lang (Tamerlane, d. 1405); Samarkand flourishes as cultural center

1380 Most of Central Asia is subdued by Tamerlane, who leads armies into the area of the Don and Volga Rivers

1389 Battle of Kosovo; Ottoman forces defeat the Serbs

1398 Tamerlane invades India, destroying Delhi and the Delhi Sultanate

1400 Islam is propagated throughout Java

1453 Mehmed II of the Ottoman Turks conquers Constantinople, seat of the Byzantine empire

1415–1471 Portuguese seize Ceuta, al-Qasr al-Saghir, and Tangier

1463 Ottomans conquer Bosnia, ruling the territory until 1878

1468 Sonni 'Ali incorporates Timbuktu into the Songhay empire. Timbuktu becomes the intellectual center of west African Islam

c. 1470 Death of Pir Hasan Kabir al-Din, Ismai'ili Shi'i preacher and composer of devotions

1475 A noble from Malacca in the Malay Peninsula introduces Islam to the Philippines

1492 Granada, last outpost in Muslim Spain, falls to Christian forces. Many Muslims and Jews are expelled from Spain Columbus voyages west

1495 In the Moluccas, Sultan of Ternate converts to Islam

1497 Zahiruddin Muhammad Babur (1483–1530), eventual founder of the Mughal empire, takes Samarkand

1498 Portuguese control Indian Ocean trade

1501–1722 Safavid empire, founded by Shah Ismail, imposes Shi'ism on the predominantly Sunni region of greater Persia and comes into frequent conflict with the Ottoman empire

1517 Sultan Selim I of the Ottoman empire conquers Mamluk Egypt and Syria and declares a new Islamic caliphate

1521 Ottomans take Belgrade

1526 The Ottoman Sultan Sulayman, "the Lawgiver," conquers Hungary

1526–1858 Mughal empire in India

1529 Vienna is put to siege by Sultan Sulayman the Magnificent, the deepest incursion of Muslim forces into Europe

1530 Aceh is founded in Sumatra

1538 Ottomans control Mediterranean Sea

ca. 1554 Death of al-Hasan al-Wazzan, diplomat, Papal captive, and author

1556–1605 Reign of the Mughal emperor Jalal al-Din Muhammad Akbar, who attempts to unite India by supporting religious pluralism

1562 Spain takes the Philippines

1572–1640 Mulla Sadra Shirazi, Shiʿi philosopher, exegete, and traditionist

1574 Selimiye Mosque is built in Edirne

1606 Islam spreads to New Guinea

1609–1614 300,000 Moriscos (secret Muslims outwardly converted to Christianity) are expelled from Spain

1611 Construction of the Shah Mosque of Isfahan is begun during the reign of Shah Abbas

1615–1659 Dara Shukoh, Mughal prince and advocate for religious pluralism

1616 Blue Mosque is completed in Istanbul under Sultan Ahmed I

1627 Shah Jahan begins constructing the Taj Mahal, a monument to his beloved wife

1627–1699 Muhammad Baqir al-Majlisi, Shiʿi scholar, expert traditionist, and prolific author

1641–1675 Sultana Taj al-ʿAlam Safiyyat al-Din Shah is queen of Aceh

1658 Aurangzeb ascends the Mughal throne, expanding imperial territories to their greatest extent and revoking pluralist reforms, thus contributing to the downfall of the empire

1585–1671 Khayr al-Din al-Ramli, Ottoman Hanafi jurist

1683 Ottoman forces fail in the Battle of Vienna. The Great Turkish War ensues

1684 Austria, Poland, Venice, and the Papacy form the Holy Alliance to resist the Ottomans

1692–1757 Al-ʿImadi, Hanafi jurist and official mufti of Damascus

1703–1762 Shah Wali Allah Dihlavi, Indian scholar, writer, and reformer

1703–1792 Muhammad ibn ʿAbd al-Wahhab, ultraconservative reformer and activist

1753–1835 or 1836 Al-Jabarti, Egyptian historian

1765 Death of Muhammad ibn Saʿud, founder of the Saudi dynasty

Atlantic Ocean
North Sea
FRANCE
Poitiers
Loire
Rhine
Rhône
Elbe
Oder
Vistula
Dneiper
Dneister
EUROPE
Vienna
ALPS
CARPATHIAN MTS.
Venice
PYRENEES
Douro
Ebro
Tagus
SPAIN
al-Andalus
Toledo
Valencia
Cordoba
Seville
Granada
Corsica
Rome
ITALY
Adriatic Sea
Sardinia
OTTOMAN
Danube
Bakhchisaray
Black Sea
Constantinople (Istanbul)
Iznik
Anatolia
Konya
TURKEY
GREECE
Aegean Sea
Athens
Rhodes
Crete
Cyprus
Mediterranean Sea
Palermo
Sicily
Malta
Algiers
ALGERIA
Tunis
Qayrawan
TUNISIA
MOROCCO
Fez
Marrakech
HIGH ATLAS MOUNTAINS
Maghrib
LIBYA
Alexandria
Cairo (Fustat)
EGYPT
Palestine
Sahara Desert
Tropic of Cancer
Nile
AFRICA
Gulf of Guinea
N
W
E
S

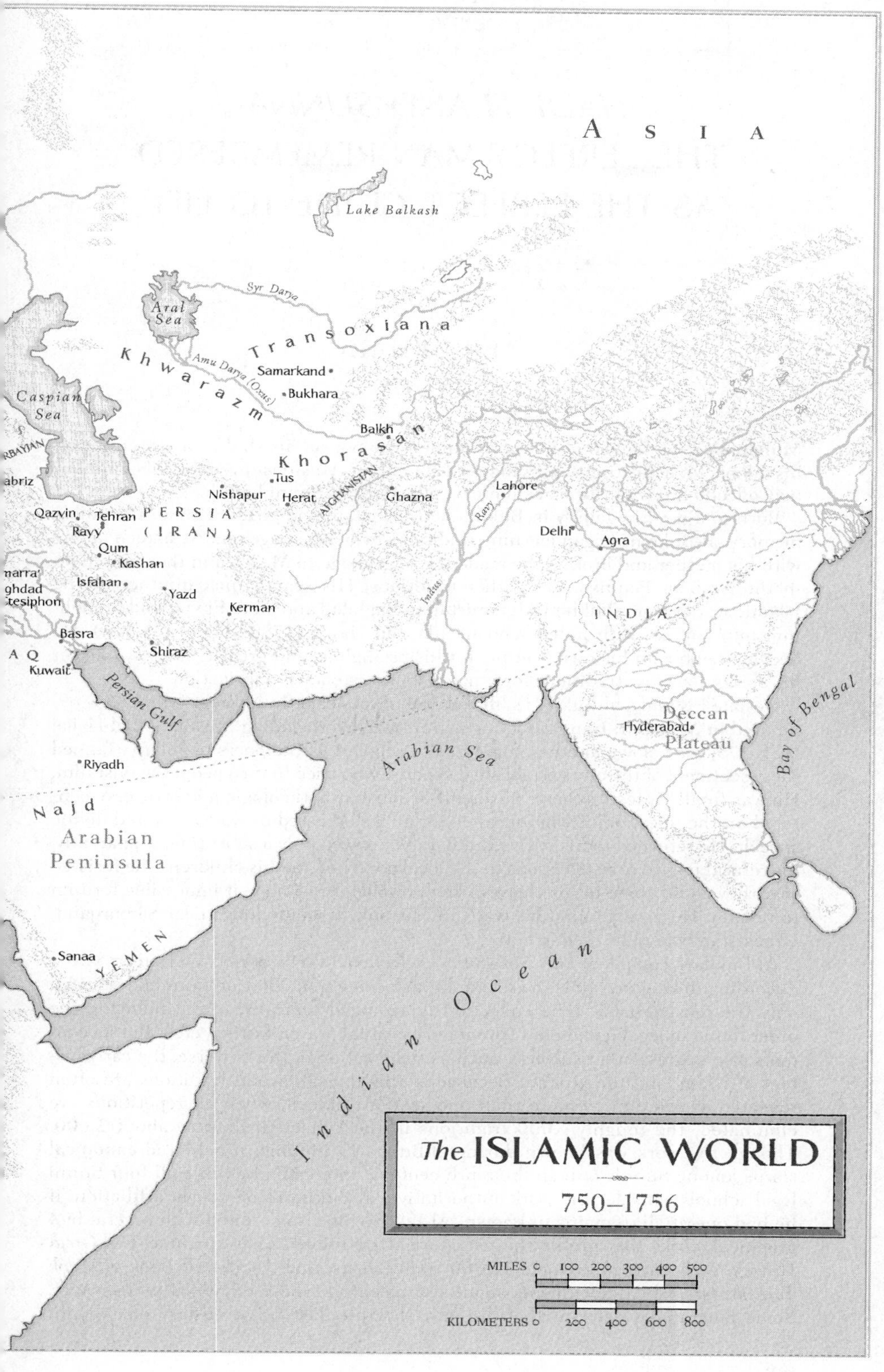

ASIA
Lake Balkash
Syr Darya
Aral Sea
Transoxiana
Khwarazm
Amu Darya (Oxus)
Samarkand
Bukhara
Caspian Sea
Balkh
Khorasan
Tus
Nishapur
Herat
AFGHANISTAN
Ghazna
Lahore
Ravy
Tehran
Qazvin
Rayy
PERSIA (IRAN)
Qum
Kashan
Delhi
Agra
Isfahan
Yazd
Kerman
Indus
INDIA
Basra
Shiraz
Kuwait
Persian Gulf
Deccan Plateau
Hyderabad
Bay of Bengal
Arabian Sea
Riyadh
Najd
Arabian Peninsula
Sanaa
YEMEN
Indian Ocean
The ISLAMIC WORLD
750–1756
MILES 0 100 200 300 400 500
KILOMETERS 0 200 400 600 800

HADITH AND *SUNNA*: THE PERFECT MAN REMEMBERED AS THE PERFECT GUIDE TO LIFE

AL-BUKHARI
810–870

Muhammad ibn Isma'il al-Bukhari's fame rests not on his skill as a writer but on his talents for collecting, codifying, and compiling. Muslims revere his *The Authentic Collection*, one of the six canonical collections of Sunni hadith.

Born to a wealthy family in Bukhara, Uzbekistan, and gifted with an incredible memory, al-Bukhari began learning traditions by heart at age ten. At sixteen, along with his mother and brother, he made the pilgrimage to Mecca and then stayed on in the Arabian Peninsula to gather traditions. His search took him across the Islamic world, from Balkh in Afghanistan to Baghdad and on to Egypt, and brought him into contact with noted scholars like Ibn Hanbal (780–855; see below). He became famous in his own lifetime for his prodigious and precise memory and for his ability to assess traditions for hints of inconsistency or fabrication.

Despite his fame, al-Bukhari's life was not always easy. In his later years (864–69) he lived in Nishapur, Iran, attracting many students, including Muslim ibn al-Hajjaj (821–875; see below), another noted hadith scholar. Al-Bukhari's popularity fanned the resentment of the city's established experts, who tried to turn people against him. He was finally forced to leave Nishapur because of a theological controversy centered on the question of whether the Qur'an was created or was uncreated divine speech. He returned to his native Bukhara but stayed only a short time. Apparently, his refusal to give private lessons to the local governor and his children—he insisted that they could come to his classes like everyone else—made it impossible for him to remain. He finally found his way to Khartank, a small village near Samarqand, Uzbekistan, where he died in 870.

Al-Bukhari compiled *The Authentic Collection* over a period of sixteen years. According to later accounts, he sifted through some 600,000 traditions and selected only the most reliable. The collection is arranged topically, often following the order found in legal handbooks (ritual purity, ritual prayer, fasting, etc.). But its contents also address other subjects, such as the creation of the universe, the early history of Islam, and the Qur'an. Because of this topical layout, traditions are often repeated as relevant to more than one section. Indeed, when all repetitions are eliminated, the roughly 7,000 traditions in the collection drop to about 2,600. Though the work was known during al-Bukhari's lifetime, it achieved canonical status among Sunnis only in the tenth century. Interestingly, while all four Sunni legal schools consider the work authoritative, al-Bukhari's own legal affiliation, if he had one at all, remains unknown. Al-Bukhari is also credited with several biographical works that profile the narrators of traditions. These include *The Great History*, with entries for some 12,300 traditionists, and *The Small Book of Weak Transmitters*, which documents about 400 narrators whose reliability was suspect. Some biographies recount that al-Bukhari wrote *The Great History* on moonlit nights during his youthful sojourn in Mecca, and that those who first saw it were amazed at its scholarly maturity.

This selection from *The Authentic Collection* narrates Muhammad's night journey from Mecca to Jerusalem and his ascension to heaven, where he encounters earlier prophets. This is a key story in Islamic literature, found repeatedly in the works of Sufis, philosophers, and poets. The translator, Muhammad Asad, is himself an interesting figure in twentieth-century Islamic history. Born Leopold Weiss (1900–1992) in what is now Ukraine, he published the autobiographical account of his conversion from Judaism to Islam as *The Road to Mecca* (1954).

PRONOUNCING GLOSSARY

Abû Ḥamzah: *a-boo ham´-zuh* (heavy *h*)
Abû Salamah ibn ʿAbd ar-Raḥmân: *a-boo sa´-la-muh ibn ab-dur-rah-man´* (heavy *h*)
al-Ḥumaydî: *al-hoo-may´-dee* (heavy *h*)
al-Jârûd: *al-ja-rood´*
al-Layth: *al-layth´*
ʿAmr: *ahmr*
Anas ibn Mâlik: *a´-nas ibn ma´-lik*
az-Zaqqûm: *az-zahq-qoom´*
Burâq: *boo-rahq´*
Hajar: *ha´-jar*
Hammâm ibn Yaḥyā: *ham-mam´ ibn yah´-ya* (heavy *h*)
Ḥaṭīm: *hah-teem´* (heavy *h*)
Ḥijr: *hejr* (heavy *h*)
Hudba ibn Khâlid: *hud´-buh ibn cha´-lid* (guttural *ch*)
Ibn ʿAbbâs: *ibn ab-bas´*
Ibn Shihâb: *ibn shee-hab´*
Idrîs: *ed-rees´*
ʿIkrimah: *ik´-ri-muh*
Jâbir ibn ʿAbd Allâh: *ja´-bir ibn ab-dul-lah´*
Kaʿbah: *ka´-buh*
Mâlik ibn Ṣaʿṣaʿa: *ma´-lik ibn sah´-sah-uh*
Qatâda: *qah-ta´-duh*
Quraysh: *qoo-raysh´*
Sufyân ibn ʿUyayna: *soof-yan´ ibn oo-yay´-nuh*
ʿUqayl: *oo-qayl´*
Yaḥyâ ibn Bukayr: *yah´-ya* (heavy *h*) *ibn boo-kayr´*

FROM THE EARLY YEARS OF ISLAM

The Story of the Night Journey

The Word of God, exalted be He: Glory be unto Him Who transported His servant by night from the Sacred Temple to the Farthest Temple . . . [1]

> Yaḥyâ ibn Bukayr related to us: Al-Layth related to us, on the authority of ʿUqayl, on the authority of Ibn Shihâb [who said]: Abû Salamah ibn ʿAbd ar-Raḥmân related to me: I heard Jâbir ibn ʿAbd Allâh [say] that

He heard the Apostle of God say: When the Quraysh accused me of lying, I remained [praying] in the enclosure of the Kaʿbah.[2] Thereupon God displayed Jerusalem before me, and I began describing it to them while I was still looking at it.

TRANSLATED BY Muhammad Asad.

1. Qur'an 17:1.
2. The Kaʿba (literally, "the Cube"), a stone shrine in Mecca—according to tradition, built by Abraham—that became the most important site in Islam (Muslims around the world face it when they pray). "Quraysh": the tribe that ruled Mecca.

The Ascension

Hudbah ibn Khâlid related to us: Hammâm ibn Yaḥyâ related to us: Qatâdah related to us, on the authority of Anas ibn Mâlik, on the authority of Mâlik ibn Ṣaʿṣaʿah [who said]:

The Prophet of God related to them the story of his Night Journey, and said: While I lay on the ground in the *Ḥaṭīm*,[3]

—or perhaps he said: in the *Ḥijr*—

lo, someone came and cut open

—[Qatâdah] said: I also heard him say: split open—

[my breast] from here to here.

[Qatâdah said:] Then I asked al-Jârûd, who was sitting by my side: What is meant thereby?—He answered: From the pit at the top of his breast to below his navel. I also heard him say: . . . from the uppermost part of his breast to below his navel.

Then he took my heart out. And a golden basin full of faith was brought unto me, and my heart was washed [therein] and was filled [with faith]; then it was restored to its place. Thereupon a white steed, smaller than a mule and larger than an ass, was brought unto me.

—Al-Jârûd asked: Was this the Burâq, O Abû Ḥamzah?[4]—Anas answered: Yea.—

Its stride was as long as the eye could reach. And I was mounted on it, and Gabriel took me with him to the nearest heaven, and demanded that it be opened. [A voice] asked: Who is it?—[Gabriel] answered: Gabriel.—And who is with thee?—Muḥammad.—And hath he received the Message?—Yea.—Welcome unto him! His is a blessed arrival!—And [the heavenly gate] was opened. When I entered [the heaven], lo! there was Adam; and [Gabriel] said: This here is thy father, Adam; offer him thy greeting.—And I greeted him, and he answered my greeting and said: Welcome unto the righteous son, the righteous Prophet!

Then [Gabriel] ascended with me still higher, and [we] reached the second heaven; and he demanded that it be opened. [A voice] asked: Who is it?—[My guide] answered: Gabriel.—And who is with thee?—Muḥammad.—And hath he received the Message?—Yea.—Welcome unto him! His is a blessed arrival!—And [the gate] was opened. When I entered, lo! [I saw] John and Jesus, the two cousins. [Gabriel] said: These here are John and Jesus; offer them thy greeting.—And I greeted [them], and they answered [my greeting] and said: Welcome unto the righteous brother, the righteous Prophet!

Then [Gabriel] ascended with me to the third heaven, and demanded that it be opened. [A voice] asked: Who is it?—Gabriel answered: Gabriel.—And who is with thee?—Muḥammad.—And hath he received the Message?—Yea. Welcome unto him! His is a blessed arrival!—And [the gate] was

3. A semicircular wall located about 7 feet from the northwest face of the Kaʿba. The space between the Kaʿba and this low-lying wall is often referred to as the *Hijr*.

4. Anas's *kunya*, or familiar name derived from his son's name. "Burâq": in Islamic mythology, a winged steed.

opened. When I entered, lo! [I saw] Joseph. Gabriel said: This here is Joseph; offer him thy greeting.—And I greeted him, and he answered [my greeting] and said: Welcome unto the righteous brother, the righteous Prophet!

Then [Gabriel] ascended with me still higher, and [we] reached the fourth heaven; and he demanded that it be opened. [A voice] asked: Who is it?—[My guide] answered: Gabriel.—And who is with thee?—Muḥammad.—And hath he received the Message?—Yea.—Welcome unto him! His is a blessed arrival!—And [the gate] was opened. When I entered, lo! I saw Idrîs.[5] Gabriel said: This here is Idrîs; offer him thy greeting.—And I greeted him, and he answered [my greeting] and said: Welcome unto the righteous brother, the righteous Prophet!

Thereafter [Gabriel] ascended with me still higher, and [we] reached the fifth heaven; and he demanded that it be opened. [A voice] asked: Who is it?—[Gabriel] answered: Gabriel.—And who is with thee?—Muḥammad.—And hath he received the Message?—Yea.—Welcome unto him! His is a blessed arrival!—And when I entered, lo! [I saw] Aaron. [Gabriel] said: This here is Aaron; offer him thy greeting.—And I greeted him, and he answered [my greeting] and said: Welcome unto the righteous brother, the righteous Prophet!

Then [my guide] ascended with me still higher, and [we] reached the sixth heaven; and he demanded that it be opened. [A voice] asked: Who is it?—[My guide] answered: Gabriel.—Who is with thee?—Muḥammad:—And hath he received the Message?—Yea.—Welcome unto him! His is a blessed arrival!—And when I entered, lo! [I saw] Moses. [Gabriel] said: This here is Moses; offer him thy greeting.—And I greeted him, and he answered [my greeting] and said: Welcome unto the righteous brother, the righteous Prophet!—And when I passed [by him], he wept. Someone asked him: What maketh thee weep?—[Moses] answered: I weep because after me there hath been sent [as Prophet] a young man whose followers will enter Paradise in greater numbers than my followers.

Thereafter Gabriel went up with me to the seventh heaven, and demanded that it be opened. [A voice] asked: Who is it?—[Gabriel] answered: Gabriel.—And who is with thee?—Muḥammad.—And hath he received the Message?—Yea.—Welcome unto him! His is a blessed arrival!—And when I entered, lo! [I saw] Abraham. [My guide] said: This here is thy father; offer him thy greeting.—And I greeted him, and he returned my greeting, saying: Welcome unto the righteous son, the righteous Prophet!

Thereafter I was made to see the Lote-Tree of the Farthest Limit:[6] its drupes were like the jars of Hajar,[7] and its leaves like elephant-ears. [Gabriel] said: This is the Lote-Tree of the Farthest Limit.—And lo! [I saw] four rivers—two hidden rivers and two manifest rivers. I said: What are these two [kinds of rivers], O Gabriel?—He answered: As to the two hidden ones, they are rivers of Paradise; and as to the two manifest ones, they are the Nile and the Euphrates.—Then I was made to see the Much-Frequented House;[8] and then a vessel full of wine, a vessel full of milk, and a vessel full of honey were brought to me; and I took the milk. Thereupon [Gabriel] said: This is [a

5. This prophet is sometimes identified with the biblical Enoch.
6. Qur'an 53:14. The lote-tree, or jujube, is a shade tree whose single-stoned fruit is usually small.
7. A town in ancient Arabia noted for producing large jars.
8. Qur'an 52:4.

symbol of] the inclination toward all that is natural in life; and it is this that thou and thy community stand for.

Thereafter prayers were elevated to a duty fifty prayers a day. When I was returning, I passed by Moses, and he said: What hath been enjoined upon thee?—I answered: Fifty prayers a day have been enjoined upon me.—[Moses] said: Behold, thy community cannot bear fifty prayers a day. By God! I have tested men before thee, and I exerted myself to the utmost with the Children of Israel. Go back, then, unto thy Sustainer, and beg of Him to lighten thy community's burden.—So I went back, and [God] granted me a remission of ten [prayers]. Then I came again to Moses, but he repeated what he had said [before]. I went back, and [the Lord] granted me a remission of ten [more]. Then I came again to Moses, but he repeated what he had said [before]. And I went back, and [the Lord] granted me a remission of ten [more]. Then I came again to Moses, but he repeated what he had said [before]. And I went back, and ten prayers a day were enjoined upon me. Then I came again [to Moses], but he repeated what he had said [before]. And I went back, and five prayers a day were enjoined upon me. Then I came again to Moses, and he asked: What hath been enjoined upon thee?—I answered: Five prayers a day have been enjoined upon me.—He said: Behold, thy community cannot bear [even] five prayers a day. I have tested men before thee, and I exerted myself to the utmost with the Children of Israel. Go back, then, unto thy Sustainer, and beg of Him to lighten thy community's burden.—I answered: I have begged so much of my Sustainer that I feel ashamed. But I am content now, and I shall submit [to God's will].—And when I left, I heard a voice: I have confirmed My injunction, and have lightened the burden of My worshippers!

Al-Ḥumaydî related to us: Sufyân related to us: ʿAmr related to us, on the authority of ʿIkrimah,

On the authority of Ibn ʿAbbâs. Concerning His Word, exalted be He, *We ordained the vision which We shewed thee but as a temptation for mankind*,[9] he said: This is [an allusion to] that which the Apostle of God was shewn in his vision on the night when he was transported to Jerusalem.

[ʿIkrimah] added:

[Concerning] *the Accursed Tree in the Qur'ân*, [Ibn ʿAbbâs] said: This is the tree of az-Zaqqûm.[1]

9. Qur'an 17:60.

1. Qur'an 17:60.

MUSLIM IBN AL-HAJJAJ
821–875

Muslim ibn al-Hajjaj, a decade younger than al-Bukhari (810–870; see above), like him published a compilation of traditions titled *The Authentic Collection*. Together these constitute the two most authoritative collections of prophetic traditions for Sunnis.

Born in Nishapur, Iran, Muslim became enamored of the study of traditions while young and, like many others, journeyed throughout the Muslim world in search of them, learning from the most notable teachers of his day. His travels took him to Iraq, Syria, the Arabian Peninsula, and Egypt, but eventually he returned to Nishapur, where he met his most famous teacher, al-Bukhari. Muslim remained in Nishapur, teaching and writing, for the rest of his life.

Muslim's collection reportedly drew from some 300,000 traditions although the work itself, when repetitions are eliminated, contains only about 3,000. While Sunnis consider al-Bukhari's work the most authoritative of hadith collections because of its more rigorous standard of authentication, some scholars prefer Muslim's collection. His method of grouping all variations of a particular tradition in a single section facilitated comparisons of content that were more difficult with al-Bukhari's arrangement. Like al-Bukhari's compendium, Muslim's *Collection* is organized by standard legal topics; it also includes sections on exegesis, theology, and character. Though the two works contain many of the same traditions, neither man borrowed from the other.

You will follow those before you—that is, the Jews and Christians—even "if they had entered into the hole of the lizard." So goes one of the Prophet's traditions recorded by Muslim. Others promise that in Paradise you will stay ever-young and your clothes will never wear out. Yet another records a divine tradition, a statement from God not found in the Qur'an: "Verily, Allah would say on the Day of Resurrection: Where are those who have mutual love for My Glory's sake? Today I shall shelter them in My shadow, when there is no other shadow but the shadow of Mine." The following selection clearly illustrates the juxtaposition of diverse subjects and the repetition of similar traditions.

PRONOUNCING GLOSSARY

ʿĀʾisha: *ah´-i-shuh*
ʿAbd al-Razzāq: *ab-dur-raz-zahq´*
ʿAbdullah ibn ʿAmr ibn ʿĀṣ: *ab-dul-lah´ ibn ahmr ibn ahs*
ʿAbdullah ibn ʿUmar: *ab-dul-lah´ ibn oh´-mar*
ʿAbdullah ibn Dīnār: *ab-dul-lah´ ibn dee-nahr´*
ʿAbdullah ibn Masʿūd: *ab-dul-lah´ ibn mas-ood´*
Abū 'l-Qāsim: *a-bool-qah´-sim*
Abū Ayyūb Anṣārī: *a-boo ai-yoob´ an-sah´-ree*
Abū Bakr ibn ʿAbdullah ibn Qais: *a-boo bakr´ ibn ab-dul-lah´ ibn qais*
Abū Bakr ibn Abū Mūsā ibn Qais: *a-boo bakr´ ibn a-boo moo´-sa ibn qais*
Abū Dharr: *a-boo dhahr*
Abū Huraira: *a-boo hoo-ray´-ruh*
Abū Idrīs Khaulānī: *a-boo ed-rees´ chaw-la´-nee* (guttural *ch*)
Abū Mūsā: *a-boo moo´-sa*
Abū Mūsā al-Ashʿarī: *a-boo moo´-sa al-ash´-ah-ree*
Abū Rabīʿ: *a-boo ra-bee´*
Abū Saʿīd al-Khudrī: *a-boo sa-eed´ al-chud´-ree* (guttural *ch*)
Abū Wāʾil (Shaqīq ibn Salama): *a-boo wa´-il (shah-qeeq´ ibn sa´-la-muh)*
aḥādīth: *a-ha-deeth´* (heavy *h*)
al-harj: *al-harj´*
ʿĀṣim al-Aḥwal: *ah´-sim al-ah´-wal* (heavy *h*)
ʿAṭāʾ ibn Yasār: *a-tah´ ibn ya-sahr´*
dirham: *dir´-ham*
Ḥabīb: *ha-beeb´* (heavy *h*)
ḥadīth: *ha-deeth´* (heavy *h*)
Hammād ibn Salama: *ham-mad´ ibn sa´-la-muh*
Ibn Abī Shaiba: *ibn a-bee´ shay´-buh*
Ibn Shubruma: *ibn shub´-roo-muh*
Jābir ibn ʿAbdullah: *ja´-bir ibn ab-dul-lah´*
Jarīr: *ja-reer´*
jihād: *ji-had´*
jinn: *jin*
Jundub ibn ʿAbdullah al-Bajalī: *jun´-dub ibn ab-dul-lah´ al-ba´-ja-lee*
Khurfat-ul-Jannah: *choor´-fat* (guttural *ch*) *al-jan´-nuh*

Muḥammad ibn Ṭalḥa: *moo-ham´-mad* (heavy *h*) *ibn tahl´-ha* (heavy *h*)
Naʿīm: *na-eem´*
Nawwās ibn Simʿān al-Anṣārī: *naw-was´ ibn sim-an´ al-an-sah´-ree*
Qutaiba: *qoo-tay´-buh*
Saʿīd: *sa-eed´*
Sahl ibn Saʿd as-Sāʿidī: *sahl* (light *h*) *ibn sad as-sa´-i-dee*
Sālim: *sa´-lim*
sharīʿa: *sha-ree´-uh*
Shuʿba: *shuh´-buh*
Thaubān: *thaw-ban´*
ʿUmar ibn al-Khaṭṭāb: *oh´-mar ibn al-chaht-tahb´* (guttural *ch*)
Umm Salama: *oom sa´-la-muh*
umma: *oom´-muh*
Wuhaib: *woo-hayb´*
Yazīd ibn Abī Ḥabīb: *ya-zeed´ ibn a-bee ha-beeb´* (heavy *h*)
zakāt: *za-kat´*
Zuhrī: *zuh´-ree* (light *h*)

FROM AUTHENTIC COLLECTION OF THE SAYINGS AND DOINGS OF THE PROPHET MUHAMMAD

From *The Book of Virtue, Good Manners and Joining of the Ties of Relationship*

POLITENESS TOWARDS PARENTS AND THEIR RIGHT TO IT

(6180) Abū Huraira reported that a person came to Allah's Messenger (may peace be upon him) and said: Who among the people is most deserving of a fine treatment from my hand? He said: Your mother. He again said: Then who (is the next one)? He said: Again it is your mother (who deserves the best treatment from you). He said: Then who (is the next one)? He (the Holy Prophet) said: Again, it is your mother. He (again) said: Then who? Thereupon he said: Then it is your father. In the ḥadīth transmitted on the authority of Qutaiba, there is no mention of the word "the people".

(6181) Abū Huraira reported that a person said: Allah's Messenger, who amongst the people is most deserving of my good treatment? He said: Your mother, again your mother, again your mother, then your father, then your nearest relatives according to the order (of nearness).

(6182) Abū Huraira reported: A person came to Allah's Apostle (may peace be upon him). The rest of the ḥadīth is the same as transmitted by Jarīr but with this addition: By your father, you would get the information.

(6183) This ḥadīth has been narrated on the authority of Ibn Shubruma with the same chain of transmitters and the ḥadīth transmitted on the authority of Wuhaib there is a slight variation of wording. Same is the case with the ḥadīth transmitted on the authority of Muḥammad b. Ṭalḥa (and the words are): "Who amongst the people deserves the best treatment from me. . . ."

(6184) ʿAbdullah b. ʿAmr reported that a person came to Allah's Apostle (may peace be upon him) and sought permission (to participate) in Jihād,[1] whereupon he (the Holy Prophet) said: Are your parents living? He said: Yes. Thereupon he (the Holy Prophet) said: You should put in your best efforts (in their) service.

(6185) This ḥadīth has been narrated on the authority of Ḥabīb with the same chain of transmitters.

TRANSLATED BY ʿAbdul Ḥamīd Ṣiddīqī.

1. Struggle to promote God's will both personally and politically or militarily.

(6186) Yazīd b. Abī Ḥabīb reported that Naʿīm, the freed slave of Umm Salama,[2] reported to him that ʿAbdullah b. ʿAmr b. ʿĀṣ said: There came to Allah's Apostle (may peace be upon him) a person and said: I owe allegiance to you for migration and Jihād seeking reward only from Allah. He (the Holy Prophet) said: Is one from amongst your parents living? He said: Yes, of course, both are living. He further asked: Do you want to seek reward from Allah? He said: Yes. Thereupon Allah's Messenger (may peace be upon him) said: Go back to your parents and accord them benevolent treatment.

KINDNESS TOWARDS THE FRIENDS OF ONE'S FATHER AND MOTHER

(6192) Ibn Dīnār reported that a desert Arab met ʿAbdullah b. ʿUmar on the way to Mecca. ʿAbdullah greeted him and mounted him upon the donkey on which he had been riding and gave him the turban that he had on his head. Ibn Dīnār (further) reported: We said to him (ʿAbdullah b. ʿUmar): May Allah do good to you, these are desert Arabs and they are satisfied even with meagre (things). Thereupon ʿAbdullah said: His father was loved dearly by ʿUmar b. Khaṭṭāb and I heard Allah's Messenger (may peace be upon him) as saying: The finest act of goodness on the part of a son is to treat kindly the loved ones of his father.

(6193) ʿAbdullah b. ʿUmar reported Allah's Apostle (may peace be upon him) as saying: The finest act of goodness is that a person should treat kindly the loved ones of his father.

(6194) ʿAbdullah b. Dīnār reported that when ʿAbdullah b. ʿUmar set out to Mecca, he kept a donkey with him which he used as a diversion from the tedium of journey on the camel's back and had a turban which he tied round his head. One day, as he was riding the donkey a desert Arab happened to pass by him. He (ʿAbdullah b. ʿUmar) said: Aren't you so and so? He said: Yes. He gave him his donkey and said: Ride it, and tie the turban round your head. Some of his companions said: May Allah pardon you, you gave to this desert Arab the donkey on which you enjoyed ride for diversion and the turban which you tied round your head. Thereupon he said: Verily I heard Allah's Messenger (may peace be upon him) as saying: The finest act of goodness is the kind treatment of a person to the loved ones of his father after his death and the father of this person was a friend of ʿUmar.

(6195) Nawwās b. Simʿān al-Anṣārī reported: I asked Allah's Messenger (may peace be upon him) about virtue and vice. He said: Virtue is a kind disposition and vice is what rankles in your heart and that you disapprove that people should come to know of it.

(6196) Nawwās b. Simʿān reported: I stayed with Allah's Messenger (may peace be upon him) for one year. What obstructed me to migrate was (nothing) but (persistent) inquiries from him (about Islam). (It was a common observation) that when any one of us migrated (to Medina) he ceased to ask (too many questions) from Allah's Messenger (may peace be upon him). So I asked him about virtue and vice. Thereupon Allah's Messenger (may peace be upon him) said: Virtue is a kind disposition and vice is what rankles in your mind and that you disapprove of its being known to the people.

2. One of Muhammad's wives.

FORBIDDANCE OF NURSING MUTUAL JEALOUSY, MUTUAL HATRED AND MUTUAL HOSTILITY

(6205) Anas b. Mālik reported Allah's Messenger (may peace be upon him) as saying: Neither nurse mutual hatred, nor jealousy, nor enmity, and become as fellow-brothers and servants of Allah. It is not lawful for a Muslim that he should keep his relations estranged with his brother beyond three days.

(6206) Anas b. Mālik reported Allah's Messenger (may peace be upon him) as saying like this. This ḥadīth has been narrated through another chain of transmitters.

(6207) This ḥadīth has been narrated on the authority of Zuhrī with the same chain of transmitters with the addition of Ibn ʿUyaina (and the words are): "Do not cut off (mutual relations)."

(6208) This ḥadīth has been narrated through another chain of transmitters and the ḥadīth transmitted on the authority of ʿAbd al-Razzāq (the words are): "Neither nurse grudge nor sever (the ties of kinship), nor nurse enmity."

(6209) Anas reported Allah's Apostle (may peace be upon him) as saying: Nurse no grudge, nurse no aversion and do not sever ties of kinship and live like fellow-brothers as servants of Allah. This ḥadīth has been narrated on the authority of Shuʿba with the same chain of transmitters but with this addition: "As Allah has commanded you."

IT IS FORBIDDEN FOR A MUSLIM TO HAVE ESTRANGED RELATIONS WITH THE OTHER MUSLIM BEYOND THREE DAYS WITHOUT ANY REASON OF SHARĪʿAH

(6210) Abū Ayyūb Anṣārī reported Allah's Messenger (may peace be upon him) as saying: It is not permissible for a Muslim to have estranged relations with his brother beyond three nights, the one turning one way and the other turning the other way when they meet; the better of the two is one who is the first to give a greeting.

(6211) This ḥadīth has been transmitted on the authority of Zuhrī with a slight variation of wording (and the words are): "The one turning away and the other turning away when they meet and one avoids the other and the other also avoids him."

(6212) ʿAbdullah b. ʿUmar reported Allah's Messenger (may peace be upon him) as saying: It is not permissible for a Muslim to have estranged relations with his brother beyond three days.

(6213) Abū Huraira reported Allah's Messenger (may peace be upon him) as saying: There should be no estranged relations beyond three days.

MERIT OF LOVE FOR THE SAKE OF ALLAH

(6225) Abū Huraira reported Allah's Messenger (may peace be upon him) as saying: Verily, Allah would say on the Day of Resurrection: Where are those who have mutual love for My Glory's sake? Today I shall shelter them in My shadow when there is no other shadow but the shadow of Mine.

(6226) Abū Huraira reported Allah's Apostle (may peace be upon him) as saying: A person visited his brother in another town and Allah deputed an

Angel to wait for him on his way and when he came to him he said: Where do you intend to go? He said: I intend to go to my brother in this town. He said: Have you done any favour to him (the repayment of which you intend to get)? He said: No, excepting this that I love him for the sake of Allah, the Exalted and Glorious. Thereupon he said: I am a messenger to you from Allah (to inform you) that Allah loves you as you love him (for His sake). This ḥadīth has been narrated on the authority of Hammād b. Salama with the same chain of transmitters.

MERIT OF VISITING THE SICK

(6227) Abū Rabīʿ reported directly from Allah's Apostle (may peace be upon him) as saying: The one who visits the sick is in fact like one who is in the fruit garden of Paradise so long as he does not return.

(6228) Thaubān, the freed slave of Allah's Messenger (may peace be upon him), reported that Allah's Messenger (may peace be upon him) said: He who visits the sick continues to remain in the fruit garden of Paradise until he returns.

(6229) Thaubān reported Allah's Apostle (may peace be upon him) as saying: Verily, when a Muslim visits his brother in Islam he is supposed to remain in the fruit garden of Paradise until he returns.

(6230) Thaubān, the freed slave of Allah's Messenger (may peace be upon him), reported Allah's Messenger (may peace be upon him) as saying: He who visits the sick is supposed to remain in the fruit garden of Paradise. It was said: Allah's Messenger, what is this *Khurfat-ul-Jannah*? He said: It is a place abounding in fruits.

(6231) This ḥadīth has been narrated on the authority of ʿĀṣim al-Aḥwal with the same chain of transmitters.

(6232) Abū Huraira reported Allah's Messenger (may peace be upon him) as saying: Verily, Allah, the Exalted and Glorious, would say on the Day of Resurrection: O son of Adam, I was sick but you did not visit Me. He would say: O my Lord, how could I visit Thee whereas Thou art the Lord of the worlds? Thereupon He would say: Didn't you know that such and such servant of Mine was sick but you did not visit him and were you not aware of this that if you had visited him, you would have found Me by him? O son of Adam, I asked food from you but you did not feed Me. He would say: My Lord, how could I feed Thee whereas Thou art the Lord of the worlds? He said: Didn't you know that such and such servant of Mine asked food from you but you did not feed him, and were you not aware that if you had fed him you would have found him by My side? (The Lord would again say:) O son of Adam, I asked drink from you but you did not provide Me. He would say: My Lord, how could I provide Thee whereas Thou art the Lord of the worlds? Thereupon He would say: Such and such of servant of Mine asked you for a drink but you did not provide him, and had you provided him drink you would have found him near Me.

IT IS FORBIDDEN TO COMMIT OPPRESSION

(6246) Abū Dharr reported Allah's Messenger (may peace be upon him) as saying that Allah, the Exalted and Glorious, said: My servants, I have made oppression unlawful for Me and unlawful for you, so do not commit oppression against one another. My servants, all of you are liable to err except one whom I guide on the right path, so seek right guidance from Me so that I should direct you to the right path. O My servants, all of you are hungry (needy) except one whom I feed, so beg food from Me, so that I may give that to you. O My servants, all of you are naked (need clothes) except one whom I provide garments, so beg clothes from Me, so that I should clothe you. O My servants, you commit error night and day and I am there to pardon your sins, so beg pardon from Me so that I should grant you pardon. O My servants, you can neither do Me any harm nor can you do Me any good. O My servants, even if the first amongst you and the last amongst you and even the whole of human race of yours, and that of Jinns even, become (equal in) God-conscious like the heart of a single person amongst you, nothing would add to My Power. O My servants, even if the first amongst you and the last amongst you and the whole human race of yours and that of the Jinns too in unison become the most wicked (all beating) like the heart of a single person, it would cause no loss to My Power. O My servants, even if the first amongst you and the last amongst you and the whole human race of yours and that of Jinns also all stand in one plain ground and you ask Me and I confer upon every person what he asks for, it would not, in any way, cause any loss to Me (even less) than that which is caused to the ocean by dipping the needle in it. My servants, these deeds of yours which I am recording for you I shall reward you for them, so he who finds good should praise Allah and he who does not find that should not blame anyone but his ownself. Saʿīd said that when Abū Idrīs Khaulāni narrated this ḥadīth he knelt upon his knees.

(6247) Abū Dharr reported Allah's Messenger (may peace be upon him) as saying that he reported it from his Lord, the Exalted and Glorious: Verily I have made oppression unlawful for Me and for My servants too, so do not commit oppression. The rest of the ḥadīth is the same.

(6248) Jābir b. ʿAbdullah reported that Allah's Messenger (may peace be upon him) said: Be on your guard against committing oppression, for oppression is a darkness on the Day of Resurrection, and be on your guard against pettimindedness for pettimindedness destroyed those who were before you, as it incited them to shed blood and make lawful what was unlawful for them.

(6249) Ibn ʿUmar reported Allah's Messenger (may peace be upon him) as saying: Oppression is the darkness on the Day of Resurrection.

(6250) Sālim reported on the authority of his father that Allah's Messenger (may peace be upon him) said: A Muslim is the brother of a fellow-Muslim. He should neither commit oppression upon him nor ruin him, and he who meets the need of a brother, Allah would meet his needs, and he who relieved a Muslim from hardship Allah would relieve him from the hardships to which he would be put on the Day of Resurrection, and he who did not expose (the follies of a Muslim) Allah would conceal his follies on the Day of Resurrection.

(6251) Abū Huraira reported Allah's Messenger (may peace be upon him) as saying: Do you know who is poor? They (the Companions of the Holy Prophet) said: A poor man amongst us is one who has neither dirham[3]

3. A silver coin.

with him nor wealth. He (the Holy Prophet) said: The poor of my Umma would be he who would come on the Day of Resurrection with prayers and fasts and Zakāt[4] but (he would find himself bankrupt on that day as he would have exhausted his funds of virtues) since he hurled abuses upon others, brought calumny against others and unlawfully consumed the wealth of others and shed the blood of others and beat others, and his virtues would be credited to the account of one (who suffered at his hand). And if his good deeds fall short to clear the account, then his sins would be entered in (his account) and he would be thrown in the Hell-Fire.

(6252) Abū Huraira reported Allah's Messenger (may peace be upon him) as saying: The claimants would get their claims on the Day of Resurrection so much so that the hornless sheep would get its claim from the horned sheep.

(6253) Abū Mūsā reported Allah's Messenger (may peace be upon him) as saying: Allah, the Exalted and Glorious, grants respite to the oppressor. But when He lays Hand upon him, He does not then let him off. He (the Holy Prophet) then recited this verse: "Such is the chastisement of thy Lord when He chastises the towns (inhabited by) wrongdoing persons. Surely, His punishment is painful, severe" (xi. 103).[5]

From *The Book of Knowledge*

PROHIBITION OF MAKING A HOT PURSUIT OF THE ALLEGORIES CONTAINED IN THE QURʾĀN, AND AVOIDING THOSE WHO DO IT, AND OF DISPUTATION IN THE QURʾĀN

(6442) ʿĀʾisha[6] reported that Allah's Messenger (may peace be upon him) recited (these verses of the Qurʾān): "He it is Who revealed to thee (Muhammad) the Book (the Qurʾān) wherein there are clear revelations—these are the substance of the Book and others are allegorical (verses). And as for those who have a yearning for error they go after the allegorical verses seeking (to cause) dissension, by seeking to explain them. And none knows their implications but Allah, and those who are sound in knowledge say: We affirm our faith in everything which is from our Lord. It is only the persons of understanding who really heed" (iii. 6).[7] ʿĀʾisha (further) reported that Allah's Messenger (may peace be upon him) said (in connection with these verses): When you see such verses, avoid them, for it is they whom Allah has pointed out (in the above-mentioned verses).

PERTAINING TO A DISPUTATIONIST

(6443) ʿAbdullah b. ʿUmar reported: I went to Allah's Messenger (may peace be upon him) in the morning and he heard the voice of two persons who had an argumentation with each other about a verse. Allah's Apostle (may peace be upon him) came to us (and) the (signs) of anger could be seen on his face. He said: Verily, the (peoples) before you were ruined because of their disputation in the Book.

4. Mandatory alms. "Umma": the Islamic community.
5. Qurʾan 11:102.
6. Muhammad's favorite wife among the many he took after the death of his first wife, Khadija.
7. Qurʾan 3:7.

(6444) Jundub b. ʿAbdullah al-Bajalī reported Allah's Messenger (may peace be upon him) as saying: Recite the Qur'ān as long as your hearts agree to do so, and when you feel variance between them (between your hearts and tongues), then get up (and leave its recital for the time being).

(6445) Jundub (i.e. Ibn ʿAbdullah) reported that Allah's Messenger (may peace be upon him) said: Recite the Qur'ān as long as your hearts agree to do so and when you find variance between them, then stand up.

(6446) Abū ʿImrān reported that Jundub told us as we were young boys living in Kūfa, that Allah's Messenger (may peace be upon him) had said: Recite the Qur'ān. The rest of the ḥadīth is the same.

(6447) ʿĀ'isha reported Allah's Messenger (may peace be upon him) as saying: The most despicable amongst persons in the eye of Allah is one who tries to fall into dispute with others (for nothing but only to display his knowledge and power of argumentation).

FOLLOWING THE FOOTSTEPS OF THE JEWS AND THE CHRISTIANS

(6448) Abū Saʿīd al-Khudrī reported Allah's Messenger (may peace be upon him) as saying: You would tread the same path as was trodden by those before you inch by inch and step by step so much so that if they had entered into the hole of the lizard, you would follow them in this also. We said: Allah's Messenger, do you mean Jews and Christians (by your words) "those before you"? He said: Who else (than those two religious groups)?

(6449) This ḥadīth has been narrated on the authority of ʿAṭā' b. Yasār through another chain of transmitters.

THOSE WHO INDULGED IN HAIR-SPLITTING WERE RUINED

(6450) ʿAbdullah reported Allah's Messenger (may peace be upon him) as saying: Ruined were those who indulged in hair-splitting. He (the Holy Prophet) repeated this thrice.

KNOWLEDGE WOULD BE TAKEN AWAY, AND IGNORANCE WOULD PREVAIL UPON PEOPLE AND THE TURMOIL AT THE END OF THE WORLD

(6451) Anas b. Mālik reported Allah's Messenger (may peace be upon him) as saying: It is from the conditions of the Last Hour that knowledge would be taken away and ignorance would prevail (upon the world), the liquor would be drunk, and adultery would become rampant.

(6452) Qatāda reported that Anas b. Mālik said: May I not narrate to you a ḥadīth which I heard from Allah's Messenger (may peace be upon him) which no one would narrate to you after me who would have personally heard it from him (the Holy Prophet) (as I have the good fortune to do so)?—"It is from the signs of the Last Hour that knowledge would be taken away, ignorance would prevail upon (the world), adultery would become common, wine would be drunk, the number of men will fall short and the women would survive (and thus such a disparity would arise in the number of men and women) that there would be one man to look after fifty women.

(6453) This ḥadīth has been transmitted on the authority of Anas b. Mālik through another chain of narrators, but with a slight variation of wording.

(6454) Abū Wā'il reported: I was sitting with ʿAbdullah and Abū Mūsā that they reported Allah's Messenger (may peace be upon him) having said:

Prior to the Last Hour, there would be a time when knowledge would be taken away, and ignorance would take its place and there would be bloodshed on a large scale.

(6455) This ḥadīth has been narrated on the authority of ʿAbdullah (b. Masʿūd) and Abū Mūsā (al-Ashaʿrī) through other chains of transmitters.

(6456) A ḥadīth like this has been narrated on the authority of Abū Mūsā through another chain of transmitters.

(6457) Abū Wā'il reported: I was sitting with Abū Mūsā and ʿAbdullah and they were conversing with each other and Abū Mūsā reported Allah's Messenger (may peace be upon him) as saying (that we find in the abovementioned aḥādīth).

(6458) Abū Huraira reported Allah's Messenger (may peace be upon him) as saying: (When) the time would draw close to the Last Hour, knowledge would be snatched away, turmoil would be rampant, miserliness would be put (in the hearts of the people) and there would be much bloodshed. They said: What is *al-harj*? Thereupon he said: It is bloodshed.

(6459) This ḥadīth has been transmitted on the authority of Abū Huraira with a slight variation of wording.

(6460) Abū Huraira reported Allah's Messenger (may peace be upon him) having said: The time would draw close to the Last Hour and knowledge would decrease. The rest of the ḥadīth is the same.

(6461) This ḥadīth has been transmitted on the authority of Abū Huraira through other chains of narrators and there is no mention of: "Miserliness would be put (in the hearts of the people)."

(6462) ʿAbdullah b. ʿAmr b. al-ʿĀṣ reported Allah's Messenger (may peace be upon him) as saying: Verily, Allah does not take away knowledge by snatching it from the people but He takes away knowledge by taking away the scholars, so that when He leaves no learned person, people turn to ignorant as their leaders; then they are asked to deliver religious verdicts and they deliver them without knowledge, they go astray, and lead others astray.

* * *

From *The Book Pertaining to Paradise, Its Description, Its Bounties and Its Intimates*

(6778) Anas b. Mālik reported: The Paradise is surrounded by hardships and the Hell-Fire is surrounded by temptations.

(6779) This ḥadīth has been narrated on the authority of Abū Huraira through another chain of transmitters.

(6780) Abū Huraira reported Allah's Apostle (may peace be upon him) as saying that Allah, the Exalted and Glorious, said: I have prepared for My pious servants which no eye has ever seen, and no ear has ever heard, and no human heart has ever perceived but it is testified by the Book of Allah. He then recited: "No soul knows what comfort has been concealed from them, as a reward for what they did" (xxxii. 17).

(6781) Abū Huraira reported that Allah's Apostle (may peace be upon him) said: Allah, the Exalted and Glorious, said: I have prepared for My pious servants which no eye (has ever) seen, no ear has (ever) heard and no human heart has ever perceived those bounties leaving apart (those bounties) about which Allah has informed you.

(6782) Abū Huraira reported Allah's Messenger (may peace be upon him) said that Allah, the Exalted and Glorious, said: I have prepared for My pious servants which the eye has seen not, and the ear has heard not and no human heart has ever perceived such bounties leaving aside those about which Allah has informed you. He then recited: "No soul knows what comfort has been hidden for them."

(6783) Sahl b. Saʿd as-Sāʿidī reported: I was in the company of Allah's Messenger (may peace be upon him) that he gave a description of Paradise and then Allah's Apostle (may peace be upon him) concluded with these words: There would be bounties which the eye has not seen and the ear has not heard and no human heart has ever perceived them. He then recited this verse. "They forsake (their) beds, calling upon their Lord in fear and in hope, and spend out of what We have given them. So no soul knows what refreshment of the eyes is hidden for them: a reward for what they did" (xxxii. 16–17).

THERE IS IN PARADISE A TREE UNDER THE SHADOW OF WHICH A RIDER CAN TRAVEL FOR A HUNDRED YEARS AND EVEN THEN HE WOULD NOT BE ABLE TO COVER IT

(6784) Abū Huraira reported Allah's Messenger (may peace be upon him) as saying: In Paradise, there is a tree under the shadow of which a rider can travel for a hundred years.

(6785) This ḥadīth has been narrated on the authority of Abū Huraira through another chain of transmitters with the addition of these words: "He will not be able to cover this distance."

(6786) Sahl b. Saʿd reported Allah's Messenger (may peace be upon him) as saying: In Paradise, there is a tree under the shadow of which a rider can travel for a hundred years without covering (the distance) completely. This ḥadīth has also been transmitted on the authority of Abū Saʿīd al-Khudrī that Allah's Apostle (may peace be upon him) is reported to have said: In Paradise, there is a tree under the shadow of which a rider of a fine and swift-footed horse would travel for a hundred years without covering the distance completely. There would be the pleasure of Allah for the inmates of Paradise and He would never be annoyed with them.

(6787) Abū Saʿīd al-Khudrī reported that Allah's Apostle (may peace be upon him) said that Allah would say to the inmates of Paradise: O, Dwellers of Paradise, and they would say in response: At thy service and pleasure, our Lord, the good is in Thy Hand. He (the Lord) would say: Are you well pleased now? They would say: Why should we not be pleased, O Lord, when Thou hast given us what Thou hast not given to any of Thy creatures? He would, however, say: May I not give you (something) even more excellent than that? And they would say: O Lord, what thing can be more excellent than this? And He would say: I shall cause My pleasure to alight upon you and I shall never be afterwards annoyed with you.

THE FIRST GROUP THAT WOULD BE ADMITTED TO PARADISE WOULD BE LIKE THE FACE OF THE FULL MOON AND THE DESCRIPTION OF THEIR QUALITIES AND THEIR SPOUSES

(6793) Muḥammad reported that some (persons) stated with a sense of pride and some discussed whether there would be more men in Paradise or more women. It was upon this that Abū Huraira reported that Abu'l-Qāsim (the Holy Prophet) (may peace be upon him) said: The (members) of the first group to get into Paradise would have their faces as bright as full moon during the night, and the next to this group would have their faces as bright as the shining stars in the sky, and every person would have two wives and the marrow of their shanks would glimmer beneath the flesh and there would be none without a wife in Paradise.

(6794) This ḥadīth has been narrated on the authority of Abū Huraira through another chain of transmitters.

(6795) This ḥadīth has been narrated on the authority of Abū Huraira through another chain of transmitters that Allah's Messenger (may peace be upon him) said: The (members of the) first group which would get into Paradise will have their faces as bright as stars in the sky. They would neither pass water, nor void excrement, nor will they suffer from catarrh, nor will they spit, and their combs would be made of gold, and their sweat will be musk, the fuel of their brazier will be aloes, and their wives will be large-eyed maidens and their form would be alike as one single person after the form of their father (Adam) sixty cubits tall.

(6796) Abū Huraira reported Allah's Messenger (may peace be upon him) as saying: The first group of my Ummah to get into Paradise would be like a full moon in the night. Then those who would be next to them; they would be like the most significantly glittering stars in regard to brightness, then after them (others) in ranks. They would neither void excrement, nor pass water, nor suffer from catarrh, nor would they spit. And their combs would be made of gold, and the fuel of their braziers would be aloes and their sweat would be musk and their form would be the form of one single person according to the length of their father sixty cubits tall. This ḥadīth has been transmitted on the authority of Ibn Abī Shaiba with a slight variation of wording.

THE EVERLASTING BLISS FOR THE INMATES OF PARADISE

(6802) Abū Huraira reported Allah's Apostle (may peace be upon him) as saying: He who would get into Paradise (would be made to enjoy such an everlasting) bliss that he would neither become destitute, nor would his clothes wear out, nor his youth would decline.

(6803) Abū Saʿīd al-Khudrī and Abū Huraira both reported Allah's Messenger (may peace be upon him) as saying: There would be an announcer (in Paradise) who would make this announcement: Verily! there is in store for you (everlasting) health and that you should never fall ill and that you live (for ever) and do not die at all. And that you would remain young and never grow old. And that you would always live in affluent circumstances and never become destitute, as words of Allah, the Exalted and Glorious, are: "And it would be announced to them: This is the Paradise. You have been made to inherit it for what you used to do" (vii. 43).

THE DESCRIPTION OF THE TENTS FOR THE INMATES OF PARADISE

(6804) Abū Bakr b. ʿAbdullah b. Qais reported on the authority of his father that Allah's Messenger (may peace be upon him) said that in Paradise there would be for a believer a tent of a single hollowed pearl the breadth of which would be sixty miles. It would be meant for a believer and the believers would go around it and none would be able to see the others.

(6805) Abū Bakr b. ʿAbdullah b. Qais reported on the authority of his father that Allah's Messenger (may peace be upon him) said that in Paradise there would be a tent made of a single hollowed pearl, the breadth of which would be sixty miles from all sides and there would live a family in each corner and the other would not be able to see the believer who goes around them.

(6806) This ḥadīth has been transmitted on the authority of Abū Bakr b. Abū Mūsā b. Qais who, on the authority of his father, reported the Apostle (may peace be upon him) to have said that there would be a tent made of a pearl whose height towards the sky would be sixty miles. In each corner, there would be a family of the believer, out of sight for the others.

AL-NAWAWI
1233–1277

A jurist and scholar of traditions (in Arabic, *hadith*), Abu Zakariyya Yahya al-Nawawi composed legal works that are considered definitive by the Shafiʿi school, and his collections of traditions are esteemed for their rigorous standards of authentication.

Al-Nawawi was born in October 1233 in Nawa, a town in southern Syria. As a youth, his father took him to Damascus to further his education and also took him on the pilgrimage to Mecca. At first he intended to pursue medicine but eventually shifted his focus to religious studies. He excelled in the Islamic sciences and by his early forties had achieved an unrivaled reputation. Al-Nawawi apparently never married and was known for his ascetic and celibate lifestyle. Biographies of al-Nawawi capture his deep dedication to learning: he studied day and night, sacrificing sleep to keep a punishing pace and drilling himself with memorized lessons even as he walked the city streets. His health suffered from these self-imposed demands, and he died at the relatively young age of forty-four in December 1277 at his father's house in Nawa.

Though best remembered for his Shafiʿi legal works, al-Nawawi was also a scholar of traditions. He composed one of the best-regarded commentaries on the authentic collection of Muslim (821–875; see above), and partial treatments of the compilations of al-Bukhari (810–870; see above) and Abu Daʾud (ca. 817–889). He also compiled his own collection, creating concise digests of the most treasured traditions. Realizing that the average Muslim would find the massive compendia of al-Bukhari and Muslim inaccessible and overwhelming, he composed handbooks that organized the material thematically. Two frequently reprinted examples are *Forty Prophetic Traditions* and *Gardens of the Righteous*.

In his introduction to *Gardens*, al-Nawawi emphasizes the moral purpose of the work. The believer is enjoined to obey God and thereby attain paradise in the next life. The best way to obey God, according to al-Nawawi, is to follow the practice of his messenger, Muhammad. To study the Prophet's words and actions prepares the believer to model his own behavior upon that of the beloved ideal. A life lived in imitation of Muhammad is a life conformed to the will and guidance of God. Just as the Prophet's life was shaped by his reception of the Qur'an, so too must the believer's life be shaped. Here al-Nawawi highlights the value of the Qur'an and the care with which it must be treated.

PRONOUNCING GLOSSARY

Abdullah ibn Amr ibn ʿAs: *ab-dul-lah´ ibn amr ibn ahs´*
Abdullah ibn Masʿud: *ab-dul-lah´ ibn mas-ood´*
Abdullah ibn Umar: *ab-dul-lah´ ibn oh´-mar*
Abu Darda': *a-boo dar-da´*
Abu Daud: *a-boo da-wood´*
Abu Hurairah: *a-boo hoo-ray´-ruh*
Abū Masʿūd Badrī: *a-boo mas-ood´ bad´-ree*
Abū Mundhir: *a-boo mun´-dhir*
Abu Musa Ashʿari: *a-boo moo´-sa ash´-ah-ree*
Abū Saʿīd al-Khudrī: *a-boo sa-eed´ al-chud´re* (guttural *ch*)
Abu Saʿid Rafiʿ: *a-boo sa-eed´ ra´-fee*
Abu Umamah: *a-boo oo-ma´-muh*
al-Baqarah: *al-bah´-qah-ruh*
al-Falaq: *al-fah´-laq*
al-Ikhlāṣ: *al-ich-lahs´* (guttural *ch*)
al-Kahf: *al-kahf´* (light *h*)
al-Mulk: *al-mulk´*
al-Nas: *an-nas´*
al-Tin: *at-teen´*
Anas ibn Malik: *a´-nas ibn ma´-lik*
Ayesha = ʿĀ'isha: *ah´-i-shuh*
Bashīr ibn Abd al-Munzir: *ba-sheer´ ibn ab-dul-mun´-dher*
Bokhari: *boo-chai-ree* (guttural *ch*)
Bra'a ibn ʿAzib: *ba-rah´ ibn ah´-zib*
Ibn Abbas: *ibn ab-bas´*
Kursi: *kur´-see*
Nawas ibn Samaʿan: *na-was´ ibn sam-an´*
Sadqa Fitr: *sah´-dah-quh fitr*
Tirmidhi: *tir´-mi-dhee*
Ubayy ibn Kaʿab: *oo-bay´ ibn kab*
Umar ibn Khattab: *oh´-mar ibn chaht-tahb´* (guttural *ch*)
Uqbah ibn ʿAmir: *uhq´-buh ibn ah´-mir*
Uthman ibn Affan: *uth-man´ ibn af-fan´*

FROM GARDENS OF THE RIGHTEOUS
On the Excellence of Reading the Quran

995. Abu Umamah relates that he heard the Holy Prophet say: Keep reading the Quran for it will intercede for its readers on the Day of Judgment (Muslim[1]).

996. Nawas ibn Samaʿan relates that he heard the Holy Prophet say: The Quran will be summoned on the Day of Judgment along with those who kept it company in this life and acted in conformity with it. It will be heralded by the second and third chapters and these will plead on behalf of those who kept company with them (Muslim).

997. Uthman ibn Affan relates that the Holy Prophet said: The best of you are those who learn the Quran and teach it (Bokhari[2]).

998. Ayesha[3] relates that the Holy Prophet said: He who recites the Quran fluently will be in the company of the noble and virtuous; and he who recites

TRANSLATED BY Muhammad Zafrulla Khan.

1. Muslim ibn al-Hajjaj (821–875); see above.
2. Muhammad ibn Ismaʿil al-Bukhari (810–870); see above.
3. Muhammad's favorite wife among the many he took after the death of his first wife, Khadija.

the Quran haltingly and with difficulty will have a double reward (Bokhari and Muslim).

999. Abu Musa Ash'ari relates that the Holy Prophet said: The case of a believer who recites the Quran is that of fruit which is fragrant and delicious; and the case of a believer who does not recite the Quran is that of fruit which has no fragrance but is sweet to the taste; and the case of a hypocrite who recites the Quran is that of fruit which is fragrant but tastes bitter; and the case of a hypocrite who does not recite the Quran is that of fruit which has no fragrance and tastes bitter (Bokhari and Muslim).

1000. Umar ibn Khattab relates that the Holy Prophet said: Allah will exalt many people through this Book, and will abase many because of it (Muslim).

1001. This *hadith* is the same as No. 575. [Ibn Umar relates that the Holy Prophet said: only two are to be envied: he upon whom Allah bestows the Quran and he conforms to it through the hours of the night and day; and he upon whom Allah bestows wealth and he spends it in the cause of Allah, through the hours of the night and day (Bokhari and Muslim).]

1002. Bra'a ibn 'Azib relates that a person was reciting *sura* Al-Kahf[4] (Chapter 18) while his horse was close to him secured by two ropes. A cloud spread over the horse and advanced towards it whereupon it began to frolic. In the morning the man came to the Holy Prophet and mentioned the incident to him. He said: This was comfort that descended by virtue of the recitation of the Quran (Bokhari and Muslim).

1003. Ibn Mas'ud relates that the Holy Prophet said that when a person recites one letter from the Book of Allah that is one good deed equal to ten good deeds the like of it. I do not say that ALM is a letter, but A is a letter, L is a letter and M is a letter (Tirmidhi[5]).

1004. Ibn Abbas relates that the Holy Prophet said: He in whose heart there is nothing of the Quran is like a house in ruin (Tirmidhi).

1005. Abdullah ibn Amr ibn 'As relates that the Holy Prophet said: One who is given to reciting the Quran will be told on the Day of Judgment: Go on reciting and ascending, and recite slowly as was thy wont in life, for thy station, will be where the last verse of thy recitation will end (Abu Daud[6] and Tirmidhi).

On Safeguarding the Quran

1006. Abu Musa relates that the Holy Prophet said: Safeguard the Quran in your memories, for by Him in Whose hands is the life of Muhammad, it escapes sooner from memory than does a camel from its rope (Bokhari and Muslim).

1007. Ibn Umar relates that the Holy Prophet said: The case of one who has the Quran by heart is like that of one who has a camel secured by a rope. If he watches it, he retains it; and if he neglects it, it wanders away (Bokhari and Muslim).

4. The Cave.
5. Muhammad ibn 'Isa al-Tirmidhi (d. 892).
6. Abu Da'ud al-Sijistani (ca. 817–899), a Persian collector of hadith.

On Good Recitation of the Quran

1008. Abu Hurairah relates that he heard the Holy Prophet say: Allah does not lend ear so joyously to anything as he does to the recitation of the Quran by a Prophet who has a beautiful voice and recites well and audibly (Bokhari and Muslim).

1009. Abu Musa Ashʿari relates that the Holy Prophet said to him: You have been granted one of the tunes of David[7] (Bokhari and Muslim). Muslim has added: I wish you could have seen me when I was listening to your recitation last night.

1010. Bra'a ibn ʿAzib relates: I heard the Holy Prophet recite *sura* Al-Tin[8] (Chapter 95) during the evening service. I have never heard anyone recite in a more beautiful voice than his (Bokhari and Muslim).

1011. Bashir ibn Abd al-Munzir relates that the Holy Prophet said: He who does not recite the Quran tunefully is not one of us (Abu Daud).

1012. This *hadith* is the same as No. 449. [Ibn Masʿud relates: The Holy Prophet asked me to recite the Quran to him. I said: Messenger of Allah, shall I recite the Quran to you, whereas it is you to whom it has been revealed? He said: I like to hear it recited by another. So I recited to him a portion from the fourth Chapter till I came to the verse: How will it be when we shall bring a witness from every people, and shall bring thee as a witness against these (4.42) [4:41]? when he said: That is enough for now. I looked at him and saw that his eyes were running (Bokhari and Muslim).]

On Special Chapters and Verses

1013. Abu Saʿid Rafiʿ relates: The Holy Prophet said to me: Shall I tell you before you go out of the mosque which is the greatest chapter of the Quran? and he took hold of my hand. When we were about to issue from the mosque I said to him: Messenger of Allah, you had said you would tell me which is the greatest chapter of the Quran. He answered: The opening chapter which contains the seven oft-repeated verses and the Great Quran which has been bestowed upon me (Bokhari).

1014. Abu Saʿid Khudri relates that the Holy Prophet said concerning the recitation of *sura* Al-Ikhlas[9] (Chapter 112): By Him in Whose hands is my life, it is equal to the recitation of one third of the Quran. Another version is: The Holy Prophet inquired from his companions: Would any of you find it burdensome to recite one third of the Quran in the course of a night? They considered it difficult and said: Which of us would have the strength to do that, Messenger of Allah? He said: *sura* Al-Ikhlas is one third of the Quran (Bokhari).

1015. Abu Saʿid Khudri relates that a man heard another recite *sura* Al-Ikhlas repeatedly. In the morning he came to the Holy Prophet and mentioned this to him belittling it. The Holy Prophet said to him: By Him in Whose hands is my life, it is equal to one third of the Quran (Bokhari).

1016. Abu Hurairah relates that the Holy Prophet said that the *sura* Al-Ikhlas (Chapter 112) equals one third of the Quran (Muslim).

7. Muslims believe that the prophet David had a melodious voice. See also Qur'an 13:18–19.

8. The Fig.

9. The Unity.

1017. Anas relates that a man said to the Holy Prophet: Messenger of Allah, I love *sura* Al-Ikhlas. He told him: Love of it will admit you to Paradise (Tirmidhi).

1018. Uqbah ibn ʿAmir relates that the Holy Prophet said: Know you not that last night certain verses were revealed the like of which has never been known; *sura* Al-Falaq and *sura* Al-Nas[1] (Chapters 113 and 114) (Muslim).

1019. Abu Saʿid Khudri relates that the Holy Prophet used to seek protection against the *jinn* and the evil eye till *suras* Al-Falaq and Al-Nas were revealed. After they were revealed he took to them and discarded everything beside them (Tirmidhi).

1020. Abu Hurairah relates that the Holy Prophet said: There is a *sura* in the Quran comprising thirty verses which continued its intercession on behalf of a man till he was forgiven. It is *sura* Al-Mulk[2] (Chapter 67) (Abu Daud and Tirmidhi).

1021. Abu Masʿud Badri relates that the Holy Prophet said: If a person recites the last two verses of *sura* Al-Baqarah[3] at night, they suffice him (Bokhari and Muslim).

1022. Abu Hurairah relates that the Holy Prophet admonished: Do not convert your houses into graves. Indeed, Satan runs away from a house in which *sura* Al-Baqarah is recited (Muslim).

1023. Ubayy ibn Kaʿab relates: The Holy Prophet asked me: Abu Mundhir, do you know which verse of the Book of Allah is the grandest? I answered: the verse of the *Kursi*[4] (2.256). He poked me in the chest and said: Felicitations on your knowledge, Abu Mundhir (Muslim).

1024. Abu Hurairah relates: The Holy Prophet had appointed me to watch over the Sadqa Fitr (alms given on the occasion of the Festival at the end of Ramadhan) and during the night one sneaked up and started stealing from the alms and I caught hold of him and said: I will take you to the Holy Prophet; but he pleaded: I am in need and I have a large family and we are in sore distress. So I let him go. Next morning the Holy Prophet asked me: Abu Hurairah, what did your prisoner do last night? I answered: Messenger of Allah, he pleaded his need and that of his family, so I took pity on him and let him go. The Holy Prophet said: He told you a lie and will return. So I realized that he would come back as the Holy Prophet had said and I kept watching for him. He sneaked up again and started taking from the alms and I said to him: I shall take you to the Holy Prophet. He pleaded: I am in need and have a large family; let me go and I shall not come back. So I took pity on him and let him go. Next morning the Holy Prophet said to me: Abu Hurairah, how did your prisoner of last night behave? I answered: Messenger of Allah, he pleaded his need and that of his family and I took pity on him and let him go. He said: He told you a lie and will come back again. So I watched for him a third time. He sneaked up to steal from the alms when I caught him and said: I shall take you to the Holy Prophet and this is the last of the three times you promised that you will not come back and you came back. He pleaded: Let me go, and I will tell you some phrases which will be of benefit to you before Allah. I asked him: What are they? He answered: When you go to bed recite the verse of the Chair (2. 256) [2:255] for it will be a guardian over you on

1. The Daybreak and Mankind.
2. The Sovereignty.
3. The Cow, the second sura of the Qur'an.
4. The Throne or Chair verse, actually 2:255 in most modern editions.

behalf of Allah and Satan will not be able to approach you till morning. So I let him go. Next morning the Holy Prophet asked me: How did your prisoner behave last night? And I answered: Messenger of Allah, he said he would teach me some phrases which would be of benefit to me before Allah. So I let him go. He asked: What are those phrases? I answered: He said to me: When you go to bed recite the verse of the Chair from its beginning to its end and told me that this would guard me on behalf of Allah and Satan would not be able to approach me till the morning. The Holy Prophet observed: This time he told you the truth and yet he is a liar. Abu Hurairah, do you realise who was speaking to you during these three nights? I answered: No. The Holy Prophet answered: It was Satan (Bokhari).

1025. Abu Darda' relates that the Holy Prophet said: He who commits to memory the first ten verses of *sura* Al-Kahf (Chapter 18) will be secure against Anti-Christ. One version is: the last ten verses of *sura* Al-Kahf (Muslim).

1026. Ibn Abbas relates: While Gabriel was sitting with the Holy Prophet a sound was heard from above and Gabriel raised his head and said: A door has been opened from heaven which had not been opened up to this day. Then an angel descended from it and Gabriel said: This angel has descended to the earth and had not descended before till this day. He saluted the Holy Prophet and said: Be glad of the two lights that have been bestowed upon you which had not been bestowed upon any Prophet before you: The opening chapter of the Book and the last verses of *sura* Al-Baqarah (Chapter 2). Whenever you recite even a word of this it will be bestowed upon you (Muslim).

On Gathering Together for Recitation of the Quran

1027. Abu Hurairah relates that the Holy Prophet said: Whenever people gather together in one of the houses of Allah for recitation of the Quran and teaching it to one another, comfort descends upon them, mercy covers them, angels spread their wings over them and Allah makes mention of them to those around Him (Muslim).

MUHAMMAD BAQIR MAJLISI
1627–1699

Muhammad Baqir Majlisi's *Oceans of Lights* may well deserve the prize as the longest book in Islamic history. A twentieth-century edition fills 110 volumes of about 400 pages each. The author of this massive work was a Persian, born in Isfahan into a family of religious scholars. After the death of his father, he assumed leadership of the Friday prayer in Isfahan and went on to become one of the most influential religious leaders in the empire. The empire was that of Safavid Iran, the Shiʿi dynasty that stood between Ottoman Anatolia and Mughal India. Safavid power was at its peak during Majlisi's lifetime, and he took full advantage of Shiʿi court patronage to create a lasting legacy of unparalleled prominence and impact.

As a youth, Majlisi became proficient in all of the religious sciences of his day, including jurisprudence, theology, philosophy, and mysticism. But he devoted most of his time to the study and collection of the hadith, or prophetic traditions (reports of what the Prophet said, did, or silently affirmed). As a Shiʿi, he held traditions from the twelve imams viewed as the Prophet's successors in highest regard, second only to those from Muhammad.

Yet as his studies took him more deeply into Shiʿi hadith, he began to realize how many had been lost, suppressed, or forgotten over the centuries. He therefore embarked upon his magnum opus as a work of recuperation, an extraordinary attempt to recover, collect, and collate every worthy aspect of Shiʿi hadith literature that he could. Secretaries were pressed into service, sponsorship was sought, and every effort expended to ensure the success of this lifelong project. An active life of teaching and other scholarly pursuits prevented Majlisi from finishing *Oceans of Lights* but he left notes and directions for its completion. While *Oceans* is written in Arabic, Majlisi also produced smaller collections of traditions in Persian, eager to make this literature accessible to those who read only his mother tongue.

As noted, Majlisi had close ties to the Safavid rulers of his day. They often underwrote his scholarly activity, and he was outspoken in his praise for them. Such praise accorded with his view that faithful Shiʿis ought to follow the king's rulings, whether he was upright or corrupt. In turn, these rulers honored Majlisi with the highest religious office in the state, giving him enormous control over the religious affairs of the entire empire. Majlisi used his power to strengthen the influence of Shiʿism in the Safavid realm, furthering the political aims of the rulers, particularly against their Sunni Ottoman rivals. While Majlisi argued forcefully against Sunni theological positions, asserting the superiority of Twelver Shiʿism, he also took aim at Sufis and Zoroastrians.

The arrangement of *Oceans* is topical and draws on a wide range of material. Following his own intellectual predilections, Majlisi tended to exclude traditions that reflected philosophical or mystical leanings. As a Shiʿi, Majlisi included traditions that were critical of the first three caliphs, signaling his rejection of Sunni Islam and bolstering the political aspirations of the Safavids against their Ottoman rivals. Appealing to a more popular audience, he inserted traditions that highlighted the miraculous nature and knowledge of the twelve imams, despite the criticism of such stories by earlier Shiʿi scholars.

The following passages from *Oceans of Lights* offer a very sophisticated series of discussions about God's nature, including his majesty, incomparability, unity, and relation to his creation, as attributed to four of the twelve imams. These four—Muhammad al-Baqir (676–ca. 732), Jaʿfar al-Sadiq (702–765), Musa al-Kazim (745–799), and ʿAli al-Rida (ca. 768–818)—lived during a critical century and a half in early Shiʿi history. Each is renowned and revered as a religious luminary, and the tombs of the latter two in Kazimayn (Baghdad), Iraq, and in Mashhad, Iran, continue to be pilgrimage sites. The graves of Muhammad al-Baqir and Jaʿfar al-Sadiq in Medina fell victim to the Wahhabi tomb destruction that was widespread in the Arabian Peninsula beginning in the early nineteenth century.

PRONOUNCING GLOSSARY

Abū ʿAbdallāh Jaʿfar al-Ṣādiq: *a-boo ab-dul-lah´ ja´-far as-sah´-diq*

Abū al-Ḥasan ʿAlī al-Riḍā: *a-bool-ha´-san* (heavy *h*) *ah´-lee ar-ri´-dah*

Abū Baṣīr: *a-boo bah-seer´*

Abū Jaʿfar Muḥammad al-Bāqir: *a-boo ja´-far moo-ham´-mad* (heavy *h*) *al-bah´-qir*

al-Maʾmūn: *al-ma-moon´*

Banū Hāshim: *ba-noo ha´-shim*

Mūsā ibn Jaʿfar: *moo´-sah ibn ja´-far*

FROM OCEANS OF LIGHTS

Al-Bāqir, the Fifth Imam

THE INCOMPARABLE LORD

Abū Baṣīr has related that a man came to Abū Jaʿfar[1] (the fifth Imam) and said to him, "O Abū Jaʿfar, tell me about thy Lord! When was He?"

He said, "Woe unto thee! Surely it is said of a thing that was not, and *then* was, 'When was it?' But my Lord—blessed is He and high exalted—was ever-living without 'how' and had no 'was'. His Being (*kawn*) had no 'how', nor had it any 'where'. He was not in anything, nor was He on anything. He did not bring into existence a place (*makān*) for His Being (*kān*). He increased not in strength *after* bringing things into being, nor was He weak *before* bringing things into being. And He was not lonely (*mustawḥish*) before creating things. He resembles nothing brought into being. He was not devoid of power over the dominion before its production that He should be devoid of the dominion after its passing. He remains Living without (created) life, a powerful King before He produces anything (over which to rule) and an all-compelling King (*malik jabbār*) after He produces the universe (*al-kawn*). His Being has no 'how', nor has it any 'where', nor has it any limit. He is not known through anything resembling Him. He ages not through the duration of His subsistence. He is thunderstruck by nothing. Nothing causes Him to fear. And all things are thunderstruck by fear of Him.

"He is Living without temporal life, without a being (*kawn*) described by attributes, without a state which can be defined (*kayf maḥdūd*), without a trace which can be followed, and without a place adjacent to anything. Nay, He is a Living One who knows, a King who ever is. His are the power and the dominion. He produces what He wills through His will (*mashiyyah*). He is neither limited nor divided into parts, and He perishes not. He was the First, without 'how', and He will be the Last, without 'where'. And 'All things perish, except His Face' (XXVIII, 88). 'His are the creation and the command. Blessed be God, the Lord of all beings!' (VII, 54).

"Woe upon thee, O questioner! As for my Lord, truly imaginations envelop Him not, uncertainties touch Him not, He is oppressed by none, none is adjacent to Him, phenomena touch Him not, He is questioned not as to anything He does, He comes not upon anything, 'Slumber seizes Him not, neither sleep' (II, 255). 'To Him belongs all that is in the heavens and the earth and all that is between them, and all that is underneath the soil' (XX, 6)."

Jaʿfar al-Ṣādiq, the Sixth Imam

1. SEEING GOD

Abū Baṣīr has related that he said to Abū ʿAbdallāh[2]—upon whom be peace—"Tell me about God, the Mighty and Majestic. Will believers see Him on the Day of Resurrection?"

TRANSLATED BY William C. Chittick. The parenthetical citations are to sura and verse of the Qurʾan.

1. Muhammad ibn ʿAli al-Baqir (676–ca. 732), the fifth Imam of the Twelver Shiʿi school. Abu Basir (fl. late 8th century), early Shiʿi scholar and companion of Jaʿfar al-Sadiq, the sixth Imam.
2. Jaʿfar al-Sadiq (702–765), the sixth Imam of the Twelver Shiʿi school.

He answered, "Yes, and they have already seen Him before the Day of Resurrection."

Abū Baṣīr asked, "When?"

The Imam answered, "When He said to them, 'Am I not your Lord?' They said: 'Yea, verily' (VII, 172)." Then he was quiet for a time. Then he said, "Truly the believers see him in this world before the Day of Resurrection. Doest thou not see Him now?"

Abū Baṣīr then said to him, "That I might be made thy sacrifice! Shall I relate this (to others) from thee?"

He answered, "No, for if thou relatest it, a denier ignorant of the meaning of what thou sayest will deny it. Then he will suppose that it is comparison and unbelief (*kufr*). But seeing with the heart (*al-ru'yah b-il-qalb*) is not like seeing with the eyes (*al-ru'yah bi-l-ʿayn*). High be God exalted above what the comparers (*mushabbihūn*) and heretics (*mulḥidūn*) describe!"

2. THE NAME THAT CAN BE NAMED . . .

It has been related that Abū ʿAbdallāh said, "The name of God is other than God, and everything that can be called by the name of a 'thing' (*shay'*) is created, except God. Therefore all that tongues express or is worked by hands is created. God is the goal of him who sets Him as his goal, but the determined goal (*al-mughayyā*, i.e., in the mind of man) is other than the (real) goal. The goal possesses attributes (*mawṣūf*), and all that possesses attributes has been fashioned (*maṣnūʿ*). But the Fashioner (*ṣāniʿ*) of things does not possess the attributes of any stated limit (*ḥadd musammā*). He has not come into being that His Being (*kaynūnah*) should be known through fashioning (*ṣunʿ*) (carried out) by other than He. He does not terminate at a limit unless it be other than He. Whoso understands this principle (*ḥukm*) will never fall into error. It is the unadulterated profession of Unity (*al-tawḥīd al-khāliṣ*), so believe in it, confirm it, and understand it well, with God's permission—the Mighty and Majestic.

"Whoso maintains that he knows God by means of a veil (*ḥijāb*) or a form (*ṣurāh*) or a likeness (*mithāl*) is an associator[3] (*mushrik*), for the veil, the likeness and the form are other than He. He is utterly and only One. So how should he who maintains that he knows Him by means of other than Him be professing Unity? Surely He alone knows God who knows Him by means of God (*billāh*). Therefore, whoso knows Him not by means of Him knows Him not. On the contrary, he only knows other than Him. There is nothing between the Creator and the created. God is the Creator of things, but not from something. He is *named* by His names, so He is other than His names, and His names are other than He. The described (*al-mawṣūf*) is other than the describer (*al-wāṣif*).

"Then whoso maintains that he has faith in that which he does not know has gone astray from knowledge (*maʿrifah*). A created thing (*makhlūq*) perceives nothing unless by means of God: the knowledge of God is perceived only by means of God. But God is empty of His creatures and His creatures are empty of Him. When He desires a thing, it is as He desires, by His command (*amr*) and without speech (*nuṭq*). His servants have no refuge from that which He decrees (*mā qaḍā*), and they have no argument against that

3. To "associate" anything with God was the fundamental sin.

which is His pleasure. They have no power to act or to deal with that which is brought about in their bodies, created (by God), except by means of their Lord. So whoso maintains that he is able to perform an act which God, the Mighty and Majestic, does not desire, has maintained that his will (*irādah*) prevails over the Will of God. 'Blessed be God' the Lord of all beings!" (VII, 54).

Mūsā, the Seventh Imam

GOD'S MIGHT AND MAJESTY

It has been related that the righteous servant, Mūsā ibn Jaʿfar,[4] said, "Surely God—there is no god but He—was the Living without 'how' (*kayf*) or 'where' (*ayn*). He was not in anything, nor was He on anything. He did not create a place (*makān*) for His grandeur (*makān*). He increased not in might after bringing things into being. Nothing brought into being resembles Him. He was not devoid of power over the dominion before its production, nor will He be devoid of power (over it) after its passing.

"He—the Mighty and Majestic—is a Living God without temporal life, King before He produces anything, Master after its production (*inshāʾ*). God has no limits (*ḥadd*). He is not known through something resembling Him. He ages not through subsistence (*baqāʾ*). He is struck not by fear of anything, and by fright before Him all things are thunderstruck. So God is Living without temporal life, without a being described by attributes, without a state which can be defined, without a designated location or fixed place. Nay, He is Living in Himself, a Master whose power does not remove. He produced what He wills when He wills through His will and His power. He was First, without 'how', and will be Last, without 'where'. And 'All things perish, except His face' (XXVIII, 88). 'His are the creation and the command. Blessed be God, the Lord of all beings!' (VII, 54)."

From *ʿAli al-Riḍā, the Eighth Imam*

1. PROFESSION OF UNITY

It has been related that when al-Maʾmūn desired to install al-Riḍā[5] (as his successor), he collected together Banū Hāshim[6] and said to them, "Verily I desire to install al-Riḍā in this affair after me."

Banū Hāshim envied al-Riḍā and said, "Thou appointest an ignorant man who possesses not the insight to direct the caliphate. Therefore send for him. He will come to us and thou wilt see how his ignorance decides thee against him." So he sent for him and he came. Banū Hāshim said to him, "O Abu-l-Ḥasan! Ascend the pulpit and display for us a sign whereby we may worship God."

4. Musa ibn Jaʿfar al-Kazim (745–799), a son of Jaʿfar al-Sadiq and the seventh Imam of the Twelver Shiʿi school.

5. ʿAli ibn Musa al-Rida (ca. 768–818), a son of Musa ibn Jaʿfar al-Kazim and the eighth Imam of the Twelver Shiʿi school. "Al-Maʾmūn": Abu Jaʿfar Abdullah al-Maʾmun ibn Harun (r. 813–33), a Sunni ʿAbbasid ruler known for his initiatives to translate Greek philosophical and scientific texts into Arabic.

6. Literally, "the sons of Hashim"; because Hashim was the great-grandfather of Muhammad and also an ancestor of the founders of the ʿAbbasid caliphate, the term can refer to the family of the Prophet or (as here) to the ʿAbbasid family.

So he ascended the pulpit and sat for a long time, his head bowed in silence. Then he trembled a great trembling and stood up straight, praised and lauded God, and asked His blessing for His prophet and his household. Then he said, "The first element in the worship of God is knowledge of Him, the root (*aṣl*) of knowledge of Him is to profess His Unity (*tawḥīd*), and the correct way (*niẓām*) to profess the Unity of God is to negate attributes from Him. For the powers of reason testify that every attribute and everything possessing an attribute (*mawṣūf*) is created. Everything possessing an attribute testifies that it has a Creator which is neither attribute nor possesses an attribute. Every attribute and everything possessing an attribute testify to connection (*iqtirān*, between the attribute and that to which it is attributed). Connection testifies to temporality (*ḥadath*). And temporality testifies that it accepts not the Beginningless, which accepts not the temporal.

"So it is not *God* whose Essence is known through comparison. It is not *His* Unity that is professed by someone who attempts to fathom Him. It is not *His* reality (*ḥaqīqah*) that is attained by someone who strikes a similitude for Him. It is not *He* who is confirmed (*taṣdīq*) by him who professes an end for Him. It is not *He* to whom repairs he who points to Him. It is not *He* who is meant by him who compares Him (to something). It is not to *Him* that he who divides Him into parts humbles himself. And it is not *He* who is desired by him who conceives of Him in his imagination.

"Everything that can be known in itself (*bi-nafsihi*) is fashioned (*maṣnūʿ*). All that stands apart from Him is an effect (*maʿlūl*). God is inferred from what He fashions (*ṣunʿ*), the knowledge of Him is made fast by the powers of reason, and the argument (*ḥujjah*) for Him is established by (man's) primordial nature (*al-fiṭrah*).

"God's creating of the creatures is a veil between Him and them. His separation (*mubāyanah*) from them is that He is disengaged from their localization (*ayniyyah*). That He is their origin (*ibtidāʾ*) is proof for them that He has no origin, for none that has an origin can originate others. That He has created them possessing means (of accomplishing things) is proof that He has no means (*adāh*), for means are witness to the poverty of those who use them.

"So His names are an expression (*taʿbīr*), His acts (*afʿāl*) are (a way) to make (Him) understood (*tafhīm*), and His Essence is Reality (*ḥaqīqah*). His inmost center (*kunh*) separates (*tafrīq*) Him from creation, and His otherness (*ghuyūr*) limits (*taḥdīd*) what is other than He. Therefore ignorant of God is he who asks for Him to be described! Transgressing against Him is he who seeks to encompass Him! Mistaken is he who imagines to have fathomed Him!

"Whoso says 'how?' has compared Him (to something). Whoso says 'why?' has professed for Him a cause (*taʿlīl*). Whoso says 'when?' has determined Him in time (*tawqīt*). Whoso says 'in what?' has enclosed Him (*taḍmīn*). Whoso says 'to what?' has professed for Him a limit (*tanhiyah*). Whoso says 'until what?' has given Him an end (*taghiyah*). Whoso gives Him an end has associated an end with Him. Whoso associates an end with Him has divided Him. Whoso divides Him has described Him. Whoso describes Him has deviated from the straight path (*ilḥād*) concerning Him.

"God does not change with the changes undergone by creation, just as He does not become limited by delimiting (*taḥdīd*) that which is limited (*al-maḥdūd*). He is One (*aḥad*), not according to the explanation offered by number (*ta'wīl 'adad*); Outward, not according to the explanation of being immediate (to the senses); Manifest, not through the appearance of a vision (of Him); Inward (*bāṭin*), not through separation (*muzāyalah*); Apart (*mubā'īn*), not through distance; Near, not through approach; Subtle, not through corporealization; Existent, not after non-existence; Active, not through coercion; Determining, not through the activity of thought (*jawl fikrah*); Directing (*mudabbir*), not through movement; Desiring, not through resolution; Willing (*shā'*), not through directing attention (*himmah*); Grasping (*mudrik*), not through touch (*majāssah*); Hearing, not through means; and Seeing, not through organs.

"Times accompany Him not, places enclose Him not, slumber seizes Him not, attributes delimit Him not, and instruments (*adawāt*) are of no use to Him. His being (*kawn*) precedes times (*al-awqāt*), His existence (*wujūd*) non-existence and His beginninglessness (*azal*) beginning (*al-ibtidā'*).

"By His giving sense to the sense organs it is known that He has no sense organs. By His giving substance to substances it is known that He has no substance. By His causing opposition among things it is known that He has no opposite. By His causing affiliation among affairs it is known that He has no affiliate. He opposed darkness to light, obscurity to clarity, moisture to solidity, and heat to cold. He joins together those things which are hostile to one another and separates those which are near. They prove (the existence of) their Separator by their separation and their Joiner by their junction. That is (the meaning of) His words—He is the Mighty and Majestic—'And of everything created We two kinds; haply you will remember' (LI, 49).

"So through them He separated 'before' and 'after' that it might be known that He has no before and after. They testify with their temperaments that He who gave them temperaments has no temperament. They prove by their disparity (*tafāwut*) that He who made them disparate has no disparity. They announce through their subjection to time that He who subjected them to time is not subject to it Himself.

"He veiled some of them from others so that it might be known that there is no veil between Him and them other than them. His is the meaning of lordship (*al-rubūbiyyah*) when there was none over whom He was Lord, the reality of godhood (*al-ilāhiyyah*) when there was nothing for whom He was God, the meaning of Knower when there was nothing to be known, the meaning of Creator (*khāliq*) when there was nothing created (*makhlūq*) and the import of hearing when there was nothing to be heard. It is not because He created that He deserves the meaning (of the term) 'Creator' and not because He brought the creatures into being that the meaning of 'making' is derived.

"How (should it not be so)? For *mudh* ('ever since') conceals Him not, *qad* ('already') brings Him not near, *la'alla* ('perhaps') veils Him not, *matā* ('when?') limits Him not in time, *ḥīn* ('at the time of') contains Him not, and *ma'* ('with') brings Him not into association. Instruments (*adawāt*) limit only themselves and means (*ālah*) allude only unto their own like. Their activities are found only in things. *Mudh* withholds things from being eternal (*qidmah*), *qad* shields them from beginninglessness, and *law lā* ('if only') wards off perfection (*al-takmilah*). Things become separate and prove (the existence of) their Separator. They become distinguished and prove their Distinguisher (*mubā'in*). Through them their Maker manifests Himself to the powers of reason. Through (these powers) He becomes veiled to sight, to them imaginations appeal for a decision, in them is substantiated (only) other than Him, from them is suspended the proof and through them He makes known to them the acknowledgement (*al-iqrār*).

"Confirmation (*tasdīq*) of God is made fast by the powers of reason, and faith (*īmān*) in Him reaches perfection through acknowledgment. There is no religiosity (*diyānah*) except after knowledge (*maʿrifah*), no knowledge except through sincerity (*ikhlāṣ*) and no sincerity along with comparison. There is no negation (*nafy*) of comparison if there is affirmation (*ithbāt*) of attributes.

"So nothing in creation is found in its Creator. All that is possible in it is impossible in its Maker. Movement (*ḥarakah*) and stillness (*sukūn*) do not affect Him. How should that which He effects (in others) have effect upon Him, or that which He has originated recur for Him? Then His Essence would be disparate, His inmost center divided, His signification (*maʿnā*) prevented from eternity. How would the Creator have a meaning different from the created?

"If something from behind limited Him, then something in front would limit Him. If perfection (*tamām*) were seeking Him, imperfection would be upon Him. How should that which does not transcend (*imtināʿ*) temporality be worthy of (the Name) 'Beginningless'? How should that which does not transcend being produced (*inshā'*) produce the things (of the world)? There then would have arisen in Him a sign of having been made (*al-maṣnūʿ*) and He would become a proof (*dalīl*) after having been the proven (*madlūl ʿalayh*).

"There is no argument in absurd opinions (such as the above), no answer when it (absurdity) is asked about, no glorification of Him in its meaning. Nor is there any ill in distinguishing Him from creation, unless it be that the Eternal accepts not to be made two, nor the Beginningless to have a beginning.

"There is no god but God, the All-high, the Tremendous. They have cried lies who ascribe equals to God! They have gone astray into far error and suffered a manifest loss! And God bless Muhammad and his household, the pure."

SHARIʿA AND *FIQH*: DIVINE WILL AND HUMAN INTERPRETATION

AL-SHAFIʿI
767–820

Only four Sunni scholars share the enduring distinction of giving their names to a major school of Islamic legal thought and practice. Muhammad ibn Idris al-Shafiʿi is one of them. For more than a thousand years, countless Muslims have identified themselves as Shafiʿis and have revered his *Epistle* as the inaugural work in the entire genre of Islamic legal theory (in Arabic, *usul al-fiqh*). Medieval jurists, who declared that "al-Shafiʿi is to legal theory what Aristotle is to logic," deemed him to be a "renewer" of the religion for his time.

Al-Shafiʿi was most likely born on the southern coast of Palestine, but he was still a child when, following the death of his father, his mother moved them to Mecca, where she had relatives. There al-Shafiʿi excelled at archery, poetry, and mastery of the Arabic language. Later in life he composed a work on archery and published a well-regarded book of poetry. A desire for religious knowledge was his primary focus, however, and he committed himself early to its lifelong pursuit. He studied with a number of Meccan scholars, among them Sufyan ibn ʿUyayana (725–813), who was sufficiently impressed with al-Shafiʿi's scholarly progress that he gave the youth permission to issue legal opinions (in Arabic, *Fatawa*, sing. *fatwa*) while still a young teenager. Ibn ʿUyayana would also later teach Ibn Hanbal (780–855; see below), another of the four famous Sunni scholars of the law.

The most renowned jurist in the Arabian Peninsula during this period of al-Shafiʿi's life was the Medinan scholar Malik ibn Anas (ca. 715–795), for whom the Maliki legal school is named. As a student in Mecca, al-Shafiʿi memorized Malik's *The Well-Trodden Path*, and then moved to Medina to study with him. He distinguished himself under Malik, with whom he studied until his teacher's death. Yet, later in life al-Shafiʿi wrote *Differences between Malik and al-Shafiʿi*, a stinging critique of methodological flaws in Malik's legal thinking: it generated a war of refutational treatises between followers of Malik and followers of al-Shafiʿi that lasted until the time of Ibn Abi Zayd al-Qayrawani (922–996; see below).

The details of al-Shafiʿi's life after leaving Medina are uncertain, but the biographical sources make it possible to construct a rough chronology. He first went to Yemen, where the local governor, who had been impressed by al-Shafiʿi upon meeting him in Mecca, offered him employment. Unfortunately, al-Shafiʿi there allied himself with a political faction that was accused of opposing the ʿAbbasid caliph, Harun al-Rashid (ca. 764–809). Consequently, he lost his position and in 803 was sent to al-Raqqa (in modern Syria) to stand trial. He received a pardon through the efforts of the Hanafi jurist al-Shaybani (ca. 750–805), a member of al-Rashid's court and a former student of both Malik and Abu Hanifa (699–767; see below), who vouched for al-Shafiʿi's credentials as a scholar. He was fortunate; a number of the other accused rebels were executed.

After being freed, al-Shafiʿi settled in Iraq and began studying the teachings of the Hanafi legal school with the most notable scholars of the region—among them the man who had engineered his pardon, al-Shaybani. As he had done after studying with Malik, al-Shafiʿi would eventually compose a critique of al-Shaybani and the Hanafi school that similarly provoked a flurry of polemical activity. During these productive years, al-Shafiʿi traveled between Iraq and the Arabian Peninsula, continuing his studies and becoming a scholar in his own right.

Eventually, he decided to settle in Egypt. By this time, according to the biographical sources, his own thought had matured to a point that it became independent of both the Maliki and Hanafi schools. The break effectively barred him from the Arabian Peninsula, where followers of Malik remained strong, as well as from Baghdad, a bastion of the Hanafi school. He was initially welcomed in Egypt as a prominent student of Malik. Once he began spreading his own views, however, he met immediate resistance. According to one account, injuries from an attack by a Maliki zealot caused his death. (Other accounts imply that he perished after a long period of poor health.) Nonetheless, his years in Egypt were tremendously successful. He attracted numerous disciples and composed most of his works there, including his monumental *Source*, a work that, like the *Epistle*, explains his legal thinking and approaches to positive law.

Al-Shafiʿi lived during the formative phase of Islamic law, when legal scholars with varying viewpoints wrestled with substantive methodological questions and sought to attract the allegiance of other jurists. It was a period rich in polemics—to which, as already noted, al-Shafiʿi added significant fuel. From these debates emerged texts devoted to matters of legal theory. Though a number of Western scholars have questioned their assessment, Muslim historians deemed al-Shafiʿi's *Epistle* to be one of the seminal works of a genre of works that seeks to explain the sources (in Arabic, *usul*) from which positive law (*al-fiqh*) can be derived. Mature works of Sunni legal theory agree on four primary sources of law: in descending order of importance, the Qurʾan, the practice of Muhammad (*sunna*), the consensus of the Muslim community, and analogical reasoning. Mature Shiʿi works accept all but the last, which they replace with intellect.

In his *Epistle*, al-Shafiʿi's main contributions to this genre are his insistence that Muhammad's practice could be ascertained only through rigorously transmitted reports (in Arabic, *hadith*), his delineation of the procedure of analogical reasoning, and his specification of the nature of consensus. His positions on these matters represented his own synthesis of the law and differed significantly from those of the Maliki and Hanafi schools of his time.

According to al-Shafiʿi, Muhammad's practice has the same authority as the Qurʾan, but the problem lies in determining what, in fact, that practice was. Al-Shafiʿi insisted that only reports that could be confidently traced back to Muhammad himself could establish his practice and that such reports superseded all other sources of the law except the Qurʾan. This position was clearly aimed at the Malikis of the time, who argued that the practice (in Arabic, *ʿamal*) of the people of Medina was a better indicator of Muhammad's behavior than a single, though well-documented, report. The Malikis reasoned that since Muhammad had spent most of his career in Medina, surely its inhabitants, who were eyewitnesses of Muhammad's actions for a longer period than any other Muslims, knew and embodied his practice most accurately. They thus were more reliable guides to the Prophet's behavior in a particular context than any report about it.

Al-Shafiʿi restricted the use of human intellect in the derivation of new laws to analogical reasoning alone. And such reasoning, in turn, could be based only on the Qurʾan, the practice of Muhammad, and the retrospectively achieved consensus of the Muslim community. By confining the use of analogical reasoning to these three sources, al-Shafiʿi resisted the Hanafi willingness to include juristic preference and public interest as having bearing on the law. Al-Shafiʿi argued that such considerations lacked a basis in the Qurʾan or the Prophet's practice and were too prone to the whims of individual jurists. Moreover, al-Shafiʿi's view that the consensus of the Muslim community was a valid source of law opposed the Maliki belief that (for the reasons given above) only the consensus of the people of Medina created a precedent binding on all Muslims.

Al-Shafiʿi's stress on the practice of the Prophet as a determinative source of the law is clearly illustrated in the following passage. The way in which Muhammad prepared for prayer and his choice of products on which to base the obligatory alms tax are to guide and govern Muslims' actions forever.

PRONOUNCING GLOSSARY

ʿAbd al-ʿAzīz ibn Muḥammad: *ab-dul-ah-zeez´ ibn moo-ham´-mad* (heavy *h*)
ʿAbd al-Raḥmān ibn Abī Saʿīd: *ab-dur-rah-man´* (heavy *h*) *ibn a-bee sa-eed´*
ʿAbdallāh ibn ʿUmar ibn Ḥafṣ: *ab-dul-lah´ ibn oh´-mar ibn hafs´* (heavy *h*)
ʿAbdallāh ibn Zayd: *ab-dul-lah´ ibn zayd*
Abū Hurayrah: *a-boo hoo-ray´-ruh*
Abū Salama ibn ʿAbd al-Raḥmān: *a-boo sa´-la-muh ibn ab-dur-rah-man´* (heavy *h*)
Abū l-Zubayr: *a-boo zoo-bayr´*
al-Maqburī: *al-mahq´-boo-ree*
al-Qāsim ibn Muḥammad: *al-qah´-sim ibn moo-ham´-mad* (heavy *h*)
al-Shāfiʿī: *ash-sha´-fi-ee*
al-Zuhrī: *az-zuh´-ree* (light *h*)
ʿAmrah: *´am-ra*
ʿAmr ibn Yaḥyā: *ahmr ibn yah´-ya* (heavy *h*)
ʿaṣr: *ahsr*
ʿAṭā' ibn Yasār: *a-tah´ ibn ya-sahr´*
Bilāl: *bee-lahl´*
Dhāt al-Riqāʿ: *that ar-ri-qah´*
Hishām: *he-sham´*
Ibn ʿAbbās: *ibn ab-bas´*
Ibn Abī Dhiʾb: *ibn a-bee dhib´*
Ibn Abī Fudayk: *ibn a-bee foo-dayk´*
Ibn al-Musayyab: *ibn al-moo-say´-yab*
Ibn Jurayj: *ibn joo-rayj´*
Jābir ibn ʿAbdallāh: *ja´-bir ibn ab-dul-lah´*
Khawwāt ibn Jubayr: *chaw-wat´* (guttural *ch*) *ibn joo-bayr´*
Nāfiʿ: *na´-fi*
Ṣāliḥ ibn Khawwāt: *sah´-lih* (heavy *h*) *ibn chaw-wat´* (guttural *ch*)
Sālim: *sa´-lim*
Sufyān: *soof-yan´*
ʿUbaydallāh ibn ʿUmar: *oo-bay-dul-lah´ ibn oh´-mar*
ʿUthmān ibn ʿAbdallāh ibn Surāqah: *uth-man´ ibn ab-dul-lah´ ibn soo-rah´-quh*
Yazīd ibn Rūmān: *ya-zeed´ ibn roo-man´*
Zayd ibn Aslam: *zayd ibn as´-lam*

FROM THE EPISTLE ON LEGAL THEORY

Obligations Established by Explicit Texts and in Regard to Which God's Emissary Provided a Parallel Practice

God (blessed and exalted) said: "When you rise to pray, wash your faces and your hands up to the elbows, and wipe your heads and wash your feet up to the ankles. If you are polluted, purify yourselves"[1] and "save when you are traveling, until you have washed yourselves."[2] He stated that ritual cleansing from major impurity is achieved through washing rather than ablutions.

TRANSLATED BY Joseph E. Lowry.

1. Qurʾan 5:6.
2. Qurʾan 4:43.

God's Emissary established practices concerning how to perform ablutions just as God revealed. He washed his face and his hands to the elbows, and wiped his head and washed his feet to the ankles.

ʿAbd al-ʿAzīz ibn Muḥammad reported to us from Zayd ibn Aslam, from ʿAṭā' ibn Yasār, from Ibn ʿAbbās, from the Prophet: The Prophet washed each place once.

Mālik[3] reported to us from ʿAmr ibn Yaḥyā, from his father, that he said to ʿAbdallāh ibn Zayd, grandfather of ʿAmr ibn Yaḥyā: "Can you show me how God's Emissary performed ablutions?" "Yes," said ʿAbdallāh. He called for a vessel for ablutions and poured it out over his hands. Then he washed his hands twice each; he rinsed his mouth and nose three times; then washed his face three times, and then his hands twice each up to the elbows. Then he wiped his head with his hands. He brought them forward and back, beginning at the front of his head, then bringing them back to the nape of his neck, and then returning them back to the place he had started. Then he washed his feet.

The apparent meaning of "wash your faces" is the least that the term "washing" can apply to, and that is once, even though it could possibly denote more. God's Emissary instituted practices according to which one performs ablutions just once, and that accords with the apparent sense of the Qur'an: it is the least that the term "washing" can apply to, even though it could possibly denote more. He also instituted practices of performing them twice and three times. Since he established the practice that one do it once, we infer that if once did not satisfy the legal obligation, he would not have performed ablutions only once and then prayed, and, moreover, that whatever exceeded once was optional, not an obligation in regard to ablutions such that doing them fewer times would not satisfy the legal obligation.

This is like what I mentioned previously about such obligations. If one did without the hadith-report, one could make do with the Book,[4] but when the hadith-report was related about the topic in question, that fact indicated that the hadith-reports followed the Book of God. Perhaps they only related the hadith-report about this because the maximum number of ablutions that God's Emissary performed was three, and they meant to indicate that three ablutions was optional, not mandatory such that fewer would not have satisfied the legal obligation. They might also have done this because of the Prophet's statement about this: "Whoever performs ablutions in this way"—and it was three times—"and then prays two bowings[5] during which he refrains from talking to himself will have his sins forgiven." They wanted to convey that there is reward in doing more in regard to ablutions, and that the extra acts are above and beyond what is required.

God's Emissary washed his elbows and ankles, but the verse could mean either that they themselves are to be washed, or that one only washes up to them without actually washing them. Perhaps they related the hadith-report as a clarifying statement for this, too. But the interpretation that is most likely, according to the apparent meaning of the verse, is that they are both to be washed.

3. The renowned Medinan legal scholar Malik ibn Anas (ca. 715–795) gave his name to the Maliki legal school and was one of al-Shafiʿi's teachers.
4. The Qur'an.
5. Arabic, *rakʿa*, refers not only to bowing down during ritual prayer, but in fact to a whole cycle or unit of the prayer that comprises sequenced bowing, prostration, and sitting up, repeated a set number of times depending on which prayer is being performed [abridged translator's note].

This is an example of a legislative statement found in an account of Prophetic Practice that is parallel to one in the Qurʾan. The examples of statements in this and in the previous topic are equivalent. By virtue of being expressed in the Qurʾan, the obligation is self-sufficient as far as scholars are concerned, but the two appear inconsistent to others. God's Emissary established practices demonstrating that the major cleansing from substantive impurity included washing the genitalia, ablutions like the ablutions for prayer, and washing—and thus do we prefer that one do it. I know of no scholar whose opinions I have learned who dissents from the proposition that however one performs the major washing, as long as it is a complete washing, it will satisfy one's legal obligation, even though those scholars might choose another way of doing it. This is because the obligation in this case is the major washing, and it was not defined as precisely as the ablutions. God's Emissary instituted practices concerning what necessitates ablutions and what kind of ritual impurity requires a major washing, because some of that was not addressed in explicit texts in the Book.

* * *

Obligations Expressed in General Terms

God (blessed and exalted) said: "Prayer is a prescription at fixed times for the believers"[6] and "Perform the prayer and pay alms."[7] He also said to His Prophet: "Take alms from their possessions by which you might purify them and make them clean."[8] And He said: "It is the people's duty to God to make the Pilgrimage to the Sacred House—for those able to do so."[9]

Al-Shāfiʿī said: God confirmed the obligations to pray, give alms, and perform the Pilgrimage in His Book, and He clarified how to perform those obligations using the words of His Prophet. God's Emissary let it be known that the number of obligatory prayers was five, and that the number of bowings for the noon, afternoon, and evening prayers was four and four again if one was in a settlement, that the sunset prayer was three, and the dawn prayer two. He also established a practice to the effect that one recite the Qurʾan in all of them, and that such recitation be made aloud in the sunset, evening, and dawn prayers, and that it be done silently in the noon and afternoon prayers. He also established the practice that one say "God is great" at the beginning of prayer and the peace at the end, and that one say "God is great," then the recitation, then the bowing, then two prostrations after the bowing, and other of their details. He established practices for those who are traveling: allowing them, if they wish, to shorten every prayer involving four bowings; confirming that the sunset and dawn prayers be done in their usual way just as when one is in a settlement; and requiring that they all be directed toward the prayer-direction, whether while traveling or resident somewhere, except that one can make do with only one bowing in case of danger.

He established practices that made extra devotional prayers equivalent to the required prayers in this regard: They are only valid in a state of ritual

6. Qurʾan 4:103.
7. Qurʾan 2:43, 83, 110, etc.
8. Qurʾan 9:103.
9. Qurʾan 3:97.

purity and may not be performed without a Qurʾanic recitation and the other things necessary for the prescribed prayers, such as prostration, bowing, and facing the prayer-direction[1] when in a settlement, in the countryside, or while traveling. Someone who is riding may perform extra devotional prayers in whatever direction his mount happens to be facing.

Ibn Abī Fudayk reported to us from Ibn Abī Dhiʾb, from ʿUthmān ibn ʿAbdallāh ibn Surāqah, from Jābir ibn ʿAbdallāh: During the raid against the Anmār tribe, God's Emissary prayed while facing east on his mount.[2]

Muslim reported something similar to that to us from Ibn Jurayj, from Abū l-Zubayr, from Jābir, from the Prophet. I do not know whether Jābir named the Anmār tribe or not, or whether he said "he prayed while traveling."

God's Emissary established practices for the number of bowings and prostrations during festival prayers and rain prayers. He also instituted practices for the eclipse prayer and added a bowing to it in addition to those in the regular prayers, making it into two bowings for each regular bowing.

Mālik reported the same account to us from Yaḥyā ibn Saʿīd, from ʿAmrah, from ʿĀʾishah, from the Prophet.

Mālik reported the same account to us from Hishām, from his father, from ʿĀʾishah, from the Prophet.

Mālik reported the same account to us from Zayd ibn Aslam, from ʿAṭāʾ ibn Yasār, from Ibn ʿAbbās, from the Prophet. The Prophet's prayer is related from ʿĀʾishah and Ibn ʿAbbās in these hadith-reports with different wordings, but they all agree that he prayed with two bowings in the eclipse prayer, two bowings for every regular bowing.

God said concerning prayer: "Prayer is a prescription at fixed times for the believers."[3] God's Emissary clarified what those times were on God's behalf, and he performed the prayers at their proper time. At the Battle of the Parties,[4] however, he was besieged and not able to pray at the proper time, so he postponed the prayer because of a valid excuse until he was able to pray the noon, afternoon, sunset, and evening prayers in one session.

Muḥammad ibn Ismāʿīl ibn Abī Fudayk reported to us from Ibn Abī Dhiʾb, from al-Maqburī, from ʿAbd al-Raḥmān ibn Abī Saʿīd, from his father: "We were prevented from praying, at the Battle of the Trench,[5] until after the sunset prayer, well into the night, until we had the fighting averted from us, as referred to in God's word "God averted fighting from the believers. God is Strong and Mighty."[6] God's Emissary called for Bilāl[7] and ordered him to make the call to prayer, and he held the noon prayer, which he led, and it was fine, just as if it had been done at its appointed time. Then he did so for the afternoon prayer and prayed it in the same way, then the sunset prayer in the same way, and then the evening prayer in the same way, too. That was before the passage about the prayer of danger was revealed: "either

1. I.e., toward Mecca, the location of the Kaʿba, the holiest shrine in Islam.
2. I.e., facing away from Mecca.
3. Qurʾan 4:103.
4. The Battle of the Parties (*yawm al-ahzab*) refers to the siege of Medina in 627. The "parties" were those allied forces—Meccans, a Jewish tribe, and a north Arabian tribe—who unsuccessfully laid the siege and after whom Sura 33 of the Qurʾan (al-Ahzab) is named. The battle is more commonly known as the Battle of the Trench (*yawm al-khandaq*) because of the defensive trench dug by Muhammad and his followers [translator's note].
5. See the preceding note.
6. Qurʾan 33:25.
7. Bilal ibn Rabah (d. ca. 640), a freed slave who was one of Muhammad's earliest and most loyal companions. He was also known as the first *muʿadhdhin* (*muezzin*), or one who calls to prayer.

on foot or mounted."[8] So Abū Saʿīd clarified that this occurred before God revealed to the Prophet the verse in which the prayer of danger is mentioned.

The verse in which the prayer of danger is mentioned is God's word "When you travel in the land, it is no sin for you to curtail your prayer, if you perceive a danger that those who disbelieve may do you mischief. Those who disbelieve are a manifest enemy for you."[9] He also said: "When you are among them and lead them in prayer, let one group of them stand with you, and let them take their weapons. Once those praying have prostrated themselves, let them fall to the rear, and let the other group who have not prayed come and pray with you."[1]

Mālik reported to us from Yazīd ibn Rūmān, from Ṣāliḥ ibn Khawwāt, from someone who prayed the prayer of danger together with God's Emissary at the Battle of Dhāt al-Riqāʿ: One group lined up with him while another group faced the enemy. He led those with him in prayer for one bowing, then he straightened up and they completed the prayer themselves and then left and lined up facing the enemy. The other group came and he led them in prayer for the one bowing that remained of his own prayer, and then he sat up in his place and they completed the prayer themselves, and then he led them in saying the peace.

Someone transmitted to us a hadith-report like that of Yazīd ibn Rūmān, having heard ʿAbdallāh ibn ʿUmar ibn Ḥafṣ mention it from his brother ʿUbaydallāh ibn ʿUmar, from al-Qāsim ibn Muḥammad, from Ṣāliḥ ibn Khawwāt, from his father Khawwāt ibn Jubayr, from the Prophet.

This provides an indication of what I have already described in this book: if God's Emissary establishes a practice, and then God creates a new ruling in regard to that practice that abrogates it or an exception that alleviates it somewhat, then God's Emissary will provide another practice by means of which he provides a binding authority that obligates people to move from his old practice to his new subsequent practice. God abrogated the postponement of the prayer until after its appointed time in cases of danger and had them pray it, instead, as God had revealed and in accordance with the practice instituted by His Emissary, at its appointed time. God's Emissary abrogated his practice concerning its postponement, pursuant to the obligation imposed by God in His book, and then God's Emissary prayed it according to his practice, as I have just explained.

Mālik reported to us from Nāfiʿ, from Ibn ʿUmar, I believe from the Prophet, that he mentioned the prayer of danger and said: "If the danger is more intense than that, then pray either on foot or mounted, facing the prayer-direction or otherwise."

Someone reported to us an account similar in import from Ibn Abī Dhiʾb, from al-Zuhrī, from Sālim, from his father, from the Prophet. He did not doubt that it was from his father and that it had been attributed to the Prophet.

So the Practice of God's Emissary indicates what I have already explained: the prayer-direction for the prescribed prayers is always in accordance with

8. Qurʾan 2:239.
9. Qurʾan 4:101.
1. Qurʾan 4:102.

the obligation respecting it except on those occasions when it is not possible to pray toward it, and that is during combat, or while fleeing, and under similar circumstances during which prayer is not possible. In this regard, Prophetic Practice also confirms that one not omit the prayer during its appointed time, and that the prayer be performed in whatever way may be feasible for the one praying.

Concerning Alms

God said: "Perform prayer and pay alms."[2] God also said: "Those performing prayer and paying alms"[3] and "Woe to the worshippers who are heedless of their prayers; who make a show, but withhold assistance."[4] A certain scholar said that this refers to obligatory alms.

God also said: "Take alms from their possessions, by which you might purify them and make them clean, and pray for them. Your prayers are a comfort for them. God is Hearing and Knowing."[5]

This verse is expressed in unrestricted terms, applying to property in general. It is possible to interpret it as pertaining to some kinds of property and not others, however, and Prophetic Practice indicates that alms are in fact due on some kinds of property and not others.

Since property is of different kinds, including livestock, God's Emissary assessed alms on camels and goats and commanded, as far as we have been informed, that one assess cattle in particular, apart from other livestock. Then he assessed them at different amounts, just as God decreed through the words of His Prophet. People had livestock that included horses, donkeys, mules, and other animals, and since God's Emissary did not assess anything from those, and established the practice that no alms be levied on horses, we infer that alms are to be assessed on that from which he took, and from what he commanded to be assessed, and not from other things.

People had produce and crops, too. God's Emissary levied alms on dates and grapes by estimating their amount while on the tree or vine, without distinguishing between them, and he took the tithe from both if they were watered by rain or a spring, and half the tithe if watered manually. Some scholars have levied them on olives, by analogy from dates and grapes. People continue to have many crops other than dates, grapes, and olives: walnuts, almonds, figs, and others. Since God's Emissary did not assess anything against those, and did not command that anyone do so, we infer that the obligation from God concerning alms was applicable to some crops and not to others.

People also used to plant wheat, barley, sorghum, and other varieties of grains as well, and we have learned that God's Emissary levied on wheat, barley, and sorghum. Those before us levied against millet, thin-husked barley, Yemeni wheat, rice, and everything else that people planted and made into provisions, such as bread, wheat flour, barley flour, and ground pulses like chickpeas and lentils, which are thus suitable for bread, gruel, and for eating with bread. All this was done following the precedent of those who went before, and based on analogies from those things on which it is confirmed that God's Emissary levied alms. These are all within the

2. Qur'an 2:43.
3. Qur'an 4:162.
4. Qur'an 107:4–7.
5. Qur'an 9:103.

scope of what he took alms from, since people plant them in order to conserve them as provisions.

People have produce other than this, but God's Emissary did not levy alms on it and neither did anyone after God's Emissary of whom we know. Such things do not belong to the category of items on which he levied alms; they are like garden-cress seeds, psyllium, coriander, safflower seeds, and similar things. One need pay no alms for them, and this fact indicates that alms are assessed against some kinds of produce but not others.

God's Emissary imposed the obligation to pay alms for silver, and the Muslims levied them on gold after him as well, either on the basis of a report from the Prophet that has not reached us or by analogy, on the grounds that gold and silver are the people's medium of exchange, which they accumulate and which they accept as payment for what they buy and sell to each other in the various countries, both before and after the coming of Islam.

People have other metals than those, to wit, copper, iron, and lead. When neither God's Emissary nor anyone after him levied alms on them, we passed them over, too, following precedent. Moreover, one may not analogize in those cases from gold and silver, which are generally recognized as a valid species of payment everywhere, to other metals that are not covered by the same rationale. One need pay no alms for them, and yet it is valid to buy those other metals using gold, silver, and other things, with delayed payment for a defined term, or at a fixed weight.

Sapphires and rubies are worth more than gold and silver, but since God's Emissary did not levy alms on them and did not command anyone else to do so, and neither did anyone after him of whom we know—for they are luxury items and cannot be used at all to set prices for consumable goods because they are not considered a medium of exchange—one does not levy alms on them.

Then there is what a large group have transmitted from God's Emissary concerning alms from livestock, to wit, that he assessed it once a year. God said: "And give its due portion on the day it is harvested"[6] and God's Emissary established the practice that alms be levied on any agricultural produce subject to them, according to God's ruling (sublime His praise), on the day one harvests it, and not at any other time.

He also established the practice that one-fifth be levied on the ore of precious metals, which indicates that it should be done on the day that it is actually mined, and not at some other time.

Sufyān reported to us from al-Zuhrī, from Ibn al-Musayyab and Abū Salamah, from Abū Hurayrah, that God's Emissary said: "One should pay the fifth for the ore of precious metals." If not for the indication from Prophetic Practice, the apparent sense of the Qur'an would be that all types of property are the same and that alms is payable for all of them, not for some rather than others.

6. Qur'an 6:141.

IBN HANBAL
780–855

Ahmad ibn Hanbal, putative founder of the Hanbali legal school, collector of traditions (*hadith*), and composer of several creeds, remains etched in Muslim memory for his refusal to capitulate during the Inquisition (*mihna*) instituted by the caliph al-Ma'mun (r. 813–33).

Ibn Hanbal's father died when he was three, and he was raised in Baghdad by his mother. Though the property he inherited from his father afforded him some degree of independence later in life, Ibn Hanbal was by all accounts a man of meager means with strong renunciant tendencies that appeared in his youth. After completing his basic schooling at about age fifteen, he decided to focus on his religious education, concentrating mainly on the study of traditions. Over the next twenty years or so, while he continued to study in Baghdad, his thirst for knowledge took him as far north as Turkey and as far south as Yemen. Various tales from his travels illustrate his asceticism: he refused aid from family members, often used books or bricks as a pillow, and traveled to many of his destinations on foot. Around 810 he was offered a judgeship but refused it because, like many pious Muslims of his time, he considered the government to be unjust and took pains to avoid any involvement with it.

By the time he was forty, Ibn Hanbal had married and ceased his travels; in Baghdad, he devoted himself to narrating traditions and responding to his students' legal questions. His first marriage produced his son Salih (819–880), who would become a judge, a biographer of his father, and a compiler of his legal responses (*fiqh*); his second marriage produced his son 'Abdallah (828–903), who also compiled his father's legal responses and traditions. Ibn Hanbal supported his family—which included six more children by his concubine—by renting out property he had inherited from his father and by selling material woven by family members.

In 827, the 'Abbasid caliph al-Ma'mun declared the Qur'an to be created rather than eternal, a belief most Muslims did not accept. This declaration initiated a period of early Islamic history known as the Inquisition. What motivated al-Ma'mun's declaration? Perhaps he was convinced that as caliph it was his duty to promulgate orthodox belief as he saw fit. Or his declaration may have been a calculated attempt to remove power from the scholars and concentrate it in the hands of the ruling authorities. If the Qur'an were created, then its pronouncements could not be viewed as binding for all of eternity and the caliph would be able to set aside its commandments.

Initially, al-Ma'mun's proclamation had little effect. It was not until 833 that the caliph ordered the interrogation of scholars to test their adherence to his declaration, thereby inaugurating the fifteen-year Inquisition. Many scholars, including Ibn Hanbal, were questioned by al-Ma'mun's representatives. Subjected to a series of progressively harsher threats, almost all of them publicly accepted the createdness of the Qur'an. Ibn Hanbal and another hadith scholar, Muhammad ibn Nuh, refused to do so and were ordered to appear before al-Ma'mun, who was then at Tarsus (in modern-day Turkey), to be tried. Before they arrived in Turkey, al-Ma'mun died, and both men were ordered back to Baghdad; Ibn Nuh passed away on the journey home.

For two years Ibn Hanbal was imprisoned in Baghdad. Then, after one of his uncles petitioned for his release, he was brought before the new caliph, al-Mu'tasim (r. 833–42), to be questioned by his representatives. For three days he debated with the court interrogators, holding fast to his position. On the third day, the caliph could no longer bear his intransigence and ordered him whipped. After more than thirty lashes, Ibn Hanbal lost consciousness. Eventually he was released and resumed teaching; but when the new caliph, al-Wathiq (r. 842–47), let it be known that he had not been forgotten, he went into hiding.

Al-Wathiq's successor, al-Mutawakkil (r. 847–61), rejected the doctrine of the Qurʾan's createdness and finally ended the Inquisition during the second year of his caliphate. He embraced scholars of hadith and welcomed them to his palace to narrate them. When Ibn Hanbal was invited to court, he realized that he had no choice and begrudgingly attended. Yet he steadfastly refused to enjoy anything the caliph's representatives offered him and managed to avoid meeting with the caliph himself: Ibn Hanbal remained as wary and distrustful of rulers as ever. Nonetheless, once he returned home his family was lavished with gifts from the caliph, and many readily accepted this largesse despite his staunch disapproval. Dismayed by their behavior, Ibn Hanbal is said to have prayed in a room apart from the rest of his family. He died in 855, and his funeral prayer in Baghdad was attended by thousands—a sign of his enduring inspiration to Muslims of his day.

Ibn Hanbal is perhaps best known for *Musnad*, a collection of traditions compiled by his son ʿAbdallah. He also composed several creeds, setting forth the articles of faith with clarity but without theological speculation. For Ibn Hanbal, almost all theological and legal matters could be resolved by a literal reading of the Qurʾan and hadith. Whatever descriptions or attributes of God these two sources presented were to be accepted on faith and not questioned.

It is unlikely that Ibn Hanbal intended to create a legal school: at times, he hesitated to let people record his responses to legal questions for fear that they would rely on these rather than closely examining the Qurʾan and traditions. Furthermore, many Muslim scholars have questioned Ibn Hanbal's stature as a jurist, preferring to regard him as a dedicated narrator of traditions. They note his assertion that most legal questions required nothing more than close examination of the tradition literature, his tendency to avoid issuing a ruling when traditions were in conflict, and the absence in his work of clear differentiation among legal categories, such as prohibited versus reprehensible acts.

Nevertheless, his legal responses were collected by his sons and students, and they formed the basis upon which a school that carried his name grew. An example of his hadith-based legal reasoning may be found in the following passage. Here he tackles questions that were raised about the legal validity of marriages contracted in a wide variety of circumstances.

PRONOUNCING GLOSSARY

ʿĀʾisha: *ah´-i-shuh*
ʿAbd Allāh ibn Aḥmad ibn Ḥanbal: *ab-dul-lah´ ibn ah´-mad* (heavy *h*) *ibn han´-bal* (heavy *h*)
ʿAmr ibn Dīnār: *ahmr ibn dee-nahr´*
ʿidda: *id´-duh*
ʿUmar ibn al-Khaṭṭāb: *oh´-mar ibn al-chaht-tahb´* (guttural *ch*)
Abū Bakr ibn ʿAbd Allāh: *a-boo bakr´ ibn ab-dul-lah´*
al-ʿAbbās: *al-ab-bas´*
al-Ḥakam: *al-ha´-kam* (heavy *h*)
amīr: *a-meer´*
amṣār: *am-sahr´*
bikr: *bikr*
ḥadīth: *ha-deeth´* (heavy *h*)
Ḥammād ibn Zaid: *ham-mad´* (heavy *h*) *ibn zayd*
Hudya ibn Khālid: *hud´-yuh ibn cha´-lid* (guttural *ch*)
Hushaim: *hoo-shaym´*
Ḥusain: *hoo-sayn´* (heavy *h*)
Maimūna bint al-Ḥārith: *may-moo´-nuh bint al-ha´-rith* (heavy *h*)
qāḍī: *qah´-dee*
Shuʿba: *shuh´-buh*
sulṭān: *sul-tahn´*
thayyib: *thay´-yib*
walī: *wa-lee´*

FROM THE BOOK OF MARRIAGE

[*What Happens When*] *a Man Marries a Woman Without a* Walī *and Who Gives a Woman in Marriage When She Has No* Walī

ʿAbd Allāh said, "I heard my father say, about a man who marries a woman without a *walī*,[1] in the presence only of witnesses, 'That is not valid (*lā yajūzu*).'"

Someone said to my father while I was listening, "Does the governor (*amīr*) or the judge (*qāḍī*) have the most right to give [a woman] in marriage?"

He said, "The judge, because he is in charge of sexual relations and legal judgments."

I asked my father about a woman who entrusts her matter to a Muslim man who thereby gives her in marriage. But she has brothers and agnates.

He said, "The marriage contract is concluded over again by her brothers or agnates."

I asked my father about a man who is one of the witnesses to a woman's marriage. Then later [after a certain period of time] the woman comes to him and says, "My husband has divorced me and my *ʿidda*[2] is over." Can the witness accept what she says and marry her [himself]?

My father said, "If he acted as a witness to her marriage with a *walī* and [other] witnesses present, then she comes and says, 'My husband divorced me,' he should inquire about her husband's divorcing her. Then if he can be certain that her husband has divorced her and that with regard to what she has claimed about the end of her *ʿidda* she is telling the truth, [he can marry her]. If, however, he turns out to be her nearest *walī*, in order to marry her he must arrange to have another man act as her *walī* and give her in marriage to him in the presence of witnesses. Further, he must award her a fair dower."

I asked my father about a secret marriage. "Do you think it is a [valid] marriage contract? If there are two witnesses and a *walī*, is it secret?"

He said, "It is preferable (*yustaḥabbu*) that a marriage be made public and not be secret, that it be with a *walī*, and that musical instruments (*duff*[3]) be played at it, so that it becomes well known and acknowledged."

I asked my father about a man who is a woman's *walī*, and puts her matter into the hands of a second man, and the second man uses that authority (*wilāya*) to marry her himself with the woman's consent. Then the marriage takes place. "Do you consider this marriage valid (*ṣaḥīḥ*)?"

My father said, "As long as he really was her nearest *walī* and there was no one nearer than he, and he gave his authority as her guardian to a second man who married her with her consent, the marriage is valid."

I said, "What if there was a *walī* nearer than he?"

He said, "Then the nearest *walī* has the right to give her in marriage with her consent."

TRASLATED BY Susan A. Spectorsky. All bracketed additions are the translator's.

1. A legal representative of a woman who has never married. According to most Muslim legal schools, the absence of the *walī*'s approval makes the marriage impermissible.

2. The waiting period of three menstrual cycles required of divorced or widowed women before they can remarry.

3. A frame drum.

[My father said,] "There is no disagreement, about the *thayyib*:[4] she is given in marriage only with her permission."

I said to my father, "What about the *bikr*?"[5]

He said, "There are those who disagree concerning the matter [of the *bikr*]."

I said, "What do you prefer?"

He said, "Her *walī* should consult her. Then if she grants permission, he can give her in marriage."

I said, "But if she does not grant it?"

He said, "If her father is [her *walī*], and she has not reached seven years of age, then her father's giving her in marriage is valid, and she has no option. But if she has reached her ninth year, neither her father nor anyone else should give her in marriage without her permission. [As for] the orphan who has not reached nine years of age, if someone other than her father is giving her in marriage, I do not like him to do so until she reaches nine years of age. When she is nine, she should be consulted. Then if she grants her permission, she has no option thereafter."

I asked my father about a woman who gives herself in marriage to a man, in the presence of two witnesses during a period in which her *walī* is absent. Then her *walī* writes that what she has done for herself is valid. "Is that permissible (*hal yaṣluḥu dhālika*)?"

He said, "The marriage contract should be concluded again."

I asked him about a woman who orders a certain man to give her daughter in marriage, and he does so.

He said, "The marriage contract should be concluded again."

I said, "[What if] the girl is five years old?"

He said, "I do not approve of such a marriage. Only her father gives an underage girl in marriage; when he does so, the marriage is valid. Only her father should give a girl in marriage, until she reaches nine years of age and can be consulted about herself. Then, if she gives her permission, her agnates may give her in marriage: her brother, her paternal uncle, his son. But if she has no agnates, then the judge (*qāḍī*) [gives her in marriage]."

I said to my father, "But if her agnates refuse to give her in marriage?"

He said, "They should not do that. [But if they do,] she brings her situation to the [attention] of the judge."

The Orphan Is Consulted about Herself

I asked my father about a minor girl who has neither a father nor a brother, but who does have a closely related paternal cousin. He goes on a pilgrimage, and while he is away, her father's paternal cousin gives her in marriage to an underage youth whose father has accepted the marriage on his behalf. Then her own paternal cousin returns from the pilgrimage and neither validates the marriage nor declares it invalid. "What do you think about this marriage? Is it valid or not? And does this young girl, when she comes of age, have an option or not?"

My father dictated to me, and he said, "The orphan is not given in marriage until she has reached nine years of age; then, when she is nine years

4. A woman considered mature enough to handle her own affairs; the term is normally used to refer to a woman who was previously married.

5. A virgin.

old, she should be consulted. If she grants permission, later on, she has no option [to turn down the marriage]. If they want to make this particular girl's marriage valid, she should be left until she reaches the age of nine, and then she should be consulted. Her closely related paternal cousin has more right to give her in marriage than a more distant agnate. Her *walī* can give her in marriage when she has reached nine years of age, but at that age she has the option [to turn down the marriage]."

I asked my father about a man who fornicates with a daughter of his wife's.

He said, "His wife is not thereby forbidden to him, but he does not have sexual intercourse with her until the *ʿidda* of the daughter with whom he has fornicated has ended."[6]

I asked my father about a girl who is given in marriage by her father when she is a minor and then marries another husband when she comes of age.

He said, "The couple are separated, and she is returned to the husband to whom her father gave her in marriage."

I said to my father, "What if the second husband has had intercourse with her?"

He said, "She receives a compensatory dower."

I said to my father, "Suppose she has had a child by him?"

He said, "The child belongs to him, but she is returned to her first husband."

I asked my father about a man who says to another, "Give me in marriage to your daughter." Then he does so, without witnesses or proof, but [in this case] her *walī* is her father.

My father said, "I prefer that a marriage be witnessed."

I said to my father, "If it is not witnessed, do you think it is invalid (*ḥarām*)?"

He said, "I prefer that it be witnessed."

My father related to me and said, "Hushaim related to us, he said, 'Ḥusain informed us on the authority of Abū Bakr b. ʿAbd Allāh who said, "ʿUmar b. al-Khaṭṭāb wrote to the *amṣār*[7] [that] any woman who marries her slave[8] or marries without proof (*bayyina*) [provided by witnesses] and without a *walī* should be beaten, and she and her spouse separated."'"

[My father continued,] "Hudya b. Khālid related to us: he said, 'Ḥammād b. Zaid related to us on the authority of ʿAmr b. Dīnār: he said, "A woman got married without a *walī*, and ʿUmar refused [to accept the validity of] her marriage."'"

I asked my father about the *ḥadīth* of Maimūna bt. al-Ḥārith, who put her matter into al-ʿAbbās's hands, and then al-ʿAbbās gave her in marriage to the Prophet. "Is this *ḥadīth* sound?"

My father said, "Shuʿba said [that] al-Ḥakam heard only four *ḥadīths* on the authority of Miqsam, and this was not among them." My father said, "This *ḥadīth* has no basis."

6. Ibn Hanbal's answer here is contrary to all his other statements on this kind of question—one about a situation in which a woman becomes a man's mother by marriage. * * * However, it does fit in with Malik's view, and Shafiʿi's, that unlawful sexual relations do not forbid lawful ones [translator's note; the Medinan Malik ibn Anas (ca. 715–795) and Muhammad ibn Idris al-Shafiʿi (767–820; see above) gave their names to Islamic legal schools].

7. Garrison cities; here, probably Kufa and Basra in Iraq.

8. A woman cannot manumit a slave on the condition that he marry her [translator's note].

What Happens If a Maternal Uncle Gives [His Niece] in Marriage

I asked my father about a minor girl given in marriage by her maternal uncle. After her husband has had intercourse with her, the couple are informed the marriage is improper (*fāsid*), and they are separated. "Is the girl due a dower? Is it lawful for the judicial authority *(sulṭān)* to give permission for her to be given in marriage to this [young] man when she has matured, or reached fifteen years of age? Or does he write to her *walīs* wherever they are? At what point is she of age if she does not menstruate? Is it lawful for her, once she has matured, or reached the [usual] age of maturity to give her maternal uncle permission to give her in marriage, if she has no other *walī*? If the couple are separated, does she wait an ʿ*idda*? If so, [for how] long?"

My father dictated to me, and he said, "If her husband has had intercourse with her, and if her maternal uncle has placed her in a situation of having a husband who is her peer, and if she has been given the full dower, then what I should like [to see done] in this [situation] is that her marriage contract be concluded again by an agnate *walī* and that she receive a dower on the basis of there having been intercourse when they conclude the marriage contract again and [decide on] a new dower.

"The point at which a girl comes of age is at the onset of menstruation, which we have called her coming of age due to menstruation.

"If she has no agnate *walī* present, her agnates should be written to, so they can give permission for her to be given in marriage, unless they are so far away, it is too hard to get in touch with them. What we have heard is that a marriage contract is concluded by a *walī*. If there is no *walī*, the judge *(sulṭān)* is the *walī* of the woman who has no other.

"A minor girl is given in marriage only by her father. Once she has reached nine years of age and can have a *walī* other than her father, she should be consulted. If she gives her consent, it is lawful for her *walī* to give her in marriage.

"If the couple are separated, she must wait an ʿ*idda*. [Regardless of] whether they are separated because the marriage is invalid, or it is not invalid—so they [are separated because they] are divorced, or they are separated for another reason, such as foster-relationship—she waits the ʿ*idda* of the divorcée. If she menstruates, her ʿ*idda* is three menstrual periods; if she does not, three months.

"Proof that a girl should be consulted when she has reached nine years of age is what is transmitted about the Prophet; that he had intercourse with ʿĀʾisha[9] when she had reached nine years of age."

When Maintenance Is Due a Woman

I heard my father say, "If a man marries a woman who withholds herself from him, she does not receive maintenance. If, however, he withholds himself from her, then he must give her maintenance. If he marries her when she is a minor, she does not receive maintenance until she is nine years of age. This is the age at which she may engage in sexual relations, because the Prophet had intercourse with ʿĀʾisha when she was nine.

9. The favorite of the Prophet's wives after the death of his first wife, Khadija.

"If a girl is an orphan, then gives permission for her marriage, she has no further option. But she should not be given in marriage until she is consulted."

If a Father Gives His Underage Daughter in Marriage, Can She Opt?

I asked my father about a man who gives his underage daughter in marriage. "Can she opt [to turn down the marriage] when she is of age?"

He said. "She cannot exercise this option if her father gave her in marriage. If she could, then ʿĀʾisha could have with regard to the Prophet, because the Prophet married her when she was six or seven years old, had intercourse with her when she was nine, and died when she was eighteen."

I asked my father about a man who gives his mature daughter in marriage without her consent. "Is the marriage valid (*yathbutu*)?"

He said, "There is disagreement on this question. I prefer that he consult her, and if she is silent, that is her consent. [However], the Madinese say her father can give her in marriage without consulting her."

I heard my father asked about a man who gives his minor son in marriage. [He was asked] whose responsibility the dower is.

He said, "The father's, if he accepts the responsibility. If he does not, the son is responsible for it."

Someone said to my father, "But the son in this case is a minor!"

He said, "I do not like it; a father should not conclude such a marriage."

I asked my father about a woman who frees her husband from the obligation of her dower, except for a pilgrimage he is to undertake on her behalf. Then she changes her mind.

He said, "She can change her mind about her dower."

AL-QAYRAWANI
922–996

Qayrawan, located in modern-day Tunisia, was a thriving intellectual and cultural center of medieval North Africa. Ibn Abi Zayd al-Qayrawani, who was named for the city of his birth, showed early promise as a scholar of Islam. His contemporaries called him "the young Malik," equating him with the renowned legal scholar Malik ibn Anas (ca. 715–795). Later biographers memorialized Ibn Abi Zayd as one of the six most important scholars, whose collective efforts prevented the Maliki school from vanishing. He led the Maliki school of Qayrawan during his lifetime and was likely a wealthy man; he was known for his generosity toward and concern for his colleagues and students.

Ibn Abi Zayd lived through a time of disruption and change. In 909, roughly a decade before his birth, the Aghlabid dynasty, which had ruled over Qayrawan and most of North Africa for the past century, was overwhelmed by forces loyal to ʿAbdallah al-Mahdi (d. 934). This victory, which inaugurated the Fatimid dynasty, marked the beginning of a period of severely reduced rights for the Malikis. The

Fatimids were Ismaʿili Shiʿis—members of a sect who believed that Ismaʿil, the son of the sixth Imam Jaʿfar al-Sadiq, and his sons should have held the office of imam—who differed significantly from the Sunni Malikis in many aspects of law and theology. As the Fatimids asserted their authority over Qayrawan and throughout North Africa, they stripped the Malikis of all governorships and judgeships, forbade the teaching of Maliki law, and denied the Malikis the right to issue legal opinions (in Arabic, *fatwas*). Further, within areas under their control they imposed Ismaʿili ritual law. Consequently, public ritual practices dear to the Malikis, such as the communal night prayer of Ramadan (*tarawih*), were banned. Other practices, like the call to prayer, were changed to bring them in line with Ismaʿili law.

Most of these restrictions lasted until 944, when a revolt begun by Abu Yazid (d. 947), leader of the Kharijis (a Muslim political and theological group formed in the seventh century that was known for its strict and puritanical views), and joined by the Maliki populace of Qayrawan threatened to bring the Fatimid empire to its knees. Although the revolt ultimately failed, the Fatimids realized that their rule was precarious and removed all restrictions on the Malikis except those relating to public rituals.

Ibn Abi Zayd addressed a range of topics, as his writings included creedal treatises and texts offering moral admonishments, but was best known for his legal works, specifically his *Rarities and Addenda* and his *Treatise on Law.* The former, completed during the last sixteen years of Ibn Abi Zayd's life, is a comprehensive encyclopedia (the modern-day edition of the work runs to fifteen large volumes) cataloging the differences of legal opinions held by early Maliki scholars on a host of issues. The *Rarities* is significant for gathering these diverse views from multiple sources and preserving them for succeeding generations of scholars.

His *Treatise*, excerpted below, is a concise handbook of Maliki law (*fiqh*). It begins with a very brief creed, summarizing the fundamentals of faith, and then treats the basics of ritual law, such as how to prepare for and perform prayers. It next addresses areas of nonritual law, such as marriage, contracts, and the rules of inheritance. The *Treatise* won immediate acceptance and acclaim in Maliki circles from Baghdad to Spain and soon was generating its own commentaries.

According to the *Treatise*'s introduction, Ibn Abi Zayd composed it for the teaching of young children, but it appealed to a far wider audience as a concise digest of Maliki law. For generations it remained a staple on the syllabi of religious schools throughout sub-Saharan Africa.

As you read the following passage, you will doubtless note its succinctness. Such concision is typical of all Islamic legal handbooks regardless of the legal school producing the work. If you memorize this selection, you will have the Maliki law on marriage and divorce on the tip of your tongue.

PRONOUNCING GLOSSARY

dīnār: *dee-nar´*
ʿiddah: *id´-duh*
k̲arʾ: *qahr*
k̲ur-ān: *qor-ahn´*
mudd: *mud*
t̲h̲ayyib: *thay´-yib*
walī: *wa-lee´*

FROM TREATISE ON LAW

Chapter I

Marriage, Divorce, Return, Injurious Assimilation, Vows of Continence, Actions of Imprecation, Release and Fosterage

CONSTITUENTS OF MARRIAGE

1. There can be no marriage, without: (a) a matrimonial guardian; (b) a dower; (c) two irreproachable witnesses.

2. If witnesses are not called to the contract, consummation should not take place till two witnesses have been called.

DOWER

3. The minimum dower is a quarter of a dīnār.[1]

RIGHT OF CONSTRAINT

4. A father may give his virgin daughter in marriage without her consent, even if she has attained puberty; but if he pleases, he may consult her.

5. Persons other than the father, (such as a testamentary guardian[2] etc.), may not give a virgin in marriage until she attains puberty and gives her consent.

6. A virgin's consent is silence.

7. Neither the father or any other can marry a woman who is not a virgin (thayyib) without her consent.

8. A woman (thayyib) must give her consent by speech.

9. A woman cannot marry without the consent (a) of her matrimonial guardian; or (b) responsible member of her family, like a man of her tribe; or (c) of the governing power.

10. There is difference of opinion whether a mean woman[3] may authorise a stranger to act as her matrimonial guardian.

11. With regard to precedence among matrimonial guardians, a son comes before a father; and a father before a brother; and generally a nearer agnate before one more remote.

12. But if a more remote agnate give the woman in marriage, the marriage will stand.

13. A testamentary guardian may give in marriage any boy who is under his guardianship.

14. He cannot marry a girl under puberty, unless where the father instructs him with regard to her marriage.

15. Maternal relations are not to be regarded as matrimonial guardians, but only relations through males.

TRANSLATED BY Alexander David Russell and Abdullah al-Ma'mūn Suhrawardy.

1. A dinar was a gold coin with the standard weight of 4.25 grams.
2. A person named in a will or deed as guardian of a minor.
3. A woman not much sought after, e.g., of humble birth, poor, a freedwoman, etc. [translator's note, edited].

COMPETITION AMONG SUITORS

16. A man shall not demand in marriage a woman previously sought by another; (just as he may not outbid the bid offered by another).

17. This applies where the first suitor's demand has been favourably received, and the parties have come to terms.

ILLEGAL MARRIAGES

18. The law forbids (1) a marriage of privation; this occurs where one bride's person is made another bride's dower:[4]

19. (2) a marriage without dower:

20. (3) an usufructuary marriage,[5] i.e. to endure till a certain date:

21. (4) a marriage during the woman's retreat:[6]

22. (5) anything which involves risk in the contract or in the dower:

23. (6) a marriage with a dower consisting of anything the sale of which would be unlawful.

24. A marriage invalid by reason of the dower falls to be annulled before consummation; after consummation, it will stand and the wife will be entitled to the customary dower.

25. A marriage invalid on account of some flaw in the contract, is to be annulled even after consummation; and the wife will be entitled to the dower stipulated.

26. A prohibition against marriage within the forbidden degrees will be established thereby, just as by a valid marriage.

27. But a marriage of this nature will not suffice to legalise for her first husband a woman trebly divorced;[7]

28. Nor will it render lawful the co-habitation of the spouses.

FORBIDDEN DEGREES

29. God forbids marriage (a) with seven classes of females on the ground of consanguinity, (b) with seven on the grounds of fosterage and affinity.

30. It is laid down in the Kur-ān—"Forbidden for you are your mothers, daughters, sisters, maternal aunts, paternal aunts, brother's daughters, sister's daughters":[8] these are prohibited on the ground of consanguinity.

31. As to those forbidden on the ground of fosterage or affinity, the passage in the Kur-ān is: "Your mothers who suckled you, and your foster-sisters, and the mothers of your wives, step-daughters that are in your laps (i. e. in your charge) through wives of yours to whom you have come in;[9] but if you have not come in to them, then there is no sin upon you: and the wives of your sons whom you have begotten:

32. And you shall not bring together (in marriage) two sisters, except what has occurred in the past."

4. Offering to marry someone else's daughter without a dower in exchange for offering one's own daughter in marriage to him without a dower: this is forbidden, because a marriage without a dower is forbidden.

5. Marriages that last for a fixed period of time; these are allowed by Shiʿi but not Sunni legal schools.

6. The mandated waiting period following the end of a marriage to ensure that a woman is not pregnant.

7. A husband who has said to his wife "I divorce you" three times cannot remarry her until she has consummated a fully legal marriage to another man. Consequently, a thrice-divorced woman whose marriage to a new husband is consummated but then annulled for a flaw in the marriage contract cannot remarry her original husband. An annulled marriage, even if consummated, does not fulfill the legal mandate.

8. Qur'an 4:23.

9. That is, with whom you have had sexual relations.

33. Elsewhere the Kur-ān says: "Do not marry women whom your fathers have married."[1]

34. Also the Prophet has forbidden on the ground of fosterage any woman who would be forbidden on the ground of consanguinity:

35. Or the bringing together in marriage of a woman and her paternal or maternal aunt.

36. On a man marrying a woman, she becomes prohibited for his ascendants and descendants, by virtue of the contract, without consummation: and her mother, grandmother etc., become unlawful for the husband:

37. But her daughters are not prohibited for him, unless the marriage has been consummated, or dalliance has taken place in wedlock or on the supposition thereof.

38. Illicit relations will not raise a prohibition against marriage with women whom it would otherwise be lawful for a man to marry.

MIXED MARRIAGES

39. God has forbidden intercourse with unbelieving women; but marriage with a scriptural woman[2] is permitted.

NON-FORBIDDEN UNIONS

40. A man may marry a daughter whom his father's wife has borne to another man; and a woman may marry a son whom her father's wife has borne to another man.

POLYGAMY

41. It is lawful for a man to marry four free Muslim or scriptural women: but let him observe justice among his wives.

HUSBAND'S DUTIES TOWARDS WIVES

42. He must give them maintenance and lodging according to his means;

43. But a wife's right to maintenance will only commence from consummation, or such time as the husband has been invited to consummate the marriage, the wife also being capable of intercourse.

MARRIAGE BY DELEGATION

44. A marriage by delegation is lawful: this occurs where the parties enter into the contract without mentioning the dower.[3]

45. The husband is not entitled to consummate the marriage until he has assigned the woman a dower.

46. If he appoints her the customary dower, the marriage is binding on her.

47. If the dower which he names is less than the customary amount, she has the option of revoking the marriage.

48. If she dislikes the dower, they are to be separated, unless the husband induces her to acquiesce, or assigns her the customary dower; in which case the marriage binds her.

1. Qur'an 4:22.
2. That is, a Jewish or Christian woman.
3. Although the dower is initially unspecified, all parties understand that it will meet societal standards.

APOSTASY

49. Where one of the spouses apostatises, the marriage is annulled by repudiation;[4] or, as other authorities maintain, without repudiation.

CONVERSION

50. When two unbelieving spouses are converted to Islam, their marriage is maintained.

51. If one only embraces Islam, their marriage is annulled without repudiation.

52. If the woman is converted, the husband is the person best entitled to her, in case he also embraces the true faith during her retreat.

53. If the man is converted, while the woman remains a scriptural woman, his right to his wife continues.

54. If she was a pagan, and enters Islam immediately after him, they remain husband and wife: if, however, her conversion be delayed, she becomes separated from her husband.

55. When a polytheist with more than four wives enters Islam, let him choose four and separate from the rest.

PERPETUAL IMPEDIMENTS

56. A perpetual prohibition against marriage arises: (1) When a man prosecutes an action of imprecation[5] against his wife;

57. (2) When a man marries a woman during her retreat, and intercourse takes place during the retreat.

THINGS FORBIDDEN

58. One woman may not be given in marriage by another woman, nor by a non-Muslim man.

59. It is not permissible for a man to marry a woman with intent to render her lawful for another man by whom she has been irrevocably repudiated; and such a marriage will not render her lawful for the former husband.

MARRIAGE ON PILGRIMAGE

60. It is not lawful for a man who has donned the pilgrim's garb to marry, or to contract marriage on behalf of another.

MARRIAGE DURING ILLNESS

61. A marriage contracted by a man during sickness is unlawful and falls to be annulled.

62. If consummation has taken place, the wife will be entitled to dower out of the disposable third in preference to his legatees.[6]

63. But she will have no right of inheritance.

64. If a sick man divorces his wife he is bound thereby; but she is entitled to share in his succession, if he dies of the same complaint.

4. The pronouncement of divorce.
5. Accusation of adultery.
6. Islamic law allows a man to distribute up to a third of his wealth as he sees fit. The remaining two-thirds must be distributed according to the rules of inheritance.

REPUDIATION

65. A man who has repudiated his wife by a triple repudiation, may not resume cohabitation with her, until she has married another husband.

66. It is heretical for a man to pronounce a triple repudiation in a single utterance; but, if it be done, it will bind the husband.

67. Repudiation in accordance with tradition is permitted.

68. A repudiation is in accordance with tradition when (a) the man repudiates his wife during a period of purity intervening between her menstrual courses; (b) when he has not approached her during that period; (c) it must be a single repudiation, and (d) one repudiation ought not to be followed by another before the expiry of the retreat resulting from the first.

69. The husband may take back a wife who menstruates so long as she has not entered upon her third monthly course.

70. If she is not menstruating, or has changed her way of life, he may repudiate her at any time when he pleases.

71. The rule is the same with regard to a pregnant woman.

72. She can be taken back by her husband at any time before childbirth.

73. A woman observing retreat by months can be taken back at any time before the retreat expires.

74. The word k̲arʾ (occurring in the K̲ur-ān)[7] has the meaning of the interval between two courses.

75. It is forbidden for a man to repudiate his wife during her courses; if he does so, it binds him; but he will be constrained to take her back so long as the retreat has not expired.

76. As for a wife with whom he has not cohabited, he may repudiate her whenever he pleases.

77. A single repudiation separates the woman from the man.

78. A triple repudiation makes relations between them unlawful, except after her marriage to another husband.

79. Whoever says to his wife, "You are repudiated", pronounces a single repudiation, unless he intended more than that.

RELEASE

80. Release[8] is an irrevocable repudiation, (even though the word "repudiation" may not have been employed), in which the wife gives a husband something in consideration of which he relinquishes his right over her.

FORMULAS OF REPUDIATION

81. When a man says to his wife, "You are repudiated finally", this is a triple repudiation, whether consummation has occurred or not.

82. If the man says, "You are free", or "You are single", or "You are prohibited", or "The rope is on your back", this is regarded as a triple divorce where consummation has occurred.

83. In the case of a wife with whom he has not cohabited regard is to be had to the husband's intention.

7. Qur'an 2:228.

8. A divorce initiated by the wife.

RIGHTS OF REPUDIATED WIVES

84. A woman repudiated before consummation is entitled to half the dower.

85. A woman who has been previously married may, however, waive her claim.

86. If the bride be a virgin, the right to waive her claim rests with her father.

87. When a man repudiates a wife, he ought to give her something by way of compensation; he is not, however, compelled to do so.

88. There is no occasion for compensation where (a) consummation has not occurred, and a dower has been assigned to the woman; nor (b) in the case of a release.

RIGHTS OF WIVES ON DEATH OF HUSBAND

89. Where the husband dies without having assigned a dower to his wife, and without having cohabited with her, she will be entitled to a share in his inheritance, but not to dower.

90. If consummation has occurred, the wife is entitled to the customary dower, unless she had agreed to something definite.

GROUNDS OF OPTION

91. A woman may be rejected on account of insanity, elephantiasis, white leprosy, and disease of the genital organs.

92. If the man consummates the marriage not being aware of the defect, he must pay the dower, but may recover it from her father or from her brother, in case it is a brother who has married her.

93. But if she is given in marriage by a walī[9] who is not one of her near relations, the husband can recover nothing from the walī; and the woman is entitled only to a fourth of a dīnār.

94. Where the bridegroom is impotent, he is allowed a year's delay: if he consummates the marriage, well and good; if not, the woman is entitled to a separation, if she pleases.

HUSBAND MISSING

95. Where a husband is missing, a delay of four years is allowed dating from the day when the matter is brought before the court, and the termination of the search for him.

96. The woman shall observe a retreat of the same duration as after a decease; thereafter she may marry if she pleases.

97. His succession will not fall to be distributed, until the expiry of such a period as would transcend the possible limits of his life.

RETREAT

98. A woman may not be sought in marriage during her ʿiddah;[1] but there is no harm in suggestions made by complimentary speeches.

9. Guardian (Arabic).
1. Her "retreat" (see n. 6, p. 213).

RESIDENCE WITH BRIDES

99. When a man marries a virgin, he may stay with her for seven days, without (having to compensate) his other wives.[2] In the case of a non-virgin, he may remain three days.

REPUDIATION BY A MINOR ETC.

100. A husband who is under age cannot repudiate his wife.

101. (a) A wife to whom the husband has given the right of repudiating herself, or (b) one to whom he has given the option of divorce, may exercise the right so long as the meeting of the parties is not broken up.

102. The husband may in the case of a wife, made mistress of her own repudiation, deny (having intended) anything beyond a single divorce.

103. A woman given the choice of her own repudiation, can only pronounce a triple repudiation, nor the husband pretend that such was not his intention.

VOW OF CONTINENCE

104. A vow of continence occurs when a man swears to discontinue relations with his wife for over four months.

105. He will not be divorced from her, until after expiry of the period allowed in the case of such vows, (which is four months), and a summons from the judge.

INJURIOUS ASSIMILATION

106. Whoever addresses an injurious assimilation[3] to his wife, must cease marital relations with her until he has made expiation.

107. (Expiation may be made) by freeing a Muslim slave, free from defect, in the ownership of whom no others are partners, and who is not already partly manumitted.

108. If the husband cannot accomplish this, he may fast for two months in succession;

109. Or, if he is unable to do that, he must feed sixty poor persons, giving them two *mudds*[4] each.

110. He ought not to have intercourse with his wife, by night or by day, until the expiation has been completed: but if he should have intercourse with her, let him ask pardon of God.

111. If the intercourse has taken place after he has begun the expiation, by feeding the poor or fasting, let him begin the expiation over again.

112. There is no objection to manumitting as expiation for an injurious assimilation, (a) an one-eyed slave, or (b) a slave below puberty.

113. But it is more commendable to pray and fast according to our view.

ACTION OF IMPRECATION

114. An action of imprecation occurs (a) where a husband repudiates the child with which his wife is pregnant, on the ground of marital relations not having preceded; or (b) where he avers having found her *in flagrante delicto*.

2. A husband is required to spend equal nights with his wives but is granted an exception when taking a new wife.

3. The act of equating one's wife to a family member with whom marriage is forbidden (e.g., a mother), intending to cut off marital relations with her.

4. *Mudd* is a dry measure equivalent to about 19 ounces [translator's note].

115. There is difference of opinion with regard to allowing an action of imprecation merely upon grounds of suspicion.

116. After separation by action of imprecation the parties may not remarry.

117. The husband begins, declaring four times, "I testify by God etc.": then a fifth time, he pronounces an imprecation upon himself, in case he has spoken falsely. The wife then declares her innocence four times; and the fifth time, she invokes the wrath of God. Thus it is prescribed in the Kur-ān.[5]

RELEASE

118. A wife may procure her release from her husband, by surrendering her dower, or more or less than her dower.

119. An exception is made where the release is arranged to the woman's detriment: in that case she receives back what she has surrendered and the release is nevertheless binding on the husband.

120. Release involves irrevocable repudiation, (precluding cohabitation); unless in case of a new marriage being entered into with the woman's consent.

FOSTERAGE

121. An impediment from fosterage will arise when the woman's milk has found its way into the child's system, during the first two years of infancy.

122. A single act of suckling will suffice to create the impediment.

123. Suckling after expiry of the first two years of infancy will not have this effect, unless when it has taken place within a month, or as some authorities say, a couple of months, from the expiry of the two years.

124. Where a child has been weaned within the first two years of infancy, so as to have become independent of milk, and capable of subsisting on food, an act of suckling thereafter will not create the impediment.

125. Milk entering the child's system, either by the mouth or the nose, will create the impediment.

126. When a woman has suckled a male child, her daughters, and her husband's daughters, whether previously or subsequently begotten, are the sisters of the suckling.

127. But a brother of the suckling may marry the foster-mother's daughters.

5. Qur'an 24:6–9.

THE INTELLECTUAL ELABORATION OF THE CLASSICAL SYNTHESIS

KALAM: THEOLOGY

ABU HANIFA
699–767

Abu Hanifa al-Nuʿman is one of the four classical scholars whose name designates a major Sunni school of law. The Hanafi school remains dominant in Central and South Asia, though its historic roots lie well to the west. Born to a wealthy family in Kufa, Iraq, a center of intellectual activity in the Muslim world, Abu Hanifa spent most of his life there. Not simply a scholar, he ran a business that produced and sold silks and he was known for spending liberally on his students and those in need. Early in his career Abu Hanifa made a name for himself as a theologian and soon attracted a circle of students. He became impatient with theological disputations, however, finding them divisive and of little value, and he therefore refocused his efforts and attention on the study of law. Abu Hanifa spent eighteen years as the principal pupil of the Kufan jurist Hammad ibn Abi Sulayman (d. 737), and upon Hammad's death, he took leadership of his mentor's circle, becoming an independent teacher. As a sign of respect and esteem for his teacher, Abu Hanifa named his eldest son after him.

Eighth-century Iraq was not a peaceful place, and Abu Hanifa lived during a time of considerable political turmoil, a witness to the decline of the Umayyads (661–750) and the ascension of the ʿAbbasids (750–1258). While he tried to avoid taking political positions, his intellectual stature did not make neutrality easy. He fled Kufa during the end of Umayyad rule and sought refuge in Mecca, having been flogged for refusing a high administrative post offered by the Umayyad governor of Kufa. He returned to Kufa once the ʿAbbasids came to power but would not accept a judgeship offered by the second ʿAbbasid caliph, al-Mansur (r. 754–75). Perhaps for this second refusal, Abu Hanifa was imprisoned sometime after 762 in the newly created capital, Baghdad, where he died in 767.

Abu Hanifa remains best known as a jurist. While no legal works from his own hand survive, his thought is preserved in the writings of two of his students, Abu Yusuf (ca. 729–798) and al-Shaybani (ca. 750–805); both men were essential to the formation of the Hanafi school. Abu Hanifa's legal thought is more systematic and more speculative than that of his contemporary, Malik ibn Anas (ca. 715–795). Willing to consider legal problems that had yet to occur, he attempted to subsume these probabilities under existing legal texts. Though he has often been accused of asserting his own opinion and ignoring relevant traditions, the charge is unfounded. Hanafi law, like that of other schools, allowed a jurist to put forward his own opinion, but not without textual anchors. Abu Hanifa's standard for accepting traditions for legal purposes was stricter than that of other scholars, however. Unlike many of his peers, he restricted the use of traditions with only a single chain of narrators as lacking in probative value.

A number of works are attributed to Abu Hanifa in his early capacity as a theologian. With the exception of his *Epistle* to ʿUthman al-Batti, a Basran jurist, the authorship of these texts remains disputed. Yet scholars agree that most do accurately reflect his theological ideas. Such is the case with *Creed I* (in Arabic, *Al-Fiqh al-Akbar I*), reproduced below. While the authenticity of the second text, *Creed II* (*Al-Fiqh al-Akbar II*), is less certain, it is included here because it provides a fuller discussion of the topics covered in the first selection.

Abu Hanifa was known for arguing against the Kharijis of his time and often traveled south to the city of Basra to debate them. The Kharijis believed that a Muslim who committed a major sin had left Islam, could never be forgiven by God, and would spend an eternity in hell. In response to them, as seen in *Creed I*, Abu Hanifa separated faith from actions at the most fundamental level. For Abu Hanifa, being a Muslim required only allegiance to the basic tenets of Islam—that there is one God and that his messenger, Muhammad, had delivered God's revelation. For Abu Hanifa, anyone who held and publicly declared these beliefs was a Muslim regardless of his actual behavior. Whatever sins a person might commit were wrong and could earn God's punishment in the next world, but they did not negate one's belief in God or membership in the Muslim community. Abu Hanifa also believed that faith could neither increase or decrease, because it consisted of simply professing the basic tenets of Islam. In contrast, those who identified faith with works held that the performance of good works actually increased an individual's faith.

As the following two creeds show, Abu Hanifa prized clarity in the declaration of doctrine and preferred conciliation to controversy. The two creeds complement rather than repeat each other; the first is very concise, and the second offers a more expansive elaboration. Together they provide a succinct primer of Sunni theology.

PRONOUNCING GLOSSARY

Abū Bakr al-Ṣiddīk: *a-boo bakr as-sid-deeq´*
al-Fārūḳ: *al-fa-rooq´*
al-Murtaḍā: *al-mur´-ta-dah*
ʿAlī ibn Abī Ṭālib: *ah´-lee ibn a-bee tah´-lib*
Djahmites: *jah´-mites* (light *h*)
Fāṭima: *fah´-te-muh*
Fiḳh Akbar: *fiqh* (light *h*) *ak´-bar*
Firʿawn: *fir-awn´*
Iblīs: *ib-lees´*
Ibrāhīm: *ib-rah-heem´*
ʿĪsā: *ee´-sah*
Ḳadarites: *qah´-da-rites*
Ḳāsim: *qah´-sim*
Kuran: *qor-ahn´*
Mādjūdj: *ma-jooj´*
Muʿtazilites: *muh-ta´-zi-lites*
Munkar: *moon´-kar*
Murdjites: *mur´-ji-ites*
Nakīr: *na-keer´*
Ramaḍān: *ra-ma-dawn´*
Ruḳaiya: *roo-qai´-yuh*
rūyi khudāy: *roo´-ye cho-die´´* (guttural *ch*)
sunna: *sun´-nuh*
Ṭāhir: *tah´-her*
ʿUmar ibn al-Khaṭṭāb: *oh´-mar ibn al-chaht-tahb´* (guttural *ch*)
Umm Kulthūm: *oom´ kul-thoom´´*
ʿUthmān ibn ʿAffān: *uth-man´ ibn af-fan´*
Yādjūdj: *ya-jooj´*
Zainab: *zay´-nab*

TWO CREEDS

The Fiḳh Akbar I

Art. 1. We do not consider anyone to be an infidel on account of sin; nor do we deny his faith.

Art. 2. We enjoin what is just and prohibit what is evil.

Translated by A. J. Wensinck.

Art. 3. What reaches you could not possibly have missed you; and what misses you could not possibly have reached you.

Art. 4. We disavow none of the Companions of the Apostle of Allah; nor do we adhere to any of them exclusively.

Art. 5. We leave the question of ʿU<u>th</u>mān and ʿAlī[1] to Allah, who knoweth the secret and hidden things.

Art. 6. Insight in matters of religion is better than insight in matters of knowledge and law.

Art. 7. Difference of opinion in the community is a token of divine mercy.

Art. 8. Whoso believeth all that he is bound to believe, except that he says, I do not know whether Moses and Jesus (peace be upon them) do or do not belong to the Apostles, is an infidel.

Art. 9. Whoso sayeth, I do not know whether Allah is in Heaven or on the earth, is an infidel.

Art. 10. Whoso sayeth, I do not know the punishment in the tomb, belongeth to the sect of the <u>Dj</u>ahmites,[2] which goeth to perdition.

The Fiḳh Akbar II

Art. 1. The heart of the confession of the unity of Allah and the true foundation of faith consist in this obligatory creed: I believe in Allah, His angels, His books, His Apostles, the resurrection after death, the decree of Allah the good and the evil thereof, computation of sins, the balance,[3] Paradise and Hell; and that all these are real.

Art. 2. Allah the exalted is one, not in the sense of number, but in the sense that He has no partner; He begetteth not and He is not begotten and there is none like unto Him. He resembles none of the created things, nor do any created things resemble Him. He has been from eternity and will be to eternity with His names and qualities, those which belong to His essence as well as those which belong to His action.

Those which belong to His essence are: life, power, knowledge, speech, hearing, sight and will. Those which belong to His action are: creating, sustaining, producing, renewing, making, and so on.

He has been from eternity and will be to eternity with His qualities and His names. None of His qualities or names has come into being; from eternity He knows by virtue of His knowledge, knowledge being an eternal quality; He is almighty by virtue of His power, His power being an eternal quality; He speaks by virtue of His speech, His speech being an eternal quality; He creates by virtue of His creative power, His creative power being an eternal quality; He acts by virtue of His power of action, His power of action being an eternal quality.

The agent is Allah and the product of His action is created, but the power of action of Allah is not created and His qualities are eternal; they have not

1. The question of who should be the third caliph, ʿUthman ibn ʿAffan (d. 656) or ʿAli ibn Abi Talib (ca. 599–661); the disagreement over succession provoked the split between Sunni and Shiʿi Muslims.

2. An early Muslim theological group, supposedly founded by Jahm ibn Safwan (d. 746); a number of its beliefs were considered heretical.

3. A reference to the scales used to weigh an individual's good and bad deeds on the Day of Judgment (e.g., Qur'an 7:8; 101:6).

come into being, nor have they been created. Whoso sayeth that they are created or have come into being, or hesitates or doubts regarding these two points, is an infidel in regard to Allah.

Art. 3. The Kuran is the speech of Allah, written in the copies, preserved in the memories, recited by the tongues, revealed to the Prophet. Our pronouncing, writing and reciting the Kuran is created, whereas the Kuran itself is uncreated.

Whatever Allah quotes in the Kuran from Moses or other Prophets, from Pharaoh or from Satan, is the speech of Allah in relation to theirs. The speech of Allah is uncreated, but the speech of Moses and other creatures is created. The Kuran is the speech of Allah and as such from eternity, not theirs. Moses heard the speech of Allah, as the Kuran saith: And Allah spoke with Moses[4]—Allah was speaking indeed before He spoke to Moses. For Allah was creating from eternity ere He had created the creatures; and when He spoke to Moses, He spoke to Him with His speech which is one of His eternal qualities.

All His qualities are different from those of the creatures. He knoweth, but not in the way of our knowledge; He is mighty, but not in the way of our power; He seeth, but not in the way of our seeing; He speaketh, but not in the way of our speaking; He heareth, but not in the way of our hearing. We speak by means of organs and letters, Allah speaks without instruments and letters. Letters are created, but the speech of Allah is uncreated.

Art. 4. Allah is thing, not as other things but in the sense of positive existence; without body, without substance, without *accidens*.[5] He has no limit, neither has He a counterpart, nor a partner, nor an equal. He has hand, face and soul, for He refers to these in the Kuran; and what He saith in the Kuran regarding face, hand and soul, this belongs to His qualities, without how.[6] It must not be said that His hand is His power or His bounty, for this would lead to the annihilation of the quality. This is the view of the Kadarites and the Muʿtazilites.[7] No, His hand is His quality, without how. Likewise His wrath and His good pleasure are two of His qualities, without how.

Art. 5. Allah has not created things from a pre-existent thing. Allah had knowledge concerning things before they existed, from eternity; He had so decreed and ordained them that nothing could happen either in this world or in the next except through His will, knowledge, decision, decree and writing on the preserved tablet. Yet His writing is of a descriptive, not of a decisive nature. Decision, decree and will are His eternal qualities, without how. Allah knoweth the non-existent things in the state of non-existence, as not existing; and He knoweth how they will be. And He knoweth the existing things in the state of existence, as existing; and He knoweth how their

4. Qur'an 4:164.
5. That is, God is without accidents. Muslims, borrowing from Greek thought, divided existents into two types—substances and accidents. Substances exist in their own right; accidents, which have no independent existence, characterize substances. Thus, a rock is a substance; but a particular rock may be characterized by such accidents as redness, largeness, and heaviness. God has no inessential (accidental) qualities.
6. That is, without any explanation being demanded or given [translator's note].
7. A school of theology influential among Shiʿis but historically repudiated by Sunnis. "Ḳadarites": the Qadarites, a sect in early Islam whose members believed in free will. Both groups rejected the ascription of human qualities to God.

vanishing will be. Allah knoweth the rising in the state of His rising, as rising. And when He sitteth down, He knoweth Himself as sitting down, in the state of His sitting down, without a change in His knowing and without His getting knowledge. But change and difference come into being in creatures.

Art. 6. Allah created the creatures free from unbelief and from belief. Then He addressed them and gave them commandments and prohibitions. Thereupon some turned to unbelief. And their denial and disavowal of the truth was caused by Allah's abandoning them. And some of them believed—as appeared in their acting, consenting and declaring—through the guidance and help of Allah.

Allah took the posterity of Adam from his loins and endowed them with intellect. Thereupon He addressed them and commanded them to believe and to abstain from unbelief. Thereupon they recognized His lordship, and this was belief on their part. And in this religion they are born. And whosoever became an unbeliever afterwards, deviated from this and changed, and whosoever believed and professed his belief, clung to it and adhered to this belief.

Allah did not compel any of His creatures to be infidels or faithful. And He did not create them either as faithful or infidels, but He created them as individuals, and faith and unbelief are the acts of men. Allah knoweth the man who turneth to belief as an infidel in the state of his unbelief; and if he turneth to belief afterwards, Allah knoweth him as faithful, in the state of his belief; and He loveth him, without change in His knowledge or His quality. All the acts of man—his moving as well as his resting—are truly his own acquisition, but Allah creates them and they are caused by His will, His knowledge, His decision, and His decree.

Art. 7. All acts of obedience are obligatory on account of Allah's command, wish, good pleasure, knowledge, will, decision and decree. All acts of disobedience happen through His knowledge, decision, decree, and will; not according to His wish, good pleasure, or command.

Art. 8. All the Prophets are exempt from sins, both light and grave, from unbelief and sordid deeds. Yet stumbling and mistakes may happen on their part.

Art. 9. Muhammad is His beloved, His servant, His Apostle, His Prophet, His chosen and elect. He did not serve idols, nor was he at any time a polytheist, even for a single moment. And he never committed a light or a grave sin.

Art. 10. The most excellent of men after the Apostle of Allah is Abū Bakr al-Ṣiddīḳ; after him, ʿUmar ibn al-Khaṭṭāb al-Fārūḳ; after him, ʿUthmān ibn ʿAffān, he of the two lights; after him, ʿAlī al-Murtaḍā,[8] may Allah encompass all of them with His good pleasure, being His servants who persevere in truth and with truth. We cling to all of them and we name all the companions of Allah's Apostle in the way of praise only.

Art. 11. We declare no Muslim an infidel on account of any sin—even though a mortal one—if he does not declare it allowed. Neither do we banish him from the field of faith, nay, we call him really faithful; he may be faithful of bad behaviour, not an infidel.

8. These are the first four caliphs following Muhammad's death.

Art. 12. The moistening of the shoes is commendable. The supererogatory prayers in the month of Ramaḍān are commendable.

Art. 13. Prayer behind every faithful man, be he of good or of bad behaviour, is valid.

Art. 14. We do not say that sins will do no harm to the Faithful; nor do we say that he will not enter the fire; nor do we say that he will remain therein for ever, although he should be of bad behaviour, after having departed this world as one of the Faithful. And we do not say—as the Murdjites[9] do—that our good deeds are accepted and our sins forgiven. But we say, that when a man performs a good deed, fulfilling all its conditions so that it is free from any blame that might spoil it, without nullifying it by unbelief, apostasy or bad morals, until he departs this world as one of the Faithful—then Allah shall not overlook it but accept it from him and reward him on account of it. As to evil deeds—apart from polytheism and unbelief—if he who commits them does not repent ere he dies as one of the Faithful, he will be dependent on Allah's will: if He willeth He punisheth him in the fire, and if He willeth He forgiveth him without punishing him in any way in the fire.

Art. 15. If any work be mixed with ostentation, its reward is forfeited thereby, and likewise if it be mixed with vainglory.

Art. 16. The signs of the Prophets and the miracles of the saints are a reality. As to those which were performed by His enemies, such as Iblīs, Firʿawn[1] and the Anti-Christ, and which, according to historical tradition, have taken place or will take place, we do not call them signs or miracles, but we call them the fulfilling of their wants. Allah fulfils the wants of His enemies, eluding them in this world and punishing them in the next. So they are betrayed and increase in error and unbelief.

All this is contingent and possible.

Allah was creator before He created, and sustainer before He sustained.

Art. 17. Allah will be seen in the world to come. The Faithful will see Him, being in Paradise, with their bodily eyes, without comparison or modality. And there will be no distance between Him and His creatures.

Art. 18. Faith consists in confessing and believing.

The faith of the inhabitants of Heaven and earth does not increase or decrease.

The Faithful are equal in faith and in the confession of the unity of Allah; they are different in degree of superiority regarding works.

Islam is absolute agreement and compliance with the commands of Allah. Language distinguishes between faith and Islam. Yet there is no faith without Islam and Islam without faith cannot be found. The two are as back and belly. Religion is a noun covering faith and Islam and all the commandments of the law.

Art. 19. We know Allah with adequate knowledge, as He describes Himself in His book, with all His qualities. Nobody, on the other hand, is able to serve Allah with adequate service, such as He may truly lay claim to. But man serves Him at His command, as He has ordered him in His book and in the *sunna* of His Apostle.

9. A Muslim political and theological group from the seventh century; its members argued that only God was fit to judge the culpability of the parties involved in the early battles for leadership of the Muslim community. In later times, the term was used to designate those who believed that faith exists independently of religious works.

1. Pharaoh. "Iblīs": the devil.

All the Faithful are equal as to knowledge, subjective certainty, trust, love, inner quiet, fear, hope and faith. They differ in all these, except in faith.

Allah lavishes His bounty on His servants and acts according to justice as well. He giveth them a reward twice as large as they have deserved, by grace, and He punisheth on account of sin, by justice. He forgiveth by grace.

Art. 20. The intercession of the Prophets is a reality.

The intercession of the Prophet on behalf of the Faithful who have committed sins, even grave sins, and who have deserved punishment, is an established reality.

Art. 21. The weighing of works in the balance on the day of resurrection is a reality.

The basin of the Prophet[2] is a reality. Retaliation between litigants by means of good works on the day of resurrection is a reality. And if they do not possess good works, the wrongs, done by them to others, are thrown upon them; this is a reality.

Paradise and Hell are created, and are in existence at the present time; they will never cease to exist.

The black-eyed ones will never die.[3] Punishment and reward by Allah will never end.

Art. 22. Allah guideth whomsoever He pleaseth, by grace, and He leadeth astray whomsoever He pleaseth, by justice. His leading astray means His abandoning, and the explanation of "abandoning" is that He does not help a man by guiding him towards deeds that please Him. This is justice on His part, and so is His punishment of those who are abandoned on account of sin. We are not allowed to say that Satan deprives the Faithful of his faith by constraint and compulsion. But we say that man gives up his faith, whereupon Satan deprives him of it.

Art. 23. The interrogation of the dead in the tomb by Munkar and Nakīr[4] is a reality and the reunion of the body with the spirit in the tomb is a reality. The pressure and the punishment in the tomb are a reality that will take place in the case of all the infidels, and a reality that may take place in the case of some sinners belonging to the Faithful.

Art. 24. It is allowable to follow scholars in expressing the qualities of Allah in Persian, in all instances except in the case of Allah's hand. It is allowable to say *rūyi khudāy*,[5] without comparison or modality.

Art. 25. Allah's being near or far is not to be understood in the sense of a shorter or longer distance, but in the sense of man's being honoured or slighted. The obedient is near to Him, without how, and the disobedient is far from Him, without how. Nearness, distance and approach are applied to man in his intimate relation with Allah, and so it is with Allah's neighbourhood in Paradise, and with man's standing before Him, without modality.

Art. 26. The Kuran is revealed to the Apostle of Allah and it is written in the copies. The verses of the Kuran, being Allah's speech, are all equal in excellence and greatness. Some, however, have a pre-eminence in regard to recitation or to their contents, *e.g.* the verse of the Throne,[6] because it deals

2. In Muslim eschatology, the basin at which the believers meet Muhammad and from where he is said to seek God's forgiveness for his community.
3. A reference to the heavenly maidens (houris) promised to Muslim men.
4. Two angels said to question the dead in their graves about their deeds.
5. That is, the face of God [translator's note].
6. Qur'an 2:255, a verse often recited or written on amulets to signify entrusting oneself to God's care.

with Allah's majesty, His greatness and His description. So in it are united excellence in regard to recitation and excellence in regard to its contents. Others possess excellence only in regard to recitation, such as the descriptions of the infidels, whereas those who are mentioned in them, that is, the infidels, have no excellence.

Likewise all of Allah's names and qualities are equal in greatness and excellence, without difference.

Art. 27. Ḳāsim, Ṭāhir and Ibrāhim were the sons of the Apostle of Allah. Fāṭima, Ruḳaiya, Zainab and Umm Kul<u>th</u>ūm were all of them daughters of the Apostle of Allah.

Art. 28. When a man is uncertain concerning any of the subtleties of theology, it is his duty to cling for the time being to the orthodox faith. When he finds a scholar, he must consult him; he is not allowed to postpone inquiry and there is no excuse for him if he should persevere in his attitude of hesitation, nay, he would incur the blame of unbelief thereby.

Art. 29. The report of the ascension is a reality, and whosoever rejects it is an erring schismatic. The appearance of the Anti-Christ, Yā<u>d</u>jū<u>d</u>j and Mā<u>d</u>jū<u>d</u>j,[7] the rising of the sun from the place where it sets, the descent of ʿIsā[8] from Heaven, as well as the other eschatological signs according to the description thereof in authentic Tradition, are a reality that will take place.

Allah guideth to the straight way whomsoever He willeth.

7. Gog and Magog, in Islamic eschatology a race of beings who are freed upon the earth near the end of time to wreak havoc.

8. Jesus.

AL-ASHʿARI
874–935

Although he was one of the most influential theologians in Islamic history, little is known about the life of Abu al-Hasan al-Ashʿari, whose name designates the theological school that defines orthodoxy for most Sunni Muslims. What is remembered is his midlife repudiation of a thoroughgoing theological rationalism and his reorientation toward an intellectual defense of traditionalism. His was one of the more consequential conversions in Islamic literature.

Born in Basra, Iraq, al-Ashʿari was the foremost pupil of al-Jubbaʾi (d. 916), the leader of a rationalist school of theology known as the Muʿtazila. At age forty, however, he created his own school. Rejecting Muʿtazili rationalism as too radical, al-Ashʿari forged a path between traditional views and dialectical argumentation. He was particularly adept at defending cherished beliefs by using Muʿtazili methodologies. His new school appealed to many Muslim scholars, but the most hadith-centered, especially the Hanbalis, considered him an unrepentant rationalist and remained opposed to him. Al-Ashʿari died in 935 in Baghdad.

More than a hundred works have been attributed to al-Ashʿari, though no more than six are extant. These six range from a treatise on heresy to a defense of dialectical reasoning in the service of theology (in Arabic, *kalam*) to tracts against the Muʿtazila to creedal expositions.

The school al-Ashʿari left behind developed in two phases and did not stay faithful to all his positions. Scholars of the school's first phase built on al-Ashʿari's writings, expanding his ideas and arguments. The second phase began in the twelfth century when Ashʿari theologians, such as al-Ghazali (1058–1111; see below) and al-Razi (1149–1210; see below), addressed the questions posed by Greek-influenced philosophers such as al-Farabi (ca. 878–950; see below) and Ibn Sina (ca. 980–1037; see below).

Al-Ashʿari's theology is grounded in the Qurʾan, the practice of Muhammad, and the consensus of the Muslim community. Human reason, which also plays a central role in his thought, can qualify those three sources but cannot supersede them. Unlike the Muʿtazila, he did not believe that human reason alone could lead to an understanding of God and his commandments. Revelation was absolutely necessary.

Al-Ashʿari disagreed with the Muʿtazila on many issues, and the debates between the two schools have a rich and fascinating history. For example, according to al-Ashʿari, God had a self, or essence; distinct from this self, he had essential attributes such as life, knowledge, volition, and the ability to act. Precisely how these attributes related to the divine self could not be fathomed by human intellects. By contrast, the Muʿtazila argued that such attributes could not be ontologically separate from God's self and dismissed al-Ashʿari's formulation of God's self as comprising a multiplicity of coexisting eternals—a theological anathema for any strict monotheist.

In al-Ashʿari's analysis, human beings could not deem God's actions just or unjust, good or evil: God's commands and actions are always inherently just and good because they are issued by God. Human notions of justice and goodness fail as measures of divine action because they assess only what causes benefit or harm to an individual, an assessment that differs from person to person. The Muʿtazila countered that reason requires that God act justly and in the best interests of his believers. For God to do otherwise and still be deemed just would be logically impossible.

While al-Ashʿari accepted the use of metaphorical interpretation for theologically difficult qurʾanic verses and traditions, he felt it was employed by the Muʿtazila haphazardly and too often in a way that negated how the earliest Muslims understood those texts. Al-Ashʿari maintained that elements of the Day of Judgment, such as the scale used to measure good deeds and the crossing of a bridge over hell, were real entities and events, not (as the Muʿtazila asserted) merely metaphorical. Although al-Ashʿari agreed with the Muʿtazila that God was incorporeal and existed outside of space and time, he was convinced that qurʾanic promises of the vision of God in the next world (e.g., Qurʾan 75:22) were literally true, a position he defended in *The Concise Remarks* (literally, *The Book of Sparks*) with linguistic and rational arguments. For the Muʿtazila, God's incorporeality made a vision of him in the next world impossible; thus Qurʾan 75:22 should be understood as an experience in the believer's heart.

Al-Ashʿari wrote *The Concise Remarks* to summarize his theology, and it became his best known and most influential work. In the following excerpts he argues against the Muʿtazila of his time, sometimes oversimplifying their positions to bolster his own.

In the first selection, al-Ashʿari tackles the problem of a Muslim who has committed a major sin. According to al-Ashʿari, the Muʿtazila consider such a person neither a Muslim nor a disbeliever. For al-Ashʿari, major sins do not discredit a believer's faith. The focus is on faith, not actions. As long as an individual professes belief, he is a believer whether his actions are in accordance with Islamic law or not.

In the second passage, al-Ashʿari contests the notion that sinful Muslims must be sent to hell, even temporarily. For the Muʿtazila, God's justice demanded that sinners be punished; but al-Ashʿari countered that such a position rested on human conceptions of justice, which limited God's omnipotence. Remember that for al-Ashʿari, all of God's acts were inherently just simply because they were God's acts. God was free to forgive sinful Muslims as he saw fit.

PRONOUNCING GLOSSARY

Khawārij: *cha-wah´-rij* (guttural *ch*)
Muʿtazila: *muh-ta´-zi-luh*
Muʿtazilī: *muh-ta´-zi-lee*
qibla: *qib´-luh*
Wāṣil ibn ʿAṭāʾ: *wah´-sil ibn a-tah´*
Zuhair: *zoo-hayr´*

FROM THE CONCISE REMARKS

Chapter 8

Discussion of Faith

Q. What, in your opinion, is faith in God?

A. It is belief in God. On that there is a consensus of those who speak the language in which the Qurʾān was revealed. God said: "We have sent no Apostle to teach, save in the language of his people" (14.4). He also said: "in plain Arabic speech" (26.195). Now faith, in the language in which God sent down the Qurʾān, is belief. God Himself said: "You do not have faith in us even though we are truthful" (12.17)—i.e. you do not believe us. And everybody says: "So-and-so has faith in the punishment of the grave and intercession", meaning that he believes in that. So faith must be that which is faith according to those who speak the language, i.e. it must be belief.

Q. What about the sinner who belongs to the People of the Qibla:[1] is he a believer?

A. Yes—a believer by reason of his faith, a sinner by reason of his sin and grave fault. Those who speak the language are agreed that he who strikes is a striker, and he who kills is a killer, and he who disbelieves is a disbeliever, and he who sins is a sinner, and he who believes is a believer. Likewise, then, he who has faith is a believer.

If the sinner were neither believer nor unbeliever, he would neither disbelieve nor believe, and consequently would neither profess God's unicity nor deny it, would be neither friend nor enemy of God. Since that cannot be, it is impossible that the sinner be, as the Muʿtazila[2] claim, neither believer nor unbeliever.

Moreover, if the sinner was a believer before he sinned, by reason of his profession of God's unicity, then adultery occurring after such profession does not annul the name which issues from the faith which he has not forsaken.

Furthermore, before the advent of Wāṣil b. ʿAṭāʾ,[3] the chief of the Muʿtazila, men followed two opinions. The Khawārij[4] among them regarded grave sinners as unbelievers, whereas the "People of Rectitude" maintained that the

TRANSLATED BY Richard J. McCarthy. The parenthetical citations are to sura and verse of the Qurʾan (the first number before the slash, where one is present).

1. The direction toward the Kaʿba shrine in Mecca, which Muslims face when they pray.
2. On the Muʿtazila and al-Ashʿari's relation to them, see the introduction to this selection.
3. An early Muslim theologian from Basra, Iraq (ca. 700–ca. 749).
4. An early Muslim political and theological group that first appeared around 657 during a battle between the fourth caliph ʿAli (ca. 599–661) and his rival Muʿawiya (ca. 602–680). Known for their puritanical views, the Kharijis believed that the commission of a major sin put a Muslim outside of the pale of Islam.

grave sinner was a believer by reason of his faith and a sinner by reason of his grave sin. But no one said that he was neither believer nor unbeliever before the advent of Wāṣil b. 'Aṭā'. The latter withdrew from the Community and departed from its view, and because of his divergence from the consensus he was called a "withdrawer" (Muʿtazilī). So from the absence of consensus on his view—for the Muslims were agreed that the disobedient member of the "People of the Prayer" must be either a believer or an unbeliever—one must conclude that Wāṣil's view is false.

Besides, if one could say that he who has faith and commits a grave sin is neither believer nor unbeliever, one could also say: Nay, but he is a believer by reason of his faith, and it should not be said that he is a sinner by reason of his sin. Since this cannot be said, because there can be no sin which does not belong to a sinner, their assertion is also impossible, for there can be no faith which does not belong to a believer.

Chapter 9

Discussion of the Particular and the Universal, and of the Promise and the Threat

Q. Tell us about God's words: "while the profligate will certainly be in a burning fire" (82.14); and: "Who does that unjustly and wrongfully, we shall roast him with fire" (4.30/34);[5] and: "Truly those who consume the wealth of orphans wrongfully are only consuming fire in their bellies, and they shall endure the blazing fire" (4.10/11).

A. God's words, "Who does that unjustly", may be interpreted as applying to *all* who do that, or as applying to *some*. For the word "who" in our language applies sometimes to all, and sometimes to some. Hence, since the form of the word occurs now with the meaning of "some", and again with the meaning of "all", one cannot affirm positively, from its form alone, that it means "all" or "some".

Likewise, one cannot conclude that God's words, "while the profligate will certainly be in a burning fire" and "those who consume", refer to "some" or "all", since those expressions sometimes refer to "all", and again to "some". If one could claim that the form means only "all" until it is proved to mean "some", he would have no more right to make this claim than another would have to say that this expression compels one to conclude that it means "some" until it is proved to mean "all". So since both claimants would have the same right of assertion, both assertions must be excluded.

The poet Zuhair[6] said: "Who is not profuse in flattery will be rent by fangs and trodden underfoot". But that is not true of everyone who does not use flattery. He also said: "Who does not wrong men will himself be wronged". But not everyone who does not wrong men is himself wronged. Moreover, a speaker says: "There came to me whom I loved"—meaning only one person. And one says: "The merchants came to me"—although all of them did not come to him. And one says: "My neighbors came to me"—although all of them

5. Where pairs of verse numbers appear, the first gives the standard (1925) Cairo edition, used by most modern translators, while the second refers to the (1834) Flügel edition.

6. A famous pre-Islamic poet [ca. 520–609]. The citations are from his *muʿallaqa*—a special prize-winning poem [translator's note].

did not come to him. And one says: "The profligate cursed me abominably"—without meaning all of them. Hence, since these expressions occur at times meaning "all", and at other times meaning "some", one cannot conclude that they mean "all" rather than "some", or "some" rather than "all", unless one has some positive indication.

Moreover, if one had to conclude from the form of these verses to the punishment of every profligate man, and of everyone who consumes the wealth of orphans wrongfully, and of everyone who consumes the wealth of men wastefully, then one would have to conclude that all those "People of the Prayer" who profess God's unicity will be in the Garden[7] from the ostensible meaning of God's words: "Those who will come with a good work will have something better than it; and on that day they will be safe from any fear" (27.89/91). And from the ostensible meaning of God's words: "Reckon not those as dead who are killed while fighting for God. On the contrary they are alive, and with their Lord have sustenance" (3.169/163), one would have to conclude that everyone killed while fighting for God is in the Gardens and there has sustenance. And from the ostensible meaning of God's words: "God indeed forgives sins, all of them!" (39.53/54), one would have to conclude that every sin can be forgiven, except the sin of which God informed the Apostle, and the Muslims are agreed, that it is unforgivable, i.e. the sin of polytheism and unbelief. So one has no more right to say that the threat-verses are universal and the others particular than one has to reverse the statement and to say that the threat-verses are particular and the others universal.

Moreover, if one had to conclude from the ostensible meanings of the verses that every profligate man and everyone who consumes the wealth of orphans wrongfully will be in hell, then one could conclude (mendaciously) from God's words: "Each time a group is cast into it its guardians ask them: 'Did no one come to warn you?' They reply: 'Yes, one came to warn us, but we belied and said: God has sent down nothing!'" (67.8–9), that only the unbeliever enters the Fire. And from the ostensible meaning of God's words: "Therefore have I warned you of a fiercely blazing Fire which only the most impious must endure, who belies and turns away" (92.14–16), one could conclude that all who endure the Fire are such. And from the ostensible meaning of God's words: Who judge not by what God has sent down, they, they are the profligate!" (5.47/51), one could conclude that only the profligate man refrains from judging by what God has sent down. Since, then, these verses do not compel one to conclude that only the unbeliever enters the Fire, the previously cited verses do not compel one to conclude that every profligate man will be in hell, and that everyone who consumes the wealth of orphans wrongfully and everyone who consumes the wealth of men wastefully will be in the Fire. And the answer to every verse which they use as an argument regarding the threat is like the answer to these verses.

God's words, "Who does that unjustly and wrongfully" (4.30/34), are to be interpreted as meaning: "Who does that while declaring it licit". So they apply to all who are such. And His words, "while the profligate will certainly be in a burning fire" (82.14), are to be interpreted as meaning "some of them", i.e. the unbelievers among them. So they apply to all who are such. One

7. Paradise.

should reply in the same way respecting every verse urged in proof of the universality of the threat.

Moreover, the Muʿtazila are constrained to admit that all "those of the Left"[8] are unbelievers because of the ostensible meaning of God's words: "The Companions of the Left! What are the Companions of the Left? They are in burning wind and boiling water and pall of smoke, neither refreshing nor rain-bearing. Once, indeed, they used to live delicately while they persisted in the Great Sin. And they were wont to say: 'When we shall have died and become dust and bones, shall we indeed be raised again?'" (56.41–47/40–47), and from His words: "But he who will be given his book in his left hand will say: 'Would that I had not been given my book!' He was indeed wont not to believe in God the Mighty and not to urge the feeding of the poor" (69.25–34).

8. One of the two groups into which people are divided on the Day of Judgment. Those who receive the book of their life's deeds in the left hand are consigned to hell; those who receive it in the right hand, to heaven.

IBN BABAWAYH [SHAYKH SADUQ]
ca. 920–991

Pilgrims still make their way to a cemetery in a southern suburb of Tehran to visit the tomb of a Shiʿi scholar who lived more than a thousand years ago. Ibn Babawayh, also known as Shaykh Saduq, was probably born in Khurasan. Details of his life are sketchy. According to legend, his birth followed his father's prayer to the Hidden Imam—the twelfth Imam, who, according to Twelver Shiʿis, disappeared as a child in 873 and will return just before the Day of Judgment—who interceded with God. Apparently, Ibn Babawayh relished telling this story of how he was the answer to his father's prayers.

Ibn Babawayh grew up in Qum—then, as now, the center of Shiʿi learning in the Muslim world. His was a family of famous scholars, several of whom counted as notable transmitters of hadith. During his youth, Ibn Babawayh's family moved to Rayy (now a suburb of Tehran), where they continued to study and teach. Ibn Babawayh's own scholarly journey took him throughout Iran, Central Asia, and Iraq. He taught for some time in Baghdad but eventually returned to Rayy, where he died in 991.

Ibn Babawayh was a prolific writer and is credited with several hundred works. His most famous book, *For the One without a Jurist Nearby*, is a collection of hadith intended to aid believers with their religious and legal duties. Shiʿi scholars count it as one of four key collections of Shiʿi traditions. The items included in this anthology come from another of his important works: *The Beliefs of the Shiʿis*, one of the earliest examples of a Twelver Shiʿi theological creed.

The creed reflects Ibn Babawayh's mastery of the sources, as he often cites qurʾanic verses and hadith to support his assertions. Despite its importance, the creed is not without its critics, including Ibn Babawayh's student al-Shaykh al-Mufid (ca. 948–1022), another major Shiʿi scholar, who challenged some of his teacher's interpretations.

The selections here present key Shiʿi beliefs. The first deals with the nature of prophetic revelation and the embodiment of continuing authority in the Shiʿi community. The infallibility of prophets and imams as an indispensable element of that authority is the thrust of the second. The third touches on a feature of Shiʿi thought and practice that is frequently misrepresented or misunderstood: a feigned friendliness with religious enemies mandated in circumstances in which Shiʿis constitute a vulnerable or persecuted minority.

PRONOUNCING GLOSSARY

Abū Jaʿfar (ibn Bābawayh): *a-boo ja´-far (ibn bah´-ba-wayh,* light *h)*
Abū Jaʿfar Muḥammad ibn ʿAlī: *a-boo ja´far moo-ham´-mad* (heavy *h*) *ibn ah´-lee*
al-Ḥasan: *al-ha´-san* (heavy *h*)
al-Ḥasan ibn ʿAlī: *al-ha´-san* (heavy *h*) *ibn ah´-lee*
al-Ḥusayn: *al-hoo-sayn´* (heavy *h*)
al-qāʾim: *al-qah´-im*
ʿAlī ibn Abī Ṭālib: *ah´-lee ibn a-bee tah´-lib*
ʿAlī ibn al-Ḥusayn: *ah´-lee ibn al-hoo-sayn´* (heavy *h*)
ʿAlī ibn Mūsā ar-Riḍā: *ah´-lee ibn moo´-sah ar-ri´-dah*
anbiyāʾ: *an-bee-ya´*
awṣiyāʾ: *aw-see-ya´*
imām: *ee-mam´*
ʿiṣma: *is´-muh*
Jaʿfar al-Ṣādiq: *ja´-far as-sah´-diq*
Jaʿfar ibn Muḥammad: *ja´-far ibn moo-ham´-mad* (heavy *h*)
kāfir: *ka´-fir*
mahdī: *mah´-dee* (light *h*)
Muḥammad ibn al-Ḥasan: *moo-ham´-mad* (heavy *h*) *ibn al-ha´-san* (heavy *h*)
Mūsā ibn Jaʿfar: *moo´-sah ibn ja´-far*
nabī: *na-bee´*
shaykh: *shaych* (guttural *ch*)
shirk: *shirk*
taqīya: *ta-qee´-yuh*
waṣī: *wah-see´*

FROM THE BELIEFS OF THE SHIʿIS

Chapter 35

The Belief Concerning the Number of Prophets (anbiyāʾ) *and Vicegerents* (awṣiyāʾ)

Says the Shaykh Abū Jaʿfar:[1] Our belief concerning their number is that in all there have been one hundred and twenty-four thousand prophets and a like number of *awṣiyāʾ*. Each *nabī* (prophet) had a waṣī[2] to whom he gave instructions by the command of Allāh. And concerning them we believe that they brought the truth from Allāh, that their word is the word of Allāh, that their command is the command of Allāh, that obedience to them is obedience to Allāh and that disobedience to them is disobedience to Allāh.

They spoke not except on behalf of Allāh, and on being inspired by Him. And verily the leaders of the prophets are five in number round whom the heavens revolve, and they are the masters of the religious paths (*aṣḥābu'sh-sharāʾiʿ*), namely, "the ones endued with firmness" [46, 35]—Noah, Abraham, Moses, Jesus and Muḥammad, on all of whom be peace. Muḥammad verily is their leader and the most excellent of them. He brought the truth and confirmed (the message of) the apostles. Those who declared him to be a liar will suffer a painful agony. And those who believed in him and honoured and helped him, and followed the light which descended with him—they are the successful and the victorious ones.

TRANSLATED BY Asaf A. A. Fyzee. The numbers in square brackets refer to sura and verse of the Qurʾan.

1. Ibn Babawayh.
2. Viceregent, and the *nabī*'s successor.

It is necessary to believe that Allāh the Mighty and Glorious did not create any created thing more excellent than Muḥammad and the Imāms, peace on them, that they are the most loved of creatures in the eyes of Allāh, and the most noble and the foremost among them, on account of their acceptance of Him (as their Lord). When Allāh took the pledge (*mīthāq*) of the prophets and "required them to bear witness of themselves (saying): Am I not your Lord? and they said: Yes, verily" [7, 172].

And verily Allāh sent His Prophet Muḥammad (with a message) to the other prophets in the world of atoms (*adh-dharr*).[3] And verily Allāh the Mighty and Glorious gave to each prophet (i.e. knowledge, power, etc.) according to the extent of his cognition (*maʿrifa*), while the cognition of our Prophet Muḥammad was greater and more sublime, for it took precedence in accepting Allāh (as the Supreme Being).

We believe that Allāh, Blessed and Exalted is He above all, created the whole of creation for him (the Prophet) and for the People of his House, and that but for them, Allāh, Glory be to Him, would not have created the heavens or the earth, Paradise or Hell, Adam or Eve, the angels or (any) created thing (*shay'*)—the Blessings of Allāh upon them all.

And our belief is that after His Prophet, the Blessings of Allāh upon him, the proofs of Allāh for the people are the Twelve Imāms,[4] the first of them being the Prince of Believers ʿAlī b. Abī Ṭālib,[5] then al-Hasan, then al-Ḥusayn, then ʿAlī b. al-Ḥusayn, then Muḥammad b. ʿAlī, then Jaʿfar b. Muḥammad, then Mūsā b. Jaʿfar, then ʿAlī b. Mūsā ar-Riḍā, then Muḥammad b. ʿAlī, then ʿAlī b. Muḥammad, then al-Ḥasan b. ʿAlī, then Muḥammad b. al-Ḥasan the Proof (*al-ḥujja*), who upholds the command of Allāh (*al-qā'im bi-amri'l-lāh*), the Master of Time (*ṣāḥibu 'z-zamān*), the Vicegerent of the Beneficent One (*khalīfatu 'r-Raḥmān*) in His earth, the one who is present in the earth but invisible (*ghā'ib*) to the eyes—the Blessings of Allāh on all of them.

Our belief regarding them is that they are in authority (*ūlū'l-amr*). It is to them that Allāh has ordained obedience, they are the witnesses for the people and they are the gates of Allāh (*abwāb*) and the road (*sabīl*) to Him and the guides (*dalīl*, pl. *adilla*) thereto, and the repositories of His knowledge and the interpreters of His revelations and the pillars of His unity (*tawḥīd*). They are immune from sins (*khaṭā'*) and errors (*zalal*); they are those from whom "Allāh has removed all impurity and made them absolutely pure" [33, 33]; they are possessed of (the power of) miracles (*muʿjizāt*) and of (irrefutable) arguments (*dalā'il*); and they are for the protection of the people of this earth just as the stars are for the inhabitants of the heavens. They may be likened, in this community, to the Ark of Noah; he who boards it obtains salvation or reaches the Gate of Repentance (*ḥiṭṭa*).

They are the most noble slaves of Allāh, who "speak not until He hath spoken; they act by His command" [21, 27]. And we believe that love for them is true belief (*īmān*) and hatred for them is unbelief (*kufr*); that their command is the command of Allāh, their prohibition is the prohibition of Allāh; obedience to them is obedience to Allāh, and disobedience to them

3. The world before God shaped its mass into different forms.
4. The successors of Muhammad, according to the Shiʿis.
5. Muhammad's cousin and son-in-law, recognized by Sunnis as the fourth caliph. What follows is a list of Muhammad's blood descendants.

is disobedience to Allāh; their friend (*walī*) is the friend of Allāh, and their enemy the enemy of Allāh.

We believe that the earth cannot be without the Proof (*ḥujja*) of Allāh to His creatures—a leader either manifest (*ẓāhir*) and well-known (*mashhūr*) or hidden (*khāfī*) and obscure (*maghmūr*).

We believe that the Proof of Allāh in His earth and His vicegerent (*khalīfa*) among His slaves in this age of ours is the Upholder (*al-Qā'im*) (of the law of Allāh), the Expected One (*al-Muntaẓar*), Muḥammad b. al-Ḥasan b. ʿAlī b. Muḥammad b. ʿAlī b. Mūsā b. Jaʿfar, b. Muḥammad b. ʿAlī b. al-Ḥusayn b. ʿAlī b. Abī Ṭālib, on them be peace. He it is concerning whose name and descent the Prophet was informed by Allāh the Mighty and Glorious, and he it is WHO WILL FILL THE EARTH WITH JUSTICE AND EQUITY, JUST AS NOW IT IS FULL OF OPPRESSION AND WRONG.[6] And he it is through whom Allāh will make His faith manifest "in order to supersede all religion, though the polytheists may dislike (it)" [9, 33; 48, 28; 61, 9]. He it is whom Allāh will make victorious over the whole world until from every place the call to prayer will be heard, and all religion will belong entirely to Allāh, Exalted is He above all. He it is, who is the Rightly Guided (*mahdī*), about whom the Prophet gave information that when he appears, Jesus, son of Mary, will descend upon the earth and pray behind him, and he who prays behind him is like one who prays behind the Prophet of Allāh, because he is his vicegerent (*khalīfa*).

And we believe that there can be no Qā'im other than him; he may live in the state of occultation (as long as he likes); and were he to live in the state of occultation for the space of the existence of this world, there would nevertheless be no Qā'im other than him. For, the Prophet and the Imām have indicated him by his name and descent; him they appointed as their successor, and of him they gave glad tidings—the Blessings of Allāh on all of them.

Chapter 36

The Belief Concerning Infallibility (ʿiṣma)

Says the Shaykh Abū Jaʿfar: Our belief concerning the prophets (*anbiyā'*), apostles (*rusul*), Imāms and angels is that they are infallible (*maʿṣūm*); purified from all defilement (*danas*), and that they do not commit any sin, whether it be minor (*ṣaghīra*) or major (*kabīra*). They do not disobey Allāh in what He has commanded them; they act in accordance with His behests. He who denies infallibility to them in any matter appertaining to their status is ignorant of them, and such a one is a *kāfir* (unbeliever).

Our belief concerning them is that they are infallible and possess the attributes of perfection, completeness and knowledge, from the beginning to the end of their careers. Defects (*naqṣ*) cannot be attributed to them, nor disobedience (*ʿiṣyān*), nor ignorance (*jahl*), in any of their actions (*aḥwāl*).

6. A common Shiʿi reference to the future Restorer—the Mahdi (Guided One), identified by Twelvers with the twelfth or Hidden Imam, who will return shortly before the Day of Judgment.

Chapter 39

The Belief Concerning Dissimulation (taqīya)

Says the Shaykh, may the mercy of Allāh be on him: Our belief concerning *taqīya* (permissible dissimulation) is that it is obligatory, and he who forsakes it is in the same position as he who forsakes prayer. Imām Jaʿfar aṣ-Ṣādiq[7] was told: O son of the Messenger of Allāh, verily we see in the mosque one who openly abuses your enemies, calling out their names. And he said: May Allāh curse him! Why does he refer to us? He, Who is Exalted above all, says: "Revile not those who invoke (deities) other than Allāh, lest wrongfully they revile Allāh through ignorance" [6, 108]. And Imām Jaʿfar in explaining this verse has said: So do not revile them, lest they revile your ʿAlī. And he also said: He who reviles the friend (*walī*) of Allāh (i.e. ʿAlī) has reviled Allāh. And the Prophet said: He who reviles thee, O ʿAlī, has verily reviled me: and he, who reviles me, has verily reviled Allāh.

Now until the Imām al-Qāʾim appears, *taqīya* is obligatory and it is not permissible to dispense with it. He, who abandons it before the appearance of the Qāʾim, has verily gone out of the religion of Allāh, Exalted is He, and the religion of the Imāms, and disobeys Allāh and His Messenger and the Imāms. Imām Jaʿfar was asked concerning the Word of Allāh, Mighty and Glorious is He: "Verily the noblest among you, in the sight of Allāh, is the most pious" [49, 13]. He said: (It means) he who adheres most scrupulously to the practice of *taqīya*.

And Allāh, the Blessed and Exalted, has described the showing of friendship to unbelievers as being (possible only) in the state of *taqīya*. And He the Mighty and Glorious says: "Let not believers take disbelievers for their friends in preference to believers. Whoso doeth that hath no connection with Allāh unless (it be) that ye but guard yourselves against them, for fear of being killed" [3, 28]. And Allāh the Mighty and Glorious says: "Allāh doth not forbid you to deal with kindness and fairness toward those who have not made war upon you on account of your religion, or driven you forth from your homes: for Allāh loveth those who act with fairness [60, 8]." "Only Allāh doth forbid you to make friends of those who, on account of your religion, have warred against you, and have driven you forth from your homes, and have aided those who drove you forth: and whoever maketh friends of them are wrong-doers" [*ibid.*, 9].

And Imām Jaʿfar said: Verily, I hear a man abusing me in the mosque: and I hide myself behind a pillar so that he may not see me. And he (Imām Jaʿfar) said: Mix with the people (enemies) outwardly, but oppose them inwardly, so long as the Amirate (*imratun*) is a matter of opinion.[8] And he also said: Verily diplomacy (*ar-riʾāʾ*) with a true believer is a form of *shirk* (polytheism); but with a hypocrite (*munāfiq*) in his own house, it is worship. And he also said: He who prays with them (hypocrites) standing in the first row, it is as though he prayed with the Prophet in the first row. And he also said: Visit their sick and attend their funerals and pray in their mosques. And he also said: (You should) become an ornament for us, and not a disgrace. And

7. The sixth Shiʿi Imam (702–765).
8. That is, until the rule of the rightful Imam is finally established [translator's note].

he said: May Allāh have mercy on a person who inculcates friendship towards us among men, and does not provoke ill-will among them.

The story-tellers (*qaṣṣāṣūn*) were mentioned before Imam Jaʿfar, and he said: May Allāh curse them, for they speak ill of us. And he was asked concerning the story-tellers, whether it is permissible to hear what they say, and he said: No. And Imām Jaʿfar said: He, who gives ear to a speaker, has verily rendered himself submissive to him; if the speaker (discourses) concerning Allāh, then the listener has verily worshipped Allāh, and if he speaks of the devil, then the listener has worshipped the devil.

And Imām Jaʿfar was asked concerning the Word of Allāh, Exalted is He above all: "As for the poets, the erring follow them" [26, 224]. He said: These are the story-tellers.

And the Prophet said: He, who goes to an innovator[9] (*dhū bidʿa*) and gives him respect, strives towards the destruction of Islam. And our belief, concerning him who opposes us in a single injunction of religion, is the like of our belief concerning him who disobeys us in all the injunctions of religion.

9. One who holds religious views judged by others to be wrong or even heretical.

AL-GHAZALI
1058–1111

Abu Hamid Muhammad ibn Muhammad al-Ghazali was born in Tus, a city in the medieval Persian province of Khurasan. What remains of that ancient city has now been swallowed by the shrine city of Mashhad, a major Iranian urban center that lies near the border of Afghanistan. Orphaned as a young child, al-Ghazali was raised by relatives who did not neglect his education. His studies began with Islamic law and jurisprudence, as was traditional. As a youth, he left Tus for Nishapur, where his most noted teacher was ʿAbd al-Malik al-Juwayni (1028–1085), a jurist of the Shafiʿi school and a proponent of Ashʿari theology whose renown earned him the sobriquet Imam al-Haramayn, the "Leader of the Two Sanctuaries" (Mecca and Medina). Al-Ghazali tells a story about his school days that underscores the importance of memorization in the world of classical Islamic scholarship. During one of his journeys, he was accosted by robbers who snatched a satchel containing the notes that he had made of the lectures he attended and the manuscripts he read. When he begged for its return, the thief chided him for relying on note taking rather than memory, leaving him vulnerable to instantaneous loss of his learning.

In 1085, at the age of twenty-seven, al-Ghazali attracted the attention of an important patron, the Seljuk vizier Nizam al-Mulk. As vizier for the sultan, who possessed political and military control while the caliph in Baghdad remained the symbolic head of the Muslim world, Nizam al-Mulk wielded enormous power and influence. To foster a strong Sunni identity for the Seljuk empire he founded colleges (*madrasas*) for the advancement of Islamic learning. The most famous of these colleges—named after him, the Nizamiyya—was in Baghdad. The vizier appointed al-Ghazali to a teaching position there in 1091, only a year before he himself was killed by the Assassins, a radical sect of Shiʿi Muslims.

At the Nizamiyya in Baghdad, al-Ghazali spent four years as a professor of law and legal theory, the fields of Islamic learning that served as the foundation of the madrasa curriculum. He was a popular teacher and his legal opinions, or fatwas, were much sought after. He also devoted himself privately to the study of philosophy, a subject that was not part of the standard teaching syllabus of the madrasa. Islamic philosophy, sparked by the major translation efforts of ninth-century Baghdad, was flourishing by the late eleventh century. Though Greek philosophy, particularly that of Plato and Aristotle, remained the most important influence, al-Ghazali paid special attention to Neoplatonism as developed by al-Farabi (ca. 878–950; see below) and Ibn Sina (ca. 980–1037; see below). Although he initially wrote a straightforward presentation of their philosophy, al-Ghazali eventually found it impossible to reconcile the basic tenets of his faith with their philosophical propositions. The recognition of this incompatibility drove him to write *The Incoherence of the Philosophers*.

During this time, his life took an unexpected turn, precipitated by a physical and psychological crisis that forced him from the classroom. Overwhelmed by religious doubt and deeply troubled by the religious hypocrisy rampant among his colleagues, al-Ghazali suddenly left Baghdad. He abandoned his professorship to his younger brother Ahmad and announced his intention to make a pilgrimage to Mecca.

Speculation about the reasons behind this abrupt departure abounds, and the details of al-Ghazali's subsequent journeys remain uncertain. But he clearly dedicated the next eleven years to far-flung travels, intense spiritual seeking, and prolific writing. From his own accounts and later biographies, we know that he stopped for varying lengths of time in Damascus, Jerusalem, and Hebron—for a visit to the prophet Abraham's tomb—as well as the pilgrimage destinations of Mecca and Medina. We also know that al-Ghazali gave himself over to the devotional practices of the Sufis and to their ascetic disciplines and deprivations. He sought to move beyond intellectual apprehension and appreciation of the divine to a complete moral and spiritual transformation, believing that only by prolonged periods of prayer and meditation, combined with severe physical mortification, could he hope to transcend the egocentrism of his human nature. Stories tell of his confining himself in the minaret of the Damascus mosque, seeking the absolute quiet of solitary seclusion.

A key concept for understanding the spiritual and psychological conversion desired by al-Ghazali is that of "heart." Within the world of medieval Sufi psychology, the Arabic term for "heart," *qalb*, connotes much more than the physical organ. Multiple uses in the Qur'an show that *qalb* designates the fully developed human capacity for understanding, through which God can act directly. Qur'an 2:97, for example, tells Muhammad that the angel Gabriel sent the Qur'an "down upon your heart." Later refinements of this notion of the heart, not the brain, as the locus of religious knowledge and sensitivity were worked out in an extensive literature on spiritual formation, a literature to which al-Ghazali was both heir and contributor.

During this extended hiatus from the responsibilities of a formal academic position, al-Ghazali did not abandon all aspects of the intellectual life. His preaching, teaching, and writing continued, and several of his major writings have been credited to this period. Among them ranks his magnum opus, *The Revival of the Religious Sciences*.

As the fifth Islamic century drew to a close, the son of Nizam al-Mulk—who, like his father, had taken service as vizier with the Seljuk ruler of Khurasan—urged al-Ghazali to return to Nishapur and resume his academic life. For several years, al-Ghazali again taught at the Nizamiyya in Nishapur. He coupled his return with the conviction that, true to a long-standing tradition, he was the one whom God was calling to be the "renewer of the religion" for the new Islamic century. That century was only five years old, however, when he died in his native city of Tus.

Al-Ghazali was a profound thinker and a prolific author. For more than a thousand years, he has stood as one of the great intellects of Islam. His writings were among the first to move from manuscript to print, and many continue to be frequently reprinted and reissued in new editions. A native speaker of Persian, he wrote primarily in Arabic—the educated scholar's language—but did not neglect his mother tongue entirely. No complete and authoritative bibliography of his writings exists, because the attribution of many is disputed and an unknown number appear under multiple titles. Nevertheless, well over fifty works are deemed authentic, falling into various categories: notably, Shafiʿi law and jurisprudence, Islamic philosophy (both works setting forth what it is and works refuting the explanations of others), dogmatic theology, Sufi theory and practice, and antiheretical polemics. As noted above his greatest work is *The Revival of the Religious Sciences.* Convinced that there had been a loss of true devotion to God due in no small part to scholars who saw the study of religion as nothing more than a means for gaining wealth and social rank, al-Ghazali aimed the *Revival* at the average believer and sought to recapture the spirit behind Islamic practices. He divides the work into four parts: "religious duties," "social customs," "blameworthy character traits," and "praiseworthy character traits." Each part is subdivided into ten books, numbered consecutively throughout the work. Part 1, "religious duties," primarily treats areas of ritual law such as prayer and fasting but also covers creedal matters. Part 2, "social customs," examines social interactions such as marriage, business dealings, and the correction of others. Part 3, "blameworthy character traits," warns against those flaws, such as lust, gluttony, and anger, that can lead to damnation, while part 4, "praiseworthy character traits," extols those virtues, such as repentance, patience, and trust in God, that led to salvation. In the first two parts al-Ghazali presents the basic requirements and prohibitions for each topic, but unlike the author of a legal handbook, he delves into the inward state of a believer and describes the ideal state of a believer's heart when these "acts of worship" and "social customs" are performed. Al-Ghazali makes clear that the point of religion is not simply to adhere to religious belief and law. Rather, one's heart should be purified in this process. Similarly, parts 3 and 4 do not merely list vices and virtues but continue al-Ghazali's exposition of the heart as the spiritual center of the human being while providing techniques for combating base tendencies and for cultivating noble ones.

Although the *Revival* stands as a landmark treatise in Islamic spirituality, al-Ghazali also composed other works on the subject, including two shorter works based on the *Revival*. *Forty Fundamentals of Faith* summarized the *Revival* (though its forty sections do not correspond to the forty books); *The Alchemy of Happiness*, a longer work, abridged the *Revival* in Persian for al-Ghazali's students. Among his other spiritual writings were his epistle *Oh Child*, which presents basic advice to one embarking on the spiritual path, and *The Noblest of Aims in the Names of God*, which explains how humans could emulate God's names and attributes.

The excerpt below is taken from book 20 of the second part of the *Revival*. In it al-Ghazali portrays Muhammad's character as well as his physical actions, including how he dressed, laughed, and spoke. Al-Ghazali's decision to end this part of the work with a description of Muhammad was deliberate. The Islamic tradition has long held that Muhammad's comportment in his relationship with God was perfect. For this reason, Muslims, out of a desire to become similarly close to God, have sought to emulate Muhammad's actions (in Arabic, *sunna*) and model themselves on his character. As al-Ghazali himself prays in the invocation at the beginning of this book, "Praised be God who guides the copying of Muhammad's attributes by them whose refinement He desires and who prevents the assuming of his character by them whose debasement He desires."

PRONOUNCING GLOSSARY

ʿĀʾisha: *ah´-i-shuh*
Abū'l-Bakhtarī: *a-bool-bach´-ta-ree* (guttural *ch*)
Anas ibn Mālik: *a´-nas ibn ma´-lik*
dīnār: *dee-nar´*
dirham: *dir´-ham*
Galen: *gay´-len*

FROM THE REVIVAL OF THE RELIGIOUS SCIENCES: THE BOOK OF THE CONDUCT OF LIFE AS EXEMPLIFIED BY THE PROPHETIC CHARACTER

A Summary Account of His Fine Qualities of Character, Which Certain of the Learned Have Gathered and Collected from the Reports

Muḥammad was the most forbearing, honest, just, and chaste of men. His hand never touched the hand of a woman over whom he did not have the right of control, with whom he did not have sexual relations, or who was unlawful for him to marry. He was the most generous of men. Neither a dinar nor a dirhem[1] was left him in the evening. If something remained, and there was not anyone to whom he could give this excess—night having fallen unexpectedly—he did retire to his lodging until he was able to give this excess to who was in need of it.

Muḥammad did not take of those things which Allāh gave him, except his yearly provisions. He gave the remaining excess of his small quantity of dates and barley to charity. He was never asked for anything but that he gave it [to him who asked]. Moreover he returned to his yearly provisions [which he stored for his family] and [taking of them] preferred him (the seeker) [over himself and his family]. Thus he was often in need before the end of the year, if nothing was presented to him. He patched his sandals and clothing, performed household duties, and ate meat with his women-folk.

Muḥammad was the most bashful of men and did not stare into anyone's face. He answered the invitation of the slave and the freeborn. He accepted presents, even if they consisted only of a draught of milk, or of a leg of rabbit; he ate them and requited equally for them. However, he did not eat of that which was offered to him as legal alms. He did not consider himself too great to answer the [ordinary] people and the poor. He became angry for Allāh and not for his own sake. He exacted the truth even though it brought harm to him and his companions.

Muḥammad, while fighting certain polytheists, was offered the help of other polytheists. However, he replied, "I do not seek assistance in conquest from a polytheist," even though he was with few men and in need of anyone who could increase his numbers.

One of the most virtuous and best of his companions was found murdered amongst the Jews, but Muḥammad did not hasten against them nor did he exceed the course of justice. Rather he accepted no more than the

TRANSLATED BY L. Zolondek. All bracketed additions are the translator's.

1. A gold and a silver coin, respectively.

blood price of a hundred female camels although his companions needed a single male camel with which they would be strengthened.

Because of hunger he at times tightened a stone around his stomach. He often ate what was at hand, did not reject what was available, nor did he refrain from lawful food. If there was available a date without bread, he ate it; if there was roast meat, he ate it; if there was wheat or barley bread, he ate it; if there was sweets or honey, he ate it; if there was milk without bread, he was content with it; if there was a melon or fresh dates, he ate it.

He did not eat reclining nor from a footed tray. He used his sole as a napkin. Until the time of his death, he did not dislike to eat wheat bread three days in succession[2] as a sign that one [should] choose neither poverty nor avarice.

He attended feasts, visited the sick, attended funerals, and walked alone without a guard amongst his enemies.

He was the humblest of men, the most silent without being insolent, and the most eloquent without being lengthy. He had the most joyful countenance, none of the affairs of the world awing him.

Muḥammad wore what was at hand—at times a cloak covering the whole body, at times a striped-cloth garment of Yemen, at times a gown of wool. He wore any permissible garment which was available. His signet was of silver which he wore now on the little finger of his right hand, now on that of his left hand.

He mounted his servant and others behind him on the same beast. He rode whatever was possible for him. At different times he rode a horse, a male camel, a gray she-mule, an ass; at times he walked on foot, barefoot without a cloak, turban, or cap.

He visited the sick in the farthest section in the city. He loved perfumes and disliked foul odors. He sat and ate with the poor. He showed regard to the people of virtue for their character and was intimate with the people of rank because of their piety. He did good for his kindred without preferring them to him who was more virtuous than they. He did not tyrannize anyone and accepted the excuse of him who begged his pardon.

He jested but he only spoke the truth. He laughed without bursting out into laughter. He witnessed the permitted games and did not disapprove of them. He raced sportingly with his family. Voices were raised against him, but he was patient.

His milch camels and sheep nourished him and his family with their milk. He did not eat better food nor wear better clothes than his male and female slave. A moment did not pass without his doing an action for Allāh or [doing] that which was indispensable for the soundness of his soul. He went to the garden of his companions. He did not despise a poor man for his poverty and misfortune, nor he did not fear a king because of his power; rather, he urged them equally to Allāh.

Allāh combined in him virtuous conduct and perfect rule of people, though he was untaught, unable to read or write, grew up poor amongst the shepherds in the land of ignorance and desert, and was an orphan without father and mother. Allāh taught him all the fine qualities of character, the praiseworthy paths, the reports of the first and last affairs, and those matters

2. Wheat bread was a luxury, while barley bread was the norm.

through which there is [obtained] salvation and reward in the future life and happiness and reward in the world. Allāh taught him to cleave to that which is as obligatory and to forsake the useless.

May Allāh direct us to obey Muḥammad in his commands and to imitate him in his actions. Amen, O Lord of the worlds.

Another Summary of His Manner and Character

Of that which Abū'l-Bakhtari related, they said that the Apostle of Allāh did not insult a Muslim but that he atoned for this and bestowed mercy. Moreover, he never cursed either a woman or a slave. While he was waging war it was said to him, "Would that you curse them (the enemy) O Apostle of Allāh!" To which he responded, "I was sent to forgive not as a curser." Whenever he was asked to wish evil against anyone whether he be a Muslim, a disbeliever, a man of the common people, or a man of worth, he turned from wishing him evil to blessing him.

Muḥammad never struck anyone except for the sake of Allāh; nor did he ever revenge himself for what was done to him except when the sanctity of Allāh was violated. He never chose between two matters but that he chose the easier; not, however, when there was a sin in this choice, or which would result in the forsaking of kindred—Muḥammad being furthest removed from that.

No person, whether he be free born, male or female, came to Muḥammad but that he supported him in his need. Anas ibn Mālik[3] said, "By Him who sent him with the truth, Muḥammad never said to me in regard to anything what he disapproved, 'why did you do it?' Moreover, his wives did not rebuke me but that he said, 'let it be'; it was written in a book and fated."

They said that the Apostle of Allāh did not regard a bed as something amiss; for if they spread out a bed for him, he reclined upon it; if not, he reclined on the earth.

Allāh had already described him in the *Torah* before he sent him in the first generation saying, "Muḥammad is the Apostle of Allāh; he is my chosen servant. He is neither harsh, coarse, nor clamorous in the market places. He does not reward evil with evil, but he forgives and examines the affair. He was born in Mecca, and his emigration was to Medina. His kingdom is in Syria. He and those with him clothe themselves with a waistband wrapper. Allāh called him for the *Qur'ān* and firm belief. He washes his extremities."[4] He is thus also described in the New Testament.

It was his nature to be the first to extend greetings to whomever he met. He was patient with anyone who asked him for help, to the point that he (Muḥammad) was the one dismissed. While hand-shaking, Muḥammad was never the first one to release his hand. When he met one of his companions he was first to commence handshaking; he then took his hand and clasped it, strengthening his grasp over his hand.

Muḥammad did not rise or sit without the mentioning of Allāh. No one sat in his company while he was praying but that he shortened his prayer and came forth to him and said, "Have you a need?" After satisfying his need, Muḥammad returned to his prayer.

3. Muhammad's personal servant and a companion.
4. The search for attestations of Muhammad in earlier scriptures generated Muslim scholarly interest in the Hebrew Bible and Christian New Testament.

Muḥammad sat most of the time with his feet together, grasping them like a cloth which is used as a support. His sitting place could not be distinguished from that of his companions because he sat in the last row of those assembled. He never was seen stretching his legs before his companions, lest he put anyone in a strait position; the exception was when there was ample space in which there was no narrowness. Most of the time Muḥammad sat facing in the direction of Mecca.

He used to show regard to his visitor to the point of often spreading his garment and seating upon it him who was neither a relative nor foster brother. He preferred his guest [over himself] by [offering him] the cushion on which he reclined; and if he refused, Muḥammad urged him until he did accept it.

No one chose Muḥammad as a friend, but that Muḥammad regarded him as the most noble of men. He shared his attention with all his guests. Moreover he sat, listened, conversed, acted gracefully, directed himself to his guest, his company being, in spite of all that, modest, humble, and sincere. Allāh said, "By the mercy of Allāh, thou hast been mild towards them, but had'st thou been harsh and hard headed, they would have certainly dispersed from around thee."

He called his companions by their "surnames" (*kunyā*)[5] so as to honor and conciliate them. He surnamed whoever did not have a surname and called him by it. Muḥammad also surnamed the women who did not have children. He surnamed the young boys, therewith softening their hearts.

Of all men he was the least angry and the readiest to be pleased. He was the most merciful, beneficial, and useful of men towards his fellow men.

No noise was raised in his company. When he arose he said, "Allāh be praised, O Allāh, I testify praising Thee that there is no God but Thou; I ask Thy pardon and repent to Thee." Then he said, "Gabriel—may Allāh bless him—taught me this."

The Account of His Speech and Laughter

Of all men Muḥammad had the most eloquent diction and the most pleasant speech. He said, "I am the most eloquent of the Arabs." He also said that the people of Paradise speak the dialect of Muḥammad. His speech was exiguous and compliant. When he spoke he was not a babbler. His speech was like a string of [matched] gems. ʿĀʾisha[6] said, "He did not construct his speech the way you do; he spoke little, and you speak a great deal." They said that of all men Muḥammad's speech was most concise, this quality having been brought to him by Gabriel.[7] However, in spite of its concision his speech expressed all that he wanted to say. He used to speak comprehensively and concisely, neither exceeding nor falling short [from his purpose]. His sentences followed each other and were cohesive, so that his listener heard and understood him.

He had a powerful and most melodious voice. He was long silent, and did not speak without necessity. He did not say that which was forbidden to say. He only spoke the truth whether he was pleased or prone to anger. He avoided whoever spoke without eloquence. Moreover he used to express himself metonymically whenever he had to say anything which he loathed expressing.

5. An epithet used as a form of familiar but polite address (often but not always derived from the name of the person's child, in the form "father of").

6. Muhammad's favorite wife among the many he took after the death of his first wife, Khadija.

7. The angel who revealed the Qur'an to Muhammad.

When he was silent, his companions spoke. One did not argue in his presence. He warned by exhortation and by advice. Muḥammad said, "Do not refute the *Qur'ān* by comparing one part by another, for the *Qur'ān* was sent down in various ways."

He was the most smiling and laughing of men in the presence of his companions, admiring what they said, and mingling with them. He often laughed so that his molar teeth showed. The laughter of his companions in his presence, in imitation of him and as a sign of their regard for him, was a smile.

They said, "One day an Arab bedouin came to Muḥammad while he was in a frame of mind of which his companions were ignorant; and he (the bedouin) desired to ask Muḥammad something. Thereupon his companions said, 'No, do not do it (ask him), O bedouin, for we do not know his frame of mind.' The bedouin answered, 'Let me! I swear by Him who sent Muḥammad as a prophet that I shall not leave him until he smiles.' Then he said, 'O Apostle of Allāh, it has reached us that the Anointed, meaning the Anti-Christ, has brought the people who were dying of hunger a bowl of soup. Do you think, you who are dearer to me than my father and mother, that I should desist from his soup, because of chastity and purity so that I die of emaciation, or do you think that I should take his soup so that when I am satiated I will believe in Allāh and deny the Anti-Christ.' Thereupon the Apostle of Allāh laughed until his molar teeth showed, and said, 'No, but Allāh will reward you with that which he rewards the Believers.'"

They said that he was the most smiling and agreeable of men except when a revelation (*Qur'ān*) was revealed to him, when he mentioned the hour of the Resurrection, and when he preached a sermon. When he rejoiced and was pleased, he was the most pleased of men. If he preached, he preached vigorously; if he were angered, being angered only for the sake of Allāh, nothing could withstand his anger. Thus he was in all his affairs.

When he undertook an affair, he entrusted the matter to Allāh, renounced his strength and power, and asked for guidance, saying, "O Allāh, show me the truth, *qua* truth, and I will follow it. Show me what is denied, *qua* denied, and cause me to shun it. Protect me, lest the truth become dubious to me, and I will follow my inclination without guidance from You. Cause my inclination to act in obedience to You, and may You be pleased with my soundness. Guide me correctly in regard to whatever I am, with Your permission, in doubt as to the truth. Verily You guide whomever You desire to the right path."

SHAH WALI ALLAH
1703–1762

A cemetery in Old Delhi attracts visitors to the shrine of an eighteenth-century scholar and writer who is honored by Indian Muslims as an intellectual revolutionary and reformer. Ahmad Abu al-Fayyad Shah Wali Allah al-Dihlavi's legacy in Indian Islamic literature has been drawn on by a wide range of successors.

Shah Wali Allah sought a coherent vision of Islam, synthesizing the often competing voices found in the works of philosophers, theologians, jurists, Sufis, and traditionists.

Central to his thought was the notion of "benefit" (in Arabic, *maslaha*), by which Islamic injunctions were understood as fulfilling a universal social purpose well beyond the betterment of the individual. He stressed the concept of "reconciliation" (*tatbiq*), seeking to harmonize multiple Sunni schools of law and theology by minimizing the differences among them. Shah Wali Allah advocated the study of traditions as a means of reviving Islamic practice and proposed a four-stage model of socioeconomic development that culminated in an ideal Muslim state.

Born four years before the death of the Mughal ruler Awrangzib, Shah Wali Allah lived during the final decades of Mughal decline. The empire was beset by internal challenges to its rule from Sikh and Hindu groups and weakened by Afghan and Persian invasions. The growing presence of colonial powers throughout India heightened the turmoil and instability of these decades. Shah Wali Allah claimed descent on his father's side from the second caliph, ʿUmar, and on his mother's side from the fourth caliph, ʿAli. He was proud of his distant lineage, and he was indebted to his father, also a scholar, for his extraordinary intellectual and spiritual training as a child. He read the entire Qurʾan by the age of seven, and when he was fifteen he began teaching at the academy in Delhi that bore his father's name, Madrasa Rahimiyya. Under his father's tutelage, Shah Wali Allah also underwent initiation into several Sufi orders. He was still a teenager when his father died and he was bequeathed leadership of the academy and permission to initiate his own Sufi disciples.

The course of his life changed in 1730 when, against family wishes, he undertook the risky journey to Mecca and Medina; he spent more than a year immersed in the study of hadith and mystical writings. During his stay in the holy cities he experienced visions, including one in which the Prophet's grandsons presented him with a pen and a robe belonging to the Prophet. He clearly interpreted this as a sign and subsequently devoted himself intensely to writing, producing most of his works after returning to India in 1732. He wrote in both Arabic and Persian, producing an annotated translation of the Qurʾan in the latter language.

The passage below is excerpted from *The Conclusive Argument*, his most significant work, which was written within the decade after his return from Mecca and Medina. This treatise, once part of the curriculum at al-Azhar—a traditional center of Islamic learning in Cairo—and still studied throughout the Middle East, South Asia, and Southeast Asia, seeks to explain the inner mysteries of Islam. It also addresses many other subjects, such as philosophy, traditions, and Shah Wali Allah's four-stage model for the ideal Muslim state.

He took the work's title from Qurʾan 6:149, which states that "the conclusive argument is from God." *The Conclusive Argument from God* represents Shah Wali Allah's effort to integrate many levels and layers of Islamic thought and practice, and it has found an enduring readership well beyond the South Asian subcontinent. Shah Wali Allah's range is encyclopedic but deeply anchored in prophetic hadith and structured to achieve harmony and balance. The importance of balance is well demonstrated in the following selection from *The Conclusive Argument from God*, which asks how religious teachings and practices become distorted and how they can be protected from such deformation.

PRONOUNCING GLOSSARY

ʿAbd Allāh Ibn ʿUmar: *abd al-lah´ ibn oh´-mar*
Ḥasan al-Baṣrī: *ha´-san* (heavy *h*) *al-bas´-ree*
Ibn Sīrīn: *ibn see-reen´*
Iblīs: *ib-lees´*
Muʿādh ibn Jabal: *moo-ahdh´ ibn ja´-bal*
mujtahid: *muj-ta´-hid*
Al-Shaʿbī: *ash-shah´-bee*
ʿUthmān Ibn Maẓ ʿūn: *uth-man´ ibn mahz-oon´*

FROM THE CONCLUSIVE ARGUMENT FROM GOD

Chapter 71

Fortifying the Religion against Distortion

It is indispensable for the man possessed of supreme authority who brings from God a religion which supersedes other religions that he fortify his religion against being penetrated by distortion, and this is because he unites many nations having manifold propensities and dissimilar goals. Often these people are misled by their self-interest or their love for the religion which they followed previously, or their deficient understanding when reasoning about something, so they miss many beneficial purposes and they neglect what the religion had explicitly assigned, or they interpolate into it something extrinsic, and the religion becomes corrupted as occurred in many religions before us. Then, since a thorough investigation in recognizing the avenues of the interpolation of unsoundness is not possible, for they are limitless and undetermined—and what cannot be completely achieved cannot be totally abandoned—he must warn them most strongly of the causes of distortion in a comprehensive way. He must single out the issues which he surmises will contain or cause laxity or distortion, or which will provoke a permanent malady among humans. He must block the entrance of corruption into them in the most complete way, and he must legislate a thing which is contrary to the familiar ways of the corrupted religions in whichever elements are most prominent among them, such as the prayers.

Among the causes of distortion is laxity, the true nature of which is that after the disciples comes a generation which neglects the prayers until they are lost and follows their lusts,[1] not giving importance to the spreading of the religion by studying, teaching, and acting; and they neither command the good nor do they forbid the evil. Thus there will coalesce, before long, customs which oppose the religion, and the desire of people's physical natures will conflict with the demand of the divine laws. Then other succeeding generations will follow, increasingly lax and careless, until they forget most of the religious knowledge, and careless neglect on the part of the leaders and the great ones of the nation is more harmful to them and further undermines them. This is the reason that the religions of Noah and Abraham disappeared, for scarcely anyone from them could be found who knew the basis of their religion correctly.

The origin of careless neglect lies in several things. Among them is the absence of transmitting from the founder of the religion and acting upon this, and this is the Prophet's saying, "It won't be long before a man with a full stomach upon his couch talks to you about this Qur'ān, saying 'what you find permitted (in the Qur'ān) allow, and what you find forbidden in it, forbid.' But what the Prophet of God forbade is what God forbade."[2] And his saying, "Indeed God does not take away knowledge, per se, by removing it from the people, but He takes away knowledge by taking away the people

Translated by Marcia K. Hermansen.

1. See Qur'an 19:59: "There came a later generation which had lost their prayers and followed their lusts" [translator's note, edited].

2. A warning about following the Qur'an only and not the Sunna [translator's note].

of knowledge, until, when no learned man remains the people will take ignorant men as leaders, and will ask them (about various cases) and they will give legal opinions without knowledge (of the religion and sharīʿa), thus they will go astray and will lead others astray."

Among the sources of distortions are corrupt intentions leading to false exegesis such as when people try to please the kings' (wishes) to follow their own desires, according to God's, may He be exalted, saying, "Those who conceal what God revealed in the scripture and purchase a small gain with this, are those who will eat nothing in their bellies except fire."[3]

Among the sources of distortion is the spread of evil things and the abandoning, on the part of the ulema, of prohibiting them, and this is God's saying, may He be exalted, "If only there had been in the generations before you people of excellence forbidding corruption on the earth, as did a few of those whom We saved. The wrongdoers followed that which made them softened by pleasure, and they were criminals."[4]

This is (also demonstrated by) what the Prophet, may the peace and blessings of God be upon him, said about the Children of Israel falling into acts of disobedience, "Their religious scholars forbade them these things, but they did not abstain from them, then they (the religious scholars) sat in their meetings and they ate in their company and they drank with them, so that God made their hearts beat in the same rhythm, and cursed them on the tongues of David and Jesus, son of Mary; and this was due to their disobedience and transgression."

Among the causes of distortion is unnecessary hair-splitting, and the nature of this is that the law-giver orders something and forbids something else, so that a man from his religion hears this and understands this as his mind is able, so that he overextends the ruling to things which resemble the (original) thing only in certain aspects or in which certain parts of the reason for the legislation (*ʿilla*) are found, or to portions of the thing, or to some of its anticipated sources or its motives. Whenever the matter becomes ambiguous for this person due to a conflict in the hadith reports, he sticks to the most stringent and makes it obligatory, and he takes everything which the Prophet, may the peace and blessings of God be upon him, used to do, as an act of worship, while the truth is that the Prophet used to do things according to the current custom. Thus he thinks that the command and the forbidding include these things so he publicly proclaims that God, may He be exalted, commanded a certain thing, and forbade some other thing. For example when the law-giver legislated fasting[5] to subdue the lower soul and forbade sexual intercourse during it, one group thought that eating before dawn was against the law because it is incompatible with subduing the lower soul, and they thought that the fasting person was forbidden to kiss his wife because this is one of the inducements to sexual intercourse, and because it is similar to intercourse in satisfying lust, and therefore the Prophet revealed the error of these statements and explained that they were distortions.

Among the causes of distortion is being excessively strict, and the true nature of this is choosing austerities in worship which the law-giver did not command such as continual fasting, praying the whole night long, retiring

3. Qur'an 2:174.
4. Qur'an 11:116.
5. Lasting from sunrise to sundown.

from the world, remaining celibate, and making the recommended practices and proper manners just as compulsory as the obligatory things. This is referred to in a hadith report of the Prophet, may the peace and blessings of God be upon him, that he forbade ʿAbd Allāh Ibn ʿUmar and ʿUthmān Ibn Maẓʿūn[6] from the arduous practices which they had in mind, and this is his saying, "No one makes religion too strict but that it overwhelms him." Thus, if this hair-splitter or strict man becomes the teacher and the leader of a group they will think that this is the command of the divine law and pleasing to God, and this is the ailment of the ascetics among the Jews and the Christian monks.

Among the causes of distortion is "preference" (*istiḥsān*). The true nature of this is that a man might see that the law-giver fixed for every rule an anticipated source related to it, and he knows that the law-giver fixed the legislation, but he appropriates certain of the inner meanings of the legislation which we have previously mentioned, so that he legislates for the people according to what he thinks is the beneficial purpose. An example of this is that the Jews believed that the Law-Giver only commanded the punishments as a deterrent from disobeying and to reform them, and they thought that stoning to death would result in altercations and fighting, so that in it there would be a greater evil, and therefore they applied (the principle of) "preference" in sanctioning blackening the face and skin (of the adulterer with coal) instead of stoning. The Prophet, may the peace and blessings of God be upon him, explained that this was a distortion and a discarding of the order of God laid down in writing in the Torah in favor of their own opinions. Ibn Sīrīn[7] said, "The first one to apply analogies was Iblīs (the devil) and the worship of the moon and sun only came about through analogy." There is a report about Ḥasan (al-Baṣrī) that he recited this verse of the Qurʾān. "You created me from fire and You created him from earth,"[8] saying that Iblīs used an analogy and he was the first to use an analogy. A report from al-Shaʿbī[9] is "By God, if you take up the use of analogies, you will forbid the permitted; and permit what is forbidden." Muʿādh ibn Jabal[1] said,

> The Qurʾān will be opened to the people so that woman, and child, and man will read it. Then the man will say, "I have read the Qurʾān, but I am not followed, by God I will implement it among them so that perhaps I will be followed." So he implemented it among them but they still did not follow him. So he said, "I will build a mosque in my house so that they will follow me." So he built a mosque in his house, but was not obeyed; so he said, "I have read the Qurʾān and was not followed, and I implemented it among them, and I was not followed, and I have built a mosque in my house and I was not followed, so now, by God, I will provide them with a discourse which they will not find in the book of God, nor have they heard it from the Prophet of God, may peace be upon him, so that perhaps I will be followed."

6. An early convert to Islam. Ibn ʿUmar (d. ca. 692), son of the second caliph.
7. The first Muslim interpreter of dreams and a respected transmitter of hadith (d. 728) translator's note, edited].
8. Qurʾan 7:12. Ḥasan al-Baṣrī (642–728), a famously pious and ascetic Islamic leader.
9. A teacher and collector of traditions (ca. 640–ca. 728).
1. A Companion of the Prophet (d. ca. 639).

> Muʿādh said, "O, you people, beware of what this person relates, for what he relates is misguidance."

It is reported of ʿUmar, may God be satisfied with him, that he said, "The lapsing of the learned man, and the arguing of the hypocrite; using the book of God, and the command of the leaders who have gone astray, will destroy Islam." What is intended by all of these examples are those things not derived from the book of God and the practice of His Prophet.

Among the causes of distortion is following the consensus (*ijmāʿ*), and the true nature of this is that a group of the bearers of the religion, whom the masses believe hold the correct opinion most of the time or always, agree; so the people think that this is a conclusive proof of the confirmation of the ruling, while this is a consensus on a matter which has no basis in the Qurʾān or the sunna. This is not the consensus which the community agreed on (*ijmāʿ al-umma*) for they agreed to call something "a consensus" which was founded on the Qurʾān or the sunna or was directly derived from one of them, and they did not allow something to be called "consensus" which was not based on one of these things. This is God's, may He be exalted, saying, "And if it is said to them, believe in what Allah has revealed, they will say, rather we follow the way upon which we found our forefathers."[2]

The Jews only persisted in denying the prophethood of Jesus and Muḥammad, may peace and blessings be upon them, because their ancestors had tested their life stories and did not find them fulfilling the conditions of prophethood, and the Christians have many divine laws which oppose both the Torah and the Gospel which they have no cause to hold onto except the consensus of their ancestors.

Among the causes of distortion is conforming to the legal decisions (*taqlīd*) of someone who is not entirely infallible, by whom I mean someone other than the Prophet whose infallibility is established. The essence of this is that when one of the learned scholars of the religion uses independent reasoning (*ijtihād*) in a problem, his followers may think that he hits the right answer assuredly or in most cases, so that due to it (his independent reasoning) they reject a sound hadith. This reliance on following (*taqlīd*) is different from that which the blessed community agreed on, for they only agreed on the permissibility of following (*taqlīd*) the experts in independent reasoning (*mujtahidūn*), knowing that the *mujtahid* may err or may be correct, and searching for the text of the report of the Prophet in the issue, with the intent that if a reliable hadith comes to the fore which opposes what is followed, then conforming with (the reasoner) should be abandoned and the hadith should be followed. The Prophet said in the interpretation of God's saying, may He be exalted, "They took their rabbis (*aḥbār*) and monks as lords besides God,"[3] that it was not that they used to worship them, but rather if they said that a thing was permitted to people, then they would take it as such, and that if they forbade them something, then they would take it to be forbidden.

Among them is the intermingling of one religion with another religion until one is not distinguishable from the other. This occurs because when a person previously professes another religion, he retains an emotional attach-

2. Qurʾan 2:170.

3. Qurʾan 9:31.

ment to the branches of knowledge of this group. Then when he joins the religion of Islam the inclination of his heart to what it had previously been attached remains, and consequently he will seek a device (to make room for those things) in this religion (Islam), even if this is weak or fabricated. Sometimes he justifies fabrication or transmitting the fabricated hadith because of this and this is the Prophet's saying, "The situation of the Children of Israel was balanced until there arose among them those of mixed descent and the children of prisoners of (other) nations so they spoke on the basis of their own opinions and went astray and led (others) astray." Among those things which have become interpolated into our religion is the lore of the Children of Israel, the exhortations of the orators of the Ignorant Age,[4] the science of the Greeks, the religious propaganda of the Babylonians, the history of the Persians, astrology, geomancy, and rationalist theology (*kalām*), and this is the ultimate cause of the anger of the Prophet, may the peace and blessings of God be upon him, when there was read before him a copy of the Torah, and the ultimate cause of ʿUmar's, may God be pleased with him, beating the man who was trying to get the books of Daniel,[5] and God knows better.

4. The pre-Islamic period, particularly in Arabia. "The Children of Israel": the Jews, or the Jews and the Christians.
5. That is, the biblical book of Daniel.

IBN ʿABD AL-WAHHAB
1703–1792

Even people with very little knowledge of Islam often recognize the term "Wahhabi Islam": in the early twenty-first century, it has become a code word and a catchphrase that raises fears around the world and attracts negative epithets—extremist, militant, fanatical, puritanical, antimodern, misogynist. Its frequent linkages with both the Afghan Taliban and Usama bin Ladin's al-Qa'ida reinforce the dark associations.

Muhammad Ibn ʿAbd al-Wahhab was born in the Najd, now an eastern province of the Kingdom of Saudi Arabia. At the time of his birth, the Arabian Peninsula was not a unified political entity with a single form of governance. Rather, it comprised a constellation of tribal societies and confederacies. Ibn ʿAbd al-Wahhab was born into a provincially educated family and his father was the chief judge (*qadi*) of al-ʿUyayna, his birthplace. Not surprisingly, his father was also his first teacher and began the instruction of his son in the Qur'an and Hanbali law. Eventually, Ibn ʿAbd al-Wahhab began to expand his educational horizons by travel to nearby Huraymila and then with hajj trips to Mecca and Medina. In Medina, where he lived for four years, he shared a teacher with Shah Wali Allah al-Dihlavi (1703–1762; see above), who was to become the most famous Indian scholar and jurist of his generation. To his time in Medina, biographers also date Ibn ʿAbd al-Wahhab's prolonged immersion in the works of Ibn Taymiyya (1263–1328; see below), an intellectual forebear of many modern and contemporary Muslim conservatives. Although Ibn ʿAbd al-Wahhab also spent time in the Iraqi city of Basra, reports of his travels to more distant cities in Iran and even India are usually considered apocryphal.

Upon his return to the Arabian Peninsula and al-ʿUyayna, Ibn ʿAbd al-Wahhab moved from preaching to political activism. He allied himself with the region's ruler, ʿUthman ibn Muʿammar, and sealed the affiliation by marrying the ruler's aunt. Protected by such patronage, Ibn ʿAbd al-Wahhab began to enforce his interpretation of true Islam by destroying objects and sites, such as shrines and saints' tombs, that had attracted veneration. Some of his actions—for example, personally stoning an alleged adulteress—proved too politically extreme. He lost ʿUthman ibn Muʿammar's support and was expelled from al-ʿUyayna. But after relocating to Darʿiyya (near the present Saudi capital of Riyadh), he found a new patron in Muhammad ibn Saʿud (d. 1765), a tribal leader who became the founder of the first Saudi dynasty. The two swore an oath of mutual loyalty (*bayʿa*), an ancient Bedouin affirmation of allegiance. While Ibn Saʿud had power over political, economic, and military matters, Ibn ʿAbd al-Wahhab controlled religious affairs. Together they created a theocratic state, which Ibn ʿAbd al-Wahhab expanded with aggressive preaching and interventions until his death in 1792.

Although various written works have been credited to Ibn ʿAbd al-Wahhab, he left no well-developed exposition of his theological and legal thought. His best-known work, *On Divine Oneness* (*Kitab al-Tawhid*), is an assemblage in sixty-seven chapters of various statements by the Prophet and other early Muslims that are relevant to that topic. Other published writings follow much the same format, though some were expanded by their twentieth-century editors. Because Ibn ʿAbd al-Wahhab's own writings provide little elaboration of his thought and scant theological argumentation, they are not easy to anthologize. Consequently, the following selection is drawn from a pamphlet published by his grandson, Sulayman ibn ʿAbd al-Wahhab, who was a strong advocate for his grandfather's teachings. Sulayman was the chief judge of Darʿiyya and fiercely opposed to the Ottomans. After the Ottoman capture of Darʿiyya in 1818, he was sentenced to death by the governor of Egypt, Ibrahim Pasha.

PRONOUNCING GLOSSARY

ʿAbdullah: *abd-ul-lah´*
ʿAbdul-Wahháb: *abd-ul-wah-hab´*
Abú Shámah al Muqrí: *a-boo-sha´-ma al-muq´-ri*
Ahl-us-Sunnat: *ahl* (light *h*) *us-sun´-nat*
ʿArsh: *ahrsh*
Al-báis fí-inkár-il-bidaʿ wal-hawádis: *al-ba´-ith fee in-kar´ al-bid´-ah wal-ha-wa´-dith*
Bidʿat: *bid´-ut*
Bismillah: *bism-il-lah´*
Çúfís: *soo´-fees*
Daff: *daff*
Daráyah: *da-ra´-yuh*
farz: *fard*
Fátihahs: *fa´-ti-hahs*
ghair-muqallid: *ghayr moo-qal´-lid*
Al-Habshí: *al-hab´-shee*
Hadíses (=hadith): *ha-deeth* (heavy *h*)
Hanafí: *han´-a-fee* (heavy *h*)
Hanbalí: *han´-ba-lee* (heavy *h*)
Hasan: *ha´-sun* (heavy *h*)
al-Hayaní: *al-ha-ya´-nee*
Husain ul-Airat'í ul-Hazramí: *hoo-sayn* (heavy *h*) *ul-ay´-rat-ee ul-had´-ra-mee*
ʿId: *eed*
Ijmáʿ: *ij-ma´*
Imám Ahmad Ibn Hanbal: *ee-mam´ ah´-mad* (heavy *h*) *ibn han´-bal* (heavy *h*)
Imám bin Qayam: *ee-mam´ bin qay-yim*
Imámiyyahs: *ee-mam´-ee-yuhs*
Iʿtikáf: *i-ti-kaf´*
al-Jamáʿat: *al-ja-ma´-at*
Khadíjah: *cha-dee´-juh* (guttural *ch*)
Makkah: *mak´-kuh*
Malakís: *ma´-la-kees*
Muhammad: *moo-ham´-mad* (heavy *h*)
Muharram: *moo-hahr´-ram* (heavy *h*)
ʿOmar ibn al Khaṭṭáb: *oh´-mar ibn al-chaht-tahb* (guttural *ch*)
Pírs: *peers*
Qorán (=Qurʾan): *qor-ahn´*
Ramazán: *ra-ma-dawn´*
Saʿúd: *sa-ood´*
Sháfiʾís: *shaf´-i-ees*
Shaikh: *shaych* (guttural *ch*)
Shaikh al-Ṭarṭúsí-al-Maghribí: *shaych* (guttural *ch*) *al-tar-too´-see al-mag´-ri-bee*
Shiʿahs: *shee´-uhs*

Sunnat: *sun´-nat*
Taráwíh: *ta-ra-weeh´* (heavy *h*)
Tafsírs: *taf-seers´*
Zaidiyyahs: *zayd-ee´-yuhs*

FROM THE HISTORY AND DOCTRINES OF THE WAHHABIS

And among the persons who presented themselves before us with the people of Makkah and witnessed our victory[1] in discussion, was Husain ul-Airat'í ul-Hazramí, afterwards al-Hayaní. He continued to visit us and sit with Saʿúd and others of the force who were well learned in the scriptures, and he asked us of those matters other than the intercession of Saints, for which our swords were unsheathed. This he did fearlessly, and without any dread, as he was guiltless of any thing wrong in our eyes. So we informed him of our belief which is as follows: We believe, our sect holds the real true religion, is the sect of the Ahl-us-Sunnat and al-Jamáʿat,[2] and that our way to salvation is that of the pious ancient departed, most easy and excellent, and opposed to the doctrines of those who hold that the modern way is the best. We construe the Qorán and Hadíṣes[3] according to the meaning apparent on the face of them, and leave the interpretation of them to God, for He is the Ruler. And for this reason that the divines[4] who have passed away, so acted in answering the question as to whether the highest heaven is level or not, which arose out of the words of the merciful God, "The *ʿArsh*[5] is level;" they held that "level" was well known, and as it was predicated of *ʿArsh*, it was lawful to believe in it, and heretical to question it. We believe that good and evil proceed from God, the exalted; that nothing happens in His kingdom, but what He commands; that created beings do not possess free will, and are not accountable for their own acts; but on the contrary they obtain rank and spiritual reward, merely as an act of grace, and suffer punishment justly, for God is not bound to do anything for His slaves.[6] We believe that the faithful will see Him in the end, but we do not know under what form, as it was beyond our comprehension. And in the same way we follow Imám Ahmad Ibn Hanbal in matters of detail; but we do not reject any one who follows any of the four Imáms,[7] as we do the Shiʿahs, the Zaidiyyahs, and the Imámiyyahs,[8] &c., who belong to no regular churches. Nor do we admit them in any way to act openly according to their vicious creeds; on the contrary, we compelled them to follow one of the four Imáms. We do not claim to exercise our reason in all matters of religion, and none of our faith demand such a position, save that we follow our judgment where a point is clearly demonstrated to us in either the Qorán or the Sunnat[9] still in force, and though there has been no special command in

Translated by J. O'Kinealy.

1. The taking of Mecca (Makkah) in 1803 by Wahhabi forces led by Sa ʿud ibn ʿAbd al- ʿAziz (1745–1814).
2. Traditional self-designation of Sunni Muslims, often translated as "People of the Tradition and Community."
3. That is, Qurʾan and hadith.
4. Religious scholars.
5. The divine throne.
6. Or "servants" (translating the Arabic word *ʿabd*).
7. The four scholars for whom the major Sunni legal traditions are named; in addition to Ahmad ibn Hanbal (780–855; see above), they are Abu Hanifa (699–767; see above), Malik ibn Anas (ca. 715–795), and Muhammad ibn Idris al-Shafiʿi (767–820; see above)—giving rise to the Hanbalis, Hanifis, Malikis, and Shafiʿis.
8. Forms of Shiʿism, here rejected as *not* belonging to one of the four acceptable legal schools ("churches").
9. Sunna.

favour of it, yet there is nothing of weight against it. As a rule, we hold the same as the four Imáms; but we reject all sects in connection with property inherited by our ancestors, and hold them preferred, although it is opposed to the Hanbalí sect. We do not enquire to what sect a person belongs, neither do we abandon the forms prescribed by the four sects, except where we find a clear decision contrary to any of them and the matter is merely an outward observance, such as the action of an Imám at prayers. Hence we direct Malakís and Hanafís equally to collect themselves an instant, when standing or sitting before prostrating themselves at prayers, for on this point the evidence is clear. On the other hand, we do not prohibit the saying of "Bismillah"[1] in a loud voice, as is the custom among Sháfiʿís, neither do we direct it to be said inwardly. Where two contrary practices were in force, and the evidence in connection with each is strong, we declare both allowable, even though this is contrary to any sect. But this occurs only very rarely. The exercise of our reason in some matters of religion is not prohibited, nor can such be deemed contradictory to repudiating the right to exercise our reason in all religious matters; for above all the four Imáms followed their own will in some minor religious observances, even so far as to act contrary to the rules of the sect which they founded.

* * *

We believe that our prophet Muhammad (may he, &c.[2]) is more exalted by God than any other created being; that he is alive, lives in his grave a life quicker than that declared by revelation unto martyrs, and that he can hear the salutations of those who salute him. We consider pilgrimage is supported by legal custom, but it should not be undertaken except to a mosque, and for the purpose of praying in it. Therefore, whoever performs pilgrimage for this purpose, is not wrong, and doubtless those who spend the precious moments of their existence in invoking the Prophet, shall, according to the Hadíṣ, obtain happiness in this world and the next, and he will dispel their sorrows. We do not deny miraculous powers to the saints, but on the contrary allow them. They are under the guidance of the Lord, so long as they continue to follow the way pointed out in the laws and obey the prescribed rules. But whether alive or dead, they must not be made the object of any form of worship. This does not prevent us from asking them or any other Muslim if living to supplicate on our behalf. Thus it is related in the Hadíṣ that Al-mar-ul-Muslim asked that his brother might be accepted by God, and 'Omar directed 'Alí to ask Uwais[3] to supplicate that he might be pardoned, and he did so. According to what has descended to us, our prophet Muhammad (may he, &c.) is empowered to intercede for us on the day of judgment, and so also are all prophets, angels, saints, and children. And we shall ask it of the Lord God, the Ruler over it, the Granter of it to whomsoever He pleases to those who are amongst the best of men, the believers in the Unity of God. Thus one of us entreating the Lord God Almighty shall say, O Lord, you have empowered our prophet Muhammad (may he, &c.) to intercede for us, &c. (in the form handed down by tradition), or we shall ask

1. Or *basmala*, the name for the phrase that prefaces all but one sura of the Qur'an: "In the name of God, the beneficent, the merciful."
2. The full Arabic invocation would read "May God's blessings and peace be upon him."
3. A Yemeni Muslim mystic (d. 657). 'Ali (ca. 599–661), the fourth caliph and Muhammad's cousin and son-in-law.

it of the Lord God, the Granter of it to us on the day of judgment. "O God, you have appointed your pure slave (mortal or angel, as may be) to intercede." Thus we shall ask God for those things which must be demanded from Him and not from them. And as regards the things over which God alone has power, no one will cry out "O prophet of God", or "O Saint of God, I ask your intercession," nor will any one say to this "help me"; or "intercede for me", or "assist me." Since calling in this manner on those who are dead, but as yet not risen to judgment, is a form of shirk.[4] There is nothing in its favour, either in the Qorán or the Sunnat. The pious departed have not urged it. On the contrary, they have decided that it is shirk of the most aggravated form, on account of which the prophet warred with the world.

* * *

Now as regards the Ahl-ul-bait,[5] a similar question, *viz* the lawfulness of marrying a Fáṭimite, was asked of the people of Daráyah,[6] and they answered in accordance with former decisions regarding them. It is right to be friendly and on good terms with them, as is stated in the Qorán and the Sunnat. But we must remember that *Islám* is the line of separation between us and the rest of mankind; and that there is neither grace nor goodness without piety which carries with it honor, respect, and reverence. All learned people are guided by it in the question of precedence, between persons nearly equal in age or knowledge, or in advancing to meet such when escorting them to the place of honor. But the custom which is prevalent in some cities, of honoring those who are young and ignorant, even so far that they are angry, beat, wound, or at least quarrel with those who do not kiss their hands instead of shaking them, is not based on any decision, nor is there any evidence in its favour. On the contrary, it is forbidden and should be abolished. If one person kisses the hand of another returning from a long journey, or if he does it to honor him for his learning, or after a long absence, it is harmless in itself, but is objectionable, as it becomes known to those who put faith in such things and creates a custom among proud people. Hence we absolutely prohibit it, especially on account of those of whom it is said as a warning: "It is not possible to close all the places where hunters watch." For this very reason we razed the house of the noble Khadíjah, the wife of our Prophet, the dwelling in which the prophet was born, and other places dedicated to certain Saints in Makkah, so that the people might be warned and flee from shirk, inconsistent with His exaltedness, and which He will never forgive. Shirk is worse even than saying God has a son;[7] the latter makes Him superior to all created beings, the former does away with this superiority. For the Lord has said, "A parable is propounded to you about yourselves:" "What your right hands have obtained, is it for you or for your companions?"[8]

* * *

Among those things which we prohibit is the custom of reciting verses in praise of the prophet, and at the same time blessing him, that of repeating

4. Arabic term for "associating" [anything with God], the fundamental sin.
5. The "People of the House," the descendants of Muhammad through his daughter Fatima and her husband, ʿAli. Fatimites are Shiʿi.
6. The capital of the Wahhabis, just west of Riyadh (sacked by the Egyptians in 1818).
7. A common accusation against the Christians.
8. Qurʾan 30:28.

his name or reading it after Taráwíh prayers[9] under the belief that it is a form of prayer. Indeed, multitudes are under the idea that this is a custom undoubtedly handed down from our ancestors, and hence we forbid it. But the Taráwíh itself is Sunnat, and there is nothing wrong in assembling to read it, or even in repeating it very often. Another form of Bidʿat[1] is the custom of reading the five prayers, which are *farz*[2] after the close of Friday in the Ramazán. This has been prohibited by Ijmáʿ,[3] and we punish it most severely. There are other forms of Bidʿat, such as taking the name of God in a loud voice, when lifting a corpse or when sprinkling the grave with water. No authority for such has descended from the pious departed. In conclusion, it is as well to point out that Shaikh Al-Ṭarṭúsí-al-Maghribí has written a book called Al-báis fí-inkár-il-bidaʿ wal-hawádiṣ,[4] and that Abú Shámah al Muqrí has compiled from it a shorter pamphlet, which should be in the hands of all who are earnest in their faith.

We prohibit those forms of Bidʿat that affect religion or pious works. Thus drinking coffee, reciting poetry, praising kings, do not affect religion or pious works and are not prohibited, so long as they are not mixed up with acts of the nature above described, neither do we prohibit *Iʿtikáf*[5] in a mosque in the belief that it is a pious act. Thus Hasan told ʿOmar ibn al Khaṭṭáb,[6] Commander of the Faithful, that he had sung before one who was better than he, and ʿOmar allowed him to sing.

All games are lawful. Our prophet (may, &c.) allowed Al-Habshí to play in his mosque on the ʿId day.[7] So it is lawful to chide and punish persons in various ways; to train them in the use of different weapons; or to use anything which tends to encourage warriors in battle, such as a war-drum. But it must not be accompanied with musical instruments. These are forbidden, and indeed the difference between them and a war drum is clear. However the Daff[8] is allowed at marriages. The prophet (may, &c.) has said, "Impurity has descended to us with purity." And again, "tell the Jews that our faith is not difficult."

We hold that Imám bin Qayam and his Shaikh[9] are true Imáms, followers of the Ahl-us-Sunnat, and we hold their writings in the greatest respect, save that as regards them we are on every point *ghair-muqallid*[1], and every one of us is allowed to accept or reject their opinions, or the opinions of any person except those of the Prophet. It is well known that we hold opinions opposed to the Imáms on several points. Thus as regards giving three divorces[2] in one assembly, in one sentence, we hold it obligatory following the four Imáms. We hold waqf[3] proper, vows allowable, and their proper performance obligatory. Among the many forms of *bidʿat* which we forbid, is offering up Fátihahs to

9. Prayers recited during the nights of Ramadan, the month of Muslim fasting (here "Ramazán").
1. Unacceptable innovation in matters of religion.
2. Obligatory (usually transliterated *fard*).
3. Scholarly consensus.
4. "The Incentive in Rejecting Innovation and Novelties," an abridgment by Abu Shama (1203–1266) of a longer work written by Muhammad ibn Walid al-Turtushi (1059/60–1126).
5. Spending the last ten days of Ramadan in a mosque.
6. The second caliph (ca. 586–644), who succeeded Abu Bakr. Hassan ibn Thabit (d. 659), a Medinan who was a favorite poet of the prophet Muhammad.
7. Eid, the holiday that marks the end of Ramadan.
8. A kind of drum.
9. Ibn Qayyim al-Jawziyya (1292–1350) and his teacher, Ibn Taymiyya (1263–1328; see below).
1. Not obligated to accept uncritically.
2. The triple repudiation by which a man divorces his wife.
3. Religious endowments and trusts.

Pírs[4] after the five daily prayers; lauding them immoderately, and seeking conjunction with them after the manner in many cities.

Consolidating prayers,[5] though considered by some as a most pious act, is as a rule a temptation towards shirk, though persons do not perceive it. For shirk is so imperceptible, that people are often unwittingly guilty of it. If not, why should our prophet (may, &c.) have sought protection from it, *viz.*, "O Lord, you have guarded me against knowingly committing shirk. Pardon me, if I have done it unwittingly. To you are known the most secret things." It is absolutely necessary that people should hold to these words, and avoid shirk as much as possible. And ʿOmar ibn ul Khaṭṭáb said, "The handle of Islám, that best of handles, will be broken." Then they asked "when," and he answered, when some Moslems know not the state of ignorance before the Prophet, &c. For these will do shirk and yet believe that it is a pious act. O God, guard us from backsliding and grant that our faith may not be impaired!

This is a short account of the heads of the conversation which, as already mentioned, we held with Husain ul-Airat'í. He often asked us to put it in writing, and as he was importunate, I have done so, but without referring to our religious books, as I have been busily employed in superintending matters connected with the Holy War. But whoever is desirous of knowing our belief, let him come to us at Daráyah, and he will see what will gladden his heart, and his eyes will be pleased in reading the compilations on the different kinds of knowledge, especially the Tafsírs[6] and Hadíṣes. He will see God praised in a pleasing manner; the assistance He gives in establishing the true faith; the kindness, which He exerts among the weak and feeble, between inhabitants and travellers.

We do not deny the doctrines of Çúfís,[7] nor the purification of a person's soul from the stains of sin in deed or thought, provided the person who holds them is firm in his religious observances, and treads the straight road as marked out. But we do not undertake to carry it out in all our acts and deeds. Nor do we turn towards, ask assistance, or beg for aid from other than the Lord God, to whom alone we turn in all our acts. He is our Agent, our Master, our Deliverer. May peace and the blessing of God be upon our prince Muhammad and on his family and his companions!

ʿAbdullah, son of Muhammad, son of ʿAbdul-Wahháb, wrote this in Muharram, 1218. [April, 1803, A. D.].

4. Spiritual teachers and masters. "Offering up Fátihahs": the practice of seeking God's blessings by repeatedly reciting the first chapter of the Qur'an, the *Fatiha*, or "Opening."

5. Combining two of the mandated five daily prayers.

6. Commentaries on the Qur'an.

7. Sufis.

FALSAFA: PHILOSOPHY

AL-FARABI
ca. 878–950

One of the most influential philosophers of the tenth century, Abu Nasr al-Farabi (known in Latin as Avennasar or Alfarabius) was often referred to in Arabic philosophical texts as the "the second teacher"—second to Aristotle himself.

Little is known about the life of al-Farabi, who was probably born in western Turkestan. As a young man, he moved to Baghdad, where he studied the Greek sciences with Nestorian Christian scholars and composed several works of his own. Sometime after 942 he moved to Syria, and in 950 he died in Damascus.

Al-Farabi's influence on later Arab philosophers, such as Ibn Sina (ca. 980–1037; see below) and Ibn Rushd (1126–1198; see below), is undeniable. His writings, most of which have been lost, dealt with logic, metaphysics, political science, and music theory. He composed commentaries on and amplifications of the logical works of Aristotle and other Greek thinkers. In metaphysics, his model of emanation influenced all subsequent Neoplatonic philosophers. Drawing on Platonic political theory, his writings on state and society left a lasting imprint on Islamic political thought. He was also a musician, and his tracts on music theory are considered indispensable for the history of Arabic music.

A number of al-Farabi's works on politics have survived, among them *On Political Government, The Attainment of Happiness*, and *The Virtuous City*, which is excerpted below. All are built upon al-Farabi's understanding of human existence and its purpose, which he viewed as the achievement of true happiness: he believed that such happiness is acquired through contemplation and self-perfection. Although philosophy is superior to religion, most people lack the capacity to achieve happiness in the way of the philosophers. Therefore revealed religions, such as Islam, present to the masses in symbolic form the realities that philosophers grasp directly.

In al-Farabi's conception of existence, creation starts from the First Cause (God), from which emanates the first created being—the First Intellect. The First Intellect contemplates the First Cause, which results in the creation of the Second Intellect. The Second Intellect contemplates itself, which results in the creation of the sphere of the highest heaven. As the Second Intellect continues this process of repeated contemplation of the First Cause and itself, the result is the creation of ten intellects and nine spheres of existence, from the fixed stars to the moon. Associated with the moon is the Tenth Intellect, which is called the Active Intellect; for al-Farabi, the angel Gabriel and the holy spirit mentioned in the Qur'an symbolize this Active Intellect. It provides a bridge between the sublunar realm—the earth and our worldly existence—and the higher levels of existence above it. The prophet and the philosopher gain access to the Active Intellect through the perfection of their imaginative and rational faculties, respectively. In al-Farabi's view, the rational faculty is superior to the imaginative faculty, which generally depends on it. The prophet is a rare being, however, with an imaginative faculty as perfect and as powerful as the rational faculty of the philosopher. The prophet can, therefore, connect with the Active Intellect independently of his rational faculty and can present the truths of the philosophers in a manner befitting the people around him.

While al-Farabi believed that the goal of human existence was to achieve happiness, he was convinced that achieving happiness was possible only in a properly structured city. Such a city had to be led by either a philosopher-ruler or a prophet-ruler who had absolute power and, through access to the Active Intellect, could administer and guide the city, making decisions and promulgating laws as required. The ruler must organize the inhabitants of the city in hierarchical classes that enabled each class to reach the highest possible level of happiness. In such a society there would be two broad classes of people: a minority, consisting of those who were philosophers or accepted the views of the philosophers, and the majority, who relied on religion. The ruler was to instruct the first class through philosophy and members of the general population through religion, using its theology, laws, and rituals to guide them.

In al-Farabi's mind, the virtuous city would mirror existence itself. The ruler, from whom all authority flowed, was akin to the First Cause. He ruled over those below him and they, in turn, ruled over those below them, replicating the hierarchy of the

Intellects. Just as this structure of existence produced harmony, the virtuous city, by mirroring it, would also be harmonious and lead to happiness for its citizens.

In the following excerpt from *The Virtuous City*, al-Farabi likens the excellent city to the perfect and healthy body as governed by its ruling organ, the heart. The ideal ruler is the heart of the city, and al-Farabi lists the twelve qualities that should characterize him. In some of the most interesting passages, the author recognizes that reality will not always match the ideal, so he offers alternative scenarios for governance when no perfectly prepared individual can be found. He also presents a telling description of those cities whose "governance" is expressed in the pursuit of diversions or depravities that can never guarantee happiness.

PRONOUNCING GLOSSARY

dīnār: *dee-nar´*
dirham: *dir´-ham*
imām: *ee-mam´*
oikumenē: *oi-ku-meh´-nay*

FROM THE VIRTUOUS CITY

Chapter 15

Perfect Associations and Perfect Ruler; Faulty Associations

In order to preserve himself and to attain his highest perfections every human being is by his very nature in need of many things which he cannot provide all by himself; he is indeed in need of people who each supply him with some particular need of his. Everybody finds himself in the same relation to everybody in this respect. Therefore man cannot attain the perfection, for the sake of which his inborn nature has been given to him, unless many (societies of) people who co-operate come together who each supply everybody else with some particular need of his, so that as a result of the contribution of the whole community all the things are brought together which everybody needs in order to preserve himself and to attain perfection. Therefore human individuals have come to exist in great numbers, and have settled in the inhabitable (inhabited?) region of the earth, so that human societies have come to exist in it, some of which are perfect, others imperfect.

There are three kinds of perfect society, great, medium and small. The great one is the union of all the societies in the inhabitable world; the medium one the union of one nation in one part of the inhabitable world; the small one the union of the people of a city in the territory of any nation whatsoever. Imperfect are the union of people in a village, the union of people in a quarter, then the union in a street, eventually the union in a house, the house being the smallest union of all. Quarter and village exist both for the sake of the city, but the relation of the village to the city is one of service whereas the quarter is related to the city as a part of it; the street is a part of the quarter, the house a part of the street. The city is a part of the territory of a nation, the nation a part of all the people of the inhabitable world.

TRANSLATED BY Richard Walzer.

The most excellent good and the utmost perfection is, in the first instance, attained in a city, not in a society which is less complete than it. But since good in its real sense is such as to be attainable through choice and will and evils are also due to will and choice only, a city may be established to enable its people to co-operate in attaining some aims that are evil. Hence felicity is not attainable in every city. The city, then, in which people aim through association at co-operating for the things by which felicity in its real and true sense can be attained, is the excellent city, and the society in which there is a co-operation to acquire felicity is the excellent society; and the nation in which all of its cities co-operate for those things through which felicity is attained is the excellent nation. In the same way, the excellent universal state will arise only when all the nations in it co-operate for the purpose of reaching felicity.

The excellent city resembles the perfect and healthy body, all of whose limbs co-operate to make the life of the animal perfect and to preserve it in this state. Now the limbs and organs of the body are different and their natural endowments and faculties are unequal in excellence, there being among them one ruling organ, namely the heart, and organs which are close in rank to that ruling organ, each having been given by nature a faculty by which it performs its proper function in conformity with the natural aim of that ruling organ. Other organs have by nature faculties by which they perform their functions according to the aims of those organs which have no intermediary between themselves and the ruling organ; they are in the second rank. Other organs, in turn, perform their functions according to the aim of those which are in the second rank, and so on until eventually organs are reached which only serve and do not rule at all. The same holds good in the case of the city. Its parts are different by nature, and their natural dispositions are unequal in excellence: there is in it a man who is the ruler, and there are others whose ranks are close to the ruler, each of them with a disposition and a habit through which he performs an action in conformity with the intention of that ruler; these are the holders of the first ranks. Below them are people who perform their actions in accordance with the aims of those people; they are in the second rank. Below them in turn are people who perform their actions according to the aims of the people mentioned in the second instance, and the parts of the city continue to be arranged in this way, until eventually parts are reached which perform their actions according to the aims of others, while there do not exist any people who perform their actions according to their aims; these, then, are the people who serve without being served in turn, and who are hence in the lowest rank and at the bottom of the scale. But the limbs and organs of the body are natural, and the dispositions which they have are natural faculties, whereas, although the parts of the city are natural, their dispositions and habits, by which they perform their actions in the city, are not natural but voluntary—notwithstanding that the parts of the city are by nature provided with endowments unequal in excellence which enable them to do one thing and not another. But they are not parts of the city by their inborn nature alone but rather by the voluntary habits which they acquire such as the arts and their likes; to the natural faculties which exist in the organs and limbs of the body correspond the voluntary habits and dispositions in the parts of the city.

The ruling organ in the body is by nature the most perfect and most complete of the organs in itself and in its specific qualification, and it also has the best of everything of which another organ has a share as well; beneath it, in turn, are other organs which rule over organs inferior to them, their rule being lower in rank than the rule of the first and indeed subordinate to the rule of the first; they rule and are ruled. In the same way, the ruler of the city is the most perfect part of the city in his specific qualification and has the best of everything which anybody else shares with him; beneath him are people who are ruled by him and rule others.

The heart comes to be first and becomes then the cause of the existence of the other organs and limbs of the body, and the cause of the existence of their faculties in them and of their arrangement in the ranks proper to them, and when one of its organs is out of order, it is the heart which provides the means to remove that disorder. In the same way the ruler of this city must come to be in the first instance, and will subsequently be the cause of the rise of the city and its parts and the cause of the presence of the voluntary habits of its parts and of their arrangement in the ranks proper to them; and when one part is out of order he provides it with the means to remove its disorder.

The parts of the body close to the ruling organ perform of the natural functions, in agreement—by nature—with the aim of the ruler, the most noble ones; the organs beneath them perform those functions which are less noble, and eventually the organs are reached which perform the meanest functions. In the same way the parts of the city which are close in authority to the ruler of the city perform the most noble voluntary actions, and those below them less noble actions, until eventually the parts are reached which perform the most ignoble actions. The inferiority of such actions is sometimes due to the inferiority of their matter, although they may be extremely useful—like the action of the bladder and the action of the lower intestine in the body; sometimes it is due to their being of little use; at other times it is due to their being very easy to perform. This applies equally to the city and equally to every whole which is composed by nature of well ordered coherent parts: they have a ruler whose relation to the other parts is like the one just described.

This applies also to all existents. For the relation of the First Cause to the other existents is like the relation of the king of the excellent city to its other parts. For the ranks of the immaterial existents are close to the First. Beneath them are the heavenly bodies, and beneath the heavenly bodies the material bodies. All these existents act in conformity with the First Cause, follow it, take it as their guide and imitate it; but each existent does that according to its capacity, choosing its aim precisely on the strength of its established rank in the universe: that is to say the last follows the aim of that which is slightly above it in rank, equally the second existent, in turn, follows what is above itself in rank, and in the same way the third existent has an aim which is above it. Eventually existents are reached which are linked with the First Cause without any intermediary whatsoever. In accordance with this order of rank all the existents permanently follow the aim of the First Cause. Those which are from the very outset provided with all the essentials of their existence are made to imitate the First (Cause) and its aim from their very outset, and hence enjoy eternal bliss and hold the highest ranks; but those which are not provided from the outset with all the essentials of their existence, are provided with a faculty by which they move towards the expected attainment of those essentials and will then be able to follow the aim of the First (Cause). The excellent city ought to be arranged in the same way: all its parts ought to imitate in their actions the aim of their first ruler according to their rank.

The ruler of the excellent city cannot just be any man, because rulership requires two conditions: (a) he should be predisposed for it by his inborn nature, (b) he should have acquired the attitude and habit of will for rulership which will develop in a man whose inborn nature is predisposed for it. Nor is every art suitable for rulership, most of the arts, indeed, are rather suited for service within the city, just as most men are by their very nature born to serve. Some of the arts rule certain (other) arts while serving others at the same time, whereas there are other arts which, not ruling anything at all, only serve. Therefore the art of ruling the excellent city cannot just be any chance art, nor due to any chance habit whatever. For just as the first ruler in a genus cannot be ruled by anything in that genus—for instance the ruler of the limbs cannot be ruled by any other limb, and this holds good for any ruler of any composite whole—so the art of the ruler in the excellent city of necessity cannot be a serving art at all and cannot be ruled by any other art, but his art must be an art towards the aim of which all the other arts tend, and for which they strive in all the actions of the excellent city.

That man is a person over whom nobody has any sovereignty whatsoever. He is a man who has reached his perfection and has become actually intellect and actually being thought (intelligized), his representative faculty having by nature reached its utmost perfection in the way stated by us; this faculty of his is predisposed by nature to receive, either in waking life or in sleep, from the Active Intellect the particulars, either as they are or by imitating them, and also the intelligibles, by imitating them. His Passive Intellect will have reached its perfection by [having apprehended] all the intelligibles, so that none of them is kept back from it, and it will have become actually intellect and actually being thought. Indeed any man whose Passive Intellect has thus been perfected by [having apprehended] all the intelligibles and has become actually intellect and actually being thought, so that the intelligible in him has become identical with that which thinks in him, acquires an actual intellect which is superior to the Passive Intellect and more perfect and more separate from matter (immaterial?) than the Passive Intellect. It is called the 'Acquired Intellect' and comes to occupy a middle position between the Passive Intellect and the Active Intellect, nothing else being between it and the Active Intellect. The Passive Intellect is thus like matter and substratum for the Acquired Intellect, and the Acquired Intellect like matter and substratum for the Active Intellect, and the rational faculty, which is a natural disposition, is a matter underlying the Passive Intellect which is actually intellect.

The first stage, then, through which man becomes man is the coming to be of the receptive natural disposition which is ready to become actually intellect; this disposition is common to all men. Between this disposition and the Active Intellect are two stages, the Passive Intellect which has become actually intellect, and [the rise of] the Acquired Intellect. There are thus two stages between the first stage of being a man and the Active Intellect. When the perfect Passive Intellect and the natural disposition become one thing in the way the compound of matter and form is one—and when the form of the humanity of this man is taken as identical with the Passive Intellect which has become actually intellect, there will be between this man and the Active Intellect only one stage. And when the natural disposition is made the matter of the Passive Intellect which has become actually intellect, and the Passive Intellect the matter of the Acquired Intellect, and the Acquired Intellect the matter of the Active Intellect, and when all this is taken as one and the same thing, then this man is the man on whom the Active Intellect has descended.

When this occurs in both parts of his rational faculty, namely the theoretical and the practical rational faculties, and also in his representative faculty, then it is this man who receives Divine Revelation, and God Almighty grants him Revelation through the mediation of the Active Intellect, so that the emanation from God Almighty to the Active Intellect is passed on to his Passive Intellect through the mediation of the Acquired Intellect, and then to the faculty of representation. Thus he is, through the emanation from the Active Intellect to his Passive Intellect, a wise man and a philosopher and an accomplished thinker who employs an intellect of divine quality, and through the emanation from the Active Intellect to his faculty of representation a visionary prophet: who warns of things to come and tells of particular things which exist at present.

This man holds the most perfect rank of humanity and has reached the highest degree of felicity. His soul is united as it were with the Active Intellect, in the way stated by us.

He is the man who knows every action by which felicity can be reached. This is the first condition for being a ruler. Moreover, he should be a good orator and able to rouse [other people's] imagination by well chosen words. He should be able to lead people well along the right path to felicity and to the actions by which felicity is reached. He should, in addition, be of tough physique, in order to shoulder the tasks of war.

This is the sovereign over whom no other human being has any sovereignty whatsoever; he is the Imām; he is the first sovereign of the excellent city, he is the sovereign of the excellent nation, and the sovereign of the universal state (the *oikumenē*).[1]

But this state can only be reached by a man in whom twelve natural qualities are found together, with which he is endowed by birth. (1) One of them is that he should have limbs and organs which are free from deficiency and strong, and that they will make him fit for the actions which depend on them; when he intends to perform an action with one of them, he accomplishes it with ease. (2) He should by nature be good at understanding and perceiving everything said to him, and grasp it in his mind according to what the speaker intends and what the thing itself demands. (3) He should be good at retaining what he comes to know and see and hear and apprehend in general, and forget almost nothing. (4) He should be well provided

1. In Greek, literally the "inhabited world" (*oikoumenē*); the whole world.

with ready intelligence and very bright; when he sees the slightest indication of a thing, he should grasp it in the way indicated. (5) He should have a fine diction, his tongue enabling him to explain to perfection all that is in the recess of his mind. (6) He should be fond of learning and acquiring knowledge, be devoted to it and grasp things easily, without finding the effort painful, nor feeling discomfort about the toil which it entails. (7) He should by nature be fond of truth and truthful men and hate falsehood and liars. (8) He should by nature not crave for food and drink and sexual intercourse, and have a natural aversion to gambling and hatred of the pleasures which these pursuits provide. (9) He should be proud of spirit [*megalopsychos*[2]] and fond of honour, his soul being by his (?) nature above everything ugly and base, and rising naturally to the most lofty things. (10) Dirham and dīnār[3] and the other worldly pursuits should be of little amount in his view. (11) He should by nature be fond of justice and of just people, and hate oppression and injustice and those who practise them, giving himself and others their due, and urging people to act justly and showing pity to those who are oppressed by injustice; he should lend his support to what he considers to be beautiful and noble and just; he should not be reluctant to give in nor should he be stubborn and obstinate if he is asked to do justice; but he should be reluctant to give in if he is asked to do injustice and evil altogether. (12) He should be strong in setting his mind firmly upon the thing which, in his view, ought to be done, and daringly and bravely carry it out without fear and weak-mindedness.

Now it is difficult to find all these qualities united in one man, and, therefore, men endowed with this nature will be found one at a time only, such men being altogether very rare. Therefore if there exists such a man in the excellent city who, after reaching maturity, fulfils the six aforementioned conditions—or five of them if one excludes the gift of visionary prophecy through the faculty of representation—he will be the sovereign. Now when it happens that, at a given time, no such man is to be found but there was previously an unbroken succession of sovereigns of this kind, the laws and the customs which were introduced will be adopted and eventually firmly established.

The next sovereign, who is the successor of the first sovereigns, will be someone in whom those [twelve] qualities are found together from the time of his birth and his early youth and who will, after reaching his maturity, be distinguished by the following six qualities: (1) He will be a philosopher. (2) He will know and remember the laws and customs (and rules of conduct) with which the first sovereigns had governed the city, conforming in all his actions to all their actions. (3) He will excel in deducing a new law by analogy where no law of his predecessors has been recorded, following for his deductions the principles laid down by the first Imāms. (4) He will be good at deliberating and be powerful in his deductions to meet new situations for which the first sovereigns could not have laid down any law; when doing this he will have in mind the good of the city. (5) He will be good at guiding the people by his speech to fulfil the laws of the first sovereigns as well as those laws which he will have deduced in conformity with their principles

2. Greek.

3. A silver and a gold coin.

after their time. (6) He should be of tough physique in order to shoulder the tasks of war, mastering the serving as well as the ruling military art.

When one single man who fulfils all these conditions cannot be found but there are two, one of whom is a philosopher and the other fulfils the remaining conditions, the two of them will be the sovereigns of this city.

But when all these six qualities exist separately in different men, philosophy in one man and the second quality in another man and so on, and when these men are all in agreement, they should all together be the excellent sovereigns.

But when it happens, at a given time, that philosophy has no share in the government, though every other condition may be present in it, the excellent city will remain without a king, the ruler actually in charge of this city will not be a king, and the city will be on the verge of destruction; and if it happens that no philosopher can be found who will be attached to the actual ruler of the city, then, after a certain interval, this city will undoubtedly perish.

In opposition to the excellent city are the 'ignorant' city, the wicked city, the city which has deliberately changed its character and the city which has missed the right path through faulty judgment. In opposition to it are also the individuals who make up the common people in the various cities.

The 'ignorant' city is the city whose inhabitants do not know true felicity, the thought of it never having occurred to them. Even if they were rightly guided to it they would either not understand it or not believe in it. The only good things they recognise are some of those which are superficially thought of as good among the things which are considered to be the aims in life such as bodily health, wealth, enjoyment of pleasures, freedom to follow one's desires, and being held in honour and esteem. According to the citizens of the ignorant city each of these is a kind of felicity, and the greatest and perfect felicity is the sum total of all of them. Things contrary to these goods are misery such as deficiency of the body, poverty, no enjoyment of pleasures, no freedom to follow one's desires, and not being held in honour.

The ignorant city is divided into a number of cities. One of them is the city of necessity, that is the city whose people strive for no more food, drink, clothes, housing and sexual intercourse than is necessary for sustaining their bodies, and they co-operate to attain this. Another is the city of meanness; the aim of its people is to co-operate in the acquisition of wealth and riches, not in order to enjoy something else which can be got through wealth, but because they regard wealth as the sole aim in life. Another is the city of depravity and baseness; the aim of its people is the enjoyment of the pleasure connected with food and drink and sexual intercourse, and in general of the pleasures of the senses and of the imagination, and to give preference to entertainment and idle play in every form and in every way. Another is the city of honour; the aim of its people is to co-operate to attain honour and distinction and fame among the nations, to be extolled and treated with respect by word and deed, and to attain (gain, achieve) glory and splendour either in the eyes of other people or amongst themselves, each according to the extent of his love of such distinction or according to the amount of it which he is able to reach. Another is the city of power; the aim of its people is to prevail over others and to prevent others from prevailing over them, their only purpose in life being the enjoyment which they get from power.

Another is the 'democratic' city:[4] the aim of its people is to be free, each of them doing what he wishes without restraining his passions in the least.

There are as many kings of ignorant cities as there are cities of this kind, each of them governing the city over which he has authority so that he can indulge in his passion and design.

We have herewith enumerated the designs which may be set up as aims for ignorant cities.

The wicked city is a city whose views are those of the excellent city; it knows felicity, God Almighty, the existents of the second order, the Active Intellect and everything which as such is to be known and believed in by the people of the excellent city; but the actions of its people are the actions of the people of the ignorant cities.

The city which has deliberately changed is a city whose views and actions were previously the views and actions of the people of the excellent city, but they have been changed and different views have taken their place, and its actions have turned into different actions.

The city which misses the right path (the 'erring' city) is the city which aims at felicity after this life, and holds about God Almighty, the existents of the second order and the Active Intellect pernicious and useless beliefs, even if they are taken as symbols and representations of true felicity. Its first ruler was a man who falsely pretended to be receiving 'revelation'; he produced this wrong impression through falsifications, cheating and deceptions.

The kings of these cities are contrary to the kings of the excellent cities: their ways of governing are contrary to the excellent ways of governing. The same applies to all the other people who live in these cities.

4. That is, ruled by the people or mob (Greek *dēmos*).

IBN SINA
980–1037

Abu ʿAli al-Husayn Ibn Sina (Avicenna in Latin) earned renown for his compendium of philosophy, *The Book of Healing*, and for his summary treatise on medicine, *The Canon of Medicine*, both of which made him famous in the world of Christian Europe as well as of Muslim scholarship. He was extraordinarily prolific and commanded many areas of scholarship, yet he was not primarily a scholar and a teacher. Rather, he made his living as a physician and an administrator for various rulers.

Ibn Sina was born in the village of Afshana in modern-day Uzbekistan, but his father soon moved the family to nearby Bukhara, capital of the Samanids (819–999). A high-ranking administrator within the Samanid government, Ibn Sina's father was able to provide him with excellent teachers and a fine education. According to his biographers, it was not too long before Ibn Sina surpassed his teachers in learning and began to educate himself in fields that were beyond their competence.

Ibn Sina's life reflects the tumult of his times. The Samanid dynasty was one of many ruling groups throughout Central and Eastern Asia who, while nominally loyal to the ʿAbbasid caliph in Baghdad, sought only to increase their own power over that of other kingdoms in their region. At age seventeen, Ibn Sina began working as a physician for the Samanid ruler Nuh ibn Mansur (r. 976–97); a few years later, following his father's death, he took an administrative position within the government.

The Samanid state's demise began in 999 when much of it was overtaken by forces of the Qarakhanid dynasty (999–1211). Ibn Sina left Bukhara and, for a number of years, led an itinerant existence; he spent time in the cities of Gurganj, Jurjan, and Rayy before finally settling in Hamadan, Iran, in 1015. There, he began working as a physician and minister for the Buyid ruler Shams al-Dawla (r. 997–1021) by day and teaching and writing at night. During this period he began his *Canon* and *Healing.* After Shams al-Dawla's death, the new ruler, Sama' al-Dawla, asked Ibn Sina to stay on in his dual roles. But Ibn Sina instead withdrew from court, seeking to find a way to join the court of the Kakuyid ruler, ʿAla' al-Dawla, in Isfahan to the south. When members of Sama' al-Dawla's court suspected Ibn Sina of secretly corresponding with ʿAla' al-Dawla, they had him imprisoned. About four months later, he was freed or escaped when ʿAla' al-Dawla launched his campaign on Hamadan and ended Sama' al-Dawla's rule. At that time, in 1024, Ibn Sina made his way to ʿAla' al-Dawla's court in Isfahan, where he received a warm welcome. Here he had more time to focus on his scholarship and completed his two great works, as well as most of the other writings attributed to him. He died in 1037 from an attack of colic while accompanying ʿAla' al-Dawla on a military campaign, probably in his capacity as a physician.

The five books of *The Canon of Medicine* are a medical encyclopedia encompassing all of the medical knowledge of Ibn Sina's day. Book 1 provides a general introduction to the humoral composition of the body, the anatomy of the body, symptoms of diseases and their treatment through diet, and maintaining one's health. The second book lists the *materia medica*, or medical substances with healing properties, while book 3 discusses the pathology of organs, beginning with the head and moving downward. Book 4 covers the identification and treatment of those conditions that affect the body as a whole (fevers) or in part (tumors, fractures). The final book is a pharmacopeia.

Ibn Sina's medical writings were well-regarded in Europe, and *The Canon* was first translated in its entirety into Latin in the latter half of the twelfth century; other whole and partial retranslations as well as versifications followed. It was the foundation of all medical instruction in European universities until the middle of the sixteenth century, when more modern works began to supersede it.

Ibn Sina's philosophical writings drew on the work of ancient Greek authors like Aristotle and of their more recent successors, like al-Farabi (ca. 878–950; see above). Borrowing al-Farabi's emanative scheme, Ibn Sina posited the existence of a Prime Cause that, although identified with the Necessary Existent (God), acted independently in the process of emanation and in the good and evil created by that process. His proof for the existence of a Necessary Existent differed from the proofs of earlier scholars. Earlier Arabic and Greek philosophers reasoned that there must be a creator or Prime Mover because everything in creation was created and changing. Ibn Sina argued from logic rather than causality. For him, existents could be of only two types: those that existed because they were possible and those that existed because they were necessary. That which existed because it was necessary could be shown to be uncaused and devoid of multiplicity (God). But that which existed because it was possible (anything in creation) could either exist or not exist: some force or power must have prevailed over its nonexistence. For Ibn Sina, this power must be a Necessary Existent, who decided what would come into existence and what would not.

Ibn Sina's contributions to Arabic philosophy were not welcomed in the western parts of the Muslim world, where al-Farabi continued to be venerated as the foremost philosopher. Many in the west, such as the Andalusian philosopher Ibn Rushd (1126–1198; see below), believed that Ibn Sina had muddled the endeavor of philosophy by straying too far from Aristotle's thought. In the eastern Muslim world, however, Ibn Sina was revered as the most advanced philosopher of his time, and even the attacks of al-Ghazali (1058–1111; see above) did nothing to blemish his reputation among the philosophers there.

Healing remains Ibn Sina's most famous philosophical work. It covers the standard topics, beginning with logic and then moving to physics, mathematics, and, finally, metaphysics. Though the work was never rendered in full into Latin, sections from it (all of "Metaphysics" and most of "Physics") were translated beginning in the middle of the twelfth century. When these translations appeared in Europe, very little of Aristotle was known, but authors such as Albertus the Great (ca. 1200–1280) and Thomas Aquinas (1225–1274) were soon engaging with both Aristotle and Ibn Sina.

The excerpt below, which presents Ibn Sina's political thought, is taken from book 10 of the *Healing*'s final section, "Metaphysics" (the first of its five chapters, not included here, summarizes the preceding nine books). These chapters demonstrate Ibn Sina's indebtedness to al-Farabi in political philosophy, showing that he too believed that the goal of existence was the attainment of happiness—a state best achieved through following the wisdom of the philosophers.

In this selection, Ibn Sina argues for the necessity of prophethood and advocates for the prophet as the best ruler. He then extols the social benefits of prayer and worship, stressing their importance in sustaining human awareness of God and anticipation of the afterlife. It is the ruler's duty to foster prayer, both its postures and its purifications. The civil duties of the legislator and the process of caliphal succession are clear. For twenty-first-century readers, however, it is Ibn Sina's thoughts on marriage, divorce, and reconciliation that may prove most striking.

PRONOUNCING GLOSSARY

ʿAlī ibn Abī Ṭālib: *ah´-lee ibn a-boo´ tah´-lib*
ʿUmar ibn al-Khaṭṭāb: *oh´-mar ibn al-chaht-tahb´* (guttural *ch*)
caliph: *ka´-lif*
dīn: *deen*
ḥajj: *haj* (heavy *h*)
ijtihād: *ij-tee-had´*
imām: *ee-mam´*
jihād: *ji-had´*
sharīʿah: *sha-ree´-uh*
sunnah: *sun´-nuh*
ummah: *oom´-muh*
Zinji: *zin´-jee*

FROM THE BOOK OF HEALING

From *Metaphysics X*

CHAPTER 2

PROOF OF PROPHECY. THE MANNER OF THE PROPHET'S CALL TO GOD, THE EXALTED. THE "RETURN" TO GOD

We now say: it is known that man differs from the other animals in that he cannot lead a proper life when isolated as a single individual, managing his affairs with no associates to help him satisfy his basic wants. One man needs to be complemented by another of his species, the other, in turn, by him and one like him. Thus, for example, one man would provide another with vege-

TRANSLATED BY Michael E. Marmura. All bracketed additions are the translator's; the numbers refer to sura and verse of the Qur'an.

tables while the other would bake for him; one man would sew for another while the other would provide him with needles. Associated in this way, they become self-sufficient. For this reason men have found it necessary to establish cities and form associations. Whoever, in the endeavor to establish his city, does not see to the requirements necessary for setting up a city and, with his companions, remains confined to forming a mere association, would be engaged in devising means [to govern] a species most dissimilar to men and lacking the perfection of men. Nevertheless, even the ones like him cannot escape associating with the citizens of a city, and imitating them.

If this is obvious, then man's existence and survival require partnership. Partnership is only achieved through reciprocal transactions, as well as through the various trades practiced by man. Reciprocal transactions demand law (*sunnah*) and justice, and law and justice demand a lawgiver and a dispenser of justice. This lawgiver must be in a position that enables him to address men and make them adhere to the law. He must, then, be a human being. Men must not be left to their private opinions concerning the law so that they disagree, each considering as just what others owe them, unjust what they owe others.

Thus, with respect to the survival and actual existence of the human species, the need for this human being is far greater than the need for such benefits as the growing of the hair on the eyebrow, the shaping of the arches in the feet, and many others that are not necessary for survival but at best are merely useful for it. Now the existence of the righteous man to legislate and to dispense justice is a possibility, as we have previously remarked. It becomes impossible, therefore, that divine providence should ordain the existence of those former benefits and not the latter, which are their bases. Nor is it possible that the First Principle and the angels after Him should know the former and not the latter. Nor yet is it possible that that which He knows to be in itself within the realm of possibility but whose realization is necessary for introducing the good order, should not exist. And how can it not exist, when that which depends and is constructed on its existence, exists? A prophet, therefore, must exist and he must be a human. He must also possess characteristics not present in others so that men could recognize in him something they do not have and which differentiates him from them. Therefore he will perform the miracles about which we have spoken.

When this man's existence comes about, he must lay down laws about men's affairs by the permission of God, the Exalted, by His command, inspiration, and the *descent of His Holy Spirit* on him [cf. xvi, 102]. The first principle governing his legislation is to let men know that they have a Maker, One and Omnipotent; that *He knows the hidden and the manifest* [cf. xvi, 19]; that obedience is due Him since *command* must belong to *Him who creates* [cf. vii, 54]; that He has prepared for those who obey Him an afterlife of bliss, but for those who disobey Him an afterlife of misery. This will induce the multitude to obey the decrees put in the prophet's mouth by the God and the angels.

But he ought not to involve them with doctrines pertaining to the knowledge of God, the Exalted, beyond the fact that He is one, the truth, and has none like Himself. To go beyond this and demand that they believe in His existence as being not referred to in place, as being not subject to verbal classifications, as being neither inside nor outside the world, or anything of this kind, is to ask too much. This will simply confuse the religion (*dīn*) they have and involve them in something from which deliverance is only possible for the one who receives guidance and is fortunate, whose existence is most rare. For it is only with great strain that they can comprehend the true states of such matters; it is only the very few among them that can understand the truth of divine "unicity" and divine "remoteness." The rest would inevitably come to deny the truth of such an existence, fall into dissensions, and indulge in disputations and analogical arguments that stand in the way of their political duties. This might even lead them to adopt views contrary to the city's welfare, opposed to the imperatives of truth. Their complaints and doubts will multiply, making it difficult for a man to control them. For divine wisdom is not easily acquired by everyone.

Nor is it proper for any man to reveal that he possesses knowledge he is hiding from the vulgar. Indeed, he must never permit any reference to this. Rather, he should let them know of God's majesty and greatness through symbols and similitudes derived from things that for them are majestic and great, adding this much—that He has neither equal, nor companion, nor likeness. Similarly, he must instill in them the belief in the resurrection in a manner they can conceive and in which their souls find rest. He must tell them about eternal bliss and misery in parables they can comprehend and conceive. Of the true nature of the afterlife he should only indicate something in general: that it is something that "no eye has seen and no ear heard," and that there are pleasures that are great possessions, and miseries that are perpetual torture.

Know that God, exalted be He, knows that the good lies in such a state of affairs. It follows, then, that that which God knows to be the good, must exist, as you have known [from the preceding discussion]. But there is no harm if the legislator's words contain symbols and signs that might stimulate the naturally apt to pursue philosophic investigation.

CHAPTER 3
ACTS OF WORSHIP: THEIR BENEFITS IN THIS WORLD AND THE NEXT

Moreover, this individual who is a prophet is not one whose like recurs in every period. For the matter that is receptive of a perfection like his occurs in few bodily compositions. It follows necessarily, then, that the prophet (may God's prayers and peace be upon him) must plan with great care to ensure the preservation of the legislation he enacts concerning man's welfare. Without doubt, the fundamental principle here is that men must continue in their knowledge of God and the resurrection and that the cause for forgetting these things with the passage of the generation succeeding [the mission of] the prophet (may God's prayers and peace be on him) must be absolutely eliminated. Hence there must be certain acts and works incumbent on people that the legislator must prescribe to be repeated at frequent specified intervals. In this way memory of the act is renewed and reappears before it can die.

These acts must be combined with what brings God and the afterlife necessarily to mind; otherwise they are useless. Remembering is achieved through words that are uttered or resolutions made in the imagination and by telling men that these acts bring them closer to God and are richly rewarded. And these acts must in reality be of such a nature. An example of these are the acts of worship imposed on people. In general, these should be reminders. Now reminders consist of either motions or the absence of motions that lead to other motions. An example of motion is prayer; of the absence of motion, fasting. For although the latter is a negative motion, it so greatly moves one's nature that he who fasts is reminded that what he is engaged in is not a jest. He will thus recall the intention of his fasting, which is to draw him close to God.

These conditions must, if possible, be mixed with others useful for strengthening and spreading the law. Adding these will also be beneficial to men's worldly interests, as in the case of war (*jihād*) and the pilgrimage (*ḥajj*). Certain areas of land must be designated as best suited for worship and as belonging solely to God, the Exalted. Certain acts, which people must perform, must be specified as belonging exclusively to God—as, for example, sacrificial offerings—for these help greatly in this connection. Should the place that is of such a benefit contain the legislator's home and abode, this will then also be a reminder of him. Remembrance of him in relation to the above benefits is only next in importance to the remembrance of God and the angels. Now, the one abode cannot be within proximate reach of the entire community (*ummah*). It therefore becomes fitting to prescribe a migration and a journey to it.

The noblest of these acts of worship, from one point of view, should be the one in which the worshiper considers himself to be addressing God, beseeching Him, drawing close to Him, and standing in His presence. This is prayer. The legislator should therefore prescribe for the worshiper in preparation for prayer those postures men traditionally adopt when they present themselves to human kings, such as purification and cleanliness (indeed, he must prescribe fully in these two things). He should also prescribe for the worshipers the behavior traditionally adopted in the presence of kings: reverence, calm, modesty, the lowering of the eyes, the contracting of the hands and feet, the avoidance of turning around, composure. Likewise, he must prescribe for each time of prayer praiseworthy manners and customs. These acts will benefit the vulgar inasmuch as they will instill in them remembrance of God and the resurrection. In this way their adherence to the statutes and laws will continue. For without such reminders they will forget all of this with the passing of a generation or two. It will also be of great benefit for them in the afterlife inasmuch as their souls will be purified in the manner you have known [in our discourse]. As for the elect, the greatest benefit they derive from these things pertains to the afterlife.

We have established the true nature of the afterlife and have proved that true happiness in the hereafter is achieved through the soul's detaching itself by piety from the acquisitions of bodily dispositions opposed to the means for happiness. This purification is realized through moral states and habits of character acquired by acts that turn the soul away from the body and the senses and perpetuate its memory of its true substance. For if the soul continues to turn unto itself, it will not be affected by the bodily states. What will remind and help the soul in this respect are certain arduous acts that lie outside natural habit—indeed they are more on the side of exertion. These tire the body and curb the [natural] animal desire for rest, for laziness, for the rejection of toil, for the quieting of the hot humor, and for avoiding all exercise except that which is conducive to bestial pleasure. In the performance of these acts the soul must be required to recall God, the angels, and the world of happiness, whether it desires to do so or not. In this way the soul is instilled with the propensity to be repelled from the body and its influences and with the positive disposition to control it. Thus it will not be affected by the body. Hence when the soul encounters bodily acts, these will not produce in it the propensities and positive disposition that they would normally produce when the soul submits to them in everything. For this reason, the one who speaks truth has said: *Surely the good deeds drive away the bad deeds* [xi, 114]. If this act persists in man, then he will acquire the positive disposition of turning in the direction of truth and away from error. He thus becomes well prepared to be delivered unto [true] happiness after bodily separation.

If these acts were performed by someone who did not believe them to be divine obligations and who, nonetheless, had to remember God in every act, rejecting everything else, this one would be worthy of some measure of this virtue. How much more worthy will be the one who performs these acts knowing that the prophet comes from God and is sent by God, that his being sent is necessitated by divine wisdom, that all the prophet's legislation is an obligation demanded of him by God, that all he legislates comes from God? For the prophet was obligated by God to impose these acts of worshiping Him. These acts benefit the worshipers in that they perpetuate in the latter adherence to the laws and religion (*sharīʿah*) that insure their existence and in that, by virtue of the goodness they inspire, they bring the worshipers closer to God in the hereafter.

Moreover, this is the man who is charged with administering the affairs of men, for insuring their livelihood in this world and their well-being in the world to come. He is a man distinguished from the rest of mankind by his godliness.

CHAPTER 4
ESTABLISHMENT OF THE CITY, THE HOUSEHOLD (THAT IS, MARRIAGE), AND THE GENERAL LAWS PERTAINING TO THESE MATTERS

The legislator's first objective in laying down the laws and organizing the city must be to divide it into three groups: administrators, artisans, and guardians. He must place at the head of each group a leader, under whom he will place other leaders, under these yet others, and so forth until he arrives at the common run of men. Thus none in the city will remain without a proper function and a specific place: each will have his use in the city. Idleness and unemployment must be prohibited. The legislator must leave the way open to no one for acquiring from another that share of a livelihood necessary for man while exempting himself from any effort in return. Such people he must vigorously restrain. If they fail to refrain from such a practice, he must then exile them from the land. But should the cause here be some physical malady or defect, the legislator must set aside a special place for such cases, under someone's charge.

There must exist in the city a common fund, part of it consisting of duties imposed on acquired and natural profits such as fruit and agricultural produce, part of it imposed as punishment, while another part should consist of property taken from those who resist the law, that is, of war-booty. Thus the fund will serve to meet the exigencies of the common good, to meet the needs of the guardians who do not work in any craft, and those prevented from earning their livelihood by maladies and chronic diseases. Some people have held the opinion that the diseased whose recovery is not to be expected should be killed. But this is base; for their sustenance will not hurt the city. If such people have relatives enjoying a superfluity of means, then the legislator must impose on these relatives the responsibility for their people.

All fines must not be imposed on the criminal alone. Some of these must be imposed on the criminal's protectors and relatives who fail to reprimand and watch over him. But the fines legislated in the latter case should be mitigated by allowing delay in payment. The same should apply to crimes committed inadvertently. These must not be ignored even though they do occur by mistake.

Just as idleness must be prohibited, so should professions like gambling, whereby properties and utilities are transferred without any benefit rendered in exchange. For the gambler takes without rendering any service at all. Rather, what one takes must always be a compensation given in return for work, a compensation that is either substance, utility, good remembrance, or any other thing considered a human good. Similarly, professions that lead to the opposite of welfare and usefulness, such as the learning of theft, brigandage, leadership of criminal bands, and the like, must be prohibited. Professions that allow people to dispense with learning those crafts pertaining to the association—professions such as usury—must be prohibited. For usury is the seeking of excess profit without practicing a craft to achieve it, even though it does render a service in return. Also those acts—which, if once permitted, would be detrimental to the city's growth—like fornication and sodomy, which dispense with the greatest pillar on which the city stands, that is, marriage, must be prohibited.

The first of the legislator's acts must pertain to marriage resulting in issue. He must call and urge people to it. For by marriage is achieved the continuity of the species, the permanence of which is proof of the existence of God, the Exalted. He must arrange it in such a way that matrimony takes place as a manifest affair, so that there will be no uncertainties concerning progeny causing defects in the proper transfer of inheritances, which are a source of wealth. For wealth is indispensable for a livelihood. Now wealth divides into source and derivatives. Sources consist of wealth that is inherited, found, or granted. Of these three sources, the best is inherited wealth; for it does not come by way of luck or chance but is of an order akin to the natural. Through this also—I mean the concealment of marriage—defects in other respects occur: for example, in the necessity that one party should undertake expenditure over the other, in rendering mutual assistance, and in other matters that will not escape the wise person after reflection.

The legislator must take firm measures to assure the permanence of the union so that not every quarrel should result in a separation that disrupts the bond between children and parents and renews the need of marriage for everyone. In this there are many sorts of harm. Also, because what is most conducive to the general good is love. Love is only achieved through friendship; friendship through habit; habit is produced only through long association. This assurance, with respect to the woman, consists in not placing in her hands the right to make the separation. For in reality she is not very rational and is quick to follow passion and anger. But a way for separation must be left open and not all doors closed. To prevent separation under all circumstances results in all kinds of harmful consequences. Of these is the fact that some natures cannot adapt themselves to others: the more they are brought together, the greater the resulting evil, aversion, and unpleasantness. Or again, someone might get an unequal partner, or one who is of bad character, or repellent in nature. This will induce the other partner to desire someone else—for desire is natural—and this in turn leads to many harmful consequences. It also might so happen that the married couple do not cooperate for procreation and if exchanged for other partners they would. Hence some means for separation is necessary. But the law must be strict about it.

The means for separation must not be placed in the hands of the less rational of the two, the one more prone to disagreement, confusion, and change. Instead, this must be relegated to the judges who will affect the separation when they ascertain the woman's mistreatment by the other partner. In the case of the man, an indemnity must be imposed on him so that he will approach separation only after ascertainment and after he finds it to be the right thing for him in every way.

The legislator must, nevertheless, leave the way open for reconciliation, without, however, emphasizing it lest this encourage thoughtless action. On the contrary, he must make reconciliation more difficult than separation. How excellent was that which [Muhammad] the greatest of legislators commanded [cf. ii, 229–30]—that the man, after thrice pronouncing the formula for divorce, is not allowed to remarry the woman until he brings himself to drink a cup unsurpassed in bitterness, which is, to first let another man marry her by a true marriage and have real relations with her. If such a prospect awaits a man, he will not approach separation recklessly, unless he has already determined that the separation is to be permanent, or unless he is of a defective character and takes perverted pleasure in scandal. But the likes of these fall outside the pale of men who deserve the seeking of their welfare.

Since woman by right must be protected inasmuch as she can share her sexual desire with many, is much inclined to draw attention to herself, and in addition to that is easily deceived and is less inclined to obey reason; and since sexual relations on her part with many men cause great disdain and shame, which are well-known harms, whereas on the part of the man they only arouse jealousy, which should be ignored as it is nothing but obedience to the devil; it is more important to legislate that the woman should be veiled and secluded from men. Thus, unlike the man, she should not be a bread-earner. It must be legislated that her needs be satisfied by the man upon whom must be imposed her sustenance. For this the man must be compensated. He must own her, but not she him. Thus she cannot be married to another at the same time. But in the case of man this avenue is not closed to him though he is forbidden from taking a number of wives whom he cannot support. Hence the compensation consists in the ownership of the woman's "genitalia." By this ownership I do not mean sexual intercourse. For both partake of its pleasure and the woman's share is even greater, as is her delight and pleasure in children. But by this I mean that no other man can make use of them.

It must be legislated with respect to the child that both parents must undertake his proper upbringing—the woman in her special area, the man by provision. Likewise it must be prescribed that the child must serve, obey, respect, and honor his parents. For they are the cause of his existence and in addition have borne his support, something we need not enlarge upon as it is evident.

CHAPTER 5
CONCERNING THE CALIPH AND THE IMAM: THE NECESSITY OF OBEYING THEM. REMARKS ON POLITICS, TRANSACTIONS, AND MORALS

Next, the legislator must impose as a duty obedience to whosoever succeeds him. He must also prescribe that designation of the successor can only be made by himself or by the consensus of the elders. The latter should verify openly to the public that the man of their choice can hold sole political authority, that he is of independent judgment, that he is endowed with the noble qualities of courage, temperance, and good governance, and that he knows the law to a degree unsurpassed by anyone else. Such a verification must be openly proclaimed and must find unanimous agreement by the entire public. The legislator must lay down in the law that should they disagree and quarrel, succumbing to passion and whim, or should they agree to designate someone other than the virtuous and deserving individual, then they would have committed an act of unbelief. Designation of the caliph through appointment by testament is best: it will not lead to partisanship, quarrels, and dissensions.

The legislator must then decree in his law that if someone secedes and lays claim to the caliphate by virtue of power or wealth, then it becomes the duty of every citizen to fight and kill him. If the citizens are capable of so doing but refrain from doing so, then they disobey God and commit an act of unbelief. The blood of anyone who can fight but refrains becomes free for the spilling after this fact is established in the assembly of all. The legislator must lay down in the law that, next to belief in the prophet, nothing brings one closer to God than the killing of such a usurper.

If the seceder, however, verifies that the one holding the caliphate is not fit for it, that he is afflicted with an imperfection, and that this imperfection is not found in the seceder, then it is best that the citizens accept the latter. The determining factor here is superiority of practical judgment and excellence in political management. The one whose attainment in the rest of the virtues [including knowledge] is moderate—although he must not be ignorant of them nor act contrary to them—but excels in these two is more fit than the one who excels in the other virtues but is not foremost in these two. Thus the one who has more knowledge must join and support the one who has better practical judgment. The latter, in turn, must accept the former's support and seek his advice, as was done by ʿUmar and ʿAlī.[1]

He must then prescribe certain acts of worship that can be performed only in the caliph's presence, in order to extol his importance and make them serve his glorification. These are the congregational affairs, such as festivals. He must prescribe such public gatherings; for these entail the call for solidarity, the use of the instruments of courage, and competition. It is by competition that virtues are achieved. Through congregations, supplications are answered and blessings are received in the manner discussed in our statements.

1. ʿUmar ibn al-Khattab (ca. 586–644) and ʿAli ibn Abi Talib (ca. 599–661), the second and fourth caliphs, respectively.

Likewise, there must be certain transactions in which the imam participates. These are the transactions that lead to the building of the city's foundation, such as marriage and communal activities. He must also prescribe, in the transactions involving exchange, laws that prevent treachery and injustices. He must forbid unsound transactions where the objects of exchange change before being actually received or paid, as with money-changing, postponement in the payment of debt, and the like.

He must also legislate that people must help and protect others, their properties, and lives, without this, however, entailing that the contributor should penalize himself as a result of his contribution.

As for enemies and those who oppose his law, the legislator must decree waging war against them and destroying them, after calling on them to accept the truth. Their property and women must be declared free for the spoil. For when such property and women are not administered according to the constitution of the virtuous city, they will not bring about the good for which property and women are sought. Rather, these would contribute to corruption and evil. Since some men have to serve others, such people must be forced to serve the people of the just city. The same applies to people not very capable of acquiring virtue. For these are slaves by nature as, for example, the Turks and the Zinjis[2] and in general all those who do not grow up in noble [that is, moderate] climes where the conditions for the most part are such that nations of good temperament, innate intelligence, and sound minds thrive. If a city other than his has praiseworthy laws, the legislator must not interfere with it unless the times are such that they require the declaration that no law is valid save the revealed law. For when nations and cities go astray and laws are prescribed for them, adherence to the law must be assured. If the adherence to the law becomes incumbent, it might very well be the case that to ensure this adherence requires the acceptance of the law by the whole world. If the people of that [other] city, which has a good way of life, find that this [new] law, too, is good and praiseworthy and that the adoption of the new law means restoring the conditions of corrupted cities to virtue, and yet proceed to proclaim that this law ought not to be accepted and reject as false the legislator's claim that this law has come to all cities, then a great weakness will afflict the law. Those opposing it could then use as argument for their rejecting it that the people of that [other] city have rejected it. In this case these latter must also be punished and war (*jihād*) waged on them; but this war must not be pursued with the same severity as against the people utterly in error. Or else an indemnity must be imposed on them in lieu of their preference. In any case, it must be enunciated as a truth that they are negators [of the true law]. For how are they not negators, when they refuse to accept the divine Law, which God, the Exalted, has sent down? Should they perish, they would have met what they deserve. For their death, though it means the end of some, results in a permanent good, particularly when the new law is more complete and better. It should also be legislated with regard to these, that if clemency on condition that they pay ransom and tax is desired, this can be done. In general, they must not be placed in the same category as the other nonbelievers.

The legislator must also impose punishments, penalties, and prohibitions to prevent disobedience to the divine Law. For not everyone is restrained

2. A people of East Africa.

from violating the law because of what he fears of the afterlife. Most of these [penalties and so forth] must pertain to acts contrary to law that are conducive to the corruption of the city's order; for example, adultery, theft, complicity with the enemies of the city, and the like. As for the acts that harm the individual himself, the law should contain helpful advice and warning, and not go beyond this to the prescription of obligatory duties. The law concerning acts of worship, marriage, and prohibitions should be moderate, neither severe nor lenient. The legislator must relegate many questions, particularly those pertaining to transactions, to the exercise of the individual judgment (*ijtihād*) of the jurists. For different times and circumstances call for decisions that cannot be predetermined. As for the further control of the city involving knowledge of the organization of guardians, income and expenditure, manufacture of armaments, legal rights, border fortifications, and the like, it must be placed in the hands of the ruler in his capacity as caliph. The legislator must not impose specific prescriptions concerning these. Such an imposition would be defective since conditions change with time. Moreover, it is impossible to make universal judgments that cover every contingency in these matters. He must leave this to the body of counsellors.

It is necessary that the legislator should also prescribe laws regarding morals and customs that advocate justice, which is the mean. The mean in morals and customs is sought for two things. The one, involving the breaking of the dominance of the passions, is for the soul's purification and for enabling it to acquire the power of self-mastery so that it can liberate itself from the body untarnished. The other, involving the use of these passions, is for worldly interests. As for the use of pleasures, these serve to conserve the body and procreation. As for courage, it is for the city's survival. The vices of excess are to be avoided for the harm they inflict in human interests, while the vices of deficiency are to be avoided for the harm they cause the city. By wisdom as a virtue, which is the third of a triad comprising in addition temperance and courage, is not meant theoretical wisdom—for the mean is not demanded in the latter at all—but, rather, practical wisdom pertaining to worldly actions and behavior. For it is deception to concentrate on the knowledge of this wisdom, carefully guarding the ingenious ways whereby one can attain through it every benefit and avoid every harm, to the extent that this would result in bringing upon one's associates the opposite of what one seeks for oneself and result in distracting oneself from the attainment of other virtues. To cause the hand to be thus fettered to the neck, means the loss of a man's soul, his whole life, the instrument of his well-being, and his survival to that moment at which he attains perfection. Since the motivating powers are three—the appetitive, the irascible, and the practical—the virtues consist of three things: (*a*) moderation in such appetites as the pleasures of sex, food, clothing, comfort, and other pleasures of sense and imagination; (*b*) moderation in all the irascible passions such as fear, anger, depression, pride, hate, jealousy, and the like; (*c*) moderation in practical matters. At the head of these virtues stand temperance, practical wisdom, and courage; their sum is justice, which, however, is extraneous to theoretical virtue. But whoever combines theoretical wisdom with justice, is indeed the happy man. And whoever, in addition to this, wins the prophetic qualities, becomes almost a human god. Worship of him, after the worship of God, becomes almost allowed. He is indeed the world's earthly king and God's deputy in it.

IBN RUSHD
1126–1198

Contemporary philosophers rarely view their profession as being politically risky, but tensions between philosophy and religious law were not infrequent in the medieval Muslim world. The life of Abu al-Walid Muhammad Ibn Rushd (known in the West as Averroës) offers a good example. Living sometimes in Spain, at other times in Morocco, he held high office, and he suffered exile. His books were venerated, and his books were burned.

Born to a distinguished family of jurists in Cordoba, Spain, Ibn Rushd was destined for a life of scholarship and legal prominence. His father was a judge in Cordoba, and his grandfather, a notable Maliki scholar, had been chief judge of the city. Little is known about Ibn Rushd's early life, but in his youth he received a thorough education in Maliki law, theology, medicine, and philosophy, as his early works in law and medicine attest. The *Beginning of the Independent Jurist*, a work on comparative law, analyzes the underlying reasons for differences of opinion among legal schools, while *General Medicine* provides a comprehensive introduction to the field.

By his early forties, Ibn Rushd was living in Marrakesh, Morocco. There he met Ibn Tufayl (d. 1185), a philosopher and the personal physician of the Almohad ruler Abu Yaʿqub (r. 1163–84). Ibn Rushd's account of his meeting with the ruler describes his initial concern and confusion at being quizzed on philosophical questions. Fearful that his responses would be interpreted as a lack of faith, Ibn Rushd was soon reassured by Abu Yaʿqub's own evident competence and interest in the subject. And Ibn Rushd clearly proved his own mastery, earning from the ruler a "donation in money, a magnificent robe of honor, and a steed." Ibn Tufayl then asked Ibn Rushd to produce an annotated summary of Aristotle's works for the benefit of Abu Yaʿqub, who had complained about the complexity of Aristotle's thought and the poor quality of available translations.

Ibn Rushd agreed and between 1169 and 1195 produced commentaries on and abridgments of most of Aristotle's works. Because these were later translated into Latin and Hebrew, Ibn Rushd became Aristotle's conduit into medieval Christian and Jewish philosophy. Not all of Ibn Rushd's philosophical writings are expositions and summaries of the works of Aristotle. Between 1174 and 1180 he also produced several important original treatises: *The Decisive Treatise on the Harmony of Religion and Philosophy, Unveiling the Methods of Proof,* and *The Incoherence of the Incoherence.* Nor was philosophical writing his only profession. He served as judge in both Seville and Cordoba, becoming chief judge in the latter city toward the end of his life.

Ibn Rushd remained in Abu Yaʿqub's favor throughout his reign, eventually becoming his physician when Ibn Tufayl retired in 1182. Abu Yaʿqub was succeeded by his son, Abu Yusuf al-Mansur (r. 1184–99), and at first Ibn Rushd enjoyed a good relationship with this new ruler. In 1195, however, he fell out of favor with Abu Yusuf, and a tribunal of prominent Cordoban scholars found Ibn Rushd guilty of unorthodox philosophical views. Abu Yusuf exiled him to Lucena, a small town near Cordoba, and ordered his philosophical works—but not his medical or legal ones—to be burned.

Ibn Rushd's banishment was politically motivated. Abu Yusuf was fighting a war against the Christians of Spain and needed the support of the jurists and theologians who controlled popular opinion. While Abu Yaʿqub and Abu Yusuf privately supported the study of philosophy, at a time of political instability they could not publicly oppose the theologians' resistance to it. Nonetheless, some two or three years after banning him, Abu Yusuf invited Ibn Rushd to join his court in Marrakesh. Ibn Rushd's vindication was short-lived, as he died in December 1198 in Marrakesh.

Ibn Rushd wanted to resuscitate the reputation of the philosophers and to harmonize the heritage of Hellenistic philosophy with orthodox Islamic beliefs. In *The Incoherence of the Incoherence* Ibn Rushd directly countered al-Ghazali (1058–1111; see above), who in *The Incoherence of the Philosophers* had attacked the philosophers, as represented by al-Farabi (ca. 878–950; see above) and Ibn Sina (980–1037; see above), on twenty counts. Of these twenty, al-Ghazali thought three warranted expulsion from the Muslim community: the philosophers' belief in a pre-eternal world, their claim that God knew only universals and not particulars, and their denial of the bodily resurrection.

In *The Incoherence of the Incoherence*, Ibn Rushd postulated that the world could be pre-eternal but created; that God knows both universals and particulars, but not as humans do; and that although physical bodies were destroyed at death, new, celestial ones were resurrected. In many of its arguments *The Incoherence of the Incoherence* acknowledged al-Ghazali's critiques, reserving its most trenchant criticisms for the expositions by al-Farabi and Ibn Sina. The work as a whole sought to present Ibn Rushd's view of true philosophy: that of Aristotle, unadulterated by the interpretations of earlier Muslim philosophers.

The Decisive Treatise, a short work of three chapters, defends the study of philosophy, arguing that philosophical investigation and analyses are a legitimate response to qur'anic verses that urge believers to consider and reflect on the world around them. But not all people are created equal, or at least not all possess the same mental equipment. Below, in chapter 3 of *The Decisive Treatise*, Ibn Rushd explains that most people are incapable of the higher levels of scriptural interpretation and can respond only to rhetorical exhortations. A much smaller group is capable of dialectical reasoning, while the scholar class alone can apprehend demonstrative (i.e., syllogistic) certainty. Exposing the masses to an interpretive strategy beyond their capacity poses grave danger to their faith and their spiritual health.

PRONOUNCING GLOSSARY

Abū Ḥāmid [al-Ghazālī]: *a-boo ha´-mid* (heavy *h*) (*al-ga-za´-lee*)

Ashʿarites: *ash´-ar-ites*

Muʿtazilites: *muh-ta´-zi-lites*

FROM THE DECISIVE TREATISE ON THE HARMONY OF RELIGION AND PHILOSOPHY

[*Chapter* 3]

[*Philosophical Interpretations of Scripture Should Not Be Taught to the Majority. The Law Provides Other Methods of Instructing Them.*]

[THE PURPOSE OF SCRIPTURE IS TO TEACH TRUE THEORETICAL AND PRACTICAL SCIENCE AND RIGHT PRACTICE AND ATTITUDES.]

You ought to know that the purpose of Scripture is simply to teach true science and right practice. True science is knowledge of God, Blessed and

TRANSLATED BY George F. Hourani. All bracketed additions are the translator's.

Exalted, and the other beings as they really are, and especially of noble beings, and knowledge of happiness and misery in the next life. Right practice consists in performing the acts which bring happiness and avoiding the acts which bring misery; and it is knowledge of these acts that is called 'practical science'. They fall into two divisions: (1) outward bodily acts; the science of these is called 'jurisprudence'; and (2) acts of the soul such as gratitude, patience and other moral attitudes which the Law enjoins or forbids; the science of these is called 'asceticism' or 'the sciences of the future life'. To these Abū Ḥāmid[1] turned his attention in his book: as people had given up this sort [of act] and become immersed in the other sort, and as this sort involves the greater fear of God, which is the cause of happiness, he called his book *'The revival of the sciences of religion'*. But we have digressed from our subject, so let us return to it.

> [Scripture teaches concepts both directly and by symbols, and uses demonstrative, dialectical and rhetorical arguments. Dialectical and rhetorical arguments are prevalent because the main aim of Scripture is to teach the majority. In these arguments concepts are indicated directly or by symbols, in various combinations in premisses and conclusion.]

We say: The purpose of Scripture is to teach true science and right practice; and teaching is of two classes, [of] concepts and [of] judgements, as the logicians have shown. Now the methods available to men of [arriving at] judgements are three: demonstrative, dialectical and rhetorical; and the methods of forming concepts are two: either [conceiving] the object itself or [conceiving] a symbol of it. But not everyone has the natural ability to take in demonstrations, or [even] dialectical arguments, let alone demonstrative arguments which are so hard to learn and need so much time [even] for those who are qualified to learn them. Therefore, since it is the purpose of Scripture simply to teach everyone, Scripture has to contain every method of [bringing about] judgements of assent and every method of forming concepts.

Now some of the methods of assent comprehend the majority of people, i.e. the occurrence of assent as a result of them [is comprehensive]: these are the rhetorical and the dialectical [methods]—and the rhetorical is more comprehensive than the dialectical. Another method is peculiar to a smaller number of people: this is the demonstrative. Therefore, since the primary purpose of Scripture is to take care of the majority (without neglecting to arouse the élite), the prevailing methods of expression in religion are the common methods by which the majority comes to form concepts and judgements.

These [common] methods in religion are of four classes:

One of them occurs where the method is common, yet specialized in two respects: i.e. where it is certain in its concepts and judgements, in spite of being rhetorical or dialectical. These syllogisms are those whose premisses, in spite of being based on accepted ideas or on opinions, are accidentally certain, and whose conclusions are accidentally to be taken in their direct

1. Abu Hamid Muhammad ibn Muhammad al-Ghazali (1058–1111); see above.

meaning without symbolization. Scriptural texts of this class have no allegorical interpretations, and anyone who denies them or interprets them allegorically is an unbeliever.

The second class occurs where the premisses, in spite of being based on accepted ideas or on opinions, are certain, and where the conclusions are symbols for the things which it was intended to conclude. [Texts of] this [class], i.e. their conclusions, admit of allegorical interpretation.

The third is the reverse of this: it occurs where the conclusions are the very things which it was intended to conclude, while the premisses are based on accepted ideas or on opinions without being accidentally certain. [Texts of] this [class] also, i.e. their conclusions, do not admit of allegorical interpretation, but their premisses may do so.

The fourth [class] occurs where the premisses are based on accepted ideas or opinions, without being accidentally certain, and where the conclusions are symbols for what it was intended to conclude. In these cases the duty of the élite is to interpret them allegorically, while the duty of the masses is to take them in their apparent meaning.

> [Where symbols are used, each class of men, demonstrative, dialectical and rhetorical, must try to understand the inner meaning symbolized or rest content with the apparent meaning, according to their capacities.]

In general, everything in these [texts] which admits of allegorical interpretation can only be understood by demonstration. The duty of the élite here is to apply such interpretation; while the duty of the masses is to take them in their apparent meaning in both respects, i.e. in concept and judgement, since their natural capacity does not allow more than that.

But there may occur to students of Scripture allegorical interpretations due to the superiority of one of the common methods over another in [bringing about] assent, i.e. when the indication contained in the allegorical interpretation is more persuasive than the indication contained in the apparent meaning. Such interpretations are popular; and [the making of them] is possibly a duty for those whose powers of theoretical understanding have attained the dialectical level. To this sort belong some of the interpretations of the Ashʿarites and Muʿtazilites[2]—though the Muʿtazilites are generally sounder in their statements. The masses on the other hand, who are incapable of more than rhetorical arguments, have the duty of taking these [texts] in their apparent meaning, and they are not permitted to know such interpretations at all.

Thus people in relation to Scripture fall into three classes:

One class is those who are not people of interpretation at all: these are the rhetorical class. They are the overwhelming mass, for no man of sound intellect is exempted from this kind of assent.

Another class is the people of dialectical interpretation: these are the dialecticians, either by nature alone or by nature and habit.

2. An 8th-century rationalist school of Islamic theology whose most controversial claim is that the Qurʾan was created. The Ashʿarites, a school founded by the former Muʿtazilite Abu al-Hasan al-Ashʿari [874–935; see above], stressed the inadequacy of human reason while maintaining the Muʿtazilite belief in free will and use of the dialectic method.

Another class is the people of certain interpretation: these are the demonstrative class, by nature and training, i.e. in the art of philosophy. This interpretation ought not to be expressed to the dialectical class, let alone to the masses.

> [To explain the inner meaning to people unable to understand it is to destroy their belief in the apparent meaning without putting anything in its place. The result is unbelief in learners and teachers. It is best for the learned to profess ignorance, quoting the *Qur'ān* on the limitations of man's understanding.]

When something of these allegorical interpretations is expressed to anyone unfit to receive them—especially demonstrative interpretations because of their remoteness from common knowledge—both he who expresses it and he to whom it is expressed are led into unbelief. The reason for that [in the case of the latter] is that allegorical interpretation comprises two things, rejection of the apparent meaning and affirmation of the allegorical one; so that if the apparent meaning is rejected in the mind of someone who can only grasp apparent meanings, without the allegorical meaning being affirmed in his mind, the result is unbelief, if it [the text in question] concerns the principles of religion.

Allegorical interpretations, then, ought not to be expressed to the masses nor set down in rhetorical or dialectical books, i.e. books containing arguments of these two sorts, as was done by Abū Ḥāmid. They should ⟨not⟩ be expressed to this class; and with regard to an apparent text, when there is a ⟨self-evident⟩ doubt whether it is apparent to everyone and whether knowledge of its interpretation is impossible for them, they should be told that it is ambiguous and [its meaning] known by no one except God; and that the stop should be put here in the sentence of the Exalted, 'And no one knows the interpretation thereof except God'.[3] The same kind of answer should also be given to a question about abstruse matters, which there is no way for the masses to understand; just as the Exalted has answered in His saying, 'And they will ask you about the Spirit. Say, "The Spirit is by the command of my Lord; you have been given only a little knowledge" '.[4]

> [Certain people have injured the masses particularly, by giving them allegorical interpretations which are false. These people are exactly analogous to bad medical advisers. The true doctor is related to bodily health in the same way as the Legislator to spiritual health, which the *Qur'ān* teaches us to pursue. The true allegory is "the deposit" mentioned in the *Qur'ān*.]

As for the man who expresses these allegories to unqualified persons, he is an unbeliever on account of his summoning people to unbelief. This is contrary to the summons of the Legislator, especially when they are false allegories concerning the principles of religion, as has happened in the case of a group of people of our time. For we have seen some of them thinking that they were being philosophic and that they perceived, with their remarkable

3. Qur'an 3:7.

4. Qur'an 17:85.

wisdom, things which conflict with Scripture in every respect, i.e. [in passages] which do not admit of allegorical interpretation; and that it was obligatory to express these things to the masses. But by expressing those false beliefs to the masses they have been a cause of perdition to the masses and themselves, in this world and the next.

The relation between the aim of these people and the aim of the Legislator [can be illustrated by] a parable, of a man who goes to a skilful doctor. [This doctor's] aim is to preserve the health and cure the diseases of all the people, by prescribing for them rules which can be commonly accepted, about the necessity of using the things which will preserve their health and cure their diseases, and avoiding the opposite things. He is unable to make them all doctors, because a doctor is one who knows by demonstrative methods the things which preserve health and cure disease. Now this [man whom we have mentioned] goes out to the people and tells them, 'These methods prescribed by this doctor for you are not right'; and he sets out to discredit them, so that they are rejected by the people. Or he says, 'They have allegorical interpretations'; but the people neither understand these nor assent to them in practice. Well, do you think that people in this condition will do any of the things which are useful for preserving health and curing disease, or that this man who has persuaded them to reject what they formerly believed in will now be able to use those [things] with them, I mean for preserving health? No, he will be unable to use those [things] with them, nor will they use them, and so they will all perish.

This [is what will happen] if he expresses to them true allegories about those matters, because of their inability to understand them; let alone if he expresses to them false allegories, because this will lead them to think that there are no such things as health which ought to be preserved and disease which ought to be cured—let alone that there are things which preserve health and cure disease. It is the same when someone expresses allegories to the masses, and to those who are not qualified to understand them, in the sphere of Scripture; thus he makes it appear false and turns people away from it; and he who turns people away from Scripture is an unbeliever.

Indeed this comparison is certain, not poetic as one might suppose. It presents a true analogy, in that the relation of the doctor to the health of bodies is [the same as] the relation of the Legislator to the health of souls: i.e. the doctor is he who seeks to preserve the health of bodies when it exists and to restore it when it is lost, while the Legislator is he who desires this [end] for the health of souls. This health is what is called 'fear of God'. The precious Book has told us to seek it by acts conformable to the Law, in several verses. Thus the Exalted has said, 'Fasting has been prescribed for you, as it was prescribed for those who were before you; perhaps you will fear God.' Again the Exalted has said, 'Their flesh and their blood shall not touch God, but your fear shall touch him'; 'Prayer prevents immorality and transgression';[5] and other verses to the same effect contained in the precious Book. Through knowledge of Scripture and practice according to

5. Qur'an 2:183; 22:37; 29:45.

Scripture the Legislator aims solely at this health; and it is from this health that happiness in the future life follows, just as misery in the future life follows from its opposite.

From this it will be clear to you that true allegories ought not to be set down in popular books, let alone false ones. The true allegory is the deposit which man was charged to hold and which he held, and from which all beings shied away, i.e. that which is mentioned in the words of the Exalted, 'We offered the deposit to the heavens, the earth and the mountains', [and so on to the end of] the verse.[6]

[It was due to the wrong use of allegorical interpretation by the Muʿtazilites and Ashʿarites that hostile sects arose in Islam.]

It was due to allegorical interpretations—especially the false ones—and the supposition that such interpretations of Scripture ought to be expressed to everyone, that the sects of Islam arose, with the result that each one accused the others of unbelief or heresy. Thus the Muʿtazilites interpreted many verses and Traditions allegorically, and expressed their interpretations to the masses, and the Ashʿarites did the same, although they used such interpretations less frequently. In consequence they threw people into hatred, mutual detestation and wars, tore the Scriptures to shreds, and completely divided people.

In addition to all this, in the methods which they followed to establish their interpretations they neither went along with the masses nor with the élite: not with the masses, because their methods were ⟨more⟩ obscure than the methods common to the majority, and not with the élite, because if these methods are inspected they are found deficient in the conditions [required] for demonstration, as will be understood after the slightest inspection by anyone acquainted with the conditions of demonstration. Further, many of the principles on which the Ashʿarites based their knowledge are sophistical, for they deny many necessary truths such as the permanence of accidents, the action of things on other things, the existence of necessary causes for effects, of substantial forms, and of secondary causes.

And their theorists wronged the Muslims in this sense, that a sect of Ashʿarites called an unbeliever anyone who did not attain knowledge of the existence of the Glorious Creator by the methods laid down by them in their books for attaining this knowledge. But in truth it is they who are the unbelievers and in error! From this point they proceeded to disagree, one group saying 'The primary obligation is theoretical study', another group saying 'It is belief'; i.e. [this happened] because they did not know which are the methods common to everyone, through whose doors the Law has summoned all people [to enter]; they supposed that there was only one method. Thus they mistook the aim of the Legislator, and were both themselves in error and led others into error.

[The proper methods for teaching the people are indicated in the *Qur'ān*, as the early Muslims knew. The popular portions of the Book are miraculous in providing for the needs of every class of mind.

6. Qur'an 33:72.

We intend to make a study of its teachings at the apparent level, and thus help to remedy the grievous harm done by ignorant partisans of philosophy and religion.]

It may be asked: 'If these methods followed by the Ashʿarites and other theorists are not the common methods by which the Legislator has aimed to teach the masses, and by which alone it is possible to teach them, then what are those [common] methods in this religion of ours'? We reply: They are exclusively the methods set down in the precious Book. For if the precious Book is inspected, there will be found in it the three methods that are available for all the people, ⟨namely⟩ the common methods for the instruction of the majority of the people and the special method. And if their merits are inspected, it becomes apparent that no better common methods for the instruction of the masses can be found than the methods mentioned in it.

Thus whoever tampers with them, by making an allegorical interpretation not apparent in itself, or [at least] not more apparent to everyone than they are (and that [greater apparency] is something non-existent), is rejecting their wisdom and rejecting their intended effects in procuring human happiness. This is very apparent from [a comparison of] the condition of the first believers with the condition of those who came after them. For the first believers arrived at perfect virtue and fear of God only by using these sayings [of Scripture] without interpreting them allegorically; and anyone of them who did find out an allegorical interpretation did not think fit to express it [to others]. But when those who came after them used allegorical interpretation, their fear of God grew less, their dissensions increased, their love for one another was removed, and they became divided into sects.

So whoever wishes to remove this heresy from religion should direct his attention to the precious Book, and glean from it the indications present [in it] concerning everything in turn that it obliges us to believe, and exercise his judgement in looking at its apparent meaning as well as he is able, without interpreting any of it allegorically, except where the allegorical meaning is apparent in itself, i.e. commonly apparent to everyone. For if the sayings set down in Scripture for the instruction of the people are inspected, it seems that in mastering their meaning one arrives at a point, beyond which none but a man of the demonstrative class can extract from their apparent wording a meaning which is not apparent in them. This property is not found in any other sayings.

For those religious sayings in the precious Book which are expressed to everyone have three properties that indicate their miraculous character: (1) There exist none more completely persuasive and convincing to everyone than they. (2) Their meaning admits naturally of mastery, up to a point beyond which their allegorical interpretation (when they are of a kind to have such an interpretation) can only be found out by the demonstrative class. (3) They contain means of drawing the attention of the people of truth to the true allegorical meaning. This [character] is not found in the doctrines of the Ashʿarites nor in those of the Muʿtazilites, i.e. their interpretations do not admit of mastery nor contain [means of] drawing attention to the truth, nor are they true; and this is why heresies have multiplied.

It is our desire to devote our time to this object and achieve it effectively, and if God grants us a respite of life we shall work steadily towards it in so far as this is made possible for us; and it may be that that work will serve as a starting point for our successors. For our soul is in the utmost sorrow and pain by reason of the evil fancies and perverted beliefs which have infiltrated this religion, and particularly such [afflictions] as have happened to it at the hands of people who claim an affinity with philosophy. For injuries from a friend are more severe than injuries from an enemy. I refer to the fact that philosophy is the friend and milk-sister of religion; thus injuries from people related to philosophy are the severest injuries [to religion]—apart from the enmity, hatred and quarrels which such [injuries] stir up between the two, which are companions by nature and lovers by essence and instinct. It has also been injured by a host of ignorant friends who claim an affinity with it: these are the sects which exist within it. But God directs all men aright and helps everyone to love Him; He unites their hearts in the fear of Him, and removes from them hatred and loathing by His grace and His mercy!

Indeed God has already removed many of these ills, ignorant ideas and misleading practices, by means of this triumphant rule. By it He has opened a way to many benefits, especially to the class of persons who have trodden the path of study and sought to know the truth. This [He has done] by summoning the masses to a middle way of knowing God the Glorious, [a way] which is raised above the low level of the followers of authority but is below the turbulence of the theologians; and by drawing the attention of the élite to their obligation to make a thorough study of the principles of religion. God is the Giver of success and the Guide by His Goodness.

ʿULUM AL-QURʾAN: SCRIPTURE SCHOLARSHIP OR "QURʾANIC SCIENCES"

FAKHR AL-DIN AL-RAZI
1149/50–1210

Muhammad ibn ʿUmar Fakhr al-Din al-Razi shares with his more famous countryman, Abu Hamid Muhammad ibn Muhammad al-Ghazali (1058–1111; see above), the epithet "renewer of religion"—in his case, a sobriquet secured for the thirteenth rather than for the twelfth century. Fakhr al-Din's later prominence was not easily predictable from his modest beginnings. He was born in the Iranian city of Rayy, a shrine city of regional importance during the ʿAbbasid caliphate (750–1258) that is today part of the greater metropolitan area of Tehran. That his father was a local preacher explains his nickname, "the preacher's son" (Ibn al-Khatib). Not surprisingly, his father was also his first teacher. But after an early education in Rayy, Fakhr al-Din continued his studies in theology, jurisprudence, and philosophy in Nishapur and Maragha.

Like many before him, Fakhr al-Din found that his own teaching career involved many locales. He began in western Iran and Azerbayjan, then returned to his hometown of Rayy, and later moved to Khwarazm (an area bordering the Amu Darya or

Oxus River in present-day Uzbekistan and Turkmenistan) and Transoxania (the land between the Amu Darya and the Syr Darya or Jaxartes River, a region that includes Uzbekistan, Tajikistan, and part of southern Kazakhstan). But the profession of madrasa teaching was not well-compensated, and a scholar's survival depended on the help of others. After he endured an early period of poverty and poor health, Fakhr al-Din's growing fame as a teacher and preacher attracted the kind of patronage that enabled him to provide for his family and continue his writing.

By all accounts, he was a powerful and charismatic preacher, capable of soaring flights of oratory and gripping, emotional rhetoric. Like the best evangelical revivalists, he could make an audience weep and in the pulpit was himself occasionally overcome by tears. Anecdotes from his biographers attest to his expressions of sentiment and passion. During one class session, a frightened bird fell at his feet and, to the surprise of his students, he interrupted his lecture to care for it. A much-repeated passage from his final "testament" speaks to a spiritual unease that may have haunted him for much of his life: "I have diligently explored the paths of theology (*kalam*) and the ways of philosophy but have not found what quenches thirst or heals the sick; but now I see that the soundest way is the way of the Qur'an read with true understanding."

During the second half of the twelfth century, the inhabitants of Fakhr al-Din's world, the eastern reaches of the Muslim empires, had no inkling of what would soon befall them. Less than a decade after his death in 1210, this area suffered the devastation of the first Mongol invasion. Subsequent assaults transformed the political geography of the entire region and culminated in the catastrophic midcentury destruction of Baghdad. Yet most of Fakhr al-Din's life passed under the patronage of dynasties that would disappear with the Mongol advance, including those that ruled Khwarazm and Khurasan, which lay southeast of Khwarazm in what is now Afghanistan, Pakistan, and northern India.

Thanks to this imperial protection from local, populist objections, the diligent explorations to which Fakhr al-Din referred in his testament resulted in a literary output of extraordinary range and size. Many of his treatises have been published but others are available only in manuscript. He wrote in both Arabic and Persian, on subjects that include alchemy, astrology, and medicine as well as the expected topics of theology, jurisprudence, and law. His magnum opus, however, to which he devoted himself in the final years of his life, is a massive commentary on the Qur'an; in a modern edition, it runs to thirty-two large volumes. It is commonly cited under two titles, *The Great Commentary* and *The Keys of the Unseen*—the latter drawn from a phrase in Qur'an 6:59.

Like most full-scale commentaries on the Qur'an, *The Great Commentary* follows the sura and verse order of the text. In other words, it begins by commenting on the first verse of the Qur'an and continues through to the concluding one. But unlike many others, its format is comparable to that of a monumental Christian medieval work, the *Summa Theologiae* of Thomas Aquinas (1225–1274). Like Aquinas, Fakhr al-Din divides his analysis of a verse into a series of "questions" (in Arabic, *masa'il*) or matters for discussion (though the sections are not numbered in the Arabic original). One of his biographers remarked upon the originality of this methodology: "He was the first one to devise this arrangement in his writings. He accomplished in them what no one before him had done, for he stated the question and then proceeded to divide it and to classify further these subdivisions. He drew conclusions on the basis of such probing and apportioning and no relevant aspect of the question eluded him."

Sections of commentary, such as the following, are often difficult to translate, for they frequently focus on precise lexical and semantic questions in the original Arabic that cannot be easily conveyed in English. For example, in the initial question that Fakhr al-Din addresses in this commentary on the first four verses of sura 98, he discusses the use of the word "until" (in Arabic, *hatta*) and the verbal constructions that it can govern. Section 10 also deals with a lexical and etymological issue that defies translation.

The attention to textual particularity captured in this small excerpt from Fakhr al-Din's *Great Commentary* is characteristic of qur'anic exegesis, and of the exegesis of other scriptural traditions as well. Each word and phrase warrants close and careful attention. Considered to be God's very word, the text of the Qur'an impresses those who study it with its aura of the sacred. Like Fakhr al-Din, they respond with a devotion to detail that is deeply reverential.

PRONOUNCING GLOSSARY

al-barī'a: *al-ba-ree´-uh*
al-bariyya: *al-ba-ree´-yuh*
al-Kashshāf: *al-kash-shaf´*
al-Wāḥidī: *al-wa´-hi-dee* (heavy *h*)
al-Zamakhsharī: *az-za-mach´-sha-ree* (guttural *ch*)
ʿaṣr: *ahsr*
barā: *ba-rah´*
dhariyya: *dha-ree´-yuh*
Gehenna: *ge-hen´-nuh*
ḥadd: *had* (heavy *h*)
hamza: *ham´-zuh*
Ibn ʿUrfa: *ibn ur´-fuh*
khābiyya: *cha-bee´-yuh* (guttural *ch*)
Khandaq: *chan´-daq* (guttural *ch*)
Kitāb al-basīṭ: *ki-tab´ al-ba-seet´*
Majūs: *ma-joos´*
nabī: *na-bee´*
Nāfiʿ: *na´-fi*
qāḍī: *qah´-dee*
sūra: *soo´-ruh*
ʿulamā': *oo-la-ma´*

FROM THE GREAT COMMENTARY
[AL-TAFSĪR AL-KABĪR: MAFĀTĪḤ AL-GHAYB]
[*On* Sūrat al-bayyina *(98), "The Clear Proof"*]

> The unbelievers of the people of the book and the idolaters would not leave off until the clear sign comes to them, a messenger from God, reading aloud pages purified, therein true books. And those who were given the book did not separate except after the clear sign came to them.[1]

Know that concerning these verses a number of problems arise.

1. Problem one. Al-Wāḥidī[2] says in his *Kitāb al-basīṭ* ('The expansive commentary') that this verse is one of the most difficult in terms of structure and interpretation. Many members of the *ʿulamā'*[3] have stumbled in dealing with it. May God Most High have mercy on whoever attempts to summarize the nature of the difficulty in the verse.

   One aspect of the difficulty occurs in re-expressing the verse, *The unbelievers . . . would not leave off until the clear sign comes to them*, which is the messenger. The Most High does not mention what it is that they 'left off' from. This, however, is known; it is the disbelief which they once had. So, one can re-express the verse in the following way. Those

Translated by Norman Calder, Jawid Mojaddedi, and Andrew Rippin.

1. Qur'an 98:1–4.
2. ʿAli ibn Ahmad ibn Muhammad al-Wahidi (d. 1076), a Persian-born commentator also known for his work on the "occasions of revelation."
3. Scholars (Arabic).

who disbelieve did not leave off their disbelief until the clear sign came to them which is the messenger. Thus the word *until* is used to indicate their reaching the end of what they were doing. So, this verse then demands that they began to leave off disbelieving when the messenger came. However, after that He said, *And those who were given the book did not separate except after the clear sign came to them.* This then demands that their disbelief increased at the time of the coming of the messenger. So, between the first verse and the second is a contradiction in the apparent sense of the verse. This results in the difficulty in these considerations.

The response to this has a number of aspects.

1.1. The first and the best is what is given by the author of *al-Kashshāf* ('The unveiling') [al-Zamakhsharī].[4] That is that the unbelievers are of two types, the people of the book[5] and the worshippers of idols. Before the mission of Muḥammad, they all used to say, 'We will not leave off from what we have in our religion. We will not leave it until the prophet who is promised and described in the Torah and the Gospel is sent.' He is Muḥammad. God reported what they used to say. Then He said, *And those who were given the book did not separate*, meaning that they promised in the agreement of their words and in conforming with the truth that when they were sent the messenger, then they would not separate from the truth. Then they established themselves in disbelief at the coming of the messenger.

1.1.1. This is parallel to what is said in speech, as when a poor and corrupt person says to someone who admonishes him, 'I will not be stopped from my evil actions until God bestows wealth upon me.' When God does bestow wealth on him, his corruption only increases. So, his admonisher says to him, 'You have not left off from your corruption even though you are able to. You slip your head into corruption even after the situation has eased.' This was said as a rebuke and a rejection of the argument.

The essence of this response rests on a single expression which is His saying, *Those who disbelieve would not leave off*—from disbelief—*until the clear sign comes to them* which mentions a story which they told among themselves. However, His saying, *Those who were given the book did not separate* is the notification of an actual outcome. The meaning is thus that what will occur is the contrary of what they claimed.

1.2. The second aspect in response to this problem is that one should re-express the verse as follows. Those who disbelieve will not leave off from their disbelief even though the clear sign has come to them. The ambiguity is removed in this re-expression and this is the way the Qāḍī[6] deals with it, although this explanation of the word *until* does not have any support in the Arabic language.

4. Mahmud ibn ʿUmar al-Zamakhshari (1075–1144), author of a Qur'an commentary that was widely cited despite criticism for its Muʿtazili tendencies. The Muʿtazilis were an early Muslim theological school, known for their use of rationality when interpreting ambiguous qur'anic verses.

5. A common qur'anic designation (*ahl al-kitab*) for the Jews and Christians.

6. Judge (Arabic); here, the Muʿtazili theologian ʿAbd al-Jabbar al-Hamadhani (937–1025).

1.3. The third aspect in response to this problem is that we do not connect His saying *leave off* to disbelief but rather to their leaving off mentioning Muḥammad and his virtues and merits. The meaning then would be that those who disbelieve would not leave off from mentioning the virtues and merits of Muḥammad until the clear sign comes to them. Ibn ʿUrfa[7] said this means 'until it came to them', such that even though the verb is in the imperfect tense, the meaning is of the perfect. That is like the saying of the Most High, *[They follow] what the devils recite [over Solomon's kingdom]* (Q 2/102) meaning 'what they recited'. So the meaning is that they did not leave off mentioning his virtues; but when Muḥammad came to them, they separated into groups regarding him. Every one of them said something about him that was incorrect. This is parallel to the saying of the Most High, *Previously they implored [God] for victory over those who disbelieve. But when there came to them what they recognized, they disbelieved in it* (Q 2/89).

The preferred answer in this is the first one.

1.4. There is a fourth aspect concerning this verse. The Most High decreed that the unbelievers would not leave off from their unbelief until the time of the coming of the messenger. The word *until* demands that it refer to a subsequent state which opposes what came before. This was the state of affairs because that specific group did not remain in unbelief but rather they separated. Among them were some who became believers while others became unbelievers. Since the state of those in the group did not remain the same after the coming of the messenger as it was before he came, that justifies the use of the word *until*.

1.5. A fifth aspect is that the unbelievers, before the sending of the messenger, had left off all hesitation about their unbelief. They were firmly convinced of it, believing in its truth. That conviction ceased at the coming of the messenger although they remained doubtful and confused about that and all other religions. This is similar to His saying, *The people were a single nation; then God sent forth the prophets as good tidings bearing warnings* (Q 2/213). The meaning of this is that the religion to which they belonged had become like the mixture of their flesh and blood. So, the Jews were firmly convinced in their Judaism, and likewise with the Christians and the idol worshippers. When Muḥammad was sent, their ideas and thoughts became troubled and all of them doubted their own religion, their teachings and their creeds. So God said, *leave off*, that is, knowing this, because 'leaving off' something for something else is being separated from the first. So the meaning is that their hearts were not freed from those creeds nor were they separated from their sound convictions. Thus, after the sending of Muḥammad, the matter did not remain in the same condition.

7. Abu al-Hasan ʿAli ibn Muhammad (d. ca. 1029), a scholar from Jurjan.

2. Problem two. The unbelievers are of two types. One consists of the people of the book, such as groups within the Jews and the Christians who are unbelievers because of their creation of their religion with elements of unbelief, as in His saying, *Ezra is the son of God* (Q 9/30) and, *The Messiah is the son of God* (Q 9/30) and their alteration of the book of God and His religion.[8] The second type are the idolaters who do not hold to a scripture. God mentioned these two types in His statement, *Those who disbelieve*, as a summation, which He then followed by a differentiation which is *of the people of the book and the idolaters*. This then provokes two questions.

2.1. One, the verse may be re-expressed as, 'The unbelievers of the people of the book and from among the idolaters. . . .' This necessitates that the people of the book be composed of some who disbelieve and some who do not. This is true. But it also suggests that the idolaters are composed of some who disbelieve and some who do not, and it is known that this is not true.

2.1.1. The answer to this has a number of possibilities. One is that the word 'from' is not to be taken as a distributive here but as an explanation as in His saying, *So avoid the abomination (which comes) from idols* (Q 22/30). Another would be that of those who disbelieve in Muḥammad, some are members of the people of the book and some are of the idolaters. So, this would be the reason for the insertion of the word 'from'. Third is that His saying *the idolaters* is a description of the people of the book. This is because Christians are tri-theists[9] and Jews are generally anthropomorphists; both of these are forms of idolatry. Someone may say, 'The intelligent ones and elegant ones came to me', meaning thereby a single group of people whose importance is indicated by these two characteristics. God has also said, *Those who bow, those who prostrate themselves, those who bid to honour and forbid dishonour, those who keep God's bounds* (Q 9/112); this is a description of a single group of people. There are many examples of this in the Qurʾān where a group of people is described by various qualities connected by the conjunctive particle. All of them describe a single entity.

2.2. The second question is in regards to the Majūs:[1] are they a part of the people of the book? Some of the *ʿulamāʾ* state that they are a part of the people of the book due to Muḥammad saying, 'We will entrust them to the practice of the people of the book', while others reject this because when God mentioned the disbelievers, He was speaking of the people in the land of the Arabs and they were the Jews and the Christians. God related a story about them, *If you say that the book was revealed to two groups before you* (Q 6/156), and the *two groups* are the Jews and the Christians.

8. Common theological objections made against the Jews and Christians.
9. As believers in the Trinity (the Father, the Son, and the Holy Spirit).

1. Zoroastrians, whose sacred writings are the Avesta (Zoroastrianism was the state religion of the Sassanids).

3. The third problem relates to why the people of the book are given precedence in disbelief over the idolaters when He says, *Those who disbelieve of the people of the book and the idolaters.* The answer here is that the connective *and* does not indicate an ordering. There are several merits to this structure, however. First, the *sūra* was revealed in Medina and the aim of the passage was to address the people of the book. Second, those knowledgeable in the scriptures had within their power the most complete knowledge of the sincerity of Muḥammad. Their persistence in disbelief is the most shameful aspect. Third, because they were learned, others copied them; so, their disbelief was the source of the disbelief of others. Thus they were mentioned first. Fourth, because they were learned and more noble than the others, they were mentioned first.

4. Problem four. Why does He say, *of the people of the book*, and not 'of the Jews and the Christians'? The answer to this is because His saying, *of the people of the book*, indicates that they are learned. Either this emphasizes a magnificent attribute which surely must describe more than just the Jews and the Christians, or it is because they are learned that this emphasizes the extent of the shamefulness of their disbelief. They are described in this way to emphasize their penalty in the hereafter as well.

. . .

They were commanded only to serve God, making the religion His sincerely as men of true faith, and to establish prayer and pay the alms; and that is the religion of the true. The unbelievers of the people of the book and the idolaters will be in the fire of Gehenna,[2] *therein dwelling forever. Those are the worst of creatures.*[3]

5. Know that when God mentioned the condition of the unbelievers first in His saying, *The unbelievers of the people of the book and the idolaters*, He followed this with a mention of the condition of the believers in His saying, *They were commanded only to serve God.* He returns at the end of this *sūra* to the mention of both groups; so, He began with the condition of *the unbelievers*, those who disbelieve. Know that God mentions only two of their conditions, one, existing in the fire of Gehenna, and two, that they are the worst of creation. Questions arise here.

6. Problem one. Why are the people of the book given precedence here over the disbelievers? The answer here has several aspects.

   6.1. One is that Muḥammad gave precedence to the truth of God over the truth of himself. Do you not see that when the community reached its fifth year, Muḥammad said, 'God, guide my community for they do not know!' When the *ʿaṣr* prayer was decreed on the day of Khandaq,[4] he said, 'God, fill their bellies and their graves with fire!' It is as if Muḥammad had himself spoken of punishment first as an illustration, and then, on the day of Khandaq, as a way of

2. Hell.
3. Qur'an 98:5–6.
4. In 627, Muhammad and his followers warded off an attack by their Meccan adversaries by digging a trench (in Arabic, *khandaq*) around Medina. "The *ʿaṣr* prayer": the late afternoon prayer (the third of the five daily compulsory prayers).

proper conduct which is prayer. Subsequently, God decreed that. God said, 'You give My truth precedence over your truth. So also I give precedence to your truth over My own. Whoever forgets prayer for all of his life does not commit disbelief, but whoever speaks evil of even one of your hairs commits disbelief. You knew that, so We say that the people of the book do not speak evil of God but only of the messenger. However, the idolaters speak evil of God.' When God wished in this verse to mention the evil of the unbelievers' condition, He began first with the offence of speaking evil of Muḥammad—and that is the offence of the people of the book. Second, He mentioned those who speak evil of Himself, and they are the idolaters.

6.2. The second point is that the crime of the people of the book in denying the truth of the messenger was greater because the idolaters saw him as a small child and he grew up among them. He then called them foolish and declared their religions corrupt. This was a difficult matter for them. The people of the book, on the other hand, started out with his coming as a prophet and they acknowledged his mission. When he came to them, however, they rejected him even though they had the knowledge. This is a serious crime.

7. Problem two. Why does He say, *the unbelievers* (lit.: '*those who disbelieve*'), using a verb but then say, *the idolaters*, using a noun? The answer is that this draws attention to the fact that the people of the book were not unbelievers from the beginning, because they believed in the Torah and the Gospel. They confirmed the mission of Muḥammad but then they disbelieved in that after his mission began. This is contrary to the idolaters who were born into the worship of idols and rejected the ideas of the assembly and the resurrection at the end of time.

8. Problem three. The idolaters rejected the ideas about the Maker, prophethood and resurrection. As for the people of the book, they accepted all of these matters but they rejected the prophethood of Muḥammad. Therefore, the disbelief of the people of the book is less than that of the idolaters. If that is so, why is the punishment of the two groups the same? The answer is as follows. One may say, 'The spring of Gehenna' when meaning a spring which comes from great depth. Thus it is as if God is saying they are proud of their search for height but they become the lowest of the low. The two groups are formed into a partnership, but their partnership in this fate is not inconsistent with there being a difference in the degree of punishment. Know that there are two aspects to sin in the appropriateness of this punishment. One is the sin of someone who does evil to you, and the other the sin of someone who benefits you. This second type is the more detestable. Benefit is likewise of two types: the benefit to the one who benefits you, and the benefit to one who does evil to you.

8.1. This benefit is of two types. The benefit of God to those disbelievers is of a greater type of benefit, and their sin and disbelief is of a more severe kind of sin. It is known that the punishment is in proportion to the crime. So, for abuse there is censure; for defamation, a *ḥadd:*[5] for stealing, amputation; for adultery, stoning; for killing, retaliation. So, the abuse of property necessitates censure, and a nasty glance at the messenger necessitates death. The crimes of these disbelievers are great, so surely they are entitled to a great punishment which is the fire of Gehenna. This fire is in a deep, dark dreadful place from which there is definitely no escape. It is as if someone said, 'Assuming there is no hope of escape, is there any hope of getting out?' So He said, 'No, they will remain in it forever.' Then it is as if someone said, 'Isn't there someone there who will have pity on them?' and He said, 'No. They blame and curse them because they are the worst of creation.'

9. Problem four. What is the reason that He does not say here, 'therein residing forever and ever'. He said in the description of the people who will be rewarded in paradise that they will be *therein residing forever and ever* (Q 98/8). The answer has several aspects, one of which is that it draws attention to the fact that God's mercy is greater than His wrath. The second is that the judgements, punishments and atonements of Hell are intertwined. As for the reward, its various aspects are not intertwined. Third, an account is related from God that He said, 'David, make me acceptable to My creation!' 'How can I do that?' he replied. He said, 'Mention the extent of My mercy to them.' This is of the same type of expression.

10. Problem five concerns the readings of the word *al-bariyya* ('creatures'). Nāfiʿ[6] read this as *al-barīʾa* with a *hamza* while everyone else read it without a *hamza*. It would be related to 'God formed [*baraʾa*] creation' with the *hamza* considered to have been left out, as in the words *nabī*, *dhariyya* and *khābiyya*. The *hamza* is present in the original root of the word in common usage, just as one can add the *hamza* to *nabī* although leaving it out is better. If *hamza* is considered a part of the root and is understood as something which was originally discarded, then this would indicate that it is false to consider that *bariyya* is from *barā* in the sense of 'dust'.

11. Problem six. What is the benefit of His saying, *the worst of creatures*? The answer is that it allows their expulsion and bears witness against them such that they are alone. Know that the worst of creatures as a whole extends its details into many aspects, for example that he is worse than a thief because he steals the description of Muḥammad from the book of God, and worse than the highway robber because he takes the way of truth from creation, and worse than the most ignorant or the boor because he pretends to have knowledge but it is really disbelief and stubbornness. And that is the absolute worst.

5. A prescribed punishment (Arabic).
6. Nafiʿ ibn ʿAbd al-Rahman ibn Abi Nuʿaym (d. ca. 785), one of the seven reciters of the Qurʾan whose recitations (leading to variant readings) all came to be deemed authoritative.

IBN TAYMIYYA
1263–1328

An uncompromising scholar, Taqi al-Din Ahmad Ibn Taymiyya held firmly to the belief that true Islam is found only in the foundational sources of the Qur'an, the traditions of the Prophet, and the practice of the earliest generations of Muslims. All that conformed to these sources, he deemed acceptable; anything that deviated from these sources he condemned.

Born in Harran, Turkey, to a family with a tradition of Hanbali scholarship, Ibn Taymiyya fled with them to Damascus in 1269, avoiding the Mongol forces advancing into the region. In Damascus, he received a traditional religious education in Hanbali texts but also read widely in those of other legal and theological schools, as well as in works on Sufism. In 1284, he became the director of the Sukkariyya school in Damascus, a post previously held by his father. This appointment marked the beginning of a successful teaching career in which he attracted students, both men and women, from a variety of legal schools.

His teachings were based directly on the Qur'an and the traditions of the Prophet, adhering closely to a literal reading of both. Consequently, his theological writings attacked the rational theologians and the philosophers for their willingness to deny the literal descriptions of God in the Qur'an and their reliance on logic for an understanding of God's nature. He also faulted the legal schools for their uncritical adherence (*taqlid*) to precedents and lack of direct engagement with the Qur'an and traditions. He was similarly wary of the concept of consensus (*ijma*ʿ) and failed to see how scholarly agreement on a matter could be of any value unless it rested on the Qur'an or the practice of the early community. He did allow the use of analogical reasoning (*qiyas*) in extending the scope of a legal judgment, provided that the basis of the legal ruling was located in the foundational sources of Islam. Following the same logic, he rejected as unorthodox such Sufi practices as visiting the shrines of saints and seeking their intercession, and he deplored the metaphysical Sufism of Ibn ʿArabi (1165–1240; see below) and his followers. Yet he was not entirely opposed to Sufism, embracing a moderate form that focused on perfecting one's faith in God.

Strong in his convictions and outspoken in their defense, Ibn Taymiyya spent long periods—more than a tenth of his life—in prison or under house arrest. Those whom he denounced often took action against him. For example, his treatises against the speculative theologians led them, in turn, to charge that his theology was essentially anthropomorphic. In the trials that followed, he was found guilty and jailed. His attacks on popular Sufi customs resulted in his imprisonment by high-ranking judges sympathetic to such practices. On one occasion, the Mamluk sultan Muhammad ibn Qalawun (1285–1341) sent him to prison for refusing to issue fatwas in accordance with the Hanbali school: Ibn Taymiyya, though trained as a Hanbali jurist, would not conform to the school on issues with which he disagreed. His stays in prison never broke his spirit, and statements from him by biographers attest to his resilience.

Yet he died incarcerated in the Citadel of Damascus in 1328. Ibn Taymiyya might have been no more than a footnote in Hanbali history books were it not for the considerable influence that his thought exercises in the contemporary period. Muhammad ibn ʿAbd al-Wahhab (1703–1792; see above), the eponym of the modern-day Wahhabi movement in Saudi Arabia, found inspiration in Ibn Taymiyya's emphasis on the foundational sources of Islam and his rejection of practices not in conformity with them. The effect of his fatwa labeling the Mongols as disbelievers (*kafirs*) for outwardly professing Islam but acting against Muslim interests can be seen in the works of individuals such as Sayyid Qutb (1906–1966; see below), who questioned the faith of modern Muslim leaders for embracing secular values. More explicitly, Ibn Taymiyya's thought appears in the writings of the Egyptian revolutionary ʿAbd al-Salam Faraj (1954–1982), who, on the basis of Ibn Taymiyya's fatwa, argued for the permissibility of assassinating any Muslim leaders who deviated from Islamic norms.

The passage below is taken from the exegetical work *Introductory Treatise on the Principles of Tafsir* (qurʾanic interpretation). In it, Ibn Taymiyya explains the ideal manner for explicating the Qurʾan: First, it should be interpreted by using one part of it to explain another. If doing so proves insufficient, prophetic traditions (*hadith*) should be consulted for clarification. If that, too, fails, then Ibn Taymiyya proposes employing the statements of the Companions of Muhammad (i.e., the first generation of Muslims), followed by those of the successors (the second generation of Muslims). He ends the passage with a stern warning to those who would interpret the Qurʾan through their own uninformed opinion.

PRONOUNCING GLOSSARY

Aban ibn Salih: *a-ban´ ibn sah´-lih* (heavy *h*)
ʿAbida as-Salmani: *ah-bee´-duh as-sal-ma´-nee*
ʿAbd al-Razzāq: *ab-dur-raz-zahq´*
ʿAbdallah ibn ʿAbbas: *ab-dul-lah´ ibn ab-bas´*
ʿAbdallah ibn ʿAmr ibn al-ʿAs: *ab-dul-lah´ ibn ahmr ibn al-ahs´*
ʿAbdallah ibn Abi as-Safar: *ab-dul-lah´ ibn a-bees-sa´-far*
ʿAbdallah ibn Masʿud: *ab-dul-lah´ ibn mas-ood´*
Abu ʿAbdallah Muhammad ibn Idris [ash-Shafiʿi]: *a-boo ab-dul-lah´ moo-ham´-mad* (heavy *h*) *ibn ed-rees´ ash-sha´-fee-ee*
Abū Bakr as-Siddiq: *a-boo bakr as-sid-deeq´*
Abu'd-Duha, Muslim ibn Subayh: *a-bood-doo´-ha* (heavy *h*) *mus´-lim ibn soo-bayh´* (heavy *h*)
Abu Jaʿfar Muḥammad ibn Jarir [at-Tabari]: *a-boo ja´-far moo-ham´-mad* (heavy *h*) *ibn ja-reer´ at-tah´-bah-ree*
Abū Kurayb: *a-boo koo-rayb´*
Abu ʿUbayd: *a-boo oo-bayd´*
Abu Waʾil Shaqiq ibn Salama: *a-boo wa´-il shah-qeeq´ ibn sa´-la-muh*
Abu'z-Zinad: *a-booz-zi-nad´*
al-Aʿmash: *al-a´-mash*
al-Bukhari: *al-boo-cha´-ree* (guttural *ch*)
al-Husayn ibn Mahdī al-Baṣrī: *al-hoo-sayn´* (heavy *h*) *ibn mah´-dee* (light *h*) *al-bahs´-ree*
ash-Shaʿbi: *ash-sha´-bee*
at-Tirmidhī: *at-tir´-mi-dhee*
Ayyub: *eye-yoob´*
Banu Isra'il: *ba-noo is-rah-eel´*
hadith: *ha-deeth´* (heavy *h*)
Hashim: *ha´-shim*
Hisham ad-Dastawa'i: *he-sham´ ad-das-ta-wah´-ee*
Ibn ʿAwn: *ibn awn´*
Ibn Abī Mulayka: *ibn a-bee moo-lay´-kuh*
Ibn Abi Umar: *ibn a-bee oh´-mar*
Ibrahim: *ib-ra-heem´*
imam: *ee-mam´*
israʾiliyat: *is-rah-ee´-lee-yat*
Jabir ibn Nuh: *ja´-bir ibn nooh* (heavy *h*)
Jundab: *joon´-dab*
Masruq: *mas-rooq´*
Muʿadh: *moo-adh´*
Muʿammar: *moo-am´-mar*
Muʾammal: *moo-am´-mal*
Mughira: *moo-gee´-ruh*
Muhammad ibn Bashshar: *moo-ham´-mad* (heavy *h*) *ibn bash-shar´*
Muhammad ibn Isḥāq: *moo-ham´-mad* (heavy *h*) *ibn is-hahq´* (heavy *h*)
Muhammad ibn Sirin: *moo-ham´-mad* (heavy *h*) *ibn see-reen´*
Mujahid ibn Jabr: *moo-ja´-hid ibn jabr*
mushaf: *mus´-haf* (heavy *h*)
Qatada: *qah-ta´-duh*
Shuʿba ibn al-Hajjaj: *shuh´-buh ibn al-haj-jaj´* (heavy *h*)
Sufyan ath-Thawri: *soof-yan´ ath-thaw´-ree*

Sufyan ibn ʿUyayna: *soof-yan´ ibn oo-yay´-nuh*
sunna: *sun´-nuh*
taʾwil: *ta-weel´*
tafsir: *taf-seer´*
Talaq ibn Ghannam: *tah´-lahq ibn gan-nam´*
ʿUbaydallah ibn Muslim ibn Yasar: *oo-bay´-dul-lah´´ ibn mus´-lim ibn ya-sar´*
ʿUmar ibn Abi Zaʾida: *oh´-mar ibn a-bee za´-i-duh*
ʿUthman al-Makki: *uth-man´ al-mak´-kee*
Yarmuk: *yar-mook´*

FROM INTRODUCTORY TREATISE ON THE PRINCIPLES OF TAFSIR

Prologue

One of the brethren asked me to write for him an introductory treatise that would include comprehensive rules prescribed for understanding the Qurʾan, for knowing its interpretation and its meanings, for distinguishing—in both what has been handed down about it and what is the result of reasoning—between the truth and various kinds of falsehood, and for drawing attention to the decisive argument [*dalil*] that distinguishes correct opinions from incorrect. For the books composed about Qurʾanic interpretation are laden with lean and fat, with obvious falsehood and evident truth. Now, true knowledge lies either in a trustworthy transmission [*naql*] from one who is protected from error [*maʿsum*] or in a statement for which there is a clearly understood argument. Anything else is either [a transmission] rejected as a forgery or remains in "suspension," neither recognized as spurious nor ever critically tested. There is a palpable need for the Muslim community to understand the Qurʾan, which is "God's strong rope, the wise remembrance, the straight path, which passions cannot divert nor tongues confuse. Despite frequent repetition, it never wears out; its wonders never cease, and learned men never become satiated with it. Whoever professes it speaks the truth; whoever acts upon it is rewarded; whoever judges by it acts justly; whoever summons [others] to [follow] it is [himself] guided to a straight path. Whoever arrogantly abandons it, God shall deal him a mortal blow. Whoever seeks guidance in anything else, God shall lead astray." . . . [1]

The Best Methods of Interpretation: Interpreting The Qurʾan Through the Qurʾan and Interpreting It Through the Sunna

If someone asks, "What is the best method of interpretation?" the answer is that the soundest method is that whereby the Qurʾan is interpreted through the Qurʾan. For what is summarily expressed in one place is expatiated upon in another. What is abridged in one place is elaborated upon in another.

If that defeats your efforts, then you should resort to the Sunna, for the Sunna is what explains the Qurʾan and elucidates it. Imam Abu ʿAbdallah

Translated by Jane Dammen McAuliffe. All bracketed additions are the translator's; the numbers refer to sura and verse of the Qurʾan. "Tafsir": qurʾanic interpretation (Arabic).

1. A hadith found in several of the major collections.

Muhammad ibn Idris ash-Shafiʿi[2] has even said, "God's Messenger based his adjudications entirely upon what he understood of the Qurʾan." God said, "We sent down to you the book with truth so that you may judge between people according to what God has shown you; do not, then, side in dispute with those who are faithless" [4:105]. And God said, "We sent down on you the remembrance so that you may make clear to people what has come down to them and perhaps they may reflect" [16:44]. And God said, "We only sent down the book on you so that you may clarify for them those matters on which they hold divergent views and [that it may be] a guidance and mercy for a people who believe" [16:64]. Because of this God's Messenger said, "Truly I was given the Qurʾan and its like together," meaning the Sunna. The Sunna, too, came down upon him by inspiration, just like the Qurʾan, except that the Sunna was not recited [to him] as was the Qurʾan. Imam ash-Shafiʿi and other leading scholars have drawn many inferences from that [hadith], but this is not the place [to discuss them].

The point is that you should seek the interpretation of the Qurʾan from the Qurʾan itself, and if you do not find it there, then from the Sunna. As God's Messenger said to Muʿadh[3] when he sent him to Yemen: "On the basis of what will you judge?" Muʿadh answered, "By the book of God." "And if you do not find anything [there]?" Muhammad pressed. Muʿadh responded, "By the Sunna of God's Messenger." "And if you still do not find anything?" Muʿadh replied, "I will give my own considered opinion." Then God's Messenger tapped Muʿadh's chest and exclaimed, "Praise belongs to God, who grants success to the messenger of God's Messenger in satisfying the Messenger of God." This hadith can be found in the various collections [*fi ʾl-masanid waʾs-sunan*] with a flawless chain of transmitters.

Interpreting the Qurʾan Through the Statements of the Companions

Then when you do not find the interpretation in the Qurʾan or in the Sunna, you should have recourse to the statements of the Companions. This is because they are particularly knowledgeable in such matters, given what they actually witnessed with regard both to the Qurʾan and to those circumstances of which they alone have cognizance. It is also because of their complete understanding and sound knowledge, especially that of the most learned and prominent among them, such as the four rightly guided and rightly guiding caliphs, and ʿAbdallah ibn Masʿud.[4] Imam Abu Jaʿfar Muhammad ibn Jarir at-Tabari[5] stated that Abu Kurayb related that Jabir ibn Nuh transmitted from al-Aʿmash, on the authority of Abu 'd-Duha [Muslim ibn Subayh], that Masruq reported ʿAbdallah, that is Ibn Masʿud, to have said: "I swear by the one and only God, no verse from the book of God came down for which I was not the most knowledgeable about when it came down and where. If I knew where there was anyone, whom riding beasts could reach, more knowledgeable about the book of God than I, I would go to him." Al-Aʿmash also, on the

2. One of the four scholars for whom the major Sunni legal traditions are named (767–820; see above).
3. Muʿadh ibn Jabal (d. 639), Companion of the Prophet.
4. A Companion of the Prophet (d. 653), and a famous reciter of the Qurʾan.
5. Historian and theologian (ca. 839–923; see below), renowned for his massive commentary on the Qurʾan as well as for his history of the world from creation to 915.

authority of Abu Wa'il [Shaqiq ibn Salama], reported Ibn Masʿud to have said: "When any one of us had learned ten verses, he would not go beyond them until he knew what they meant and how to put them into practice."

Among them (that is, those particularly knowledgeable in interpretation) stands the learned man and scholar ʿAbdallah ibn ʿAbbas,[6] cousin of God's Messenger and expositor of the Qurʾan by virtue of the blessing obtained for him by the supplication of God's Messenger when he prayed, "O God, give him understanding in religion and teach him the interpretation [*taʾwil*] of the Qurʾan." . . .

Yet sometimes sayings which they used to recount from the "people of the Book"[7] are transmitted on the Companions' authority, [a practice] which was approved by God's Messenger when he said, "Convey on my authority even a single verse and narrate [traditions] about the Banu Israʾil [i.e., Jews and Christians] without constraint. But whoever tells lies against me intentionally, let him take his seat in the Fire." Al-Bukhari related this on the authority of ʿAbdallah ibn ʿAmr [ibn al-ʿAs].[8]

Because of this, on the day of [the battle of] Yarmuk[9] ʿAbdallah ibn ʿAmr acquired two camel loads of books belonging to the "people of the Book." He then used to transmit information from them, based on what he understood of this hadith to be the permission to do so.

Yet these Jewish and Christian accounts [*al-ahadith al-israʾiliyat*] should only be mentioned for purposes of attestation, not as a basis for belief. These accounts are essentially of three kinds. The first kind is what we know to be true because we already possess that which attests to its authenticity. That kind is sound. The second sort is that which we know to be untrue because of what we possess which contradicts it. The third type is that about which nothing can be said, being neither of the first kind nor the second. We should neither believe it nor declare it to be false. It is permissible to recount it, given what has just been said, but most of it provides no benefit in matters religious.

Among the "people of the Book" the scholars themselves disagree greatly in such matters and consequently disagreement is conveyed through the interpreters of the Qurʾan [who utilize *israʾiliyat*]. . . .

The best thing to do in reporting matters about which there is disagreement is this: all of the views pertinent to that case should be included; the reader should be made aware of those that are valid and the erroneous ones should be refuted; and the extent to which the diversity of opinion is useful or fruitful should be mentioned lest prolonged controversy and disagreement over useless matters distract one from what is more important.

Anyone who reports a disputed question without including everything that people have said about it is acting deficiently, since the correct view may be in what he ignores. Whoever simply reports disputed matters and lets it go at that, without drawing attention to which views are sound, also acts deficiently. If he deliberately defines as sound what is not, he has supported falsehood. If he does so out of ignorance, then he has committed an error.

6. The most prominent early exegete (ca. 619–687).
7. A common qurʾanic designation (*ahl al-kitab*) for the Jews and Christians.
8. A Companion of the Prophet (d. ca. 684), and one of the earliest collectors of hadith. Al-Bukhari (810–870; see above), author of one of the most authoritative Sunni collections of hadith.
9. The first major victory of the Muslim forces after the death of Muhammad; fought near the Yarmuk River (which forms part of the border between Syria and Jordan) in 636, it ended Byzantine rule of Syria.

The same can be said for one who generates disagreement about useless matters or transmits statements under many different wordings, the gist of which conveys but one or two views as far as sense is concerned. He, too, has certainly wasted his time and made much of what is unsound. He is like someone dressed in "the two garments of a lie" [*thawbay zur*].[1] But God is the One who leads us to the right answer.

Interpreting the Qurʾan Through the Statements of the Followers

When you find the interpretation in neither the Qurʾan nor the Sunna, nor on the authority of the Companions, in that case much that is reported on the authority of the leading scholars goes back to the statements of the Followers, for example Mujahid ibn Jabr,[2] for he was a prodigy [*aya*] in interpretation. Muhammad ibn Ishaq recounted from Aban ibn Salih that Mujahid said, "I spread out the *mushaf* [i.e., the text of the Qurʾan] before Ibn ʿAbbas three times, from its opening sura to its concluding one. At each and every verse I stopped him and asked him about it." At-Tirmidhi[3] included a report about it from al-Husayn ibn Mahdi al-Basri, who received it from ʿAbd ar-Razzaq, who was told by Muʿammar that Qatada[4] said, "There is no verse in the Qurʾan about which I have not heard something [significant]." At-Tirmidhi also included a report about it from Ibn Abi ʿUmar, who received it from Sufyan ibn ʿUyayna on the authority of al-Aʿmash, who heard Mujahid say, "If I had read Ibn Masʿud's version of the *mushaf* [*qiraʾata Ibn Masʿud*], I would not have needed to ask Ibn ʿAbbas about many of the qurʾanic matters on which I sought information." Ibn Jarir [at-Tabari] reported from Abu Kurayb, who related from Talaq ibn Ghannam on the authority of ʿUthman al-Makki, that Ibn Abi Mulayka said, "I saw Mujahid, with his slates in hand, asking about the interpretation of the Qurʾan. [Whenever he posed a question] Ibn ʿAbbas said to him, 'Write.' This went on until Mujahid had asked Ibn ʿAbbas about the interpretation of the whole text." For this reason Sufyan ath-Thawri[5] used to say, "When interpretation comes to you from Mujahid, it is sufficient for you."

[After listing a number of Followers, he continues:] You may mention their statements about a particular verse. But when a difference of wording occurs in what they have expressed, the unknowledgeable person counts it as a divergence of opinion and conveys it as a plurality of views. That, however, is not the case. For among this group are those who express something in its exact wording [*bi-lazimihi*], or the equivalent of that [*nazirihi*], and those who render the essence of it [*bi-ʿaynihi*]. Taken as a whole, this amounts to a single idea expressed in many [different] passages. The intelligent person should certainly understand that. God, however, is the supreme Guide.

Shuʿba ibn al-Hajjaj[6] and others said, "In legal stipulations [*al-furuʿ*] the statements of the Followers do not constitute sufficient proof [*hujja*], so how can they do so in matters of interpretation?" That is to say, they are not

1. This expression, which can refer to someone who pretends to have more than he possesses, occurs in a prophetic hadith recorded in the collections of both al-Bukhari and Muslim (821–875; see above) (q.v.) [translator's note].
2. A famous exegete (d. ca. 720). "The Followers": members of generation after those who personally accompanied the Prophet (the Companions); they are also called "the Successors."
3. Author of one of the six canonical collections of traditions (d. 892).
4. A famous exegete among the Successors (d. 735).
5. A famous traditionist of Kufa (ca. 715–778).
6. A Basran transmitter of traditions (d. 776/77).

considered a sufficient proof against the statements of other Followers who disagree with them. This, in fact, is a sound argument. When the Followers are in agreement, it unquestionably constitutes sufficient proof. If, however, they disagree, the statement of one does not disprove either the statement of another Follower or that of succeeding generations. In that situation one must resort to the language of the Qur'an or to the Sunna or to Arabic usage generally or to the statements of the Companions about the matter.

Interpreting the Qur'an on the Basis of Personal Opinion

Interpreting the Qur'an solely on the basis of personal opinion [*ra'y*] is strictly forbidden. . . . Ibn 'Abbas reported, "God's Messenger said, 'Whoever speaks about the Qur'an without knowledge will assuredly take his seat in the Fire.'" Jundab[7] related, "God's Messenger said, 'Whoever speaks about the Qur'an on the basis of his personal opinion, even if he gets it right, has still erred.'" . . .

Similarly, it has been reported that some scholars, both Companions and others, spoke harshly about the interpretation of the Qur'an without well-founded knowledge. No one should suggest, however, that to say Mujahid, Qatada, and other such scholars interpreted the Qur'an means that they spoke about the Qur'an or interpreted it without well-founded knowledge or on their own accord. What, in fact, has been recounted of them definitely confirms what we have said, that is, that they did not speak of their own accord or without knowledge. Whoever *does* speak about the Qur'an on the basis of his own personal opinion feigns a knowledge that he does not possess and acts contrary to the command he has been given. Even if, in actuality, he were to get the meaning right, he would still be erring, because he did not come at the matter in the proper way.

The same can be said for anyone who, in a state of ignorance, judges between people. He, too, is in the Fire, even if, in actuality, his judgment accords with the right one. Still, he is less blameworthy than one who makes a wrongful judgment. God, however, knows best. In similar fashion did God call those who make slanderous accusations liars when He said, "Since they did not bring witnesses, in God's eyes they are liars" [24:13]. For one who utters slander is a liar, even were he to slander someone who has actually committed adultery. That is because he has made a statement about something on which he has no right to comment, and because he has feigned a knowledge which he does not possess. But, again, God knows best.

For this reason a group of our distinguished predecessors refrained from any interpretation of which they had no knowledge. . . . Abu Bakr as-Siddiq[8] exclaimed, "What earth would support me and what heaven would overshadow me were I to say about the book of God what I knew not." . . .

Ayyub, Ibn 'Awn, and Hisham ad-Dastawa'i reported that Muhammad ibn Sirin said, "I asked 'Abida as-Salmani about a verse of the Qur'an and he replied, 'Those who know why the Qur'an was sent down (that is, the circumstances of revelation) have died, so fear God and follow the right course.'"

7. Samura ibn Jundab (d. 679), a Companion of the Prophet.

8. Muhammad's chief adviser and father-in-law, and the first Caliph (573–634).

Abu ʿUbayd related from Muʿadh, who transmitted from Ibn ʿAwn that ʿUbaydallah ibn Muslim ibn Yasar reported that his father said, "When you speak about God stop to consider the premises and the consequences of what you say."

Hashim related from Mughira that Ibrahim said, "Our associates have always feared and dreaded interpreting the Qur'an."

Shuʿba related from ʿAbdallah ibn Abi as-Safar that ash-Shaʿbi said, "By God, there is not a single verse about which I have not asked, and yet it is God's own transmission!"

Abu ʿUbayd reported from Hashim, who related from ʿUmar ibn Abi Za'ida on the authority of ash-Shaʿbi that Masruq said, "Beware of interpreting the Qur'an because it is nothing less than God's own transmission!"

These and other well-founded reports, which come down to us from our leading predecessors, are concerned with their refusal to say anything of which they have no knowledge about the interpretation of the Qur'an. There is no objection, however, to one who speaks from a basis of [sound] linguistic and legal knowledge.

There is no contradiction, consequently, in the fact that statements about the interpretation of the Qur'an have been reported from these and others, because they talked about what they knew and kept quiet about what they did not know. This is what everyone should do. Just as one should remain silent about what he knows not, one should speak when asked about what he knows. This is supported by God's saying, "You shall expound it to people and not suppress it" (3:187), and by the hadith that is handed down through various lines of transmission: "Whoever is asked about something he knows but suppresses it, will be bridled on the Day of Resurrection with a bridle of fire."

Ibn Jarir [at-Tabari] reported from Muhammad ibn Bashshar, who transmitted from Mu'ammal on the authority of Sufyan who reported from Abu 'z-Zinad that Ibn ʿAbbas said, "Interpretation of the Qur'an is of four kinds: a kind that the Arabs recognize on the basis of their [native] speech; interpretation that no one can be excused for not knowing; interpretation that the scholars [alone] know; and interpretation that only God knows." For God, may He be exalted and glorified, is all-knowing.

ʿ*ILM AL-AKHLAQ*: PRIVATE ETHICS AND PUBLIC GOVERNANCE

MISKAWAYH
ca. 932–1030

The Buyid dynasty (952–1062) in Iran and Iraq, known for its cultural patronage and support of public works, fostered a particularly lively intellectual and literary culture, as the eminent Abu ʿAli Ahmad ibn Muhammad Miskawayh exemplifies. While the medieval Muslim world produced a number of renowned historians and important philosophers, Miskawayh's prominence in both fields was unusual.

Miskawayh was born in Rayy, a suburb of modern-day Tehran, and in 952 he began his career in Baghdad as a secretary for Hasan al-Muhallabi (d. 963), vizier of the Buyid prince Muʿizz al-Dawla (r. 945–67). Later, in Rayy, he served Ibn al-ʿAmid (d. 971), vizier of the Buyid prince Rukn al-Dawla (r. 935–76), as a librarian, manager of the state archives, and teacher for the vizier's son. By his late forties he became attached to the court of ʿAdud al-Dawla (r. 949–83) in Baghdad. Miskawayh lived to be almost one hundred years old, but his later years were passed in relative obscurity as he devoted himself to reflection and to the writing that was to be his legacy.

His fame derives from two of his works: one on history, *Experiences of the Nations and Consequences of High Ambitions*, and the other on philosophical ethics, *The Refinement of Character*. *Experiences* is a universal history that begins from the time of Noah and the Flood and continues to the death of the Buyid prince ʿAdud al-Dawla. Miskawayh had an ethicist's interest in history, seeing a knowledge of the past as useful for the lessons it could teach. Miskawayh would have understood George Santayana's famous aphorism, "Those who cannot remember the past are condemned to repeat it." The first part of *Experiences* relies heavily on *History of Messengers and Kings*, by Abu Jaʿfar ibn Jarir al-Tabari (ca. 839–923; see below). From the point where al-Tabari's history ends in 915, Miskawayh uses lesser-known works and the reports of his contemporaries, such as those of the Buyid viziers, to bring his account up to 983.

His influential *The Refinement of Character*, from which the excerpt below is taken, lays out a conception of the soul and offers practical methods of disciplining it in the pursuit of ultimate happiness. Grounded in Greek philosophical thought, especially the Platonic theory of the soul and Aristotelian notions of virtue, *Refinement* demonstrates the compatibility of these conceptions with Islamic ideals. Miskawayh begins with a supplication to God and explicitly connects the pursuit of spiritual purification to the Qurʾan. He proposes a spiritual psychology that identifies the various parts of the human soul: the irascible, the lustful, and the rational. As the rational soul achieves supremacy over the other elements, the four virtues—wisdom, temperance, courage, and justice—are brought into balance and the soul progresses toward perfection.

Miskawayh's *Refinement* lays a foundation for subsequent works of philosophical ethics. It inspires the chapter on self-control in *Revival of the Religious Sciences* by al-Ghazali (1058–1111; see above), as well as his *Balance of Action*. *The Nasirean Ethics*, by Nasir al-Din al-Tusi (1201–1274; see below), summarizes it in Persian with additional sections on economics and politics. Even modern Muslim reformers such as Muhammad ʿAbduh (1849–1905; see below) incorporated it into their teaching.

What follows are instructions for child rearing that would surprise most modern parents. The natural state of the child is described as "generally bad," and only "education, age and experience" can ameliorate it. Table manners might strike many as a curious place to begin the "training of the soul," but Miskawayh argues that all else is built upon a discipline of the appetites.

PRONOUNCING GLOSSARY

sultan: *sul-tahn´*

vizier: *viz-eer´*

FROM THE REFINEMENT OF CHARACTER

A Section on the Education of the Young, and of Boys in Particular, Most of Which I Have Copied from the Work of 'Bryson'[1]

We have said previously that the first faculty that appears in man when he is first formed is the faculty with which he desires the food that keeps him alive. He instinctively asks for milk and seeks it from its source, the breast, without any previous instruction or direction. Along with this, he comes to possess the faculty by which he asks for it with the voice, which is his resource and the sign with which he shows pleasure or pain. Then this faculty grows in him, and it induces him to continually desire its growth and to use it in the pursuit of all sorts of pleasures. Following this, he acquires the faculty with which he seeks those pleasures through the organs which are formed in him, and this is followed by the desire to perform the actions which give him those pleasures. Then he obtains through the senses the faculty of imagination, and he begins to desire the images which are formed in it. Next comes the irascible faculty by means of which he tries to ward off what injures him and to resist what hinders him from his benefits. If he is able by himself to take his revenge from what injures him, he goes ahead and does it; otherwise, he seeks the assistance of others or asks the help of his parents by shouting and crying.

Following this, he acquires gradually the desire to discern those actions which are characteristically human, until he reaches his perfection in this respect, at which stage he is called a rational being.

These faculties are many in number, and some of them are necessary for the formation of others, until one attains the final end, the one which is sought by man *qua* man. The first feature of this faculty which occurs in man is bashfulness, which is fear on his part lest he commit anything disgraceful. This is why we have said that bashfulness is the first sign which should be looked for in a boy and taken as a symptom of his reason. For it shows that he has begun to perceive what is disgraceful and, at the same time, to be on his guard against it, to avoid it, and to be cautious lest it appear from him or in him. If, then, you look at the boy and find him bashful, with his eyes lowered towards the ground, neither having an insolent face nor staring at you, take this as the first evidence of his intelligence and as the testimony that his soul has discerned what is good and what is bad, and that his bashfulness is no more than self-restraint caused by his fear lest anything disgraceful should come out of him. This, in turn, is no more than the choice of the good and the abandonment of the disgraceful through judgment and reason. Such a soul is apt to be educated and fit to be taken care of. It should not be neglected or left to association with people of opposite character who would corrupt, through companionship and intercourse, anyone who has this fitness to receive virtue. For the boy's soul is still simple and has not yet received the impress of any form, nor does it possess any

TRANSLATED BY Constantine K. Zurayk. All bracketed additions are the translator's.

1. A late Greek text, *Oikonomikos*, attributed to a neo-Pythagorean named Bryson (1st or 2nd century C.E.), whose work survives largely in Arabic.

view or determination which would turn it from one thing to another. Should it, however, receive the impress of a particular form and assume it, the boy would grow in accordance with it and become accustomed to it.

It is appropriate, therefore, that such a soul be roused to the love of honor, especially that which comes to the boy through religion and the observance of its traditions and duties, rather than through money. Further, good men should be praised in his presence, and he himself should be commended for any good thing which he may perform and warned of reproach for the least disgraceful thing which he may demonstrate. He should be blamed for any desire on his part for food, drink, or splendid clothes, and he should hear the praise of self-restraint and of disdain of greed for food in particular and pleasures in general.

He should be trained to like giving others preference over himself in food and to be content with what is moderate and frugal in seeking it. He should be taught that the people who are most fit to wear colored and embroidered clothes are, first, women who adorn themselves for the sake of men and, second, slaves and servants, and that the dress which is most becoming to noble and honorable people is white or its like. Thus, being brought up on these teachings and hearing them repeatedly from everybody around him, he should also be prevented from mixing with those who tell him the contrary, especially if they happen to be his companions or his associates and playmates of the same age. For, in his early life, the boy is generally bad in all or most of his actions: he is a liar, telling and relating what he has not heard or seen; he is jealous; he steals and slanders; he is importune, meddlesome, spiteful, and malicious; and he is most harmful to himself as well as to everything that touches him. Later, under the constant influence of education, age, and experience, he changes from one state to another. That is why he should be trained as long as he is a child along the lines which we have described and are describing.

He should then be required to learn by heart good traditions[2] and poems which corroborate what he has practiced in his education, so that by reciting, learning, and discussing them, all that we have described may become confirmed in him. He should also be put on his guard against the study of frivolous poetry and what it contains about love and lovers, and against the impression which its authors give that it is a form of elegance and of refinement. For this kind of poetry has, indeed, a strong corrupting influence on youth.

The boy should also be praised and honored for any good trait or any good deed which he may show. If, at times, he violates what I have described, it is preferable that he not be reproached for it or openly told that he has committed it. One should feign not to have noticed it, as if it would not occur to him that the boy would ever dare such a thing or attempt to do it. This is especially necessary when the boy conceals it and endeavors to hide what he has done from other people. If he repeats it, let him be reproached for it secretly, shown the seriousness of his action and warned against doing it again. For if you accustom him to reproach and disclosure, you will make him impudent and incite him to repeat what he has detested. It will become easy for him to hear blame for indulging in the detestable pleasures to which his nature urges him. And these pleasures are very numerous.

2. That is, hadith.

The training of the soul should begin with [the formation of] good manners in eating. The boy should first be made to understand that eating is meant only for health and not for pleasure and that all the kinds of food have been created and prepared for us solely to make our bodies healthy and to sustain our life. They should be considered as medicines with which we remedy hunger and the pain resulting from it. Just as we do not seek medicine for pleasure and are not driven by greed to take more and more of it, so it is also with food: we should take only as much of it as would preserve the health of the body, remove the pain of hunger, and guard against disease. Thus, the boy should be made to despise the value of food, which gluttonous people extol, and to disdain those who covet it and take more of it than is necessary for their bodies or indulge in what does not agree with them. In this way, he would get to be satisfied with only one course of food and would not desire many courses. When he sits in the company of others, he should not be the first to start eating, nor should he stare constantly and fixedly at the courses of food but should be content with whatever is near him. He should not eat in a hurry or take rapidly one mouthful after another. The mouthfuls should not be too big or swallowed before they are well chewed. He should not soil his hands, or his clothing, or his table companions, nor follow with his eyes the movements of their hands in eating. He should be trained to offer to others the food that lies near him if it is the kind that he prefers, and to control his appetite so as to be content with the least and poorest of food, eating once in a while dry bread without anything else. These manners, if commendable when shown by poor people, are even more commendable when shown by the rich.

The boy should have his full meal in the evening, for, if he has it during the day, he will feel lazy and sleepy and also his understanding will become slow. If he is forbidden to eat meat most of the time, the result will be favorable to him in [stirring] his activity and attentiveness, in reducing his dullness, and in arousing him to liveliness and agility. As for sweets and fruits, he should abstain from them entirely if possible; otherwise, let him take as little of them as possible because they become transformed in his body, thus hastening the process of dissolution, and, at the same time, they accustom him to gluttony and to the desire for excessive food. He should be trained to avoid drinking water during his meals. As for wine and the different kinds of intoxicating beverages, let him indeed beware of them, for they injure him in his body and in his soul and incite him to quick anger, foolhardiness, the performance of vile deeds, impudence, and the other blameworthy dispositions. Nor should he attend drinking parties, except when the company is well-bred and virtuous; otherwise, he might hear vile speech and silly things that usually take place in such parties. [Finally,] he should not begin to eat until he has performed the educational tasks which he is pursuing and has become sufficiently tired.

Furthermore, the boy should be forbidden to do anything which he hides or conceals, for, if he hides anything, it is only because he either thinks or knows that it is disgraceful. He should not be allowed to sleep too long because too much sleep makes him flabby, dulls his mind, and deadens his thinking. So much for night sleep; as for sleep during the day, he should never become accustomed to it. Similarly, he should not be given a soft bed or any other means of luxury and flabbiness, so as to harden his body and to habituate him to a rough life. For the same reasons, he should be denied moistened canvas [to cool off the air] and living underground in summer, and camel furs and fire in winter. Let him develop the habits of walking, movement, riding, and exercise lest he succumb to their opposites.

The boy should be taught not to uncover the extremities of his body, nor to walk fast, nor to hang his hands loose but to join them together at his chest. He should not let his hair grow long, nor adorn himself with dresses fit for women, nor wear a ring except when necessary. Let him not boast to his companions of something which his parents possess, or of his food, clothing, or the like. On the contrary, let him be humble towards everybody and honor all those who associate with him. Should he possess any honor, or any power derived from his kin, he must not arouse the anger of those who are below him, or attempt to guide those whom he cannot divert from their whims, or deal with them high-handedly. If, for instance, his maternal uncle happens to be a vizier or his paternal uncle a sultan, this must not lead him to do injustice to his companions, or to defame his friends, or to seize the property of his neighbors and acquaintances.

He should be taught, when in the company of others, not to spit, or blow his nose, or yawn, or cross his legs, or beat his chin with his forearm, or support his head with his hand, for this is an indication of laziness and a proof that he has become so flabby that he is no longer able to carry his head without the help of his hand. Further, he should be trained not to tell lies and never to swear, whether truthfully or falsely, for swearing is disgraceful to men, though they may need it at times, but it is never needed by boys. He should also be taught to keep silent, to talk sparingly, and only to answer questions. If he is in the company of older people, his duty is to listen to them and to keep silent in their presence. He should be forbidden to utter vile or improper speech, to insult, curse, or talk nonsense. On the contrary, he should be taught to utter good and elegant speech and to greet gracefully and kindly, and should not be allowed to hear the opposite of this from others. He should also be accustomed to serve himself, his master, and older people. The children of the rich and of those who live in luxury need, more than others, to cultivate these good manners.

If the boy is beaten by his teacher, he should not cry or ask the intercession of any one, for such is the conduct of slaves and those who are feeble and weak. He should not reproach others except for disgraceful and bad manners. He should be accustomed not to treat other boys harshly, but to show kindness to them and to repay their favors with bigger ones lest he make it a habit to seek gain from boys and from friends. He should be made to detest silver and gold and to fear them more than he does lions, snakes, scorpions, and serpents. For the love of silver and gold is more harmful than poison. He should be allowed from time to time to play nice games in order that he may thus rest from the toil of education, but his play should not involve pain or intense fatigue. And, finally, he should be trained to obey his parents, teachers, and educators and to honor, extol, and revere them.

AL-MAWARDI
974–1058

Abu al-Hasan ʿAli ibn Muhammad ibn Habib al-Mawardi is widely acknowledged to be among the greatest writers on politics and government that the Muslim world ever produced, yet he lived at a time when his own government, the ʿAbbasid caliphate, saw its power recede.

Al-Mawardi started his studies in his hometown of Basra, Iraq, where his father made and sold rose water. He continued his education in Baghdad, where he eventually became a teacher. His intellectual prowess soon attracted the attention of those in power and he was appointed a judge. He rose through the judicial ranks, serving in a number of towns, then moving to a post in Baghdad, and finally receiving the honorific of "supreme judge" (*aqda al-qudat*) in 1038. Recognizing his talent, the ʿAbbasid caliphs al-Qadir (r. 991–1031) and al-Qaʾim (r. 1031–74) sought his counsel and deployed him on several occasions as a diplomat and negotiator. Though best known for his writings on government, in particular *The Ordinances of Government*, he also composed works on judgeship, qurʾanic exegesis, and grammar.

The ʿAbbasid caliphate, long in decline, had held only titular power since 945. In the lands formerly ruled by the caliph, true power now lay in the hands of the Buyids. The Buyids, who were Imami Shiʿis, offered nominal allegiance to the caliph in Baghdad; in return for this acknowledgment, he granted them the title of *amir*, or governor. The Buyid governors ruled their territories as they wished, neither consulting nor seeking approval from the caliph, whom they could replace at will. The caliph's only real authority lay in the administration of the palace and the appointment of Sunni religious officials and judges, especially in Baghdad. Al-Mawardi diligently served the ʿAbbasids but was also respected by the Buyid governors—whose downfall he lived to see when they lost Baghdad in 1055 to the Seljuk Tughril Beg. (The Seljuks, descended from Turkish tribes from Central Asia, were viewed as champions of Sunni beliefs; at its height, their empire extended from modern-day Turkey past Iran.)

Al-Mawardi's *The Ordinances of Government*, from which the excerpt below is taken, is generally recognized as the most authoritative treatment of Sunni political theory. Though *The Ordinances* is viewed as a classic, al-Mawardi was by no means the first or last Sunni author to wrestle with questions of governance. Notable contributions were also made by al-Baqillani (d. 1013), ʿAbd al-Qahir al-Baghdadi (d. 1037), al-Ghazali (1058–1111; see above), and Ibn Taymiyya (1263–1328; see above). In addition to its synthesis and expansion of earlier writings, what distinguishes al-Mawardi's *Ordinances* is the comprehensive detail of its plan for a functioning Islamic government.

While *The Ordinances* may be read as the definitive exposition of an ideal Sunni government, it can also be read as al-Mawardi's attempt to preserve the fading relevance of the caliphate by placing the imprimatur of Islamic law on current political realities. For example, after discussing those governors freely appointed by the caliph, he turns to the case of the governor who gains his appointment through force. According to al-Mawardi, provided that such a governor upholds the law of Islam in the lands under his control, the caliph *must* recognize him—thus forestalling a possible rebellion. Though he names no one in specific, al-Mawardi can only be referring to the Buyids, who had coerced recognition from the caliph. Al-Mawardi seems aware that his ruling has no genuine legal basis and contradicts earlier authors, yet he argues that the caliph's impotence coupled with the need for public protection requires that the standards for appointing a governor must be relaxed.

The *Ordinances* seeks to delineate the duties of the caliph, and its introduction suggests that it may have been written at the request of one of the two ʿAbbasid caliphs mentioned above. Its underlying assumption is that the caliphate is a divinely ordered form of government, as the caliph continues Muhammad's role of preserving the Muslim community. The caliph derives his authority from God and channels it to those whom he appoints. According to al-Mawardi, the caliph must fulfill obligations in three areas: defense of religion, administration of the state, and security of the state. As defender of the faith he must preserve Islamic practice in the lands under his control and punish those who disrupt the public peace by questioning matters of religion. As an administrator, he must appoint competent deputies and levy fair taxes. As guardian of state security, he is responsible both for internal matters, such as prosecuting criminals and securing roads, and for external matters, such as defending the borders of the empire. Finally, al-Mawardi charges the caliph with personal oversight of these responsibilities, noting that he cannot delegate them to others and live a life of leisure.

This selection from chapter 9 of *The Ordinances* describes, in characteristic detail, the caliph's role in appointing prayer leaders, one of the few powers he retained during Buyid rule. Note how al-Mawardi expounds the ritual differences among the Sunni schools of law and attempts to address a range of variations and exceptions to the basic mandates. Note also the prayer leader's requisite qualities, both of learning and gender.

PRONOUNCING GLOSSARY

Abū Ḥanīfa: *a-boo ha-nee´-fuh* (heavy *h*)
Abū Thawr: *a-boo thawr´*
Abū Yūsuf: *a-boo yoo´-suf*
al-Layth: *al-layth´*
al-Muzanī: *al-moo´-za-nee*
al-Zuhrī: *az-zuh´-ree* (light *h*)
ʿAmr ibn Maslama: *ahmr ibn mas´-la-muh*
Baṣra: *bahs´-ruh*
caliph: *ka´-lif*
Dāwūd (ibn Khalaf): *da-wood´*
Ḥanafite: *ha´-na-fite* (heavy *h*)
Ḥijāz: *he-jaz´* (heavy *h*)
imām: *ee-mam´*
Mālik ibn Anas: *ma´-lik ibn a´-nas*
muezzin: *moo-ez´-zin*
Muḥammad ibn al-Ḥasan: *moo-ham´-mad* (heavy *h*) *ibn al-ha´-san* (heavy *h*)
Shāfiʿī: *sha´-fi-ee*
Shāfiʿite: *sha´-fee-ite*
sūra: *soo´-ruh*

FROM THE ORDINANCES OF GOVERNMENT

From *Chapter 9*

On the Appointment of Prayer Leaders

Leadership at prayer falls into three divisions, depending on whether we are concerned with the five daily prayers, the Friday prayer, or the optional prayers. Appointment of leaders for the five prescribed prayers is a function of the status of the mosques wherein they are performed. Mosques are either built by the state or dedicated by members of the public. State mosques, central mosques, and shrines are relatively large structures which accommodate great numbers of people and are maintained by the government. It is inappropriate, therefore, for someone other than the official appointed by the sovereign to lead the worshippers at prayer in them, as that would constitute

TRANSLATED BY Wafaa H. Wahba.

an infringement of the rights of sovereignty. The Caliph's nominee has a stronger title to the office than anyone else, however more virtuous or knowledgeable.

Unlike judgeships and the syndicate,[1] this appointment is made because it is desirable rather than obligatory or necessary. There are two reasons for this. The first is that if a group of people choose a man to lead them at prayer, his leadership is valid and their collective worship is acceptable. The second is that group performance of the five daily prayers is an optional tradition and a commendable practice, albeit not a mandatory duty in the opinion of all authorities, with the sole exception of Dāwūd[2] who makes it obligatory unless for an excuse.

If it is certain that the sovereign has appointed an official for those mosques, no one else is entitled to lead the worship while he is present, and the person deputised by him alone should lead it in his absence. Should there be no deputy, his permission should be sought if possible regarding anyone who offers to perform this function; otherwise the people must agree on a leader so that their group worship may not be interrupted. If the appointed prayer leader is still absent by the time of the next prayer, the one who replaced him at the previous worship may according to some authorities continue to do so at the next prayer and the next until he returns, while others suggest that a different leader should be chosen for each prayer so that the impression may not be given that a new appointment has been made by the Caliph. Personally, I believe that, rather than adopting one of these two approaches unquestioningly, the situation at the second prayer should be considered; if the same people who attended the first are present, the same leader may officiate, otherwise a new choice is made with the former leader being like any other member of the congregation. Once a group prayer has been started, however, any newcomers who were not there from the beginning may not worship as a group but only as individuals in order to avoid seeming at odds with the original group and guard against suspicion of quarrelsomeness and contradiction.

It is the prerogative of the sovereign, however, to appoint two prayer leaders for a certain mosque, assigning a number of prayers to each, such as ordering one to lead the daytime and the other the night prayers, in which case they should stick to their assignments. He may, on the other hand, assign them different days of the week, each then having more claim to lead all of the prayers on his specific days; or he may leave it open so that both nominees have equal claim to lead, and the one who is earlier to start the service becomes the sole leader at that particular prayer. In that case, the other may not simultaneously lead another group in worship, for it is not permissible to have two separate congregations at one prayer in state mosques.

There are two views regarding how much earlier one leader has to be in order to have priority over his counterpart in conducting the service: one saying that the leader who arrives first at the mosque has precedence, the other that the one who begins the service does. If both men arrive simultaneously and there is no way to give either precedence over the other, they

1. A judge who is appointed to settle the disputes of a particular clan (in contrast, a normal judge hears cases from a variety of claimants regardless of their genealogy).

2. Dawud ibn Khalaf (d. 884), founder of the Zahiri or literalist school of law.

may settle the matter amicably between them. Failing this, some authorities would settle the dispute by drawing lots, others by asking the worshippers to choose one of the two.

The mandate of this prayer leader covers the appointment of muezzins unless authorised to do without one, because calling the prayer hours is one of the traditions pertaining to the prayer he is charged to lead. He has the right to direct those muezzins as to what he deems the proper timing and manner of the call to prayer. A Shāfiʿite[3] *Imām* may, for instance, prefer holding the prayers soon after they are announced, repeating phrases of the set call at first announcement, and pronouncing them without repetition in the second announcement proclaiming the actual commencement of the service. A Ḥanafite,[4] on the other hand, may think differently, preferring a delayed performance of the prayer, except the fourth one at sundown, no repetition in the first announcement, and repetition in the second. In either case, he tells the muezzins what to do, even if they disagree with him. The same thing applies in the actual performance of the divine service: the *Imām* or leader following his own discretion. Should he, therefore, as a Shāfiʿī, find it proper to utter the invocation of the name of the Lord, the Benign, the Merciful, audibly and add the special invocation of God's mercy on the Prophet in the morning prayer, neither may the sovereign rebuke nor the congregation object to him. A Ḥanafite leader would similarly be unopposed for omitting the latter morning ritual and silent invocation of the Lord's name. The difference between the service and the call for it lies in the fact that the former is performed on one's own behalf, and that is why the leader's discretion in it is not questioned, while the call is performed by the muezzin on behalf of other people, so that his discretion in uttering it stands subject to questioning, and if he still feels he should perform it his own way, he may utter a second call on his own behalf in the manner he likes, but only after the public call is finished, and only inaudibly.

SECTION

The qualities pertinent to this office are five in number: manhood, probity, knowledge of the Qurʾān, authority in religious matters, and freedom from speech defects. A minor, a slave, or an otherwise inequitable person may lead Muslims in prayer, but may not be appointed as the *Imām* of a mosque, because he would be disqualified from holding the office, although not from actually leading at prayer, by his minority, bondage, or inequity. The Messenger, God bless him and grant him salvation, did, for instance, order ʿAmr ibn Maslama at a tender age to lead his people in prayer because he was the most knowledgeable of the Qurʾān among them, and God's Messenger himself prayed with a slave of his leading, and commented: "Pray after any leader, pious or depraved."

This *Imām* may not be a woman, a hermaphrodite, a mute, or a person with a lisp. The prayer of both men and hermaphrodites in a congregation is invalidated if the leader is a woman or a hermaphrodite, and that of the entire congregation is invalidated if the *Imām* is a mute or has a lisp that causes him to substitute certain sounds for others, except for worshippers

3. A follower of the Shafiʿi legal school, named after Muhammad ibn Idris al-Shafiʿi (767–820; see above).

4. A follower of the Hanafi school of law, founded by Abu Hanifa al-Nuʿman ibn Thabit (699–767; see above).

suffering from the same speech defect. The minimum knowledge of the Qur'ān and religious learning this prayer leader must possess is thorough memorisation of the whole Book and mastery of the rules pertaining to prayer, as that is the portion relevant to his office, although it would be preferable to know the Qur'ān by heart and be familiar with the entire field of jurisprudence. If a choice has to be made between a religious authority who has not memorised the Qur'ān and one who can recite the Qur'ān but is otherwise no authority, the former is preferable so long as he knows the first *sūrahs* of the scripture, because the portion of the Qur'ān that needs to be recited is limited, while unexpected incidents in prayer are not. This *Imām* and his muezzin are entitled to remuneration by the treasury for their duties out of the allocations for public welfare, although Abū Ḥanīfa dissents on this point.

The sovereign, however, does not interfere with the choice of *Imāms*, or prayer leaders, for privately dedicated mosques built by citizens on the streets where they live or by tribesmen for their tribes. The office in this case belongs to the person approved by the congregation, who may not then dispense with his services unless some change in him causes him to be no longer qualified, nor may they replace him with a deputy after nomination. The congregation of a particular mosque have the most title to the choice of their prayer leader, the election to be determined according to the majority of votes in the case of disagreement. A tied vote is settled by the sovereign, who in the interest of peace may select the candidate of most piety, seniority in years, knowledge of the Qur'ān, and religious learning. As to whether he should limit his choice to the candidates in question or select from the congregation at large, one view suggests he should not go beyond the candidates under consideration, the others having already been excluded, while another viewpoint argues that he should choose the most suitable member of the mosque's congregation to be the prayer leader, because the sovereign's choice should be subject to no limits. Meanwhile, a man who has a mosque built is not privileged to be its *Imām*, but has an equal claim to serving as prayer leader or muezzin there to the rest of the neighbourhood, although Abū Ḥanīfa accords him greater title in that respect. On the other hand, the host in a household has more right to lead the prayer in his own house than any of his visitors, even if he is not their equal in merit. If the sovereign is one of the visitors, however, he is more entitled in one opinion to lead at prayer since he has authority over the landlord in all matters, while the latter is held in the second view to have more right to lead, on the ground that he is sole master in his own property.

SECTION

Jurists are disagreed regarding the necessity of appointing leaders for the Friday prayers. Abū Ḥanīfa and the Iraqis consider such appointment as obligatory, arguing that the Friday prayer is invalid unless attended by the sovereign personally or his representative. Al-Shāfiʿī, may God be pleased with him, and the Ḥijāz authorities, however, maintain that permanent appointment is optional, that the presence of the sovereign is unnecessary, and that the prayer would be valid so long as the congregation perform it with due observance of its conditions. A slave may lead the Friday prayer, even though he is not eligible for investment, while there is disagreement regarding the validity of a minor leading. This service may only be performed in a settled area, such as a town or village, with houses grouped together, which people do not leave in winter or summer unless temporarily for a need. Abū Ḥanīfa maintains that the Friday prayer belongs only in the cities, but not in villages, a city being marked by a ruler who enforces the legal punishments and a judge who upholds the law. There has been disagreement whether those outside a town have to perform the Friday prayer, Abū Ḥanīfa exempting them from it, and al-Shāfiʿī requiring them to perform it if they hear the call to it coming from the town.

Authorities are also of different opinions regarding the minimum number of worshippers required for holding the Friday service. Al-Shāfiʿī, God approve of him, has set it at forty men of the permanent congregation, excluding women, slaves, and travellers. His followers disagreed whether to count the *Imām* as one of the forty or as an addition to the number, some stipulating forty worshippers other than the leader for the prayer to be valid, but most allowing for forty including him. Al-Zuhrī and Muḥammad ibn al-Ḥasan[5] make the number necessary a minimum of twelve, excluding the *Imām*, Abū Ḥanīfa and al-Muzanī[6] say the service takes place with four worshippers including the *Imām*, al-Layth and Abū Yūsuf[7] say it is valid with three including him, Abū Thawr[8] says two worshippers are enough as for other Community prayers, and Mālik[9] argues that number is immaterial so long as it is normally sufficient for a town to be built.

The Friday service may take place neither on a journey nor outside of a city, unless its buildings extend that far. It may be performed in the old districts of a city, like Baghdad, that has grown large enough to encompass surrounding towns, although it has to be held only in one place in a city like Mecca which has retained its character and where the mosque can accommodate all of the population. In a city like Baṣra, however, which is also coherent but has too many people to fit into a single mosque, Shāfiʿis have entertained two views regarding the holding of Friday services in two places rather than one, some allowing it on account of the large population, others rejecting this solution on the ground that the congregation could flow out into the streets surrounding the mosque and in this way the service does not have to be scattered over several locations.

If the Friday service is held in two locations in a city where service in scattered places is not permitted, one view maintains that only the earlier service counts, while the other congregation of the later service have to make it up as a regular noon prayer. Others believe that the service held at the greater mosque attended by the governor is the proper Friday service whether it takes place before or after the other, and that whoever performs it at the smaller mosque must make up.

An *Imām* appointed to lead the Friday service may not also lead at the five daily prayers. There is disagreement, however, concerning the right of the appointed leader of the five services to lead the Friday prayer as well; those who regard the latter prayer as an independent service do not allow

5. A Hanafi jurist (ca. 750–805). Ibn Shihab al-Zuhri (d. 742), an authority on hadith.
6. An Egyptian Shafiʿi collector of hadith (d. 878).
7. A Hanafi jurist (ca. 729–798). Al-Layth ibn Saʿd (713–791), Egyptian hadith scholar.
8. A prominent jurist (764–854).
9. Malik ibn Anas (ca. 715–795), the renowned Medinan legal scholar who gave his name to the Maliki legal school and was one of al-Shafiʿi's teachers.

him to do so, while those who consider it a variation on the noon service do. If the Friday service leader believes that a congregation of forty is the minimum required for holding it, even though the fewer-than-forty worshippers assembled want to hold it, he may not lead them himself, but should let one of them lead the worship. If the leader believes, on the other hand, that the service may be held with fewer than forty assembled for it, while the few gathered worshippers do not share his view, neither the *Imām* nor the congregation is obliged to hold it, as the latter do not want to, and consequently the *Imām* would have no one to lead. Should the sovereign order the *Imām* to lead the Friday prayer only if forty worshippers are assembled, he may not hold it for fewer than forty, even if he is convinced it should be held, because his mandate is conditional upon a congregation of forty and no less, but he may get someone else to hold the service. Ordered by the person in authority to lead a congregation of fewer than forty while he disapproves, the *Imām*'s mandate is considered by some to be invalid because he cannot fulfil it, and considered valid by others who recommend that he delegate somebody else to lead the worship.

NIZAM AL-MULK
1018–1092

Al-Hasan ibn ʿAli ibn Ishaq al-Tusi, known by his honorific Nizam al-Mulk, was born in a village outside of Tus (northeastern Iran). Trained in Islamic law and hadith in his youth, he fled with his father to Ghazna in eastern Afghanistan when the Seljuks—descended from Turkish tribes from Central Asia—advanced into Khurasan in 1040. Like his father, Nizam al-Mulk took a position with the Ghaznawid government, but after several years he returned to Khurasan to serve the Seljuks.

Nizam al-Mulk worked first in Balkh, and then made his way to Marw, serving under the minister of the Seljuk prince Alp Arslan and eventually becoming minister himself. Despite some scheming by a competitor, Nizam al-Mulk was retained as minister when Alp Arslan in 1063 became sultan of the Seljuk empire, which at its height included modern-day Turkey, Syria, and Iran. Nizam al-Mulk worked closely with the sultan, joining him on ongoing military campaigns and leading some himself. Alp Arslan, assassinated in 1072, was succeeded by his eighteen-year-old son Malikshah. It was during Malikshah's reign that Nizam al-Mulk essentially wielded full authority over the Seljuk empire.

Nizam al-Mulk was a renowned patron. Most famously, he supported religious scholars by founding a series of Islamic colleges (in Arabic, *madrasa*) throughout the eastern Islamic lands. These were known as Nizamiyya, and the most famous was built in Baghdad in 1067. It was there that Nizam al-Mulk sent al-Ghazali (1058–1111; see above) to teach in 1091, and there that al-Ghazali would have his transformative spiritual crisis four years later.

These colleges promoted Nizam al-Mulk's preferred schools of Islamic thought, emphasizing Ashʿari theology and Shafiʿi law in particular, though also teaching Hanafi law. The institutions were intended to strengthen this stream of Sunnism against the Muʿtazili and Shiʿi intellectual and political influences of the time. Nizam al-Mulk was particularly opposed to the Ismaʿili branch of Shiʿism favored by the rival Fatimid dynasty in Egypt, whom he considered to be enemies of Islam and the state. Nizam al-Mulk is also remembered for the considerable improvements that he made to the Meccan pilgrimage, which substantially reduced costs for pilgrims and greatly increased their security from bandits.

Weathering the occasional intrigue against him, especially as Malikshah attempted to exercise his own power, Nizam al-Mulk continued to flourish until the later years of his life. In 1091 the Qarmatis, another group of Isma'ilis, sacked Basra while Hasan-i Sabbah, head of the Assassins, took control of the Alamut fortress high in the Iranian mountains and then used it as a base to attack the Seljuks. In 1092 Nizam al-Mulk was assassinated while traveling between Isfahan and Baghdad. It is unclear whether Hasan-i Sabbah alone sent the assassin, disguised as a Sufi, or he and Nizam al-Mulk's enemies in the court—perhaps even including Malikshah—conspired in the murder.

In 1086–87 Malikshah ordered Nizam al-Mulk and others to write a treatise for him setting forth the nature and meaning of kingship and proper rule, the current problems of the government, and useful points from the histories of earlier kings. It was Nizam al-Mulk's book that won the sultan's approval. Known as the *Siyasat-nama* (*The Book of Government*) in Persian and as *Siyar al-muluk* (*Manners of the Kings*) in Arabic, it was written in or before 1091, with another eleven chapters added in 1091 or 1092. Those additions, mainly focused on the Isma'ili threat, brought the total number of chapters to fifty and completed the work.

Most chapters begin with practical advice to the king on some particular aspect of governance. The focus was not theory but practice. Because of its initial chapter, the *Siyasat-nama* is considered a key source on the medieval Persian theory of government, but Nizam al-Mulk was more interested in the realities of governing. And while much of his thought on governance reflects that of the Sassanids, his advice is quite original and not derivative of earlier books in the same genre.

Nizam al-Mulk does not spend much time justifying political power or the sultan's position. Because he held the Sassanian notion that the sultan is chosen by God, Nizam al-Mulk's goal is to help the sultan carry out his duty properly. This includes organizing the society so that its members can pursue their lives and livelihoods in safety, an idea based on the Sassanian understanding that every person in the society had a particular function, which the ruler ought to regulate. Looking after the people also called for the ruler to be vigilant in supervising his tax collectors, as they were the main point of interaction between the people and the state, and were the most likely to create injustice by demanding bribes or imposing repressive taxes. The king ought to reduce injustice and ill will by holding court so that people could complain against government officials—another Sassanian practice. Likewise, the ruler should appoint a person to regulate the affairs of the bazaar, such as ensuring the validity of weights and measures in order to protect the people against fraud. Finally, the ruler should maintain a strong military as the ultimate support of his rule, and he ought to institute a far-reaching intelligence service; spies in all manner of disguises should report to him from throughout the empire, even about the highest government officials.

The ruler himself should possess such qualities as a pleasing appearance, modesty, intelligence, justice, mercy, a good nature, and expertise in horsemanship and the use of weapons. He should also practice the obligatory and customary elements of religion and meet with and learn from religious scholars several times each week. He should never issue frivolous orders, but should act only in a way that commands respect and awe.

The selections here cover the range of Nizam al-Mulk's vision of governance, including the intelligence apparatus, solutions for the ruler's quotidian concerns, and ways in which the sultan can cultivate good qualities in himself and project them to his subjects. They make clear that Nizam al-Mulk was concerned about all aspects of the ruler's life. In addition to more mundane matters, such as the need for a secure and dependable communication system and for a well-run royal household, he addresses the need for royal friends. Their role is not an easy one, and its requirements are many. As a group, they simulate the sovereign. If they are "good-natured, affable, liberal, patient, merciful and gracious" the king will be seen as the same. "If they are sour-faced, haughty, foolish, miserly and wanton," the royal reputation will suffer.

PRONOUNCING GLOSSARY

divan: *dee-vahn´*
farsang: *far´-sang*
Ghaznain: *gaz-nayn´*
Jikili: *ji´-ki-lee*
Samanids: *sah-mah´-nids*
Samarqand: *sa-mar-qand´*
sultan: *sul-tahn´*
Tughril: *toog´-ril*
Turkistan: *tur-ke-stahn´*
Uzgand: *ooz-gand´*
wazir: *wa-zeer´*

FROM THE BOOK OF GOVERNMENT, OR MANNERS OF THE KINGS

Chapter 14

Concerning Constant Employment of Messengers and Carriers

Messengers must be posted along the principal highways, and they must be paid monthly salaries and allowances. When this is done, everything that happens throughout the twenty-four hours within a radius of fifty farsangs[1] will come [to their knowledge]. In accordance with established custom they must have sergeants to see that they do not fail in their duties.

Chapter 15

On Being Careful about Giving Verbal Orders in Drunkenness and Sobriety

Verbal orders [from the king] reach the divan[2] and the treasury concerning matters of state, fiefs or gifts. It may be that some of these commands are [given] in a state of merriment. Now this is a delicate matter and it needs the utmost caution. Or possibly the bearers of the message may not agree, or have not heard correctly. Such a mission must be entrusted to one person only, and he must deliver the message personally, not through a deputy. And it must be the rule in those cases [where there is doubt about an order] that, in spite of the fact that an order has been delivered, it must not be executed or acted upon until its substance has been referred by the divan back to The Sublime Intellect[3] [for confirmation].

TRANSLATED BY Hubert Darke. All bracketed additions are the translator's.

1. About 183 miles (one farsang is roughly 3 2/3 miles).
2. A state secretary who records all government transactions.
3. The ruler himself. This is one of the titles used by Nizam al-Mulk to address Malik-shah.

Chapter 16

Concerning the Steward of the Household and the Importance of His Post

The office of steward of the household has fallen into disuse nowadays. This work always used to be entrusted to someone well-known and respected, for a person whose duties concern the royal palace, the kitchen, cellars and stables, the king's children and his retainers, must have daily access to The Lofty Throne for discourse with the sovereign. He must [be free to] present himself at any hour of the day to report on all matters, to ask advice and to render account of all his arrangements and transactions. So he needs to command complete respect in order to be able to do his work and discharge his duties successfully.

Chapter 17

Concerning Boon-Companions and Intimates of the King and the Conduct of Their Affairs

A king cannot do without suitable boon-companions with whom he can enjoy complete freedom and intimacy. The constant society of nobles [such as] margraves[4] and generals tends to diminish the king's majesty and dignity because they become too arrogant. As a general rule people who are employed in any official capacity should not be admitted as boon-companions nor should those who are accepted for companionship be appointed to any public office, because by virtue of the liberty they enjoy in the king's company they will indulge in high-handed practices and oppress the people. Officers should always be in a state of fear of the king, while boon-companions need to be familiar. If an officer is familiar he tends to oppress the peasantry; but if a boon-companion is not familiar the king will not find any pleasure or relaxation in his company. Boon-companions should have a fixed time for their appearance; after the king has given audience and the nobles have retired, then comes the time for their turn.

There are several advantages in having boon-companions: firstly they are company for the king; secondly since they are with him day and night, they are in the position of bodyguards, and if any danger (we take refuge with Allah!) should appear, they will not hesitate to shield the king from it with their own bodies; and thirdly the king can say thousands of different things, frivolous and serious, to his boon-companions which would not be suitable for the ears of his wazir[5] or other nobles, for they are his officials and functionaries; and fourthly all sorts of sundry tidings can be heard from boon-companions, for through their freedom they can report on matters, good and bad, whether drunk or sober; and in this there is advantage and benefit.

A boon-companion should be well-bred, accomplished and of cheerful face. He should have pure faith, be able to keep secrets and wear good clothes. He must possess an ample fund of stories and strange tales both amusing and

4. Noblemen who had military responsibilities.

5. Vizier (Arabic).

serious, and be able to tell them well. He must always be a good talker and a pleasant partner; he should know how to play backgammon and chess, and if he can play a musical instrument and use a weapon, so much the better. He must always agree with the king, and whatever the king says or does, he must exclaim, 'Bravo!' and 'Well done!' He should not be didactic with 'Do this' and 'Don't do that' for it will displease the king and lead to dislike. Where pleasure and entertainment are concerned, as in feasting, drinking, hunting, polo and wrestling—in all matters like these it is right that the king should consult with his boon-companions, for they are there for this purpose. On the other hand in everything to do with the country and its cultivation, the military and the peasantry, warfare, raids, punishments, gifts, stores and travels, it is better that he should take counsel with the ministers and nobles of the state and with experienced elders, for they are more skilled in these subjects. In this way matters will take their proper course.

Some kings have in the past made their physicians or their astrologers boon-companions, so that their opinions could always be sought about what was advisable and what was inadvisable. The physician looked after the king's health, and the astrologer gave warning of good and bad auguries; he kept watch on the time and the hour, and chose the right moment for every enterprise. Other kings have refused to have them and said, 'The physician forbids us to eat the things we like and gives us medicine when we are not ill and bleeds us when we have no pain; likewise the astrologer prevents us from doing what we want to do and hinders us from important business; and when you consider, both of them do nothing but keep us back from the pleasures, appetites and desires of this world, and make our life miserable; so it is better that we should call for them only when we need them.'

A boon-companion is more highly esteemed if he is a man of experience and has travelled widely and served great people. When people want to know the character and disposition of the sovereign they judge by his boon-companions; if they are good-natured, affable, liberal, patient, merciful and gracious, they will know that the king has a kindly nature, a pleasant disposition, good morals and acceptable manners; but if his boon-companions are sour-faced, haughty, foolish, miserly and wanton, people will judge that the king is of unpleasant disposition, evil nature, bad temper and bad morals.

And further every one of the boon-companions should have a rank and degree; some have sitting status, others standing status.[6] From ancient times this has been the custom at the courts of kings and caliphs; and it is a custom that is still observed. The present caliph has as many boon-companions as his fathers had before him; and the sultans of Ghaznain[7] have always had twenty companions, ten standing and ten sitting; they took the custom and procedure from the Samanids.[8] The king's boon-companions must be given salaries, and treated with the highest respect among the retinue; they must know how to control themselves, be polite and shew affection for the king.

6. Court officials allowed to sit while the king sat had a higher rank than those who had to remain standing; this behavior reflects pre-Islamic Persian court custom.

7. A Turkish empire that at its height stretched over Iran, Afghanistan, and Pakistan (977–1186).

8. A Persian dynasty that ruled over parts of Iran and Central Asia (819–1005).

Chapter 35

Concerning the Arrangements for Setting a Good Table

Kings have always paid attention to having well supplied tables [lit: trays] in the mornings so that those who come to the royal presence may find something to eat there. If the nobles have no desire for it at the time, there is no objection to their eating their own provisions in due course, but it is essential to have the table well spread in the mornings.

Sultan Tughril[9] paid the utmost attention to having good tables and various kinds of eatables. If he mounted his horse in the early morning to go for a ride or to hunt, food was prepared, and when it was served out in the country, there was so much that all the nobles and amirs were astonished. [Almost] the whole system of government of the khans of Turkistan consists in having abundant food in the hands of servants and in their kitchens. When we went to Samarqand and Uzgand[1] certain meddlesome persons were heard to declare that the Jikilis and people of Transoxiana[2] were constantly repeating that never from the arrival of the sultan until his departure did they eat a single morsel at his table.

A man's magnanimity and generosity must be [judged] according to [the excellence of] his household management. The sultan is the head of the family of the world; all kings are in his power. Therefore it is necessary that his housekeeping, his magnanimity and generosity, his table and his largesse should accord with his state and be greater and better than that of other kings.

It says in a tradition that providing abundant bread and food for the creatures of God (to Him be power and glory) increases the duration of a king's life, his reign and good fortune.

9. The founder of the Seljuk dynasty (ca. 990–1063).

1. Malikshah made two expeditions to these parts in the course of his reign, in about 1078 and in 1088 [translator's note, edited]. The city and town are both in present-day Uzbekistan, and under Turkish rule they were administrative centers.

2. The region in which Samarqand is located. "Jikilis": the eastern Turks who formed the core of the army of the Qarakhanids, who ruled Transoxiana from 999 to 1211 (for part of that time as vassals of the Seljuks).

NASIR AL-DIN AL-TUSI
1201–1274

Abu Jaʿfar Muhammad Nasir al-Din al-Tusi, one of the most prolific authors in Muslim history and a major thirteenth-century intellectual, wrote roughly 165 works in Arabic and Persian. His range was broad as he treated both religious and scientific subjects and produced significant treatises in philosophy, mathematics, law, medicine, and astronomy.

Even during his lifetime, al-Tusi's scholarly impact was extraordinary. His defense of and commentaries on the philosophical works of Ibn Sina (ca. 980–1037; see above) revived the study of philosophy in the thirteenth century. His *Abstract of Theology* left an indelible stamp on Shiʿi thought and inspired subsequent Shiʿi theologians to adopt his metaphysical terminology and to write commentaries on the work. He advanced the scientific studies of his day by publishing definitive Arabic editions of notable works by such authors as Ptolemy and Euclid. His most significant scientific contributions were in astronomy, as he devised sophisticated tables of celestial motion and created an astronomical model to explain the Ptolemaic system of planetary movement.

Al-Tusi witnessed the watershed moment of medieval Islamic history—the Mongol destruction of Baghdad in 1258—and throughout his life proved exceptionally adept at adjusting to tumultuous events. His ability to thrive during such upheavals underscores his considerable talents outside scholarship. Born in Tus (northeastern Iran), he began his studies under the tutelage of his open-minded father, a noted Shiʿi jurist, who not only instructed him in traditional subjects such as the Qurʾan, hadith, and law but also encouraged him to explore fields beyond religious learning. From Tus, he went to Nishapur, where he spent eight years, (1213–21) under the guidance of scholars who had studied with Fakhr al-Din al-Razi (1149/50–1210; see above). He next traveled to Iraq for further training in mathematics, astronomy, and jurisprudence, completing his education there in 1233.

Returning to Iran, al-Tusi entered the court of Muhtasham Nasir al-Din ʿAbd al-Rahim ibn Abi Mansur (d. 1257), the Ismaʿili governor of Quhistan, a province in northeast Iran. He remained with the Ismaʿilis for about twenty years and may have embraced their beliefs (either sincerely or for reasons of political expediency). In 1255 the Ismaʿili leadership sent him to negotiate with the advancing Mongol army and its leader, Hulegu (ca. 1217–1265). Negotiations failed, and the Ismaʿili capital of Alamut fell in 1256. Impressed by al-Tusi's reputation and abilities, however, Hulegu invited him to join his retinue.

Hulegu entrusted al-Tusi with the administration of religious endowments and appointed him court astrologer. After the capture of Baghdad, al-Tusi began construction, under Mongol patronage, of an observatory at Maragha, in modern-day Azerbayjan. Upon its completion in 1262, he became its first director. He spent most of his remaining years at Maragha, whose observatory and important library made it a scholarly center, and wrote some of his most important astronomical treatises there. In 1274, al-Tusi died in Baghdad.

Al-Tusi initially undertook *The Nasirean Ethics* at the behest of his first major patron, the Ismaʿili governor Muhtasham Nasir al-Din. According to al-Tusi, the governor asked him to translate *The Refinement of Character* by Miskawayh (ca. 932–1030; see above) into Persian for the benefit of his people. Al-Tusi suggested that a mere translation would not be enough and proposed an expanded treatise. The governor approved this suggestion, and al-Tusi completed the first version in 1235. After joining Hulegu's retinue, he revised *The Nasirean Ethics*, changing its introduction and conclusion. In this new version he apologized for having earlier glorified Ismaʿilism, explaining that he had felt compelled to do so.

The *Nasirean Ethics* consists of three parts: the first deals with personal ethics, the second with the correct way to organize and manage a household, and the third with politics and government. This framework—ethics, household management, and politics and government—served as a model for many later works on ethics that strove for a similar level of comprehensiveness.

The passage below, taken from the second part of *The Nasirean Ethics*, urges husbands to rule their wives by inspiring awe, showing favor, and occupying their minds. Should these strategies prove unsuccessful, al-Tusi is ready with suggestions for managing less-than-satisfactory marital situations.

PRONOUNCING GLOSSARY

sūra: *soo´-ruh*

FROM THE NASIREAN ETHICS

Concerning the Chastisement and Regulation of Wives

The motive for taking a wife should be twofold, the preservation of property and the quest of progeny; it should not be at the instigation of appetite or for any other purpose.

A good wife is the man's partner in property, his colleague in housekeeping and the regulation of the household, and his deputy during his absence. The best of wives is the wife adorned with intelligence, piety, continence,[1] shrewdness, modesty, tenderness, a loving disposition, control of her tongue, obedience to her husband, self-devotion in his service and a preference for his pleasure, gravity, and the respect of her own family. She must not be barren, and she should be both alert and capable in the arrangement of the household and in observing a proper allotment of expenditure. In her courteous and affable behaviour and in her pleasantness of disposition, she must cultivate the companionship of her husband, consoling him in his cares and driving away his sorrows.

A free woman is preferable to a slave, as possessing greater intimacy with both strangers and kinfolk, being better able to enlist the support of relatives and to conciliate enemies, rendering greater co-operation and assistance in the matters of daily life, and being more apprehensive of degradation in respect of society, progeny and offspring. A virgin is preferable to one who is not, for she will be more likely to accept discipline, and to assimilate herself to the husband in disposition and custom, and to follow and obey him. If, over and above these attributes, she wears the adornments of beauty, race[2] and wealth, she unites in herself all the varieties of merits and nothing can conceivably be added thereto.

If, however, some of these qualities be lacking, (at least) intelligence, continence and modesty should be present; for to prefer beauty, race and wealth to these three qualities is to invite trouble and ruin and disorder in matters spiritual and temporal. Let not a woman's beauty, above all, be an incentive to ask for her in marriage: beauty is seldom allied with continence, for a beautiful woman will have many admirers and suitors; at the same time, the weakness of women's intelligences offers no obstacle or hindrance to their compliance, so that they embark upon disgraceful proceedings; so, the outcome of addressing oneself to them in marriage is either lack of self-respect and endurance of their disgraceful conduct (which involves wretchedness in both worlds) or the dissipation of property and wealth and the suffering of all manner of griefs and cares. Thus, as regards beauty, one should confine oneself to symmetry of frame, and even in this respect one should observe the exact requirement of moderation.

Likewise, a woman's property should not become a reason for desiring her, for when women own property it invites their domination and authority, a tendency to use others and to assume superiority. Even if the husband controls the wife's property, the wife accounts him as in the position of a servant and an assistant, according him no regard or esteem; thus, absolute

Translated by G. M. Wickens.

1. Chastity.

2. *Nasab*, more accurately translated "lineage."

upset follows as a necessary consequence, until, with the corruption of affairs, household and livelihood lapse utterly.

Once the bond of union is effected between husband and wife, the husband's procedure in ruling his wife should be along three lines: to inspire awe, to show favour, and to occupy her mind.

Inspiring awe means that he maintains himself as a formidable figure in the eyes of the wife, so that she would not account it allowable to be remiss in heeding his commands and prohibitions. This is the foremost condition for ruling womenfolk, for if any upset befall this one condition, the way is open for the wife to follow her fancy and her will. Nor will she confine herself to this, but rather bring the husband into subjection, making him the means of attaining her desires and realizing her purposes by reducing him to subjugation and servitude. Thus the one who should command is commanded, the one who should obey is obeyed, and the regulator is regulated; and the end of such a state is the realization of shame and disgrace, of reproach and destruction to both, for so many ignominies and villainies result that it becomes inconceivable to make reparations and amends therefor.

As for showing favour, this means that one confers on the wife those things that call for love and sympathy, so that when she feels apprehensive as to the removal of that state, she solicitously undertakes the affairs of the household together with submission to her husband; whereby the desired organization results. The various categories of favours in this connection are six in number.

First, to keep her fair of aspect. Secondly, one should go to extreme lengths to keep her veiled and secluded from those having no right of entry to the female quarters, so contriving that no outsider ever learns of her marks or qualities or reputation. Thirdly, one may consult her in the early stages of household affairs, provided that this does not give her the desire to be obeyed. Fourthly, she may be given a free hand in control of provisions in the best interest of the household, and in the employment of servants on important tasks. Fifthly, one should establish close ties with her relatives and members of her family, considering it a necessary obligation to observe the exact requirements of co-operation and mutual support. Sixthly, when the husband senses the effect of her integrity and propriety, he should not prefer another wife to her, albeit the former be her superior in beauty, property, race and family; for women are impelled, by the jealousy rooted in their natures, operating together with their deficiency in intelligence, to give way to abominations and ignominies, and to such other acts as necessarily bring about the corruption of the household, evil association, a disagreeable existence, and a want of order. Indeed, no indulgence is allowed in this regard to any save kings, whose purpose in taking a wife is the quest of progeny and numerous descendants, and in whose service wives are virtually slaves. Even in their case, caution is to be preferred; for the man in the household is like the heart in the body, and just as one heart cannot be the source of life in two bodies, so one man cannot easily organize two households.

As for occupying the mind, this means that one should keep the wife's mind constantly busy with the assumption of responsibility for the important affairs of the household, for consideration of its best interests, and for the performance of those things that inevitably affect the organization of daily life; for the human soul will not suffer idleness, and lack of concern with necessities inevitably leads to a regard for unnecessary matters. Thus, if a wife have no part in the arrangement of the household or the rearing of children or concern with the welfare of the servants, she will confine her attention to matters inevitably bringing disorder into the household: she will busy herself with excursions, with decking herself out for excursions, with going to see the sights, and with looking at strange men, so that not only are the affairs of the household disordered, but her husband even comes to enjoy no esteem or awe in her eyes. Indeed, when she sees other men, she despises him and holds him of little account, and she is emboldened to embark on abominable courses, and even to provoke admirers to quest after her; so that in the long run, in addition to disorganization of daily life and loss of manhood and the acquisition of disgrace, destruction and misery supervene in both this world and the next.

However, in the matter of ruling a wife, a husband must be on his guard against three things. First comes excessive love of the wife, for if this be present, it necessarily follows that the wife will become dominant and that her fancy will be preferred to his own best interests. If he is, however, afflicted with the trial of love for her, he should keep it concealed from her and so contrive that she never becomes aware thereof. Then, if he cannot contain himself, he must employ the remedies prescribed in the case of Love.[3] In no case should he remain in that state, for such a calamity inevitably produces the aforementioned corruptions. Secondly, the husband should not consult the wife on affairs of universal importance, and certainly not inform her of his own secrets. He should, moreover, keep hidden from her the amount of his property and his capital, for women's inaccurate opinions and their want of discrimination in such matters can only invite numerous calamities. Thirdly, he should restrain the wife from foolish pastimes, from looking at strangers, and from listening to tales about men from women characterized by acts of this kind. Certainly he must never give her any easy way thereto, for such notions inevitably bring grave corruptions. The most destructive (activity of all in this respect) is the frequentation of old women who have been admitted to male gatherings and retail stories from these (experiences).

There is a Tradition to the effect that women should be prevented from learning the Joseph Sūra,[4] inasmuch as listening to such narratives may cause them to deviate from the law of continence. From strong drink they should be restrained totally, for this, in however small an amount, may be the cause of impudent behaviour and of excitation of appetite; and in women, no characteristics are worse than these two.

The way by which women may become worthy of their husbands' satisfaction, and gain esteem in their eyes, comprises five heads: the practice of continence; a display of efficiency; standing in awe of them; compatibility in marriage and avoidance of disputes; and, finally, a minimum of scolding, with a courteous manner in their society. The philosophers have said that a worthy wife will take on the role of mother, friend and mistress, while a bad wife will adopt those of despot, enemy and thief.

3. A reference to the first part of this work, in which al-Tusi warns that excessive love for another is destructive. The cure for such love is to avoid thinking of one's beloved by developing other virtues and associating with virtuous friends. If this fails, al-Tusi prescribes strenuous physical exertion and, as a final resort, fasting to weaken the body.

4. The twelfth chapter of the Qur'an. "Tradition": a hadith.

As for the worthy wife's attempt to assimilate to a mother, this means that she desires the husband's proximity and presence, while hating his absence; and that she will bear the burden of her own suffering in the course of attaining his desire and satisfaction, for this is the very course followed by a mother with a child. Assuming the part of a friend means that the wife should be content with whatever the husband gives her, while excusing him for whatever he withholds from her or does not give to her; at the same time, she should not grudge him (the use of) her own property, and she should conform to him in character. Playing the part of a mistress involves humbling herself in the manner of a maidservant, giving a pledge of service, and enduring the husband's sharp temper; she must also endeavour to publicize his praiseworthy side and to conceal his faults; let her, further, give thanks for his graciousness, while forbearing to scold him for whatever (in him) is uncongenial to her nature.

When the unworthy wife becomes like a despot, this means that she loves sloth and idleness, utters foul abuse, frequently makes false accusations, and gives way to violent rages; at the same time, she is heedless of those things that necessarily bring about her husband's satisfaction or enragement, and she inflicts much distress on the servants, both male and female. When she behaves like an enemy, she shows contempt for her husband and treats him lightly; she displays a harsh temper, and disavows his benevolence; she becomes rancorous towards him, complains of him and repeats his faults. When she assumes the part of a thief, it means that she betrays him with respect to his property, asking from him without need and making little of his kindness; she likewise persists in courses which he detests, falsely affects friendship, and places her own advantage above his.

The prudent course for one afflicted with an unworthy wife is to seek release from her, for the proximity of a bad wife is worse than that of wild beasts and serpents. If, however, release be virtually impossible of attainment, four sorts of stratagem may be applied to the situation.

First, the expenditure of wealth, for the preservation of one's soul and manhood and good repute is better than the preservation of wealth; indeed, if it is necessary to spend a great deal of wealth to redeem oneself from her, that wealth should be accounted of little consequence. Secondly, one may resort to disputes, displays of bad temper, and a separation of sleeping-quarters, albeit in such a manner as not to lead to any mischief. Thirdly, one may adopt subtle wiles, such as encouraging old women to inspire her with an aversion to oneself and a desire for another husband, at the same time oneself outwardly professing desire for her and unwillingness to leave her—so that it may come about that she herself conceives an eagerness to leave the husband; in short, one may use, as one sees fit, all manner of connivance or obstruction, encouragement or deterrence, in order to effect a separation. Fourthly, and after finding oneself unable to implement the other measures, one may leave her, choosing to go on a far journey, so long as one shall have made arrangements to prevent her from embarking on any ignominies: this, to the end that she may lose hope, and herself choose separation.

The wise men of the Arabs have said that one should be on one's guard against five types of woman: the lamenting widow, the wife who trades on her wealth, the wife bemoaning her fallen estate, the one who is like a brand on the back of the neck, and the one who is like vegetation growing on a dunghill.

The lamenting widow is the woman who has children by another husband, and who is continually showing them favours with the wealth of that husband. The wife trading on her wealth is the well-endowed woman who by means of her wealth places her husband under an obligation. The wife bemoaning her fallen estate is the woman who, before the time of her present husband, enjoyed better circumstances or had a more eminent husband, and is continually complaining and moaning about (the loss of) those circumstances and that husband. The wife like a brand on the back of the neck is the incontinent woman: whenever her husband leaves a gathering, men speak of her in such a way as to affix a mark to the nape of his neck. The wife like vegetation on a dunghill is the fair woman of bad origin,[5] who is accordingly compared to herbage on a midden.

Whoever is incapable of fulfilling the conditions for the chastisement of wives should rather remain a bachelor, drawing his skirt clear of contact with their affairs; for the mischief of associating with women, quite apart from its disorder, can only result in an infinite number of calamities: one of these may be the wife's intention to bring about the man's destruction, or the intention of another with regard to the wife. God it is who prospers and assists!

5. That is, of disreputable family and lineage.

TA'RIKH: HISTORY, GEOGRAPHY, AND TRAVEL WRITING

IBN AL-KALBI
ca. 737–821

Ibn al-Kalbi made a name for himself writing about idols, an interest that did not endear him to those classical Muslim scholars intent on erasing all awareness of pre-Islamic paganism. Although he is credited with about 150 titles, few survive except as excerpts in later works. Yet his *Book of Idols* continues to be read as a source for the history of Arabia before Islam. Hisham ibn Muhammad ibn al-Sa'ib al-Kalbi was born in Kufa, Iraq. His was a notable family of scholars, teachers, and writers. In addition to composing historical and antiquarian studies, Ibn al-Kalbi was a master genealogist whose work was indispensable to his successors in this subject area.

The Book of Idols, which has been translated into several European languages, starts with a short introduction about the beginning of idol worship in the Arabian Peninsula and then describes twenty deities that were worshipped in the region. Each description details the origin of devotion to that deity, its location, the tribes that worshipped it, and some specifics about the form of veneration.

Reproduced below are Ibn al-Kalbi's introduction and his entries on three particularly important deities: al-Lat, al-ʿUzza, and Manat. These three female goddesses are mentioned in the Qur'an and are the subject of a controversy over the "satanic verses." In brief: while Muhammad was leading his followers in prayer and reciting Qur'an 53:19–20, Satan altered the Prophet's recitation by inserting two verses which suggested that supplication could be made to al-Lat, al-ʿUzza, and Manat, in addition to God (Allah). Worshippers of these goddesses, who had thus far vehemently opposed Muhammad's monotheistic message, were understandably pleased at their mention. When he realized his misrecitation, Muhammad became upset but was reassured by the revelation of Qur'an 22:52–54:

> We never sent a messenger or a prophet before you but when He recited (the message) Satan proposed (opposition) in respect of what he recited of it. But God abolishes what Satan proposes. Then God establishes His revelations. God is knower, wise;
>
> That He may make what the devil proposes a temptation for those in whose hearts is a disease, and those whose hearts are hardened—the evildoers are in open schism—
>
> And that those who have been given knowledge may know that it is the truth from your Lord, so that they may believe in it and their hearts may submit humbly to Him. God is guiding those who believe to a right path.

Thus comforted, Muhammad disavowed the mistaken verses, denying them any place in the Qur'an.

Although prominent Muslim exegetes and historians of the first two Islamic centuries (the seventh and eighth centuries C.E.) recorded the incident of the satanic verses, as did some scholars of the classical period, many others, even as early as the tenth century, rejected the authenticity of these reports. The current orthodox position, held by both Sunnis and Shi'is, finds them ahistorical and unbelievable because they call into question the nature of revelation and the integrity of the Qur'an. The accounts of this episode have also been dismissed on technical grounds, such as being transmitted by dubious narrators or not going back to an eyewitness.

PRONOUNCING GLOSSARY

'Abd-al-'Uzza ibn-Ka'b ibn-Sa'd ibn-Zayd-Manāh ibn Tamīm: *ab-dul-uz´-zuh ibn kab ibn sad ibn zayd ma-nah´ ibn ta-meem´*
'Abd-al-'Uzza ibn Wadī'ah al-Muzani: *ab-dul-uz´-zuh ibn wa-dee´-uh al-moo´-za-nee*
'Abd-Manāh: *abd ma-nah´*
Abu-al-Mundhir Hishām ibn Muḥammad al-Kalbī: *a-bool-mun´-dhir he-sham´ ibn moo-ham´-mad* (heavy *h*) *al-kal´-bee*
abu-'Ubaydah 'Abdullāh ibn-abi-'Ubaydah ibn 'Ammār ibn-Yāsir: *a-boo oo-bay´-duh ab-dul-lah´ ibn a-bee oo-bay´-duh ibn am-mar´ ibn ya´-sir*
Abu-Jundub al-Hudhali al-Qirdi: *a-boo jun´-doob al-hoo´-dha-lee al-qir´-dee*
'al-'Uzza: *al-uz´-zuh*
al-Bustān: *al-boo-stan´*
al-Fals: *al-fals´*
al-Ghabghab: *al-gab´-gab*
al-Ghumayr: *al-goo-mayr´*
al-Ḥārith ibn abi Shamir al-Ghassānī: *al-ha´-rith* (heavy *h*) *ibn a-bee sha´-mir al-gas-sa´-nee*
(al-)Muzdalifah: *(al-)mooz-da´-li-fuh*
'al-Mughīrah ibn Shu'bah: *al-moo-gee´-ruh ibn shuh´-buh*
al-Mushallal: *al-moo-shal´-lal*
al-Mutalammis: *al-moo-ta-lam´-mis*
al-Ṭā'if: *at-tah´-if*
'Alī (ibn Abī Ṭālib): *ah´-lee ibn a-bee tah´-lib*
Allāt: *al-lat´*
'Alqamah: *al´-qah-muh*
'Amr ibn-al-Ju'ayd: *ahmr ibn al-joo-ayd´*
'Arafah: *ah´-ra-fuh*
Asmā': *as-ma´*
Aws: *aws*
Aws ibn Ḥajar: *aws ibn ha´-jar* (heavy *h*)
banu 'Attāb ibn Mālik: *ba-noo at-tahb´ ibn ma´-lik*
banu-Ghanm: *ba-noo ganm´*
Buss: *bus*
Dhāt-'Irq: *dhat irq´*
Dhu-al-Faqār: *dhul´-al-fa-qahr´*
Dirham ibn-Zayd al-Awsi: *dir´-ham ibn zayd al-aw´-see*
Ghassān: *gas-san´*
hijrah: *hij´-ruh*
Hudhayl: *hoo-dhayl´*

Ḥurāḍ: *hoo-rahd´* (heavy *h*)
Ḥuwayrith: *hoo-way´-rith* (heavy *h*)
Jāhilīyah: *ja´-he-lee´´-yuh*
Kaʿbah: *ka´-buh*
Khazraj: *chaz´-raj* (guttural *ch*)
Khuzāʿah: *choo-za´-ah* (guttural *ch*)
Maʿadd: *ma-ad´*
Manāh: *ma-nah´*
Mikhdham: *mich´-dham* (guttural *ch*)
Muḍar: *moo-dahr´*
Nakhlat al-Shaʾmīyah: *nach´-lat* (guttural *ch*) *ash-sha´-mee-yuh*
Nizār: *nee-zar´*
Qudayd: *qoo-dayd´*
Quraysh: *qoo-raysh´*
Rabīʿah: *ra-bee´-uh*
Rasūb: *ra-soob´*
Sarif: *sa´-rif*
Shaddād ibn ʿĀriḍ al-Jushami: *shad-dad´ ibn ah´-rid al-joo´-sha-mee*
Suqām: *soo-qahm´*
taḥlīl: *tah-leel´* (heavy *h*)
talbiyah: *tal-bee´-yuh*
Tamīm ibn-Murr: *ta-meem´ ibn mur*
Taym-Allāt: *taym al-lat´*
Taym-Allāt ibn-al-Namir ibn-Qāsiṭ: *taym al-lat´ ibn an-na´-mir ibn qah´-sit*
Taym-Allāt ibn Rufaydah ibn Thawr: *taym al-lat´ ibn roo-fay´-duh ibn thawr*
Ṭayyr': *tay´-yeh*
Thaʿlabah ibn ʿUkābah: *tha´-la-buh ibn oo-ka´-buh*
Thaqīf: *tha-qeef´*
ʿUbaydah ʿAbdullāh ibn abi ʿUbaydah ibn ʿAmmār ibn Yāsir: *oo-bay´-duh ab-dul-lah´ ibn a-bee oo-bay´-duh ibn am-mahr´ ibn ya´-sir*
Yathrib: *yath´-rib*
Ẓālim ibn Asʿad: *zah´-lim ibn as´-ad*
Zayd-Allāt: *zayd al-lat´*
Zayd-Allāt ibn Rufaydah ibn Thawr ibn Wabarah ibn Murr ibn Udd ibn Ṭābikhah: *zayd al-lat´ ibn roo-fay´-duh ibn thawr ibn wa´-ba-ruh ibn mur ibn ud ibn tah´-bi-chah* (guttural *ch*)
Zayd-Manāh: *zayd ma-nah´*
Zayd-Manāh ibn Tamīm ibn Udd ibn Ṭābikhah: *zayd ma-nah´ ibn ta-meem´ ibn ud ibn tah´-bi-chah* (guttural *ch*)

FROM THE BOOK OF IDOLS

From *Introduction*

Hishām ibn-Muḥammad al-Kalbi said: I was informed by my father and others, and I personally checked and ascertained their report, that when Ishmael, the son of Abraham, settled in Mecca, he begot many children. [Their descendants] multiplied so much that they crowded the city and supplanted its original inhabitants, the Amalekites. Later on Mecca became overcrowded with them, and dissension and strife arose among them, causing them to fight among themselves and consequently be dispersed throughout the land where they roamed seeking a livelihood.

The reason which led them to the worship of images and stones was the following: No one left Mecca without carrying away with him a stone from the stones of the Sacred House (al-Ḥaram) as a token of reverence to it, and as a sign of deep affection to Mecca. Wherever he settled he would erect that stone and circumambulate it in the same manner he used to circumambulate the Kaʿbah[1] [before his departure from Mecca], seeking thereby its blessing and affirming his deep affection for the Sacred House. In fact,

Translated by Nabih Amin Faris. All bracketed additions are the translator's.

1. Literally, "the Cube," a stone shrine in Mecca—according to tradition, built by Abraham—that became the most important site in Islam (Muslims around the world face it when they pray). It is also called "the Sacred House," and as part of the required pilgrimage to Mecca, worshippers walk around it seven times.

the Arabs still venerate the Kaʿbah and Mecca and journey to them in order to perform the pilgrimage and visitation, conforming thereby to the time-honored custom which they inherited from Abraham and Ishmael.

In time this led them to the worship of whatever took their fancy, and caused them to forget their former worship. They exchanged the religion of Abraham and Ishmael for another. Consequently they took to the worship of images, becoming like the nations before them. They sought and determined what the people of Noah had worshipped of these images and adopted the worship of those which were still remembered among them. Among these devotional practices were some which came down from the time of Abraham and Ishmael, such as the veneration of the House and its circumambulation, the pilgrimage, the visitation or the lesser pilgrimage (*al-ʿumrah*), the vigil (*al-wuqūf*) on ʿArafah and [al-]Muzdalifah,[2] sacrificing she-camels, and raising the voice in the acclamation of the name of the deity (*tahlīl*) at the pilgrimage and the visitation, introducing thereinto things not belonging to it. Thus whenever the Nizār[3] raised their voice in the *tahlīl*, they were wont to say:

> "Here we are O Lord! Here we are! Here we are!
> Thou hast no associate save one who is thine.
> Thou hast dominion over him and over what he possesseth."

They would thus declare His unity through the *talbiyah*,[4] and at the same time associate their gods with Him, placing their affairs in His hands. Consequently, God said to His Prophet, "And most of them believe not in God, without also associating other deities with Him."[5] In other words, they would not declare His unity through the knowledge of His rightful dues, without associating with Him some of His own creatures.

* * *

Manāh

The most ancient of all these idols was Manāh. The Arabs used to name [their children] ʿAbd-Manāh and Zayd-Manāh.[6] Manāh was erected on the seashore in the vicinity of al-Mushallal in Qudayd, between Medina and Mecca. All the Arabs used to venerate her and sacrifice before her. [In particular] the Aws and the Khazraj,[7] as well as the inhabitants of Medina and Mecca and their vicinities, used to venerate Manāh, sacrifice before her, and bring unto her their offerings.

The children of the Maʿadd were followers of a faith which still preserved a little of the religion of Ishmael. The Rabīʿah and the Muḍar,[8] too, were followers of a similar faith. But none venerated her more than the Aws and the Khazraj.

Abu-al-Mundhir Hishām ibn-Muḥammad said: I was told by a man from the Quraysh,[9] on the authority of abu-ʿUbaydah ʿAbdullāh ibn-abi-ʿUbaydah

2. Two locations near Mecca. Muslim pilgrims stand on the plain of ʿArafah during the second day of the pilgrimage, praying to God for forgiveness, and next stop in Muzdalifah for a night to perform other rites of the pilgrimage.
3. A tribal group in north Arabia.
4. A prayer of greeting to the deity.
5. Qur'an 12:106.
6. Literally, Servant of Manat and Abundance of Manat.
7. Two tribes of south Arabia.
8. Three north Arabian tribes.
9. The tribe that ruled Mecca in Muhammad's time.

ibn-ʿAmmār ibn-Yāsir[1] who was the best informed man on the subject of the Aws and the Khazraj, that the Aws and the Khazraj, as well as those Arabs among the people of Yathrib[2] and other places who took to their way of life, were wont to go on pilgrimage and observe the vigil at all the appointed places, but not shave their heads. At the end of the pilgrimage, however, when they were about to return home, they would set out to the place where Manāh stood, shave their heads, and stay there a while. They did not consider their pilgrimage completed until they visited Manāh. Because of this veneration of Manāh by the Aws and the Khazraj, ʿAbd-al-ʿUzza ibn-Wadīʿah al-Muzani, or some other Arab, said:

> "An oath, truthful and just, I swore
> By Manāh, at the sacred place of the Khazraj."

During the Jāhiliyah[3] days, the Arabs were wont to call both the Aws and the Khazraj by the single generic name, al-Khazraj. For this reason the poet said, "at the sacred place of the Khazraj."

This Manāh is that which God mentioned when He said, "And Manāh, the third idol besides."[4] She was the [goddess] of the Hudhayl and the Khuzāʿah.[5]

The Quraysh as well as the rest of the Arabs continued to venerate Manāh until the Apostle of God set out from Medina in the eighth year of the Hijrah, the year in which God accorded him the victory.[6] When he was at a distance of four or five nights from Medina, he dispatched ʿAli[7] to destroy her. ʿAli demolished her, took away all her [treasures], and carried them back to the Prophet. Among the treasures which ʿAli carried away were two swords which had been presented to [Manāh] by al-Ḥārith ibn-abi-Shamir al-Ghassāni, the king of Ghassān.[8] The one sword was called Mikhdham and the other Rasūb. They are the two swords of al-Ḥārith which ʿAlqamah[9] mentions in one of his poems. He said:

> "Wearing two coats of mail as well as
> Two studded swords, Mikhdham and Raṣūb."

The Prophet gave these two swords to ʿAli. It is, therefore, said that dhu-al-Faqār, the sword of ʿAli, was one of them.

It is also said that ʿAli found these two swords in [the temple of] al-Fals, the idol of the Ṭayyiʾ,[1] whither the Prophet had sent him, and which he also destroyed.

Allāt

They then adopted Allāt as their goddess. Allāt stood in al-Ṭāʾif,[2] and was more recent than Manāh. She was a cubic rock beside which a certain Jew

1. A hadith relater (d. 785).
2. Former name of Medina.
3. The age of ignorance (the literal meaning of *jāhiliyah*); that is, the time before Islam.
4. Qurʾan 53:20.
5. Two tribes living near Mecca.
6. That is, the conquest of Mecca in 630.
7. ʿAli ibn Abi Talib (ca. 599–661), the Prophet's cousin and son-in-law, who became the fourth caliph.
8. An Arab Christian kingdom in present-day Syria and Jordan, conquered by the Muslims in the 7th century.
9. Pre-Islamic Arab poet (6th century; see below), associated with the Ghassanid court.
1. A prominent pre-Islamic Arab tribe.
2. A city 50 miles east of Mecca. Some scholars think that the name al-Lat is derived from a verb for the mixing of barley and that mixing barley was part of a pre-Islamic ritual that took place near the "cubic rock" mentioned here, which eventually took on the name al-Lat.

used to prepare his barley porridge (*sawīq*). Her custody was in the hands of the banu-ʿAttāb ibn-Mālik of the Thaqīf,[3] who had built an edifice over her. The Quraysh, as well as all the Arabs, were wont to venerate Allāt. They also used to name their children after her, calling them Zayd-Allāt and Taym-Allāt.[4]

She stood in the place of the left-hand side minaret of the present-day mosque of al-Ṭāʾif. She is the idol which God mentioned when He said, "Have you seen Allāt and al-ʿUzza?"[5] It was this same Allāt which ʿAmr ibn-al-Juʾayd[6] had in mind when he said:

> "In forswearing wine I am like him who hath abjured Allāt,
> although he had been at one time her devotee."

Likewise it was the same idol to which al-Mutalammis alluded in his satire of ʿAmr ibn-al-Mundhir[7] when he said:

> "Thou hast banished me for fear of lampoon and satire.
> No! By Allāt and all the sacred baetyls[8] (anṣāb), thou
> shalt not escape."

Allāt continued to be venerated until the Thaqīf embraced Islam, when the Apostle of God dispatched al-Mughīrah ibn-Shuʿbah,[9] who destroyed her and burnt her [temple] to the ground.

In this connection, when Allāt was destroyed and burnt to the ground, Shaddād ibn-ʿĀriḍ al-Jushami[1] said warning the Thaqīf not to return to her worship nor attempt to avenge her destruction:

> "Come not to Allāt, for God hath doomed her to destruction;
> How can you stand by one which doth not triumph?
> Verily that which, when set on fire, resisted not the flames,
> Nor saved her stones, is inglorious and worthless.
> Hence when the Apostle in your place shall arrive
> And then leave, not one of her votaries shall be left."

Aws ibn-Ḥajar,[2] swearing by Allāt, said:

> "By Allāt and al-ʿUzza and those who in them believe,
> And by Allah, verily He is greater than both."

From *Al-ʿUzza*

They then adopted al-ʿUzza as their goddess. She is, in point of time, more recent than either Allāt or Manāh, since I have heard that the Arabs named their children after the latter two before they named them after al-ʿUzza. Thus I have found that Tamīm ibn-Murr had called his son[s] Zayd-Manāh

3. The main tribe of al-Ta'if, who opposed Muhammad. "Banu": children of.
4. Servant of Allat.
5. Qur'an 53:19.
6. A pre-Islamic poet considered to be a soothsayer; he was known as the sayyid (chief) of the Rabi'a tribe.
7. King of the Lakhmids (r. 554–69), Christian Arabs of southern Arabia, whom the poet al-Mutalammis left to join their rivals, the Ghassanids.
8. Stones that are worshipped.
9. A Thaqafi from al-Ta'if (d. 670).
1. A pre-Islamic poet; his poetry is quoted in *Life of the Prophet* by Ibn Hisham (d. 833; see above).
2. Pre-Islamic panegyrist (6th century).

ibn-Tamīm ibn-Murr ibn-Udd ibn-Ṭābikhah and ʿAbd-Manāh ibn-Udd. Similarly Thaʿlabah ibn-ʿUkābah named his son after Allāt, calling him Taym-Allāt. [Others were]: Taym-Allāt ibn-Rufaydah ibn-Thawr, Zayd-Allāt ibn-Rufaydah ibn-Thawr ibn-Wabarah ibn-Murr ibn-Udd ibn-Ṭābikhah, Taym-Allāt ibn-al-Namir ibn-Qāsiṭ, and ʿAbd-al-ʿUzza ibn-Kaʿb ibn-Saʿd ibn-Zayd-Manāh ibn-Tamīm. It is therefore more recent than the first two. ʿAbd-al-ʿUzza ibn-Kaʿb is among the earliest compounded names the Arabs used in conjunction with al-ʿUzza.

The person who introduced al-ʿUzza was Ẓālim ibn-Asʿad. Her idol was situated in a valley in Nakhlat al-Shaʿmīyah called Ḥurāḍ, alongside al-Ghumayr to the right of the road from Mecca to al-ʿIrāq, above Dhāt-ʿIrq and nine miles from al-Bustān.[3] Over her [Ẓālim] built a house called Buss in which the people used to receive oracular communications. The Arabs as well as the Quraysh were wont to name their children ʿAbd-al-ʿUzza. Furthermore al-ʿUzza was the greatest idol among the Quraysh. They used to journey to her, offer gifts unto her, and seek her favours through sacrifice.

We have been told that the Apostle of God once mentioned al-ʿUzza saying, "I have offered a white sheep to al-ʿUzza, while I was a follower of the religion of my people."

The Quraysh were wont to circumambulate the Kaʿbah and say:

"By Allāt and al-ʿUzza,
And Manāh, the third idol besides.
Verily they are the most exalted females
Whose intercession is to be sought."[4]

These were also called "the Daughters of Allah," and were supposed to intercede before God. When the Apostle of God was sent, God revealed unto him [concerning them] the following:

> "Have you seen Allāt and al-ʿUzza, and Manāh the third idol besides? What? Shall ye have male progeny and God female? This indeed were an unfair partition! These are mere names: ye and your fathers named them thus: God hath not sent down any warranty in their regard."[5]

The Quraysh had dedicated to it, in the valley of Ḥurāḍ, a ravine (*shiʿb*) called Suqām and were wont to vie there with the Sacred Territory of the Kaʿbah. Abu-Jundub al-Hudhali (also al-Qirdi), describing a woman with whom he was in love, composed the following verses and mentioned in them a vow which she made to him swearing by al-ʿUzza:

"She swore an earnest and solemn oath
By her to whom the vales of Suqām were dedicated:
'If thou wouldst not return my clothes, go,
For the rest of my life I would hate thee.'
Since it was hard for him to part with umm-Ḥuwayrith,
He became eager to fulfil her desire."

3. That is, on a road between Mecca and al-Ta'if.
4. The last two lines are "satanic verses."
5. Qur'an 53:19-23.

Dirham ibn-Zayd al-Awsi also said:

> "By the Lord of al-ʿUzza, the propitious,
> And by God betwixt whose House [and Suqām] Sarif stands."

She also had a place of sacrifice called al-Ghabghab where they offered their oblations. Al-Hudhali speaks of it in a satire which he composed against a certain man who had married a beautiful woman whose name was Asmā'. He said:

> "Asmā' was married to the jawbone of a little cow
> Which one of the banu-Ghanm had offered for sacrifice.
> As he led it to the Ghabghab of al-ʿUzza,
> He noticed some defects in its eyes;
> And when the cow was offered upon the altar,
> And its flesh divided, his portion was foul."

It was customary to divide the flesh of the sacrifice among those who had offered it and among those present at the ceremony.

* * *

AL-BALADHURI
d. ca. 892

To Ahmad ibn Yahya al-Baladhuri we owe much of our knowledge of early Islamic military history, its campaigns and battles, and its catalogue of notables who fought and then governed the conquered territories. He was probably born in Baghdad and, except for limited travel, spent his life there. Al-Baladhuri was close to the ʿAbbasid caliphs al-Mutawakkil (r. 847–61) and al-Mustaʿin (r. 862–66) but lost favor during the reign of al-Muʿtamid (r. 870–92). His fame rests chiefly on two historical works: *The Origins of the Islamic State* and *The Lineage of the Nobles.*

Al-Baladhuri's *Origins* abridges a longer historical work that is now lost. It describes the battles and expansion of the Muslim community, beginning with the lifetime of Muhammad, and documents the later conquests that led Muslim forces as far west as Spain and as far east as Iran. Its value lies in its historical detail and its attention to the changes these expansions wrought in the societies of the conqueror and conquered. Al-Baladhuri's *Lineage* presents the biographies of prominent Arab notables in genealogical arrangement. Beginning with the life of Muhammad and his family, *Lineage* profiles the elites of Umayyad and ʿAbbasid Islam. Along with *Origins*, it remained an important and reliable source for centuries to come, one to which later historians repeatedly refer.

The passage below from al-Baladhuri's *Origins* describes the conquest of Syria. A key figure in this narrative is Khalid ibn al-Walid (d. 642). Al-Walid had initially opposed Muhammad but later converted to Islam. After his conversion, he proved himself an able military commander, initially under Muhammad and then under the first and second caliphs, Abu Bakr (573–634) and ʿUmar (ca. 586–644).

PRONOUNCING GLOSSARY

ʿAbdullāh ibn-al-Muṭâʿ al-Kindi: *ab-dul-lah´ ibn al-moo-tah´ al-kin´-dee*
abu-ʿUbaidah ibn-al-Jarrâḥ: *a-boo oo-bay´-duh ibn al-jar-rah´* (heavy *h*)
abu-Arwa ad-Dausi: *a-boo ar´-wah ad-daw´-see*
abu-Bakr: *a-boo bakr*
abu-Ḥafṣ ash-Shâmi: *a-boo hafs´* (heavy *h*) *ash-sha´-mee*
Abu-Mikhnaf: *a-boo mich´-naf* (guttural *ch*)
abu-ʿUbaidah Âmir ibn-ʿAbdallâh ibn-al-Jarrâḥ al-Fihri: *a-boo oo-bay´-duh ah´-mir ibn ab-dul´lah´ ibn al-jar-rah´* (heavy *h*) *al-fih´-ree* (light *h*)
abu-Umâmah aṣ-Ṣudai ibn-ʿAjlân al-Bâhili: *a-boo oo-ma´-muh as-soo-dai´ ibn aj-lan´ al-ba´-he-lee*
ad-Dubbiyah (=ad-Dâbiyah): *ad-da´-bee-yuh*
Ailah: *ay-luh*
ʿAin at-Tamr: *ain´ at-tamr´´*
al-ʿArabah: *al-ah´-ra-buh*
al-Ghauth ibn-Murr ibn-Udd ibn Ṭâbikhah: *al-gawth´ ibn mur ibn ud ibn tah´-bi-chah* (guttural *ch*)
al-Ḥijâz: *al-he-jaz´* (heavy *h*)
al-Ḥuṣaid: *al-hoo-said´* (heavy *h*)
al-Jurf: *al-jurf´*
al-Ḳaryatain: *al-qar´-ya-tayn*
al-Kawâthil: *al-ka-wa´-thil*
al-Kûfah (=Kûfah): *al-koo´-fuh*
al-Madînah (=Medina): *al-ma-dee´-nuh*
al-Muḍaiyah: *al-moo-dai´-yuh*
al-Muthanna ibn-Ḥârithah ash-Shaibâni: *al-moo-than´-nuh ibn ha´-ri-thuh* (heavy *h*) *ash-shay-ba´-nee*
al-Wâḳidi: *al-wah´-qi-dee*
al-Yaman (=Yemen): *al-ya´-man*
ʿAmir ibn-al-ʿÂṣi ibn-Wâʾll as-Sahmi: *ahmr ibn al-ah´-si ibn wa´-il as-sah´-mee* (light *h*)
Arakah: *a´-ra-kuh*
Baʿlabakk: *bah´-luh-bak* (modern: *ba-ahl´-bak*)
Bahrāʾ: *bah-rah´* (light *h*)
banu-Jumaḥ: *ba-noo joo´-mah* (heavy *h*)
banu-Mashjaʿah ibn-at-Taim ibn-an-Namir ibn Wabarah ibn-Taghlib ibn-Ḥulwân ibn-ʿImrân ibn-al-Ḥâfi ibn-Ḳuḍâʿah: *ba-noo mash´-ja-ah ibn at-taym´ ibn an-na´-mir ibn wa´-ba-ruh ibn tag´-lib ibn hul-wan´* (heavy *h*) *ibn im-ran´ ibn al-ha´-fee* (heavy *h*) *ibn qoo-dah´-ah*
banu-Taghlib ibn-Wâʾil: *ba-noo tag´-lib ibn wa´-il*
Busr ibn-abi-Arṭāt al-ʿÂmiri: *busr ibn a-bee ar-that´ al-ah´-mi-ree*
Buṣra: *bus´-ruh*
Dâthin: *da´-thin*
dhimmah: *dhim´-muh*
dhu-l-Marwah: *dhul-mar´-wah*
Dûmat al-Jandal: *doo´-mat al-jan´-dal*
Ghazzah: *gaz´-zuh*
Ghûṭah: *goo´-tah*
Ḥabîb ibn-Maslamah-l-Fihri: *ha-beeb´* (heavy *h*) *ibn mas´-la-muh al-fih´-ree* (light *h*)
Ḥaurân: *how-ran´* (heavy *h*)
Ḥurḳûṣ ibn-an-Nuʿmân al-Bahrâni: *hur-qoos´* (heavy *h*) *ibn an-nuh-man´ al-bah-rah´-nee* (light *h*)
Ḥûwârîn: *hoo-wa-reen´* (heavy *h*)
Iyâd: *ee-yahd´*
Jâbiyah: *ja´-bee-yuh*
Kalb: *kalb*
Ḳanât Buṣra: *qah-naht´ bus´-ruh*
Ḳarḳîsiya: *qar-qee-see´-yuh*
Khâlid ibn-al-Walîd ibn-al-Mughîrah-l-Makhzûmi: *cha´-lid* (guttural *ch*) *ibn al-wa-leed´ ibn al-moo-gee´-ruh al-mach-zoo´-mee* (guttural *ch*)
Khâlid ibn-Saʿîd ibn-al-ʿÂṣi ibn-Umaiyah: *cha´-lid* (guttural *ch*) *ibn sa-eed´ ibn al-ah´-si ibn oo-mai-yuh*
Kindah: *kin´-duh*
Ḳuḍâʿah: *qoo-dah´-ah*
Ḳuraish = Quraysh: *qoo-raysh´*
Ḳurâḳir: *quh-rah´-qir*
Ḳuṣam: *qoo´-sahm*
Maʿmar ibn-Ḥabîb ibn Wahb ibn Ḥud-hâfah ibn-Jumaḥ: *mah´-mar ibn ha-beeb´* (heavy *h*) *ibn wahb* (light *h*) *ibn hoo-dha´-fuh* (heavy *h*) *ibn joo´-mah* (heavy *h*)
Makkah (=Mecca): *mak´-kuh*
Marj Râhiṭ: *marj rah´-hit*
Muʿâwiyah: *moo-ah´-we-yuh*
Muḥarram: *moo-har´-ram* (heavy *h*)
Rabîʿ: *ra-bee´*

Rabî'ah ibn-al-Muṭā': *ra-bee´-uh ibn al-moo-tah´*
Rabî'ah ibn-Bujair: *ra-bee´-uh ibn boo-jayr´*
Râfi' ibn-'Umair aṭ-Ṭā'i: *ra´-fi ibn oo-mayr´ at-tah´-ee*
Sa'd ibn-'Amr ibn-Ḥarâm al-Anṣâri: *sad ibn ahmr ibn ha-rahm´* (heavy *h*) *al-an-sah´-ree*
Ṣafar: *sah´-far*
Ṣandauda': *sahn-daw-da´*
Sanir: *sa´-nir*
sheikh = shaykh: *shaych* (guttural *ch*)
Shuraḥbîl ibn-Ḥasanah: *shoo-rah´-bil* (heavy *h*) *ibn ha´-sa-nuh* (heavy *h*)
Ṣûfah: *soo-fuh´*
Suwa: *soo-wa´*
Tabûk: *ta-bouk´*
Tadmur: *tad´-mur*
Thaniyat al-'Uḳâb: *tha-nee´-yat al-oo-qahb´*
'Umar (ibn al-Khaṭṭâb): *oh´-mar ibn al-chaht-tahb´* (guttural *ch*)
'Umar ibn-'Ali ibn-abi-Ṭâlib: *oh´-mar ibn ah´-lee ibn a-bee tah´-lib*
umm-Ḥabîb aṣ-Ṣahbâ: *oom ha-beeb´* (heavy *h*) *as-sah-ba´* (heavy *h*)
Yazîd ibn-abi-Sufyân: *ya-zeed´ ibn a-bee soof-yan´*

FROM THE ORIGINS OF THE ISLAMIC STATE

The Conquest of Syria

The "tying of the three banners." When abu-Bakr[1] was done with the case of those who apostatized, he saw fit to direct his troops against Syria. To this effect he wrote to the people of Makkah, at-Ṭâ'if, al-Yaman, and all the Arabs in Najd and al-Ḥijâz[2] calling them for a "holy war" and arousing their desire in it and in the obtainable booty from the Greeks.[3] Accordingly, people, including those actuated by greed as well as those actuated by the hope of divine remuneration, hastened to abu-Bakr from all quarters, and flocked to al-Madînah. Abu-Bakr gave three banners to three men [appointed them commanders] namely: Khâlid ibn-Sa'id ibn-al-'Âṣi ibn-Umaiyah, Shuraḥbîl ibn-Ḥasanah, an ally of the banu-Jumaḥ[4] and 'Amr ibn-al-'Âṣi ibn-Wâ'il as-Sahmi. (Shuraḥbîl, according to al-Wâḳidi,[5] was the son of 'Abdallâh ibn-al-Muṭâ' al-Kindi, Ḥasanah being his mother and a freedmaid of Ma'mar ibn-Ḥabíb ibn-Wahb ibn-Ḥudhâfah ibn-Jumaḥ. But according to al-Kalbi,[6] Shuraḥbîl was the son of Rabî'ah ibn-al-Muṭâ' descended from Ṣûfah, i. e., al-Ghauth ibn-Murr ibn-Udd ibn-Ṭâbikhah.) The tying of these banners took place on Thursday the first of Ṣafar, year 13,[7] after the troops had camped at al-Jurf throughout the month of Muḥarram with abu-'Ubaidah ibn-al-Jarrâḥ leading their prayers. Abu-Bakr wanted to give a banner to abu-'Ubaidah; but the latter begged to be relieved. Others claim that he did give one to him, but that report is not confirmed. The fact is that when 'Umar[8] became caliph, he conferred on him the governorship of all Syria.

TRANSLATED BY Philip Khûri Hitti. All bracketed additions are the translator's.

1. The first caliph (573–634), who had been Muhammad's chief adviser and father-in-law.
2. A region of the Arabian Peninsula that borders the Red Sea and contains Medina, Mecca, and at-Ta'if. Najd, to its east, is the central region of the peninsula. Al-Yaman, or Yemen, is the southwest corner of the peninsula.
3. As part of the Byzantine Empire, Syria was at that time under Greek control.
4. A tribe (literally, "the sons of Jumah").
5. Abu 'Abdallah Muhammad ibn 'Umar al-Waqidi (747–822), an early historian of the Muslim conquests.
6. Hisham ibn al-Kalbi (ca. 737–821); see above.
7. That is, April 634 C.E.; the Muslim calendar begins with Muhammad's hijra to Medina in 622 (Muharram and Safar are the first two months).
8. 'Umar ibn al-Khattab (ca. 586–644), who would become the second caliph and greatly expand the Muslim empire.

Abu-ʿUbaidah commander-in-chief. Abu-Mikhnaf[9] states that ʿUmar said to the commanders, "If ye altogether are to lead a fight, your commander will be abu-ʿUbaidah ʿÂmir ibn-ʿAbdallâh ibn-al-Jarrâḥ al-Fihri, otherwise Yazîd ibn-abi-Sufyân." Others assert that ʿAmr ibn-al-ʿÂṣi acted only as a reinforcement for the Moslems and commanded only those who joined him.

Abu-Bakr replaces Khâlid by Arwa. The assignment of Khâlid ibn-Saʿid by abu-Bakr to the leadership displeased ʿUmar who approached abu-Bakr with a view to dismissing him, charging him with being "a vain-seeking man who tries to make his way through dispute and bigotry." Accordingly abu-Bakr dismissed Khâlid and directed abu-Arwa ad-Dausi to take the banner from his hand. Abu-Arwa met him at dhu-l-Marwah where he received the banner from him and carried it back to abu-Bakr. Abu-Bakr handed it to Yazîd ibn-abi-Sufyân who left, with his brother Muʿâwiyah carrying the banner before him. Others say that the banner was delivered to Yazîd at dhu-l-Marwah whence he started at the head of Khâlid's army. Khâlid went with the army of Shuraḥbîl for the divine remuneration.[1]

Abu-Bakr gives instructions to the commanders. Abu-Bakr instructed ʿAmr ibn-al-ʿÂṣi to follow the way of Ailah[2] with Palestine for objective. Yazîd he instructed to follow the way of Tabûk.[3] To Shuraḥbîl, he wrote to follow the way of Tabûk, too. At the outset each one of the commanders had three thousand men under his leadership, but abu-Bakr kept on sending reinforcements until each one had 7,500. Later the total was increased to 24,000.

It is reported on the authority of al-Wâḳidi that abu-Bakr assigned ʿAmr to Palestine, Shuraḥbîl to the Jordan, and Yazîd to Damascus saying, "When ye all fight together, your commander is the one in whose province ye are fighting." It is also reported that to ʿAmr he gave oral instructions to lead the prayers in case the armies are united, and to have each commander lead the prayer of his own army when the armies are separate. Abu-Bakr ordered the commanders to see that each tribe flies a banner of its own.

Abu-Bakr directs Khâlid ibn-al-Walîd to Syria. On his arrival in the first district of Palestine, ʿAmr ibn-al-ʿÂṣi sent a message to abu-Bakr informing him of the great number of the enemy, their great armament, the wide extent of their land and the enthusiasm of their troops. Abu-Bakr, thereupon, wrote to Khâlid ibn-al-Walîd ibn-al-Mughīrah-l-Makhzûmi—who was at that time in al-ʿIrâḳ[4]—directing him to go to Syria. According to some, he thereby made him a commander over the commanders in the war. According to others, Khâlid only commanded his men who accompanied him; but whenever the Moslems met for a battle, the commanders would choose him as their chief for his valor and strategy and the auspiciousness of his counsel.

The battle of Dâthin. The first conflict between the Moslems and the enemy took place in Dâthin, one of the villages of Ghazzah,[5] which lay on the way between the Moslems and the residence of the patrician[6] of Ghazzah. Here the battle raged furiously, but at last Allah gave victory to his friends and defeat to his enemies whom he dispersed. All this took place before the arrival of Khâlid ibn al-Walîd in Syria.

9. A Shiʿi historian (d. 774).
1. As a volunteer [translator's note].
2. Town in the northern Hijaz.
3. Another town in the northern Hijaz.
4. Iraq.
5. Gaza.
6. An army leader.

The battle of al-ʿArabah. Thence Yazîd ibn-abi-Sufyân went in quest of the patrician, but hearing that a large host of Greeks were gathered in al-ʿArabah,[7] which lay in Palestine, he directed against them abu-Umâmah aṣ-Ṣudai ibn-ʿAjlân al-Bâhili, who, falling upon them, put most of them to the sword and went his way. Regarding this battle of al-ʿArabah, abu-Mikhnaf reports that six of the Greek leaders at the head of 3,000 men camped at al-ʿArabah when abu-Umâmah with a body of Moslems advanced against them and defeated them, killing one of their leaders. Thence he pursued them to ad-Dubbiyah[8] (i. e. ad-Dâbiyah) where he inflicted another defeat on them, and the Moslems carried off a large booty.

According to a tradition communicated by abu-Ḥafṣ ash-Shâmi on the authority of certain *sheikhs* from Syria, the first conflict of the Moslems was the Battle of al-ʿArabah before which no fighting at all took place since they left al-Ḥijâz. In no place between al-Ḥijâz and al-ʿArabah did they pass without establishing their authority and taking possession of it without resistance.

The Advance of Khâlid ibn-al-Walîd on Syria and the Places He Reduced on His Way

Khâlid takes ʿAin at-Tamr and Sandaudâʾ by force. When Khâlid ibn-al-Walîd received abu-Bakr's letter at al-Ḥîrah,[9] he left in his place al-Muthanna ibn-Ḥârithah ash-Shaibâni over the district of al-Kûfah, and set out at the head of 800 men in Rabîʿ II,[1] year 13. (Some give 600 and others 500 as the number of men.) On his way, he passed through ʿAin at-Tamr and reduced it by force. (According to others, he received abu-Bakr's message in ʿAin at-Tamr after having subdued it.) From ʿAin al-Tamr Khâlid made his way to Ṣandaudâʾ[2] in which lived some of the Kindah and Iyâd tribes and non-Arabs. These people fought against him; but Khâlid won the victory and left in the city Saʿd ibn-ʿAmr ibn-Ḥarâm al-Anṣâri whose descendants still live in it. Khâlid, having learnt that a body of the banu-Taghlib ibn-Wâʾil at al-Muḍaiyaḥ and al-Ḥuṣaid had apostatized[3] and were led by Rabîʿah ibn-Bujair, made his way to them. They fought against him; but he put them to flight and took captives and booty. The captives he sent to abu-Bakr, and among them was umm-Ḥabîb aṣ-Ṣahbâʾ, daughter of Ḥabîb ibn-Bujair, and [later] the mother of ʿUmar ibn-ʿAli ibn-abi-Ṭâlib.[4]

Khâlid crosses the desert to Suwa. Then Khâlid made an incursion on Ḳurâḳir[5] which was a spring belonging to the Kalb tribe, and thence crossed the desert to Suwa[6] which was also a spring held conjointly by the Kalb and some men of the Bahrâʾ. Here Khâlid killed Ḥurḳûṣ ibn-an-Nuʿmân al-Bahrâni of the Ḳuḍâʿah tribe and swept off all their possessions. When Khâlid wanted to cross the desert, he gave the camels all the water they could drink and then thrust into the camels' lips spears, which he left for them to drag, lest they should ruminate and get thirsty again. The quantity of water he carried along, though big, was exhausted on the way. So Khâlid

7. In modern-day Lebanon.
8. Also in Lebanon, southwest of al-ʿAraba.
9. A city in south-central Iraq, south of Kufa.
1. The fourth month of the Islamic calendar (i.e., June in 634).
2. Khalid went northwest from Hira to ʿAyn al-Tamr, then northeast to Sandawda'.
3. Had renounced their allegiance to Islam.
4. A son of ʿAli ibn Abi Talib (ca. 599–661), the fourth caliph.
5. Quraqir, due west of Sandawda', on the border of Iraq and Syria.
6. In Syria, northwest of Quraqir. "The Kalb": a Christian Arab tribe.

had to slay the camels one after the other and drink with his men the water from their bellies. Khâlid had a guide named Râfiʿ ibn-ʿUmair aṭ-Ṭâʾi whom the poet meant when he said:

"How wonderful has Râfiʿ been,
who succeeded in finding the way from Ḳurâḳir to Suwa,
to the water from which the coward who attempts to reach it
returns before attaining it.
No human being before thee ever did that!"

When the Moslems arrived in Suwa they found Ḥurḳûṣ and a band of men drinking and singing. Ḥurḳûṣ himself was saying:

"Again give me to drink before abu-Bakr's army is on,
our death may be at hand while we are unaware."

As the Moslems killed him, his blood flowed into the basin from which he had been drinking; and some report that his head, too, fell therein. It is claimed by others, however, that the one who sang this verse was one of those of the banu-Taghlib whom Khâlid had attacked with Rabîʿah ibn-Bujair.

Khâlid in Ḳarḳîsiya. According to al-Wâḳidi, Khâlid started from Suwa to al-Kawâthil thence to Ḳarḳîsiya[7] whose chief met him with a large host. Khâlid left him alone, turned to the mainland and went his way.

Arakah makes terms. Another place to which Khâlid came was Arakah (i.e. Arak) whose people he attacked and besieged. The city surrendered and made terms, offering a certain sum for the Moslems.

Dûmat al-Jandal, Ḳuṣam, Tadmur and al-Ḳaryatain taken. Dûmat al-Jandal[8] he then reached and conquered. Then he came to Ḳuṣam in which the banu-Mashjaʿah ibn-at-Taim ibn-an-Namir ibn-Wabarah ibn-Taghlib ibn-Ḥulwân ibn-ʿImrân ibn-al-Ḥâfi ibn-Ḳuḍâʿah came to terms with him. Khâlid wrote them a promise of security and advanced to Tadmur [Palmyra]. Tadmur's inhabitants held out against him and took to their fortifications. At last they sought to surrender and he wrote them a statement guaranteeing their safety on condition that they be considered *dhimmah* people,[9] that they entertain Moslems and that they submit to them. Khâlid then pushed to al-Ḳaryatain, whose people resisted him but were defeated, losing a large booty.

Ḥûwârîn reduced. Khâlid proceeded to Ḥûwârîn in Sanir and made a raid on its cattle. Its inhabitants, having been reinforced by the inhabitants of Baʿlabakk and of Buṣra[1] (the capital of Ḥaurân) stood out against him. The victory was won by Khâlid who took some as captives and killed others.

Ghassân attacked. Thence he came to Marj Râhiṭ and led an incursion against Ghassân[2] on their Easter day—they being Christians. He took some captive and killed others.

Thanîyat al-ʿUḳâb. Khâlid then directed Busr ibn-abi-Arṭât al-ʿÂmiri of the Ḳuraish and Ḥabîb ibn-Maslamah-l-Fihri to the Ghûṭah[3] of Damascus where they attacked many villages. Khâlid arrived at Thanîyat in Damascus, the Thanîyat al-ʿUḳâb of to-day, and stood there for one hour, spreading his

7. A fortress town on the bank of the Euphrates.
8. A commercial town at an important strategic position in what is now northwestern Saudi Arabia.
9. A category of people, usually Jews and Christians, who pay a tax to Muslim overlords in exchange for military protection.
1. A caravan juncture point in southwest Syria.
2. An Arab Christian kingdom, a vassal of Byzantium, in present-day Syria and Jordan.
3. A place in Damascus noted for its orchards [translator's note].

banner. This banner was the one the Prophet used, and was black in color; and because the Arabs call a banner "*uḳâb*," the Thanîyat was known since as Thanîyat al-ʿUḳâb. Others say that it was thus called because a vulture [Ar. *ʿuḳâb*] happened to descend on it at that time. But the first explanation is more reliable. I heard it said by some that at that place stood a stone image of a vulture. But there is no truth in that statement.

Khâlid meets abu-ʿUbaidah. Khâlid camped at the East [Sharḳi] gate of Damascus; and according to others, at the Jâbiyah gate. The bishop of Damascus offered him gifts and homage and said to Khâlid, "Keep this covenant for me." Khâlid promised to do so. Then Khâlid went until he met the Moslems who were at Ḳanât Buṣra. According to others, however, he came to the Jâbiyah where abu-ʿUbaidah was with a band of Moslems. Here they met and went together to Buṣra.

AL-TABARI
ca. 839–923

Stop by a bookstore in any part of the Muslim world and you're likely to find two massive works by Abu Jaʿfar Muhammad ibn Jarir al-Tabari. Each runs to dozens of volumes, and both remain foundational sources in their respective fields of early Islamic history and commentary on the Qur'an.

Born in Amul, a city in northern Iran, al-Tabari came from a wealthy family who supported his educational endeavors. He was a young prodigy of the Qur'an, memorizing it by the time he was seven and able to lead the prayer as an eight-year-old. At twelve he moved to Rayy, today a suburb of Tehran, for further study and from there to the major academic hub, Baghdad. Eleven years later, al-Tabari left for Egypt, Syria, and Palestine, but he returned to Baghdad in 870 to begin a career of teaching and writing.

Al-Tabari's familial wealth ensured that he did not have to seek a patron, and by all accounts he never accepted an official government role. Thus freed, he could pursue research and writing that ranged across many fields of Islamic scholarship. He founded his own law school, the Jariri school, and wrote *Differences among the Jurists*, analyzing the methods and opinions of the most important legal scholars in Islamic history. His work extended beyond the founders of the four Sunni schools but, much to the chagrin of the Baghdad Hanbalis, notably failed to include Ahmad ibn Hanbal (780–855; see above), whom al-Tabari considered a great scholar of traditions but not a jurist.

The precision and balance of an accomplished jurisprudent are clearly displayed in al-Tabari's most influential work, his commentary on the Qur'an. Completed in the early tenth century, *The Comprehensive Clarification of the Interpretation of the Verses of the Qur'an* presents a vast and cumulative summation of the first three centuries of qur'anic exegesis. Much of future Sunni commentary tradition would build upon this foundation.

In his *History of Messengers and Kings* al-Tabari opens with the world's creation and concludes with the decades before his death. His vision is theological, as he shapes a salvation history replete with the long succession of prophets and the peoples who rejected their preaching. After setting the stage with this sequence of narratives, al-Tabari then tightens his focus with the advent of Muhammad's prophethood.

From that point on, his format becomes annalistic as he chronicles the major events of Muhammad's life and the lives of the caliphs who carried on his mandate and mission. Again, his encyclopedic bent expresses itself as he gathers diverse accounts of the events he records and sets them side by side with no attempt to achieve either synthesis or harmony.

The passage below from al-Tabari's *History* recounts the events that led the second ʿAbbasid caliph, Abu Jaʿfar al-Mansur (r. 754–75), to build the city of Baghdad in 762. Al-Mansur decided to move his capital from Hashimiyya—which, for a time, had been the capital city of the first ʿAbbasid caliph, Abu al-ʿAbbas al-Saffah (r. 750–54)—because of the agitation of groups opposed to him in nearby Kufa and because of a riot in the city of Hashimiyya led by the Rawandiyya, a renegade sect convinced that he was a deity incarnate. Al-Mansur picked the site of Baghdad for defensive, economic, and environmental reasons. The site's waterways and location near major trading routes gave it immediate defensive and economic advantages. In addition, the area's fertility and temperate climate were obvious attractions.

Situated within three circular walls, al-Mansur's capital was also called the "City of Peace." It quickly expanded beyond the city walls, and Baghdad's cultural and economic importance also grew from the later part of the eighth century, reaching a peak in the mid-ninth century. During its heyday Baghdad was the wealthiest city in the world, welcoming trading ships from regions as far-flung as China and East Africa; a center for scientists, religious scholars, litterateurs, and artisans; and an urban paradise of grand mosques, lush gardens, and magnificent palaces.

PRONOUNCING GLOSSARY

ʿAbd al-Malik ibn Ḥumayd: *ab-dul-ma´-lik ibn hoo-mayd´* (heavy *h*)
Abū al-ʿAbbās al-Faḍl ibn Sulaymān al-Ṭūsī: *a-bool-ab-bas´ al-fadl´ ibn soo-lay-man´ at-too´-see*
Abū Ayyūb al-Khūzī: *a-boo eye-yoob´ al-choo´-zee* (guttural *ch*)
Abū Ḥanīfah al-Nuʿmān ibn Thābit: *a-boo ha-nee´-fuh* (heavy *h*) *an-noo-man´ ibn tha´-bit*
Abū Jaʿfar al-Manṣūr: *a-boo ja´-far al-man-soor´*
al-ʿAtīqah: *al-ah-tee´-quh*
al-Baṣrah: *al-bas´-ruh*
al-Ḥajjāj ibn Arṭāh: *al-haj-jaj´* (heavy *h*) *ibn ar-tah´*
al-Hāshimiyyah: *al-ha´-shi-mee´´-yuh*
al-Haytham ibn ʿAdī: *al-hay´-tham ibn a-dee´*
al-Jabal: *al-ja´-bal*
al-Jibāl: *al-ji-bal´*
al-Khuld: *al-chuld´* (guttural *ch*)
al-Kūfah: *al-koo´-fuh*
al-Madāʾin: *al-ma-da´-in*
al-Mawṣil: *al-mou´-sil*
al-Mukharrim: *al-moo-char´-rim* (guttural *ch*)
al-Raqqah: *ar-rahq´-quh*
al-Ruṣāfah: *ar-roo-sah´-fuh*
al-Sarī: *as-sa´-ree*
al-Zawrāʾ: *as-zaw-ra´*
Āmid: *a´-mid*
Bādūrayā: *ba-doo´-rah-yah´´*
Bārimmā: *ba´-rim-ma*
Bishr ibn Maymūn al-Sharawī: *bishr ibn may-moon´ ash-sha´-ra-wee*
Bustān al-Qass: *boo-stan´ al-qahs´´*
dihqān: *dih-qahn´*
Ḥijāz: *he-jaz´* (heavy *h*)
Ibn ʿAyyāsh: *ibn eye-yash´*
Jarjarāyā: *jar-ja-rah´-yah*
Jazīrah: *ja-zee´-ruh*
Kalwādhā: *kal-wa´-dha*
Madīnat Ibn Hubayrah: *ma-dee´-nat ibn hoo-bay´-ruh*
Miqlāṣ: *miq-lahs´*
Muḥammad ibn Maʿrūf ibn Suwayd: *moo-ham´-mad* (heavy *h*) *ibn ma-roof´ ibn soo-wayd´*
Nahr Būq: *nahr bouq´*
Qaṣr al-Salām: *qasr´ as-sa-lam´´*
Quṭrabbul: *qoot-rab´-bul*
Raḥā al-Biṭrīq: *ra´-hal-bit-reeq´* (heavy *h*)
Rāwandiyyah: *ra´-wan-dee´´-yuh*
Sābāṭ: *sa-baht´*
Ṣarāt: *sah-raht´*

Sawād: *sa-wad´*
Sulaymān ibn Mujālid: *soo-lay-man´ ibn moo-ja´-lid*
Tāmarrā: *ta´-mar-rah*
ʿUmar ibn Shabbah: *oh´-mar ibn shab´-buh*
Wāsiṭ: *wah´-sit*
Zāb: *zab*

FROM THE HISTORY OF MESSENGERS AND KINGS

From *ʿAbbāsid Authority Affirmed*

THE REASON ABŪ JAʿFAR BUILT BAGHDAD

The reason for that is as follows: Tradition has it that at the time when the caliphate devolved upon Abū Jaʿfar al-Manṣūr,[1] he built al-Hāshimiyyah opposite Madīnat Ibn Hubayrah. Between the two was the whole extent of the road. Madīnat Ibn Hubayrah, opposite which stood Abū Jaʿfar's al-Hāshimiyyah, lay toward al-Kūfah.[2] Al-Manṣūr also built a city behind al-Kūfah by the name of al-Ruṣāfah. When the Rāwandiyyah[3] were stirred up by [their beliefs about] Abū Jaʿfar in his city called al-Hāshimiyyah—the one that lies opposite Madīnat Ibn Hubayrah—the caliph began to dislike living there. His dislike was due to the disturbance that various of the Rāwandiyyah set in motion against him as well as to the city's close proximity to al-Kūfah. Abū Jaʿfar had no confidence in the loyalty of its inhabitants and wanted to distance himself from them. He is said to have gone out personally, exploring for a site that he could use as a settlement for himself and for his army, and where he could build a city. He began by going down to Jarjarāyā.[4] From there he went to Baghdad and then on to al-Mawṣil.[5] Finally, he went back to Baghdad and said, "This is a good place for an army camp. Here's the Tigris, with nothing between us and China, and on it arrives all that the sea can bring, as well as provisions from the Jazīrah,[6] Armenia and surrounding areas. Further, there is the Euphrates on which can arrive everything from Syria, al-Raqqah,[7] and surrounding areas. The caliph therefore dismounted and pitched his camp on the Ṣarāt Canal.[8] He sketched a plan of the city and put an army commander in charge of each quarter.

According to ʿUmar b. Shabbah—Muḥammad b. Maʿrūf b. Suwayd—his father—Sulaymān b. Mujālid: The people of al-Kūfah fomented rebellion against him in the Commander of the Faithful's, i.e., al-Manṣūr's, army. Therefore he headed for al-Jabal[9] in search of a place to settle. At that time

TRANSLATED BY Jane Dammen McAuliffe. All bracketed additions are the translator's.

1. The second ʿAbbasid caliph (ca. 710–775); he succeeded his brother in 754.
2. A garrison town in Iraq that became an early center of Sunni jurisprudence and philology; the first ʿAbbasid caliph, al-Saffah, was proclaimed in its mosque in 749.
3. A radical sect whose extreme support for al-Mansur—whom they believed to be a divine prophet—was an embarrassment and a political liability.
4. A town on the east bank of the Tigris roughly 65 miles southeast of Baghdad.
5. Mosul.
6. Region of high agricultural production between the Tigris and Euphrates Rivers (now in northern Iraq, eastern Turkey, and northeastern Syria); it was also a trading crossroads.
7. A town in north-central Syria, on the Euphrates.
8. A branch of the great ʿIsa Canal that flowed eastward through the upper Karkh section of Baghdad; the ʿIsa itself flowed through the lower part of this section [translator's note, edited].
9. Located in northern Mesopotamia, about 90 miles west of Mosul.

the road went by way of al-Madā'in.[1] We left via Sābāt, but one of our companions fell behind, afflicted with an eye inflammation. As he stayed there to have his eyes treated, the physician asked him where the Commander of the Faithful was heading. "He is looking for a place to settle," the man replied. To this the physician responded: "In one of our books we find it written that a man named Miqlāṣ will build a city called al-Zawrā' between the Tigris and the Ṣarāt. After he has laid its foundation and built one course of its walls, a problem will erupt for him in the Ḥijāz,[2] and he will interrupt construction of the city and turn his attention to repairing that breach of the peace. When this is almost done, trouble will arise for him in al-Baṣrah,[3] this one more difficult for him than the first. Before long, however, the two breaches will be mended, and he will return to building the city and will complete it. Then will he be given a long life and sovereignty shall remain in his progeny."[4] Sulaymān continued: The Commander of the Faithful was on the outskirts of al-Jibāl searching for a place to settle when my companion reached me and gave me this account. I reported this to the Commander of the Faithful, and he summoned the man, who repeated the story to Abū Ja'far. At this the caliph turned right around and went back to his starting point, saying, "By God, I'm that very man! I was called Miqlāṣ as a lad but then the name for me fell into disuse."

According to al-Haytham b. 'Adī—Ibn 'Ayyāsh: Intending to move from al-Hāshimiyyah, Abū Ja'far sent scouts to search out a site for him, a place where he could settle that would be centrally located and comfortable for both the common people and the army. A site near Bārimmā[5] was described to him, and it was commended to him as having excellent victuals. He went to take a look at it himself and even spent the night there. Searchingly he scanned the site, seeing it to be a good place, and then questioned a group of his associates, including Sulaymān b. Mujālid, Abū Ayyūb al-Khūzī, 'Abd al-Malik b. Ḥumayd, the secretary, and others, about their opinion of it. "We've not seen anything to equal it," they replied; "it is pleasant, fitting, and congenial." To this the caliph responded, "You are right; it is just as you say, yet it could not support the army, the people, and the various groups. What I want is a place that is comfortable for the people and congenial for them as well as for me, a place where the prices will not become too high for them and the food supplies will not prove too hard to obtain. If I live in a place where it is impossible to import anything by land or sea, the prices will be high, goods will be scarce, and shortages in the food supply will cause hardship for the people. On the way here, I actually passed a place that combines these various natural qualities, so I shall stop and stay overnight there. If I find it to be the precise combination that I want, i.e., a healthful nocturnal environment, convenience, and the capacity to support both the army and the people, I shall build there."

1. Literally, "the Cities" (which included Sabat), a metropolis about 12 miles south of Baghdad, on both sides of the Tigris.
2. The western region of the Arabian Peninsula; it borders the Red Sea and contains Mecca and Medina.
3. Basra, in southeast Iraq near the mouth of the Persian Gulf.
4. Among other prophecies associated with Baghdad is one predicting that no caliph would die a natural death there [translator's note].
5. A town on the Tigris north of Baghdad, near Tikrit.

According to al-Haytham b. ʿAdī: I was told that Abū Jaʿfar came toward the bridge, crossed over at [what is now] Qaṣr al-Salām,[6] and then performed the late-afternoon prayer. It was summertime, and at the site of al-Qaṣr was a priest's church. The caliph stayed there all night and into the next morning, enjoying the most pleasant and refreshing night's rest on earth. The caliph then remained for the rest of the day without seeing anything he did not like. Consequently he declared, "This is the site on which I shall build. Goods can come here via the Tigris, the Euphrates, and various canals. Only a place like this can support both the army and the populace." He marked the boundaries of the city and calculated the extent of its construction. With his own hand he set the first brick in place while saying the words "In the name of God" and "Praise God" and "The earth belongs to God who makes heirs of it those of His servants whom He wishes, and the outcome is to the upright."[7] He concluded with the statement "Build, then, with God's blessing."

According to Bishr b. Maymūn al-Sharawī—Sulaymān b. Mujālid: Upon al-Manṣūr's return from the region of al-Jibāl, he asked about the account that the army commander had heard from the physician. This was the physician who had told him about the report of a certain Miqlāṣ that they had found in their books. He stopped at the monastery that lay opposite his [future] palace known as al-Khuld.[8] Al-Manṣūr summoned the head of the monastery and had the Patricius,[9] the master of Raḥā al-Biṭrīq ("Mills of the Patricius"), brought to him as well. Others whom he summoned were the overlord of [the village of] Baghdad, the overlord of al-Mukharrim, and head of the monastery known as Bustān al-Qass ("Garden of the Priest") and the overlord of al-ʿAtīqah.[1] The caliph questioned them about the places where they lived, asking what they were like in heat and cold, in rainy and muddy weather, and in terms of bugs and vermin. Each one told him what he knew from personal experience. Next, the caliph dispatched men on his own behest and ordered each of them to spend the night in one of these villages. Accordingly, each of these men passed the night in one of these villages and brought the caliph information about it. Al-Manṣūr next sought the advice of those whom he had summoned and examined carefully what they said. Their unanimous choice fell upon the overlord of Baghdad, so the caliph had him brought for consultation and careful questioning. (Now he was the *dihqān*[2] whose village still stands in the quarter known as that of Abū al-ʿAbbās al-Faḍl b. Sulaymān al-Ṭūsī. To this very day the domes of the village are still maintained in good repair, and his house survives intact.) The overlord of Baghdad said, "O Commander of the Faithful, you have asked me about these places, about their [relative] suitability, and about which of them should be chosen. What I think, O Commander of the Faithful, is that you should settle in four sectors, the two on the west side being Quṭrabbul and Bādūrayā, and the two on the east side being Nahr Būq and Kalwādhā. There you would be among date palms and

6. East of Baghdad.
7. Qur'an 7:128.
8. The name means "Eternity," and the palace complex that al-Mansur began to build there around 774 included gardens thought to rival those of paradise [translator's note, edited].
9. An administrator from Byzantium.
1. That is, those who governed districts and suburbs of Baghdad.
2. Literally, "head of the village" (Persian), a member of the land-owning nobility of Sassanid Persia.

near water. If one sector suffers from drought and its productivity is delayed, the other could be cultivated. Further, O Commander of the Faithful, you would be on the Ṣarāt Canal, permitting provisions to come to you along the Euphrates in ships from the west, as well as the choice products of Egypt and Syria. Supplies would also come to you along the Tigris in ships from China, India, al-Baṣrah and Wāsit.[3] Finally, stores would reach you from Armenia and those adjacent areas via the Tāmarrā Canal connecting to the Zāb,[4] as well as from Byzantium, Āmid,[5] the Jazīrah, and al-Mawṣil down the Tigris. You would be among waterways where no enemy of yours could reach you except by a floating or fixed bridge. When you cut the floating bridge and destroy the fixed bridges, your enemy will not be able to reach you at all. You would be between the Tigris and Euphrates, where no one could come to you from either the east or west without having to make a crossing. You would be midway among al-Baṣrah, Wāsiṭ, al-Kūfah, al-Mawṣil, and the whole Sawād.[6] You would be near land, sea, and mountain." Al-Manṣūr became ever more determined to settle on the site that he had selected. The overlord of Baghdad added, "Furthermore, O Commander of the Faithful, God has blessed the Commander of the Faithful with such a great quantity of forces, commanders, and troops that not one of his enemies, would aspire to come anywhere near him. The proper organization of cities requires you to make walls, moats and forts, but the Tigris and Euphrates shall be the moats for the Commander of the Faithful's city."

* * *

According to al-Sarī—Sulaymān b. Mujālid: Al-Manṣūr sent for a host of craftsmen and laborers from Syria, al-Mawṣil, al-Jabal, al-Kūfah, Wāsiṭ, and al-Baṣrah to be brought to him, commanding [also] the selection of a group of people endowed with virtue, integrity, intelligence, fidelity, and surveying competence. Consequently, among those brought to him were al-Ḥajjāj b. Arṭāh and Abū Ḥanīfah al-Nuʿmān b. Thābit. The caliph ordered the city to be marked out, its foundations excavated, its mud bricks shaped, and its baked bricks fired. Thus was it begun, the first stage of the project being initiated in 145.[7]

It is said: When al-Manṣūr decided to build Baghdad, he wanted to see for himself what it would look like, so he commanded that its outline be drawn with ashes. He then proceeded to enter through each gate and to walk among its outside walls, its arched areas, and its courtyards, all of which were outlined in ashes. He made the rounds, looking at the workmen and at the trenches that had been sketched. Having done that, he ordered cotton seeds placed on this outline and oil poured on it. Then he watched as the fire flared up, seeing the city as a whole and recognizing its full plan. Subsequently, he ordered the foundations to be excavated along those lines and commenced its construction.

* * *

3. A neighboring province to Baghdad's southeast.
4. A river that joins the Tigris north of Mosul.
5. A major commercial city on the Tigris in the far north of the Jazira (in present-day Turkey).
6. Fertile lands of southern Iraq.
7. 762 C.E.

IBN AL-NADIM
d. ca. 990

The tenth-century Shiʿi bookseller Abu al-Faraj Muhammad, commonly called Ibn al-Nadim, gained renown for his work *The Catalogue* in which he attempted to document every known Arabic book of his time. Because of the wealth of information Ibn al-Nadim provides in *The Catalogue*, it has been an invaluable historical source for scholars since it first appeared.

Like his father, Ibn al-Nadim copied and sold books in Baghdad and was clearly well educated. He knew the city's intellectual elite—everyone from leading poets and scholars of traditions to Christian philosophers and priests. He had studied with many of them and used them as sources for his work. Unlike many of his contemporaries, however, he does not seem to have traveled much. Other than a trip to the city of al-Mawsil (Mosul) in the north of Iraq, there are no reports of his leaving Baghdad.

Ibn al-Nadim wrote *The Catalogue* fairly late in life, completing the work by 988. Each of its ten chapters concentrates on a different subject area: the first on the scripts of different languages and the sacred texts of the Jews, Christians, and Muslims; the second on early grammarians; the third on the writings of historians and government officials; the fourth on poets; the fifth through eighth on theologians, jurists, philosophers, scientists, and storytellers; the ninth on religions and beliefs in India and China; and the tenth on alchemy.

Ibn al-Nadim introduces each chapter with a succinct survey of the history and current state of the subject area. An annotated listing of authors and their works follows. As a snapshot of scholarship and intellectual inquiry in tenth-century Baghdad, *The Catalogue* is of unique worth. It also offers the only information we have for some authors and preserves excerpts and descriptions of many lost works.

Below is the second section of *The Catalogue*'s first chapter, in which Ibn al-Nadim describes religious writings and scriptures that preceded the Qur'an. Note the careful approach to translation that Ibn al-Nadim cites and the sequence of revelation through the prophets, beginning with Adam.

PRONOUNCING GLOSSARY

ʿAbd Allāh ibn Salām: *ab-dul-lah´ ibn sa-lam´*
ʿAbd Yasūʿ ibn Bahrīz: *abd ya-soo´ ibn bah-reez´* (light *h*)
absūqāt: *ab-soo-qaht´*
Abū ʿIzzah: *a-boo iz´-zuh*
Aḥmad ibn ʿAbd Allāh ibn Salām: *ah´-mad* (heavy *h*) *ibn ab-dul-lah´ ibn sa-lam´*
Aḥmad ibn Isḥāq: *ah´-mad* (heavy *h*) *ibn is-hahq´* (heavy *h*)
al-Ma'mūn: *al-ma-moon´*
al-Mawṣil: *al-mou´-sil*
al-Nikut: *an-nee´-koot*
al-Ṣābiyūn al-Ibrāhīmīyah: *as-sah´-be-yoon al-ib-rah-hee´-mee-yuh*
al-Ṣūra: *as-soo´s-ruh*
al-zabūr: *az-za-bour´*
Baḥīr al-Rāhib: *ba-heer´* (heavy *h*) *ar-ra´-hib*
Dā'ūd: *da-ood´*
farāsah, farāsāt: *fa-ra´-suh, fa-ra-sat´*
Frāksīs: (=*praxeis*)
ḥadīth: *ha-deeth´* (heavy *h*)
Hafṭārōth: *haf-tah-rote´*
Ḥarrān: *har-ran´* (heavy *h*)
Hārūn al-Rashīd: *ha-roon´ ar-ra-sheed´*
Hazqīl: *haz-qeel´*
ḥunafā': *hoo-na-fa´* (heavy *h*)
Ibn al-Tīhān: *ibn at-tee-han´*
Ibrāhīm: *ib-rah-heem´*
Idrīs: *id-rees´*
Ikhnūkh: *ich-nooch´* (guttural *ch*)
Ilyās: *il-yas´*
Kaʿb al-Aḥbār: *kab al-ah-bar´* (heavy *h*)
Kasdānī: *kas-da´-nee*

Malkhā al-Mulūk: *mal-chahl-moo-louk´* (guttural *ch*)
Marqus al-Badawī: *mar´-qus al-ba´-da-wee*
Mishna: *mish´-nah*
Muḥammad ibn Isḥāq al-Nadīm: *moo-ham´-mad* (heavy *h*) *ibn is-hahq´* (heavy *h*) *an-na-deem´*
Mūsā: *moo´-sah*
Sa'īd (or Sa'dīya) al-Fayyūmī: *sa-eed´ (sad´-ya) al-feye-yoo´-mee*
Shīth: *sheeth*
Tawmā al-Ruhāwī: *taw-ma´ ar-roo-ha´-wee*
Wahb ibn Munabbih: *wahb* (light *h*) *ibn moo-nab´-bih* (light *h*)
Yāmīn ibn Yāmīn: *ya-meen´ ibn ya-meen´*
Yūnus: *yoo´-nus*
Yūsha' ibn Nūn: *yoo´-sha ibn noon´*
Yūsha' Yaḥb: *yoo´-sha yahb* (heavy *h*)

FROM THE CATALOGUE

The Second Section of the First Chapter, with the Titles of the Books of the Laws Revealed to the Community of Muslims and the Sects of the Peoples [through Revealed Books]

Thus saith Muḥammad ibn Isḥāq [al *Nadīm*]: I once read a book which fell into my hands, and which was an ancient transcription, apparently from the library of al-*Ma'mūn*.[1] In it the copyist mentions the names and numbers of the scriptures and revealed books, with their scope and with the things which most of the common people and the populace feel sure of and believe. I have recorded from it what is related to this book of mine. This statement in the wording of the [ancient] book is [the passage] from it which is needed by me. *Aḥmad* ibn 'Abd Allāh ibn Salām, a protégé of the Commander of the Faithful Hārūn,[2] whom I esteem as al-*Rashīd*, said:

> I have translated this book from a book of the *ḥunafā'* of al-Ṣābiyūn al-Ibrāhīmīyah,[3] who believed in *Ibrāhīm* [Abraham], for whom may there be peace, and who received from him the scripture revealed to him by Allāh.
>
> It is a long book, but I have deleted such material as is unnecessary for an understanding of the reasons which are mentioned for their disagreements and differences. I have introduced into it what is needed for proof of these things from the Qur'ān and the Ḥadīth coming from the Apostle, may Allāh bless him and give him peace, and from his Companions, as well as from the People of the Book[4] who became Muslims, among whom were *'Abd Allāh* ibn Salām,

TRANSLATED BY Bayard Dodge. All bracketed additions are the translator's.

1. Abu al-'Abbas 'Abdallah al-Ma'mun (786–833), the seventh 'Abbasid caliph, who supported the translation of Greek works into Arabic. He also proclaimed—contrary to the orthodox view—that the Qur'an was created and, in the last months of his rule, instituted a theological test referred to as the Inquisition.
2. Harun al-Rashid (763 or 766–809), the fifth 'Abbasid caliph, under whom the dynasty attained its greatest power. "Al-Rashid" means "the Upright"; "Commander of the Faithful" is a title often given to the caliph.
3. Likely a group of Sabians who were opposed to idolatry. *Hunafa'* is the plural of *hanif*, a term used for a pre-Islamic monotheist; see Qur'an 3:67 and Qur'an 6:74 [translator's note, edited].
4. A common qur'anic designation for the Jews and Christians.

Yāmīn ibn Yāmīn, *Wahb* ibn Munabbih, *Kaʿb* al-Aḥbār, Ibn al-*Tīhān*, and *Baḥīr* al-Rāhib (the Monk).

Aḥmad ibn ʿAbd Allāh ibn Salām [also] said:

I have translated the beginning of this book, and the Torah, the Gospels, and the books of the prophets and disciples from Hebrew, Greek, and Ṣābian, which are the languages of the people of each book, into Arabic, letter for letter. In so doing I did not wish to beautify or embellish the style for fear of inaccuracy. I added nothing to what I found in the book which I was translating and I subtracted nothing, unless there were words presented by the language of the people of that book with meanings which could not be clearly translated into Arabic except by transposing. Thus something coming last may not be clear unless it is placed first, so as to be understood in Arabic. For example, the words of one who says *āt māym tān* I have translated into Arabic as *māʾ hāt*, only I have placed *māʾ* (water) last and *hāt* (bring) first. So in translating these languages correctly into Arabic I seek the protection of Allāh lest I add or subtract, except in the manner which I have recorded and explained in this book.

In another place in the book he said:

The total number of prophets was one hundred and twenty-four thousand, three hundred and fifteen, among whom were those sent forth with revelation on their lips. The total number of books which Allāh Almighty revealed was one hundred and four. Among these Allāh Almighty revealed one hundred of the sacred scriptures between the times of *Adam* and *Mūsā* (Moses).

The first of these books revealed by Him [Allāh], honor to His name, were the sacred writings of Adam, for whom be peace, twenty-one in number. Allāh revealed to *Shīth* (Seth) for whom be peace, the second book, twenty-nine sacred writings. Allāh, may He be exalted, revealed the third book, thirty sacred writings, to *Ikhnūkh* (Enoch) who is Idrīs, may peace rest with him. The fourth book of ten sacred writings He, honor to His name, revealed to *Ibrāhīm* (Abraham), for whom be peace, and the fifth book of ten sacred writings to *Mūsā* (Moses). These are five books of one hundred sacred writings. Some time subsequent to these scriptures He, may He be blessed and exalted, revealed the Torah on ten tables to Mūsā (Moses), for whom be peace.

Aḥmad ibn ʿAbd Allāh recorded that the tables were green with the writing on them red like the rays of the sun, but *Aḥmad* ibn Isḥāq said that the Jews do not know about this characteristic. Aḥmad [ibn ʿAbd Allāh] also said:

When *Mūsā* (Moses) descended from the mountain and learned that his companions had been worshipping a calf, he threw down [the tables of stone] so that they were broken. Then he repented and asked Allāh, may He be glorified and honored, to give them to him again. So Allāh, honor to His name, revealed, "I will do it again with two tables." This Allāh did for him, one of the tablets being the "Table of the Covenant" and the other the "Table of Witnessing."[5]

Then Allāh, may He be glorified and honored, revealed to *Dāʾūd* (David) the Psalms, that is *al-zabūr*, which are one hundred and fifty in number and in the hands of the Jews and Christians.[6]

A STATEMENT ABOUT THE TORAH, WHICH IS IN THE HANDS OF THE JEWS, WITH THE NAMES OF THEIR BOOKS AND INFORMATION ABOUT THEIR SCHOLARS AND AUTHORS

When I asked one of their notable men about these matters, he said, "God, honor to His name, revealed to Moses the Torah in five fifths, each fifth divided into two parts and each part into a number of *farāsāt*, which means sūrahs, with every *farāsah* divided into a number of *absūqāt*, meaning verses."

He said that there is a book of Moses called the *Mishna*,[7] from which the Jews derive the science of the law, with the religious ordinances and judgments. It is a large book, its languages being Kasdānī and Hebrew.[8] In addition to that there were among the books of the prophets:

> Joshua; Judges; Samuel; the scripture of Isaiah; the scripture of Jeremiah; the scripture of Ezekiel; Kings, which is the scripture of David and his associates, known as "Malkhā al-Mulūk"[9]; the Prophets, comprising twelve minor scriptures. There are also books called Hafṭārōth derived from the books of the twelve prophets.

Among their books there are also:

> Ezra; Daniel; Job; Song of Songs; Lamentations; Ruth; Ecclesiastes; Psalms of David; Proverbs of Solomon; Record of the Days [Chronicles], containing the history of the kings and accounts about them; Ahasuerus, called the Megillah [Esther].[1]

Al-*Fayyūmī*[2] was one of the most eminent of the Jews and of their scholars who were versed in the Hebrew language. In fact the Jews consider that there was nobody else like al-Fayyūmī. His name was Saʿīd, also said to be Saʿdīyā, and he lived so recently that some of our contemporaries were alive before he died. Among his books there were:

> Origins; Sacred Laws; Commentary on Isaiah; Commentary on the Torah, arranged without explanation, Proverbs, in ten chapters; Commentary on the Decrees of David; Commentary on "Al-Nikut,"[3] which is an exposition of the Psalms of David, for whom be peace; Commentary on the Third Sacred Book of the Last Half of the Torah, with explanation; Commentary on the Book of

5. See Exodus 24:12; 31:18; 32:15. See also Qurʾan 7:148–54 [translator's note].
6. See Qurʾan 3:184 (181); 4:163 (161) [translator's note, edited].
7. The collection of oral rabbinic law that was codified ca. 200 C.E.
8. *Kaśdu* was an old Babylonian form for the people of Chaldea. This probably means that the languages were a Chaldean dialect and Hebrew [translator's note].
9. King of kings.

1. This book was evidently Esther, which was known in Hebrew as *Megilloth*. Sometimes, however, this term was used for Esther and four other books [translator's note].
2. The Arabic name of Saʿadia ben Joseph (882–942); born in Egypt, he became head of the Talmudic academy in Sura, Babylonia, and was one of the most important Jewish scholars of his time.
3. Evidently a transliteration of the Hebrew word *nekoth* ("treasure house") [translator's note].

Job; Establishment of Prayers and Sacred Laws; Events, which is a history.

REMARKS ABOUT THE GOSPEL OF THE CHRISTIANS, THE NAMES OF THEIR BOOKS, THEIR SCHOLARS, AND THEIR AUTHORS

I asked *Yūnus* the priest, who was an excellent man, about the books translated into the Arabic language which they expound and according to which they act. He replied, "Among them is the book *Al-Ṣūrah* (The Form) which is divided into two parts, the 'Old Form' and the 'New Form.'" He stated that the "Old [Form]" was the ancient basis for the Jewish sect and the "New [Form]" for the sect of the Christians. He also said that the "Old [Form]" depends upon a number of books, the first of which is the Torah, which is five sacred writings. [Then follows] a compilation comprising a number of books, among which are:

> Joshua, the Son of Nūn; The Tribes, which is the book of Judges; Samuel and the Judgment of David; Traditions of the Children of Israel; The Story of Ruth; Solomon, the Son of David, about wise sayings; Ecclesiastes [Qoheleth]; The Song of Songs; The Wisdom of Jesus, the Son of Sirach [Ecclesiasticus]. The Prophets, composed of four books: Isaiah the Prophet, for whom be peace; Jeremiah the Prophet, for whom be peace; The Twelve Prophets, for whom be peace; Ezekiel. The New Form, which is composed of four gospels: The Gospel of Matthew; The Gospel of Mark; The Gospel of Luke; The Gospel of John. Book of the Disciples, known as Frāksīs [Acts]; Paul the Apostle, twenty-four epistles.

They also have books about the religious law and the judgments of their community, among which are the books of the synods, western and eastern,[4] each of which contains a number of chapters of legal decisions.

One of their authorities on the religious law and judicial interpretations was Ibn *Bahrīz*,[5] whose name was ʿAbd Yasūʿ. He was at first the metropolitan of Ḥarrān and subsequently became the metropolitan of al-Mawṣil and Ḥarrah.[6] He wrote epistles and books.

There was also the book of *Marqus* the Jacobite,[7] who was known as al-Bādawī. It was a reply to two books, which refuted his doctrine and denying the oneness of the Trinity professed by the Jacobites and Melchites.[8]

Ibn Bahrīz was learned, his scholarship approaching that of Islām. He translated a great deal of material from books about logic and philosophy. There was also *Pethiōn*, who was the most accurate of the translators from the point of view of translation, also the best of them for style and diction. There were *Theodorus* and *Yūshaʿ* Yaḥb, *Hazqīl* (Ezekiel), *Timotheus*, and *Yūshaʿ* ibn Nūn, who were translators and commentators. We shall give accounts about them in the chapter on the ancient sciences [Chapter VII].

4. Associated with Catholic Christianity and Orthodox Christianity, respectively.
5. A Syrian (d. 833).
6. Mosul and al-Harra are in Iraq. Harran, an ancient city on a major trade route, is in present-day southeast Turkey.
7. Jacob Burdeana [or Baradeus; d. 578], a metropolitan of the Syrian Orthodox Church, after whom the Jacobite church is called [translator's note].
8. Those Christians of Syria and Egypt who, like the Byzantine emperor, accepted that Christ had two distinct but unified natures, human and divine.

Among their learned men there was *Tawmā* al-Ruhāwī (Thomas of Ruhā' *or* Edessa),[9] who wrote an epistle to his sister about what took place between him and the opposition at Alexandria. There was also *Ilyās* (Elias), the metropolitan of Damascus, who wrote a book, *The Call*, as well as Abū *'Izzah*, the Melchite bishop of Ḥarrān, among whose works there was a book in which he defamed *Nestorius*[1] the leader. A group has denounced him.

9. The apostle also known as "Doubting Thomas" or "the Twin" (d. 53); his proselytizing took him as far east as India.

1. The patriarch of Constantinople (428–31; d. ca. 451), banished for teaching that Christ had human and divine natures that remained independent.

IBN MUNQIDH
1095–1188

Although Usama Ibn Munqidh served as a diplomat and soldier for several rulers in Syria and Egypt, he is best known as a literary figure. His poetry became famous in his own lifetime, as did his literary and historical works, most of which have now been lost. Yet we still have his *Book of Instruction by Example*, a memoir of anecdotes and reflections that continues to attract the interest of historians.

Ibn Munqidh was a member of the Banu Munqidh, a notable Syrian clan that played an important role in the country's political life from the middle of the eleventh to the end of the twelfth century. Their loss of power was hastened by a natural disaster. In 1157 many in the clan had assembled for a feast in Shayzar, their hometown and Ibn Munqidh's birthplace, when a massive earthquake struck, devastating large parts of Syria and destroying the building in which they had congregated. Ibn Munqidh was absent from the gathering, but most members of the Banu Munqidh died.

The territory controlled by the Munqidh clan was centered in an area contested by stronger powers in the region, such as the Christian Franks, the Nizari Isma'ili Assassins, and the Turkish Seljuks. The Banu Munqidh frequently had to defend their territory from attacks launched by competing Muslim, Christian, and combined Muslim and Christian forces. To protect its interests, in 1122 the clan allied itself with 'Imad al-Din Zangi (r. 1127–46), founder of the Syrian Zangid dynasty. Ibn Munqidh entered Zangi's service in 1131 and remained with him until 1138, when a clan power struggle led to Ibn Munqidh's banishment, and that of his brothers, from Shayzar.

Next, Ibn Munqidh went to Damascus, where he joined the retinue of Mu'in al-Din Unur (d. 1149), the administrator of the city for the Turkish Burid dynasty (1104–54). Mu'in al-Din maintained cordial relations with the Christian Frankish kingdoms in the region, such as those of Jerusalem, Antioch, and Edessa. As a military officer and diplomat for Mu'in al-Din, Ibn Munqidh traveled to these Christian kingdoms to negotiate security arrangements (organizing defenses against common Muslim foes) or to ransom hostages. He was forced to leave Damascus in 1144, perhaps because of involvement in political intrigues.

By that time nearly fifty, and effectively blacklisted from service in Syria, Ibn Munqidh found employment in Egypt, functioning as a diplomat for the Fatimid minister Ibn al-Sallar (d. 1153). Ibn al-Sallar asked Ibn Munqidh to form an alliance with the new Zangid ruler, Nur al-Din Mahmud (the son of 'Imad al-Din Zangi;

d. 1174), to defend Fatimid interests against the Franks. Ibn Munqidh remained in the service of the Fatimids until 1154, when accusations of complicity in the plots leading to the murder of Ibn al-Sallar in 1153 and the Fatimid caliph Zafir in 1154 forced him to flee.

Approaching his seventh decade, he joined the retinue of Nur al-Din Mahmud, who had recently gained control of Damascus, and apparently worked to promote Nur al-Din's policies in the region. He stayed with Nur al-Din until 1164, when he accepted an offer to join the court of the Turkish Artukid dynasty and moved to their capital city of Hisn Kayfa, located about 500 miles east of Konya in modern-day Turkey. In Hisn Kayfa he devoted himself to writing and began to frequent the city's Sufi circles. In 1174, at almost eighty years of age, he returned to Damascus by invitation of the famous Salah al-Din (1137/38–1193), known in the West as Saladin, who had taken control of the city following Nur al-Din's death. There, he completed some of his most noted works, including the *Book of Instruction by Example.*

The *Book of Instruction by Example* is the work of a man in the final years of his life. A few sections are arranged chronologically, but it consists primarily of interesting anecdotes and observations from Ibn Munqidh's life, a few of which he uses to illustrate some larger point. For example, he provides stories that point to the predestination of life or the tribulations of living too long, a subject of his complaints. His time in Egypt, his interaction with the Franks, his battles, and his hunting experiences were all sources for his stories.

As the selection that follows demonstrates, Ibn Munqidh clearly found the Christian Crusaders, who had conquered and colonized cities in Syria and Palestine, both fascinating and repellant. His keen eye and quick sensibility captured details that have delighted centuries of readers.

PRONOUNCING GLOSSARY

abu-al-Fatḥ: *a-bul-fat'h* (heavy *h*)
al-Amīr Muʿīn-al-Dīn: *al-a-meer´ moo-ee´-nad-deen*
al-Munayṭirah: *al-moo-nay´-ti-ruh*
Aqṣa: *ahq´-suh*
Muʿizz: *moo-iz´*
Nāblus: *nab´-loos*
qiblah: *qib´-luh*
Shayzar: *shay´-zar*
Thābit: *tha´-bit*
Usāmah: *oo-sa´-muh*

FROM THE BOOK OF INSTRUCTION BY EXAMPLE

From *An Appreciation of the Frankish Character*

Their lack of sense.—Mysterious are the works of the Creator, the author of all things! When one comes to recount cases regarding the Franks,[1] he cannot but glorify Allah (exalted is he!) and sanctify him, for he sees them as animals possessing the virtues of courage and fighting, but nothing else; just as animals have only the virtues of strength and carrying loads. I shall now give some instances of their doings and their curious mentality.

In the army of King Fulk,[2] son of Fulk, was a Frankish reverend knight who had just arrived from their land in order to make the holy pilgrimage[3]

TRANSLATED BY Philip K. Hitti.

1. A label applied by Arabs of the eastern Mediterranean to all Europeans.
2. King of Jerusalem (r. 1131–43), and count of Anjou and Maine.
3. To Jerusalem and other sites associated with the life of Jesus.

and then return home. He was of my intimate fellowship and kept such constant company with me that he began to call me "my brother." Between us were mutual bonds of amity and friendship. When he resolved to return by sea to his homeland, he said to me:

> My brother, I am leaving for my country and I want thee to send with me thy son (my son, who was then fourteen years old, was at that time in my company) to our country, where he can see the knights and learn wisdom and chivalry. When he returns, he will be like a wise man.

Thus there fell upon my ears words which would never come out of the head of a sensible man; for even if my son were to be taken captive, his captivity could not bring him a worse misfortune than carrying him into the lands of the Franks. However, I said to the man:

> By thy life, this has exactly been my idea. But the only thing that prevented me from carrying it out was the fact that his grandmother, my mother, is so fond of him and did not this time let him come out with me until she exacted an oath from me to the effect that I would return him to her.

Thereupon he asked, "Is thy mother still alive?" "Yes." I replied. "Well," said he, "disobey her not."

Their curious medication.—A case illustrating their curious medicine is the following:

The lord of al-Munayṭirah[4] wrote to my uncle asking him to dispatch a physician to treat certain sick persons among his people. My uncle sent him a Christian physician named Thābit. Thābit was absent but ten days when he returned. So we said to him, "How quickly hast thou healed thy patients!" He said:

> They brought before me a knight in whose leg an abscess had grown; and a woman afflicted with imbecility. To the knight I applied a small poultice until the abscess opened and became well; and the woman I put on diet and made her humor wet. Then a Frankish physician came to them and said, "This man knows nothing about treating them." He then said to the knight, "Which wouldst thou prefer, living with one leg or dying with two?" The latter replied, "Living with one leg." The physician said, "Bring me a strong knight and a sharp ax." A knight came with the ax. And I was standing by. Then the physician laid the leg of the patient on a block of wood and bade the knight strike his leg with the ax and chop it off at one blow. Accordingly he struck it—while I was looking on—one blow, but the leg was not severed. He dealt another blow, upon which the marrow of the leg flowed out and the patient died on the spot. He then examined the woman and said, "This is a woman in whose head there is a devil which has possessed her. Shave off her hair." Accordingly they shaved it off and the woman began once more to eat their ordinary diet—garlic and mustard. Her

4. A city in Lebanon west of the Bekaa Valley.

> imbecility took a turn for the worse. The physician then said, "The devil has penetrated through her head." He therefore took a razor, made a deep cruciform incision on it, peeled off the skin at the middle of the incision until the bone of the skull was exposed and rubbed it with salt. The woman also expired instantly. Thereupon I asked them whether my services were needed any longer, and when they replied in the negative I returned home, having learned of their medicine what I knew not before.

I have, however, witnessed a case of their medicine which was quite different from that.

The king of the Franks had for treasurer a knight named Bernard [*barnād*], who (may Allah's curse be upon him!) was one of the most accursed and wicked among the Franks. A horse kicked him in the leg, which was subsequently infected and which opened in fourteen different places. Every time one of these cuts would close in one place, another would open in another place. All this happened while I was praying for his perdition. Then came to him a Frankish physician and removed from the leg all the ointments which were on it and began to wash it with very strong vinegar. By this treatment all the cuts were healed and the man became well again. He was up again like a devil.

Another case illustrating their curious medicine is the following:

In Shayzar we had an artisan named abu-al-Fatḥ, who had a boy whose neck was afflicted with scrofula. Every time a part of it would close, another part would open. This man happened to go to Antioch on business of his, accompanied by his son. A Frank noticed the boy and asked his father about him. Abu-al-Fatḥ replied, "This is my son." The Frank said to him, "Wilt thou swear by thy religion that if I prescribe to thee a medicine which will cure thy boy, thou wilt charge nobody fees for prescribing it thyself? In that case, I shall prescribe to thee a medicine which will cure the boy." The man took the oath and the Frank said:

> Take uncrushed leaves of glasswort, burn them, then soak the ashes in olive oil and sharp vinegar. Treat the scrofula with them until the spot on which it is growing is eaten up. Then take burnt lead, soak it in ghee butter [*samn*] and treat him with it. That will cure him.

The father treated the boy accordingly, and the boy was cured. The sores closed and the boy returned to his normal condition of health.

I have myself treated with this medicine many who were afflicted with such disease, and the treatment was successful in removing the cause of the complaint.

Newly arrived Franks are especially rough: One insists that Usāmah should pray eastward.—Everyone who is a fresh emigrant from the Frankish lands is ruder in character than those who have become acclimatized and have held long association with the Moslems. Here is an illustration of their rude character.

Whenever I visited Jerusalem I always entered the Aqṣa Mosque, beside which stood a small mosque which the Franks had converted into a church. When I used to enter the Aqṣa Mosque, which was occupied by the

Templars[5] [*al-dāwiyyah*], who were my friends, the Templars would evacuate the little adjoining mosque so that I might pray in it. One day I entered this mosque, repeated the first formula, "Allah is great," and stood up in the act of praying, upon which one of the Franks rushed on me, got hold of me and turned my face eastward saying, "This is the way thou shouldst pray!" A group of Templars hastened to him, seized him and repelled him from me. I resumed my prayer. The same man, while the others were otherwise busy, rushed once more on me and turned my face eastward, saying, "This is the way thou shouldst pray!" The Templars again came in to him and expelled him. They apologized to me, saying, "This is a stranger who has only recently arrived from the land of the Franks and he has never before seen anyone praying except eastward." Thereupon I said to myself, "I have had enough prayer." So I went out and have ever been surprised at the conduct of this devil of a man, at the change in the color of his face, his trembling and his sentiment at the sight of one praying towards the *qiblah*.[6]

Another wants to show to a Moslem God as a child.—I saw one of the Franks come to al-Amīr Muʿīn-al-Dīn (may Allah's mercy rest upon his soul!) when he was in the Dome of the Rock[7] and say to him, "Dost thou want to see God as a child?" Muʿīn-al-Dīn said, "Yes." The Frank walked ahead of us until he showed us the picture of Mary with Christ (may peace be upon him!) as an infant in her lap. He then said, "This is God as a child." But Allah is exalted far above what the infidels say about him!

Franks lack jealousy in sex affairs.—The Franks are void of all zeal and jealousy. One of them may be walking along with his wife. He meets another man who takes the wife by the hand and steps aside to converse with her while the husband is standing on one side waiting for his wife to conclude the conversation. If she lingers too long for him, he leaves her alone with the conversant and goes away.

Here is an illustration which I myself witnessed:

When I used to visit Nāblus,[8] I always took lodging with a man named Muʿizz, whose home was a lodging house for the Moslems. The house had windows which opened to the road, and there stood opposite to it on the other side of the road a house belonging to a Frank who sold wine for the merchants. He would take some wine in a bottle and go around announcing it by shouting, "So and so, the merchant, has just opened a cask full of this wine. He who wants to buy some of it will find it in such and such a place." The Frank's pay for the announcement made would be the wine in that bottle. One day this Frank went home and found a man with his wife in the same bed. He asked him, "What could have made thee enter into my wife's room?" The man replied, "I was tired, so I went in to rest." "But how," asked he, "didst thou get into my bed?" The other replied, "I found a bed that was

5. Members of a military and religious order, originally founded ca. 1120 to protect Christian pilgrims to the Holy Land.
6. The point that Muslims face in prayer—toward the Kaʿba, the stone shrine in Mecca that is Islam's most important shrine.
7. A shrine on the site from which Muhammad was believed to have made his night flight to heaven (see "The Story of the Night Journey," p. 167). Muʿin al-Din Unur (d. 1149), administrator of Damascus (1140–49).
8. A city 30 miles north of Jerusalem, in what is now the West Bank.

spread, so I slept in it." "But," said he, "my wife was sleeping together with thee!" The other replied, "Well, the bed is hers. How could I therefore have prevented her from using her own bed?" "By the truth of my religion," said the husband, "if thou shouldst do it again, thou and I would have a quarrel." Such was for the Frank the entire expression of his disapproval and the limit of his jealousy.

* * *

IBN JUBAYR
1145–1217

Muhammad ibn Ahmad Ibn Jubayr's *Travels* is among the most famous examples of a genre of Islamic literature that chronicled and celebrated journeys undertaken for learning, for spiritual seeking, and for religious pilgrimage.

Born in Valencia, Spain, Ibn Jubayr was the son of a government administrator, and after completing his education, he obtained a secretarial position with the governor of Granada. As legend has it, Ibn Jubayr was meeting with the governor when the latter offered him some wine. Although he at first refused, he eventually felt compelled to accept. A devout Muslim, Ibn Jubayr regretted his decision and sought to atone for it by making the pilgrimage to Mecca.

In February 1183 he embarked from Ceuta, Spain, on a Genoese ship. A month later, the ship docked in Alexandria, Egypt, and after passing through Cairo and crossing the Red Sea, Ibn Jubayr reached Mecca. He completed the pilgrimage in March 1183 and remained in Mecca for about nine months. Afterward, he traveled to other cities in the region, including Baghdad and Damascus. He began his return in October 1184, departing from Acre, located in the Crusader kingdom of Jerusalem, on a Genoese ship filled with Christian pilgrims and a smaller number of Muslims. Ibn Jubayr was shipwrecked off the coast of Sicily but was later able to gain passage on another ship to Spain. He reached Granada at the end of April 1185, after more than two years of traveling. He returned to the East twice—in his mid-forties (1189–91) and in his seventies, when he left Spain in 1217 for Alexandria, where he died—but he left no report of those journeys.

Ibn Jubayr's *Travels* is a meticulous account of his pilgrimage to Mecca and the trips associated with it. The work serves as a model for later writers, such as Ibn Battuta (1304–ca. 1368; see below), who record their travels while on a quest for learning or making the pilgrimage. The work is of great historical value because of Ibn Jubayr's precise record keeping (he provides monthly entries with both Christian and Muslim dates), his detailed descriptions of the locales he visits, and his balanced commentary on the events that befall him and on the cultures he encounters. For example, his description of the thriving Arab-Norman culture of Sicily, which he experienced while shipwrecked there, documents the policies of William II (r. 1166–89) toward his Muslim subjects and the degree to which Muslim practices pervaded the life of the island.

The passage below is Ibn Jubayr's detailed and rich description of the Kaʿba and the mosque surrounding it. The entry was composed during the nine months Ibn Jubayr remained in Mecca after completing his pilgrimage.

PRONOUNCING GLOSSAY

ʿAbbas: *ab-bas´*
ʿAbbaside: *ab-bas´-id*
Abu'l-Abbas Ahmad al-Nasir ibn al-Mustadi' billah Abu Muhammad al-Hasan ibn al-Mustanjid billah Abu'l-Muzaffar Yusuf al-ʿAbbasi: *a-bool-ab-bas´ ah´-mad* (heavy *h*) *an-nah´-sir ibn al-moos-tah´-di bil-lah´ a-boo moo-ham´-mad* (heavy *h*) *al-ha´-san* (heavy *h*) *ibn al-moos-tan´-jid bil-lah´ a-bool-moo-dhahf´-far you´-suf al-ab-ba´-see*
al-Maʿjan: *al-ma´-jan*
al-Mustajar: *al-moos-ta-jar´*
al-Sharabiyyah: *ash-sha-rah´-bee-yuh*
Bab al-Rahmah: *bab ar-rah´-muh* (heavy *h*)
Bab al-Safa: *bab as-sa-fah´*
Bab al-Taubah: *bab at-taw´-buh*
Bakkah: *bak´-kuh*
Banu Shayba: *ba-noo shay´-buh*
dawraq: *daw´-rahq*
dīnār: *dee-nar´*
Hajar: *ha´-jar*
Haram: *ha´-ram* (heavy *h*)
Hijr: *hijr* (heavy *h*)
Imam al-Nasir li Din Ilah: *ee-mam´ al-na´-sir li-deen i-laa´*
Ismaʿil: *is-mah-eel´*
Jumada 'l-Ula: *joo-ma´-dal-oo´´-luh*
Kaʿbah: *ka´-buh*
Khurasan: *choo-ra-sahn´* (guttural *ch*)
maqam: *ma-qahm´*
mihrab: *mih-rahb´* (heavy *h*)
Mizab: *mee-zab´*
Muhammad ibn Ismaʿil ibn ʿAbd al-Rahman: *moo-ham´-mad* (heavy *h*) *ibn is-mah-eel´ ibn ab-dur-rah-man´* (heavy *h*)
Multazam: *mool-ta´-zam*
musalla: *moo-sahl´-luh*
qabbat al-Sharab: *qah´-bat ash-sha-rab´*
Qarmata: *qar´-mah-tah*
Quraysh: *qoo-raysh´*
Rukn al-Yamani: *rook´-nal-ya´´-ma-nee*
shaut: *shout*
tawaf: *tah-wahf´*
ʿUthman ibn Talhah ibn Shaybah ibn Talhah ibn ʿAbd al-Dar: *uth-man´ ibn tahl´-hah* (heavy *h*) *ibn shay´-buh ibn tahl´-hah* (heavy *h*) *ibn ab-dad-dahr´*
Zamzam: *zam´-zam*

FROM THE TRAVELS

From *The Month of Jumada 'l-Ula* (579)

[*22nd of August–20th of September,* 1183]

May God let us know His favour

The new moon rose on the night of Monday the 22nd of August, when we had been in Mecca—may God Most High exalt it—eighteen days. The new moon of this month was the most auspicious our eyes had seen in all that had passed of our life. It rose after we had already entered the seat of the venerable enclosure, the sacred Haram of God,[1] the dome in which is the maqam[2] of Abraham, the place from whence the Prophet's mission (was sent out), and the alighting place of the faithful spirit Gabriel with inspiration and revelation. May God with His power and strength inspire us to

Translated by R. J. C. Broadhurst. All bracketed additions are the translator's.

1. The Great Mosque in Mecca, which surrounds the Kaʿba ("the Cube"—a stone shrine that became the most important site in Islam; Muslims around the world face it when they pray).
2. Station (Arabic): a stone slab near the Kaʿba bearing Abraham's footprints. Supplications made near this stone are believed to be particularly efficacious, and Muhammad is said to have prayed near this stone when performing the pilgrimage.

ISLAM

Minaret of the Kalyan Mosque, Bukhara, Central Asia, 1127

This minaret exemplifies the architectural style of brick layering that creates textured surfaces resembling weaving. As in any mosque, a muezzin would stand at the minaret's summit, calling Muslims to prayer at the appointed times. ALAMY

Interior view, Shah Mosque, Isfahan, Iran, 1611

The Shah Mosque was built by the Safavid ruler Shah 'Abbas. Islamic architecture typically attempts to manifest certain symbolisms, and the geometrical precision of this dome's interior represents celestial order. The tiled ornamentation illustrates the propensity of Persian artists to infuse floral motifs into their designs.

Shi'i mihrab rug, likely from central Iran, ca. 1570–80

Small rugs were sometimes hung on walls facing Mecca to serve as a mihrab, or a niche that indicates the direction of prayer. Embroidered into this rug are the Throne Verse (2:255) and 33:56 ("Truly God and His angels bless the Prophet; oh, you who believe, bless him and surrender to his guidance"): both feature prominently in daily Shi'i prayer. © THE NASSER D. KHALILI COLLECTION OF ISLAMIC ART / NOUR FOUNDATION. COURTESY OF THE KHALILI FAMILY TRUST

e ladies of Zulaykha astonished by the uty of Joseph. From a "Falnamah," India, Deccam, probably Golconda, ca. 1610–30

s illustration from the Chapter of Joseph (Q12: a Yusef) depicts the amazement of the Egyptian nen who laid eyes on the beauty of Joseph. The r'an explains that they were so overcome as they dining that they inadvertently cut themselves h the knives placed before them. © THE NASSER HALILI COLLECTION OF ISLAMIC ART / NOUR NDATION. COURTESY OF THE KHALILI FAMILY TRUST

Cursive calligraphy adorning the Wazir Khan Mosque in Lahore, 1634

The Arabic reads, "A believer in the mosque is like a fish in water, and the hypocrite in the mosque is like a bird in a cage." This adage is found in the book of prophetic sayings, or *jami'*, compiled by the Persian hadith collector Muhammad ibn 'Isa al-Tirmidhi (d. ca. 892).
AKG-IMAGES / GERARD DEGEORGE

Muslim pilgrims touching door of the Ka'ba, Mecca, Saudi Arabia, 2012

Muslims during the hajj have the opportunity to be close to the Ka'ba, the cubical house of worship that embodies the center of Muslim spiritual consciousness. The structure's history mirrors Islam's self-presentation as a continuation of the monotheistic traditions that came before. It is believed to have been originally sent down from heaven for use by Adam, destroyed by Noah's flood, rebuilt by Abraham and his son Ishmael, and eventually purified of idolatrous accretions by Muhammad. It is toward this cube that the globe's Muslims, in a display of unity, direct their earthly prayers.
MEHMET BIBER

African pilgrims at the Mosque of the prophet in Medina, 1999

It is now traditional for those undertaking the hajj to journey to the Mosque of the prophet Muhammad. The original mosque, which Muhammad helped build, was adjacent to his simple living quarters. The elaborate mosque that replaced that open-air structure houses the tombs of Muhammad and of Abu Bakr (573–634) and 'Umar (ca. 586–644), his companions and successors.

Mirador de Lindaraja, the Alhambra, Spain, mid-14th century

The Alhambra (a name derived from the Arabic phrase meaning "red fortress") is a palatial complex that has adorned the highest hill in Granada since Muslim rule. Completed in the mid-14th century, it is now a major tourist attraction; its ornamental Arabic inscriptions are masterpieces of epigraphic art in Andalusia. This photograph shows a detail from the Mirador de Lindaraja, or the "Gazebo of the Fountain of the Home of A'isha." LUCAS VALLECILLOS / AGE FOTOSTOCK / SUPERSTOCK

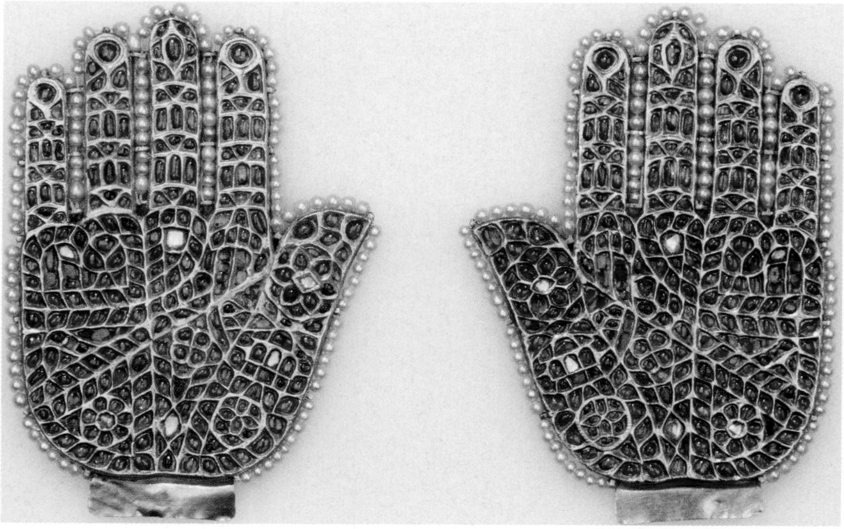

Shi'i amulets representing the hands of Fatima, India (possibly Hyderabad, Deccan), late 18th or early 19th century

The pair of amulets symbolize reverence for the holy family of Muhammad through his daughter Fatima (d. 633), who was married to 'Ali (d. 661), the spiritual father of Shi'ism and the father of Hasan (624–680) and Husayn (Shi'ism's great martyr, 626–680). In many Eastern cultures, the hand symbol was believed to offer protection against the evil eye. THE NASSER D. KHALILI COLLECTION

Sain Zahoor, Oslo, Norway, 2011

In Hindi, *mela* means "gathering." The mela festival is a cultural gathering that has spread worldwide as a celebration of global arts and entertainment. Here, the famed Sufi Sain Zahoor performs at one such international festival in Norway. Zahoor, who is illiterate, entrances his listeners by singing Sufi poetry. He won an international artist award from the British Broadcasting Corporation in 2006, and he has released several albums. © PÅL BERGSTAD / DEMOTIX / CORBIS

Indonesian boy practicing calligraphy, 2006

Muslims have taken the art of calligraphy very seriously since at least the ninth and tenth centuries, when Arabic writing and rules of grammar were standardized. Many beautiful examples of Arabic script adorn mosques and artworks throughout the Islamic world, and even non-Muslims have been known to pursue the art, most notably in Japan. This photograph was taken at the Lemka Qur'anic Calligraphy Boarding School in Sukabami, West Java. © ENNY NURAHENI / REUTERS / CORBIS

Hassan II Mosque, Casablanca, Morocco

In 1993, the Hassan II Mosque was completed in Casablanca, Morocco. The French builders engaged local artisans and master craftsmen to attend to the elaborately detailed adornments of the highest mosque in the world (ca. 690 feet). Hassan II ruled Morocco as king from 1961 until his death in 1999. © JP LAFFONT / SYGMA / CORBIS thanks for His favour and make us sensible of that amount of privilege He has made our portion, finally accepting us (into Paradise) and rewarding us with the accustomed generosity of His beneficent works, and giving us of His gracious help and support. There is no God but He.

A DESCRIPTION OF THE SACRED MOSQUE AND THE ANCIENT HOUSE

May God bless and exalt it

The venerable House[3] has four corners and is almost square. The chief of the Banu Shayba[4] who are the custodians of the House, one Muhammad ibn Isma'il ibn 'Abd al-Rahman ibn * * * * of the stock of 'Uthman ibn Talhah ibn Shaybah ibn Talhah ibn 'Abd al-Dar, the Companion of the Prophet—may God bless and preserve him—and the incumbent of the chamberlainship of the House, informed me that its height, on the side which faces the Bab [Gate] al-Safa and which extends from the Black Stone[5] to the Rukn al-Yamani [Yemen Corner], is twenty-nine cubits.[6] The remaining sides are twenty-eight cubits because of the slope of the roof towards the water-spout.

The principal corner is the one containing the Black Stone. There the circumambulation begins,[7] the circumambulator drawing back (a little) from it so that all of his body might pass by it, the blessed House being on his left. The first thing that is met after that is the 'Iraq corner, which faces the north, then the Syrian corner which faces west, then the Yemen corner which faces south, and then back to the Black corner which faces east. That completes one *shaut* [single course]. The door of the blessed House is on the side between the 'Iraq corner and the Black Stone corner, and is close to the Stone at a distance of barely ten spans.[8] That part of the side of the House which is between them is called the Multazam: a place where prayers are answered.

The venerable door is raised above the ground eleven and a half spans. It is of silver gilt and of exquisite workmanship and beautiful design, holding the eyes for its excellence and in emotion for the awe God has clothed His House in. After the same fashion are the two posts, and the upper lintel over which is a slab of pure gold about two spans long. The door has two large silver staples on which is hung the lock. It faces to the east, and is eight spans wide and thirteen high. The thickness of the wall in which it turns is five spans. The inside of the blessed House is overlaid with variegated marbles, and the walls are all variegated marbles. (The ceiling) is sustained by three teak pillars of great height, four paces apart, and punctuating the length of the House, and down its middle. One of these columns, the first, faces the centre of the side enclosed by the two Yemen corners, and is three paces distant from it. The third column, the last, faces the side enclosed by the 'Iraq and Syrian corners.

3. The Ka'ba.
4. A Meccan family ("Banu" means "the sons of" or "the children of").
5. A stone fixed in a setting of silver metal in the eastern corner of the Ka'ba. Because Muhammad kissed it while performing the pilgrimage, Muslims do the same.
6. About 50 feet (1 cubit=ca. 21 inches).
7. As part of the hajj, Muslims walk around the Ka'ba seven times.
8. About 90 inches.

The whole circuit of the upper half of the House is plated with silver, thickly gilt, which the beholder would imagine, from its thickness, to be a sheet of gold. It encompasses the four sides and covers the upper half of the walls. The ceiling of the House is covered by a veil of coloured silk.

The outside of the Kaʿbah, on all its four sides, is clothed in coverings of green silk with cotton warps; and on their upper parts is a band of red silk on which is written the verse, 'Verily the first House founded for mankind was that at Bakkah [Mecca]' [Koran III, 96]. The name of the Imam al-Nasir li Din Ilah,[9] in depth three cubits, encircles it all. On these coverings there has been shaped remarkable designs resembling handsome pulpits, and inscriptions entertaining the name of God Most High and calling blessings on Nasir, the aforementioned ʿAbbaside (Caliph) who had ordered its instalment. With all this, there was no clash of colour. The number of covers on all four sides is thirty-four, there being eighteen on the two long sides, and sixteen on the two short sides.

The Kaʿbah has five windows of ʿIraq glass, richly stained. One of them is in the middle of the ceiling, and at each corner is a window, one of which is not seen because it is beneath the vaulted passage described later. Between the pillars (hang) thirteen vessels, of silver save one that is gold.

The first thing which he who enters at the door will find to his left is the corner outside which is the Black Stone. Here are two chests containing Korans. Above them in the corner are two small silver doors like windows set in the angle of the corner, and more than a man's stature from the ground. In the angle which follows, the Yemen, it is the same, but the doors have been torn out and only the wood to which they were attached remains. In the Syrian corner it is the same and the small doors remain. It is the same in the ʿIraq corner, which is to the right of him who enters. In the ʿIraq corner is a door called the Bab al-Rahmah [Door of Mercy, usually called the Door of Repentance, Bab al-Taubah] from which ascent is made to the roof of the blessed House. It leads to a vaulted passage connecting with the roof of the House and having in it a stairway and, at its beginning, the vault containing the venerable maqam [the standing-stone of Abraham]. Because of this passage the Ancient House has five corners. The height of both its sides is two statures[1] and it encloses the ʿIraq corner with the halves of each of those two sides. Two-thirds of the circuit of this passage is dressed with pieces of coloured silk, as if it had been previously wrapped in them and then set in place.

This venerable maqam that is inside the passage is the maqam of Abraham—God's blessings on our Prophet and on him—and is a stone covered with silver. Its height is three spans, its width two and its upper part is larger than the lower. If it is not frivolous to draw the comparison it is like a large potter's oven, its middle being narrower than its top or bottom. We gazed upon it and were blessed by touching and kissing it. The water of Zamzam[2] was poured for us into the imprints of the two blessed feet [of Abraham who stood on this stone when he built the Kaʿbah], and we drank it—may God profit us by it. The traces of both feet are visible, as are the traces of the honoured and blessed big toes. Glory to God who softened the

9. The thirty-fourth ʿAbbasid caliph (r. 1180–1225).

1. That is, twice a man's height.

2. A venerated well about 65 feet east of the Kaʿba.

stone beneath the tread so that it left its trace as no trace of foot is left in the soft sand. Glory to God who made it a manifest sign. The contemplation of this maqam and the venerable House is an awful sight which distracts the senses in amazement, and ravishes the heart and mind. You will see only reverent gazes, flowing tears, eyes dissolved in weeping, and tongues in humble entreaty to Great and Glorious God.

Between the venerable door and the ʿIraq corner is a basin twelve spans long, five and a half spans wide, and about one in depth. It runs from opposite the door post, on the side of the ʿIraq corner, towards that corner, and is the mark of the place of the maqam at the time of Abraham—on whom be (eternal) happiness—until the Prophet—may God bless and preserve him—moved it to the place where now it is a musalla [place of worship]. The basin remained as a conduit for the water of the House when it is washed. It is a blessed spot [called al-Maʿjan] and is said to be one of the pools of Paradise, with men crowding to pray at it. Its bottom is spread with soft white sand.

The place of the venerated Maqam, behind which prayers are said, faces the space between the blessed door and the ʿIraq corner, well towards the side of the door. Over it is a wooden dome, a man's stature or more high, angulated and sharp-edged [i.e. pyramidal], of excellent modelling, and having four spans from one angle to another. It was erected on the place where once was the maqam [standing-stone], and around it is a stone projection built on the edge like an oblong basin about a span deep, five paces long, and three paces wide. The maqam was put into the place we have described in the blessed House as a measure of safety. Between the maqam and the side of the House opposite it lie seventeen paces, a pace being three spans. The place of the Maqam also has a dome made of steel and placed beside the dome of Zamzam. During the months of the pilgrimage, when many men have assembled and those from ʿIraq and Khurasan[3] have arrived, the wooden dome is removed and the steel dome put in its place that it might better support the press of men.

From the corner containing the Black Stone to the ʿIraq corner is scarcely fifty-four spans. From the Black Stone to the ground is six spans, so that the tall man must bend to it and the short man raise himself (to kiss it). From the ʿIraq corner to the Syrian corner is scarcely forty-eight spans, and that is through the inside of the Hijr[4] [an adjacent enclosure]; but around it from the one corner to the other is forty paces or almost one hundred and twenty spans. The *tawaf* [circumambulator] moves outside. (The distance from) the Syrian corner to the Yemen corner is the same as that from the Black corner to the ʿIraq corner for they are opposite sides. From the Yemen to the Black is the same, inside the Hijr, as from the ʿIraq to the Syrian for they are opposite sides.

The place of circumambulation is paved with wide stones like marble [they are in fact of fine polished granite] and very beautiful, some black, some brown and some white. They are joined to each other, and reach nine paces from the House save in the part facing the Maqam where they reach out to embrace it. The remainder of the Haram, including the colonnades,

3. The northeast region of Iran.
4. The area between the Kaʿba and the Hatim, a low-lying semicircular wall (3 feet high and 5 feet wide) that starts 6 feet from the northern corner of the Kaʿba and curves symmetrically to its western corner.

is wholly spread with white sand. The place of circumambulation for the women is at the edge of the paved stones.

Between the ʿIraq corner and the beginning of the wall of the Hijr is the entrance to the Hijr; it is four paces wide, that is six cubits exactly, for we measured it by hand. This place is not enclosed in the Hijr, and is that part of the House which the Quraysh[5] left, and is, as true tradition has it, six cubits. Opposite this entrance, at the Syrian corner, is another of the same size. Between that part of the wall of the House which is under the Mizab [waterspout] and the wall of the Hijr opposite, following the straight line which cuts through the middle of the aforementioned Hijr, lie forty spans. The distance from entrance to entrance is sixteen paces, which is forty-eight spans. This place, I mean the surroundings of the wall (of the Kaʿbah, under the Mizab), is all tessellated marble, wonderfully joined * * * * with bands of gilded copper worked into its surface like a chess-board, being interlaced with each other and with shapes of *mihrabs*.[6] When the sun strikes them, such light and brightness shine from them that the beholder conceives them to be gold, dazzling the eyes with their rays. The height of the marble wall of this Hijr is five and a half spans and its width four and a half. Inside the Hijr is a wide paving, round which the Hijr bends as it were in two-thirds of a circle. It is laid with tessellated marble, cut in discs the size of the palm of the hand, of a dinar and more minute than that, and joined with remarkable precision. It is composed with wonderful art, is of singular perfection, beautifully inlaid and checkered, and is superbly set and laid. The beholder will see bendings, inlays, mosaics of tiles, chess-board forms and the like, of various forms and attributes, such as will fix his gaze for their beauty. Or let his looks roam from the carpet of flowers of many colours to the mihrabs over which bend arches of marble, and in which are these forms we have described and the arts we have mentioned.

Beside it are two slabs of marble adjacent to the wall of the Hijr opposite the Mizab, on which art has worked such delicate leaves, branches, and trees as could not be done by skilled hands cutting with scissors from paper. It is a remarkable sight. The one who decreed that they should be worked in this fashion is the Imam of the East, Abu 'l-ʿAbbas Ahmad al-Nasir ibn al-Mustadiʾ billah Abu Muhammad al-Hasan ibn al-Mustanjid billah Abu 'l-Muzaffar Yusif al-ʿAbbasi[7]—may God hold him in His favour. Facing the waterspout, in the middle of the Hijr and the centre of the marble wall, is a marble slab of most excellent chiselling with a cornice round it bearing an inscription in striking black in which is written, '(This is) among the things ordered to be done by the servant and Caliph of God Abu 'l-ʿAbbas Ahmad al-Nasir li dini Ilah, Prince of the Faithful, in the year 576 [1180]'.

The Mizab is on the top of the wall which overlooks the Hijr. It is of gilded copper and projects four cubits over the Hijr, its breadth being a span. This place under the waterspout is also considered as being a place where, by the favour of God Most High, prayers are answered. The Yemen corner is the same. The wall connecting this place with the Syrian corner is called al-Mustajar [The Place of Refuge]. Underneath the waterspout, and in the

5. The tribe that ruled Mecca in Muhammad's time.
6. Niches in the walls of a mosque that indicate the direction of Mecca.
7. That is, al-Nasir li-Din Allah, the thirty-fourth ʿAbbasid caliph.

court of the Hijr near to the wall of the blessed House, is the tomb of Isma'il [Ishmael]—may God bless and preserve him. Its mark is a slab of green marble, almost oblong and in the form of a mihrab. Beside it is a round green slab of marble, and both [they are *verde antico*[8]] are remarkable to look upon. There are spots on them both which turns them from their colour to something of yellow so that they are like a mosaic of colours, and I compare them to the spots that are left in the crucible after the gold has been melted in it. Beside this tomb, and on the side towards the 'Iraq corner, is the tomb of his mother Hajar [Hagar]—may God hold her in His favour—its mark being a green stone a span and a half wide. Men are blessed by praying in these two places in the Hijr, and men are right to do so, for they are part of the Ancient House and shelter the two holy and venerated bodies. May God cast His light upon them and advantage with their blessings all who pray over them. Seven spans lie between the two holy tombs.

The dome of the Well of Zamzam is opposite the Black Corner, and lies twenty-four paces from it. The Maqam, which we have already mentioned and behind which prayers are said, is to the right of this dome, from the corner of which to the other is ten paces. The inside of the dome is paved with pure white marble. The orifice of the blessed well is in the centre of the dome deviating towards the wall which faces the venerated House. Its depth is eleven statures of a man as we measured it, and the depth of the water is seven statures, as it is said. The door of this dome faces east, and the door of the dome of 'Abbas[9] and that of the Jewish dome face north. The angle of that side of the dome named after the Jews, which faces the Ancient House, reaches the left corner of the back wall of the 'Abbaside corner which faces east. Between them lies that amount of deviation. Beside the dome of the Well of Zamzam and behind it stands the qabbat al-Sharab [the dome of drinking], which was erected by 'Abbas—may God hold him in His favour. Beside this 'Abbaside dome, obliquely to it, is the dome named after the Jews. These two domes are used as storerooms for pious endowments made to the blessed House, such as Korans, books, candlesticks, and the like. The 'Abbaside dome is still called al-Sharabiyyah because it was a place of drinking for the pilgrims; and there, until to-day, the water of Zamzam is put therein to cool in earthenware jars and brought forth at eventide for the pilgrims to drink. These jars are called *dawraq* and have one handle only. The orifice of the Well of Zamzam is of marble stones so well joined, with lead poured into the interstices, that time will not ravage them. The inside of the orifice is similar, and round it are lead props attached to it to reinforce the strength of the binding and the lead overlay. These props number thirty-two, and their tops protrude to hold the brim of the well round the whole of the orifice. The circumference of the orifice is forty spans, its depth four spans and a half, and its thickness a span and a half. Round the inside of the dome runs a trough of width one span, and depth about two spans and raised five spans from the ground, and it is filled with water for the ritual ablutions. Around it runs a stone block on which men mount to perform the ablutions.

The blessed Black Stone is enchased in the corner facing east. The depth to which it penetrates it is not known, but it is said to extend two cubits into

8. Literally, "antique green," an ornamental variety of green veined marble.
9. 'Abbas ibn 'Abd al-Muttalib (566–ca. 653), Muhammad's uncle; his descendants founded the 'Abbasid caliphate.

the wall. Its breadth is two-thirds of a span, its length one span and a finger joint. It has four pieces, joined together, and it is said that it was the Qarmata[1] [Carmathians]—may God curse them—who broke it. Its edges have been braced with a sheet of silver whose white shines brightly against the black sheen and polished brilliance of the Stone, presenting the observer a striking spectacle which will hold his looks. The Stone, when kissed, has a softness and moistness which so enchants the mouth that he who puts his lips to it would wish them never to be removed. This is one of the special favours of Divine Providence, and it is enough that the Prophet—may God bless and preserve him—declare to be a covenant of God on earth. May God profit us by the kissing and touching of it. By His favour may all who yearn fervently for it be brought to it. In the sound piece of the stone, to the right of him who presents himself to kiss it, is a small white spot that shines and appears like a mole on the blessed surface. Concerning this white mole, there is a tradition that he who looks upon it clears his vision, and when kissing it one should direct one's lips as closely as one can to the place of the mole.

* * *

1. A Shiʿi sect in Iraq, Yemen, and especially Bahrain; in 930, Bahraini adherents sacked Mecca and took the Black Stone.

IBN BATTUTA
1304–1368

Born in the port city of Tangier, Morocco, Muhammad ibn Battuta became famous for his travels. Over the course of almost thirty years, they took him to nearly every known Muslim country of his day, as well as to many non-Muslim ones. After returning to his native Morocco, he published a memoir of his journeys, *The Travels of Ibn Battuta*, which is considered the pinnacle of the Arabic travel literature genre.

Ibn Battuta came from a long line of Maliki jurists, many of whom served as judges. In 1325, after completing his education, he decided to make the pilgrimage to Mecca. By his own account, however, once on his way he became consumed by a desire to travel throughout the world, and after completing his pilgrimage, he did just that. His travels can be grouped into two phases. Until 1332 he used Mecca as a base city from which he journeyed as far south as Tanzania and as far east as Iran. During this time, including three years spent in Mecca (1327–30), he enhanced his scholarly credentials by studying with many teachers.

The second phase of his travels began after 1332, when Ibn Battuta decided to travel to India, drawn by reports of the munificence of the ruler of Delhi, Ibn Tughluq (r. 1325–51), and his active recruitment of foreign scholars. Rather than going directly by sea, Ibn Battuta took a circuitous overland route that allowed him visits to several countries and cities, including Constantinople. Well-received by Ibn Tughluq, he was made a judge and served in Delhi for nearly a decade. Eventually, Ibn Battuta's standing with the ruler declined, and he left for the Maldives. Next, he decided to visit China, possibly reaching Beijing, before heading back to Morocco. Even after returning to Morocco in his mid-forties (in 1349), he continued to travel until 1353, when the ruler of Morocco, Abu ʿInan (r. 1349–58), asked Ibn Battuta to dictate an account of his journeys to a court scribe, Ibn Juzayy (1321–ca. 1356). The two men worked together on the *Travels* for two years. On its completion, Ibn Battuta settled into the quiet life of a small-town provincial judge.

Modern scholars generally accept the *Travels* as authentic and accurate, having independently verified many of its details. Still, there are inconsistencies in the work, and some of Ibn Battuta's travels—for example, his voyage to China—have been questioned. Ibn Battuta himself readily admits that in many cases he has lost his notes and is recalling events from memory. And Ibn Juzayy's transcription and editing of the work further complicates assessments of its accuracy. Yet Ibn Battuta's descriptions of the lands, societies, peoples, and customs encountered in the 75,000 miles he covered remain valuable. Ibn Battuta's *Travels* provides a significant firsthand account of many regions, such as Asia Minor, the western coast of India, the Maldives, and East and West Africa, and for a few locales his description is the only eyewitness source available.

In the passage below, chapter 10 of *Travels*, Ibn Battuta recounts his time in Southeast Asia before he left for China. Previously he had been appointed to a judgeship in Delhi by Ibn Tughluq, whose partiality for foreign scholars was rooted in a desire to have total control over his domain—relying on foreigners both ensured that those in his administration were wholly dependent on him and marginalized locals who opposed him. Known for his extremes of both generosity and viciousness, Ibn Tughluq granted Ibn Battuta not just the revenue from his judgeship and four villages but also an annual salary of 12,000 dinars (by comparison, in a year the average family in the region survived on 60 dinars; the average royal soldier earned 2,400 dinars). But like so many others who served Ibn Tughluq, Ibn Battuta fell out of favor; he was then appointed to lead a delegation to China. He was responsible for ensuring that Ibn Tughluq's many gifts—including slaves, concubines, and horses—safely made the long and difficult journey to China. Unfortunately for Ibn Battuta, just after these presents had been loaded onto ships in the port of Calicut in western India, a fierce storm sent all of them and most of the delegation to the bottom of the sea. Ibn Battuta, who had made plans to travel separately (on a ship with better accommodations), survived. Fearing Ibn Tughluq's wrath, Ibn Battuta decided to make a name for himself on the western coast of India rather than return to Delhi. When this attempt failed, he moved on to the Maldives. There, he was favorably received because of his ties to Delhi and his knowledge of Maliki law, on which Maldive courts relied. He was appointed a judge on Male, the central administrative island, and within two months married a local noblewoman. Using his new position and connections, he was soon enmeshed in local politics; but after finding himself on the losing side in a power struggle, he was forced to leave the Maldives.

Chapter 10 begins after Ibn Battuta's departure from Male and narrates his stops in Burma and Sumatra. These events likely occurred about 1345, but Ibn Battuta's exact itinerary and the identification of the locales mentioned here continue to vex modern scholars. Nonetheless, his ability to ingratiate himself with his hosts and his penchant for recording the customs of those he met are amply illustrated in this selection. In Sumatra, likely the easternmost Muslim land of the time, he was offered hospitality by the ruler, Ahmad al-Malik al-Zahir (d. ca. 1404), who also supplied him with provisions when he revealed his intention to visit China. In the city of Qaqula, possibly on the eastern coast of the Malay Peninsula, Ibn Battuta was received as the guest of a local ruler whose subjects demonstrated their devotion by cutting off their own heads, a feat that he witnessed and recounts below.

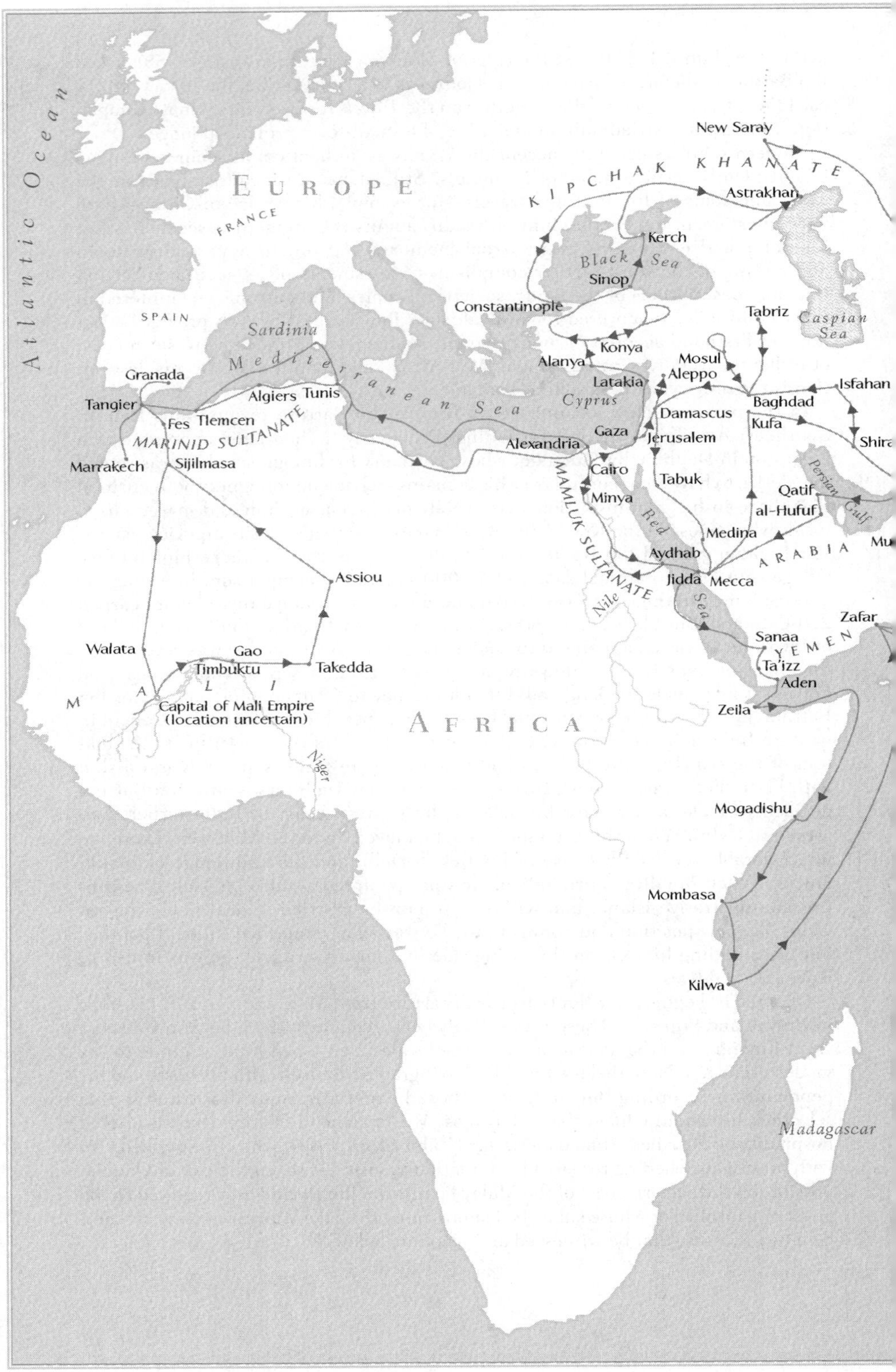
Atlantic Ocean
EUROPE
FRANCE
SPAIN
Sardinia
Mediterranean Sea
Granada
Tangier
Algiers
Tunis
Fes
Tlemcen
MARINID SULTANATE
Marrakech
Sijilmasa
Assiou
Walata
Gao
Timbuktu
Takedda
MALI
Capital of Mali Empire
(location uncertain)
Niger
AFRICA
New Saray
KIPCHAK KHANATE
Astrakhan
Kerch
Black Sea
Sinop
Constantinople
Tabriz
Caspian Sea
Konya
Alanya
Mosul
Aleppo
Latakia
Cyprus
Isfahan
Baghdad
Damascus
Kufa
Gaza
Jerusalem
Alexandria
Shira
Cairo
Tabuk
MAMLUK SULTANATE
Persian Gulf
Minya
Qatif
al-Hufuf
Red Sea
Medina
ARABIA
Mu
Aydhab
Jidda
Mecca
Nile
Zafar
Sanaa
YEMEN
Ta'izz
Aden
Zeila
Mogadishu
Mombasa
Kilwa
Madagascar

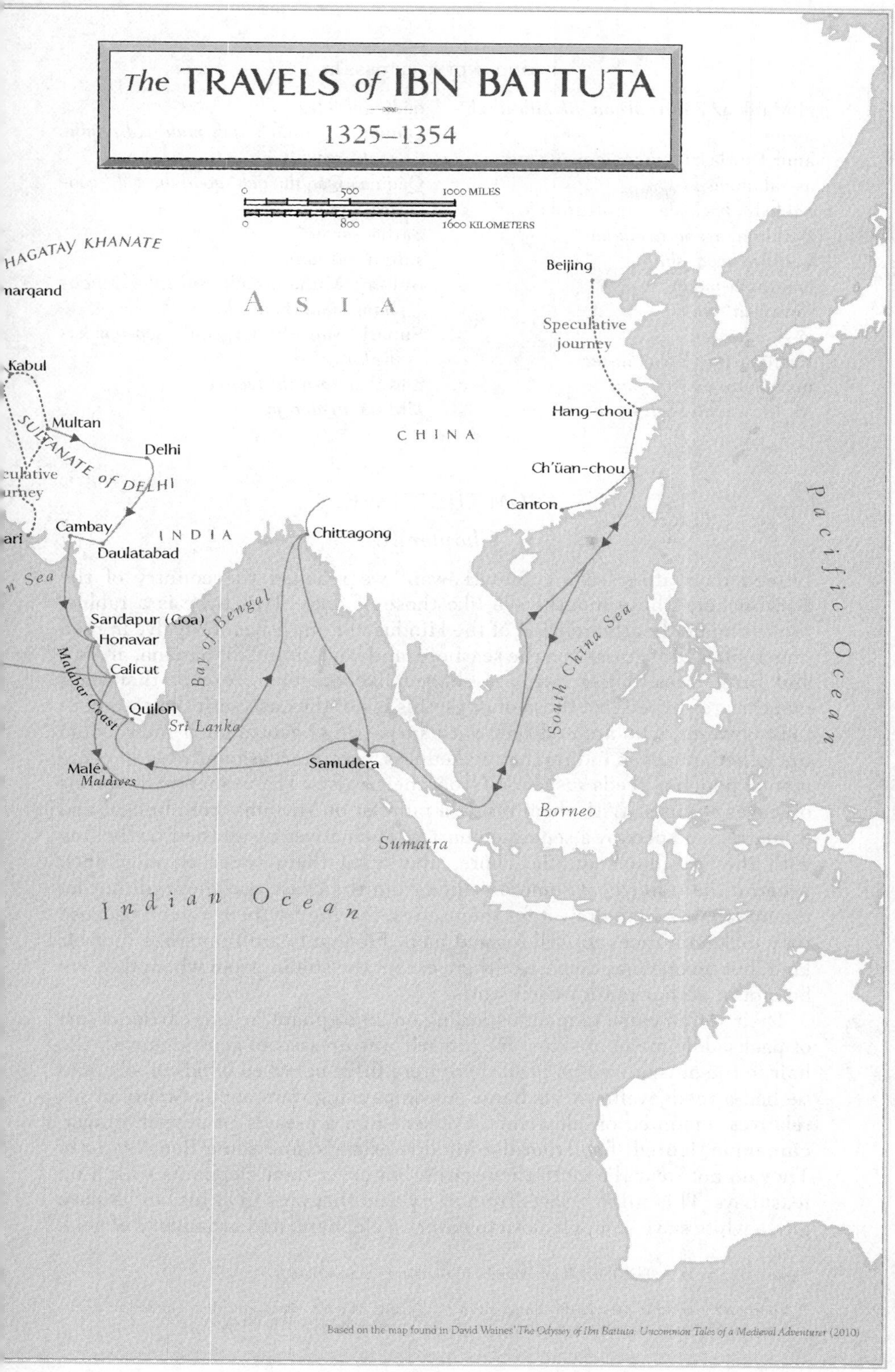
The TRAVELS of IBN BATTUTA
1325–1354
0
500
1000 MILES
0
800
1600 KILOMETERS
HAGATAY KHANATE
marqand
ASIA
Kabul
Multan
SULTANATE of DELHI
Delhi
culative
urney
Cambay
ari
Daulatabad
INDIA
n Sea
Sandapur (Goa)
Honavar
Malabar Coast
Calicut
Quilon
Sri Lanka
Malé
Maldives
Bay of Bengal
Chittagong
Samudera
CHINA
Beijing
Speculative
journey
Hang-chou
Ch'üan-chou
Canton
South China Sea
Borneo
Sumatra
Indian Ocean
Pacific Ocean
Based on the map found in David Waines' The Odyssey of Ibn Battuta: Uncommon Tales of a Medieval Adventurer (2010)

PRONOUNCING GLOSSARY

al-Malik az-Záhir: *al-ma´-lik adh-dhah´-hir*
amír Dawlasa: *a-meer´ daw´-la-suh*
as-salám: *as-sa-lam´*
bakhshí: *bach-shee´* (guttural *ch*)
Barahnakár: *ba-ra-na-kar´*
buqsha: *booq´-shuh*
jamún: *ja-moon´*
Jáwa: *jah´-wuh*
jáwí: *jah´-wee*
Kaylúkarí: *kay-loo´-ka-ree*
martabán: *mar-ta´-ban´*
Mul-Jáwa: *mul-jah´-wuh*
qádí: *qah´-dee*
Qamára, Qamárí: *qah-mah´-ruh, qah-mah´-ree*
Qáqula, Qáqulí: *qah´-qoo-luh, qah´-qoo-lee*
Sarhá: *sar-ha´*
sultan: *sul-tahn´*
Sultan Muhammad: *sul-tahn´ moo-ham´-mad* (heavy *h*)
Sunarkáwán (Sunargaon): *soo-nar-ka-wahn´*
Tawálisí: *ta-wah´-lee-see*
Urdujá: *ur-doo-ja´*

FROM THE TRAVELS

Chapter 10

Fifteen days after leaving Sunarkáwán[1] we reached the country of the Barahnakár, whose mouths are like those of dogs. This tribe is a rabble, professing neither the religion of the Hindus nor any other. They live in reed huts roofed with grasses on the seashore, and have abundant banana, areca,[2] and betel trees. Their men are shaped like ourselves, except that their mouths are shaped like those of dogs; this is not the case with their women-folk, however, who are endowed with surpassing beauty. Their men too go unclothed, not even hiding their nakedness, except occasionally for an ornamental pouch of reeds suspended from their waists. The women wear aprons of leaves of trees. With them reside a number of Muslims from Bengal and Sumatra, who occupy a separate quarter. The natives do all their trafficking with the merchants on the shore, and bring them water on elephants, because the water is at some distance from the coast and they will not let the merchants go to draw it for themselves, fearing for their women because they make advances to well-formed men. Elephants are numerous in their land, but no one may dispose of them except the sultan, from whom they are bought in exchange for woven stuffs.

Their sultan came to meet us, riding on an elephant, which carried a sort of packsaddle made of skins. He himself was dressed in goatskins with the hair to the outside; on his head there were three coloured bands of silk, and he had a reed javelin in his hand. Accompanying were about twenty of his relatives, mounted on elephants. We sent him a present of pepper, ginger, cinnamon, [cured] fish from the Maldive Islands, and some Bengali cloth. They do not wear the cloth themselves, but cover their elephants with it on feast days. This sultan exacts from every ship that puts in at his land a slave girl, a white slave, enough cloth to cover an elephant, and ornaments of gold,

Translated by H. A. R. Gibb. All bracketed additions are the translator's.

1. A port on the coast of present-day Bangladesh.
2. A 40- to 50-foot-high palm tree known for its fruit, which is dried and then chewed in a mixture wrapped in a betel leaf.

which his wife wears on her girdle and her toes. If anyone withholds this tribute, they put a spell on him which raises a storm on sea, so that he perishes or all but perishes.

Twenty-five days after leaving these people we reached the island of Jáwa [Sumatra], from which the incense called *jáwí* takes its name. We saw the island when we were still half a day's journey from it. It is verdant and fertile; the commonest trees there are the coco-palm, areca, clove, Indian aloe, jack-tree, mango, jamún,[3] sweet orange, and camphor cane. The commerce of its inhabitants is carried on with pieces of tin and native Chinese gold, unsmelted. The majority of the aromatic plants which grow there are found only in the districts occupied by the infidels; in the Muslim districts they are less plentiful. When we reached the harbour its people came out to us in small boats with coconuts, bananas, mangoes, and fish. Their custom is to present these to the merchants, who recompense them, each according to his means. The admiral's representative also came on board, and after interviewing the merchants who were with us gave us permission to land. So we went ashore to the port, a large village on the coast with a number of houses, called Sarhá. It is four miles distant from the town. The admiral's representative having written to the sultan to inform him of my arrival, the latter ordered the amir Dawlasa to meet me, along with the qádí[4] and other doctors of the law. They came out for that purpose, bringing one of the sultan's horses and some other horses as well. I and my companions mounted, and we rode in to the sultan's capital, the town of Sumutra, a large and beautiful city encompassed by a wooden wall with wooden towers.

The sultan of Jáwa, al-Malik az-Záhir,[5] is a most illustrious and open-handed ruler, and a lover of theologians. He is constantly engaged in warring for the Faith [against the infidels] and in raiding expeditions, but is withal a humble-hearted man, who walks on foot to the Friday prayers. His subjects also take a pleasure in warring for the Faith and voluntarily accompany him on his expeditions. They have the upper hand over all the infidels in their vicinity, who pay them a poll-tax[6] to secure peace.

As we went towards the palace we found near by it some spears stuck in the ground on both sides of the road. These are to indicate to the people to dismount; no one who is riding may go beyond them, so we dismounted there. On entering the audience-hall we found the sultan's lieutenant, who rose and greeted us with a handshake. We sat down with him and he wrote a note to the sultan informing him of our arrival, sealed it and gave it to a page, who brought the reply written on the back. After this a page brought a *buqsha*, that is, a linen bag. The lieutenant taking this led me by the hand into a small house, where he spends his hours of leisure during the day. He then brought out of the *buqsha* three aprons, one of pure silk, one of silk and cotton and the third of silk and linen, three garments like aprons which they call underclothing, three garments of different kinds called middleclothing, three woollen mantles, one of them being white, and three turbans. I put on one of the aprons in place of trousers, according to their custom, and one

3. A tall tree with an edible fruit. "Jack-tree": jackfruit, a tree with a large edible fruit.
4. Judge (Arabic). Amir (Commander) Dawlasa was an official in the court of the ruler of Sumatra.
5. A title used by a number of Sumatran rulers; here, it most likely refers to Ahmad al-Malik al-Zahir (d. ca. 1404).
6. The jizya, levied on non-Muslim subjects of a Muslim state.

garment of each kind, and my companions took the rest of them. After food had been served we left the palace and rode in company with the lieutenant to a garden surrounded by a wooden wall. In the midst of the garden there was a house built of wood and carpeted with strips of cotton velvet, some dyed and others undyed. We sat down here along with the lieutenant. The amír Dawlasa then came bringing two slave girls and two men servants, and said to me "The sultan says to you that this present is in proportion to his means, not to those of Sultan Muhammad[7] [of India]." The lieutenant left after this, and the amír Dawlasa remained with me.

The amír and I were acquainted with one another, as he had come as an envoy to the sultan at Delhi. I said to him "When can I see the sultan?" and he replied "It is the custom of our country that a newcomer waits three nights before saluting[8] the sultan, that he may recover from the fatigue of his journey." We stayed for three days, food being sent to us thrice a day and fruits and rare sweetmeats every evening and morning. On the fourth day, which was a Friday, the amír Dawlasa came to me and said "You will salute the sultan [today] in the royal enclosure of the cathedral mosque after the service." After the prayer I went in to the sultan; he shook me by the hand and I saluted him, whereupon he bade me sit down upon his left and asked me about Sultan Muhammad and about my travels. He remained in the mosque until the afternoon prayers had been recited, after which he went into a chamber there, put off the garments he was wearing (these were robes of the kind worn by theologians, which he puts on when he comes to the mosque on Fridays), and dressed in his royal robes, which are mantles of silk and cotton. On leaving the mosque he found elephants and horses at the gate. Their custom is that if the sultan rides on an elephant his suite ride on horses, and *vice versa*. On this occasion he mounted an elephant, so we rode on horses, and went with him to the audience hall. We dismounted at the usual place [where the lances were] and the sultan rode on into the palace, where a ceremonial audience was held, the sultan remaining on his elephant opposite the pavilion where he sits [at receptions]. Male musicians came in and sang before him, after which they led in horses with silk caparisons, golden anklets, and halters of embroidered silk. These horses danced before him, a thing which astonished me, though I had seen the same performance at the court of the king of India.

My stay at his court in Sumutra lasted fifteen days, after which I asked his permission to continue my journey, since it was now the sailing season, and because it is not possible to travel to China at all times of the year. He fitted out a junk for us, provisioned us, and made us rich presents—may God reward him!—sending one of his courtiers with us to bring his hospitality gift to us on the junk. We sailed along the coast of his territories for twenty-one nights, and arrived at Mul-Jáwa, an infidel land, two months' journey in length, and containing aromatic spices and the excellent aloes called *Qáqulí* and *Qamárí*. Qáqula and Qamára[9] [after which these aloes are named] form part of the territories of this land. In the territories of the sultan of Sumutra there is only incense, camphor, and a little cloves and Indian aloes, whereas the largest quantity of these is found in Mul-Jáwa.

On reaching the port of Qáqula, we found there a number of junks ready for making piratical raids, and also for dealing with any junks that might

7. Muhammad ibn Tughluq (r. 1325–51).
8. Courteously greeting.
9. Khmer, or Cambodia. "Qáqula": a city probably located on the Malay Peninsula's eastern coast.

attempt to resist their exactions, for they impose a tribute on each junk [calling at that place]. We went ashore to Qáqula, which is a fine town with a wall of hewn stones, broad enough for three elephants to walk abreast on it. The first thing I saw outside the town was elephants bearing loads of Indian aloes, which they burn in their houses and which fetches the same price as firewood with us, or even less. That is when they are selling amongst themselves; to the merchants, on the other hand, they sell a load of it for a roll of cotton cloth, which is dearer in their land than silk. Elephants are very numerous there; they ride on them and use them to carry loads. Every person has his elephants picketed at his door, and every shopkeeper his elephant picketed near him, for riding on to his house and for carrying loads. The same is the case with all the people of China and Cathay [Northern China].

The sultan of Mul-Jáwa is an infidel; I saw him outside his palace sitting beside a pavilion on the bare ground. With him were the officers of state, and the troops were passing in review before him—foot-soldiers, for there are no horses there except those belonging to the sultan, and they have no beasts but elephants on which to ride and fight. He was told about me and summoned me, whereupon I came forward and said "Peace [*as-salám*] be upon those who follow the true religion." They understood nothing but the word *as-salám*. The sultan then welcomed me and ordered a piece of cloth to be spread for me to sit upon. I said to the interpreter "How can I sit on the cloth when the sultan is sitting on the ground?" He replied "Such is his habit; he sits on the ground out of humility. You are a guest and have come from a great sultan, so he wishes to show you honour." Thereupon I sat down, and having asked me very briefly about the sultan [of India] he said to me "You shall stay with us as a guest for three days, and after that you may go."

While this sultan was sitting in audience, I saw a man with a knife in his hand resembling a bookbinder's tool. He put this knife to his own neck, and delivered a long speech which I did not understand, then gripped it with both hands and cut his own throat. So sharp was the knife and so strong his grip that his head fell to the ground. I was amazed at his action. The sultan said to me "Does anyone do this in your country?" I replied "I have never seen such a thing." Then he laughed and said "These are our slaves, who kill themselves for love of us." He gave orders that the body should be carried away and burned, and the sultan's lieutenants, the officers of state, the troops, and the citizens went out to his cremation. The sultan assigned a large pension to his children, wife, and brothers, and they were held in high esteem because of this act. One of those present at this audience told me that the speech made by the man was a declaration of his affection for the sultan, and that he was slaying himself for love of him, as his father had slain himself for love of the sultan's father, and his grandfather for love of the sultan's grandfather. Thereafter I withdrew from the audience and he sent me a guest's portion for three days.

We continued our journey by sea and thirty-four days later came to the sluggish or motionless sea.[1] There is a reddish tinge in its waters, which, they say, is due to soil from a country in the vicinity. There are no winds or waves or movement at all in it, in spite of its wide extent. It is on account of this sea that each Chinese junk is accompanied by three vessels, as we have mentioned, which take it in tow and row it forwards. Besides this every junk

1. The China Sea or some of the neighboring waters [translator's note, edited].

has about twenty oars as big as masts, each of which is manned by a muster of thirty men or so, who stand in two ranks facing one another. Attached to the oars are two enormous ropes as thick as cables; one of the ranks pulls on the cable [at its side], then lets go, and the other rank pulls [on the cable at its side]. They chant in musical voices as they do this, most commonly saying *la'lá, la'lá.* We passed thirty-seven days on this sea, and the sailors were surprised at the facility of our crossing, for they [usually] spend forty to fifty days on it, and forty days is the shortest time required under the most favourable circumstances.

Thereafter we reached the land of Tawálisí, it being their king who is called by that name. It is a vast country and its king is a rival of the king of China. He possesses many junks, with which he makes war on the Chinese until they come to terms with him on certain conditions. The inhabitants of this land are idolaters; they are handsome men and closely resemble the Turks in figure. Their skin is most commonly of a reddish hue, and they are brave and warlike. Their women ride on horseback and are skilful archers, and fight exactly like men. We put in at one of their ports, at the town of Kaylúkarí, which is among their finest and largest cities. It was formerly the residence of the son of their king. When we anchored in the port their troops came down and the captain went ashore to them, taking with him a present for the prince. When he enquired of them about him, however, they told him that the prince's father had appointed him governor of another district and had made his daughter, whose name was Urdujá, governor of this city.

The day following our arrival at the port of Kaylúkarí, this princess summoned the ship's captain and clerk, the merchants and pilots, the commander of the footsoldiers, and the commanders of the archers to a banquet which she had prepared for them, according to her custom. The captain wished me to go with them, but I declined, because, being infidels, it is not lawful to eat their food. When they came into her presence she asked them if there was any one else of their company who had not come. The captain replied "There is only one man left, a *bakhshí* (that is, a qádí, in their tongue), and he will not eat your food." Thereupon she said "Call him," so her guards came [to me] along with the captain's party and said "Comply with the princess's wish." I went to her then, and found her sitting in full state. On my saluting her she replied to me in Turkish, and asked me from what land I had come. I said to her "From the land of India." "From the pepper country?" she asked, and I replied "Yes." She questioned me about this land and events there, and when I had answered she said "I must positively make an expedition to it and take possession of it for myself, for the quantity of its riches and its troops attracts me." I replied "Do so." She ordered me to be given robes, two elephant loads of rice, two buffaloes, ten sheep, four pounds of syrup, and four *martabáns* (that is, large jars) filled with ginger, pepper, lemons, and mangoes, all of them salted, these being among the things prepared for sea voyages.

The captain told that this princess has in her army women, female servants and slave-girls, who fight like men. She goes out in person with her troops, male and female, makes raids on her enemies, takes part in the fighting, and engages in single combat with picked warriors. He told me too that during a fierce engagement with certain of her enemies, many of her troops were killed and they were all but defeated, when she dashed forward and broke through the ranks until she reached the king against whom she was fighting, and dealt him a mortal blow with her lance. He fell dead and his army took to flight. She brought back his head on the point of a spear, and his relatives redeemed it from her for a large sum of money. When she returned to her father he gave her this town, which had formerly been in her brother's hands. The captain told me also that she is sought in marriage by various princes, but she says "I shall marry none but him who fights and overcomes me in single combat," and they avoid fighting with her for fear of the disgrace [that would attach to them] if she overcame them.

We then left the land of Tawálisí and after seventeen days at sea with a favouring wind, sailing with maximum speed and ease, reached the land of China.

IBN KHALDUN
1332–1406

Ibn Khaldun's monumental *Introduction* to his universal history is one of the milestones and masterpieces of Islamic literature. It earned him fame as the first Muslim sociologist and social theorist, because he drew from historical data a meta-analysis of cultural progression and decline. Ibn Khaldun was alert to the multiple forces and factors that shape a civilization and its history. His scope was broad and his influence immense.

Yet Ibn Khaldun did not live in scholarly seclusion. His early decades were tumultuous, driven by unabashed political ambition and the ability to shift alliances quickly—traits necessary for survival in the political life of his time.

Born under Hafsid rule in Tunis to a well-established family with roots in Spain, Ibn Khaldun received a thorough education in the standard subjects of his day, including law, traditions, and the Arabic language. His education was enhanced by the influx of scholars, who arrived with the occupation of Tunis (1347–49) by the Merinid dynasty, which was centered in Fez, Morocco. At about that time, the Black Death reached Tunis—and carried off both his parents. Ibn Khaldun was seventeen, and the loss haunted him for the rest of his life. About three years later, he obtained a government post that could have led to higher positions. Yet the opportunities for advanced education were limited and the future of the Hafsids—now restored to power—was uncertain, so Ibn Khaldun left Tunis for a series of westward destinations.

In 1354 the new Merinid ruler, Abu ʿInan (r. 1351–58), invited Ibn Khaldun to join his study circle at court in Fez. Ibn Khaldun continued his studies there and soon received a minor clerical post, but Abu ʿInan came to question his clerk's loyalties. Perhaps suspicious of Ibn Khaldun's friendship with a former Hafsid ruler named Abu ʿAbdallah, then resident in Fez, Abu ʿInan had him imprisoned in 1357. Almost two years later, when the Merinid ruler died, Ibn Khaldun was freed and took part in the ensuing power struggle. The candidate he supported, Abu Salim, ascended to the throne, and Ibn Khaldun was made an administrative secretary and later given a judicial appointment. But Abu Salim's death in 1361 left Ibn Khaldun in a precarious position once again, and he sought a new home.

In 1362 he was welcomed to Granada, Spain, by Muhammad V (1338–1391) and his minister, Ibn al-Khatib (d. 1375); both men had met Ibn Khaldun while taking refuge in Fez during a temporary fall from power. Indeed, Ibn al-Khatib became a lifelong friend, though Ibn Khaldun began to fear that his own swift rise in influence—his successful completion of whatever tasks Muhammad V assigned him soon made him a favorite—was provoking the minister's envy. Fortunately, his old ally from Fez, the Hafsid ruler Abu ʿAbdallah, had regained his throne in Bougie, Algeria, and offered Ibn Khaldun a high-ranking position in his administration (having already appointed Ibn Khaldun's younger brother as a minister). Ibn Khaldun accepted, leaving on good terms with the authorities in Granada, and arrived in Bougie in March of 1365. However, Abu ʿAbdallah's reign was cut short when he was killed in 1366 in an attack led by his cousin, the ruler of nearby Constantine.

For nearly a decade Ibn Khaldun continued to serve various rulers in North Africa and Spain who wanted his aid but viewed him with growing suspicion. Finally, well into his forties, Ibn Khaldun had had enough of the vicissitudes of political life; around 1375 he sought refuge with an Arab tribe in Oran, Algeria. There, over the course of three years, he completed the first draft of his *Introduction* and large portions of his universal history. To finish the work he moved back to his hometown in 1378, needing access to its libraries. He continued his research in Tunis, revised the *Introduction*, and taught Maliki law. Although he avoided political activities in the city, the ruling class remained distrustful of him because of his history.

Using the excuse of the pilgrimage, Ibn Khaldun departed Tunis in October 1382; he traveled only as far as Cairo, which he reached in January 1383. He lived there for the remaining twenty-three years of his life. He was well received by the Mamluk ruler of Egypt, Barquq (r. 1382–99), who appointed him to teaching and administrative positions. Ibn Khaldun was also made the chief Maliki judge of Cairo. Though apparently not always in favor—he would lose and regain the judgeship a total of six times—he kept his distance from politics and led a relatively uneventful life. One notable exception to this calm was his meeting with Timur (1336–1405) during the Turkic conqueror's capture of Damascus in 1400.

The selection below is taken from Ibn Khaldun's *An Introduction to History*, which formed the prelude to his universal history but stands as a literary and scholarly masterpiece in its own right. The *Introduction* comprises six chapters; in order, they analyze human civilizations through the lens of geography; describe nomadic societies and their characteristics; examine different forms of governments, detailing their strengths and weaknesses; present sedentary societies and their distinctive features; enumerate and describe various professions, with general observations on commerce; and discuss different fields of knowledge, such as medicine and law. As these topics suggest, Ibn Khaldun's focus is not specific historical events but the enduring forces that shape these events. His attention to the factors of physical geography, of environmental constraints and opportunities, of sedentary and nomadic social groupings, and of the cohesive solidarity that secured ethnic loyalties earned him accolades as an intellectual innovator and credit for providing the foundational insights of future academic disciplines. While the *Introduction* was lauded during Ibn Khaldun's lifetime, its discovery some centuries later by European scholars and its translation into several European languages greatly enhanced its influence and prestige.

In the section of his first chapter reproduced here, Ibn Khaldun talks about food and its effects on the human body and personality. At times, he sounds eerily akin to contemporary diet gurus who promote particular food choices and even full or partial fasting.

PRONOUNCING GLOSSARY

Algeciras: *al-he-see´-ras*
as-Sûs: *as-soos´*
Ghumârah: *goo-mah´-ruh*
Ḥijâz: *he-jaz´* (heavy *h*)
Ifrîqiyah: *if-ree-qee´-yuh*
Maghrib: *mag´-rib*
Maṣmûdah: *mas-moo´-duh*
shaykh: *shaych* (guttural *ch*)
Ṣinhâjah: *sin-ha´-juh*
Sultan Abû 'l-Ḥasan: *sul-tahn´ a-bool-ha´-san* (heavy *h*)

FROM AN INTRODUCTION TO HISTORY

From *Chapter 1. Human Civilization in General*

FIFTH PREFATORY DISCUSSION

DIFFERENCES WITH REGARD TO ABUNDANCE AND SCARCITY OF FOOD IN THE VARIOUS INHABITED REGIONS (ʿUMRÂN) AND HOW THEY AFFECT THE HUMAN BODY AND CHARACTER

It should be known that not all the temperate zones have an abundance of food, nor do all their inhabitants lead a comfortable life. In some parts, the inhabitants enjoy an abundance of grain, seasonings, wheat, and fruits, because the soil is well balanced and good for plants and there is an abundant civilization. And then, in other parts, the land is strewn with rocks, and no seeds or herbs grow at all. There, the inhabitants have a very hard time. Instances of such people are the inhabitants of the Ḥijâz and the Yemen, or the Veiled Ṣinhâjah who live in the desert of the Maghrib[1] on the fringes of the sandy deserts which lie between the Berbers and the Sudanese Negroes. All of them lack all grain and seasonings. Their nourishment and food is milk and meat. Another such people is the Arabs who roam the waste regions. They may get grain and seasonings from the hills, but this is the case only at certain times and is possible only under the eyes of the militia which protects (the hill country). Whatever they get is little, because they have little money. They obtain no more than the bare necessity, and sometimes less, and in no case enough for a comfortable or abundant life. They are mostly found restricted to milk, which is for them a very good substitute for wheat. In spite of this, the desert people who lack grain and seasonings are found to be healthier in body and better in character than the hill people who have plenty of everything. Their complexions are clearer, their bodies cleaner, their figures more perfect and better, their characters less intemperate, and their minds keener as far as knowledge and perception are concerned. This is attested by experience in all these groups. There is a great difference in this respect between the Arabs and Berbers (on the one hand), and the Veiled (Berbers) and the inhabitants of the hills (on the other). This fact is known to those who have investigated the matter.

As to the reason for it, it may be tentatively suggested that a great amount of food and the moisture it contains generate pernicious superfluous matters in the body, which, in turn, produce a disproportionate widening of the body, as well as many corrupt, putrid humors. The result is a pale complexion and an ugly figure, because the person has too much flesh, as we have stated. When the moisture with its evil vapors ascends to the brain, the mind and the ability to think are dulled. The result is stupidity, carelessness, and a general intemperance. This can be exemplified by comparing the animals of waste regions and barren habitats, such as gazelles, wild cows (*mahâ*), ostriches, giraffes, onagers, and (wild) buffaloes (cows, *baqar*), with their counterparts among the animals that live in hills, coastal plains, and fertile

TRANSLATED BY Franz Rosenthal.

1. The Mediterranean coastal plain of Morocco, Algeria, Tunisia, and Libya. "The Ḥijâz": the western region of the Arabian Peninsula; it borders the Red Sea and contains Mecca and Medina. "The Veiled Ṣinhâjah": Berber tribes of the Sahara who covered their faces for protection from the sand.

pastures. There is a big difference between them with regard to the glossiness of their coat, their shape and appearance, the proportions of their limbs, and their sharpness of perception. The gazelle is the counterpart of the goat, and the giraffe that of the camel; the onagers and (wild) buffaloes (cows) are identical with (domestic) donkeys and oxen (and cows). Still, there is a wide difference between them. The only reason for it is the fact that the abundance of food in the hills produces pernicious superfluous matters and corrupt humors in the bodies of the domestic animals, the influence of which shows on them. Hunger, on the other hand, may greatly improve the physique and shape of the animals of the waste regions.

The same observations apply to human beings. We find that the inhabitants of fertile zones where the products of agriculture and animal husbandry as well as seasonings and fruits are plentiful, are, as a rule, described as stupid in mind and coarse in body. This is the case with those Berbers who have plenty of seasonings and wheat, as compared with those who lead a frugal life and are restricted to barley or durra, such as the Maṣmûdah Berbers and the inhabitants of as-Sûs and the Ghumârah.[2] The latter are superior both intellectually and physically. The same applies in general to the inhabitants of the Maghrib who have plenty of seasonings and fine wheat, as compared with the inhabitants of Spain in whose country butter is altogether lacking and whose principal food is durra. The Spaniards are found to have a sharpness of intellect, a nimbleness of body, and a receptivity for instruction such as no one else has. The same also applies to the inhabitants of rural regions of the Maghrib as compared with the inhabitants of settled areas and cities. Both use many seasonings and live in abundance, but the town dwellers only use them after they have been prepared and cooked and softened by admixtures. They thus lose their heaviness and become less substantial. Principal foods are the meat of sheep and chickens. They do not use butter because of its tastelessness. Therefore the moisture in their food is small, and it brings only a few pernicious superfluous matters into their bodies. Consequently, the bodies of the urban population are found to be more delicate than those of the inhabitants of the desert who live a hard life. Likewise, those inhabitants of the desert who are used to hunger are found to have in their bodies no superfluous matters, thick or thin.

It should be known that the influence of abundance upon the body is apparent even in matters of religion and divine worship. The frugal inhabitants of the desert and those of settled areas who have accustomed themselves to hunger and to abstinence from pleasures are found to be more religious and more ready for divine worship than people who live in luxury and abundance. Indeed, it can be observed that there are few religious people in towns and cities, in as much as people there are for the most part obdurate and careless, which is connected with the use of much meat, seasonings, and fine wheat. The existence of pious men and ascetics is, therefore, restricted to the desert, whose inhabitants eat frugally. Likewise, the condition of the inhabitants within a single city can be observed to differ according to the different distribution of luxury and abundance.

2. The hilly region in northwestern Morocco. "The Maṣmûdah": one of the major Berber tribal confederations. "As-Sûs": southern Morocco.

It can also be noted that those people who, whether they inhabit the desert or settled areas and cities, live a life of abundance and have all the good things to eat, die more quickly than others when a drought or famine comes upon them. This is the case, for instance, with the Berbers of the Maghrib and the inhabitants of the city of Fez and, as we hear, of Egypt (Cairo). It is not so with the Arabs who inhabit waste regions and deserts, or with the inhabitants of regions where the date palm grows and whose principal food is dates, or with the present-day inhabitants of Ifrîqiyah[3] whose principal food is barley and olive oil, or with the inhabitants of Spain whose principal food is durra and olive oil. When a drought or a famine strikes them, it does not kill as many of them as of the other group of people, and few, if any, die of hunger. As a reason for that, it may tentatively be suggested that the stomachs of those who have everything in abundance and are used to seasonings and, in particular, to butter, acquire moisture in addition to their basic constitutional moisture, and (the moisture they are used to) eventually becomes excessive. Then, when (eating) habits are thwarted by small quantities of food, by lack of seasonings, and by the use of coarse food to which it is unaccustomed, the stomach, which is a very weak part of the body and for that reason considered one of the vital parts, soon dries out and contracts. Sickness and sudden death are prompt consequences to the man whose stomach is in this condition. Those who die in famines are victims of their previous habitual state of satiation, not of the hunger that now afflicts them for the first time. In those who are accustomed to thirst and to doing without seasonings and butter, the basic moisture, which is good for all natural foods, always stays within its proper limits and does not increase. Thus, their stomachs are not affected by dryness or intemperance in consequence of a change of nourishment. As a rule, they escape the fate that awaits others on account of the abundance of their food and the great amount of seasonings in it.

The basic thing to know is that foodstuffs, and whether to use or not to use them, are matters of custom. Whoever accustoms himself to a particular type of food that agrees with him becomes used to it. He finds it painful to give it up or to make any changes (in his diet), provided (the type of food) is not something that does not fulfill the (real) purpose of food, such as poison, or alkaloids, or anything excessively intemperate. Whatever can be used as food and is agreeable may be used as customary food. If a man accustoms himself to the use of milk and vegetables instead of wheat, until (the use of them) gets to be his custom, milk and vegetables become for him (his habitual) food, and he definitely has no longer any need for wheat or grains.

The same applies to those who have accustomed themselves to suffer hunger and do without food. Such things are reported about trained (ascetics). We hear remarkable things about men of this type. Those who have no knowledge of things of the sort can scarcely believe them. The explanation lies in custom. Once the soul gets used to something, it becomes part of its make-up and nature, because (the soul) is able to take on many colorings. If through gradual training it has become used to hunger, (hunger) becomes a natural custom of the soul.

The assumption of physicians that hunger causes death is not correct, except when a person is exposed suddenly to hunger and is entirely cut off

3. The area of present-day Tunisia and Libya.

from food. Then, the stomach is isolated, and contracts an illness that may be fatal. When, however, the amount of food one eats is slowly decreased by gradual training, there is no danger of death. The adepts of Sufism practice (such gradual abstinence from food). Gradualness is also necessary when one gives up the training. Were a person suddenly to return to his original diet, he might die. Therefore, he must end the training as he started it, that is, gradually.

We personally saw a person who had taken no food for forty or more consecutive days. Our *shaykhs* were present at the court of Sultan Abû l-Ḥasan[4] when two women from Algeciras and Ronda were presented to him, who had for years abstained from all food. Their story became known. They were examined, and the matter was found to be correct. The women continued this way until they died. Many persons we used to know restricted themselves to (a diet of) goat's milk. They drank from the udder sometime during the day or at breakfast. This was their only food for fifteen years. There are many others (who live similarly). It should not be considered unlikely.

It should be known that everybody who is able to suffer hunger or eat only little, is physically better off if he stays hungry than if he eats too much. Hunger has a favorable influence on the health and well-being of body and intellect, as we have stated. This may be exemplified by the different influence of various kinds of food upon the body. We observe that those persons who live on the meat of strong, large-bodied animals grow up as a (strong and large-bodied) race. Comparison of the inhabitants of the desert with those of settled areas shows this. The same applies to persons who live on the milk and meat of camels. This influences their character, so that they become patient, persevering, and able to carry loads, as is the case with camels. Their stomachs also grow to be healthy and tough as the stomachs of camels. They are not beset by any feebleness or weakness, nor are they affected by unwholesome food, as others are. They may take strong (alkaloid) cathartics unadulterated to purify their bellies, such as, for instance, unripe colocynths, *Thapsia garganica*, and Euphorbia.[5] Their stomachs do not suffer any harm from them. But if the inhabitants of settled areas, whose stomachs have become delicate because of their soft diet, were to partake of them, death would come to them instantly, because (these cathartics) have poisonous qualities.

An indication of the influence of food upon the body is a fact that has been mentioned by agricultural scholars and observed by men of experience, that when the eggs of chickens which have been fed on grain cooked in camel dung, are set to hatch, the chicks come out as large as can be imagined. One does not even have to cook any grain to feed them; one merely smears camel dung on the eggs set to hatch, and the chickens that come out are extremely large. There are many similar things.

When we observe the various ways in which food exercises an influence upon bodies, there can be no doubt that hunger also exercises an influence upon them, because two opposites follow the same pattern with regard to exercising an influence or not exercising an influence. Hunger influences

4. The Merinid Sultan who ruled Morocco from 1331 to 1351; he was deposed by his son Abu 'Inan (r. 1351–57), who invited Ibn Khaldun to come to Fez.

5. Plants that are strong purgatives.

the body in that it keeps it free from corrupt superfluities and mixed fluids that destroy body and intellect, in the same way that food influenced the (original) existence of the body.

God is omniscient.

AL-HASAN AL-WAZZAN
between 1489 and 1496–ca. 1554

Captured in the Mediterranean by privateers, al-Hasan ibn Muhammad al-Wazzan, or Leo Africanus as he is known in the West, wrote a famous Italian treatise on the geography, people, and customs of Africa titled *Description of Africa* (*Descrittione dell' Africa*).

Soon after al-Hasan's birth in Granada, Spain, most likely after Granada fell to Christian forces in 1492, his family emigrated south to the Moroccan city of Fez. There, he is believed to have been educated at the Qarawiyyin University, one of the oldest schools in the Islamic world. As a student, he worked part-time in a hospital; after completing his education, he obtained an administrative appointment with the sultan of Morocco, Muhammad al-Burtuqali (r. 1505–26). This position allowed him to travel widely on behalf of the sultan, and al-Hasan's diplomatic travels took him to much of North Africa, Saharan Africa (e.g., Mali and Sudan), and parts of the Middle East. Al-Hasan al-Wazzan was an observant traveler, making notes and writing descriptions of the places he visited. During the last of his North African journeys, he was returning to Fez across the Mediterranean when, in June 1518, he was captured by Spanish privateers who targeted Ottoman ships.

Most Muslims captured in the Mediterranean had one of two options. If they could afford the ransom demanded by their captors, they were freed and repatriated. If not, they were enslaved and forced to serve on Christian ships. The case of al-Hasan, however, proved to be exceptional. His captors recognized his intelligence and realized they could benefit from the knowledge of African geography and culture he had gained as a diplomat. At that time, Rome was planning to attack North Africa to protect its interests in the region and needed as much intelligence as possible about the area. Al-Hasan al-Wazzan was presented to Leo X (pope 1513–21) in October 1518 and soon thereafter was freed and given a generous stipend to entice him to stay in Italy. Al-Hasan did so and was baptized in January 1520, taking the name Johannes Leo de Medicis or Giovanni Leone Africano. Al-Hasan did not spend all of his time in Rome; after Leo X's death in December 1521, he lived in Bologna for a while. He taught Arabic there, and during his years in Italy he learned Italian and Latin. In 1526 he returned to Rome, where he completed his *Description of Africa* in March of that year. Al-Hasan al-Wazzan's later years are shrouded in mystery. In all likelihood he left Italy for Tunis sometime after 1528 and reconverted to Islam. Although he may have returned to Fez, where his friends and family lived, no evidence of his movements survives. He is believed to have died after 1550.

While in Italy he composed other works in addition to his *Description*. These include an Arabic-Hebrew-Latin medical dictionary, an Arabic translation of the Epistles of St. Paul, and a biographical work about notable Muslim and Jewish scholars. Yet his *Description of Africa*, which consists of nine books, stands as his masterwork. The first book is a general overview, introducing the reader to the lands, people, languages, and beliefs of Africa. Books 2 through 6 focus on specific regions and cities in North Africa: Morocco (in particular Fez and Marrakesh), Algeria, Libya, and Tunisia. Book 7 treats the area of present-day Sudan, and book 8 deals with Egypt. Book 9 examines the rivers, plants, and wildlife found in Africa.

The *Description* is neither comprehensive nor completely accurate, and clearly al-Hasan devotes most of his attention to those areas, such as Fez and Morocco, with which he was most familiar. Nonetheless, the work was considered authoritative in Europe and remained well-regarded for centuries. After its completion, al-Hasan al-Wazzan's *Description* likely circulated for two decades in handwritten copies until it was first published in Venice in 1550. It was soon translated into French and Latin (1556) and eventually into English (1600). The *Description* had an impact on later European culture. For example, many have suggested that Shakespeare's Othello was based on al-Hasan, and the poet William Butler Yeats (1865–1939) was convinced that he was communing with the spirit of al-Hasan during séances in which he participated from 1912 to 1917.

The passage below, from the third book of the *Description*, describes religious beliefs and practices in the city of Fez. Al-Hasan al-Wazzan is obviously intrigued and repelled by what he experienced there. He sets his depictions against the larger backdrop of sectarian differences in the Muslim world. In doing so, he demonstrates an educated familiarity with many genres of Islamic literature and the principal works in them.

PRONOUNCING GLOSSARY

al-Afkani: *al-af-ka´-nee*
al-Ashʿari: *al-ash´-ah-ree*
al-awtad: *al-aw-tad´*
al-Buni: *al-boo´-nee*
al-Ghazali: *al-ga-za´-lee*
al-Harith ibn Asad: *al-ha´-rith* (heavy *h*) *ibn a´-sad*
al-Hasan al-Basri: *al-ha´-san* (heavy *h*) *al-bahs´-ree*
al-kannazin: *al-kan-na-zeen´*
al-Lumaʿ al-Nuraniyya: *al-loo´-mah an-noo-rah´-nee-yuh*
al-Maghrabi: *al-mag´-ra-bee*
al-qutb: *al-qutb´*
al-Suhrawardi: *as-suh-ra-war´-dee* (light *h*)
al-Tughraʾi: *at-tug-rah´-ee*
Bayn al-Qasrayn: *bayn al-qahs-rayn´*
caliph: *ka´-lif*
Farghani: *far-gah´-nee*
hijra: *hij´-ruh*
Ibn al-Farid: *ibn al-fah´-rid*
Jabir: *ja´-bir*
Khorasan: *khoo-ruh-sahn´*
Malik Shah: *ma´-lik shah*
Mamluk: *mam-louk´*
Nizam al-Mulk: *nee-dhahm´ al-mulk´*
Shams al-Maʿarif: *sham´-sal-ma-ah˝-rif*
Sirr al-Asmaʾ al-Husna: *sir al-as-ma´ al-hus´-nuh* (heavy *h*)
sultan: *sul-tahn´*
suwwah: *soo´-wah* (heavy *h*)

FROM DESCRIPTION OF AFRICA

Rules and Differences Observed by Some in the Law of Muhammad

Here, too, there are many learned men, who call themselves sages and moral philosophers, and who observe some additional laws not imposed by Muhammad. And some are held to be orthodox and some not, but common people consider them saints even though they desire that many things be allowed which are prohibited by Mohammadan law: as, for example, it is forbidden

TRANSLATED FROM THE ITALIAN BY Dennis McAuliffe.

in the law to sing love songs accompanied by music, and they say that it is permitted. In their law there are many commandments and many rules each of which has its proponent who defends it and they have jurists that defend said rules and who have produced many writings on spiritual living. This sect[1] began eighty years after Muhammad, and its first and most famous author was called al-Hasan al-Basri,[2] from the city of Basra, who began to give his disciples certain rules, but left no writings.

A hundred years later, there was another man very capable in this matter whose name was al-Harith ibn Asad,[3] from the city of Baghdad, who wrote a beautiful work universally intended for all his disciples. From then on this sect was severely criticized by the jurists to the clerics in charge, and anyone who observed the rules of this man was condemned. The same sect rose up eighty years later and its head was another very worthy man[4] who was followed by many disciples and preached his beliefs publicly so that all the jurists together with the caliph condemned him and his followers to death by beheading. When the leader heard this, he immediately wrote a letter to the caliph begging him to grant him the favor of being allowed to dispute with the jurists and, if they prevailed over him, that he would gladly die; but if he showed to them that his doctrine was superior to theirs, it was not right that so many poor innocent men should perish on account of false calumny. The caliph found his request fair and granted it. When thus the learned man came to the disputation, he easily overcame all the jurists to the extent that the caliph tearfully converted to the sect of this same man, and for the rest of his life he favored it, ordering convents and colleges to be built for the sect's followers.

This sect lasted another hundred years until the Emperor Malik Shah,[5] a Turk in origin, arrived from Asia and persecuted the sect. Some fled to Cairo, others to Arabia, and they remained exiled for twenty years, until the reign of Caselsah,[6] Malik Shah's nephew. Caselsah's counselor, a man of great spirit, whose name was Nizam al-Mulk,[7] was a member of this sect and caused it to be reinstated and respected and it flourished due to a very learned man named al-Ghazali, who wrote a noble volume divided into seven books[8] and brought about peace between the jurists and the followers of this sect. Thus, the jurists held the title of doctors and preservers of the law of the Prophet, and the followers of this sect were named interpreters and reformers of this law. This union lasted until Baghdad was destroyed by the Tartars, which was in the six hundred and fifty-sixth year of the Hijra.[9] But the division in no way harmed them since all Africa and Asia were already full of the sect's disciples.

In those days the only ones who used to enter this sect were men learned in every discipline, and above all those well versed in scripture, in order to be able to defend it ably and refute the opposite. Now for the past hundred years every ignoramus wants to enter, and they say that doctrine is not needed, because the holy spirit opens understanding of the truth to those

1. Sufis.
2. An ascetic, writer, and preacher who focused on the inner life (642–728).
3. Al-Harith ibn Asad al-Muhasibi (ca. 781–857), known for his writings on spirituality and mysticism.
4. Abu 'l-Husayn al-Nuri (d. 907), a prominent Baghdadi Sufi.
5. The most powerful sultan of the Seljuk dynasty (r. 1072–92).
6. The name "Caselsah" does not correspond to known nephews of Malik Shah (d. 1092); Nizam al-Mulk (d. 1092) died before Malik Shah.
7. A powerful vizier (1018–1092; see above), he served two of the most notable Seljuk sultans, Alp Arslan (r. 1063–72) and his successor, Malik Shah.
8. *The Revival of the Religious Sciences*, by al-Ghazali (d. 1111; see above).
9. 1258 CE.

who have a pure heart, and they adduce various other weak rationales. From here, leaving aside the commandments as excessive and unnecessary for the law, they do not preserve duties other than those done by the doctors of law: but they take all the pleasures that they deem licit under the rule, with the result that they hold frequent banquets, they sing love songs and dance for hours, some of them at times opening their clothing, according to the verses they are singing and according to the fantasies that play on the minds of these indecent men. They say that in those moments they are heated by the flames of divine love; but I think they are heated by the excessive amount of food, since each of them takes an amount of food that would be too much for three men. Or, that which seems more true, they make these shouts very often accompanied by cries of love that they make to certain beardless youths, wherefore not infrequently it happens that some gentleman invites to his wedding one of these shaykhs and masters with all his disciples, who, when they enter the banquet, say their divine prayers and songs; and when the dinner is over, the more advanced in age immediately begin to open their skirts, and during the dance, if any of these old fellows falls he is immediately caught and set on his feet by one of his young disciples, whom he most often wantonly kisses. For this reason a proverb was coined that in Fez is on everyone's tongue, that is to say, "the banquet of the hermits." It means that after the banquet, each of those young men becomes the bride of his master, and it is for this reason that they cannot take wives and are called hermits.

Various Other Rules and Sects, and Superstitious Credulity of Many

Among these sects there are many rules considered heretical by one or another sort of doctors of the law, since they differ from others not only in the law, but also in the faith. There are indeed some who firmly hold the opinion that man, by means of his good works, his fasts and abstinences, may acquire an angelic nature: wherefore they say that he purifies his intellect and his heart, in such a way that he cannot sin even if he wanted to. But it is necessary that he first pass through fifty steps of discipline: and though he may sin before he pass all fifty, God no longer counts his sin. And these men indeed do strange and countless fasts in the beginning; afterward they take all the pleasures of the world. They also have a strict rule, set down in four volumes by an eloquent and educated man, whose name was al-Suhrawardi of Suhraward, a city in Khorasan.[1]

There is another author, called Ibn al-Farid,[2] who rendered all his learning in very graceful verses; but the afore-mentioned verses are so full of allegories that they seem to treat of nothing but love. Thus someone called Farghani[3] commented on the work and drew from it the stages that one must pass through. This poet was so elegant that the followers of this sect do not sing anyone else's verses but his at their banquets, whence for the last three hundred years there has not been a language more cultivated

1. The northeastern region of Iran. Shihab al-Din Abu Hafs ʿUmar al-Suhrawardi (1145–1234), Persian author of the influential Sufi manual *ʿAwarif al-maʿarif* (*Knowledge of the Spiritually Learned*).
2. Abu Hafs ʿUmar ibn al-Farid (1181/82–1235), a famous Sufi who lived in Egypt; he was renowned for his mystical poetry.
3. Saʿid al-Din Muhammad ibn Ahmad Farghani (d. ca. 1290s), best-known for his commentary on Ibn al-Farid's poem *Nazm al-Suluk* (*Poem of the Spiritual Path*).

than the one preserved of his. Those followers hold that the spheres and the firmament, the elements, planets and all the stars are one god, and no faith or law can be in error, since all men in their soul think they should adore him who is worthy of being adored. And they believe that God's science is contained in one man, who is called *al-qutb*,[4] elected and participant in God, and like God in knowledge. There are forty other men among them, who are called *al-awtad*, that is, the trunks, since they are of lesser grade and lesser science. When the *al-qutb* dies, another is created from among these forty, and this one is chosen from the number of seventy. There are seven hundred and sixty-five others, whose title I do not remember; but when one of the seventy dies, another is added from that number.

Their rule states that they go through the world unrecognized, as crazy people or big sinners or the worst man possible. Under such disguise, many fraudulent and evil men go running around Africa naked, showing their shame, and they are so wild and without any respect that, as beasts do, they sometimes use women in the middle of the public squares: and nevertheless they are considered by the masses to be saints. Of this rabble there is a great quantity in Tunis, but many more in Egypt and mostly in Cairo. And I in said Cairo, in the square called Bayn al-Qasrayn,[5] saw with my own eyes one of them take a beautiful young woman, who was just coming out of the bathing house, and lay her down in the middle of the square and have intercourse with her. And as soon as he left the woman, everyone rushed to touch her clothing, as if she were a devout thing and touched by a holy man, and they said among themselves that this holy man pretended to commit sin, but that he didn't commit it. When her husband heard of it, he considered it a rare grace and thanked God, holding banquets and solemn feasts, and giving alms for such a grace. The judges and learned men of the law wanted in every way to castigate the ruffian, but were in danger of being killed by the populace, because, as I said, each of these types is in great veneration among the masses and continually receives countless gifts and presents, and I have seen more things like this that I am ashamed to narrate.

Cabalists and Other Sects

There is another rule of some who can be called cabalists, who fast in an unusual manner, and do not eat any meat from animals, but have certain food and clothing ordered and prescribed for each hour of the day and night, and certain particular prayers according to the days and months, retrieving such prayers by means of numbers; and they habitually carry around with them some little paintings, with characters and numbers carved in them. Also they say that good spirits appear to them and speak with them, and give them universal news of the things of the world. One of these men was an excellent scholar called al-Buni,[6] who composed their rule and prayers, and

4. Pole or axis (Arabic). According to the Sufis, there is a hierarchy of pious figures—hidden from most of the world yet integral to its order—topped by the *qutb*, the most perfect human in his relationship with God. Under him, in order, are two individuals at the rank of *imam*, five *awtad* (pillars), seven *afrad* (incomparables), forty *abdal* (substitutes), and other lower ranks (details vary). Vacancies in higher ranks are filled from below.

5. Literally, "Between the Two Palaces" (Arabic); the square is located between two of the first palaces built by the Fatimids after they founded Cairo in 969.

6. Ahmad ibn ʿAli ibn Yusuf al-Buni (d. 1225), an Egyptian Sufi who composed treatises on the power of qurʾanic verses, secrets in the names of God, numerology, and other esoteric subjects. His most famous work was *Shams al-Maʿarif* (*Sun of Knowledge*), from which many of the compositions ascribed to him are excerpted.

how the said little paintings were to be made; and I saw his work, and this science seemed to be more about magic than about cabala. His most famous works were approximately eight in number: The first is called *al-Luma'al-Nuraniyya*, that is, "The Demonstration of Light,"[7] and in this work are arranged the prayers and fasts; the second is called *Shams al-Ma'arif*, that is, "The Sun of the Sciences," in which is contained the manner of making the little paintings and it shows the usefulness that is to be found in them; the third is titled *Sirr al-Asma' al-Husna*, "The Secret of the Ninety-nine Names of God,"[8] and this work I saw in Rome in the hands of a Venetian Jew. There is another rule in this sect, that is called the rule of *suwwah*,[9] that is, certain recluses who live in woods and solitary places, and who eat only wild fruits and herbs; and no one can understand the particulars of their life, since they flee every human intercourse.

But I would stray too far from the purpose of my work, if I wanted to follow minutely all the different Mohammaden sects. Let anyone who wishes to learn more read the work of a man whose name is al-Afkani,[1] who amply treats of the various sects that proceed from the Mohammaden faith, which are seventy-two principal ones; and each of them maintains that his is the good and true one, in which man can be saved. It is true that in the present age hardly more than two can be found: one is that of al-Ash'ari, which extends throughout all Africa, Egypt, Soria,[2] and Arabia and all of Turkey; the other is that of Imamiyya, and it is found all over Persia and in some cities of Khorasan.[3] The Sophi[4] king of Persia adheres to this latter sect, and for this sect practically all of Asia is destroyed, since beforehand they adhered to the sect of al-Ash'ari; several times the said king wanted to force them by means of arms to belong to his sect. It is true that ordinarily only a single sect embraces the domain of the Mohammadans.

Treasure Hunters

There are also in Fez some men called *al-kannazin*, whose business it is to search for treasure that they believe buried in the foundations of ancient ruins. These silly people go out of the city and enter grottoes and caves in order to find said treasure, being firmly of the opinion that when the Romans lost control of Africa and were fleeing toward Bética[5] in Spain, they buried in those regions many precious and costly things, which they could not carry with them; and for this reason they try to procure magicians for said treasure. And there is no lack of people who claim that they saw gold in such and such a cave, and others silver, but that they could not dig them up because they didn't have the appropriate magic spells and perfumes; and

7. Or *Radiant Sparks*, a work on God's names.
8. Or *The Secret of the Most Beautiful Names of God*, likely extracted from *Shams al-Ma'arif*.
9. Wanderers (Arabic), a label often applied to traveling renunciants.
1. Probably the physician and anthologist Abu 'Abdallah Muhammad al-Ansari (ca. 1285–1348), known as Ibn al-Akfani, whose *Irshad al-Qasid ila Asna al-Maqasid* (*The Guidance of the Aspirant to the Highest Goals*) has a section on Islamic heresiography cited by later historians.
2. Syria. Abu al-Hasan al-Ash'ari (874–935; see above), whose writings form the basis for Sunni theology.
3. The northeast region of Iran. "The Imamiyya": Twelver or Imami Shi'ism, established as the state religion by the Safavid empire (1501–1733), which ruled over much of modern-day Iran and parts of other nearby countries.
4. Or Sophy, a title formerly given by Europeans to the ruler of the Safavid empire.
5. Baetica, a Roman province in Southern Spain (western Andalusia).

with this empty belief of theirs they frequently ruin buildings and tombs with their digging, and at times they travel ten or twelve days' distance from Fez. And the business has gone so far that they hold as oracles certain books they possess that mention some mountains and places where there are many hidden treasures. And before I left Fez, these people created a consul to govern their madness and asking permission from the owners of the places, when they had dug as much as they wanted, they paid them for any damage done.

Alchemists

And do not think that there is a lack of alchemists; on the contrary there are in abundance those who strive in that foolish vanity, and they are the dirtiest of men and the ones who smell the worst in the world, on account of the sulfur and other unhappy odors. And in the evening, almost as a rule, many of them get together in the most important temple, and they discuss these false imaginings of theirs. And there are many works on the above-mentioned art, composed by eloquent men: and the first is written by Jabir,[6] who lived a hundred years after Mohammad, who was said to be a disavowed Greek, and all his formulas are written as allegory. There is still another author who wrote another important work, called al-Tughra'i,[7] who was the secretary of the Sultan of Baghdad, as we described in the life of the Arabic philosophers. And another work composed in canticles, I say all the articles of this art, and the master was named al-Maghrabi,[8] who was from Granada: and it was annotated by a Mamluk of Damascus,[9] a man very learned in this art, but the comment is more difficult to understand than is the text. These alchemists are of two sorts: some go looking for elixir, that is, the material that changes every metal and vein (of ore); and others dedicate themselves to investigating the multiplication of the quantities of metal, by mixing the one with the other. But I have seen that the objective of these men is most frequently to take up the counterfeiting of money; most of those who belong to this group in Fez are recognizable because they are missing a hand.[1]

Bewitchers and Snake Charmers

Lastly there are in this city many of that useless rabble who in Italy are called bewitchers. And men of this sort sing in the squares romances, songs, and such nonsense, playing a certain kind of drums, violas, harps, and other instruments, and sell to the ignorant crowd certain charms and amulets that, as they claim, are against various evils. To this sort must be added another sort of very vile men, who are all of the same family and go through the city making monkeys dance, and carrying many snakes around their neck and hands. They also make many figures of divination, and foretell the future of women. They bring with them some, as they say in Italy, stallions, and for a price they impregnate the mares of anyone who wishes.

6. Jabir ibn Hayyan (ca. 721–ca. 815), the court physician of the caliph and a noted alchemist.
7. Abu Ismail al-Husayn al-Tughra'i (1061–1121), renowned for his poetry and works on alchemy.
8. Abu al-Hasan ʿAli (d. 1197); the work referred to is his long poem on alchemy, *Shudhur al-Dhahab* (*Shavings of Gold*).
9. ʿIzz al-Din Aydamir al-Jildaki (d. ca. 1342), the last of the great Muslim alchemists; he wrote extensive commentaries on his predecessors.
1. The punishment for counterfeiting was amputation of the hand.

Now I could keep going with other particulars about the men of this city: but let it be enough to say that they are for the most part unpleasant and have little love for foreigners, albeit there is not any great number of foreigners, because the city is about a hundred miles from the sea, and between the sea and the city the roads are very rough and unpleasant for a foreigner. Furthermore I will say that the nobility are very haughty, such that few frequent them; doctors and judges behave in the same way and have the reputation of not wanting to associate with any but a few. Nevertheless the conclusion is that the city is beautiful, commodious, and well organized. And although in the springtime there is a great quantity of mud, such that in order to walk it is necessary to wear certain wooden shoes that they use, nevertheless they make certain outlets from their canals so that these wash the mud from all the quarters of the city. And where there are no canals they gather up the mud and, piling it onto beasts of burden, they throw it into the river.

TASAWWUF: THE MYSTICAL INTERIORITY OF SUFISM

ZAYN AL-ʿABIDIN ʿALI B. AL-HUSAYN

ca. 658–ca. 713

ʿAli ibn al-Husayn, the fourth Imam of Twelver Shiʿis, is more commonly known by his honorifics Zayn al-ʿAbidin ("The Ornament of the Worshippers") or al-Sajjad ("He Who Constantly Prostrates Himself"). He was born in Medina, the son of Husayn (and so the great-grandson of Muhammad) and, many believe, of the daughter of the last Sassanid Persian king.

Though present at the massacre of his father, his father's followers, and other family members at Karbalaʾ in 680, Zayn al-ʿAbidin was confined to his tent by serious illness for the battle's duration. Only the intervention of his aunt Zaynab saved him from execution at Karbalaʾ and again in Kufa when he was brought there en route to Damascus with the other prisoners. After imprisonment in Damascus, Zayn al-ʿAbidin was sent by the Umayyad caliph Yazid (r. 680–83) back to Medina, where he spent his life in worship and teaching. According to Shiʿi sources, around 713 he was poisoned at the hands of the caliph al-Walid (r. 705–15) or the caliph's brother Hisham. It is said that upon his death one hundred families in Medina realized that he had been the one delivering food and sustenance to them each night while covering his face to remain anonymous.

The period after the Karbalaʾ massacre gave rise to various Shiʿi movements, several of which took an activist stance against the Umayyads. Zayn al-ʿAbidin maintained a quietist position on politics and thus many Shiʿis did not acknowledge him as an imam. He was, however, widely respected throughout the Muslim community as Muhammad's great-grandson, as a victim and witness at Karbalaʾ, as a teacher of Islamic sciences, and, most importantly, as a pious, prayerful individual. He is reported to have performed 1,000 cycles of the supererogatory prayers each day, increasing his devotions during the fasting month of Ramadan.

The most outstanding example of his piety is *The Book of the Constant Prostrator.* Considered the oldest Muslim prayer manual, it has an importance to Shiʿis rivaled only by the Qurʾan itself and the collection of writings by the first Imam ʿAli ibn Abi Talib (ca. 599–661) titled *The Peak of Eloquence.* It is still used daily by millions of Muslims, both Shiʿi and Sunni.

Both Muslim and Western scholars accept the overall authenticity of this work, though some of the latter question a series of "whispered prayers" that modern editions add to the original fifty-four supplications. These supplications are thought to have been first taught to Zayn al-ʿAbidin's children; they then spread into the Muslim community at large. The book became even more popular during the Safavid era (1501–1733), when it was translated into Persian.

The prayer forms of *The Book of the Constant Prostrator* would be familiar to many Christians. These are supplications, or *duʿaʾ*, in contrast to the obligatory ritual prostrations and formulas that observant Muslims perform five times daily. Typically, in supplications one personally invokes God, praising him and seeking his aid. Such prayers are often spontaneous, and those in the *Constant Prostrator* were probably composed on impulse and later became more widely adopted by the community.

The prayers in Zayn al-ʿAbidin's book focus on particular times and occasions, members of family and community, morally challenging situations, and other topics. Themes in the supplications include fostering a personal relationship with God, praising him extensively, requesting divine guidance and protection, and seeking his forgiveness. The prayers manifest a particular emphasis on God's love and mercy and often—as do the supplications below—incorporate qurʾanic verses. Indeed, *The Constant Prostrator* is sometimes called "the Sister of the Qurʾan."

PRONOUNCING GLOSSARY

sharīʿa: *sha-ree´-uh*

sunna: *sun´-nuh*

FROM THE BOOK OF THE CONSTANT PROSTRATOR

Supplication 6

His Supplication in Morning and Evening

Praise belongs to God,
who created night and day
through His strength,
set them apart
through His power,
and appointed for each
a determined limit
and a drawn-out period.
He makes each of the two enter into its companion,
and makes its companion enter into it,
as an ordainment from Him for His servants
in that through which He feeds them
and with which He makes them grow.
He created for them the night,
that they might rest in it[1]
from tiring movements
and wearisome exertions
and He made it a garment for them

TRANSLATED BY William C. Chittick.

1. Qurʾan 10:67.

that they might be clothed
in its ease and its sleep,
that it might be for them refreshment and strength,
that they might reach therein pleasure and passion.
He created for them *the daytime, giving sight,*
that they might seek within it of His *bounty*,[2]
find the means to His provision,
and roam freely in His earth,
searching for that through which
to attain the immediate in their life in this world
and to achieve the deferred in their life to come.
Through all of this He sets right their situation,
tries their records,
and watches their state in
the times for obeying Him,
the waystations of His obligations,
and the places of His ordinances,
That He may repay those who do evil with what they have done
and repay those who do good with goodness.[3]
O God,
to Thee belongs praise
for the sky Thou hast split into dawn for us,[4]
giving us to enjoy thereby the brightness of daytime,
showing us sought-after nourishments,
and protecting us from the striking of blights.
In the morning we and all things, every one, rise for Thee,
the heaven and the earth
and what Thou hast scattered in each,
the still and the moving.
the resident and the journeying,
what towers up in the air and what hides under the ground.
We rise in the morning in Thy grasp:
Thy kingdom and authority contain us
and Thy will embraces us.
We move about by Thy command
and turn this way and that through Thy governing,
We own nothing of the affair
except what Thou hast decreed
and nothing of the good
except what Thou hast given.
This is a fresh, new day,
over us a ready witness.
If we do good,
it will take leave from us with praise,
and if we do evil,
it will part from us in blame.
O God,
bless Muḥammad and his Household,
provide us with the day's good companionship

2. Qur'an 17:12.
3. Qur'an 53:31.
4. An allusion to Qur'an 6:96 [translator's note].

and preserve us against parting from it badly
by doing a misdeed
or committing a sin, whether small or a great!
Make our good deeds within it plentiful
empty us therein of evil deeds,
and fill what lies between its two sides for us
with praise and thanksgiving,
wages and stores,
bounty and beneficence!
O God,
ease our burden on the Noble Writers,[5]
fill our pages for us
with our good deeds,
and degrade us not before them
with our evil works!
O God,
appoint for us in each of the day's hours
a share from Thy servants,
a portion of giving thanks to Thee,
and a truthful witness among Thy angels!
O God,
bless Muḥammad and his Household
and safeguard us from before us and behind us,
from our right hands and our left hands
and from all our directions,
a safeguarding that will preserve from disobeying Thee,
guide to obeying Thee,
and be employed for Thy love!
O God,
bless Muḥammad and his Household
and give us success in this day of ours,
this night of ours,
and in all our days,
to employ the good,
stay away from the evil,
give thanks for favours,
follow the *Sunna*'s norms,
avoid innovations,
enjoin good behavior,
forbid the disapproved,
defend Islam,
diminish falsehood and abase it,
help the truth and exalt it,
guide the misguided,
assist the weak,
and reach out to the troubled!
O God,
bless Muḥammad and his Household
and make this
the most fortunate day we have known,

5. The angels mentioned in Qur'an 3:18 who record the good and bad deeds of humankind.

the most excellent companion we have accompanied,
and the best time in which we have lingered!
Place us among
the most satisfied of all Thy creatures
whom night and day have passed by,
the most thankful of them
for the favours Thou hast done,
the firmest of them
in the laws Thou hast set down in the *Sharīʿa*,
and the most unyielding of them
toward the prohibited acts
against which Thou hast cautioned!
O God,
I call Thee to witness
—and Thou art sufficient witness—
and I call Thy heaven and Thy earth to witness
and Thy angels and Thy other creatures who inhabit them
in this my day,
this my hour,
this my night,
and this my resting place,
that I bear witness
that Thou art God,
other than whom there is no god,
Upholding justice,
Equitable in judgment,
Clement to the servants,[6]
Master of the kingdom,[7]
Compassionate to the creatures,
and that Muḥammad is Thy servant and Thy messenger,
Thy chosen from among Thy creatures.
Thou didst charge him with Thy message
and he delivered it;
Thou didst command him to counsel his community
and he counselled it.
O God,
so bless Muḥammad and his Household
more than Thou hast blessed any of Thy creatures!
Give him for our sake the best Thou hast given any
of Thy servants,
and repay him on our behalf better and more generously
than Thou hast repaid any of Thy prophets
on behalf of his community!
Thou art All-kind with immensity,
the Forgiver of the great,
and Thou art more merciful
than every possessor of mercy!
So bless Muḥammad and his Household,
the good, the pure, the chosen, the most distinguished!

6. Qurʾan 2:207.

7. Qurʾan 3:26.

Supplication 8

His Supplication in Seeking Refuge from Hateful Things, Bad Moral Qualities, and Blameworthy Acts

O God, I seek refuge in Thee from
the agitation of craving,
the violence of wrath,
the domination of envy,
the frailty of patience,
the lack of contentment,
surliness of character,
urgency of passion,
the disposition to vehemence,
following caprice,
opposing guidance,
the sleep of heedlessness,
undertaking the toilsome,
preferring falsehood over truth,
persisting in sin,
making little of disobedience,
making much of obedience,
vying with the wealthy,
disparaging the poor,
guarding badly over those in our hands,
failing to thank those who have done good to us,
aiding a wrongdoer,
abandoning someone troubled,
wanting what is not rightfully ours,
and speaking about knowledge without knowing.
We seek refuge in Thee from
harbouring dishonesty toward anyone,
being pleased with our works,
and stretching out our expectations.
We seek refuge in Thee from
ill-mindedness,
looking down on the small,
Satan's gaining mastery over us,
time's afflicting us,
and the sovereign's oppressing us.
We seek refuge in Thee from
acting with prodigality
and not having sufficiency.
We seek refuge in Thee from
the gloating of enemies,
indigent need for equals,
living in hardship,
and dying without readiness.
We seek refuge in Thee from
the most dreadful remorse,
the greatest affliction,
the most wretched wretchedness,

the evil end to the journey,
the deprivation of reward,
and the advent of punishment.
O God,
bless Muḥammad and his Household
and through Thy mercy, give to me refuge from all of that,
and to all the faithful, both men and women!
O Most Merciful of the merciful!

AL-BISTAMI
d. ca. 875

Abu Yazid Tayfur ibn ʿIsa ibn Surushan al-Bistami, a representative of "drunken" Sufism, gained renown for expressing his relationship with the divine through ecstatic utterances (in Arabic, *shatahat*). While these utterances may appear blasphemous when read literally, many Muslims found them a sincere expression of spiritual unification with God.

Born in northern Iran, Abu Yazid spent his entire life—barring his brief flights to escape persecution by local religious scholars—in the town of Bistam. According to most historical sources, he died there in 875, though substantial evidence suggests a date almost thirty years earlier.

The historical literature preserves only brief mentions of Abu Yazid, but those reveal a man who took seriously his religious and spiritual practices. He was known for assiduously performing his prayer ablutions and always cleaning his mouth as preparation for the Sufi practice of repeated invocations of God's name (in Arabic, *dhikr*). Before meditating he closed every window and door so that nothing would disturb him. Sufi hagiography portrays Abu Yazid as a self-effacing individual who minimized the importance of the miraculous acts attributed to him and disparaged those who took themselves too seriously.

The teacher who introduced Abu Yazid to the mystical ideas of Sufism was Abu ʿAli al-Sindi; he lacked knowledge of the basic rituals of Islam and received instruction in them from Abu Yazid who had studied Hanafi law. Abu ʿAli may have been from India, and on the basis of this hypothesis, a few modern scholars have argued that Abu Yazid's ecstatic utterances were influenced by Buddhist and Hindu religious ideas.

Though Abu Yazid wrote nothing, roughly five hundred of his statements were collected and then passed down to later generations through two lines of transmission. One collection was handed on by his family members, beginning with Abu Musa ʿIsa ibn Adam, his nephew and disciple. These sayings were later translated from Persian into Arabic by the famous "sober" Sufi jurist of Baghdad, Abu al-Qasim al-Junayd (d. 910). Another collection was disseminated by those Sufis who frequented Abu Yazid's circle. Both collections were preserved and commented on in the writings of later Sufi authors, such as al-Sulami (d. 1021; see below), Farid al-Din ʿAttar (ca. 1142–ca. 1220), and Ibn al-ʿArabi (1165–1240; see below).

Abu Yazid's fame stemmed primarily from such ecstatic exclamations as "Glory be to Me! How great is My majesty!" and "I am He." Both declarations would leave the average Muslim listener with the impression that Abu Yazid was claiming to be God. While his detractors heard only heresy or insanity in his statements, his supporters understood them as an attempt to convey the experience of being so united with the divine that there ceased to be either a human self or a divine being.

All that existed in such moments was a mystical union of both, and Abu Yazid's ecstatic statements were an effort, however imperfect, to express this reality.

Because of such statements, Abu Yazid was regularly represented in Sufi literature as an exemplar of "drunken" Sufism, which viewed losing the self in God as the highest attainable state. At the other end of the spectrum, al-Junayd of Baghdad was cited as an example of "sober" Sufism, which viewed mystical self-effacement in God as a sign of spiritual immaturity. For this group, the highest state was remaining sober and seeing the world as it truly is.

Among the transmissions from Abu Yazid's followers is a description of mystical union experienced as an ascent through ever-higher heavens. This narrative has been preserved in several Sufi works, among them al-Junayd's *Quest for God*, which is reproduced below. Abu Yazid's account was molded on that of the most famous ascension in Islamic history—the prophet Muhammad's. Versions of this story depict the stages of Muhammad's journey as he rose through the heavens until he reached the seventh heaven, where he finally met God.

Abu Yazid begins his narrative by explaining that his entire ascent occurred during a dreamlike state. He rose through the seven heavens and at each one was tested by God with the promise of dominion beyond description. On every occasion, however, he realized that God was trying him, and he testifies that his goal is nothing but God. This pattern enables his account to serve a didactic purpose, cautioning other Sufis to be mindful of the temptations that might befall them during their own mystical journey to God but also encouraging them in their endeavor. After passing the tests of the seventh heaven, Abu Yazid finally attained his goal—a mystical union with God. He describes the experience of union as being beyond words, recalling that he was closer to God "than the spirit is to the body."

PRONOUNCING GLOSSARY

Abū l-Qāsim al-ʿ Arif: *a-bool-qah´-sim al-ah´-rif*
Abū Yazīd al-Bisṭāmī: *a-boo ya-zeed´ al-bis-tah´-mee*
al-Qaṣd ilā Allāh: *al-qasd´ ee-lal-la´*
Baryāʾīl: *bar-ya-eel´*
Jabarūt: *ja-ba-root´*
Lawīdh: *la-weedh´*
maʿrifa: *mah´-ri-fuh*
Malakūt: *ma-la-koot´*
Nayāʾīl: *na-ya-eel´*

THE *MIʿRAJ*

Abū l-Qāsim al-ʿArif,[1] may Allah be pleased with him, said: Know, O you tribes in quest of Allah Most High and Glorious, that Abu Yazid has had states and stations which the hearts of the neglectful and the common people would not be able to bear. He also has secrets with Allah which would astonish the heedless if they could come to know them. In a book containing the virtues of Abu Yazid I have seen things concerning his states and moments and words that would wear out the tongue to describe and depict. Whoever wishes to know Abu Yazid's completeness and rank should regard Abu Yazid's dream and vision, which is sounder in content and more verifiable than is the waking state of others. This is what has been related from the retainer of Abu Yazid, that he said: I heard Abu Yazid al-Bistami, may Allah be pleased with him, say:

TRANSLATED BY Michael A. Sells.

1. Abu al-Qasim al-Junayd (d. 910), mystic and author of *Quest for God*.

I saw myself in the dream as if I had risen to the heavens in quest of Allah, seeking union with Allah Most High that I might abide with him forever. I was tried in a trial that the heavens and earth and everything in them could not stand. He spread out before me gifts of every kind and showed me dominion over every heaven. Throughout, I kept my gaze lowered from these things. I knew he was testing me with them. Through all of this I kept saying: O my dear one, my goal is other than what you are showing me.

He said: I said to him, may Allah have compassion on you! Describe for me some of what he showed you of the dominion over every heaven!

The First Heaven

He said: I saw myself in the dream, as if I had risen to the heavens. When I came to the lowest heaven, I was in the presence of a green bird. It spread out one of its wings and bore me away, taking me as far as some legions of angels who were standing with their feet aflame amidst the stars, praising Allah morning and evening. I saluted them and they returned my salutation. The bird set me down among them and departed. I remained among them and continued to recite Allah's praises and to glorify Allah Most High (*taʿālā*) in their tongue, while they were saying: This is an Adamite, not a Luminary,[2] who comes among us and speaks to us. He said: I was inspired with words and said: In the name of Allah who is able to release me from all need for you! Then he continued to show me dominion that would wear out the tongue to describe and depict. I knew that he was testing me with it in that. I was saying: My goal is other than what you are showing me. I did not turn toward it out of respect for his sanctity.

The Second Heaven

Then I saw myself as if I had risen to the second heaven. Droves of angels came upon me, gazing at me like people gazing upon a prince who is entering their city. Then the chief of the angels approached me. His name was Lawīdh. He said: O Abu Yazid, your lord offers you salutations and says: You have loved me and I have loved you. He took me as far as a green garden. In it was a flowing river surrounded by flying angels. Every day they would fly to the earth one thousand times to look upon the friends of God, faces radiant as the sun, who had known me according to the *maʿrifa*[3] of the earth, that is, on the earth. Then they approached me, greeted me, and took me down to the shore of that river. Upon its banks were trees of light with numerous boughs hanging out into the air. Upon each bough was the nest of a bird, that is, of one of the angels. And in every nest was an angel bowing down in prayer. Throughout all that, I was saying: O my dear one, my goal is other than what you are showing me. Be for me, dear one, a protector of protectors and a companion of companions. Then there surged up in the secret of my heart something like the thirst of the flame of longing, so that the angels with their trees were reduced to a gnat alongside my aspiration. They were all gazing at me, amazed and astonished at the grandeur of what they saw in me. When Allah Most High knew the sincerity of my will in the

2. That is, a human, not an inhabitant of heaven.

3. A direct spiritual knowledge of God.

quest for him and my self-divestment of everyone beside him, behold, there was an angel extending his hand, drawing me toward him.

The Third Heaven

Then I saw myself as if I had risen to the third heaven. All the angels with all their qualities and attributes had approached me and greeted me. Suddenly from among them an angel stood with four faces: a face turned toward the heaven that wept tears without cease; a face turned toward the earth that cried out: O servants of Allah, the day of cessation! the day of seizure! the day of reckoning![4] a face whose right side was turned toward angels reciting Allah's praises; and a face whose left side sent forth an army into the quarters of the heavens to chant throughout them the praises of Allah. I saluted him and he returned my salutation. Then he said: Who are you to be preferred over us? I said: a servant whom Allah Most High (*taʿālā*) has granted a share of his favor. He said: Do you wish to look upon the marvels of Allah? I said "Of course!" He spread out one of his wings and behold: On each of his feathers there was a lamp whose light would darken the sun. Then he said: Come up (*taʿāli*), O Abu Yazid, and take shade in the shade of my wing where you can recite the praises of Allah until death. Then I said to him: Allah is able to release me from all need for you. Then there surged up from the secret of my heart the bright light of my *maʿrifa*, the brightness of which clouded over theirs, that is, the brightness of the lamps, and the angel was reduced to a gnat alongside my completeness. He continued to show me dominion that would wear out the tongue to describe. Through all that, I knew that he was testing me. I did not turn toward that out of respect for his sanctity. Throughout I was saying: O my dear one! My goal is not what you are showing me. When Allah knew the sincerity of my will in quest for him, behold there was an angel extending his hand and raising me up.

The Fourth Heaven

Then I saw myself as if I had risen to the fourth heaven. There were all the angels with their attributes, figures, and qualities. They approached me, greeted me, and gazed at me like a people gazing at their prince the moment he enters their country. They raised their voices in praise and affirmation of divine unity because of the grandeur they saw in my cutting myself off for him and my refusal to turn to them. An angel greeted me who was said to be named Nayāʾīl. He extended his hand and sat me upon a throne (*kursī*) placed upon the shore of a roaring sea whose beginning and end could not be seen. I was inspired with his recitation of praise and found myself pronouncing in his tongue. Still, I did not turn to him. He continued to show me dominion that would wear out the tongue to describe. Through all that, I knew that he was testing me with it. I did not turn to him out of respect for his sanctity. I kept saying: O my dear one! My goal is other than that which you are showing me. When Allah Most High knew the sincerity of my aloneness for him in the quest toward him, behold, there was an angel extending his hand and raising me up to him.

4. All references to the Day of Judgment.

The Fifth Heaven

Then I saw myself as if I had risen to the fifth heaven. There I was in the presence of angels who stood in the fifth heaven with their heads in the sixth, which dropped down light that would make the heavens flash. They all saluted me in various languages and I returned the salutations to them in every language in which they had saluted me. They were amazed at that. They said: O Abu Yazid, come up (*taʿāli*) to recite Allah's praises and unity and we will set aside for you whatever you wish. I did not turn to them out of respect for my lord. At that point, there surged up, in the secret of my heart, springs of longing, and the light of the angels became, in the light that radiated from me, like a lamp placed on the sun. He continued to show me dominion that would wear out the tongue to describe. Through all that, I knew that he was testing me. I kept saying: O my dear one! My goal is other than that which you are showing me. When Allah Most High (*taʿālā*) knew the sincerity of my will in quest for him, behold there was an angel raising me up to himself.

The Sixth Heaven

Then I saw myself as if I had ascended to the sixth heaven and stood before the angels of longing. They approached me, greeted me, and boasted over me of their longing, so I boasted over them with something of the secret of my heart. He continued to show me dominion that would wear out the tongue to describe. Throughout all that, I knew that he was testing me in these things and I did not turn to them. When Allah Most High saw the sincerity of my will in my quest for him, behold an angel was extending his arm and raising me up to himself.

The Seventh Heaven

Then I saw myself as if I had risen to the seventh heaven. There were a hundred thousand legions of angels greeting me, each legion like the two heavy ones[5] one thousand thousand times. With every angel was a standard of light and under every standard were one thousand thousand angels, the height of each angel a journey of five hundred years. At their front was an angel named Baryāʾīl. They saluted me in their language and I returned the salutation in their language. They were amazed at that. Then behold, a crier was crying out: O Abu Yazid, stop, stop, you have arrived at the end! I did not turn toward his words. He continued to show me dominion that would wear out the tongue to describe. Through all that, I knew that he was testing me in it. I kept saying: O my dear one! My goal is other than that which you are showing me. When Allah knew the sincerity of my will in quest for him, he turned me into a bird, each wing feather of which was greater than the distance from East to West one thousand thousand times. I continued flying

5. This enigmatic qurʾanic expression has been interpreted in a number of ways, as referring to the jinn and human beings (the two heavy "earth creatures"), or as referring to Jupiter and Saturn, to give two common interpretations [translator's note].

through the *Malakūt* and roaming through the *Jabarūt*.[6] I cut across kingdom after kingdom, veils after veils, domains after domains, seas after seas, curtains after curtains, until I stood before the angel of the throne (*kursī*), who received me.

He had a column of light as he greeted me. He said: Take the column. As soon as I took it, the heavens and everything in them were sheltered in the shade of my *maʿrifa* and were illuminated in the light of my longing. All the angels were reduced to a gnat alongside the completeness of my aspiration in quest for him. Through all that, I knew he was testing me with it and I did not turn to it out of respect for the sanctity of my lord, Allah Most High.

I continued to fly and roam kingdom after kingdom, veil after veil, domain after domain, sea after sea, curtain after curtain, until I ended up at a throne. I was received by angels with eyes as numerous as the stars of the heavens. From each eye there was flashing a light that would illumine the viewer. Those lights became lamps. From the interior of the lamps I heard chants of praise and divine unity.

I continued to fly like that until I ended up at a sea of light with crashing waves. Alongside it the light of the sun was darkened. There on the sea was a ship of light. Alongside its light the lights of those seas were darkened.

I continued to cross sea after sea until I ended up at the greatest sea on which was the royal throne (*ʿarsh*) of the Compassionate. I continued to recite his praises until I saw that all that there was—from the throne to the earth, of Cherubim (*karūbiyyīn*), angels, and the bearers of the royal throne and others created by Allah Most High and Glorious in the heavens and the earth—was smaller, from the perspective of the flight of the secret of my heart in quest for him, than a mustard seed between sky and earth. Then he continued to show me of the subtleties of his beneficence and the fullness of his power and the greatness of his sovereignty what would wear out the tongue to depict and describe. Through all that, I kept saying: O my dear one! My goal is other than that which you are showing me, and I did not turn toward it out of respect for his sanctity. And when Allah Most High and Glorious knew the sincerity of my will in quest for him, he called out "To me, to me!" and said O my chosen one (*ṣafī*), come near to me and look upon the plains of my splendor and the domains of my brightness. Sit upon the carpet of my holiness until you see the subtleties of my artisanship I-ness. You are my chosen one, my beloved, and the best of my creatures.

Upon hearing that, it was as if I were melting like melting lead. Then he gave me a drink from the spring of graciousness (*luṭf*) with the cup of intimacy. Then he brought me to a state that I am unable to describe. Then he brought me closer and closer to him until I was nearer to him than the spirit is to the body.

Then the spirit of each prophet received me, saluted me, and glorified my situation. They spoke to me and I spoke to them. Then the spirit of Muhammad, the blessings and peace of God be upon him, received me, saluted me, and said: O Abu Yazid: welcome! welcome! Allah has preferred you over

6. Many scholars understand the *Malakut* as an angelic realm that holds unchanging spiritual truths and the *Jabarut* as a higher world that contains God's names and attributes, but the terms have no agreed-on definitions.

many of his creatures. When you return to earth, bear to my community my salutation and give them sincere advice as much as you can and call them to Allah Most High and Glorious. I kept on in this way until I was like he was before creation and only the real remained *(baqiya)* without being or relation or place or position or quality. May his glory be glorified and his names held transcendent!

Abu l-Qāsim al-ʿArif said: O tribes of my brothers, I have shown this vision to the most venerable among the people of *maʿrifa*. All of them support it, none deny it. Rather, they accept it as one of the levels of the people who cut themselves off in quest for him. Then they cited the word of the Prophet, the blessings and peace of Allah upon him, that "the servant remains from Allah and Allah is never from him as long as he does not panic. If he panics, then he incurs blame and reckoning." It is also related from the Prophet, blessings and peace of Allah upon him, that "of knowledge there is something like a hidden figure which is known only by the people of knowledge in Allah and which is denied only by the people of heedlessness of Allah." And were it not for a dislike of going on at too much length, we would have mentioned support of the soundness of the story through the sound reports and known and accepted accounts. However, I know that whoever is ignorant of the levels of the chosen and the people of *maʿrifa* will not know (*yaʿraf*) their destiny and nobility. Multiplying proofs and elucidation will not suffice them and multiplying arguments and demonstrations will not avail them. In this regard, Allah Most High said (10:101): "Signs and warnings will not avail those who do not believe"; and [7:146]: "I will turn away from my signs those who act proud on the earth without reality"; and [29:49]: "These are clear signs in the breasts of those to whom knowledge is given. No one ignores our signs except the unjust"; and [24:40]: "Whomever Allah does not provide light will have no light." Allah is most knowing of the right.

AL-HAKIM AL-TIRMIDHI
fl. 9th century

Abu ʿAbdallah Muhammad ibn ʿAli al-Hakim al-Tirmidhi, a prolific Sufi author, is noted for his idea of a hierarchy of saints and for his concept of the seal of the saints.

Al-Hakim al-Tirmidhi was born before 830 in Tirmidh, Uzbekistan, and his father—a scholar specializing in traditions (*hadith*)—was his first teacher. He began studying when he was eight and quite early was pursuing a range of subjects, including law and theology. Following a pilgrimage to Mecca at age twenty-eight, he reached a turning point in his life and felt drawn to ascetic and renunciant practices. Soon thereafter he began experiencing mystical states. He attracted a small circle of like-minded individuals in his hometown, but many found his discourse and writings blasphemous. Though at one point al-Hakim al-Tirmidhi was forced to stand trial before the governor of the region, he was eventually exonerated and came to be revered in his city.

He is credited with more than eighty titles, covering such themes as traditions, ritual practices, and religious laws, all viewed through the lens of his heightened spiritual insight. In some works he treats mysticism more directly and addresses topics such as the mystical path, its pitfalls, and the means of gaining certain belief in God. His contributions to Sufism were enduring; he is the earliest author to propose a hierarchy of saints and one of the earliest to discuss the notion of a seal of the saints.

Al-Hakim al-Tirmidhi's hierarchy of saints starts with the group of general believers whom he calls "the Friends of Oneness." Above them are "the Truthful," who—unlike general believers—truly aspire to God, but find spiritual advancement difficult because they remain engrossed with daily life. Next are "the Noble Generous Ones," whose spiritual advancement protects their hearts but who have yet to master their souls. Above this group are the "the Forty Truthful," in whom only love for God remains and who have the ability to take on certain names of God. Finally, there stands "the Solitary One" (in Arabic, *al-munfarid*), the highest saint. Though not among the prophets, he is closer to them than he is to the Forty Truthful below him, sharing in many of their abilities—such as insight into the minds of others and truthful dreams—to which other saints have only limited access. Al-Hakim al-Tirmidhi's concept of the seal of the saints mirrors the notion that Muhammad was the seal of the prophets. Just as Muhammad was the final prophet, so too there will eventually appear a seal of the saints who will be God's greatest saint and whom no other saint can surpass. This idea is later developed by Ibn al-ʿArabi (1165–1240; see below), who expands on it in his writings, claiming that he himself is the seal of the saints.

The passage below is taken from *The Seal of the Saints.* In this excerpt al-Hakim al-Tirmidhi describes his early years, his spiritual awakening, the trials he endured, and his subsequent spiritual growth, which begins with two series of dreams: first his own, and then those that his wife has about him. He views these truthful dreams as a sign of sainthood. Two points stand out in this passage. First, closeness to God is not attained through works, seclusion, or ascetic practices; rather, the secret lies in having goodness in one's heart. Second, in one of the early dreams of al-Hakim al-Tirmidhi's wife, an angel informs her that she is her husband's equal in spiritual rank. This is striking not because of her sex but because of her total lack of scholarly training. It reinforces the view that purity of heart—not works or knowledge—is paramount in spiritual development.

PRONOUNCING GLOSSARY

Abū Dawūd: *a-boo da-woud´*
Aḥmad ibn Jibrīl: *ah´-mad* (heavy *h*) *ibn jib-reel´*
al-Anṭākī: *al-an-tah´-kee*
al-ḥubb: *al-hub´* (heavy *h*)
Balkh: balch (guttural *ch*)
Dawdabad: *daw-dah´-bahd*
Dhū al-Qaʿda: *dhool-qah´-duh*
furuzd: *fo-roozd´*
kaʿba: *ka´-buh*
Muḥmmad ibn ʿAlī al-Tirmidhī: *moo-ham´-mad* (heavy *h*) *ibn ah´-lee at-tir´-mi-dhee*
Muḥammad ibn Najm: *moo-ham´-mad* (heavy *h*) *ibn najm´*
multazan: *mul-tuh´-zum*
qibla: *qib´-luh*
Rajab: *Ra´-jub*
Ramadan: *ra-ma-dawn´*
Shaʿbān: *Sha-ban´*

FROM THE SEAL OF THE SAINTS

The Beginning of the Career of Abī ʿAbd Allāh [the Sage of Tirmidh]

My career began because God favored me with a father—God rest his soul—who pressed me to take up the pursuit of knowledge. When I was

TRANSLATED BY Dwight F. Reynolds, Kristen E. Brustad, et al. All bracketed additions are the translator's.

eight years old, he began to instruct me and to encourage me to study. This he did with unvarying vigor both when I was disposed to heed him and when I was not, until study became a habit for me and took the place of the games and play of childhood. He thus acquainted me, still a youth, with the sciences of *ḥadīth* and legal reasoning.

When I reached the age of twenty-seven, or thereabouts, I suddenly felt the need to make the pilgrimage. Fortunately, the means to do so became available to me, and I set off, stopping for a time in Iraq to collect *ḥadīth.* I then traveled to Basra and from there I left for Mecca in the month of Rajab, arriving toward the end of Shaʿbān.[1] God provided me with the means to remain in Mecca until pilgrimage time.[2] I came, by God's grace, to pray at the *multazam* [the area near the door of the Kaʿba[3] where all prayers are said to be answered], every morning at the first light of dawn. There I was truly converted in my heart, and made to see past the clash of questions great and small. I performed the pilgrimage and returned, having effected in myself a change of heart.

At those times when I prayed at the *multazam*, I would ask God to make me righteous, inspire me with an aversion for the things of the world, and grant me the ability to know His Book by heart. At that time, this was all I felt the need to ask for.

I set off for home, God having instilled in me the desire to memorize the Qurʾān while on the road. I learned a good portion of it while traveling, and, after I had returned home, God by His grace eased my task, and I succeeded in memorizing all of it. I would stay up late reading, but I never wearied of the Qurʾān, even when I had been up all night, and I discovered the sweetness of it.

I began reading books of the praises of God—blessed be His name—and collecting phrases with which to admonish myself and to inspire thoughts of the Hereafter. Meanwhile, I was searching the nearby towns, but could find no one to guide me along the path, or preach to me and strengthen my resolve. I was confused; I did not know what God wished for me. Nevertheless, I pursued my fasting and my prayer, until at last the words of a man of [mystical] knowledge reached my ears. I came across the book of al-Anṭākī[4] and examined it, and was thus guided to some knowledge of the discipline of the soul. I took up this practice and God helped me. Inspired to deny myself my desires, I found that I could train myself to do one thing after another, even to the point of denying myself cool water. I would refrain from drinking from the river, thinking, "Perhaps this water had flowed here wrongfully." So I would drink from a well or from a big watercourse.

I became enamored of solitude at home and of walking in the wilderness. I took to wandering amid the ruins and the cemeteries on the outskirts of town. I sought for trustworthy friends to support me, but could find none, and so I withdrew to those ruins and lonely places.

While in this state, I dreamt that the Prophet—God bless him and grant him peace—entered the Friday mosque in our town. I followed him inside. He continued walking until he reached the enclosed area[5] with me close

1. The eighth month of the Islamic calendar (because it is a lunar calendar, its dates in relation to the Gregorian calendar vary from year to year). Rajab is the previous month.
2. Four months later, during the final month of the Islamic calendar, Dhu al-Hijja.
3. Literally, "the Cube," a stone shrine in Mecca—according to tradition, built by Abraham—that became the most important site in Islam (Muslims around the world face it when they pray).
4. Ahmad ibn ʿAsim al-Antaki (d. ca. 845?), a Muslim mystic known for narrating the works of the famous Sufi al-Muhasibi (ca. 781–857).
5. The area reserved for the ruler.

behind him, almost touching his back, and placing my feet exactly where he had placed his, until I too reached the enclosed area. The Prophet ascended the pulpit, and I followed behind him, step for step. He reached the top step and sat down, and I sat on the next step down. To my right was the Prophet, in front of me were the doors that open onto the market, and to my left was the congregation. I then woke up while I was still in that state.

One night, a little time later, I was praying and felt sleepy, so I put my head down on the prayer rug next to my bed. I saw an enormous stretch of desert, in some place I did not know, and I saw an enormous court, with a place prepared at the head, and a tent or booth set up there, made of cloths and curtains I cannot describe. Then I seemed to hear someone saying, "You are being taken to your Lord." I entered the tent. I could see no one at all, no shape or figure, but I was terrified as I passed behind the curtains. I was certain, even as I slept, that I was standing in His presence. Soon after, I saw myself emerging from the tent, standing near the outermost curtain, and saying, "He has forgiven me" [or: "May He forgive me!"]. I found that I had stopped breathing, I was so terrified.

I continued in my practice of self-denial, pushing aside my desires, staying at home to be away from people, and constantly addressing myself to God in supplication. In this way, one thing after another was opened up to me. I discovered strength and awareness in myself, and I sought out those who could help me. We would meet at night, practicing the remembrance of God, praying, and abasing ourselves in supplication at the first light of dawn.

At this time I fell into trouble on account of slander and baseless rumors about me. Certain persons, of the sort who pretend to knowledge, made themselves heard at my expense. They slandered and persecuted me, accusing me of freethinking and heresy. Rumors spread, but I was indifferent. I remained on my own course, day and night, never changing, always the same. But matters took a turn for the worse: I was denounced to the governor at Balkh,[6] who sent someone to investigate. "Here," it was reported to the governor, "is someone who talks of Love [*al-ḥubb*], corrupts the people, preaches heresy, and claims to be a prophet," and other things that I had never even thought, much less said. Finally, I went to Balkh, where I was forbidden by the governor to speak of Love.

Sorrow purifies the heart, and thus did God—blessed be His name—provide me with the means to purify myself. I recalled the saying of David—God bless him and grant him peace: "O Lord, Thou hast commanded me to purify my body by fasting and prayer, but how do I purify my heart?" God said: "With trouble and sorrow, David!" [cf. II Samuel 16]. Troubles came upon me from all sides, but I finally found in them the path to the mortification of my soul. In the past, I had tried to mortify my soul in various ways: I had ridden a donkey through the marketplace, walked barefoot through the streets, worn shabby clothes, and carried burdens like a poor man or a slave; but my soul would recoil and refuse to submit. This was upsetting to me, but when these slanders came to afflict me, the perversity of my soul disappeared. My soul bore all these things and was humbled, and obeyed me; and at last, I experienced in my heart the sweetness of humility.

6. A region in northern Afghanistan.

One night during this time, a group of us gathered for the remembrance of God, on the occasion of a visit by one of our brethren. After some part of the night had passed, I left to return home. On the road, my heart opened up in a manner I cannot describe: as if something had touched my heart, something which cheered and delighted my soul. I was so happy that, as I walked, I feared nothing in my path: the dogs barked at me and I treasured their barking, because of some delight I felt in my heart. It even seemed to me that the sky with its moon and all its stars had drawn near the earth. All the while, I was invoking God, and I felt as if something had been set firmly within my heart. As I experienced this sweetness, my stomach wriggled and twisted and turned over on itself, and contracted, so powerful was this delight. The sweetness spread down my spine and through my veins. It seemed to me as if I were as close to God as His throne.

Every night I would stay awake until morning, unable to sleep, and I grew to bear this easily. I was still perplexed, however; I did not know what this experience was, but I grew stronger and more assiduous in my activities.

At that time an insurrection occurred in the area and civil strife ensued. All those who were persecuting and defaming me in the nearby towns fled. They suffered in the conflict and were forced into exile, and the country was rid of them.

It was during this period that my wife said to me:

> I dreamt I saw someone walking in the air, coming out of our house and walking above the path. He looked like a young man with curly hair, dressed in white, wearing sandals. He was calling to me from the air, and I was opposite him on the bench. He said, "Where is your husband?" "He has gone out," I replied. He said, "Tell him the Prince commands him to act justly." Then he was gone.

A short while later, a large number of people, including the elders of the town, gathered at my doorstep. I did not realize they were there until they started banging on the door. I went out and found them asking me to teach and hold assemblies for them on a regular basis. These people were the very same ones who had been spreading nasty rumors about me among the population, rumors so malicious that I had come to think of these people—or most of them in any case—as a sort of infectious disease. They had cast aspersions on my way of life and accused me of heretical beliefs that I had never held or even imagined holding.

Now here they were asking me to do this for them. Eventually, I gave in. When I spoke to them, it was as if the words came to me like ladlefuls of water from the sea and captivated their hearts. More and more people gathered round me. They filled the house and formed crowds in the street and the mosque. Finally, they carried me off to the mosque and it was as if all those lies and falsehoods about me had never been. Then the conversions began and disciples appeared and leadership, with all of its trials, fell to me as a Divine tribulation.

When the aforementioned slanderers returned from exile, they found that I had become a powerful man with many students and followers. In the past, they had turned the government and the people against me so effectively that I did not dare show my face in public, but God saw to it that their plots came to nothing. Now it was clear that they had acted out of malice and envy, and that no one was listening to them any more, so they gave up hope of harming me further.

In the meantime, my wife continued to have visions. They always came before dawn, and they came one after the other, like a Divine message. They were always so clear and so obvious in their meaning that they need no interpretation. One of these visions went like this:

> I saw a big pool, in a place I had never been before. The water in the pool was as clear as spring water. Where the water was flowing into the pool, we saw bunches of grapes; all white. My two sisters and I were sitting at the head of the pool eating the grapes, with our legs in the water, but floating without sinking or disappearing from sight. I said to my little sister, "Here we are eating grapes, but who do you think is sending them to us?"
>
> Suddenly a man appeared, curly haired, dressed in white, with a white turban on his head and his hair hanging loose behind him. He asked me, "Who would have a pool like this or grapes like these?"
>
> Then he took my hand and helped me to my feet, and, leading me away from my sisters, said: "Tell [your husband] Muḥammad ibn ʿAlī [al-Tirmidhī] to stop reading the verse, 'We have placed the balanced scales for the Day of Resurrection . . .'" [Q 21:47] and so on to the end of the verse. "Those scales are not for flour nor for bread; they weigh the speech that comes from here"—pointing to his tongue—"and the deeds that come from here and here"—pointing to his hands and feet. "You do not know that an excess of words, like the drinking of wine, produces a kind of intoxication."
>
> I asked him: "Who are you?"
>
> He replied: "I am an angel. We roam the earth, and we reside in the Holy Temple at Jerusalem." In his right hand, I saw a sprig of fresh green myrtle, and in his other hand, sweet basil. He was holding these as he spoke to me.
>
> "We walk the earth," he said, "and seek out the servants of God. We place this basil on the hearts of the servants of God, that they arise to serve and worship Him. And we place the myrtle on the hearts of the True and Certain Ones, that they may know sincerity. Sweet basil is green even in summer, and the myrtle never changes, no matter what the season. So ask [your husband] Muḥammad ibn ʿAlī, 'Would you not be happy to have these?'—pointing to the myrtle and the basil. "God can increase the piety of the God-fearing to the point that they need fear no longer, but He places these on their hearts to teach them piety first."
>
> Then he continued, "Tell him to purify his home."
>
> I replied, "I have small children and it is hard to keep the house clean."
>
> He answered, "I don't mean free of urine. I mean this"—pointing to his tongue.
>
> "Why don't you tell him all this yourself?" I asked him.
>
> "I will not tell him myself," he said, "because the matter is not important enough for that, at least, not for other people. When he transgresses, though, it is important. Why does he trangress, then?

Because this"—he gestured with the myrtle—"is still a long way off for him."

Then he pulled off some of the myrtle from the bunch in his hand and gave it to me.

"Should I keep this for myself, or give it to him?" I asked.

He laughed and his teeth sparkled like pearls. "Take it," he said, "and I'll bring the rest to him myself. What you have is for both of you—the two of you are of equal rank. And tell him, 'Let this be my last exhortation to you.' Peace be with you." But then he added, "God will give you, you and your sisters, a garden, but not because of your fasting and prayer; rather, because of the goodness of your hearts, and because you love good and shun evil"—or, in Persian, "You do not accept evil and you love the good."

"Why didn't you say this in front of my sisters?" I asked him.

"Because neither of them measures up to you." Then he said, "Peace be with you," and was gone, and I woke up.

Another time she dreamt that she was in the big room of our house:

In the room were couches upholstered with silk. One of these big couches was next to the prayer room. I looked and behind the couch I saw a tree growing out of the *qibla* end of the prayer room [the wall facing Mecca]. The tree grew as high as the height of a man, and then stopped. It was dry and shriveled up, with branches like a palm tree, looking like tent-pegs or shavings. Then fresh green branches, about five in number, sprouted from the trunk. When the new branches started growing about halfway up the trunk, the tree suddenly shot up into the air, about three times as high as a man, carrying the new sprouts up with it. Then bunches of fresh dates appeared on the branches.

I said to myself in my sleep, "This tree is mine. No one in the world, even in Mecca, has a tree like this." I stepped closer to it, and I heard a voice coming out of the trunk of the tree. I could see no one, so I looked at the trunk of the tree, and I noticed that it was growing out of a rock. It was a big rock and it filled half the room, with the tree growing out of the center of it. Next to this rock was another one, hollowed out like a basin. Water was flowing from the trunk of the tree into the hollow rock. This water was utterly clear and pure, like sap.

Then I heard a voice calling to me from somewhere near the tree: "Do you promise to watch over this tree and to make sure that no one touches it? For this tree is yours. Once it grew in sandy soil, and so many hands touched it that its fruit drooped and withered, but we placed a rock around it and sent a bird to watch over its fruit. Look!"

I looked and I saw a green bird the size of a dove on one of the branches of the tree, not on one of the fresh shoots that had sprouted from the trunk, but on one of the withered limbs just above. The bird flew from branch to branch, working its way upward. Whenever it landed on one of the dry branches that looked like pegs, the branch would turn green and fresh, and sprout bunches of dates.

The voice said, "Guard this tree until the bird reaches the top and makes the whole tree green or else it will have to stop there in the middle."

"I will guard it," I said, not seeing who I was speaking to. The bird went up the tree branch by branch, and each one turned green. When the bird reached the top of the tree, I said in wonder, "There is no god but God! Where is everybody? Don't they see this tree? Don't they know where it is?"

From the top of the tree the bird cried, "There is no god but God!"

I wanted to pull a date from the tree, but the voice said, "Not yet! Wait until they ripen." Then I woke up.

Then another time she dreamt she was sleeping next to me on the roof:

I heard voices from the garden. I cried aloud in dismay, "We've neglected our guests! I'd better go and give them something to eat." I walked over to the edge of the roof to find my way down, and then the whole side of the house simply lowered itself and left me standing upright on the ground.

Two men were sitting there, awe-inspiring in their dignity. I approached them and apologized, but they smiled back. One of them said, "Ask your husband why he is so preoccupied with this *furuzd,*[7] meaning 'grass.' Your duty is to succor the weak, and be a support to them. And tell him, 'You are one of the pegs [that hold up] the earth, and a large segment of mankind is in your care.'"

"Who are you?" I asked.

"I am the Prophet Muḥammad Aḥmad, and this is Jesus." Then he said, "Tell him: 'When you say—O King! O Holiness! Have mercy on us!—you bring holiness upon yourself. Every land you bless will grow strong and mighty, and every land you do not bless will grow weak and feeble.' And tell him: 'We have given you a dwelling place and the *frequented house* [Q 52:4—a reference to the Ka'ba in Mecca], so treat them well.'" Then I woke up.

Then, on the twenty-fourth night of the month of Ramadan,[8] she dreamt that she heard my voice from afar . . .

. . . but sounding like no voice I had ever heard. I followed the sound and came to the door of a palace full of light. I went in. The prayer room was raised up, higher than the congregation and higher than the building around it. There you were, in something that resembled a prayer niche, standing and facing Mecca. You were praying, with the light shining all around you. I thought, "His voice is enough to save the people, but he keeps himself from them."

Abū Dawūd the tailor dreamt he saw people gathering around a stairway, or ladder, set in a wall that rose to the skies:

I approached and found a crowd of people at the base of the ladder. I wanted to climb up, but a voice said, "You shall not ascend until

7. A Persian word; eating grass seems to have been a practice of ascetics [translator's note].
8. The ninth month of the Islamic calendar, in which the first verses of the Qur'an were revealed to Muhammad; it is the month of fasting.

you obtain permission." I looked up and there was a man standing in my way.

I thought to myself, "How am I supposed to obtain permission?" Then I noticed a piece of paper in my hand. I showed it to the man, and he stepped aside. I climbed the high wall. At the top, I saw only a few other people. Beyond the wall was a sea, and beyond the sea was an enormous, dizzying expanse of emptiness. I said to the others at the top of the wall, "Who are you? What are you doing here?"

"On the other side of the sea," they said, "in that great space, is Muḥammad ibn ʿAlī [al-Tirmidhī]." I stared as if staring at the crescent moon, until at last I saw you a great distance away. Again and again I rubbed my eyes and stared. I noticed the people with me were keeping away from the sea. I threw myself into it and almost immediately found myself on the other side. I walked until I found you, and there you were, sitting in that emptiness with your hood wrapped around your head. I wondered how I had come to find you in this place. Then I woke up.

Then Ahmad ibn Jibrīl the whole-cloth dealer told me that he had dreamt of me as well:

I saw you walking around the Holy Kaʿba. Something like a shelf, or a wing, had come out of the walls, about two cubits below the roof. You were making your circumambulations[9] on this shelf, with the top of the wall just higher than your waist. Then you rose up into the air until you were higher than the roof, and you kept on walking around the Kaʿba, up in the air like that. Then, astonished, I woke up.

And Muḥammad ibn Najm the lumber dealer had a dream:

I saw the Prophet—may God bless and grant him peace—surrounded by light and praying with Muḥammad ibn ʿAlī [al-Tirmidhī] right behind him, praying along with him.

At one point during those years, I became much occupied with computing the declinations and learning to calculate using the zodiac and the astrolabe, and had become immersed in these matters. Then Muḥammad ibn Najm told me of a dream he had had:

I heard a voice say, "Tell Muḥammad ibn ʿAlī [al-Tirmidhī], 'These things you are doing are not part of your calling or your way, so avoid them!'" I was terror-stricken by the awful splendor of the man who spoke these words. He appeared to me as an old man with white hair and beard, sweet smelling, handsome, and I imagined somehow that he was an angel.

Then he said, "Tell Muḥammad ibn ʿAlī to cast those things aside, for I suspect they will become a veil between him and the Lord of Majesty. Remember to fear God in this world—you are not a base wretch, you are merely distracted [?]. Tell him this and do not neglect to pass on God's counsel to His creatures."

9. As part of the hajj, Muslims walk around the Kaʿba seven times.

Then my wife dreamt that the two of us were sleeping in one bed and the Prophet of God—may God bless him and grant him peace—entered and lay down in our bed with us. Another time she dreamt that he came to our house. She said:

> I was overjoyed and bent to kiss his feet, but he stopped me. He gave me his hand and I kissed it. I was trying to think of what to ask him for. I used to suffer from an inflammation in one of my eyes, so I said, "O Prophet of God, sometimes my eye becomes inflamed." He replied, "Whenever that happens, put your hand over your eye and say, 'There is no god but God, alone, without partner; His is the power and His is the praise. He brings life and death. Goodness is in His hands, for He is All-Powerful.'" Then I woke up. After that, whenever my eye became inflamed, I would say these words and the inflammation would subside.

Then my wife dreamt that she was on Sakiba Street, looking at the cemetery, a long way off:

> Then suddenly I could see even farther—as far as Dawdabad,[1] it seemed—and I saw an uncountable number of people, as if the world had suddenly become crowded with people, even clinging to walls and treetops, like birds. I thought, "What is all this?"
>
> A voice said, "The prince has invaded without warning. No one knew he was coming. For twelve days his armies were advancing upon us, and we sensed nothing, and now they have covered the earth."
>
> I looked at all the people. They were pale-faced and speechless with terror. Then I saw you coming into the room. You undressed, asked for water, and then washed yourself with water from the brass ewer. You put on a waist-wrapper and a cloak. You were wearing sandals. I asked you, "What are you doing?" You replied, "What a marvel! Do you know what this prince wants?"
>
> The people had fallen into a stunned and terror-stricken silence. It was as if they no longer knew one another—as if, in their fear, they had all become strangers. But you were calm and fearless. You were saying to me, "What a marvel! The prince will choose, from all the people on the earth, forty souls to speak to."
>
> I said, "Why aren't you going?"
>
> "God's will be done," you replied.
>
> The whole world was watching you (this she said in Persian). The people were saying, "Unless Muḥammad ibn ʿAlī comes to our rescue we shall all perish. He must find these forty people, wherever they are, and if he does not take his place among them, then all these people will be destroyed."

She said that forty people were to be found, from all over the world, and if I was not among them, then all these people would go to ruin. But how would the prince know me and when would he find me? At any rate, it seemed I was needed to complete the forty myself, for there was still one missing. The story was that the prince had come with Turkish troops to

1. In Iran.

search out these people. She said that I put on a white shirt and cowl, and sandals, and went out:

> It seemed to me in my dream—she said—that when you reached the prince, you found the people jostling to get away from the Turks, but the Turks were not beating anyone, and the people's fear seemed to have disappeared. I called out, as I stood at the end of the street, "Are you one of the forty?"
>
> Someone said, "By those forty we shall be saved."
>
> "Muḥammad ibn ʿAlī will save us," said someone else. I started to weep. "What are you weeping about? He's the one who is going to save us," they said. "Not because something bad is going to happen to him," I said, "but because of his kind heart. How can he bear to look at the sword?" I was thinking that the forty would be executed, so I wept.
>
> Then I went back to the house. I felt that somehow a whole day had passed. When I reached the front door, I turned and I saw you there. "Thank God!" I said. "How were you spared?"
>
> You gestured as if to say, "If only I had been!" Then, "Just wait until you hear the whole story."
>
> You seemed to be covered in white, and you seemed twice your normal height. Your cheeks were flushed and shining, and your forehead and eyebrows were covered with something that looked like dust. I looked more closely and saw that there was no dust, only the traces of your terror. "How were you spared?" I asked again.
>
> "Don't you realize? I am the first of the forty. It was me he recognized and me he chose. He touched me here"—you pointed to your chest—"and he shook me so hard I thought my whole body was going to be torn apart. Then he said to me in Persian, 'You are a great lord. . . . You are at the head of the world.'"
>
> "You saw the prince? You actually saw him?!"
>
> "No. I got as far as the pavilion, where there was an enclosure set up before his door, and the prince put his hand out—or so it seemed—and he touched me, and shook me, and spoke to me. Then we went out into the courtyard, which looked like the festival enclosure they set up in the cemetery. The prince said, 'Take these forty souls out to the courtyard, and hold them there. Keep them standing, do not let them sit.'
>
> "So I went out with the others into the courtyard. The prince said to the others, 'Send this one'—meaning me—'out to pray.' So I entered with them and then I was sent out to pray. It was as if we had been chosen from all the souls on earth. I walked on past the prince's troops and past the Turks, and no one laid a hand on me. I realized then that the prince thought well of me, and that he had assembled all those people for my sake. He had sought out those forty souls only because I would be among them."
>
> "Now you can rest," I said.
>
> "I am saved from myself," you said, and went up to the mosque. I watched you move away, borne above the heads of the people. Then I woke up.

Later she had another dream, this time in Persian. At the end she said, "Then I woke up." Then she was seized by an ardent desire to listen to sermons and to exact obedience from her soul. The first validation of her visions came on the twenty-seventh of the month of Dhū al-Qaʿda,[2] five or six days after her last vision. While sitting in the garden, she heard in her heart the words, "O Light and Guidance to all things! O You Whose light cleaves the darkness!"

She said:

> I felt as if something had entered my breast and wrapped itself about my heart. My chest and throat were full, so full that I felt near to choking, full of something hot that scorched my heart. All things seemed beautiful to me. Everything I looked at—the earth, the sky, the creatures—had taken on a new and different shape, a shape lovely, glorious and sweet. There came to me then words in Persian: "We have given you a seal-ring." I was filled with joy, contentment and cheer.

She told me of this experience and the next day she told me of another:

> I heard the words, "We have given you three things"—in Persian—"My glory, My greatness, and My majesty." A light appeared above me, and remained there above my head, as I had seen once before in a dream. And in the light appeared the mark of glory, the mark of greatness, and the light of majesty. Of this glory, I saw a house that moved [in Persian] with something in it, with all of mankind moving along in it, and the greatness of the kingdom and of all things, and the majesty of all things, and their grandeur, were in it. I saw clearly a flame spreading through the heavens . . . and then downwards.

Then on the third day she heard in her heart: "I have bestowed upon you the knowledge of those who have gone before and those who are to come." And in this state, she spoke the knowledge of the [99] Names of God.[3] Every day, names were revealed to her. A light would shine upon her heart and reveal the hidden meaning of the Names to her. This continued until, on Friday, the tenth of the month, she attended our gathering and told us that God's Beneficent [100th] Name had been revealed to her.

2. The eleventh month of the Islamic calendar.
3. According to a hadith, the Prophet said that there were ninety-nine names (or attributes) of God.

AL-SULAMI
937–1021

Abu ʿAbd al-Rahman Muhammad al-Sulami's significance for the history and development of Sufi thought is proven by the frequency with which he is cited by later luminaries, such as al-Ghazali (1058–1111; see below) and Ibn ʿArabi (1165–1240; see below).

Upon his birth in Nishapur to a pious Sufi family, al-Sulami was reportedly blessed by his father's donation of all of his possessions to the poor. Soon thereafter his father emigrated to Mecca, entrusting al-Sulami's education to Ismaʿil ibn Nujayd, his maternal grandfather, whose wealth ensured that the family would suffer no financial hardship. Ibn Nujayd was also a Sufi and a specialist in hadith, having been taught by the son of Ibn Hanbal (780–855; see above). In his youth, al-Sulami studied Sufism, theology, and Shafiʿi law, and he traveled as far west as the Arabian Peninsula in search of traditions. He completed the pilgrimage to Mecca in 976, but Ibn Nujayd died before his return to Nishapur in 978. Al-Sulami inherited his grandfather's extensive library and founded a Sufi retreat and teaching center in Nishapur.

Al-Sulami's writings, which exceed more than a hundred titles, were quite popular during his lifetime; even poorly copied editions fetched high prices from buyers. He wrote for a wide range of audiences, from general readers to those advanced on the Sufi path, and his legacy has been both direct and indirect. Manuscripts of some of his most important works exist, even if only in single copies, while other writings are available solely in the extracts reproduced by subsequent authors. In whichever form it has reached us, al-Sulami's work can be divided into three genres of Sufi literature: biography, Qurʾan commentary, and handbooks of custom and practice.

He produced a major commentary on the Qurʾan, *Realities of Exegesis* and the *Appendix to the Realities of Exegesis*, both of which are now in print (though only the latter in a scholarly edition). Nasir ibn Sebuktigin, a Ghaznavid prince, was so enamored of the *Realities* that he commissioned a copy of it in which passages from the Qurʾan were written in gold and then besieged al-Sulami with repeated requests to teach him the work; al-Sulami eventually acquiesced.

His most famous biographical work, *History of the Sufis*, exists only in the compositions of later authors, but an abridgment titled *Classes of the Sufis* is extant and contains biographical notices for some hundred Sufi men. He also produced a companion piece to *Classes* titled *Memorial of Pious Sufi Women*.

Though al-Sulami was widely respected as a scholar and Sufi, he faced opposition during his lifetime and after his death, especially from Hanbali scholars. His critics judged his knowledge of traditions to be insufficient, disliked his use of allegorical interpretations in Qurʾan commentary, and found his references to Shiʿi sources, such as Jaʿfar al-Sadiq (the sixth Shiʿi imam; 702–765), unacceptable.

The text below is taken from al-Sulami's *Memorial of Pious Sufi Women*. A unique compilation of eighty-two biographical notices, it provides insight into the role of women during the formative phase of Sufi thought. Al-Sulami wanted to preserve the memory and example of these pious women for later generations because he believed that women could attain the same spiritual rank as men, and that the women he profiled were "masters of the realities of divine oneness, recipients of divine discourse, possessors of true visions and exemplary conduct, and followers of the ways of the Prophet."

PRONOUNCING GLOSSARY

ʿAbd al-ʿAzīz ibn ʿUmayr: *ab-dul-a-zeez´ ibn oo-mayr´*

ʿAbd al-Qays: *ab-dul-qays´*

ʿAbd ar-Razzāq: *ab-dur-raz-zahq´*

ʿAbd al-Wāḥid ibn Zayd: *ab-dul-wa´-hid* (heavy *h*) *ibn zayd*

ʿAbd ar-Raḥmān ibn Jabala: *ab-dur-rah-man´* (heavy *h*) *ibn ja´-ba-luh*

ʿAbdallāh ibn Ayyūb al-Muqriʾ: *ab-dul-lah´ ibn eye-yoob´ al-muq´-ri*

ʿAbdallāh ibn Yūsuf: *ab-dul-lah´ ibn you´-suf*

Abū al-Faḍl Muḥammad ibn Ibrāhīm ibn al-Faḍl al-Muzakkī: *a-bool-fahdl moo-ham´-mad* (heavy *h*) *ibn ib-rah-heem´ ibn al-fahdl al-moo-zak´-kee*

Abū al-Fatḥ Yūsuf ibn ʿUmar al-Qawwās: *a-bool-fath´* (heavy *h*) *you´-suf ibn oh´-mar al-qahw-was´*

Abū ʿAwn Muʿādh ibn al-Faḍl: *a-boo awn moo-adh´ ibn al-fahdl´*

Abū ʿUmar aḍ-Ḍarīr: *a-boo oh´-mar ad-dah-reer´*

Abū al-Mufaḍḍal ash-Shaybānī: *a-bool-moo-fahd´-dahl ash-shay-ba´-nee*

Abū Bakr ibn Shādhān ar-Rāzī: *a-boo bakr´ ibn shah-dhan´ ar-ra´-zee*

Abū Hishām ar-Rāzī: *a-boo he-sham´ ar-ra´-zee*

Abū Jaʿfar Muḥammad ibn Aḥmad ibn Saʿid ar-Rāzī: *a-boo ja´-far moo-ham´-mad* (heavy *h*) *ibn ah´-mad* (heavy *h*) *ibn sa-eed´ ar-ra´-zee*

Abū Muʿādh: *a-boo moo-adh´*

Abū Saʿid ibn al-Aʿrābī: *a-boo sa-eed´ ibn al-ah-rah´-bee*

Abū Salama al-ʿAtakī: *a-boo sa´-la-muh al-ah´-ta-kee*

Abū Salama al-Baladī: *a-boo sa-la-muh al-ba´-la-dee*

Abū Sulaymān ad-Dārānī: *a-boo su-lay-man´ ad-da-ra´-nee*

ʿĀfiyya: *ah´-fee-yuh*

Aḥmad ibn Abī al-Ḥawārī: *ah´-mad* (heavy *h*) *ibn a-bil-ha-wa´-ree* (heavy *h*)

Aḥmad ibn Isḥāq ibn Wahb: *ah´-mad* (heavy *h*) *ibn is-hahq´* (heavy *h*) *ibn wahb* (light *h*)

Aḥmad ibn Muḥammad: *ah´-mad* (heavy *h*) *ibn moo-ham´-mad* (heavy *h*)

Aḥmad ibn Muḥammad ibn Masrūq: *ah´-mad* (heavy *h*) *ibn moo-ham´-mad* (heavy *h*) *ibn mas-rooq´*

ʿAjrada: *aj´-ra-duh*

Āl ʿAtīk: *al ah-teek´*

al-ʿAbbās ibn al-Walīd al-Mashriqī: *al-ab-bas´ ibn al-wa-leed´ al-mash´-ri-qee*

al-ʿAbbās ibn Ḥamza: *al-ab-bas´ ibn ham´-zuh* (heavy *h*)

al-Ahwāz: *al-ah-waz´* (light *h*)

al-ḥūr al-ʿayn: *al-hoor´ al-ain´*

al-Ḥusayn ibn ʿAbd al-ʿAzīz ibn al-Wazīr al-Judhamī: *al-hoo-sayn´* (heavy *h*) *ibn ab-dul-a-zeez´ ibn al-wa-zeer´ al-joo´-dha-mee*

al-Ḥusayn ibn Muḥmmad ibn Isḥāq: *al-hoo-sayn´* (heavy *h*) *ibn moo-ham´-mad* (heavy *h*) *ibn is-hahq´* (heavy *h*)

al-Ubulla: *al-oo-bul´-luh*

ʿAlqama an-Nakhaʿī: *al´-qah-muh an-na´-cha-ee* (guttural *ch*)

ʿĀṣim al-Jaḥdarī: *ah´-sim al-jah´-da-ree* (heavy *h*)

aṭ-Ṭufāwā: *at-too-fah´-wah*

ʿAthāma: *ah-tha´-muh*

Basra: *bahs´-ruh*

Bikr ibn ʿAbdallāh ibn Muḥammad: *bikr ibn ab-dul-lah´ ibn moo-ham´-mad* (heavy *h*)

Bilāl ibn Abī ad-Dardāʾ: *bee-lal´ ibn a-bid-dar-dah´*

Dāwūd aṭ-Ṭāʾī: *da-wood´ at-tah´-ee*

Dāwūd ibn al-Muḥabbir: *da-wood´ ibn al-moo-hab´-bir* (heavy *h*)

Ghufayra al-ʿĀbida: *goo-fay´-ruh al-ah´-bi-duh*

Ḥafṣa bint Sīrīn: *haf´-suh* (heavy *h*) *bint see-reen´*

ḥajj: *haj* (heavy *h*)

Ḥammād ibn Zayd: *ham-mad´* (heavy *h*) *ibn zayd*

Hārūn ar-Rashīd: *ha-roon´ ar-ra-sheed´*

Ḥasnā bint Fayrūz: *has-nah´* (heavy *h*) *bint fay-rooz´*

Hind bint al-Muhallab: *hind bint al-moo-hal´-lab*

Hishām ibn Ḥassān: *he-sham´ ibn has-san´* (heavy *h*)

houri: *hoo´-ree*

Ḥukayma: *hoo-kay´-muh* (heavy *h*)

Ibrāhīm ibn al-Azhar: *ib-rah-heem´ ibn al-az´-har*

Ibrāhīm ibn al-Junayd: *ib-rah-heem´ ibn al-joo-nayd´*

iḥrām: *ih-ram´* (heavy *h*)

ʿImrān ibn Khālid: *im-ran´ ibn cha´-lid* (guttural *ch*)

Isḥāq ibn Manṣūr as-Salūlī: *is-hahq´* (heavy *h*) *ibn man-soor´ as-sa-loo´-lee*

Ismāʿīl ibn ʿAyyāsh: *is-mah-eel´ ibn eye-yash´*

Ismāʿīl ibn Nujayd: *is-mah-eel´ ibn noo-jayd´*

Jaʿfar ibn Muḥammad ibn Nuṣayr al-Khuldī: *ja´-far ibn moo-ham´-mad ibn noo-sayr´ al-chul´-dee* (guttural *ch*)

Jaʿfar ibn Sulaymān: *ja´-far ibn soo-lay-man´*

Jaʿfar ibn Sulaymān aḍ-Ḍubʿī: *ja´-far ibn su-lay-man´ ad-dub´-ee*

jinn: *jin*
Khālid ibn Maʿdān: *cha´-lid ibn mah-dan´* (guttural *ch*)
Kitāb aṭ-ṭabaqāt: *ki-tab´ at-tah-bah-qaht´*
Kurdiyya bint ʿAmr: *kur-dee´-yuh bint ahmr*
Lubāba al-ʿĀbida: *loo-ba´-buh al-ah´-bi-duh*
Lubāba al-Mutaʿabbida: *loo-ba´-buh al-moo-ta-ab´-bi-duh*
Maryam: *mar´-yam*
Maymūn ibn al-Aṣbagh: *may-moon´ ibn al-ahs´-bag*
Muʿādha bint ʿAbdallāh al-ʿAdawiyya: *moo-ah´-dhuh bint ab-dul-lah´ al-a-da-wee´-yuh*
Muʾmina bint Bahlūl: *muh´-mi-nuh bint bah-lool´* (light *h*)
muezzin: *moo-ez´-zin*
Muḥammad ibn ʿAbdallāh ibn Akhī Mīmī: *moo-ham´-mad* (heavy *h*) *ibn ab-dul-lah´ ibn achee mee´-mee* (guttural *ch*)
Muḥammad ibn Abī Dāwūd al-Azdī: *moo-ham´-mad* (heavy *h*) *ibn a-bee da-wood´ al-az´-dee*
Muḥammad ibn al-Ḥusayn al-Burjulānī: *moo-ham´-mad* (heavy *h*) *ibn al-hoo-sayn´* (heavy *h*) *al-bur-joo-la´-nee*
Muḥammad ibn Ismāʿīl al-Ismāʿīlī: *moo-ham´-mad* (heavy *h*) *ibn is-mah-eel´ al-is-mah-ee´-lee*
Muḥammad ibn Ismāʿīl ibn ʿAyyāsh: *moo-ham´-mad* (heavy *h*) *ibn is-mah-eel´ ibn eye-yash´*
Muḥammad ibn Rawḥ: *moo-ham´-mad* (heavy *h*) *ibn rauh* (heavy *h*)
Muḥammad ibn Sīrīn: *moo-ham´-mad* (heavy *h*) *ibn see-reen´*
Muḥammad ibn Sulaym ibn Hilāl ar-Rāsibī: *moo-ham´-mad* (heavy *h*) *ibn soo-laym´ ibn he-lal´ ar-ra´-si-bee*
Muḥammad ibn Wāsiʿ: *moo-ham´-mad* (heavy *h*) *ibn wa´-si*
Musaddad ibn Qaṭan: *moo-sad´-dad ibn qah´-tahn*
Nusiyya bint Salmān: *noo-see´-yuh bint sal-man´*
Qaṭīʿat ad-Daqīq: *qah-tee´-at ad-dah-qeeq´*
Rabāḥ al-Qaysī: *ra-bah´* (heavy *h*) *al-qay´-see*
Rābiʿa al-ʿAdawiyya: *ra´-bi-uh al-a-da-wee´-yuh*
Rābiʿa al-Azdiyya: *ra´-bi-uh al-az-dee´-yuh*
Rābiʿa bint Ismāʿīl: *ra´-bi-uh bint is-mah-eel´*
Rayḥāna: *ray-ha´-nuh* (heavy *h*)
Saʿīd ibn ʿUthmān al-Ḥannāṭ: *sa-eed´ ibn uth-man´ al-han-naht´* (heavy *h*)
Saʿīda bint Zayd: *sa-ee´-duh bint zayd*
Salama al-Afqam: *sa´-la-muh al-af´-qahm*
Ṣāliḥ al-Murrī: *sah´-lih* (heavy *h*) *al-mur´-ree*
Sayyār ibn Ḥāṭim: *seye-yar´ ibn hah´-tim* (heavy *h*)
Shaʿwanā: *shah-wa-nah´*
Shabaka: *sha´-ba-kuh*
Shaybān al-Ubullī: *shay-ban´ al-oo-bul´-lee*
Shaybān ibn Farrūkh: *shay-ban´ ibn far-rooch´* (guttural *ch*)
Shuʿba ibn al-Ḥajjāj: *shuh´-buh ibn al-haj-jaj´* (heavy *h*)
Sufyān ath-Thawrī: *soof-yan´ ath-thaw´-ree*
sunna: *sun´-nuh*
Ṭāhir al-Wazīrī: *tah´-hir al-wa-zee´-ree*
ʿUbayda bint Abī Kilāb: *oo-bay´-duh bint a-bee ki-lab´*
Umm ʿAbdallāh: *oom ab-dul-lah´*
Umm al-Aswad bint Zayd al-ʿAdawiyya: *oom al-as´-wad bint zayd al-a-da-wee´-yuh*
Umm Saʿīd an-Nakhaʿiyya: *oom sa-eed´ an-na´-cha-ee-yuh* (guttural ch)
Umm Sālim ar-Rāsibiyya: *oom sa´-lim ar-ra´-si-bee-yuh*
Umm Ṭalq: *oom tahlq´*
Unaysa bint ʿAmr al-ʿAdawiyya: *oo-nay´-suh bint ahmr al-a-da-wee´-yuh*
Wahb al-Bazzāz: *wahb* (light *h*) *al-baz-zaz´*
Yaḥyā ibn Bisṭām: *yah´-ya* (heavy *h*) *ibn bis-tahm´*
Yūsuf ibn al-Ḥusayn ar-Rāzī: *you´-suf ibn al-hoo-sayn´* (heavy *h*) *ar-ra´-zee*
Yūsuf ibn Asbāṭ: *you´-suf ibn as-baht´*

FROM THE MEMORIAL OF PIOUS SUFI WOMEN

I. RĀBIʿA AL-ʿADAWIYYA[1]

Rābiʿa was from Basra and was a client (*mawlāt*) of the clan of Āl ʿAtīk. Sufyān ath-Thawrī[2] (may God have mercy upon him) sought her advice on legal matters and referred such issues to her. He also sought her spiritual advice and supplications. Both ath-Thawrī and Shuʿba [ibn al-Ḥajjāj][3] transmitted Rābiʿa's words of wisdom.

Muḥammad ibn ʿAbdallāh b. Akhī Mīmī personally reported from Aḥmad ibn Isḥāq b. Wahb that his father [Wahb al-Bazzāz] reported through ʿAbdallāh ibn Ayyūb al-Muqriʾ (the Qurʾān Reciter) through Shaybān ibn Farrūkh, that Jaʿfar ibn Sulaymān related: Sufyān ath-Thawrī took me by the hand and said about Rābiʿa: "Take me to the mentor. For when I am apart from her, I can find no solace." When we entered her abode, Sufyān raised his hand and said, "Oh God, grant me safety!" At this, Rābiʿa wept. "What makes you weep?" he asked. "You caused me to weep," she replied. "How?" he asked. She answered, "Have you not learned that true safety from the world is to abandon all that is in it? So how can you ask such a thing while you are still soiled with the world?"

Abū Jaʿfar Muḥammad ibn Aḥmad b. Saʿīd ar-Rāzī reported from al-ʿAbbās ibn Ḥamza through Aḥmad ibn Abī al-Ḥawārī through al-ʿAbbās ibn al-Walīd al-Mashriqī that Shaybān al-Ubullī related: I heard Rābiʿa say: "For everything there is a fruit (*thamara*), and the fruit of the knowledge of God (*maʿrifa*) is in orienting oneself toward God at all times (*iqbāl*)."

Also on his authority, Rābiʿa said: "I ask God's forgiveness for my lack of truthfulness in saying, 'I ask God's forgiveness.'"

Also on his authority, Rābiʿa was asked: "How is your love for the Prophet (may God bless and preserve him)?" To which she replied, "Verily, I love him. But love for the Creator has turned me away from love for created things."

[Shaybān al-Ubullī] also said: One day, Rābiʿa saw Rabāḥ [al-Qaysī][4] kissing a young boy. "Do you love him?" she asked. "Yes," he said. To which she replied, "I did not imagine that there was room in your heart to love anything other than God, the Glorious and Mighty!" Rabāḥ was overcome at this and fainted. When he awoke, he said, "On the contrary, this is a mercy that God Most High has put into the hearts of His slaves."

I heard Abū Bakr ar-Rāzī report from Abū Salama al-Baladī that Maymūn ibn al-Aṣbagh related through Sayyār from Jaʿfar [ibn Sulaymān]: Muḥammad ibn Wāsiʿ[5] came upon Rābiʿa while she was staggering like one inebriated. "What causes you to stagger?" he asked. "Last night I became intoxicated with love for my Lord and woke up inebriated from it," she replied.

In a quarter of Baghdad named Qaṭīʿat ad-Daqīq, I heard Muḥammad ibn ʿAbdallāh b. Akhī Mīmī report from Aḥmad ibn Isḥāq b. Wahb al-Bazzāz (the Cloth Merchant) through ʿAbdallāh ibn Ayyūb al-Muqriʾ through Shaybān ibn Farrūkh that Jaʿfar ibn Sulaymān said: I heard Rābiʿa al-ʿAdawiyya say that Sufyān ath-Thawrī asked her, "What is the best way

TRANSLATED BY Rkia Elaroui Cornell. All bracketed additions are the translator's.

1. Born ca. 714 and died in 801.
2. Best known as a collector of traditions [ca. 715–778), but also an influential commentator on the Qurʾan and on religious law.
3. A Basran transmitter of hadith (d. 776/77).
4. A Sufi ascetic (d. 796).
5. A Sufi ascetic and judge (d. ca. 735).

for the slave (*ʿabd*) to come close to God, the Glorious and Mighty?" She wept and replied: "How can the likes of me be asked such a thing? The best way for the slave to come close to God Most High is for him to know that he must not love anything in this world or the Hereafter other than Him."

Also on [Jaʿfar ibn Sulaymān's] authority it is reported that ath-Thawrī said in Rābiʿa's presence, "How sorrowful I am!" "Do not lie!" she said. "Say instead, 'How little is my sorrow!' If you were truly sorrowful, life itself would not please you."

Also on his authority Rābiʿa said: "My sorrow is not from feeling sad. Rather, my sorrow is from not feeling sad enough."

Also on his authority: In Basra, Rābiʿa came across a man who had been arrested and crucified for immorality. She said: "Upon my father! With that tongue you used to say, 'There is no god but God!'" Sufyān said: "Then she mentioned the good works that the man had done."

Also on his authority: Ṣāliḥ al-Murrī[6] said in her presence, "He who persists in knocking at the door will have it opened for him." "The door is already open," she replied. "But the question is: Who wishes to enter it?"

II. LUBĀBA AL-MUTAʿABBIDA (LUBĀBA THE DEVOTEE) FROM JERUSALEM

Lubāba was a specialist in the ways of gnosis (*maʿrifa*) and self-denial (*mujāhadāt*).

Abū Jaʿfar Muḥammad ibn Aḥmad b. Saʿīd ar-Rāzī reported from al-ʿAbbās ibn Ḥamza through Aḥmad ibn Abī al-Ḥawārī that Muḥammad ibn Rawḥ related: Lubāba the Worshipper said: "I am ashamed lest God see me preoccupied with other than Him."

Lubāba also said: "The more I observe self-denial, the more comfortable I become with its practice. Thus, when I get tired from human encounter, I find intimacy in the remembrance of God. And when human discourse tires me, I take my rest in dedication to the worship of God and fulfilling His service."

A man said to her: "This is the question. I want to perform the pilgrimage to Mecca, so what invocation should I make during this period?" She said: "Ask God Most High for two things: that He will be pleased with you, so that He will make you attain the station of those who find their satisfaction in Him, and that He will magnify your reputation among His friends (*awliyāʾ*)."

III. MARYAM OF BASRA FROM THE NATIVES OF BASRA

Maryam was a contemporary of Rābiʿa [al-ʿAdawiyya] and survived her. She was also her companion and served her. She used to lecture on the subject of love (*maḥabba*), and whenever she listened to discourses on the doctrine of love, she went into ecstasy.

It was said: One day she attended the session of a preacher. When he started to speak about love, her spleen ruptured and she died during the session.

6. A preacher, Qurʾan reciter, and transmitter of early Muslim traditions (d. 792/93) [translator's note, edited].

Muḥammad ibn Aḥmad b. Saʿīd ar-Rāzī reported from al-ʿAbbās ibn Ḥamza through Aḥmad ibn Abī al-Ḥawārī that ʿAbd al-ʿAzīz ibn ʿUmayr related: Maryam of Basra would remain standing in worship from the beginning of the night, saying, "Gracious is God toward His servants" [Qur'ān 42 (*ash-Shūrā*), 19], and did not go beyond this verse until daylight.

Maryam said: "I have never been preoccupied with my sustenance, nor have I exhausted myself in seeking it from the day when I heard the statement of God the Glorious and Mighty: 'For in heaven is your sustenance, as is that which you are promised' [Qur'ān 51 (*adh-Dhāriyāt*), 22]."

IV. MUʾMINA THE DAUGHTER OF BAHLŪL FROM THE FEMALE WORSHIPPERS OF DAMASCUS

Mu'mina was one of the most important female gnostics (*ʿārifāt*) of her age.[7] I found this in the handwriting of my father, who related: It was reported that Mu'mina bint Bahlūl said: "This world and the Hereafter are not pleasurable except through God or through contemplation of the effects of His artifice and His power. He who is denied closeness to God experiences intimacy through these effects. How desolate is the hour in which God is not mentioned!"

[My father] also related: Mu'mina was asked, "From whence did you acquire these spiritual states (*aḥwāl*)?" She replied, "By following God's commands according to the Sunna of the Prophet Muḥammad (may God bless and preserve him), by magnifying the rights of the Muslims, and by rendering service to the righteous and the virtuous."

I heard Abū al-Mufaḍḍal ash-Shaybānī (report from Ibrāhīm ibn al-Azhar through Abū Hāshim ar-Rāzī through Ibn Abī al-Ḥawārī) who said: I heard Mu'mina bint Bahlūl (the quintessential female ascetic of Damascus) say: "Oh most Beloved! This world and the Hereafter are not pleasurable except through You. So do not overwhelm me with the loss of You and the punishment that results from it!"

V. MUʿĀDHA BINT ʿABDALLĀH AL-ʿADAWIYYA

Muʿādha was a contemporary of Rābiʿa [al-ʿAdawiyya] and was her close companion.

She did not lift up her gaze toward the sky for forty years. She did not eat during the day and did not sleep at night. For this she was told, "You are causing yourself harm." To which she replied, "No. I have postponed one time for the other. I have postponed sleep from night until day and have postponed food from day until night."

I found this in the handwriting of my father (may God have mercy upon him). It says: A woman used to take care of Muʿādha al-ʿAdawiyya, who used to stay up all night praying. When overcome by the need for sleep, she would get up and wander around the house, saying, "Oh, soul! Eternal sleep is ahead of you. If I were to die, your repose in the grave would be a long one, whether it be sorrowful or happy." She would remain that way until daylight.

VI. SHABAKA OF BASRA

Shabaka was a companion of her brother and like him specialized in the way of scrupulousness (*waraʿ*).

7. Perhaps the 9th century CE.

There were underground cells (*sarādīb*) in her house for her female students and disciples, where they learned the ways of self-denial and spiritual practice.

She used to say: "Souls are purified by acts of worship (*riyāḍāt*). When they are purified, they find peace in worship, just as before they were burdened by it." Abū Saʿīd ibn al-Aʿrābī also mentioned this statement in *Kitāb aṭ-ṭabaqāt.*[8]

VII. NUSIYYA BINT SALMĀN

Nusiyya was the wife of Yūsuf ibn Asbāṭ.[9] She once said to Yūsuf ibn Asbāṭ: "You will be asked by God on my behalf whether you have provided me with any food other than that which is lawful, and whether you might be suspected of any wrongdoing for my sake."

[Yūsuf ibn Asbāṭ] said; When Nusiyya gave birth to a son she said: "Oh, Lord! You do not see me as someone worthy of Your worship. So for this You have preoccupied me with a child!"

VIII. RAYHĀNA THE ENRAPTURED FROM THE ASCETICS OF BASRA

Rayḥāna was a contemporary of Ṣāliḥ al-Murrī.[1] The following verses were written beneath her collar:

You are my Intimate Companion, my Aspiration, and my Happiness,
And my heart refuses to love anything but You.

Oh, my Dear, my Aspiration, and Object of my desire,
My yearning is endless! When will I finally meet You?

My request is not for Heaven's pleasures;
I desire only to encounter You!

IX. GHUFAYRA AL-ʿĀBIDA (GHUFAYRA THE WORSHIPPER) FROM THE NATIVES OF BASRA

Ghufayra was a companion of Muʿādha al-ʿAdawiyya. Ibrāhīm ibn al-Junayd reported from Muḥammad ibn al Ḥusayn [al-Burjulānī] that Yaḥyā ibn Bisṭām related: Ghufayra the Worshipper wept until she became blind. A man said to her: "How devastating is blindness!" To which Ghufayra replied: "Being veiled from God is worse. And the blindness of the heart from understanding the intent of God's commands is even greater!"

X. ʿĀFIYYA THE INFATUATED FROM THE TRIBE OF ʿABD AL-QAYS FROM THE NATIVES OF BASRA

ʿĀfiyya was constantly enraptured (*wāliha*) and lost in the love of God (*hā'ima*). Most of her time was spent in remembrance of God and she seldom associated with anyone.

Ibrāhīm ibn al-Junayd[2] mentioned that she would spend all night awake, and during the day she would seek refuge from human contact in cemeter-

8. *Book of Classes* (or *Levels*); al-Aʿrabi (d. 952) was a famous scholar of hadith.
9. An ascetic preacher and traditionist (d. 814/15) [translator's note, edited].

1. That is, d. ca. 792/93 (see n. 6, p. 410).
2. Abu al-Qasim Ibrahim al-Junayd (d. 910), Sufi jurist of Baghdad.

ies. She used to say: "The lover is never weary from confiding in his Beloved, and nothing is of interest to him other than the Beloved. Oh, desire! Oh, desire! Oh desire!" (three times).

XI. UMM ʿABDALLĀH THE DAUGHTER OF KHĀLID IBN MAʿDĀN[3]

Umm ʿAbdallāh was the mother of Ismāʿīl ibn ʿAyyāsh. Muḥammad ibn Ismāʿīl b. ʿAyyāsh related that he heard his father say: I heard my mother Umm ʿAbdallāh say: "Were I certain that God Most High would grant me Heaven, I would have increased my self-denial and service to Him. Truly, [the best legacy] for slaves is excellence in their service to their masters."

XII. UNAYSA BINT ʿAMR AL-ʿADAWIYYA

Unaysa was a native of Basra and was a student (*tilmīdha*) of Muʿādha al-ʿAdawiyya.

I heard my grandfather Ismāʿīl ibn Nujayd[4] report from Musaddad ibn Qaṭan through Muḥammad ibn al-Ḥusayn [al-Burjulānī] that ʿAbd ar-Raḥmān ibn Jabala related: Unaysa bint ʿAmr was a servant of Muʿādha al-ʿAdawiyya. She used to say: "My spirit has never resisted anything that I compelled it to do more strongly than the avoidance of eating that which is permissible and earning a living."

XIII. UMM AL-ASWAD BINT ZAYD [YAZĪD] AL-ʿADAWIYYA OF BASRA

Muʿādha [al-ʿAdawiyya] was Umm al-Aswad's wet-nurse. Musaddad ibn Qaṭan reported from Muḥammad ibn al-Ḥusayn [al-Burjulānī] through Yaḥyā ibn Bisṭām that ʿImrān ibn Khālid related: Umm al-Aswad bint Zayd told me that she was asked about the statement of God the Glorious and Mighty: "So forgive with gracious forgiveness" [Qur'ān 15 (*al-Ḥijr*), 85]. Commenting on this verse, she said: "Acceptance without blame."

XIV. SHAʿWĀNA[5]

Shaʿwāna used to live in al-Ubulla.[6] She was a remarkable person, and had a beautiful and melodious voice. She preached to the people and recited the Qur'ān to them. Her sessions were attended by ascetics, worshippers, those who were close to God, and the masters of hearts and self-denial.

She was one of those known for self-denial, who fear God, who weep, and influence others to weep.

Musaddad ibn Qaṭan reported through Muḥammad ibn al-Ḥusayn [al-Burjulānī] through Abū Muʿādh that Abū ʿAwn [Muʿādh ibn al-Faḍl] related: Shaʿwāna wept until we feared that she would become blind. So we said to her, "We are afraid that you might become blind." She wept and replied: "'We are afraid?' By God! Becoming blind in this world from weeping is more desirable to me than being blinded by Hellfire in the Hereafter!"

Shaʿwāna used to say: "Can an eye be separated from its Beloved and yearn to be united with Him without weeping? This is not right!"

3. A Syrian scholar (d. ca. 772/73).
4. Al-Sulami's maternal grandfather (d. 976/77).
5. An ascetic of the 8th century.
6. A port in Iraq, near Basra; it was an important commercial center.

XV. SAʿĪDA BINT ZAYD THE SISTER OF ḤAMMĀD IBN ZAYD[7]

Saʿīda was one of the female gnostics of Basra. She was similar to Rābiʿa [al-ʿAdawiyya]. She frequently practiced self-denial, and was always in a meditative state (*tafakkur*).

It was reported that she used to say: "When one reflects upon the bounties that God has bestowed on him, and how little he is thankful for them, he becomes ashamed of asking for more because of how much he has attained thus far."

XVI. ʿATHĀMA THE DAUGHTER [NIECE?] OF BILĀL IBN ABĪ AD-DARDĀʾ[8]

ʿAthāma was a devotee and practitioner of female chivalry (*min mutaʿabbidāt an-niswān*). She was stricken by blindness but bore it patiently.

The ascetic Abū al-Fatḥ Yūsuf ibn ʿUmar [al-Qawwās] of Baghdad reported from Jaʿfar ibn Muḥammad b. Nuṣayr [al-Khuldī] through Aḥmad ibn Muḥammad b. Masrūq through Muḥammad ibn al-Ḥusayn al-Burjulānī through al-Ḥusayn ibn ʿAbd al-ʿAzīz b. al-Wazīr al-Judhāmī that ʿAbdallāh ibn Yūsuf of Damascus related: ʿAthāma the daughter of Bilāl b. Abī ad-Dardāʾ lost her eyesight. One day she was engaged in worship and her son came into the house after finishing his prayers. She said, "Have you prayed, my son?" "Yes," he said. And she replied:

> "Oh ʿAthāma, why are you so distracted?
> "Your house must have been invaded by a trickster!
>
> "Weep so that you may complete your prayers on time,
> "If you are to weep at all today!
>
> "And weep while the Qurʾān is being recited,
> "For once you too, used to recite it.
>
> "You used to recite it with reflection,
> "While tears streamed down from your eyes.
>
> "I shall lament for you with fervent love,
> "For as long as I shall live!"

XVII. UMM SAʿĪD THE DAUGHTER OF ʿALQAMA AN-NAKHAʿĪ[9]

Umm Saʿīd was one of the ascetics of Basra. Abū al-Fatḥ al-Qawwās related from Jaʿfar ibn Muḥammad b. Nuṣayr [al-Khuldī] through Ibn Masrūq through Muḥammad ibn al-Ḥusayn [al-Burjulānī] through Isḥāq ibn Manṣūr as-Salūlī that Umm Saʿīd an-Nakhaʿiyya related that she heard Dāwūd aṭ-Ṭāʾī say: "Your grace [oh God] has put an end to my worries and came between me and my insomnia. And my longing to gaze upon You banished my desires." Umm Saʿid used to serve Dāwūd aṭ-Ṭāʾī.[1]

Her path of servitude followed that of aṭ-Ṭāʾī. She used to weep ceaselessly, following Dāwūd aṭ-Ṭāʾī's example.

7. A famous scholar of traditions (d. ca. 795).
8. A transmitter of hadith (d. 714/15), son of a well-known Companion of the Prophet [translator's note, edited].
9. An early ascetic of Kufa and a Successor of the Prophet (d. before 728) [translator's note, edited].
1. An ascetic scholar and disciple of Abu Hanifa (see above).

XVIII. KURDIYYA BINT ʿAMR

Kurdiyya was either from Basra or al-Ahwāz. She used to serve Shaʿwāna. She said: "Once I spent the night at Shaʿwāna's. When I fell asleep, she kicked me and said, 'Get up, oh, Kurdiyya! This is not the abode of sleep! Verily, sleep is reserved for cemeteries!'"

It was said to Kurdiyya: "What blessings did you attain from serving Shaʿwāna?" She replied, "Since serving her I have never loved the world; I have never preoccupied myself with my sustenance; I have never exalted in my sight any of the greats of the world out of greed for what they possess; and I have never shortchanged any Muslim in the least."

XIX. UMM ṬALQ

Umm Ṭalq was one of the female devotees and specialists in the ways of self-denial and gnosis.

Musaddad reported from Muḥammad ibn al-Ḥusayn [al-Burjulānī] through Yaḥyā ibn Bisṭām that Salama al-Afqam related that he heard ʿĀṣim al-Jaḥdarī[2] say: Umm Ṭalq used to say: "Whenever I prevent my lower soul from attaining its desires, God makes me a ruler over it."

Umm Ṭalq also said: "The lower soul is a king if you indulge it, but it is a slave if you torment it."

XX. ḤASNĀ BINT FAYRŪZ

Ḥasnā was one of the female devotees of Yemen and a specialist in the way of desire. She was endowed with great spiritual states.

Abū al-Faḍl Muḥammad ibn Ibrāhīm b. al-Faḍl al-Muzakkī related from Muḥammad ibn Ismāʿīl al-Ismāʿīlī through Aḥmad ibn Abī al-Ḥawārī of Damascus through Muḥammad ibn Abī Dāwūd al-Azdī, who reported that ʿAbd ar-Razzāq said: There was a woman in Yemen who was called Ḥasnā bint Fayrūz and she used to say: "Oh, God! How long will you keep Your friends buried in the ground and under the earth? Why don't You bring about the Day of Resurrection so that You can fulfill that which You have promised them?"

XXI. ḤAFṢA BINT SĪRĪN THE SISTER OF MUḤAMMAD IBN SĪRĪN[3]

Ḥafṣa was one of the female devotees of Basra. Like her brother, Muḥammad ibn Sīrīn, she was a specialist in the ways of asceticism and scrupulousness. She used to manifest exemplary signs and miracles.

I heard Muḥammad ibn Ṭāhir al-Wazīrī report from al-Ḥusayn ibn Muḥammad b. Isḥāq through Saʿīd ibn ʿUthmān al-Ḥannāṭ of Baghdad through Sayyār ibn Ḥātim that Hishām ibn Ḥassān related: Ḥafṣa bint Sīrīn used to light her lamp at night, and then would rise to pray in her prayer area. At times, the lamp would go out, but it would continue to illuminate her house until daylight.

2. A famous Qur'an reciter from Basra (d. before 748/49) [translator's note, edited].

3. A leading Muslim interpreter of dreams (d. 728).

XXII. LUBĀBA AL-ʿĀBIDA[4] (LUBĀBA THE WORSHIPPER) FROM THE NATIVES OF SYRIA

Lubāba was a specialist in the ways of scrupulousness (*waraʿ*) and reclusiveness (*nusuk*).

Aḥmad [ʿAbdallāh] ibn Muḥammad of Antioch reported from Aḥmad ibn Abī al-Ḥawārī that Aḥmad ibn Muḥammad related: Lubāba said, "I am ashamed lest God see me preoccupied with other than Him after having known Him."

He also related that she said: "Knowledge of God bequeaths love for Him; love for Him bequeaths longing for Him; longing for Him bequeaths intimacy with Him; and intimacy with Him bequeaths constancy in serving Him and conforming to His laws."

XXIII. ḤUKAYMA OF DAMASCUS FROM THE NOBLE WOMEN OF SYRIA

Ḥukayma was Rābiʿa [bint Ismāʿīl's][5] teacher (*ustādh*) and companion. Abū Jaʿfar Muḥammad ibn Aḥmad b. Saʿīd ar-Rāzī reported from al-ʿAbbās ibn Ḥamza that Aḥmad ibn Abī al-Ḥawārī related that his wife Rābiʿa [bint Ismāʿīl] said to him: I entered Ḥukayma's room while she was reading the Qur'ān and she said to me, "Oh, Rābiʿa! I have heard that your husband is taking another wife." "Yes," I said. "How could he?" she replied. "Given what I have been told about his good judgment, how could his heart be distracted from God by two women? Have you not learned the interpretation of this verse: 'Except one who comes to God with a sound heart' [Qur'an 26 (*ash-Shuʿarā'*), 89]?" "No," I said. Ḥukayma said, "It means that when one encounters God, there should be nothing in his heart other than Him." Abū Sulaymān [ad-Dārānī] said: "In thirty years I have not heard an account more excellent than this."

Rābiʿa said: "When I heard her words I went out, staggering, into the streets. I was embarrassed lest men see me and assume that I was inebriated."

Aḥmad [ibn Abī al-Ḥawārī] said: "By my father! This is true intoxication!"

XXIV. RĀBIʿA AL-AZDIYYA FROM THE NATIVES OF BASRA

Rābiʿa was one of the greatest companions of the Sufis of Basra and was a specialist in the way of scrupulousness.

ʿAbd al-Wāḥid ibn Zayd[6] was her companion and transmitted reports about her.

Abū Jaʿfar [ar-Rāzī] reported from al-ʿAbbās [ibn Ḥamza] through Aḥmad [ibn Abī al-Ḥawārī] that Bikr [ibn ʿAbdallāh] b. Muḥammad of Basra related: ʿAbd al-Wāḥid ibn Zayd asked Rābiʿa al-Azdiyya to marry him. She refused and kept away from him, and he was greatly distressed. However, he bore her refusal patiently until one day she gave him permission to see her. When he entered her house she said, "Oh lustful one! What did you see in

4. The same individual as "Lubāba the Devotee," above (II).
5. See below (XXIX).
6. Apparently the same person as Hammad ibn Zayd (see n. 7, p. 414).

me that aroused your desire? Why don't you ask a lustful person like yourself to marry you?"

XXV. ʿAJRADA THE BLIND FROM THE NATIVES OF BASRA

ʿAjrada was one of the masters of self-denial. Sayyār reported from Jaʿfar ibn Sulaymān [aḍ-Ḍubʿī],[7] who said: I heard one of our women (either my mother or someone else) relate: ʿAjrada the Blind did not break her fast for sixty years. She would only sleep for part of the night, and when she awoke she would say: "Oh my! Daytime cuts us off from intimate discourse with our Lord and returns us to the human discourse of which we are most worthy, both in our hearing and our speech."

XXVI. UMM SĀLIM AR-RĀSIBIYYA FROM THE NATIVES OF BASRA

Umm Sālim was one of the greatest masters of self-denial (*ijtihād*). Muḥammad ibn Sulaym b. Hilāl ar-Rāsibī said: Umm Sālim ar-Rāsibiyya fulfilled the requirements of *iḥrām* [i.e., the Ḥajj pilgrimage to Mecca] from Basra seventeen times.

Another person mentioned that Umm Sālim said when she made the intention to perform the Ḥajj in a state of *iḥrām*: "A slave should not seek his Lord unless he resolves to see himself fulfill all of his service to God. For if the slave delays fulfilling his service near to his goal, it is as if he has failed to fulfill all of it."

XXVII. ʿUBAYDA BINT ABĪ KILĀB[8] FROM THE NATIVES OF BASRA

ʿUbayda used to live in aṭ-Ṭufāwā [a bedouin village near Basra]. She was sound in judgment (*ʿāqila*) and practiced the way of self-denial (*mujtahida*). She was an excellent preacher.

Dāwūd ibn al-Muḥabbir (Son of the Ink-Maker) related: After ʿUbayda bint Abī Kilāb died, Basra never produced a woman better than she was.

It was reported that she said: "When one perfects his consciousness of God and knowledge of Him, nothing is more beloved to him than meeting his Lord and coming near to Him."

XXVIII. HIND BINT AL-MUHALLAB FROM BASRA

Musaddad [ibn Qaṭan] reported from Muḥammad ibn al-Ḥusayn [al-Burjulānī] through Abū ʿUmar aḍ-Ḍarīr (The Blind),[9] who related: I heard their client (*mawlā*) Abū Salama al-ʿAtakī say: Hind bint al-Muhallab said: "If you are granted a blessing from God, hurry toward it with thankfulness before it disappears."

XXIX. RĀBIʿA [RABĪʿA] BINT ISMĀʿĪL THE WIFE OF AḤMAD IBN ABĪ AL-ḤAWĀRĪ[1]

Rābiʿa was one of the great women of Syria. She was extremely rich and spent all of her wealth on Aḥmad [ibn Abī al-Ḥawārī] and his companions.

7. A transmitter of hadith (d. 794).
8. Eighth century C.E.
9. This chain of transmission indicates that Hind bint al-Muhallab lived at the beginning of the 9th century [translator's note, edited].
1. An ascetic Sufi of Damascus (d. 844/45).

Abū Jaʿfar ar-Rāzī reported from al-ʿAbbās ibn Ḥamza that Aḥmad ibn Abī al-Ḥawārī related: Rābiʿa said to me one day: "I used to pray to God Most High that someone like you or your companions would consume my fortune."

I heard Abū Bakr ibn Shādhān [ar-Rāzī] report from Yūsuf ibn al-Ḥusayn [ar-Rāzī] that Aḥmad ibn Abī al-Ḥawārī related: Rābiʿa said to us: "Take that wash basin away from me! For I see written on it: 'Hārūn [ar-Rashīd], the Commander of the Believers[2] has died.'"

Aḥmad said: We looked into the matter, and found that Hārūn had indeed died on that day.

Muḥammad ibn Aḥmad b. Saʿid reported from al-ʿAbbās ibn Ḥamza that Aḥmad ibn Abī al-Ḥawārī related: I heard Rābiʿa say: "Sometimes I see spirits (*al-jinn*) in the house coming and going. At times they are houris (*al-ḥūr al-ʿayn*), who veil themselves from me with their sleeves." She said this swearing with her hand upon her head.

[Aḥmad ibn Abī al-Ḥawārī] said: I heard Rābiʿa say: "I never look at blowing snow without thinking of the dispersal of the pages of destiny; I never look at a swarm of locusts without thinking of the gathering of souls at the Resurrection; and I never hear the muezzin without thinking of the Caller of Souls on Judgment Day."

And on the same authority Aḥmad said: Once I called for Rābiʿa and she did not answer. After an hour had passed she answered me: "What prevented me from answering you was that my heart was filled with happiness from God Most High. For this reason, I could not answer you."

2. Or "Commander of the Faithful," a title often given to the caliph; Harun al-Rashid (ca. 764–809) was the fifth ʿAbbasid caliph, under whom the dynasty attained its greatest power.

AL-GHAZALI
1058–1111

The life and works of Abu Hamid Muhammad ibn Muhammad al-Ghazali have already been outlined. In addition to his monumental *The Revival of the Religious Sciences*, excerpted above, he wrote an autobiographical work in the final years of his life that for centuries has captured special attention.

Deliverance from Error, which exists in hundreds of manuscripts and in a significant number of printed translations, has no exact correlate in the full corpus of either Islamic literature or classical Western writings. As a personal exploration of al-Ghazali's spiritual and philosophical development, it has frequently been compared to the great autobiographical work of the patristic period, St. Augustine's *Confessions* (ca. 400). Yet it does not read like a conventional autobiography. Many periods and parts of al-Ghazali's life are left unmentioned. Although *Deliverance* stands as the primary source for what we can know of his life, it omits much that would please and interest the historian. Even what is stated has become the subject of considerable controversy. Did al-Ghazali really leave Baghdad because he found himself in acute psychological and spiritual turmoil, or was he motivated by the fear of political reprisal? Did he really undergo the spiritual transformations that he describes, or was he simply trying to burnish his image as the new "renewer of the religion"? Although scholarly speculation continues, the abiding consensus accepts *Deliverance* as the sincere recollection of a spiritual and intellectual journey. At some points in the narrative, the personal interweaves with the polemical. In other parts, extended theological digressions are prominent.

The section from *Deliverance* presented here is not the work's first English translation, but Richard McCarthy's contemporary rendering draws on a more expanded manuscript tradition than that used by earlier efforts, thereby solving a number of textual difficulties.

The perennial appeal of *Deliverance* is rooted largely in how it repeats the age-old wisdom of spiritual transformation. Knowledge must be married to action. Discipline of the body frees the soul. Inner conversion is a process, not an event. Interiority flourishes in silence and seclusion. Al-Ghazali describes his own fascination with Sufism as being of long duration. First he sought clarification and guidance in the writings of famous mystics from earlier centuries. This effort whetted his appetite and appealed to his scholarly bent. But even as he continued to immerse himself in the classics of Sufi spirituality, al-Ghazali began to realize that words were not enough. At some point, he would have to move from words to action. At some point, he would have to make the commitment to push from knowledge to practice.

To describe this difference between knowing and doing, al-Ghazali uses the homely metaphor of inebriation. You can define "drunkenness," he tells us, you can read countless descriptions of it—but you don't really *know* drunkenness until you've imbibed to the point of stupefaction. This metaphor is particularly apt because, al-Ghazali alerts us, a person in a state of complete inebriation forgets the definition of drunkenness and would be at a loss to provide a scholarly explanation. The same holds true for the state of spiritual inebriation. The soul that is totally transported loses the capacity to convey that experience in words. The ever-deepening realization that he must forsake his current professional and personal life, with all its responsibilities and concerns, in order to devote himself wholeheartedly to the practice of those physical and spiritual disciplines that could prepare him for inner transformation led to the watershed moment in al-Ghazali's life. By his own account, this moment came not by choice but by compulsion: "God put a lock upon my tongue so that I was impeded from public teaching. I struggled with myself to teach for a single day, to gratify the hearts of the students who were frequenting my lectures, but my tongue would not utter a single word: I was completely unable to say anything."

As this selection from *Deliverance* makes clear, al-Ghazali recognizes and makes explicit different ways of knowing. What has just been described is the form of knowledge that McCarthy translates as "fruitional experience." It is ordinarily preceded by propositional knowledge—the form of human understanding that depends on linear exposition, rational analysis, and logical proof. The heartfelt embrace of *faith* represents the third way of knowing, a way that is opened through prophet-mediated forms of revelation. For al-Ghazali, Qur'an 58:11 provides a scriptural warrant for these modalities and degrees of understanding, and he offers a rudimentary human psychology to explain the progression from sensate experience to those insights that lie beyond the range of ordinary human intellection, those accessible only to the divinely designated prophet. The human heart, the vital center of spiritual consciousness, can be healed and made whole only by fruitional experience and faith. Reason can serve a preparatory function, but reason is not enough. Our hearts need prophets just as our bodies need physicians, because only prophets can provide the remedies required by our hearts.

Deliverance has served for many as both a testimony to spiritual transformation and a manual—even a self-help book—for the healing of the heart. Its author has long been celebrated as among the most revered Muslims of any age. Biographers of al-Ghazali delight in compiling such comments as "if there had been a prophet after Muhammad, it would have been al-Ghazali" or in calling him "a man who stands on a level with Augustine and Luther in religious insight and intellectual vigor" or "an Imam by whose name breasts are dilated and souls revived, in whose literary productions the ink horn exults and the paper quivers with joy, and at the hearing of whose message voices are hushed and heads are bowed."

PRONOUNCING GLOSSARY

Abū Naṣr al-Fārābī: *a-boo nasr´ al-fah-ra´-bee*
Abū Ṭālib al-Makkī: *a-boo tah´-lib al-mak´-kee*
Abū Yazīd al-Bisṭāmī: *a-boo ya-zeed´ al-bis-tah´-mee*
al-Ḥārith al-Muḥāsibī: *al-ha´-rith* (heavy *h*) *al-moo-ha´-si-bee* (heavy *h*)
al-Junayd: *al-joo-nayd´*
al-Shāfiʿī: *ash-sha´-fi-ee*
al-Shiblī: *ash-shib´-lee*
caliph: *ka-lif*
Galen: *gay´-len*
Ḥijāz: *he-jaz´* (heavy *h*)
Ḥirāʾ: *hi-ra´* (heavy *h*)
Ibn Sīnā: *ibn see´-nah*
Rajab: *ra´-jab*
sharīʿa: *sha-ree´-uh*
Sufi: *soo´-fee*
sultan: *sul-tahn´*

FROM DELIVERANCE FROM ERROR

Discussion of the Ways of the Sufis

When I had finished with all those kinds of lore,[1] I brought my mind to bear on the way of the sufis. I knew that their particular Way is consummated [realized] only by knowledge and by activity [by the union of theory and practice]. The aim of their knowledge is to lop off the obstacles present in the soul and to rid oneself of its reprehensible habits and vicious qualities in order to attain thereby a heart empty of all save God and adorned with the constant remembrance of God.

Theory was easier for me than practice. Therefore I began to learn their lore from the perusal of their books, such as *The Food of Hearts* by Abū Ṭālib al-Makkī (God's mercy be upon him!) and the writings of al-Ḥārith al-Muḥāsibī, and the miscellaneous items handed down from al-Junayd and al-Shiblī and Abū Yazīd al-Bisṭāmī[2] (God hallow their spirits!) and others of their masters. As a result I came to know the core of their theoretical aims and I learned all that could be learned of their way by study and hearing.

Then it became clear to me that their most distinctive characteristic is something that can be attained, not by study, but rather by fruitional experience[3] and the state of ecstasy and "the exchange of qualities." How great a difference there is between your *knowing* the definitions and causes

TRANSLATED BY Richard Joseph McCarthy. The parenthetical citations are to sura and verse of the Qurʾan; all bracketed additions are the translator's.

1. Al-Ghazali has just refuted the doctrines of the scholastic theologians, the Ismaʿili Shiʿis, and the philosophers.
2. Noted Sufi authors of the 9th and 10th centuries. For al-Bistami, see above.
3. A translation of the Arabic *al-dhawq* (literally, "taste"), an experience that goes beyond the cognitive and touches the deepest emotions. Compare Psalm 34:8, "O taste and see that the Lord is good."

and conditions of health and satiety and your *being* healthy and sated! And how great a difference there is between your knowing the definition of drunkenness—viz. that it is a term denoting a state resulting from the predominance of vapors which rise from the stomach to the centers of thought—and your actually being drunk! Indeed, a drunken man, while he is drunk, does not know the definition and concept of drunkenness and has no knowledge of it. But a physician knows the definition and the elements of drunkenness, though he is experiencing no actual drunkenness. So also, when a physician is ill, he knows the definition and causes of health and the remedies which procure it, though he is then actually bereft of health. Similarly, too, there is a difference between your knowing the true nature and conditions and causes of asceticism and your actually practicing asceticism and personally shunning the things of this world.

I knew with certainty that the sufis were masters of states,[4] not purveyors of words, and that I had learned all I could by way of theory. There remained, then, only what was attainable, not by hearing and study, but by fruitional experience and actually engaging in the way. From the sciences which I had practiced and the methods which I had followed in my inquiry into the two kinds of knowledge, revealed and rational, I had already acquired a sure and certain faith in God Most High, in the prophetic mediation of revelation, and in the Last Day. These three fundamentals of our Faith had become deeply rooted in my soul, not because of any specific, precisely formulated proofs, but because of reasons and circumstances and experiences too many to list in detail.

It had already become clear to me that my only hope of attaining beatitude in the afterlife lay in piety and restraining my soul from passion. The beginning of all that, I knew, was to sever my heart's attachment to the world by withdrawing from this abode of delusion and turning to the mansion of immortality and devoting myself with total ardor to God Most High. That, I knew, could be achieved only by shunning fame and fortune and fleeing from my preoccupations and attachments.

Next I attentively considered my circumstances, and I saw that I was immersed in attachments which had encompassed me from all sides. I also considered my activities—the best of them being public and private instruction—and saw that in them I was applying myself to sciences unimportant and useless in this pilgrimage to the hereafter. Then I reflected on my intention in my public teaching, and I saw that it was not directed purely to God, but rather was instigated and motivated by the quest for fame and widespread prestige. So I became certain that I was on the brink of a crumbling bank and already on the verge of falling into the Fire, unless I set about mending my ways.

I therefore reflected unceasingly on this for some time, while I still had freedom of choice. One day I would firmly resolve to leave Baghdad and disengage myself from those circumstances, and another day I would revoke my resolution. I would put one foot forward, and the other backward. In the morning I would have a sincere desire to seek the things of the afterlife; but by evening the hosts of passion would assail it and render it lukewarm. Mundane desires began tugging me with their chains to remain as I was,

4. Stages of spiritual experience.

while the herald of faith was crying out: "Away! Up and away! Only a little is left of your life, and a long journey lies before you! All the theory and practice in which you are engrossed is eyeservice and fakery! If you do not prepare now for the afterlife, when will you do so? And if you do not sever these attachments now, then when will you sever them?"

At such thoughts the call would reassert itself and I would make an irrevocable decision to run off and escape. Then Satan would return to the attack and say: "This is a passing state: beware, then, of yielding to it! For it will quickly vanish. Once you have given in to it and given up your present renown and splendid position free from vexation and renounced your secure situation untroubled by the contention of your adversaries, your soul might again look longingly at all that—but it would not be easy to return to it!"

Thus I incessantly vacillated between the contending pull of worldly desires and the appeals of the afterlife for about six months, starting with Rajab of the year 488 (July, 1095 A.D.). In this month the matter passed from choice to compulsion. For God put a lock upon my tongue so that I was impeded from public teaching. I struggled with myself to teach for a single day, to gratify the hearts of the students who were frequenting my lectures, but my tongue would not utter a single word: I was completely unable to say anything. As a result that impediment of my speech caused a sadness in my heart accompanied by an inability to digest; food and drink became unpalatable to me so that I could neither swallow broth easily nor digest a mouthful of solid food. That led to such a weakening of my powers that the physicians lost hope of treating me and said: "This is something which has settled in his heart and crept from it into his humors; there is no way to treat it unless his heart be eased of the anxiety which has visited it."

Then, when I perceived my powerlessness, and when my capacity to make a choice had completely collapsed, I had recourse to God Most High as does a hard pressed man who has no way out of his difficulty. And I was answered by Him Who "answers the needy man when he calls on Him" (27.63/62) and He made it easy for my heart to turn away from fame and fortune, family, children, and associates. I announced that I had resolved to leave for Mecca, all the while planning secretly to travel to Syria. This I did as a precaution, lest the Caliph and the group of my associates might learn of my resolve to settle in Damascus. Therefore I made clever use of subtle stratagems about leaving Baghdad, while firmly resolved never to return to it. I was much talked about by the religious leaders of the Iraqis, since none among them could allow that giving up my career had a religious motive. For they thought that my post was the highest dignity in our religion—and "that was the farthest limit they had attained in learning!" (53.31/30).

Thereupon people got involved in devising explanations of my conduct. Those at some distance from Iraq thought I was acting so because I was afraid of the authorities. But those close to the authorities, who saw their attachment and devotion to me, and how I shunned them and paid no attention to what they said, were saying: "This is something supernal: its only cause is an evil eye which has afflicted Muslims and the coterie of the learned!"

I departed from Baghdad after I had distributed what wealth I had, laying by only the amount needed for my support and the sustenance of my children. My excuse for that was that the money of Iraq was earmarked for the welfare of the people, because it was a pious bequest in favor of Muslims. Nowhere in the world have I seen a more beneficial arrangement regarding money which the scholar can use for his family.

Then I entered Damascus and resided there for nearly two years. My only occupation was seclusion and solitude and spiritual exercise and combat with a view to devoting myself to the purification of my soul and the cultivation of virtues and cleansing my heart for the remembrance of God Most High, in the way I had learned from the writings of the sufis. I used to pray in seclusion for a time in the Mosque, mounting to its minaret for the whole day and shutting myself in. Then I traveled from Damascus to Jerusalem, where I would go daily into the Dome of the Rock[5] and shut myself in. Then I was inwardly moved by an urge to perform the duty of the pilgrimage and to draw succor from the blessings of Mecca and Medina and the visit to the tomb of the Apostle of God—God's blessing and peace be upon him!—after finishing my visit to the Friend of God—God's blessings and peace be upon him! So I traveled to the Ḥijāz.[6]

Then certain concerns and the appeals of my children drew me to my native land; so I came back to it after being the person most unlikely to return to it. There I also chose seclusion out of a desire for solitude and the purification of my heart for the remembrance of God. But current events and important family matters and gaining the necessities for daily living had an effect on the way to realize my desire and troubled the serenity of my solitude, and the pure state of ecstasy occurred only intermittently. But nonetheless I did not cease to aspire to it. Obstacles would keep me away from it, but I would return to it.

For ten years I remained in that condition. In the course of those periods of solitude things impossible to enumerate or detail in depth were disclosed to me. This much I shall mention, that profit may be derived from it: I knew with certainty that the sufis are those who uniquely follow the way to God Most High, their mode of life is the best of all, their way the most direct of ways, and their ethic the purest. Indeed, were one to combine the insight of the intellectuals, the wisdom of the wise, and the lore of scholars versed in the mysteries of revelation in order to change a single item of sufi conduct and ethic and to replace it with something better, no way to do so would be found! For all their motions and quiescences, exterior and interior, are learned from the light of the niche of prophecy. And beyond the light of prophecy there is no light on earth from which illumination can be obtained.

In general, how can men describe such a way as this? Its purity—the first of its requirements—is the total purification of the heart from everything other than God Most High. Its key, which is analogous to the beginning of the Prayer,[7] is the utter absorption of the heart in the remembrance of God. Its end is being completely lost in God. But the latter is its end with reference to its initial stages which just barely fall under the power of choice and personal acquisition. But these are really the beginning of the

5. An ancient shrine in Jerusalem. Many Muslims believe that the stone over which the Dome of the Rock was built was the point from which Muhammad ascended into heaven.

6. The region of the Arabian Peninsula that borders the Red Sea and contains Mecca and Medina.

7. The opening formula is "God is greater" (than anything else), said in the obligatory prayers recited five times daily as well as in all other prayers.

Way, and everything prior to it is like an antechamber for him who follows the path to it.

From the very start of the Way revelations and visions begin, so that, even when awake, the sufis see the angels and the spirits of the prophets and hear voices coming from them and learn useful things from them. Then their "state" ascends from the vision of forms and likenesses to stages beyond the narrow range of words: so if anyone tries to express them, his words contain evident error against which he cannot guard himself. But speaking in general, the matter comes ultimately to a closeness to God which one group almost conceives of as "indwelling," and another as "union," and another as "reaching": but all that, is wrong. We have already shown why it is wrong in our book *The Noblest Aim.*[8] But really one intimately possessed by that state ought not to go beyond saying:

> There was what was of what I do not mention:
> So think well of it, and ask for no account![9]

Generally speaking, anyone who is granted nothing of that through fruitional experience grasps, of the reality of prophecy, only the name. The charisms of the "saints" are in reality the first stages passed through by the prophets. Such was the initial state of the Apostle of God—God's blessing and peace be upon him!—when he went to Mount Ḥirāʾ,[1] where he would be alone with his Lord and perform acts of worship, so that the Arabs of the desert said: "Muḥammad indeed passionately loves his Lord!"

This is a state which one following the way leading to it will verify by fruitional experience. But one to whom such experience is not granted can acquire certain knowledge of that state through experience of others and hearsay, if he frequents the company of the sufis so as to have a sure understanding of that from observing the circumstances accompanying their ecstatic states. Whoever associates with them will derive this faith from them, for they are the men whose associate is never wretched. But whoever is not favored with their company must learn the certain possibility of such mystical states through the evidence of apodeictic demonstration in the way we have mentioned in "The Book of the Marvels of the Heart," one of the books of *The Revivification of the Religious Sciences.*[2]

Ascertainment by apodeictic proof leads to *knowledge.* Intimate experience of that very state is *fruitional experience.* Favorable acceptance of it based on hearsay and experience of others is *faith.* These, then, are three degrees, or levels, of knowledge—"God raises in degrees those of you who believe and those to whom knowledge is given" (58.12/11).

In addition to the men with such levels of knowledge there are a number of ignorant men who deny its very foundation and are astonished at such words. They listen and scoff, saying: "Extraordinary! How they rave!" Of such as these God Most High said: "And among them (infidels) are those who listen to you, then, when they have left you, they say to those who have been given knowledge: 'What did he just say?' Those are men whose hearts

8. An exposition of the ninety-nine names or attributes of God (a number specified by the Prophet).
9. The verse is by the poet Ibn al-Muʿtazz (861–908) [translator's note, edited].
1. A hill near Mecca to which the prophet Muhammad withdrew in prayer.
2. On al-Ghazali's *Revival of the Religious Sciences*, see the introduction to the excerpt in this volume, above.

God has sealed and who follow their own vain desires" (47.18/16)—so God renders them deaf and blinds their eyes.

What became clear to me of necessity from practicing their Way was the true nature and special character of prophecy. So attention must be called to its basis because of the urgent need for it.

The True Nature of Prophecy and the Need All Men Have for It

Know that man's essence, in his original condition, is created in blank simplicity without any information about the "worlds" of God Most High. These "worlds" are so many that only God Most High can number them, as He has said: "No one knows the hosts of your Lord but He" (74.34/31). Man gets his information about the "worlds" by means of perception. Each one of his kinds of perception is created in order that man may get to know thereby a "world" of the existents—and by "worlds" we mean the categories of existing things.

The first thing created in man is the sense of touch: by this he perceives certain classes of existents such as heat and cold, wetness and dryness, smoothness and roughness, etc. But touch is definitely unable to perceive colors and sounds; indeed, these are, as it were, nonexistent with respect to touch.

Next the sense of sight is created for man, by which he perceives colors and shapes: this is the most extensive of the "worlds" of the sensibles.

Then the sense of hearing is opened, so that man hears sounds and tones.

Next the sense of taste is created for man; and so on until he passes beyond the "world" of the sensibles. Then, when he is about seven years old, *discernment* is created for him. This is another of the stages of man's existence; in it he perceives things beyond the "world" of the sensibles, none of which are found in the "world" of sensation.

Then man ascends to another stage, and *intellect* is created for him, so that he perceives the necessary, the possible, the impossible, and things not found in the previous stages.

Beyond the stage of intellect there is another stage. In this another eye is opened, by which man sees the hidden, and what will take place in the future, and other things, from which the intellect is as far removed as the power of discernment is from the perception of intelligibles and the power of sensation is from things perceived by discernment. And just as one able only to discern, if presented with the things perceptible to the intellect, would reject them and consider them outlandish, so some men endowed with intellect have rejected the things perceptible to the prophetic power and considered them wildly improbable. That is the very essence of ignorance! For such a man has no supporting reason except that it is a stage he himself has not attained and for him it does not exist: so he supposes that it does not exist in itself.

Now if a man born blind did not know about colors and shapes from constant report and hearsay, and were to be told about them abruptly, he would neither understand them nor acknowledge their existence. But God Most High has brought the matter within the purview of His creatures by giving them a sample of the special character of the prophetic power: sleeping. For the sleeper perceives the unknown that will take place, either plainly, or in the guise of an image the meaning of which is disclosed by interpretation.

If a man had had no personal experience of dreaming and someone were to tell him: "There are some men who fall down unconscious as though they were dead, and their perception, hearing, and sight leave them, and they then perceive what is 'hidden,'" he would deny it and give apodeictic proof of its impossibility by saying: "The sensory powers are the causes of perception. Therefore one who does not perceive such things when his powers are present and functioning a fortiori will not perceive them when his powers are suspended."

This is a kind of analogy which is belied by factual experience and observation. Just as the intellect is one of man's stages in which he receives an "eye" by which he "sees" various species of intelligibles from which the senses are far removed, the prophetic power is an expression signifying a stage in which man receives an "eye" possessed of a light, and in its light the unknown and other phenomena not normally perceived by the intellect become visible.

Doubt about prophecy touches either its possibility, or its actual existence, or its belonging to a specific individual.

The proof of its *possibility* is its existence. And the proof of its *existence* is the existence in the world of knowledge which could not conceivably be obtained by the intellect alone—such as the knowledge of medicine and of astronomy. For whoever examines such knowledge knows of necessity that it can be obtained only by a divine inspiration and a special help from God Most High, and that there is no empirical way to it. Thus among astronomical phenomena there is a phenomenon which occurs only once every thousand years. How, then, could knowledge of that be obtained empirically? The same is true of the properties of medicaments.

From this proof it is clearly within the bounds of possibility that a way exists to grasp these things which the intellect does not normally grasp. This is what is meant by prophecy. Not that prophecy signifies such knowledge only. Rather, the perception of this kind of thing which is outside the things normally perceived by the intellect is one of the properties of prophecy. It also has many other properties; what we have mentioned is a drop from its sea. We have mentioned it only because you have in your own experience an example of it, viz. the things you perceive while asleep. You also have knowledge of the same sort in medicine and astronomy. These, too, belong to the category of the prophets' apologetic miracles—the blessing and peace of God be upon them! But men endowed with intellect have no way at all of attaining such knowledge by intellectual resources alone.

The properties of prophecy beyond those just mentioned can be perceived only by fruitional experience as a result of following the way of sufism. For you have understood that only because of an example you have been given, viz. sleep; were it not for this, you would not assent to that. If, then, the prophet has a special quality of which you have no example and which you in no wise understand, how can you find it credible? Assent comes only after understanding. But the example needed occurs in the first stages of the way of sufism. Then, through this example, one obtains a kind of fruitional experience commensurate with the progress made plus a kind of assent to what has not been attained based on analogy with what has been attained. So this single property we have mentioned is enough ground for you to believe in the basis of prophecy.

If it occurs to you to doubt whether a particular individual is a prophet or not, certainty will be gained only by becoming acquainted with his circumstances, either through personal observation or from impeccable tradition and hearsay. For when you are familiar with medicine and jurisprudence, you can recognize jurisprudents and physicians by observing their circumstances, and also by hearing their dicta, even if you have not seen them yourself. Moreover, you are quite capable of knowing that al-Shāfiʿī (God's mercy be upon him!) was a jurisprudent and that Galen[3] was a physician—and that with a knowledge based on fact, not on uncritical acceptance of someone's say-so—by your learning something about jurisprudence and medicine and then perusing their writings and works: thus you will acquire a necessary knowledge of their scientific status.

Likewise, when you understand the meaning of prophecy and devote much study to the Qurʾān and the traditions, you will acquire the necessary knowledge of the fact that Muḥammad—God's blessing and peace be upon him!—had attained the loftiest level of prophecy. Then back that up by sampling what he said about the acts of worship and their effect on the purification of hearts. Consider, for example, how right he was—God's blessing and peace be upon him!—in his saying: "Whoever acts according to what he knows, God will make him heir to what he does not know"; and how right he was in his saying: "Whoever aids an unjust man, God gives the latter dominion over him"; and how right he was in his saying: "Whoever reaches the point where all his cares are a single care, God Most High will save him from all cares in this life and the next." When you have had that experience in a thousand, two thousand, and many thousands of instances, you will have acquired a necessary knowledge which will be indisputable.

Therefore, seek sure and certain knowledge of prophecy in this way, not from the changing of the staff into a serpent and the splitting of the moon.[4] For if you consider that sort of thing alone, without adding the many, indeed innumerable, circumstances accompanying it, you might think it was a case of magic and deception, and that it was a "leading astray" coming from God Most High, because "He leads astray whom He will and rightly guides whom He will" (16.95/93), and the problems connected with apologetic miracles[5] would confront you.

Furthermore, if your faith were based on a carefully ordered argument about the way the apologetic miracle affords proof of prophecy, your faith would be broken by an equally well-ordered argument showing how difficulty and doubt may affect that mode of proof. Therefore, let such preternatural events be one of the proofs and concomitants that make up your total reflection on the matter. As a result, you will acquire such necessary knowledge that you will be unable to cite its specific basis. It would be like the case of a man to whom many men report an unimpeachable tradition. He cannot aver that his sure and certain knowledge is derived from the statement of one specific individual. Rather, he does not know whence it comes:

3. Greek physician (129–ca. 199), the primary authority on medicine in Europe and the Middle East until the 17th century. On al-Shafiʿi (767–820), eponymous founder of one of the major Islamic schools of law, see above.

4. Two events mentioned in the Qurʾan; the staff belongs to Moses, who throws it down to defeat the sorcery of Pharaoh's magicians (20:69–70), while Muslims see Muhammad as responsible for splitting the moon (54:1).

5. That is, miracles done as a means of defense or vindication.

but it is neither outside the group testimony, nor is it due to pinpointing individuals. This, then, is the strong belief based on knowledge. Fruitional experience, on the other hand, is comparable to actual seeing and handling: this is found only in the way of the sufis.

This much, then, of the real meaning of prophecy is sufficient for my present purpose. Now I shall mention the reason why it is needed.

From *The Reason for Resuming Teaching After Having Given It Up*

A. DOCTORS OF HEARTS

For nearly ten years I assiduously cultivated seclusion and solitude. During that time several points became clear to me of necessity for reasons I cannot enumerate—at one time by fruitional experience, at another time by knowledge based on apodeictic proof, and again by acceptance founded on faith. These points were: that man is formed of a body and a heart—and by the "heart" I mean the essence of man's spirit which is the seat of the knowledge of God, not the flesh which man has in common with corpse and beast; that his body may have a health which will result in its happiness, and a malady in which lies its ruin; that his heart, likewise, may have a health and soundness—and only he will be saved "who comes to God with a sound heart" (26.89), and it may have a malady which will lead to his everlasting perdition in the next life, as God Most High has said: "In their hearts is a malady" (2.9/10); that ignorance of God is the heart's deadly poison, disobedience to God its incapacitating malady, knowledge of God Most High its quickening antidote, and obedience to Him by resisting passion its healing remedy; that the only way to treat the heart by removing its malady and regaining its health lies in the use of remedies, just as that is the only way to treat the body.

Remedies for the body effectively procure health because of a property in them which men endowed with intellect cannot perceive by virtue of their intellectual resources, but rather it must be the object of blind obedience to the physicians who learned it from the prophets, who, because of the special attribute of prophecy, came to know the special properties of things. In a similar fashion it became necessarily evident to me that the reason for the effectiveness of the remedies of the acts of worship, with their prescriptions and determined quantities ordained by the prophets, cannot be perceived by means of the intellectual resources of men endowed with intellect. On the contrary, they must be the object of blind obedience to the prophets who perceived those qualities by the light of prophecy, not by intellectual resources.

Moreover, just as medicaments are composed of mixtures of elements differing in kind and quantity, some of them being double others in weight and quantity, and just as the difference of their quantities is not without a profound significance pertaining to the kind of the properties, so, likewise, the acts of worship, which are the remedies of hearts, are composed of actions differing in kind and quantity, so that a prostration is the double of a bowing, and the morning prayer is half as long as the afternoon prayer. This difference is not without a profound significance which pertains to the kind of the properties knowable only by the light of the prophecy. Very stupid and ignorant would be the man who would wish to discover in them a wisdom by means of reason, or who would suppose that they had been mentioned by chance, and not because of a profound divine significance in them which requires them to be such because of the special property in them. And just as in medicaments there are basic elements which are their chief ingredients and additional substances which are their complements, each of them having a special effect on the workings of their basic elements, so, likewise, supererogatory prayers and customary practices[6] are complements for perfecting the effects of the principal elements of the acts of worship.

In general, then, the prophets (Peace be upon them!) are the physicians for treating the maladies of hearts. By its activity reason is useful simply to acquaint us with this fact, to bear witness to prophecy by giving assent to its reality, to certify its own blindness to perceiving what the "eye" of prophecy perceives, and to take us by our hands and turn us over to the prophets as blind men are handed over to guides and as troubled sick men are handed over to sympathetic physicians. To this point reason can proceed and advance, but it is far removed from anything beyond that except for understanding what the physician prescribes. These, then, are the insights we gained with a necessity analogous to direct vision during the period of our solitude and seclusion.

B. THE SLACKNESS OF FAITH

Then we saw the lukewarmness of men's beliefs in the basis of prophecy, and consequently, in the reality of prophecy and in action in accord with the data of prophecy. We also ascertained that this was widespread among men. I then reflected on the reasons for men's lukewarmness and the weakness of their faith, and found them to be four in number:

1. A reason stemming from those engrossed in the science of philosophy.
2. A reason stemming from those absorbed in the way of sufism.
3. A reason stemming from those attached to the claim of authoritative teaching.
4. A reason stemming from the behavior of those popularly regarded as preeminent in learning.

For a period of time I next addressed myself successively to individuals, questioning those who were remiss in fulfilling the Law. I would ask a man about his specious reason for that and inquire into his belief and his inner convictions, asking him: "Why are you so remiss? If you believe in the afterlife, but do not prepare yourself for it and barter it for this life—why, this is stupidity! You would not ordinarily barter two things for one. How, then, can you barter what is unending for a limited number of days? And if you do not believe, then you are an infidel! So act wisely in the quest for faith and look into the cause of your hidden unbelief! For this is your real inner conviction and the cause of your outward boldness, even though you do not openly express it, because you want to bedeck yourself with the trappings of faith and to be respected for paying lip service to the law!"

One man would reply: "If this were a matter one was bound to observe, then the learned would be those most properly bound to do it. But of those

6. Prayers and practices that supplement those that are mandatory.

most renowned among the learned, so-and-so does not perform the prescribed Prayer, and such a one drinks wine, and another devours the assets of religious endowments and the property of orphans, and another feathers his nest with the lavish largesse of the Sultan without being wary of what is illicit, and another accepts bribes for judgment and testimony, and so on in many similar instances!"

A second man would claim to be an adept in the science of sufism and allege that he had attained a degree beyond the need for formal worship. And a third would offer as his excuse one of the specious reasons advanced by the licentious. These are the erring who profess the way of sufism.

A fourth respondent would have had contact with the Taʿlīmites.[7] So he would declare: "The truth is doubtful, the way to it hard, there is much disagreement about it, and no one view is preferable to any other. Moreover, rational proofs contradict one another so that no reliance can be placed on the opinion of independent thinkers. But the advocate of authoritative teaching makes categorical pronouncements without needing any proof. How, then, can we give up the certain because of the uncertain?"

A fifth man would say: "I do not do this out of servile conformism, but I have studied the science of philosophy and I have grasped the real meaning of prophecy. I know that it comes down to what is wise and beneficial and that the aim of its religious prescriptions is to control the common people and to curb them from internecine strife and contention and from unrestrained indulgence in their passions. Hence I am not one of the ignorant masses and therefore subject to commandment. Rather, I am one of the wise, following the way of wisdom and well versed in it, and in my wisdom I can get along without servile conformism!" This is the limit reached by the faith of those who have studied the philosophy of the theistic philosophers: that is known from the books of Ibn Sīnā and Abū Naṣr al-Fārābī.[8]

These are the men who bedeck themselves with the trappings of Islam. Often you may see one of them reciting the Qur'ān and attending the assemblies and public prayers and paying great lip service to the Sharīʿa. But despite that he does not give up his winebibbing and various kinds of depravity and debauchery. If he is asked: "If prophecy is not authentic, why do you pray?" he may reply: "It is an askesis of the body and the custom of the local people and a way to preserve fortune and family." And he may say: "The Sharīʿa is authentic and prophecy is genuine." Then one should say: "Why, then, do you drink wine?" And he may say: "Wine was prohibited simply because it causes enmity and hatred. But I, by my wisdom, can guard against that. My only aim in drinking is to stimulate my mind."

Indeed, Ibn Sīnā went so far as to write in a testament of his that he made a pact with God to do certain things, and that he would extol the ordinances of the Law and would not be remiss in performing the religious acts of worship, nor would he drink for pleasure, but only for medicinal purposes and to promote his health. So the furthest he got respecting purity of faith and the obligation of acts of worship was to make an exception for winebibbing on the score of promoting his health! Such is the faith of those philosophers who pretend to have faith! Many, indeed, have been deceived by them, and their

7. Literally, "Instructionists," a Shiʿi sect who believed that truth rests on the authority of a leader.

8. On the philosophers Ibn Sina (980–1037) and al-Farabi (ca. 878–950), see above.

deception has been intensified by the weak arguments of those who opposed the philosophers. For their opposition was to repudiate the sciences of geometry and logic and others which, for the philosophers, are true of necessity, according to the reasoned explanation we have set forth previously.

IBN AL-ʿARABI
1165–1240

One of the most prolific, influential, and controversial figures in the history of Sufism, Muhyi al-Din Ibn al-ʿArabi constructed his mystical philosophy around the "oneness of being," a concept with profound resonance within the strict monotheism of Islam but one that also carried the potential for blurring the human/divine boundary. Consequently, Ibn al-ʿArabi's writings sparked some controversy during his lifetime even though he was well-regarded as a religious scholar and student of traditions. For the most part, his mystical writings remained limited to a select audience. After his death, however, his works gained popularity through the teachings of his students. Some people staunchly opposed his ideas and saw no value in them; others embraced them, believing that Ibn al-ʿArabi had been blessed with unique insights into God and his creation. It is to this latter group that he owes his recognition as the seal of the saints.

Born in Murcia, Spain, in August 1165, Ibn al-ʿArabi had a peripatetic life. His father, a government employee, left Murcia in 1172 and moved to Seville to take another administrative position. Ibn al-ʿArabi had the normal upbringing of one whose family was employed by the government and appears to have had no special religious training beyond what any educated person in his society would have received. During his youth—possibly while ill—Ibn al-ʿArabi experienced an overwhelming vision of God. He would later note that everything he had written was an attempt to explain the insights gained during this vision. Hearing of Ibn al-ʿArabi's experiences, the famous philosopher Ibn Rushd (or Averroës, 1126–1198; see above) asked Ibn al-ʿArabi's father to arrange a meeting for him with the boy. Ibn Rushd and Ibn al-ʿArabi discussed their respective approaches to the divine, the rational versus the mystical. According to Ibn al-ʿArabi's retelling of the event, by the end of the discussion Ibn Rushd had turned pale, shaken by the depth of Ibn al-ʿArabi's insight.

Following his spiritual awakening, Ibn al-ʿArabi continued to live in Seville but traveled throughout Spain and North Africa, studying with Sufi teachers and with specialists in traditions, law, and the Qurʾan. At age thirty, he left Seville and moved to Tunis, making it the base for more study and travel. In 1202, the pilgrimage took him to Mecca, where visionary experiences inspired new writings, including his magnum opus, *The Meccan Openings.* He left Mecca after two years to travel throughout Turkey, Syria, and Egypt, going as far east as Baghdad (1211–12). He was welcomed to the courts of regional rulers, serving as a scholar and adviser. In 1223, Ibn al-ʿArabi settled in Damascus, where he would remain until his death in 1240. His reasons for moving there remain obscure, but he undoubtedly had the support of powerful backers, including some among the ruling Ayyubids. In Damascus he attracted disciples, taught his esoteric and mystical philosophy, and continued to write. He completed *The Meccan Openings* and, inspired by another vision, composed *The Ringstones of Wisdom.*

The Ringstones of Wisdom summarizes Ibn al-ʿArabi's most important ideas and was intended for those on the Sufi path, not the general public. Using qurʾanic verses and traditions, he described how a particular aspect of divine wisdom was manifest by a specific prophet. He chose twenty-seven prophets, from Adam to Muhammad, to construct this spiritual typology.

Like *The Ringstones*, *The Meccan Openings* was not intended for a general audience. Inspired by visions received during his Meccan pilgrimage, Ibn al-ʿArabi composed this work over many years; its size and topical heterogeneity bear witness to this lengthy generation. Ranging from metaphysics and cosmology to psychology and eschatology, *The Meccan Openings* contains 560 chapters divided into six sections, which treat divinely inspired knowledge, correct actions, spiritual states, spiritual way stations, spiritual encounters, and spiritual ranks.

Ibn al-ʿArabi's writings are complex, and scholars of his thought trace his ever-evolving understanding. But one of his key concepts is that all of existence is a reflection and manifestation of the divine names, a notion often termed the "oneness of being." The challenge for humans who seek the divine lies in perfectly balancing how they manifest these names. Reflecting an abundance of God's harsher names may make a person cruel, but overly expressing the merciful may create an excessively compliant individual. The human soul's perfection and its closer alignment to the divine rest on proper proportionality. Tied to this understanding of God's names is Ibn al-ʿArabi's observation that both creation and humankind reflect the divine. Creation taken as a whole displays the multiplicity of God's names, while the totality of God's names is embodied in each individual. The cosmos is a macrocosmic expression and human beings are a microcosmic expression of the divine names.

Ibn al-ʿArabi's controversial claim to be the seal of God's saints was not intended to have temporal force; he was not asserting that he would be the last saint in Islamic history. Rather, he believed that he would be the last person to fully inherit all of the spiritual insights, gifts, and powers that a saint could receive. No saints following him would possess all aspects of sainthood in their fullness. Ibn al-ʿArabi saw his sainthood as mirroring the prophethood of Muhammad. Just as Muhammad, the last prophet, was the seal of the prophets, so Ibn al-ʿArabi was sainthood's final seal. As might be expected, many people, Sufis and non-Sufis alike, rejected Ibn al-ʿArabi's claim and questioned whether the very notion had any validity.

The following selection from *The Meccan Openings* is not easy reading. Ibn al-ʿArabi makes complex linguistic arguments about how the descriptions and characterization known as the ninety-nine divine names are derived. His discourse on the name "Allah" continues and expands a theological-mystical tradition that finds the generative essence of all beings in this single word. Ibn al-ʿArabi himself acknowledges the inherent difficulty of this discourse: "So the fact that we have professed God's Incomparability has taken us to bewilderment, since all the paths are muddled. Both intellectual and law-inspired speculation lead to a single center which is bewilderment. . . . So rational speculation leads to bewilderment and theophany leads to bewilderment. There is nothing but a bewildered one. There is nothing exercising properties but bewilderment. There is nothing but Allah."

FROM THE MECCAN OPENINGS

From *The Most Beautiful Names*
Chapter 558

I see the ladder of the Names, rising and falling, through it blowing a wind from south and north.

Translated by Michel Chodkiewicz, in collaboration with William C. Chittick and James W. Morris. All bracketed additions are the translators'.

I wonder—how to reach safety? For blindness is the brother of guidance and affairs are not separate.

Do you not see that in the Fire God is Just? That in the Garden of Firdaws[1] He favors and obliges?

If you say, "This one is an infidel," I say, "God is Just." If you say, "This one a man of faith," I say, "He gives preference."

Here is proof that my Lord is one: God appoints and removes whom He will.

So our entities are His Names, they are nothing other, for in His own Self he decrees and differentiates affairs.

God says, *"To God belong the Most Beautiful Names"* (Qur'an 7:180). These are none other than the Divine Presences *(al-hadarât al-ilâhiyya)* that are sought and entified[2] by the properties of the possible things *(ahkâm al-mumkinât)*. And these properties are none other than the forms manifest within True Being *(al-wujûd al-haqq)*. Hence "Divine Presence" is a name belonging to an Essence, Attributes, and Acts; or, if you like, you can say: to the Attributes of Acts *(sifa fi'l)* and the Attributes of Incomparability *(sifa tanzîh)*.

The Acts derive from the Attributes. No doubt the Acts are Names, but some of the Names He ascribes *(itlâq)* to Himself, while others He does not ascribe, though they have come in words [indicating] Acts, such as, *"[They deceived] and God deceived"* (Qur'an 3:54); *"God derides [them]"* (Qur'an 9:79); *"[They scheme a scheme] and I scheme a scheme"* (Qur'an 86:16); *"God mocks them"* Qur'an 2:15). In these cases it is not impossible for an active noun *(ism fâ'il)* to be built from the words.

A similar case is provided by indirect expressions (*kinâyât*), such as, *"[He has appointed for you] shirts to protect you from the heat"* (Qur'an 16:81). In fact He is the Protector, while the shirt here is the deputy. And so on with other verses.

There are also pronouns, whether referring to the first, third, or second person, or to all things *('âmm)*, as in God's words, *"Oh people, you are the poor toward Allah"* (Qur'an 35:15), where He is named by everything toward which people are poor. Hence, everything toward which someone is poor is a Name of God, since [as stated in this verse] there is no poverty except toward Him; though no word is ascribed to Him here, we take into account the meanings given us by the sciences.

As for prohibition *(tahjîr)* and lack of it in the ascription [of Names] to Him, that depends on God. Hence, if He has restricted Himself to certain words in ascription, we also restrict ourselves, since we only name Him by what He has named Himself. Those Names which are forbidden, we forbid, out of courtesy *(adab)* toward God. For we are in Him and we belong to Him. Hence in this chapter we will mention, Presence by Presence, the Divine Presences that God has alluded to as the Most Beautiful Names. We will restrict ourselves to one hundred Presences. Then we will follow that with sections, each of which will refer back to this chapter. Among the Presences is:

1. The highest level of heaven. 2. Reified.

The Divine Presence, that is, The Name "Allah"

Allah, Allah, Allah—His signs *(âyât)* have passed judgment that He is Allah.
Glory be to Him!—He is greater than that any of the servants should win Him, for there is no god but He.
He alone possesses a Name not shared by any other: that is the speaker's word, "Allah."

This is the Presence that comprehends *(jâmiʿ)* all Presences. Hence no worshipper of God worships anything but this Presence. God judges *(hukm)* this in His words, *"Thy Lord has decreed that you shall not worship any but Him"* (Qurʾan 17:23), and His words, *"You are the poor toward Allah."*

To God belongs what is hidden, to God belongs what appears,
How excellent is that which is God, that which is none other than He.

You should know that since the power *(quwwa)* of the Name Allah contains, according to the original coinage *(al-wadʿ al-awwal)*, every Divine Name, or rather, every Name having an effect *(athar)* within engendered existence, it takes, on behalf of what it names, the place of every Name of God. So when someone says, "Oh Allah," look at the state which incited him to make this call and consider which Divine Name is specifically connected to that state. That specific Name *(al-ism al-khâss)* is what the caller is calling with his words, "Oh Allah." For the Name Allah, by its original coinage, names the Essence of God Itself, *"in whose hand is the dominion of everything"* (Qurʾan 36:83). That is why the Name which refers specifically to the Essence takes the place of every Divine Name.

To the One who is named by this Name, in respect of the fact that *"To Him the whole matter will be returned"* (Qurʾan 11:123), belongs the name of every named thing toward which there is poverty, whether mineral, plant, animal, man, celestial sphere, angel, or any such thing, whatever name is applied to it, that of a creature *(makhlûq)* or an originated thing *(mubdaʿ)*. Hence He is named by every name which is possessed by a named thing in the world and which has an effect within engendered existence *(al-kawn)*; and there is nothing that does not have an effect in engendered existence.

As for the fact that the Name Allah includes the Names of Incomparability, the source for this is near at hand: though every Divine Name is the same in respect of denoting the Essence of God, nevertheless, since every Name other than Allah while denoting the Essence of God also denotes—because of its derivation *(ishtiqâq)* [from a specific root having a specific meaning]—a meaning of negation *(salb)* or affirmation *(ithbât)*, it cannot be as strong as this Name in the unity of its denotation *(ahadiyyat al-dalâla)* of the Essence; such is the case with the All-Merciful *(al-rahmân)* and others of the Most Beautiful Names. It is true that in the Qurʾan God says to the Prophet, commanding him, *"Say: 'Call upon Allah or call upon the All-Merciful; whichever you call upon, to Him belong the Most Beautiful Names'"* (Qurʾan 17:110), but the pronoun "Him" refers back to Him who is called upon, since He who is originally named, outside of derivation, is but One Self *(ʿayn wâhid)*.

God has preserved this proper name *(ism 'alam)* from naming any but the Essence of God. Therefore God says, as an argument against those who had ascribed divinity to something other than this Named One, *"[They ascribe to Allah associates.] Say: 'Name them!'"* (Qur'an 13:33), and those who had held such a view were rendered speechless, for if they had named that thing, they would have named it by other than the Name Allah.

As for the all-comprehensiveness *(jam'iyya)* of this Name, that is because the objects denoted *(madlûlât)* by the Names, which are superadded *(zâ'id)* to what is understood *(mafhûm)* by the "Essence," are multiple and diverse. We do not have any pure proper name for the Essence except the Name Allah, since the Name Allah denotes the Essence by exact congruence *(bi hukm mutâbaqa)*, in the same way that proper names denote the objects they name.

There are Names which denote Incomparability.

There are Names which denote the affirmation of the entities of the Attributes, though the Essence of God does not allow that numbers should subsist *(qiyâm al-'adad)*. These are the Names that make known *(i'tâ')* the entities of the affirmative Attributes of the Essence *(a'yân al-sifât al-thubûtiyyat al-dhâtiyya)*, such as the Knower, the Powerful, the Willing, the Hearing, the Seeing, the Living, the Responder, and the Thankful; the Names that make known descriptions *(nu'ût)*, so that nothing is understood from their ascription except relations *(nisab)* and correlations *(idâfât)*, like the First and the Last, the Manifest and the Nonmanifest; and the Names that make known Acts, such as Creator, Provider, Author, Shaper, etc.

In this way everything has been classified. All the Divine Names, as many as there may be, can be reduced to one of these kinds, or to more than one; while everyone of them must unquestionably denote the Essence.

So this Presence contains all the Presences. He who knows Allah knows all things. But he does not know Allah who does not know one thing, whatever named possible thing it might be, since the property of one of these things is the property of them all in denoting knowledge of God, in respect to the specific fact that He is God over the world. Then when you receive unveiling *(kashf)* in respect to works set down in the Law *(al-'amal al-mashrû')*, you will see that you did not know Him except through Him. The denotation *(dalîl)* is identical to what is denoted through that denotation and denoter.

Though this Presence comprehends all realities, the states which pertain to it most specifically are bewilderment *(hayra)*, worship *('ibâda)*, and the profession of Incomparability *(tanzîh)*. As for Incomparability, which is the fact that He stands high above similarity *(tashabbuh)* with His creatures, it leads to bewilderment in Him and also to worship. God gave us the power of reflection *(quwwat al-fikr)* so that we might speculate *(nazar)* upon what we know of ourselves and of Him. The property of this power demands that there be no likeness *(mumâthala)* between us and Him in any respect, except specifically our dependence *(istinâd)* upon Him for the bestowal of existence upon our entities. The most that the profession of Incomparability gives is the affirmation of relations *(nisab)* that He possesses toward us, because of what the concomitants of our entities' existence demands. These relations are called Attributes.

If we say that these relations are things superadded to His Essence, that they are ontological *(wujûdî)*, and that He possesses no perfection except through them—even were He not to have them—this would mean that He is imperfect in essence but perfect through the superadded ontological thing.

If we say, "They [the relations] are neither He nor other than He," this would be a contradictory statement *(khulf min al-kalâm)*, words with no life that denote a deficiency of intelligence and a lack of speculative power in the speaker far more than they denote God's Incomparability.

If I say that they are not He, that they have no existence, and that they are only relations, while relations are nonexistent things *(umûr ʿadamiyya)*, then we would have given nonexistence an effect within existence, while the relations are multiple because of the multiplicity of the properties bestowed by the entities of the possible things.

If we say none of this whatsoever, we will have rendered the speculative power ineffectual *(muʿattal)*.

If we say that nothing has any reality, that things are illusions *(awhâm)* and sophistry *(safsata)* and of no avail, and that no one can trust any of them, whether [they are known] by way of sense perception or rational reflection—then if this position is correct and known, what is the proof *(dalîl)* that can have led us to it? If it is not correct, how can we know that it is not correct?

Since the intellect is incapable of reaching knowledge of any of these matters, we return to the Law *(al-sharʿ)*, but we only accept it through the intellect. The Law is a branch *(farʿ)* of a root *(asl)* that we know through the Lawgiver *(shâriʿ)*. But through which attribute has the existence of the Law reached us, when we are incapable of knowing the root? So we are even more incapable of [knowing] and affirming the branch. If we pretend to be blind and accept the Lawgiver's words through faith in something self-evident *(darûrî)* within ourselves which we cannot repel, we will hear him attributing to God things depreciated by speculative proofs. No matter which proof we grasp hold of, another stands opposed to it. If we interpret *(ta'awwul)* what he has brought, we will be taking it back to rational speculation. Hence we will have worshipped our own intellects and based His Being upon our existence; but He cannot be perceived by reasoning *(qiyâs)*. So the fact that we have professed God's Incomparability has taken us to bewilderment, since all the paths are muddled *(tashawwush)*. Both intellectual and Law-inspired speculation lead to a single center, which is bewilderment.

As for worship: In respect of its being directed at the Essence it is nothing but the possible thing's poverty *(iftiqâr)* toward Him who gives preponderance *(al-murajjih* [i.e., to existence over nonexistence]). I mean by worship only prescription *(taklîf)*; no one can have prescriptions made for him unless he has power over the acts that are prescribed for him and over the prohibited things from which he must hold himself back. In one respect, we negate acts from created things and give them back to Him who has made the prescriptions; but a thing cannot prescribe for itself, so there must be a locus that receives the address *(khitâb)* for it to be correct. In another respect we affirm acts for created things because of what the wisdom in prescription demands. But negation stands opposed to affirmation, so this view throws us into bewilderment, as did the profession of Incomparability. But bewilderment yields nothing.

So rational speculation leads to bewilderment and theophany leads to bewilderment. There is nothing but a bewildered one. There is nothing exercising properties but bewilderment. There is nothing but Allah.

When one of them was faced in his inmost consciousness *(sirr)* with all these conflicting properties, he used to say, "Oh bewilderment! Oh confusion! Oh conflagration that cannot be fathomed!" This property does not belong to any Presence but the Presence of the Name Allah.

RUMI
1207–1273

Jalal al-Din Rumi is a thirteenth-century mystic and poet whose works are perennial best sellers in the United States. Born in Balkh, in what is today Afghanistan, he moved with his family first to Samarkand (in today's Uzbekistan), and then to Anatolia (Turkey). Traditionally they were believed to have fled in fear of the Mongol armies (whose onslaught included the destruction of Baghdad, the symbolic center of Muslim political power, in 1258), though recent research points to a much earlier departure for other reasons. The family ultimately settled in the city of Konya, where Rumi's father, also a Sufi mystic, taught in a religious school and served as a highly respected preacher. Their location gave Rumi the name by which he is known in the West: Anatolia was then known as "Rum" (Rome), the Arabic term for the Byzantine and Latin empires. Persian speakers more often call him "Mowlana" (Our Master) or "Mowlavi" (My Master), which in Turkish becomes "Mevlana," giving the Sufi order of the Mevlevis its name.

Rumi received a traditional education in the Islamic sciences, including mysticism, first in Konya and later in Aleppo and Damascus. Returning to Konya, he served as a preacher and religious teacher as well as a Sufi guide for many disciples. But his life changed in 1244, when he crossed paths with a wandering Sufi named Shams al-Din of Tabriz (d. 1247). Stories of this fateful meeting stress the instant spiritual rapport that sprang up between the two, who immediately went into seclusion together. Rumi never divulged what happened during the year and a half that Shams lived in his house, later telling an inquiring friend that nobody would understand.

As a master of his own Sufi order, Rumi was not quite Shams's disciple but was probably prodded by him to deeper levels as the men together explored mystical insights. Many, including Rumi's sons, have compared Rumi and Shams to the prophet Moses and the mysterious "servant of God" identified as Khidr, though nameless in the Qur'an. Khidr teaches Moses about deeper religious truths by taking some highly unorthodox actions: he sinks a boat, kills a young man, and repairs a wall on the verge of collapse. Moses cannot see the divine wisdom behind these deeds until Khidr provides their rationale (Qur'an 18:65–82).

His intimacy with Shams made Rumi's disciples jealous, and they drove Shams out of Konya. His absence made poignantly real the theme of lost love, which Rumi expressed in poetry as he mourned. Hearing that Shams had gone to Damascus, Rumi sent one of his sons to bring him back to Konya, but the return was brief. After Shams disappeared again, Rumi himself went to Syria but never found his beloved friend and guide. Though it has long been held that Rumi's students murdered Shams, more recent scholarship contests that belief.

By this time Rumi had become a mystical and performative poet, often breaking into spontaneous outbursts of verse or of spinning or dancing, sometimes accompanied by music. These practices would later be formalized in the rituals of the Mevlevi order, famous for its "whirling dervishes." Rumi also continued his search for another spiritual companion who, like Shams, could mirror the divine presence. The first to fulfill this role was Salah al-Din Zarkub, a blacksmith in Konya; at the sound of his rhythmic hammering, Rumi is said to have fallen into an ecstatic swoon. When Zarkub died in 1258, Rumi found another companion on the mystical path, Husam al-Din Celebi. It was at Husam's urging that Rumi began to recite *The Mathnavi*, and it was he who recorded Rumi's words for the nearly ten years during which the work was composed. Not long after its completion, Rumi contracted an illness; he died in December 1273. His funeral was attended by many of Konya's non-Muslims, some of whom had participated in his classes and lectures. His shrine remains a major multifaith pilgrimage site in Konya.

The Mathnavi, also known as the *Masnavi* (following the Persian pronunciation of the Arabic alphabet), is regarded as the greatest work of mystical poetry in Islamic literature. Often called "the Qur'an in Persian," it is an Iranian cultural icon familiar to all speakers of Persian and frequently quoted from memory. "Mathnavi" is simply the name of the poetic meter used, a form of rhyming couplet (here translated into English heroic couplets, the closest equivalent to Persian mathnavi style). The full title of the work, *Mathnavi al-Maʿnavi*, is best translated as *Spiritual Couplets*. While many Persian poets and mystics wrote in the mathnavi style, Rumi's text of more than 25,000 couplets is the only one called simply *The Mathnavi*.

Rumi's disciples wanted their own mathnavi, like the ones written by Sanaʾi (1050–1131) and ʿAttar (ca. 1142–ca. 1220), two renowned Persian mystics. Despite his stated distaste for poetry, Rumi acquiesced and orally composed the verses whenever the impulse struck him. Husam al-Din would accompany Rumi on these occasions, transcribing the poetry as it was recited. He would then read the verses back to Rumi for corrections. Although the first volume was likely written sometime between 1258 and 1263, only the second volume—begun in 1264 after a two-year period of mourning for the death of Husam al-Din's wife—can be dated with certainty.

Rumi's poetic style was unorthodox and idiosyncratic, straying from the expected formalities of Persian poetry. Because he composed spontaneously, he did not impose an ordered structure or overarching narrative. Typically, the end of one section connects loosely to the beginning of the next, but the work is full of digressions—a story begun at one point is sometimes resumed much later in the work. Moreover, *The Mathnavi* draws from a wide range of sources and genres. Rumi made extensive use of the oral and written works popular in his day, ranging from pious anecdotes to ribald stories. He also took inspiration from all of the contemporary religious sciences, including theology, law, hadith, qur'anic exegesis, philosophy, and medicine. That *The Mathnavi* is bursting with references to the Qur'an itself (which are clearly marked in the translation below) is yet another consequence of Rumi's firm grounding in Islamic thought and tradition.

Rumi's highly entertaining stories serve as the hook for his deeper purpose: to make his Sufi teachings accessible and memorable to his followers. *The Mathnavi* was probably intended for recitation in communal mystical sessions that used music and poetry to induce controlled movement and ecstatic trance, practices that Rumi likely cultivated under the tutelage of Shams al-Din.

Laments of longing introduce *The Mathnavi*, and few poets have captured a sense of spiritual yearning more vividly than does Rumi in "The Song of the Reed": "How can my mind stay calm this lonely night / When I can't find here my beloved's light?" According to some biographical accounts, Rumi pulled from his turban a paper on which this poem was already written when Husam al-Din requested that he produce the work that would become *The Mathnavi*. It and the second selection reproduced here depict the seeker's deep sense of separation from God; the final selection—about the prophet Joseph, who was renowned for his beauty (see Qur'an 12:23–31)—makes explicit the need for purification under the guidance of a Sufi master so that the seeking soul can reflect the image of God.

PRONOUNCING GLOSSARY

Galen: *gay´-len*
kohl: *kohl* (heavy *h*)
Majnun: *maj-noon´*

FROM THE MATHNAVI

BOOK ONE

Exordium: The Song of the Reed

Now listen to this reed-flute's deep lament
   About the heartache being apart has meant:
'Since from the reed-bed they uprooted me
   My song's expressed each human's agony,
A breast which separation's split in two
   Is what I seek, to share this pain with you:
When kept from their true origin, all yearn
   For union on the day they can return.
Amongst the crowd, alone I mourn my fate,
   With good and bad I've learnt to integrate,
That we were friends each one was satisfied
   But none sought out my secrets from inside;
My deepest secret's in this song I wail
   But eyes and ears can't penetrate the veil:
Body and soul are joined to form one whole
   But no one is allowed to see the soul.'
It's fire not just hot air the reed-flute's cry,
   If you don't have this fire then you should die!
Love's fire is what makes every reed-flute pine,
   Love's fervour thus lends potency to wine;
The reed consoles those forced to be apart,
   Its notes will lift the veil upon your heart,
Where's antidote or poison like its song,
   Or confidant, or one who's pined so long?

TRANSLATED BY Jawid Mojaddedi.

This reed relates a tortuous path ahead,
  Recalls the love with which Majnun's[1] heart bled:
The few who hear the truths the reed has sung
  Have lost their wits so they can speak this tongue.
The day is wasted if it's spent in grief,
  Consumed by burning aches without relief—
Good times have long passed, but we couldn't care
  When you're with us, our friend beyond compare!
While ordinary men on drops can thrive
  A fish needs oceans daily to survive:
The way the ripe must feel the raw can't tell,
  My speech must be concise, and so farewell!

Unchain yourself, my son, escape its hold!
  How long will you remain a slave of gold?
You've tried to fit inside a jug the sea—
  It only has a day's capacity:
A greedy eye is never satisfied;
  Shells only when content grow pearls inside,
While men whose clothes are ripped to shreds by love
  Are cleansed of greed like this to rise above.
Be joyful, love, our sweetest bliss is you,
  Physician for all kinds of ailments too,
The cure for our conceit and stubborn pride
  Like Plato here with Galen,[2] side by side;
Through love the earthly form soars heavenward,
  The mountain dances nimbly like a bird:
Love made Mount Sinai drunken visibly,
  So *Moses fell and swooned*[3] immediately!
With my own confidant if I'd been paired,
  Just like the reed, such stories I'd have shared:
Without a kindred spirit there to hear
  The storyteller's voice must disappear,
And if the rose should vanish from its sight
  The nightingale[4] will keep its beak shut tight—
The loved one's all, the lover's just a screen,
  A dead thing, while the loved one lives, unseen.
When shunned by love you're left with emptiness,
  A bird without its wings knows such distress:
'How can my mind stay calm this lonely night
  When I can't find here my beloved's light?'
Love wants its tale revealed to everyone,
  But your heart's mirror won't reflect this sun,
Don't you know why we can't perceive it here?
  Your mirror's face is rusty—scrape it clear!

1. A figure from early Arabic literature who became insane when separated from his love, Layla.
2. Greek physician (129–ca. 199), the primary authority on medicine in Europe and the Middle East until the 17th century. The Greek philosopher Plato (429–347 B.C.E) was held in high regard by Sufis.
3. Qur'an 7:143: after Moses asks to see God, God reveals himself to a nearby mountain, the mountain is destroyed, and Moses falls unconscious.
4. The type of the lover, in classical Persian poetry; the rose stands for the beloved.

From *The Lion, the Wolf, and the Fox*

STORY ABOUT THE PERSON WHO KNOCKED ON THE DOOR OF HIS BELOVED, WHO ASKED HIM FROM INSIDE, 'WHO IS IT?' HE REPLIED 'IT IS I!' SHE RESPONDED, 'SINCE YOU ARE YOU, I WON'T OPEN THE DOOR: I DON'T KNOW ANY FRIEND WHO IS "I"—GO AWAY!'

A man knocked on his lover's door one day,
'Who is it?' he heard his beloved say.
He said, 'It's me.' She answered, 'Leave at once!
There isn't room for such raw arrogance.'
Raw meat's cooked just by separation's flame—
What else can cure hypocrisy's deep shame?
He wandered off in pain as his heart burnt,
In exile from the one for whom he yearned,
Matured before then going back once more
And walking to and fro outside her door.
He tapped the door, now suffering nerves inside,
Not to let slip a wrong word how he tried!
His sweetheart then responded, asking who
Was at the door—he said, 'None, love, but you.'
'Now you are I, please enter in this place
Because for two I's here there isn't space.'
A needle can't accommodate split thread,
To enter thread must have a single head.
To fit a needle thread is suitable,
For camels, needle eyes are much too small![5]
A camel's being must be cut to size
With scissors of religious exercise—
For that to work God's hand is necessary—
His *'Be!'*[6] solves each impossibility.
With His hand everything is possible—
Fear of Him tames each stubborn animal;
He doesn't heal just lepers and the blind
But he can raise the dead too you will find,
And non-existents, more dead than the dead,
Towards existence by His will are led.
Recite, *'He works on something new each day'*[7]
And never think He idles time away.
His least achievement daily is to send
Three armies, each to a specific end;
One from men's loins to mothers has to go
So in their wombs they'll form an embryo;
One from the wombs towards the world outside—
Thus males and females have been multiplied;
One army's sent above straight from the earth
So all can see good actions have much worth—
This talk is endless, so come quickly here
To friends and followers who are sincere!

5. See Qur'an 7:40, where the context (as in Matthew 19:24) is the likelihood of entering heaven.
6. A number of qur'anic verses emphasize God's omnipotence by noting he creates simply by saying "Be!" (e.g., Qur'an 2:117; 3:47).
7. Qur'an 55:29, a reference to God as constantly creating.

His sweetheart said, 'Come in, all of my heart,
Not like the rose and thorn that are apart.'
Make fewer errors now there's just one thread—
If you see two, know there's just one ahead.
Just like a noose, '*Be!*' draws you from a distance
And thus brings non-existence to existence,
Although in form the noose may look like two
There's just one rope and one thing it will do!
With pairs of legs all men must cross the street,
Two scissor-blades together cut one sheet;
Look at this pair of laundry-men, for instance,
Between them there is obviously a difference:
One washed your clothes in water with some soap,
To dry the other hangs them on a rope,
But then the first one rinses them again
As though there is a fight between these men!
But these two who may seem to be apart
Both act and think as one—they're one at heart;
Each prophet and each saint has his own way,
But all lead to the One to whom they pray.
Sleep overcame the audience for a while,
Water then bore their millstones for a mile—
This water comes from up beyond the mill,
For your sake it flows down here by God's will,
When you don't need to have mills any more
It then will flow above you as before.

To teach, this truthful speech comes to your tongue
Or else to its own course it could have clung;
It smoothly travels, so one wouldn't know,
To gardens *under which the rivers flow.*[8]
That place to my soul, God, won't you disclose
Where speech without a word is born and grows,
So that the pure soul headlong then will race
To non-existence's vast open space!
A wide and vast realm of magnificence
From which this false world gains its sustenance.
Tighter than non-existence is thought's realm,
That's why it causes griefs that overwhelm.
Temporal existence is more cramped than thought,
That's why the moon shrinks almost to a dot;
The sensual world's more cramped than this as well,
It is the most restrictive prison cell.
What makes it narrow? Multiplicity:
Our senses drag us to plurality.
Unity's not what senses can perceive—
If that's your goal, then this realm you must leave;
Though 'B' and 'e' formed it, '*Be*' was one act—
The meaning was still pure and kept intact.
Let's now return, though this is incomplete,
To see what fate that old wolf had to meet.

8. Qur'an 2:25, a reference to heaven.

A Guest Came to Joseph, and Joseph Demanded a Gift from Him

To truthful Joseph came from the world's end
To be his guest, a generous loving friend;
They were so close in childhood that the pair
Would often share the seat of one small chair.
The friend asked of his brothers' jealousy,
Joseph said, 'They were like a chain round me:
The lion's not ashamed bound in a chain—
About the Lord's decree I don't complain.'
Although the lion's neck with chains is bound
He rules all chain-makers that can be found.
'In gaol and in the well, how were those days?'
'Just like the moon when in its waning phase.'
Though when it wanes, it's seen to shrink and bend,
Still it becomes a full moon in the end;
In mortars, pearls are ground and mixed with kohl
To grant sight to the eye inside the soul;
If seeds are planted firmly in the ground,
Wheat will eventually grow all around;
Then in the mill they grind it to make bread—
Its value soars now with it men are fed;
Next by men's teeth the bread is ground again,
Life, wisdom, and intelligence they gain,
And when in love that life becomes effaced
Farmers rejoice[9] the seed's not gone to waste!
This discourse could go on, so let's find out
What that good friend and Joseph talked about.
Joseph, on telling his biography,
Asked, 'Friend, what present have you brought for me?'
Going empty-handed to a friend's worse still
Than setting off without wheat to the mill,
For at *the Gathering* God then will say,
'So where's your gift for *Resurrection Day*?[1]
Are you alone, without a present too,
In the same shape as I created you?[2]
Or have you brought with you a souvenir,
Knowing that you'd be resurrected here?
Perhaps you thought you'd not reach home again,
That promises about today were vain?'
Deniers of this day have brains so numb
That from His kitchen they won't gain a crumb!
If you don't disbelieve, how can you go
To your friend empty-handed like a foe!
Sleep less, reduce too the amount you eat,
Take then a present when you're due to meet—
Be of those who *sleep little when they sleep*,
At dawn *seek his forgiveness*,[3] truly weep!

9. Qur'an 48:29, where they rejoice at a crop of believers.
1. Like "the Gathering," a reference to Judgment Day (see, e.g., Qur'an 11:103; 75:6–15).
2. Qur'an 6:94.
3. Qur'an 51:17–18, describing those who will be admitted into heaven.

Move just a little like a foetus, so
The sense which sees the light He'll then bestow;
And when you step outside this womb-like place
You'll leave the world for a much wider space:
They said, '*God's land is vast*,'[4] and thus they meant
The lofty realm of prophets He has sent;
Hearts don't become depressed there, since they're free;
You won't see shrivel up a fresh, young tree.
The burden of your senses you now bear,
You're weary, tired, and falling everywhere,
But when you sleep you're carried off instead,
Free then of tiredness, injury, and dread—
Consider sleep's state just a little taste
Of how the saints are borne when they're effaced:
They are Companions of the Cave[5]—you'll learn
That *they're asleep* although they stand and turn;
Without them seeking it, He draws them there
First right, then left though they are unaware:
What is that *right side*? Proper and good action,
The left?[6] The body's own source of distraction;
From all the prophets these two both flow out,
Though they don't sense the echo of their shout:
Echoes bring good and evil sounds to you
Though mountains stay oblivious to these two.

THE GUEST SAYS TO JOSEPH, 'I'VE BROUGHT YOU A MIRROR, SO THAT EACH TIME YOU LOOK IN IT YOU'LL SEE YOUR OWN HANDSOME FACE AND REMEMBER ME'

Joseph asked, 'Where's the gift with which you came?'
This question made his guest then moan with shame,
He said, 'How many gifts I sought for you,
But none seemed worthy in my humble view:
How could I bring a nugget to the mine,
A single drop to a vast sea of wine?
I'm taking cumin to Kerman,[7] it's true,
By bringing here my heart and soul for you.
No seed is missing from the storehouse here
Except your perfect form which has no peer—
To bring a mirror thus appeared just right,
One that's as radiant as your pure breast's light,
So you can see in it the face I love,
Just like the sun, that candle up above—
I've brought a mirror, so that when you see
Your handsome face you'll then remember me.'
He showed the mirror he'd kept by his side,
With mirrors good men are preoccupied;

4. Qur'an 29:56; 39:10.
5. The story of these young men is told in Qur'an 18:9–26. After they fled their polytheistic society, seeking refuge in a cave, God put them (and their dog) into a deep slumber, turning them to their left and right while they slept so that they would appear awake if discovered, and awakened them some three centuries later.
6. The Qur'an imbues the right hand with positive connotations and the left with negative ones (see, e.g., Qur'an 9:17–20; 17:71).
7. A city in southeastern Iran; it was a major source of cumin.

Non-being serves as Being's mirror, friend,
  So choose non-being if you comprehend:
In this way, Being will be clear to see,
  Like in the poor, when men give generously:
Food is the mirror of the hungry and
  The tinder's mirror is the flame that's fanned;
Emptiness and non-being serve to show
  The virtue of the crafts that skilled men know:
When garments are already so well sewn
  How can they let the mender's skill be shown?
Tree trunks must be left for the carpenter
  Untouched, so he can make some furniture;
The doctor who mends broken bones heads straight
  For that place where the injured men all wait:
If there's no casualty, who needs your aid?
  Medicine's virtue can't then be displayed!
If copper's faults aren't plain for all to see
  How can one tell the worth of alchemy?
Defects reflect perfection's purest light,
  They mirror God's own glory and His might;
All things thus make their opposites appear—
  In vinegar the taste of honey's clear.

Whoever recognizes his own faults
  Towards perfection rapidly then vaults,
But if you think you're perfect as you are,
  You won't reach God for you have strayed too far—
Imagining you're perfect is the worst
  Of faults, you show-off—learn this lesson first!
Much blood will flow out from your heart and eyes
  Before your self-conceit completely dies;
Claiming, *'I'm better'*[8] was cursed Satan's error
  And this same defect lies in every creature:
Although they like to show themselves as meek,
  There's dung beneath the surface—smell the reek!
When, as a test, the Lord should stir them round,
  Their water then immediately is browned:
There's dung in your stream's bed that you've not seen,
  And to your eyes the stream looks pure and clean!

The guide who's knowing has a special role—
  To join streams to the Universal Soul,
The streams can't clean themselves—the point's been made
  That from God's knowledge man receives much aid;
How can a sword carve its own hilt? You show
  The surgeon wounds you've suffered from your foe;
Flies gather on men's wounds, so none can see
  His own wound's putrid foulness normally—
Such flies are fancies and possessions too,
  The wounds the dark states that emerge in you.

8. Qur'an 7:12: this was how Iblis [Satan] explained his refusal to bow down before Adam, as commanded by God.

The guide puts on your wound a salve to heal
  The pain and misery that you now feel—
Don't think the pain's forever gone away,
  The salve has been sent down as just one ray!
Don't turn away, fool, from this salve again,
  Not you but that guide's ray has soothed the pain!

ISMAʿILI DEVOTIONAL SONGS

O Lord, since you have taken my hand, uphold any honor
O ineffable One, tell me how far our love should go
Love me and marry me
Even though I am sinful . . .

The spiritual longing expressed in the devotional songs of Nizari Ismaʿilis make them treasures of world Islamic literature. These songs play an active role in the life of the community and are still recited when members congregate for daily ritual prayers.

Nizari Ismaʿilis, like all Ismaʿilis, are Shiʿi Muslims who believe that after the death of Muhammad, guidance for the Muslim community continued through the descendants of his daughter Fatima (ca. 605 or 616–633) and her husband ʿAli ibn Abi Talib (ca. 599–661). Shiʿi Muslims regard ʿAli as their first imam while Sunni Muslims honor him as the fourth caliph. Shiʿi Islam has several branches, and the Ismaʿili branch developed out of the dispute over succession to the sixth Imam, Jaʿfar al-Sadiq (702–765). Ismaʿili Shiʿis supported his oldest son, Ismaʿil (d. before 765), while another group, who became known as Twelver Shiʿis, believed that his true successor was the younger son, Musa al-Kazim (745–799). The Nizari Ismaʿilis were born of a later split among Ismaʿili Shiʿis over succession to the Fatimid caliph and imam al-Mustansir (1029–1094). The Nizari Ismaʿilis held that his oldest son Nizar (d. 1095) should follow him, while other Ismaʿilis regarded al-Mustansir's younger son, al-Mustaʿli (d. 1101), as his true successor.

There are two groups of Nizari Ismaʿilis in South Asia: the first is concentrated in the north of Pakistan, the second in the western parts of India. Nizari Ismaʿili thought reached the Indian subcontinent through the work of preachers (*daʿis/pirs*) from Iran who arrived as early as the eleventh century. As successful missionaries, these pirs sought to express the key theological concepts of Persian Ismaʿili thought in a manner appropriate to the cultural context they had entered. Out of this impulse developed the unique devotional genre of the *ginan*: religious poems set to the melodies and rhythms of Indian ragas.

Most of the extant *ginans* are attributed to four preachers who lived between the twelfth and fifteenth centuries, including Sadr al-Din and Hasan Kabir al-Din, who were father and son. Biographical information on them is sketchy. Sadr al-Din is said to have died sometime between 1369 and 1416, and the death dates of his eldest son, Hasan Kabir al-Din, range between 1449 and 1490/91. Both composed *ginans* as a teaching device, conveying Ismaʿili beliefs in the languages and symbols of the indigenous Indian religions.

The incorporation of heterogeneous religious elements is not limited to the *ginans*. For example, in Ismaʿili thought the imam is a central figure: he provides spiritual direction and continuing guidance from God. To explain this significance in an Indian context, the pirs portrayed ʿAli ibn Abi Talib, the first imam, as the tenth incarnation of the god Vishnu. Similarly, they applied the Vedic label "true path" (*santpath*) to

Isma'ili beliefs. Using the notion of cycles of existence common to many Indic religions, these preachers taught that the only way to escape the world of repeated rebirth was to follow a "true guide" (*sat guru*)—that is, the imam or one of his preachers.

The *ginans* presented here draw on a common Indian trope, representing the relationship between the imam and his follower as that of a woman seeking her beloved or a bride awaiting her groom.

PRONOUNCING GLOSSARY

chedo: *chay´-doe*
chori: *choor´-ee*
cok bazār: *chok ba-zar´*
dūhāg: *zoo-hahg´*
nikāḥ: *ni-káh* (heavy *h*)
Pīr Ḥasan Kabīr al-Dīn: *peer ha´-san* (heavy *h*) *ka-beer´ ad-deen´´*
Pīr Ṣadr al-Dīn: *peer sad-rad-deen´*
Rūḥānī Visāl: *roo-han-ee vee-sal´*
shāh: *shah*
Sol thar: *sol´ tar*
sūhāg: *soq-hahg*
viraha: *vi´-ruh-hak*
yugas: *yoo´-geh*

TWO *GINANS*

From *Venti* (*Supplication*)*Rūḥānī Visāl,* attributed to Pir Hasan Kabir al-Din

In the beginning there was God without attributes,
He who was without qualities and without form.
You are our (true) origin,
Although we have been separated from You by form.

Refrain:
This weak creature is at Your mercy;
My Lord, be kind to us; we are at Your mercy.

Countless ages have gone by
And we have continued to change form.
We have been petitioning (You) for ages;
O Lord let us be reunited. . . . (*refrain*).

Lord, in the midst of nothingness,
You gave rise to infinite astonishing acts;
In the form of the unseen, You played.
You, ancient Yogi, why this delay?
O Lord, how long can I remain like this? . . . (*refrain*).

In the sixteen states (*sol thar*),[1] O Lord,
You played and played;
How can I praise this enough?
Since that very day I have been petitioning;
Lord at least now pay heed to me. . . . (*refrain*).

Translated by Ali S. Asani.

1. The sixteen cosmological states (*sol thar*) of divine creative activity [translator's note, edited].

In the void You were in the unseen form;
Lord, You were in contemplation.
Whoever in that gathering recognized You,
Him You will make return. . . . (*refrain*).

Age upon age I have been waiting anxiously,
But yet the marriage (*nikāḥ*) has not taken place!
Now I am in the full bloom of youth.
O Ruler of the three worlds, preserve my honour . . . (*refrain*).

Having filled my water pots (*hail*),
I have come before You, Lord.
Lord, take down my water pots,
Lest my water pots be rejected.
Forgive my sins. . . . (*refrain*).

Lord, cover me with a veil (*chedo*) and watch over me,
For I have come (to you as) a sinner.
I am but a weak and humble creature.
O Ruler, it is Your honour (that is at stake)! . . . (*refrain*).

For countless ages I have been waiting with hope;
O Ruler of three worlds,[2] hear me!
The bloom of youth is upon me,
So now I will be ashamed (if You do not marry me) . . . (*refrain*).

In the four ages (*yugas*), I have experienced
cycles of countless forms;
Yet my marriage has not taken place.
Lord, please marry me!
Be merciful, O Lord of miracles! . . . (*refrain*).

O, Lord, how long must I remain alone?
The days pass in separation (*dūhāg*) from You;
Change my state of separation (*dūhāg*) into married
bliss (*sūhāg*).
Lord of the fourteen heavens,
preserve my honour . . . (*refrain*).

Mother, father, sister and relatives,
No one wants to keep me.
I have come and thrown myself on Your mercy.
Lord, my honour depends on You . . . (*refrain*).

O Lord, if my honour is not protected,
Then You will have to bear the loss!
When You have a festive gathering,
Do not humiliate me (through separation) . . . (*refrain*).

O Ruler, as You seat Yourself on the throne,
Then and there I will cry out for You.

2. In Hinduism, the physical universe, the mental and emotional sphere inhabited by demigods and spirits, and the causal realm of the gods.

From the beginning You have been holding my hand,
So how can You abandon me today? . . . (*refrain*).

Lord, do not look at my misdeeds;
(I confess that) I am a sinner.
Lord cover me with a veil and watch over me:
I am only an innocent maiden . . . (*refrain*).

Lord, my parents gave birth to me
(And) entrusted me to Your mercy.
Now have the decency to fulfil Your part of this trust.
O Saviour, save me . . . (*refrain*).

O Lord, there are countless maidens for You;
There are thousands like me.
You are the Ineffable and the Unseen;
I am but humble dust . . . (*refrain*).

O Lord, since You have taken my hand,
  uphold my honour.
O ineffable One, tell me how far our love should go.
Love me and marry me,
Even though I am sinful . . . (*refrain*).

Lord, the bloom of youth is upon me;
I cannot remain alone;
It is shameful for me to look upon outside(rs).
O Lord, let the marriage ceremony be performed . . . (*refrain*).

Lord, come with the marriage procession;
Do not delay (Your arrival).
Be merciful and come, O Lord,
For I am Your devoted spouse . . . (*refrain*).

O Lord, speaking your name I ascend,
Ascend the *cok bazār*,[3]
Where souls from countless ages will meet,
Soul upon soul in infinite number . . . (*refrain*).

The countless souls of ages will gather.
You, come there Yourself.
As You come in, look around and search
And come to Your humble spouse . . . (*refrain*).

After having walked and walked I am worn out;
I can walk no more.
Do not look upon my evil deeds.
I can live no more . . . (*refrain*).

3. An ornamented square of colored flour in which a bride and bridegroom are seated for a short while during a number of nights before the wedding [translator's note].

Just as a fish without water writhes in agony,
So also a wife without her husband.
Lord, bring whatever is needed for the marriage.
Delay not Your coming anymore . . . (*refrain*).

O Lord, You are the Perfect One, beyond Brahma[4]
And in indescribable form.
How can I adequately praise Your brilliance?
Your countless (heavenly) wives are
  dazzling and beautiful . . . (*refrain*).

Lord, these women are heavenly;
Great and indescribable is their beauty,
(Whereas) I am but ugly and humble;
Husband, preserve mine honour. . . . (*refrain*).

Lord, my attention is fixed upon You;
It is You who occupy my thoughts:
How can I capture another (like You)?
Lord, return to fulfil Your promise to me;
  do not forsake me even for a moment . . . (*refrain*).

Lord, preserve my honour.
How can it be entrusted to anyone else?
On Your behalf the coconut[5] has already been sent.
How can I gaze upon another? . . . (*refrain*).

Lord, most humbly I petition You;
Hear my cries.
For the sake of my humble state, forgive me.
Lord, You are the Protector of the unprotected . . . (*refrain*).

Lord, this weak creature pines for You;
Tears flow incessantly from my eyes.
You, my Lord, have many women;
Won't You try to understand my agony? . . . (*refrain*).

Having pleaded and pleaded,
  how much more shall I plead?
You are the Ruler, immanent in all.
Take pity on me and meet me,
So that my honour be saved. . . . (*refrain*).

Lord, do not take my sins to heart;
I am only a weak and humble woman.
I have reached the bloom of youth;
I am an innocent maiden. . . . (*refrain*).

Any clothes and ornaments that may be required,
Lord, I will bring them all (for You).

4. The Hindu god of creation.

5. Frequently part of wedding ceremonies in India.

I will make myself beautiful
For my Lord whom I am meeting. . . . (*refrain*).

Lord, from the beginning of the beginning
I have been petitioning (You);
Breath upon breath I contemplate.
In every nook and cranny of my being You are playing,
So that my sins flee from me. . . . (*refrain*).

With the aid of Your name,
I can reach heaven.
There are so many thieves obstructing my way,
But with Your name they disappear. . . . (*refrain*).

The road to heaven is full of pain,
But with Your name these pains are removed.
The one Lord is (my) true master (*sat guru*).
With the secret name He can be recognized. . . . (*refrain*).

Lord, with the aid of Your name,
The great oceans give way.
Come Husband, be merciful!
I fall at Your feet. . . . (*refrain*).

Lord, sobbing and sighing I plead with You.
My heart pines in longing.
O Lord, come soon,
Lest (it is too late and) the (bloom of my youth) fades
away. . . . (*refrain*).

Lord, the eyes of this evil age (*Kalyug*)[6] are all contrary;
They look (upon me) with evil eyes.
Lord, sometimes I make mistakes;
Then I have to begin all over. . . . (*refrain*).

My Lord Yogi, be merciful;
Take me to safety.
This evil age is full of deceit and falsehood,
So rescue me soon from it. . . . (*refrain*).

(My) parents and all are happy
With my marriage to You.
O Lord, come quickly and marry me;
Do not take too long. . . . (*refrain*).

Lord, my youth has matured;
I am embarrassed to go out (alone).
In this evil age there is much ignorance,
In which I may become trapped. . . . (*refrain*).

6. In Hindu cosmology, the universe repeatedly goes through cycles of creation and destruction; each cycle consists of four ages, the last and most degenerate of which is the Kali yuga.

Lord, (for us) set up a sacred space (*chorī*);
In the midst of the universe marry me.
Become manifest and marry me,
So that I can experience the bliss of marriage . . . (*refrain*).

Lord, my marriage bliss lies with You,
Of which you have been in charge for countless ages.
The perfect and the imperfect, and even those
who simply wish—
To all (of them) grant salvation. . . . (*refrain*).

(But) whoever indulges in backbiting,
He will have to stay away from the Lord;
He will be surrounded by Satan
And will not acquire the true knowledge. . . . (*refrain*).

Any discourse without true knowledge
Shreds (into pieces) the heart.
Lord, keep me away from such beings,
So that I can be certain of my marriage (to You). . . . (*refrain*).

Listen, O believers, be virtuous,
So that you become dear to the Lord.
If you recognize Him by good deeds
and (meditation on) the Word,
Then He will come to you. . . . (*refrain*).

Abide by the true Word and the scriptures,
So that you acquire the Lord's friendship.
Believers, give the Lord a place in your hearts,
So that love (for Him) is kindled. . . . (*refrain*).

Pīr Ḥasan Kabīr al-Dīn, like a woman, supplicates
And holds the hand of her Husband and Lord.
Whoever in these days of the evil age recognizes Shāh Pīr,
Will never be abandoned. . . . (*refrain*).

Sakhī mārī ātama nā odhār (O Friend, the Saviour of My Soul), attributed to Pir Sadr al-Din

O Friend, the saviour of my soul,
do not go away and stay apart from me.
I have built such a beautifully decorated house for you,
come and reside in it.

O Friend, I have prepared for You a bed of incomparable beauty;
return (to rest) on this bed.
(Lying) next to the Beloved, overwhelmed by love,
I forget all of my sorrows.

O Friend, the bed-swing sways back and forth,
with (the rhythm of) my every breath.

What ecstasy is aroused in my body
when I am with the Beloved.

O Friend, to whom can I describe
the pangs of separation (*viraha*) from the Beloved?
(Perhaps if) I were to meet a wise sage
he would understand.

O Friend, the Creator of the creation
is the One who has saved me.
Pīr Ṣadr al-Dīn, grasping me by the hand,
takes me across the ocean (to salvation).

MULLA SADRA SHIRAZI
ca. 1572–1640

Mulla Sadra, one of the most influential Shiʿi philosophers of his time, lived during the Safavid dynasty (1501–1733), a period of Persian history that produced an extraordinary florescence of art, architecture, literature, and philosophy—the Islamic intellectual pursuits that had stagnated in the wake of the Mongol conquests of the thirteenth century. While Sadra wrote primarily on philosophical matters, he also composed works on exegesis and traditions.

The only child of a wealthy family, Sadra was born in Shiraz, Iran. Displaying a precocious intellect, he completed his basic studies under the guidance of his father. In 1597, to further his education, he moved to Isfahan, renowned for its schools of philosophy, where he learned from two of the most esteemed scholars of his day, Mir Damad (d. 1631) and Shaykh Baha'i (ca. 1546–1621). Under Mir Damad's tutelage, Sadra read the works of Ibn Sina (ca. 980–1037; see above) and Suhrawardi (ca. 1155–1191). He formed an enduring bond with this teacher, exchanging letters with him and seeking his spiritual counsel throughout his life. With Shaykh Baha'i, Sadra devoted himself to the study of qur'anic exegesis and Shiʿi traditions.

Sadra completed his training in Isfahan after 1602 and returned to Shiraz, but for some reason did not settle there. Most reports suggest that he ran afoul of the established Shiʿi authorities, who found his philosophical views objectionable. In any event, he relocated to the village of Kahak, near the city of Qum. During his years there—and sources differ as to their number—he kept in close contact with Mir Damad, seeking his spiritual guidance and often visiting him in Isfahan. Sadra focused his teaching and writing on philosophy. His magnum opus, *Transcendent Wisdom in the Four Intellectual Journeys*, was begun in 1606 and completed thirty-two years later.

By that time, at the request of Imamqoli Khan (d. 1633), the influential governor of Fars, Sadra had returned to his native Shiraz, where he settled permanently in 1631. Khan's father had established a school there, Madrasa-yi Khan, with the goal of educating students in philosophy and scientific subjects (e.g., math, chemistry, physics). As a madrasa professor, Sadra earned great fame in Shiraz as he continued his academic and spiritual pursuits. He died in 1640 in Basra, Iraq, while on a journey to Mecca.

All of Sadra's works, save for a few letters and a single treatise in Persian, were written in Arabic. They target an educated audience of scholars, well-versed in religious subjects and sympathetic to philosophical and mystical thought. As Sadra's writings spawned commentaries, they attracted a broader, less educated audience who could access his ideas via these elaborations and interpretations.

Sadra's contribution to the Shiʿi intellectual tradition is tremendous, and he is celebrated for his ability to harmonize divergent views into a coherent whole. For Sadra, neither the philosopher's reliance on intellect nor the mystic's on spiritual practice can achieve a true understanding of God. True knowledge can be gained only through a mix of intellectual and spiritual practices. Sadra's synthesis draws heavily on works of dogmatic theology, on the metaphysical works of Ibn Sina, on the writings of Ibn al-ʿArabi (1165–1240; see above), and on the Illuminationist philosophy of Suhrawardi.

In the twentieth century, there was a surge of Western scholarship on Sadra. Henry Corbin's translations and studies of Sadra brought his philosophy to the attention of French-speaking intellectuals. First in Iran and then in United States, Seyyid Hossein Nasr has been a major expositor and exponent of Sadra's thought.

The Four Journeys, which runs to nine volumes in its modern printed edition, is Sadra's most famous work and the most authoritative source for his thought. It covers topics normally addressed in philosophical works (everything from ontology to eschatology) but not in their standard order of presentation. Instead, Sadra structures his work around the four intellectual journeys that lead to true knowledge. He introduces basic philosophical and metaphysical concepts in the first journey, that of the traveler moving from this world to God. Sadra uses the second journey, which is in God with God, to examine theological issues, including the divine names and proofs for God's existence. Next, the journey from God back to the world offers a means to examine God's relationship to his creation and the ontology of creation itself. In the last journey, which is in this world with God, Sadra addresses issues relating to the soul and eschatology.

The excerpts below are from *The Wisdom of the Throne*, Sadra's major treatment of eschatology, the area of thought that deals with the final events of human life and human history. The first part examines God's names and attributes. In the second part, which focuses on the resurrection, Sadra provides philosophical proofs for the possibility of a bodily resurrection; he thus opposes al-Farabi (ca. 878–950; see above) and Ibn Sina, who rejected such a belief. Although certain sections of the work are quite difficult and can be understood only in relation to Sadra's longer philosophical works, these passages can be read independently and provide insight into Sadra's views on the preexistence of the soul and its role in eschatology.

PRONOUNCING GLOSSARY

Abū ʿAbdallāh Jaʿfar al-Ṣādiq: *a-boo ab-dul-lah´ ja´-far as-sah´-diq*

Abū al-Ḥasan al-ʿĀmirī: *a-bool-ha´-san* (heavy *h*) *al-ah´-mi-ree*

Abū Jaʿfar Muḥammad al-Bāqir: *a-boo ja´-far moo-ham´-mad* (heavy *h*) *al-bah´-qir*

al-Ḥujaj al-ʿAshara: *al-hu´-jaj* (heavy *h*) *al-ash´-a-ruh*

al-Shawāhid al-Rubūbīya: *ash-sha-wa´-hid ar-roo-boo´-bee-yuh*

al-Talwīḥāt: *at-tal-wee-hat´* (heavy *h*)

Ḥikmat al-Ishrāq: *hik´-mat* (heavy *h*) *al-ish-rahq´*

Kitāb al-Shifāʾ: *ki-tab´ ash-shi-fa´*

Kitāb al-Tawḥīd: *ki-tab´ at-taw-heed´* (heavy *h*)

Muḥammad ibn Bābawayh: *moo-ham´-mad* (heavy *h*) *ibn bah´-ba-wayh* (light *h*)

Suhrawardi: *suh-ra-war´-dee* (light *h*)

FROM THE WISDOM OF THE THRONE

Principle (Concerning the Pre-Existence of Soul)

The "Adamic" soul has a form of existence preceding the body, without this entailing the transmigration of souls, and without necessitating the pre-eternity of the (individual) soul, which is the well-known view of Plato.[1] This (mode of pre-existence) does not require a multiplicity of individuals of a single species or their differentiation without reference to any matter or (material) preparedness; nor does it entail the soul's being divided after having been one, in the manner of continuous quantities; nor does it presume the soul's inactivity before (being connected with) bodies. Rather, (soul's pre-existence) is as we have indicated and explained in our commentary on *Ḥikmat al-Ishrāq* (Suhrawardi's[2] "Philosophy of Illumination") in a way that cannot be surpassed, (so that here we shall offer only scriptural allusions).

It is to this (noetic pre-existence of soul) that His saying—May He be exalted!—refers: *And when your Lord took out from the loins of the children of Adam their descendants, and caused them to bear witness against themselves,* (saying) *"Am I not your Lord?" they said: "Indeed (You are)!"* (7:172). Similarly with the Prophetic tradition: "The spirits (of men) are armies drawn up in ranks: [Those who recognize one another are in harmony, and those who dislike one another are in disagreement]."

And likewise (this saying) from Abū ʿAbdallāh (the Shiite Imam Jaʿfar al-Ṣādiq[3])—Peace be with him!: "God created us from the Light of His Majesty and Grandeur. Then He fashioned our created form from Clay concealed underneath the divine Throne, and caused that Light to dwell therein. So we were all men of Light, and He created our party [*shīʿa*] from our Clay." And the following statement of Abū ʿAbdallāh is related by Muḥammad Ibn Bābawayh[4]—May God have mercy on him!—in his *Kitab al-Tawḥīd* ("Book of the divine Unity"): "God—May He be exalted and glorified!—created the truly faithful from the Clay of the Gardens [of Paradise] and caused His Spirit to flow into them." And from Abū Jaʿfar (the Shiite Imam Muḥammad al-Bāqir[5])—Peace be with him!—he related something similar: "God created the truly faithful from the Clay of the Gardens and poured into their forms the breeze of the Gardens." From Abū ʿAbdallāh (it is also related): "The truly faithful are brothers, since their spirits are from the Spirit of God—May He be exalted and glorified! Indeed, the spirit of the truly faithful [person] is more intensely connected to the Spirit of God than the connection of the sun with its rays." The traditions handed down on this subject by our fellow (Shiites) are so innumerable that it is as though the existence of the spirits prior to (their) bodies were one of the essential premises of the Imamite (Shiite) school—May God's pleasure be with them!

TRANSLATED BY James Winston Morris. The parenthetical citations are to sura and verse of the Qur'an; all bracketed additions are the translator's.

1. In his *Phaedo* and *Phaedrus*, the Greek philosopher (429–347 B.C.E.) argues that knowledge is possible because of souls' "recollection" of eternal realities glimpsed before they were embodied.
2. Shihab al-Din Suhrawardi (ca. 1155–1191), a Persian mystic and philosopher; he founded the Illuminationist school, which privileges knowledge by presence—a form of knowledge that provides immediate access to the truth, brought to awareness by the light of the self.
3. The sixth Imam (702–765).
4. A famous Shiʿi traditionist and legal scholar (ca. 920–991); for an excerpt from his *Creed*, see above.
5. The fifth Imam (676–ca. 732).

Principle (Concerning the Soul as the Key to Eschatology)

Know that souls which have emerged from potentiality to actuality with regard to the Intellect and the intelligible are extremely few in number and rarely to be found among individual human beings. The vast majority of individual souls are imperfect, not having become Intellect in actuality. But this does not entail the annihilation of these souls after death, as Alexander Aphrodisias[6] supposed, since his supposition was based on (the supposition) that there are only two worlds (of being), the world of material bodies and the world of intellects.

But it is not like that. Instead, there is another world of being, alive and sensible by essence, unlike this (physical) world—a world that is perceived by these true (inner) senses, not by these transient external ones. That world is divided into a sensible Garden (or "Paradise") containing the felicities of the blessed, including food, drink, marriage, sensual desire, intercourse, and all that could delight the soul and give pleasure to the eyes; and a sensible "Hell" containing the punishments of the wretched, including hellfire, torments, serpents, and scorpions. If this world (of soul) did not exist, what Alexander mentioned would be undeniably true, and that would mean that the sacred Laws and divine Books were lying when they maintained the resurrection for everyone.

The master of philosophers, Abū ʿAlī (Avicenna[7]) reported what Alexander had maintained and what could be said in refutation of that view in his treatise *al-Ḥujaj al-ʿAshara* ("The Ten Arguments") and elsewhere. But he himself seems to have been inclined towards Alexander's view in another work, in his replies to the questions put to him by Abū al-Ḥasan al-ʿĀmirī.[8] And in general, what is reported of the leader of the Peripatetics (that is, Aristotle), according to Alexander, is the belief that imperfect, material souls are dissolved after death. (Admittedly), according to Themistius'[9] account, they do have a survival. But this is difficult to maintain according to their (Peripatetic) principles, since it implies that these souls have a survival even though they cannot retain any vice of the soul that might torment them, or any intellective virtue that might give them pleasure—and yet (if they do survive) it is impossible that they be deprived of all ability to act and be acted upon. These people (that is, Themistius and other philosophers who maintained some kind of survival for imperfect souls) said that God's providence is all-encompassing, and that therefore these souls must necessarily have some sort of weak, imaginary happiness, of the sort that comes from apprehending the first principles (of all reasoning), such as the saying that the whole is greater than the part, and similar notions. Therefore (on their view) it is said that "the souls of dead infants are between Paradise and Hell." This was what Avicenna had to say.

But I wonder what happiness there could be in the perception of these elementary notions?! As for those ordinary, honest souls who did not acquire

6. A Greek Peripatetic philosopher (fl. early 3rd century C.E.); he wrote the most authoritative commentaries on the works of the Greek philosopher Aristotle (384–322 B.C.E.).
7. Ibn Sina (980–1037); see above.
8. Iranian philosopher (d. 992).
9. Greek philosopher and rhetorician (ca. 317–ca. 388), author of explanatory paraphrases of many works by Aristotle.

a desire for the theoretical sciences, the (Peripatetic) philosophers do not tell us anything about their afterlife or about the sayings concerning their Return and that of the other souls of their rank, since they do not have the rank of ascent to the world of noetic Sanctity.

One cannot say that such souls return in the bodies of animals, because of the impossibility of reincarnation. Nor can one claim that they totally disappear, because of what we know concerning the impossibility of corruption in things (like souls) that are not disposed to it by nature. Accordingly, one group (of philosophers) was driven to the hypothesis that the souls of the pious and of ascetics become connected (after death) with a body composed of vapor and smoke in the atmosphere, and that this body serves as a substrate for what they imagine, through which they attain a sort of imagined happiness; and the wretched likewise (attain their punishment) this way. Still another group disagreed, rejecting this theory of a vaporous body, and corrected it by placing that substrate instead in the body of the heavens. The author of *Kitāb al-Shifāʾ*[1] (that is, Avicenna) reported this view on the part of a certain learned man, and described it as not a rash conjecture.

The author (Suhrawardi) of *al-Talwīhāt* ("The Intimations") agreed with this view about the connection of the soul with the body of the spheres in the case of the blessed. "But as for the wretched," he said that they lacked the power to rise up to the world of the heavens because "the heavenly spheres possess [only] luminous souls and noble bodies. Rather," he said, "the powers [of these sinful souls] demand that they have corporeal imaginations [which would be incompatible with the lofty state of the souls of the heavenly spheres]. So it is not impossible that there may exist, beneath the sphere of the moon and above that of [the element] fire, still another unbroken spherical body, a distinctive species that would be . . . a substrate for their imagined hellfires, biting snakes, stinging scorpions, and bitter drink."

But all the sayings of these worthy men are many stages removed from the path of the reality of true inner knowing and the way of Lights of the Koran. We have shown the many intellectual errors that their theories entail in (our book) *al-Shawāhid al-Rubūbīya* ("The Divine Witnesses").

1. *The Book of Healing.*

BELLES LETTRES: THE FINE ARTS OF POETRY AND PROSE

Qasida: *The Arabic Ode*

ʿALQAMA
fl. sixth century

ʿAlqama, a famous poet from the Arabian Peninsula, lived during the sixth century, but beyond that fact little else is known about him. One of the few reports we do possess describes how, by reciting one of his odes, he won from a rival tribe the release of captured members of his own tribe—including his brother. It is generally believed that he died about the time of Muhammad's birth (ca. 570), but some modern scholars place his death about twenty years before the hijra, Muhammad's emigration from Mecca to Medina in 622.

Poetry was a vibrant oral tradition in pre-Islamic Arabia, considered the highest form of artistic expression. The most respected poetic form was the ode (in Arabic, *qasida*), which has a tripartite structure. The best poets would gather for a competition during a yearly Meccan trade fair; after they recited their poetry, the winner's ode would be embroidered with gold thread on a fabric hung from the central shrine, the Kaʿba. The odes ordinarily begin with the remembrance of a lost beloved, a recollection often triggered by something in the protagonist's environment, such as a ruined campsite. The next section of the ode frequently describes a journey undertaken by the protagonist, a conventional topic that enables the poet to showcase his descriptive skill. The ode's third and culminating section presents its primary theme, such as the protagonist's prowess in battle, the weakness of his enemies, or the virtue of a notable individual.

Reproduced below is ʿAlqama's favorite, "Is What You Knew Kept Secret." The ode begins with the protagonist lamenting the loss of his Salma. A remembrance of his journey is sparked by the mention of a "night courser," which launches a description of the animals he has seen while traveling. Interestingly, these animals are not named but described: the "tuck-bellied brindle-leg" is a type of antelope (a bull oryx) and the "red-legged clump-wing" is an ostrich. The narrator transitions into the third and final section of the ode, which recounts tales of his bravery and hardiness, by first offering a series of ruminations on fate and destiny and then providing tales of wine drinking.

PRONOUNCING GLOSSARY

ʿAnah: *ah´-nuh*
Náhdi: *nah´-dee* (light *h*)
Qúrran: *qoor-ran´*
Sálma: *sal´-muh*
Tazidi: *ta-zee´-dee*
utrújja: *ut-rooj´-juh*

IS WHAT YOU KNEW KEPT SECRET

Is what you came to know,
   given in trust,
kept secret? Is her bond to you
   broken, now that she is far?

Does a grown man weeping
   tears without end for those he loved,
   the dawn of parting,
receive his fair reward?

By the time I knew,
   they had set their leave,
all the camel stallions
   standing bridled before dawn,

Translated by Michael A. Sells.

Camel stallions of her tribe
led in by maiden servants,
then loaded,
bundles bound in Tazídi brocade,[1]

While birds hung in the air
plucking at dye streaks and tassels
as if they'd been stained
heartsblood crimson.

They carried an *utrújja*[2] away.
A saffron-scented perfume trailed.
Before the senses even now
her fragrance lingers,

The folds of her hair
redolent as musk when the pod is opened.
Reaching out to touch it
even the stuff-nosed is overcome.

Liken my weeping eye to a water bag
dragged down the well slope
by a roan mare, withers
bound to the saddle-stay,

For a full season unsaddled,
until her hump hardened,
firm as the rounded side
of a smith's bellows,

Cured of the mange
and covered
with a resinous balm,
clear and pure,

Spilling water into channels
as grain husks part
from the ripening fruit,
the flooded slopes flowing over.

To remember Sálma! to recall
times spent with her
is folly, conjecture about the other side,
a casting of stones,

Breast sash crossed
and falling, gown folds
at the hip, clinging, tender
as a gazelle fawn reared within the yard.

---

1. The distinctive streaked cloth produced by the Tazid tribe, which belonged to the Quda'a grouping of northern Arabian tribes.
2. A citron.

Will I overtake
her far-flung tribe's rear guard
on a night courser,
solid as a worn boulder in a stream,

Dromedarian lips,
tinged by a wash of green mallow
that foams up
over cheek and jaw?

On one like that,
borne through the desert,
ranging far, while in the shadows
the owl sends forth a muffled cry.

She side-eyes the whip,
silent as a tuck-bellied brindle-leg,
ears sharpened
to the softest sound,

Or like a red-legged clump-wing,
bitterapple and castorberry
ripening for him
behind the twisting dune.

At the black-banded colocynth[3]
he lingers,
cracking pods,
and snipping sprouts of grey castor.

Mouth like the split in a stick—
you barely make it out—
and ears, tufted markings,
as if he'd been docked,

Until he remembers some eggs,
disquieted by a day
of drizzle and wind
and a covering of cloud.

He quickens his pace,
without strain,
whisking along just short of all out,
untiring,

Split-foot flying
past his bulging eye,
as if he were wary of ill luck,
fear-quickened,

3. The bitter apple, a gourd whose fruit is a well-known purgative.

A strider, forechest
like the string of a lyre,
like a water bird
in a meadow pool.

He doubles back to a down-cropped
brood of nestlings
that appear when they tumble over
like a clod-covered root.

Circling the nest hollow,
circling again,
searching for tracks . . .

Until he reaches
as the sun's horn rises
the nest hollow
and a heap of eggs,

Beckoning to them
with a cackling and clucking
like the babble of Greeks
in their fortresses,

Small-headed, thin-necked,
wings and chest
like a caved-in heap of a tent
set up wrong by a clumsy maid.

A female draws near,
long neck lowered,
responding
with a warbling cry.

Every tribe,
though great, though many,
will one day see its chief
struck down by the hearthstones of evil.

Praise can't be purchased
except for a price
men begrudge,
one that is well known.

Generosity is a blight on riches,
an abode of loss.
What you hoard is left over,
the object of scorn.

What you own
is a wooly plaything,

growing long on stubby sheep,
then shorn.

He who gains his quarry
the day of the raid
finds it wherever he turns.
He who misses, misses out.

Hot-neck folly will cross your path.
You don't have to track it down.
Foresight and self-command
make themselves scarce in the crowd.

Whoever comes upon crows
and scatters them for an omen
though secure at the time
is fated to ruin.

Every fortress,
long safe on great pillars,
will one day
be razed to the ground.

I could well see the drinkers,
among them a ringing lyre,
men laid low
by golden, foaming wine,

The drink of a potentate,
aged by tavernkeepers
for a special occasion.
It'll take you up and spin you around.

For the headache it's a cure.
A jolt of it won't harm you.
No dizziness from it
will mix in your brain,

A vintage of ʿAnah,[4] a slammer,
for a full year unexposed,
kept in a clay-stoppered jug
with a waxen seal,

Glistening in its decanter,
while a foreign-born page,
mouth covered with a cotton band,
pours it.

4. A city on the Euphrates in the Iraqi province of al-Anba.

Flagon like a gazelle
high on the cliff face,
neck and spout sealed
with a linen sieve.

Its keeper brings it out into the sun.
It flashes white,
ringed by branches of sweet basil,
fragrance brimming over.

Many times have I set out early
against a peer,
accompanied by a firm,
fine-honed, piercing blade.

Many times have I gambled,
trusting hunger to an arrow
carved from hard wood,
bound with sinew and notched.

They put their stallions up for wager.
I offered mine first.
Whatever the stakes,
the loser pays.

I might well ride with a band of braves,
no provisions
but a food sack green with mold
and some stinking meat.

Many times have I mounted the saddle frame,
face seared
by a day of the Gemini[5]
and pestilent, blistering winds,

Burning,
as if one were cloaked
and turbaned, wrap on wrap
in the kindled air.

I might well lead before the tribe
a tall mare,
as if her lineage, known to all,
were leading her.

With a flawless splint bone
and a flawless pastern,
with hoof walls
trimmed and intact,

5. The extreme heat of the Arabian Peninsula begins in June, which falls under the zodiacal sign associated with the Gemini, a constellation.

With shanks like the base of a palm branch,
legs like a Náhdi's[6] staff,
feet with a hoof frog as tough
as a hard-gnawed date pit from Qúrran,[7]

She follows a troop of black dromedaries
that cry out when driven
like a tambourine
torn on the heights.

On one side a spring-born calf
is pleading, while on the other
the old camels, humps high,
bellow,

Led by a stallion,
worn and tried,
an old-timer,
meaty, huge.

6. A tribe in a region known for wood that was smooth and robust.
7. A settlement in the ʿArid mountains, located about 50 miles northwest of present-day Riyadh, Saudi Arabia.

Persian Lyricism and Further Poetic Permutations

NIZAMI
ca. 1141–1209

Born in Ganja, Azerbaijan, Nizami Ganjawi was a Persian poet whose epic poems are a treasure of world literature. In 1991 UNESCO celebrated the 850th anniversary of his birth and conferences in his honor were held in cities around the world. Little is known about him, but by all accounts Nizami spent his life in his birthplace. Although not a major city, Ganja was known for its silk production, and its location near the confluence of several important trading routes attracted many travelers and merchants. The larger region was nominally ruled by the Seljuks, who strongly supported Sunnism and were generally wary of any non-Sunni thought, especially that of Ismaʿili Shiʿism. Nonetheless, Nizami lived during a period marked by a spirit of inclusivity among the Muslims of his region, when the arts flourished with the support of local rulers. Many patrons commissioned works from Nizami, and he also dedicated poems to nearby rulers. Yet he never became a member of any court, carefully preserving his artistic independence and integrity.

Many of Nizami's works have been lost, but his fame endures because of five epic poems collectively known as the "Five Treasures" (in Persian, *Panj Ganj*) or the "Quintet" (in Arabic, *Khamsa*). Composed in rhyming couplets, they offer deft psychological portrayals of their protagonists and subtle moral exhortations to develop virtuous character traits. In many cases, the Five Treasures blend pre-Islamic Persian themes with contemporary Islamic ones, all of them filled with rich symbolism. This symbolism appealed (and continues to appeal) to a range of audiences, each understanding his works through the lens of its own beliefs. These poems are so deeply allusive that it remains impossible for any one group to claim Nizami as its own or to establish a definitive interpretation of all of his symbols. His poems reached a vast readership, prompting imitations from later authors in Persian, Turkish, and Urdu.

The first of this quintet, *The Treasury of Mysteries*, was likely composed around 1175; it consists of twenty stories, each of which emphasizes a particular moral lesson, such as remaining unattached to the world. The second poem is Nizami's *Khusraw and Shirin*, composed about 1180 and based on the love story of the Sassanid ruler Khusraw II (r. 590–628). Nizami was by no means the first to use Khusraw II's attempts to meet with his beloved Shirin in a literary piece, but his tale is especially poignant, instructing the reader on the power of love and the need for just leaders. The third poem, *Layla and Majnun*, penned about a decade later, retells the tribulations of two well-known, ill-fated lovers from seventh-century Arabic poetry, Qays and Layla. They are madly in love with each other but events conspire to keep them apart. Qays expresses his longing and despondency through poetry and eventually goes mad, thereby earning the name Majnun, the Arabic word for one possessed or insane. The fourth poem is *Seven Beauties* (in Persian, *Haft Paykar*), completed in 1197, from which the selection here is taken. The last of these poems is *The Book of Alexander*, finished about 1200, which tells the story of Alexander the Great (356–323 B.C.E.), a figure often encountered in Persian literature. It presents him first as a conqueror and ruler and then as a prophet and philosopher.

Nizami's *Seven Beauties* explores the evolution of Bahram Gur, a character loosely drawn from the Sassanid ruler of the same name (r. 421–39), who was renowned for his love of hunting and revelry but also respected as a just ruler. The main portion of the poem focuses on seven beautiful women, from seven different countries, whom the fictional Bahram ordered brought to him. In the special palace he has built for the women, each has her own dome-covered quarters. The seven women are highly symbolic, and each is associated with a specific day of the week, color, and celestial planet. In the poem, Bahram visits each woman, intently listening as she tells a tale possessing a moral, such as the value of patience, forgiveness, or justice. Bahram spends considerable time listening to these tales—seven years, according to scholars of the poem. When he finally returns to his duties as a king he discovers that the minister to whom he had entrusted his kingdom has brought it to the brink of war with China. Withdrawing to reflect, Bahram goes hunting and chances to meet a shepherd who has hanged his once-faithful dog, because the dog had surrendered the sheep in his care to a she-wolf in exchange for copulation with her. Bahram realizes that his task as ruler is to protect his people—an insight he could grasp only because he had heard the seven tales. With a new sense of purpose, Bahram investigates the misdeeds of his minister and has him executed, averts the impending war with China, and rids himself of the seven beauties, turning each of their domes into a temple for worship. Taken as a whole, the epic emphasizes a theme common to several of Nizami's works: a ruler's cultivation of an exemplary character. The excerpt below, from Nizami's introduction to *Seven Beauties*, praises Muhammad and describes his ascent (in Arabic, *mi'raj*) through the seven heavens until he meets God (compare the selection from Bistami, above). By foreshadowing and framing Bahram Gur's own enlightenment, Nizami's introduction adds another layer of symbolism to the poem and exemplifies his amalgamation of Persian and Islamic traditions.

PRONOUNCING GLOSSARY

Burāq: *boo-rahq´*
caliph: *ka´-lif*
Isrāfīl: *is-rah-feel´*
Kāvūs: *kah-voos´*
Nizāmī: *ne-zah-mee´*
Rafraf: *raf´-raf*
sāqī: *sah´-qee*

FROM SEVEN BEAUTIES

In Praise of the Chief among Prophets

BENEDICTIONS AND PEACE BE UPON HIM!

The primal Circle's centre, and
the Seal upon Creation's line;
The ancient sphere's first fruits; the crown
of lofty discourse; reason's gem:
Who, but the lord of confirmed faith,
God's Prophet, Messenger most praised.
By sword and crown the prophets' lord:
the Ascent his crown, the Law[1] his sword.
Unlettered,[2] source of all that's made,
the Carpet's light, the High Throne's[3] shade,
Who sounds the Law's five turns;[4] arrays
his fourfold rule[5] o'er earthly clay.
He foremost goal, we all in need:
Muhammad he, his mission praised.
Of that first clay that Adam pressed,[6]
he essence pure, all others dregs;
And when Heaven turns its final round,
his word shall seal its final sound.
On right are based his yeas and nays,
enjoining good, and banning base.
His boast, of poverty; no pain
to him, who such a treasure gained!
He put day's brightness in the shade:
what talk of shade,[7] with sun displayed!
Of worldly rule the godly stay,
he worldly rulers mates and slays,
Abasing all who would rebel,
grasping the hand of those who fell.
With righteous men he dealt aright,
but anger showed towards evil might.
His vengeful sword struck evil down;
for good his kindness mixed sweet balm,
Elixir to sore hearts; his blade
to hearts of stone his wrath displayed.
Those foes who barred the road of faith,
and girded up their loins with hate,

TRANSLATED BY Julie Scott Meisami. Except as indicated, all notes are the translator's (most have been edited).

1. Islamic law (in Arabic, *shariʿa*). "Ascent": the Prophet's ascent to Heaven (*miʿraj*).
2. The Prophet was said to have been illiterate (Qurʾan 7:158; 29:48).
3. The throne of God (in Arabic, *ʿarsh*), in Islamic cosmology equated with the ninth sphere (the encompassing sphere), and in esoteric thought with the Universal Intellect. "Carpet": a metaphor for the earth.
4. The five daily prayers in Islam.
5. The first four caliphs who rule following Muhammad's death in 632 (Abu Bakr [573–634], ʿUmar [ca. 586–644], ʿUthman [d. 656], and ʿAli [ca. 599–661]). Together, the "five turns" and the "fourfold rule" signify the combination of spiritual and temporal rule.
6. A reference to the creation of Adam, the first man and the first prophet, who was made of clay (Qurʾan 38:71).
7. According to legend, Muhammad did not cast a shadow.

Now beat their thongs upon his drum,
and, after years, all follow him.
Though God chose him from every age;
created this world for his sake;
'Turned not aside'[8] his eyes hath sealed,
a garden beyond this revealed.
From seven hundred thousand years,
seven thousand servitude declare.
The servants[9] of the blue-robed sphere
his service's ring wear in their ear.
His four true friends,[1] both root and branch,
are walls for the Law's treasure, staunch.
From the divine Creator came
his eyes' bright light—blessings on him!
His soul life's every breath maintains;
his body both earth and Heaven spans.
This soul that body's life does bring;
all others throne, he Solomon.
His breath like musk the air perfumes,
and shakes moist dates from dry date-palms.
His miracle: dates from dry thorns,
that for his foes to sharp barbs turn!
His nail did split the moon in twain,[2]
a two-halved apple in his hand.
Despite its fear, he rent away
the cataract that blinds the sky.
He was most blessed by the Creator,
the chosen one of that Elector;
And may on both our praises fall,
longer than the blue sphere shall roll.

On the Prophet's Ascent to Heaven

Since this world compassed not his crown,
his Ladder[3] bore him to God's Throne.
To raise him high from low degree
came Gabriel with Burâq,[4] his steed.
'Place now on air your foot of clay,
that your earth be made heavenly.
The Holy Presence you will guard
tonight; be purity's staunch ward.
Yours now is Burâq's lightning speed;
mount, to perform your watchman's deed.
Since I've conveyed your guardian's lot,
Burâq, your mount, I've also brought.
Traverse the sphere, for you're its moon;
speed o'er the stars, for you're their king;
From their seven roots, uproot the six

8. Qur'an 53:17.
9. The planets.
1. The first four caliphs.
2. See Qur'an 54:1–2 [editor's note].
3. Some accounts of Muhammad's ascension describe the ladder on which he ascends to heaven.
4. The magical mount brought by Gabriel to the Prophet on which he made his ascent.

directions;[5] the nine spheres[6] unfix
From their four nails; pass by the Fish,[7]
and bend the heavens to your wish.
The stars blend night's dark musk for you;
the green-robed angels wait for you.
The Egyptian beauties of this sphere
adore you, like a Joseph fair.[8]
Rise, that your face they all may see,
and wound themselves in ecstasy.
Beneath you, form new vaulted whorls
for Heaven, from your shadow's curls.
Lamp-like,[9] give the stars blooms of light;
fresh-faced as garden flowers, shine bright.
This night is yours; this hour, of prayer;
you'll gain whatever you desire.
Make new the angels' carpet; raise
your tent at the Divine Throne's base;
Brighten the Throne's eyes with your light;
fold up the carpet in your flight;
Then grasp the crown, for you are king;
exalted, rule created things.
Raise high your head in grandeur; make
both worlds[1] your own, through your attack.
Then cleanse your path of dust; speed on
to the court of the Eternal One,
So that—your meed for coming nigh—
your flag may over both worlds fly.'
When he, in secret converse, heard
from Gabriel these soul-moving words,
His intellect perfect thereby,
the Prophet hastened to obey.
One God's trustee in revelation,
the other in wise deliberation:
Both guardians of a wealthy trust:
no demon this, no sinner that.
One brought the message as decreed;
the other did its secrets heed.
In dark night, that light-giving lamp
was sealed by his high wish's stamp.
He shook not off that lasso's bond;
no yoke of gold but this is known.
Like lightning on Burâq he leapt;

5. North, south, east, west, up, and down. "Seven roots": seven earths.
6. In Islamic cosmology the universe consists of the seven spheres of the planets, the fixed stars, and the encompassing outer sphere.
7. The two stars Arcturus ("Lancer") and Spica Virginis ("the Unarmed"), the fourteenth lunar station, whose auroral rising in central Arabia in early October coincides with the date of the Prophet's emigration from Mecca to Medina in 622. "Four nails": the four pivots from which stem the four imaginary lines that divide the celestial vault into four quadrants.
8. In the qur'anic story of Joseph and the Egyptian ruler's wife (later called Zulaykha), when the Egyptian women mocked Zulaykha for her love of Joseph, she invited them to a banquet to observe him; they were so amazed at his beauty that they cut their hands with the knives with which they were peeling citrons (Qur'an 12:31–32).
9. The Prophet is described in Qur'an 33:46 as a "light-giving lamp."
1. This world and the next.

his steed beneath, he grasped his whip.
He mounted; that celestial steed
traversed the sky with eagle's speed.
Like peacocks' wings his striking hoofs;
the moon like Kâvûs'[2] throne above;
And in its flight—so quick it climbed—
the four eagles shed their wings behind.
It quickly passed o'er all it found;
the night was spurned, the moon reined in.
Have you seen how swift a fancy speeds?
how lightning quick unsheathes its blade?
Both world-traversing Reason's speed
and the soul's leap towards generous deed:
All, by its flight, were left as lame;
all by its lengthy stride constrained.
Its speed outstripped the Poles' swift course:
one moment south, the other north.
The Fish in that swift rushing stream
showed now as Lancer, now unarmed.[3]
When he with Burâq's dancing feet
inscribed that volume, sheet by sheet,
He left behind the worldly road,
and far above the heavens soared;
Cut through the stations of the sky,
with angel's wings, a broad highway.
From his own verdant nature, he
gave to the moon new verdancy.
His silver-work to Mercury gave
the bluish shade of leaden glaze.
O'er Venus, from the moon's bright light,
he drew a veil of silvery white.
His dust, as he attacked the heavens,
set on the sun a golden crown.
Green-robed like Caliph of the West,[4]
red garments bright to Mars he left;
And, finding Jupiter consumed
by pain, rubbed sandalwood thereon.
When Saturn's crown his feet had kissed,
he placed its flag in ambergris.
As he rushed on like morning's wind,
astride a mount like raging lion,
His comrade left off his attack,
and in his course Burâq grew slack.
For he had reached a stage so far
that Gabriel dared not come near.
From Michael's[5] couch he rose, until
he reached the tower of Isrâfîl.[6]

2. The king of the semi-mythical pre-Islamic Persian Kayanid dynasty. Legend states that he attempted, unsuccessfully, to ascend to heaven on a throne borne by eagles.
3. See n. 7, p. 468.
4. The Prophet is clad in green, the sacred color of Islam and royal color of the Umayyad caliphs. The phrase "Caliph of the West" can also refer to the setting sun.
5. The angel Michael.
6. The angel whose trumpet blast heralds the Day of Judgment.

He left that throne behind, and soared
beyond both Rafraf and the Lote.[7]
Companions left behind, he pressed
on to the Sea of Selflessness;
Passed o'er that ocean, drop by drop;
traversed all Being, step by step.
When he came to the Throne's support,
he made a ladder from prayer's rope.
He went beyond the radiant Throne,
to the mystery of 'Praise be Mine'.[8]
When, lost in his bewilderment,
God's Mercy came and seized his reins,
His distance of *'two bowlengths'* went
from *'he came near'* to *'nearer yet'*.[9]
Rending the veil of thousand lights,
that unveiled Brilliance reached his sight.
Beyond his being's bounds he trod,
till he achieved the sight of God.
He saw outright the Worshipped One,
and cleansed his eyes of all but Him;
Nor did in one place rest his sight,
as greetings came from left and right.
All one—front, back, left, right, high, low;
the six directions were no more.
When Non-direction's flame burns high,
world and direction swiftly flee.
God, without form, knows no direction;
and so he turned towards Non-direction.
When sight is veiled by direction,
the heart's not free from false perception;
But when direction's hid from sight,
He who has none is seen aright.
Nought but the Prophet's breath remained;
for God alone then dwelled in him.
How can direction compass Him,
the All and All-encompassing?
When the Prophet saw God thus,
he heard words spoken without voice.
He drank a special draught; attained
great honour; from his closeness gained
The way to Truth; Fortune his cup,
Wisdom his sâqî:[1] nought else left.
With myriad prayers in tribute rendered,
from that high summit he descended;
Spent all he brought upon his friends;

7. The lote tree is considered by many exegetes to be the boundary beyond which no one can travel (Qur'an 53:14). "Rafraf": often interpreted as green cushions or carpet (Qur'an 55:76); Nizami uses it to mean a mount or a litter that carries Muhammad on the final stage of his ascent.
8. An allusion to Qur'an 17:1, in which God praises himself ("Praise be to Him who made His servant ascend by night").
9. A reference to Qur'an 53:9–11, which indicates that Muhammad came within two bow lengths or closer to God ("Then he [Muhammad] approached closer, and [God] leaned down toward him, so that it was [like] two bows with one string [or: twin bows], or closer still. Then He revealed to his servant that which He had willed to reveal").
1. Cup-bearer (Arabic) [editor's note].

placed it in trust for sinful men.
How long, Nizâmî, love this world?
How long be base? Raise high your head!
The eternal realm strive to attain,
which through Muhammad's faith you'll gain.
If reason guard your faith aright,
you'll cleave to Truth through the Law's light.

SAʿDI
ca. 1215–early 1290s

Abu ʿAbdallah Saʿdi, a master of Persian literature perhaps equaled only by Hafiz (1325/26–1390; see below), is best known for his poetical work *The Fragrant Herb Garden*, his prose work *The Rose Garden*, and his unique love poems (in Persian, *ghazals*).

Saʿdi was born in the city of Shiraz, Iran, which he left in 1225—perhaps prompted by Mongol incursions in the surrounding region—to begin his scholarly journeys. He received financial support to study at the Nizamiyya University in Baghdad (on which see the introduction to Nizam al-Mulk, above) and, if his autobiographical accounts are taken at face value, then traveled extensively. Saʿdi tells us that he finally returned to Shiraz in 1257 and composed *The Fragrant Herb Garden* as a gift to the city's inhabitants. The following year he completed *The Rose Garden*, and he continued writing poetry and prose until his death. Colorful details about Saʿdi's life abound, such as visits to a Hindu temple in India and travels to Kashgar, China, but scholars question the reliability of such reports, even those attributed to Saʿdi himself. They judge them to be not accounts of actual episodes but the author's efforts to fashion a compelling persona.

Saʿdi lived in a period of great turmoil and quickly shifting alliances. The Mongols were the primary threat, and in the year of *The Rose Garden's* completion they destroyed Baghdad and killed the last ʿAbbasid caliph. The themes and dedications of Saʿdi's writings reflect these upheavals. For example, after the deaths of the last ʿAbbasid caliph and the last independent ruler of his home province, Saʿdi composed poems praising both. As a precautionary measure, he also composed poems praising the Mongol leader Hulegu (ca. 1217–1265), who had killed both men, as well as poems lauding other Mongol officials.

Saʿdi's *Herb Garden* is a work of poetry, while his *Rose Garden* is prose punctuated by poetry. Yet they are similar in their topical arrangement and presentation of stories designed to impart life lessons and popular wisdom. Ever alert to context and situation, Saʿdi offers some anecdotes that counsel honesty in the face of despotic rule and forgiveness to wrong doers, while other tales encourage the reverse.

Saʿdi's writings won him acclaim during his lifetime, and *The Rose Garden* quickly became the model for Persian prose. As his work spread to Turkey and India, it inspired commentaries and imitations, and translations soon appeared beyond the Persian-speaking world. In the mid-seventeenth century, European translations were published in French, German, and Latin. An English translation was issued in 1774, and by the nineteenth century some American writers were aware of his compositions.

Saʿdi's *Rose Garden* consists of an introduction and eight chapters: (1) "On the Conduct of Kings," (2) "On the Morals of Dervishes," (3) "On the Excellence of Contentment," (4) "On the Benefits of Silence," (5) "On Love and Youth," (6) "On

Frailty and Old Age," (7) "On the Effects of Education," and finally (8) "On Manners." The wide reception and enduring appeal of this book lie in the timelessness of the themes addressed. The two stories presented below, from the fifth chapter, speak of love and its effects; the first tells of a judge who becomes enamored of a blacksmith's male assistant. Saʿdi wrote openly about the love lives of men and women in all of their manifestations, aware that such frankness would inevitably offend some members of his audience.

PRONOUNCING GLOSSARY

atabeg: *a-ta-beg´*
cadi: *kah´-dee*
Hamadan: *ha-ma-dahn´*
Layla: *lay´-luh*
Majnun: *maj-noon´*
Saʿdi: *sa-dee´*

FROM THE ROSE GARDEN

From *Chapter 5. Love and Youth*

STORY 20

The story is told of the cadi[1] of Hamadan who was consumed by love for a blacksmith's boy. For a long time he sought him out and pursued him.

> Into my eyes came that tall, elegant cypress. He stole my heart and trampled it under foot.
> This impudent eye draws in hearts with a lasso. If you want not to lose your heart to anyone, shut your eyes.

I have heard that the boy met the cadi in a lane. Having heard something of the cadi's attentions, and being insulted beyond description, he cursed him soundly, called him vile names, threw rocks at him, and did everything he could to embarrass him.

The cadi said to a learned man who was with him,

> "See that beauty and anger. See how sweet is that furrow on a sour brow."

In the Arab countries they say, "A blow from the beloved is as sweet as a raisin."

> To receive a blow on the mouth from a fist of your hand is nicer than to eat bread with one's own hand.

And behold, from the boy's wounded dignity came the scent of leniency.

> Newly produced grapes are sour in taste. Wait two or three days, and they'll turn sweet.

This the cadi said as he returned to his seat of judgment. Several dignified witnesses who were in his chambers kissed the ground in servitude and said, "With your permission we would say a few words to you, although it may be a breach of etiquette and the great have said,

TRANSLATED BY Wheeler M. Thackston. The bracketed addition is the translator's.

1. That is, a qadi, or Muslim judge. Hamadan is a city in northwestern Iran.

> Not every word should be debated; it is a mistake to point out great men's faults.

However, inasmuch as our lord has always shown us favor in the past, it would be an act of ingratitude to see where your best interests lie and not to mention it. The correct manner of proceeding would be for you not to set your sights on this lad but rather to roll up the carpet of enflamed desire. The office of a judge should be an unassailable position, and you should not sully it with a hideous offense. You have seen and heard the type of person you are up against."

> What concern has he for another's honor who has severely disgraced himself?
> Many a good repute of fifty years has been trampled into the dust by one bad name.

The cadi approved of his devoted friends' advice and praised their good opinion, saying, "Your valued advice on the best manner in which to proceed is absolutely correct, and the matter cannot be challenged. However,

> Blame me as much as you want, but you can't wash the black from a Negro.
> Nothing will make me stop thinking of you. I am a snake that has been hit on the head: I cannot keep from writhing."

He said this, and it prompted some persons to have him investigated, and thus he lost boundless wealth. They say that he who has gold in the scales has power in his arm, and he who cannot put his hand on a dinar has no one in all the world.

> Everyone who sees gold lowers his head—even a scale with its iron shoulder.

In short, he managed to achieve one night of intimacy, and that very night the police were informed. All that night the cadi had wine in his head and the youth in his embrace, enjoying himself and singing:

> Tonight perhaps the cock will not crow at dawn: lovers have not had enough of embracing and kissing.
> The beloved's breasts in the crook of curly locks, like ivory balls in the crook of an ebony polo-stick.
> Beware of one instant when the eye of sedition is asleep. Be awake lest you live to regret it.
> Until you hear the dawn call to prayer from the Friday mosque or the beat of war drums from the atabeg's[2] palace gate,
> It is foolish to take your mouth from lips puckered like a cock's eye just because of the vain cry of the cock.

The cadi was in this state when one of his retainers came in and said, "Why are you sitting here? Get up! Flee as fast as you can, for the envious have informed on you—indeed, they have done no more than tell the truth. Let us quench the fire of sedition with the water of strategic action while it is still small, before it grows larger to consume the world tomorrow."

The cadi looked at him with a smile and said,

2. A high-ranking provincial ruler (Turkish).

"What does it matter to a lion that has put its claw into its prey if
the dogs bark?
Face your beloved, and let your enemies seethe with regret."

That very night the king was also informed that such an abomination had been committed in the kingdom. "What do you command?" he was asked.

"I considered him one of the most learned men of the age," he said, "and unique in his time. Possibly detractors have maligned him. I will not believe it of him until the matter is investigated, for the wise have said:

To put your hand to the sword too quickly means to bite the hand
in regret."

I heard that at dawn the king went with several of his courtiers to the cadi's bedroom. There he saw a candle standing, a beauty sitting, wine spilled, goblets broken, and the cadi in a stupor of intoxication, oblivious to the world. Gently he roused him, saying, "Get up! The sun has risen."

The cadi realized what a situation he was in. "From which direction did the sun rise?" he asked.

"From the east," the king said.

"Thank God!" said the cadi. "The gates of repentance are still open in accordance with the Prophet's dictum, 'The gates of repentance will not be closed to God's servants until the sun rises in the west.' I seek your forgiveness, O God, and I repent!"

These two things instigated me to sin: bad luck and a weak mind.
If you take me to task, I deserve it. If you forgive me, pardon is
better than revenge.

"To repent when you know you are going to die avails you nothing," said the king. *But their faith availed them not, after they had beholden our vengeance* [Kor. 40:85].

Of what benefit is it to repent of theft when you can't throw your
lasso over the palace?
If the fruit is too high, lower your hand, for a short person cannot
reach the branch.

It is impossible to release you, given the abomination you have committed." This the king said as the jailers began to haul him off to extract retribution from him.

"I have one word left to say to the king," said the cadi.

The king heard him and said, "What is it?"

He said:

"You may shake me off in boredom, but do not expect that I will
let go of your skirt.
Even though release is impossible because of the crime I have
committed, there is yet hope of the generosity you possess."

"You have produced a novel analogy and spoken a rare anecdote," said the king, "but it is logically absurd and contrary to the law for your erudition and eloquence to get you released from the grip of my punishment. I think the best thing would be for me to have you thrown down from the fortress so that others will learn a lesson."

"O lord of the world," he said, "I have been nourished by the benefaction of this dynasty, and I am not the only one to have committed this crime. Have someone else thrown down so that I may learn a lesson."

The king burst out laughing and pardoned his crime, and to the detractors who had insisted that he be killed he said,

"You who admit to your own guilt, do not taunt others for their faults."

STORY 21

There was an honest and chaste young man who was pledged to a
fair face.
I have read that they fell into a whirlpool together in the great
ocean.
When a sailor came to take him by the hand lest he perish in that
condition,
From the midst of the waves and maelstrom he said, "Leave me
and take my friend's hand."
As he spoke, the waves crashed over him, and he was heard to say
as he perished,
"Listen not to the tale of love from that worthless one who forgets
a friend in difficulty."
Thus the friends lived. Listen to this worthless one that you may
know,
For Saʿdi knows the path and custom of love as well as he knows
Arabic in Baghdad.
Set your hopes on the beloved you possess, and forget about all the
rest of the world.
If Layla's Majnun[3] were alive, he would pen the tale of love from
this notebook.

3. A reference to a well-known tragic love story: Majnun, (literally, "One Possessed") was driven mad following his separation from Layla.

HAFIZ
1325/26–1390

Shams al-Din Muhammad Shirazi was born in the Iranian city of Shiraz. Known by his pen name Hafiz meaning "one who has memorized the Qur'an," he is the most popular Persian poet, and many of his lines have assumed the status of proverbs. Even today his most notable work, the *Diwan*, is used as a tool for divining the future.

Though Hafiz's childhood is thought to have been relatively impoverished, he received a traditional education in the religious sciences and was quite familiar with Persian literature. He may have worked as a baker's apprentice and probably served as a scribe for poets and others. Eventually he began writing his own poetry in the courtly circles of Shiraz, and from that day forward he placed his imprint on Persian poetry.

Hafiz is considered the master of a form of lyric poetry known in Persian as the *ghazal*. Though this poetical style had existed for several centuries before him, Hafiz took the ghazal in a new direction. Typically seven to nine lines long, Hafiz's ghazals address many themes, often—and unusually, in this genre—in a single poem. Love, the standard ghazal topic, certainly plays a central role in his work, but he took the novel step of also making the criticism of moral and religious hypocrisy a major theme. In elaborating these and other topics, he extensively uses mystical language and symbolism.

In Hafiz's time, Shiraz was a site of political instability and turmoil. At the beginning of his career, the Inju dynasty controlled Shiraz, but in 1353 a rival dynasty, the Muzaffarids, assumed power. Thus it was under Muzaffarid rule—which was marked by constant strife among the Muzaffarids themselves—that Hafiz spent most of his career. In addition to this general political uncertainty, Hafiz also had to endure a period of strict Islamic rule in Shiraz under one of the shahs, and later lost the favor of another for a decade. Yet this was the era in which he did his best work, some of which referred to these events. Hafiz spent the last few years of his life under the rule of Timur (1336–1405), descendent of the Mongols and founder of the Timurid dynasty, who conquered the city in 1387.

Even during his lifetime, Hafiz's poems found an appreciative audience at least as far away as India and Iraq, but travel did not tempt him. Aside from a short sojourn in the Iranian desert city of Yazd, Hafiz stayed in Shiraz, where he died in 1390. His tomb was erected about sixty years after his death; located in a garden of flowers and orange trees, it continues to be a major attraction for locals and tourists alike.

In his collection of poetry (in Persian, *Diwan*), along with treating traditional love themes Hafiz targets religious leaders, false mystics, and others who claim moral authority yet violate the values they preach. To illustrate his point, he elevates those groups normally seen as immoral and socially marginalized—wine drinkers, Zoroastrians, the poor, and various scoundrels—above such hypocritical authorities. He does this all with a sense of humor and wit, rather than relying on direct attacks or self-righteousness.

Hafiz's celebration of love and beauty, of wine and the drinking tavern, of Muslim and non-Muslim alike has led to an unresolved debate among scholars about how to interpret his *Diwan*. Was he a libertine whose writings were to be taken literally, or was he a Sufi mystic engaging in allegory? It does seem likely that Hafiz had an affinity for Islamic mysticism that went beyond mere familiarity with the Sufi themes and imagery of the time. His condemnation of religious hypocrisy is not a dismissal of religion. On the other hand, reducing his poetry to veiled mysticism would be an overreach. A better approach is to see the ambiguity of his work as an attempt to reconcile the diversity of human nature and the challenges of life with religious and spiritual ideals.

The poems below, from an anthology compiled by the British scholar A. J. Arberry, are by different translators and thus are in various styles. In his editorial annotations, Arberry notes that the poem "Where Are the Tidings of Union?" is inscribed on Hafiz's tomb.

PRONOUNCING GLOSSARY

Anca: *an-qah´*
Hafiz: *hah´-fiz*
Jamshid: *jam-sheed´*
saki: *sah´-kee*

FROM THE COLLECTION *A Mad Heart*[1]

I

Long years my heart had made request
Of me, a stranger, hopefully
(Not knowing that itself possessed
The treasure that it sought of me),
That Jamshid's chalice[2] I should win
And it would see the world therein.

That is a pearl by far too rare
To be contained within the shell
Of time and space; lost vagrants there
Upon the ocean's margin, well
We know it is a vain surmise
That we should hold so great a prize.

II

There was a man that loved God well;
In every motion of his mind
God dwelt; and yet he could not tell
That God was in him, being blind:
Wherefore as if afar he stood
And cried, "Have mercy, O my God!"

III

This problem that had vexed me long
Last night unto the taverner
I carried; for my hope was strong
His judgement sure, that could not err,
Might swiftly solve infallibly
The riddle that had baffled me.

I saw him standing in his place,
A goblet in his grasp, a smile
Of right good cheer upon his face,
As in the glass he gazed awhile
And seemed to view in vision clear
A hundred truths reflected there.

IV

"That friend who, being raised sublime
Upon the gallows, glorified
The tree that slew him for his crime,
This was the sin for which he died,
That, having secrets in his charge,
He told them to the world at large."

1. Translated by Arthur J. Arberry.
2. A cup that enabled the legendary Persian king Jamshid to see anywhere in the universe in the past, present, and future.

So spake he; adding, "But the heart
That has the truth within its hold
And, practising the rosebud's art,
Conceals a mystery in each fold,
That heart hath well this comment lined
Upon the margin of the mind.

"When Moses unto Pharaoh stood,
The men of magic strove in vain
Against his miracle of wood;[3]
So every subtlety of brain
Must surely fail and feeble be
Before the soul's supremacy.

"And if the Holy Ghost descend
In grace and power infinite
His comfort in these days to lend
To them that humbly wait on it,
Theirs too the wondrous works can be
That Jesus wrought in Galilee."

V

"What season did the Spirit wise
This all-revealing cup assign
Within thy keeping?" "When the skies
Were painted by the Hand Divine
And heaven's mighty void was spanned,
Then gave He this into my hand."

"Yon twisted coil, yon chain of hair
Why doth the lovely Idol spread
To keep me fast and fettered there?"
"Ah, Hafiz!", so the wise man said,
"'Tis a mad heart, and needs restraint
That speaks within thee this complaint."

Where Are the Tidings of Union?[4]

Where are the tidings of union? that I may arise—
Forth from the dust I will rise up to welcome thee!
My soul, like a homing bird, yearning for Paradise,
Shall arise and soar, from the snares of the world set free.
When the voice of thy love shall call me to be thy slave,
I shall rise to a greater far than the mastery
Of life and the living, time and the mortal span:
Pour down, oh Lord! from the clouds of thy guiding grace
The rain of a mercy that quickeneth on my grave,
Before, like dust that the wind bears from place to place,

3. When the magicians of Pharaoh competed against Moses, he cast down his staff at the command of God and defeated their illusions (Qur'an 7:113–19).

4. Translated by Gertrude Bell.

I arise and flee beyond the knowledge of man.
When to my grave thou turnest thy blessed feet,
Wine and the lute thou shalt bring in thine hand to me,
Thy voice shall ring through the folds of my winding-sheet,
And I will arise and dance to thy minstrelsy.
Though I be old, clasp me one night to thy breast,
And I, when the dawn shall come to awaken me.
With the flush of youth on my cheek from thy bosom will rise.
Rise up! let mine eyes delight in thy stately grace!
Thou art the goal to which all men's endeavour has pressed,
And thou the idol of Hafiz' worship; thy face
From the world and life shall bid him come forth and arise!

The Riddle of Life[5]

With last night's wine still singing in my head,
I sought the tavern at the break of day,
Though half the world was still asleep in bed;
The harp and flute were up and in full swing,
And a most pleasant morning sound made they;
Already was the wine-cup on the wing.
"Reason", said I, "'tis past the time to start,
If you would reach your daily destination,
The holy city of intoxication."
So did I pack him off, and he depart
With a stout flask for fellow-traveller.

Left to myself, the tavern-wench I spied,
And sought to win her love by speaking fair;
Alas! she turned upon me, scornful-eyed,
And mocked my foolish hopes of winning her.
Said she, her arching eyebrows like a bow:
"Thou mark for all the shafts of evil tongues!
Thou shalt not round my middle clasp me so,
Like my good girdle—not for all thy songs!—
So long as thou in all created things
Seest but thyself the centre and the end.
Go spread thy dainty nets for other wings—
Too high the Anca's[6] nest for thee, my friend."

Then took I shelter from that stormy sea
In the good ark of wine; yet, woe is me!
Saki[7] and comrade and minstrel all by turns,
She is of maidens the compendium
Who my poor heart in such a fashion spurns.
Self, HAFIZ, self! That must thou overcome!
Hearken the wisdom of the tavern-daughter!
Vain little baggage—well, upon my word!

5. Translated by Richard Le Gallienne.
6. A legendary species of bird (often identified with the phoenix), known for its destructiveness and said to live on mountains.
7. Cup-bearer (Arabic).

Thou fairy figment made of clay and water,
As busy with thy beauty as a bird.

Well, HAFIZ, Life's a riddle—give it up:
There is no answer to it but this cup.

Adab: *Fable, Aphorism, and Essay*

AL-JAHIZ

ca. 776–868/69

Abu ʿUthman ʿAmr ibn Bahr al-Jahiz was the most famous man of letters of his era. He wrote on all topics, from politics to theology, and was renowned for his distinctive prose style. His nickname, al-Jahiz, means "pop-eyed," a reference to his bulging corneas, and Arabic historical sources, perhaps to make him a more interesting figure, record anecdotes that highlight his unattractiveness. According to one probably apocryphal tale, his ugliness led the caliph al-Mutawakkil (r. 847–61) to refuse to hire al-Jahiz to teach his children.

Al-Jahiz was born in Basra, Iraq, a city with a thriving intellectual community. His family was of North African origin and not wealthy, and during his time in Basra he seems to have supported himself by selling fish and accepting the largess of patrons. Historical sources note that he studied with some of the city's foremost literary and theological scholars, but there is scant information about his formal education and how he gained access to such teachers. Perhaps his sharp intellect and verbal facility attracted their attention in their public classes.

Al-Jahiz lived during a time of political and theological turmoil. He wrote political tracts defending the ruling ʿAbbasids against Shiʿi and Umayyad claimants and was a member of the rationalist Muʿtazili theological school, which was embraced by several ʿAbbasid caliphs who reigned during his lifetime. One of his early political works, written near 816, caught the eye of the caliph al-Ma'mun (r. 813–33). Heartened by that positive reception, al-Jahiz decided to move to Baghdad. There he lived primarily on the support provided by influential patrons, often senior ministers and judges, who offered him land and money when he dedicated works to them. Al-Jahiz's skills were always in demand, and his talent—coupled with the backing of well-placed patrons—protected him from shifts in power within the ʿAbbasid administration. In addition to writing, he continued his studies in Baghdad, where he had access to Greek texts whose translation into Arabic had been funded by the caliphs. Toward the end of his life, likely under the rule of al-Mutawakkil, al-Jahiz returned to his native Basra; there he retired, semi-paralyzed, and died in December 868 or January of 869. His return to Basra should not be taken as a sign that he had fallen into disfavor. By all accounts, al-Mutawakkil respected al-Jahiz and sought his attendance at court, though the caliph had renounced Muʿtazili thought.

Of al-Jahiz's prolific output—about two hundred works on a wide range of subjects—his literary writings, both anthologies and essays, won him the most lasting fame. In his anthologies he selected and commented on the material with which he believed an educated person of his day should be familiar. He chose from the best of the Arabic literary tradition, as well as from translations of Greek and Persian sources. His best-known anthology is the seven volume *Book of Animals*, begun toward the end of his life but never completed; it contains poetry, prose, and anecdotes on some 350 different animals. As he presents material on these animals, al-Jahiz delves into other subjects, especially theological and sociological ones. Another important anthology is the *Book of Elegance of Expression and Clarity of Exposition*, whose selections from Arabic literature showcase the excellence of Arabic rhetoric and poetry. Al-Jahiz's literary essays focus on manners and ethical concerns, and thus reflect the interests of other eighth- and ninth-century Arabic and Persian authors. He examines topics such as speech and silence, hostility and envy, and the keeping of secrets.

Here are excerpts from al-Jahiz's essay "The Art of Keeping Secrets and Holding One's Tongue." The piece is a meditation on the twin faults of garrulousness and the inability to keep a confidence. As he reflects on their causes and their cure, al-Jahiz's digressive writing style leads him to other discussions, especially on the nature of the human soul.

PRONOUNCING GLOSSARY

ʿaql: *ahql*
al-Aʿmash: *al-a´-mash*
Bakr: *bakr*
ḥijr: *hejr* (heavy *h*)
ḥilm: *hilm* (heavy *h*)
Muʿāwiya: *moo-ah´-we-yuh*
Taghlib: *tag´-lib*
ʿUmar ibn al-Khaṭṭāb: *oh´-mar ibn al-chaht-tahb´* (guttural *ch*)

FROM THE ART OF KEEPING SECRETS AND HOLDING ONE'S TONGUE

The author sings the praises of his correspondent—not identified for certain—and then goes on to say that he has noted two failings in him,

I. GARRULITY AND INDISCRETION

. . . The two things I have against you are talking idly and giving away secrets. The qualities I think desirable and strive to inculcate in you are not easy to acquire or simple to practice; how could it be otherwise, seeing that nowadays I do not know a single one of our many contemporaries, those who belong to the aristocracy, are reckoned among the élite, aspire to power and authority, pride themselves on their learning, and make a great point of their dignified, staid, judicial, solemn demeanour—I do not know a single one of them who is able to control his tongue to my satisfaction or can keep secrets properly? Nothing is harder than the battle of wits with one's own instincts and the struggle to subdue one's own emotions. Throughout one's life judgment is subordinated to emotion, and it is the latter that makes people betray secrets and let their tongues run away with them. If reason has been called *ʿaql* (shackle) and *ḥijr* (prohibition) . . . it is because it ties down, bridles, shackles and restrains the tongue and binds and shackles unnecessary words to keep them from becoming senselessly, wrongfully or harmfully excessive, as a camel is hobbled or an orphan put under restraint. The tongue is an interpreter for the heart, and the heart a casket wherein thoughts and secrets are carefully stored away, as well as everything else, good or bad, that is entrusted to it by the senses, engendered by the desires and emotions, or begotten by wisdom and learning. The human breast is not constructed as a receptacle for tangible matter, but is destined by providence to be a vessel

Translated by Charles Pellat; translated from the French by D. M. Hawke. The summaries of omitted material are by Pellat.

for material unknown to man; and hence it becomes so oppressed by what it contains, and finds its load so heavy, that it seeks relief by unburdening itself and takes pleasure in unloading itself on to the tongue. But it is no help to a man to speak of his secret to himself in private: contrariwise, he needs to share it with someone else who is incapable of keeping it safe. The outcome of it all is that emotion takes over control of the tongue, and an excess of thought leads to an excess of words.

The tongue is made for proclaiming the glory of God, but is often used for speaking evil. It is, however, merely an organ, and deserves neither praise nor blame.

2. SELF-CONTROL (*ḤILM*)

. . . It is self-control that deserves praise, and the lack of it that deserves blame. The word *ḥilm* is a noun that encompasses all the qualities: it means the power of reason to restrain emotion. To restrain one's wrath, suppress evil impulses and clip the wings of hotheadedness—all this merits the name of *ḥilm*, and comes close to the essence of it; no less, to repress exuberant satisfaction, control one's desires and refrain from malicious glee, insolent merriment, inappropriate grief or excessive anxiety, over-hasty compliments or reproaches, evil propensities and base covetousness, unwholesome greed for a bargain, excess of covetousness for one's objective, whining and snivelling, being full of complaints and repining, shifting too suddenly from anger to pleasure or pleasure to anger, and from making either body or tongue perform meaningless, useless, pointless evolutions.

It is easier to be silent than to say something of value, but man enjoys imparting and acquiring information. Indeed, the transmission of traditions is due to this instinctive human tendency.

3. IT IS HARD TO KEEP A SECRET

. . . Man finds it difficult to keep secrets because of the strength of this urge and his proneness to yield to this instinct. It would be easier for him to move well-established mountains than to fight against his own instincts. When he has a secret to keep, he falls into the grip of melancholy, grows ill and haggard, and feels deep down inside himself a sort of tingling or mangy itching, or as though he were being stung by a swarm of hornets, or prodded with gimlets; but these feelings vary in intensity according to the amount of self-control a man exercises and his natural levelheadedness or emotivity. When a man divulges his secret, he feels as though a yoke has been lifted off his shoulders.

The author then gives examples to illustrate the difficulty of keeping secrets, notably the case of al-Aʿmash, who was so anxious to keep to himself the traditions of the Prophet he had collected that he recited them to a sheep. Then he goes on to

4. THE DISSEMINATION OF SECRETS

. . . When a secret emerges from its holder's breast, escapes from his tongue and reaches a single ear, it is thenceforth no longer a secret but a piece of news destined to spread, opening the door to evil and scandal. For all it needs to speed it on its way headlong is to reach a second ear; and seeing how few people there are that can be trusted, and the discomfort that discretion entails, this is likely to happen in the twinkling of an eye. The owner of the second ear finds it even harder to keep: he is more readily disposed to divulge it, more willing to be lavish with it, and finds it more excusable to speak of it and easier to refute the accusation he risks incurring. The same is true of the third by comparison with the second, of the fourth by comparison with the third, and so on. This happens even when the confidant has been sworn to secrecy and is an intelligent, level-headed, sensible and kindly person. It is all the worse if silence is not enjoined on him and he is a man given to peddling slanders and broadcasting other people's blemishes, always on the look-out for a piece of swindling or double-dealing, or in a position to use the betrayal of the secret for his own profit or the avoidance of loss. In this case it is the first holder of the secret who is to blame rather than his confidant; for it was his secret, and by removing its shackles, unfastening the bolt and opening the door for it he has allowed it to escape from custody. In this way he has made himself the slave of his confidant, and has put his neck beneath the latter's yoke. It is open to the confidant to be a good owner and look after the secret, at the same time keeping the imprudent one at his mercy as a hostage against the day when he himself is blamed. But good owners who control themselves and do not abuse their freedom are rare; and in any case they may divulge their secret simply out of stupidity or weakness, without meaning to betray it. Bad owners, on the other hand, break their pledge and disclose the secret, confiding it to people who will be even less disposed to keep it—thus giving rise to bloodshed, calamity, scandal and strife. But the most blameworthy is still the man who failed to keep the secret in the first place . . . Indeed, who could be more degraded, more ill-starred or more of a weakling than the man who, being free and his own master, voluntarily makes himself another man's slave, choosing servitude without having been captured or coerced? For slaves only tolerate their yoke because they have been weakened by being captured and reduced to slavery. This man, who has the secret safe in his heart but lets it go the moment he is asked about it, puts himself in the position of needing to go cap in hand to beg a favour from someone who has no duty to him, no thought of sparing him unpleasant consequences, and no incentive to help him out of trouble. The more widely he disseminates his secrets, the more masters he makes for himself and the more trouble he will have in serving them. Once the secret is known to many, or even to only a few, how hard it becomes to conceal! But the blame should not be laid at the door of the man who passes it on, for he did not start the dissemination of the secret, and it is not thanks to him that it has become known.

But even the most circumspect of men, who guards his tongue, fences in his secret and weighs his words, cannot—at any rate without a tremendous effort and constant vigilance—control his expression or the muscles of his face, or stop himself blushing or turning pale, or smiling or frowning, when the secret is alluded to in his presence or happens to cross his mind; nor can he prevent the play of his features betraying him when the subject of the secret, or something akin to it, is casually mentioned in conversation, or even when someone concerned in it enters the room. Since the secret can be deduced from these signs or others like them, guessed by shrewd people seeking to interpret words and gestures, or found out by scrutiny of the indirect causes of behaviour and actions—since it can spread in these ways better than on the tongues of chatterboxes, it is bound to be even worse when the tongue is completely at liberty to do as it wills with it and the mind is accustomed to spread it (for training is known to be reinforced by habit). Sometimes a secret may be penetrated by intuition or discovered by guesswork; in that case the mention of a part of it to the holder, giving him the impression that it is noised abroad and widely known, will be enough to hoodwink him and get him to confirm and corroborate the hypothesis, explain in detail what was previously only known in outline, and ruin and condemn himself out of his own mouth.

> The author refers to people who customarily give away secrets, and concludes that it is best to trust no one: for the conditions needed for perfect discretion are but rarely met with, and the qualities needed for it seldom found in one person.

5. THE APPEAL OF FORBIDDEN FRUIT

. . . These virtues exist in words but not in deeds. Only a fool would be taken in by a promise in this field without testing it against the known facts. We have found by experience that the majority of confidants disseminate and broadcast secrets entrusted to them more efficiently than a messenger charged to learn by heart a message he is to carry, and rewarded with thanks and a tip for so doing. So much so that the best way to disseminate a piece of news is often to entrust it to somebody well known for his fondness for slander, telling him to keep it secret; the news will at once stream from his mouth like a light in the darkness. That is how ʿUmar b. al-Khaṭṭāb[1] went about it when he wanted his conversion to Islam known: he inquired for the worst mischief-maker in Mecca, went to see the person in question, told him he had been converted, and begged him to keep the news secret. By nightfall there was no one in Mecca who did not know that ʿUmar had become a Muslim.

Another very good way of disseminating a secret is to make your confidant promise to keep it, at the same time warning him of the consequences of divulging it. The prohibition stimulates envy, for it imposes a restriction, and restrictions are hard to bear: they are heavy, whereas the mind is light and volatile, loves to unbosom itself, and burns with eagerness to confide in others. It is sufficient to say to someone: 'Do not rub your hands against this wall' for him to want to do so, though he never did it before. Conversely, if you pass a secret on to someone without telling him to keep it, it may not occur to him to divulge it; for a man naturally tends to covet that which is forbidden and to weary of that which he possesses. We should dearly like to know why it is that, for no apparent reason, he sets greater store by that which is forbidden, even if it is of no use to him, than by that which is permitted—unless it be that he grows weary of whatever he has in plenty and is attracted by whatever he lacks. We should also like to know why he pursues those that will have none of him and will have none of those that pursue him; why it is said: 'The more pressing the request the firmer the

1. The second caliph (ca. 586–644).

refusal'; why a man hankers after something, mentions it in his prayers, and yearns for it with all his might, and then has no sooner obtained it than it loses its lustre for him and he abandons it; and why kings are indifferent to their own wealth and covet other men's possessions. In our view God gave every individual a certain capacity, such that he cannot exceed it or encompass anything beyond it. Within this limit he is aware of want and of danger, beyond it he experiences the power of wealth and the certainty that he is secure from destitution. It is because of this feeling, and of avarice and greed which are akin to it, that a person despises those who have need of him and esteems those who can do without him. God created the soul to be inflamed by desire, greedy for novelty, easily wearied, tugged in different directions, volatile, constantly shattered and distressed but resilient and quickly comforted. Were the soul not made thus, there would be no more testing. It prizes whatever it lacks, either through necessity, as in the case of some foodstuff, or through perversity and capriciousness, as in the case of some covetous whim. Covetousness is of many kinds, and each has its devotees, who engage in nothing else. The soul esteems the unusual and rare, and enjoys the strange and fortuitous; but when the unusual is multiplied it becomes familiar, and when the coveted object becomes abundantly available, so as to exceed the soul's capacity and needs and become otiose and superfluous, the soul no longer esteems it, and disdains the abundance of it. For it prizes most highly whatever it feels most need of, even if to do without it is not really harmful, and most despises whatever it can do without, even if it is something important. When a man obtains what he covets and slakes his thirst for it, he forsakes and rejects the object of his desire: his love for it changes to hate and his covetousness to weariness. The reason for all this is that the world is the abode of the ephemeral and of weariness: by its nature neither it nor anything in it can endure unchanged. Continuance and durability belong only to the abode of stability.

After some thoughts about the capacity of the senses and the mishaps caused by excesses, the author reverts to the disclosure of secrets, and then goes on to

6. BACKBITING

. . . We have no reason to suppose that God allowed anyone to backbite Believers: on the contrary, He represented backbiting in the most hideous guise, such as to make death preferable to life, saying: 'Do not spy, and do not backbite each other. Would one of you like to eat his dead brother's flesh? You would abhor it!'[2] Throughout mankind backbiting is an attitude that betrays deep-seated unfairness, inherent baseness, meanness and deliberate wickedness based on envy and jealousy; it has taken hold of the world, governed men's instincts, and flourished on habitual misdeeds, the victory of evil over good, and the abounding seeds of discord, depravity and envy in men's hearts. No one is free of it. One man looks around him in justice and fairness, then espies things that displease him and shows his disapproval in looks and words. Another, actuated by hatred and hostility, often finds faults

2. Qur'an 49:12.

in his enemy that help him to invent others: he expands and enlarges the existing ones, and if the reality seems insufficient turns to fabrication, making the good points out as bad ones and the merely bad ones as atrocious. Any conversation of any importance revolves entirely around the subject of other people, and is nothing but gossip, tittle-tattle, drivel, ravings, backbiting, calumny and defamation of character.

. . . 'Do you know', asked Muʿāwiya,[3] 'who is the noble soul? He is the man you fear to his face and backbite behind his back.' By my life, such is the fate great men suffer among the common people, kings from their subjects and masters from their slaves. Any advantage the backbiter may gain over his victim by maligning him is always less than the reverential awe he shows to his face! If the backbiter only used backbiting in self-defence against those whose power he feared, it would be excusable; but his overweening baseness spurs him on to backbite not only his fellow-men and equals but his male or female slave. He will backbite So-and-so to his detested rival, making himself his accessory out of stupidity and his servant out of flabby weakness of character: yet he is under no compulsion to do this, and can expect neither reward nor thanks for his pains. Then he will go at once, the very same day, to the man he has just been maligning and tearing to shreds, and say similar or even worse things to him about the rival to whom he has maligned him—once again for no reason, and with no advantage or profit in view such as would easily outweigh the humiliation and degradation he feels in his heart of hearts. In the same way he gratuitously extols the rich, and despises the poor for no reason at all. When such a man is unmasked or accused, he suffers yet another humiliation as he chokes over lying excuses and is driven to take refuge in false oaths. Anyone who behaves in this way deserves to be unmasked, and then for people to accept no excuse from him and trust neither his word nor his oath; for he has taken vileness as his garment, and obsequiousness covers him from head to foot.

Some thoughts on the subject of excuses are followed by maxims about idle chatter, and then by a disquisition on

7. THE HARM DONE BY WORDS

. . . This is a subject that we would have dealt with fully, were it not for our reluctance to involve the reader in a subject extraneous to our main theme and purpose. It is a huge topic, and material for it abounds; but a single sentence will suffice, for the difference lies only in the words that clothe the ideas. Observe each of the ills of this world, and you will see that they stem from a word that gained ground, starting strife as endless as the feud of the Bakr and the Taghlib[4] . . . Study the traditions about the ancients, and you will lose count of those that were killed by their tongues and died because of a word they let fall. The surprising thing is not that we entrust our secrets to persons unworthy of them, picked out from old acquaintances above suspicion; the surprising, the really astonishing thing is for a man to entrust a secret to someone he barely knows, someone he has taken up with after one

3. The first caliph of the Umayyad dynasty (ca. 602–680).
4. Two Arabian tribes; according to legend, their long war began when a member of the Bakr tribe murdered the chief of the Taghlib tribe in retaliation for the Taghlib's intentional killing of the Bakr's camel, which was grazing on his land.

or two meetings without finding out who or what he is, where he comes from or who his family are, thus allowing himself to be duped from the outset and cheated intellectually before being cheated materially or spiritually; the result is disaster aggravated by lifelong remorse.

The book ends with a postcript about its usefulness.

IBN HAZM
994–1064

Abu Muhammad ʿAli Ibn Hazm, an Andalusian scholar of legal theory, law, and theology, is most famous for his comprehensive treatise on love, *The Ring of the Dove.*

Born in Cordoba, Spain, Ibn Hazm spent his first fifteen years in peace and security in the household of his father, Ahmad, who had attained a high-ranking position in the administration of the Spanish Umayyad caliph, Hisham II (r. 976–1009, 1010–13). In 1009, however, political intrigues led to the caliph's abdication, followed by warfare among claimants to the caliphate. The fortunes of Ibn Hazm's family declined with Hisham II's abdication. Some of the family's wealth was seized, and his father, who was imprisoned for a time, died only three years after the abdication. In 1013 the family's house was destroyed during the siege of Cordoba, and Ibn Hazm left for the city of Almeria in southern Spain. Ibn Hazm continued to align himself with Umayyad claimants to the caliphate, an allegiance that was not without consequences: in 1016 he was imprisoned for a few months. In 1018 he became a minister in the administration of ʿAbd al-Rahman IV (r. 1018), an Umayyad claimant, and fought in his army. But ʿAbd al-Rahman IV was betrayed by his own troops and assassinated; Ibn Hazm was captured by opposing forces and later released.

For a time, Ibn Hazm retired from politics and lived in Jativa, a city in eastern Spain. But the lure of power remained strong, and he became a minister for another Umayyad caliphal claimant, ʿAbd al-Rahman V (r. 1023). ʿAbd al-Rahman V lasted forty-seven days before being assassinated; Ibn Hazm was once again held prisoner, and then returned to Jativa. Whether this was Ibn Hazm's last foray into politics remains unclear. Some sources indicate that he served as a minister for the last Umayyad caliph of Spain, Hisham III (r. 1027–31), whose forcible removal constituted the end of the Umayyad caliphate.

By 1031, in his late thirties, Ibn Hazm had unquestionably retired from politics and embarked on a second career as a scholar. He is most closely associated with a legal school known as Zahiri, whose adherents believed that the general, apparent (in Arabic, *zahir*) meaning of qur'anic texts and prophetic traditions must be given primacy. A particular verse or tradition could be read in a restricted or nonliteral manner if compelling evidence was presented to support doing so.

Yet it would be a disservice to call Ibn Hazm a simple "literalist"; his writings consistently reveal a man who had thought deeply about problems of language, meaning, and textual interpretation. Ibn Hazm, who had been educated in the Maliki and Shafiʿi legal schools, also argued against using analogical reasoning (in Arabic, *qiyas*) and the consensus of the Muslim community (*ijmaʿ*) as sources for law. He believed that only the consensus of the Companions of the Prophet—those believers who personally knew Muhammad—had any legal weight. Western scholars view Ibn Hazm as the first Zahiri scholar to apply the school's linguistic reasoning to theological questions, thereby creating for it a more consistent and coherent theology. Finally, historical sources portray Ibn Hazm as a relentlessly outspoken man, a trait that did not endear him to those in positions of authority—especially members of the dominant Maliki school. His intransigence did not go unnoticed, and at times his books were burned and students forbidden to study with him.

Ibn Hazm's *The Ring of the Dove*, which is excerpted below, treats love comprehensively, analyzing its signs, causes, and results. It is quite unlike the rest of Ibn Hazm's oeuvre, and Ibn Hazm himself realized that some might find it shocking. In his introduction he declares that his intentions in pursuing the topic of love are irreproachable and provides qur'anic verses and prophetic traditions to defend himself and his choice of subject matter. Ibn Hazm likely started the work early in his scholarly career—either between the rule of ʿAbd al-Rahman IV and that of ʿAbd al-Rahman V or after Hisham III was deposed in 1031.

The Ring fits into a larger genre of Arabic literature that deals with love, usually by drawing on a common stock of earlier Arabic tales and poems to illustrate particular points. But Ibn Hazm's approach is unique, as he uses anecdotes collected from his acquaintances in Andalusia and poems of his own composition. These features make *The Ring* valuable as a work of social history that provides a window into the Andalusian culture of Ibn Hazm's time.

The thirty chapters of *The Ring* break down as follows. In the first chapter Ibn Hazm sketches his plan for the work. After chapter 2, examining the signs of love, he analyzes how individuals fall in love (3–7) and communicate their love (9–11). Next, Ibn Hazm discusses actions and outside actors who may help or hinder a blossoming love (12–19). Chapter 20, the high point of the work, presents the union, or meeting, between lovers; chapter 21 recounts their breaking off, or separation. Chapter 22 explores fidelity, while the following chapters (23–28) speak of the myriad ways a love can end. The last two chapters of *The Ring*, titled "The Vileness of Sinning" and "The Virtue of Chastity," constitute one-fifth of the work and examine legal and moral questions surrounding human love.

The passage below is taken from the beginning of the second chapter of *The Ring*. In it Ibn Hazm's considerable powers of observation and sensitivity to detail—which served him well as a scholar—are turned to the signs that indicate love.

FROM THE RING OF THE DOVE

From *The Signs of Love*

Love has certain signs which the intelligent man quickly detects, and the shrewd man readily recognizes. Of these the first is the brooding gaze: the eye is the wide gateway of the soul, the scrutinizer of its secrets, conveying its most private thoughts, and giving expression to its deepest-hid feelings. You will see the lover gazing at the beloved unblinkingly; his eyes follow the loved one's every movement, withdrawing as he[1] withdraws, inclining as he inclines, just as the chameleon's stare shifts with the shifting of the sun. I have written a poem on this topic, from which the following may be quoted.

My eye no other place of rest
  Discovers, save with thee;

TRANSLATED BY A. J. Arberry.

1. As is typical in Arabic poetry, Ibn Hazm sometimes leaves the gender of his pronouns ambiguous. Some translators have substituted feminine pronouns, but Arberry has chosen not to do so.

Men say the lodestone is possessed
  Of a like property.

To right or left it doth pursue
  Thy movements, up or down,
As adjectives in grammar do
  Accord them with their noun.

The lover will direct his conversation to the beloved, even when he purports however earnestly to address another: the affectation is apparent to anyone with eyes to see. When the loved one speaks, the lover listens with rapt attention to his every word; he marvels at everything the beloved says, however extraordinary and absurd his observations may be; he believes him implicitly even when he is clearly lying, agrees with him though he is obviously in the wrong, testifies on his behalf for all that he may be unjust, follows after him however he may proceed and whatever line of argument he may adopt. The lover hurries to the spot where the beloved is at the moment, endeavours to sit as near to him as possible, sidles up close to him, lays aside all occupations that might oblige him to leave his company, makes light of any matter however weighty that would demand his parting from him, is very slow to move when he takes his leave of him. I have put this somewhere into verse.

No captive for the gallows bound
  With more reluctance quits his cell
Than I thy presence, in profound
  Regret to say farewell.

But when, my darling, comes the time
  That we may be together, I
Run swiftly as the moon doth climb
  The ramparts of the sky.

At last, alas! that sweet delight
  Must end anew; I, lingering yet,
Turn slowly, as from heaven's height
  The fixed stars creep to set.

Other signs of love are that sudden confusion and excitement betrayed by the lover when he unexpectedly sees the one he loves coming upon him unawares, that agitation which overmasters him on beholding someone who resembles his beloved or on hearing his name suddenly pronounced. This I have put into verse, as the following extract indicates.

Whene'er my ranging eyes descry
  A person clad in red,
My heart is split with agony
  And sore discomforted.

His roguish glance, as I conclude,
  Has shed such human blood
That now his garments are imbrued
  All saffron from the flood.

A man in love will give prodigally to the limit of his capacity, in a way that formerly he would have refused; as if he were the one receiving the donation, he the one whose happiness is the object in view; all this in order that he may show off his good points, and make himself desirable. How often has the miser opened his purse-strings, the scowler relaxed his frown, the coward leapt heroically into the fray, the clod suddenly become sharp-witted, the boor turned into the perfect gentleman, the stinker transformed himself into the elegant dandy, the sloucher smartened up, the decrepit recaptured his lost youth, the godly gone wild, the self-respecting kicked over the traces—and all because of love!

All these signs are to be observed even before the fire of Love is properly kindled, ere its conflagration truly bursts forth, its blaze waxes fierce, its flames leap up. But when the fire really takes a hold and is firmly established, then you will see the secret whispering, the unconcealed turning away from all present but the beloved. I have some verses in which I have contrived to bring together many of these signs, and will now quote from these.

I love to hear when men converse
And in the midst his name rehearse;
The air I breathe seems redolent
That moment with the amber's scent.
But when he speaketh, I give ear
Unto no other sitting near,
But lean to catch delightedly
His pretty talk and coquetry,
Nor yet, though my companion there
The Prince of All the Faithful[2] were,
Permit my mind to be removed
On his account from my beloved.
And if, through dire compulsion, I
Stand up at last to say good-bye,
Still glancing fondly at my sweet
I stumble, as on wounded feet;
My eyes upon his features play
The while my body drifts away,
As one the billows tumble o'er
Yet gazes, drowning, on the shore.
When I recall how distant he
Now is, I choke in sorrow's sea,
Weary as one who sinks, to expire
In some deep bog, or raging fire.
Yet, if thou sayest, "Canst thou still
Aspire to heaven?" "That I will",
I answer boldly, "and I know
The stairs that to its summit go!"

Other outward signs and tokens of love are the following, which are apparent to all having eyes in their heads: abundant and exceeding cheerfulness at finding oneself with the beloved in a narrow space, and a corresponding depression on being together in a wide expanse; to engage in a playful tug-

2. A title commonly applied to the caliph.

of-war for anything the one or the other lays hold of; much clandestine winking; leaning sideways and supporting oneself against the object of one's affection; endeavouring to touch his hand, and whatever other part of his body one can reach, while engaged in conversation; and drinking the remainder of what the beloved has left in his cup, seeking out the very spot against which his lips were pressed.

There are also contrary signs, that occur according to casual provocations and accidental incitements, and a variety of motivating causes and stimulating thoughts. Opposites are of course likes, in reality; when things reach the limit of contrariety, and stand at the furthest bounds of divergency, they come to resemble one another. This is decreed by God's omnipotent power, in a manner that baffles entirely the human imagination. Thus, when ice is pressed a long time in the hand, it finally produces the same effect as fire. We find that extreme joy and extreme sorrow kill equally; excessive and violent laughter sends the tears coursing from the eyes. It is a very common phenomenon in the world about us. Similarly with lovers: when they love each other with an equal ardour, and their mutual affection is intensely strong, they will turn against one another without any valid reason, each purposely contradicting the other in whatever he may say; they quarrel violently over the smallest things, each picking up every word that the other lets fall and wilfully misinterpreting it. All these devices are aimed at testing and proving what each is seeking in the other.

Now the difference between this sham, and real aversion and contrariness born of deep-seated hatred and inveterate contention, is that lovers are very quickly reconciled after their disputes. You will see a pair of lovers seeming to have reached the extreme limit of contrariety, to the point that you would reckon not to be mended even in the instance of a person of most tranquil spirit, wholly exempt from rancour, save after a long interval, and wholly irreparable in the case of a quarrelsome man; yet in next to no time you will observe them to have become the best of friends once more; silenced are those mutual reproaches, vanished that disharmony; forthwith they are laughing again and playfully sporting together. The same scene may be enacted several times at a single session. When you see a pair of lovers behaving in such a fashion, let no doubt enter your mind, no uncertainty invade your thoughts; you may be sure without hesitation, and convinced as by an unshakable certainty, that there lies between them a deep and hidden secret—the secret of true love. Take this then for a sure test, a universally valid experiment: it is the product only of an equal partnership in love, and a true concord of hearts. I myself have observed it frequently.

Another sign is when you find the lover almost entreating to hear the loved one's name pronounced, taking an extreme delight in speaking about him, so that the subject is a positive obsession with him; nothing so much rejoices him, and he is not in the least restrained by the fear that someone listening may realise what he is about, and someone present will understand his true motives. Love for a thing renders you blind and deaf. If the lover could so contrive, that in the place where he happens to be there should be no talk of anything but his beloved, he would never leave that spot for any other in the whole world.

It can happen that a man sincerely affected by love will start to eat his meal with an excellent appetite; yet the instant the recollection of his loved one is excited, the food sticks in his throat and chokes his gullet. It is the same if he is drinking, or talking—he begins to converse with you gaily enough, then all at once he is invaded by a chance thought of his dear one. You will notice the change in his manner of speaking, the instantaneous failure of his conversational powers; the sure signs are his long silences, the way he stares at the ground, his extreme taciturnity. One moment he is all smiles, lightly gesticulating; the next, and he has become completely boxed up, sluggish, distrait, rigid, too weary to utter a single word, irritated by the most innocent question.

* * *

THE THOUSAND AND ONE NIGHTS
fourteenth century

The Thousand and One Nights, often called the *Arabian Nights,* is a collection of entertaining tales of mostly Indian, Persian, and Arab provenance. Their worldwide fame began with an eighteenth-century translation into French, which brought them to the notice of European readers and spurred translation into other languages. This interest, in turn, drew renewed attention from Arab readers and scholars.

The Nights is a composite work whose origin is murky. Its earliest physical evidence is a ninth-century Arabic manuscript fragment that records a portion of one of its tales. In addition, tenth-century Arabic historical sources, such as *The Catalogue* of Ibn al-Nadim (d. ca. 990; see above), note the existence of a Persian work titled *A Thousand Tales* that was translated into Arabic as *A Thousand Nights.* Modern historians believe that this Arabic work was subsequently expanded by Arab authors until, around the latter half of the thirteenth century, the 200 to 282 tales that form the core of what we now know as *The Thousand and One Nights* coalesced.

From 1704 to 1712, a French translation of the *Nights* was published in twelve volumes. The first seven volumes were translated from a medieval manuscript of the *Nights*, but popular demand prompted the translator and publisher to publish other tales "from the East" in subsequent volumes, further confusing the work's textual history. This immediate success had many causes, not least being the Western belief that these tales accurately portrayed life in the East. Its popularity encouraged scholarly study of the *Nights*, and led to several critical editions of the work. The translation below is based on an edition produced from a fourteenth-century Syrian manuscript.

All the stories in *The Thousand and One Nights* are told within a larger frame tale of a king named Shahrayar, who killed his wife after discovering her unfaithfulness. He then proceeded to marry a new wife each day, killing her the next. After three years of such murders, he married a woman named Shahrazad, the daughter of one of his ministers, who had devised a scheme that she believed would stop him. Each night she wove him a wonderful tale that she left incomplete, always assuring him that she would finish it the next night. The king would spare her life so that he could hear the rest of her story. The following night she would either continue the story or complete it—and immediately start on another. She continued in this manner for a thousand and one nights until she had no more tales to tell him. By that time, the king's anger over his first wife's adultery had subsided, and he had fallen in love with Shahrazad.

Presented below are the first four tales spun by Shahrazad to save her life and spark the king's affection.

PRONOUNCING GLOSSARY

Dinarzad: *dee-nar-zad´*
Shahrayar: *shah-ra-yar´*
Shahrazad: *shah-ra-zad´*

[*The Story of the Merchant and the Demon*]

THE FIRST NIGHT

It is said, O wise and happy King, that once there was a prosperous merchant who had abundant wealth and investments and commitments in every country. He had many women and children and kept many servants and slaves. One day, having resolved to visit another country, he took provisions, filling his saddlebag with loaves of bread and with dates, mounted his horse, and set out on his journey. For many days and nights, he journeyed under God's care until he reached his destination. When he finished his business, he turned back to his home and family. He journeyed for three days, and on the fourth day, chancing to come to an orchard, went in to avoid the heat and shade himself from the sun of the open country. He came to a spring under a walnut tree and, tying his horse, sat by the spring, pulled out from the saddlebag some loaves of bread and a handful of dates, and began to eat, throwing the date pits right and left until he had had enough. Then he got up, performed his ablutions, and performed his prayers.

But hardly had he finished when he saw an old demon, with sword in hand, standing with his feet on the ground and his head in the clouds. The demon approached until he stood before him and screamed, saying, "Get up, so that I may kill you with this sword, just as you have killed my son." When the merchant saw and heard the demon, he was terrified and awestricken. He asked, "Master, for what crime do you wish to kill me?" The demon replied, "I wish to kill you because you have killed my son." The merchant asked, "Who has killed your son?" The demon replied, "You have killed my son." The merchant said, "By God, I did not kill your son. When and how could that have been?" The demon said, "Didn't you sit down, take out some dates from your saddlebag, and eat, throwing the pits right and left?" The merchant replied, "Yes, I did." The demon said, "You killed my son, for as you were throwing the stones right and left, my son happened to be walking by and was struck and killed by one of them, and I must now kill you." The merchant said, "O my lord, please don't kill me." The demon replied, "I must kill you as you killed him—blood for blood." The merchant said, "To God we belong and to God we return. There is no power or strength, save in God the Almighty, the Magnificent. If I killed him, I did it by mistake. Please forgive me." The demon replied, "By God, I must kill you, as you killed my son." Then he seized him and, throwing him to the ground, raised the sword to

TRANSLATED BY Husain Haddawy; based on the text of the fourteenth-century Syrian manuscript edited by Muhsin Mahdi.

The Merchant and the Genie. This image of the vengeful genie whose story is included in this volume was drawn by T. Morten for *Dalziel's Illustrated Arabian Nights' Entertainments*, a mid-19th-century edition of a work that had captured European and American imaginations for more than a hundred years.

strike him. The merchant began to weep and mourn his family and his wife and children. Again, the demon raised his sword to strike, while the merchant cried until he was drenched with tears, saying, "There is no power or strength, save in God the Almighty, the Magnificent." Then he began to recite the following verses:

> Life has two days: one peace, one wariness,
> And has two sides: worry and happiness.

Ask him who taunts us with adversity,
"Does fate, save those worthy of note, oppress?
Don't you see that the blowing, raging storms
Only the tallest of the trees beset,
And of earth's many green and barren lots,
Only the ones with fruits with stones are hit,
And of the countless stars in heaven's vault
None is eclipsed except the moon and sun?
You thought well of the days, when they were good,
Oblivious to the ills destined for one.
You were deluded by the peaceful nights,
Yet in the peace of night does sorrow stun."

When the merchant finished and stopped weeping, the demon said, "By God, I must kill you, as you killed my son, even if you weep blood." The merchant asked, "Must you?" The demon replied, "I must," and raised his sword to strike.

But morning overtook Shahrazad, and she lapsed into silence, leaving King Shahrayar burning with curiosity to hear the rest of the story. Then Dinarzad said to her sister Shahrazad, "What a strange and lovely story!" Shahrazad replied, "What is this compared with what I shall tell you tomorrow night if the king spares me and lets me live? It will be even better and more entertaining." The king thought to himself, "I will spare her until I hear the rest of the story; then I will have her put to death the next day." When morning broke, the day dawned, and the sun rose; the king left to attend to the affairs of the kingdom, and the vizier, Shahrazad's father, was amazed and delighted. King Shahrayar governed all day and returned home at night to his quarters and got into bed with Shahrazad. Then Dinarzad said to her sister Shahrazad, "Please, sister, if you are not sleepy, tell us one of your lovely little tales to while away the night." The king added, "Let it be the conclusion of the story of the demon and the merchant, for I would like to hear it." Shahrazad replied, "With the greatest pleasure, dear, happy King":

THE SECOND NIGHT

It is related, O wise and happy King, that when the demon raised his sword, the merchant asked the demon again, "Must you kill me?" and the demon replied, "Yes." Then the merchant said, "Please give me time to say good-bye to my family and my wife and children, divide my property among them, and appoint guardians. Then I shall come back, so that you may kill me." The demon replied, "I am afraid that if I release you and grant you time, you will go and do what you wish, but will not come back." The merchant said, "I swear to keep my pledge to come back, as the God of Heaven and earth is my witness." The demon asked, "How much time do you need?" The merchant replied, "One year, so that I may see enough of my children, bid my wife good-bye, discharge my obligations to people, and come back on New Year's Day." The demon asked, "Do you swear to God that if I let you go, you will come back on New Year's Day?" The merchant replied, "Yes, I swear to God."

After the merchant swore, the demon released him, and he mounted his horse sadly and went on his way. He journeyed until he reached his home and came to his wife and children. When he saw them, he wept bitterly, and when his family saw his sorrow and grief, they began to reproach him for his behavior, and his wife said, "Husband, what is the matter with you? Why do you mourn, when we are happy, celebrating your return?" He replied, "Why not mourn when I have only one year to live?" Then he told her of his encounter with the demon and informed her that he had sworn to return on New Year's Day, so that the demon might kill him.

When they heard what he said, everyone began to cry. His wife struck her face in lamentation and cut her hair, his daughters wailed, and his little children cried. It was a day of mourning, as all the children gathered around their father to weep and exchange good-byes. The next day he wrote his will, dividing his property, discharged his obligations to people, left bequests and gifts, distributed alms, and engaged reciters to read portions of the Quran in his house. Then he summoned legal witnesses and in their presence freed his slaves and slave-girls, divided among his elder children their shares of the property, appointed guardians for his little ones, and gave his wife her share, according to her marriage contract. He spent the rest of the time with his family, and when the year came to an end, save for the time needed for the journey, he performed his ablutions, performed his prayers, and, carrying his burial shroud, began to bid his family good-bye. His sons hung around his neck, his daughters wept, and his wife wailed. Their mourning scared him, and he began to weep, as he embraced and kissed his children good-bye. He said to them, "Children, this is God's will and decree, for man was created to die." Then he turned away and, mounting his horse, journeyed day and night until he reached the orchard on New Year's Day.

He sat at the place where he had eaten the dates, waiting for the demon, with a heavy heart and tearful eyes. As he waited, an old man, leading a deer on a leash, approached and greeted him, and he returned the greeting. The old man inquired, "Friend, why do you sit here in this place of demons and devils? For in this haunted orchard none come to good." The merchant replied by telling him what had happened to him and the demon, from beginning to end. The old man was amazed at the merchant's fidelity and said, "Yours is a magnificent pledge," adding, "By God, I shall not leave until I see what will happen to you with the demon." Then he sat down beside him and chatted with him. As they talked . . .

But morning overtook Shahrazad, and she lapsed into silence. As the day dawned, and it was light, her sister Dinarzad said, "What a strange and wonderful story!" Shahrazad replied, "Tomorrow night I shall tell something even stranger and more wonderful than this."

THE THIRD NIGHT

When it was night and Shahrazad was in bed with the king, Dinarzad said to her sister Shahrazad, "Please, if you are not sleepy, tell us one of your lovely little tales to while away the night." The king added, "Let it be the conclusion of the merchant's story." Shahrazad replied, "As you wish":

I heard, O happy King, that as the merchant and the man with the deer sat talking, another old man approached, with two black hounds, and when he reached them, he greeted them, and they returned his greeting. Then he asked them about themselves, and the man with the deer told him the story of the merchant and the demon, how the merchant had sworn to return on

New Year's Day, and how the demon was waiting to kill him. He added that when he himself heard the story, he swore never to leave until he saw what would happen between the merchant and the demon. When the man with the two dogs heard the story, he was amazed, and he too swore never to leave them until he saw what would happen between them. Then he questioned the merchant, and the merchant repeated to him what had happened to him with the demon.

While they were engaged in conversation, a third old man approached and greeted them, and they returned his greeting. He asked, "Why do I see the two of you sitting here, with this merchant between you, looking abject, sad, and dejected?" They told him the merchant's story and explained that they were sitting and waiting to see what would happen to him with the demon. When he heard the story, he sat down with them, saying, "By God, I too like you will not leave, until I see what happens to this man with the demon." As they sat, conversing with one another, they suddenly saw the dust rising from the open country, and when it cleared, they saw the demon approaching, with a drawn steel sword in his hand. He stood before them without greeting them, yanked the merchant with his left hand, and, holding him fast before him, said, "Get ready to die." The merchant and the three old men began to weep and wail.

But dawn broke and morning overtook Shahrazad, and she lapsed into silence. Then Dinarzad said, "Sister, what a lovely story!" Shahrazad replied, "What is this compared with what I shall tell you tomorrow night? It will be even better; it will be more wonderful, delightful, entertaining, and delectable if the king spares me and lets me live." The king was all curiosity to hear the rest of the story and said to himself, "By God, I will not have her put to death until I hear the rest of the story and find out what happened to the merchant with the demon. Then I will have her put to death the next morning, as I did with the others." Then he went out to attend to the affairs of his kingdom, and when he saw Shahrazad's father, he treated him kindly and showed him favors, and the vizier was amazed. When night came, the king went home, and when he was in bed with Shahrazad, Dinarzad said, "Sister, if you are not sleepy, tell us one of your lovely little tales to while away the night." Shahrazad replied, "With the greatest pleasure":

THE FOURTH NIGHT

It is related, O happy King, that the first old man with the deer approached the demon and, kissing his hands and feet, said, "Fiend and King of the demon kings, if I tell you what happened to me and that deer, and you find it strange and amazing, indeed stranger and more amazing than what happened to you and the merchant, will you grant me a third of your claim on him for his crime and guilt?" The demon replied, "I will." The old man said:

[From *The First Old Man's Tale*]

Demon, this deer is my cousin, my flesh and blood. I married her when I was very young, and she a girl of twelve, who reached womanhood only afterward. For thirty years we lived together, but I was not blessed with children, for she bore neither boy nor girl. Yet I continued to be kind to her, to care for her, and to treat her generously. Then I took a mistress, and she bore me a son, who grew up to look like a slice of the moon.[1] Meanwhile, my wife grew jealous of my mistress and my son. One day, when he was ten, I had to go on a journey. I entrusted my wife, this one here, with my mistress and son, bade her take good care of them, and was gone for a whole year. In my absence my wife, this cousin of mine, learned soothsaying and magic and cast a spell on my son and turned him into a young bull. Then she summoned my shepherd, gave my son to him, and said, "Tend this bull with the rest of the cattle." The shepherd took him and tended him for a while. Then she cast a spell on the mother, turning her into a cow, and gave her also to the shepherd.

When I came back, after all this was done, and inquired about my mistress and my son, she answered, "Your mistress died, and your son ran away two months ago, and I have had no news from him ever since." When I heard her, I grieved for my mistress, and with an anguished heart I mourned for my son for nearly a year. When the Great Feast of the Immolation[2] drew near, I summoned the shepherd and ordered him to bring me a fat cow for the sacrifice. The cow he brought me was in reality my enchanted mistress. When I bound her and pressed against her to cut her throat, she wept and cried, as if saying, "My son, my son," and her tears coursed down her cheeks. Astonished and seized with pity, I turned away and asked the shepherd to bring me a different cow. But my wife shouted, "Go on. Butcher her, for he has none better or fatter. Let us enjoy her meat at feast time." I approached the cow to cut her throat, and again she cried, as if saying, "My son, my son." Then I turned away from her and said to the shepherd, "Butcher her for me." The shepherd butchered her, and when he skinned her, he found neither meat nor fat but only skin and bone. I regretted having her butchered and said to the shepherd, "Take her all for yourself, or give her as alms to whomever you wish, and find me a fat young bull from among the flock." The shepherd took her away and disappeared, and I never knew what he did with her.

Then he brought me my son, my heartblood, in the guise of a fat young bull. When my son saw me, he shook his head loose from the rope, ran toward me, and, throwing himself at my feet, kept rubbing his head against me. I was astonished and touched with sympathy, pity, and mercy, for the blood hearkened to the blood and the divine bond, and my heart throbbed within me when I saw the tears coursing over the cheeks of my son the young bull, as he dug the earth with his hoofs. I turned away and said to the shepherd, "Let him go with the rest of the flock, and be kind to him, for I have decided to spare him. Bring me another one instead of him." My wife, this very deer, shouted, "You shall sacrifice none but this bull." I got angry and replied, "I listened to you and butchered the cow uselessly. I will not listen to you and kill this bull, for I have decided to spare him." But she pressed me, saying, "You must butcher this bull," and I bound him and took the knife . . .

1. That is, he was beautiful.
2. Or Feast of Sacrifice ('Id al-Adha), which marks the end of the pilgrimage to Mecca and commemorates the willingness of Ibrahim (Abraham) to sacrifice his son at God's command; to celebrate it, sheep and cattle are slaughtered and offered to God.

But dawn broke, and morning overtook Shahrazad, and she lapsed into silence, leaving the king all curiosity for the rest of the story. Then her sister Dinarzad said, "What an entertaining story!" Shahrazad replied, "Tomorrow night I shall tell you something even stranger, more wonderful, and more entertaining if the king spares me and lets me live."

* * *

DARA SHUKOH
1615–1659

A Mughal prince and Sufi executed on charges of heresy, Dara Shukoh (or Shikoh or Shikuh) believed that Islam and Hinduism shared the same core beliefs and differed only in their expression of them.

Shukoh was the oldest of the four sons of Shah Jahan (1592–1666; r. 1628–57), the Mughal ruler who commissioned the construction of the Taj Mahal, and was groomed by his father to succeed him. When Shah Jahan fell ill in 1657, Shukoh's brothers immediately began a battle for the throne. Shukoh's forces suffered debilitating defeats, and his brother Awrangzib (r. 1658–1707) emerged as the next Mughal ruler. Awrangzib imprisoned his father, who had recovered from his illness and still supported Shukoh; Shah Jahan spent the next eight years until his death under house arrest in the palatial Agra Fort, cared for by his oldest daughter. Soon after assuming power, Awrangzib ordered Shukoh to be tried on charges of heresy. Unsurprisingly, Shukoh was found guilty; he was executed in Delhi in September 1659.

Shukoh was to gain lasting renown not for his military prowess but for his writings. A member of the Qadiri Sufi order, he was also quite close to leading Hindu mystics of his time. Shukoh's earliest works explored Sufism, and his later ones studied the relationship between Islam and Hinduism.

Ship of the Saints (1640), which borrows from earlier Sufi biographical writings, contains short reports on famous Sufis and other luminaries from Islamic history. The work starts with Muhammad and the first four caliphs, and includes notices for the founders of the Sunni legal schools and the Shiʿi imams. It also describes various Sufi orders, and in the final chapter examines prominent Sufi women. Another of Shukoh's biographical works, *Tranquility of the Saints* (1643), documents the history of his Sufi order, the Qadiris, and argues for its superiority while also presenting other Sufis of his era. Shukoh attributes *Compass of Truth* (1647), his introductory work on Sufism, to divine inspiration. In this presentation of basic Sufi doctrines and practices for spiritual aspirants, he describes the stages through which a Sufi goes on the path to union with God and expounds his belief that everything in creation is a manifestation of God. Fascinatingly, Shukoh also draws a number of correspondences between Islamic beliefs and Hindu ones. For example, he connects the four levels of existence embraced by many Sufis—that is, the world of matter, the world of angels and spirits, the world of divine attributes, and the world of the divine essence—with the multilevel reality described in the Upanishads.

His works on Islam and Hinduism promote the idea that the two religions share essential beliefs, with citations from the sacred texts of both religions to support this claim. *Confluence of the Two Oceans* (1655), arguably Shukoh's most significant work in this area, offers a comparative analysis of terms from Sufi and Vedantic literature, drawing multiple connections. It equates Allah with Om, the most sacred syllable in

Hinduism, and Adam, viewed by Muslims as the first man and prophet, with Brahma, the Hindu god of creation. Moreover, it finds analogues for the angels Jibril, Mikaʾil, and Israfil in the Hindu deities Brahma, Vishnu, and Shiva.

Shukoh's *The Greatest Secret* (1657) renders fifty-two Upanishads into Persian. This highly accessible translation, which he completed with the help of Hindu scholars and holy men, was aimed at the average literate Muslim in the Indian subcontinent who had no background in Hindu thought. The excerpt below explains his motives for translating the work. Referring to himself in the third person, he observes that the Upanishads are "a treasure of monotheism" and laments that "there are few thoroughly conversant with it even among the [Hindus]." He promises that one who truly studies his translation "shall become imperishable, fearless, unsolicitous, and eternally liberated."

Shukoh's conviction of the underlying harmony between Islam and Hinduism, his desire to inspire mutual understanding among members of both faiths, and his wish to see a country that did not privilege one religion above the other prompted this translation and several others that he commissioned. The endurance of these works, despite his execution for apostasy, is a testament to his efforts and vision.

PRONOUNCING GLOSSARY

Atharva Veda: *a-tar´-vuh vay´-duh*
bismallāh: *bis-mil-la´*
Dārā Shikōh: *dah-rah´ shi-koh´*
hijra: *hij´-ruh*
Kashmir: *kash-meer´*
Mullā Shāh: *mul´-luh shah*
pandit: *pan´-dit*
Rig Veda: *rig vay´-duh*
Sama Veda: *sah´-muh vay´-duh*
sannyasi: *san-ya´-see*
Yajur Veda: *ya´-jur vay´-duh*

FROM THE GREATEST SECRET

Praised be the Being, that one among whose eternal secrets is the dot in the [letter] ب of the bismallāh[1] in all the heavenly books, and glorified be the mother of books. In the holy Qurʾān is the token of His glorious name; and the angels and the heavenly books and the prophets and the saints are all comprehended in this name. And be the blessings of the Almighty upon the best of His creatures, Muhammad, and upon all his children and upon his companions universally!

To proceed; whereas this unsolicitous faqīr [a religious mendicant], Muhammad Dārā Shikōh in the year 1050 after Hijra [A.D. 1640] went to Kashmir, the resemblance of paradise, and by the grace of God and the favor of the Infinite, he there obtained the auspicious opportunity of meeting the most perfect of the perfects, the flower of the gnostics, the tutor of the tutors, the sage of the sages, the guide of the guides, the unitarian accomplished in the Truth, Mullā Shāh,[2] on whom be the peace of God.

And whereas, he was impressed with a longing to behold the gnostics of every sect, and to hear the lofty expressions of monotheism, and had cast his

TRANSLATED BY Bikrania Jit Hasrat.

1. Literally, "in the name of Allah": the name of the Arabic phrase that begins all but one sura of the Qurʾan, "In the name of God, the beneficent, the merciful."
2. Shah Muhammad b. ʿAbd Ahmad (d. 1661), a Sufi guide.

eyes upon many books of mysticism and had written a number of treatises thereon, and as the thirst of investigation for unity, which is a boundless ocean, became every moment increased, subtle doubts came into his mind for which he had no possibility of solution, except by the word of the Lord and the direction of the Infinite. And whereas the holy Qurʾān is mostly allegorical, and at the present day, persons thoroughly conversant with the subtleties thereof are very rare, he became desirous of bringing in view all the heavenly books, for the very words of God themselves are their own commentary; and what might be in one book compendious, in another might be found diffusive, and from the detail of one the conciseness of the other might become comprehensible. He had, therefore, cast his eyes on the Book of Moses,[3] the Gospels, the Psalms, and other scriptures, but the explanation of monotheism in them also was compendious and enigmatical, and from the slovenly translations that selfish persons had made, their purport was not intelligible.

Thereafter he considered, as to why the discussion about monotheism is so conspicuous in India, and why the Indian theologians and mystics of the ancient school do not disavow the Unity of God nor do they find any fault with the unitarians, but their belief is perfect in this respect; on the other hand, the ignoramuses of the present age—the highwaymen in the path of God—who have established themselves for erudites and who, falling into the traces of polemics and molestation, and apostatizing through disavowal of the true proficients in God and monotheism, display resistance against all the words of unitarianism, which are most evident from the glorious Qurʾān and the authentic traditions of indubitable prophecy.

And after verifications of these circumstances, it appeared that among this most ancient people, of all their heavenly books, which are the *Rig Veda*, the *Yajur Veda*, the *Sama Veda*, and the *Atharva Veda*,[4] together with a number of ordinances, descended upon the prophets of those times, the most ancient of whom was Brahman or Adam, on whom be the peace of God, this purport is manifest from these books. And it can also be ascertained from the holy Qurʾān, that there is no nation without a prophet and without a revealed scripture, for it hath been said: "Nor do We chastise until We raise an apostle" (Qurʾān 17.15). And in another verse: "And there is not a people but a Warner has gone among them" (Qurʾān 35.24). And at another place: "Certainly We sent Our apostles with clear arguments, and sent down with them the Book and the measure" (Qurʾān 57.25).

And the *summum bonum* of these four books, which contain all the secrets of the Path and the contemplative exercises of pure monotheism, are called the *Upanekhats [Upanishads]*,[5] and the people of that time have written commentaries with complete and diffusive interpretations thereon; and being still understood as the best part of their religious worship, they are always studied. And whereas this unsolicitous seeker after the Truth had in view the principle of the fundamental unity of the personality and not Arabic, Syriac, Hebrew, and Sanskrit languages, he wanted to make without any worldly motive, in a clear style, an exact and literal translation of

3. That is, the Pentateuch (the first five books of the Hebrew Bible), which traditionally were attributed to Moses.
4. The four collections of poems and hymns (composed between 1500 and 1000 B.C.E.) that are the earliest Hindi sacred texts.
5. The speculative and mystical scriptures that conclude each Veda.

the *Upanekhats* into Persian. For it is a treasure of monotheism and there are few thoroughly conversant with it even among the Indians. Thereby he also wanted to solve the mystery that underlies their efforts to conceal it from the Muslims.

And as at this period the city of Banares,[6] which is the center of the sciences of this community, was in certain relations with this seeker of the Truth, he assembled together the pandits [Hindu scholars] and the sannyasis [Hindu ascetics or monks], who were the most learned of their time and proficient in the *Upanekhats* . . . in the year 1067 after Hijra;[7] and thus every difficulty and every sublime topic that he had desired or thought and had looked for and not found, he obtained from these essences of the most ancient books, and without doubt or suspicion, these books are first of all heavenly books in point of time, and the source and the fountainhead of the ocean of unity, in conformity with the holy Qurʾān.

Happy is he, who having abandoned the prejudices of vile selfishness, sincerely and with the grace of God, renouncing all partiality, shall study and comprehend this translation entitled *The Great Secret (Sirr-i-Akbar)*, knowing it to be a translation of the words of God. He shall become imperishable, fearless, unsolicitous, and eternally liberated.

6. Varanasi, an ancient city that is sacred to Hindus, located on the Ganges in northern India.

7. 1657 C.E.

The Classical Synthesis Encounters Modernity

1765 to the Present

In 1765, when Britain established its first true Asian colony in Bengal (modern Bangladesh plus India's West Bengal), the classic Islamic synthesis had reached its maturity: Arabic in religion, it was largely Persian in culture and quite often Turkish in matters political and military. But behind that mingled heritage and that social fact was a story virtually all Muslims had embraced without reflection, making it part of their psychological and theological self-understanding. As European colonialism began unexpectedly to encroach upon *dar al-islam*, the House of Islam, this master narrative encountered a different master narrative—one that had become part of the psychological and philosophical self-understanding of the Europeans who were fashioning what we now call modernity.

The Muslim story began with God, who, while revealing the Qur'an to Muhammad, had guided him to Medina and made him not just the supreme religious authority for the community

A Karachi child sets out trays of food for the breaking of the Ramadan fast. From dawn until sunset during Ramadan, Muslims attempt to enhance spiritual discipline through taming bodily urges such as the desire to eat and drink, express anger, or engage in sexual relations. Ending the fast with a meal (*iftar*) at sunset is often done communally in the homes of friends or relatives; charitable organizations organize large *iftars* for the poor outside of mosques or in the public squares of towns and cities.

that gathered around him there but also the chief executive, the lawgiver and final court of judicial appeal, and the commander in chief of the armed forces. God's power and the authority of the Qur'an had been proved by the Medinan Muslims' astonishingly swift conquest of all Arabia. Indeed, in the final decade of Muhammad's lifetime the Arabs, abandoning further resistance, submitted at one and the same time to God and to Muhammad in all his roles. As they did so, Medina in effect grew to encompass the entire Arabian Peninsula. After Muhammad's death, God's power and the truth of the Qur'an had been proved again and again as his successors, the first caliphs, still operating within the same fusion of roles, vaulted from one unprecedented and spectacular victory to the next. Troubling as it may have been when, as repeatedly happened, two or more Muslim leaders claimed to be the true caliph, God's invincible power had steadfastly remained with his Muslim people, according to the received story. The principal European chapter in this story, after ʿUmar's early victories over the Roman Empire, had been the demonstration of God's power in the ultimate defeat of the Crusaders: the initial success of the European invaders had been only temporary and illusory. Any other ostensibly permanent Muslim losses, as in northern Spain, had come at the margins of the House of Islam. The House as a whole continued to stand, still impregnable, still growing, a visible and daily manifestation of the master narrative's truth.

Bengal, located where India shades off into Indochina and China, might have seemed in 1765 like a Spain at the opposite margin of the Islamic world—a kind of eastern vestibule of the House of Islam. The creation of a British colony there, so far from England, perhaps struck those nearby as a bizarre and regrettable but finally minor development. Yet less than a century ahead, Muslim rule would be progressively replaced by non-Muslim British sovereignty over all of India, which then included what are today Pakistan and Bangladesh. The population of Muslims affected by that enormous change was anything but marginal. Moreover, as their control over India expanded, the British were also intruding on Muslim East Africa, Muslim northern Nigeria, the Muslim Sudan, and even Muslim Egypt. At its peak, the British Empire would include close to half a billion people—a major portion of the world's population—some half or more of them Muslim. While all this was happening, similar intrusions were occurring elsewhere in Muslim Africa, by the French and sometimes the Spanish; in Muslim Central Asia, by the Russians; and in Muslim Indonesia, by the Dutch. In all these areas, Muslim sovereignty was being rolled back in a process that would not end until European colonialism itself was brought to an end after World War II. But in the decades since 1945, Muslim sovereignty has returned to the former European colonies in a scarcely recognizable form, evincing a nationalism far more reflective of the European master narrative and political worldview than of the Islamic one.

At the dawn of the era of European colonialism, world Islam was divided into three great empires: the Ottoman in the Middle East, southeast Europe, and North Africa; the Safavid in Iran and southwest Asia; and the Mughal in India. Each of these had a corresponding sphere of influence lying just beyond its formal imperial control. Southeast of the Mughal empire lived the Muslims of Malaya (modern Malaysia and southern Thailand), Indonesia, and the southern Philippines. North and northeast of the Safavid empire lived the Turkic Muslim peoples of Central Asia. South of Ottoman North Africa lived the sometimes but not always Arabized Muslim populations of coastal and sub-Saharan Africa.

The Mughal empire was the first of these three to succumb to European colonialism. British control over India grew steadily during the first half of the nineteenth century, and local discontent increased as well, until only a spark was needed to ignite widespread conflict. That spark came in 1857, when Indian soldiers in the service of the British were given new rifles that used greased cartridges. Hearing rumors that the grease was a mix of pig and cow tallow, the soldiers mutinied: for Muslims, the pig is unclean; for Hindus, the cow is sacred. The mutiny grew into a national uprising, but it was quelled within a year; and in its aftermath, the British deposed the last Mughal shah and established direct British rule over all of India. In 1877, Queen Victoria would add the title "Empress of India" to the others that she bore. India would not regain its independence until 1947.

Baiturrahman, the Great Mosque of Banda Aceh, Indonesia, was built by the Dutch as a gesture of reconciliation for their 1873 razing of the original mosque in the Aceh wars. The mosque was designed by an Italian architect in the North Indian Moghul style. Many people sheltered there during the tsunami that devastated Indonesia in 2004. The mosque, which served as an emergency shelter, hospital, and morgue, sustained only minor damages.

The Ottoman empire was the next to crumble. Through the later nineteenth and into the early twentieth century, the empire lost its southeast European holdings either to ethnic liberation and independence movements, often backed by western European powers, or to the southward expansion of the Russian empire, which was also expanding eastward to the Pacific through Turkic Central Asia. During the same period, the Ottoman sultan lost control of his North African domains to Spanish, French, and British colonial forces or to such forces in collaboration with restive or opportunistic locals. Finally, after its defeat as an ally of Germany and Italy in World War I (1914–18), the empire was stripped of its Middle Eastern holdings by the victorious French and British. Syria, Lebanon, Iraq, Palestine, and the Hijaz in western Arabia became French or British "protectorates," in the euphemistic language of the postwar agreements.

The Safavid empire fared slightly better, as Iran never entirely lost its political independence. However, the Qajar dynasty, which had succeeded the Safavid, saw its autonomy severely hedged about with territorial and other concessions made both to imperial Russia, encroaching from the north, and to imperial Britain, manipulating events from its Indian colony to the east. In what the British novelist and poet Rudyard Kipling would call "the Great Game," the two nominally Christian empires competed for control of what had been the Safavid empire, each determined to foil the designs of the other. The Persian Muslims became pawns rather than dominant players in this geopolitical chess game.

For Muslims living in these three regions that once had seemed to be divinely ordained Islamic empires, what did this humiliating transformation mean? How could such a change be accommodated within the collective Muslim self-understanding? Did it mean that God, for some reason, had abandoned his Muslim people? Muhammad Iqbal (1877–1938), Pakistan's national poet, boldly entertained this idea and more boldly voiced this complaint to God in a poem excerpted here. More shocking still, did this shift of sovereignty validate another master story, in which Christianity—the religious heritage of the Europeans—was to be victorious over Islam?

That is not what it meant to the pioneering Portuguese, Dutch, and British colonialists themselves, at least at the start. Those in Britain's East India Company did not plant the cross on an island in the Ganges Delta and claim Bengal, or all India, for Christ and the Anglican Church. Indeed, that notion might have prompted mild amusement, for theirs was a *trading* company, not a missionary fellowship. Though Christian nominally and sometimes (in private) even fervently, they did not allow religion to intrude upon business. They regarded it, increasingly, as a private pursuit and not a topic that men of affairs should discuss at length. Rather than school themselves in the careful distinctions of theology, they turned their attention to developments in technology and to how such advances might be implemented for commercial gain. In all these regards, their fight was on behalf of modernity or perhaps sovereign nationality. It was neither waged nor—to the extent that they were victorious—won for Christianity.

If the founding colonists had been declared fighters for Christianity, if they had been neo-Crusaders, their story would have been more nearly congruent with the received Muslim story. But such was not the case. Christian missions certainly did exist, but the agenda of modernity—the agenda forced upon the House of Islam in Asia and in Africa by rampant European colonialism—did not by any means begin and end with the triumph of Christianity. Instead, the colonists understood themselves as primarily acting either in their commercial self-interest or in the interest of their respective *nations*. And the national interests they served in the formative phase of Europe's colonialization of Asia and Africa were overwhelmingly commercial rather than religious, much less philanthropic. As nationalist commercial adventurers rather than Christian missionaries, they no longer celebrated martyrdom for the Christian faith. Instead, they celebrated the heroism of dying for king or country, and they bravely confronted enormous dangers for the sake of the enormous potential rewards of overseas business. Their respect for the master merchant and venture capitalist verged on religious reverence.

Repeatedly, after a Western colony was established, a Christian missionary effort would follow—perhaps most notably in British India and in the Ottoman empire. There, under pressure, the sultan extended extraterritorial diplomatic immunity to Christian missions: thus merchant and missionary certainly appeared to be part of a single foreign offensive. Yet these efforts were not necessarily encouraged or even welcomed by the more secular and profit-minded architects of the colonies, who might well expect business relations with the Muslims to go more smoothly if fewer Christians with a potentially offensive missionary agenda were on the scene. In any case, to appreciate the encounter of the classic Islamic synthesis with modernity, which arose in Europe in the late seventeenth century, it helps to recall that it was *not* primarily an encounter between religions—and it was confounding precisely for that reason.

For if the invaders were not neo-Crusaders, what were they? If they were not true Christians, they were infidels of a stripe not easily comprehended: not idolaters, not polytheists, only rarely (if you asked them) atheists, these foreigners lacked any pronounced hostility to Islam but also lacked any interest in it or any evident desire to confront it. Rather than seeking to debate their Muslim subjects about religion, the British wished to strike deals with them about goods and money. And behind that desire—that readiness to change the subject—lay a story as integral to their own history as the Muslim self-understanding and the story behind it were to Muslim history. The subsequent record of this encounter, down to our own day, largely details the failure of either side to achieve any deep appreciation of how the other's story could appeal and seem intuitively right to those whom it has shaped.

Christians had no equivalent, in their story, to Medina nor any inspirational figure who combined all major civic and religious roles in himself as Muhammad had done. Instead, they had their church, a unique social entity without any sacred territory, any sacred language, or, in its early centuries, any sponsoring government or army. Christianity had begun as an essentially private movement; though it would repeatedly fuse with state power of one sort or another during its later history, it would never entirely lose the understanding of itself as finally separable from any such partner. By the same token, a status as private or underground could never feel entirely alien to Christians, and such a privatizing shift had in fact begun in European Christianity in the mid-seventeenth century.

The secularization of European public life in the modern era and the attendant confinement of Christianity to private life are in large part the result of Europe's religious wars. In the sixteenth and seventeenth centuries, the Protestants and Roman Catholics of western Europe had fought each other to an extremely bloody draw whose aftermath was culturally momentous. By signing the Peace of Westphalia, which ended the ghastly Thirty Years' War in 1648, each sovereign party was empowered to determine his country's religion while agreeing not to seek to impose that religion *outside* his country. This agreement to disagree about religion, as well as other key assertions, had such long-term political importance that the modern system of nation-states is labeled the Westphalian system—a system that undergirds the United Nations. Any political entity that accepts membership in that organization is required or at least expected to respect this first crucial step in the privatization of religion.

At the same time, this confinement of national faiths within national borders set a course toward further religious privatizations, down to the level of the home and even of the individual person—a change reflected in such words as *individual* and *person*, which then were coined or took on new meanings that are now entirely taken for granted. These multiple privatizations at the national level and below also fostered religious pluralization. Complicating the still-perceived unity of Christianity was increased fragmentation and a growing sense that rather than one international Christianity, there now existed a variety of national Christianities. As religious choice became ever more personal, this sense of religious plurality became even stronger. Thus there emerged—in the full flower of the European Enlightenment—the nascent sense of a global religious pluralism, extending beyond Christianity to other religions in other countries that could become part of the same international system of mutual forbearance. From this process was born the "freedom of religion" of which the West came to boast.

From another perspective, however, this freedom could as easily be seen as religious disintegration. And what were Muslims to think when the exponents of this semi-Christian or post-Christian or inconsistently Christian religious disintegration arrived, determined to assume power through their superior military technology, cunningly innovative economic organization, and confidence in their own cultural entitlement? Their certainty was mainly rooted not in religious faith but in pride in the grandeur of what at the peak of the colonial project would be called "the white man's burden" or "la mission civilisatrice" or "progress" or "development." Though these aggressive newcomers might often seem to be nominally Christian, practically they were something else—but what? and what was to be made of it and of them? How were they different from the Christian missionaries who often arrived in their wake? How were they to be accommodated in the story that had begun so inspiringly at Medina? Because Islam's story included no cultural critique comparable to the Enlightenment critique of Christianity, because it included no comparable moment at which religious privatization began, the accommodation entailed a coming to terms for which no actual terms—no usable and adequate language—were readily available.

Each of the six traditions included in the full *Norton Anthology of World Religions* documents some sort of engagement between its focal religion and modernity. And because this multifaceted encounter is ongoing and unresolved, its inconclusive explorations toward a resolution are most accurately captured by representative examples. *What were Muslims to think?* was asked in the previous paragraph. Lamentation before the Almighty was one kind of reaction, already noted in the instance of Muhammad Iqbal. Indignation at the invaders both for the unwarranted and criminal invasion itself and for their vulgar or contemptible mores was another, as displayed by the Egyptian chronicler al-Jabarti (1753–1826) in describing Napoleon's invasion of Egypt in 1798. Indignation against Muslims themselves for a lax or otherwise defective practice of Islam, taken as the root of all other ills, has been another and more common response. Rashid Ahmad Gangohi (1829–1905), co-founder of a conservative seminary at Deoband, India, took the imposition of direct British rule on India as a call not to rebel but rather to withdraw from political life and intensify the private life of religious observance. That response appealed to others, as was (and is) proved by the multiplication of Deobandi seminaries modeled on Rashid Ahmad's original.

Related to Deobandi conservatism but with important and controversial differences was the reaction of the Egyptian Qur'an scholar Sayyid Qutb (1906–1966). Like Rashid Ahmad, Qutb blamed Muslims for bringing disaster upon the House of Islam by deserting the "straight path" of Shariʿa, but he took two further bold steps. First, he insisted that many alleged Muslims should not be considered Muslims at all, thereby explicitly harking back to the fourteenth-century thought of Ibn Taymiyya (d. 1328), who regarded the Mongols as non-Muslim despite their conversion. Second, Qutb went beyond Ahmad in urging his Muslim readers and hearers to take up arms against their oppressors, foreign as well as domestic. The Saudi Usama bin Ladin (1957–2011) stood in a clear line of descent from Qutb, adding an agenda of terrorist retaliation against the oppressive West to Qutb's demotion of Muslims he found defective to the status of *kafir*, or non-Muslim.

Given the centrality of nationalism to modernity as a kind of surrogate religion, the Iranian Ruhollah Khomeini's (1902–1989) vision of an "Islamic Republic" is striking as a self-conscious and explicit repudiation of nationhood as the basis for statehood—the core notion of the Westphalian system, to which much of the Muslim world has superficially adapted, even though (as often noted) many of the national borders of post–World War II Muslim states were drawn by the colonial powers. Khomeinism asserts the superiority of a statehood based on religious rather than national identity. For Ayatollah Khomeini—unlike his predecessor, Shah Muhammad Reza Pahlavi, who celebrated the past glories of Persia—the glories of Iran were purely Muslim. What mattered for him was the greatness not of the Persian imperial past but only of the Muslim religious past.

We might dub these thinkers members of the House of Rejection, but others have belonged to a House of Acceptance. The nineteenth-century Egyptian cultural visionary Muhammad ʿAbduh (1849–1905) saw no conflict between Western science or education, which he actively promoted, and Muslim religion. Unlike Rashid Ahmad, his contemporary, he believed that reform had to look forward as well as backward. In India, Sayyid Ahmad Khan (1817–1898), another contemporary, responded to British dominance by acquiring a British as well as a traditional Islamic education and founding not a seminary but a university. More recently, the American Muslim convert Amina Wadud (b. 1952), a noted feminist, has achieved a groundbreaking engagement with Western methods even in the crucial and highly charged theater of qurʾanic scholarship. Her "holistic" method of qurʾanic interpretation controversially asserts that the reforms instituted by the Qurʾan have goals whose realization necessarily must come long after its revelation, thus giving her overall interpretation of Islam—like that of Muhammad ʿAbduh—a prospective rather than a retrospective emphasis.

The more recent writers anthologized here are distinguished by a stance that is simultaneously appreciative and critical of both modernity and Islam. The Franco-Algerian historian Mohammed Arkoun (1928–2010) is perhaps the most radical in his refusal to make the thinking of any one period normative for all time, idealizing neither our own historical moment nor any supposed high-water mark in past Muslim achievement. In a kindred spirit, both the Swiss Tariq Ramadan (b. 1962) and the Canadian Ebrahim Moosa (b. 1957) engage their double heritage dialectically—that is, they undertake an ongoing inner conversation between modernity and Islam, an open-ended dialogue in service to a future that will be partly constructed but also partly inherited.

The reactions to modernity variously characterized above as rejection, acceptance, and critical appreciation are grouped differently in the table of contents, where they appear under four headings that correspond to four

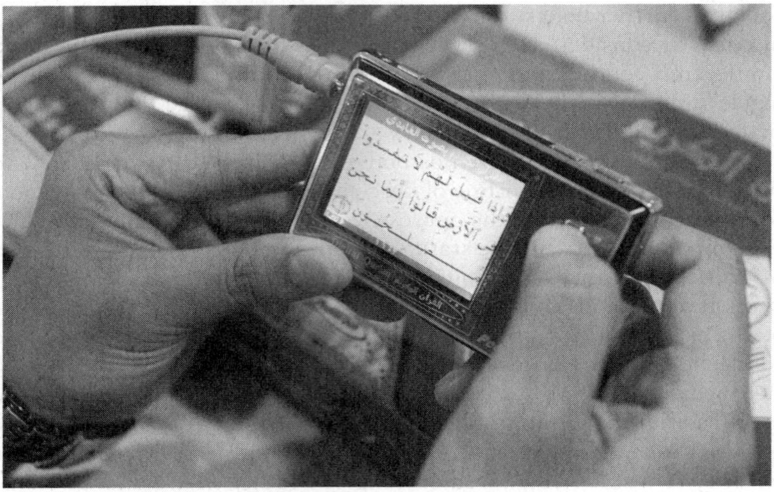

In a Jakarta bookstore, a young Muslim uses a digital device to display the text of the Qur'an. Muslims the world over can access the Qur'an through smartphone and tablet applications that allow them to switch between different translations and different popular reciters and to replay verses or passages multiple times as a memorization aid.

key components in what may be a new Islamic identity in the making. Those components are nationality ("Colonialism and Postcolonialism"), secularity ("The Religious Reassertion"), sexuality ("The Emergence of Women's Voices"), and what we might call minority—the recognition that Islam, like every other religion, seems destined to remain a minority of the world's population ("Negotiating Religious Pluralism").

The modern understanding of national identity as capable of subsuming and subordinating religious identity ("You're a Jew, I'm a Hindu, but, hey, we're both Americans!") is easily taken for granted not just in the United States but, by and large, throughout the West and the rest of the international community to the extent that the West dominates its thinking. The Muslim encounter with "nation" in this sense of the word, which is far from being universal or intuitive, is still unfinished.

Our contemporary understanding of secularity as an autonomous cultural space distinct from and equal to the cultural space occupied by religion is, again, a familiar component of modernity. But the implicit elevation of culture to a conceptual rank above religion, assigning religion a position alongside secular pursuits such as science, sports, art, or business, is as problematic for Muslims as the political elevation of national above religious identity. The Iranian Revolution, in addition to repudiating nationality as a basis for statehood, recognizes no secular realm within the Islamic Republic to which Shari'a does not apply.

With regard to sexuality and the Muslim encounter with modernity, the popular Afghani American writer Tamim Ansary has observed perceptively in *Destiny Disrupted* (2009):

> On this point, the disagreement between Islamic and Western culture is not about whether women should be oppressed, as is often repre-

> sented in the West. Well-meaning folk on both sides believe that no human beings should be oppressed. This is not to deny that women suffer grievously from oppressive law in many Muslim countries. It is only to say that the principle on which Muslims stand is not the "right" to oppress women. Rather, what the Muslim world has reified over the course of history is the idea that society should be divided into a men's and a women's realm and that the point of connection between the two should only be in the private arena, so that sexuality can be eliminated as a factor in the public life of the community.

The notion that sexuality should be privatized in this way, so intuitively self-evident in many Muslim-majority countries and so incomprehensible in many Western countries, can be seen as a mirror image of the notion that religion should be privatized, so intuitively self-evident at this point in the West but so baffling elsewhere.

What was called above the challenge of minority might also be called the challenge of hospitality, if we remember that the Latin word *hospes*, from which we derive *hospitality*, can mean either "guest" or "host." Muslims have long prided themselves on being good hosts, with a historical record of treating the Jewish and Christian minorities of Muslim-majority communities better than Jewish or Muslim minorities were treated in, for example, fifteenth-century Christian Spain, from which both Jews and Muslims were expelled as unworthy to be Spanish. But what we call "the West," as the child of Christianity and the parent of what we call "the international community," prides itself on being not just a good host but the historically inevitable last host standing. The notion that something larger may be coming into existence to which today's international community might have to accommodate as guest rather than host is every bit as discomfiting to its proponents as the ongoing accommodation to world religious pluralism is to the Muslim community. The challenge in the contemporary world may be less how to be a good host than how to be a good guest in a world without a host.

Who among the world's Muslims has the authority to resolve such difficult contradictions as these? The short answer to that question is no one now has that authority. Earlier in Muslim history, wherever Islamic wisdom and political sovereignty temporarily appeared to coincide in one man, the conditions for a Sunni caliphate seemed to be in place. But no actual claim of such authority has lasted for long. Moreover, twice—first in Fatimid Egypt and later in Safavid Iran—a sustained, if finally unsuccessful, effort was launched to replace the caliphate with a different institution embodying Islamic authority, the imamate as inaugurated by the martyred ʿAli. After the Mongol sack of Baghdad, the last ʿAbbasid caliph fled to Egypt; a "shadow caliphate" lingered there until the Ottoman empire moved the office to Istanbul, where it remained until its abolition in 1924 by the secularist reformer Mustafa Kemal Atatürk, the father of modern Turkey. Whatever Atatürk's immediate motivation, his action can be seen in retrospect as a prescient recognition that Islamic wisdom and political sovereignty may never again coincide in one man for the Muslims of our world as they did in Muhammad for the Muslims of Medina. The Muslim future may be now collectively owned—the property not of a latter-day *khalifa* but of a Muslim *umma* whose voices the rest of the world has only now begun to hear.

Chronology

THE CLASSICAL SYNTHESIS ENCOUNTERS MODERNITY, 1756–2012

1757 The Battle of Plassey in Bengal allows the British East India Company to begin exercising power and the first British governor of Bengal to be installed

1765 Mughal emperor Shah Alam cedes Bengal revenue management rights to British East India Company

1787–1859 Muhammad Ali ibn al-Sanusi, founder of a Sufi order and an Islamic state in Libya

1793–1864 Nana Asmaʾu, poet, scholar, and princess of the Sokoto Caliphate

1798 Napoleon invades Egypt, to be expelled in 1801 by Muhammad Ali

1803 British take Delhi
Saudi-Wahhabi alliance takes Mecca and Medina

1804–present Sokoto Caliphate, founded by Uthman Dan Fodio in northern Nigeria

1817–1898 Sayyid Ahmad Khan, scholar and Islamic modernist reformer

1829–1905 Rashid Ahmad Gangohi, Indian jurist

1839 Tanzimat Reforms in the Ottoman empire affect education, the judiciary, military conscription, and tax collection

1849–1905 Muhammad ʿAbduh, Egyptian reformer activist

1853–1856 Crimean War

1857 Indian uprising against the British presence. The final Mughal emperor is exiled, and the British government takes formal control of the country from the British East India Company

1877 Queen Victoria adds "Empress of India" to her title

1877–1938 Muhammad Iqbal, poet, philosopher, and early advocate for separate nation of Pakistan

1893–1963 Mahmud Shaltut, Egyptian scholar, educator, and eventual rector of al-Azhar

1902–1989 Khomeini, Shiʿi cleric and voice of the Iranian Revolution

1906–1966 Sayyid Qutb, Egyptian intellectual and Muslim Brotherhood activist

1911 Italy invades Libya in the Tripolitanian War. The Sanusi Sufi brotherhood leads resistance, to be replaced by Bedouin leaders like ʿUmar al-Mukhtar

1914–1918 World War I
Britain and France seize Ottoman holdings in the Middle East as punishment for the empire's alliance with German and Italian forces

1915 ʿAbd al-ʿAziz ibn Saʿud signs treaty with British guaranteeing financial and military support for his campaign to control the Arabian peninsula (the Hijaz)

1924 The Ottoman caliphate is abolished and secular rule affirmed in Turkey. Nationalist movements flourish in former Ottoman lands

1925–1979 Pahlavi dynasty rules Iran

1925–1965 Malcolm X, African-American Muslim activist

1926 ʿAbd al-ʿAziz ibn Saʿud assumes (un-Islamic) title of King of the Hijaz

1928–2010 Mohammed Arkoun, Franco-Algerian intellectual

1928 Hasan al-Banna of Egypt founds Muslim Brotherhood

1933–1977 Ali Sharia'ti, sociologist and ideologue of the Iranian revolution

1939–2005 Nurcholish Madjid, modernist Indonesian scholar

1940– Fatima Mernissi, Moroccan scholar and feminist activist

1941– Fethullah Gulen, Turkish reformer who emphasizes universal religious values

1945 With the end of WWII, Japanese occupation of Indonesia ceases, and independence is declared

1947 British rule ends in India. The State of Pakistan is established, and massacres of Muslims and Hindus occur in the wake of the partition of India

1948 State of Israel is established. Arab armies fail in their offensive against the new state. The Palestinian refugee crisis ensues

1949 Hasan al-Banna is assassinated

1952 Egyptian Free Officers take power from King Farouk in a bloodless revolution

1952– Amina Wadud, African-American scholar-activist

1954 Muslim Brotherhood in Sudan begins agitating for Islamic state and implementation of Islamic law

1956 Pakistan declares itself an Islamic Republic

1957–2011 Usama bin Ladin, Saudi Islamist and violent extremist

1957– Ebrahim Moosa, Indian-born American scholar

1962– Tariq Ramadan, Oxford professor and reformer

1963 Islamic Center of Dearborn, largest mosque in North America, is established

1965 Gamal Abdel Nasser begins widescale repression of Muslim Brotherhood in Egypt

1967 Arab armies' attempt to regain land lost in 1948 fails and results in even greater territorial loss, referred to as the "Naksa" (setback)

1969 Muammar Qaddafi takes power in Libya

1971 East Pakistan asserts its independence and, after civil war, becomes the nation of Bangladesh

1975 Civil war erupts in Lebanon

1979 Soviets enter Afghanistan
Islamic Republic of Iran is established

1980–1988 Iran-Iraq War

1981 Anwar al-Sadat is assassinated

1982 Hafiz al-Asad brutally represses Muslim Brotherhood–supported opposition movement in Syria
Sabra and Shatila massacre in Lebanon

1988 Benazir Bhutto becomes first Muslim female elected head of state
Mujahidin (backed by U.S. funds and arms) eject Soviets from Afghanistan

1990–1991 First Persian Gulf War

1993 Oslo Accords between Israel and the PLO

2001 Usama bin Laden engineers attacks on the Twin Towers in New York. United States military forces enter Afghanistan

2003 U.S. forces enter Iraq

2010–2012 Arab Spring

2012 Muslim Brotherhood's Mohammed Morsi is elected president of Egypt

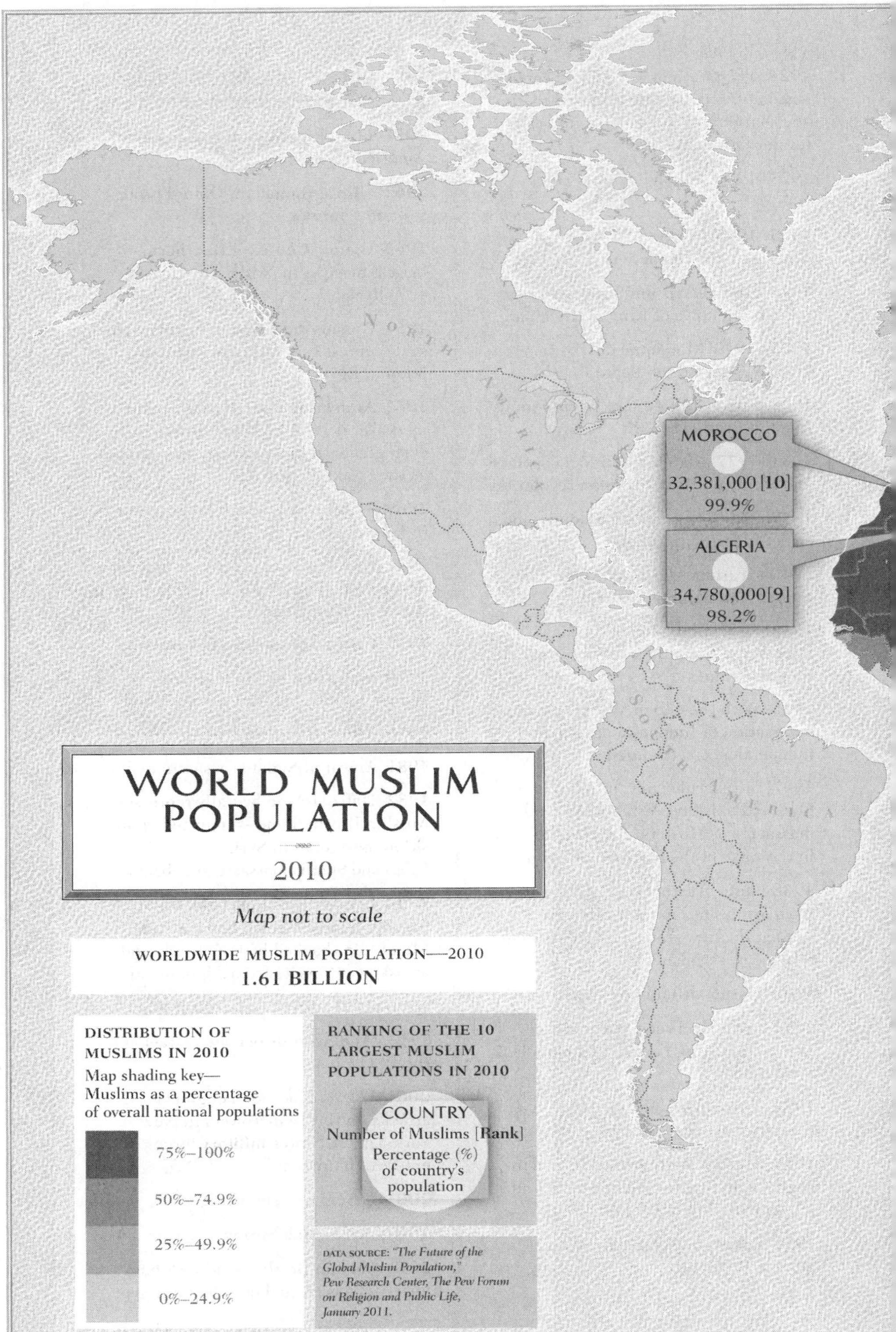
WORLD MUSLIM POPULATION
2010
Map not to scale
WORLDWIDE MUSLIM POPULATION—2010
1.61 BILLION
DISTRIBUTION OF MUSLIMS IN 2010
Map shading key—
Muslims as a percentage of overall national populations
75%–100%
50%–74.9%
25%–49.9%
0%–24.9%
RANKING OF THE 10 LARGEST MUSLIM POPULATIONS IN 2010
COUNTRY
Number of Muslims [Rank]
Percentage (%) of country's population
DATA SOURCE: "The Future of the Global Muslim Population," Pew Research Center, The Pew Forum on Religion and Public Life, January 2011.
NORTH AMERICA
SOUTH AMERICA
MOROCCO
32,381,000 [10]
99.9%
ALGERIA
34,780,000[9]
98.2%

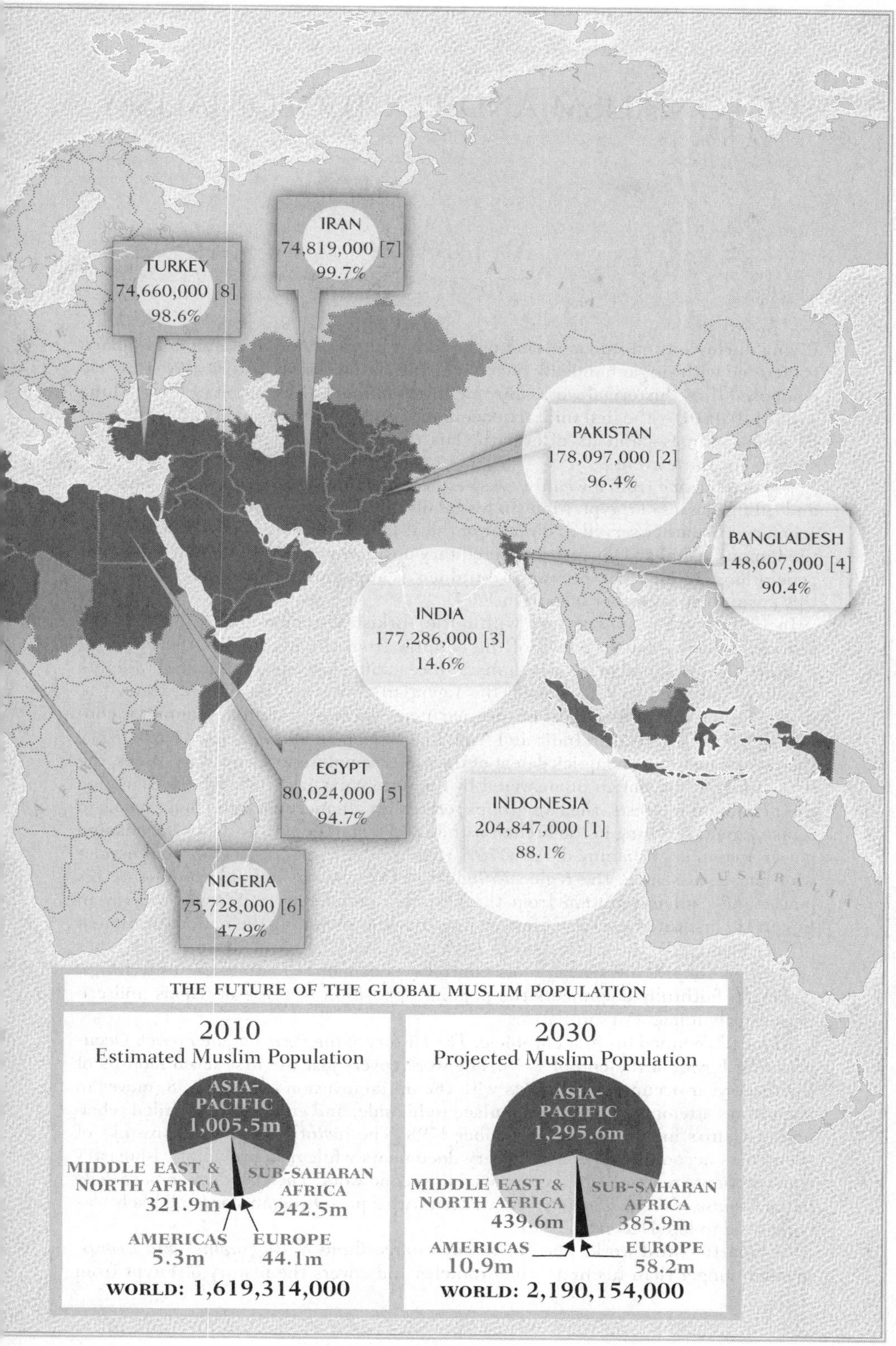

TURKEY
74,660,000 [8]
98.6%
IRAN
74,819,000 [7]
99.7%
PAKISTAN
178,097,000 [2]
96.4%
BANGLADESH
148,607,000 [4]
90.4%
INDIA
177,286,000 [3]
14.6%
EGYPT
80,024,000 [5]
94.7%
INDONESIA
204,847,000 [1]
88.1%
NIGERIA
75,728,000 [6]
47.9%
THE FUTURE OF THE GLOBAL MUSLIM POPULATION
2010
Estimated Muslim Population
ASIA-PACIFIC 1,005.5m
MIDDLE EAST & NORTH AFRICA 321.9m
SUB-SAHARAN AFRICA 242.5m
AMERICAS 5.3m
EUROPE 44.1m
WORLD: 1,619,314,000
2030
Projected Muslim Population
ASIA-PACIFIC 1,295.6m
MIDDLE EAST & NORTH AFRICA 439.6m
SUB-SAHARAN AFRICA 385.9m
AMERICAS 10.9m
EUROPE 58.2m
WORLD: 2,190,154,000

COLONIALISM AND POSTCOLONIALISM

AL-JABARTI
1753–1825/26

Living during a tumultuous period of Egyptian history, ʿAbd al-Rahman al-Jabarti is credited with single-handedly reviving Egyptian interest in historical writing. He composed three historical works chronicling the French occupation of Egypt (June 1798–July 1801)—the first military encounter between Europe and the Middle East in modern times—and its aftermath. His three chronicles are among the best sources for these events.

Al-Jabarti came from a wealthy, well-established family with ties to the scholarly and ruling classes of Egypt. Many in his family, like his father, were Hanafi religious scholars. His father served as director of the al-Jabarti residence hall for students at the famous al-Azhar University, a hereditary position passed from father to son for generations. Al-Jabarti, who was also trained as a religious scholar, likely inherited this position at his father's death in 1774.

In 1798 Egypt was a province within the Turkish Ottoman empire. In 1517 the Ottomans had wrested control of the country from the Mamluks—the powerful military class that had held the sultanate since 1250—but many influential Mamluk families continued to rank among the Egyptian elite. In 1798 France decided to invade Egypt, one of its largest trading partners, to create a staging ground for contesting British interests in India and Asia. Led by Napoleon Bonaparte (1769–1821), the French invasion and quick defeat of the professional Mamluk military forces, the best in Egypt, did not go unanswered by the Ottomans or the British. Recognizing their common interests, the two groups formed an alliance and launched attacks to retake Egypt, resulting in the French withdrawal from Egypt in 1801. In the ensuing power vacuum, Muhammad ʿAli (1769–1849), an Albanian Ottoman commander who had been sent to the region to fight the French, was able to consolidate his power and gain recognition from the Ottoman empire in 1805 as its viceroy in Egypt. He instituted a series of far-ranging changes, including the nationalization of private farmlands, the cultivation of cash crops, and the reorganization of Egypt's government to give the viceroy more control over economic matters. In his writings, Al-Jabarti faithfully documents the popular opposition to these decisions and critiques Muhammad ʿAli's initiatives.

Al-Jabarti penned his first chronicle, *The History of the Period of the French Occupation in Egypt*, at the end of 1798. The work covers just the first seven months of the three-year occupation. It starts with the initial invasion in June 1798, moves to Napoleon's attempts to win the populace to his side, and ends with the failed rebellion of Cairo's inhabitants in December 1798. The history makes extensive use of eyewitness accounts and contemporary documents while also providing al-Jabarti's own emotional reaction to these events. His second work, *The Demonstration of Piety in the Demise of French Society*, was written with a pro-Ottoman slant and likely was completed in late December 1801.

Al-Jabarti's third work, *The Marvelous Compositions of Biographies and Events*, is much longer than his first two chronicles and covers the history of Egypt from

1688 to 1821. It includes Muhammad ʿAli's ascent to power and the first ten years of his rule. Though its tone is more scholarly than the first two histories, it still contained severe criticisms of Muhammad ʿAli's leadership. Because of these critiques, the work was banned in Egypt until 1870 and not published in full until 1880.

The following excerpt from *The History of the Period of the French Occupation* captures al-Jabarti's outrage at the massive invasion of his homeland. Furious at the French attempt to alienate the populace from its Mamluk leadership, he castigates the social and cultural depravity of these vulgarians, while also correcting the Arabic of their emancipatory proclamation.

PRONOUNCING GLOSSARY

ʿadala: *ah´-da-luh*
ʿalā ʾl-bashar: *al-lal-ba´-shar*
al-ān: *al-an´*
alladhī yūwjad: *al-la´-dhee yoo´-jad*
alladhī lā yūwjad: *al-la´-dhee la yoo´-jad*
ʿaṣr: *ahsr*
bi-ʿawnih: *bi-awn´-ih*
bi ʾl-bashar: *bil-ba´-shar*
Burnayṭa: *bur-nay´-tuh*
btāʿ al-Mamālīk: *bi-ta´-l-ma-ma-leek´*
Damanhūr: *da-mahn-hoor´*
fa-amma Rabb al-ʿālamīn: *fa-am-ma rab al-a-la-meen´*
fa-huwa al-ʿaql: *fa-hoo-wal-ahql´*
fa ʾl-yuwarrūnā: *fal-yoo-war-roo´-na*
fī hādhā ʾl-ṭaraf: *fee ha´-dha ta´-ruf*
Fuwwa: *foo´-wuh*
ḥāl: *hal* (heavy *h*)
Ḥaythumā: *hay-thoo-ma´* (heavy *h*)
Hijra: *hij´-ruh*
Imāms: *ee-mams´*
innanī aʿbudu Allāh akthar min al-Mamālīk: *in-na-nee ah´-boo-doo ul-lah´ ak´-thar min al-ma-ma-leek´*
kamā yaḥlū: *ka-ma yah´-loo* (heavy *h*)
kufr: *koofr*
lākin: *la´-kin*
lā yustathnā aḥad: *la yoos-tath´-na a´-had* (heavy *h*)
al-majlūbīn: *al-maj-loo-been´*
al-majlūbūn: *al-maj-loo-boon´*
mā ʾl-ʿaql: *mal-ahql´*
Mamlūks: *mam-looks´*
al-manāṣib al-sāmiya: *al-ma-nah´-sib as-sa´-mee-ya*
min al-yawm: *min al-yawm´*
al-Miṣriyyūn: *al-mis-ree-yoon´*
muftarī: *moof-ta´-ree*
Muḥarram: *moo-hahr´-ram* (heavy *h*)
al-murtafiʿa: *al-mur-ta´-fi-a*
muṭmaʾin: *moot-mah-in´*
muṭmaʾinan: *moot-mah-in´-an*
naṣb: *nahsb*
naʿt maqṭūʿ: *naht maq-too´*
nūn: *noon*
Qāḍīs: *qah´-dees*
qad ḥattama: *qad hat´-ta-muh* (heavy *h*)
qad yaqūlū lakum: *qad ya-qoo´-loo la-koom*
al-Qurʾān al-ʿaẓīm: *al-qor-ahn´ al-ah-zeem´*
raʾafa: *rah´-fuh*
sanjāq: *san-jaq´*
ṣanjaq: *sahn-jaq´*
Ṣanjaqs: *sahn-jax´*
Shaykhs: *shaychs* (guttural *ch*)
Shurbājiyya: *shur-ba-jee´-yuh*
ʿuṣūr: *oo-soor´*
wa-bayn al-Mamālīk: *wa-bayn al-ma-ma-leek´*
Wā ḥasratan: *wa has´-ra-tan* (heavy *h*)
wa-khuṣūṣan: *wa-choo-soo´-san* (guttural *ch*)
wa-qūlū li ʾl-muftariyīn: *wa-qoo´-loo lil-moof-ta-ree-yeen´*
Yā ayyuhā ʾl-Miṣriyyīn: *ya ay-yoo´-hal mis-ree-yeen´*
yatamallakū: *ya-ta-mal´-la-koo*
yufsidūn min muddat ʿuṣūr: *yoof-si-doon´ min mud-dat oo-soor´*
zumra: *zoom´-ruh*

FROM THE HISTORY OF THE PERIOD OF THE FRENCH OCCUPATION

On Monday news arrived that the French had reached Damanhūr and Rosetta, bringing about the flight of their inhabitants to Fuwwa[1] and its surroundings. Contained in this news was mention of the French sending notices throughout the country demanding impost for the upkeep of the military. Furthermore they printed a large proclamation in Arabic, calling on the people to obey them and to raise their 'Bandiera'.[2] In this proclamation were inducements, warnings, all manner of wiliness and stipulations. Some copies were sent from the provinces to Cairo and its text is:

In the name of God, the Merciful, the Compassionate. There is no god but God. He has no son, nor has He an associate in His Dominion.

On behalf of the French Republic which is based upon the foundation of liberty and equality, General Bonaparte, Commander-in-Chief of the French armies makes known to all the Egyptian people that for a long time the Ṣanjaqs[3] who lorded it over Egypt have treated the French community basely and contemptuously and have persecuted its merchants with all manner of extortion and violence. Therefore the hour of punishment has now come.

Unfortunately this group of Mamlūks,[4] imported from the mountains of Circassia and Georgia have acted corruptly for ages in the fairest land that is to be found upon the face of the globe. However, the Lord of the Universe, the Almighty, has decreed the end of their power.

O ye Egyptians, they may say to you that I have not made an expedition hither for any other object than that of abolishing your religion: but this is a pure falsehood and you must not give credit to it, but tell the slanderers that I have not come to you except for the purpose of restoring your rights from the hands of the oppressors and that I more than the Mamlūks, serve God—may He be praised and exalted—and revere His Prophet Muḥammad and the glorious Qur'ān.

And tell them also that all people are equal in the eyes of God and the only circumstances which distinguish one from the other are reason, virtue, and knowledge. But amongst the Mamlūks, what is there of reason, virtue, and knowledge, which would distinguish them from others and qualify them alone to possess everything which sweetens life in this world? Wherever fertile land is found it is appropriated to the Mamlūks; and the handsomest female slaves, and the best horses, and the most desirable dwelling-places, all these belong to them exclusively. If the land of Egypt is a fief of the Mamlūks, let them then produce the title-deed, which God conferred upon them. But the Lord of the Universe is compassionate and equitable toward mankind, and with the help of the Exalted, from this day

TRANSLATED BY S. Moreh. All bracketed additions are the translator's.

1. An Egyptian city about 50 miles east of Alexandria; it lies between Damanhur, about 40 miles southeast of Alexandria, and Rosetta, on the coast of the Mediterranean about 40 miles northeast of Alexandria.
2. Flag (Italian).
3. Ottoman governors who ruled over Egypt. Napoleon Bonaparte (1769–1821) became commander of the army of the Interior in 1795 and would become emperor of the French in 1805.
4. The military class that ruled Egypt from 1250 to 1517; originally they were slaves (in Arabic, "slave" is *mamluk*) who served the 'Abbasid caliphs. Under the Ottomans, who conquered Egypt in 1517, they acted as governors.

forward no Egyptian shall be excluded from admission to eminent positions nor from acquiring high ranks, therefore the intelligent and virtuous and learned (*ʿulamāʾ*) amongst them, will regulate their affairs, and thus the state of the whole population will be rightly adjusted.

Formerly, in the lands of Egypt there were great cities, and wide canals and extensive commerce and nothing ruined all this but the avarice and the tyranny of the Mamlūks.

O ye Qāḍīs,[5] Shaykhs and Imāms; O ye Shurbājiyya[6] and men of circumstance tell your nation that the French are also faithful Muslims, and in confirmation of this they invaded Rome and destroyed there the Papal See, which was always exhorting the Christians to make war with Islam. And then they went to the island of Malta, from where they expelled the Knights,[7] who claimed that God the Exalted required them to fight the Muslims. Furthermore, the French at all times have declared themselves to be the most sincere friends of the Ottoman Sultan and the enemy of his enemies, may God ever perpetuate his empire! And on the contrary the Mamlūks have withheld their obeisance from the Sultan, and have not followed his orders. Indeed they never obeyed anything but their own greed!

Blessing on blessing to the Egyptians who will act in concert with us, without any delay, for their condition shall be rightly adjusted, and their rank raised. Blessing also, upon those who will abide in their habitations, not siding with either of the two hostile parties, yet when they know us better, they will hasten to us with all their hearts. But woe upon woe to those who will unite with the Mamlūks and assist them in the war against us, for they will not find the way of escape, and no trace of them shall remain.

First Article

All the villages, situated within three hours' distance from the places through which the French army passes, are required to send to the Commander-in-Chief some persons, deputed by them, to announce to the aforesaid, that they submit and that they have hoisted the French flag, which is white, blue, and red.

Second Article

Every village that shall rise against the French army, shall be burnt down.

Third Article

Every village that submits to the French army must hoist the French flag and also the flag of our friend the Ottoman Sultan, may he continue for ever.

Fourth Article

The Shaykh of each village must immediately seal all property, houses, and possessions, belonging to the Mamlūks, making the most strenuous effort that not the least thing be lost.

Fifth Article

The Shaykhs, Qāḍīs, and Imāms must remain at their posts, and every countryman shall remain peaceably in his dwelling, and also prayers shall be performed in the mosques as customary and the Egyptians, all of them

5. Judges.
6. Military officers in Ottoman Egypt's most elite regiment.
7. The Knights of Malta or Hospitallers, a religious military order founded in Jerusalem in the 11th century and charged with the defense of the Holy Land; they had sovereignty on Malta from 1530 until 1798, when Napoleon expelled them.

shall render thanks for God's graciousness, praise be to Him and may He be exalted, in extirpating the power of the Mamlūks, saying with a loud voice, May God perpetuate the glory of the Ottoman Sultan! May God preserve the glory of the French army! May God curse the Mamlūks and rightly adjust the condition of the Egyptian people.

Written in the Camp at Alexandria on the 13th of the month Messidor[8] [the 6th year] of the founding of the French Republic, that is to say toward the end of the month Muḥarram in the year [1213] of the Hijra [2 July 1798].

It ends here word for word. Here is an explanation of the incoherent words and vulgar constructions which he put into this miserable letter.

His statement 'In the name of God, the Merciful, the Compassionate. There is no god but God. He has no son, nor has He an associate in His Dominion'. In mentioning these three sentences there is an indication that the French agree with the three religions, but at the same time they do not agree with them, nor with any religion. They are consistent with the Muslims in stating the formula 'In the name of God', in denying that He has a son or an associate. They disagree with the Muslims in not mentioning the two Articles of Faith,[9] in rejecting the mission of Muḥammad, and the legal words and deeds which are necessarily recognized by religion. They agree with the Christians in most of their words and deeds, but disagree with them by not mentioning the Trinity, and denying the mission and furthermore in rejecting their beliefs, killing the priests, and destroying the churches. Then, their statement 'On behalf of the French Republic, etc.', that is, this proclamation is sent from their Republic, that means their body politic, because they have no chief or sultan with whom they all agree, like others, whose function is to speak on their behalf. For when they rebelled against their sultan[1] six years ago and killed him, the people agreed unanimously that there was not to be a single ruler but that their state, territories, laws, and administration of their affairs, should be in the hands of the intelligent and wise men among them. They appointed persons chosen by them and made them heads of the army, and below them generals and commanders of thousands, two hundreds, and tens, administrators and advisers, on condition that they were all to be equal and none superior to any other in view of the equality of creation and nature. They made this the foundation and basis of their system. This is the meaning of their statement 'based upon the foundation of liberty and equality'. Their term 'liberty' means that they are not slaves like the Mamlūks; 'equality' has the aforesaid meaning. Their officials are distinguished by the cleanliness of their garments. They wear emblems on their uniforms and upon their heads. For example an Amīr of ten has a large rosette of silk upon his head like a big rose. If he is a commander of twenty-five his rosette is of two colours, and if he is a commander of a hundred his rosette is of three colours. His hat which is known as *burnayṭa* (It. *borreta*) is embroidered with gold brocade, or he may bear upon his shoulders an emblem of the same. If he has a reputation for daring and is well-known for his heroism and has been wounded several times he receives two badges on his shoulder. They follow this rule: great and small, high and

8. The tenth month in the French Revolutionary calendar, used from 1793 until 1805.
9. There is no God but God, and Muhammad is his messenger.
1. That is, Louis XVI (1754–1793; r. 1774–92).

low, male and female are all equal. Sometimes they break this rule according to their whims and inclinations or reasoning. Their women do not veil themselves and have no modesty; they do not care whether they uncover their private parts. Whenever a Frenchman has to perform an act of nature he does so wherever he happens to be, even in full view of people, and he goes away as he is, without washing his private parts after defecation. If he is a man of taste and refinement he wipes himself with whatever he finds, even with a paper with writing on it, otherwise he remains as he is. They have intercourse with any woman who pleases them and vice versa. Sometimes one of their women goes into a barber's shop, and invites him to shave her pubic hair. If he wishes he can take his fee in kind. It is their custom to shave both their moustaches and beard. Some of them leave the hair of their cheeks only.

They do not shave their heads nor their pubic hair. They mix their foods. Some might even put together in one dish coffee, sugar, arrack,[2] raw eggs, limes, and so on. As for the name 'Bonaparté' this is the title of their general, it is not a name.[3] Its meaning is 'the pleasant gathering', because *Bona* (*Būnā*) means 'pleasant' and *parté* means 'gathering'. His statement 'for a long time' is a redundant adverb (*ẓarf laghw*) connected with his saying 'have treated' and the implication underlying the statement is that the Ṣanjaqs who are ruling over Egypt have been treating for a long time, etc. *Ṣanājiq* is the plural of *Ṣanjāq*, he is so called with reference to the banner which is displayed over his head. Sometimes the *ṣād* is changed into *sīn*. The correct form of '*yatasalṭanū*' is *yatasalṭanūn* (to rule), because there is no reason to omit the *nūn*. The same applies to *yataʿāmalū* (to treat). His statement 'basely and contemptuously' is connected with an elision which again is connected with his statement *fī ḥaqq*, and the implication is that 'they give treatment with baseness and contempt'. But if he were to say *yuʿāmilūn al-Faransāwiyya bi'l-dhull wa'l-iḥtiqār* (they treat the French basely and contemptuously), it would be most excellently and succinctly expressed. In fact the French are more deserving of such a treatment. His statement *Faḥaḍara* (Therefore has come) there is no reason for this *fā* here. Good style would require *wa-qad ḥaḍara* (it has come). The word *al-ān* (now) is in the accusative, being an adverb modifying the verb *ḥaḍara* (has come) and *sāʿa* (the hour) is a subject. So the meaning is: 'the hour of their punishment has now come'. It is much better to delete the word now (*al-ān*), the adverb being redundant, because *al-ān* is a noun denoting present time, and it is the same as the hour of punishment. It requires some constraint to turn it into a simple adverb of time, may God afflict them with every calamity. His statement *Wā ḥasratan* (Unfortunately), probably it is *wa-khuṣuṣan* (especially), because this word has no place here, for *wā ḥasratan* is a word expressing affliction and the context does not permit it here. Its occurrence here is like animal droppings on the road or a boulder in a mountain pass, may God afflict the man who composed it with break-bone fever and may God expose him to all sorts of destruction. His statement 'for ages' is connected with his statement 'have acted corruptly' (*yufsidū*) which is corrupt like all former and later verbs in the imperfect, because the *nūn* has been

2. An alcoholic drink.
3. Napoleon's father was in fact named Buonaparte; he belonged to a Corsican family of Italian origin.

omitted. The expression should be read as *yufsidūn min muddat ʿuṣūr* (they have been corrupting for ages). He qualifies the ages as long in order to clarify and explain. However, *ʿuṣūr* is the plural of *ʿaṣr* (age), *ʿaṣr* means time, and so if they are numerous ages they are long. The correct form of *al-majlūbīn* is *al-majlūbūn* (imported), because it is an adjective qualifying the *zumra* (group), or it is *naʿt maqṭūʿ* (an adjective cut off from its qualified noun).

His statement *alladhī yūwjad* (that is to be found) should be *alladhī lā yūwjad* (that is not to be found). The expression is not complete without *lā*.

His statement *fa-ammā Rabb al-ʿālamīn* (However the Lord of the Universe) is recommencement: 'the Almighty', (indeed He is), and one aspect and clear sign of His great power is bringing these devils to the fertile land of the kings and sultans, and their discomfiture and their destruction.

His saying *qad ḥattama* etc. (has decreed) shows that they are appointing themselves controllers of God's secrets, but there is no disgrace worse than disbelief. *Yā ayyuhā 'l-Miṣriyyīn* should be *al-Miṣriyyūn*, because it is a vocative.

His statement *'qad yaqūlū lakum'* (they may say) refers to those who fabricate lies against us.

His saying *fī hādhā 'l-ṭaraf* (hither), means 'this part of the earth'. His statement *wa-qūlū li 'l-muftariyīn* (but tell the slanderers) is the plural of *muftarī* (slanderer) which means liar, and how worthy of this description they are. The proof of that is his saying 'I have not come to you except for the purpose of restoring your rights from the hands of the oppressors', which is the first lie he uttered and a falsehood which he invented. Then he proceeds to something even worse than that, may God cast him into perdition, with his words: 'I more than the Mamlūks serve God . . .'. There is no doubt that this is a derangement of his mind, and an excess of foolishness. What a worship he is speaking about, however great its intensity, *kufr* (disbelief) had dulled his heart, and prevented him from reaching the way of his salvation. There is inversion in the words which should read *innanī aʿbudu Allāh akthar min al-Mamālik* (I serve God more than the Mamlūks do). However, it is possible that there is no inversion, and that the meaning is 'I have more troops or more money than the Mamlūks' and that the accusative of specification has been omitted. So his words 'I serve God' are a new sentence and a new lie.

His statement '[I] revere His Prophet' is conjoined to what goes before, as one lie joined to another, because if he respected him he would believe in him, accept his truth, and respect his nation. His statement *al-Qurʾān al-ʿaẓim* (the glorious Qurʾān) is joined to 'His Prophet', that is, 'I respect the glorious Qurʾān', and this too is a lie, because to respect the Qurʾān means to glorify it, and one glorifies it by believing in what it contains. The Qurʾān is one of the miracles of the Prophet which proves his truth, and that he is the Prophet to the end of time, and that his nation is the most noble of all nations. These people deny all that and lie in every thing they enumerate. 'And many as are the signs in the Heavens and on the Earth, yet they will pass them by, and turn aside from them'.[4]

His saying '[all people] are equal in the eyes of God' the Almighty, this is a lie and stupidity. How can this be when God has made some superior to others as is testified by the dwellers in the Heavens and on the Earth?

4. Qurʾan 12:105.

In his statement *fa-huwa al-ʿaql* (it is the reason), there is no place for the *fā*, except that it is put in through the ignorance of the writer.

His statement *wa-bayn al-Mamālīk*, the word *bayn* is out of place and makes the language even more corrupt.

His saying *mā 'l-ʿaql* (what is there of reason), is a subject and predicate, and a rhetorical question. In this sentence there is an omission, that is 'to them', and the meaning is that the Mamlūks have no Reason.

His statement *kamā yaḥlū* (everything which sweetens) is an object to his word *yatamallakū* (to possess). His statement *Ḥaythumā* (wherever) is a new sentence, mentioned to enumerate the favours which the Mamlūks obtained.

His statement *fa 'l-yuwarrūnā* (let them then produce), this is a colloquial word which is not in accordance with Arabic style. His saying 'the title-deed, which God conferred upon them': this is base ignorance and *kufr* (heresy), because God does not give men possession of anything by writing a title-deed. What he means is that the people pass the country from hand to hand from their masters as these Mamlūks did, or from their masters' successors, or by conquest and compulsion. Prefixing *lākin* with *fa* is proof of ungrammatical language. The word *lākin* is as ungrammatical language as is the prefixing of *fa*.

As for his statement *ʿalā 'l-bashar* (toward mankind), it is more correct to say *bi 'l-bashar*, because the verb *raʾafa* (to show mercy) introduces its object with *bi*, but the verb *ʿadala* is intransitive.

His saying *bi-ʿawnih* (with the help of) is connected with his statement *lā yustathnā aḥad* (no one shall be excluded from) and so is his saying *min al-yawm* (from this day).

His statement *al-manāṣib al-sāmiya* (eminent positions), that means *al-murtafiʿa* (elevated). This is in order to avert blame from themselves by giving high posts of authority to the low and vulgar people among them, as for example their appointment of Barṭulmān (Barthélemy) the artilleryman to the post of Katkhudā Mustaḥfiẓān.[5] He says 'and thus the state of the whole population will be rightly adjusted'. Yes, that is to say, under the administration of wise and intelligent men. But they did not appoint them. The word *Muslimīn* should be *Muslimūn* in the nominative. The point of putting the word in the *naṣb* (accusative) has already been mentioned. There is another point namely: that their Islam is *naṣb* (fraud).

As for his statement 'and destroyed there the Papal See', by this deed they have gone against the Christians as has already been pointed out. So those people are opposed to both Christians and Muslims, and do not hold fast to any religion. You see that they are materialists, who deny all God's attributes, the Hereafter and Resurrection, and who reject Prophethood and Messengership. They believe that the world was not created, and that the heavenly bodies and the occurrences of the Universe are influenced by the movement of the stars, and that nations appear and states decline, according to the nature of the conjunctions and the aspects of the moon. Some believe in transmigration of souls, or other fantasies. For this reason they do not slaughter ritually any animal they eat or behead any man, before having killed them, so that the parts of his soul may not be separated and scattered,

5. A powerful second-in-command among regimental officers in the infantry regiment known as the Janissaries.

so as not to be whole in another body, and similar nonsense and erroneous beliefs. The word *sanjāq* should be *ṣanjaq* without the *ā*.

His statement *btāʿ al-Mamālīk* (belonging to the Mamlūks) is despicable and a banal and trite word. The word *muṭmaʾin* should be *muṭmaʾinan* because it is *ḥāl* (circumstantial expression), and converting it to the nominative (*rafʿ*) incorrectly is an indication of their state, and their insignificance. May God hurry misfortune and punishment upon them, may He strike their tongues with dumbness, may He scatter their hosts, and disperse them, confound their intelligence, and cause their breath to cease. He has the power to do that, and it is up to Him to answer.

NANA ASMAʾU
1793–1864

A daughter of the famous nineteenth-century West African scholar and warrior Usman dan Fodio (1754–1817), Nana Asmaʾu was learned in her own right and championed women's education in West Africa.

Asmaʾu's contributions can only be understood in the context of the holy war (in Arabic, *jihad*) that her father waged in Gobir, an area located in the northwest of present-day Nigeria. Usman dan Fodio, often known as the Shehu (shaykh), came from a long line of West African Muslim scholars, and like them he received a standard Islamic education. After completing his studies, he began his career in Gobir as a teacher and public preacher around 1775. While many in this kingdom were nominally Muslim, animistic religions flourished in the region and some fusion of practices was common. Dan Fodio preached a populist, inclusive message that challenged this syncretism that had crept into Islamic practices while promoting Islam as a religion of morality and social justice. Through the 1780s and '90s his message enjoyed a positive reception, and he quickly attracted a large popular following, especially among the kingdom's poor and enslaved. Local rulers were understandably worried by his burgeoning popular support—new converts refused to pay taxes, were unwilling to serve in the military, and fled their slave masters. Further, Dan Fodio's followers had started arming themselves, ostensibly for self-defense. In 1797, the then ruler of Gobir, who was nominally a Muslim, banned Dan Fodio's disciples from preaching in public, forbade the conversion of non-Muslim males to Islam, and prohibited the wearing of turbans and veils. Dan Fodio's supporters were harassed and targeted by the kingdom's security apparatus, and relations between the two sides deteriorated.

As a result, Dan Fodio and many of his followers emigrated from the kingdom in 1804 to a region northwest of Gobir and outside of its control. Now in his fifties, Dan Fodio declared a holy war against Gobir and its rulers, whom he condemned as being non-Muslims by virtue of their attacks on Muslims. Against formidable odds, he established a functioning state, usually referred to as the Sokoto caliphate, and by 1808 his military commanders had captured the capital of Gobir. Within a few years, Dan Fodio, while remaining the titular caliph, devolved authority to his two most trusted ministers: his son Muhammad Bello (d. 1837), who ruled the eastern half of the state, and his brother Abdullahi, who ruled the western half. Dan Fodio himself returned to teaching and preaching, and criticized, as did his two ministers, any shortcomings he found in the new state.

Nana Asmaʾu was one of her father's thirty-six children and received a thorough Islamic education. She memorized the Qurʾan while young; studied foundational texts on law, exegesis, and spirituality; and knew four languages (including Arabic). At about age eleven she emigrated with her family from Gobir; in the ensuing years of war and after, she continued her studies, bore children, wrote, and taught both men and women. She was instrumental in preserving her father's extensive corpus of writings, which she started collating soon after his death, while simultaneously managing a household of several hundred individuals. She was consulted on the political decisions of the state and was well-known as far west as Mauritania, whose scholars sent her greetings. Like her father, she championed the education of women, and this is where her real strength lay. She built a network to instruct the underprivileged, rural women of the region in the basic tenets of Islam and its teachings on moral rectitude. This network was designed to enable women to run their households while continuing to receive education and instruction from local teachers. Out of gratitude, participants in the program would send Asmaʾu donations, often consisting of foodstuffs, which she would then distribute among the needy of the state.

Though the full range of Asmaʾu's written works is not known, some didactic poems for her students and a number of elegies survive. Reproduced below are two elegies she composed after the death of her brother Muhammad Bello, who became head of the Sokoto caliphate upon Dan Fodio's death. The poems reveal the depth of sorrow at the loss of Bello, her reverence for his character, and the close bond the two shared throughout their lives. The first poem exists in two versions, Arabic and Fulfulde; the second was composed in Fulfulde.

PRONOUNCING GLOSSARY

Caliph: *ka´-lif*
ḥadīth: *ha-deeth´* (heavy *h*)
Sharʿīa: *sha-ree´-uh*
Shaikh: *shaych* (guttural *ch*)

ELEGY FOR BELLO

I rely on God the Enthroned, the Pure, the Omnipotent,
To help me to accept what He has inflicted on me.
May He help in my loneliness. Only God
Can ease this loneliness, for He is All-Powerful.
        God the Almighty can work all things.
I rely on the most Excellent of mortals[1]
I invoke peace upon him
Whose benevolence is free from taint
Also on his Relatives and Companions may there fall
        The peace of him whose guidance illuminates our Path.
Calling on him, I weep and compose this poem
Shedding tears for the passing of the Caliph[2]
I seek to soothe my heart
In this world of sadness and confusion
        I relive the loss of my Shaikh.

Translated by Jean Boyd and Beverly B. Mack.

1. The prophet Muhammad [translator's note].
2. Asmaʾu's brother Muhammad Bello became head of the Sokoto caliphate after the death of their father, Usman dan Fodio, who established it.

I am alone, missing the eternal love, the companionship
Of my brother, we were confidants,
He was my mentor;
I shall never have that again.
    I cannot tell all, but will explain some points.
Restless and agitated I turn again to God the Pure on whom I rely
I weep over my prayer beads[3]
And when I try to sleep I toss and turn
In grief as I remember Bello.
    May God reunite us with him.
Reunite me with him in the realms of Heaven,
Oh God most Holy, Gracious, You can do this.
My sins terrify me
But I still hope for Your mercy.
    For Your Generosity is limitless.
I am like a small chicken
Whose mother died, leaving him crying forlornly.
Or like someone abandoned in the wilderness,
Howling until his ears are closed forever.
    God alone can wipe away my grief.
I am like an abandoned infant,
Left piteous and vulnerable,
Like a mother and father he cared for me,
That is how I remember him.
    Only the grace of God can help me.
He helped me in every respect as far as my religion and my worldly affairs,
    everything,
God knows, and so do the people.
He was my teacher.
He helped all people with their affairs:
    He had concern for their welfare and he did things
      according to Religion.
He was upright, exceedingly generous, patient:
He spread learning and explained matters.
He was wise. He could turn back prodigals
And used his wits to remedy any situation.
    Oh God help us, for You are merciful.
In his day he was unique in his status
Among scholars and non-scholars alike.
He assuaged people's griefs and fears,
He was a refuge, a haven
    In our time. Listen to what I say.
He had a fine character, he was merciful to the poor, he honored
And befriended people.
He was gracious to strangers and generous to them,
Looked after their interests, fed them.
    It was his nature to be very generous.
He was never ill-tempered, he was pleasant to everyone,
Only if the law was broken did he become angry.
In that case he was implacable and could not be appeased.

3. Stringed beads used in reciting prayer litanies or the ninety-nine names or descriptions of God.

When he regained equanimity he was calm.
These were his characteristics from his boyhood.
Oh God bestow on him Your blessings,
Your mercy, and perfume him
In his grave with Your favors;
Light up his tomb;[4] give him honor
For the honor of he who exceeds honor,[5] I make my plea.
On the Day of Resurrection may he be saved
By the grace of the Prophet
And drink from the Pool,[6]
And be taken to Paradise the abode of the Prophet.
By the grace of Ahmad.[7]
May he see the face of the Prophet the Chosen One,
And may he be with those who see God's Majesty.
May he be united with his father and mother and all Muslims
Who have followed Muhammad's way.
In the name of the Prophet, our leader.
Let us pray that God will help us now that Bello is gone
And give victory to his successor.
May he have a long life
And defend religion, as Bello did,
In the name of the Prophet I make this plea.
My poem is completed. May God accept it.
I give thanks
And invoke blessings on the Prophet,
His Companions and the Saints.
I ask for enlightenment through the Prophet.
Count on good news from the Hijra of the Prophet
To Medina, the date is fixed.
Count and see, take care. Reflect.
You know where he went,
And remember "God is our helper". Here the poem is complete.'

BELLO'S CHARACTER

I give thanks to the King of Heaven, the One God
I invoke blessings on the Prophet and set down my poem.
The Lord made Heaven and earth and created all things,
sent prophets to enlighten mankind.
Believe in them for your own sake, learn from them and be saved,
believe in and act upon their sayings.
I invoke blessings on the Prophet who brought the Book, the Qur'an:
he brought the *hadith* to complete the enlightenment.
Muslim scholars have explained knowledge and used it,
following in the footsteps of the Prophet.

4. The graves of the good are said to be aromatic and light, reflecting the positive spiritual attributes of the deceased [translator's note].
5. The prophet Muhammad [translator's note].
6. Kawthar, a pool from which the inhabitants of paradise drink.
7. Another name of Muhammad.

It is my intention to set down Bello's characteristics
and explain his ways.
For I wish to assuage my loneliness, requite my love,
find peace of mind through my religion.
These are his characteristics: he was learned in all branches of knowledge
and feared God in public and in private.
He obeyed religious injunctions and distanced himself from forbidden things:
this is what is known about him.
He concentrated on understanding what is right to know
about the Oneness of God.
He preached to people and instructed them about God:
he caused them to long for Paradise.
He set an example in his focus on eternal values:
he strove to end oppression and sin.
He upheld the *Sharī'a*, honored it, implemented it aright,
that was his way, everyone knows.
And he made his views known to those who visited him:
he said to them "Follow the *Sharī'a*, which is sacred."
He eschewed worldly things and discriminated against anything of ill-repute;
he was modest and a repository of useful knowledge.
He was exceedingly level-headed and generous, he enjoyed periods of quietude:
but was energetic when he put his hand to things.
He was thoughtful, calm, a confident statesman, and quick-witted.
He honored people's status: he could sort out difficulties
and advise those who sought his help.
He had nothing to do with worldly concerns, but tried to restore to a healthy state
things which he could. These were his characteristics.
He never broke promises, but faithfully kept them:
he sought out righteous things. Ask and you will hear.
He divorced himself entirely from bribery and was totally scrupulous:
He flung back at the givers money offered for titles.
One day Garange sent him a splendid gift,
but Bello told the messenger Zitaro to take it back.[1]
He said to the envoy who had brought the bribe,
"Have nothing to do with forbidden things."
And furthermore he said, "Tell him that the gift was sent for unlawful purposes;
it is wrong to respond to evil intent."
He was able to expedite matters: he facilitated learning, commerce,
and defense, and encouraged everything good.
He propagated good relationships between different tribes
and between kinsmen. He afforded protection; everyone knows this.
When strangers came he met them, and taught about religious matters,
explaining things: he tried to enlighten them.

1. Garange was the Chief of Mafara in Bukkwuyam or Bukkuyum District (located in present-day Zamfara State, in northwest Nigeria); Zitaro was the envoy [translator's note, edited].

He lived in a state of preparedness, he had his affairs in order
and had an excellent intelligence service.
He had nothing to do with double agents and said it was better to ignore them,
for they pervert Islamic principles.
He was a very pleasant companion to friends and acquaintances:
he was intelligent, with a lively mind.
He fulfilled promises and took care of affairs, but he did not act hastily.
He shouldered responsibilities and patiently endured adversities.
He was watchful and capable of restoring to good order
matters which had gone wrong.
He was resourceful and could undo mischief, no matter how serious,
because he was a man of ideas.
He was gracious to important people and was hospitable to all visitors,
including non-Muslims.
He drew good people close to him and
distanced himself from people of ill-repute.
Those are his characteristics. I have recounted a few examples
that are sufficient to provide a model for emulation and benefit.
May God forgive him and have mercy on him:
May we be united with him in Paradise, the place we aspire to.
For the sake of the Prophet, the Compassionate,
who was sent with mercy to mankind.
May God pour blessings on the Prophet and
his Kinsmen and all other Followers.
May God accept this poem. I have concluded it in the year 1254.

MUHAMMAD ʿABDUH
1849–1905

Muhammad ʿAbduh, a major modern thinker, devoted his teaching, writing, and organizational leadership to the reform and renewal of Muslim thought and institutional structures. Although he lived during an era of European dominance and colonial dislocation, ʿAbduh recognized and embraced Western advances in science and education.

Born to a peasant family in Mahallat Nasr, Egypt, ʿAbduh did not begin his formal schooling until age thirteen—and he quit before fifteen, dismayed by the reliance on rote memorization. One of his uncles, Shaykh Darwish, introduced him to Sufism and persuaded him to recommit to his studies. In 1866 he enrolled at al-Azhar University in Cairo, where, in addition to his other subjects, he quickly became immersed in the study of Sufi thought.

In 1870, while still at al-Azhar, ʿAbduh met Jamal al-Din al-Afghani (1838–1897), who would become one of the most significant influences on his life. The anticolonial ideologue and activist had attracted many followers in Cairo, and a number in his circle would later figure prominently in twentieth-century Egyptian history. His lectures on philosophical and literary topics opened their eyes to the problems facing Egypt and the Muslim world. ʿAbduh was captivated by al-Afghani's visionary rhetoric and embraced the more expansive intellectual horizon it opened for him. Upon completing his program at al-Azhar in 1877, ʿAbduh began teaching; he was appointed to two separate positions, one at a training college for teachers and the other at a school for Arabic language and literature. His courses soon showed his characteristic blend of classical Muslim sources, such as *The Refinement of Character* by Miskawayh (ca. 930–1030; see above) and *Introduction to History* by Ibn Khaldun (1332–1406; see above), with contemporary European works like François Guizot's *General History of Civilization in Europe* (1828). During this time he also began writing newspaper articles with a reformist agenda, an activity he sustained throughout his life, on subjects covering everything from the advantages of modern science to the important role of a free press.

In 1879 the Ottoman sultan, at the behest of the French and British, appointed Muhammad Tawfiq (r. 1879–92) as Khedive (ruler) of Egypt. Tawfiq promptly banished al-Afghani, while ʿAbduh—almost certainly because of his connection to the outspoken activist—was dismissed from his teaching position and ordered to return to his native town. But about a year later, he was invited back to Cairo as an editor of the official state paper, *Egyptian Events*. In it, he wrote articles criticizing the moral and social decay in Egyptian society and voicing anew his commitment to reform. For ʿAbduh, reform could occur only if individuals were educated; he promoted the study of science, but insisted that the foundations of pedagogy were religious and moral teachings.

In December 1882 ʿAbduh's fortunes changed again. He was sentenced to three years in exile for allegedly supporting Ahmad ʿUrabi Pasha (1839–1911), the minister of war, who had rebelled against Khedive Tawfiq and his colonial backers; he would in fact be gone for six years. In 1884 he left Beirut for Paris, where he reconnected with al-Afghani and with him founded a society and journal called *The Strongest Bond* that advocated a pan-Islamism, urging Muslim unity as a counterforce to colonial domination. Though it did not survive a year, this journal had an enduring influence. After traveling to England and throughout the Middle East promoting the journal, in 1885 ʿAbduh decided to settle in Beirut. He taught at a high school and attracted a large circle of students and scholars whom he addressed on various topics. A series of lectures on theology formed the basis for his most famous work, *The Theology of Unity*. He also edited several works of classical Muslim scholarship for publication and continued to write for journals and newspapers.

In 1889 ʿAbduh was allowed to return to Egypt; initially barred from teaching, he was appointed to a series of judgeships, until in 1899 he was made the chief jurisconsult (*mufti*) of Egypt, a position he held until his death. By 1894, however, he was permitted to resume his work as an educator, and in 1895 he inaugurated a process of academic reforms at al-Azhar. His recommendations, which included expanding the curriculum to incorporate the study of ethics and history, were only partially implemented, but they provided a foundation for many later reformers. Even after his return to Egypt he continued to travel extensively and write prolifically. Many of his thoughts are preserved in the articles he wrote for *The Lighthouse*, a monthly journal launched in 1898 by his student Rashid Rida (1865–1935); it published sections of ʿAbduh's unfinished Qur'an commentary, based on Rida's lecture notes.

Several themes dominate ʿAbduh's life and work. Most apparent was his call to religious reform. ʿAbduh was convinced that many Muslim scholars had abandoned the abiding beliefs and values of Islam for legal and theological hairsplitting. Thus he rejected the traditional notions of binding, communal consensus (*ijmaʿ*) and adherence to precedents set by earlier legal scholars (*taqlid*). Instead, he urged scholars to a fresh engagement with issues (*ijtihad*), unburdened by the weight of tradition. ʿAbduh himself felt free to draw on multiple legal schools (a process called *talfiq*) in his fatwas, some of which were controversial. For example, he permitted the consumption of meat from animals slaughtered by Christians who did not follow Muslim rituals.

ʿAbduh was concerned with social and institutional reform as well. Though he blamed many of the problems of Muslim societies on their tyrannical rulers, he also criticized the citizens for their love of wealth, acceptance of corruption, and embrace of nepotism. He promoted institutional reform in the areas most familiar to him, the educational and judicial systems.

Yet another theme to which ʿAbduh constantly returned was the absence of conflict between modern science and Islam, the pinnacle of all religions—which, he argued, was founded on and appealed to rational thought. His emphasis on interpreting Islamic texts in harmony with modern science whenever possible likely explains why, despite his early infatuation with Sufism, he was skeptical toward miracles and the purported abilities of the saints, which in his view contradict the laws of science.

The excerpt below is taken from ʿAbduh's *The Theology of Unity*, published in 1897 after his return to Egypt. The *Theology* has been translated into several languages and used in many Muslim universities, including al-Azhar. In its introduction, ʿAbduh asserts that he composed the work because he was unsatisfied with the available theological literature. The classical works were "beyond the comprehension" of his students, and the intermediate-level books were stylistically outdated. The *Theology* covers not just topics familiar from earlier works, such as God's names and attributes, and proofs for his existence, but also subjects not normally found, such as a general theory of religious evolution and a history of Islam's expansion. In this passage, history is put to the service of theology. Islam's rapid and successful spread was directly due to the compelling clarity and rationality of its message. Reason, not the sword, was the spur.

PRONOUNCING GLOSSARY

ʿAlī ibn Abī Ṭālib: *ah´-lee ibn a-bee-tah´-lib*
Ismāʿīl: *is-mah´-eel*
jizyah: *jiz´-yuh*
Surah: *soo´-ruh*
ʿUmar ibn ʿAbd al-ʿAzīz: *oh´-mar ibn abd-ul-ah-zeez´*

FROM THE THEOLOGY OF UNITY

Chapter 15. The Expansion of Islam: Its Unparalleled Speed

The need of the nations for reformation was one which they all shared, so God made the mission-message of the final Prophet universal. Even so the intelligent observer of human events is left in utter amazement at the way in which Islam gathered the whole of the Arab nation from end to end into its allegiance in less than thirty years, and then embraced other nations from the western ocean to the borders of China in less than one century. No other religion has a comparable story and for that very reason many have missed the real explanation. But the fair-minded understood and left no cause for idle wonderment.

Like other religions, Islam began with its message. But it encountered a quite unprecedented enmity on the part of those who in their perversity oppressed the truth. No prophet had such antagonism or faced such humiliation as Muḥammad—trials which he would never have survived

TRANSLATED BY Isḥāq Musaʿad and Kenneth Cragg.

without God's protection. Those who responded to his message were brow-beaten, denied food and ejected from their homes. Much blood was shed. When blood seals faith it is as if springs of high resolves are set flowing from the hard rocks of patient endurance. At the sight of it, God strengthened the righteous and struck misgiving into the obdurate. It might be compared to a surgeon's blood-letting by which the body is rid of its corruption. For at the sight of it some of the dubious folk were melted in heart and their evil purged: 'That God may separate the bad from the good and gathering the bad together cast them as one into hell. Truly these are the lost.' (Surah 8.37.)

The different religious sects inhabiting the Arabian peninsula and neighbouring areas joined forces against Islam to root it out and strangle its message. It was a case of the strong against the weak, the wealthy against the poor. Islam in its steadfast self-defence had nothing to rely on save its inherent truth, pitted against error and the light of its guidance in the darkness of falsehood, to bring it to victory. Thus it gathered strength. Tribes in the Arabian peninsula of other religious allegiance were very active in propagating their creeds and had rulers, power and authority all on their side, and stooping to cunning devices to further their ends. Nevertheless they achieved little and their forceful methods proved barren.

Islam cemented the desert peoples of Arabia into a unity hitherto unknown. There was nothing like it in their history. The Prophet extended his mission by God's command, to neighbouring territories, to the emperors of Persia and of Greece. But they scorned him, proscribed his message and evil-intreated both him and his people. They intimidated the caravans and waylaid the merchandise, to which Muḥammad replied with raids, sending deputations to their countries, as did the Caliphs his companions after his death, demanding safe passage and the acceptance of his message. The Muslims, despite their weakness and poverty, took the truth in their hands and went forth in its defence. They waged war against the superior enemy and overcame them, for all their vast numbers, strength and advanced equipment. When the distresses of war were spent and sovereignty passed to the victor, Islam treated the vanquished with kindly gentleness, allowed them to maintain their religions and their rites in security and peace. They gave them protection and safeguarded their possessions, as they did their own people and their property, levying for this service a slight tax on their incomes according to stipulated rates.

When non-Muslim powers conquered a kingdom they used to follow the army of conquest with an army of preachers of their faith, who took up quarters in the houses and occupied their councils, in order to impose the conqueror's religion. Their argument was force and their evidence conquest. It was not so with Muslim victors: such things were quite unknown in all their history. There were no preachers with the official and special duty to undertake propaganda and give their whole energies to urging their creed on non-Muslims. Instead the Muslims contented themselves with mixing among other peoples and treating them kindly. The entire world witnessed that Islam counted the proper treatment of conquered peoples a meritorious and virtuous thing, whereas Europeans regard such behaviour as weak and despicable.

Islam lightened the heavy burden of tribute payment and restored plundered property to its owners and dispossessed those who had extorted their unlawful gains. It gave equality before the law to Muslim and non-Muslim.

Subsequently it became a regulation that no one be accepted into Islam except before a judge of the sacred law who required from the new Muslim a declaration that he had become a Muslim without duress and without personal self-interest. Under some of the Umayyad Caliphs it even happened that the district administrators looked with strong disfavour on Islamizing because of the resultant decrease in the tax yield of the *jizyah*,[1] or tribute. Such officials were undoubtedly a deterrent to the spread of the faith and for that reason ʿUmar ibn ʿAbd al-ʿAzīz[2] ordered that they should be reprimanded.

The Muslim Caliphs and rulers in all periods recognized the skills of various kinds which some of the people of the Book,[3] and others too, possessed. They brought them into their service and gave them the highest positions even to the point of putting them in command of the armies in Spain.

Such was the fame of Islamic lands for freedom of religion that Jews from Europe migrated, as for example to Andalusia, and elsewhere, seeking sanctuary for their religion.

So much for the benign policy of Muslims towards those whom their swords guarded. Their only concern was to bring to these peoples the Book of God[4] and His holy law, which they offered them in full freedom either to accept or refuse. They did not preach among them and used no forcible methods to induce faith. Nor was the tribute tax in any way onerous. What then was it which drew the adherents of the various faiths into Islam and convinced them that in Islam, rather than in their ancestral beliefs, the truth lay, so that they espoused it en masse and even outdid the Arabs themselves in its zealous service?

The triumph of Islam over the various pagan rites of the Arabian peninsula, its victory over the vicious pagan practices and evil ways, and its success in leading the inhabitants to uprightness and excellence of character, made the readers of earlier scriptures realize that here was the fulfilment of God's promise to Abraham or Ismāʿīl.[5] Herein was the answer to the prayer of the former, the friend of God: 'O our Lord, send among them a messenger from their own ranks.' (Surah 2.129.) This is the religion which the prophets proclaimed to their peoples after them. The just folk among them could no longer hold out in obstinate resistance to it, but gratefully embraced it and patiently abandoned their patrimony.

These conversions occasioned much heart-searching among those who held by their traditions and aroused them to look into Islam, where they met with kindliness and compassion, with goodness and grace, not a creed which scared away reason. For reason is the pioneer of authentic belief. Nor is it in any way onerous for human nature, which is the true criterion of what best serves and befits human needs. They saw that Islam lifts the souls of men by an awareness of the Divine to a point where men almost

1. A tax levied on non-Muslim subjects of a Muslim state.
2. An Umayyad caliph who was a pious reformer (682/83–720; r. 717–20).
3. A common qurʾanic designation for the Jews and Christians (members of religions that have scripture).
4. The Qurʾan.
5. Ishmael.

transcend the lower world and become a part of the heavenly kingdom. Islam invites men to the daily renewal of that awareness of God through the five times of prayer,[6] yet for all that it does not impede the delight of pleasurable things. It does not impose disciplines and acts of asceticism that would be a burden upon natural human proclivities. It considers that the body should have its rights consistently with pure conscience and proper intention and takes such an attitude to be pleasing to God and meritorious. If any man is carried away by passion and succumbs, there is Divine forgiveness for him when he duly repents and turns back.

Readers of the Qurʾān were much impressed with the simplicity of this religion and the way of life of its true and pure followers had great appeal. They realized the difference between the incomprehensible creeds and one whose essentials could be taken in at a glance. They almost stampeded into it to be free of the heavy, oppressive thing they endured.

Now the nations had what they were looking for—a religion with a mind to think. Now they had a faith which gave justice its due place. The main factor which deterred a massive and spontaneous accession to Islam to enjoy these things long-desired lay in the system of class privilege under which the nations laboured. By this some classes lorded it over others, without right. Rulers recked nothing of the interests of the common people if the desires of the higher classes conflicted with them. Here was a religion which regulated human rights and gave equal respect to persons of all classes, their beliefs, their dignity and their property. It gave, for example, to a poor non-Muslim woman the perfect right to refuse to sell her small dwelling, at any price, to some great amir, ruling absolutely over a large territory, who wanted it, not for private purposes, but in order to enlarge a mosque. When, in this particular case, he doubled the price and took forcible steps to acquire it and she raised a complaint to the Caliph, he issued an order to ensure her possession and reproached the amir for his action. Islamic justice permitted a Jew to take up a case before the judge against no less a person than ʿAlī ibn Abī Ṭālib,[7] who was made to stand with the plaintiff in the court-process until judgement was given.

The foregoing makes clear how the message and relationships Islam brought endeared even its enemies to it, and so revolutionized their outlook as to make them its allies and protégés.

Muslims were consistently motivated by the spirit of Islam through all periods. They were naturally disposed to friendship with their non-Muslim neighbours. Nor did they harbour enmity in their hearts towards those who differed from them, as long as the latter refrained from coercing them. It was from such hostile neighbours that the Muslims learned hatred and then only in a transient way. Once the causes of the animosity were terminated their hearts reverted readily to the earlier benevolence and easy relationships. Thus despite the negligence of their faith on the part of Muslims and their disloyalties and despite the efforts of many, intelligently or otherwise, to undermine it, Islam continued to expand, especially in China and Africa. The spectacle of numerous people of other communities coming into Islam

6. Before dawn, at noon, in the late afternoon, at sunset, and before retiring.

7. The fourth caliph (ca. 599–661), who was also Muhammad's cousin and son-in-law.

was an uninterrupted phenomenon—and adopting doctrines with open eyes, with no sword behind them and no inciter before them. They were prompted only by what they had seen of Islam's precepts with as yet little intellectual scrutiny of its laws.

Thus the speed of Islam's expansion and the welcome men of every community gave to its doctrine derived from the ease with which it could be understood, the simplicity of its principles and the justice of its laws. In a word, human nature in its need for a religion, demands one that is nearest to the interests of human nature and most akin to their hearts' emotions, one which offers security in both worlds. A religion meeting these criteria will find an effective way into the hearts and minds of men, without recourse to propagators consuming large sums and much time in order to multiply means and devise stratagems to way-lay people into accepting it.

This was the case with Islam in its original simplicity and the pristine purity in which God shaped it, and which it has continued in large measure to maintain in many parts of the world to this day.

Those who do not understand, or have no will to understand, all this say that Islam only expanded at this pace by dint of the sword. The Muslims conquered the territories of men with the Qur'ān in one hand and the sword in the other. They offered the Qur'ān to the defeated and if it was not accepted their life was forfeit. Forsooth! this is a great slander. Our earlier account of the way Muslims handled accessions to their authority is steadily authenticated by the chronicles and there can in general be no doubt whatever about it, even if there are disparities of detail. The Muslims only used the sword in self-defence and in retaliation against aggression. Subsequently opening up of those territories to conquest was a necessity of statecraft. Otherwise good neighbourliness and immunity was the principle of Muslim relationships and a way whereby Islam came to be known for what it was. The need for better intellectual and practical standards was a powerful factor leading men to adopt it.

Were the sword to propagate religion, the pursuit of such violent methods of compulsion would constitute a threat to every nation not accepting it—a mortal threat of annihilation from the face of the earth. This would need overwhelmingly large armies and the utmost expenditure of force. Such things had been initiated three whole centuries before the rise of Islam and continued for seven centuries more after Islam appeared. But those ten entire centuries of sword-propagation did not achieve what Islam accomplished in respect of accession of believers in less than one century. Add to that vain sword in those centuries, and following it at every step, the preachers saying what they will behind the security of the sword, and, withal, a spate of zeal and eloquence, and money to turn the hearts of the wavering—and all in vain! Surely all that is sign enough for those who are open to conviction.

How splendid is the wisdom of God in the pattern of Islam. It was a river of life welling up in the desert of Arabia, the remotest part of God's earth from civilization. It flowed out to cover and to embrace in one the territories it renewed, bringing to them a vitality, both popular and communal, so far-reaching that it included kingdoms whose people boasted of even heaven's glories and whose cultural achievements had no earthly equals. The reverberations of Islam gently loosened the stony hardness of men's spirits, releasing the vital secrets that lay within them. To the charge that Islam was not innocent of militant conquest provocatively, we reply that there is a Divine imperative by which the struggle in the created world between right and wrong, good and evil, is unrelenting, until God gives the verdict. If God brings spring upon the barren land to renew its dead wastes, and with moisture slakes its thirst so that fertility returns, will that be of less worth because in the course of it He removes some obstacles in His path and even a fine built house has to be destroyed?

The light of Islam shone in the lands where its devotees went, and the only factor at work in their relation with the local people was the Word of God heard and apprehended. At times the Muslims were pre-occupied with their own affairs and fell away from the right path. Then Islam halted like a commander whose allies have disappointed him and is about to give ground. 'God brings about what He intends.' (Surah 65.3.) The Islamic lands were invaded by the Tartar peoples, led by Jenghiz Khan,[8] pagans who despoiled the Muslims and were bent on total conquest, plunder and rapine. But it was not long before their successors adopted Islam as their religion and propagated it among their kin with the same consequences as elsewhere. They came to conquer the Muslims and they stayed to do them good.

The west made a sustained attack against the east,[9] involving all the kings and peoples, and continuing more than two hundred years, during which time the west engendered a quite unprecedented zeal and fervour for religion. With military forces and preparations to the utmost of their capacity, they advanced towards the Muslim hearth-lands, fired by religious devotion. They overran many countries of Islamic allegiance. Yet in the end these violent wars closed with their evacuation.

Why did they come and why did they return? The religious leaders of the west successfully aroused their peoples to make havoc of the eastern world and to seize the sovereignty over those nations on what they believed to be their prescriptive right to tyrannize over masses of men. They came in great numbers of all sorts of men, estimated in millions, many settling in Muslim territory as residents. There were periods of truce in which the angry fires abated and quieter tempers prevailed, when there was even time to take a look at the surrounding culture, pick up something from the medley of ideas and react to what was to be seen and heard. It became clear that the exaggerations of their idle dreams which had shaped into such grievous efforts had no vestige of truth. And, furthermore, they found freedom in a religion where knowledge, law and art could be possessed with entire certitude. They discovered that liberty of thought and breadth of knowledge were means to faith and not its foes. By God's will they acquired some experience of refined culture and went off to their own territories thrilled with what they had gained from their wars—not to mention the great gains the travellers gathered in the lands of Andalusia by intercourse with its learned and polished society, whence they returned to their own peoples to taste the sweet fruits they had reaped. From that time on, there began to be much more traffic in ideas. In the west the desire for knowledge intensified and concern grew to break the entail of obscurantism. A strong resolve was

8. Ghenghis Khan (ca. 1162–1227) unified the Mongols; their forces led by his grandson Hulegu (ca. 1217–1265) sacked Baghdad in 1258.

9. That is, the Crusades (1095–1291).

generated to curb the authority of religious leaders and keep them from exceeding the proper precepts of religion and corrupting its valid meanings. It was not long after that a party made its appearance in the west calling for reform and a return to the simplicities of the faith—a reformation which included elements by no means unlike Islam. Indeed, some of the reforming groups brought their doctrines to a point closely in line with the dogma of Islam, with the exception of belief in the prophetic mission of Muḥammad. Their religion was in all but name the religion of Muḥammad; it differed only in the shape of worship, not in meaning or anything else.

Then it was that the nations of Europe began to throw off their bondage and reform their condition, re-ordering the affairs of their life in a manner akin to the message of Islam, though oblivious of who their real guide and leader was. So were enunciated the fundamental principles of modern civilization in which subsequent generations as compared with the peoples of earlier days have found their pride and glory.

All this was like a copious dew falling on the welcoming earth, which stirs and brings forth a glad growth of every kind. Those who had come for strife, stayed to benefit and returned to benefit others in turn. Their rulers thought that in stirring up their peoples they would find an outlet for their rancour and secure their own power. Instead they were shown up for what they were and their authority foundered. What we have shown about the nature of Islam, well enough known to every thoughtful student, is acknowledged by many scholars in western countries and they know its validity and confess that Islam has been the greatest of their mentors in attaining their present position. 'God's is the final issue of all things.' (Surah 22.41.)

RASHID AHMAD GANGOHI
1829–1905

Rashid Ahmad Gangohi, a scholar and Sufi, came from a religiously minded family with close ties to the intellectual elite in India. His father, a noted scholar, died when he was seven. Raised by relatives, he studied the religious sciences with many teachers, including the Delhi luminaries of his time. After completing his studies he returned to his birth place, Gangoh, to teach, but by 1867 he was living in Deoband, a city roughly 90 miles northeast of Delhi. There he collaborated with Muhammad Qasim Nanautawi (1833–1877) to found the now famous Dar al-ʿUlum (Institute of Knowledge), a religious seminary that emphasized core Islamic subjects and trained its students in Hanafi law. The influence of the school quickly spread through South Asia; before the end of the century there were more than twenty schools identified as "Deobandi" as far east as Chittagong, Bangladesh, and as far south as Madras, India. At the beginning of the twenty-first century, more than three thousand students were enrolling annually at the Dar al-ʿUlum in Deoband, and hundreds of Deobandi schools were thriving throughout South Asia.

Rashid Ahmad and the two legal judgments (fatwas) reproduced below can be understood only in the context of British colonialism in India. Following the abortive Indian Rebellion of 1857 in which both Hindus and Muslims challenged the control exercised by the British East India Company, Britain declared direct rule over India, officially ending the Mughal empire (1528–1858). In the aftermath of this revolt, many Sunni scholars in India saw no benefit in political engagement or in further antagonizing the government. Viewing their role as safeguarding Islam, they focused their energy on educating Muslims from all strata of society so that they might resist the pressure of Western customs. While these scholars all strove to preserve Islam, they differed over definitions of the "true" Islam in theory and practice. Three of the most famous reform groups to emerge in this milieu were the Deobandis, the Ahl al-hadith, and the Barelwis.

Rashid Ahmad and others of the Deobandi school believed that to save Islam, they must produce a class of formally educated scholars who could fulfill the religious needs of society, whether as prayer leaders, teachers, or public advocates. The Deobandis drew on classical Islamic texts to provide proper guidance for Muslims on the requirements of Islamic law. They followed and taught the Hanafi legal school, though they recognized all Sunni legal schools as valid. In addition to being jurists (their primary role), they were spiritual leaders who embraced Sufism and drew guidance from some of its famous figures, such as Abu Yazid (al-Bistami, d. 875; see above) and Junayd (d. 910).

Given their emphasis on Sunni orthodox practices, the Deobandis vigorously opposed many customs in India, which they judged to lack a foundation in Islamic tradition. They denounced the lavish ceremonies that often accompanied births, marriages, and funerals. They inveighed against the custom of refusing to marry widows. They rejected numerous rites performed at saints' shrines and Rashid Ahmad himself condemned belief in the intercessory power of saints after their death. They frowned upon those who would portray Muhammad as something more than a human being or believed that God shared with him the knowledge of the unseen.

The Ahl al-hadith also wanted to reform many customary practices, but they derived their understanding of Islam from a literal and restrictive reading of the Qur'an and hadith alone. They also rejected all four Sunni legal schools and denied Sufism and any practice associated with it.

Emerging in opposition to both groups were the Barelwis, who possessed the same scholarly training as the Deobandis and like them adhered to Hanafi law. Unlike the Deobandis, however, they embraced the customary practices associated with saints' shrines and believed in seeking the intercession of saints, both living and dead, as key to becoming closer to Muhammad and God. Furthermore, for the Barelwis, Muhammad was no mere mortal but was created of a special light and possessed knowledge of everything, even the unseen.

The two fatwas below are taken from a three-volume collection of Rashid Ahmad's legal rulings. This Urdu collection, as well as others from South Asian scholars of the late nineteenth century, have become classics and are reprinted to this day. Rashid Ahmad's fatwas reflect the context of his time, but they are generally unconcerned with British colonialism, focusing instead on matters of belief and the correct performance of ritual acts. Both fatwas were replies to queries received in 1893 from an individual named ʿAzizuddin. The first is directed against the Ahl al-hadith, who opposed the visiting of all graves, including Muhammad's grave in Medina. Rashid Ahmad's comment about raising the hands during the ritual prayer as well as saying "amin" out loud was also aimed at the Ahl al-hadith, who, contrary to Hanafi ritual, insisted on these movements. The second fatwa subtly discourages the questioner from leaving British-controlled India for a Muslim-ruled land and illustrates the Deobandis' avoidance of political issues.

PRONOUNCING GLOSSARY

āmīn: *a´-meen*
hijrat: *hij´-rut*

TWO FATWAS ON HAJJ IN BRITISH INDIA

Query. What of a person who goes to Noble Mecca on hajj and does not go to Medina the Radiant, thinking, "To go to Noble Medina is not a required duty [*farz-i wājib*] but rather a worthy act [*kār-i khayr*]. Moreover, why should I needlessly take such a dangerous route where there are marauding tribes from place to place and risk to property and life. A great deal of money would be spent as well—so what is the point?" Is such a person sinful or not?

Answer. Not to go to Medina because of such apprehension is a mark of lack of love for the Pride of the World,[1] on whom be peace. No one abandons a worldly task out of such apprehension, so why abandon this pilgrimage? The road is not plundered every day; [safety] is a matter of chance—so that is no argument. Certainly, to go is not obligatory. Some people, at any rate, think this pilgrimage is a greater source of reward and blessing than lifting the hands in prayer and saying "āmīn" out loud. Do not give up going out of fear of controversy or concern for your reputation. Should you abandon this pilgrimage from such apprehension and supposition, or put it off, consider, then, which portion is that of full faith. It is a joy to spend money on good acts. To go from Mecca to Medina, traveling first class, costs only fifty rupees.[2] Whoever takes account of fifty rupees and does not take account of the blessed sepulchre of the lord is a person of undoubtedly defective faith and love. Even if not a sinner, this person lacks faith in his basic nature. The end. Almighty Allah knows better. Rashid Ahmad, may he be forgiven.[3]

Query. A person is such that he brings many religious benefits, for example, he teaches the Word of Allah, hadith, commentary, etc. Thanks to him, any mosque he is in is full. Is it better for him to undertake *hijrat* [migration] to the Noble Holy Places,[4] or is his current occupation better? (Marginal note: from ʿAzizuddin Sahih, Moradahadi, 1311/1893)

Answer. If there is no harm to the religion of this learned person, and the populace receives religious benefit from him, it is better for him to stay than to undertake *hijrat* to Arabia. But Almighty Allah knows better. Rashid Ahmad, may he be forgiven (Rashid Ahmad Gangohi 1362/1943, 1:43–44).

TRANSLATED BY Barbara D. Metcalf. All bracketed additions are the translator's.

1. Muhammad.
2. In 1893, there were about 3 rupees to a U.S. dollar.
3. A customary pious close.
4. Mecca and Medina.

MUHAMMAD IQBAL
1877–1938

Regarded by many as the spiritual father of Pakistan, Muhammad Iqbal was a poet and philosopher whose writings captured the angst Muslims felt at their greatly diminished status in the colonial world. Considered the best Urdu poet of his time, he is still Pakistan's national poet, and his birthday is officially commemorated.

Iqbal was born in Sialkot, India (in present-day Pakistan), and spent his entire life under British colonial rule. His linguistic and scholarly abilities were apparent early. During his studies, he mastered Urdu and Persian, became fluent in English and Arabic, and was taught by some of the foremost poets of his time. In 1899 he graduated with an MA in philosophy from Government College in Lahore, an urban literary and scholarly center. He was particularly close to and influenced by a teacher named Sir Thomas Arnold (1864–1930), a scholar of both modern philosophy and Islamic studies who encouraged him to pursue further education in Europe. Arnold had previously taught at the Mohammedan Anglo-Oriental College in Aligarh and was known among Indian Muslims for treating Islam sympathetically and for promoting indigenous culture, values, and educational reforms.

Shortly after graduation, Iqbal began teaching Arabic and English at colleges in Lahore. He was already a noted Urdu poet when he decided to travel to Europe in 1905 to further his studies. He enrolled in Cambridge University, where he earned a BA in Western philosophy and forged ties with scholars of the Near East. He also studied law in London at Lincoln's Inn and qualified as a barrister. At the same time, he was registered as a doctoral student at the University of Munich; in 1907 he received a PhD, and he dedicated his dissertation—"The Development of Metaphysics in Persia"—to Arnold.

When Iqbal returned to Pakistan in 1908, he pursued a legal career and wrote poetry as an avocation. He also developed a strong interest in politics and became involved in local legislative assemblies as well as the All-India Muslim League, an organization formed in 1906 to promote the interests of Indian Muslims. In the presidential address delivered to the All-India Muslim League in 1930, he proposed that a separate nation be created for India's Muslims. Though all of the organization's leadership did not agree with that goal, it was achieved with the partition of India and Pakistan in 1947.

Iqbal's poetry is suffused with certain persistent themes. He laments the state of Muslims throughout the world who had come to be dominated by foreign powers, blaming their condition on Muslim laziness and resistance to internal reform. Iqbal inveighs against the notion that Muslims should contentedly and willingly accept whatever God had decreed for them. Instead, he argues that they should actively develop their own selves and better the world around them. Only through such efforts could Muslims gain control of their own countries and destinies. Such arguments shocked many, especially those inclined to contemplative and mystical interpretations of Islam, but a large audience received his works positively. Iqbal's most notable work of poetry is *The Book of Eternity* (1932), a long poem in which he imagines his ascension through the various heavens led by the poet Rumi (1207–1273; see above). His most famous prose work is *The Reconstruction of Religious Thought in Islam* (1934), based on a series of lectures he delivered from 1928 to 1929. These essays, which represent Iqbal's mature views, urge that all areas of Islamic thought undergo constant reevaluation (in Arabic, *ijtihad*) so that they remain responsive to the current needs of Muslims.

A pair of poems, "Complaint" (in Urdu, "Shikwa"), and its companion piece, "Answer to the Complaint," were both written within four years of Iqbal's return to India in 1908. In "Complaint" (included here) Iqbal assumes the role of spokesman for the Muslim community and boldly complains to God, reminding him that although his religion was spread and continues to survive to this day because of faithful Muslims, he appears to have withdrawn his favor from the Muslim community. Iqbal entreats God for its return. "Answer to the Complaint" provides a response from God's perspective, noting the failings of the Muslim community as a whole but promising that if Muslims remain faithful they will rise again in the world. Both poems are undergirded by familiar Iqbalian themes, such as the need for moral uprightness and for the resolve to act.

PRONOUNCING GLOSSARY

Ahmad: *ah´-mad* (heavy *h*)
Allahu Akbar: *al-lah´-hu ak´-bar*
Ayaz: *ay-yahz´*
Bilal: *bi-lal´*
Hejaz: *hi-jaz´* (heavy *h*)
Kaaba: *kah´-buh*
Laila: *lay´-luh*
Mahmud: *mah-mood´* (heavy *h*)
Qais: *qays*
Qarani: *qah´-rah-nee*
saki: *sah´-kee*
Salman: *sal-man´*

COMPLAINT

Why must I forever suffer loss, oblivious to gain,
Why think not upon the morrow, drowned in grief for yesterday?
Why must I attentive heed the nightingale's lament of pain?
Fellow-bard, am I a rose, condemned to silence all the way?
No; the burning power of song bids me be bold and not to faint;
Dust be in my mouth, but God—He is the theme of my complaint.

True, we are forever, famous for our habit to submit;
Yet we tell our tale of grief, as by our grief we are constrained.
We are but a muted lyre; yet a lament inhabits it—
If a sigh escapes our lips, no more can sorrow be contained.
God, give ear to the complaint of us, Thy servants tried and true;
Thou art used to songs of praise; now hear a note of protest too.

In Thy everlasting Essence Thou wast from eternity;
Bright the bloom bedecked the garden; undiffused the scent abode;
Lord of universal favour, let impartial justice be—
Could the rose's perfume scatter with no breeze to waft abroad?
Peace of mind and quiet spirit won we of our labours glad,
Else the folk of Thy Beloved[1]—should they be accounted mad?

Strange indeed the spectacle Thy world supplied before our days,
Here men bowed them down to stones, there paid they reverence
    to trees;

TRANSLATED BY A. J. Arberry.

1. Muhammad.

Only to the visual image was attuned the human gaze—
How could hearts adore a God no eye percipient may seize?
Well Thou knowest, was there any anywhere to name Thy Name?
By the Muslim's strong right arm Thy purpose to fulfilment came.

Though the Seljuks had their emire,[2] the Turanians[3] their sway,
Though the Chinese ruled in China, the Sassanians in Iran,
Though the Greeks inhabited broad, fruitful acres in their day
And the Jews possessed their cubit, and the Christians owned
    their span,
Who upraised the sword of battle in Thy Name's most sacred cause,
Or who strove to right the ruined world by Thy most hallowed laws?

It was we and we alone who marched Thy soldiers to the fight,
Now upon the land engaging, now embattled on the sea,
The triumphant Call to Prayer in Europe's churches to recite,
Through the wastes of Africa to summon men to worship Thee.
All the glittering splendour of great emperors we reckoned none;
In the shadow of our glinting swords we shouted, "God is One!"

All our life we dedicated to the dire distress of war;
When we died, we died exultant for the glory of Thy Name;
Not to win a private empire did we draw the swords we bore—
Was it in the quest of riches to earth's frontiers that we came?
Had our people striven for the sake of wordly goods and gold
Would they then have shattered idols they might gainfully
    have sold?

We were rocks immovable when in the field we took our stand,
And the bravest-hearted warriors by our thrust were swept away;
It sufficed us to enrage, if any gainsaid Thy command,
Then we hurled us on their cannons, took their swordpoints
    but for play.
Into every heart we struck the impress of Thy Unity
And beneath the dagger's lightning preached the Message, Lord,
    of Thee.

Tell us this, and tell us truly—who uprooted Khyber's gate?[4]
Or who overthrew the city where great Caesar reigned in pride?
Who destroyed the gods that hands of others laboured to create,
Who the marshalled armies of the unbelievers drove aside?
Who extinguished from the altars of Iran that sacred flame,
Who revived the dimmed remembrance of Yazdan's[5] immortal
    Name?

2. That is, emir. The Seljuks were a Turkish Muslim dynasty, stretching at its height (11th–12th centuries) from Turkey through the Middle East to Central Asia.
3. A people mentioned in the Avesta, which is the scripture of Zoroastrianism (the dominant religion of pre-Islamic Iran), and in the Persian national epic written by Firdawsi (ca. 935–ca. 1020), the *Shah Nameh*. There they are presented as having an empire beyond northeastern Iran, with which they were often at war.
4. The tribes of Khyber, located about 95 miles north of Medina, were defeated by Muhammad (ca. 628/29).
5. God (Persian).

Strove there ever other nation in the cause of Thee alone,
Bore there ever other people battle's anguish for Thy sake?
Whose the sword that seized the world, and ruled it as its very own?
Whose the loud Allahu Akbar[6] that compelled the earth to wake?
Whose the dread that kept the idols cowering and terrified
So that, heads cast down and humbled, "He is God, the One,"
they cried?

In the press of mortal combat if the hour of worship came
Then the people of Hejaz,[7] to Mecca turning, bowed in prayer;
King Mahmud, Ayaz the slave[8]—their rank in service was the same,
Lord and servant—at devotion never difference was there.
Slave and master, rich and needy—all the old distinctions gone,
Unified in adoration of Thy Presence, they were one.

In the Hall of Space and Being, at the dawn and eventide
Circulated we like goblets with the Wine of Faith replete;
Still we roved o'er plain and mountain, spread Thy Message far
and wide—
Is it known to Thee, if ever we returned to own defeat?
Desert after desert spanning, faring on through sea on sea,
In the Ocean of the Shadows our strong coursers watered we.

We erased the smudge of falsehood from the parchment
firmament,
We redeemed the human species from the chains of slavery;
And we filled the Holy Kaaba[9] with our foreheads humbly bent,
Clutching to our fervent bosoms the Koran in ecstasy.
Yet the charge is laid against us we have played the faithless part;
If disloyal we have proved, hast Thou deserved to win our heart?

Other creeds claim other peoples, and they have their sinners too;
There are lowly men among them, and men drunken with conceit;
Some are sluggards, some neglectful, some are vigilant and true;
Multitudes disdain Thy Name in loathing utter and complete;
But the showers of Thy mercy other thirsting souls assuage,
Only on the hapless Muslims falls the lightning of Thy rage.

Hark, the idols in the temples shout, "The Muslims are no more,"
Jubilant to see the guardians of the Kaaba's shrine depart;
The world's inn is emptied of those singing cameleers of yore,
Vanished is their caravan, Koran close-pressed to reverent heart.
Disbelief is loud with laughter; art Thou deaf, indifferent?
Disregardest Thou Thy Unity, as if it nothing meant?

6. God is Great (Arabic), a phrase said in prayer that is also used as a battle cry.
7. The western region of the Arabian Peninsula; it borders the Red Sea and contains Mecca and Medina.
8. The friendship or love affair between Mahmud (971–1030), king of Ghazni—whose rule eventually extended from Afghanistan over northwestern India and most of Iran—and his slave-boy Ayaz was legendary; it was celebrated by a number of Sufi poets, including Rumi (1207–1273; see above).
9. Literally, "the Cube," a stone shrine in Mecca that became the most important site in Islam (Muslims around the world face it when they pray).

Not of this are we complaining, that their coffers overflow
Who have not the wit or grace of converse in society;
But that infidels should own the houris and the palaces—ah, woe!
While the wretched Muslims must with promises contented be.
Now no more for us Thy favours and Thy old benevolence—
How and wherefore is Thy pristine kindliness departed hence?

Why no more are wordly riches among Muslims to be found,
Since Thy power is as of old beyond compute and unconfined?
If Thou willest, foaming fountains from the desert's breast
can bound
And the rippling mirage may the traveller in the forest blind.
All we have is jeers from strangers, public shame, and poverty—
Is disgrace our recompense for laying down our lives for Thee?

So; it is on others only that the world its love bestows;
We, who walk Thy chosen path—to us a phantom world is left.
Be it so; bid us be gone, and let the earth belong to those;
Yet protest not that the earth of Unity is now bereft.
For no other cause we live but Thy remembrance to maintain;
When the saki[1] is departed, can the winecup yet remain?

Gone is now the thronged assembly, and Thy lovers too are gone,
Ended are the midnight sighings, silenced dawn's deep threnody;
They bestowed their hearts upon Thee, and with their reward
passed on;
Scarcely were Thy faithful seated when they were dismissed
from Thee.
So Thy lovers came, so with the promise of "To-morrow" went—
Now come, seek them with the lantern of Thy beauty's
blandishment;

Laila's pangs are still the same, Qais yearns as fiercely as of old,[2]
Still amid the forests and the vales of Nejd[3] the fleet deer run,
Beauty rules the same as ever, hearts deep passions still enfold,
Still abide the folk of Ahmad,[4] still Thou art their Lord, the One;
Then what means Thy high displeasure, since its cause is
all unknown?
What denotes it, that Thine eye is turned in wrath upon Thy own?

Did we ever shun Thee, or Arabia's Messenger forsake?
Did we tire of idol-breaking, and to idol-making turn?
Did we cry an end to passion, growing weary of love's ache?
Did we quit the path of Salman,[5] cease from Qarani[6] to learn?

1. Cup-bearer (Arabic).
2. Layla and Qays were tragic lovers of Persian legend; driven mad by their separation, Qays is given the nickname Majnun, "One Possessed."
3. The central region of Saudi Arabia, which is a plateau.
4. Another name of Muhammad.
5. Salman al-Farisi (d. ca. 656), by Muslim tradition the first Persian convert to Islam; he was also regarded by many Muslim scholars as a key figure in the origins of Sufism.
6. ʿUways al-Qarani (d. 657), a Muslim Yemeni mystic; according to a legend recorded in *Memorial of the Saints* by the Persian mystic poet Farid al-Din ʿAttar (ca. 1142–ca. 1220), he was able to communicate telepathically with Muhammad.

Still the fire of "God is Greatest" in our hearts we keep ablaze,
Still Bilal the Abyssinian[7] guides us in our daily ways.

It may be that Love's sweet manners are perchance no more
observed,
And the path of acquiescence leads no longer hearts resigned;
Haply the heart's Qibla-pointing[8] compass from its course
has swerved,
And the ancient law of faithfulness has lost its power to bind;
Yet Thou too, alas, art changed, now us, now others favouring:
Monstrous as it is to say, Thy love is such a fickle thing!

On the summit of Faran[9] Thou madest Faith complete and whole,
Tookest captive hearts a thousand with a single, simple sign;
Thou it was that Love's quintessence set afire, a blazing coal,
Flamed the assembly with the ardour of Thy loveliness divine.
Why is it, that in our bosoms not a spark remains to-day?
We are still the same burnt chattels, what, hast Thou forgotten,
pray?

In the vale of Nejd no longer may those clanging chains be heard,
Qais no more awaits distracted Laila's litter to behold;
Vanished are those passionate yearnings; we are dead, our
hearts interred;
Gone the light of the assembly, the abode is dark and cold.
Joyous day, when Thou returnest in Thy beauty and grace
And unbashfully revealst to our gathering Thy face!

Strangers sit within the garden, quaffing wine beside the stream;
Glass in hand they sit and listen to the cuckoo song of Spring.
Far from the commotioned meadow we sit silently and dream,
Dream, Thy lovers, of Thy coming, and the cry of "He, the King!"
Reawaken in Thy moths the eager joy to be aflame,
Bid again the ancient lightnings brand our bosoms with Thy Name!

Turns anew the wandering people to Hejaz their bridle-string,
Skyward lifts the wingless nightingale the lilting love of flight,
In the garden every blossom fragrance—drenched is quivering.
Strike the silent lute, long eager for Thy plectrum to alight—
String-imprisoned melodies await Thy touch to sing in choir;
Sinai is trembling, trembling to be ravished by Thy fire.

Grant at last Thy sore-tried people in their difficulties ease,
Make the ant of little substance peer of Solomon to be;[1]
Love is grown too rare and costly—cheapen its exalted fees;

7. A freed black slave of Ethiopian (Abyssinian) origin; an early convert to Islam, he was chosen by Muhammad to be the first to give the daily call to prayer.
8. That is, pointing in the direction toward Mecca, faced by Muslims when they pray.
9. An alternative spelling of Paran, the dwelling place of Ishmael (Genesis 21:21); it is also mentioned as a place where God "shone forth" in Deuteronomy 33:2, a biblical verse regularly cited by medieval Muslim scholars as a prediction that Islam would replace Judaism and Christianity.
1. In a story told in Qur'an 27:17–19, Solomon heeds the words of an ant whom he hears ordering the other ants of the valley to seek shelter from the feet of his army.

Turn our India temple-squatters into Muslims true to Thee.
See, the stream of blood is pouring from our griefs, so long suppressed;
Hark, the cry of pain is throbbing in our dagger-riven breast.

Now the secret of the garden by the rose's scent is spread;
Shame it is, the garden's blossoms should themselves the traitor play!
Now the garden's Lyre is broken, and the rose's bloom-time sped,
And the minstrels of the garden from their twigs have winged away;
Yet one nightingale sings on there, rapt by his own melody,
In his breast the plangent music tosses still tempestuously.

All the ring-doves from the branches of the cypresses have flown,
And the petals of the blossoms flutter down and take to flight;
And the garden's ancient walks, how desolate they are and lone;
Ravished of their leafy robes, the boughs stand naked to the light.
Still he sings forlorn, all heedless of the season's changing mood;
Oh, that someone in the garden his sad anthem understood!

Life is joyless now, and death no comfort promises to bring;
To remember ancient sorrows is the sole delight I know.
In the mirror of my mind what gems of thought are shimmering,
In the darkness of my breast what shining revelations glow!
Yet no witness in the garden may the miracle attest;
Not a tulip there lies bleeding with a brand upon its breast.

Break, hard hearts, to hear the carol of this nightingale forlorn;
Wake, dull hearts, to heed the clamour and the clangour of this bell;
Rise, dead hearts, by this new compact of fidelity reborn;
Thirst, dry hearts, for the old vintage whose sweet tang you knew so well.
Though the jar was cast in Persia, in Hejaz the wine first flowed;
And though Indian the song be, from Hejaz derives the mode.

MAHMUD SHALTUT
1893–1963

Mahmud Shaltut, a scholar and educator, enjoyed the unusual experience of leading a university from which he had earlier been dismissed. During the last five years of his life, he served as rector (*shaykh*) of al-Azhar, the oldest and most venerated university in the Muslim world. Yet as a young faculty member there, he had lost his position because of his reformist activism.

Born in Lower Egypt in 1893, Shaltut was raised under British occupation and experienced firsthand the changes it brought to Egypt. He obtained a traditional Islamic education and graduated from a religious academy in Alexandria in 1918 at the top of his class. He began his teaching career there the following year, but in 1927 was appointed to a more prestigious lectureship at al-Azhar. Shaltut supported efforts to modernize the university that were initially resisted, and he was dismissed in 1931. In 1935, under a reformist rector, he was rehired as vice dean of the Islamic law faculty. Shaltut continued to rise in scholarly reputation and academic status until his appointment as rector in 1958.

Several key concerns preoccupied Shaltut throughout his life: the need for educational reform at al-Azhar, the cultivation of an ecumenical spirit among all Muslims, and the importance for the Muslim community of an open and inclusive engagement with contemporary issues.

In Shaltut's view, the curriculum of al-Azhar was outdated. Its graduates were unable to think independently, to understand the modern world, or to serve the needs of Muslims. He called for revising the curriculum and updating the standard teaching texts, for eliminating any hint of religious factionalism, and for ending al-Azhar's self-isolation. Shaltut fostered his university's participation in national and world affairs by promoting institutional cooperation with relevant organizations and by responding to requests for legal opinions from Muslims all over the world.

Shaltut sought to unify the *umma*, the worldwide Muslim community. In his own writings he stressed the essentials of faith and action and avoided sectarian debates and digressions. More importantly, he fostered harmony among all schools of law and cofounded an organization of Sunni and Shiʿi jurists to end the enmity between them. He was not, however, intent on creating a single legal school. As rector, he introduced the study of Shiʿi law into the curriculum of al-Azhar and declared in a controversial 1959 fatwa that ritual acts performed according to Shiʿi law were as valid as those performed according to Sunni law. Shaltut's catholic views embraced even those with no religion: provided that they did no harm to Muslims, he considered them "brothers in humanity."

Shaltut insisted on engaging contemporary issues in an accessible manner. His fatwas treated topics clearly and provided the evidence and analysis underlying his judgments. With a similar insistence on accessibility, he wrote a commentary arranged thematically to better convey the central messages of the Qurʾan; he felt that the traditional verse-by-verse format distracted the reader with unnecessary details. His desire to engage contemporary issues afresh was most evident in his attack on the doctrine of consensus (*ijmaʿ*), the belief that scholars' earlier accord could be trusted to guide the community. In his criticism, Shaltut pointed to the lack of scholarly agreement on the doctrine's specifics and its use to stifle debate and intimidate opponents.

Representative of the topics he treated were questions of female testimony, interest-bearing transactions, and jihad. Many scholars viewed Qurʾan 2:282 as proof that a woman's testimony was always worth only half that of a man. Shaltut disagreed, arguing that the verse applied to a specific context. If a woman had expertise in a field normally dominated by men, her testimony could be as valid as that of any man. On the subject of interest, Shaltut's views evolved. He initially forbade any interest-bearing transactions but in later writings sanctioned the interest accrued in a savings account on the grounds that it is a nonexploitive transaction freely undertaken by both parties.

In the passage that follows, excerpted from his book *The Qurʾan and Fighting* (1948), Shaltut examines the relevant qurʾanic verses surrounding jihad, which he understands to be a defensive measure. His motivation for writing the book, explained in the introduction, was the many wars in his time. He particularly wanted to correct those who misunderstand the concept of jihad and use it to denigrate Islam.

PRONOUNCING GLOSSARY

Sūrat al-Anfāl: *soo´-rut al-an-fal´*
Sūrat al-Baqara: *soo´-rut al-bah´-qa-ruh*
Sūrat al-Ḥudjurāt: *soo´-rut al-hu-ju-rat´* (heavy *h*)
Sūrat al-Māʾida: *soo´-rut al-ma´-i-duh*
Sūrat al-Mumtaḥana: *soo´-rut al-mum-ta´-ha-nuh* (heavy *h*)
Sūrat al-Nisāʾ: *soo´-rut an-ni-sa´*
Sūrat al-Tawba: *soo´-rut at-taw´-buh*

FROM THE QUR'AN AND FIGHTING

The Verses of Fighting

In this chapter we shall expound the Verses of Fighting in the Koran, in order to understand their meaning and purpose and to learn their relation to one another. After that we shall arrive at a conclusion which, together with the conclusions reached in the preceding chapter, will elucidate those verses that order fighting.

The Koran is concerned with two kinds of fighting: the fighting of Muslims against Muslims and the fighting of Muslims against non-Muslims.

The first kind belongs to the internal affairs of the Islamic state (*umma*)[1] and concerns only this state with the exclusion of any other state. The Koran deals with the event of rebellion and breach of public order, either between two groups of subjects or between subjects and rulers. It gives certain provisions for this event with a view to preserve the unity of the Islamic state (*umma*) and the power of and the respect for the ruling class, and to protect the community against the evils of rebellion and mutual hostility. These provisions are to be found in *Sūrat al-Ḥudjurāt*[2] [49:9–10]: *"If two parties of the believers fight, put things right between them; then, if one of them is insolent against the other, fight the insolent one till it reverts to God's commandment. If it reverts, set things right between them equitably, and be just. Surely, God loves the just. The believers indeed are brothers; set things right between your brothers, and fear God; haply so you will find mercy."*

This verse assumes a case of disagreement between two groups of believers that cannot be solved by peaceful means, so that both groups resort to the use of force and leave the final decision to the sword. In this case it prescribes, that the Islamic state *(umma)* represented by its government, investigate the causes of discord and endeavour to set things right between the parties. If this can be attained by means of negotiations, and both parties obtain what is due to them so that rebellion is warded off and safety and peace prevail, then God saves the believers the trouble of fighting. However, if one of the parties continues to oppress the other, refuses to return to the affair of God and attacks the authority of the believers, then they have become rebels against the legal power and public order. In that case the community of Muslims is obliged to fight them until they submit and return to what is right. Further, this verse points out the secret of success in solving discord arising between different groups. This secret is that the return of one of the parties to what is right, should not be used as a means to oppress them or to deprive them of their rights. Instead, justice must prevail and each party must have its due. Consider the end of the verse [49:9]: *"Surely, God loves the just."* Furthermore the second verse teaches that what these provisions aim at is to preserve the unity and undivisibility of the Islamic state and to safeguard the religious brotherhood which is one of the most important matters of faith, for it reads [49:10]: *"The believers indeed are*

TRANSLATED BY Rudolph Peters. Shaltut's notes are omitted.

1. That is, the Islamic community (not "nation-state").

2. The Private Apartments.

brothers; set things right between your brothers, and fear God; haply so you will find mercy."

These wise Koranic provisions were revealed by the mouth of the illiterate Prophet,[3] as instruments to secure peace and in order to exterminate rebellion and aggression, more than thirteen centuries before the human mind invented what is called the "League of Nations" or the "Security Council" to serve as a means of preservation of peace, consolidation of liberties and enjoyment by all states of their rights.

Had the nations understood these wise provisions with true understanding, had they given them the attention they deserve and had they followed their purport, then these nations would never have gone astray from the path of wisdom and they would have been saved from the frequent disasters caused by rebellion and aggression on the one hand and disagreement and discord on the other.

These are the rules the Koran gives with regard to fighting between Muslims. It is evident that they bear no relation whatsoever to the principles of the Islamic Mission and faith.

The second kind of fighting, viz. fighting between Muslims and non-Muslims, has been dealt with comprehensively in many Koranic verses and chapters. The Koran goes into the causes which may lead to it, its aim, upon the attainment of which fighting must stop, the obligatory preparations for it by the Muslims and the necessary caution against an unexpected outbreak of it. It treats of many provisions and regulations and enters upon connected subjects like armistices or treaties. In the following we shall discuss the verses dealing with the cause of fighting, and with the aim of fighting, upon the attainment of which the fighting must stop and finally we shall go into the relation between the Verses of Forgiveness and the Verses of Fighting.

In Mecca, the Muslims suffered for several years under the worst kinds of punishment, oppressed in their religious freedom, persecuted for the sake of the creed in which they found reassurance and terrorized with regard to property and personal safety. For all these reasons they were compelled to emigrate. They left their dwellings and settled in Medina, patiently submitting to God's orders and gladly accepting His authority. Whenever they felt the urge to resist the oppression and to revenge themselves on the oppressors, the Prophet held them back, bidding them to be patient in expectation of a command from God. "I have not been ordered to fight" he used to say. This lasted so long that they were almost overcome by desperation, and consequently by doubts and misgivings. And just then God revealed the first verses of fighting [22:39–41]: *"Leave is given to those who are fought because they were wronged—surely God is able to help them—who were expelled from their habitations without right, except that they say 'Our Lord is God.' Had God not driven back the people, some by the means of others, there had been destroyed cloisters and churches, oratories and mosques, wherein God's name is much mentioned. Assuredly God will help him who helps Him—surely God is all-strong, all-mighty—who, if We establish them in the land, perform the*

3. Many Muslims see the description of Muhammad as an "unlettered prophet" (Qur'an 2:157) as evidence of his illiteracy, and thus as further proof of the divine origin of the Qur'an.

prayer, and pay the alms, and bid to honour, and forbid dishonour; and unto God belongs the issue of all affairs." These verses deal with the permission to fight. This permission was motivated by the fact that the Muslims suffered injustice and were forced to emigrate and to leave their dwellings without justification.

They then explain that this permission corresponds with the customary practice that people ward each other off so that a certain equilibrium is attained, oppression is averted, and adherents of the different creeds and cults can perform their religious observances and keep believing in the pure doctrine of monotheism. Finally these verses point out that God only helps those who help and fear Him and therefore do not use war as an instrument for destruction and corruption, for subjecting the weak and satisfying their own desires and lust, but cultivate the land when it falls into their hands, obey God's orders and summon people to do what is good and reputable and not to do what is disreputable and wicked. God distinguishes between those who act destructively and those who act constructively [22:41]: *"And unto God belongs the issue of all affairs."* These verses are, as we have said, the first Verses of Fighting. They are very clear and do not contain even the slightest evidence of religious compulsion. On the contrary, they confirm that the practice that people ward each other off is one of God's principles of creation, inevitable for the preservation of order and for the continuation of righteousness and civilization. Were it not for this principle, the earth would have been ruined and all the different places of worship would have been destroyed. This would have happened if powerful tyrants would have held sway over religions, free to abuse them without restraint and to force people to conversion, without anyone to interfere. These verses are not only concerned with Muslims, but have clearly a general impact [22:40]: *"(. . .) there had been destroyed cloisters and churches, oratories and mosques (. . .)"*

Let us now have a look at the Verses of Fighting that are to be found in *Sūrat al-Baqara*[4] [2:190–194]: *"And fight in the way of God with those who fight you, but aggress not: God loves not the aggressors. And slay them wherever you come upon them, and expel them from where they expelled you; persecution is more grievous than slaying. But fight them not by the Holy Mosque until they should fight you there; then, if they fight you, slay them—such is the recompense of unbelievers—but if they give over, surely God is All-forgiving, All-compassionate. Fight them, till there is no persecution and the religion is God's; then if they give over, there shall be no enmity save for the evildoers. The holy month for the holy month; holy things demand retaliation. Whoso commits aggression against you, do you commit aggression against him like as he has committed against you; and fear you God, and know that God is with the godfearing."*

These verses order the Muslims to fight in the way of God those who fight them, to pursue them wherever they find them and to scatter them just as they had once scattered the Muslims. They prohibit the provocation of hostility and this prohibition is reinforced by God's repugnance to aggression and by his dislike of those who provoke hostility. Then they point out that expelling people from their homes, frightening them while they are

4. The Cow (sura 2).

safe and preventing them from living peacefully without fear for their lives or possessions is persecution worse than persecution by means of murder and bloodshed. Therefore those who practise or provoke these things must be fought just like those who actually fight. These verses also prohibit fighting in holy places or in holy periods, unless the Muslims are under attack. For if their sacred protection is violated and fighting becomes lawful for them, they are allowed to meet the hostility by the same means by way of retaliation. These points having been explained, the verses finally define the aim upon the attainment of which the war must end. This aim is accomplished when there is no more persecution in matters of religion, and religion is God's [cf. K 2:193 and 8:39], so that people obtain religious freedom and are not oppressed or tortured, because of their religion. As soon as this aim has been accomplished and people feel safe, fighting must cease.

In these verses and the principle they contain with regard to the reason and the aim of fighting, there is not a single trace to be found of any idea of conversion by force. On the contrary, these verses, like the previous ones, say in plain and distinct words that the reason for which the Muslims have been ordered to fight is the aggression directed against them, expulsion from their dwellings, violation of God's sacred institutions and attempts to persecute people for what they believe. At the same time they say that the aim upon the attainment of which Muslims must cease fighting is the termination of the aggression and the establishment of religious liberty devoted to God and free from any pressure or force.

The principles expounded in these verses can be found, in the same or similar words, in many other verses of fighting, e.g., in *Sūrat al-Nisā'*, *Sūrat al-Anfāl* and *Sūrat al-Tawba*[5] [4:75]:

"How is it with you, that you do not fight in the way of God, and for the men, women, and children who, being abased, say, 'Our Lord, bring us forth from this city whose people are evildoers, and appoint to us a protector from Thee, and appoint to us from Thee a helper.'" [4:84]: *"So do thou fight in the way of God; thou art charged only with thyself. And urge on the believers; haply God will restrain the unbelievers' might; God is stronger in might, more terrible in punishing."* [4:90–91]: *"If they withdraw from you, and do not fight you, and offer you peace, then God assigns not any way to you against them (. . .). If they withdraw not from you, and offer you peace, and restrain their hands, take them, and slay them wherever you come on them."*

Read these verses and have a closer look at the following phrases: *"(. . .) haply God will restrain the unbelievers' might (. . .)"* and *"If they withdraw not from you, (. . .),"* then you will realize the spirit of persecution that the people harboured against the Muslims and on account of which the Muslims were ordered to fight. This is exactly the same principle as that which has been expounded in *Sūrat al-Baqara*, as we have seen, and we will find this principle also in *Sūrat al-Anfāl* [8:39]: *"Fight them until there is no persecution and the religion is God's entirely; then, if they give over, surely God sees the things they do,"* and in *Sūrat al-Tawba* [9:12–13]: *"But if they break their oaths after their covenant and thrust at your religion, then fight the leaders of unbelief; they have no sacred oaths; haply they will give over. Will you not fight*

5. Women (sura 4), the Spoils (sura 8), and Repentance (sura 9).

a people who broke their oaths and purposed to expel the Messenger, beginning the first time against you? Are you afraid of them? You would do better to be afraid of God, if you are believers." And [9:36]: *"And fight the unbelievers totally even as they fight you totally; and know that God is with the godfearing."* Read these verses and consider firstly the phrase: *"But if they break their oaths after their covenant and thrust at your religion . . ."*, then the phrase: *". . . beginning the first time against you . . ."* and finally the phrase: *". . . as they fight you totally . . ."* then you will realize that these verses were revealed with regard to people recalcitrantly practising persecution, amongst whom the elements of depravation were so deeply rooted that they did not respect pledges anymore and that virtue became meaningless to them. There is no doubt that to fight these people, to purify the earth from them and to put an end to their persecution, is to serve the commonweal and a benefaction to mankind as a whole.

After the aforementioned verses, we find in *Sūrat al-Tawba* two verses which, at first sight, seem to contain prescriptions contradicting the just mentioned principles concerning fighting. We shall quote them here and reveal their true meaning in the light of the previous verses which, because of their frequency and unequivocalness, must be considered fundamental with regard to the legality of fighting and the reasons for it. Therefore, other verses should be compared with the principles they contain and interpreted accordingly.

The first verse reads [9:29]: *"Fight those who believe not in God and the Last Day and do not forbid what God and His Messenger have forbidden—such men as practice not the religion of truth, being of those who have been given the Book*[6]—until they pay the tribute out of hand and have been humbled." The second one goes [9:123]: *"O believers, fight the unbelievers who are near to you and let them find in you a harshness; and know that God is with the godfearing."* The first verse commands the Muslims to fight a certain group which is characterized by the fact that *"they do not believe in God etc."* Previously they had broken their pledges and hindered and assailed the propagation of the Islamic Mission [cf. K 9:7–16]. These acts constitute for the Muslims reasons for fighting them. Therefore this verse does not say that the quality of being an unbeliever etc. constitutes a sufficient reason for fighting, but mentions the characteristics peculiar to them in order to give a factual description and as a further incitement to attack them once their aggression will have materialized. They modified the religion of God and took their scholars and monks for Lords apart from Him [cf. K 9:30], while making things allowed and forbidden according to their whims, since they did not accept that only God can do so. There was nothing to hold them back from breaking pledges, and violating rights, and they were not inclined to desist from aggression and tyranny.

These are the people which, according to this verse, must be fought continuously until, by being thoroughly subjected, they can do no more harm and will desist from the persecution they used to practise. The Koran introduced a special token for this submission, viz. the payment of poll-tax (*jizya*),[7]

6. That is, Jews and Christians, who have a revealed scripture.

7. A tax levied on non-Muslim subjects of a Muslim state.

which means that they actually participate in carrying the burdens of the state and providing the means for the commonweal, both for Muslims and non-Muslims.

Two phrases in this verse indicate the reason for fighting which we have already pointed out. These phrases are: *"and have been humbled"* and *"out of hand"*. They determine the state wherein they will come when poll-tax (*jizya*) is collected from them, viz. a state of submission to the authority of the Muslims and subjection to their laws. There is no doubt that this implies that previously they had been recalcitrant and that there had been reasons for the Muslims to fight them. This is how this verse is to be understood. This interpretation is supported by the context and brings this verse in agreement with the other verses. For if this verse had meant that they must be fought because of their unbelief and that unbelief had been the reason why they should be fought, then it would have been laid down that the aim of fighting then consisted in their conversion to Islam. Collecting poll-tax (*jizya*) from them would not have been allowed in that case and they would not have been allowed to abide by their own religion.

The second verse: *"fight the unbelievers that are near to you"* is not to be compared with the previous verses because those verses indicate the reason and motive for fighting, whereas this verse has been revealed as a directive for a practical war plan, to be followed when legitimate fighting actually breaks out. Thus it informs the Muslims that, when the enemies are manifold, it is imperative to fight the nearest first of all, then the nearest but one and so on, in order to clear the road from enemies and to facilitate the victory.

This principle, formulated by the Koran, is still being followed today by belligerent states, for attacking states do not advance unless they have cleared the roads before them and are sure that there are no more obstacles in their way. Thus it is clear that these two verses have no link with the reason for fighting, as formulated by the other verses.

From the preceding words one may infer:

1. That there is not a single verse in the Koran which could support the opinion that the aim of fighting in Islam is conversion;

2. That, as explained by the verses mentioned above, there are only three reasons for fighting, viz. to stop aggression, to protect the Mission of Islam and to defend religious freedom;

3. That in giving its prescriptions for fighting, the Koran did not admit of avidity, selfishness and humiliation of the poor as motives for it, but intended it as an instrument for peace and tranquillity and for a life founded on justice and equality.

4. That poll-tax (*jizya*) is not a financial compensation for the granting of one's life or preservation of one's own religion, but a symbol of submission and desistance from harmful acts and a contribution in carrying the burdens of the state.

After this exposé nobody can vilify Islam anymore or misinterpret the Koranic verses and maintain as some ignoramuses have done, that Islam has taken up fighting as a means of propagating its Mission and as an instrument for conversion, and that its Mission and creed were founded on and propagated by suppression and the use of force.

Here we shall cite a verse from *Sūrat al-Mumtaḥana*[8] which may be considered as an Islamic charter concerning the relations between Muslims and non-Muslims [60:8]: *"God forbids you not, as regards those who have not fought you in religion's cause, nor expelled you from your habitations, that you should be kindly to them, and act justly towards them; surely God loves the just."*

Read this charter and then turn your attention to *Sūrat al-Mā'ida*,[9] one of the parts of the Koran that were revealed most recently. There you may read the following with regard to the relations between Muslims and non-Muslims [5:5]: *"Today the good things are permitted to you, and the food of those who were given the Book is permitted to you, and permitted to them is your food. Likewise believing women in wedlock, and in wedlock women of them who were given the Book before you if you give them their wages, in wedlock and not in license. Whoso disbelieves in the faith, his work has failed, and in the world to come he shall be among the losers."*

Read all this and you will know the lofty spirit of righteousness, equity, co-operation and affinity that Islam cherishes with regard to its relations with non-Muslims. It is a kind of relationship so magnificent that, compared with it the most modern principle known to the human mind in international relations wanes into insignificance.

8. She Who Is to Be Examined (sura 60).

9. The Table Spread (sura 5).

SAYYID QUTB
1906–1966

A prolific author whose early work included poetry and literary criticism, in his later writings Sayyid Qutb focused on the contemporary issues confronting Muslims. These later works, particularly *In the Shade of the Qur'an* and *Milestones*, have served as a theoretical foundation for militant Sunni movements inspired by both Qutb's life and his writings.

Born in Musha, a small village in the center of Egypt, Qutb was the eldest child in a socially conservative and politically active family. His father, a nationalist, opposed the British occupation of Egypt and met in their house with like-minded compatriots. Influenced by this atmosphere of political activism, Qutb, one brother, and two of his sisters were drawn to Islamic concerns.

As a child, Qutb attended a modern elementary school as well as the village religious school, where he memorized the Qur'an by age ten. This, and perhaps a few classes taken some years later, appears to be the extent of his training in Islamic studies. He continued his studies in Cairo, and in 1933 he earned a degree in Arabic language and literature from the Dar al-ʿUlum (Institute of Knowledge), a university established in the late nineteenth century to bridge the divide between modern and traditional models of higher education.

Qutb began working for the Egyptian Department of Education, first as a teacher and then as an inspector of schools. In 1948 he was sent to the United States to study teaching and administrative practices at several institutions, and he earned an MA in education from what was then Colorado State College of Education (the University of Northern Colorado). Qutb's impressions were largely negative. Though awed by U.S. industrial and technological prowess, he saw American society as morally bankrupt, appallingly sexualized, and overly concerned with brutish displays of strength. He would voice these criticisms in "The America I Have Seen" (1951), an essay published after his departure in August 1950.

Back in Egypt, Qutb became more politically engaged. He had close ties to the Muslim Brotherhood, an Egyptian religio-political organization founded in 1928, and to the Free Officers, a group of military officers who came to power in 1952 after overthrowing King Faruq; Gamal Abdel Nasser (1918–1970), their leader who in 1954 became prime minister, knew Qutb personally. During the early 1950s there was probably some overlap between the two groups: members of both had similar backgrounds (mainly lower-middle-class) and shared the ultimate goal of removing all Western influence from Egyptian affairs. Following the coup, Qutb became the only civilian on the Revolutionary Command Council (RCC) set up by the Free Officers to temporarily govern the country, serving as cultural adviser.

But relations between the Muslim Brotherhood and Free Officers quickly soured. The Muslim Brothers wanted some form of Islamic law and, believing that most Egyptians supported them, called for a general referendum to approve the new constitution, but the RCC—committed to a vision of secular nationalism—rejected their demand. Qutb's sympathies lay with the Muslim Brotherhood; by 1953 he was the editor of its weekly paper, and he was soon appointed to the Brotherhood's most significant groups—the Working Committee and Guidance Council. The decisive break came when shots were fired as Nasser gave a speech in Alexandria in October 1954. Though the Brotherhood denied any involvement, the government banned the organization and arrested more than a thousand of its members—Qutb among them. Sentenced to a fifteen-year term, he would not be freed until 1964.

Already in poor health, Qutb served most of his time in the prison infirmary; like many Muslim Brothers, he was brutalized in jail, and he witnessed the continued abuse, torture, and murder of others. His years in prison deeply informed his two most famous works, a thirty-volume commentary on the Qur'an titled *In the Shade of the Qur'an* (of which sixteen volumes were completed and published before January 1954) and *Milestones*, published shortly after the efforts of the Iraqi president ʿAbd al-Salam ʿArif (1921–1966) won his release in May 1964. He was rearrested in August 1965 on charges of sedition and plotting to overthrow the government, and the text of *Milestones* was used as evidence against him. After a sham trial that attracted international attention and condemnation, Qutb was executed on August 29, 1966.

A line divides Qutb's writings before and after the mid-1940s. His early work includes collections of poetry, literary criticism, and articles on current political and social issues. His later work focuses chiefly on Islam, presented mainly as a solution to the ills plaguing society, and is his most significant—especially *In the Shade* and *Milestones*.

Qutb is particularly noted for two concepts: his interpretation of the sovereignty of God (in Arabic, *hakamiyya*) and his definition of "ignorance" and "ignorant" (*jahiliyya* and *jahili*). Both cases involve reconceptualizations that diverge from traditional understandings. For Qutb, God's sovereignty demanded that Islamic law—that is, God's law—be applied throughout the land. To do otherwise would place the rule of men above that of God. In this reading, he relied on key qur'anic verses (e.g., 5:44, 45, 47; 12:40, 67) that rebuke those who "judge [*yahkumu*; the same root (*h-k-m*) from which the term *hakamiyya* is derived] by other than what God has revealed." Most traditional exegetes did not draw general conclusions about non-Islamic law from such verses, instead limiting their application to the specific incidents that prompted their revelation.

Similarly, Qutb decontextualized the terms *jahiliyya* and *jahili*, which were ordinarily applied by Muslim exegetes to Arabia before the Islamic revelation. For him, they referred to any society or people who were heedless of God or opposed to him, who were unjust, or who were polytheistic. Yet such a broad definition might condemn many Muslims as unbelievers or apostates. Apostasy, a charge that most Muslim scholars throughout history have been reluctant to level against those who identify themselves as Muslim, is punishable by death. Qutb never explicitly labeled fellow Muslims as apostates or directly called for the overthrow of the government, but others have extended his arguments to do both.

Qutb was executed before he could fully develop his theological and political analysis. Those in the Muslim Brotherhood whom he influenced split into three main camps: those who believed that ignorance was everywhere and condemned everyone, save themselves, as apostates; those who blamed only the rulers of Muslim states and considered them apostates; and those who understood Qutb's references to *jahiliyya* as a figurative description of the moral breakdown of society. Among the first group were members of Al-Takfir wa-al-Hijra (Excommunication and Emigration) under the leadership of Shukri Mustafa (1942–1978): building on Qutb's thought, he concluded that he and his followers were the only true Muslims. Among the last group were those members of the Muslim Brotherhood who were not imprisoned and who, outside Egypt, had gained status and financial success that would be threatened by any social upheaval.

Qutb wrote *Milestones* to provide markers (milestones) for the vanguard of Muslims who wished to revive Islam. Parts of it are informed by the exegetical analysis in his much larger Qur'an commentary and develop insights from that earlier work. The excerpt below from *Milestones* presents his thoughts on jihad.

Milestones was perceived as a security threat by the Egyptian government. As noted above, it led to Qutb's arrest, and copies were confiscated, impounded, and then burned. Nonetheless, since its publication it has been read around the world and translated into many languages, including Urdu and Malay, and Qutb's writings remain influential. A recent study reveals that after Ibn Taymiyya (1263–1328; see above), who had some impact on Qutb's thought, Qutb is the author cited most often on militant Sunni websites.

PRONOUNCING GLOSSARY

Braʿt: *bi-rah´-ut*
Dhimmies: *dhim´-mees*
Iqraa, bisme Rabbika alladhee: *iq´-rah bis-mi-rab´-bi-kuh al-la´-dhee*
jizyah: *jiz´-yuh*
Jihaad: *ji-had´*
Jahili: *ja´-he-lee*
Jahiliyyah: *ja´-he-lee´-yuh*
Ya ayyuha al-Muddathir, qum fandhir: *ya ay-yoo´-hal-mud-dath´-thir qoom fan´-dhir*
Zad al-Miʿad: *zad al-mi-ad´*

FROM MILESTONES

From *Chapter 4.* Jihaad *in the Cause of God*

The great scholar Ibn Qayyim, in his book *Zad al-Miʿad*,[1] has a chapter entitled "The Prophet's Treatment of the Unbelievers and the Hypocrites from the Beginning of His Messengership Until His Death," In this chapter, this scholar has summed up the nature of Islamic *Jihaad*.

Translator unidentified. The translator's footnotes and parenthetical Qur'an citations have been omitted.

1. *Provisions for the Hereafter* (Arabic); Ibn Qayyim al-Jawziyya (1292–1350), a scholar with wide-ranging interests (especially in the area of spirituality), was one of the most famous students of Ibn Taymiyya (1263–1328; see above).

"The first revelation from God which came to the Prophet—peace be on him—was *'Iqraa, bisme Rabbika alladhee. . . .'* ('Read, in the name of Your Sustainer, Who created . . .').[2] This was the beginning of the Prophethood. God commanded the Prophet—peace be on him—to recite this in his heart. The commandment to preach had not yet come. Then God revealed *'Ya ayyuha al-Muddathir, qum fandhir'* ('O you who are enwrapped in your mantle, arise and warn').[3] Thus, the revelation of *'Iqraa'* was his appointment to Prophet-hood, while *'Ya ayyuha al-muddathir'* was his appointment to Messengership. Later God commanded the Prophet—peace be on him—to warn his near relatives, then his people, then the Arabs who were around them, then all of Arabia, and finally the whole world. Thus for thirteen years after the beginning of his Messengership, he called people to God through preaching, without fighting or *Jizyah*,[4] and was commanded to restrain himself and to practice patience and forbearance. Then he was commanded to migrate, and later permission was given to fight. Then he was commanded to fight those who fought him, and to restrain himself from those who did not make war with him. Later he was commanded to fight the polytheists until God's religion was fully established. After the command for *Jihaad* came, the non-believers were divided into three categories: one, those with whom there was peace; two, the people with whom the Muslims were at war; and three, the *Dhimmies*.[5] It was commanded that as long as the non-believers with whom he had a peace treaty met their obligations, he should fulfill the articles of the treaty, but if they broke this treaty, then they should be given notice of having broken it; until then, no war should be declared. If they persisted, then he should fight with them. When the chapter entitled *'Bra't'*[6] was revealed, the details of treatment of these three kinds of non-believers were described. It was also explained that war should be declared against those from among the 'People of the Book'[7] who declare open enmity, until they agree to pay *Jizyah* or accept Islam. Concerning the polytheists and the hypocrites, it was commanded in this chapter that *Jihaad* be declared against them and that they be treated harshly. The Prophet—peace be on him—carried on *Jihaad* against the polytheists by fighting and against the hypocrites by preaching and argument. In the same chapter, it was commanded that the treaties with the polytheists be brought to an end at the period of their expiration. In this respect, the people with whom there were treaties were divided into three categories: The first, those who broke the treaty and did not fulfill its terms. He was ordered to fight against them; he fought with them and was victorious. The second were those with whom the treaty was made for a stated term; they had not broken this treaty nor helped anyone against the Prophet—peace be on him. Concerning them, God ordered that these treaties be completed to their full term. The third kind were those with whom there was neither a treaty nor were they fighting against the Prophet—peace be on him—or those with whom no term of expiration was stated.

2. Qur'an 96:1.
3. Qur'an 74:1.
4. A tax levied on non-Muslim subjects of a Muslim state.
5. Non-Muslim subjects of a Muslim state who enjoy the state's protection as long as they pay a tax specific to them, the jizya.
6. Disavowal (Arabic), the ninth chapter of the Qur'an (also called *al-Tawba*, "Repentance").
7. A common qur'anic designation for the Jews and Christians (members of religions that have scripture).

Concerning these, it was commanded that they be given four months' notice of expiration, at the end of which they should be considered open enemies and fought with. Thus, those who broke the treaty were fought against, and those who did not have any treaty or had an indeterminate period of expiration were given four months' period of grace, and terms were kept with those with whom the treaty was due to expire. All the latter people embraced Islam even before the term expired, and the non-Muslims of the state paid *Jizyah*. Thus, after the revelation of the chapter *'Bra't'*, the unbelievers were of three kinds: adversaries in war, people with treaties, and *Dhimmies*. The people with treaties eventually became Muslims, so there were only two kinds left: people at war and *Dhimmies*. The people at war were always afraid of him. Now the people of the whole world were of three kinds: One, the Muslims who believed in him; two, those with whom he had peace; and three, the opponents who kept fighting him. As far as the hypocrites were concerned, God commanded the Prophet—peace be on him—to accept their appearances and leave their intentions to God, and carry on *Jihaad* against them by argument and persuasion. He was commanded not to pray at their funerals nor to pray at their graves, nor should he ask forgiveness from God for them, as their affair was with God. So this was the practice of the Prophet—peace be on him—concerning his enemies among the non-believers and the hypocrites."

In this description we find a summary of the stages of Islamic *Jihaad* presented in an excellent manner. In this summary we find all the distinctive and far-reaching characteristics of the dynamic movement of the true religion; we should ponder over them for deep study. Here, however, we will confine ourselves to a few explanatory remarks.

First, the method of this religion is very practical. This movement treats people as they actually are and uses resources which are in accordance with practical conditions. Since this movement comes into conflict with the *Jahiliyyah*[8] which prevails over ideas and beliefs, and which has a practical system of life and a political and material authority behind it, the Islamic movement had to produce parallel resources to confront this *Jahiliyyah*. This movement uses the methods of preaching and persuasion for reforming ideas and beliefs; and it uses physical power and *Jihaad* for abolishing the organizations and authorities of the *Jahili*[9] system which prevents people from reforming their ideas and beliefs but forces them to obey their erroneous ways and make them serve human lords instead of the Almighty Lord. This movement does not confine itself to mere preaching to confront physical power, as it also does not use compulsion for changing the ideas of people. These two principles are equally important in the method of this religion. Its purpose is to free those people who wish to be freed from enslavement to men so that they may serve God alone.

The second aspect of this religion is that it is a practical movement which progresses stage by stage, and at every stage it provides resources according to the practical needs of the situation and prepares the ground for the next one. It does not face practical problems with abstract theories, nor does it confront various stages with unchangeable means. Those who talk about

8. Ignorance (Arabic).

9. Ignorant (Arabic).

Jihaad in Islam and quote Qur'anic verses do not take into account this aspect, nor do they understand the nature of the various stages through which this movement develops, or the relationship of the verses revealed at various occasions with each stage. Thus, when they speak about *Jihaad*, they speak clumsily and mix up the various stages, distorting the whole concept of *Jihaad* and deriving from the Qur'anic verses final principles and generalities for which there is no justification. This is because they regard every verse of the Qur'an as if it were the final principle of this religion. This group of thinkers, who are a product of the sorry state of the present Muslim generation, have nothing but the label of Islam and have laid down their spiritual and rational arms in defeat. They say, "Islam has prescribed only defensive war"! and think that they have done some good for their religion by depriving it of its method, which is to abolish all injustice from the earth, to bring people to the worship of God alone, and to bring them out of servitude to others into the servants of the Lord. Islam does not force people to accept its belief, but it wants to provide a free environment in which they will have the choice of beliefs. What it wants is to abolish those oppressive political systems under which people are prevented from expressing their freedom to choose whatever beliefs they want, and after that it gives them complete freedom to decide whether they will accept Islam or not.

A third aspect of this religion is that the new resources or methods which it uses during its progressive movement do not take it away from its fundamental principles and aims. From the very first day, whether the Prophet—peace be on him—addressed his near relatives, or the Quraish,[1] or the Arabs, or the entire world, his call was one and the same. He called them to the submission to One God and rejection of the lordship of other men. On this principle there is no compromise nor any flexibility. To attain this purpose, it proceeds according to a plan, which has a few stages, and every stage has its new resources, as we have described earlier.

A fourth aspect is that Islam provides a legal basis for the relationship of the Muslim community with other groups, as is clear from the quotation from *Zad al-Mi'ad*. This legal formulation is based on the principle that Islam—that is, submission to God—is a universal Message which the whole of mankind should accept or make peace with. No political system or material power should put hindrances in the way of preaching Islam. It should leave every individual free to accept or reject it, and if someone wants to accept it, it should not prevent him or fight against him. If someone does this, then it is the duty of Islam to fight him until either he is killed or until he declares his submission.

When writers with defeatist and apologetic mentalities write about "*Jihaad* in Islam," trying to remove this 'blot' from Islam, then they are mixing up two things: first, that this religion forbids the imposition of its belief by force, as is clear from the verse, "There is no compulsion in religion,"[2] while on the other hand it tries to annihilate all those political and material powers which stand between people and Islam, which force one people to

1. The tribe that ruled Mecca in Muhammad's time.

2. Qur'an 2:256.

bow before another people and prevent them from accepting the sovereignty of God. These two principles have no relation to one another nor is there room to mix them. In spite of this, these defeatist-type people try to mix the two aspects and want to confine *Jihaad* to what today is called 'defensive war'. The Islamic *Jihaad* has no relationship to modern warfare, either in its causes or in the way in which it is conducted. The causes of Islamic *Jihaad* should be sought in the very nature of Islam and its role in the world, in its high principles, which have been given to it by God and for the implementation of which God appointed the Prophet—peace be on him—as His Messenger and declared him to be the last of all prophets and messengers.

This religion is really a universal declaration of the freedom of man from servitude to other men and from servitude to his own desires, which is also a form of human servitude; it is a declaration that sovereignty belongs to God alone and that He is the Lord of all the worlds. It means a challenge to all kinds and forms of systems which are based on the concept of the sovereignty of man; in other words, where man has usurped the Divine attribute. Any system in which the final decisions are referred to human beings, and in which the sources of all authority are human, deifies human beings by designating others than God as lords over men. This declaration means that the usurped authority of God be returned to Him and the usurpers be thrown out—those who by themselves devise laws for others to follow, thus elevating themselves to the status of lords and reducing others to the status of slaves. In short, to proclaim the authority and sovereignty of God means to eliminate all human kingship and to announce the rule of the Sustainer of the universe over the entire earth. In the words of the Qur'an:

> "He alone is God in the heavens and in the earth."[3]
>
> "The command belongs to God alone. He commands you not to worship anyone except Him. This is the right way of life."[4]
>
> "Say: O People of the Book, come to what is common between us: that we will not worship anyone except God, and will not associate anything with Him, and will not take lords from among ourselves besides God; and if they turn away then tell them to bear witness that we are those who have submitted to God."[5]

The way to establish God's rule on earth is not that some consecrated people—the priests—be given the authority to rule, as was the case with the rule of the Church, nor that some spokesmen of God become rulers, as is the case in a 'theocracy'. To establish God's rule means that His laws be enforced and that the final decision in all affairs be according to these laws.

The establishing of the dominion of God on earth, the abolishing of the dominion of man, the taking away of sovereignty from the usurper to revert it to God, and the bringing about of the enforcement of the Divine Law (*Shari'ah*) and the abolition of man-made laws cannot be achieved only through preaching. Those who have usurped the authority of God and are oppressing God's creatures are not going to give up their power merely through preaching; if it had been so, the task of establishing God's religion

3. Qur'an 43:84.
4. Qur'an 12:40.
5. Qur'an 3:64.

in the world would have been very easy for the Prophets of God! This is contrary to the evidence from the history of the Prophets and the story of the struggle of the true religion, spread over generations.

This universal declaration of the freedom of man on the earth from every authority except that of God, and the declaration that sovereignty is God's alone and that He is the Lord of the universe, is not merely a theoretical, philosophical and passive proclamation. It is a positive, practical and dynamic message with a view to bringing about the implementation of the *Shari'ah* of God and actually freeing people from their servitude to other men to bring them into the service of God, the One without associates. This cannot be attained unless both 'preaching' and 'the movement' are used. This is so because appropriate means are needed to meet any and every practical situation.

Because this religion proclaims the freedom of man on the earth from all authority except that of God, it is confronted in every period of human history—yesterday, today, or tomorrow—with obstacles of beliefs and concepts, physical power, and the obstacles of political, social, economic, racial and class structures. In addition, corrupted beliefs and superstitions become mixed with this religion, working side by side with it and taking root in peoples' hearts.

If through 'preaching' beliefs and ideas are confronted, through 'the movement' material obstacles are tackled. Foremost among these is that political power which rests on a complex yet interrelated ideological, racial, class, social and economic support. Thus these two—preaching and the movement—united, confront 'the human situation' with all the necessary methods. For the achievement of the freedom of man on earth—of all mankind throughout the earth—it is necessary that these two methods should work side by side. This is a very important point and cannot be overemphasized.

This religion is not merely a declaration of the freedom of the Arabs, nor is its message confined to the Arabs. It addresses itself to the whole of mankind, and its sphere of work is the whole earth. God is the Sustainer not merely of the Arabs, nor is His providence limited to those who believe in the faith of Islam. God is the Sustainer of the whole world. This religion wants to bring back the whole world to its Sustainer and free it from servitude to anyone other than God.

* * *

MALCOLM X
1925–1965

Malcolm X, born Malcolm Little in Omaha, Nebraska, was one of the most influential African Americans of the twentieth century. Through both his life and his *Autobiography*, he significantly changed how Americans thought about race and religion.

Malcolm's parents were followers of the Pan-Africanist thinker Marcus Garvey (1887–1940) and raised their children in a home steeped in black activism and the philosophy of empowerment. Malcolm's early life was plagued by racist encounters. In 1929, soon after the Littles moved to Lansing, Michigan, their home was firebombed. In 1931 Malcolm's father, a Baptist minister, died in a suspicious streetcar accident. A few years later, his mother was institutionalized and the children were sent into foster care.

As a youth, Malcolm proved himself an excellent student but left school in the eighth grade after one of his teachers suggested that he forget his dream of studying law and pursue carpentry instead. Malcolm started to hang out in black nightclubs, first in Lansing and then in Boston, where he had moved to live with his half-sister. During these years, he survived largely on petty crime and hustling, living in Harlem from 1942 to 1944. After returning to Boston, Malcolm was arrested in January 1946 for robbery and sentenced to an eight- to ten-year prison term.

From 1946 to 1952, while in prison, Malcolm considered himself "beyond atheism." As a child, he had been exposed by his mother to a range of Christian groups, from mainline churches to the Seventh-Day Adventists and Jehovah's Witnesses. Yet his own observations and religious questioning left him dissatisfied with all of the Christian groups he encountered.

During his imprisonment, all of Malcolm's siblings in Detroit and Chicago became members of the Nation of Islam (NOI), an organization that used a version of Islam to promote black nationalism. Aware of his antipathy toward Christianity, Malcolm's family encouraged him to learn about and join the NOI by emphasizing its social and racial teachings rather than its religious ideas. At the suggestion of one of his sisters, Malcolm began corresponding with the leader of the NOI, Elijah Muhammad (1897–1975), and soon became a convert himself. Once released, Malcolm met with Elijah Muhammad and was given a new last name—the "X" assumed by NOI members to replace their "slave" names and to indicate their membership in the organization.

The Nation of Islam was established after W. D. Fard, a merchant who sold household goods, appeared in Detroit in 1930. In addition to handing out health and dietary advice, Fard used the Bible and the Qur'an to preach what he claimed were the "Asiatic" origins of his black patrons' true religion. He also taught that the cruel and evil domination of the "blue-eyed devils" was merely temporary, declaring that God was black and would liberate the black people. Fard soon established a temple and won many adherents. He instituted a dietary code that, like traditional Islam, forbade pork and alcohol; he banned tobacco as well. He also claimed both mystical powers and a messianic status. An early disciple was Elijah Poole, who took the name Elijah Muhammad and became a leader in the new organization; a gifted minister, he began to proclaim Fard's divinity in his sermons.

When Fard mysteriously disappeared in 1934, the movement splintered, and Elijah Muhammad emerged as the head of one of its branches. He further elaborated the movement's theology, claiming Fard was God, incarnated in a black man, and that he was Fard's messenger and successor. Elijah Muhammad told his followers that the white race, weak and evil by nature, was created by a black scientist named Yacub in an act of rebellion against God. Though whites had power now, a coming apocalypse would destroy them and give power back to blacks. He also preached a black nationalist message, promoting black economic self-sufficiency and full separation from whites.

As a younger ally of Elijah Muhammad's, Malcolm was an active and inspiring preacher, quickly expanding the Nation's membership base and the number of its temples. His success secured him the position of minister of Temple No. 7 in Harlem. Much sought-after by the media, Malcolm frequently gave interviews and participated in debates on behalf of the Nation of Islam. His voice was prominent in the civil rights movement, and his call for separation and direct action served as a counterpoint to Martin Luther King Jr.'s pleas for integration and nonviolent protest.

In the early 1960s Malcolm and Elijah Muhammad became increasingly estranged, as Malcolm's popularity began to eclipse Elijah Muhammad's. In addition, Malcolm discovered that Elijah Muhammad was engaging in extramarital affairs with young female members of the NOI. Malcolm was also becoming more politically radical, and the Nation of Islam suspended his speaking engagements when he described President Kennedy's assassination as "the chickens coming home to roost." Eventually, ejected from the NOI by Elijah Muhammad himself, Malcolm created his own organization, the Muslim Mosque, Inc., which maintained many of Elijah Muhammad's religious ideas but promoted a more activist black nationalist agenda.

Malcolm's own religious thinking was evolving. On the college lecture circuit, he met white students whose strong support challenged his stereotypes of white racism. At the same time, he was criticized by Sunni Muslims living in the United States who insisted that his racist rhetoric was contrary to authentic Muslim thought. Malcolm corresponded with some of his critics, and watched as one of Elijah Muhammad's own sons left the Nation of Islam for mainstream Sunni Islam, and began studying at al-Azhar University in Cairo, the famous center of Sunni learning.

In 1964 Malcolm had the opportunity to participate in the hajj—the pilgrimage to Mecca that all Muslims must, if possible, make in their lifetime. This proved to be a pivotal experience, as described in the passage below. His encounter with the pilgrimage rituals with people of all colors and ethnicities gave credence to what Malcolm's Sunni correspondents had been arguing for years, namely that Islam's message was one of racial harmony. Malcolm allied himself with Sunni Islam, changed his name to El-Hajj Malik El-Shabazz, and redirected his sociopolitical message toward condemning the oppressive individuals and institutions of white America rather than attacking whites as a race.

After returning to the United States, Malcolm X faced new criticism and at times threats of violence, which he attributed to the Nation of Islam. His home was firebombed, and seven days later, on February 21, 1965, he was assassinated while speaking at the Audubon Ballroom in Harlem. *The Autobiography of Malcolm X*, which charts his transformation from a school dropout to a charismatic religious leader, has become a contemporary classic of American Muslim literature.

PRONOUNCING GLOSSARY

Allah Akbar: *al-lah´-hu ak´-bar*
asr: *ahsr*
Hajar: *ha´-jar* (heavy *h*)
Ihram: *ih-rahm´* (heavy *h*)
Labbayka: *lab-bay´-kuh*
Maghrib: *mag´-rib*
Al-Marwah: *al-mar´-wuh*
Mina: *mee´-nuh*
Mutawaf (muṭawwif): *moo-taw´-wif*
Rakʿa: *rak´-ah*
Safa/Al-Safa: *sa-fah´; as-sa-fah´*
Takbir: *tak-beer´*
Zem Zem: *zam´-zam*

FROM THE AUTOBIOGRAPHY OF MALCOLM X

From *Chapter 17. Mecca*

* * *

Mecca, when we entered, seemed as ancient as time itself. Our car slowed through the winding streets, lined by shops on both sides and with buses, cars, and trucks, and tens of thousands of pilgrims from all over the earth were everywhere.

The car halted briefly at a place where a *Mutawaf*[1] was waiting for me. He wore the white skullcap and long nightshirt garb that I had seen at the airport. He was a short, dark-skinned Arab, named Muhammad. He spoke no English whatever.

We parked near the Great Mosque. We performed our ablution and entered. Pilgrims seemed to be on top of each other, there were so many, lying, sitting, sleeping, praying, walking.

My vocabulary cannot describe the new mosque that was being built around the Kaʿba.[2] I was thrilled to realize that it was only one of the tremendous rebuilding tasks under the direction of young Dr. Azzam, who had just been my host. The Great Mosque of Mecca, when it is finished, will surpass the architectural beauty of India's Taj Mahal.

Carrying my sandals, I followed the *Mutawaf.* Then I saw the Kaʿba, a huge black stone house in the middle of the Great Mosque. It was being circumambulated by thousands upon thousands of praying pilgrims, both sexes, and every size, shape, color, and race in the world. I knew the prayer to be uttered when the pilgrim's eyes first perceive the Kaʿba. Translated, it is "O God, You are peace, and peace derives from You. So greet us, O Lord, with peace." Upon entering the Mosque, the pilgrim should try to kiss the Kaʿba if possible, but if the crowds prevent him getting that close, he touches it, and if the crowds prevent that, he raises his hand and cries out "Takbir!"[3] ("God is great!") I could not get within yards. "Takbir!"

My feeling there in the House of God was a numbness. My *Mutawaf* led me in the crowd of praying, chanting pilgrims, moving seven times around the Kaʾba. Some were bent and wizened with age; it was a sight that stamped itself on the brain. I saw incapacitated pilgrims being carried by others. Faces were enraptured in their faith. The seventh time around, I prayed two *Rakʿa*,[4] prostrating myself, my head on the floor. The first prostration, I prayed the Quran verse "Say He is God, the one and only"; the second prostration: "Say O you who are unbelievers, I worship not that which you worship. . . ."[5]

As I prostrated, the *Mutawaf* fended pilgrims off to keep me from being trampled.

The *Mutawaf* and I next drank water from the well of Zem Zem. Then we ran between the two hills, Safa and Marwa, where Hajar wandered over the same earth searching for water for her child Ishmael.

Three separate times, after that, I visited the Great Mosque and circumambulated the Kaʿba. The next day we set out after sunrise toward Mount Arafat, thousands of us, crying in unison: "Labbayka![6] Labbayka!" and "Allah Akbar!" Mecca is surrounded by the crudest-looking mountains I have ever seen; they seem to be made of the slag from a blast furnace. No vegetation is on them at all. Arriving about noon, we prayed and chanted from noon until sunset, and the *asr* (afternoon) and *Maghrib* (sunset) special prayers were performed.

1. A guide who leads pilgrims on the hajj and instructs them in the rites.
2. Literally, "the Cube," a stone shrine in Mecca that became the most important site in Islam (Muslims around the world face it when they pray). It is also called "the Sacred House," and as part of the required pilgrimage to Mecca, worshippers walk around it seven times.
3. The Arabic name of the phrase "Allahu Akbar," which means "God is greater."
4. Two cycles of Muslim ritual prayer.
5. Qur'an 112:1–2; 109:1–2.
6. Here I am.

Finally, we lifted our hands in prayer and thanksgiving, repeating Allah's words: "There is no God but Allah. He has no partner. His are authority and praise. Good emanates from Him, and He has power over all things."[7]

Standing on Mount Arafat had concluded the essential rites of being a pilgrim to Mecca. No one who missed it could consider himself a pilgrim.

The *Ihram*[8] had ended. We cast the traditional seven stones at the devil. Some had their hair and beards cut. I decided that I was going to let my beard remain. I wondered what my wife Betty, and our little daughters, were going to say when they saw me with a beard, when I got back to New York. New York seemed a million miles away. I hadn't seen a newspaper that I could read since I left New York. I had no idea what was happening there. A Negro rifle club that had been in existence for over twelve years in Harlem had been "discovered" by the police; it was being trumpeted that I was "behind it." Elijah Muhammad's[9] Nation of Islam had a lawsuit going against me, to force me and my family to vacate the house in which we lived on Long Island.

The major press, radio, and television media in America had representatives in Cairo hunting all over, trying to locate me, to interview me about the furor in New York that I had allegedly caused—when I knew nothing about any of it.

I only knew what I had left in America, and how it contrasted with what I had found in the Muslim world. About twenty of us Muslims who had finished the Hajj were sitting in a huge tent on Mount Arafat. As a Muslim from America, I was the center of attention. They asked me what about the Hajj had impressed me the most. One of the several who spoke English asked; they translated my answers for the others. My answer to that question was not the one they expected, but it drove home my point.

I said, "The *brotherhood!* The people of all races, colors, from all over the world coming together as *one!* It has proved to me the power of the One God."

It may have been out of taste, but that gave me an opportunity, and I used it, to preach them a quick little sermon on America's racism, and its evils.

I could tell the impact of this upon them. They had been aware that the plight of the black man in America was "bad," but they had not been aware that it was inhuman, that it was a psychological castration. These people from elsewhere around the world were shocked. As Muslims, they had a very tender heart for all unfortunates, and very sensitive feelings for truth and justice. And in everything I said to them, as long as we talked, they were aware of the yardstick that I was using to measure everything—that to me the earth's most explosive and pernicious evil is racism, the inability of God's creatures to live as One, especially in the Western world.

I have reflected since that the letter I finally sat down to compose had been subconsciously shaping itself in my mind.

The *color-blindness* of the Muslim world's religious society and the *color-blindness* of the Muslim world's human society: these two influences had

7. A prayer of the Prophet, slightly altered, that can be found in the *Sahih* of al-Bukhari (see above).

8. The restricted state a pilgrim enters when beginning the hajj.

9. Born Elijah Poole (1897–1975), he led the Nation of Islam from 1934 until his death; Malcolm X had been expelled from the organization shortly before he went to Mecca.

each day been making a greater impact, and an increasing persuasion against my previous way of thinking.

The first letter was, of course, to my wife, Betty. I never had a moment's question that Betty, after initial amazement, would change her thinking to join mine. I had known a thousand reassurances that Betty's faith in me was total. I knew that she would see what I had seen—that in the land of Muhammad and the land of Abraham, I had been blessed by Allah with a new insight into the true religion of Islam, and a better understanding of America's entire racial dilemma.

After the letter to my wife, I wrote next essentially the same letter to my sister Ella. And I knew where Ella would stand. She had been saving to make the pilgrimage to Mecca herself.

I wrote to Dr. Shawarbi,[1] whose belief in my sincerity had enabled me to get a passport to Mecca.

All through the night, I copied similar long letters for others who were very close to me. Among them was Elijah Muhammad's son Wallace Muhammad, who had expressed to me his conviction that the only possible salvation for the Nation of Islam would be its accepting and projecting a better understanding of Orthodox Islam.

And I wrote to my loyal assistants at my newly formed Muslim Mosque, Inc. in Harlem, with a note appended, asking that my letter be duplicated and distributed to the press.

I knew that when my letter became public knowledge back in America, many would be astounded—loved ones, friends, and enemies alike. And no less astounded would be millions whom I did not know—who had gained during my twelve years with Elijah Muhammad a "hate" image of Malcolm X.

Even I was myself astounded. But there was precedent in my life for this letter. My whole life had been a chronology of—*changes.*

Here is what I wrote . . . from my heart:

"Never have I witnessed such sincere hospitality and the overwhelming spirit of true brotherhood as is practiced by people of all colors and races here in this Ancient Holy Land, the home of Abraham, Muhammad, and all the other prophets of the Holy Scriptures. For the past week, I have been utterly speechless and spellbound by the graciousness I see displayed all around me by people *of all colors.*

"I have been blessed to visit the Holy City of Mecca. I have made my seven circuits around the Kaʿba, led by a young *Mutawaf* named Muhammad. I drank water from the well of Zem Zem. I ran seven times back and forth between the hills of Mt. Al-Safa and Al-Marwah. I have prayed in the ancient city of Mina, and I have prayed on Mt. Arafat.

"There were tens of thousands of pilgrims, from all over the world. They were of all colors, from blue-eyed blonds to black-skinned Africans. But we were all participating in the same ritual, displaying a spirit of unity and brotherhood that my experiences in America had led me to believe never could exist between the white and the non-white.

"America needs to understand Islam, because this is the one religion that erases from its society the race problem. Throughout my travels in the Mus-

1. Mahmoud Youssef Shawarbi, an Egyptian Muslim professor at the University of Cairo (then living in New York) who encouraged and facilitated his undertaking the hajj.

lim world, I have met, talked to, and even eaten with people who in America would have been considered 'white'—but the 'white' attitude was removed from their minds by the religion of Islam. I have never before seen *sincere* and *true* brotherhood practiced by all colors together, irrespective of their color.

"You may be shocked by these words coming from me. But on this pilgrimage, what I have seen, and experienced, has forced me to *re-arrange* much of my thought-patterns previously held, and to *toss aside* some of my previous conclusions. This was not too difficult for me. Despite my firm convictions, I have been always a man who tries to face facts, and to accept the reality of life as new experience and new knowledge unfolds it. I have always kept an open mind, which is necessary to the flexibility that must go hand in hand with every form of intelligent search for truth.

"During the past eleven days here in the Muslim world, I have eaten from the same plate, drunk from the same glass, and slept in the same bed (or on the same rug)—while praying to the *same God*—with fellow Muslims, whose eyes were the bluest of blue, whose hair was the blondest of blond, and whose skin was the whitest of white. And in the *words* and in the *actions* and in the *deeds* of the 'white' Muslims, I felt the same sincerity that I felt among the black African Muslims of Nigeria, Sudan, and Ghana.

"We were *truly* all the same (brothers)—because their belief in one God had removed the 'white' from their *minds*, the 'white' from their *behavior*, and the 'white' from their *attitude*.

"I could see from this, that perhaps if white Americans could accept the Oneness of God, then perhaps, too, they could accept *in reality* the Oneness of Man—and cease to measure, and hinder, and harm others in terms of their 'differences' in color.

"With racism plaguing America like an incurable cancer, the so-called 'Christian' white American heart should be more receptive to a proven solution to such a destructive problem. Perhaps it could be in time to save America from imminent disaster—the same destruction brought upon Germany by racism that eventually destroyed the Germans themselves.

"Each hour here in the Holy Land enables me to have greater spiritual insights into what is happening in America between black and white. The American Negro never can be blamed for his racial animosities—he is only reacting to four hundred years of the conscious racism of the American whites. But as racism leads America up the suicide path, I do believe, from the experiences that I have had with them, that the whites of the younger generation, in the colleges and universities, will see the handwriting on the wall and many of them will turn to the *spiritual* path of *truth*—the *only* way left to America to ward off the disaster that racism inevitably must lead to.

"Never have I been so highly honored. Never have I been made to feel more humble and unworthy. Who would believe the blessings that have been heaped upon an *American Negro?* A few nights ago, a man who would be called in America a 'white' man, a United Nations diplomat, an ambassador, a companion of kings, gave me *his* hotel suite, *his* bed. By this man, His Excellency Prince Faisal,[2] who rules this Holy Land, was made aware of my presence here

2. Faisal ibn ʿAbd al-ʿAziz ibn Saʿud (ca. 1906–1975); he was regent of Saudi Arabia when Malcolm X met him and became king before the end of 1964.

in Jedda. The very next morning, Prince Faisal's son, in person, informed me that by the will and decree of his esteemed father, I was to be a State Guest.

"The Deputy Chief of Protocol himself took me before the Hajj Court. His Holiness Sheikh Muhammad Harkon himself okayed my visit to Mecca. His Holiness gave me two books on Islam, with his personal seal and autograph, and he told me that he prayed that I would be a successful preacher of Islam in America. A car, a driver, and a guide, have been placed at my disposal, making it possible for me to travel about this Holy Land almost at will. The government provides air-conditioned quarters and servants in each city that I visit. Never would I have even thought of dreaming that I would ever be a recipient of such honors—honors that in America would be bestowed upon a King—not a Negro.

"All praise is due to Allah, the Lord of all the Worlds.

"Sincerely,

"El-Hajj Malik El-Shabazz[3]
"(Malcolm X)"

3. Elsewhere in the *Autobiography*, Malcolm X relates the teaching of Elijah Muhammad that African Americans are all descendants of the tribe of Shabazz.

THE RELIGIOUS REASSERTION

RUHOLLAH KHOMEINI
1902–1989

Ayatollah Ruhollah Khomeini was born in Khomein, a village in central Iran. When he was about five months old, his father was murdered, and his mother and aunt, who helped raise him, both died when he was in his teens. His brother, a religious scholar, supervised Komeini's early education until he was nineteen, when he was sent to the town of Arak to study under the Iraqi-trained Shaykh Abd al-Karim Ha'iri (1859–1936). Soon after, Ha'iri was invited to reorganize the system of religious education in Qom, a center of Shiʿism, and Khomeini moved there with him.

Known for his piety even as a youth, Khomeini was mainly interested in ethics and mysticism. When he eventually began to teach classes in both, they drew many students. For Khomeini, mysticism was a set of spiritual practices that shaped the individual for service to society, rather than for a life of seclusion and severe asceticism. Yet he himself lived in poverty and simplicity, carefully adhering to the religious law. Later, he would argue that such moral and spiritual purification was a vital foundation for political leadership.

Khomeini studied in Qom at the same time that a new shah (king) of Iran, Reza Shah Pahlavi (1878–1944; r. 1925–41) was consolidating his power and seeking to modernize the country—efforts that would be taken up more urgently by his son Mohammad Reza (1919–1980; r. 1944–79). The Pahlavis' emphasis on Westernization alienated much of the populace and drew the denunciation of many religious scholars. The reforms included legislation to ban the veil and to mandate Western dress, as well as efforts to bring the seminaries and other religious institutions under state control.

The death in 1962 of the highest-ranking Iranian cleric, Ayatollah Burujirdi, created a leadership vacuum in the religious establishment. Though several other ayatollahs commanded general respect, it was Khomeini who rose to prominence, primarily through his willingness to challenge the Pahlavi regime. His criticism of the reforms drew a strong response from the government, including violence against students at the religious seminary in Qom, and ultimately he was arrested. These events sparked a popular uprising in June 1963 that was brutally suppressed by the Shah, causing upward of 15,000 deaths.

Because he continued to denounce the Shah after his release, Khomeini was deported to Turkey in 1964. In 1965, he moved to Najaf, a site of Shiʿi learning in Iraq, where he was able to maintain his influence at home through lectures that were smuggled into Iran.

It was during this period that Khomeini developed his concept of *wilayat al-faqih*, or the "guardianship of the jurist." This theory of political and religious leadership diverged from most earlier Shiʿi teaching, which had held that only one of the twelve infallible imams could establish a political order. The lineage of imams began with Muhammad's son-in-law, ʿAli ibn Abi Talib (ca. 599–661), and ended with Muhammad al-Mahdi—the "Hidden Imam" (b. ca. 869), who disappeared but is expected to return to bring justice to the world. Some eighteenth- and nineteenth-century Shiʿi thinkers argued that in the absence of the infallible imam, a portion

An image from the 1979 Iranian Revolution, which brought to power the Shi'i cleric Ayatollah Ruhollah Khomeini. The Iranian people surprised many by throwing their support behind the religious leader instead of the American-supported dictator, the Shah.

of his authority falls to the jurist; Khomeini extended this authority beyond religious issues to include the political arena and matters of governance. Ultimately, Khomeini claimed that if a qualified and morally upright jurist attempted to form a government, the support of that effort was not just permissible but the duty of all Muslims.

In Iran, the Shah continued to provoke popular anger by exalting the legacy of ancient Persia and disregarding the country's Islamic identity. His lavish expenditures to celebrate 2,500 years of Iranian monarchy at a time when the gap between rich and poor was rapidly growing fueled popular discontent. In 1977, the notorious Iranian secret police assassinated Khomeini's eldest son in Najaf, and soon thereafter ordered a prominent newspaper to print an article attacking Khomeini. These events prompted widespread protests, and demonstrators were killed by the hundreds. Khomeini declared his support for the actions of the people and was forced to leave Najaf; in October 1978, he took up temporary residence in France. In December, during the holy month of Muharram, mass demonstrations raged against the Shah, and in January 1979 he fled Iran. The way was open for Khomeini's triumphant return.

Upon his arrival on February 1, 1979, Khomeini was enthusiastically greeted as a symbol of the revolution and welcomed as a leader. He gradually increased his direct involvement in the government, as he successfully incorporated his theory of guardianship of the jurist into Iran's new political structure by filling the role himself.

The years between his return to Iran and his death in 1989 were challenging for Khomeini. He faced internal opposition to the newly formed republic, the Iranian student takeover of the U.S. Embassy in Tehran, and a prolonged war with Iraq. The writings printed below reflect some of these themes. The first, a formal declaration of the founding of the Islamic Republic of Iran, notes the circumstances leading up to the revolution; the second, a speech delivered in Tehran, highlights the cultural issues that Khomeini felt needed to be addressed in the universities. Despite the country's significant social, political, and religious changes since Khomeini's death, his works and legacy continue to influence discourse in Iran.

PRONOUNCING GLOSSARY

Baluch: *bah-looch´*
fiqh: *fiqh*
mujtahid: *muj-ta´-hid*
madrasa: *mad-ra´-sa*
Shah: *shaw*
usul: *oo-sool´*

THE FIRST DAY OF GOD'S GOVERNMENT

[*April 1, 1979*]

> "We desired to grant Our favor to those that were oppressed in the land, and to make of them leaders and the inheritors" (Qur'an, 28:4).[1]

I offer my sincere congratulations to the great people of Iran, who were despised and oppressed by arrogant kings throughout the history of the monarchy. God Almighty has granted us His favor and destroyed the regime of arrogance by His powerful hand, which has shown itself as the power of the oppressed. He has made our great people into leaders and exemplars for all the world's oppressed, and He has granted them their just heritage by the establishment of this Islamic Republic.

On this blessed day, the day the Islamic community assumes leadership, the day of the victory and triumph of our people, I declare the Islamic Republic of Iran.

I declare to the whole world that never has the history of Iran witnessed such a referendum, where the whole country rushed to the polls with ardor, enthusiasm, and love in order to cast their affirmative votes and bury the tyrannical regime forever in the garbage heap of history. I value highly this unparalleled solidarity by virtue of which the entire population—with the exception of a handful of adventurers and godless individuals—responded to the heavenly call of "Hold firm to the rope of God, all together" (Qur'an, 3:103) and cast a virtually unanimous vote in favor of the Islamic Republic, thus demonstrating its political and social maturity to both the East and the West.

Blessed for you be the day on which, after the martyrdom of your upright young people, the sorrow of their grieving mothers and fathers, and the suffering of the whole nation, you have overthrown your ghoulish enemy, the pharaoh of the age. By casting a decisive vote in favor of the Islamic Republic, you have established a government of divine justice, a government in which all segments of the population shall enjoy equal consideration, the light of divine justice shall shine uniformly on all, and the divine mercy of the Qur'an and the Sunna shall embrace all, like life-giving rain. Blessed for you be this government that knows no difference of race, whether between black and white, or between Turk, Persian, Kurd, and Baluch.[2] All

TRANSLATED BY Hamid Algar.

1. In most editions, Qur'an 28:5.
2. Most of Iran's population are Persian; less than a third are Turkic, Kurdish, Baluchi, or other ethnicity.

are brothers and equal; nobility lies only in the fear of God, and superiority may be attained only by acquiring virtues and performing good deeds. Blessed for you be the day on which all segments of the population have attained their legitimate rights; in the implementation of justice, there will be no difference between women and men, or between the religious minorities and the Muslims. Tyranny has been buried, and all forms of transgression will be buried along with it.

The country has been delivered from the clutches of domestic and foreign enemies, from the thieves and plunderers, and you, courageous people, are now the guardians of the Islamic Republic. It is you who must preserve this divine legacy with strength and determination and must not permit the remnants of the putrid regime of the Shah who now lie in wait, or the supporters of the international thieves and oil-bandits, to penetrate your serried ranks. You must now assume control of your own destiny and not give the opportunists any occasion to assert themselves. Relying on the divine power that is manifested in communal solidarity, take the next steps by sending virtuous, trustworthy representatives to the Constituent Assembly, so that they may revise the Constitution of the Islamic Republic. Just as you voted with ardor and enthusiasm for the Islamic Republic, vote, too, for your representatives, so that the malevolent will have no excuse to object.

This day of Farvardin 12,[3] the first day of God's government, is to be one of our foremost religious and national festivals; the people must celebrate this day and keep its remembrance alive, for it is the day on which the battlements of the twenty-five hundred-year old fortress of tyrannical government crumbled, a satanic power departed forever, and the government of the oppressed—which is the government of God—was established in its place.

Beloved people! Cherish and protect the rights you have attained through the blood of your young people and help to enact Islamic justice under the banner of Islam and the flag of the Qur'an. I stand ready to serve you and Islam with all the strength at my disposal during these last days of my life, and I expect the nation to devote itself similarly to guarding Islam and the Islamic Republic.

I ask the government that, fearing neither East nor West and cultivating an independent outlook and will, it purge all remnants of the tyrannical regime, which left deep traces upon all the affairs of our country. It should transform our educational and judicial systems, as well as all the ministries and government offices that are now run on Western lines or in slavish imitation of Western models, and make them compatible to Islam, thus demonstrating to the world true social justice and true cultural, economic, and political independence.

I ask God Almighty that He grant dignity and independence to our country and the nation of Islam.

Peace be upon you, and also the blessings and mercy of God.

3. April 1, 1979, now celebrated as Islamic Republic Day.

THE MEANING OF THE CULTURAL REVOLUTION
[*April 26, 1980*]

Greetings to the great nation of Islam, greetings to all Muslims in the world! Greetings to the people of Iran! Greetings to the students of Iran's universities!

It is necessary for me to clarify what our aim is in reforming the universities. Some people have imagined that those who are calling for the reform of our universities and wish to make them Islamic regard every science as consisting of two sectors, one Islamic and the other non-Islamic, so that, for example, there is an Islamic mathematics and a non-Islamic mathematics, or an Islamic physics and a non-Islamic physics. On the basis of this assumption, they have protested that the sciences are not divisible into Islamic and non-Islamic. Others have assumed that the call for the Islamization of the universities means that only *fiqh*, Qur'anic exegesis, and *usul*[1] would be taught there, that, in other words, the universities would adopt the same curriculum as the traditional madrasas. These ideas that some people hold, or pretend to hold, are erroneous. When we speak of the reform of the universities, what we mean is that our universities are at present in a state of dependence; they are imperialist universities, and those whom they educate and train are infatuated with the West. Many university teachers suffer from this infatuation, and they transmit it to their students, our young people. That is why we say that our universities in their present state are of no use to our people.

We have had universities in our country for fifty years now, and throughout this period, the backbreaking expenditures that have been lavished upon them have been borne by our toiling masses. But we have been unable to attain self-sufficiency in any of the subjects taught in our universities. After fifty years of universities, when someone falls sick, many of our doctors will recommend that he go to England for treatment; we do not have doctors that can meet the needs of our people. We have had universities, but we are still dependent on the West for all that a nation needs.

It is for these reasons that fundamental changes must take place in the universities and it is in this sense that they must become Islamic. We do not mean that only Islamic learning should be taught in them, or that each science comes in two varieties, one Islamic and the other non-Islamic. But show us the achievements of our universities during their fifty years of existence! Our universities have served to impede the progress of the sons and daughters of this land; they have become propaganda arenas. Our young people may have succeeded in acquiring some knowledge, but they have not received an education, an Islamic education. Those who go to our universities to study do so in order to acquire a piece of paper and then become a burden to the people. The universities do not impart an education that corresponds to the needs of the people and the country; instead they squander the energies of whole generations of our beloved youth, or oblige them to serve the foreigners.

1. *Fiqh* is jurisprudence. *Usul* (*al-din*), the foundations of the religion, refers to dogmatic theology [translator's note, edited].

Teachers in our schools, as a class, have not conceived of their profession in Islamic terms; they have imparted knowledge, but not an education. Our university system, therefore, has not produced committed individuals, people concerned with the welfare of their country and prepared to overlook their narrow personal interests.

So, to repeat, we demand fundamental changes in our university system so that the universities come to serve the nation and its needs instead of serving foreigners. Many of our schoolteachers and university professors are now effectively serving the West by brainwashing and miseducating our youth. We are not rejecting modern science, nor are we saying that each science exists in two varieties, one Islamic and the other non-Islamic; this notion is attributed to us by some people out of malice or ignorance. Our universities lack Islamic morality and fail to impart an Islamic education; if this were not so, our universities would not have been transformed into a battlefield for ideologies harmful to the nation. If Islamic morality existed in the universities, these shameful clashes would not occur. They reflect a lack of Islamic education and true understanding of Islam. The universities, then, must change fundamentally. They must be reconstructed in such a way that our young people will receive a correct Islamic education side-by-side with their acquisition of formal learning, not a Western education.

This is our aim, to prevent one group of our young people from being drawn to the West and another group to the East. We do not wish even one group among our university students and young people to aid those who are actively at war with us, who wish to impose an economic embargo on us. If the Iranian people stand up to the West, we want our university students to join them in their resistance. Similarly, if the people take a stand against the communists, we want our university students to do the same.

Some of our young people have been simple-minded enough to assimilate the wrong education that was given by their teachers. As a result, now that we wish to carry out fundamental changes in the universities in order to make them independent both of the West and of the communist East, they oppose us. This is in itself an indication that our universities have not been Islamic or given our young people a proper education. Many of our university students not only lack an Islamic education, they also fail to pursue their studies; they spend all their time on sloganeering, false propaganda, and expressions of support for America or the Soviet Union. We want our young people to be truly independent and to perceive their own real needs instead of following the East or the West.

Those who are creating disturbances on the streets or in the universities and creating problems for the government and the nation are followers of the West or the East. In my opinion, they are mostly followers of the West, of America. For today it is the superpower America that we are confronting, and at a time when we need our youth to participate in this confrontation, we see them confronting each other instead and thus serving America. But we want to reconstruct our universities in such a way that our young people work for themselves and the nation.

Certain gentlemen sitting on the sidelines are raising all kinds of objections and imagine that the members of the Revolutionary Council do not know what they are doing. They pretend, for example, that the Islamization of the universities rests on the assumption that the sciences are divisible into Islamic and non-Islamic varieties, so that we have Islamic mathematics and non-Islamic mathematics. Do they not know that some members of the Revolutionary Council hold doctorates and some are *mujtahids*?[2] The place for the strictly Islamic sciences is the traditional *madrasa*; the other sciences are to be taught at the university. However, the universities must become Islamic in the sense that the subjects studied in them are to be pursued in accordance with the needs of the nation and for the sake of strengthening it. The curricula that have been followed up to now at the universities have resulted in the gravitation of one part of our young people toward communism and another part toward the West. Some university professors, moreover, have prevented our young people from progressing in their various fields of study; being in the service of the West, they want us to remain in a state of perpetual dependence on the West. To Islamize the universities means to make them autonomous, independent of the West and independent of the East, so that we have an independent country with an independent university system and an independent culture.

My beloved listeners! We fear neither economic boycott nor military intervention. What we fear is cultural dependence and imperialist universities that propel our young people into the service of communism. We do not wish our universities to produce more people of the same type as those who are now objecting to the Islamization of the universities. They do not understand what is meant by making the universities independent and Islamic.

I support all that has been said by the Revolutionary Council and the President of the Republic concerning the necessity for a purge of the universities and a change in the atmosphere prevailing in them in order to make them fully independent. I request that all of our young people not resist or try to sabotage the reform of the universities; if any of them do so, I will instruct the nation as to how to respond.

I beseech God Almighty to grant happiness to the nation of Islam and to our young people, and I hope that our universities will be cleared of all elements of dependency, so that, God willing, we will come to have a university system based on Islamic morality and an Islamic culture.

Peace be upon you, and also the mercy and blessings of God.

2. Scholars who, according to Shiʿism, are qualified to answer religious questions in the absence of the twelve infallible imams. But unlike the imams, a *mujtahid* is fallible, and his decisions are effective only during his lifetime.

MOHAMMED ARKOUN
1928–2010

A seminal thinker willing to range widely in the humanities and social sciences, Mohammed Arkoun drew on his deep knowledge of critical theory and his training in medieval Islam to urge a rethinking of the methodological approaches to early Islamic history and the study of the Qur'an.

Born in the northern Algerian village of Taourirt Mimoun, Arkoun came from a poor Berber family of no social prominence. He left his village at nine to work in his father's successful grocery store in a prosperous town whose population was largely French. Through the generosity of one of his uncles, Arkoun was able to attend a French school there, an advantage enjoyed by few Muslim students. After completing high school, he began advanced education at the University of Algiers but then transferred to the Sorbonne in Paris, where he completed his studies. His 1970 PhD thesis on the thought of Miskawayh (ca. 930–1030; see above) established his credentials in classical Islamic thought.

Arkoun published most of his work in French but also oversaw the translation into English and Arabic of selected titles. One of his most enduring contributions is his *Lectures du Coran* (1982, *Readings on the Quran*), a collection of seven articles originally published between 1970 and 1980 and introduced with a survey of the principal problems in the field of qur'anic studies as well as directions for future research. He reengages many of these ideas in his 2002 article for the *Encyclopedia of the Qur'an* titled "Contemporary Critical Practices and the Qur'an."

Arkoun's analysis is undergirded by several key concepts, especially his notions of the "thinkable," "unthinkable," and "unthought." Arkoun argues that certain interpretations and understandings are thinkable at a specific moment in time because factors such as one's society, language, culture, and science allow them to be conceived and expressed. In an Islamic context, these thinkable ideas are equivalent to the "orthodox" ideas promulgated by those in authority, particularly scholars and religious leaders. Conversely, some ideas fall so far beyond the realm of acceptable views in a society that individuals dare not entertain them—they remain unthinkable. In Arkoun's view, Muslim historians, theologians, and jurists built a bounded orthodoxy that prevented the emergence of heterodox (unthinkable) views. The unthought consists of all that is in the category of the unthinkable plus all those notions that a society lacks the capacity to even consider at a particular moment in history. For example, for millennia the possibility that something other than the earth was the center of the universe was unthought. Thus the unthinkable and unthought in Islam include interrogating the textual integrity of the Qur'an, questioning aspects of Islamic history (such as the standard biographies of Muhammad), and, in broadest terms, challenging anything deemed to be "orthodox."

Convinced that Islamic thought has stagnated and has lost an essential dynamism because of the hegemonic power of the thinkable, Arkoun urges an examination of all that remains unthought. In exploring the dominance of the thinkable, he identifies two key dates in Islamic history. The first is the death of Muhammad in 632, which effectively ended qur'anic revelation. The second is 936, which marks the final transformation of the Qur'an from an originally open, oral text into a fixed, closed text denuded of variant readings, as well as the formation and rise of orthodoxy (the thinkable) in Islamic thought, which closed off avenues to the unthought.

For instance, Arkoun questions the work of accepted Muslim historians such as al-Tabari (ca. 839–923; see above), whom he sees as simply reinforcing the orthodoxy imposed by those in power. He rejects much of the qur'anic commentary tradition as propagating a set of accepted orthodox beliefs to the exclusion of others. He criticizes most modern Muslim and non-Muslim scholars of Islam and the Qur'an for their near exclusive focus on philology, the dating of historical events, and the texts deemed canonical by the Islamic tradition. To accurately reconstruct the history of Islam, Arkoun urges a creative encounter with the unthought and the consideration of all types of evidence and texts, regardless of how marginalized or neglected they have been by Islamic orthodoxy.

The reception of Arkoun's work has been mixed. While his proponents see a scholar with an active and innovative intellect and a prodigious level of publication, his critics complain that his arguments lack any systematic and coherent elaboration and are couched in complicated terminology that clouds clear explanation.

The passage below, in which Arkoun assesses the concept of human rights within the Islamic and Western tradition, was originally published in French in *Ouvertures sur Islam* (1989, *Rethinking Islam*). Intended for a general audience, the book addresses French and European fears about Islam and Muslims. Arkoun responds to twenty questions, on topics ranging from women to nationalism, that were posed to him by two French intellectuals. His stated goal is "to defuse the issue and to open intellectual, historical, anthropological, theological, and philosophical perspectives on Islamic studies, which have so often been confined in the West (Europe and North America) to static descriptions of beliefs, life-styles, images, institutions, and practices unique to 'Islam' and 'Muslims.'"

PRONOUNCING GLOSSARY

al-ḥaqq: *al-hahq* (heavy *h*)
ḥuqūq: *hoo-qooq´* (heavy *h*)
salafī: *sa´-la-fee*
umma: *oom´-muh*

FROM RETHINKING ISLAM

Chapter 22. Human Rights

Who is the audience for an "Islamic" discourse on human rights? What relationship can be established between what we call Islam with a capital "I" and nation-states founded for the most part after World War II? Still more generally, what meaning can be assigned to the idea of an exclusively divine origin of human rights? What is one to make of the "philosophical" or "secular" assertion that human beings win their rights by sociopolitical struggle and cultural progress—without external help? In what philosophical direction can we or should we orient research on the foundations of human rights and the means of assuring their implementation?

Like Jews and Christians, contemporary Muslims have shown concern for human rights, but they have attempted to demonstrate that the original matrix for a culture based on human rights comes from the Qurʾan and the teaching of the Prophet Muhammad. This drive to reclaim for Islam a vision of human beings and a practice of law and politics that, in fact, only gained credence with the English, American, and especially the French revolutions was clearly demonstrated at a UNESCO meeting of September 19, 1981, where a Universal Islamic Declaration of Human Rights was prepared on the initiative of the Islamic Council and its secretary general, Salem Azzam. In the West there has always been a tendency to exclude Islam from the cultural domain where human rights were conceived and proclaimed and where they retain meaning. The Universal Islamic Declaration of Human Rights was a response to that exclusion. "Eminent scholars, Muslim jurists, and representatives of movements and currents of Islamic thought" prepared the text of this declaration, and all twenty-three articles are based on verses of the Qurʾan or on selections from official Sunni compilations of hadith. No reference is made to the canonic corpus of Shiʿi hadith.

TRANSLATED BY Robert D. Lee.

The principles asserted in the introduction permit us to identify the theological postulates dictating the very notion of rights:

> Islam gave humanity an ideal code of human rights 1400 years ago. The purpose of these rights is to confer honor and dignity on humanity and to eliminate exploitation, oppression, and injustice. Human rights in Islam are deeply rooted in the conviction that God, and God alone, is the author of Law and the source of all human rights. Given this divine origin, no leader, no government, no assembly or any other authority can restrict, abrogate or violate in any manner the rights conferred by God.

The great virtue of this declaration is that it expresses the convictions, modes of thought, and demands that contemporary Muslims are coming to embrace. Historians may decry the anachronism of projecting modern concepts backward toward the founding age, the mythical age of Islam; the jurist may emphasize the ethical idealism of articles that are dead letters and even openly violated in all Muslim countries. Such exercises are only too easy, but one could also apply them to a variety of statements made in the West since the American Declaration of Independence of 1776 (a philosophical exposition of human rights by Thomas Jefferson) and the more elaborate declaration of 1789 in France. History continues to represent suffering for a majority of human beings, and even in countries that have already struggled hard for human rights, such as France, examples of shortcomings and backwardness continue to surface. Moreover, to cloak such precious rights as religious freedom, freedom of association, freedom of thought, and freedom of travel in the full authority of the Islamic tradition is not a negligible accomplishment.

The questions posed at the beginning of this chapter do not arise in the context of intelligibility invoked by the authors of the Islamic Declaration. The divine origin of all creation cannot be the object of questioning, and legislation is for God alone. In a militantly secular context, the religious origin of human rights does not constitute a pertinent question, either; if evoked at all, it serves to emphasize a revolutionary break that, in the view of reductionist positivists, rescues human beings from "alienation."

A critical reexamination and reworking of the concept of Truth-Right (*al-ḥaqq*) and of its foundations are both possible and necessary. Let's keep in mind that the Qur'anic term *al-ḥaqq* applies to God himself as well as to absolute, transcendent Truth, sender and receiver of the "rights of God" (*ḥuqūq allah*). By respecting these rights one puts oneself in the right, *al-ḥaqq*, sees the true reality, and benefits from the rights that follow from it. In the Arabic language, the movement from the singular *ḥaqq* to the plural *ḥuqūq* translates a desacralization of right extracted from the religious force of *al-ḥaqq* and dispersed in the management of contingent, profane, individual rights. Analysis must proceed in two directions:

1. The apologetic function and inspiration of the text are undeniable. It is a matter of showing not only that Islam as a religion is open to the proclamation and defense of human rights but also that the Qur'an, the Word of God, defined these rights at the beginning of the seventh century, well before Western revolutions. The desire for and process of recuperation employed by contemporary Judaism and Christianity translate the same apologetic

tendency. Although this practice quite rightly shocks the historian, one must not lose sight of the current utility of finding authorities within the religious tradition to consecrate rights that need to be taught and defended in the oppressive political contexts unfortunately so widespread in today's world.

2. The critical and historical reexamination of the actual contents of the Holy Scriptures, on the one hand, and of the modern culture of human rights, on the other, is still an urgent and indispensable intellectual task. It offers an excellent opportunity to shore up religious thought in general by forcing it to recognize that the highest religious teachings and revelation itself in the three monotheistic religions are subject to *historicity*.

The ideological conditions and the cultural limits that distinguished the birth and development of human rights in the West must be the object of the same sort of critical reexamination to illuminate the weaknesses not only in the traditional religious imaginary but in the imaginary of civil religion secreted by Western secular revolutions. It is time to open a new field of intelligibility and go beyond the mimetic competition, essentially ideological, between traditional religions and civil religion, itself bound to the powerful phenomenon described by Fernand Braudel[1] under the title of material civilization.

Islamic thought has always included a discourse on the rights of God and the rights of man (*ḥuqūq allah/ḥuqūq adam*), with the former having primacy and priority over the latter. That is why traditional thought insists that each believer perform the five canonical obligations: profession of faith (*shahāda*), prayer, almsgiving, fasting at Ramadan, and the pilgrimage to Mecca. It is through obedience that the faithful internalize the notion of the rights of God; summoned to obey in this way, all creatures find themselves constrained to respect the social and political conditions for living completely this relationship between rights of God and rights of man. In other words, the respect of human rights is an aspect of, and a basic condition for, respecting the rights of God.

However, the rights thus defined within the fundamental Pact (*ʿahd*) or Covenant (*mīthāq*) between creature and Creator concern first the believers who form a spiritual community (*umma*). Potentially these rights touch all human beings and are universal insofar as all human beings are called upon to enter the Covenant. In the real world, theological categories have conveyed different legal statuses. The great schism creating a simple dichotomy between faithful and infidel gave way to complication and several types of status:

1. Inside the *umma*, a great split (*al-fitna-l-kubrā*) produced competing communities: Sunni, Shiʿa, and Khariji,[2] each with its claim to a monopoly of *ḥaqq*, of the Truth-Right that governed the members of the ideal orthodox community in their earthly relations and in their relationship with God.

1. French historian (1902–1985), a leader of the Annales school, which focused on everyday life and on social and environmental factors and forces; one of his most famous works is *Civilisation matérielle, économie, et capitalisme* (3 vols., 1979).

2. Literally, the Seceders, a sect that formed in the late 7th century; members held that any worthy believer, regardless of lineage, could be caliph, that all believers (Arab and non-Arab) are equal, and that any believer who commits a mortal sin is an apostate.

2. Beyond believers, there were peoples of the Book[3] (*ahl al-kitāb*) who enjoyed a status (*dhimmī*) protected by the Islamic government. Polytheists (*mushrikūn*) lived outside the guarantees offered by the Divine Law. In legal terms there was thus a clear demarcation between the living space of Islam (*dār al-islām*), where the Divine Law (*sharīʿa*) was applied, and the land of war (*dār al-ḥarb*), where the Divine Law could potentially be applied some day.

3. Inside the orthodox *umma* itself, there were obviously important differences among free men, slaves, women, and children. Those distinctions are found in other legal systems and linked to the general development of law and the transition from traditional systems of law, all more or less influenced by dogmatic theologies, to modern positive law.[4]

What we call "modernity" made a brutal eruption into the "living space of Islam" with the intrusion of colonialism as a historical fact. Seen strictly in terms of the development and diffusion of human rights in the framework of intellectual modernity, the colonial fact poses problems for both the West and Muslim countries. We must pause here to untangle what is a very confused ideological situation for both sides.

Colonial endeavors of nineteenth-century Europe sought justification in what was called a civilizing mission. It was a matter of raising "backward" peoples to the level of a "universal" culture and civilization. According to this perspective, for colonizing countries such as France, human rights appeared to be exported along with modern culture and civilization. The Catholic and Protestant churches participated in this movement by implanting missionary outposts even in the land of Islam.

The colonial adventure ended badly. It is difficult to speak to a Muslim audience today about the Western origin of human rights without provoking indignant protests. We must not lose sight of the wars of liberation and the ongoing, postcolonial battle against Western "imperialism" if we want to understand the psychological and ideological climate in which an Islamic discourse on human rights has developed in the past ten or fifteen years.

The development of that discourse is without doubt based on mimetic overbidding; it picks up the enunciations of Western declarations and confers upon them an Islamic origin. The operation, essentially ideological, conceals a crucial difference: A powerful movement of Enlightenment philosophy had already prepared the way for a declaration of human rights in eighteenth-century England, America, and France. Moreover, the rise of the bourgeoisie to rival the nobility and clergy created a social and economic force capable of insuring that political application of the new ideas of equality, liberty, and fraternity would at least begin.

In the nineteenth century, Muslim countries encountered only fragments, or heard only faint echoes, of the philosophical Enlightenment. A very small number of intellectuals, scholars, journalists, politicians, and travelers had access to the schools, universities, and literatures of the West. It was the so-called liberal epoch. Arab, Indian, Indonesian, Turkish, and Iranian elites believed they could cause their countries to benefit from the light cast

3. A common qur'anic designation for the Jews and Christians (members of religions that have scripture).

4. That is, statutes established by governments, as distinct from natural or divine law.

by science and the political revolutions of Europe. Even the reformist movement known as *salafī* ("orthodox") initiated by Jamal al-Din al-Afghani and then continued by Muhammad ʿAbdu,[5] showed itself hospitable to the philosophy of human freedom that inspired the discourse on human rights. Nationalist leaders such as Farhat ʿAbbas (Algeria), Habib Bourguiba (Tunisia), Allal al-Fassi (Morocco), Michel Aflaq (Syria), and even Gamal abdel Nasser (Egypt), as well as the first leaders of the Algerian war of liberation,[6] referred to the great principles of 1789. As for Turkey, Atatürk, with excessive zeal, imposed a secular revolution on a country of long-standing Islamic tradition.[7]

The intellectual and political elites of the Muslim world, unlike those in France and England, could not find support in a rather enlightened and dynamic social class capable of animating secular institutions and of creating a state apparatus corresponding to the new ideas. In the new states linked to the Islamic tradition, much more than in the countries where such conceptions were born, human rights based in Enlightenment philosophy remain a set of idealistic demands and a theme for the anticolonial struggle, but they lack cultural and social rootedness.

Classical Islam (seventh to the thirteenth centuries) had lost its dynamism and its capacity for self-renewal long before the advent of colonialism in all these countries. With the triumph of the ideology of national liberation in the 1950s, a great historical confusion beset many minds: The breach with the civilization of classical Islam was attributed exclusively to colonial intrusion and then in turn to the "imperial" domination that took its place after the reconquest of political sovereignties. The discourse of the so-called Islamic revolution in Iran[8] took up the great themes of the ideology of national liberation, which retained a socialist, secular coloration, and reworked them to include Islamic sources and to encompass struggle against Westernization.

The new states all developed a political willfulness that nationalized religion along with education, information, and other sectors of social life. Supervision of religion by a minister of religious affairs became necessary as a result of increasing pressure from two sides:

1. Demography amplified social and economic demands. It conferred upon Islam a primordial role in structuring, channeling, and inaugurating a discourse of demands, which were not tolerated in direct political form.
2. Unable to legitimate its authority by democratic procedures, the state resorted to Islam to legitimate its presence and its policy of modernization, all the while keeping open a line of communication to the masses. In this way, the necessary recourse to material civilization and technology as bearers of modernity could be reconciled with inevitable traditionalization through a return to the Islamic model of legislation, government, and culture.

5. On the Egyptian reformer Muhammad ʿAbduh (1849–1905), a student of al-Afghani (1838–1897), see above.
6. Waged against the French (1954–62).
7. In 1924, a year after being elected president of the new Turkish republic, Atatürk (1881–1938) abolished the caliphate and removed Islam from its position as state religion. He also introduced a secular law code and a secular system of schools controlled by the government.
8. In 1979.

The reconciliation was above all a do-it-yourself ideology. It suggested submitting societies to all the processes of economic development imported from the West while reestablishing or reinforcing the cultural *signals* of Islamic identity: construction of mosques, encouragement of religious education, foundation of Islamic universities or theological schools, wearing of traditional dress, and the application of the *shari'a*.

Where jurists tried, as in Algeria, to form a league for human rights to protect citizens, the state itself felt under attack and retaliated by refusing to grant permission to organize and prosecuting the instigators. It solicited the formation of a competing association to seize the initiative in this domain without threatening the establishment. At that moment the Islamic Declaration of Human Rights acquired its ideological and psychological purpose: to reassure, in effect, believer-citizens by proclaiming that God guaranteed rights, to undercut secular demands of Western origin, and to reestablish confidence in the "modernity" of Islamic law and its universal and intangible character.

There is a profound and indestructible conspiracy between states in search of legitimacy; the collective conscience eager for justice, civil liberties, and political participation; and nations aroused by an old, mythic desire for unity. (The eschatological expectation of the spiritual *umma* converges with the political hopes for national unity according to the Western, nationalist model of the nineteenth century.) I see Islamic difficulties with human rights within a specific set of historical circumstances and social complexities. Therefore, I appreciate the pertinence of research on the meaning of the opposition between divine and secular origins of human rights.

The question about human rights is first historical, then philosophical. Its heightened importance in our time reflects the return to religion and lack of intellectual and cultural preparation to discuss the question in all its dimensions: historic rupture with the conditions for the emergence of human rights in different cultures; development of the very notion of right; political decisions on the separation of spheres of human existence—temporal and spiritual, secular and religious; "scientific" judgments about the intelligence of the totality called "world" and our place in it; extension of so-called "rational" political groupings, which are in fact highly ideological.

Language is a social link, an irreducible force prescribed for all. For Muslim societies, language remains impregnated with "values" and religious references, whereas in the West, so-called scientific rationality and the therapeutic, even messianic, virtue of human rights discourse in a secular, desacralized context have replaced religious language. In both cases, critical reevaluations and new types of intelligibility are indispensable to show that, even in modern secularized culture cut off from the divine, human rights presuppose the sacredness of human beings. I am not speaking of the traditional notion of the sacred proclaimed by contemporary Islamic discourse but utterly violated in the most widespread of political, social, and economic practices; I am not speaking either of an artificial resacralization in the style of the cult of the Supreme Being installed by the French Revolution.[9]

9. A form of Deism established in 1794 and intended to be the new state religion.

The sacredness of human beings must result from a cultivation and an even broader and richer implementation of human rights.

To think simultaneously in an Islamic context about the positive contributions of secularism and the enduring values of religion is surely possible, but only for the very long term. Current political and sociological circumstances militate against that enterprise. Modes of intelligibility in classical Islamic thought are much too tied to medieval mental space to permit a correct interpretation and an integration of modernity. The models put to work by Western thought are themselves either inadequate or perceived as a strategy of cultural domination from which Muslims must protect themselves. This situation fully justifies the question posed at the outset: In what philosophical direction can we or should we orient research on the foundations of human rights and the means of assuring their implementation?

Current Islamic thought believes it can confront and defy the thought and historical experience of the West where the philosophical foundations of human rights have been progressively eroded. To proclaim human rights, or even to guarantee them on a strictly legal level, is not enough if the human calling to transcend the human condition and human achievement is not founded on undebatable, universal, transhistoric teachings. Islam, like the Christianity of the early Church Fathers, insists on the spiritual calling of human beings. Created in the image of God, human beings are summoned to join God in eternal life. Muslim law first defines the rights of God (*ḥuqūq allah*); the legal manuals begin by treating rules for the fulfillment of canonical obligations (*ʿibādāt*) before passing to a discussion of worldly transactions (*mu ʿamalāt*). Thus, all rights accorded to others in business transactions and other civil matters are linked to the rights of God, which impart value as well as sacred and ontological guarantees.

The methodology of Muslim law (*uṣūl al-fiqh*) defines intellectual and "scientific" procedures that prescribe a religious way of perceiving the whole of the law elaborated by the jurists. That theoretical structure permits law to be sacralized by locating its roots (*taʾṣīl*) in sacred texts: the Qurʾan and the prophetic traditions (*uṣūl*). In effect, the faithful still perceive religious law (*shariʿa*) as a Divine Law rooted in revelation. That is why people demand a political regime that protects and applies this law and rejects all legislation of human origin.

The rights enumerated in the American Declaration of Independence remain linked to their religious origins. The English and French revolutions took more decisive steps toward secular philosophical foundations without completely breaking away from a rationalizing spirituality. The massive return to religious affirmation, even in the West, forces me to pose or repose the problem of revelation in the three monotheistic religions, no longer starting with traditional theological definitions but with the data and requirements of a modern hermeneutic. We can think about human rights in a secular framework today only if we can intellectually and culturally get a hold on all the problems, old and new, linked to the phenomenon of revelation. This work has not yet been undertaken or even perceived in the terms and framework that I am suggesting here. It is indeed a fact that the streams of theological discourse coming from the three communities continue to function as strategies of self-justification and thus of reciprocal exclusion aimed at preserving a monopoly on control of revelation and of all the symbolic capital that flows from it. The prevalent attitudes of these religious traditions toward the origins of human rights illustrate perfectly these self-serving tendencies. Historical criticism is too often missing; all seek in particular to annex for themselves the ethical-legal privileges and the ideological functions that now more than ever are attached to the bewitching theme of human rights. I have tried hard to keep from falling into this error myself.

To approach the question of how to insure implementation of human rights in contemporary Muslim societies, one can work from the constitutions adopted by various regimes. By integrating the principle of respect for human rights, a large number of states have created a legal arena where it is theoretically possible for citizens to respond to violations by initiating protest procedures. Here as elsewhere, reality differs greatly from principle, but creating a legal arsenal for potential future use is not a negligible achievement. With the exception of Turkey, launched by Atatürk into a radical, secular experiment, the first constituent assemblies in the Muslim countries all tried to reconcile Islam and modern legislation. One would have to analyze each case to be able to assess the differences, the bold steps, the successes, the delays, and the breaches with Islam and continuity.

These developments are far from complete. The Islamist movements have brought about an ideological hardening that rejects modernity and restores elements of the *shari'a*—utterly out of context and juxtaposed with legal codes borrowed from the West. The status of women suffers most, especially from legislation where intent diverges widely from effect. That is why questions about human rights cannot be posed in the same way for women as for men. A set of provisions called the "personal statutes" (*al-aḥwal al-shakhsiyya*) continues to govern the condition of women in many countries. To touch that would generate theological problems heretofore ill- or unformulated. Above and beyond theological objections, the philosophical status of the person is at stake.

Much remains to be done in all societies so that "human rights" are not mere words designed to assuage the thirst for liberty, justice, dignity, and equality all human beings experience. Religions have performed significant educative and therapeutic functions over the centuries, but their effectiveness has always been limited either by misuse at the hands of clerics or by weaknesses inherent in traditional cultural systems. One cannot, indeed, judge the effect of religious teachings on the emancipation of the human condition without evaluating the cultures that have refined, diffused, and applied those teachings.

Religion, like language, is a collective force that governs the life of societies. Secular religions have taken over for traditional religions in this regard. It is illusory and dangerous to ask of religions more than they can give. Only human beings, with their creativity and their innovative boldness, can constantly renew and augment opportunities for their own liberation.

USAMA BIN LADIN
1957–2011

Usama Bin Ladin's father was an uneducated manual laborer from the southern coast of Yemen. After emigrating to Saudi Arabia and opening a construction business that caught the attention of the ruling family, he parlayed his contacts with them into a construction empire that was valued at $11 billion by the time of his death in 1968.

Bin Ladin was one of his father's fifty-four children from more than twenty wives. He studied at King Abd al-Aziz University's Management and Economics School in Saudi Arabia, where he was drawn to classes on Islamic topics and was influenced by two teachers who were members of the Muslim Brotherhood. Bin Ladin entered the family's construction business before completing his degree and did well. He clearly possessed his father's acumen and earned a small fortune running several of the company's enterprises.

Following the Soviet invasion of Afghanistan in 1979, Bin Ladin (like thousands of other non-Afghani Muslims) joined the Afghan resistance. Although only twenty-three, he was charged with setting up a facility in Peshawar, Pakistan, to house new Arab recruits who had come to fight in Afghanistan. During this time he worked with several intelligence agencies, including the CIA. Aided by Saudi and American funding, he used his construction experience to help build bases and training camps in Afghanistan to fight the Soviets. Bin Ladin did more than provide logistical support for the war: he also fought in it, earning the respect of other fighters.

The Soviets withdrew from Afghanistan in 1989, and Bin Ladin was received warmly upon his return to Saudi Arabia. Nonetheless, he quickly grew disillusioned with the Saudi ruling family, whom he judged to be corrupt and unconcerned with Islam. He was particularly dismayed by the Saudi response to Saddam Hussein's invasion of Kuwait. The Saudis refused Bin Ladin's offer to provide fighters from the Afghan war; instead, they invited U.S. troops into the country to defend it against a possible attack by Saddam Hussein. Bin Ladin openly criticized the Saudis for this decision, was placed under house arrest for a time, and then left for Sudan in 1991.

He spent the next five years in Sudan, where he continued to train fighters and expand his network, and began plotting attacks against Saudi and Western interests. It was during this time that Bin Ladin first began issuing pronouncements criticizing the Saudi leadership and declaring them to be non-Muslims. Assassination attempts against him multiplied, and in 1994 the Saudi government revoked his citizenship. In the face of increasing pressure from the United States and Saudi Arabia, Sudan was forced to expel Bin Ladin in 1996. He promptly set up operations in Tora Bora, Afghanistan, at a camp he had previously helped to build, and secured the support of his hosts, the Taliban.

From 1996 onward Bin Ladin and his network, al-Qaʿida (literally, "the Base"), founded in 1988, carried out attacks on Western targets and allies. In 1999 they bombed U.S. embassies in Kenya and Tanzania; in 2000 they attacked the USS *Cole* in Yemen; and in 2001 they commandeered four passenger jetliners and crashed them into the World Trade Center in New York City, the Pentagon near Washington, DC, and a field near Shanksville, Pennsylvania. Following the attacks of September 11, U.S. intelligence and military forces sought the capture or death of Bin Ladin; he was found and killed in Pakistan in May 2011.

Bin Ladin issued the statement below in 1998 from Afghanistan. Its context was Saddam Hussein's 1990 invasion of Kuwait and the Saudi request that U.S. forces bolster its defensive preparations. More generally, this pronouncement counters

U.S. foreign policy in the Middle East, particularly its increased military action against Iraq. Bin Ladin calls on Muslims throughout the world "to kill the Americans and their allies—civilians and military," insisting that such killing is necessary "to liberate" Muslim lands "from their grip." To support his proclamation, Bin Ladin selectively cites Islamic legal works and qur'anic verses.

PRONOUNCING GLOSSARY

Abu-Yasir Rifʿai Ahmad Taha: *a-boo ya´-sir ri-fah´-ee ah´-mad* (heavy *h*) *ta´-ha*
amir: *a-meer´*
al-Aqsa: *al-ahq´-sah*
Ayman al-Zawahiri: *ay´-man az-za-wah´-hi-ree*
Fazlur Rahman: *fahz´-ler rah´-mahn* (heavy *h*)
Imam al-Kisa'i: *ee-mam´ al-ki-sa´-ee*
Imam ibn Qudama: *ee-mam´ ibn qoo-da´-muh*
Jamiat–ul-Ulema-e-Pakistan: *ja´-mee-ut-ul-oo-le-ma´-ee-pahk-is-tahn´*
al-Qurtubi: *al-qur´-tu-bee*
Sheikh Osamah bin Muhammad bin Laden: *shaych* (guttural *ch*) *u-sah-muh bin moo-ha´-mad* (heavy *h*) *bin la´-din*
Sheikh Mir Hamzah: *shaych* (guttural *ch*) *meer ham´-zuh* (heavy *h*)

THE WORLD ISLAMIC FRONT

[*February 23, 1998*]

Sheikh Osamah bin Muhammad bin Laden
Ayman al-Zawahiri,[1] amir of the Jihad Group in Egypt
Abu-Yasir Rifʿai Ahmad Taha,[2] Egyptian Islamic Group
Sheikh Mir Hamzah, secretary of the Jamiat-ul-Ulema-e-Pakistan[3]
Fazlur Rahman,[4] amir of the Jihad Movement in Bangladesh

Praise be to God, revealer of the Book, controller of the clouds, defeater of factionalism, who says in His Book: "When the forbidden months are over, wherever you find the polytheists, kill them, seize them, besiege them, ambush them."[5] Prayers and peace be upon our Prophet Muhammad bin Abdallah, who said: "I have been sent with a sword in my hands so that only God may be worshipped, God who placed my livelihood under the shadow of my spear and who condemns those who disobey my orders to servility and humiliation."[6]

TRANSLATED BY James Howarth and edited by Bruce Lawrence.

1. An Egyptian physician (b. 1951), who was radicalized as a teenager. He was not just a leader of Egyptian Islamic Jihad but also a founding member of al-Qaʿida; after the two organizations merged, he became Bin Ladin's chief deputy.
2. Leader of the militant Islamic Group (1954–2001?), following the U.S. arrest (and, in 1995, life sentence) of its spiritual leader, Shaykh Omar Abdel-Rahman, for conspiring to bomb New York landmarks.
3. The Party of the Religious Scholars of Pakistan, an Islamic political party dominated by Barelwis, one of the Sunni groups that emerged in the 19th century with the aim of preserving Islam in South Asia without directly challenging the British. The Barelwis embraced popular religious practices such as venerating saints and visiting their shrines.
4. Abdul Salam Muhammad, who like Bin Ladin fought to drive the Soviets out of Afghanistan; he subsequently returned to Bangladesh to organize youth in an organization called Harakat ul-Jihad al-Islami (Movement of Islamic Holy War) Bangladesh.
5. Qur'an 9:5. The second half of the verse reads, "but if they turn [to God], maintain the prayer, and pay the prescribed alms, let them go on their way, for God is most forgiving and merciful" [translator's note].
6. A prophetic tradition from the hadith collection of Ibn Hanbal (780–855; see above).

Ever since God made the Arabian peninsula flat, created desert in it and surrounded it with seas, it has never suffered such a calamity as these Crusader hordes that have spread through it like locusts, consuming its wealth and destroying its fertility. All this at a time when nations have joined forces against the Muslims as if fighting over a bowl of food. When the matter is this grave and support is scarce, we must discuss current events and agree collectively on how best to settle the issue.

There is now no longer any debate about three well acknowledged and commonly agreed facts that require no further proof, but we will repeat them so that people remember them. They are as follows:

Firstly, for over seven years America has occupied the holiest parts of the Islamic lands, the Arabian peninsula, plundering its wealth, dictating to its leaders, humiliating its people, terrorizing its neighbours and turning its bases there into a spearhead with which to fight the neighbouring Muslim peoples.

Some might have disputed the reality of this occupation before, but all the people of the Arabian peninsula have now acknowledged it. There is no clearer proof than America's excessive aggression against the people of Iraq, using the Peninsula as a base. It is true that all its leaders have rejected such use of their lands, but they are powerless.

Secondly, despite the great devastation inflicted upon the Iraqi people at the hands of the Judeo-Crusader alliance, and despite the terrible number of deaths—over one million—despite all this, the Americans are trying to repeat these horrific massacres again, as if they are not satisfied with the long period of sanctions after the vicious war, or with all the fragmentation and destruction.

Today they come to annihilate what is left of this people and humiliate their Muslim neighbours.

Thirdly, while these wars are being waged by the Americans for religious and economic purposes, they also serve the interests of the petty Jewish state, diverting attention from its occupation of Jerusalem and its murder of Muslims there.

There is no better proof of this than their eagerness to destroy Iraq, the strongest neighbouring Arab state, and their efforts to fragment all the states in the region, like Iraq, Saudi Arabia, Egypt, and Sudan, into paper ministates whose weakness and disunity will guarantee Israel's survival and the continuation of the brutal Crusader occupation of the Peninsula.

All these American crimes and sins are a clear proclamation of war against God, his Messenger, and the Muslims. Religious scholars throughout Islamic history have agreed that *jihad* is an individual duty when an enemy attacks Muslim countries. This was related by the Imam ibn Qudama in "The Resource," by Imam al-Kisa'i in "The Marvels," by al-Qurtubi in his exegesis, and by the Sheikh of Islam[7] when he states in his chronicles that "As for fighting to repel an enemy, which is the strongest way to defend freedom and religion, it is agreed that this is a duty. After faith, there is no greater duty than fighting an enemy who is corrupting religion and the world."

7. Ibn Taymiyya (1263–1328; see above), a conservative scholar frequently cited by Sunni militants; he urged resistance to the Mongol invasion into Muslim territory. Muwaffaq al-Din ibn Qudama al-Maqdisi (1147–1223), a Hanbali legal scholar from Jerusalem "often cited by modern radicals for enumerating the situations in which *jihad* becomes compulsory" [translator's note]. Al-Kisa'i is properly al-Kasani (d. 1189), a prominent Hanafi jurist. Muhammad ibn Ahmad al-Qurtubi (d. 1272), a Maliki scholar from Spain whose Qur'anic commentary focuses on jurisprudence.

On this basis, and in accordance with God's will, we pronounce to all Muslims the following judgment:[8]

To kill the American and their allies—civilians and military—is an individual duty incumbent upon every Muslim in all countries, in order to liberate the al-Aqsa Mosque and the Holy Mosque[9] from their grip, so that their armies leave all the territory of Islam, defeated, broken, and unable to threaten any Muslim. This is in accordance with the words of God Almighty: "Fight the idolators at any time, if they first fight you;"[1] "Fight them until there is no more persecution and until worship is devoted to God;"[2] "Why should you not fight in God's cause and for those oppressed men, women, and children who cry out: 'Lord, rescue us from this town whose people are oppressors! By Your grace, give us a protector and a helper!'?"[3]

With God's permission we call on everyone who believes in God and wants reward to comply with His will to kill the Americans and seize their money wherever and whenever they find them. We also call on the religious scholars, their leaders, their youth, and their soldiers, to launch the raid on the soldiers of Satan, the Americans, and whichever devil's supporters are allied with them, to rout those behind them so that they will not forget it.

God Almighty said: "Believers, respond to God and His Messenger when he calls you to that which gives you life. Know that God comes between a man and his heart, and that you will be gathered to Him."[4]

God Almighty said: "Believers, why, when it is said to you, 'Go and fight in God's way,' do you dig your heels into the earth? Do you prefer this world to the life to come? How small the enjoyment of this world is, compared with the life to come! If you do not go out and fight, God will punish you severely and put others in your place, but you cannot harm Him in any way: God has power over all things."[5]

God Almighty also said: "Do not lose heart or despair—if you are true believers you will have the upper hand."[6]

8. The word Bin Ladin uses here means "considered judgment" (*hukm*) which carries a less binding authority than a "juridical decree" (*fatwa*) [translator's note].

9. The mosque in Mecca that houses the Kaʿba, the cubical stone shrine that is the most important site in Islam, visited by Muslims during the pilgrimage. "Al-Aqsa Mosque": the mosque in Jerusalem to which Muhammad traveled from the Kaʿba during the Night Journey (Qurʾan 17:1) and from which he undertook his ascent to heaven.

1. Qurʾan 9:36.

2. Qurʾan 2:193; 8:39. The conclusion to the first reads: "If they cease hostilities, there can be no [further] hostility, except towards aggressors"; and to the second: "if they desist, then God sees all that they do" [translator's note, edited].

3. Qurʾan 4:75.

4. Qurʾan 8:24.

5. Qurʾan 9:38–39.

6. Qurʾan 3:139.

EBRAHIM MOOSA
b. 1957

Born in South Africa, Ebrahim Moosa received a traditional religious education at seminaries (in Arabic, *madrasa*) in India, worked in England as a journalist, and then in 1995 completed his PhD at the University of Capetown. In 2001 he was appointed a professor of religion and Islamic studies at Duke University, where his work focuses on Islamic ethics, the encounter with modernity, and the madrasas of South Asia. Moosa has received a number of prestigious awards in support of his research and publications.

The excerpt below is taken from a 2003 essay in which Moosa explores the difficulties of being a modern Muslim intellectual. He identifies the core problem faced by such thinkers as the tension created by the need to offer new solutions to often intractable and long-standing problems affecting the Muslim community without completely breaking with tradition. If the Muslim intellectual veers too far from the tradition, his or her faith is called into question. Moosa recognizes that this tension is not unique to modern thinkers: it can be found throughout Islamic history, as seen in earlier debates about the assimilation of Greek, Indian, and Persian thought.

Though Moosa offers no definitive solutions to this dilemma, he does offer a number of thoughtful suggestions. In particular, he warns against two moves often made by modern Muslim thinkers that gloss over the complexity of Islamic thought. He inveighs against essentializing statements about the nature of Islam, such as "Islam is for justice" or "Islam is a religion of peace." He also urges a wary attitude toward "text fundamentalism," the belief that the norms that a community should follow are provided by a text. For Moosa, the community surrounding a text, in conversation with it, imbues the text with meaning, and the community, not the text itself, must decide its norms.

Moosa encourages modern thinkers to study the creativity of past scholars and their multiple interpretive strategies while at the same time producing new hermeneutic approaches to Islamic texts to keep them relevant to modern society.

PRONOUNCING GLOSSARY

Abu Hanifa: *a-boo ha-nee´-fuh* (heavy *h*)
Caliph ʿUmar: *ka´-lif oh´-mar*
al-Shafiʿi: *ash-sha´-fi-ee*
Tabari: *tah´-ba-ree*

FROM THE DEBTS AND BURDENS OF CRITICAL ISLAM

Critical Islam: Beyond Apologia

Of all the intellectual issues facing Muslim communities, the one area that is most troubling is the area of Islamic law (*Shariʿah*). This is especially problematic when the Qurʾan endorses elements of the law. In a tradition where the revelation is viewed as the eternal word of God, the law framed in such terms does present a conundrum. The verses dealing with the law do not exceed six hundred (out of over six thousand verses in the whole of the Qurʾan) yet somehow receive disproportionate scholarly attention. The bulk of the verses that more importantly address the aesthetics of the Muslim imagination get neglected. Ordinary Muslims of course feel obligated to act upon the mandate of these legal verses. However, untrained in the various exegetical and interpretive traditions, lay people are not aware that a complex methodology is applicable to materials dealing with law, even if these are stated in the revelation.

One of the features of the dominant Muslim discourse in almost all its variants, including modernist discourse, is reification. This is where Muslim traditions, by which I mean living subjective experiences and practices, are reduced and transformed into various concepts, ideas, and things. Thus the way the Qurʾan offers women a share in inheritance or assuages their position in seventh-century Arabia is reduced to meaning that the Qur'an advocates justice as personified in that historical model. Flowing from that is an inference that the form of justice as embodied in the Qur'anic statement is applicable to all times and places. For instance, the limited measures introduced to manumit slaves as penances for certain moral violations as stated in the Qur'an, or the measures adopted by the Caliph ʿUmar[1] to prohibit the sale of slave women who have children by their masters are all held up as instances that are indicative of notions of freedom.

These can be deemed as essentialist categories, reducing complex problems and practices to their bare essentials in order to score an ideological point. Terms such as the "spirit" of Islam are employed in order to argue that the spirit of Islam is justice, egalitarianism, equality, or humanism—either as single signifiers or combinations of these qualities. These qualities are held metonymically to represent the entirety of Islam. Often history is invoked to argue that these ideals were evident at the very inception of Islam as a tradition in the seventh century. This is of course done at the expense of exploring exactly *how* these ideas became manifest in the practices and behavior of early Muslims.

It is not very clear whether ʿUmar was actuated by concerns of freedom in limiting the sale of female slaves who had offspring or whether he wanted to prevent the proliferation of incest. For there were real concerns that a young female slave separated from her offspring when sold off could years later unknowingly be sold as a concubine to her wealthy offspring. It is also uncertain whether the inheritance system intended to further justice. However, there are clear indications that the new system of intergenerational succession attempted to further a specific form and system of kinship based on patriarchy.

Nowadays, not only Muslim modernists make these arguments, but even orthodox traditionalists and revivalist groups are becoming expert in such apologetics. The real problem with these kinds of arguments is a more acute one. For one thing, they are apologetic and try to justify the past by today's standards. In the process, they inevitably distort history. Since modern Muslim sensibilities are offended by the rules regulating women, such as corporal punishment or the minimum marriageable age for women in Muslim antiquity, they try either to wish them away or to argue them away. There is of course the misplaced belief that the past is embarrassing. For, surely, closer scrutiny shows that in all patriarchal cultures—Christian, Jewish, and Hindu—during antiquity, women were married off at a very early age, in some cases even before they showed their first signs of menstruation.

If we have changed these practices in our world, then we have done so for our own reasons: our sense of justice, equality, and reasons consistent with our political-economy. For a whole set of reasons, we no longer consider marriage to what our modern culture deems minors, corporal punishment, and the death penalty to be acceptable practices. But surely in changing our practices we are not condemning millions of people before us and judging them as reprobate for being different from us? So why should we debate the past as if it is the present? The predisposition among many Muslim apologists is not to understand history, but rather to try to fix or correct it, with the enormous condescension of posterity.

1. ʿUmar ibn al-Khattab (ca. 586–644), the second caliph.

But this desire to find justification in the past, in a text or the practice of a founder, suggests that Muslims can act confidently in the present only if the matter in question was already prefigured in the past. Such a perpetually retrospective approach to religious understanding is the sign of a profound lack of dynamism among the contemporary adherents of the tradition. At best, this is reverse science fiction; at worst, it is a sad commentary on the state of Muslim self-confidence in the modern period. Does this mean that Muslims can engage in discourses of justice, egalitarianism, freedom, and equality only if there is some semblance that the scripture or the Prophet or some of the learned savants (imams) of the past endorsed, hinted, or fantasized about the possibility of such discourses?

What this mentality suggests is that Muslims discredit the legitimacy of their experience in the present and refuse to allow this experience to be the grounds for innovation, change, and adaptation. In order to persuade people in public discourse today, the most effective psychological trick to play on unsuspecting Muslim audiences is to say that some past authority—Tabari, Abu Hanifa, or al-Shafiʿi[2]—held such an enlightening position on matter X, so why do you lesser mortals not adopt it? The greater the vintage of the authority, the more persuasive the argument will sound to folks, even if the rationale of the argument and its substance make no sense at all. These may sound like anecdotal stereotypes, but this happens repeatedly in Muslim communities, even among secularly educated lay Muslims. Now what happens if we are faced with problems and issues that al-Shafiʿi et al. never even dreamt of, let alone confronted in their lives? Are we going to fictionalize and fabricate statements and attribute these to them in good faith? This is exactly how a great deal of prophetic reports (*ahadith*, sing. *hadith*) were invented and attributed to the Prophet and the early authorities of Islam in order to give new ideas and changing practices some credibility, legitimacy, and authority.

If this kind of mentality has a longer history, then it certainly has reached pathological proportions among modern Muslims. Among the many reasons for this is the outlook that only the past was good in Muslim history; indeed it was perfect, if not a utopia. This suggests that Muslims lack confidence in their abilities and is symptomatic of their despair. It implies that the present is always despised and viewed as fallen. Ironically, despite the amazing and brilliant success Muslims had in history, for many modern Muslims the present, their time and opportunity in history, is viewed to be as dreadful as the original sin. Perhaps the words of Charles Baudelaire, who said that "you have no right to despise the present,"[3] have more relevance than ever before.

Some contemporary readings of the Qurʾan are predisposed to text fundamentalism, a feature evident among modernists, fundamentalists, and neotraditionalists. There are several problems attached to text fundamentalism. Sure, some of these interpretations do provide rhetorical allegiance to history by arguing that the verses of the Qurʾan are accompanied by historical contextualization that locates the revelation within a material context, called "occasions of revelation" (*asbab al-nuzul*). The doctrine of textual abrogation (*naskh*) is also employed to show that a very rudimentary form of historiography is at work in the commentary tradition of the Qurʾan. While this does provide some help, it still falls far short of making the complexity

2. Three foundational scholars of Islam's early centuries; see above.
3. From "The Painter in Modern Life" (1983) by the French poet and critic Baudelaire (1821–1867); the phrase was famously quoted by Michel Foucault in "What Is Enlightenment?" (1984).

of the text understandable and intelligible to modern audiences, especially if the past is presented in apologetic and defensive terms. Such an approach prevents an honest, critical, and open understanding of how the revelation functioned in societies radically different than ours.

On other occasions there has been a predilection to provide a purposive interpretation of the text. This follows the method developed in jurisprudence called the purposive approach (*maqasid*) to legal passages in the Qur'an. Each legal verse or cluster of verses, scholars argue, attempts to fulfill a larger social, ethical, or religious function that is the real intention of the verse. It is these intentions that one must take seriously and not the literal intent of the verse. While this approach has no doubt brought some relief to really knotty problems, it remains inadequate. For without adequate historical support this approach can lead to the bowdlerization of the text. For then it means the more equipped the interpreter, the more effectively he or she could read meanings and intentions *into* the text or read meanings *off* the text as derivations from the text. In this case, the text remains sovereign, ignoring the reader or marginalizing the "community of the text" and their experiences as credible participants in the textual process. After all, what is a sacred scripture worth if it does not have a community of participants, listeners, and readers? All the sacred scriptures already exist in the mythical Preserved Tablet (*al-lawh al-mahfuz*) anyway, so why send it to humans when the angels already adore it more perfectly than us humans? From the misplaced pre-occupation with the sovereignty of the text *sans* community of the text, it is but a small step to the deification of the text that unfortunately already occurs. What many Muslims fail to discern is that the Qur'an is not God; the word of God can never be God, and to imagine it as such certainly raises very serious problems of a theological nature.

On further reflection, it will become apparent that the Qur'an itself prefigures a community of listeners and participants: without this audience it ceases to be the Qur'an. Let me explain. Literally the word *qur'an* means a "recitation." As a revelation it is recited by the human voice and heard by the human ear. In the final instance the message must both be heard and understood by the "heart," as the Qur'an literally puts it.[4] In all this a fundamental presumption persists: the Qur'an as revelation requires an audience of listeners and speakers. In other words, a community is integral to it being a revelation. If one does not take that audience and community seriously, implicitly one has not taken revelation seriously. This audience is not a passive audience, but an interactive audience that engages with a performative revelation.

Something has happened in the reading of the Qur'an in modern Islam that goes in the opposite direction. Many Muslim audiences have little sensibility for the complex ways a revealed and performance text like the Qur'an is interpreted. The fact is that how the interpretation of the Qur'an is to be approached is not as easily available as free copies of the holy book. Instead many people read it like one reads a medical textbook or an engineering manual. So the Qur'an has been turned into a sovereign, passive, non-interactive text. In other words, it ceases to be a revelation that melts the heart of the reciter and/or listener. It no longer makes reverent readers' skin shiver in awe of the Divine. Instead of having readers being in awe of God, fierce warrior-readers of the Qur'an these days scare the wits out of

4. As in Qur'an 47:24: "Will they not then meditate on the Qur'an or are there locks on the hearts?"

believers and non-believers alike. Gone is how the Qur'an itself describes its effect on listeners and reciters. "God bestows from on high, the best of all teachings in the shape of a divine writ, fully consistent with itself, repeating each statement in manifold forms—[a Divine writ] that makes the flesh [literally, skin] of all those who stand in awe of their Sustainer shiver; but in the end their flesh and their hearts soften at the remembrance of the grace of God" (Q. 39:23).

Several attempts to introduce an element of complexity in the understanding of the Qur'an are beginning to lift our veil of ignorance. The work of Mohammed Arkoun, Nasr Hamid Abu Zayd, Khaled Abou El Fadl, Farid Esack, and Abdulkader Tayob[5] among others is doing just that. A commonsensical reading of this complex text would be far too inadequate. The Qur'an as a text is alive within contemporary Muslim communities and is subject to multiple uses. In the past too it had contexts where it negotiated multiple agendas of the society in which it was first revealed; in short it has a political history. By "political history," I mean it also occurs against the backdrop of power and history. In its multiple iterations, the Qur'an continues to develop new and multiple histories as it is embodied in communities. In other words, we need to know not only the detailed social contexts in which God's revelation is played out in history but also how it plays out in history. For this reason it is so crucial to study the different communities of the Qur'an. Without that voice of the communities engaged with their scripture, we can hardly make sense of revelation and the various communities of revelation.

There has been a pattern in contemporary Muslim scholarship to let the sovereign voice of the Qur'an speak without the community of the Qur'an speaking and interacting with the Qur'an in deep and life-transforming conversations. For instance, modern Muslim interpreters, especially Muslim feminists, make too much of a few verses of the Qur'an that suggest reciprocal rights and duties between unequal spouses and then hasten to suggest that the Qur'an advocates egalitarianism as norm. In order to accept this one must pretend to be blind to the welter of evidence that suggests an outright patriarchy as the "textual" norm. Generations of Muslim scholars have correctly stated that the Qur'an advocates patriarchal norms, since that was the historical condition in which the Qur'an was revealed. By privileging a few verses and then suggesting that these isolated and singular verses should control the meaning and interpretation of numerous other verses, using the adage that "part of the Qur'an explains other parts" (*al-qur'an yufassiru ba'duhu ba'dan*) is nothing short of hermeneutical acrobatics or a hermeneutics of wishful thinking. It may be preferable to hear the Qur'an in its patriarchal voice but to understand it with the sensibility of an actor/reader/listener/reciter immersed in the process of revelation. It is that listener/reciter who discovers through her or his history, experience, and transformed inner sensibility that gender justice, equality, and fairness is a norm for our time, and not patriarchy.

Having once done the former kind of interpretation myself, I increasingly find it unfulfilling and unsatisfactory. I am more inclined to give history and the performative role of the revelation a greater place in an interpretive schema. A closer look at text fundamentalism suggests that it sustains several fictions.

5. All scholars of Islam active in the late 20th and early 21st century; for Arkoun, see above.

Such interpretations attempt to exclusively seek authority in some founding text. However, in doing so they fail to engage the revelatory text in an interactive manner. It is precisely such interactivity that transforms the human being who is ultimately the subject of revelation, and who has to embody the qualities that combat patriarchy and endorse justice and equality. Glossing the text with anti-patriarchal virtues is not the warrant of liberation or egalitarianism. Text fundamentalism in part perpetuates the fiction that the text actually provides the norms, and we merely "discover" the norms. The truth is that we "make" the norms in conversation with the revelatory text. If one reads medieval Muslim legal texts, one will note how the discursive formation orchestrated by the jurists constructs the norms. For this reason, many people are surprised how early Muslim jurists could give verdicts seemingly contrary to the explicit sense of the revealed text.

The answer is both simple and revealing: the earlier scholars gave greater credence to their specific social context and often gave the context decisive authority in the interpretation of the text by employing a very sophisticated hermeneutic. Thus, we find that some classical jurists argue that causing injury to the wife by means of beating is a ground for divorce, despite the Qur'an saying that a disobedient spouse can be chastized. Abu Hanifa has no objections to non-Muslims entering the holy city of Mecca, despite an explicit text of the Qur'an that deems the polytheists to be unclean and prevents them from entering the sacred mosque. For him the Qur'anic passage had a once-only application at the inception of Islam, when the holy sanctuary had to be dedicated to the faith of Islam, and has no subsequent mandate.

What is required is to explore the multiple interpretive methods that were employed by scholars in the past to discover the creativity they invested. In addition, we need to explore and develop new ways of interpretation of especially the revealed text in order to allow its full breadth and vision to speak to us in a transformative way.

Conclusion

This moment in history, more than any other, places an extraordinary burden on Muslim intellectuals. In short, there is an almost impossible expectation on us to provide solutions in places where none appears on the horizon, offer hope in times of utter despair, and address issues that are overwhelming in their magnitude and proportions. And yet, we dare not retreat. If anything we need to offer hope. Hope, as the novelist Anne Lamott says, is a revolutionary patience.[6] The painstaking and soul-searching intellectual quest must be embraced boldly, creatively, and patiently. The uncomfortable questions have to be asked. If we do not, then the responsibility of learning and faith has gone unanswered.

6. Quoted from *Bird by Bird: Some Instructions on Writing and Life* (1994), by the American novelist and nonfiction writer (b. 1954).

THE EMERGENCE OF WOMEN'S VOICES

SAYYID AHMAD KHAN
1817–1898

One of the founders of Islamic modernism, Sayyid Ahmad Khan came from a family with well-established ties to India's Mughal dynasty (1528–1858). His maternal grandfather had twice served as prime minister for the Mughals, and ties to the dynasty earned Khan's father a stipend from them. But Khan's privileged life in Delhi abruptly ended when his father's death in 1838 left his family in financial straits.

Forced to leave school and seek work, Khan began his career as a clerk for the judicial department of the British East India Company. He became a "subjudge" in 1841, and served in various places; at his retirement from the company in 1876, he was a judge in Benares, India.

Even while he worked for the East India Company, Khan pursued other activities. By 1857, he had published a number of Urdu works on religious and historical topics—most notably, *Monuments of the Great* (1847), a study of the architecture of Delhi. Its French translation helped build Khan's reputation, and he was appointed a fellow of the Royal Asiatic Society of Great Britain in 1864.

The defining event of Khan's life was the Indian Rebellion of 1857. Although both Hindus and Muslims participated in this unsuccessful revolt, the British chiefly blamed the Muslims, and they bore the brunt of British reprisals. Khan remained loyal to the British and at great risk to himself, saved members of the British colony in the district where he was stationed. Yet he lost relatives in the uprising, including his mother.

In the aftermath, Khan tried simultaneously to defend Indian Muslims and to dispel misunderstandings between them and the British. He blamed the revolt on Britain's misadministration of India and its failure to understand the people it governed, as he explained in *Reasons for the Indian Rebellion* (1858), a pamphet he published in Urdu. Khan sent copies to British officials in England and India; it influenced subsequent British policy in India but was not publicly available until its translation into English in 1873. He next sought to demonstrate that the vast majority of Muslims in positions of authority had remained loyal to the British throughout the rebellion, writing a series of articles that were later published as *An Account of the Loyal Mahomedans of India* (1861). To enhance Muslims' understanding of Christianity, Khan published *The Mahomedan Commentary on the Holy Bible* (1862). Tellingly, he appends a legal opinion from the Hanafi mufti of Mecca that states, "As long as even some of the peculiar observances of Islam prevail in [India], it is the Daru'l-Islam (land of Islam)."

It was during this period that Khan began to embrace modern thought. He established a number of elementary schools in which he could test educational theories and in 1864 founded the Scientific Society to encourage the translation of modern European writings on science and the humanities for the benefit of Indians.

In May 1869 Khan traveled to England and was utterly awed by its technological superiority and its educational system; he was to devote much of the remainder of his life to urging Muslims to adopt Western advances. Within a few months of his return to India in October 1870, he founded a journal called *The Refinement of*

Character that strove, in the broadest way possible, to modernize the Muslims of India. The journal promoted modern civilization, the sciences, and technology, and it called on Muslims to reform their own cultural practices. Khan also wished to develop a modern university to match what he had observed at Oxford and Cambridge, and in 1877 he established the Muhammadan Anglo-Oriental College in Aligarh, which in 1920 became Aligarh Muslim University.

Khan's argument that embracing modernity required the reform of certain aspects of Islam drew fierce resistance from some Indian Muslim scholars, who criticized his lack of formal religious training. They condemned his insistence on demythologizing traditional Islamic beliefs and labeled him a "naturist" for his position that the laws of nature and God's revelation were both divine creations and thus could never contradict each other. Nevertheless, Khan had undeniable influence over Indian Muslims. When he objected to their joining the All-India National Congress in 1887, most Muslims heeded his advice.

The essay below, originally published in *The Refinement of Character* in 1871, contrasts the role of women in England and in Muslim societies. While arguing that Islamic law elevates the status of women above that of women in "developed countries," Khan nevertheless laments that Muslim societies have failed to respect this law and instead "have treated women so badly that all the nations laugh at the condition of Muslim women."

PRONOUNCING GLOSSARY

ummah: *oom´-muh*

THE RIGHTS OF WOMEN

Developed countries loudly proclaim that men and women are created equal and that both hold equal rights. They also proclaim that there is no reason why women should be thought of as less important or less worthy of respect than men. They do not even accept that, by way of illustration, it can be said that a woman is like the left hand and a man the right hand, or that in value a woman adds up to 12 and a man to a dozen. Nevertheless, even today we observe that in no developed country have women been bestowed with the same stature and parity in rights and authority to men as has been bestowed upon them in the religion of Islam. England greatly favors the freedom of women, yet when its laws relating to women are examined, it is obvious that the English consider women quite insignificant, unintelligent, and valueless.

According to English laws, when a woman marries, she is considered to have lost her separate existence, and her distinctive individuality is absorbed into that of her husband. She does not stand in the capacity of a separate member to a contract, and thus she is not able to hold responsibility for any legal instrument she may have signed according to her own will and without the agreement of her husband. The personal possessions, wealth, cash, and property that were hers before marriage all belong to the husband after marriage. That property that comes to a woman by inheritance either before or after marriage is also possessed by the husband for as long as he lives, and he also receives any earnings produced from it. Her status is like that

TRANSLATED BY Kamran Talattof. All bracketed additions are the translator's.

of a feeble-minded incompetent: She cannot bring a lawsuit against anyone, nor can anyone [directly] bring a lawsuit against her. She cannot buy or sell anything without the permission of her husband. Except for the expenses of food, clothing, and living in one house, that is, the basic expenses necessary for daily living, she cannot spend money on anything without her husband's permission.

In 1870 a bill was presented in Parliament regarding the property of married women. Only this much was desired, that the law be rescinded by means of which after marriage a woman's property becomes lost to her. This bill was presented by the Honorable Mr. Russell Gurney, M. P. On this occasion he made some exquisite remarks. He observed that, according to the law then active, whatever a woman had before marriage and received after marriage, and all that she earned by her ability and hard work, left her hands after marriage. Her husband became the owner of it all. Thus the effect of marriage upon a woman was like that of a crime whose prescribed punishment was the confiscation of property! At this, the whole House of Commons burst into laughter and most of the members supported him. Thus, this is the state of English law regarding women, and probably no other law is more deplorable, damaging, and unjust.[1]

Muslim Law Concerning Women

Now consider how women are honored in Muslim law, and how their rights and authority have been conceded to be equal to those of men. Before adulthood, just like men, women are considered to be without authority and unqualified to enter into official agreements. But upon reaching adulthood she assumes the same authority as a man and is qualified to enter into a contract. Just like men, women have the authority to marry. Just like a man's, a woman's marriage cannot take place without her consent. She herself is the owner and controller of all her personal property, and has full authority over it. She has the capability, like a man, of executing any kind of contract, and her person and her property stand accountable with respect to any contracts and documents that she may have written. She is the owner of any property that may have come into her possession before or after marriage, and she herself is the claimant to its benefits. Like men, women can file suits or be sued in the courts. She can purchase anything she wants to with her wealth, and can sell anything she wishes. Like a man, she can give, will, or donate any kind of inheritance. In accordance with regular procedures she can inherit from the property of her relatives and her husband. She can gain, then, all the materials a man may gain. All of the pious merits a man may gain, she may gain as well. Likewise, she receives the same rewards or punishments for her behavior in this world on Judgment Day.

There is no special restriction placed upon a woman that is not also placed upon a man, except that which she has taken upon herself in terms of the wedding contract, or the restriction relating to the private parts of her body that differ by nature from man's.

1. The Married Women's Property Act passed in 1882.

Thus, in truth, in no religion and in no nation's law have women and men been considered as equal as in the religion of Islam. But it is a most astonishing fact that all developed countries strongly criticize the condition of women in Islam. Yet there is no doubt that the condition of the women of developed countries is many levels better than that of Muslim women and women of Muslim countries, although the situation ought to be the reverse.

In admitting the superiority of the state of women in developed countries, we have not considered the matter of their freedom from the veil, because in our opinion, to the same extent as there is excess in this respect in India, there is excess [of another kind] in advanced countries. And as far as man can bring his intellect to bear on this matter, the limit set by the shari'ah law certainly seems to be perfectly correct.

At this point, what we wish to argue for is simply: good treatment of women by men; good fellowship; courtesy; consideration; love; encouragement; paying attention to their comfort, ease, happiness, and pleasure; keeping them happy in every way. Instead of considering them servants, to consider them as companions, comrades, and partners in both sorrow and happiness and to consider each other the cause of mutual joy and strength is best. Doubtless, as far as we know, considerable progress is being made in areas on these particulars regarding women, in the advanced countries. But in Muslim countries there is no progress in these areas and in India there are perpetrated such unworthy and humiliating events that one can only cry out, "May God have mercy on us!"

People who associate these evils with the religion of Islam are surely mistaken. To the extent that there is deterioration in the condition of women in India, it is due to a failure to observe the regulations of Islam fully. If its principles were brought into practice, no doubt all of these evils would be eliminated.

In addition, there is another important reason for this: Muslims today remain in large part uncivilized. Despite the fact that the laws of the developed nations regarding women were extremely defective and miserable, those nations have elevated the position of their women to an extremely high level while Muslims, despite the fact that the laws of the rest of the world are less generous, on account of being uncivilized have treated women so badly that all the nations laugh at the condition of Muslim women. Because of our inherent evils, and because the whole *ummah*[2] is in a sorry state (with perhaps some minimal exceptions willed by God!), all nations criticize our religion.

Therefore, this is not the time for us to ignore these truths and delay correcting our conduct or to fail to show by the light of our behavior that Islam is an enlightened religion.

2. The Muslim community.

MUHAMMAD ʿABDUH
1849–1905

As the introduction to his selection earlier in this volume noted, Muhammad ʿAbduh is one of the most important figures in the history of modern-day Muslim reform movements; he worked tirelessly through his writings and his involvement in a range of organizations and committees to reverse the decline of Muslim institutions and societies. While his *Theology of Unity* is his most significant publication, he also made notable contributions to the genre of qurʾanic exegesis (in Arabic, *tafsir*). Traditional qurʾanic exegesis proceeded verse by verse or even phrase by phrase and often focused on linguistic, legal, or theological points. While not ignoring these detailed technical discussions, ʿAbduh's exegesis does not become mired in them and often addresses larger themes and ideas within the Qurʾan.

During his own lifetime, ʿAbduh published a commentary on the last section of the Qurʾan (suras 78–114, commonly referred to in Arabic as *juzʾ ʿamma*), as well as separate commentaries on sura 1 (*al-Fatiha*, or "The Opening") and 103 (*al-ʿAsr*, or "The Declining Day"). But his best-known exegetical work is the *Al-Manar Commentary* (named for the journal in which sections of it were published), which is based on his lectures as transcribed by his student Rashid Rida (1865–1935). From the first sura of the Qurʾan to Qurʾan 4:125, the commentary combines these lecture notes with additions by Rashid Rida that were approved by ʿAbduh. Following ʿAbduh's death in 1905, Rida continued the commentary up to 12:107, using his own exegesis as well as ʿAbduh's notes and clearly identifying each.

For example, in the following passage Rashid Rida includes a fatwa he wrote in response to the query of a Muslim student in America, who found himself repeatedly questioned about Islam's permission for polygamy and desired an answer that was more satisfying than his own replies. Rashid Rida introduces his response with a description of the differences between male and female sexual desire. Both he and Muhammad ʿAbduh judge polygamy to be a concession to circumstances or character flaws that make it impossible to attain the matrimonial ideal, monogamy. ʿAbduh does suggest, however, that if women received the right kind of religious education, they could control their jealousy of another wife and their families could thereby escape damage.

PRONOUNCING GLOSSARY

Al-Manār: *al-ma-nahr´*
Muḥammad ʿAbduh: *moo-ham´-mad* (heavy *h*) *ahb´-doo*
Muḥammad Rashīd Riḍā: *moo-ham´-mad* (heavy *h*) *ra-sheed´ ri´-dah*
Najīb Āfandī Qonawī: *na-jeeb´ a-fan´-dee qoh´-na-wee*
Sūra: *soo´-ruh*
Ustādh-Imām: *oo-stadh´ ee-mam´*

FROM AL-MANAR COMMENTARY

From *Polygamy*

MUḤAMMAD ʿABDUH AND MUḤAMMAD RASHĪD RIḌĀ ON SŪRA 4:3

> If you fear that you will not be able to act justly towards orphans (who are to be the first choice in marriage, then instead of them) marry two, three, or four of such women as seem good to you, but if you fear you will not be equitable, then (marry) only one, or what your right hands own (as slaves). Thus it will be more likely that you will not be partial.

. . . The Ustādh-Imām[1] (Muḥammad ʿAbduh) has said: Polygamy is mentioned in connection with the words (of the present verse) concerning orphans and with the prohibition against spending all their wealth, even though it be through marriage. He said: If you feel within yourself the fear that by marrying the orphaned girl (*al-yatīma*) you will spend all her wealth, then you may (choose) not (to) marry her, since here God has given to you a possibility of avoiding (your duty) concerning (marriage to) the orphan. He has given you the choice of marrying other wives, up to (the number of) four. If you fear, however, that you will not be able to treat two or more wives justly, you must restrict yourself to one. Moreover, (justifiable) fear that a proper act will not be done is present whenever there is adequate presumption and adequate doubt, indeed even when there is adequate suspicion. The law may nevertheless justify suspicion since where knowledge of this kind of thing exists there is seldom freedom from it. The marriage of two or more wives is therefore allowed as an option (only) to one who has the conviction in himself that he will deal justly, (indeed) in such a way that he has no doubt about it, or that he suspects it but shelters (only) a small doubt about it.

Muḥammad ʿAbduh has said: After God said *But if you fear you will not be equitable, then (marry) only one*, he gives a reason for this in his words: *Thus, it will be more likely that you will not be partial*, that is, thus you will come more closely to the condition in which neither injustice nor oppression will occur. Consequently, God has made the condition that one keep far from injustice to be the basis for his giving of a law (concerning marriage). This confirms the fact that justice is enjoined as a condition and that duty consists in striving for it. Further, it shows that justice is something difficult to attain. God says in another verse of this sūra: 'You will not be able to treat your wives equally, regardless of how eager you are (to do so)' (Sūra 4:129/128). This refers to justice in the inclination of the heart, since otherwise the two verses taken together would have the result that there would be no permission for polygamy at all. And then also the meaning of his words in (another) part of the verse just cited, (namely) 'Yet do not follow your inclination to the extreme (thus completely severing your relations with any of them) so that you leave her as it were deserted' (Sūra 4:129/128), would not be clear. God forgives the servant when something in the inclination of his heart goes beyond his power, even as, towards the end of his life,

TRANSLATED BY Helmut Gätje (from the Arabic) and Alford T. Welch (from the German).

1. Professor-Leader (Arabic).

the Prophet felt a stronger inclination for ʿĀʾisha than for his other wives. To be sure, he did not treat her with any distinction above them, that is, not without their consent and authorization. He used to say: 'God, this is my share of what lies in my power. Do not call me to account for what does not lie in my power!' That is: (This is my share) regarding the inclination of the heart.

Muḥammad ʿAbduh has said: Whoever considers the two verses correctly acknowledges that permission for polygamy in Islam applies (only) with the most severe restriction. Polygamy is like one of those necessities which is permitted to the one to whom it is allowed (only) with the stipulation that he act fairly with trustworthiness and that he be immune from injustice (*al-jaur*). In view of this restriction, when one now considers what corruption results from polygamy in modern times, then one will know for certain that a people (*umma*) cannot be trained so that their remedy lies in polygamy, since, in a family in which a single man has two wives, no beneficial situation and no order prevail. Rather, the man and his wives each mutually assist in the ruin of the family, as if each of them were the enemy of the other; and also the children then become enemies to one another. The corruption of polygamy carries over from the individual to the family and from the family to the (entire) people.

Muḥammad ʿAbduh has said: Polygamy had advantages in the early period of Islam, among the most important at that time being that it brought about the bond of blood relationship and of relationship by marriage, so that the feeling of tribal solidarity was strengthened. Also, at that time it did not lead to the same harm (*ḍarar*) that it does today, since at that time the religion was firmly rooted in the souls of women and men, and the insult (*adhan*) of taking an additional wife (*ḍarra*) did not go beyond her rival (in its effect). Today, on the other hand, the harm (*ḍarar*) of every additional wife (*ḍarra*) carries over to her child, its father, and its other relatives. The wife stirs up enmity and hatred among them; she incites her child to enmity against his brothers and sisters, and she incites her husband to suppress the rights of the children which he has from the other wives. The husband, on the other hand, follows in the folly of the wife whom he loves the most, and thus ruin creeps into the entire family. If one wished to enumerate specifically the disadvantages and mishaps that result from polygamy, then one would present something that would cause the blood of the believers to curdle. This includes theft and adultery, lies and deceit, cowardice and deception, indeed even murder, so that the child kills the father, the father kills the child, the wife kills the husband, and the husband kills the wife. All this is tangible and is demonstrated from the (records of the) courts of justice.

It may suffice here to refer to the (poor) education of the (modern) woman, who knows neither the worth (*qīma*) of the husband nor that of the child and finds herself in ignorance concerning herself and her religion, knowing of religion only legends and errors which she has snatched up from others like herself and which are not found either in the scriptures or in (the sayings of) the prophets who have been sent. If women had the benefit of a proper religious education, so that religion had the highest power over their hearts and would prevail over jealousy, then no harm would grow out of polygamy for the people today, but the harm would remain limited as a rule to the women (who are concerned). However, since the matter now stands as we see and hear it, there is no possibility of educating the people so long as polygamy is widespread among them. Thus, it is the duty of scholars to investigate this problem, (that is) especially the Ḥanafite scholars, in whose hand the matter lies (in the Ottoman empire and its sphere of influence), and whose opinion is determinative (here). They do not deny that religion was sent down for the use and benefit of mankind and that it belongs to the principles of religion to prevent harm and injury. Now if at a (certain) time (that is, the present), corruption results from something that was not connected with it earlier, it is without doubt necessary to alter the laws and to adapt them to the actual situation, that is, according to the principle that one must prevent the deterioration beforehand in order then to bring about the well-being (of the community). Muḥammad ʿAbduh has said: Hence, it is recognized that polygamy is strictly forbidden when the fear exists that one cannot act fairly.

This is what the Ustādh-Imām (Muḥammad ʿAbduh) said in the first lecture in which he interpreted the present verse. In the second lecture he then said: It has been said before that permission for polygamy is restricted since a stipulation is imposed which is so difficult to realize that it represents the same as a prohibition against polygamy. Further, it has been said that to him who fears that he is unable to act equitably it is forbidden to marry more than one wife. This is not, as has been done by some students (of al-Azhar University[2]), to be understood in the sense that a marriage settlement is null and void when it has been completed under such circumstances, since the prohibition (given here) is not so firm that it could require the negation of the marriage settlement. The husband may indeed fear that he will act unjustly, but yet not do so. And he may act unjustly, but then repent and act equitably and thus lead a legitimate life. . . .

I (Muḥammad Rashīd Riḍā) say: Add to this that polygamy is at variance with the natural fundamental rule (*aṣl*) in the nature of marriage, since the fundamental rule is that the man is to have a single wife and that he is her mate just as she is his. Polygamy is, however, a necessity that befalls human society (under certain circumstances, that is) especially in warlike peoples (*al-umam al-ḥarbiyya*) like the Islamic community. Polygamy is permitted to them only in the case of necessity, and then only with the stipulation that neither injustice nor oppression will occur thereby. This problem requires further discussion. So the wisdom of the plurality and number (of wives) is discussed, and there must be discussion as to the extent to which the administrators of the law are in a position to impede the perversions of polygamy through restraint when the harm done through polygamy becomes widespread, as is seen to be the case in Egypt. For those men who marry more than one wife are numerous here, while in Syria and Turkey this is not the case; and at the same time, the customs in Egypt ordinarily are more corrupted than there. We have published a legal opinion (*fatwa*) concerning the wisdom of polygamy in the seventh volume of (the journal) *Al-manār.* It reads as follows:

THE WISDOM OF POLYGAMY

Question . . . from Najīb Āfandī Qonawī, a student in America: Many American physicians and others ask me about the verse: *Then marry two,*

2. One of the leading universities in the Islamic world, founded in Cairo in the 10th century.

three, or four of such women as seem good to you, but if you fear you will not be equitable, then (marry) only one. And they say: 'How can a Muslim join together four women (to form a family unit)?' I have answered them, so far as I understand this verse, in support of my religion, and have said: It is impossible to treat two (wives) equitably. For if one marries a new (wife), the old one must be resentful. How is one to treat them equitably? But God has commanded that one treat (them) equitably. Therefore, it is best when one has (only) one (wife). I have said this and usually those who inquire are satisfied with this answer. However, I would appreciate your interpretation and explanation of this verse, and I would like to know what you say to those who marry two or three (wives).

Answer: The general public in the West regard the problem of polygamy to be the most serious deficiency in Islam, because this general public are influenced by their customs, their religious traditions, their excessive esteem for women, and by what they have heard and learned about the conduct of many Muslims who marry several wives only for the release of their animal desires, without holding to the restrictions that have been imposed upon them concerning permission for it. (Further, the general public in the West are of this opinion because they are influenced) by what appears to them to be corruption in a family which consists of one husband and several wives, whose children confront each other with jealousy, strife, and hatred. This kind of view, however, does not suffice in order to resolve so serious a problem as this for human society. Rather, before making a decision one must reflect about the nature of man and woman, about (the question) of whether there is a larger number of men or women, (further) about the problem of domestic life and the care of men for women or vice versa, or the independence of both marriage partners from each other, and (finally) about the history of human development, in order to know whether people in the stage of nomadic life were satisfied for each man to have (only) a single wife. After all this, one has to see whether the Qur'ān has made the problem of polygamy a religious matter worthy of striving after or a concession that is allowed in the case of necessity and under limiting restrictions.

You who are occupied with the medical sciences know best among mankind the distinction between the nature of man and that of woman as well as the most important difference between the two. According to what we all know, man has by nature a greater desire for woman than she has for him. There is (only) seldom an impotent man who (because of this impotence) by nature has no desire for women; but there are many women who by nature have no desire for men. If the woman were not to become enamoured with being loved by the man, and if she did not undertake considerable reflection regarding esteem by the man, then there would be many more women today who would forgo marriage. This passion in the woman is something other than the inclination that grows out of the natural craving for procreation in her and in the man. This passion is sheltered also by the old woman and by those who cannot hope for a wedding with the customary adornments of the virgin bride. In my opinion, the most important reason for it is a social one, consisting of the fact that many centuries have established in the nature and belief of women the desire to have the benefit of the protection and care of men, (further) in the fact that the provision of the man for the woman arises according to the measure of esteem which she has for him and the inclination which he has for her. Women felt this in primitive times (by necessity) and have continued it so that it has become a hereditary factor with them. This is so much the case that, even when a woman hates a man, it hurts her if he turns away from her and treats her contemptuously, and it hurts the woman when she sees a man—even a stricken old man or a monk who has turned away from the world—who feels no inclination for the woman, does not succumb to her charms, and does not show a reaction to her glamour. Hence it follows that the procreative instinct is stronger in the man than in the woman, and this is a primary premise (for the solution of the problem).

* * *

When one considers all these premises[3] correctly and knows them according to branch and root, the following conclusion or the following conclusions become clear: The basis for happiness in marriage and family life consists in the man having (only) a single wife. This is the final aim of human development in its kind and the perfection into which the people grow up and with which they should be satisfied. Over against this, however, stands the fact that not all men can reach this stage and that conditions (often) require that a particular man care for more than a single woman. This can be to the benefit of the particular men as well as of the particular women. Thus, a man may marry a barren wife and then for the sake of posterity be obliged to (marry) another woman. Here it is then to the benefit of the (first) wife or to the benefit of both together, provided he does not separate from her and she declares herself agreed that he should marry another woman, especially in the case of a king or prince. Or, the woman may reach the change of life when the man is in the position to have more than a single wife and to care for many children and to rear them, and he perceives that he still could witness offspring with another woman. Or, he may perceive that one woman does not suffice for him to continue blameless (in marriage fidelity), since his temperament drives him to frequent sexual intercourse while it is the opposite with her, or she absolutely cannot endure it, or her menstrual period extends for a long time and lasts up to fifteen days in a month. Then the man sees himself faced with the alternative of marrying a second woman or being forced into unchastity; but the religion (Islam) prohibits the possibility and wholesomeness of unchastity, which signifies a greater evil for the wife than when one adds to her another (woman) and at the same time treats both properly, as is the stipulation in Islam for the sanction (of polygamy). For this reason unchastity is regarded as legal in countries in which polygamy is forbidden.

Polygamy is sometimes also of benefit for the people (as a whole), as perhaps when a large surplus of women exists in a society, as for example in England and in any country that has suffered a devastating war[4] to which the men are carried off, up to many thousands, leading to a large surplus of women and forcing the women to seek employment and to be concerned for their means of livelihood. In such cases most of them have as an object of value in exchange for earnings nothing other than their sexual parts. If she surrenders these, then no observer can remain unaware of the misery that results from this surrender for the woman who is without a breadwinner, if

3. In the omitted passage, six more "premises" are specified.
4. That is, World War I.

she is forced to grieve for herself and a fatherless child, especially just after the birth and during the time of nursing, but also during the entire period of infancy. When many women writers of England have spoken of the necessity of polygamy, they have done this (only) after first gaining insight into the situation of the girls who work in the factories and other public places and (after seeing) what shame, what need, and what misery these girls have suffered. Now since the grounds for allowing polygamy lie in the extent of the necessities for which it is permitted, and since men as a rule are inclined to it in order to satisfy their eager desire rather than to promote the (general) welfare, and (finally) since perfection (in family life), which is to be aspired to as a basic principle, knows no multiple marriage, polygamy has been approved in Islam, but not as an obligation nor as something that would be recommended as desirable in itself. It is tied to the stipulation that is declared in the noble verse (Sūra 4:3—'But if you fear you will not be equitable, then [marry] only one') and is confirmed and repeated (in the statement: 'Thus, it will be more likely that you will not be partial'). One should contemplate this verse thoughtfully. . . .

ʿALI SHARIʿATI
1933–1977

ʿAli Shariʿati, an Iranian activist and intellectual, was born in the village of Mazinan in Khurasan, in northeastern Iran. His father was a traditionally trained Muslim scholar, and other members of his family served as clerics in Mashhad, the burial site of the eighth Shiʿi imam and an important center of Shiʿi learning. Shariʿati was educated in government schools rather than in the religious seminaries, but studied Islam with his father. His father, who had become dissatisfied with what he saw as the shortsightedness and irrelevance of many religious scholars in modern times, set up an organization to fashion a response both to traditional scholarship and to communism, Marxism, and other imported ideologies, whose influence was growing.

After completing a teachers' training program, Shariʿati taught in rural villages for a number of years; he later received a BA in Persian and French from the University of Mashhad. During these years he was active in several organizations opposed to the Iranian monarchy, at one point spending about six months in jail in Tehran for his political resistance. In 1960 he went to the Sorbonne in Paris to pursue his PhD. Though the terms of his scholarship required that he focus on Persian literature—which he did, working with the famous Orientalist Louis Massignon—he also studied the works of French intellectuals such as the sociologist Georges Gurvitch and the philosopher Jean-Paul Sartre. He joined in local activism for the liberation of Algeria, earning a six-month stay in a Paris jail (where he became familiar with the theories of the revolutionary Frantz Fanon); and because he continued his work in the movement against the shah, Mohammad Reza (1919–1980; r. 1941–79), he was again imprisoned for six months when he returned to Iran in 1964.

Eventually Shariʿati was able to secure a teaching position in history at the University of Mashhad, where his classes quickly swelled. His novel sociological approach to Islam appealed to students and young people, and he was invited to speak at other universities and at religious events. In 1965 a group of reformers in Tehran established the Husayniyya-yi Irshad (the Husayniyya of Guidance), a center of Islamic learning named after Muhammad's grandson Husayn, where Shariʿati became a frequent lecturer, and publications of his lectures reached a national audience. These talks became increasingly political, and in 1973 the Shah's government closed the center and jailed Shariʿati. Even after his release two years later, he remained under house arrest.

Unable to teach or travel in Iran, Shariʿati decided to head for the United States (where his son was studying), but his family was not allowed to accompany him. He was at his brother's house in England, waiting for them to get permission to leave Iran, when he suddenly died in June 1977. Though the official cause of death was a heart attack, it is widely believed that the Shah's secret police assassinated him. He was buried in Damascus next to Zaynab, the most important female figure of the massacre of Karbala'. Both Zaynab and her brother Husayn, who was killed in that battle in 680, were central figures in Shariʿati's articulation of Islam.

Shariʿati lived during a time of great ferment in Iranian history. The Shah's increasingly arbitrary and unjust actions, along with his advocacy of Westernization, provoked the anger not just of traditional clergy but also of Iranian secularists. Events such as the U.S.-aided coup against the nationalist prime minister Mohammed Mossadegh in 1953 also fed popular outrage against the Shah. Like his father, Shariʿati sought to articulate a way of being both modern and religious that rejected the Shah's equation of modernization with Westernization. It also differed from the concerns of traditional Islamic scholars, who were more focused on the religio-legal minutiae of inherited understandings of Islam than on the practical religious guidance sought by contemporary Muslims.

A major component of his thought was a revolutionary view of Shiʿism. Shariʿati saw important events like Karbala' not as memorial occasions that elicited only weeping but as shining beacons in the struggle against injustice and corruption that compelled believers to action. Similarly, important figures in Islamic history—especially Muhammad, his household, and their supporters—were portrayed as revolutionaries who acted against social injustice. Thus Shariʿati's participation in the Husayniyya-yi Irshad was a natural complement to his Islamic thought, as traditionally Shiʿis retold the story of Karbala' in such institutional settings. This approach appealed strongly to many Iranians living under the Shah, and contributed significantly to the Iranian Revolution in 1979.

Fatima Is Fatima, from which the selection below is drawn, was first given as a lecture at the Husayniyya-yi Irshad. Here, as in his treatment of other contemporary Iranian issues, Shariati criticizes the traditional religious and cultural roles assigned to women as well as the new Westernized roles advanced by some segments of the Iranian population. As an alternative, he presents Fatima as the ideal model for Muslim women.

Fatima, the daughter of Muhammad and his first wife Khadija, was the only one of his children to survive him. She married Muhammad's cousin ʿAli, venerated as the first Shiʿi imam, and was the mother of their two sons, Hasan and Husayn (the second and third imams, respectively). Shariʿati presents her here as the ideal combination of wife, mother, and outspoken activist against social injustice, intimately aligned with the message and actions of her father.

PRONOUNCING GLOSSARY

dar al-madweh: *dahr al-mad´-wuh*
faqih: *fa-qeeh´*
Fatima: *fah´-ti-muh*
Haji Agha: *ha´-jee ah´-gah*
Imam Husayn: *ee-mam´ hoo-sayn´*
Karbala: *kar-ba-la´*
Khadija: *cha-dee´-juh* (guttural *ch*)
Makkah: *mak´-kuh*
Masjid al-Haram: *mas´-jid al-ha-rahm´* (heavy *h*)
mujtahid: *muj´-ta-hid*
Quraysh: *qoo-raysh*
Taif: *tah´-if*
Zaynab: *zay´-nab*

FROM FATIMA IS FATIMA

Chapter 1. Who Am I?

In our society, women change rapidly. The tyranny of our times and the influence of institutions take women away from 'what she is'. All her traditional characteristics and values are taken away from her until she is made into a creature 'they want', 'they build'. We see that 'they have built'! This is why the most important and relevant question for the awakened woman at this time is, 'Who am I?' She knows full well that she cannot remain what she is. Actually, she does not want to accept modern masks to replace the traditional ones. She wants to decide for herself. Her contemporaries choose for themselves. They consciously adorn their personalities with awareness and independence. They dress themselves. They manifest an essence. They reflect a sketch. But they do not know how. They do not know the design of the real human aspect of their personality which is neither a reflection of their ethnic heritage nor an artificially imposed imitative mask. With which of these do they identify??

The second question which arises from this, stems from the following: we are Muslims, women of a society, who wish to make decisions through reason and choice and to relate them to a history, religion and society which received its spirit and basis from Islam. A woman in this society wants to be herself. She wants to build herself, 'herself'. She wants to be reborn. In this re-birth, she wants to be her own midwife. She neither wants to be a product of her ethnic heritage nor to adopt a superficial facade. She cannot remain heedless of Islam, and she cannot remain indifferent to it.

Thus, it is natural that this question should arise for the Muslim woman. Our people continue to speak about Fatima.[1] Every year, hundreds of thousands of Muslims cry for her. There are hundreds of thousands of gatherings, prayer meetings, festivals and mourning ceremonies in her memory. There are ceremonies of praise, joy, honor and majesty for her in which her generosity is remembered through unusual customs. They hold rituals of lamentation where they re-create her sorrows and speak ill of and damn those who offended her. In spite of all of this, her real personality is not known.

Yet, in spite of the little Muslims know about her, they accept Fatima, her majesty and power, with their whole hearts. They offer her their hearts with all the spiritual strength, faith and will that a people can have or a human community build.

WISDOM AND LOVE

Each religion, school of thought, movement or revolution is made up of two elements: wisdom and love. One is light and the other is motion. One gives common sense and understanding, the other, strength, enthusiasm and movement. In the words of Alexis Carrel,[2] 'Wisdom is like the lights of a car which show the way. Love is like the motor which makes it move.' Each is nothing without the other. A motor, without lights, is blind love—dangerous, tragic and potentially fatal.

TRANSLATED BY Laleh Bakhtiar. All bracketed additions are the translator's.

1. The daughter (ca. 605 or 616–633) of the prophet Muhammad and his first wife, Khadija.

2. Nobel Prize–winning French surgeon and experimental biologist (1873–1944).

In a society, in a movement of thought or in a revolutionary school of thought, men of letters (who are clear thinkers, who are aware and responsible) show, through their works, that there is a way to come to know a school of thought or a religion. They show that there is a way to give awareness to people. The responsibility of the people, on the other hand, is to give their spirits and their strength to a movement. They are responsible for giving the starting push.

A movement is like a living body. It thinks with the brain of scholars and loves through the hearts of its people. If faith, sincerity, love and sacrifice seldom found in a society, people are responsible. But where correct understanding of a school of thought is at a low level (where vision, awareness, logical consciousness and deep familiarity with the goals of a school of thought are lacking, where the meaning, purpose and truths of a school of thought are missing) the scholars are responsible. Religion, in particular, needs both. In religion, knowledge and feelings are not treated as separate entities. They are transformed into understanding and faith by means of common sense and knowledge.

This is Islam. More than any other religion, it is a religion of the recitation of the book, a religion of struggle in God's Way (*jihad*), a religion of thought and love. In the Koran, one cannot find the boundaries between love and faith. The Koran considers martyrdom to be eternal life. It blinds one to the pen and writing. If Muslims are unaware of this, who is responsible?

From *Chapter 2. Who Is Responsible?*

Religious scholars! It is they who do not perform their responsibilities in respect to the people. They should give awareness, consciousness and direction to the people. They do not.

All our geniuses and great talents occupy themselves with philosophy, theology, Sufism, jurisprudence, conjugation and syntax. Through all the years of research, thought and their own scholarly anguish, they write nothing other than 'practical treatises' on such subjects as purity for the prescribed prayer, types of ritual impurities, rules of menstruation, and doubts which arise in prescribed prayer.

They leave aside writing treatises on how to speak with people, treatises on how to communicate the religious truths and the philosophy of the pillars of the religion, treatises on how to communicate consciousness and awareness to people, treatises on the understanding of the traditions of the Prophet and the personalities of the Companions, treatises on the revolutionary purpose behind Karbala,[3] treatises on the family of the Prophet, and treatises on the faith of the people. All of these treatises are written, but all of them are written without responsibility, without the role of a commander. They pass their responsibilities on to the ordinary speakers in the mosques, not to the religious leaders whose directions for the practice of the faith are followed (*mujtahids*[4]).

3. The site in central Iraq of the battle in 680 at which the forces of the Umayyad caliph Yazid I killed Husayn, the grandson of Muhammad, and all the men in his small party of supporters; according to Shiʿis, Husayn was resisting the corruption of Islam, as represented by Yazid. "Companions": those followers of the Prophet who were close to him in his lifetime and who memorized and transmitted the Qurʾan and hadith before their written compilations.

4. Scholars who are capable of answering questions posed to them without relying on the opinions of other scholars.

This is why the task of introducing the Prophet's family, the task of understanding religion and the task of studying the truths of Islam fall prone to the 'failures of the old schools of religion'. It is for this reason that a group of young people, in order to study Islamic sciences and to carry jurisprudence forward, enter the schools. If talented, through great efforts, they become jurisprudents or *mujtahids* or *faqihs* [theologians]. This group is imprisoned as teachers and removed from the community. Those who do not succeed in studying properly, because they do not have the ability, talent or spiritual strength but rather have warm, often artistic, voices, are obliged to propagate and advertise the truths of the religion. The third group, who have neither this nor that, neither the science nor at least a voice, take the third way. They become dumb and speechless. They take themselves to the 'sacred door' and move ahead of both *mujtahids* and speakers in the mosques.

In the midst of this, be just! What will the fate of the people be? What is the fate of their religion? It is not necessary to think very hard. No. Just look.

We know a dream appeared to Joan of Arc,[5] a sensitive and imaginative girl, commanding her to fight in order to have her king returned. For centuries, her dream has given a vision of freedom, of sacrifice and of revolutionary courage to enlightened, aware and progressive French people. Compare Joan to Zaynab, the sister of Imam Husayn,[6] who carried a heavier mandate. Zaynab's mandate was to continue the movement of Karbala. She opposed murders, terror and hysterics. She continued the movement at a time when all the heroes of the revolution were dead, when the heroism and wisdom of the commanders of Islam at the time of the Prophet were gone. But she has been turned into only a 'sister who mourns'.

I hear reproachful cries towards the scholars who are responsible for these beliefs, ideas and thoughts of the people. I do not know whether these cries come from the throats of people or from the depths of their consciences.

With what are you busy? From where do you speak? Throughout all of these years, where is one book for people telling them what is in the Koran? In place of praise, eulogy, prayer, poetry, song, lamentation and the love of Rumi,[7] why have you sealed your lips among people? An English speaking person cannot easily understand what the Prophet has said, but can he read all of the works of La Martine,[8] the French lover. What do you say? All the songs of the ancient Greek woman, Bilitis,[9] of dubious morals, can be read, but the words of the Prophet, one saying of the Prophet, cannot be read.

You speak so much about the generosity and miracles of the Prophet's family but where are the books about them? You recount their miracles on their birthdays and days of their deaths. You have festivals and mourning ceremonies. Where are the treatises for Muslims, enamored of the Prophet, which say who he was and who Fatima was, which say how their children lived and how they thought, which say what they did and what they said?

Our people, who spend their lives in love with the Companions and who cry over the difficulties they faced, who serve them for months and years, who glorify their name, spend money and give sincerity and patience to them,

5. The national heroine of France (ca. 1412–1431); she led the French in battle against the English, who burned her at the stake.

6. The third Imam of the Shiʿa (626–680); he was the son of ʿAli (ca. 599–661), the fourth caliph and first Imam, and Fatima. Zaynab survived the massacre at Karbala'.

7. Persian mystic and poet (1207–1273); see above.

8. Alphonse de Lamartine (1790–1869), an extremely popular French poet.

9. The imaginary classical Greek writer to whom Pierre Louÿs falsely attributed the prose poems he published in French as *The Songs of Bilitis* (1894).

deserve to know the real lives of each one of them. Their lives, thoughts, words, silences, freedoms, imprisonments, and martrydoms should give awareness, chastity and humanness to people.

If an ordinary person mourns for Husayn and on the anniversary of his death [*ashura*][1] strikes his head with his dagger and bears the pain—even with pleasure—and still knows Husayn only in an oblique way and misunderstands Karbala, who is responsible? If a woman cries with her whole being, if the recollection of the name of Fatima and Zaynab burns her to her bones and if she would, with complete love, give her life for them, and yet, if she does not thoroughly know Fatima and Zaynab, who is responsible?

* * *

From *Chapter 4. What Should Be Done?*

Islam distributes freedom. People are in love with Islam and yet, the young intellectuals realize the weakness and decline of Islam's followers. The main reason for this contradiction is 'not having come to know'. It is coming to know which has value. Love and faith have no value if they precede coming to know and precede choice or commitment. If the Koran is read but not understood, it is no different from a blank book. The Prophet gave his followers awareness, greatness, chastity and freedom when they came to know who he was. When one reads a book mis-stating the Prophet's character or when a book of his sayings is not given to his longing people, what effect can loving him, praising and eulogizing him have?

Love and faith follow coming to know something. It is that which moves the spirit and brings up the nation. This is why the face of Fatima has remained unknown behind the constant praise, eulogies, and lamentations of her followers.

In Muslim societies there are three faces of woman. One is the face of the traditional woman. Another is the face of the new woman, European-like, who has just begun to grow and introduce herself. The third is the face of Fatima which has no resemblance whatsoever to that of the ethnically Muslim woman. The face of the ethnically Muslim woman, which has taken form in the minds of those loyal to religion in our society, is as far away from the face of Fatima as Fatima's face is from the modern woman's.

The crises which we are facing in the world today, in the East, and in particular in Islamic society, the contradictions which have appeared are all the result of the break-down of human qualities. It has come from the agitation which affects the way a society behaves and thinks. Principally, the changing human form has produced a particular type of intellectually educated man and woman, modernists, who contradict the religious man or woman. No power could have prevented the appearance of this contradiction.

* * *

Those who act as guides, who give explanations, in the name of faith, religion and charity are also mistaken in trying to save forms inherited from the past. They try to preserve old customs and habits. They are referred to in the

1. A Muslim holy day, which among Shiʿis is a major festival and day of mourning.

Koran as 'tales of the ancients', 'the ancients,' 'legends of the ancients', 'fathers of old', 'fables of the ancients', and 'stories of yore'.

These words all refer to the first myths and first fathers. But those who act as guides see old as synonymous with traditional. As a result, they call every change, including even change in dress or hair-do, infidelity. They mistakenly believe that the spiritual source and the belief in submission to God (*islam*) can only be preserved through the worship of anything which is old. They turn away from anything new, from any change and from any re-birth.

Woman, in their view, must also remain as she is today because, simply enough, her form existed in the past and has become part of social traditions. It may be 19th century, 17th century or even pre-Islamic, but it is considered to be religious and Islamic. It must, therefore, be preserved. Those who seek to guide accept this view because it has become part of their way of life and because it suits their interests. They try to remain the same and hold onto things of the past forever. They say, "Islam wanted it to be this way. Religion has taken this form. It should remain like this until Judgment Day."

But the world changes. Everything changes. Mr. X and his son change. But a woman must retain her permanent form. In general terms, their point of view is that the Prophet sealed woman into her traditional form and that she must retain the characteristics which Haji Agha,[2] [her husband], inscribed in her.

This type of thinking tends to lead us astray. If we wish to keep the forms because of our own inexperience, time itself will outrun us. We must realize that destruction is also a reality. Insistence upon keeping these forms will bear no fruit as society will never listen. It cannot listen because these are mortal transient customs.

Those who seek to guide try to explain social traditions, which have come into being through habit, in religious terms. When we equate religion with social or cultural traditions, we make Islam the guardian of declining forms of life and society. We confuse cultural and historical phenomena with inherited, superstitious beliefs. Time changes habits, social relationships, indigenous, historical phenomena and ancient, cultural signs. We mistakenly believe the Islamic religion to be only these social traditions. Aren't these great errors committed today? Aren't we seeing them with our own eyes?

From *Chapter 6. What Role Did Women Play in the Attack!?*

THE CRIES OF EXPLOITATION

* * *

Women in Islamic societies must not only be transformed into consumers of goods exported from Europe and America but they must also become active participants within their households. They must learn to relate according to today and tomorrow's generations. They must change the form of society. They must have an effect upon ethics, values, literature and art. They

2. The title character of a 1945 Iranian novel by Sadeq-e Hedayat; a hypocrite, in popular culture he became the personification of one version of religious masculinity. "Haji" is a title of respect, given to one who has made the obligatory pilgrimage to Mecca.

must have a deep revolutionary effect upon everything. They should be put to work upon this way.

Time, culture, social possibilities, new economics, changes in social relationships, new thoughts—all of these conditions in an Islamic society, themselves, change the types and traditions. Women become obliged to change internal and external conditions because past modes are no longer practical nor sufficient.

Now that things must be changed, isn't it logical that capitalists should get busy and prepare their moulds so that as soon as a woman puts aside her traditional mould, their mould can be forced upon her? They make her into a form they want and then place her, instead of themselves, in a position to corrupt society.

WHAT SHOULD WE DO?

In the midst of this disruption—which has been imposed upon us and will continue to impose itself upon us—what can we do? Who is it that can take up the mandate?

The one who can do something, and, in saving us plays an active role, is not the traditional woman asleep in her quiet, tame, ancient mould nor is it the new woman, the modern doll who has assumed the mould of the enemy. Rather, she is the one who can choose the new human characteristics, who can break old traditions (presented as religion, but in fact, only national and tribal traditions ruling the spirit, thoughts and behavior of society). She is a person who is not satisfied with old advice. Slogans which are given by doubtful sources do not interest her. Behind the prepackaged slogans of freedom [of the monarchy], she sees ugly, frightening faces which act against the spiritual, and which oppose the human. She sees that they contradict the spiritual, the rational, the human. They are against women and the human reverence of women.

It is such people who know where those things which are forced upon us come from. They know from where they get their orders. What creatures they have sent to the market place! Creatures without sensitivities, without knowledge, without pain, without understanding, without responsibility and, even, without human feelings. Fresh, clean dolls—'worthy ones'. It is obvious what their worthiness is in and for. Their means of support and its derivation are also obvious. This is tossed to our women and they know why.

It is because of them that "Who am I? Who should I be?" is pertinent, since they neither want to remain this nor become that. They cannot surrender themselves to whatever was and is without their own will and choice playing a role.

They want a model.

Who?

Fatima.

From *Chapter 13. Why Fatima?*

RECALLING FATIMA'S LIFE

Fatima's childhood occurred after her mother had given all of her wealth for the cause of Islam. The peacefulness of the life of her father and the happiness of her youth with her sisters had passed. Her mother had become old and broken. Her mother's age was beyond sixty-five. Happiness, wealth and the good fortune of life were replaced by weakness, poverty, difficulties, an environment of hatred, and the treachery of strangers.

Her mother, Khadija,[3] before being the mother of Fatima and wife of the Prophet, had been the first associate and the greatest companion of a man on whom the heavy mission of heaven had fallen, the mission of removing the blackness of ignorance, the mission of returning the fire of God to mankind, the mission of freeing people from the chains of bondage by changing the economic system of slavery and the mission of freeing people from the mental prison of idol worship, Khadija was now the mother of Fatima, but completely occupied with the Prophet who had received inner inspiration about that which is above life and happiness. Around Khadija a fire full of hatred, the troubles of the worship of materialism and enmity spread. The mother of Fatima was busy with the difficulties and the revolution of the Prophet. The Prophet lived amidst his troubles and his revolution giving the message of God to his people.

There is no heart which could sense what Fatima was feeling. The love of Fatima for the Prophet was much more than the love of a daughter for her father. She was the daughter who was also the mother of her father, the sympathizer with him in his exile and loneliness, the acceptor of his troubles and his sorrow, the companion in the religious struggle, the link in the chain of his line; his last daughter and, during the last years of his life, his only child. After his death, she was his only survivor, the light of his home, the only pillar of his family and, finally, the only mother of his children, his inheritors.

Just when Fatima needed the love of her mother and the kindness of her father, she sensed that her mother and father, (both of whom had lived only with pain, loneliness and misery) needed her child-like kindness and caresses.

There is a saying that a heart which finds a friend through trouble and sorrow develops a friendship which, when compared to a love based on happiness and pleasure, is much deeper and more certain. The feeling with which one views how one has lived one's life and how one's friend has answered one's needs is not the same as the feeling of familiarity one senses from the friend in one's own being. For when one sees that one has sacrificed one's life and that the needs of the friend have been met, the spirit—in the heights of its subtleness and the depths of its feelings—forms another spirit within the self—the spirit of friendship.

And Fatima gave such friendship to the Prophet that there is no comparison to one who gives love to one's father. The intimacy and purity of feelings which she had for him created a continuous link and a situation incapable of being described. With the spirit of her father within herself, she was able to bear the years of difficulties, hatred, fear and torture. She bore the fact that her hero father was sacrificed and remained a stranger in his own country, unknown in his own city, alone among his family, alone among those who spoke his language. He remained without anyone to whom he

3. The widow of a wealthy merchant (d. 619); Muhammad took no other wives while she was alive.

could talk. He had to stand face to face with ignorance and idol worship. He had to stand face to face in savage conflicts with untamed elders, petty aristocrats and hated slave dealers.

His shoulders were bent under the heavy weight of the divine mission of the One God. He was alone in this long walk from slavery to freedom, from the dark valleys of Makkah[4] to the peaks of the mountain of light, alone and without a companion while his soul was suffering from the hatred, plots and blindness of the people. His body was wounded from the troubles and blows of the enemy. He tried harder than anyone else to bring happiness and salvation to his tribe, and yet he and his family suffered because of the trouble his tribe caused him. They treated him as a stranger.

On the one hand, he was alone, a suffering spirit, bearer of the revelation and on the other, he was a storm of love and fiery faith. Tribal enmity, the blindness of the people, the loneliness of not having anyone and the heavy weight of the load of the 'trust' he had brought caused him anguish. God had offered the burden of bearing this weight to the heavens and the earth, but they had rejected it. Only mankind was willing to accept the responsibility. In following this, the Prophet, every day from morning until night, cried out a warning (to whomever passed by the Safa hill[5]) of danger to people who were asleep and passive. He did this under the rain of problems that sought him out each day.

He announced the message in the sacred precinct of the Masjid al-Haram beside the *dar al-madweh*,[6] the meeting place of the wealthy Quraysh[7] aristocrats and before the eyes of 330 dumb, senseless, spiritless idols who were the gods of the people. He called the people to awaken. He cried for freedom. At the end of the day, tired and exhausted, wounded internally, his heart overflowing with pain, he returned to a silent home empty-handed, followed by mockery. Within his home there was a woman broken by the sufferings of life, her body and her whole existence full of love, her two eyes waiting in anticipation, watching the door.

Fatima, a young girl, weak, moved step by step with her father through the streets of hatred to the *Masjid al-haram* under the taunts of curses, mockery, and contempt. Whenever he fell he became like a bird that had fallen out of the nest. When a bird falls from its nest, the possibility arises that it will fall into the claws and beaks of wild animals or birds. Fatima threw herself upon her father. With all of her strength, she protected him. With her small, fine hands, she took her hero into her arms. With the edge of her small, fine fingers, alive with kindness, she cleaned the blood from her father's head and hands. She healed his wounds with her soft words. She encouraged the man who carried the Word of God. She returned him to their home.

She was a link of kindness, attraction and love between a suffering mother and a suffering father. When her bloodied father returned from Taif,[8] she alone came forward to greet him and with her child-like, endearing efforts,

4. That is, Mecca.
5. A hill in Mecca.
6. A meeting place just north of the Kaʿba, the cubical stone shrine in Mecca that became the most important site in Islam (Muslims around the world face it when they pray); it is located within the Masjid al-Haram (the Sacred Mosque), which also contains the Safa Hill.
7. The tribe that ruled Mecca in Muhammad's time.
8. A town 40 miles southeast of Mecca. In 620 Muhammad preached to its inhabitants, but they rejected his message and pelted him with stones, forcing him to return to Mecca.

attracted him to herself, despite of all of his worries and troubles. She attracted his heart towards her warm reception.

In the valley of the confine she lived three years beside her sad, bed-ridden, elderly mother and her suffering father covered with difficulties. She bore hunger, sorrow and loneliness. After the death of her mother and the death of the uncle[9] of the great Prophet, she filled the sudden emptiness in his life with her kindness and endless understanding. The Prophet was now alone both inside the home and outside of it.

She acted as a mother to her father who was now very much alone. She devoted love, faith and all the moments of her life to her father. Through her kindness, the feelings of her father were satisfied. Through her devotion and faith in the mission of her father, she gave him energy and honor.

By going to Ali's house and by accepting his noble poverty, she gave him hope. Through Hasan,[1] Husayn and Zaynab she offered her father the sweetest and dearest fruits of her life. Her children compensated the Prophet for his terrible losses: the deaths of his three infant sons and the deaths of his three grown daughters. The roots of Fatima's lifelong love were deeper than the feelings of a child of eighteen or twenty-eight years. She was stronger than life, purer than will and faith. All the golden webs of the beyond were created in the soul, depth and conscience of Fatima. They joined her with the spirit of her father.

And now this delicate web was torn by the thorn of the death of her father. Fatima must 'remain' without him and 'live'. How terrifying and heavy was this blow to the frail heart and weak body of Fatima, this girl who lived only through love of her father, faith in her father. She lived because of her father.

It is no accident that the Prophet, upon his deathbed, consoled her and gave her the strength, the strength to bear her father's death. This strength was the only gift from the death of her dear one. The special news was that she would join him sooner than any of the others.

From *Epilogue*

Fatima lived like this and died like this. After her death, she began a new life in history. Fatima appeared as a halo around the faces of all of the oppressed who later became the multitudes of Islam. All of the sufferers, all of those whose rights had been destroyed, all who had been deceived, all took the name of Fatima as their emblem.

The memory of Fatima grew with the love and wonderful faith of the men and women, who throughout the history of Islam, fought for freedom and justice. Throughout the centuries they were punished under the merciless and bloody lash of the caliphates. Their cries and anger grew and overflowed from their wounded hearts.

This is why in the history of all Muslim nations and among the deprived masses of the Islamic community, Fatima has been the source of inspiration for those who desire their rights, for those who seek justice, for those who resist oppression, cruelty, crime and discrimination.

9. Abu Talib (d. 619), an influential leader among the Quraysh who protected Muhammad after his preaching began to cause hostility.

1. Her oldest son (625–669).

It is most difficult to speak about the personality of Fatima. Fatima was the ideal that Islam wanted a woman to be. The form of her face was fashioned by the Prophet himself. He melted her and made her pure in the fires of difficulties, poverty, revolution, deep understanding and the wonder of humanity.

She was a symbol for all the various dimensions of womanhood. She was the perfect model of a daughter when dealing with her father. She was the perfect model of a wife when dealing with her husband. She was the perfect model of a mother when raising her children. She was the perfect model of a responsible, fighting woman when confronting her time and the fate of her society.

* * *

FATIMA MERNISSI
b. 1940

Born in Fez, Morocco, Fatima Mernissi is an internationally known Muslim feminist whose numerous publications focus chiefly on women's issues. During the late 1990s Mernissi's research expanded to examine the impact of modern communications, such as satellite television and the Internet, on Arab nations and the role of such technology in making Arab societies more transparent. Nonetheless, the place of women in Islam and the Arab world continues to be an important research interest. After completing her undergraduate education in Morocco, she studied at the Sorbonne and earned a PhD in sociology from Brandeis University. She then returned to Morocco to teach, first at the University of Rabat and since 1980 at the Mohammed V University in Rabat. Her writings have been translated into many languages, including Japanese and English.

Mernissi's most noted works address the reasons behind gender inequality in Muslim societies. *Beyond the Veil* (1975) is regarded as a groundbreaking work that introduced feminist readings of Islamic texts and Muslim history to the world. In it, Mernissi argues that Islamic texts view women as threatening to men because of their seductiveness and sexuality. To contain this threat, Islam relegates women to a separate sphere through social practices such as veiling and the separation of sexes. It assigns economic responsibility in a marriage to the husband and deemphasizes the value of marriage by permitting men to have multiple wives and by giving them the power of unilateral divorce. Mernissi astutely observes that in modern Arab countries—her research focuses principally on Morocco—such a disparity in roles can no longer be sustained. Modern society's requirement that women work and enter the male space complicates the vision of male-female relations provided in Islamic texts.

The Veil and the Male Elite, published a dozen years after *Beyond the Veil*, continues Mernissi's study of the place of women in Muslim societies. She was prompted to write, she tells us, by her grocer's insistence that a woman could not lead Muslims. To counter this assertion she first examines a series of prophetic traditions (in Arabic, *hadith*) that appear to demean women and negate the possibility of their leadership. She then investigates the events during three years of

A demonstration of Muslim and Christian Iraqis. The Muslim woman (covering her hair with a black scarf) and the Christian woman (covering her hair with a white scarf) are marching to support the rights of Christian Iraqis, who are often the victims of violent persecution. Each woman is holding a copy of her respective holy book.

Muhammad's career (627–29) when the matters of veiling and the separation of men from women were revealed. Using her own logic as well as the interpretive tools and research methods of classical Muslim scholars, Mernissi argues that the earliest message of Islam, that preached and practiced by Muhammad himself, was one of equality among men and women. Her close rereading of the Qur'an, hadith, and early historical sources finds an Islam in which women led vigorous, outspoken lives. But according to Mernissi, patriarchal agendas soon intruded, as first seen in Muhammad's own lifetime during the years 627–29. Quite quickly, male scholars offered interpretations of Qur'anic and hadith texts that cemented the superior position of males in society. She observes, "Not only have the sacred texts always been manipulated, but manipulation of them is a structural characteristic of the practice of power in Muslim societies. Since all power, from the seventh century on, was only legitimated by religion, political forces and economic interests pushed for the fabrication of false traditions."

In a third book, *Forgotten Queens of Islam* (1990), Mernissi sifts through Islamic history to find examples of female Muslim rulers. Many of these women, such as the Indian queen Radiyya (r. 1236–40) and the Egyptian queen Shajar al-Durr (r. 1250), had coins struck in their names and had their names pronounced from the pulpit during the Friday prayer—both signs that their rule was accepted by their subjects. These women managed to wield power and govern effectively in spite of the patriarchal structures opposing them.

Mernissi's studies are not without detractors. Her observations have been criticized as ahistorical and too sweeping in their reach. Others have pointed to errors in her knowledge of Islamic history, her failure to fully understand the method of the Muslim scholars she critiques, and the internal contradictions in her own writings attributable to insufficient data and evidence. Nonetheless, even her critics admit that she has tackled a vast subject, using data from and tools of several disciplines.

The passage below from *The Veil and the Male Elite* brings to life the household of the Prophet with deft portrayals of several of his wives. Far from being stereotypes of demure docility, these women expressed strong emotion and asked him challenging questions. One such question, about women's relative absence from the Qur'an, prompts the revelation of Qur'an 33:35, a ringing declaration of the spiritual equality of the sexes.

PRONOUNCING GLOSSARY

ʿA'isha: *ah´-i-shuh*
Al-ghazawa: *al-ga-za´-wuh*
ghazi: *ga´-zee*
hijab: *hi-jab´*
Hind Bint ʿUtba: *hind bint ut´-buh*
Al-Isaba: *al-i-sah´-buh*
minbar: *min´-bar*
jahiliyya: *ja´-he-lee'-yuh*
Lisan al-ʿArab: *li-san´ al-ah´-rub*
Quraysh: *qoo-raysh´*
Umm Salama: *oom sa´-la-ma*
Zaynab: *zay´-nab*
Zunub: *zu´-nub*

FROM THE VEIL AND THE MALE ELITE

From *Chapter 7. The Prophet and Women*

The Muslim God is the only monotheistic God whose sacred place, the mosque, opens on to the bedroom, the only one to have chosen a Prophet who does not keep silent about his concerns as a man, but who, on the contrary, voices his thoughts about sexuality and desire.

Clearly, the imams were able to take advantage of our ignorance of the sacred texts to weave a *hijab*—a screen—to hide the mosque/dwelling. But everyone knows that, as the Koran tells us, "of use is the reminder,"[1] and all we have to do is pore over the yellowed pages of our history to bring to life ʿA'isha's[2] laughter, Umm Salama's[3] fiery challenges, and to be present to hear their political demands in a fabulous Muslim city—Medina open to the heavens.

THE WIVES OF THE PROPHET: THE HAPPY YEARS

When the Prophet asked for the hand of Umm Salama in year 4 of the Hejira (AD 626), ʿA'isha was very jealous because she had heard about Umm Salama's beauty. When she saw her for the first time, she caught her breath: "She is more beautiful than they led me to believe!" The author of *Al-Isaba*[4] describes Umm Salama as "a woman of uncommon beauty, very sound judgment, rapid powers of reasoning, and unparalleled ability to formulate correct opinions."

Umm Salama, like Muhammad, belonged to the Quraysh[5] aristocracy. She had four children by her first marriage when the Prophet asked for her hand. At first she refused, for, she said, "I already have children, and I am very jeal-

TRANSLATED BY Mary Jo Lakeland. Mernissi's notes have been omitted.

1. Qur'an 87:9.
2. Regarded by many Muslims as Muhammad's favorite wife (d. 678).
3. Another of Muhammad's wives (d. ca. 679), whom he married in 626.
4. A biographical dictionary of the Companions of the Prophet, by Ibn Hajar al-ʿAsqalani (1372–1449), an Egyptian Sunni historian and scholar of traditions. It is the source of the quotations in this and the following paragraph.
5. The tribe that ruled Mecca in Muhammad's time.

ous." To persuade her, the Prophet told her that he was going to ask God to rid her of her jealousy, and as for the question of age, in any case he was much older than she was. It was Umm Salama's son who gave her in marriage to the Prophet. The bride was nursing her last-born, Zaynab, when she joined the Prophet's household, and he used to greet her when he came to her apartment by saying, "Where is Zunab?", the affectionate nickname of Zaynab.

Umm Salama was one of those women of the Quraysh aristocracy in whom physical beauty and intelligence assured them as they grew older a special ascendancy over their entourage, and the privilege of being consulted on matters of vital concern to the community. The Prophet's first wife, Khadija, was also typical of such women, full of initiative in public life as well as private life. Khadija had had two husbands before the Prophet and had borne a child by each. It was she who "asked for the hand of the Prophet," because she found that he had the qualities she most appreciated in a man. She was also, as we have seen, the heiress of a large fortune left to her by her previous husband, a fortune that she augmented by investing it in wide-ranging trading operations. Tradition stresses the difference in age at the time of marriage between Muhammad (25) and Khadija (40), but one may question whether she really was that old, since in 15 years of marriage together she bore seven children to the Prophet.

A typical example of the dynamic, influential, enterprising woman in public as well as private life is Hind Bint ʿUtba, who played such a central role in the Meccan opposition to Muhammad that, when he conquered Mecca, her name was on the list of the few Meccans condemned to death by the Prophet. He never forgave her the songs and dances she performed among the dead Muslims on the battlefield of Uhud:[6] "The women, coming down from the mountain, stood behind the army, beating their tambourines to spur on the soldiers. Hind, the wife of Abu Sufyan, skipped and danced as she sang this verse:

> We are daughters of the morning star.
> We trample cushions underfoot.
> Our necks are adorned with pearls.
> Our hair is perfumed with musk.
> If you battle us, we will crush you in our arms.
> If you retreat, we will let you go.
> Farewell to love."[7]

One of women's roles in pre-Islamic Arahia was to spur men on during war to fight to the end, to not flinch, to brave death on the battlefield. This role obviously has nothing to do with the image of the nurturing woman who bandages wounds and comforts the dying. Hind and her war song express, on the contrary, an image of woman as exhorter to death. In addition, Hind is described as a cannibal, because she is supposed to have eaten the liver of Hamza, the Prophet's uncle, whom she particularly detested. Al-ʿAsqalani justifies Hind's excessive behavior on the battlefield of Uhud by recalling that she had a grudge against the Prophet's uncle because he had killed *her* uncle, Shayba, and taken part in the intrigues that led to the death of her father,

6. A mountain near Medina; in the battle by its side (624/25), the Meccan forces (led by Abu Sufyan) defeated the Muslims and wounded Muhammad.

7. Quoted from *History of the Prophets and Kings*, by the Muslim historian al-Tabari (ca. 839–923; see above).

ʿUtba. Her hatred of Islam was not just simply acknowledged, but considered justified because Islam had decimated her clan.

So it is understandable that the Prophet demanded her head upon his triumphal entry into Mecca in year 8 of the Hejira (AD 630). But she was the wife of Abu Sufyan, the chief of the city, who pleaded mercy for her from Muhammad. Once it was granted, she had to appear before Muhammad with a delegation of the female population of Mecca to swear the oath of allegiance, after, of course, having recited the declaration of faith. Hind's oath of allegiance, which has been transcribed word for word by the historians, is a masterpiece of humor and political insolence by a woman forced to submit, but in no way renouncing her right to self-expression. When the Prophet commanded her to swear to "not commit adultery," Hind replied: "A free woman never commits adultery." The Prophet is supposed to have thrown an amused glance at ʿUmar, "because he was aware of Hind's love affairs and her relations with ʿUmar before his conversion to Islam." The historians have been so fascinated by Hind's personality that they have devoted pages and pages to her. How do they speak about Hind, that woman who accepted Islam with so much reluctance? As strange as it may seem today, and to the great honor of the Muslim historians, Hind's personality emerges in all its complexity, with her excessive hate and her cannibalism on the one hand, but also with her undeniable gifts on the other: "Hind became Muslim the day of the conquest of Mecca. She was one of the women most gifted in judgment."

The Prophet then was not surprised to hear a woman like Umm Salama, in contrast to the still adolescent ʿAʾisha, raise very political questions that only mature women were in a position to do: "'Why,' she asked the Prophet one day, 'are men mentioned in the Koran and why are we not?'"[8] Once her question was asked, she awaited the reply from Heaven.

One day when she was calmly combing her hair, worried about her question still not having been answered (in those days God used to respond when a woman or a man asked a question about his or her status and position in the new community), she heard the Prophet recite in the mosque the latest verse that had been revealed to him and that concerned her:

> I had asked the Prophet why the Koran did not speak of us as it did of men. And what was my surprise one afternoon, when I was combing my hair, to hear his voice from the *minbar*.[9] I hastily did up my hair and ran to one of the apartments from where I could hear better. I pressed my ear to the wall, and here is what the Prophet said:
>
> "O people! Allah has said in his book: 'Men who surrender unto Allah, and women who surrender, and men who believe and women who believe,'" etc. And he continued in this vein until he came to the end of the passage where it is said: "Allah hath prepared for them forgiveness and a vast reward."[1]

The answer of the Muslim God to Umm Salama was very clear: Allah spoke of the two sexes in terms of total equality as believers, that is, as members of the community. God identifies those who are part of his

8. Quoted from from al-Tabari's Qur'an commentary, *Tafsir* (from the same passage as the longer extract, below).

9. Pulpit (Arabic).

1. Qur'an 33:35.

kingdom, those who have a right to his "vast reward." And it is not sex that determines who earns his grace; it is faith and the desire to serve and obey him. The verse that Umm Salama heard is revolutionary, and reading it leaves no doubt about it:

> Lo! Men who surrender unto Allah, and women who surrender, and men who believe and women who believe, and men who obey and women who obey, and men who speak the truth and women who speak the truth, and men who persevere (in righteousness) and women who persevere, and men who are humble and women who are humble, and men who give alms and women who give alms, and men who fast and women who fast, and men who guard their modesty and women who guard (their modesty), and men who remember Allah much and women who remember—Allah hath prepared for them forgiveness and a vast reward.[2]

* * *

WOMEN AND BOOTY

After Umm Salama's success and the verses affirming women's equality and especially their right to inheritance, a critical period followed. Other verses came, which temporized on the principle of equality of the sexes and reaffirmed male supremacy, without, however, nullifying the dispositions in favor of women. This created an ambiguity in the Koran that would be exploited by governing elites right up until the present day. In fact, women's triumph was of very short duration. Not only did Heaven no longer respond to their pleas, but every time they formulated a new demand, revelations did not, as before, come to their rescue.

Encouraged by the fact that Allah considered them to be believers just like men, women were emboldened to claim the right to go to war in order to gain booty and the right to have a say with regard to the sex act. These claims were surely going to be perceived by men for what they were: a challenge to the very foundations of male supremacy. The heads of family, realizing that what women were demanding was eminently political, mobilized a veritable opposition movement with an elite leader: ʿUmar Ibn al-Khattab,[3] a military chief without peer. His courage had always galvanized the Muslim troops, and the Prophet himself recognized that "the conversion of ʿUmar to Islam was a conquest and a triumph in itself." ʿUmar had boundless admiration for the Prophet and his projects for change, for the creation of an Arab society. He was prepared to go far with the Prophet, to follow him in his desire to change society in general. But the point at which he was no longer prepared to follow him came when it was a question of relations between the sexes. ʿUmar could not imagine an Islam that overturned the traditional—that is, pre-Islamic—relations between men and women. Women's demands to bear arms and to participate actively in military operations instead of passively waiting to be taken prisoner, as the *jahiliyya*[4] tradition required, seemed absurd to him. He was ready to destroy the gods of polytheistic Mecca that his ancestors had worshipped and thus to upset the

2. Qur'an 33:35.
3. The second caliph (ca. 586–644), who was also a close companion of Muhammad.
4. Literally, "ignorance" (Arabic); that is, pre-Islamic.

equilibrium of the heavens. But to envisage that the Arab woman could claim a different status on earth seemed an intolerable change to him.

This was happening at the moment when the women, in a triumphant mood, were taking action. The most virulent of them became openly provocative by declaring that the Koranic verse that said that "a man's share is double that of a woman"[5] did not apply only to inheritance, but also to sin. At the last judgment, they said, every man would have the surprise of seeing the number of his sins multiplied by two: "Since they have two shares of inheritance, let them have the same for sins!" The situation was heating up!

To the great surprise of women, Heaven intervened this time on the side of men and affirmed their privileges. Verse 32 of the sura on women[6] is divided into two arguments and responds to two requests that must be carefully distinguished: women's desire to have the same privileges as men, and their declaration that real equality is achieved in terms of wealth. So, for them to be really the equals of men, Allah had to give them the right to go to war and thus to gain booty. Allah answered in terms of the obvious: since the rights of each are proportional to what they earn, women, who are exempted from going to war, cannot claim to be treated equally: "Unto men a fortune from that which they have earned, and unto women a fortune from that which they have earned."[7] This part of the verse, al-Tabari tells us, is an answer to women's demand to bear arms. They then pushed the reasoning about equality to its logical limit. Since the share of each person is equal to what he or she acquires, and since men only grow rich through war, they demanded the right to this privilege.

To understand women's insistence on this point, we have to have some appreciation of the mechanisms of war and booty and their importance to Medina's economy. *Al-ghazawa*, according to the *Lisan al-'Arab*[8] dictionary, were "raids on an enemy to strip him of his possessions." The dictionary says that a "failed raid is one in which no booty is seized." *Al-ghazawa* were one of the most common means of "creating" wealth. They were intertribal forays, extremely ritualized, whose primary aim was to capture "the wealth of the other," camels most of the time, while avoiding bloodshed. Causing bloodshed was a very serious act which was to be avoided at all costs, because the *ghazi* (attacker) would then be exposed to revenge by the tribe of the person killed. Bloodshed unleashed a chain of reprisals with interminable vendettas governed by the law of an eye for an eye. Nevertheless, two kinds of *ghazawa* coexisted, one that we have just discussed for possessions, and the other for war, in which no quarter was given. War with access to booty, along with the trading of the Meccans and the agriculture of the Medinese, was one of the possible and important sources of revenue. Muhammad himself engaged in it, while using it, however, for an objective that went beyond the traditional *ghazawa*. If he had done otherwise, he would have become just one of the many small tribal chieftains of Arabia whom history would have forgotten or noted only briefly. However, the Prophet quickly discovered the limits and contradictions of such an activity. The laws of *ghazawa* were implacable and left to the victor only a choice

5. See Qur'an 4:11.
6. Sura 4.
7. Qur'an 4:32.
8. *The Tongue of the Arabs* (Arabic), by the Tunisian lexicographer Ibn Manzur (1232–1311).

between two equally inhumane alternatives with regard to the defeated: kill the men and reduce the women (occasionally the men too) to slavery, or, if the men and women were of aristocratic origin, exchange them for a large ransom. But the question Muslims had to face was: What should be done with prisoners who declare themselves converts to Islam? Although one gains a believer, one also loses booty, which was the original aim of the enterprise.

The women took advantage of the new questions that arose to slip in their own demands. "During the pre-Islamic period, men excluded women and children from inheriting, because, they said, they did not go on raids and did not share in booty." Umm Salama, in her usual clear and concise way, formulated in a petition the essential point of women's new claim: "Messenger of God, men make war, and we do not have the right to do it although we have the right to inheritance!" In another version Umm Salama is supposed to have said: "Messenger of God, why do men make war and we do not?"

AMINA WADUD
b. 1952

Amina Wadud, a scholar, activist, and author of works examining the role of women in Islam, captured the attention of Muslims worldwide when she led mixed congregations of men and women in the ritual prayer. Wadud's speeches, actions, and writings have been controversial, and many within the Muslim community—both within the United States and abroad—have criticized her severely.

Born in Bethesda, Maryland, Amina Wadud converted to Islam at the age of twenty. After completing her PhD in 1988 at the University of Michigan, she began teaching at the International Islamic University in Malaysia, where she remained until 1992. While there, she published her most influential work, *Qur'an and Woman* (1991); the passage below is taken from its second edition. Frequently reprinted, this book has been translated into Indonesian, Turkish, Persian, and Arabic.

In *Qur'an and Woman*, Wadud sets the Qur'an as the standard of Islamic values and then measures the treatment of women in Muslim societies against the ideal it promulgates. Her central contention is that the Qur'an, while noting biological differences between men and women, teaches the ontological and spiritual equality of the sexes. As Wadud sees it, the centuries-long relegation of women to second-class roles in Islamic societies is a function of patriarchal social practices that are antithetical to the Islam of the Qur'an.

Wadud employs what she calls a "holistic" method of reading, which seeks to understand the Qur'an in its totality. She criticizes traditional exegesis for producing piecemeal commentaries: in explaining the Qur'an verse by verse, they engage only a few topics broadly—such as grammar, rhetoric, or law—while ignoring the Qur'an's larger themes of justice and equality. In addition, she argues that traditional exegetes were male and reproduced the patriarchy of their societies, wittingly or not, in their interpretations. Another feature of her holistic reading is that she distinguishes between those qur'anic texts that are specific in their application and those that provide guiding principles. For example, Qur'an 2:228 states that men are given a "degree" over women. Since this "degree" is mentioned in the context of divorce, Wadud contends that the verse means only that men can more easily obtain a divorce than women, and not as most commentaries have held—that men as a gender are superior to women. A final salient feature of Wadud's exegetical method is her notion that reforms instituted by the Qurʾan have long-term goals that could not be realized at the time of its revelation. For example, Wadud points to reforms that sought to improve the conditions of women to argue that the Qurʾan intends that women's and men's testimony be weighted equally and that inheritances be distributed equitably among family members, although it does not explicitly command either outcome.

Wadud's exegesis prompts her activism. Though not the first woman to do so, she garnered international headlines in March 2005 by leading a mixed congregation of men and women in ritual prayer at a church in New York City. Despite harsh criticism, Wadud defended her decision, declaring, "The issue of gender equality is a very important one in Islam, and Muslims have unfortunately used highly restrictive interpretations of history to move backward." Speaking before the service began, she affirmed, "With this prayer service we are moving forward. This single act is symbolic of the possibilities within Islam."

PRONOUNCING GLOSSARY

khilafah: *chi-la´-fuh* (guttural *ch*)
sharʿiah: *sha-ree´-uh*
tawhid: *taw-heed´* (heavy *h*)

FROM QUR'AN AND WOMAN

From *Preface*

GENDER DISCOURSE AND ISLAM

The process of identity formation is pivotal in current Islamic resurgence. As more women take part in this resurgence, increasing attention has been paid to gender in identity formation. Issues of women in society, economics, politics, or spirituality play an important part in the Muslim goal in modernity to preserve the past and benefit appropriately from the new. Before new ideas can be accepted, their legitimacy within Islam must be clearly established. Establishing legitimacy is most often achieved by drawing an analogy between the new idea and the preserved tradition as exemplified in cultural practices, *shariʿah* law, or text. The textual method is vicarious and haphazard because similar passages can yield divergent conclusions—depending on the point of view of the reader.

Not unlike all premodern and modern discourses, the underlying presumption that the male person is the normative human being restricts women from full consideration in the construction of ethical-spiritual and social-political postulates in Islamic thought. Because women were nearly completely excluded from the foundational discourse that established the paradigmatic basis for what it means to be Muslim, they are often relegated to the role of subject without agency. Are women the same as men; different or distinct from; alike and unequal to; or unlike and equal to? Each of these questions rests on a single rhetorical flaw—that women must be measured against men—that inadvertently reinforces the erroneous notion that men are the standard-bearers, which, by extension, means that only men are fully human.

In modern and postmodern discourses about Islam, extensive attention has been given to how women have been reduced from full humanity and moral agency, or *khilafah*, to subjects. However, the scarcity of works that challenge the underlying paradigmatic basis of Islamic thought for the absence of gender, as a principal category of thought and as an aspect of analysis in the articulation of Islamic ideals, could not be more glaring. Most of the books and articles concerned with issues of Islam and gender are dedicated to the role of women in society, culture, or history. Although *Qur'an and Woman* assumes the basis of knowledge to be the one established in the Qur'an, it contributes to the post-colonial, postmodern field of Islamic studies by its focus on gender as a category of thought—not just a subject for discourse.

HERMENEUTICS AND METHODOLOGY

Since the publication of *Qur'an and Woman*, my interests in interpretive methodologies have increased. I am hoping to explicate certain underlying hermeneutical assumptions about the significance of female inclusive exegesis, which ultimately will need to be incorporated into the main corpus of Qur'anic exegesis. In what ways does this female inclusive reading augment the exegetical process as previously understood? Although some areas have been clarified for me in my research, other questions remain unanswered. Throughout this line of inquiry, I continue to see the significance of gender in interpretative methodology.

My criticism of the limitations in the atomistic approach of almost all traditional exegesis remains. To help move beyond its limitations, I propose a hermeneutics of *tawhid*[1] to emphasize how the unity of the Qur'an permeates all its parts. Rather than simply applying meanings to one verse at a time, with occasional references to various verses elsewhere, a framework may be developed that includes a systematic rationale for making correlations and sufficiently exemplifies the full impact of Qur'anic coherence.

One goal of a hermeneutics of *tawhid* would be to address the dynamics between Qur'anic universals and particulars. Above all, the Qur'an seeks to establish a universal basis of moral guidance. Certainly, the circumstance of seventh-century Arabia sets the backdrop for the Qur'an and its goal of universal guidance. Later generations of Muslims must consider how the text was restricted by the particulars of that time. For example, the language of that context is used, not to make Arabic sacred, but to make the revelation comprehensible. It is unfathomable that the Lord of all the worlds is not potentially multilingual. Meanwhile, since every term in Arabic—whether referring to inanimate or animate things, physical or metaphysical realms or dimensions—is expressed in gendered terms, some ideas continue to include gender markers and others ignore them. How can ideas that transcend gender be expressed in a gendered language? To lead the reader to ungendered spheres of reality is complicated by the limitations of language.

1. Oneness (Arabic), a term used in Muslim theological texts to emphasize monotheism and deny any notion that might impugn the oneness of God. In borrowing the term to describe her exegesis, Wadud emphasizes that to be properly understood, the Qur'an must be viewed as a single whole.

Except in the case of formal rituals—which are necessarily invariant—for any part of the text to be deemed universal, it cannot require mere mimicry. Seventh-century Arabian particulars in the Qurʾan should be restricted to that context unless a broader basis of understanding and application can be developed from them. In the social, political, and moral arena, a reciprocal relationship must be made between particular historical or cultural practices during the time of the Qurʾanic revelation as reflections of the underlying principles and the diverse reflections of those principles in other historical and cultural contexts. This is one reasonable proposal for the continual following of textual guidance.

Systematic attention to the relationship between universals and particulars would also bear on our understanding the Qurʾan's usage of particular terms, since it establishes its own paradigmatic field of meaning for key terms. Both the whole revelation and the particular context in which each term is used bear on its meaning. Each term should therefore be examined on the basis of its language act, syntactical structures, and textual context in order to more fully determine the parameters of meaning. This requires a dual process: keeping words in context and referring to the larger textual development of the term.

One way this focus on languaging[2] is relevant to the issue of women is that the text establishes a trajectory of social, political, and moral possibilities, but does not articulate them definitively. The textual precedent for this sense of momentum is explicit with regard to the drinking of wine. For a complex social, cultural, and historical phenomenon like slavery, for example, following only the explicit references in the Qurʾan would never have led to the eradication of it as an institution. The Qurʾanic ethos of equity, justice, and human dignity, however, might contribute to such a reform.

In the area of gender, conservative thinkers read explicit Qurʾanic reforms of existing historical and cultural practices as the literal and definitive statement on these practices for all times and places. What I am calling for is a reading that regards those reforms as establishing precedent for continual development toward a just social order. A comprehensive just social order not only emphasizes fair treatment of women, but also includes women as agents, responsible for contributing to all matters of relevance to human society. Despite so much Qurʾanic evidence about the significance of women, gender reform in Muslim society has been most stubbornly resisted.

My concerns for *what* the Qurʾan says, *how* it says it, what is said *about* the Qurʾan, and *who* is doing the saying, have been supplemented by a recent concern over what is left *unsaid*: the ellipses and silences. I have been developing certain linguistic measures for constructing categories of thought that although not actually articulated in the Qurʾan can be deduced from existing structural forms. By noting how and where the Qurʾan uses certain grammatical constructs, some light might be shed on a more subtle encoding for the construction of its trajectories.

2. The term is taken from Alton Becker's *Beyond Translation* (Ann Arbor: University of Michigan Press, 1995), in which he distinguished "language for the code image" from "languaging . . . the view that combines shaping, storing, retrieving and communicating knowledge into one open-ended process" or to the more diffuse "context shaping" (p. 9) [Wadud's note].

Verbs, gerunds, and participles in Arabic are built on a trilateral root with strictly established rules. Potentially, every Arabic word can have each of these possible forms. Some are never used in the Qur'an. Some were not common in the language. Are certain constructs preferred in different textual circumstances? The Qur'an might use only the verbal noun of a word and never its verb, or vice versa. Does the very occurrence of a noun form have implications that a verb form might not? Although both the verb and verbal noun are used in some cases, are they equally interchangeable? Which have been emphasized in Qur'anic interpretation? Are there "do" passages and "be" passages? How do various Qur'anic passages on similar themes correspond to each other? Are there passages that set up hierarchies of meaning through which we can analyze increased parameters of meaning on specific themes, despite the absence of explicit mention in the text? How much is left unsaid? How many forms are excluded absolutely? Can we fill in the gaps of these exclusions by charting the inclusions along the lines of some schematic chart?

My continued philological interest in the subtleties of the Qur'an and in the depth of exegetical analysis has led me to emphasize reading for the construction of Qur'anic ambiguities. For example, how is one thing brought into relief and another ignored, since both effect textual coherence? What can be learned through the relationship between foreground and background in the Qur'an? In detailing these aspects of textual analysis, I hope to articulate ways of reading for gender and then to advocate how such a reading is central to comprehensive Qur'anic analysis.

Such a Qur'anic analysis might facilitate a movement away from preoccupations with particulars and focus on policy-oriented hierarchy and power-based dichotomies such as have characterized traditional and neoconservative, mainstream interpretation. A female-centered or female-inclusive reading might finally lend itself to more that just syntactical structures, legal articulations, and historical renditions and help to weave a symbiotic relationship between the Qur'an and the reader, as indicated by the Qur'an's own statement about believers who read the text and "their eyes over-flow with tears" (5:83). The Qur'an is not just descriptive; it is prescriptive, with a goal of achieving some response from readers as part of the process of surrender and belief. This responsive efficacy increases in proportion to the complexity and totality of human motivation, which extends beyond mere rational cognition to include emotive impact.

One simple indicator of these Qur'anic aesthetics would be found in a reading that validates the female voice and brings it out of the shadows. If the way we view the text has been predominantly articulated on the basis of male experiences and through the male psyche, then visions that respond to the male-center of being would have been considered in greatest detail, over and above any differences, inherent or contrived, in the female-center of experience. The extent to which women are seen as distinct from men, therefore, implies the necessity for a female-centered consideration of the Qur'an as the only means by which that distinctiveness will be justly considered in the formulas of basic Islamic identity.

NEGOTIATING RELIGIOUS PLURALISM

NURCHOLISH MADJID
1939–2005

The beneficiary of a strong traditional Islamic education in addition to a thoroughly modern one, the Indonesian scholar Nurcholish Madjid questioned the contemporary applicability of much of the received canon of medieval Islamic thought. Though loved by many in Indonesia, particularly its middle-class professionals, he was a somewhat controversial figure—especially among more conservative Muslims who refused to accept his insistence on subsuming Indonesia's Christian, Hindu, and Buddhist minorities under the qur'anic category of "People of the Book" (in Arabic, *ahl al-kitab*).

Born in East Java, Madjid spent his early years attending a secular school during the mornings and his father's Islamic school (in Arabic, *madrasa*; in Bahasa, *pesantren*) in the afternoon. He then enrolled in a series of Islamic boarding schools. The school from which he would eventually graduate, located in Gontor, East Java, was fairly advanced: it taught secular subjects such as economics and history, presented Arabic as a modern language, and used both Arabic and English as languages of instruction. To further his religious and secular studies, in 1960 Madjid enrolled in the State Institute of Islamic Studies (IAIN) in Jakarta—one of several universities that relied on modern pedagogy to provide a religious and secular education for those seeking a career in the religious administration of Indonesia. Working in IAIN's Department of Arabic Literature and the History of Islamic Thought, he graduated in 1968 having written a thesis titled "The Qur'an: Arabic in Language, Universal in Significance."

At IAIN, Madjid was active in Muslim student political organizations that had national power and international connections. He himself came to national prominence: he was elected the general chairman of the Islamic Student Organization (HMI), serving two terms (1966–69, 1969–71), and he made a number of statements advocating that Muslim political parties, which he described as moribund and ineffectual, cease to participate in Indonesian politics. Most famously, in a speech on January 3, 1970, he proclaimed, "Islam, yes! Islamic parties? No!" He argued that Islam in Indonesia needed to be revitalized and reconceptualized, in an approach that did not involve applying the Qur'an and hadith literally or turning Indonesia into a Muslim state. His comments immediately drew fire from members of the established Muslim political parties, who viewed them as a betrayal. They were welcomed, however, by the New Order administration of General Suharto, who had come to power in 1966 and sought to marginalize the influence of Indonesia's Islamic parties.

After his graduation Madjid taught at IAIN, directed a magazine devoted to revitalizing Islam, collaborated with organizations that sought to present a new vision of Islam, and continued to publish his thoughts on a reformed Islam. In 1976 two professors from the University of Chicago, Fazlur Rahman and Leonard Binder, whom he had met in Jakarta, invited him to the university to take part in their seminar on Islam and social change; he impressed them enough that in 1978 he returned to the United States and entered the PhD program at Chicago. His dissertation, completed in 1984 under the supervision of Fazlur Rahman, was titled "Ibn Taymiyya on *Kalām* and *Falsafa* (A Problem of Reason and Revelation in

Islam)." He argued that Ibn Taymiyya (1263–1328; see above), often esteemed by Muslim political parties in Indonesia as a champion of conservativism, should also be understood as a reformer.

Upon returning to Indonesia, Madjid resumed his previous activities and, at the urging of like-minded friends, focused his efforts on presenting a renewed vision of Islam to Indonesia's rising middle class. With the help of his colleagues and friends, he set up an extremely successful organization, Paramandia, devoted to disseminating reformist thought throughout Indonesian society. In addition to publishing Madjid's works, it hosted a well-received lecture series that showcased Indonesia's foremost intellectuals, speaking on religious topics. The format of these lectures contributed to their popularity: following the remarks of the invited speaker, Madjid would present his response, which then flowed into open, uncensored discussion involving the audience.

For Madjid, Islam fundamentally involves a belief in God and an attitude of surrender and submission to him. Beyond these essentials, Madjid proposed that the received tradition of Islamic thought—whether legal, theological, or spiritual—must always be reassessed and reevaluated to examine its contemporary relevance. Undergirding this reassessment is Madjid's contention that the laws drawn from the Qur'an can be understood only in their historical context. That is, what is important about the Qur'an is not the laws themselves but rather the larger reasons behind particular qur'anic commandments—reasons that are eternal and indicate what God desires. Madjid therefore rejected the traditional view, held by most Muslim scholars, that the historical context of the Qur'an should matter little to those deriving rulings from it.

Madjid roots his view of qur'anic interpretation in the practice of Muhammad's Companions themselves. As an example, he notes the case of ʿUmar (ca. 586–644), the second caliph, who, following the conquest of Syria, forbade the distribution of the newly captured territory among the conquering soldiers. This decree contradicted the literal meaning of Qur'an 8:41, which explicitly states that the spoils of war should be divided among the conquerors. ʿUmar refused to do so, according to Madjid, because he realized that dividing up the newly conquered land would only create economic distress and social chaos in the region—results that were both contrary to the general message of the Qur'an. According to Madjid, ʿUmar was willing to act against the letter of the law, as interpreted by some Muslims of his own time, to uphold what he believed to be the Qur'an's true message. Reading the Qur'an in this way, Madjid argued for changes in Islamic law, including in the punishment for apostasy and the rules surrounding inheritance.

The following text from an article by Madjid originally published in 2003 makes an interesting argument for the simultaneous plurality and oneness of revealed religions. Finding the essence of religion in human submission to God—what Muslims would call *islam*—Madjid sees a core commonality underlying the diverse expressions of belief and practice. He further connects political practices of religious freedom and tolerance to this core commonality, suggesting that "religious freedom in the modern times is a consistent advanced development of that of the classical Islam."

PRONOUNCING GLOSSARY

Aelia: *ay´-lee-uh*
ʿAbd al-Rahmân ibn ʿAwf: *abd al-rah-mahn´* (heavy *h*) *ibn awf*
Ahl al-Kitâb: *ahl* (light *h*) *al-ki-tab´*
ʿAmr ibn al-ʿÂs: *ahmr ibn al-ahs´*
Bayt al-Maqdis: *bayt al-maq´-dis*
Hijâz: *hi-jaz´* (heavy *h*)
Hijrîya: *hij-ree´-yuh*
Ibn Taymîyah: *ibn tay-mee´-yuh*
al-ikhlâs: *al-ich-lahs´* (guttural *ch*)
al-islâm: *al-is-lam´*
al-istislâm: *al-is-tis-lam´*
al-inqiyâd: *al-in-qee-yad´*
jizyah: *jiz´-yuh*

kalimah sawâʾ: *ka-lee-muh sa-wa´*
Khâlid ibn al-Walîd: *cha´-lid* (guttural *ch*) *ibn al-wah-leed´*
Muʿâwiyah ibn Abî Sufyân: *moo-aw´-ee-yuh ibn a-bee soof-yan´*
Muhammad ibn ʿAbd Allâh: *moo-ham´-mad* (heavy *h*) *ibn abd-al-lah´*
mustaʾmin: *moos´-ta-min*
Pancasila: *pan-ka-see´-luh*
al-Quds: *al-quds´*
sharîʿah: *sha-ree´-yuh*
tawhîd: *taw-heed´*
ʿUmar ibn al-Khattâb: *oh´-mar ibn al-chaht-tahb* (guttural *ch*)
Wahhâbî: *wa-ha´-bee*

FROM ISLAMIC FAITH AND THE PROBLEM OF PLURALISM: RELATIONS AMONG THE BELIEVERS

Almost all universal religions, particularly those with a great number of followers (Islam, Christianity, Hinduism and Buddhism), have adherents in Indonesia. This makes Indonesia, as Indonesians themselves usually acknowledge, a plural society. Also, Indonesians often proudly refer to the high degree of the religious tolerance they have. Given this situation, they even consider themselves unique among the nations in this world. And one—if not the most important—fundamental factor that is considered to contribute to this positive situation is *Pancasila* (Five Principles),[1] the ideology of the nation. . . .

Actually, the plurality in Indonesian society is not unique. Particularly during the modern era, in practice there is no society that is not unique in terms of having different groups of believers (consisting of a great number of religious followers), except in certain cities like the Vatican, Mecca, and Medina. Even in Islamic countries in the Arab World, which were formerly the centers of Christianity and Judaism, the significant religious minorities of Christians and Jews have remained there up until now. In fact, those countries developed into the countries in which Muslims became the majority citizen, only after they had undergone a long natural process of Islamization, which took place for centuries. Though it appears that the Arab Muslims managed to liberate those countries when they brought Islam with them, what they actually carried out was socio-political reforms. One of the most important reforms was the affirmation of religious freedom, instead of the compulsory conversion of non-Muslim subjects into Islam (which would certainly oppose the basic principles of Islam).

The only exclusivist policy is that non-Muslims are not allowed to live in the compounds of Mecca and Medina (Hijâz[2]). This policy, which was initiated by ʿUmar ibn al-Khattâb,[3] was expanded by the Wahhâbî Saudis, who established modern Saudi Arabia. Apart from these two compounds, however, Christian and Jewish minorities still can be found in almost all Islamic countries. This can be explained not only from the historical and sociological points of view, but also more fundamentally from the perspective of Islamic doctrine. It shows the consistency of Muslim societies in practicing the Islamic teachings on religious plurality.

1. The Indonesian state philosophy; as written into the preamble of the 1945 constitution, the principles are belief in one God, just and civilized humanity, Indonesian unity, democracy, and social justice.
2. The western region of the Arabian Peninsula; it borders the Red Sea and contains Mecca and Medina.
3. The second caliph (ca. 586–644); under his leadership, the lands under Muslim control expanded greatly.

Concepts of the Oneness and the Truth

Deeply rooted in the consciousness of the Muslim worldview is that Islam is a universal religion, a religion for everyone. It is true that this awareness also belongs to believers of other religions (the Jews deny the universal validity of Christianity and Islam, and Christians deny the universal validity of Judaism and Islam). However, it is only fair to say that for Muslims, this awareness bears with it a socio-religious attitude that is unique, which is very different from the attitudes of other religious believers, except since the beginning of the twentieth century.

Without depreciating the depth of Muslim faith regarding the truth of their belief (an attitude that will necessarily be held by a believer of any religious system), the unique attitude of Muslim believers in relation to other religions is characterized by tolerance, freedom, transparency, justice, fairness and honesty. To date, these principles have been quite clearly observable in the contemporary Muslim societies, but quite phenomenally so in the classical Muslims (*salaf*). The basic principles are derived from teaching points in the Holy Book which explain that the universal Truth is naturally one, though the physical manifestations of it may vary. Additionally, anthropology explains that in the beginning man was one, because man held onto the truth, which is only one. But later this view started to differ because many interpretations of the oneness of the truth developed. These differences became sharper because of certain vested interests, that is, the desire of certain groups to succeed at the expense of others. The unity of the origin of human beings is visualized in God's saying: "All mankind were once but one single community, and only later did they begin to hold divergent views," and His saying:

> All mankind were once one single community; then God raised up the prophets as bearers of glad tidings and of warnings, and with them revealed the Scripture with the truth, that it might judge between mankind concerning that wherein they differed. And only those unto whom (the Scripture) was given differed concerning it, after clear proofs had come unto them, through hatred one of another. And God by His leave guided those who believe unto the truth of that concerning which they differed: for God guides unto a straight path him that wills [to be guided].[4]

The starting point of the oneness of the universal truth is the concept of God as One or *tawhîd* (which literally means "to believe in One"). From the beginning of their existence, humans professed *tawhîd*, which is symbolized both in Adam and by his faith. Adam is considered the first human and the first prophet and messenger on earth by the Semitic religions (Judaism, Christianity, and Islam). * * *

The most important consequence of pure *tawhîd* is the complete submission or self-surrender to God the One, without doing the same for any other purpose, object, or person except Him. This is *al-islâm*, the essence of all true religions. The following is an explanation by Ibn Taymîyah,[5] a famous figure of Islamic reform:

4. Qur'an 2:213.
5. Ibn Taymiyya (1263–1328; see above), a noted Hanbali jurist and theologian.

> The (Arabic) word "al-islâm" contains the meaning of the words "al-istislâm" (self-surrender) and "al-inqiyâd" (submission, obedience) and also contains the meaning of the word "al-ikhlâs" (sincerity). . . . Therefore it is necessary in Islam to submit oneself to God the One, leaving behind submission to others. This is the essence of our saying, "There is no god but God" (*lâ ilâh illa 'l-Lâh*). If one submits to God, while at the same time submitting himself to others, then he is a polytheist.

Therefore, it is emphasized in the Qur'ân that the tasks of God's messengers are to deliver the teachings of God the Almighty or *tawhîd* as well as the teachings regarding man's obligation to obey God alone:

> We never sent any apostle before you [O, Muhammad] without having revealed to him that there is no god save Me, therefore worship Me [alone].[6]

Since the principles taught by the messengers and the prophets are the same, the followers of them are one single community. In other words, the concept of the unity of the basic teachings lays a foundation for the concept of the unity of prophecy, which then brings about the concept of one faithful community. This is affirmed by God's saying:

> Verily, this community of yours is one single community, since I am the Sustainer of you all. Therefore worship Me [alone].[7]

It has been mentioned by Ibn Taymîyah that the word *al-islâm* carries the meaning of the words *al-istislâm* (self-surrender) and *al-inqiyâd* (submission, obedience). From the formal aspect of religious obligation, this is expressed in the act of worshiping nothing but the One, that is, God. Briefly and in conclusion, *al-islâm* teaching in the generic sense is the core and the essence of all religions of the prophets and the messengers. Ibn Taymîyah states:

> Because the origin of religion, that is *al-islâm*, is one, even though its *sharîʿah* varies, the Prophet Muhammad says in valid hadiths, "Our religion and the religion of the prophets is one," and "All the prophets are paternal brothers, [even though] their mothers are different," and "The nearest of all the people to Jesus, the son of Mary, is me."

From this perspective, we begin to understand better the description in the Qur'ân that to hold on to any religion except *al-islâm* or to devote oneself without total submission and surrender to God is not genuine and is therefore illegitimate. What I would like to argue here is that although someone may be socially dubbed "Islamic" or "Muslim," if their attitude is not *al-islâm*, they are categorized religiously as ingenuine and are denied legitimacy. Affirmation of this in the Qur'ân is found in the famous saying of God: "*The only true faith in God's sight is* al-islâm."[8] For a comparative study regarding the meaning of Islâm, the following is the complete translation of the verse by Muhammad Asad, one of the best-known modern commentators on the Qur'ân:

> Behold, the only [true] religion in the sight of God is (man's) self-surrender unto Him (*al-islâm*); and those who were vouchsafed

6. Qur'an 21:25.
7. Qur'an 21:92; 23:52.
8. Qur'an 3:19.

> revelation aforetime took, out of mutual jealousy, to divergent views [on this point] only after knowledge [thereof] had come unto them. But as for him who denies the truth of God's messages—behold, God is swift in reckoning![9]

If we look at the above verse carefully, the implication is that the former communities who received scriptures from God through His messengers and prophets, namely, those were technically called *Ahl al-Kitâb* (People of the Book), did know and understand that the core of the true religion is the act of total submission to God, which is the original meaning of the Arabic word *islâm.* On this matter, Muhammad Asad writes:

> Most of the classical commentators are of the opinion that the people referred to are followers of the Bible, or of parts of it—i.e., the Jews and the Christians. It is, however, highly probable that this passage bears a wider import and relates to all communities which base their views on a revealed scripture, extant in a partially corrupted form, with parts of it entirely lost.
>
> . . . All these communities at first subscribed to the doctrine of God's oneness and held that man's self-surrender to Him (*islâm* in its original connotation) is the essence of all true religion. Their subsequent divergences were an outcome of sectarian pride and mutual exclusiveness.[1]

Religious Plurality

Given the principles above, it can be argued that the Qur'ân essentially teaches the concept of religious plurality. To be sure, this does not necessarily mean an affirmation of the truth of all religions in their actual practices (in this respect, many of the actual religious practices of the Muslims are not correct because they basically contradict the teachings of the Qur'ân, such as their practice of deifying other human beings or creatures, whether they are dead or alive). However, the teaching of religious plurality emphasizes the basic understanding that all religions are free to be practiced, yet the believers, individually or collectively, have to be responsible for their practices. This attitude can be interpreted as an expectation of all religions: because—as mentioned above—all religions initially upheld the same principle, that is, the necessity of man to submit totally to God the One, those religions whether due to their internal dynamism or their encounter with one another, would eventually find their own original truth, leading them all to "one meeting point," "a common platform," or using the Qur'ânic term, "*kalîmah sawâ*," as indicated by one of the God's commands to the Prophet Muhammad:

> Say: "People of the Book, let us come to an agreement (*kalîmah sawâ'*): that we will worship none but God, that we will associate none with Him, and that none of us shall set up mortals as deities besides God."[2]

For a comparison, the following is Asad's translation of the verse:

9. Qur'an 3:19, translated in Muhammad Asad, *The Message of the Qur'an* (Gibraltar: Dar al-Andalus, 1984), 69. Asad (1900–1992), born a Jew named Leopold Weiss in what is now Ukraine, was a convert to Islam.

1. Asad, *Message*, 69 nn. 12, 13.

2. Qur'an 3:64.

> Say: "O followers of earlier revelations! Come unto that tenet which we and you hold in common (*kalîmah sawâʾ*): that we shall worship none but God, and that we shall not ascribe divinity to aught beside Him, and that we shall not take human beings for our lords beside God."[3]

Because of the parallelism between the attitude to "worship none but God" and the concept of *al-islâm* in terms of its generic meaning explained by Ibn Taymîyah (that is, before *islâm* becomes the proper noun for the Prophet Muhammad's religion), thus the meeting point for all religions is *al-islâm* in that generic sense. In other words, the total and genuine submission to God the One, without association to anything else, is the only correct and true religious act. Thus others are denied and hence the affirmation in the Qurʾân:

> He that chooses a religion other than *islâm* (self-surrender to God), it will not be accepted from him and in the world to come he will surely be among the losers.[4]

* * *

The principles discussed above[5] serve as the basis of a great number of political policies of religious freedom in the Islamic world. The principles of religious freedom in the classical Muslim society are similar to modern ideals. It is even not exaggerating to suggest that religious freedom in the modern times is a consistent advanced development of that of the classical Islam. An example of the practices of religious freedom during the classical period of Islam was reflected in an agreement between ʿUmar Ibn al-Khattâb and the people of Jerusalem or Bayt al-Maqdis, al-Quds (it was also called Aelia), after that holy city had been liberated by Muslim soldiers. The following is a complete translation of the agreement:

> In the name of God, the Most Compassionate, the Most Merciful.
>
> This is the guarantee of safety granted by the servant of God, ʿUmar, the Commander of the believers, to the people of Aelia (al-Quds):
>
> He guarantees their personal safety, and the safety of their belongings, their churches and crosses—whether they are in a good or a bad condition—and for all their co-religionists! Their churches shall not be seized or damaged, and nothing shall be taken from their churches or from their property, nor shall their crosses or even the smallest possession be removed from their churches. They shall not be harassed because of their religion, and none of them shall be harmed. No Jew will be allowed to live with them in Aelia.
>
> The people of Aelia will have to pay a poll-tax (*jizyah*)[6] as the inhabitants of other cities (in Syria) do. They have the authority to expel from Aelia the Romans and brigands (*al-Lasût*). Those (of the Romans) who leave shall be granted safety for themselves and their belongings until they reach a safe destination, and those among them who want to stay shall be safe on the condition that they pay

3. Asad, *Message*, 76.
4. Qurʾan 3:85.
5. That is, plurality, openness, respect, and tolerance.
6. A tax levied on non-Muslim subjects of a Muslim state.

> the *jizyah* like the people of Aelia. If any of the people of Aelia want to leave with the Romans, take their belongings with them, and leave behind their churches and crosses, they and their churches and crosses shall be protected until they reach their own place of safety (Byzantium). Those among the local inhabitants (the Syrians) who have been in the city (Aelia) since before the war (i.e. the war in which Syria was liberated by the Muslim soldiers—NM) shall have the option of either staying on condition that they pay the *jizyah* like the people of Aelia or if they so wish, they shall be allowed to live with the Romans or go back to their original homes. No tax shall be collected from them until they have gathered their harvest (i.e. they are able to pay it—NM).
>
> This writing is placed under the guarantee of God and the covenant of the Prophet, of the caliphs, and of the believers, on condition that the people of Aelia pay their due tax.
>
> Witnessed by: Khâlid ibn al-Walîd, Amr ibn al-ʿAss, ʿAbd al-Rahmân ibn ʿAwf, Muʿâwiyah ibn Abî Sufyān. Written in the year 15 (Hijrîyah).[7]

The agreement between ʿUmar and the people of Jerusalem was actually consistent with the spirit of the agreement that the Prophet Muhammad had made with the people of Medina, including the Jews, immediately after he returned from Mecca during the Hijrah (migration). This agreement was later known as the Medina Charter. Modern scholars are very impressed with it because it is the first official political document that put forward the principles of religious and economic freedoms. Moreover, the Prophet made a particular agreement that guarantees the freedom and safety of the Christians at all times and in all places. In order to get a brief overview of the agreement, the following is a quote from the first part of the agreement made by the Prophet:

> In the name of God, the Most Compassionate, the Most Merciful, and from Whom comes all help. This agreement was written by Muhammad ibn ʿAbd Allâh, the messenger of God.
>
> To all Christians,
>
> This is the document for humankind written by Muhammad ibn ʿAbd Allâh, as a bearer of glad tidings and of warnings, as a holder of God's trust for His creatures, so that man shall have no reason against God after (the coming of) God's apostles, as God is the Most Exalted and the Most Wise.
>
> This is written for the followers of Islam and those who adopt Christianity from the East and the West, near and far, Arabs and non-Arabs, the known and the unknown, a document made by him (the Prophet) as a covenant for them (the Christians).
>
> Whoever violates the agreement in this document, deviates from it, and disobeys what has been stipulated, then spoils God's agreement, breaks His covenant, insults His religion, which will result

7. *The History of al-Ṭabarī,* vol. 12, *The Battle of al-Qādisiyyah and the Conquest of Syria and Palestine*, trans. Yohanan Friedmann (Albany: State University of New York Press, 1992), 191–92. Al-Tabari (ca. 839–923; see above) is among the earliest historians to preserve a copy of the pacts made between ʿUmar and the groups that he conquered. Jerusalem surrendered in 637 C.E.

> in a curse upon him, whether he is a ruler or not among the Muslims and the Believers.
>
> If a priest or a traveler takes shelter in a mountain or in a valley or in a cave or in a building or in a desert or in a church, I am behind them to protect them from any hostility towards them, by my soul, my supporters, the holders of my religion, my followers, as they (the Christians) are my citizens and under my protection.
>
> I will protect them against anything that displeases them according to the obligations placed upon the supporters of this covenant, that is, to pay the *jizyah* (the poll-tax), except those who are *musta'min* (i.e. those who are treated as non-residents, and therefore are exempt from paying tax—NM).
>
> They (the Christians) shall not be forced or coerced. There shall be no change to their buildings, or to their monasteries, or to their shrines, or to their surroundings. No building within their synagogues or churches shall be demolished, nor shall the property of their churches be taken to build mosques or houses for Muslims. Whoever commits such things breaks God's covenant and opposes His messenger.[8]

Such is the way the Prophet Muhammad provided the example of how to live life according to one of the Islamic ideals, which is brotherhood among human beings with faith in God. As mentioned above, the Muslims have the obligation to bring as many people as possible to God's way in order to achieve their ideals. However, acts should be in accord with the soul and the spirit of the ideals of brotherhood; hence God Himself reminded the Prophet and all of the believers that to force others to accept the truth is not right. The faithful have been commanded to accept the plurality of human society as a reality as well as a challenge.

8. For a translation of the charter or Constitution of Medina, see the selection above from Ibn Hisham (d. 833), whose biography of Muhammad preserves the account of this document by Ibn Ishaq (d. 767).

FETHULLAH GÜLEN
b. 1941

Fethullah Gülen is a Turkish scholar who has created an international outreach operation to promote his own understanding of Islam. His many publications and public appearances have attracted an extensive network of supporters.

Born in eastern Turkey, he attended both religious and secular schools as a child and was tutored in the study of Islam by his parents. His mother guided him and the women of their village in memorization of the Qur'an, while his father, an imam, taught him Arabic and introduced him to the world of classical Islamic thought. Gülen read extensively and also absorbed the works of more recent Muslim thinkers such as the Indian theologian Shah Wali Allah (1703–1762; see above) and the Kurdish-Turkish scholar Saʿid Nursi (ca. 1876–1960).

Gülen received a government-approved preacher's license in 1958 and in 1966 was transferred to a mosque in Turkey's third-largest province, Izmir. There, he started to draw a following with his message that Islam emphasized universal values shared by all of humanity and was thoroughly compatible with modernity. He found a base of support among prosperous Turks, whom he inspired to begin building a network of institutions, including primary and secondary schools, universities, media outlets, businesses, and public interest groups.

Though the particular focus of individual schools founded by members of Gülen's network may differ, they are open to anyone (not just Muslims), emphasize tolerance for all, and focus on academic subjects rather than on religious indoctrination. Gülen's supporters have founded schools where Muslim and Christian students can study peacefully together in nearby regions such as Azerbayjan and the Balkans and in distant locales like the Philippines. In Pakistan, they are an option for parents who wish to provide their children with an education that is rigorous and modern without being completely secular.

Gülen's Islam emphasizes morality, promotes tolerance, encourages dialogue among all faith communities, and embraces forgiveness, love, and compassion for all. He finds support for his presentation in the Qur'an, in the practice of Muhammad, and in the classical intellectual tradition. Because his message is deliberately apolitical, it poses no threat to the state's authority—a significant reason for his success in Turkey. Nonetheless, his commitment to interfaith communication, such as his 1998 meeting with Pope John Paul II at the Vatican, has sometimes been criticized by both committed secularists and Islamist groups. Secularists argued that he was encroaching on state authority by meeting the pope without the government's permission; conservative Muslims considered visiting a non-Muslim religious leader an affront to Islam. Finally, Gülen, while acknowledging the causes of terrorism, has unequivocally condemned terrorist acts and declared that "a terrorist cannot be a Muslim and a Muslim cannot be a terrorist."

In the following selection Gulen draws a distinction between what he considers to be the fundamental principles of Islam (peace, love, forgiveness, and tolerance) and secondary elements (execution, exile, and war) that are situation and circumstance dependent. The distinction enables him to advocate constructive dialogue among adherents of different religions when conducted in good faith on both sides. But Gülen warns that a certain degree of care is required: "Being merciful to a cobra means being unjust to the people the cobra has bitten."

PRONOUNCING GLOSSARY

Abu Sufyan: *a-boo soof-yan´*
Al-Anam: *al-an-ahm´*
Al-Ankabut: *al-ahn-ka-boot´*
Al-Baqara: *al-bah-qa-ruh*
Al-Furqan: *al-fur-qahn´*
Al-Imran: *al-im-rahn´*
Al-Isra: *al-is-rah´*
Al-Jathiya: *al-ja´-thee-yuh*
Al-Mumtahana: *al-mum-ta´-ha-na* (heavy *h*)
Al-Qasas: *al-qah´-sus*
An-Nisa: *an-ni-sa´*
Bediüzzaman: *be-dee-uh-za-man´*
Bi'r Al-Maunah: *bir al-ma-oo´-nuh*
Habibullah: *ha-beeb´-ul-lah´* (heavy *h*)
Kaʿba: *kah´-buh*
Madina: *ma-dee´-nuh*
Makka: *mak´-kuh*
Yunus Emre: *yoo´-nus em´-re*
Zahiris: *zah´-hi-rees*

FROM TOWARD A GLOBAL CIVILIZATION OF LOVE AND TOLERANCE

Tolerance and Dialogue in the Qur'an and the Sunna

The Qur'an always accepts forgiveness and tolerance as basic principles, so much so that "the servants of the All-Merciful" are introduced in the following manner:

> And the servants of (God) the All-Merciful are those who move on the Earth in humility, and when the ignorant address them, they say: "Peace." (Al-Furqan[1] 25:63)
>
> When they meet hollow words or unseemly behavior, they pass them by with dignity. (Al-Furqan 25:72)
>
> And when they hear vain talk, they turn away therefrom and say: "To us our deeds, and to you yours." (Al-Qasas[2] 28:55)

The general gist of these verses is that when those who have been favored with true servanthood to God encounter meaningless and ugly words or behavior they say nothing unbecoming, but rather pass by in a dignified manner. In short: "Everyone acts according to his own disposition," (Al-Isra[3] 17:84) and thus displays his or her own character. The character of heroes of tolerance is gentleness, consideration, and tolerance. When God sent Moses and Aaron to a man who claimed to possess divinity, as the Pharaoh had done, He commanded them to behave tolerantly and to speak softly (Ta Ha[4] 20:44)

The life of the Pride of Humanity, peace and blessings be upon him, was led in an orbit of forgiveness and forbearance. He even behaved in such a manner toward Abu Sufyan,[5] who persecuted him throughout his lifetime. During the conquest of Makka,[6] even though Abu Sufyan said he still was not sure about Islam, the Messenger said: "Those who take refuge in Abu Sufyan's house are safe, just as those who take refuge in the Ka'ba[7] are safe." Thus, in respect of providing refuge and safety, Abu Sufyan's house was mentioned alongside the Ka'ba. In my humble opinion, such tolerance was more valuable than if tons of gold had been given to Abu Sufyan, a man in his seventies, in whom egoism and chieftainship had become ingrained.

In addition to being commanded to take tolerance and to use dialogue as his basis while performing his duties, the Prophet was directed to those aspects in which he had things in common with the People of the Book (Jews and Christians):

> Say: "O People of the Book! Come to common terms as between us and you: that we worship none but God; that we speculate no

TRANSLATED BY Mehmet Ünal, Nagihan Haliloğlu, and Mükerrem Faniküçükmehmedoğlu.

1. The Criterion (Arabic).
2. The Story (Arabic).
3. The Night Journey (Arabic); this sura is also called Banu Isra'il, "The Children of Israel."
4. These are isolated Arabic letters. Twenty-nine suras begin with such letter combinations.
5. A Meccan leader (d. ca. 654), who headed the opposition to Muhammad before he converted to Islam.
6. That is, Mecca.
7. Literally, "the Cube," a stone shrine in Mecca that became the most important site in Islam (Muslims around the world face it when they pray).

> partners with Him; that we take not some from among ourselves for Lords other than God." (Al-Imran[8] 3:64)

In another verse, those whose hearts are exuberant with belief and love are commanded to behave with forgiveness and tolerance, even to those who do not believe in the afterlife:

> Tell those who believe to forgive those who do not look forward to the Days of God: It is for Him to recompense each people according to what they have earned. (Al-Jathiya[9] 45:14)

Those who consider themselves addressed by these verses, all devotees of love who dream of becoming true servants of God merely because they are human beings, those who have declared their faith and thereby become Muslims and performed the mandated religious duties, must behave with tolerance and forbearance and expect nothing from other people. They must take the approach of Yunus Emre:[1] not to strike those who hit them, not to respond harshly to those who curse them, and not to hold any secret grudge against those who abuse them.

Dialogue in the Muhammadan Spirit and Meaning

I do not like to make claims and I have a poor memory, but in spite of this I can recite tens of verses, one after the other, that are concerned with forgiveness, dialogue and opening one's heart to all. This demonstrates the all-embracing nature or universality of Islam.

For example, the Qur'an states, "peace is good" (An-Nisa[2] 4:128). The verse does not necessitate its being particular to a certain event, meaning or framework. The rule is general. Moreover, does not the root of the noun "Islam" express soundness, surrender, peace, safety, and trust? Then it is not possible for us to be true Muslims without fully representing and establishing these characteristics. In addition to this, underlying the meaning of this sacred name is an essence that incorporates embracing all and approaching everything with love. But if we do not approach the subject in this spirit, then we cannot be considered as having understood Islam or having made its call or having represented it.

In addition to rules that guarantee peace and security, there are also verses in the Qur'an related to attitudes that should be taken against criminals and people who cause anarchy and terror; for such people there are legal sanctions, punishments, and retaliations. However, whether regarding verses and hadiths on these subjects or their implementations, if we do not take into consideration the conditions, if we do not separate the essence from the detail and the goal from the means, if we do not evaluate the verses in the context of the situation both before and after they were revealed, then we will always arrive at false conclusions.

I can and do say that peace, love, forgiveness, and tolerance are fundamental to Islam; other things are accidental. Yet, it is necessary to give priority to basic Muslim issues according to their degree of importance. For

8. The Family of ʿImran (Arabic), usually Al-ʿImran.
9. Crouching (Arabic).
1. Esteemed Turkish poet (ca. 1238–ca. 1320), a Sufi known for his mystical verse.
2. Women (Arabic).

example, if God gives importance to love, if he has informed us that He loves those who love Him, and if he has given to the person He loved most the name "Habibullah," i.e. one who loves God and is loved by Him, then we have to take this as a fundamental principle. Rules like jihad against hypocrites and unbelievers are secondary matters that are necessitated by circumstances. Rules are tied to various reasons and conditions. If there are no such reasons, then the rules will not be enforced.

Rules regarding things like execution, exile and war have been tied to various reasons. What is essential here is explaining and conveying the principles of Islam with kind words and gentle behavior. Also, peace, justice and stability are essential in Islam, war being a by-product of circumstances and dependent on certain conditions. Unfortunately, those who ignore the essence and do so without taking into consideration the reasons for the secondary rules and regulations, those who (by reading the Qur'an in the manner of a crude kind of *Zahiris* [3]) emphasize violence—these people have not understood the rules, the reasons for them nor their source, nor have they understood Islam.

When the relevant reasons appear, of course the rules necessitated by the reasons become operative. For example, when foreign enemy armies attack our country, we will, of course, not be expected to sit passively in a corner and say to the attackers, "How nice of you to come."

Look at the world in which we find ourselves! According to some news recently reported in one of the newspapers, "bloody wars" are continuing in 56 places in the world. There are still floods of tears and blood flowing in many parts of the world. In many of these wars, some of the countries that defend democracy and human rights are on both sides. In that case, opposing war means opposing a human reality. For this reason, the moment someone touches our democratic rights and freedoms, we are, of course, going to defend ourselves and fight when necessary. But as I mentioned at the beginning, these are secondary things. The basis of Islam is peace and embracing humankind with love.

A CALL TO THE COMMON WORD

Another aspect of establishing and maintaining dialogue is the necessity of increasing the interests we have in common with other people. In fact, even if the people we talk with are Jews and Christians, this approach still should be adopted and issues that can separate us should be avoided altogether. For example, when the Qur'an calls the People of the Book, it says, "O People of the Book! Come to a word (that is) common between us and you." What is that word? "Let us not worship anything but God." Because real freedom is realized only by being saved from being someone else's slave. When someone becomes a servant of God they are rescued from being anyone else's slave. So come and let us unite on this matter. The Qur'an continues, "Let us not take some of us for Lords." (Al-Imran 3:64) What is meant here is that our primary common point is belief in God; mentioning the Messengership of Muhammad has not even been mentioned yet. In another verse: "Say to those who believe: Let them forgive those who have no hope

3. *Zahiris* approach the Qur'an and Sunna only from the perspective of their outward meaning, devoid of insight and proper perception. They are very few in number [Gülen's note].

for the afterlife." What is being said here is let those who do not believe in the afterlife and resurrection after death be forgiven, because "God only rewards or punishes a people with what they have earned," (Al-Jathiya 45:14) i.e., if someone is going to be punished, then God will punish them and this matter does not concern anyone else.

Another clear example of this issue is related in particular to our Prophet who received a mild warning from God regarding the time he prayed against some guilty pagans. According to a report, a Bedouin Arab tribe requested that the Messenger send them teachers of the Qur'an. The Messenger sent them some, but they were ambushed and cruelly martyred at Bi'r Al-Maunah (the well of Al-Mauna).[4] After this event, God's Messenger prayed to God for their punishment. However, God revealed the following verse:

> Not for you, (but for God), is the judgment concerning My servants: whether He turns in mercy to them, or punishes them because they are indeed wrongdoers. (Al-Imran 3:127–128)

Today there is an interest in religion all over the world. In my opinion, representing faith with its true values has gained an even greater importance than before. Today there is a need for people who are virtuous, self-possessed, cautious, sincere and pure of heart, people who do not steal or think too highly of themselves, and who prefer the well-being of others to their own, and who have no worldly expectations. If society can educate people with these characteristics, then it means that a much better future is imminent.

Dialogue with the People of the Book

The attitude of believers is determined according to the degree of their faith. I believe that if the message is put across properly, then an environment conducive to dialogue will be able to emerge in our country and throughout the world. Thus, as in every subject, we should approach this issue as indicated in the Qur'an and by the Prophet, peace and blessings be upon him. God says in the Qur'an:

> This is the Book; in it is sure guidance, without doubt, to those who are God-conscious, pious. (Al-Baqara[5] 2:2)

Later on, these pious ones are identified as follows:

> Who believe in the Unseen, are steadfast in prayer, and spend out of what We have provided for them; and who believe in the Revelation sent to you and sent before your time, and (in their hearts) have the reassurance of the Hereafter. (Al-Baqara 2:3–4)

Using a very gentle and slightly oblique style, the Qur'an calls people to accept the former Prophets and their books. The fact that such a condition has been placed at the very beginning of the Qur'an seems to be very significant to me when it comes to talking about the establishment of a dialogue with Jews and Christians. In another verse God commands:

4. A well located on the route between Mecca and Medina.

5. The Cow (Arabic).

> And argue not with the People of the Book unless it be in (a way) that is better. (Al-Ankabut[6] 29:46)

In this verse, the Qur'an describes the method and approach we should use and the behavior we should display. Bediüzzaman[7] said some extremely significant words in order to clarify this: "Those who are happy about their opponent's defeat in debate have no mercy." He explains the reason for this: "You gain nothing by defeating someone. If you are defeated and the other person is victorious, then you would have corrected one of your mistakes."

Debate should not be for the sake of ego, but rather to enable the truth to appear. When we look at political debates in which the only thought is to vanquish the other person, there can be no positive result. For the truth to emerge in a debate of ideas, such principles as mutual understanding, respect, and dedication to justice cannot be ignored. As a Qur'anic rule, debate can only take place in an environment that is conducive to dialogue.

Reading the above verse (29:46) further, we notice that the condition "unless it be with those who disbelieve and inflict wrong (and injury)" is placed. Wrong is also mentioned in another verse:

> It is those who believe and confuse not their beliefs with wrong—that are (truly) in security, for they are on (right) guidance. (Al-Anam[8] 6:82)

According to the interpretation of this above verse by the Prophet, associating partners with God is equal to unbelief in the sense that one has contempt for the universe. The greatest tyranny is to silence all the voices in one's conscience that express God. Tyranny also means committing an injustice against others, oppressing them, and imposing one's ideas onto others. In that respect, as tyranny includes both polytheism and unbelief, it is the greater sin. Every polytheist or unbeliever may not be a wrongdoer in the sense outlined above. However, those who oppress others, who arm themselves in the name of committing evil, and who violate the rights of other people and the justice of God must be confronted within the framework of the law.

When dealing with People of the Book who are not oppressors, we have no right to behave violently against them or to think about how to destroy them. Such behavior is non-Islamic, contrary to Islamic rules and principles, and it can even be said that it is anti-Islamic. Elsewhere in the Qur'an it is stated:

> God does not forbid you, regarding those who did not fight you on account of religion and did not drive you out of your homes, to show kindness and deal with them justly. (Al-Mumtahana[9] 60:8)

This verse was revealed when an emigrant lady called Asma asked the Prophet if she should meet with her polytheistic mother, who wanted to come from Makka to Madina to see her daughter. The verse suggests that such a meeting was perfectly acceptable, and that Asma could also be kind

6. The Spider (Arabic).
7. Wonder of the Age (Turkish), a title of the Turkish religious scholar Saʿid Nursi (ca. 1876–1960).
8. Cattle (Arabic).
9. She Who Is to Be Examined (Arabic).

to her mother. I leave it to your discretion as to what approach should be used toward those who believe in God, the Judgment Day, and the prophets.

Hundreds of Qur'anic verses deal with social dialogue and tolerance. But care must be taken to establish balance in one's tolerance. Being merciful to a cobra means being unjust to the people the cobra has bitten. Claiming that "humanism" is more merciful than Divine Mercy is disrespectful to mercy and violates the rights of others. In truth, except in certain special cases, the Qur'an and the Sunna always advocate tolerance. The shielding canopy of this tolerance extends not only to the People of the Book, but, in a sense, to all people.

Sports and the Process of Dialogue

It is a fact that the concepts of democracy, peace, dialogue, and tolerance have spread and are now being taken seriously with the expansion of communication networks throughout the world. In order for these concepts to become more widespread and for everyone to benefit from them, a number of responsibilities fall on all people, both as individuals and as societies.

In connection with this matter, one important source of power and means of communication that can influence society is without a doubt sports. All manner of sports programs, indeed, anything that pertains to sports, are instantly transmitted from one side of the globe to the other. Of course, there are other, more conventional ways to spread ideas, but by employing this means we can help the ideas of dialogue and tolerance spread; ideas that we believe to be so essential that they must be made known to everyone can be publicized by this means for the sake of the well-being of both our own people and all of humanity.

For example, the 90 minutes spent on the field during a football[1] match could be well utilized. The game itself will give pleasure to the spectators in the stands and, at the same time, without any objections, a number of human virtues could be easily displayed. It is important to utilize this 90 minutes in this way. For example, as was formerly done in sports matches, the victors and the defeated would come together, embrace, shake hands and radiate sportsmanship to all around them. Such behavior would in time be reflected by the behavior of the people in the stands. This would be an important lesson to the people who occasionally feel inclined to burn their seats, curse one another, or even attack one another with weapons; for them it would be highly beneficial to see and show the sports profession in a light that radiates good feelings and thoughts. Even if the spectators of today do not respect the fact that the players are shaking hands before leaving the stadium, in time the behavior of the players will break the cycle of hate and vengefulness, or at least, neutralize it. At this time, this is what the world desperately needs.

Both internally and externally certain people have a desire for conflict and have been brought up in an environment of conflict, and therefore they do not desire dialogue or the improvement of human relationships. It is for this reason that we must act very cautiously. In every task undertaken, there should be a certain meaning, sincerity should be sought, and reason and

1. That is, association football (soccer).

good judgment should be the priority. In addition, every profession should be given its due and it should behave accordingly. An imam uses his voice in the mosque, but a film star, an actor, or an author does not act in the same way. The actor gives precedence to body language or acting ability and the author to writing style and the writing of ideas in a literary way. This is how it should be; otherwise, the impact of the message and its effect is diminished and the message is of no benefit. The same thing is true for sports. An athlete should demonstrate his or her abilities through success, good behavior, and an exemplary lifestyle.

Unfortunately, today the importance of some values has not been perceived. People have a greater need for religion than they do for bread and water, for the peace and security provided by religion, and for the guarantee of an afterlife; I believe that when these facts have been properly explained, then there will be no doubting this matter. There are many people throughout the world who want to do something in the name of Islam. But when this important subject is approached in a crude manner, hate is evoked in the place of love, and unbridgeable abysses appear between people. Yet, what is expected and needed is for Islam to be a bridge and a road between people, as well as a factor that breaches the abysses.

If we do not respond to those who are extending their hands in order to express their love and respect, we will become unlovable. In fact, we will cause some undesirable negative developments to occur. In short, we can say that as an important factor in realizing social dialogue and tolerance, sports can also be utilized, if done so in a well-thought out manner.

TARIQ RAMADAN
b. 1962

Born in Switzerland, Tariq Ramadan is a Muslim intellectual who insists that Muslims living in the West must carve out their own unique identity, respecting both their religious affiliation and their position as citizens of Western democracies.

Ramadan's father and grandfather were both prominent members of the Muslim Brotherhood, a social and political organization created in 1928 to curb the growing foreign influence in Egypt. Indeed, Ramadan's grandfather, Hasan al-Banna, was its founder; he was assassinated in 1949, presumably by government agents. His son-in-law—Ramadan's father—was exiled from Egypt in 1954 for his involvement with the group.

Ramadan received a thoroughly European education, obtaining a master of arts in philosophy and French literature as well as a PhD in Arabic and Islamic studies from the University of Geneva. He has studied traditional Islamic thought with scholars from al-Azhar University in Egypt. Ramadan has earned many awards, has taught Islamic studies at several universities, is affiliated with a number of research institutions, and works with various Muslim organizations at the grassroots level.

Ramadan addresses his writings primarily to European Muslims, who live in nations where they are in the minority. He urges congregations in those nations to operate independently and become "financially, politically, and intellectually" free of any ties to Muslim-majority countries. Among the key ideas undergirding his

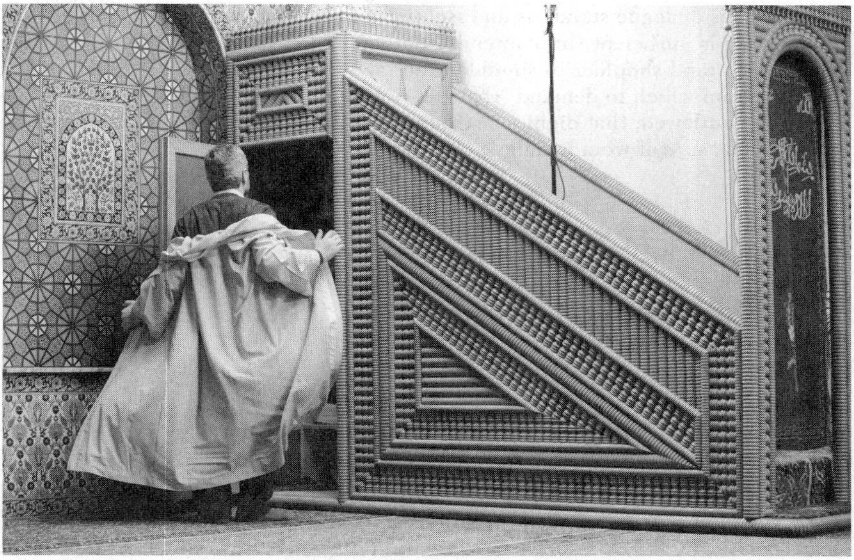

Imam Ibrahim Soekmen removes his clerical robes to store them within the minbar, or pulpit, of a modern mosque in Hamburg, Germany. In Muslim-ruled countries, the minbar was often a symbol of the relationship between religion and state power; the imam would deliver the Friday sermon and invoke blessings on the ruler, thereby contributing to his (or her) legitimacy. Often the ruler would ascend the minbar himself to deliver an address. More than 4 million Muslims live in Germany—twice as many as in the United Kingdom, and roughly as many as live in France. March 2011.

thought is a conviction that pluralism must be respected and accepted because the Qur'an itself states that God wanted multiple faiths to exist and that there can never be any coerced conversion to Islam. Ramadan emphasizes that anything "not in opposition to an Islamic principle (or a recognized prohibition) on the level of human and social affairs is to be considered Islamic," an important position from which to construct Muslim identities that are specifically European.

The admiration of Ramadan by Muslims living in Europe and elsewhere owes much to his family's renown as well as to his training with both academic and religious scholars. Furthermore, he is respected for his command of Arabic, his oratorical gifts, and his intellect. Yet he is no stranger to controversy. In 2004, just as Ramadan was about to begin a professorship at the University of Notre Dame, the U.S. Department of State used a provision of the Patriot Act to revoke his visa. After years of legal action by the American Civil Liberties Union and other groups, the revocation was reversed in 2010 by Secretary of State Hillary Clinton, and Ramadan has since accepted speaking engagements in the United States. He has also been attacked by traditionalist Muslim critics who reject his readings of classical theological and legal texts and accuse him of pandering to young and disaffected Muslims. His supporters counsel that he also attracts middle-class Muslims by articulating the tensions they feel as residents of Europe in a pluralist and secularist century.

In the passage that follows (from a book originally published in French in 2003), Ramadan builds a powerful argument for a Muslim mandate for interreligious dialogue and, more urgently, for interfaith action. After thoughtfully assessing the qur'anic verses that have been used to promote dialogue and those that have been used to proscribe it, Ramadan turns traditions upon themselves, insisting that intrareligious dialogue stands as an essential counterpoint to interreligious efforts. But neither is sufficient, he contends. Rather, faiths in conversation with each other must stand shoulder to shoulder and face forward. They must find a public platform from which to demand "that the rights of all be respected, that discriminations be outlawed, that dignity be protected, and that economic efficiency cease to be the measure of what is right."

PRONOUNCING GLOSSARY

aslamtu: *as-lam´-too*
aslim: *as´-lim*
Bhagavad Gita: *ba-ga-vad gee´-tuh*
dawa: *da´-wa*
Iblis: *ib-lees´*
kafir: *ka´-fir*
kuffar: *koof-far´*
kufr: *koofr*
rida: *ri´-dah*
tawhid: *taw-heed* (heavy *h*)

FROM WESTERN MUSLIMS AND THE FUTURE OF ISLAM

Chapter 9. Interreligious Dialogue

There is a very long tradition of interreligious dialogue. At various times in history, in very diverse contexts, people of various religions have engaged in interreligious exchanges to try to understand one another better; they have succeeded in gaining one another's respect and have managed not only to live but also to work together on shared endeavors. Today, we feel the need to engage even more in this process: Western societies' religious pluralism makes mutual knowledge essential. At the same time, technical developments have changed our view of the world, and daily images of societies and customs different from our own arouse our curiosity. More dramatically, acts of violence perpetrated in the name of religion challenge our awareness: how can such horror be justified in the name of religion? How can we understand it? How can we prevent it?

Many groups of specialists have been formed in recent years. At colloquia, conferences, and seminars, they meet to try to build bridges, discuss sensitive subjects, and prevent conflicts. With time, these specialists in dialogue have come to know one another and to enjoy excellent relationships founded on courtesy and respect. This is an important gain. Nevertheless, the problem remains that these are fairly closed circles whose members are not always in real contact with their own religious groups, and this makes it difficult to convey to the heart of each religious community the advances made in these numerous meetings. Moreover, whole sections of these communities are neither concerned with nor touched by the various dialogues that are taking place. Those who meet do not represent the various denominations, schools of thought, or tendencies of the adherents of their religion. Those who hold the most closed opinions, which in daily life are the cause of the real problem, never meet. Thus, we have, on both the national and international levels, a very uneven picture: dialogue is well under way between specialists from each religion who are more or less open-minded,

Except as indicated, notes are Ramadan's, as are bracketed additions to the text; some of his notes are omitted.

while ordinary believers meet only rarely and the most entrenched and radical views are never voiced. Common sense and logic would encourage us to hope for the opposite: the specialists do not, or no longer, really need dialogue, and it is within religious communities and between those with the most radical views that the debate should take place. It is a vicious circle: it is precisely because people do not know one another, or reject one another, that dialogue is impossible.

The responsibility of people involved in dialogue between religions is in fact doubly important: whether they have become specialists or are simply members of an interreligious group, it is vital that they play the role of mediators between their partners in dialogue and their coreligionists. It is a question of listening to the other side, challenging it and questioning it in order to increase understanding and then of getting involved in working within one's own community, informing, explaining, even teaching. At the same time, participants in dialogue should express their own convictions, clarify the place of their own sense of religion among other views held within their religious family, and respond as well as they can to the questions of their partners in dialogue. By acting in this way they create, between the various traditions, areas of trust, sustained by shared convictions and values that, even though they certainly do not bring the extremes together, do open real horizons for living together and at least allow ruptures to be avoided and conflicts better managed.

The need for interreligious dialogue is not doubted, but some people still do not understand its real usefulness and purpose. What exactly is it about? Does one want to convert the other? Can one get involved with a clear conscience? What is the real impact of these fine words about respect and living together when we look at how believers from each religion behave? Is there not a place for being doubtful or suspicious about the intentions of one or the other side if we take the time to read the scriptural sources? These questions cannot simply be swept under the carpet. They are of primary importance, because, unless they are clearly and succinctly answered, we run the risk of having an outwardly agreeable dialogue that does not eliminate the mistrust and suspicion and that in the end leads nowhere. Let us try, from within the Muslim tradition, to suggest possible answers to these questions, beginning with the last.

THE ISLAMIC TRADITION AND INTERRELIGIOUS DIALOGUE

We recalled in part I[1] that, according to Muslims, the last Revelation taught them to recognize all the books of the prophets who had gone before. They all had the same purpose: to remind human beings of the presence of the Creator and the finiteness of life on earth. The Islamic tradition's concept of humankind emerged through this teaching: after forgiving Adam his sin, God told men: "A guidance will certainly come to you from me. Those who follow my guidance will have nothing to fear and will not grieve."[2] This guidance is the series of Revelations that came throughout human history, each to confirm, complete, and correct the preceding.

1. The first four chapters of the book, where Ramadan notes that for Muslims, the "last Revelation" is the Qur'an itself [editor's note].
2. Qur'an 2:38.

NECESSARY DIVERSITY

So individuals, innocent and free, have to make their choices (either to accept or to reject the Revelation); there will necessarily be diversity among people, and so these three seemingly similar verses contain teachings that augment and complete each other: "Had God so willed. He would have united them [human beings] in guidance, so do not be among the ignorant";[3] "If your Lord had so willed, everyone on earth would have believed. Is it for you to compel people to be believers?";[4] "If God had willed, He would have made you one community but things are as they are to test you in what He has given you. So compete with each other in doing good."[5] The first verse instructs us that diversity is willed by the Transcendent, the second makes clear that, in the name of that will, compulsion in matters of religion is forbidden,[6] and the Revelation teaches that the purpose of these differences is to *test* us in order to discover what we are going to do with what has been revealed to us: the last commandment is to use these differences to "compete in doing good." Diversity of religions, nations, and peoples is a test because it requires that we learn to manage difference, which is in itself essential: "If God did not enable some men to keep back others, the world would be corrupt. But God is the One who gives grace to the worlds";[7] "If God did not enable some men to keep back others, hermitages, synagogues, chapels and mosques where the name of God is often called upon, would have been demolished."[8] These two verses give complementary information that is of prime importance: if there were no differences between people, if power were in the hands of one group alone (one nation, one race, or one religion), the earth would be corrupt because human beings need others to limit their impulsive desire for expansion and domination. The last verse is more precise with regard to our present discussion; it refers to places of worship to indicate that if there is to be a diversity of religions, the purpose is to safeguard them all: the fact that the list of places begins with hermitages, synagogues, and chapels before referring to mosques shows recognition of all these places of worship and their inviolability and, of course, respect for those who pray there. So, just as diversity is the source of our test, the balance of power is a requirement for our destiny.

Difference might naturally lead to conflict; therefore, the responsibility of humankind is to make use of difference by establishing a relationship based on excelling one another in doing good. It is vital that the balance of power is based not on a tension born of rejection or mutual ignorance but fundamentally on knowledge: "O people, we have created you from a male and a female, we have divided you into nations and tribes so that you might know one another."[9] Knowing the other is a process that is unavoidable if fear of difference is to be overcome and mutual respect is to be attained. So human beings live a test that is necessary for their nature but that they can—and must—master by making the effort to know and recognize those who are not of their tribe, their country, their race, or their religion.[1] Dialogue, particularly interreligious dialogue, is indispensable.

3. Qur'an 6:35.
4. Qur'an 10:99.
5. Qur'an 5:48.
6. The Qur'an confirms this in a clear general rule: "No compulsion in religion" (2:256).
7. Qur'an 2:251.
8. Qur'an 22:40.
9. Qur'an 49:13.
1. Read and understood globally, these Qur'anic references bring together all the dimensions of "difference" among human beings: tribe, nation, race, religion.

GENERAL PRINCIPLES OF DIALOGUE

All believers who participate in interreligious dialogue do so having been nourished by a faith or a conviction on the basis of which they understand themselves, perceive the world, and build relations with those around them. Their connection with Truth, with the beliefs of others, and with diversity in general is directly influenced by the content and nature of that faith or conviction. The centrality of *tawhid*[2] in the message of Islam has been strongly emphasized in part I. It is the principle on which the whole of Islamic teaching rests and is the axis and point of reference on which Muslims rely in dialogue. The intimate awareness of *tawhid* forms the perception of the believer, who understands that plurality has been chosen by the One, that He is the God of all beings, and that He requires that each be respected: ". . . and say: 'We believe in what has been revealed to us and what has been revealed to you; our God and your God is the One.'"[3] It is out of this conviction that Muslims engage in dialogue, and this is assumed in forming relations with the other. What establishes difference from the other, and consequently the direction and terms of the dialogue that is to be built, is whether or not there is commitment to the expression of absolute monotheism. This is why the Qur'anic call to the Jews and Christians begins with: "O people of the book, come to agreed terms between us and you: that we worship none but God, that we do not attribute any associate to Him and that none of us takes other divinities apart from Him. If they turn away, say: 'Be witnesses that we are submitting ourselves [*muslimun*].'"[4] Firmly asserting this principle indicates that *tawhid* is the point of reference on the basis of which a Muslim engages in discussion: if there are differences on this central point, it is then necessary that dialogue be entered into and developed on the basis of shared values and teachings, since the last Revelation recognizes those that came before: "God, there is no god but God. It is He who sent down the Book [the Qur'an] upon you [Muhammad] in all truth confirming what came before. And He sent down the Torah and the Gospel before as a guidance for people, and He sent down the Discernment [*al-furqan*] the Qur'an."[5] This recognition is fundamental and opens up the way for dialogue, which, although it forces us to see our differences, is bound to establish bridges between convictions and traditions.

The Qur'an not only issues a call to dialogue but is also insistent about the form it should take and the way in which it should be conducted. It should not simply be an exchange of information: It should also be a way of being and of speaking, an attitude: "And discuss with them in the best way."[6] and again: "Do not discuss with the people of the Book except in the best of ways, apart from those who are unjust among themselves."[7] In this last verse, the restriction is not at all upon dialogue as such, but as it pertains to the repressive attitude some Jews and Christians adopted toward the Muslim community, which was at that time facing serious adversity. This contextualized approach is what gives meaning to the often quoted verse "You will certainly see that those most hardened in hostility toward the Muslims are the Jews

2. The oneness of God (Arabic) [editor's note].
3. Qur'an 29:46.
4. Qur'an 3:64.
5. Qur'an 3:2–4.
6. Qur'an 16:125.
7. Qur'an 29:46.

and the polytheists and you will certainly see that those closest to you in affection are those who say: 'We are Christians,' because there are among them priests and monks who are not swollen with pride."[8] Here again, it is the attitude of people and potential partners in dialogue that is at issue, and not dialogue in itself. To those who choose to understand this contextualized teaching (warning us to be concerned about injustice, adversity, and the pride of human beings) as an absolute prohibition on dialogue, the Revelation replies clearly: "God does not forbid you from establishing relations of generosity and just behavior with those who have not fought against you over your religion and who have not evicted you from your dwellings. God loves those who act fairly."[9] This verse goes even further than all the others: if dialogue is necessary and if the way of speaking about oneself is important, we are here clearly called to establish relations of generosity and justice with all who respect our freedom of conscience and our human dignity. Dialogue is an act of conviction, of listening, of self-awareness, of self-knowledge, and of the heart: together, these qualities constitute wisdom.

VERSES INTERPRETED VARIOUSLY

When we speak of interreligious dialogue, it would not be honest to refer only to the verses we have quoted without mentioning a series of other passages in the Qur'an that can be equivocal and that are moreover variously interpreted by Muslim scholars. Some of the ulama of the literalist traditions read them restrictively, which basically does not leave any real room for discussion. A sincere involvement in dialogue must stop to consider these verses. Thus, one finds in the Qur'an verses that define Jews and Christians, even though they are among the "people of the Book," as *kuffar* (plural of *kafir*), most often translated as "infidels" or "miscreants": "They are certainly *in a state of denial* [*kafara*], those who have said that God was the Messiah the son of Mary"[1] or again, "Those among the people of the Book and the polytheists who *have denied* [*kafaru*]."[2] According to the perspective of the majority of literalist scholars, this leaves no doubt as to their fate, especially since the Qur'an says explicitly: "Religion in the sight of God is Islam"[3] and again: "He who desires religion other than Islam will not find himself accepted and in the hereafter he will be among the losers."[4] Other verses seem to tell us that we should not trust Jews and Christians: "And the Jews and Christians will not be pleased with you unless you follow their religion"[5] or take them as allies except in extreme circumstances: "Let the believers [Muslims] not take as allies the deniers [*kafirin*] rather than believers; those who do so will receive no help from God, unless you feel yourselves to be in danger from them."[6] Such an avalanche of verses has the effect of causing perplexity and raises questions about whether any real place for dialogue remains, the more so since these same scholars clearly explain that they do not believe there is any virtue in discussion unless the intention is to convince the other party of the strength and truth of our arguments. Interreligious dialogue would then become a call to our truth, a *dawa* (call, invitation, preaching), with no meaning beyond that.

8. Qur'an 5:82.
9. Qur'an 60:8.
1. Qur'an 5:17.
2. Qur'an 98:1.
3. Qur'an 3:19.
4. Qur'an 3:85.
5. Qur'an 2:120.
6. Qur'an 3:28.

Here we are at the heart of the problem of the types of "reading" to which we referred in part I where the various schools of thought were described. The advantage of the literalist reading over all the others is that it stops at the primary meaning of the text that, as soon as it is quoted, seems to make immediate sense and gives weight to the argument. No trouble is taken to work out a reading based on critical distance, contextualized interpretation, or determination of the meaning of a verse in light of the message as a whole. As a literalist, what I read is what was said, and God speaks through me as long as my quotations are from His word. It is nevertheless advisable to take each of the verses mentioned earlier and to try to discover whether the literalist reading is the only appropriate one.

It must be said, to begin with, that the Arabic notion of *kufr* or *kafir* has often been mistranslated, quite apart from the fact that many Muslims in the West use it as a definite insult. But the word has a central sense in the Islamic sciences, and it is clearly perceived at various levels. Without going into technical details here, we may say that, according to the root, the general meaning of *kafir* could be rendered as "a denier with a veiled heart": this refers to those whose original longing for the Transcendent has been stifled, veiled, shut off in their hearts to the extent that they deny the presence of the Creator. But *kafir* may also indicate one who denies the evidence of the truth, like the satanic figure of Iblis in the Qurʾan, who *knows* that God is, since he speaks to Him, but refuses to obey: "He [Iblis] refused, became proud and was among the deniers [*min al-kafirin*]."[7] To this must be added various kinds of negation, *kufr*, which are determined according to what is denied; God, the truth of the message, one of the pillars of faith, the nature of a particular commandment, and so on. So to apply the term *kafir* to Jews and Christians in a neutral sense is justified in that, in a quite natural way, they do not recognize the Qurʾan as the last revealed book. They deny [*yakfuru*] the truth of the message and its Prophet, but this does not mean we may call them "miscreants" in the sense that their faith in God is not recognized, which would be an inaccurate assertion: this would be as senseless as to say that Iblis, who had a dialogue with the Most High, did not *believe* in Him and was a *miscreant*. This is neither logical understanding nor a consistent translation. We must add that it is never legitimate to use the word as an insult.

The verse indicating that the religion in the sight of God is Islam has caused a lot of ink to flow. Here again we are dealing with a question of interpretation. We know that in the Qurʾan the word *islam* has two meanings. The first is universal and generic: all the elements, as we have said in part I, are in "submission" to God because they respect the order of creation; in the same sense, all the revelations and prophets came with a message of the oneness of God and the need to "submit oneself" to Him. Thus, Abraham, well before the revelation of the Qurʾan, is commanded by God: "And when his Lord said to him: 'Submit [*aslim*]!' he replied: 'I submit [*aslamtu*] to the Lord of the worlds.'"[8] The words *aslim* and *aslamtu* come from *islam* in the sense of recognition of the one God and acceptance of the obedience due to Him. The second meaning of the word *islam* is the religion whose text is the Qurʾan and whose prophet is Muhammad. Literalist scholars

7. Qurʾan 2:34.

8. Qurʾan 2:131.

have interpreted these verses giving the word the restricted meaning of the second definition, while the generic definition makes better sense of the Islamic message as a whole, which, apart from being the final revelation, identifies natural religion, one and unique throughout history, as the recognition of the existence of a Creator and conformance to His messages. This is also confirmed by the verse "Certainly those who have believed, the Jews, the Christians, and the Sabaeans,[9] all those who have believed in God and in the last day of judgment and who have done good—they will have their reward from God. They will not be afraid and they will not grieve."[1] The generic meaning is clear here, and those scholars who have claimed that this verse has been abrogated [*mansukh*] pay no regard to the rule of abrogation, which specifies that only verses stipulating obligations or prohibitions (which may change in the course of revelation) can be abrogated but not information, which cannot be true one day and untrue the next. This verse is clearly giving information.

The verse "The Jews and the Christians will not be pleased with you unless you follow their religion [*milla*]" is quoted at will in times of trouble or simply when people want to justify mistrusting some Jews or Christians. The verse is heard from mosque pulpits, in conferences, and at seminars, with the implication that it explains the attitude of Jews and Christians toward Muslims: their rejection of Islam, their double dealing, not to say deceitfulness, and colonization, proselytism, wars, Bosnia, Palestine, and so on. But that is not what the verse says: the phrase "will not be pleased with you" [*lan tarda anka*] translates here the idea of full and absolute satisfaction, expressed with the heart as well as the mind. For Jews and Christians convinced, like a Muslim, of the truth of their own message, complete satisfaction with the other is attained when the experience of faith and truth is shared. One has the feeling of living and sharing this essential element that gives meaning and light to one's life. This does not imply that in the absence of this full satisfaction one can live in and express only rejection, mistrust, and conflict. One can feel and manifest deep and sincere respect toward a human being with whom one does not share this full spiritual communion. It is a matter of being sincere and of recognizing the states of our souls and hearts. It is within our communities of faith that we live most deeply the fullness of the meaning of (*rida*) with the other who shares our truth, even if it is possible (though it is the exception rather than the rule) that we might experience a unique spiritual relationship with a woman or a man from another tradition. The Qur'an here is speaking only of the intimate and very natural inclination of people of faith toward one another. At a deeper level, believers must be conscious that ultimately what they must seek before all else is to please God [*rida Allah*], not other people. It is good for believers to remember that the full satisfaction shared with their coreligionists is still only a stage along the way. Seeking the pleasure of God is a demanding path punctuated by testing stations, but this initiation is ultimately the only way that it is possible to become, in humility, fully content with oneself.

9. Mentioned three times in the Qur'an (2:62; 5:69; 22:17), the Sabians were identified by commentators with various religious communities in Iraq and generally included within the People of the Book as monotheists [editor's note].

1. Qur'an 2:62.

With regard to the verse referring to the seemingly impossible alliance with Jews and Christians, we have already referred to it. From the context of the verse, and others like it, we derive that Muslims are commanded in situations of potential conflict not to take deniers as allies against Muslims [*min dun al-muminin*],[2] that is to say, to make an alliance unjustly or treacherously in opposition to their spiritual community. It does not apply absolutely, and the following verse specifies clearly those with whom relations are banned: "God forbids you to turn in friendship toward [or take as allies] only such as fight against you because of your faith, and drive you forth from your homelands, or aid [others] in driving you forth: and as for those [from among you] who turn toward them in friendship [or alliance], it is they, they who are truly wrongdoers!"[3]

Here a word is needed on that concept of *dawa*, often translated as "preaching," "call," or "invitation to Islam" and which has thus come to express the missionary character of Islam. It cannot be denied that some Muslims, on the basis of a certain number of verses, are engaged in straightforward missionary activity, and in their minds dialogue is only a form of mission. To deny this would be dishonest. One must then look at how the Qur'an presents the act of "inviting" or "calling" to Islam. The verse that follows is well known: "Call [invite] to the path of your Lord using wisdom and good exhortation, and debate with them in the best of manner."[4] If we meditate on this verse, we understand that emphasis is put first on the Muslim who "invites." He has to have acquired a certain wisdom, know to speak well, and have mastered the best way of expressing things: three injunctions bring together the requirements related to being a good speaker, the content of the message, and the way in which it must be delivered. In other words, to "invite" is first to "bear witness," as much by one's behavior as by the content and form of what one says, what the message of Islam is. It is not a matter of wanting to convert, because people's hearts are God's domain and secret. It is a matter of bearing witness, which is an invitation to remember and meditate. This meaning also is captured by another verse: "And thus have We willed you to be a community of the middle way, so that [with your lives] you might bear witness to the truth before mankind."[5] Interreligious dialogue should be a meeting of "witnesses" who are seeking to live their faiths, to share their convictions, and to engage with one another for a more humane, more just world, closer to what God expects of humanity.

At the end of this section, we note that the verses mentioned earlier are indeed variously interpreted. All religious traditions experience these differences, and, depending on the type of reading that is accepted, one may be open to dialogue or absolutely opposed to it. The nature of these difficulties has to be taken into account in order to avoid any illusions about the possible results of our meetings.

TOWARD EXACTING AND CONSTRUCTIVE DIALOGUE

The dialogue we engage in must be anything but complaisant. The lack of trust that permeates our Western societies and the situations of religious

2. In Qur'anic usage, the word *mu'min* (believer; pl. *muminin*) usually means *Muslim*.
3. Qur'an 60:9.
4. Qur'an 16:125.
5. Qur'an 2:143.

conflict throughout the world mean that our task must be far-reaching, exacting, and rigorous. First of all, dialogue must be based on mutual knowledge achieved by our seeking to make clear our shared convictions, values, and hopes, while clearly defining and circumscribing our specificities, our differences, and what may even be our disagreements. This is what is done in most interreligious groups, and I believe it is necessary to move in this direction. But this will not be enough: we have already said that the majority of women and men engaged in this kind of meetings are rather open and ready for the encounter. It is crucial that they describe and explain what they really represent in their religious families—what trend, the extent of it, their relations with the community as a whole, and so forth. It is important to know to whom one is speaking: it is no less essential to know to whom one is not speaking, and why. Interreligious dialogue should make it possible for each partner better to understand the various theories, the points shared, the differences and conflicts that are present in other traditions. It is a matter first of not deluding oneself that the other "represents," for example, the *whole* of Hinduism, the *whole* of Buddhism, the *whole* of Judaism, the *whole* of Christianity, or the *whole* of Islam, and second of knowing what links and types of relations our partners have with their coreligionists.

To be involved in dialogue between religions while being completely cut off from the believers of one's own religion is problematic and can be illusory. Many "specialists" in interreligious dialogue, who go from conference to conference, are totally disconnected from their religious community, as well as from grass-roots realities. This might be conceivable if it were a matter of purely theological discussions, but in most cases, unfortunately, that is not the case. How is it possible to have a real understanding of religious traditions and the dynamics that permeate them on the ground if those who dialogue are not actively involved in their communities? Again, how can one hope to influence believers more widely if the specialists' circle is isolated in an ivory tower and does not report back on the nature of its work to each of the respective religious communities?

So, two fundamental conditions for dialogue with the other emerge: first, to commit oneself, as far as possible, to giving an account of the shared work to one's own faith community and second, in order to achieve that, to devote part of one's energy to opening up intracommunal dialogue, which will make possible the advancement of real pluralism. This dialogue is extremely difficult, sometimes much more difficult than interreligious dialogue itself, because discussion with one's nearest and dearest is so risky. This commitment is nevertheless essential if we want to break down internal ghettoes and sectarianism and try, within manageable limits, to respect one another more. It can never be said enough that intracommunal dialogue between Muslims is virtually nonexistent. Groups know one another, know how to identify one another, and work out where they are in relation to one another, but then they immediately ignore one another, exclude one another, or insult one another, without any attempt at discussion. Within one religious understanding, one current of thought, divisions are maintained by intervening organizations. The culture of dialogue has practically abandoned Muslim communities and the respect for diversity, which always has been and should have continued to be their source of richness, has been replaced by dueling disagreements that contribute to maintaining the division, which causes their weakness. Some still tentative initiatives have taken off, but the movement must become more general and must naturally go alongside involvement in dialogue with other traditions.

Apart from getting to know one another, it is also necessary to establish relationships of trust and respect. Trust is lacking today: we meet often, listen sometimes, and distrust each other often. Trust needs time and support. The frequency and quality of meetings and the nature of the exchanges certainly help to create spaces for sincere encounter. However, it seems to me that four rules should be applied which may be quite demanding as preliminaries, but which are fundamentally constructive:

1. Recognition of the legitimacy of each other's convictions and respect for them;
2. Listening to what people say about their own scriptural sources and not what we understand (or want to understand) from them;
3. The right, in the name of trust and respect, to ask all possible questions, sometimes even the most embarrassing;
4. The practice of self-criticism, which consists in knowing how to discern the difference between what the texts say and what our coreligionists make of them, and deciding clearly what our personal position is.

These rules are essential. One cannot enter into dialogue if one does not recognize the legitimacy of other people's convictions. Not to share them is one thing, but not to recognize, deep in one's heart, their right to be is another. Nor is it fitting to try to become an exegete of one's partner's scriptures. This is not our role or our area of expertise. It is for our partners to tell us what they understand or what their coreligionists understand, from such and such a text. Reading the Torah or the Bible for a Muslim, the Qur'an for a Jew or a Christian, or the Bhagavad Gita[6] for all three is certainly useful and necessary in order to try to understand others' convictions, but these readings should inspire meditation and questions, not a simplistic accusation. We must also give ourselves the right to dare to ask all the questions that occur to us. The answers may or may not be satisfying, they may or may not suit us, but they will have been clearly stated. Trust can be born only from this frankness and clarity: in the meantime, without the latter, courtesy is artificial or even a masquerade. At a deeper level, these are all questions that help people to go further in understanding their own traditions. Looking for a way to give a deep explanation means making the effort to understand better. The relevance of the question to my partner in dialogue is a gift, an intellectual and spiritual tonic, because I learn to express better what I believe and so to understand more deeply the meaning of what I am. Finally, dialogue involves clarity and courage: our scriptural sources have sometimes been used, or have legitimized (and still legitimize) discourses, behavior, and actions toward others about which we need to make clear statements. This is not always easy, but it is nevertheless vital, and all the religious traditions should be involved in this self-criticism. Some see it as a kind of disloyalty toward their own community; it should instead be a matter of self-respect and dignity before God and each person's conscience.

6. Literally, "Song of the Lord" (Sanskrit), a poem (1st or 2nd century C.E.?) that is incorporated within the Mahabharata, one of the religious classics of Hinduism [editor's note].

SHARED INVOLVEMENT

Dialogue is not enough. Even if it is rigorous, even if it is necessary to give time to knowing, trusting, and respecting each other, even if we should take on ourselves the widest possible responsibility to report back, it is only one stage or one aspect of the encounter among the various religious traditions. In Western societies, it is urgent that we commit ourselves to joint action.

In dialogue, we soon realize that we hold a great number of convictions and values in common. We understand very quickly that we are facing the same difficulties and challenges. But we very rarely move outside these circles of reflection. Together we say "God," awareness, spirituality, responsibility, ethics, solidarity, but we live and experience, each one on one's own, the problems of education, transmission of spirituality, individualism, consumerism, and moral bankruptcy. In philosophical terms, we could say that we know one another in words but not *in action.* Our experience of fifteen years of joint action in South America, Africa, and Asia has convinced us not only that this path is necessary but also that it is the only way to eventually change minds and build mutual respect and trust.

In the West, there are many shared challenges, first among them being education. How can we pass on to our children the sense of the divine, for the monotheistic faiths, or of spiritual practice for Buddhism, for example? In a society that pushes people to own, how are we to form individuals whose awareness of being illumines and guides their mastery of possession? Again, how are we to explain morality and boundaries, to pass on principles of life that do not confuse liberty with carelessness and that consider neither fashion nor quantity of possessions as the measure of goodness? All the religious and spiritual traditions are experiencing these difficulties, but we still see few examples of shared commitment to proposing alternatives. And there is so much to do—working together, as parents and as citizens, so that schools will provide more and more courses on the religions; suggesting ways of providing educational modules outside the school structures to teach the general population about the religions—their fundamental beliefs, particular topics, and social realities. Such modules need to be thought out together, not only by inviting a partner from the other religion to come to give a course as part of a program we have put together for and by ourselves. By way of example, the Interreligious Platform in Geneva has launched an interesting "school of religions," and there is the Center for Muslim-Christian Studies, in Copenhagen, which, under the leadership of Lissi Rasmussen,[7] has scored a first in Europe in establishing a real partnership within an institution promoting and practicing dialogue.

Acts of solidarity take place from within each religious family, but the examples of shared initiatives are rare. People sometimes invite others, but do not act in collaboration. One of the best testimonies that a religious or spiritual tradition can give of itself lies in acts of solidarity between its adherents and others. To defend the dignity of the latter, to fight so that our

7. A Danish theologian and historian of religion; she is the chairman of the board of the Islamisk-Kristent Studiecenter, founded in 1996 to build positive relations between Muslims and Christians. The Interreligious Platform was founded in 1992 to promote encounters between members of Geneva's various religious communities [editor's note].

societies do not produce indignity, to work together to support marginalized and neglected people, will certainly help us know one another better, but it will, above all, make known the essential message that shines at the heart of our traditions: never neglect your brother in humanity and learn to love him or at least to serve him.

More broadly, we have to act together so that the body of values that forms the basis of our ethics is not relegated to such a private and secluded sphere that it becomes inoperative and socially dead. Our philosophies of life must continue to inspire our civil commitment, with all due respect to the supporters of a postmodernism whose aim seems to be to deny any legitimacy to all reference to a universal ethic. We need to find together a civil role, inspired by our convictions, in which we will work to demand that the rights of all be respected, that discriminations be outlawed, that dignity be protected, and that economic efficiency cease to be the measure of what is right. Differentiating between public and private space does not mean that women and men of faith, or women and men of conscience, have to shrink to the point of disappearance and fear to express themselves publicly in the name of what they believe. When a society has gone so far as to disqualify, in public debate, faith and what it inspires, the odds are that its system is founded only on materialism and ruled only by materialist logic—the self-centered accumulation of goods and profit.

We must dare to express our faith, its demands, and its ethics, to involve ourselves as citizens in order to make known our human concerns, our desire for justice and dignity, our moral standards, our fears as consumers and televiewers, our hopes as mothers and fathers—to commit ourselves to do the best possible, together, to reform what might be. All our religious traditions have a social message that invites us to work together on a practical level. We are still far from this. In spite of thousands of dialogue circles and meetings, we still seem to know one another very little and to be very lacking in trust. Perhaps we must reconsider our methods and formulate a mutual demand: to behave in such a way that our actions, as much as possible, mirror our words, and then to act together.

APPENDICES

Glossary

Words in SMALL CAPS are defined in their own entries.

ʿAbbasid dynasty. The dynasty that ruled the MUSLIM empire from 750 to 1258, the period typically referred to as the classical era of Islamic history. The line is traced back to al-ʿAbbas ibn ʿAbd al-Muttalib (d. ca. 653), the Prophet's uncle.

adab (Arabic, "etiquette"). A broad category covering the proper forms of self-discipline and correct social behavior. Instructions on it are provided in sections of HADITH literature, with further elaboration in the later literary tradition. In modern usage, *adab* is synonymous with "literature."

Ahl al-bayt (Arabic, "the people of the house"). A qurʾanic term (33:33) that is understood to refer to the family of the Prophet, limited by the SHIʿA to five individuals: Muhammad; his daughter Fatima (d. 632); his cousin and her husband, ʿAli ibn Abi Talib (d. 661); and their two sons, al-Hasan (d. 669/70) and al-Husayn (d. 680).

Ahl al-hadith (Arabic, "the partisans of HADITH" or "traditionists"). Those who link law exclusively to prophetic authority as embodied in the HADITH: specifically, one of the scholarly reformist groups (cf. DEOBANDIS, BARELWIS) that emerged in India in the eighteenth century. It offered a restrictive reading of the QURʾAN and HADITH and denied any authority to the SUNNI legal schools or to SUFISM.

Ahl al-kitab. See PEOPLE OF THE BOOK.

akhbar (Arabic, "reports"). Narrative records, encompassing prophetic and historical reports, travel writing, and biographical accounts. As a genre, it usually means "history." In modern usage it often means "news."

Allah (Arabic, "God"). A contraction of *al-Ilah*, "the God," and thus an implicit denial of other gods: used by Arabic-speaking Jews and Christians as well as MUSLIMS.

Allahu akbar (Arabic, "God is greater"; i.e., none is greater than God). A phrase frequently uttered by MUSLIMS during prayer; also, an expression of approval, enthusiasm, or encouragement.

Arab Spring. A series of pro-democracy demonstrations and uprisings in the Middle East and North Africa that began in late 2010 in Tunisia (whose prime minister resigned) and spread, resulting in the overthrow of several other governments (Egypt, Yemen, Libya), widespread protests (e.g., Bahrain, Algeria), and, in the case of Syria, a prolonged civil war.

ʿAshuraʾ. Holiday celebrated on the 10th of Muharram (the first month of the Islamic calendar). For SHIʿIS, it is the commemoration of the martyrdom of al-Husayn, grandson of the Prophet, at KARBALAʾ in 680. For SUNNIS, it is observed as a voluntary fast in commemoration of the Prophet's practice.

as-salaamʿalaykum (Arabic, "Peace be upon you"). A salutation commonly used by MUSLIMS. It is considered the greeting of Paradise (see QURʾAN 14:23).

ayat (Arabic, "verses"; sing., *aya*). Literally, "signs" or "miracles" (i.e., from God), such as natural wonders and extraordinary events. Each chapter (SURA) of the QURʾAN is composed of as few as 3 to as many as 286 *ayat*.

ayatollah (Persian, "sign of God"; from Arabic *aya*, "sign," + ALLAH). In TWELVER SHIʿISM, an honorific for high-ranking religious authorities.

banu (Arabic, "children of"). A term that appears before the name of a tribal progenitor, often used to designate a people. Thus the QURʾAN refers to the Jews as the "Children of Israel" (*Banu Israʾil*).

Barelwis. Along with the DEOBANDIS and AHL AL-HADITH, a scholarly reformist group that emerged in India in the eighteenth century. Adherents of HANAFI law, the Barelwis also embraced many popular practices and beliefs, such as the intercession of saints and the conviction that the prophet Muhammad was not mortal.

basmalla (Arabic, "In the name of God"). In its entirety, the *Basmalla* reads, "In the name of God, the beneficent, the merciful." It begins all SURAS of the QURʾAN but the ninth, and is also used as an opening prayer for a wide range of sacred and mundane activities.

bidʿa (Arabic, "innovation"). A departure from orthodoxy. In common usage *bidʿa* is synonymous with heresy, although scholars classify some acts as "good innovation."

caliph. Anglicized version of the Arabic term *khalifa* (lit., "successor"; vicegerent), applied to the supreme MUSLIM civil and religious ruler. The first four MUSLIM rulers are known as the Rightly Guided Successors (*al-khulafaʾ al-RASHIDUN*).

Companions. Followers of Muhammad who had personal contact with him (*sahaba*).

Crusades. A series of religio-military expeditions launched by western European powers against MUSLIM holdings in the east, specifically areas of Palestine and Syria held sacred by Christians. The First Crusade (1096–99) established the four states of the Latin East: Jerusalem, Tripoli, Antioch, and Edessa. The last major (eighth) crusade ended unsuccessfully in 1270.

dar al-harb (Arabic, "house of war"). All areas beyond MUSLIM governance, considered unsafe because MUSLIMS could not practice their religion freely: a premodern term.

dar al-Islam (Arabic, "house of Islam"). All areas under MUSLIM rule, where MUSLIMS considered themselves assured of full human and legal rights: a premodern term.

Deobandis. Along with the BARELWIS and AHL AL-HADITH, a scholarly reformist group that emerged in India in the eighteenth century. The Deobandis were rigorous scholars of Islam, trained in HANAFI law at the famed Dar al-ʿUlum seminary in Deoband, India.

dhimmi (Arabic, from *dhimma*, "covenant of protection"). A non-Muslim living in a MUSLIM state who, in return for paying a tax (the *JIZYA*), is accorded a protected status and allowed to practice his or her religion.

Dome of the Rock. The first major expression of Islamic architecture and qurʾanic epigraphy, completed ca. 692 on the site from which, according to HADITH reports, Muhammad ascended into heaven (the *MIʿRAJ*) during his Night Journey (*israʾ*). Because its site is also considered holy by Jews, controversy has surrounded the structure for centuries.

Eid (ʿId) al-Adha (Arabic, "The Feast of the Sacrifice"). A three-day celebration marking the end of the HAJJ pilgrimage and commemorating the willingness of the prophet Ibrahim (Abraham) to sacrifice his son (usually understood to be Ismaʿil/Ishmael rather than Isaac) at God's command.

Eid (ʿId) al-Fitr (Arabic, "The Feast of Fast-Breaking"). A three-day celebration marking the end of the month-long RAMADAN fast. MUSLIMS celebrate with group prayer at the MOSQUE and feasting with family and friends.

falsafa (Arabic, "philosophy"). The study and methods of logical reasoning and metaphysical speculation. Initially inspired by Greek precedents, it eventually influenced all areas of Islamic thought.

Fatimid dynasty. An ISMAʿILI SHIʿI dynasty that claimed descent from Fatima (d. 632), daughter of the prophet Muhammad; it ruled portions of North Africa and the Middle East from 909 to 1171. The Fatimids founded the city of Cairo in 969, and al-Azhar University in 970.

fatwa (Arabic, "legal opinion"; pl. *fatawa*). An Islamic legal decision issued by a qualified jurist called a *MUFTI*. These decisions are provided in response to queries about issues ranging from personal to professional to political.

fiqh (Arabic, "understanding"). Islamic jurisprudence: articulation of the divine law (SHARIʿA) and its elaboration as rules designed to guide human conduct. There are two divisions of *fiqh*: devotional acts (*ʿibadat*) and social interactions (*muʿamalat*).

Five Pillars (in Arabic, *arkan al-din*, "supports of the religion"). The fundamental requirements of MUSLIM religious observance: confession of faith (*SHAHADA*), ritual prayer (*SALAT*), almsgiving (*ZAKAT*), fasting (*sawm*), and pilgrimage (*HAJJ*).

hadith (Arabic, "statement" or "report"; pl., *ahadith*). Traditions that convey the deeds and utterances of the prophet Muhammad. Collectively, the hadith form the second basis, after the QURʾAN, of Islamic law. Both SUNNIS and SHIʿIS consider certain collections of hadith to be authoritative.

hadith qudsi (Arabic, "sacred report"). Traditions deemed to have come directly from God to the Prophet (in contrast with the QURʾAN, which reached Muhammad through the medium of the angel Gabriel). They exist within the canonical HADITH collections and in separate compilations.

hajj (Arabic, "pilgrimage"). A complex combination of rituals performed in Mecca and its surrounding areas, mainly enacted between the 8th and the 12th of the Islamic month of Dhu al-Hijja. All adult MUSLIMS are obligated to perform the hajj at least once, health and finances permitting.

halal (Arabic, "allowed, permissible"). Activities in which MUSLIMS can engage or things they can eat and drink without violating Islamic legal dictates. For example, meat slaughtered according to Islamic legal prescriptions is called "halal meat."

Hanafi. The school of religious law within SUNNI Islam named for the Kufan scholar Abu Hanifa (d. 767). Predominant in India, Pakistan, Turkey, Central Asia, Russia, and China, it also has many adherents in Egypt, Syria, and Iraq, its birthplace.

Hanbali. The school of religious law within SUNNI Islam named for the Baghdadi scholar Ahmad ibn Hanbal (d. 855). Known for its strict interpretations, this school predominates in the Arabian peninsula (especially Saudi Arabia).

Hejaz. The western region of the Arabian peninsula (also spelled "Hijaz"); it borders the Red Sea and contains Mecca and Medina.

hijab (Arabic, "barrier"). In contemporary usage, the headscarf and full-cover clothing worn by MUSLIM women for reasons of modesty, God-consciousness, and MUSLIM identity. How women "practice" hijab, including how the scarf is wrapped and what clothing accompanies it, varies according to region and individual taste.

hijra (Arabic, "emigration"). The emigration of Muhammad and his followers to the city of Medina in 622 C.E. (also spelled "hegira"); this event marks the start of the Islamic calendar.

ijmaʿ (Arabic, "consensus"). Agreement on a legal ruling or on the meaning or authenticity of a tradition or interpretation. It is one of the "four sources" of *FIQH* (along with the QURʾAN, SUNNA, and *QIYAS*), and its scope is a major concern of Islamic legal literature.

ijtihad (Arabic, "exertion"). The independent reasoning by a legal scholar (*mujtahid*) to draw a new deduction from the fundamental sources of religious law.

ʿilm (Arabic, "knowledge," "science"; pl., *ʿulum*). According to a famed HADITH, "Seeking knowledge is obligatory upon each MUSLIM." Some interpret this statement as referring only to the knowledge contained in the QURʾAN, while others apply it to every area of learning.

imam (Arabic, "leader"). Most commonly, the person who leads the ritual prayer, whether for a small group in a private home or a large congregation in a MOSQUE. The SHIʿIS associate the term with specific descendants of ʿAli ibn Abi Talib (d. 661), revered as infallible interpreters of the religion.

Imami (Arabic, from IMAM). TWELVER SHIʿISM is also known as Imami SHIʿISM. Unlike the other branches of Shiʿism, which recognize five or seven IMAMS, the Imami SHIʿIS revere twelve successive leaders of the house of ʿAli ibn Abi Talib (d. 661).

Iranian Revolution. A broad-based social movement in 1978–79 that overthrew Mohammad Reza, SHAH of Iran (d. 1980), widely despised for his oppressive policies and lavish lifestyle.

islam (Arabic, "submission"). Purposeful surrender to the will of God. See also MUSLIM.

Islamist. One who seeks revival as a catalyst for sweeping social change anchored in often-contested interpretations of the QURʾAN and the SUNNA.

Ismaʿili. Member of the branch of Shiʿism who believes that Ismaʿil, son of the sixth IMAM, Jaʿfar al-Sadiq (d. 765), should have held the office of IMAM. Ismaʿilis, who founded the FATAMID DYNASTY, are thus known as "Seveners."

Jahiliya (Arabic, "Ignorance"). The period of time prior to Muhammad's seventh-century call to prophecy. Some reformers use this term to frame their call for a return to Islamic values by suggesting that the modern era is a moral equivalent to the pre-Islamic "Age of Ignorance."

jihad (Arabic, "striving," "exertion"). In full, "striving in the way of God": spiritual, financial, or military effort to bring about God's will. When referring to military action, it is often translated "holy war."

Jinn (Arabic, "demons," "invisible beings"). The third class of intelligent beings for whom salvation is possible (the others are humankind and angels). According to QURʾAN 55:15, God made the jinn—who cannot be seen by humans—from smokeless fire.

jizya (Arabic, "tax," "tribute"). The head tax paid by non-Muslims living under MUSLIM rule. See DHIMMI.

juzʾ (Arabic, "part"; pl., *ajzaʾ*). One-thirtieth of the QURʾAN: these units of division, roughly equal in length, facilitate the recitation of the text in a single month.

Kaʿba (Arabic, "cube"). The stone shrine in Mecca, believed to have been built by Adam and then rebuilt by Ibrahim (Abraham) and Ismaʿil (Ishmael), that became the most important site in Islam. MUSLIMS around the world face it when they pray, and pilgrims circumambulate it during the HAJJ.

kafir (Arabic, "ungrateful"; "infidel"). One who shows ingratitude to God by rejecting his divine revelation through the prophet Muhammad. Sometimes the term refers generally to all non-Muslims as unbelievers, but occasionally the PEOPLE OF THE BOOK, who are usually recognized as monotheists, are excluded.

kalam (Arabic, "discourse," "speech"). The study of (divine) speech. *ʿIlm al-kalam* refers properly to dialectical theology—the application of reasoned argument to a broad range of religious questions and issues.

Karbalaʾ. Site in Iraq of the pivotal battle in 680 in which UMAYYAD forces massacred SHIʿI revolutionaries. The battle and the martyrdom of al-Husayn, grandson of Muhammad and son of ʿAli ibn Abi Talib (d. 661), are commemorated every year by SHIʿIS around the world in the festival of ʿASHURAʾ.

khalifa. See CALIPH.

Khariji (Arabic, literally "outsider"). A strict and puritanical MUSLIM political and theological faction that emerged in the seventh century. The Kharijis held that through grave sin—such as allowing human arbitration rather than the divine decision given by battle—one ceased to be a MUSLIM and was liable to execution.

kufr (Arabic, "covering up"). Ingratitude, infidelity: willful disbelief in God after having been shown signs of his existence. See also *KAFIR*.

madhhab (Arabic, "a direction"; pl., *madhahib*). An intellectual orientation or way of thinking, particularly on legal matters; dozens of such "schools" emerged in the first centuries of Islam. The most famous remaining SUNNI legal schools are the HANAFI, MALIKI, SHAFIʿI, and HANBALI; the term *Jaʿfari* is often used to refer to SHIʿI legal theory and practice.

madrasa (Arabic, "place of study"). A traditional institution of learning to train students in the religious sciences of QURʾAN, HADITH, and Islamic jurisprudence.

Mahdi (Arabic, "the guided one"). For the SHIʿIS, the Twelfth IMAM whose messianic return will herald the Day of Judgment. Numerous historical figures have claimed this epithet in their campaigns of Islamic reformation.

Maliki. The school of religious law within SUNNI Islam named for the Medinan scholar Malik ibn Anas (d. 795), currently predominant in North Africa.

mihrab (Arabic, "niche"). Recess in the wall of a MOSQUE indicating the direction of Mecca (*QIBLA*), and thus the direction of prayer.

miʿraj (Arabic, "ascension"). The Night Journey during which the prophet Muhammad ascended into the heavens. A MOSQUE was built at the site of that ascension (the Temple Mount in Jerusalem), the DOME OF THE ROCK.

minaret (Arabic, from *manara*, "lighthouse," or *maʾdhana*, "place of calling to prayer"). A MOSQUE tower. Historically, a muezzin would stand on a balcony of the minaret to call MUSLIMS to daily prayer at five appointed times.

minbar (Arabic, "pulpit"). The pulpit of a MOSQUE, most often an elevated space accessed by a small staircase.

mosque (Arabic, from *masjid*, "place of prostration"). The site of congregational worship. Purpose-built mosques are typically large open spaces, often with separate areas for men and for women.

Mughal empire. The line of rulers, descended from the Turkic-Mongol conqueror Timur Lenk (Tamerlane, d. 1405), who ruled India from 1526 to 1759.

mufti (Arabic, "one who issues a FATWA"). A qualified and experienced legal scholar who issues nonbinding legal opinions (*fatawa*, sing. *FATWA*) in response to queries. Before the modern era of centralized governments, the local *mufti* was frequently the main articulator of Islamic legal procedure.

muhaddith (Arabic, "scholar of HADITH," "TRADITIONIST"). One who compiles and evaluates HADITH, as well as one devoted to using the HADITH (rather than subjective personal opinion) in forming juridical decisions.

mulla, mullah (Persian, "master"). An honorific given to a member of the learned class, or ulama, who is an expert in the religious sciences.

mu'min (Arabic, "believer"). One who believes in the precepts of ISLAM (often juxtaposed to *KAFIR*). A *mu'min* is often differentiated from a MUSLIM (one who practices ISLAM) as having a higher relationship with ALLAH. See also *IMAM*.

Muslim (Arabic, "one who submits"). The active participle of the word ISLAM. A Muslim is someone who confesses belief in the oneness of God and the prophethood of Muhammad and who attempts to live in conscious deference to the divine will.

Muʿtazila (Arabic, "those who withdraw"). Rationalist theologians who called themselves "the People of Justice and Divine Unity" and denied that God has eternal attributes, including the QUR'AN as his uncreated word; influential among SHIʿIS, this position was historically repudiated by SUNNIS.

Nation of Islam. African American sect, originally founded in 1930, that blends black nationalist ideologies and traditional Islamic elements. Most of its members became SUNNIS in the late 1980s; Louis Farrakhan (b. 1933) heads the estimated 10,000–50,000 members who remain.

Nestorians. Members of a branch of Christianity named for Nestorius, a fifth-century patriarch of Constantinople who professed that in Jesus there were two persons, one human and one divine (one of the major Catholic heresies). Evidence of Nestorian missionary activity can be found as far east as China.

Ottoman empire. A Turkic dynasty that ruled from the late thirteenth to the early twentieth century; it traced its lineage to Osman (1258–1324), its Anatolian founder. At its peak, it stretched from Algiers to Yemen, from the borders of Austria to Upper Egypt, and from Russia to the Persian Gulf.

People of the Book. Qur'anic designation for the adherents of monotheist, scripture-based religions—that is, mainly Jews and Christians.

Persia. Earlier name for the contemporary state of Iran, derived from a region of Iran known as Pars or Fars. Consequently, the Persian language is called Farsi. The name "Iran," officially adopted in 1935, means "land of the Aryans."

Pir (Persian, "elder"). In SUFISM, a spiritual master or teacher who, having already advanced on the path of nearness to God, can serve as a guide to the novice. In Persian and Indian SUFISM, the term usually replaces the Arabic *SHAYKH*.

positive law. Human law (as distinguished from "natural" or "divine" law).

qadi (Arabic, "judge" or "magistrate"). An official appointed by the ruler or government to render legally binding decisions.

Qajar dynasty. An ethnically Turkish dynasty that ruled Persia from 1794 to 1925. The final Qajar ruler was deposed by Reza SHAH Pahlavi (d. 1941), whose Pahlavi dynasty ruled until the IRANIAN REVOLUTION (1978–79).

qasida (Arabic, "ode" or "poem"). A poetic form often composed of three parts: typically, a beginning focused on longing for a lost love, a middle describing a difficult journey or trial, and a conclusion culminating in elaborate boasting about oneself or one's tribe.

qibla (Arabic, "direction of the KA'BA"). The direction toward which MUSLIMS face during prayer. MOSQUES have a niche called a MIHRAB to orient worshippers, and today various technologies, including digital compasses, enable MUSLIMS anywhere to direct themselves toward the KA'BA.

qiyas (Arabic, "analogy"). Analogical reasoning in Islamic law. By extrapolating from what is covered by the QUR'AN and SUNNA, legal scholars bring new circumstances and situations within the law's scope.

Qur'an (Arabic, "recitation"). The MUSLIM scripture. In Islamic belief, the Qur'an is the direct speech of God, revealed by the angel Gabriel to the prophet Muhammad, who in turn recited it to his followers. It is preserved on a heavenly tablet whose earthly reproduction, a *mushaf* (codex), contains 114 chapters, arranged roughly from longest to shortest.

Quraysh. The Meccan tribe of the prophet Muhammad. An oft-quoted HADITH states that Islam's leaders would be of the Quraysh, and both the UMAYYAD and 'ABBASID dynasties were descended from Qurayshi clans.

Ramadan. The ninth month of the Islamic calendar and the MUSLIM month of fasting; according to QUR'AN 2:185, during this month the QUR'AN was first revealed.

rashidun (Arabic, "rightly guided"). Collective honorific of the first four CALIPHS who ruled after the death of the prophet Muhammad: Abu Bakr al-Siddiq (r. 632–34), 'Umar ibn al-Khattab (r. 634–44), 'Uthman ibn 'Affan (r. 644–56), and 'Ali ibn Abi Talib (r. 656–61).

Safavid dynasty. The dynasty that ruled Persia from 1501 to 1722. Founded by SHAH Isma'il (d. 1524), it made TWELVER SHI'ISM the state religion.

sahih (Arabic, "authentic" or "sound"). A characterization of HADITH viewed as having a high degree of probability and therefore authority: their chains of transmission have been closely scrutinized and can be traced back to the Prophet himself. Two of the most famous collections of HADITH are *Sahih al-Bukhari* and *Sahih Muslim*.

salaf (Arabic, "predecessors"). The pious ancestors of the MUSLIM community, most often understood to be the COMPANIONS of the Prophet and the two generations of SUCCESSORS. These early MUSLIMS are viewed as the best representatives of lived Islam.

salat (Arabic, "prescribed prayer ritual"). Ritual prayer is prescribed five times daily: dawn (*fajr*), noon (*zuhr*), late afternoon (*'asr*), sunset (*maghrib*), and before retiring (*'isha'*). The *salat* is performed by reciting the first along with other SURAS of the QUR'AN, followed by two to four cycles of bowing and prostration.

Sassanid dynasty. The last pre-Islamic Persian empire (224–651), and the main rival of the Byzantine or Roman empire.

Sayyid (Arabic, "master, overlord"; pl., *sada*). An honorific originally bestowed on those who trace descent from the Prophet's family (see also AHL AL-BAYT). Today, it is commonly used in Arabic-speaking countries as the equivalent of "Mister."

seal. The last or final one, whether a prophet or saint. Muhammad is considered the "Seal of the Prophets" (*khatam al-nabiyyin*): i.e., there can be no authentic prophet after him.

Seljuk dynasty. A Turkish SUNNI military dynasty (also Seljuqs, Saljuqs) that ruled large portions of the Middle East from the eleventh century until the early thirteenth century (destroyed largely by internecine power struggles).

Shafiʿi. The school of religious law within SUNNI Islam named for al-Shafiʿi (d. 820), a scholar who could trace his lineage to the Prophet's tribe (QURAYSH). The Shafiʿi school, a tradition-based approach to legal sources, predominates in Indonesia and Malaysia, as well as in portions of East Africa.

shah. King (Persian).

shahada (Arabic, "witnessing"). The profession of faith that is the first of the FIVE PILLARS of ISLAM: "There is no god but God, and Muhammad is his Emissary."

Shariʿa (Arabic, "path to a watering hole"). Islamic law; the guidance of human conduct, including law, belief, and morals, as revealed by God to the MUSLIMS through the QURʾAN and the practice of Muhammad (as expressed in HADITH).

shaykh (Arabic, "elder" or "chief"). A title associated with authority and venerability. A *shaykh* can also be a tribal leader, a learned person, or a spiritual master (especially a SUFI mystical guide).

Shiʿi. A member of *shiʿat ʿAli* (Arabic, the "party of ʿAli")—those who believe that ʿAli ibn Abi Talib (d. 661), the cousin, son-in-law, and confidant of the Prophet, should have assumed leadership directly after his death. Different Shiʿi groups acknowledge somewhat different lineages of IMAMS, whose words in books of HADITH they (unlike SUNNIS) consider authoritative.

sira (Arabic, "way of living" or "noteworthy action"). Biographies, especially the traditional biographies of Muhammad.

Successors (Arabic, *tabiʿun*). Those of the generation following the generation of the Prophet's COMPANIONS (*tabiʿun* is also translated "Followers").

Sufi. A practitioner of SUFISM.

Sufism. Mystical Islam, or the quest for inner meaning in the practice and rituals of Islam. See also *TASAWWUF*.

sultan (Arabic, "ruler" or "one who has authority [*sulta*]"). MUSLIM sovereign. Originally a title broadly applied to those holding political authority, by the time of the SELJUKS it was the highest title conferred on rulers by the CALIPH.

sunna (Arabic, "way," "example"). The behavior and practice of the Prophet, held by MUSLIMS to be exemplary and worthy of imitation. The HADITH are the recorded accounts of the Prophet's sunna.

Sunni (Arabic, "follower of the SUNNA"). Self-described followers of the SUNNA of the Prophet (ca. 90 percent of the world's MUSLIMS; the others identify as SHIʿI). They look only to the QURʾAN and canonical books of HADITH for authority, and acknowledge four major legal schools: HANAFI, MALIKI, SHAFIʿI, and HANBALI.

sura (Arabic, "chapter"). A chapter of the QURʾAN; it contains 114 suras.

tafsir (Arabic, "interpretation"). QUR'AN exegesis.

taqlid (Arabic, "imitation"). In *FIQH*, the willingness to accept a legal position on the authority of earlier scholars, without independent investigation of its validity.

tasawwuf (Arabic, "to put on wool"). SUFISM; the Arabic is etymologically linked to the word for the coarse wool garments (*suf*) of ascetics. The SUFI path can be described as the quest for inner meaning in the practice and rituals of Islam.

tradition. See HADITH.

traditionist. See *MUHADDITH*.

Twelver Shi'ism. The branch of Shi'ism (also known as IMAMI Shi'ism) whose members revere twelve successive leaders of the house of 'Ali ibn Abi Talib (d. 661); other branches recognize only five or seven IMAMS.

Umayyad dynasty. The first great MUSLIM dynasty (661–750), founded by Mu'awiya ibn Abi Sufyan. The Umayyads traced their heritage to a clan of QURAYSH, the 'Abd Shams; they were overthrown by the 'ABBASIDS.

umma (Arabic, "community, nation"). The MUSLIM community as a whole. QUR'AN 2:143 refers to the MUSLIMS as a community of "the middle way" or of "moderation."

Wahhabi movement. The puritanical reformist movement founded in the Arabian peninsula by Muhammad ibn 'Abd al-Wahhab (d. 1792). Adopted in 1744 by the Sa'udi family, it helped the Sa'udis create Saudi Arabia as an absolute monarchy in 1932.

Yathrib. The ancient Arabic name for Medina. The city was renamed Madinat al-Nabi (City of the Prophet) after Muhammad's emigration there in 622.

zakat (Arabic, "purity," "integrity," "alms"). The obligatory tax paid by MUSLIMS as a religious and spiritual duty and used for charitable purposes. Once overseen by agents of the Islamic empire, the payment of *zakat* is now left to the individual conscience (though its collection is still a government function in Saudi Arabia).

Zoroastrianism. Religion founded by Zoroaster in 6 B.C.E. It flourished in SASSANID Iran until the rise of Islam; many Zoroastrians fled to India, where the religion's adherents are still called Parsis ("Persians"). Like Manichaeans, Zoroastrians have a dualistic worldview.

Selected Bibliography

INTRODUCTIONS, REFERENCE WORKS, AND HISTORICAL SURVEYS

Introductions

Several surveys present basic information about the Islamic religious tradition that is accessible to the interested general reader and suited to classroom use. Fazlur Rahman's *Islam*, 2nd ed. (Chicago: University of Chicago Press, 1979), a longtime favorite by a renowned Muslim scholar, deftly sketches the major themes of Islamic history and its enduring intellectual traditions. Three textbooks that have served thousands of students are David Waines, *An Introduction to Islam*, 2nd ed. (Cambridge: Cambridge University Press, 2003); Frederick Denny, *Introduction to Islam*, 4th ed. (Upper Saddle River, N.J.: Pearson Prentice Hall, 2011); and Andrew Rippin, *Muslims: Their Religious Beliefs and Practices*, 4th ed. (Abingdon, Oxon.: Routledge, 2011). A succinct but still valuable introduction by H. A. R. Gibb continues to be published under the outmoded title *Mohammedanism: An Historical Survey*, 2nd ed. (New York: Oxford University Press, 1962). Moojan Momen's *An Introduction to Shi῾i Islam: The History and Doctrines of Twelver Shi῾ism* (New Haven: Yale University Press, 1987) offers a solid overview of this important form of Islamic thought and practice.

Reference Works

The third edition of *The Encyclopaedia of Islam*, available to subscribers at http://referenceworks.brillonline.com, builds on two earlier multivolume print editions. The subject range is vast, covering historical, geographic, conceptual, ethnographic, and architectural topics with an emphasis on the classical, medieval, and early modern periods of Muslim civilization. In the new online edition, which is still being developed, the entry titles use English terminology where possible. The two previous editions (also online) were arranged alphabetically by transliterated Arabic subject headings. An English-language key to the entries of most interest for the religion of Islam in those editions may be found in the "Registry of Subjects" in the *Shorter Encyclopaedia of Islam*, ed. H. A. R. Gibb and J. H. Kramers (Ithaca, N.Y.: Cornell University Press, 1953). John Esposito, ed., *The Oxford Encyclopedia of the Modern Islamic World*, 4 vols. (New York: Oxford University Press, 1995), covers major figures, political movements, and religious orientations of modern and contemporary Islam. His *Oxford Islamic Studies Online*, www.oxfordislamicstudies.com, provides a searchable source for this and many other works. It also includes timelines, maps, and translations/interpretations of the Qur'an, as well as a concordance of the Qur'an.

The major English-language reference work on the Qur'an is Jane Dammen McAuliffe, ed., *Encyclopaedia of the Qur'ān*, 6 vols. (Leiden: Brill, 2001–06), also available at http://referenceworks.brillonline.com. In addition to articles on important figures, places, and concepts in the Qur'an, it contains extended essays on major topics and areas of research importance to the study of the Qur'an. Hugh Kennedy, ed., *An Historical Atlas of Islam*, 2nd rev. ed. (Leiden: Brill, 2002), updates an essential source on the historical cartography of the Muslim world. Suad Joseph, ed., *The Encyclopedia of Women and Islamic Cultures*, 6 vol. (Leiden: Brill, 2003–07), represents a substantial source of information on gender studies and the Muslim world. Important articles in the major areas of Islamic thought and practice have been collected in Mona Siddiqui, ed., *Islam*, 4 vols. (London: Sage, 2010).

Historical Surveys

Marshall G. S. Hodgson, *The Venture of Islam: Conscience and History in a World Civilization* (Chicago: University of Chicago Press, 1974), is a virtuoso three-volume work—*The Classical Age of Islam, The Expansion of Islam in the Middle Periods*, and *The Gunpowder Empires and Modern Times*—published several decades ago that is still studied and cited. Hodgson developed a vocabulary and a methodology for assessing Islam across many geographic and cultural zones, bringing a global perspective into more common scholarly use. His *Rethinking World History: Essays on Europe, Islam and World History* (Cambridge: Cambridge University Press, 1993) argues for such a global history and rejects efforts to create direct links between Greek history and the European Renaissance that exclude the influences of Islamic civilization. Although now somewhat dated, the best bibliographical guide to primary and secondary sources is R. Stephen Humphreys' *Islamic History: A Framework for Inquiry*, rev. ed. (Princeton: Princeton University Press, 1991). Ira Lapidus, *A History of Islamic Societies*, 2nd ed. (Cambridge: Cambridge University Press, 2002), offers an excellent, single-volume synthesis of the transformations wrought by the rise of Islam. As its many editions indicate, Philip K. Hitti, *History of the Arabs: From the Earliest Times to the Present*, rev. 10th ed. (New York: Palgrave Macmillan, 2002), remains an indispensable overview of the Arab role in Islamic civilization.

THE FOUNDATIONAL EPOCH, 610–750

Qurʾan

Several English translations enjoy wide acceptance and popularity. Marmaduke Pickthall's *Meaning of the Glorious Koran: An Explanatory Translation* (London: A. A. Knopf, 1930), is a reliable rendering by a British convert to Islam who chose to reproduce a biblically toned verbal register. A revised version in more contemporary English will soon be released as part of Jane Dammen McAuliffe, ed., *The Qurʾan*, Norton Critical Edition (New York: W. W. Norton, forthcoming). Richard Bell, *The Qurʾān: Translated, with a Critical Rearrangement of the Surahs*, 2 vols. (Edinburgh: T. T. Clark, 1937–39), develops the translator's hypothesis about the chronology of the Qurʾan's composition. Arthur Arberry, *The Koran Interpreted*, 2 vols. (London: Allen & Unwin; New York: Macmillan, 1955), strove to convey the literary power of qurʾanic Arabic, particularly in the shorter suras. Abdullah Yusuf Ali's 1946 translation, available under various titles in a wide range of editions and revisions, has been popular among English-speaking Muslims for decades. Muhammad Asad, *The Message of the Qurʾān* (Gibraltar: Dar al-Andalus, 1980), relies heavily on the rationalist interpretations of both medieval and modern scholars. A more recent translation by a well-regarded British scholar is M. A. S. Abdel Haleem's *The Qurʾān*, [corr. ed.] (Oxford: Oxford University Press, 2008).

W. Montgomery Watt's revision of *Bell's Introduction to the Qurʾan* (Edinburgh: Edinburgh University Press, 1970), a work originally published in 1950, provides a good mid-twentieth-century survey of qurʾanic studies, and its tables and indexes remain useful scholarly tools. M. A. Cook, *The Koran: A Very Short Introduction* (Oxford: Oxford University Press, 2000), is a succinct survey that reflects contemporary scholarly debates, while Ingrid Mattson, *The Story of the Qurʾan: Its History and Place in Muslim Life*, 2nd ed. (Malden, Mass.: Wiley-Blackwell, 2013), provides the insight of a contemporary believer and scholar. A time-tested and accessible overview of qurʾanic contents is Fazlur Rahman's *Major Themes of the Qurʾān*, 2nd ed. (Minneapolis: Bibliotheca Islamica, 1989). Jane Dammen McAuliffe, ed., *The Cambridge Companion to the Qurʾān* (Cambridge: Cambridge University Press, 2006), and Andrew Rippin, ed., *The Blackwell Companion to the Qurʾan* (Malden, Mass.: Blackwell, 2006), present helpful collections of contemporary scholarship on the Qurʾan.

Muhammad

For decades the standard English-language study comprised two volumes by W. Montgomery Watt, *Muhammad at Mecca* (Oxford: Clarendon Press, 1953) and *Muhammad at Medina* (Oxford: Clarendon Press, 1956). Jonathan Brown's *Muhammad: A Very Short Introduction* (Oxford: Oxford University Press, 2011) is an updated and more succinct presentation. Fred M. Donner, *Muhammad and the Believers: At the Origins of Islam* (Cambridge, Mass: Belknap, 2010), offers a major historian's rethinking of the life of

Muhammad and the events following his death. The standard classical source is Alfred Guillaume's translation of Ibn Ishaq's *The Life of Muhammad: A Translation of Ishāq's Sīrat Rasūl Allāh* (London: Oxford University Press, 1955). A modern biography that draws extensively on Ibn Ishaq's *Sira* was published by a British Muslim convert, Martin Lings, as *Muhammad: His Life Based on the Earliest Sources*, rev. ed. (Rochester, VT: Inner Traditions International, 2006). A more controversial work is that of the Iranian journalist and politician ʿAli Dashti, *Twenty-Three Years: A Study of the Prophetic Career of Mohammad*, trans. F. R. C. Bagley (London: Allan & Unwin, 1985). Harald Motzki, ed., *The Biography of Muhammad: The Issue of the Sources* (Leiden: Brill, 2000), is a major work on the sources for the biography of Muhammad.

Early History

Wilferd Madelung's *The Succession to Muhammad: A Study of the Early Caliphate* (Cambridge: Cambridge University Press, 1997) is an engaging yet solid historical narrative depicting the succession crisis after Muhammad's death. Jonathan P. Berkey's *The Formation of Islam: Religion and Society in the Near East, 600–1800* (Cambridge: Cambridge University Press, 2003) spans the centuries from the birth of Islam to the early modern period. For a rich and detailed account of early political history, see Hugh Kennedy's *The Prophet and the Age of the Caliphates: The Islamic Near East from the 6th to the 11th Century*, 2nd ed. (London: Longman, 2004). Patricia Crone's *Meccan Trade and the Rise of Islam* (Princeton: Princeton University Press, 1987) provocatively disputes the claim that Muhammad's Mecca was a major trading center.

THE CLASSICAL SYNTHESIS, 750–1756

Hadith* and *Sunna

Jonathan A. C. Brown, *Hadith: Muhammad's Legacy in the Medieval and Modern World* (London: Oneworld, 2009), offers an accessible introduction to traditional Muslim understandings of this genre of religious literature as well as to Western scholarship that challenges its historicity. Brown's *The Canonization of al-Bukhārī and Muslim: The Formation and Function of the Sunnī Ḥadīth Canon* (Leiden: Brill, 2007) is a more detailed and scholarly study of two major sources of classical hadith. John Burton's *An Introduction to the Hadith* (Edinburgh: Edinburgh University Press, 1994) has become a foundational work for the field of hadith studies, and Harald Motzki, ed., *Hadith: Origins and Development* (Aldershot: Ashgate/Variorum, 2004), collects the articles of major Western scholars of hadith.

Law

Wael B. Hallaq, *An Introduction to Islamic Law* (Cambridge: Cambridge University Press, 2009), is an excellent overview, complete with glossary and chronology, by a major scholar. Hallaq's *Sharīʿa: Theory, Practice, Transformations* (Cambridge: Cambridge University Press, 2009) builds on it with even more attention to social theory and regional context. Knut S. Vikor's *Between God and the Sultan: A History of Islamic Law* (Oxford: Oxford University Press, 2005) presents a useful overview of this vast topic. Bernard G. Weiss's *The Spirit of Islamic Law* (Athens: University of Georgia Press, 1998) develops the chief features of Muslim juristic thought. Devin J. Stewart, *Islamic Legal Orthodoxy: Twelver Shiite Responses to the Sunni Legal System* (Salt Lake City: University of Utah Press, 1998), draws the connections between Sunni and Shiʿi legal development. Michael Cook, *Commanding Right and Forbidding Wrong in Islamic Thought* (Cambridge: Cambridge University Press, 2000), is an encyclopedic work on a key concept in Islamic law and moral philosophy. Harald Motzki's *The Origins of Islamic Jurisprudence: Meccan Fiqh before the Classical Schools*, trans. Marion H. Katz (Leiden: Brill, 2001), challenges the prevailing skepticism about the earliest sources of Islamic legal reasoning.

Theology

An older work but one of enduring value is Arendt Jan Wensinck, *The Muslim Creed: Its Genesis and Historical Development* (Cambridge: The University Press, 1932). W. Montgomery Watt's *Islamic Philosophy and Theology: An Extended Survey*, 2nd ed. (Edinburgh: Edinburgh University Press, 1985) offers a chronological overview of these interrelated disciplines with attention to the social contexts within which individual thinkers worked. Tilman Nagel's *The History of Islamic Theology from Muhammad to the Present*, trans. Thomas Thornton (Princeton: Markus Wiener, 2000), draws from primary sources and explores major theological concepts. Tim Winter, ed., *The Cambridge Companion to Classical Islamic Theology* (Cambridge: Cambridge University Press, 2008), collects an important group of essays by noted scholars that address both historical and thematic study of classical Islamic theology.

Philosophy

Two standard surveys are Majid Fakhry, *A History of Islamic Philosophy*, 2nd ed. (New York: Columbia University Press, 1983), and Harry Austryn Wolfson, *The Philosophy of Kalam* (Cambridge, Mass.: Harvard University Press, 1976). More recent is Oliver Leaman, *An Introduction to Classical Islamic Philosophy*, 2nd ed. (Cambridge: Cambridge University Press, 2002). Seyyed Hossein Nasr, a venerable Shiʿi scholar, draws on a lifetime of learning in his *Islamic Philosophy from Its Origin to the Present: Philosophy in the Land of Prophecy* (Albany: State University of New York Press, 2006). Comparative work can be found in Lenn E. Goodman's *Jewish and Islamic Philosophy: Crosspollinations in the Classical Age* (New Brunswick, N.J.: Rutgers University Press, 1999). Two excellent essay collections are Michael E. Marmura, ed., *Islamic Theology and Philosophy: Studies in Honor of George F. Hourani* (Albany: State University of New York Press, 1984), and Peter Adamson and Richard C. Taylor, eds., *Cambridge Companion to Arabic Philosophy* (Cambridge: Cambridge University Press, 2005).

Scripture Scholarship

No scholarly translation of a multivolume work of qurʾanic exegesis has yet been published in English, but John Cooper translated the introduction and first part of al-Tabari's (d. 923) commentary as *A Commentary on the Qurʾān* (London: Oxford University Press, 1987). Selections from many commentators, both classical and modern, may be found in Helmut Gätje, *The Qurʾān and Its Exegesis: Selected Texts with Classical and Modern Muslim Interpretation*, trans. Alford T. Welch (Berkeley: University of California Press, 1976), while the two volumes of Mahmoud Ayoub's *The Qurʾan and Its Interpreters* (Albany: State University of New York Press, 1984–92) provide summaries of major exegetical works on verses from the first few suras. An edited volume of enduring value is Andrew Rippen, ed., *Approaches to the History of the Interpretation of the Qurʾān* (Oxford: Clarendon Press; New York: Oxford University Press, 1988). More recent collections are those by Gabriel Said Reynolds, ed., *The Qurʾān in its Historical Context* (London: Routledge, 2008); Angelika Neuwirth, Nicolai Sinai and Michael Marx, eds., *The Qurʾān in Context: Historical and Literary Investigations into the Qurʾānic Milieu* (Leiden: Brill, 2010); and Mustafa Shah, ed., *Tafsīr: Interpreting the Qurʾān*, 4 vols. (London: Routledge, 2013). Comparative studies on the interpretation of the Qurʾan and the Bible have been published in Jane Dammen McAuliffe, Barry D. Walfish, and Joseph W. Goering, eds., *With Reverence for the Word: Medieval Scriptural Exegesis in Judaism, Christianity, and Islam* (Oxford: Oxford University Press, 2003), and John C. Reeves, ed., *Bible and Qurʾān: Essays in Scriptural Intertexuality* (Atlanta: Society of Biblical Literature, 2003).

Private Ethics and Public Governance

George F. Hourani, *Reason and Tradition in Islamic Ethics* (Cambridge: Cambridge University Press, 1985), collects the essays of a major scholar of Islamic philosophy and ethics. Majid Fakhry's *Ethical Theories in Islam*, 2nd expanded ed. (Leiden: E. J. Brill, 1994), categorizes the developments within classical ethical theory as scriptural, theological, philosophical, and religious. A. Kevin Reinhart, *Before Revelation: The Boundaries of Muslim Moral Thought* (Albany: State University of New York Press, 1995), studies a millennium of Islamic writing on the question of the moral value of those actions performed before the revelations of the Qurʾan. Jonathan E. Brockopp, ed., *Islamic Ethics of Life: Abortion, War, and Euthanasia* (Columbia: University of South Carolina Press, 2003), gathers scholarly studies of these important contemporary issues.

For the study of Islamic governance a good beginning can be made with a still-standard survey, E. I. Rosenthal, *Political Thought in Medieval Islam: An Introductory Outline* (Cambridge: Cambridge University Press, 1958), and with Roy Mottahedeh's *Loyalty and Leadership in an Early Islamic Society*, rev. ed. (London: I. B. Tauris, 2001). Patricia Crone's *God's Rule: Government and Islam* (New York: Columbia University Press, 2004) explores early Islamic political thought until the advent of the Mongols, describing its diversity and how it seeds the development of modern political structures. An earlier book that she coauthored with Martin Hinds argues for a concept of power in Sunni Islam that was originally far closer to the Shiʿi model featuring the imam as both head of state and definitive source of religious authority: *God's Caliph: Religious Authority in the First Centuries of Islam* (Cambridge: Cambridge University Press, 1986). Shiʿi political theory is admirably detailed in Abdulaziz Abdulhussein Sachedina, *The Just Ruler (al-sultān al-ʿādil) in Shīʿite Islam: The Comprehensive Authority of the Jurist in Imamite Jurisprudence* (New York: Oxford University Press, 1988). A collection of important essays on state and society has been edited by Fred M. Donner as *The Articulation of Early Islamic State Structures* (Farnham, Eng.: Variorum, 2012).

History, Geography, and Travel Writing

In addition to those already noted, an excellent presentation of the sweep of Islamic history from the period of the early conquests through the premodern period is Michael Cook, ed., *The New Cambridge History of Islam*, 6 vols. (Cambridge: Cambridge University Press, 2010). Two good, single-volume surveys are Albert Hourani, *A History of the Arab Peoples* (Cambridge, Mass.: Belknap Press of Harvard University Press, 1991), and Hugh Kennedy, *When Baghdad Ruled the Muslim World: The Rise and Fall of Islam's Greatest Dynasty* (Cambridge, Mass.: Da Capo Press, 2004). The preeminent classical historian Abu Jaʾfar ibn Jarir al-Tabari is the subject of an excellent volume of essays: Hugh Kennedy, ed., *Al-Ṭabarī: A Medieval Muslim Historian and His Work* (Princeton: Darwin Press, 2008). For Muslim sources on the Crusades, one may consult Francesco Gabrieli's *Arab Historians of the Crusades: Selected and Translated from the Arabic Sources*, trans. E. J. Costello (Berkeley: University of California Press, 1969), and Carole Hillenbrand's *The Crusades—Islamic Perspectives* (Chicago: Fitzroy Dearborn, 1999). Monographs on several of the authors featured in this anthology have been published. For example, Ross E. Dunn, *The Adventures of Ibn Battuta: A Muslim Traveler of the Fourteenth Century*, rev. ed. (Berkeley: University of California Press, 2005); Paul M. Cobb, *Usama ibn Munqidh: Warrior-Poet of the Age of the Crusades* (Oxford: Oneworld, 2005); and Natalie Zemon Davis, *Trickster Travels: A Sixteenth-Century Muslim between Worlds* (New York: Hill and Wang, 2006). Two recent works of social history are Yossef Rapoport, *Marriage, Money and Divorce in Medieval Islamic Society* (Cambridge: Cambridge University Press, 2005), and Khaled El-Rouayheb, *Before Homosexuality in the Arab-Islamic World, 1500–1800* (Chicago: University of Chicago Press, 2005). Good regional histories include S. D. Goitein's monumental *A Mediterranean Society: The Jewish Communities of the Arab World as Portrayed in the Documents of the Cairo Geniza*, 6 vols. (Berkeley: University of California Press, 1967–93); Harold Bailey, ed., *The Cambridge History of Iran*, 7 vols. (Cambridge: Cambridge University Press, 1993); Annemarie Schimmel, *Islam in the Indian Subcontinent* (Leiden: E. J. Brill, 1980); David Morgan, *Medieval Persia, 1040–1797* (London: Longman, 1988); Salma Khadra Jayyusi, ed., *The Legacy of Muslim Spain*, 2nd ed., 2 vols. (Leiden: E. J. Brill, 1994); Nehemiah Levtzion and Randall L. Pouwels, *The History of Islam in Africa* (Athens: Ohio University Press, 2000).

The Mystical Interiority of Islam

Three standard introductions are A. J. Arberry, *An Introduction to the History of Ṣūfism: The Sir Abdullah Suhrawady Lectures for 1942* (London: Longman, 1942), his *Sufism: An Account of the Mystics of Islam* (London: Allen & Unwin, 1950), and Annemarie Schimmel's *Mystical Dimensions of Islam* (Chapel Hill: University of North Carolina Press, 1975). Toshihiko Izutsu's *Sufism and Taoism: A Comparative Study of Key Philosophical Concepts* (Berkeley: University of California Press, 1983) presents an insightful comparison of major philosophical concepts in both traditions. Two fine source books of Sufi writings are Michael Sells, *Early Islamic Mysticism: Sufi, Qurʾan, Miraj, Poetic and Theological Writings* (New York: Paulist Press, 1996), and John Renard, *Tales of God's Friends: Islamic Hagiography in Translation* (Berkeley: University of California Press, 2009). Among the excellent studies of early modern and modern Sufism are Martin Lings, *A Sufi Saint of the Twentieth Century: Shaikh Aḥmad al-ʿAlawi, His Spiritual Heritage and Legacy*, 3rd ed. (Cambridge: Islamic Texts So, 1993); Valerie

J. Hoffman, *Sufism, Mystics, and Saints in Modern Egypt* (Columbia: University of South Carolina Press, 1995); and Vincent J. Cornell, *Realm of the Saint: Power and Authority in Moroccan Sufism* (Austin: University of Texas Press, 1998). Studies of individual Sufis abound, such as Margaret Smith, *Rabiʿa the Mystic and Her Fellow-Saints in Islām* (Cambridge: The University Press, 1928); Louis Massignon, *The Passion of al-Hallāj: Mystic and Martyr of Islam*, trans. Herbert Mason, 4 vols. (Princeton: Princeton University Press, 1983); and William C. Chittick, *The Sufi Path of Knowledge: Ibn al-ʿArabi's Metaphysics of Imagination* (Albany: State University of New York Press, 1989).

Literature

Roger M. A. Allen, *An Introduction to Arabic Literature* (Cambridge: Cambridge University Press, 2000), is an excellent introductory work that spans the full chronology of literary output as well as the diverse genres of this production. The individual volumes of *The Cambridge History of Arabic Literature*, ed. A. F. L. Beeston et al., 6 vols. (Cambridge: Cambridge University Press, 1983–2006), treat the pre-Islamic through Umayyad period, the era of the ʿAbbasids, and the literature of al-Andalus, as well as the post-classical, postcolonial, and modern periods. Two good surveys of the literature of Muslim Spain are María Rosa Menocal, Raymond P. Scheindlin, and Michael Sells, eds., *The Literature of Al-Andalus* (Cambridge: Cambridge University Press, 2000), and James T. Monroe, comp., *Hispano-Arabic Poetry: A Student Anthology* (Berkeley: University of California Press, 1974).

Much important Islamic literature was written in Persian. A major publishing program on the history of Persian literature has been launched at Columbia University. The first volume is J. T. P. de Bruijn, ed., *General Introduction to Persian Literature* (London: I. B. Tauris, 2009).

Finally, an extensive literature has been generated by the collected tales known as *The Thousand and One Nights* and *The Arabian Nights*. Two helpful guides are Robert Irwin's *The Arabian Nights: A Companion* (London: Allen Lane, 1994) and *The Arabian Nights*, ed. Daniel Heller-Roazen, Norton Critical Edition (New York: Norton, 2010), which includes the Husain Haddawy translation of Muhsin Mahdi's authoritative text.

THE CLASSICAL SYNTHESIS ENCOUNTERS MODERNITY, 1756–to the Present

Colonialism and Postcolonialism

Numerous works provide important contextualization for the literatures of the colonial and postcolonial periods. These include Barbara Daly Metcalf, *Islamic Revival in British India: Deoband, 1860–1900* (Princeton: Princeton University Press, 1982); Timothy Mitchell, *Colonising Egypt* (Cambridge: Cambridge University Press, 1988); Almut Höfert and Armando Salvatore, eds., *Between Europe and Islam: Shaping Modernity in a Transcultural Space*, (Brussels: Peter Lang, 2000); and Michael Francis Laffan, *Islamic Nationhood and Colonial Indonesia: The Umma below the Winds* (London: RoutledgeCurzon, 2003). For the American Muslim experience, a good place to start is Zahid H. Bukhari, Sulayman S. Nyang, Mumtaz Ahmad, and John L. Esposito, eds., *Muslims' Place in the American Public Square: Hope, Fears, and Aspirations* (Walnut Creek, Calif.: AltaMira Press, 2004).

Studies of particular writers in this period are plentiful. A good example is Annemarie Schimmel's *Gabriel's Wing: A Study into the Religious Ideas of Sir Muhammad Iqbal*, 2nd ed. (Lahore: Iqbal Academy Pakistan, 1989). Beverly B. Mack and Jean Boyd, *One Woman's Jihad: Nana Asmaʾu, Scholar and Scribe* (Bloomington: Indiana University Press, 2000), bring this important voice to a broader audience. Mark Sedgwick, *Muhammad Abduh* (Oxford: Oneworld, 2010), profiles this prominent Muslim modernist as part of the series "Makers of the Muslim World." A later Egyptian reformer, Sayyid Qutb, has been the subject of a spate of books, more recently because of his ideological connections with al-Qaʿida. These include William E. Shepard, *Sayyid Qutb and Islamic Activism: A Translation and Critical Analysis of "Social Justice in Islam"* (Leiden: E. J. Brill, 1996); Paul Berman, *Terror and Liberalism* (New York: Norton, 2003); Adnan A. Musallam, *From Secularism to Jihad: Sayyid Qutb and the Foundations of Radical Islamism* (Westport, Conn.: Praeger, 2005); and John Calvert, *Sayyid Qutb and the Origins of Radical Islamism* (New York: Columbia University Press, 2010).

The Religious Reassertion

In the past two decades, particularly since the tragedy of September 11, 2001, a flood of publications dealing with forms of religious revival in the Muslim world has been produced in the fields of comparative politics, international relations, religious studies, and recent Middle Eastern history. In many works in each of these fields, revised understandings of the "secularization hypothesis" are central. Two studies of particular relevance to this debate within the study of Muslim societies are Talal Asad, *Formations of the Secular: Christianity, Islam, Modernity* (Stanford, Calif.: Stanford University Press, 2003), and Abdullahi Ahmed an-Naʿim, *Islam and the Secular State: Negotiating the Future of Shariʿa* (Cambridge, Mass.: Harvard University Press, 2008). Studies of particular countries and societies include Daniel Brumberg, *Reinventing Khomeini: The Struggle for Reform in Iran* (Chicago: University of Chicago Press, 2001); Stephen Philip Cohen, *The Idea of Pakistan* (Washington, D.C.: Brookings Institution Press, 2004); and Loren D. Lybarger, *Identity and Religion in Palestine: The Struggle between Islamism and Secularism in the Occupied Territories* (Princeton: Princeton University Press, 2007). Rudolph Peters, *Jihad in Classical and Modern Islam: A Reader*, 2nd ed. (Princeton: Markus Wiener, 2005), provides important background for a contemporary understanding of this concept. A valuable reference work that covers the formative periods of Islamic political thought, as well as its contemporary manifestations, is Gerhard Bowering, ed., *The Princeton Encyclopedia of Islamic Political Thought* (Princeton: Princeton University Press, 2013).

The Emergence of Women's Voices

Three works that deal with the historical development of gender views in the early sources are Leila Ahmad, *Women and Gender in Islam: Historical Roots of a Modern Debate* (New Haven: Yale University Press, 1992); Barbara Freyer Stowasser, *Women in the Qur'an, Traditions, and Interpretation* (New York: Oxford University Press, 1994); and D. A. Spellberg, *Politics, Gender and the Islamic Past: The Legacy of ʿA'isha bint Abi Bakr* (New York: Columbia University Press, 1994). Prominent contemporary voices on gender equity include Asma Barlas, *"Believing Women" in Islam: Unreading Patriarchal Interpretations of the Qur'ān* (Austin: University of Texas Press, 2002); Khaled Abou El Fadl, *Speaking in God's Name: Islamic Law, Authority and Women* (Oxford: Oneworld, 2001); Amina Wadud, *Inside the Gender Jihad: Women's Reform in Islam* (Oxford: Oneworld, 2006); Kecia Ali, *Sexual Ethics and Islam: Feminist Reflections on Qur'an, Hadith, and Jurisprudence* (Oxford: Oneworld, 2006); and Margot Badran, *Feminism in Islam: Secular and Religious Convergences* (Oxford: Oneworld, 2009).

Negotiating Religious Pluralism

Yohanan Friedmann's *Tolerance and Coercion in Islam: Interfaith Relations in the Muslim Tradition* (Cambridge: Cambridge University Press, 2003) offers a sensitive historical analysis of Muslim perspectives on other religious faiths. Sohail H. Hashmi, ed., *Islamic Political Ethics: Civil Society, Pluralism, and Conflict* (Princeton: Princeton University Press, 2002), and Robert W. Hefner, ed., *Remaking Muslim Politics: Pluralism, Contestation, Democratization* (Princeton: Princeton University Press, 2005), explore contemporary themes and issues. A comparative study of Europe and North America may be found in Jocelyne Cesari, *When Islam and Democracy Meet: Muslims in Europe and in the United States* (New York: Palgrave Macmillan, 2004). Two helpful entries among many books on interfaith dialogue between Muslims and people of other faiths are Michael Ipgrave, ed., *Scriptures in Dialogue: Christians and Muslims Studying the Bible and the Qur'an Together* (London: Church House, 2004), and Jane Idleman Smith, *Muslims, Christians, and the Challenge of Interfaith Dialogue* (Oxford: Oxford University Press, 2007).

Permissions Acknowledgments

GENERAL INTRODUCTION

Kay Ryan, "On the Nature of Understanding": From *The New Yorker*, July 25, 2011. Copyright © 2011 by Kay Ryan. Reprinted by permission of the author.

TEXT

THE CONFERENCE OF THE BIRDS by Farid Ud-Din Attar, tr. Afkham Darbandi and Dick Davis (Penguin Books Ltd, 1984). Copyright © Afkham Darbandi and Dick Davis, 1984. Reprinted by permission of Penguin Group (UK).

Qur'an 1, 4, 12, 55, 78–114: From QUR'AN: A NORTON CRITICAL EDITION, edited by Jane Dammen McAuliffe. Copyright © 2014 by W. W. Norton & Company, Inc. Used by permission of W. W. Norton & Company, Inc.

Ibn Hisham: From THE LIFE OF MUHAMMAD: A TRANSLATION OF ISHAQ'S SIRAT RASUL ALLAH, translated by Alfred Guillaume. Published by Oxford University Press, Pakistan.

Al-Bukhari, "The Story of the Night Journey" and "The Ascension": From SAHIH AL-BUKHARI: THE EARLY YEARS OF ISLAM, translated by Muhammad Asad.

Muslim ibn al-Hajjaj, *The Book of Virtue, The Book of Knowledge,* and *The Book Pertaining to Paradise:* From SAHIH MUSLIM: BEING TRADITIONS OF THE SAYINGS AND DOINGS OF THE PROPHET MUHAMMAD AS NARRATED BY HIS COMPANIONS AND COMPILED UNDER THE TITLE AL-JAMI'-US-SAHIH, N.D., VOLUME IV, translated by 'Abdul Hamid Siddiqi. Published by Adam Publisher. Used by permission of the publisher.

Al-Nawawi: From GARDENS OF THE RIGHTEOUS: RIYADH AS-SALIHIN OF IMAM NAWAWI, translated by Muhammad Zafrulla Khan. Copyright © 1974 by Muhammad Zafrulla Khan. Reproduced with permission of Rowman & Littlefield Publishing Group, Inc. in the format textbook via Copyright Clearance Center.

Muhammad Baqir Majlisi, "The Incomparable Lord," "Seeing God and the Name That Can Be Named," "God's Might and Majesty," and "Profession of Unity": From A SHI'ITE ANTHOLOGY, edited by Allamah Sayyid M.Husayn Tabatabai, translated by William Chittick. Copyright © 1980 by Muhammadi Trust of Great Britain and Northern Ireland. Reprinted by permission of Muhammadi Trust of Great Britain and Northern Ireland.

Al-Shafi'i: From THE EPISTLE ON LEGAL THEORY, translated by Joseph E. Lowry. Published by New York University Press.

Ibn Hanbal: From CHAPTERS ON MARRIAGE AND DIVORCE: RESPONSES OF IBN HANBAL AND IBN RAHWAYH, translated and with an introduction by Susan A. Spectorsky. Copyright © 1993 by University of Texas Press. Reprinted by permission of University of Texas Press.

Al-Qayrawani: From *Treatise on Law.* Translated by Alexander David Russell and Abdullah al-Ma'mun Suhrawardy. Public domain.

Abu Hanifa, *The Fikh Akbar I* and *Fikh Akbar II*: From THE MUSLIM CREED: ITS GENESIS AND HISTORICAL DEVELOPMENT, translated by A. J. Wensinck. Copyright © 1932 by Cambridge University Press. Reprinted with permission of Cambridge University Press.

Al-Ash'ari, *The Concise Remarks*: From THE THEOLOGY OF AL-ASH'ARI, translated by Richard H. McCarthy.

Ibn Babawayh: From A SHI'ITE CREED: A TRANSLATION OF I'TIQADAT AL-IMAMIYYA (THE BELIEFS OF THE IMAMIYYA), translated by Asaf A. A. Fyzee. Reprinted by permission of World Organization for Islamic Studies.

Al-Ghazali, The *Revival of the Religious Sciences: The Book of the Conduct of Life as Exemplified by the Prophetic Character:* From BOOK XX OF AL- GHAZĀLĪ'S IHYĀ' 'ULŪM AL-DĪN, translated by L. Zolondek.

Shah Wali Allah, "Fortifying the Religion Against Distortion": From THE CONCLUSIVE ARGUMENT FROM GOD, translated by Marcia Hermansen. Copyright © 1996 by E. J. Brill, Leiden, Netherlands. Reprinted by permission of Brill.

Ibn 'Abd al-Wahhab: From *The History and Doctrines of the Wahhabis.* Public domain.

Al-Farabi, *The Virtuous City*: From AL-FĀRĀBĪ ON THE PERFECT STATE, translated by Richard Walzer. Copyright © 1985 by Oxford University Press. By permission of Oxford University Press.

Ibn Sina (Avicenna), *Healing, Metaphysics X,* chapter 2–5: From MEDIEVAL POLITICAL PHILOSOPHY: A SOURCEBOOK, translated by Michael E. Marmura and edited by Ralph Lerner and Muhsin Mahdi. Copyright © 1963 by the Free Press of Glencoe. Reprinted by permission of Ralph Lerner.

Ibn Rushd (Averroes), "Philosophical Interpretations of Scripture Should Not Be Taught to the Majority": From AVERROES ON THE HARMONY OF RELIGION AND PHILOSOPHY, translated by George F. Hourani. Copyright © 1961. Reprinted with the permission of the E. J. W. Gibb Memorial Trust.

Fakhr al-Din al-Razi, *The Great Commentary*: From CLASSICAL ISLAM: A SOURCEBOOK OF RELIGIOUS LITERATURE, edited and translated by Norman Calder, Jawid Mojaddedi, and Andrew Rippin. Copyright © 2003 by Norman Calder, Jawid Mojaddedi, and Andrew Rippin. Reproduced by permission of Taylor & Francis UK.

Ibn Taymiyya, *Introductory Treatise on the Principles of Tafsir*: From WINDOWS ON THE HOUSE OF ISLAM: MUSLIM SOURCES ON SPIRITUALITY AND RELIGIOUS LIFE, edited by John Renard. Copyright © 1998 by the Regents of the University of California. Published by the University of California Press.

Miskawayh: From THE REFINEMENT OF CHARACTER: A TRANSLATION FROM THE ARABIC OF AHMAD IBN-MUHAMMAD MISKAWAYH'S TAHDHĪB AL-AKHLĀQ, translated by Constantine K. Zurayk (Beirut: American University of Beirut, 1968). Reproduced with permission from the American University of Beirut Press.

Al-Mawardi, "On the Appointment of Prayer Leaders": From THE ORDINANCES OF GOVERNMENT, translated by Wafaa H. Wahba. Copyright © 1996 by Garnet Publishing Ltd. Reading UK. Reprinted by permission of Garnet Publishing Ltd.

Nizam al-Mulk: From THE BOOK OF GOVERNMENT, OR RULES FOR KINGS, translated by Hubert Darke. Copyright © 1960 by Routledge & Kegan Paul. Reproduced by permission of Taylor & Francis Books UK.

Nasir al-Din al-Tusi: From THE NASIREAN ETHICS, translated by G. M. Wickens. Copyright © 1964 by George Allen Unwin Ltd. Reproduced by permission of Taylor & Francis UK.

Ibn al-Kalbi: From THE BOOK OF IDOLS. Translated by Nabih Amin Faris. Public domain.

Al-Baladhuri: From THE ORIGINS OF THE ISLAMIC STATE. Translated by Philip K. Hitti. Public domain.

Al-Tabari: From THE HISTORY OF AL-TABARĪ: 'ABBASID AUTHORITY AFFIRMED, VOLUME XXVIII: 'ABBASID AUTHORITY AFFIRMED: THE EARLY YEARS OF AL-MANSUR A.D. 753–763/A.H., translated by Jane Dammen McAuliffe, the State University of New York Press © 1995, State University of New York. All rights reserved.

Ibn al-Nadim: From THE FIHRIST OF AL-NADIM: A TENTH-CENTURY SURVEY OF MUSLIM CULTURE, edited and translated by Bayard Dodge. Copyright © 1970 by Columbia University Press. Used by permission of Columbia University Press.

Ibn Munqidh: From AN ARAB-SYRIAN GENTLEMAN AND WARRIOR IN THE PERIOD OF THE CRUSADES, translated by Philip K. Hitti. Copyright © 2000 by Columbia University Press. Used by permission of Columbia University Press.

Ibn Jubayr: From THE TRAVELS OF IBN JUBAYR, translated by R. J. C. Broadhurst. Published by Jonathan Cape. Reprinted by permission of The Random House Group Limited.

Ibn Battuta: From TRAVELS IN ASIA AND AFRICA, 1325–1354, translated by H. A. R. Gibb. Copyright © 1929 by Routlege & Kegan Paul. Reproduced by permission of Taylor & Francis UK.

Ibn Khaldun, "Fifth Prefatory Discussion": From THE MUQADDIMAH: AN INTRODUCTION TO HISTORY, translated by Franz Rosenthal. Copyright © 2005 by Princeton University Press. Reprinted by permission of Princeton University Press.

Al-Hasan al-Wazzan: From DESCRIPTION OF AFRICA. Translated from the Italian by Dennis McAuliffe.

Zayn al-'Abidin: From THE PSALMS OF ISLAM, translated by William C. Chittick. Copyright © 1988 by Muhammadi Trust of Great Britain and Northern Ireland. Reprinted by permission of Muhammadi Trust of Great Britain and Northern Ireland.

Al-Bistami, *The Mi'raj*: From EARLY ISLAMIC MYSTICISM, edited and translated by Michael Sells. Copyright © 1996 by Michael Sells. Reproduced with permission of Paulist Press in the format textbook via Copyright Clearance Center.

Al-Hakim al-Tirmidhi, *The Seal of the Saints*: From INTERPRETING THE SELF: AUTOBIOGRAPHY IN THE ARABIC LITERARY TRADITION, edited by Dwight F. Reynolds et al. Copyright © 2001 by the Regents of the University of California. Published by the University of California Press.

Al-Sulami, *Memorial of Pious Sufi Women*: From EARLY SUFI WOMEN: DHIKR AN-NISWA AL-MUTA'ABBIDĀT AS-SŪFIYYAT, edited and translated by Rkia Elaroui Cornell. Reprinted by permission of Fons Vitae Publishing

Al-Ghazali: From DELIVERANCE FROM ERROR: AN ANNOTATED TRANSLATION OF AL-MUNQIDH MIN AL DALĀL WORKS OF AL-GHAZĀLĪ, translated and edited by Richard Joseph McCarthy. Reprinted by permission of Fons Vitae Publishing.

Ibn al-'Arabi, "The Most Beautiful Names": From THE MECCAN REVELATIONS, VOLUME I, translated and edited by Michael Chodkiewicz, William C. Chittick, and James W. Morris. Copyright © 2002. Reprinted by permission of William C. Chittick and Pir Press.

Rumi, "The Song of the Reed," "The Lion, the Wolf, and the Fox," and "A Guest Came to Joseph, and Joseph Demanded a Gift from Him": From THE MASNAVI: BOOK ONE, translated by Jawid Mojaddedi. Copyright © 2004 by Jawid Mojaddedi. By permission of Oxford University Press.

Two *Ginans*: From ECSTASY AND ENLIGHTENMENT: THE ISMAILI DEVOTIONAL LITERATURE OF SOUTH ASIA by Pir Hasan Kabir al-Din, edited and translated by Ali S. Asani. Copyright © 2002 by Islamic Publications. Reprinted by permission of I. B. Tauris Publishers.

Mulla Sadra Shirazi: From THE WISDOM OF THE THRONE: AN INTRODUCTION TO THE PHILOSOPHY OF MULLA SADRA, translated by James Winston Morris. Reprinted by permission of the translator.

'Alqama ibn Abada, "Is What You Knew Kept Secret": From DESERT TRACINGS: SIX CLASSIC ARABIAN ODES, translated and edited by Michael A. Sells. Copyright © 1989 by Michael A. Sells. Reprinted by permission of Wesleyan University Press.

Nizami Ganjavi, "In Praise of the Chief among Prophets" and "On the Prophet's Ascent to Heaven": From THE HAFT PAYKAR: A MEDIEVAL PERSIAN ROMANCE, translated by Julie Scott Meisami. Copyright © 1995 by Julie Scott Meisami. By permission of Oxford University Press.

Sa'di, "Love and Youth," Stories 20 and 21: From THE GULISTAN (ROSE GARDEN) OF SA'DI, translated by Wheeler M. Thackston. Copyright © 2008 by Ibex Publishers, Inc. Courtesy of Ibex Publishers.

Hafiz, "A Mad Heart" (trans. A. J. Arberry), "Where Are the Tidings of Union?" (trans. G. Bell), "The Riddle of Life" (trans. R. Le Gallienne): From FIFTY POEMS OF HAFIZ. Copyright © 1947 Cambridge University Press. Reprinted with permission of Cambridge University Press.

Al-Jahiz, "The Art of Keeping Secrets and Holding One's Tongue": From THE LIFE AND WORKS OF JĀHIZ, edited by Charles Pellat. Copyright © 1969 by Routledge & Kegan Paul. Reproduced by permission of Taylor & Francis Books UK.

Ibn Hazm, "The Signs of Love": From THE RING OF THE DOVE: A TREATISE ON THE ART AND PRACTICE OF ARAB LOVE, translated by A. J. Arberry. Reprinted by permission of Luzac Oriental.

From **THE ARABIAN NIGHTS**: THE THOUSAND AND ONE NIGHTS, translated by Husain Haddawy. Copyright © 1990 by W. W. Norton & Company, Inc. Used by permission of W. W. Norton & Company, Inc.

Dara Shukoh, *The Greatest Secret*: From SOURCES OF INDIAN TRADITION, SECOND EDITION, VOLUME ONE: FROM THE BEGINNING TO 1800, edited by Ainslie T. Embree. Copyright © 1988 by Columbia University Press. Reprinted by permission of Columbia University Press.

Al-Jabarti: From AL-JABARTĪ'S CHRONICLE OF THE FIRST SEVEN MONTHS OF THE FRENCH OCCUPATION OF EGYPT, edited and translated by S. Moreh. Copyright © 1975 by E. J. Brill, Leiden, Netherlands. Reprinted by permission of Brill.

Nana Asma'u, "Elegy for Bello" and "Bello's Character": From COLLECTED WORKS OF NANA ASMA'U, DAUGHTER OF USMAN D'AN FODIYO (1793–1864), edited and translated by Jean Boyd and Beverly B. Mack. Reprinted by permission of Michigan State University Press.

Muhammad 'Abduh: From THE THEOLOGY OF UNITY, translated by Ishaq Musa'ad and Kenneth Cragg.

Rashid Ahmad Gangohi, "Two Fatwas on Hajj in British India" (pp. 184–85; translated by Barbara D. Metcalf): From ISLAMIC LEGAL INTERPRETATION: MUFTIS AND THEIR FATWAS, edited by Muhammad Khalid Masud, Brinkley Messick, and David S. Powers. Cambridge, MA: Harvard University Press. Copyright © 1996 by the President and Fellows of Harvard College. Reprinted by permission of the publisher.

Muhammad Iqbal, "Complaint": From THE COMPLAINT AND ANSWERS, translated by A. J. Arberry.

Mahmud Shaltut, "The Verses of Fighting": From JIHAD IN CLASSICAL AND MODERN ISLAM: A READER, Second Edition, pp. 70–80, edited by Rudolph Peters (Princeton Series on the Middle East: Bernard Lewis and Andras Hamori, editors). Copyright © 2005 by Rudolph Peters for the updated and expanded edition. Reprinted by permission of Markus Wiener Publishers.

Sayyid Qutb, "*Jihaad* in the Cause of God": From MILESTONES. Copyright © 2007. Reprinted by permission of KAZI Publications, Inc.

Malcolm X, "Mecca": From THE AUTOBIOGRAPHY OF MALCOLM X by Malcolm X and Alex Haley. Copyright © 1964 by Alex Haley and Malcolm X. Copyright © 1965 by Alex Haley and Betty Shabazz. Used by permission of Random House, Inc., and the Random House Group Limited.

Ruhollah Khomeini, "The First Day of God's Government": From ISLAM AND REVOLUTION, translated by Hamid Algar. Copyright © 2002 Kegan Paul. Reproduced by permission of Taylor & Francis UK.

Mohammed Arkoun: From RETHINKING ISLAM: COMMON QUESTIONS, UNCOMMON ANSWERS, translated by Robert D. Lee. Reprinted by permission of Editeur/Les editions Garncher.

Usama Bin Ladin, "The World Islamic Front": From MESSAGES TO THE WORLD: THE STATEMENTS OF OSAMA BIN LADEN, edited by Bruce Lawrence, translated by James Howarth. Reprinted by permission of Verso.

Ebrahim Moosa, "Critical Islam: Beyond Apologia": From PROGRESSIVE MUSLIMS: ON JUSTICE, GENDER AND PLURALISM, edited by Omid Safi. Copyright © 2003 by Omid Safi. Reprinted with permission of Oneworld Publications Ltd. in the format textbook via Copyright Clearance Center.

Sayyid Ahmad Khan, "The Rights of Women": From MODERNIST AND FUNDAMENTALIST DEBATES IN ISLAM: A READER, translated by Kamran Talattof, edited by Mansoor Moaddel and Kamran Talattof. Copyright © 2002 by Palgrave Macmillan. Reproduced with permission of Palgrave Macmillan.

Muhammad 'Abduh, "Polygamy": From THE QUR'ĀN AND ITS EXEGESIS: SELECTED TEXTS WITH CLASSICAL AND MODERN MUSLIM INTERPRETATIONS by Helmut Gätje, translated by Alford T. Welch. Copyright © 1971 by Artemis Verlag. Translation copyright © 1976 by Routledge & Kegan Paul, Ltd. Reproduced with permission of Oneworld Publications, Ltd. in format textbook via Copyright Clearance Center.

'Ali Shari'ati, "Fatima Is Fatima": From SHARIATI ON SHARIATI AND THE MUSLIM WOMAN, translated by Laleh Bakhtiar. Copyright © by Laleh Bakhtiar. Reprinted by permission of KAZI Publications and the translator.

Fatima Mernissi, "The Prophet and Women": From THE VEIL AND THE MALE ELITE: A FEMINIST INTERPRETATION OF WOMEN'S RIGHTS IN ISLAM, translated by Mary Jo Lakeland. Copyright © 1987 by Editions Albin Michel S. A. Translation copyright © 1991 by Addison-Wesley Publishing Company. Reprinted by permission of Edite Kroll Literary Agency on behalf of the author.

Anima Wadud: From QUR'AN AND WOMAN: REREADING THE SACRED TEXT FROM A WOMAN'S PERSPECTIVE. Copyright © by Oxford University Press. By permission of Oxford University Press.

Nurcholish Madjid, "Islamic Faith and the Problem of Pluralism": From THE TRUE FACE OF ISLAM: ESSAYS ON ISLAM AND MODERNITY IN INDONESIA, edited by John J. Donohue and John L. Esposito.

Fethullah Gülen: From TOWARD A GLOBAL CIVILIZATION OF LOVE AND TOLERANCE, translated by Mehmet Ünal, Naghihan Halilojlu, and Mükerrem Faniküçükmehmedojlu, edited by Jane Louise Kandur and Hakan Yeşilova. Copyright © by The Light, Inc., and Işik Yayinlan. Reproduced by permission of The Light, Inc.

Tariq Ramadan: From WESTERN MUSLIMS AND THE FUTURE OF ISLAM. Copyright © 2003 by Oxford University Press. By permission of Oxford University Press.

ILLUSTRATIONS

Tiled calligraphic roundel: Princeton University Press, 2005
Title page of the first English edition of the Qur'an: Open Library

Tower of the al-Mutawakkili Mosque: © Tips Images/Tips Italia Srl a socio unico/Alamy
Syrian tray, mid-13th century: Imperial Archaeological Commission, St. Petersburg, 1898
Hissa Hilal, Saudi poetess: © ALI HAIDER/epa/Corbis
Adam and Eve, from a *Book of Omens*: Smithsonian, Freer Gallery of Art and Arthur M. Sackler Gallery
Pakistani women at peace demonstration: AP Photo/Anjum Naveed
Folio from a late 7th- or 8th-century Qur'an: © The British Library Board, OR. 2165 f77
View of Mecca (1788): © Victoria and Albert Museum, London
Leaf from a Turkish translation of Ibn Ishaq's *Life of the Prophet*: Spencer Collection, The New York Public Library, Astor, Lenox and Tilden Foundations
Imam Mosque: © Paule Seux/Hemis/Corbis
Qal'a Madrasa, Iraq: © Universal Images Group/DeAgostini/Alamy
Mihrab in Jami' Mosque, Iran: © Roger Wood/CORBIS
Mosque lamp, ca. 1557: © Victoria and Albert Museum, London
Merchant and Genie, from *Illustrated Arabian Nights* (mid-19th century): © The Trustees of the British Museum/Art Resource, NY
Break of Ramadan fast, Karachi: © ATHAR HUSSAIN/Reuters/Corbis
Great Mosque of Banda Aceh, Indonesia: © Fadil/Corbis
Reading the Qur'an on a digital device: © CRACK PALINGGI/Reuters/Corbis
Iranian Revolution (1979): © Bettmann/CORBIS
Muslim and Christian women demonstrate: Karim Kadim/AP
Minbar of mosque in Hamburg, Germany: © Angelika Warmuth/dpa/Corbis

Index